The United States: Physical–Political

America
and
Its People

America and Its People

James Kirby Martin
University of Houston

Randy Roberts
Purdue University

Steven Mintz
University of Houston

Linda O. McMurry
North Carolina State University

James H. Jones
University of Houston

HarperCollins*Publishers*

For our students

Cover and Chapter Opener art:
Steven Karchin

Acknowledgments for the copyrighted materials not
credited on the page where they appear are listed in
the "Credits" section beginning on page A-33. This
section is to be considered an extension of the
copyright page.

Library of Congress Cataloging-in-Publication Data

America and its people/James Kirby Martin . . . [et al.].
    p. cm.
  Bibliography: p.
  Includes index.
  ISBN 0-673-18302-5 (set). ISBN 0-673-18315-7 (v. 1).
ISBN 0-673-18316-5 (v. 2)
  1. United States—History. I. Martin, James Kirby,
1943– .
E178.1.A4886 1989   88-18546
973—dc19   CIP

  23456-RRW-93929190

About the Authors

JAMES KIRBY MARTIN is a member of the Department of History at the University of Houston. A graduate of Hiram College in Ohio, he earned his Ph.D. degree from the University of Wisconsin in 1969, specializing in early American history, and taught for several years at Rutgers University. His interests also include American social and military history. Among his publications are *Men in Rebellion* (1973), *In the Course of Human Events* (1979), *A Respectable Army* (1982), and *Drinking in America* (rev. ed., 1987), the latter two volumes written in collaboration with Mark E. Lender. Martin serves as general editor for the American Social Experience Series, New York University Press. He is affiliated with the Rutgers Center of Alcohol Studies and recently was scholar-in-residence at the David Library of the American Revolution in Pennsylvania. He is currently finishing a biography of Revolutionary-period hero and villain, Benedict Arnold.

RANDY ROBERTS earned his Ph.D. degree in 1978 from Louisiana State University. His areas of specialization include modern United States history and the history of American popular culture and sports. He is a member of the Department of History at Purdue University, having previously taught at the University of Maryland and Sam Houston State University. His publications include *Jack Dempsey: The Manassa Mauler* (1979), *Papa Jack: Jack Johnson and the Era of White Hopes* (1983), and with James S. Olson *Winning Is the Only Thing: Sports and American Society, 1945 to the Present* (1989). Roberts serves as co-editor of the Illinois Series on Sports and Society, University of Illinois Press, and he is on the editorial board of the *Journal of Sport History*. His current writing project is an investigation of the life of Muhammad Ali and black activism during the 1960s and 1970s.

STEVEN MINTZ graduated from Oberlin College in Ohio before earning his Ph.D. degree at Yale University in 1979. His special interests include American social history with particular reference to families, women, children, and communities. Mintz is a member of the Department of History at the University of Houston, and he has also taught at Oberlin College and the Universitat-Gesamthochschule-Siegen in West Germany. His books include *A Prison of Expectations: The Family in Victorian Culture* (1983), and *Domestic Revolutions: A Social History of American Family Life* (1988), written in collaboration with Susan Kellogg. While at Yale, he received training in psychoanalytic theory from the Kanzer Fellowship for Psychoanalytic Studies in the Humanities. Currently he serves as an editor of the American Social Experience Series, New York University Press, and is researching a book on the history of private life in the United States.

LINDA O. McMURRY is a member of the Department of History at North Carolina State University. She completed her undergraduate studies at Auburn University, where she also earned her Ph.D. degree in 1976. Her fields of specialization include nineteenth- and twentieth-century United States history with an emphasis on the Afro-American experience and the New South. Before joining the history faculty at North Carolina State, McMurry taught at Valdosta State College in Georgia. A recipient of a Rockefeller Foundation Humanities Fellowship, she has written *George Washington Carver: Scientist and Symbol* (1981), and *Recorder of the Black Experience: A Biography of Monroe Nathan Work* (1985). McMurry has been active as a consultant to public television stations and museums on topics relating to black history, and she is currently completing a study of the role college-educated blacks played in the South from 1880 to 1920.

JAMES H. JONES completed his undergraduate studies at Henderson State College in Arkansas and then earned his Ph.D. degree at Indiana University in 1972. His areas of specialization include modern U.S. history, the history of medical ethics and medicine, and the history of sexual behavior. A member of the Department of History at the University of Houston, Jones has been a Senior Fellow of the National Endowment for the Humanities, a Kennedy Fellow at Harvard University, and a Senior Research Fellow at the Kennedy Institute of Ethics, Georgetown University. His writings include *Bad Blood: The Tuskegee Syphilis Experiment* (1981), and he is currently finishing a book on Alfred C. Kinsey and the rise of scientific research dealing with human sexual behavior. Jones also serves as a member of the Scientific Board of Advisors, Kinsey Institute for Research in Sex, Gender, and Reproduction, Indiana University.

Preface

The survey textbook in United States history is an essential learning instrument. It must do much more than present a chronological rendering of names, dates, and facts. It must gain the attention of students; it must overcome stereotypes of boredom; and it must challenge students intellectually. It must show real people confronting real problems, complete with their triumphs and failures, and it must increase the tolerance of students for differing interpretations of formative historical change. As such, it must encourage thinking in historical perspective while seeking to enhance such fundamental skills as the recognition of key issues and the solving of difficult problems. The U.S. survey text, in sum, must function as a work of synthesis that will assist course instructors in making history interesting and meaningful for students.

This is not an easy set of assignments for any textbook. In our increasingly technocratic culture, students have been repeatedly advised to concentrate their academic energies in disciplines that will assure them steady incomes as workers in society. An exciting, intelligently-conceived textbook, we are convinced, can assist course instructors in challenging this mentality by demonstrating that the subject of history does function as a central laboratory for learning about life and for acquiring knowledge and skills essential for successful living.

As instructors actively involved in teaching U.S. survey history, we began the development of *America and Its People* with these thoughts in mind. The most compelling works of history, we concluded, focus on people, both the great and the ordinary. They establish the importance of time, place, and circumstance in evaluating various forms of human behavior. They do not smooth over but highlight the dramatic conflict among people that has so often produced meaningful change. They frame their themes rigorously, and they tell their story with a strong narrative pulse. The most effective works of history, we believe, encourage readers to comprehend their own times and themselves more clearly in the light of what has come before them.

In writing *America and Its People* we have followed these guidelines. We have sought to impart to today's generation of college students our enthusiasm for the value of historical inquiry and our sense of what fundamentals a well-educated person needs to know about the American experience. In our opinion, the story of the United States—of colonization, the Revolution, slavery, Indian removal, social reform, the Civil War, global expansion, the Great Depression, and the civil rights and women's liberation movements—is best told by focusing on the struggle and dilemmas faced by passing generations of Americans. Thus, our "people-oriented" approach encourages students to grasp and evaluate the difficult choices human beings have made in molding the texture of life in the United States.

Besides encouraging student involvement, we have tried to keep the needs of history faculty members very much in mind. The text's structure conforms to the course outlines used by most instructors. It offers a clear narrative rendering of essential political, diplomatic, cultural, social, intellectual, and military history and concisely identifies major historical concepts and themes.

And finally, we have taken great care to present a text offering breadth and balance. We have found that the oft-expressed dichotomy between political/diplomatic history and social/cultural history disappears when the text is people-centered from its inception. Materials on ethnicity, gender, and race belong at the core of our narrative, not as adjunct information, and we have attempted to balance the important findings and insights of more traditional and newer historical subjects. It is our hope that we have achieved a sensitive and compelling presentation.

The book's structure is fashioned to heighten and sustain student interest. To borrow a phrase associated with computer programming, we have aimed at the production of a "user friendly" text. Each chapter begins with an **outline of contents** and a carefully-selected **anecdote or incident** that frames the chapter's themes while drawing students into the material. A chronological and topical narrative follows, building toward a **conclusion** and a **summary statement** in outline form highlighting and reinforcing essential points. In addition, each chapter contains a **chronology** of key issues and events, a thorough **bibliography** of suggested additional readings, and a **feature essay** designed to offer students an in-depth look at an important topic in one of the following people-oriented categories that illustrates change over time: Experiencing Combat, Aspects of Family Life, Sports and Leisure, The American Mosaic, Perspectives on Lawbreaking, and Medicine.

Other features of the text include four **picture essays** on the Changing Landscape and Popular Protest, combining insightful narrative with high-impact visual expression; an extensive **full-color map, photo, figure, and artwork program** including four full-page battlefield picture maps; a **multidimensional timeline** at the front of the book that is replete with high-interest items; and valuable tables, charts, graphs, and maps in the **Appendix.**

A comprehensive and up-to-date supplement package accompanies *America and Its People*. It includes a two-volume *Study Guide* and a *Test Item File* (both include map questions), an *Instructor's Manual* with much text author input, an outstanding **reference and source map transparency program** comprising 110 maps with extensive instructional material, and a complete **text map transparency packet.**

ACKNOWLEDGMENTS

Any textbook project is very much a team effort. We are indebted to many individuals who have worked with us on this book, beginning with the talented historians who served as reviewers, and whose valuable critiques contributed greatly to the final product.

Larry Balsamo
Western Illinois University
Lois W. Banner
University of Southern California
Delmar L. Beene
Glendale Community College
Albert Camarillo
Stanford University
Clayborne Carson
Stanford University
Jay Caughtry
University of Nevada, Las Vegas
John P. Crevelli
Santa Rosa Junior College
James P. Gormly
Pan American University
Elliott Gorn
Miami University
Nancy Hewitt
University of South Florida
Alphine W. Jefferson
Southern Methodist University

David R. Johnson
University of Texas at San Antonio
Steven F. Lawson
University of South Florida
Myron Marty
Drake University
Michael Perman
University of Illinois at Chicago
George Rable
Anderson College
Max Reichard
Delgado Junior College
John Ray Skates
University of Southern Mississippi
Sheila Skemp
University of Mississippi
Kathryn Kish Sklar
University of California, Los Angeles
Robert Striplin
American River College

The dedicated staff at Scott, Foresman provided us great support and expert guidance. From the beginning, Bruce D. Borland, Barbara Muller, and Charlotte Iglarsh worked with us to produce a student-oriented text, to improve our ideas and sharpen our writing. In later stages, Ann-Marie Buesing, Barbara Schneider, Lucy Lesiak, Nina Page, Leslie Coopersmith, and Paul Yatabe brought their skills to the editorial, art and design, photo research, and cartographic processes. To all of them, we offer our sincere appreciation.

Each author has received invaluable help from friends, colleagues, and family. James Kirby Martin thanks Larry E. Cable, Joseph T. Glatthaar, Jeffrey T. Sammons, Hal T. Shelton, and especially Karen W. Martin, whose talents as an editor and critic are too often overlooked. Randy Roberts thanks Terry Bilhart and Joan Randall, and especially James S. Olson and Suzy Roberts. Steven Mintz thanks James McCaffrey for fact-checking help, and Susan Kellogg for her encouragement, support, and counsel. Linda O. McMurry thanks Joseph P. Hobbs, John David Smith, Richard McMurry, and William C. Harris. James H. Jones thanks James S. Olson, Terry Rugeley, Laura B. Auwers for expert punctuation assistance, and especially Linda S. Auwers, who contributed both ideas and criticisms. All of the authors thank Gerald F. McCauley, whose infectious enthusiasm for this project has never wavered. And above all else, we wish to thank our students to whom we have dedicated this book.

The Authors

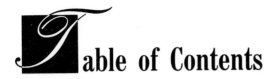

able of Contents

Maps

Tables and Graphs

COMPARATIVE CHRONOLOGIES

70,000 B.C.–1450	**1450–1550**

POLITICAL / DIPLOMATIC

300–900 Mayan civilization flourishes in Mexico's Yucatan peninsula and in Guatemala.

900 Toltecs rise to power in the Valley of Mexico.

1000 Seljuk Turks conquer the Holy Land.

1000 Norsemen under Leif Ericson land on coast of North America.

1095 Crusades begin.

1200 Aztecs conquer the Toltecs.

1400 Incas dominate western South America.

1494 Line of Demarcation divides the "New World" between Spain and Portugal.

1519 Hernando Cortés and 400 soldiers begin conquest of the Aztec empire.

1530–1535 A.D. Francisco Pizarro and 180 soldiers conquer the Inca empire.

SOCIAL / ECONOMIC

70,000–8000 B.C. Migrants come across tundra land bridges from Asia to people North and South America.

c. 8000 B.C. Glaciers recede, temperatures warm, and many large mammals die off.

1418 Prince Henry the Navigator of Portugal founds a school of navigation and sends expeditions to Africa.

1487 Dias sails around the Cape of Good Hope.

1492–1504 Columbus makes four voyages to the New World.

1496 Columbus introduces cattle, sugar cane, and wheat to the West Indies.

1497–1498 Portuguese explorer Vasco da Gama reaches India.

1507 The New World is named America after Florentine navigator Amerigo Vespucci.

1508 First sugar mill in the New World is built in the West Indies.

1513 Balboa is the first white man to view the western coast of the Pacific Ocean.

1517 Coffee is introduced in Europe.

1519–1522 Magellan's fleet circumnavigates the globe.

1531 Tobacco cultivation in the West Indies begins.

CULTURAL

1271 Seventeen-year old Marco Polo sets off for China.

1517 Martin Luther's public protest against the sale of indulgences (pardons of punishment in purgatory) marks the beginning of the Protestant Reformation.

1518 Bartolomé de Las Casas proposes that Spain replace Indian laborers with African slaves.

1539 First printing press in the New World is established in Mexico City.

1550–1650

1650–1750

1588 English fleet defeats the Spanish Armada.

1607 First permanent English colony in North America is founded at Jamestown.

1608 Samuel de Champlain claims Quebec for France.

1610 Spanish found Santa Fe, New Mexico.

1620 102 Pilgrims arrive at Cape Cod from England on the *Mayflower* and establish a colony at Plymouth.

1624 Dutch establish New Netherland.

1630 The Puritans establish Massachusetts Bay Colony.

1632 Maryland, the first proprietary colony, is established as a refuge for Roman Catholics.

1636 Roger Williams founds Providence, Rhode Island.

1649 Charles I of England beheaded.

1660, 1663 Navigation Acts monopolize colonial trade and shipping for England.

1663 Carolina is founded.

1664 England conquers New Netherland.

1665 New Jersey is founded.

1673 Joliet and Marquette explore Mississippi River.

1675–1676 King Philip's War in New England.

1682 William Penn founds Pennsylvania as a haven for Quakers.

1682 La Salle reaches Mississippi delta.

1688 Glorious Revolution in England deposes James II.

1732 Georgia is founded as a haven for debtors and a barrier against the Spanish.

1733 The Molasses Act restricts colonial imports of sugar goods from the French West Indians.

1553 Europeans learn about the potato.

1585 Walter Raleigh tries to colonize Roanoke Island, North Carolina.

1612 John Rolfe of Virginia discovers a method of curing the tobacco leaf.

1616 Chickenpox wipes out most New England Indians.

1617 England begins transporting criminals to Virginia as punishment.

1619 Englishwomen arrive in Virginia.

1619 A Dutch ship brings the first Africans to Jamestown.

1619 Virginia's population numbers approximately 2000.

1624 Cattle are introduced into New England.

1630 Colonial population totals about 5700.

1638 Anne Hutchinson convicted of heresy in Massachusetts.

1670 Colonial population totals about 114,500, including 4535 slaves.

1673 Regular mail service between Boston and New York begins.

1690 Massachusetts begins printing paper money.

1700 Colonial population is about 250,000. About 7000 people live in Boston, the colonies' largest city.

1714 Tea is introduced in the colonies.

1720 Colonial population totals about 474,000, including 68,839 slaves.

1731 Parliament forbids English factory workers to emigrate to America.

1576 Some 40,000 slaves brought to South America.

1582 Richard Hakluyt's *Divers Voyages* encourages English exploration, conquest, and colonization.

1613 Pocahontas becomes the first Indian convert to Christianity in Virginia.

1636 Harvard College founded.

1640 The first book is published in the colonies, the *Bay Psalm Book.*

1647 Massachusetts Bay Colony adopts the first public school law in the colonies.

1649 Maryland Toleration Act affirms religious freedom for all Christians in the colony.

1650 Anne Bradstreet, New England's first poet, publishes *The Tenth Muse.*

1691 New Massachusetts charter permits freedom of worship.

1692 Salem witch trials result in the execution of 20 people.

1719 The Great Awakening, a series of religious revivals, sweeps the colonies over the next three decades.

1731 Benjamin Franklin founds the first circulating library in Philadelphia.

1735 John Peter Zenger trial decides truth cannot be libel.

1739–1740 George Whitefield leads religious revivals in the colonies.

	1750	1760	1770

POLITICAL / DIPLOMATIC

1750 The Iron act restricts production of finished iron goods in the colonies.

1754 Albany Congress draws up a plan to unite the 13 colonies under a single government.

1754–1763 French and Indian War.

1760 George III accedes to the throne.

1763 Ottawa chief Pontiac captures British forts in Indiana, Michigan, and Wisconsin.

1763 The Proclamation of 1763 forbids settlement west of the Appalachian Mountains.

1764 The Sugar Act levies new duties on cloth, coffee, indigo, sugar, and wine.

1765 Quartering Act required colonists to provide barracks to British troops.

1765 Representatives from nine colonies convene in the Stamp Act Congress.

1766 Parliament repeals the Stamp Act.

1767 Townsend Act place duties on glass, lead, paint, paper, silk, and tea.

1770 The Townshend Act is repealed except for the tax on tea.

1773 The Boston Tea Party. A band of "Indians" dumps 342 chests of tea into Boston Harbor.

1774 The Coercive Acts close Boston harbor, revoke Massachusetts charter, and forbid town meetings.

1775 George III issues Prohibitory Act, declaring that a state of rebellion exists in the colonies.

1776 The Continental Congress formally declares independence.

1777 The "Stars and Stripes" is adopted as the official flag of the U.S.

SOCIAL / ECONOMIC

1750 The flatboat and the Conestoga wagon appear in Pennsylvania.

1756 Stagecoach line is established between New York and Philadelphia.

1760 Colonial population numbers about 1.6 million, including 325,000 slaves.

1763 English surveyors Charles Mason and Jeremiah Dixon set the boundary between Pennsylvania and Maryland—the Mason-Dixon line.

1765 The first medical school in the colonies is established in Philadelphia.

1766 Mastadon bones are discovered along the Ohio River.

1767 Daniel Boone undertakes his first exploration west of the Appalachians.

1770 The colonial population is about 2.1 million.

1773 Harvard College announces that it will no longer rank students in order of social prominence.

1774 Mother Ann Lee, founder of the Shakers in America, lands in New York City.

CULTURAL

1756 Wolfgang Amadeus Mozart born in Salzburg, Austria.

1758 A British army surgeon, Dr. Richard Shuckburgh, composes Yankee Doodle during the French and Indian war.

1760 Touro Synagogue in Newport, Rhode Island, is built. It is the first synagogue in the thirteen colonies.

1761 *The Complete Housewife*, a cookbook, is published in New York City.

1766 Robert Rogers writes the first play on a native American subject, *Ponteach, or the Savages of America*.

1771 Historical painter Benjamin West renders *Death of Wolfe* and *Penn's Treaty with the Indians*.

1773 Phillis Wheatley, the slave of a Boston merchant, publishes *Poems on Various Subjects*.

1776 Thomas Paine publishes *Common Sense*, a political treatise urging immediate separation from England.

1780	1790	1800

1781 Lord Cornwallis surrenders to George Washington at Yorktown.

1781 The states approve the nation's first constitution, the Articles of Confederation.

1783 Congress ratifies the Treaty of Paris.

1784 Spain closes the Mississippi River to American shipping.

1787 Congress passes the Northwest Ordinance, providing an orderly system for settling and developing the Old Northwest.

1787 Constitutional convention convenes in Philadelphia.

1788 Constitution wins ratification.

1789 George Washington elected first President of the U.S.

1791 Congress charters a national bank.

1791 The Bill of Rights is ratified.

1793 After Britain declares war on France, President Washington issues a Proclamation of Neutrality.

1794 General Anthony Wayne defeats the Indians at the Battle of Fallen Timber, opening Ohio to white settlement.

1796 Washington issues his Farewell Address, in which he warns the country not to form "permanent alliances."

1798 Congress adopts the Alien and Sedition Acts.

1798–1799 Kentucky and Virginia resolutions, declaring the Alien and Sedition Acts unconstitutional, are adopted.

1800 Thomas Jefferson elected President.

1801 John Marshall appointed Chief Justice of the Supreme Court.

1803 Thomas Jefferson purchases Louisiana Territory from Napoleon for $15 million or 4 cents an acre.

1803 In *Marbury* v. *Madison* the Supreme Court establishes judicial review.

1804 Vice-President Aaron Burr kills Alexander Hamilton in a duel.

1807 Jefferson imposes an embargo against trade with Britain and France.

1807 Congress prohibits the African slave trade.

1809 Embargo Act repealed; Non-Intercourse Act passed.

1780 U.S. population is about 2,780,400.

1783 Former Continental Army officers form the Cincinnati Society.

1784 The *Empress of China* inaugurates sea trade with China.

1785 Benjamin Franklin invents bifocals.

1787 Western Massachusetts farmers, led by Daniel Shays, seize a county courthouse to protest taxes.

1787 Levi Hutchins, a Concord, New Hampshire, clockmaker invents the alarm clock.

1790 The U.S. population is 3,929,214.

1790 Samuel Slater constructs the first textile factory in the U.S.

1793 Eli Whitney invents the cotton gin.

1794 The Whiskey rebellion, protesting the federal excise tax on whiskey, is put down.

1800 U.S. population is 5,308,483 including 896,849 slaves.

1800 John Chapman, better known as Johnny Appleseed, passes out religious tracts and apple seeds throughout the Ohio Valley.

1804–1806 Lewis and Clark expedition explores Louisiana Territory.

1807 Seth Thomas and Eli Terry begin to manufacture clocks out of interchangeable parts.

1807 Robert Fulton sails the steamboat *Clermont* from New York City to Albany in 32 hours.

1808 John Jacob Astor establishes the American Fur Company in the West.

1782 J. Hector St. John Crèvecoeur publishes *Letters from an American Farmer.*

1786 Virginia legislature enacts separation of church and state.

1786 Charles Willson Peale opens the first art gallery in Philadelphia.

1789 William Hill Brown's *The Power of Sympathy* is the first novel published in the U.S.

1793 Louis XVI of France sent to the guillotine.

1794 Thomas Paine publishes *The Age of Reason.*

1796 Houdon's marble statue of Washington is on display in Virginia's State capitol.

1798 Charles Brockden Brown publishes *Wieland.*

1800 Mason Locke Weems publishes his *Life of Washington,* the source of the legend about Washington chopping down the cherry tree.

1806 Noah Webster's *Compendious Dictionary of the English Language* is published.

COMPARATIVE CHRONOLOGIES

| | 1810 | 1820 | 1830 |

POLITICAL / DIPLOMATIC

1811 Western Indians led by the Shawnee "Prophet" are defeated at Tippecanoe.

1812 Congress declares war against Britain.

1813–1814 Creek War.

1814 Treaty of Ghent ends War of 1812.

1816 Congress charters the second Bank of the United States.

1818 U.S. and Britain agree to joint occupation of Oregon.

1819 Spain cedes Florida to the U.S.

1819 "A Firebell in the Night," Jefferson's phrase describing the crisis over slavery after Missouri applies for admission to the Union as a slave state.

1820 The Missouri Compromise admits Missouri as a slave state, Maine as a free state, and prohibits slavery in the northern half of the Louisiana Purchase.

1821 Mexico wins independence from Spain.

1823 President James Monroe opposes any further European colonization or interference in the Americas, establishing the principle now known as the Monroe Doctrine. It was actually written by J.Q. Adams.

1830 Indian Removal Act purchases Indian homelands in exchange for land in present-day Oklahoma and Arkansas.

1832 South Carolina "nullifies" the federal tariff.

1833 Nullification crisis ends.

1836 Texans under Sam Houston defeat the Mexican army at the Battle of San Jacinto.

1837 Panic of 1837 begins.

SOCIAL / ECONOMIC

1810 U.S. population is 7,239,881.

1810 In *Fletcher* v. *Peck* the Supreme Court finds a state law unconstitutional for the first time.

1814 The first totally mechanized factory producing cotton cloth from raw cotton opens in Waltham, Massachusetts.

1817 American Colonization Society is founded to resettle free blacks in Africa.

1819 Financial Panic of 1819.

1819 An asylum for the deaf, dumb, and blind is set up in Hartford, inaugurating a new era of humanitarian concern for the handicapped.

1819 The *Savannah* becomes the first steamship to cross the Atlantic.

1820 The U.S. population is 9,638,453.

1820 Congress reduces the price for public land to $1.25 an acre.

1821 Stephen Austin founds the first American colony in Texas.

1822 Liberia founded as a colony for free blacks from the U.S.

1825 Erie Canal completed.

1826 Jedidiah Smith blazes the first overland trail to California.

1827 *Freedom's Journal*, the first black newspaper, begins publication in New York City.

1828 The *Cherokee Phoenix*, the first Indian newspaper, begins publication.

1830 The U.S. population is 12,866,020.

1830 America's first commercially successful steam locomotive, the Tom Thumb, loses a race against a horse.

1831 Oberlin College opens its doors as the nation's first coeducational college. In 1835, it becomes the first American college to admit blacks.

1832 Samuel F. B. Morse invents the telegraph.

1835 The Liberty Bell cracks as it tolls the death of Chief Justice John Marshall.

1837 Horace Mann becomes Massachusetts's first superintendent of education.

1839 Charles Goodyear successfully vulcanizes rubber.

CULTURAL

1814 Francis Scott Key writes the lyrics to "The Star-Spangled Banner" during the British assault on Fort McHenry, Maryland.

1818 Washington Irving publishes *Rip Van Winkle*.

RIP VAN WINKLE

1821 Emma Willard founds the Troy Female Seminary, one of the first academies to offer women a higher education.

1823 John Howard Payne and Henry Bishop compose the song "Home, Sweet Home."

1823 James Fenimore Cooper publishes *The Pioneer*, the first of his leatherstocking tales.

1827 James Audubon publishes *Birds of America*, consisting of 435 lifelike paintings of native birds.

1829 David Walker issues his militant *Appeal to the Colored Citizens of the World*.

1831 Samuel Francis Smith composes the words to the song "America."

1834 *A Narrative of the Life of David Crockett* is published.

1836 William Holmes McGuffey publishes his First and Second Reader.

1838 Sarah Grimke publishes one of the earliest public defenses of sexual equality.

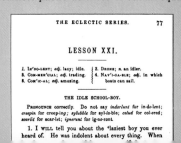

1840	1850	1860

POLITICAL / DIPLOMATIC

1846 Oregon divided along the 49th parallel.

1846 The U.S. declares war on Mexico.

1848 The Treaty of Guadalupe Hidalgo cedes to the U.S. California, Nevada, New Mexico, and Utah, and parts of Arizona, Colorado, Kansas, and Wyoming.

1850 The Compromise of 1850 provides for the admission of California as a free state. It also includes a strict law for the return of fugitive slaves.

1854 Abolitionist William Lloyd Garrison publicly burns the U.S. Constitution in Framingham, Massachusetts, calling it "agreement with hell and a covenant with death."

1854 Stephen Douglas introduces the Kansas-Nebraska Act. Opponents of the act form the new Republican Party.

1854 Commodore Matthew C. Perry negotiates a treaty opening Japan to the West.

1859 John Brown raids Harpers Ferry.

1860 Fifty-one-year-old Abraham Lincoln becomes the nation's sixteenth president.

1860 South Carolina secedes from the Union.

1861 Confederate States of America is formed.

1863 President Lincoln signs the Emancipation Proclamation.

1865 John Wilkes Booth assassinates President Lincoln at Ford's Theater in Washington.

1865 The 13th Amendment to the Constitution abolishing slavery and involuntary servitude, is ratified.

1868 Andrew Johnson is acquitted by just one vote in his Senate impeachment trial.

SOCIAL / ECONOMIC

1840 The U.S. population is 17,069,453.

1841 The first wagon train arrives in California.

1842 The Massachusetts Supreme Court upholds workers' right to organize.

1845 A potato blight strikes Ireland.

1846 Elias Howe constructs and patents the first reliable sewing machine.

1846 William Morton, a Boston dentist, uses an anesthetic for the first time during a surgical operation.

1848 Alexander T. Stewart opens the first department store in New York City.

1849 New York State grants married women property rights.

1850 U.S. population is 23,191,876.

1850 The U.S. Navy outlaws flogging.

1851 Isaac Singer patents an improved sewing machine.

1851 The Young Men's Christian Association opens its first American chapter in Boston.

1854 13,000 Chinese arrive to work on transcontinental railroad.

1856 Gail Borden patents condensed milk.

1857 Elisha Graves Otis installs the first passenger elevator in a New York City department store.

1859 Edwin L. Drake drills the first commercial oil well at Titusville, Pennsylvania.

1860 U.S. population is 31,443,321.

1860 The Pony Express begins carrying mail between St. Joseph, Missouri, and Sacramento, California.

1862 To help raise revenue for the Civil War, the first federal income tax goes into effect.

1866 The potato chip is invented by a Saratoga, New York chef.

1866 Cyrus W. Field lays the first permanent transatlantic telegraph cable.

1867 Christopher Latham Sholes and Carlos Glidden invent the first practical typewriter.

1869 William Semple of Mount Vernon, Ohio, receives a patent for chewing gum.

CULTURAL

1841 Edgar Allan Poe publishes *Murders in the Rue Morgue*, the first modern detective story.

1843 New word *millionaire* is coined to describe Pierre Lorillard, tobacco magnate.

1848 Karl Marx and Friedrich Engels write the *Communist Manifesto*.

1850 Nathaniel Hawthorne publishes *The Scarlet Letter*.

1851 Herman Melville completes *Moby Dick*.

1852 Harriet Beecher Stowe's *Uncle Tom's Cabin* sells a million copies its first year and a half.

1854 Henry David Thoreau publishes *Walden*.

1855 Walt Whitman publishes *Leaves of Grass*.

1859 Charles Blondin crosses over Niagara Falls on a 110-foot tightrope.

1859 Charles Darwin publishes *Origin of Species*.

1860 Erastus and Irwin Beadle issue the first dime novels, featuring such figures as Kit Carson and Calamity Jane.

1865 Mark Twain publishes his first story, "The Celebrated Jumping Frog of Calaveras County."

1865 Lewis Carroll publishes *Alice's Adventures in Wonderland*.

	1870	1880	1890

POLITICAL / DIPLOMATIC

1870 Hiram R. Revels of Mississippi is the first black U.S. Senator.

1876 Disputed Presidential election. Democrat Samuel J. Tilden receives 250,000 more popular votes than Republican Rutherford Hayes in the popular vote.

1877 Electoral Commission awards the electoral votes to Rutherford Hayes, who is inaugurated president.

1877 Hayes withdraws the last federal troops from the South, marking the end of Reconstruction.

1881 President James A. Garfield is mortally wounded at a Washington train station.

1882 Congress suspends Chinese immigration for 10 years.

1883 Pendleton Act establishes Civil Service Commission to administer competitive examinations to federal job seekers.

1883 Supreme Court declares Civil Rights Act of 1875 unconstitutional.

1887 Dawes Allotment act subdivides all Indian reservations into individual plots of land and opens "surplus" land to white settlers.

1888 Department of Labor established.

1889 First Pan-American Conference meets in Washington.

1890 Congress passes the Sherman Anti-Trust Act, forbidding restraints on trade.

1891 Federal Courts of Appeal are created to relieve the Supreme Court's case load.

1892 Populists demonstrate elective strength.

1896 William McKinley defeats William Jennings Bryan for the presidency.

1897 President Cleveland vetoes a bill that would have required all immigrants to take literacy tests.

1898 Spanish-American war.

1898 Eugene Debs helps found the Social Democratic Party, later the Socialist party.

1899 Anti-Imperialist League founded to oppose American expansion.

SOCIAL / ECONOMIC

1870 U.S. population is 39,818,449.

1873 Congress passes the Comstock Act, banning birth control devices and information from the mails.

1875 The first Kentucky Derby.

1876 Sioux and Cheyenne Indians overwhelm Gen. George A. Custer and 264 cavalrymen at the Battle of the Little Big Horn.

1876 Alexander Graham Bell patents the telephone.

1876 The nation celebrates its centennial at an exposition in Philadelphia.

1878 James J. Ritty of Dayton, Ohio, invents the cash register.

1878 A. A. Pope begins to manufacture early bicycles, called "wheels."

1880 U.S. population is 50,155,783.

1881 Clara Barton founds the American National Red Cross.

1883 U.S. railroads adopt four standard time zones.

1886 Supreme Court extends protection of due process to corporations.

1886 Apache Chief Geronimo surrenders.

1886 The Statue of Liberty is dedicated.

1886 Pharmacist James S. Pemberton invents Coca-Cola.

1888 William S. Burroughs patents the first practical adding machine.

1888 The first incubators are used for premature infants.

1889 The Johnstown Flood kills 2300.

1890 U.S. population is 62,947,714.

1890 At Auburn State prison in New York, executions by the electric chair begin.

1893 Cherokee land between Colorado and Oklahoma opened to white settlement.

1893 Chlorine is first used to treat sewage in Brewster, New York.

1895 Supreme Court declares income tax unconstitutional in *Pollack* v. *Farmers Loan and Trust Company.*

1895 Lewis B. Halsey begins commercial production of pasteurized milk.

1897 A high society ball, costing $370,000 is held at New York's Waldorf Astoria Hotel despite serious economic depression.

CULTURAL

1871 P. T. Barnum opens his circus, which he calls "The Greatest Show on Earth."

1871 James Whistler paints the *Arrangement in Gray and Black No. 1,* better known as *Whistler's Mother.*

1875 Mary Baker Eddy publishes *Science and Health,* the basic text of Christian Science.

1876 Mark Twain publishes *The Adventures of Tom Sawyer.*

1876 Baseball's National League is founded.

1879 Henry George publishes *Progress and Poverty.*

1883 Joseph Pulitzer purchases the *New York World* and converts it into a successful 2 cent mass circulation newspaper.

1883 "Buffalo Bill" Cody organizes his first Wild West Show.

1884 Mark Twain publishes *The Adventures of Huckleberry Finn.*

1888 Edward Bellamy publishes *Looking Backward,* describing life in Boston in the year 2000.

1895 Stephen Crane, 24, publishes *The Red Badge of Courage.*

1896 John Philip Sousa composes "The Stars and Stripes Forever."

1896 The first comic strip appears in Joseph Pulitzer's *New York World.*

1896 Billy Sunday begins his career as an evangelist.

1899 Composer Scott Joplin's "Maple Leaf Rag" helps popularize ragtime.

1899 In *The School and Society,* philosopher John Dewey outlines his ideas about "progressive education."

1900	1910	1920

1900 "Gentleman's Agreement" between the U.S. and Japan limits Japanese immigration to the U.S.

1900 U.S. forces take part in putting down the Boxer Rebellion in China.

1901 Emilio Aguinaldo, leader of the Philippine revolt is captured.

1902 Oregon adopts the initiative and referendum.

1907 President Theodore Roosevelt dispatches 16 battleships ("the great white fleet") on an around-the-world cruise.

1913 The Sixteenth Amendment creates legal authority for an income tax.

1914 World War I begins following the assassination of Archduke Francis Ferdinand, heir to the Austro-Hungarian throne in Sarajevo in present-day Yugoslavia.

1917 The U.S. declares war on Germany.

1917 The first woman, Jeanette Rankin of Wyoming, is elected to Congress.

1920 Palmer Raids result in the deportation of 556 aliens because of their leftist political beliefs.

1920 Prohibition begins.

1920 The 19th Amendment is ratified, giving women the right to vote.

1920 The Panama Canal officially opens.

1928 Kellogg-Briand Treaty renounces war "as an instrument of national policy."

New York Tribune

Berlin Orders Ruthless U-Boat War; Puts Rigid Limit on American Ships; Washington Fears Break Will Follow

1900 U.S. population is 75,994,575.

1901 King C. Gillette of Chicago patents the first safety razor.

1903 The Wright Brothers make the first piloted flight on a powered airplane.

1904 The ice cream cone and iced tea are introduced at the St. Louis World's Fair.

1906 The Great San Francisco earthquake leaves 600 people dead and 300,000 homeless.

1908 Henry Ford introduces the Model T at a cost of $850.

1908 Jack Johnson becomes the first black man to hold the heavyweight boxing title.

1909 Explorers Robert E. Peary and Matthew Henson reach the North Pole.

1910 U.S. population is 91,972,266.

1911 145 female garment workers die in a fire at the Triangle Shirtwaist Company.

1912 The Titanic sinks on its maiden voyage, and 1500 of the ship's 2200 passengers drown.

1918 Influenza epidemic begins. It claims more than 20 million lives worldwide.

1918 Germany surrenders.

1920 The U.S. population is 105,710,620.

1920 A grand jury indicts 8 Chicago "Black Sox" players for throwing the 1919 World Series.

1924 Clarence Birdseye develops the first packaged frozen foods.

1926 Nineteen-year-old Gertrude Ederle swims the English channel.

1926 National Broadcasting Company becomes the first nationwide radio network.

1929 Stock Market Crash.

1900 Theodore Dreiser publishes his first novel, *Sister Carrie*.

1900 L. Frank Baum publishes *The Wonderful Wizard of Oz*.

1903 W. E. B. DuBois publishes *The Souls of Black Folk*, declaring that "The problem of the twentieth century is the color line."

1904 *The Great Train Robbery* is the first American film to tell a story.

1906 Upton Sinclair publishes *The Jungle*, an expose of conditions in Chicago's meat packing industry.

1913 The first crossword puzzle appears in a U.S. newspaper.

1914 Edgar Rice Burrough publishes *Tarzan of the Apes*.

1915 Margaret Sanger is arrested in New York City for teaching methods of contraception.

1918 The U.S. Post Office confiscates copies of *The Little Review* on the grounds of obscenity. It contained an episode from James Joyce's *Ulysses*.

1920 F. Scott Fitzgerald publishes his first novel, *This Side of Paradise*.

1921 The first bathing beauty pageant is held in Atlantic City, New Jersey.

1922 Tomb of Egyptian Pharaoh Tutankhamen ("King Tut") discovered.

1925 The first motel opens in San Luis Obispo, California.

1927 The first talking motion picture *The Jazz Singer*, starring Al Jolson, opens.

1928 Walt Disney releases the first Mickey Mouse cartoon.

1930	1940	1950

POLITICAL / DIPLOMATIC

1932 Near the Capitol U.S. army units led by General Douglas MacArthur drive out an encampment of 15,000 World War I vets who demanded a bonus from Congress.

1933 Adolf Hitler, Nazi party leader, is appointed Chancellor of Germany.

1935 Italy invades Ethiopia.

1935 Louisiana Governor Huey Long assassinated.

1936 Civil War breaks out in Spain.

1938 Munich Pact hands over a third of Czechoslovakia to Nazi Germany.

1939 Germany and Soviet Union sign non-aggression pact.

1939 World War II begins following Germany's invasion of Poland.

1940 British Royal Air Force fights off Hitler's Luftwaffe in the Battle of Britain.

1940 The Smith Act outlaws organizations advocating the overthrow of the U.S. government.

1944 D-day.

1945 V-E Day.

1945 V-J Day.

1946 Winston Churchill, delivers his "iron curtain" metaphor about Eastern Europe.

1948 The United Nations declares Israel an independent nation.

1949 Communists led by Mao Tse-Tung gain control of China.

1950 North Korean troops cross the 38th parallel, beginning the Korean War.

1950 Senator Joseph McCarthy brandishes a "list" of "members of the Communist party."

1951 Julius and Ethel Rosenberg are sentenced to death for atomic espionage.

1954 The French garrison at Dien Bien Phu falls to Vietnamese nationalists led by Ho Chi Minh.

1954 The Supreme Court rules in *Brown* v. *Board of Education* that segregated education is unconstitutional.

1959 Fidel Castro leads a successful revolution in Cuba against the regime of Fulgencio Batista.

SOCIAL / ECONOMIC

1930 The U.S. population is 122,775,046.

1933 Prohibition repealed.

1934 Public Enemy Number One, John Dillinger, shot and killed by FBI agents at a Chicago movie theater.

1935 Wagner Act guarantee's workers' right to bargain collectively.

1936 The last public hanging in the U.S. takes place in Owenboro, Kentucky.

1937 Patent issued for nylon.

1937 Following a 44-day sit-down strike, General Motors recognizes the United Automobile Workers.

1940 U.S. population is 131,669,275.

1942 Physicist Enrico Fermi sets off the first atomic chain reaction.

1942 Gasoline rationing goes into effect.

1943 A race riot in Detroit leaves 25 blacks and 9 whites dead.

1944 GI Bill of Rights provides educational benefits for servicemen.

1946 The first electronic computer, begins service.

1947 Air Force Captain Charles Yeager flies faster than the speed of sound.

1947 The transistor is invented.

1950 U.S. population is 150,697,361.

1952 The U.S. detonates the first hydrogen bomb.

1954 Dr. Jonas Salk invents a vaccine against polio.

1954 The birth control pill is invented.

1954 Roger Bannister runs a mile in 3 minutes 59.4 seconds, breaking the four-minute barrier.

1957 The Soviet Union rockets the first artificial satellite, Sputnik, into space.

1958 Six countries form the European Common Market.

CULTURAL

1931 CBS inaugurates the first regular schedule of television broadcasting.

1935 Charles Darrow, an unemployed engineer, markets a new board game, Monopoly.

1936 Jesse Owens wins four gold medals in track events at the Berlin Olympics.

1937 The German zeppelin Hindenberg bursts into flames at Lakehurst, New Jersey, killing 35 passengers.

1938 Action Comics #1 presents the Man of Steel, Superman.

1938 Orson Welles broadcasts reports of a Martian invasion.

1939 John Steinbeck's *The Grapes of Wrath* published.

1941 Richard Wright, black author, publishes *Native Son.*

1948 Miles Davis pioneers "cool" jazz.

1948 Alfred Kinsey publishes *Sexual Behavior in the Human Male,* which is followed five years later by *Sexual Behavior in the Human Female.*

1948 The first successful long-playing phonograph record is developed.

1949 French fashion designers introduce the bikini bathing suit.

1949 Playwright Arthur Miller completes *Death of a Salesman.*

1950 Charles Shulz creates the cartoon strip "Peanuts."

1951 J. D. Salinger publishes *Catcher in the Rye.*

1952 Ralph Ellison publishes *The Invisible Man.*

1956 Elvis Presley's first hit "Heartbreak Hotel" is released.

1957 Jack Kerouac's *On the Road* is published.

1957 Dr. Seuss publishes *The Cat in the Hat.*

1960	1970	1980

1960 U-2 reconaissance pilot Francis Gary Powers is shot down over the U.S.S.R.

1962 Cuban Missile Crisis.

1963 The U.S. and Soviet Union sign first nuclear test ban treaty.

1963 President Kennedy assassinated.

1964 Gulf of Tonkin incident.

1965 The first U.S. combat troops arrive in South Vietnam.

1968 Dr. Martin Luther King, Jr., assassinated.

1968 Senator Robert F. Kennedy assassinated.

1968 Violence breaks out at the Democratic National Convention in Chicago.

1973 The U.S. ends direct American military involvement in Vietnam.

1973 Vice-President Spiro Agnew resigns and pleads no contest to a charge of income tax evasion.

1974 Richard Nixon becomes the first president to resign from office.

1975 The Vietnam War ends as communist troops occupy Saigon.

1977 President Anwar el-Sadat of Egypt is the first Arab leader to visit Israel.

1978 Camp David Accords.

1979 Iranian militants seize 52 hostages at the U.S. embassy in Teheran, Iran.

1981 American hostages in Iran released after 444 days of captivity.

1981 Sandra Day O'Connor is appointed to the Supreme Court.

1984 Democrats nominate Geraldine Ferraro for vice president.

1985 Mikhail Gorbachev becomes leader of the Soviet Union.

1987 House and Senate panels investigate the Iran-*Contra* Affair.

1987 Black Monday on Wall Street, October 19 records the worst decline in Wall Street history.

1988 The U.S. and Soviet Union forges medium range nuclear arms agreement.

1960 U.S. population is 179,323,175.

1960 U.S. scientists invent the laser.

1960 The U.S. submarine *Triton* circumnavigates the globe under water.

1961 Russian Cosmonaut Yuri Gagarin becomes the first human to orbit the earth.

1961 FCC Chairman Newton Minow calls TV "a vast wasteland."

1963 Jean Nidetch incorporates Weight Watchers, an organization of diet clubs.

1964 Martin Luther King receives the Nobel Peace Prize.

1965 Congress requires cigarette packages and ads to contain health warnings.

1969 Astronaut Neil Armstrong becomes the first human to walk on the moon.

1970 The U.S. population is 203,235,175.

1971 The Twenty-sixth Amendment gives eighteen-year-olds the right to vote.

1973 Arab countries impose an oil embargo against the U.S.

1977 The U.S. ends a 10-year moratorium on capital punishment.

1978 California voters approve Proposition 13, sharply cutting property taxes.

1979 A serious nuclear power accident occurs at the Three Mile Island nuclear plant.

1979 Oil prices go from $10 a barrel to over $20 a barrel.

1980 U.S. population is 226,545,805.

1981 Doctors diagnose the first cases of AIDS.

1981 President Reagan decertifies air traffic controllers' union.

1982–1983 Recession raises the unemployment to 10.2 percent but reduces inflation and interest rates.

1986 Crack, a highly addictive form of cocaine, appears in American cities, heightening public concern about drug abuse.

1960 A House subcommittee accuses disk jockeys of accepting "payola" to play certain records on the air.

1962 Illinois becomes the first state to decriminalize all private sexual conduct between consenting adults.

1963 Twenty-two-year-old Bob Dylan composes "Blowin' in the Wind."

1964 The Beatles make their first U.S. tour.

1969 500,000 young people attend a four-day rock concert near Woodstock, New York.

1970 Satirical comic strip *Doonesbury* begins appearing in 30 newspapers.

1971 Controversial situation comedy series *All in the Family* debuts.

1977 Record TV audiences watch the dramatization of Alex Haley's black family history *Roots*.

1977 The film *Saturday Night Fever* popularizes disco music.

1985 Live Aid, organized by musician Bob Geldof, is broadcast live from London and Philadelphia and raises over $100 million for African famine relief.

1987 *Platoon*, a film showing the plight of American troops in Vietnam, wins the Academy Award for best picture.

1987 The publication of Allan Bloom's *The Closing of the American Mind* and E. D. Hirsch, Jr.'s *Cultural Literacy* triggers widespread debate about American education.

1987 Baby M case raises moral and ethical issues involved in surrogate parenting.

America
and
Its People

CHAPTER 1

The Peopling and Unpeopling of America

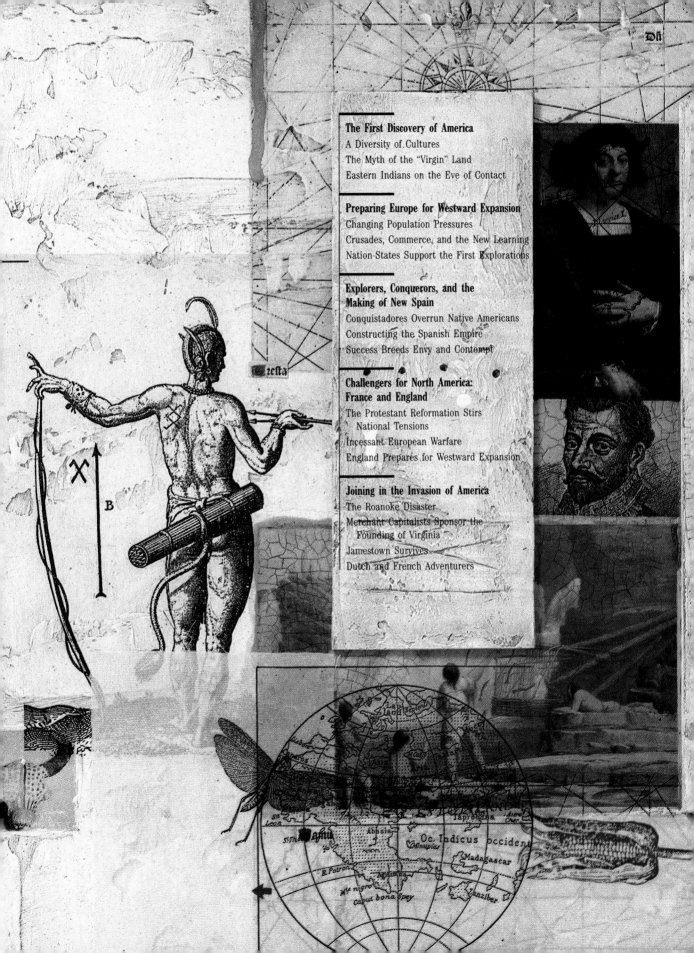

*E*ach Thanksgiving Americans remember Squanto as the valued Indian friend who saved the suffering Pilgrims from starvation. Few know the other ways in which Squanto's life reflected the disastrous collision of human beings occurring in the wake of Christopher Columbus's first voyage of discovery to America in 1492. European explorers believed they had stumbled upon two empty continents, which they referred to as the "new world." In actuality, the new world was very old and home to millions of Native Americans. A little more than 100 years after Columbus, at the time of the Pilgrims, Indian numbers had been reduced by as much as 90 percent. For Squanto and his tribe, the Patuxets of eastern Massachusetts, and for many other natives, the appearance of the Europeans meant mayhem and death.

Born about 1590, Squanto acquired the values of his Algonquian-speaking elders before experiencing much contact with adventurers from overseas. Tribal fathers taught him that personal dignity came from respecting the bounties of nature and serving his clan and village, not from acquiring material possessions. He also learned the importance of physical and mental endurance. To be accepted as an adult, he spent a harrowing winter surviving alone in the wilderness. When he returned the next spring, his Patuxet fathers fed him poisonous herbs for days on end, which he unflinchingly ate—and survived by forced vomiting. Having demonstrated his fortitude, tribal members declared him a man.

Living among 2000 souls in the Patuxet's principal village, located on the very spot where the Pilgrims settled in 1620, Squanto may well have foreseen trouble ahead when fair-skinned Europeans started visiting the region. First there were fishermen; then in 1605 the French explorer, Samuel de Champlain, stopped at Plymouth Bay. More fatefully, Captain John Smith, late of the Virginia colony, passed through in 1614. Smith's party treated the Patuxets with respect, but they viewed the natives as little more than wild beasts, to be exploited if necessary. Before sailing away, Smith ordered one of his lieutenants, Captain Thomas Hunt, to stay behind with a crew of men and gather a rich harvest of fish. After completing his assignment, Hunt lured twenty Indians, among them Squanto, on board his vessel and, without warning, set his course for the slave market in Malaga, Spain.

Somehow Squanto avoided a lifetime of slavery. By 1617, he was in England, where he devoted himself to mastering the English tongue. One of his sponsors, Captain Thomas Dermer, who had been with Smith in 1614, asked him to serve as an interpreter and guide for yet another New England expedition. Anxious to return home, Squanto readily agreed and sailed back to America in 1619.

When Dermer's party landed at Plymouth Bay, a shocked Squanto discovered that nothing but overgrown fields and rotting human bones remained of his once-thriving village. As if swept away by some unnamed force, the Patuxets had disappeared from the face of the earth. Trained to show no emotion, Squanto grieved privately. Soon he learned of a great epidemic; thousands of Indians had died in the Cape Cod vicinity. They were victims of diseases previously unknown in New England—probably in this case chicken pox carried from Europe by fishermen and explorers. When these micro-organisms struck, the native populace, lacking antibodies, had no way to protect themselves.

Squanto soon left Dermer's party and went in search of possible survivors. He was living with the Pokanoket Indians when the Pilgrims stepped ashore in December 1620 at the site of his old village. The Pilgrims endured a terrible winter in which half their numbers died. Then in the early spring of 1621 a lone Indian, Samoset, appeared in Plymouth Colony. He spoke halting English and told of another who had actually lived in England. Within a week Squanto arrived and agreed to stay and help the Pilgrims produce the necessities of life.

Squanto taught them how to grow Indian corn (maize), a crop unknown in Europe, and how to catch great quantities of fish. His efforts resulted in an abundance of food, celebrated in the first Thanksgiving feast during the fall of 1621. To future Pilgrim Governor William Bradford, Squanto "was a special instrument sent of God for their good beyond their expectation."

The story does not have a pleasant ending. Contact with the English had changed Squanto, and he adopted some of their practices. He became greedy. Violating his childhood training, he started to serve himself. As Bradford recorded, Squanto told neighboring Indian tribes that the Pilgrims would make war on them unless they gave him gifts. Further, he would unleash the plague, which the English "kept . . . buried in the ground, and could send it among whom they would." By the summer of 1622 Squanto had become a problem for the Pilgrims, who were anxious for peace. Within a short time, he fell sick, "bleeding much at the nose," and died within a few days—another victim of some European disease.

Squanto

As shown by Squanto's life, white-Indian contacts did not point toward a fusing of Native American and European customs, values, and ideals. Rather, the westward movement of peoples destroyed Indian cultures and replaced them with European-based communities. The history of the Americas (and of the United States) cannot be fully appreciated without understanding why thousands of Europeans crossed the Atlantic Ocean and sought dominance over the American continents. Three groups in particular, the Spanish, French, and English, succeeded in this life-and-death struggle that forever changed the course of human history.

THE FIRST DISCOVERY OF AMERICA

The world was a much colder place 75,000 years ago. A great ice age, known as the Wisconsin glaciation, had begun. Year after year, water being drawn from the oceans formed into mighty ice caps, which in turn spread over vast reaches of land. This process dramatically lowered ocean levels. In the area of the Bering Straits, where today fifty-six miles of ocean separates Siberia from Alaska, a land bridge emerged. At times this link between Asia and America, *Beringia,* may have been 1000 miles wide. This corridor, most experts believe, provided the pathway used by early humans to enter a new world.

These people, known as Paleo-Indians, were nomads and predators. With stone-tipped spears, they hunted mastadons, woolly mammoths, giant beavers, giant sloths, and bighorn bison, as well as many smaller animals. The mammals led prehistoric men and women to America 20,000 or more years ago. For generations, these humans roamed Alaska in small bands, gathering seeds and berries when not hunting the big game or attacking and killing one another.

Eventually, corridors opened through the Rocky Mountains as the ice began to recede. The migratory cycle began again. Humans and animals trekked southward and eastward, reaching the bottom of South America and the east coast of North America by about 8000 B.C. It had been a long journey, covering thousands of miles, and in the process Paleo-Indians had become Native Americans.

A Diversity of Cultures

As these first Americans fanned out over two continents, they improved their weapons by flaking and crafting maleable stones such as flint into sharper spear points, which allowed them to slaughter the big game more easily. Also with the passing of time, the atmosphere began to warm as the ice age came to an end. Mammoths, mastodons, and other giant mammals did not survive the warming climate and needless overkilling.

The first Americans now faced a serious food crisis. Their solution showed ingenuity. Beginning in Central America between roughly 8000 and 5000 B.C., groups of humans started cultivating plant life as an alternate food source. They soon mastered the basics of agriculture. They raked the earth with stone hoes and produced crops as varied as maize, potatoes, squashes, pumpkins, and tomatoes.

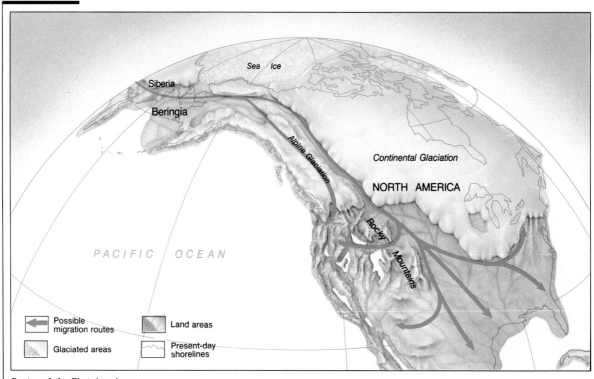

Routes of the First Americans

This agricultural revolution profoundly affected Native American life. Those who engaged in farming became more sedentary. They constructed villages and ordered their religious beliefs around such elements of nature as the sun and rain. With dependable food supplies, they had more children, resulting in a population explosion. Work roles became differentiated by gender. Men still hunted and fished for game, but they also prepared the fields for crops. When not caring for children, women did the planting, weeding, and harvesting.

Ultimately out of these agriculturally-oriented groups evolved complex Native American cultures, the most sophisticated of which appeared in Central America and the Ohio and Mississippi river valleys. Emerging before 300 A.D., the Mayas of Mexico and Guatemala based their civilization on abundant agricultural pro-

duction. They also built elaborate cities and temples. Their craft workers produced jewelry of gold and silver, and their merchants developed extensive trading networks. Their intellectuals devised forms of hieroglyphic writing, mathematical systems, and several calendars, one of which was the most accurate in the world at that time.

Although their society was highly stratified with powerful kings and priests ruling over the ordinary citizens, the Mayas did not develop a warrior class. After 1000 A.D., warlike peoples from the North began to conquer their cities. First came the Toltecs, then the Aztecs. The Aztecs called their principal city Tenochtitlán (the site of present-day Mexico City). At its zenith just before the Spanish conquerors (conquistadores) appeared in 1519, it contained a population of 300,000.

Mayas, Aztecs, and Incas

Tlaloc (above), the Aztec rain god, represented fertility and emphasized the importance of water and moisture as a basis for agricultural abundance. This mural (left) depicts the many facets of the Mayan civilization. Their culture revolved around agricultural production, elaborate architecture, jewelry making, and complex trade networks. Located on the site of present-day Mexico City, Tenochtitlán (below) served as the metropolitan center of the Aztec empire.

While imitators of Mayan culture, the Aztecs brutally extracted tribute, both in wealth and lives, from subject tribes. Their priests reveled in human sacrifice, since Huitzilopochtli, the Aztec war god, voraciously craved human hearts. At one temple dedication, Aztec priests sacrificed some 20,000 subject peoples. Not surprisingly, these tribes hated their oppressors. Many cooperated with the Spanish in destroying the Aztecs.

Other mighty civilizations also emerged, such as the Incas of Peru, who came into prominence after 1100 A.D. Settling in the Andes Mountains, they developed a sophisticated food supply network. They trained all young males as warriors to protect the empire and their kings, whom they thought of as gods and to whom all riches belonged. The Incas were even wealthier than the Aztecs, and they particularly prized gold and silver, which they mined in huge quantities—and which made them a special target for the conquistadores.

In North America, the Mound Builders (Adena and Hopewell peoples) appeared in the Ohio River valley around 1000 B.C. and lasted until 700 A.D. These natives hunted and gathered food as much as they farmed, and they grew crops like tobacco for ceremonial functions. Their merchants traded far and wide. Fascinated with death, they built elaborate burial sites, such as the Great Serpent Mound in Ohio. In time they gave way to the Temple Mound Builders (Mississippian peoples), who were more sedentary and agriculturally-minded. They too were great traders, and they constructed large cities, including a huge site near Cahokia, Illinois, where as many as 75,000 people lived amidst 85 large temple mounds, the most prominent of which had a base larger than the Great Pyramid of Egypt.

For unknown reasons the Mississippian culture broke apart before European contact. Remnant groups may have included the Choctaws and Creeks of Mississippi and Alabama, as

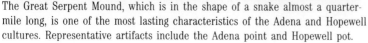

The Great Serpent Mound, which is in the shape of a snake almost a quarter-mile long, is one of the most lasting characteristics of the Adena and Hopewell cultures. Representative artifacts include the Adena point and Hopewell pot.

well as the Natchez Indians. In the rigidly stratified Natchez society the Great Sun was the all-powerful chief, and he ruled over nobles and commoners, the latter being called "stinkards." As with their Mississippian predecessors, when important individuals died, others gave up their lives so that central figures would have company as they passed into eternity. Eventually exterminated by the French, the Natchez were the last of the Mound Builders in North America.

The Myth of the "Virgin" Land

Beginning with the agricultural revolution, population in the Americas increased rapidly. Estimates vary widely, and one authority has claimed a native populace of up to 120 million persons by the 1490s. Other experts consider this estimate too high, suggesting a figure of 50 to 80 million, with 5 to 8 million inhabitants of North America. Europe's population, by comparison, was roughly 75 million at the time of Columbus, which undercuts the mistaken impression among European explorers that America was a "virgin" or vacant land.

Over several centuries Indian groups developed as many as 2200 different languages, some 550 to 650 of which were in use in Central and North America at the time of Columbian contact. So many languages implied great cultural diversity. While there were sophisticated civilizations of enormous wealth, most natives belonged to smaller, less complex groups in which families formed into clans—and clans into tribes.

Native groups varied greatly, developing life-styles to fit their environments. Tribes in Oregon and Washington, such as the Chinooks, did some farming, but fishing for salmon was their primary means of subsistence. In the Great Plains region, Indians like the Arapahos and Pawnees, while wandering less aimlessly than their ancestors, still pursued wild game within more or less fixed hunting zones. Men concentrated on bringing in meat, and women functioned as gatherers of berries and seeds. In the Southwest, Hopi and Zuni tribes relied upon agriculture, since edible plant and animal life

Tribes like the Micmac Indians of eastern Canada were corrupted by the arrival of the Europeans. The Indians began killing animals not only for food, but also for fur to supply clothing for markets in Europe. Also, many medicine men lost tribal favor when they could no longer combat devastating European diseases.

was scarce in their desert environment. These Indians even practiced irrigation. Perhaps they are best known for their multi-tiered villages which the Spanish called *pueblos.*

Eastern Indians on the Eve of Contact

In the East, where English explorers and settlers first made contact with Native Americans, there were dozens of small tribal groups. Southeastern natives, including Cherokees, Chickasaws, Creeks, Choctaws, and Seminoles, were more attuned to agriculture because of lengthy growing seasons. Northeastern tribes, like the Mahicans and Micmacs, placed more emphasis upon hunting and gathering. This is not to say that southeastern Indians never hunted or that northeastern peoples never planted crops. In each case, it was a matter of emphasis.

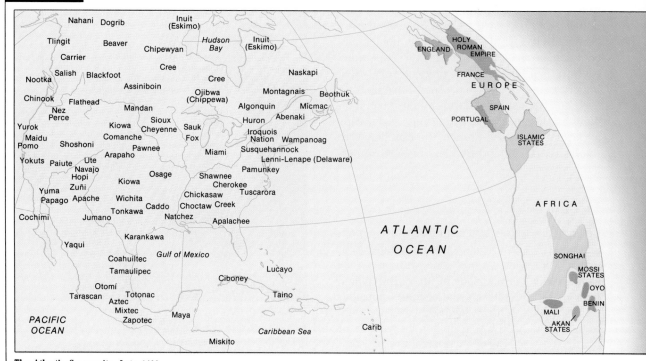

The Atlantic Community, Late 1400s
Indian groups in America and kingdom/states in Europe and Africa made up a triad around the
Atlantic Ocean.

Eastern Woodland Indians spoke several different languages but held many cultural traits in common. Perhaps linked to memories of the period of overkilling, they treated plant and animal life with respect. Essential to their religious values was the notion of an animate universe. They considered trees, plants, and animals to be spiritually alive (filled with *manitou*). Animals were not inferior to humans, as they, too, organized themselves into nations, and through their "boss spirits," permitted some thinning of their numbers for humans to survive. Boss spirits, however, would never accept overkilling. If tribes became gluttonous, animal nations could either leave the region or declare war, causing starvation and death.

Tribal *shamans*, or medicine men, communicated with the boss spirits and prescribed elaborate rules, or taboos, regarding the treatment of plants and animals. Indian parents, having mastered such customs, taught children like Squanto that nature contained the resources of life. While there was intertribal trading and much gift-giving of pottery, baskets, metals,

furs, and wampum (conch and clam shells), spiritual values deterred tribal members from exploiting the landscape for the sake of acquiring great personal wealth.

Eastern Woodland parents did not introduce their children to the concept of individual ownership of land. Tribal boundaries consisted of geographic locales large enough to provide for basic food supplies. Although individual dignity did matter, cooperation with tribal members rather than individual competitiveness was the essential ideal, even in sports. Eastern Woodland tribes enjoyed squaring off with one another in lacrosse matches, archery contests, and foot races. Betting and bragging occurred regularly, as did serious injuries in the heat of competition, but it was all group-oriented. Individuals did not enter events for personal honor, but rather to bring glory to their tribe.

Sports and the refinement of athletic skills also represented useful training for intertribal warfare. Wars were sporadic and could be caused by any number of factors, such as competition over valued hunting grounds. Skirmishes and the taking of a few lives by roving bands of warriors usually ended the contest, but not necessarily the ill will, especially among different language groups. Festering tensions and language barriers worked against intertribal cooperation in repelling the Europeans.

Even though males served as warriors, they did not always control tribal decision-making. Among the powerful Five Nations of Iroquois (Mohawks, Oneidas, Onondagas, Cayugas, and Senecas) in central New York, tribal organization was matrilineal. Women headed individual family units, which in turn formed into clans. Clan leaders were also women, and they decided which males would sit on tribal councils, which considered policies regarding diplomacy and war. Women held the power of removal as well, so males had no choice but to respect the authority of female clan heads. Among other Eastern Woodland Indians, women occasionally served as tribal *sachems* (chiefs), much to the shock of Europeans.

When European fishermen and explorers started making contact, there were 500,000 to 800,000 Indians inhabiting the region between the Atlantic coastline and the Appalachian Mountains. The Europeans, in a pattern that was essentially the same throughout the Americas, were initially curious as well as fearful, but these feelings soon gave way to expressions of contempt. Judging all people by European standards, they regarded the Indians as inferior. Native Americans looked and dressed differently. Their religious conceptions did not relate to European forms of Christianity. The men seemed lazy, since women did the bulk of the farming, and there was no consuming drive to acquire personal wealth, leaving the mistaken impression of much "want in a land of plenty," as one historian has summarized European perceptions.

To make matters worse, Native Americans, like those of Squanto's Patuxet tribe, began to die in huge numbers, which further confirmed European impressions that Indian peoples were inferior rather than merely different. Native Americans became "savages" who were blocking the path of a more advanced civilization desiring expansion. Thus commenced what many historians now call the European "invasion" of America.

PREPARING EUROPE FOR WESTWARD EXPANSION

Nearly five hundred years before Columbus's first westward voyage, Europeans made their first known contacts with North America. Around 1000 A.D., the Vikings (Scandinavians) explored barren regions of the North Atlantic. Eric the Red led an expedition of Vikings to Greenland, and one of his sons, Leif Ericson, continued exploring south and westward, stopping at Baffin Island, Labrador, and Newfoundland (described as *Vinland*). There were some settlement attempts, but they did not survive. The Viking voyages had no long-term impact because Europe was not yet ripe for westward expansion.

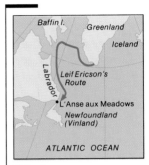

Vinland

Changing Population Pressures

Europeans of the Middle Ages lived short, difficult lives. Most tilled the soil as peasants, owing allegiance to manor lords and eking out a meager subsistence. Their crops, grown on overworked soil, were not nutritious, and because they rarely ate fruits, they suffered from constipation and rickets among other diseases. Peasants worshiped as Roman Catholics, regularly attending divine services that emphasized the importance of preparing for a better life after death. In the meantime, the dominant concern was to live long enough to see the next generation begin the cycle anew.

A variety of factors, including rapid population growth, gradually altered the established rhythms of medieval life. Between 1000 and 1350 A.D., Europe's population doubled, reaching over 70 million people. Even with improved methods of agricultural production, a new problem—overcrowding on the land—emerged. Overcrowding represents a condition in which too many individuals try to provide for themselves and their families on fixed supplies of farmland. To ease the pressure, some peasants were forced off the land. Some joined the Crusades; others became highway bandits; and many moved to the developing towns where they sought to acquire craft skills. Only a handful advanced beyond marginal existences.

By 1350 Europe was bulging at the seams, but the knowledge and technology was not yet in place to move some people to other regions. Then, suddenly, a frightening disaster relieved the pressure. Mediterranean merchant ships trading in the Muslim world hauled rats as well as cargoes back to their home ports. These rats carried fleas infested with microbes that caused bubonic plague. The plague, or Black Death, spread mercilessly through a populace existing on an inadequate diet. Between 1347 and 1353, one-third of all Europeans died in a medical calamity not to be outdone until the plague and other killer diseases wiped out large numbers of Native Americans.

The Black Death temporarily eliminated any compelling need to find and inhabit new territories. By the late 1500s, overcrowding was again a problem in many locales. As the English expansionist Richard Hakluyt wrote in his *Dis-*

One of the greatest depictions of the disease and destruction of the Black Death was Hans Holbein's *Dance of Death.*

course of Western Planting (1584), "infinite numbers may be set to work" in America, "to the unburdening of the realm . . . at home."

Crusades, Commerce, and the New Learning

While the population boomed, Europeans gathered knowledge about previously unknown people and places. The Crusades, designed to oust the Muslim "infidels" from Christian holy sites like Jerusalem, enhanced the broadening of horizons. Begun in 1095, the Crusades lasted for two centuries. European knights and peasant warriors failed to break Muslim power but, as a side benefit, they discovered that trade with the Orient was possible. They learned of spices that would preserve meats over long winters, fruits that would bring greater balance to diets, silk and velvet clothing, hand-crafted rugs, delicate glassware, and dozens of other commodities that would make European lives more comfortable.

The Italians, with city-states like Venice and Genoa taking the lead, seized upon the Mediterranean trade. Other European cities mushroomed in size at key trading points when Oriental goods started making their way from Italy into Switzerland, France, and Germany. While the new trade provided some work for dislocated peasants, a more lasting outcome was the rise of great merchants who concentrated on securing scarce commodities—and selling them for handsome profits.

The new wealth displayed by the great merchants promoted a pervasive spirit of material acquisition. The merchants, however, did more than merely reinvest profits in additional trading ventures. They also fostered and underwrote a resurgence in learning, known as the *Renaissance.* Beginning in Italy, the Renaissance soon captivated much of Continental Europe. There were new probings in all subjects. Learned individuals rediscovered the writings of such ancient scholars as Ptolemy, who had mapped the Earth, and Eratosthenes, who had estimated its circumference. By the early fifteenth century educated Europeans knew the world was not flat. Indeed, early in

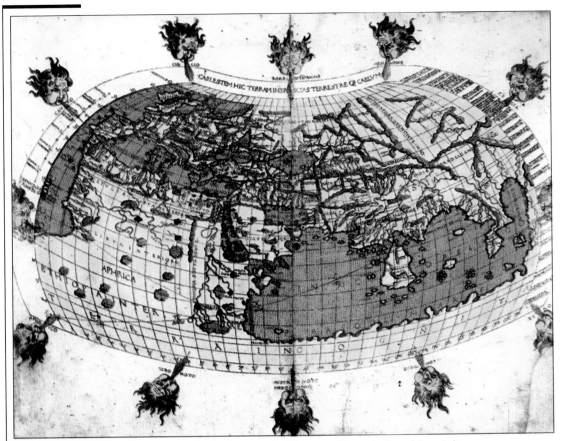

Ptolemy prepared his *Guide to Geography* in the second century A.D. His work showed knowledge that the world was round, but he underestimated the circumference and imagined Asia to be a larger continent than it actually was. Ptolemy's work was widely reprinted in Europe after 1475 as part of the New Learning.

1492, just a few months before Columbus sailed, a German geographer, Martin Behaim, constructed a round globe for all to see.

Enhanced geographical knowledge went hand in hand with developments in naval science. Before the fifteenth century, Europeans risked their lives if they did not sail close to land. The Muslims provided knowledge about the astrolabe and sextant and their use as basic navigational instruments. Contact with the Arabs also introduced Europeans to more advanced ship designs. Europeans soon abandoned their outmoded galleys, which required oarsmen to maneuver them, in favor of three-masted, lateen-rigged caravels. These vessels were not only faster and more mobile, but they

also could sail against the wind. All of these advances heightened prospects for worldwide exploration in the ongoing quest for valuable trading commodities.

The adventures of Marco Polo underscored the new learning and exemplified its relationship to commerce and exploration. Late in the thirteenth century, this young Venetian trader traveled throughout the Orient. He later recorded his findings and told of unbelievably great wealth in Asian kingdoms like Cathay (China). Around 1450, Johann Gutenberg, a German printer, perfected movable type, making it possible to reprint limitless numbers of manuscripts, heretofore laboriously copied by hand. The first printed edition of Marco Polo's

The invention of movable type meant that many writings could be printed rapidly rather than laboriously copied by hand. The printing press sped up the circulation of knowledge and helped spur explorations.

Journals appeared in 1477. Merchants and explorers alike, among them Christopher Columbus, read Polo's *Journals,* which spurred them on in the prospect of gaining complete access to Oriental riches.

Nation-States Support the First Explorations

Although there was a new vitality in Europe, it did not pervade all elements of society. Powerful manor lords still controlled the countryside, and they made it difficult for merchants to move goods across their lands, unless traders paid heavy tolls. These nobles also sneered at monarchs wanting to collect taxes. Tapping into peasant manpower, manor lords quite often had

stronger armies, leaving royal figures unable to enforce their will. Over time, merchants and monarchs began to work together to centralize political authority. Using mercantile capital, they formed armies that challenged the nobility.

The process of creating nation-states happened in the fifteenth century. The marriage of Ferdinand of Aragon to Isabella of Castile in 1469 represented the beginnings of national unity in Spain. These joint monarchs hired mercenary soldiers to break the power of defiant nobles. In 1492 they also crushed the Muslims (Moors) inhabiting southern Spain, driving them as well as Jewish inhabitants out of the country. Working closely with the Roman Catholic church, Ferdinand and Isabella used Inquisition torture chambers to break the spirit of others whose loyalty they doubted. By 1500, their subjects no longer owed first allegiance to local manor lords. Whether or not they liked it, they had become full-fledged Spaniards expected to serve their nation loyally.

Portugal, France, and England also faced the turbulence of nation-making. John I led the way by consolidating Portugal in the 1380s. Louis XI, known as the Spider King, was responsible for unifying France in the 1450s, after the Hundred Years' War with England. In England, two great noble lines, the houses of York and Lancaster, fought endlessly and devastated themselves in the Wars of the Roses (1455–85). Henry Tudor, who became Henry VII (1485–1509), emerged victorious from the chaos and initiated a lengthy internal unification process that set the stage for England's westward expansion.

Unification was critical to focusing national efforts on exploration, as demonstrated by Portugal. Secure in his throne, King John I was able to support his son, Prince Henry the Navigator (1394–1460), in the latter's efforts to learn more about the world. Henry set up a school of navigation at Sagres on the rocky, southwestern coast of Portugal. With official state support, he sent out ships on exploratory missions. When the crews returned, they worked to improve maps, sailing techniques, navigational procedures, and ship designs.

Initially, the emphasis was on learning, but then it shifted to a quest for valuable trade goods as Henry's mariners conquered island groups like the Azores and brought back raw wealth (gold, silver, and ivory) from the west coast of Africa. Trading ties developed with Africans, including the first dealings in black slaves by early modern Europeans. The lure of wealth drove Portuguese ships farther south along the African coast. Bartholomew Dias made it to the Cape of Good Hope in 1487. Ten years later, Vasco da Gama took a small flotilla around the southern tip of Africa and onto the riches of India.

Besides returning a four hundred percent profit, da Gama's expedition led to the development of Portugal's Far Eastern empire. It also proved that the Muslim world, with its heavy tolls on trade, could be circumvented in getting European hands on Oriental riches. None of this would have been possible without a unified Portuguese government able to tax the populace and thus sponsor Prince Henry's attempts to probe the boundaries of the unknown.

Ferdinand and Isabella were intensely aware of Portugal's triumphs when a young Genoese mariner, Christoforo Columbo (1451–1506), asked them to underwrite his dream of sailing west to reach the Orient. Too consumed with their struggle for internal unification, they refused him, but Columbus persisted. He had already contacted King John II of Portugal, who rebuffed him as "a big talker and boastful." Columbus also turned to France and England but gained no sponsorship. Finally, Queen Isabella reconsidered. She met Columbus's terms, which included ten percent of all profits from his discoveries, and proclaimed him "Admiral of the Ocean Sea." It was a monumental decision, made possible by Spain's unification.

On August 3, 1492, Columbus and some ninety mariners set sail from Palos, Spain, in the *Niña*, *Pinta*, and *Santa Maria*. Based on faulty calculations, the Admiral estimated Asia to be no more than 4500 miles to the west (the actual distance is closer to 12,000 miles). Some 3000 miles out, his crew became fearful and wanted to return home. But he convinced them to keep

Columbus first landed on the Bahamian island that he named San Salvador. He described the local natives as peaceful and generous, an image that changed rapidly as conquistadores swept over the native populace in their rush to tap into the riches of the Americas.

sailing west. Just two days later, on October 12, they landed on a small island in the Bahamas, which Columbus named San Salvador (holy savior). There they found hospitable natives, the Arawaks, whom Columbus described as "a loving people without covetousness." He called them Indians, a misnomer to this day, because he believed that he was nearing the Indies and the Asian mainland. Sailing on, Columbus landed on Cuba, which he thought was Japan, and then on to Hispaniola, where he traded for gold-laden native jewelry. Columbus and his crew returned home to a hero's welcome in 1493 and to funding for three more expeditions to America.

EXPLORERS, CONQUERORS, AND THE MAKING OF NEW SPAIN

A fearless explorer, Columbus turned out to be an ineffective administrator and a poor geographer. He ended up in debtor's prison, and to his dying day in 1506 he never admitted to locating a world unknown to Europeans. Geographers overlooked his contribution and named the western continents after another mariner, Amerigo Vespucci, a merchant from Florence who participated in a Portuguese expedition to South America in 1501. In a widely reprinted letter, Vespucci claimed that a new world had been found, and it was his name that caught on.

Columbus's significance lay elsewhere. His 1492 venture garnered enough extractable wealth to excite the Spanish monarchs. They did not care whether Columbus had reached Asia, only that further exploratory voyages might produce unimaginable riches. Because they feared Portuguese interference, Ferdinand and Isabella moved quickly to solidify their interests. They went to Pope Alexander VI, who issued a papal bull, *Inter Caetera*, which divided the unknown world between Portugal and Spain. In 1494 they worked out a formal agreement with Portugal in the Treaty of Tordesillas, drawing a line some 1100 miles west of the Cape Verde Islands.

All undiscovered lands to the west of the demarcation line belonged to Spain. Those to the east were Portugal's. Inadvertently, Ferdinand and Isabella had given away the easternmost portion of South America. In 1500 a Portuguese mariner, Pedro Alvares Cabral, laid claim to this territory, which came to be known as Brazil. The Spanish monarchs claimed title to everything else, which of course left nothing for emerging nation-states like France and England.

The Spanish monarchs used their strong army, seasoned by its struggle for unification, as a weapon to conquer the Americas. These conquistadores did so with relish. Befitting their crusader's ideology, they agreed to subdue the natives and, with the support of church leaders, convert them to Roman Catholicism. Bravery and courage, these warriors believed, would bring distinction to themselves and to their nation. Further, they could gain much personal wealth, even if shared with the Crown. Gold, glory, and the gospel formed a triad of factors motivating the Spanish conquistadores, and their efforts resulted in a far-flung empire known as New Spain.

Conquistadores Overrun Native Americans

Before 1510, the Spanish confined their explorations and settlements to the Caribbean islands. The conquistadores met with Indians, searched diligently for rare metals and spices, and listened to tales of fabulous cities of gold somewhere over the horizon. Most natives remained friendly, but in some locales they were hostile; in the Lesser Antilles the cannibalistic Caribs dined on more than one Spanish warrior.

Unwittingly, the conquistadores carried their own weapons of retaliation against all Indians—friend and foe alike. Natives on all the islands lacked the antibodies to fend off European diseases. Smallpox, typhoid, diphtheria, the measles, and various plagues and fevers took a rapid and devastating toll. In 1492 more than 200,000 Indians inhabited Hispaniola. Just twenty years later, there were fewer than 30,000.

After 1510, the conquistadores moved onto the mainland. Vasco Núñez de Balboa reached Panama in 1513. He organized an exploratory party, cut across the isthmus, and became the first European to see the Pacific Ocean, which he dutifully claimed for Spain. The same year Juan Ponce de Léon, governor of Puerto Rico, led a party to Florida in search of gold and a rumored fountain of youth. Although disappointed on both counts, he claimed Florida for Spain.

Then in 1519 Hernando Cortés, a leader of great bravado, mounted his dramatic expedition against the Aztecs. Landing on the Mexican coast with 600 soldiers, his party began a difficult overland march toward Tenochtitlán. Along the way Cortés won tribes subservient to the Aztecs to his side. These natives may have thought him a god. They certainly admired his

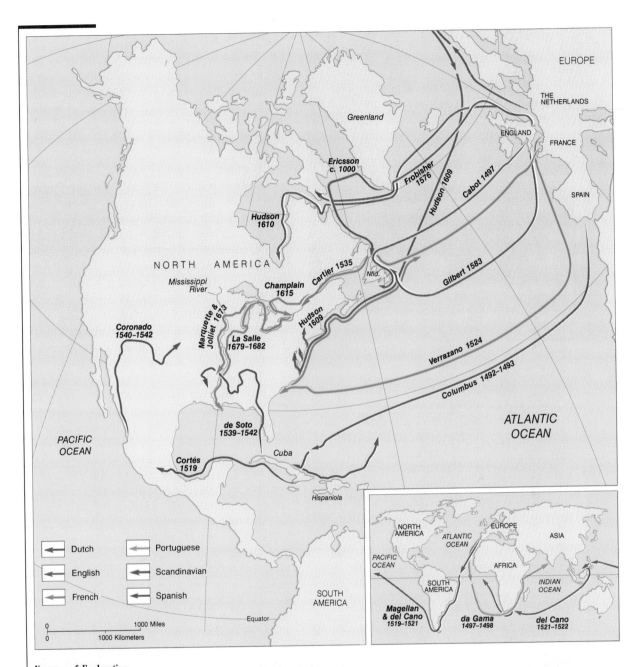

Voyages of Exploration

Except for an abortive attempt by Norsemen in the tenth century, contact between North America and Europe began at the end of the 1400s. In the 1500s settlements were founded by Spain in Mexico and Florida, and in the early 1600s France, England, Sweden, and Holland claimed settlements along the Atlantic coast.

This Aztec drawing presumably represents Cortés's conquering of Tenochtitlán in 1519–22.

Even Cortés was sick from the stench in his nostrils." It has been estimated that the spread of European diseases resulted in seventeen major epidemics in the Americas during the sixteenth century—there were fourteen in Europe. One of these seventeen epidemics wreaked such havoc among the Aztecs that it destroyed their ability to continue effective resistance.

Cortés's stunning triumph spurred on many other soldiers, such as Francisco Pizarro. With fewer than 200 men, he overwhelmed thousands of Incas in Peru, seizing the capital city of Cuzco in 1533 with hardly any fighting. Again, diseases stalked wherever Pizarro went. The Incan rulers, paralyzed by fear, provided little leadership in fending off the Spanish and their powerful germ allies. Pizarro showed no mercy; he executed the great chief Atahualpa and proclaimed Spain's sovereignty. By the 1550s, conquistadores had conquered much of the rest of South America.

To the north, various expeditions scoured the landscape but found nothing comparable to the wealth of the Aztecs and Incas. Four hundred men under Pánfilo de Narváez began a disastrous adventure in 1528; they landed in Florida and searched the Gulf Coast region before being shipwrecked in Texas. Only four men survived, and one, Cabeza de Vaca, wrote a tract telling of seven great cities laden with gold. Vaca's writings stimulated Hernando de Soto and 600 others, beginning in 1539, to investigate the lower Mississippi River valley. In 1540 another party under Francisco Vásquez de Coronado began exploring parts of New Mexico, Texas, Oklahoma, and Kansas. They were the first Europeans to see the Grand Canyon. In 1542–43 sailors under Juan Rodriguez Cabrillo sailed along the California coast as far north as Oregon. None of these groups ever located the fabled cities, but they advanced geographic knowledge of North America while claiming everything before them for Spain.

horses—unknown to America—as well as the armor and weapons of his soldiers. Yet so small a party, even if well-armed, could never have prevailed over thousands of Aztec warriors, if other factors had not intervened.

Aztec emperor Montezuma II, who feared that Cortés was the old Toltec war god Quetzalcoatl coming back to destroy the Aztecs, tried to keep the Spaniards out of Tenochtitlán. He offered mounds of gold and silver, but this gesture only magnified the conquistadores' greed. They boldly marched into the city and took Montezuma prisoner. The Aztecs finally drove off Cortés's party in 1520, but not before smallpox had broken out. Less than a year later, the Spaniards retook Tenochtitlán and claimed all Aztec wealth and political authority as their prize.

Carried away with success, Cortés's soldiers razed the city. They boasted of their great prowess as warriors and the superiority of their weapons. They even claimed that God had willed their victory. But the germs they brought were the true victors. As one participant wrote, when they reentered the city, "the streets, squares, houses, and courts were filled with bodies, so that it was almost impossible to pass.

Constructing the Spanish Empire

To keep out intruders and to maintain order in New Spain, the Spanish Crown set up two home-based administrative agencies in Madrid.

Made in 1551, this Spanish map shows that the unknown interior of America was filled with Indians, birds, and deer. More details were filled in as various explorations continued.

The House of Trade formulated economic policies and provided for annual convoys of galleons, called plate fleets, to haul American booty back to Spain. The Council for the Indies controlled all political matters in what became an autocratic, rigidly managed empire for the exclusive benefit of the parent state.

The Council for the Indies ruled through viceroys heading four regional areas of administration. Viceroys, in turn, consulted with *audiencias* (appointed councils) on matters of local concern, but there were no popularly-based representative assemblies. Normally, only pure-blooded Spaniards could influence decision-making—and only if they had ties to councilors or viceroys. Those who questioned their political superiors found little tolerance for divergent opinions.

During the sixteenth century about 200,000 Spaniards, a modest number, migrated to the Americas. There was plenty of work at home, and Spain's population was in decline, reflecting the government's constant warfare in Europe. Most migrants were young males looking for adventure and quick profits. They found little of each, but some became wealthy as manor holders, ranchers, miners, and government officials.

From the very outset, Spanish settlers complained about a shortage of laborers. One solution was the *encomienda* system, initially approved by the Crown to reward conquistadores for outstanding service. Favored warriors and settlers received land titles to Indian villages and the surrounding countryside. As *encomenderos,* or landlords, they agreed to educate the natives under their jurisdiction and guarantee instruction in the Roman Catholic faith. In return, the landlords gained control of the labor of whole villages of Indians and received portions of annual crops and other forms of tribute in recognition of their efforts to "civilize" the native populace.

There were serious problems with the *encomienda* system. Landlords regularly abused the Indians, treating them like slave property. They maimed or put troublemakers to death and bought and sold many others as if they were commodities. There was so much exploitation and death that one Dominican priest, Bartolomé de Las Casas (1474–1566), later a bishop in southern Mexico, repeatedly begged officials in Madrid to stop such barbarities.

In 1542 the Crown settled the issue by outlawing both the *encomienda* system and the enslavement of Indians. This ruling did not change matters that much. Governing officials continued to award pure-blooded Spaniards vast estates *(haciendas),* on which Indians lived in a state of peonage, cultivating the soil and sharing their crops with their *hacienda* landlords *(hacendados).*

Since the native populace also kept dying from contact with European diseases, another solution to the labor problem was to import Africans. In 1501 the Crown authorized the first shipment of slaves to the Caribbean islands, a small beginning to what became a vast, forced migration of some 10 million human beings to the Americas.

Slavery as it developed in New Spain was harsh. *Hacienda* owners and mine operators

Intermarriage between Spanish men and Indian noblewomen was encouraged in Colonial Spanish America. However, children of mixed blood did not have the same rights as full-blooded Spaniards, who were at the apex of Spanish-American society.

wanted only young males who could literally be worked to death, then replaced by new shiploads of Africans. On the other hand, Spanish law and Roman Catholic doctrine curbed some brutality. The church believed that all souls should be saved, and it recognized marriage as a sacrament, meaning that slaves could aspire to family life. Spanish law even allowed slaves to purchase their freedom. Many blacks, particularly those who became artisans and house servants in the cities, did manage to gain their independence.

Also easing slavery's harsh realities was the matter of skin color gradation. The lighter the skin, the greater were the privileges. Pure-blooded natives of Spain *(peninsulares)* were at the apex of society. Next came the creoles *(criollos),* or whites born in New Spain. Since so many of the first Spanish migrants were males, they often intermarried with Indians, their children forming the *mestizo* class; or they intermarried with Africans, their children making up the *mulatto* class. The mixture of skin colors in New Spain helped Africans escape some of the racial contempt experienced by blacks in English North America, where there was less skin color variation because of legal restrictions against racial intermarriage.

Success Breeds Envy and Contempt

Still, most slaves and Indians lived in privation at the bottom of society. Many church officials, as suggested by the pleas of Las Casas, sought to ease their burdens. As Spanish authority spread north into areas like New Mexico, Arizona, and California, Dominican and Jesuit friars opened missions and offered protection to all those natives who would accept Roman Catholic beliefs. Las Casas even went so far as to denounce the enslavement of Africans, but the Crown ignored him, realizing that without slavery there would be fewer shipments of gold, silver, and other commodities back to Spain.

As it took shape, then, New Spain contained many sharp contrasts. Great cathedrals and universities could not overshadow the endemic poverty of Indian and *mestizo* villagers on the *haciendas* and the brutal treatment of slaves in the mines. These contrasts reflected the acquisitive beginnings of Spain's American empire, which operated first and foremost as a treasure chest for the Spanish monarchs back in Madrid.

The flow of wealth made Spain the most powerful—and envied—nation in Europe during the sixteenth century. Such success also became a source of contempt. When Las Casas, for example, published *A Very Brief Relation of the Destruction of the Indies* (1552), he described the Indians as "patient, meek, and peaceful . . . lambs" whom bloodthirsty conquistadores had "cruelly and inhumanely butchered." Las Casas's list of atrocities became the basis of the "Black Legend," a tale that other Europeans started using as a rationale for challenging Spain's New World supremacy. The other Europeans promised to treat Native Americans more humanely, but in reality, their primary motivation was to garner some of America's riches for themselves.

CHALLENGERS FOR NORTH AMERICA: FRANCE AND ENGLAND

When Henry VII of England realized how successful Columbus had been, he chose to ignore the Treaty of Tordesillas and underwrote another Italian explorer, Giovanni Caboto (John Cabot), to seek Cathay on behalf of the Tudor monarchy. Cabot's expedition was the first to touch North America since the Viking voyages. He landed on Newfoundland and Cape Breton Island in 1497. A second expedition in 1498 ended in disaster when Cabot was lost at sea, but his voyages became the basis for English claims to North America.

France soon joined the exploration race. In 1524 King Francis I authorized yet another Italian mariner, Giovanni da Verrazzano, to sail westward. He tracked along the American coast from North Carolina to Maine. Unfortunately, during another voyage in 1528, he died somewhere in the Lesser Antilles where the Caribs dined on his carcass. More important for later French claims, Jacques Cartier mounted three expeditions to the St. Lawrence River area, beginning in 1534. He scouted as far inland as modern-day Quebec and Montreal. Cartier even started a colony in 1541–42, but there was too much internal turmoil in France to sustain support for permanent settlements.

Verrazzano and Cartier were among the first to show interest in finding an all-water route—the "Northwest Passage"—through North America to the Orient. This was a response to the epic voyage of Ferdinand Magellan (1519–22) under the Spanish flag. Magellan's party circumnavigated the globe around South America and proved, once and for all, that the world was round and that there was vast ocean space between America and Asia. Searching for the Northwest Passage was a means of avoiding New Spain while gaining access to Oriental wealth, since no one, as yet, had found readily extractable riches in North America. It was also a way of dismissing the worldwide pretensions of Portugal and Spain, particularly after 1529 when these two powers extended the demarcation line down through the Pacific Ocean.

The Protestant Reformation Stirs National Tensions

Throughout the sixteenth century, England and France did not directly challenge Spain's supremacy in the Americas. There were too many problems at home, especially those related to religious turmoil. The Protestant Reformation shattered the unity of the Roman Catholic church, convulsed Europe, and provoked national wars. At the same time, the Reformation helped stimulate many Europeans, feeling repression because of their new-found beliefs, to think about westward expansion. This would be particularly true in England.

The Catholic church was the most powerful institution in medieval Europe. On occasion, dissenters emerged, but they invariably burned at the stake for their heresies. Then in 1517 Martin Luther, an obscure monk and close student of the Bible, tacked "Ninety-Five Theses" on a church door in Wittenberg, Germany. He wanted to reform what he thought were unscriptural practices, in particular the selling of indulgences, or payments to assure prayers easing the

Martin Luther

journeys of loved ones through purgatory to heaven. After some consideration, the church excommunicated him, but the German monk refused to recant.

Luther's ideas caught on quickly. Many Europeans resented the worldly political ambitions of church leaders and the haughtiness of poorly-trained village priests. Luther insisted that people did not need priests to interpret scriptures but should be allowed to read the Bible for themselves. Faith in God, not good works, was essential to gaining divine favor. He thus advocated a "priesthood of all believers" in comprehending the mysteries of Christianity. By the 1550s, Lutheranism had spread over much of Germany and the Scandinavian countries, accompanied by enormous social turmoil.

Once underway, the Reformation gained rapid momentum. It also took on many forms. In England, politics rather than theology dictated the split with Rome. Henry VIII (1509–1547) prided himself on his devotion to Catholicism.

In 1521 he published a *Defense of the Seven Sacraments,* which castigated Luther for arguing in favor of only two sacraments—baptism and communion. The Pope responded by awarding Henry a new title, "Defender of the Faith." At the same time, Henry worried about the succession to his throne. His queen, Catherine of Aragon, daughter of Ferdinand and Isabella, bore him a daughter named Mary. Henry needed a male heir to assure perpetuation of the Tudor line. In 1527 he asked the Pope to annul his marriage. When the Pope refused, Henry severed all ties with Rome.

Henry's actions were also spurred by his infatuation with Anne Boleyn, who bore him Elizabeth before being beheaded as an accused adulteress. Through a series of parliamentary acts, Henry closed monasteries and seized church property. In the 1534 Act of Supremacy, he formally repudiated the Pope and declared himself God's regent over England. Henceforth, all subjects would belong to the Anglican (English) church. The Church of England, unlike Lutheranism, was similar to Roman Catholicism in doctrine and ritual.

After his death, Henry's reformation became a source of internal political chaos. When "Bloody" Mary I (1553–58) came to the throne, she tried to return England to the Roman Catholic faith. Her government persecuted Protestants relentlessly, sending hundreds to the stake. Many church leaders fled the land, and some of these "Marian exiles" went to Geneva, Switzerland, to study with John Calvin, whose biblical ideas formed the basis of the Reformed Protestant tradition.

John Calvin was a French lawyer who had fled to Switzerland because of his controversial theological ideas. A brilliant and persuasive man, he soon controlled Geneva and ordered life there according to his understanding of scripture. Calvin believed God to be both all-powerful and wrathful. To avoid eternal damnation, it was necessary to gain His grace through a conversion experience denoted by accepting Jesus Christ as one's savior. However, while all had to seek, God had already predestined who would be saved and who would be damned. Since it was difficult to discern God's chosen "saints," Calvin taught that correct moral be-

Figure 1.1
The Tudor Monarchy of England

Henry VII (1485-1509) m.
Elizabeth of York,
daughter of Edward IV

Henry VIII (1509-1547) m.
various wives

by Catherine of Aragon   by Anne Boleyn   by Jane Seymour

Mary I
(1553-1558)

Edward VI
(1547-1553)

Elizabeth I (1558-1603)

havior according to the Bible and outward prosperity, physical and mental as well as material, represented possible signs of divine favor.

John Calvin

Individuals disenchanted with Catholicism studied Calvin's famous *Institutes of the Christian Religion* (1536). Many, like the Marian exiles, went to Geneva to learn more. Then they returned to their homelands determined to set up godly communities. Their numbers included founders of the German and Dutch Reformed churches, as well as Huguenots in France who eventually suffered from organized state persecution. John Knox, another disciple of Calvin, set up the Presbyterian church in Scotland.

The Marian exiles began reappearing in England after 1558. In time, they developed a large following, calling themselves Puritans. They wanted to advance Henry's reformation along theological lines. Fiercely dedicated to their beliefs, they had a startling impact on the course of English history, particularly after the reign of Elizabeth I (1558–1603), when some of them moved to North America and others caused a civil war.

Incessant European Warfare

Spain's success in the Americas in combination with religious disagreements between Catholics and Protestants fostered unending turmoil among sixteenth-century nation-states. Some of the tension related to America, where French, Dutch, and English "sea dogs" attacked Spanish commerce or traded covertly within the empire. Some related to attempted French Huguenot settlements in South Carolina and Florida. Spain, cast as the primary defender of Roman Catholicism, fought back, using wealth extracted from America to support military forces capable of protecting its interests.

France remained overwhelmingly Roman Catholic but was at first tolerant of the Hugue-

nots. Leaders, however, did encourage Huguenot settlements in America as a way of ridding the realm of these zealous dissenters. During the 1550s, the Crown permitted a party to colonize off the coast of Brazil, but the Portuguese wiped them out. In 1562 another group located in South Carolina, but food shortages finished off that effort. Then in 1564 there was a third colonization attempt, this time involving 142 men, women, and children. They chose northern Florida for their Fort Caroline settlement.

Spanish officials responded decisively. In 1565 they sent out a small army under Pedro Menéndez de Aviles, who first constructed a Spanish fort at St. Augustine (the beginnings of the oldest city in North America), then turned on the Huguenots. Menéndez's party massacred the Fort Caroline settlers. Just to make sure other outsiders, especially Protestants, understood the danger of locating so close to New Spain, Menéndez ordered his soldiers to hack up the bodies before dumping the remains into a river. The butchery of Menéndez helped put an end to sixteenth-century French settlement ventures.

Raids on Spanish treasure ships created another source of tension. As early as the 1520s, French freebooters started attacking Spanish vessels. But the most daring of the sea dogs were Englishmen like John Hawkins and Francis Drake. During the 1560s and 1570s, Hawkins traded illegally and raided for booty in New Spain. Drake's adventures were even more dramatic. With private financial backing, including funds from the Queen, he began a voyage in 1577 that took him around the globe. Drake attacked wherever Spanish ports-of-call existed before returning home in 1580. Elizabeth gratefully dubbed him a knight, not only for being the first Englishman to circle the globe, but also for securing a 4600 percent profit for investors.

Elizabeth's professions of innocence to the contrary, King Philip II of Spain suspected her of actively supporting the sea dogs, whom he considered piratical scum. Further, he was furious with the English for giving military aid to the Protestant Dutch, who since 1567 had been fighting to free themselves of Spanish rule. Philip so despised Elizabeth that he conspired with her Catholic cousin Mary Stuart, Queen of

With the defeat of the Spanish Armada in 1588, England established itself as a naval power in Europe and helped clear the way for much of the expansion in the west.

Scots, to overthrow the English Protestant government. Always wary of plots, Elizabeth had Mary beheaded in 1587, at which point Philip decided to conquer the troublesome English heretics.

Philip and his military advisers pulled together an armada of Spanish ships. They planned to sail through the English Channel, pick up thousands of troops fighting the Dutch, and then invade England. The expedition ended in disaster, however, when English vessels under Drake's command appeared in the Channel and offered battle. Then the famous "Protestant Wind" took over and blew the Spanish Armada to bits. The war with Spain did not officially end until 1604, but the destruction of the Armada in 1588 established England's

reputation as a naval power. It also demonstrated that little England, heretofore a minor country, could prevail over Europe's most powerful nation, which encouraged taking the risk of founding settlements in America.

England Prepares for Westward Expansion

England's population grew dramatically in the sixteenth century, doubling in size and reaching nearly 4 million people by the 1590s. Yet opportunities for employment lagged behind the population explosion. The phenomenal growth of the woolens industry, for instance, forced peasants from the land as manor lords enclosed their farmland fields to make pastures for sheep. By 1600, there were three times as many sheep as people in England. Cities like London became havens for unemployed persons, many of whom now subsisted by begging and stealing.

Not only displaced peasants faced serious economic difficulties. Farmers owning their own land confronted a major problem of rapid inflation. The cost of many necessities rose by up to five times between 1500 and 1600, but agricultural produce, despite the enclosure movement, did not increase as fast. Real income declined, and heavy taxes under the Tudors left many yeoman farmers destitute. In time, the abundant land of America attracted many of England's failing independent farmers and permanently poor (or sturdy beggars).

A few citizens did prosper in the wake of economic dislocation and inflation, among them manufacturers of woolen goods and merchants who made all of Europe a marketplace for English products. With their profits, these gentlemen of capital gained social respectability by purchasing landed estates and by marrying into England's nobility. Now members of the gentry class, they started pooling their capital and sponsoring risky overseas business ventures by investing in joint-stock trading companies.

In 1555 the Crown chartered the Muscovy Company, giving it the exclusive right to develop England's trade with Russia. Having a monopoly made the venture more attractive to potential stockholders, who could invest according to their personal willingness to take risks. The tight-fisted Tudors liked this model of business organization because private capital rather than royal funds would be employed to underwrite England's economic—and eventually political—expansion abroad. The Crown, of course, would share in any profits.

The Muscovy Company was a success, and other joint-stock ventures followed, such as the East India Company, chartered in 1600 to develop England's Far Eastern interests. Then in 1606 a charter for the Virginia Company gained royal approval. Ironically, even though this business venture failed its stockholders, its efforts did produce England's first enduring colony in North America.

JOINING IN THE INVASION OF AMERICA

England's path to America lay through Ireland. On and off over four centuries, there had been sporadic raids on the "wild" Irish, as the English thought of their Gaelic-speaking neighbors. During Elizabeth's reign, these forays became routine. The goal was to gain political control of Ireland. The queen and her favorites also hoped to establish agricultural colonies because ample food supplies had become a problem at home with the spreading enclosure movement.

Elizabeth named as governor one of her favorites, Sir Humphrey Gilbert, and instructed him to subdue the Irish. Gilbert did so with a vengeance, operating as if the only good Irish subject was one whose head had been cut off. The Irish, a million strong, fought back relentlessly, causing the English "plantations" there to exist precariously as military outposts in an alien environment.

For Elizabethan courtiers, Ireland became a laboratory for learning how to crush one's adversaries. Assumptions of cultural superiority abetted the onslaught. The English conquerors castigated the Irish, who were Roman Catholics, calling them religious heathens. They faulted them for using the land improperly, since the Irish were not sedentary farmers but

Sir Humphrey Gilbert

people of migratory habits who tilled the soil only when they needed food. England's expansionists held these same attitudes when they began American settlements. This time, though, the Indians would be the wild, unkempt people in need of subjugation or eradication.

The Roanoke Disaster

Sir Humphrey Gilbert was as intolerant and contemptuous of the Spanish as he was of the

Irish. It bothered him that Spain claimed everything in America. He dreamed of finding the Northwest Passage to facilitate a flow of Oriental riches to England, and he was willing to risk his personal fortune in the quest. Gilbert had other dreams as well, including the effective occupation of North America and the founding of American colonies. He appealed to Elizabeth for exclusive rights to carry out his plans, and she acceded in 1578.

Gilbert's patent represented an important statement of future guidelines for England's westward expansion. On the monarch's authority, he could occupy "heathen and barbarous lands . . . not actually possessed of any Christian prince or people." He would share in profits from extractable wealth, as would the Crown. Even more significant, prospective settlers would be assured the same rights of Englishmen "as if they were born and personally resident" at home. Not guaranteeing fundamental liberties would have inhibited the development of English colonies.

Gilbert did not live to see his dreams fulfilled. He disappeared in a North Atlantic storm after searching for the Northwest Passage. In 1584 his half-brother, Sir Walter Raleigh, requested permission to carry on Gilbert's work. Elizabeth agreed, and Raleigh went into motion. He sent out a reconnoitering party, which explored the North Carolina coast and surveyed Roanoke Island. Then in 1585 he sponsored an expedition of 600 men, many of them veterans of the Irish wars. After some raiding for booty in New Spain, Raleigh's adventurers sailed north and dropped off 107 men under Governor Ralph Lane at the chosen site.

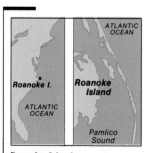

Roanoke Island

Lane's party found the local Croatoan and Roanoak Indians to be friendly. Then diseases struck. "That people," an eyewitness wrote, "began to die very fast, and many in short space." In the spring of 1586, a local chief, Wingina, probably trying to get his tribe away from an illness "so strange that they neither knew what it was, nor how to cure it," moved inland. Ralph Lane went after the natives and ordered an attack, during which one of his men beheaded Wingina, in the tradition of dealing with "wild" Irishmen. Fortunately for Lane, Sir Francis Drake, completing a raiding expedition against New Spain, appeared and carried the English party away before the Indians counterattacked.

Raleigh persisted; he decided to send out families in 1587, with John White, a capable, gentle person, as their governor. White had been on the 1585 expedition. Besides preparing many famous drawings of native life in the Roanoke area, he had spoken out against butchering the Indians. White and the other 114 settlers arrived on Roanoke Island in late July. In mid-August, his daughter Elinor gave birth to Virginia Dare, the first English subject born in America. A few days later, White sailed back to England to obtain additional supplies. The war with Spain delayed his return, and he did not get back to Roanoke until 1590. Nothing was left, except the word CROATOAN carved on a tree.

What happened to the lost colony will never be known. No European ever saw the settlers again. Local Indians either killed them or absorbed them into their tribes. As for Raleigh, he found himself in desperate financial straits. All that was left was a patent that Raleigh turned over to others during the 1590s, a sense that colonizing in America was a hazardous undertaking at best, and a name, Virginia, which Raleigh had offered in thanks to his patron, Elizabeth, the Virgin Queen.

Merchant Capitalists Sponsor the Founding of Virginia

During the 1590s, English courtiers and merchant capitalists disdained further American ventures. The ongoing war with Spain took precedence, and profits came easily from capturing Spanish vessels on the high seas. But once the war ended, influential merchants were anxious to pool their capital, spread the financial risk, and pursue Raleigh's patent. They took their case to Elizabeth's successor, the Stuart monarch James I (1603–1625), who willingly

John White captured the life-style of natives of Roanoke Island in his famous drawings. This one, depicting the Village of Secoton, shows a fire built for solemn prayer at the bottom left, and a ceremony of prayer bottom right.

granted them a generous trading company charter.

James, like his predecessor, accepted the rationale for English expansion as articulated in Richard Hakluyt's *Discourse* (1584) and other influential writings. Hakluyt had written of American settlements as the key to national greatness. Besides putting sturdy beggars and other indigents back to work, colonies would be a source of valuable commodities. They would stimulate the shipbuilding industry. They would help "enlarge the glory of the gospel" by offering the Indians "sincere religion" in the form of the Anglican church. Furthermore, Hakluyt argued, there could never be "humanity, courtesy,

and freedom" in America, unless England challenged Spain's supremacy and offered "liberty" to oppressed Native Americans. As with other New World colonizers, the English considered their motives to be pure on all counts, but what really mattered most were profits for investors.

This is hardly surprising, since joint-stock companies existed to make profits. The Virginia Company was no exception. There were two sets of investors. The first, a group of London merchants, held Raleigh's patent. They had made profits by investing in other joint-stock ventures and were ready to take further risks. Foolishly, they dreamed of heaping piles of gold and silver, but more realistically, they hoped to trade for valuable commodities with the Indians and to plant vineyards and silk-producing mulberry trees. The London merchants had first claim to all land between the Cape Fear River in southern North Carolina and present-day New York City.

In December 1606, they sent out 144 adventurers under Captain Christopher Newport on the *Susan Constant, Godspeed,* and *Discovery.* The crossing was difficult, and thirty-nine men died. In May 1607, the survivors located on an island some forty miles up the James River off Chesapeake Bay. They called their settlement Jamestown.

The second set of investors were from West Country port towns like Plymouth. In response to bitter complaints over the years about London's dominance of joint-stock ventures, the Virginia Company charter granted the merchants of Plymouth lands lying between the mouth of the Potomac River and northern Maine, which meant there was an

ATLANTIC OCEAN

Overlapping Grants

Grant to Virginia Co. of London, 1606

Grant to Virginia Co. of Plymouth, 1606

Map shows present-day boundaries

Conflicting Land Claims

overlapping middle zone that both investor groups could develop, as long as their settlements were at least 100 miles apart.

The West Country merchants hoped to reap profits from harvesting America's timber,

INDIAN SCALPING AND EUROPEAN WAR DOGS

When Native Americans and Europeans first came into contact, each seemed genuinely curious about the other. Curiosity, however, soon turned to mistrust, and mistrust to a state of unending warfare. Both sides employed "the tactics of remorseless terrorism" in their combat, as one student of early white-Indian relations has written, because both were fighting for control of the landscape— the Indians to retain their ancient tribal homes and the Europeans to inhabit the same.

In their life-and-death struggle, Europeans and Indians drew upon long-accepted styles of waging combat. Neither showed much mercy toward the other. Europeans rationalized their acts of butchery by claiming that they were dealing with "savages" who were at best "inhumanely cruel" and at worst "carnivorous beasts of the forest." Because of language barriers, the thoughts of Native Americans are not known, but they learned to hate the invaders from across the ocean, and they too fought with a vengeance, although often with more mercy than Europeans.

Long before the English first made contact, Eastern Woodland Indians regularly engaged in small-scale, intertribal wars. Their weapons included bows and arrows, knives, tomahawks, spears, and clubs. War parties did not attack in battle formations but used the forest as their cover as they ambushed enemies in surprise, guerilla-like raids. Employing hit-and-run tactics, intertribal combat rarely resulted in much bloodshed, since battles invariably lasted a few minutes before attacking warriors melted back into the forest.

When possible, Indian war parties celebrated their victories by the taking of enemy scalps, which for them were war trophies filled with religious meaning. Native Americans believed that the piece of scalp and hair carefully sliced from an enemy's head contained the victim's living spirit, which now belonged to the holder of the scalp. To take a scalp, then, was to gain control over that person's spirit *(manitou)*. Even if victims survived scalping, which happened on occasion, they were spiritually dead, since they no longer possessed the essence of human life.

Because of their spiritual meaning and power, scalps were treated with great respect. Indians decorated them with jewelry and paint, and warriors kept them on display, even strapping them on their belts as symbols of individual prowess. In other instances, warriors gave scalps to families who had lost relatives in battle. Since they contained life, scalps took the place of deceased tribal members.

When Europeans first saw scalps, they did not know what to think. They certainly attached no spiritual significance to them. Frenchman Jacques Cartier, exploring along the St. Lawrence River in 1535, wrote about local Indians who showed him "the skins of five men's heads, stretched on hoops, like parchment." The local chief explained that the scalps were from Micmacs living to "the south, who waged war continually against his peo-

28

ple." Just five years later in west Florida, natives killed two Spanish conquistadores exploring with Hernando de Soto. The Indians then "removed" the "head" of one victim, "or rather all around his skull—it is unknown with what skill they removed it with great ease—and carried it off as evidence of their deed."

Europeans quickly concluded that scalping was typical of the barbarous cultural practices of "savage" Native Americans. Also frightening was the way in which Indians conducted combat. They would not stand and fight in "civilized" fashion, holding to linear formations as Europeans did. Rather, "they are always running and traversing from one place to another," complained de Soto, making it impossible for musket-wielding Europeans to shoot them down. Worse yet, an expert Indian bowman could easily "discharge three or four arrows" with great accuracy by the time musketeers went through the elaborate steps of preparing their cumbersome weapons for firing. This made combat with Native Americans particularly dangerous because, as de Soto concluded, an Indian bowman "seldom misses what he shoots at."

The Indian style of fighting caused a stream of negative commentary from the first European New World adventurers. Natives did not fight fairly but used "cunning tricks" and "slippery designs" to defeat their adversaries. Rather than engaging in manly combat, they were "as greedy after their prey as a wolf," wanting above all else to mutilate their opponents by taking their scalps. The only effective way to counter Indian tactics, reasoned the Europeans, was to employ the most brutal forms of

corporal punishment in use during the sixteenth and seventeenth centuries.

In times of combat, the Europeans treated Indians as if they were criminals. This meant that natives, in various combinations, would be hanged, drawn and quartered, disemboweled, and like the "savage" and "wild" Irish, beheaded. Captain Miles Standish, charged with protecting the Pilgrims, killed one troublesome Indian and then carried his head back to Plymouth where he had it publicly displayed. When the Dutch in New Netherland went to war with local natives in the 1640s, they regularly beheaded their opponents and had their "gory heads . . . laid in the streets of New Amsterdam, where the governor's mother kicked them like footballs."

Such wanton cruelty, when measured by modern standards, recently resulted in claims from some students of Native American history that Indians, before making contact with Europeans, did not scalp their enemies. Scalping, they claimed, was modeled on beheading but was a more efficient means of gaining war trophies for highly-mobile Indian warriors not wanting to carry the extra weight of human heads.

Designed to demonstrate the "barbarous" influence of "civilized" Europeans expanding westward, this line of reasoning has been thoroughly refuted. Among other forms of evidence, Indian cultural traditions and the surprise of explorers who first saw scalps support the conclusion that Europeans learned about scalping from Indians and soon incorporated the practice into their arsenal of punishments.

In at least one area, however, European adventurers reached

beyond accepted methods for exacting terror, pain, and death. The Spanish conquistadores used war dogs to maim and kill their victims. The English, who during the sixteenth century reveled in horror stories about Spanish New World barbarities (the so-called "Black Legend"), thought of war dogs as a new low point in human warfare. Yet within a few years of founding their first settlements, the English were training and unleashing war dogs on Native Americans.

Apparently the favored breed was the English Mastiff. These were huge, ugly dogs, weighing up to 150 pounds and naturally protective of their masters. In sixteenth-century England their owners trained them to "bait the bear, to bait the bull and other such like cruel and bloody beasts." The next logical step was to turn these dogs loose on the "heavy beast" in America. In retaliation for Opechancanough's 1622 massacre of Virginians, surviving settlers used dogs, presumably mastiffs, to track and kill local Indians. War dogs participated in the slaughter of Pequot Indians of New England during the 1630s and performed similar duty throughout the colonial period.

If prospects of facing the scalping knife filled European New World settlers with fear, war dogs, whether on guard duty or on the attack, represented an "extreme terror to the Indians," as one New England minister wrote in the early eighteenth century. This clergyman wanted yet more dogs "trained up to hunt Indians as they do the bear." He understood the nature of "total war" between whites and Indians in the bloody contest for the Americas, and he wanted to survive.

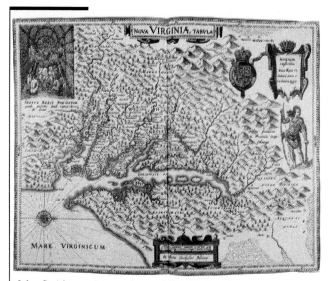

John Smith, a prime explorer of Virginia, published this map with an accompanying description of the country in 1612.

from fur trading with the natives, and from fishing off the New England coast, which had been going on for a century. They dispatched a party in 1607, which located at Sagadahoc, Maine, near the mouth of the Kennebec River. These forty-four adventurers squabbled incessantly among themselves and did not maintain good relations with the Indians. Those who survived the first winter gave up and returned home in 1608. The Plymouth investors refused to expend more funds, and their patent fell dormant—to be revived at a later date.

As with the Irish invasion, both groups of adventurers arrived in military fashion. They built forts to protect themselves from unfriendly natives and Spanish raiding parties. In its early days, Jamestown functioned as an outpost in another alien environment. Most of the participants wanted to get in, gain access to some easy form of wealth, and get out before losing their lives.

Jamestown Survives

It is amazing that Jamestown lasted at all; Newport's adventurers were miscast for survival in the wilderness. Many were the second or third sons of English noblemen. Because of primogeniture and entail (laws which specified that only first-born male heirs could inherit landed estates and family titles), these younger sons had to choose alternate careers. Many became lawyers, clergymen, or high-ranking military officers, but few toiled in the fields, as that was not a gentleman's calling. When Jamestown ran short of food, this type of company adventurer still avoided agricultural work, preferring to search for gold and silver, or the Northwest Passage. Some starved to death as a result.

Besides gentleman-adventurers, other equally ill-prepared individuals, such as valets and footmen, joined the expedition, and their duties extended only to waiting on their masters. Then there were goldsmiths and jewelers, plus a collection of ne'er-do-wells who knew no occupation but apparently functioned as soldiers under gentleman officers in dealings with the natives.

The social and economic makeup of these first adventurers suggests that the London investors may have modeled the expedition after the early Spanish conquests—with the idea of forcing the local Indians to become agricultural workers as peons or slaves. As it turned out, the natives supplied food, but even with their assistance, only thirty-eight Englishmen were still alive by the early spring of 1608.

Another problem was the settlement site. Company directors had ordered the adventurers to locate on high ground far enough inland so as to go undetected by the Spanish. Jamestown Island met the second requirement, but it was a low, swampy place lying at a point on the James River where salt and fresh water mingled. The brackish water was "full of slime and filth," one observer noted. The water could cause salt poisoning and was a breeding ground for malaria, typhoid fever, and dysentery.

Several factors saved the Jamestown settlement. The local Indians under Powhatan, an Algonquian-speaking Pamunkey, initially offered sustenance. Powhatan had organized a confederacy of some thirty coastal tribes, involving 20,000 people, to defend themselves against aggressive interior neighbors. The defensive alliance may also have resulted from a serious population decline because of killer diseases long since introduced into the area by Europeans like those at Roanoke.

Powhatan tried to stay clear of the Jamestown adventurers, but when he was around them, he could not help but notice their large ships, shiny body armor, and noisy (though less-than-deadly) firearms. He viewed the English as potential allies in warfare with interior tribes, a faulty evaluation but one that kept him from wiping out the weakened adventurers.

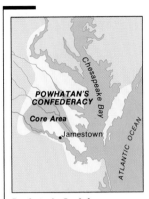

Powhatan's Confederacy

At the same time, company investors in London refused to quit. They kept sending out supplies and adventurers, as many as 800 more young men plus a few women in 1608 and 1609. Upon their arrival, however, many quickly died from diseases such as malaria, and others were too debilitated from warding off illnesses to work, and they became a drain on Jamestown's precarious food supply.

At that time, the dynamic and ruthless local leadership of Captain John Smith kept the colony from totally collapsing. Smith, who loved to boast about his far-flung military exploits, had crossed the Atlantic with the original adventurers. Once in Jamestown, he emerged as a virtual dictator, and he saved many lives by imposing discipline and forcing everyone—gentleman or servant, sick or well—to adhere to one rule: "He who works not, eats not."

In October 1609, Smith returned to England after suffering burns in an accidental explosion of gunpowder. Lacking authoritarian leadership, the settlers experienced a tragic "starving time" during the winter of 1609–10. Hundreds died as food supplies, described as "moldy, rotten, full of cobwebs and maggots," gave out. Only about sixty persons survived by eating everything from rats to snakes, and there was even cannibalism. One man completely lost his mind; he murdered his wife, then "powdered [salted] her up to eat her, for which he was burned" at the stake.

Smith's presence might not have averted the disaster. Too often, he, like the other early adventurers, had treated the Indians with contempt, and bad relations caused Powhatan to shut off food supplies. Yet, for some reason, Powhatan did not seize the opportunity to wipe out Jamestown. Perhaps still hoping for an alliance, he simply allowed the feeble English to die on their own.

Back home, Virginia Company stockholders refused to concede defeat. By 1610, they realized that mineral wealth was an illusion, but still they sent out more people. One of them, John Rolfe, experimented with local tobacco plants, which produced a harsh-tasting crop. Rolfe, too, persisted. He procured some plants from Trinidad in the West Indies and grew a milder, more flavorful leaf. Tobacco soon became Virginia's gold and silver. The colony now had a valuable trading commodity, and settlements quickly spread along the banks of the James River. English subjects had found a reason to stay in the Americas.

Dutch and French Adventurers

In the early 1600s, the Spanish contented themselves with drawing wealth from their Caribbean basin empire. They did not challenge various European interlopers who sought to stake North American claims. Ultimately, Dutch settlements in New York were seized by the English, but France's efforts resulted in a Canadian empire capable of rivaling those of Spain and England.

Once fully liberated from Spanish domination at home, the Dutch grabbed at a portion of North America. In 1609 they sent out an English sea captain, Henry Hudson, to search for the Northwest Passage. He explored Delaware Bay, then the New York waterway that bears his name. Hudson made contact with the Iroquois Indians, probably the Mohawks, and talked of trade in furs. Broad-rimmed beaver hats were the fashion rage in Europe, but fur supplies were giving out. North America could become a new source of pelts, if the Indians would cooperate. The Dutch established trading stations

 HRONOLOGY
OF KEY EVENTS

30,000–20,000 B.C.	Paleo-Indians pass across *Beringia* and enter North America
8000–5000 B.C.	Native Americans face food crisis but save themselves through an agricultural revolution
300 A.D.	(Ca.) Mayan civilization begins to develop
1000	(Ca.) Toltecs and later the Aztecs overrun the Mayas; (Ca.) Vikings explore and briefly settle in Newfoundland
1095	Europeans launch crusades against the Muslim world
1100	(Ca.) Incas construct a wealthy empire
1298–1299	Polo composes a journal about his travels to the Orient
1347–1353	"Black Death" kills one-third of Europe's population

1420s	Prince Henry of Portugal first sends out mariners to explore the west coast of Africa
1450	(Ca.) Gutenberg develops movable type
1469	Ferdinand and Isabella marry and start to unify Spain
1485	Henry Tudor emerges from the Wars of the Roses as king of England

1492	Columbus sails to America, reaches Caribbean islands
1494	Treaty of Tordesillas divides the unknown world between Spain and Portugal
1497	Da Gama begins Portuguese voyage around Africa to India; Cabot coasts along Newfoundland, laying the basis for England's claim to American territory
1517	Luther challenges the Roman Catholic church
1519	Cortés invades Mexico; Magellen begins voyage that circumnavigates globe
1529–1533	Henry VIII leads English Reformation against Roman Catholicism
1533	Pizarro conquers the Incan empire
1534	Cartier reaches the St. Lawrence River and claims region for France
1536	Calvin publishes his *Institutes of the Christian Religion*
1539	De Soto begins Spanish exploration of the lower Mississippi Valley
1540	Coronado launches Spanish exploration of the Southwest
1558	Elizabeth I becomes queen of England
1585	Raleigh sponsors first English attempt to settle Roanoke Island
1588	England defeats the Spanish Armada
1603	James I becomes king of England
1606	Virginia Company receives a joint-stock charter
1607	English adventurers land on Jamestown Island
1608	Champlain establishes a French fur trading post at Quebec
1616–1618	(Ca.) Squanto's Patuxets wiped out by chicken pox
1620	Pilgrims settle in New England

on Manhattan Island (later called New Amsterdam), and Fort Orange (Albany) in 1624. The Iroquois did their part in delivering furs, and the colony of New Netherland took hold under the auspices of the Dutch West India Company.

Profits from furs also helped to motivate the French. In 1608 Samuel de Champlain set up an outpost at Quebec on the St. Lawrence River, and he found local Indians ready to trade. Quebec was the base from which New France spread. Yet only after 1663 when the Crown took control did the French population grow significantly, reaching 10,000 people by the 1680s.

The French Canadians were energetic. Following Champlain's lead, they explored everywhere and claimed everything in sight. They also maintained harmonious relations with dozens of different Indian tribes. They even joined in native wars as a way of solidifying trading ties. The French, with their small numbers, could not impose their cultural values. They did use the natives for their own purposes, but they also showed respect, which paid off handsomely when their many Indian allies willingly fought beside them in a series of imperial wars that beset America beginning in 1689.

CONCLUSION

Except in Canada, the Europeans who explored the Americas and began colonies after 1492 acted as foreign invaders. At first curious, they soon viewed the natives as their adversaries, describing them as "worse than those beasts which are of the most wild and savage nature." Judgments of cultural superiority seemed to justify the destruction of Native Americans.

Still, there was a "Columbian exchange" of sorts. The Indians taught the Europeans about tobacco, corn, potatoes, varieties of beans, peanuts, tomatoes, and many other crops then unknown in Europe. In return, Europeans introduced the native populace to wheat, oats, barley, and rice, as well as to grapes for wine and various melons. The Europeans also brought in domesticated animals, including horses, pigs, sheep, goats, and cattle. Horses

proved to be important, particularly for Great Plains Indians, who used them later in fighting against the encroachment of white settlers, just as tobacco production in the Chesapeake area had the unintended effect of attracting enough Europeans to end native control of that area.

Killer diseases, most of all, served to unbalance the exchange. From the first moments of contact, great civilizations like the Aztecs and more humble groups like Squanto's Patuxets faced devastation. In some cases, the Indians who survived, as in New Spain, had to accept the status of peons. Along the Atlantic coastline, survivors were drawn into the European trading network. In exchange for furs, the Indians wanted firearms to kill yet more animals whose pelts could be traded for still more guns and for alcohol to help them forget, even for a moment, what was happening to them in the wake of European westward expansion.

The English would send the most settlers. They left home for various reasons. Some, like the Pilgrims, crossed the Atlantic to avoid further religious persecution. Others, such as the Puritans, sought to build a holy community that would shine as a light upon Europe. Still others, such as colonists in the Chesapeake Bay area, desired land for growing tobacco. The latter group wanted laborers to help them raise their crops. Unable to enslave the Indians, they ultimately borrowed from the Spanish model and enslaved Africans. In so doing, they forced blacks to enter their settlements in chains and to become a part of a peopling and unpeopling process that shaped the contours of life in colonial America.

REVIEW SUMMARY

During the age of exploration, Europeans expanded outward and discovered new land. At the same time religious and social movements convulsed much of Europe.

> the Portuguese charted Africa and Asia
> the Spanish colonized Latin America
> the English and the French laid claims to sections of North America
> the Protestant Reformation challenged the Roman Catholic church

nation states rose to power

humanism and capitalism altered medieval thinking

The result of the exploration and colonization was a clash between Europeans and Native American populations, which were heirs of different cultures and ways of thinking.

SUGGESTIONS FOR FURTHER READING

OVERVIEWS AND SURVEYS

Charles M. Andrews, *The Colonial Period of American History*, 4 vols. (1934–1938); Daniel J. Boorstin, *The Americans: The Colonial Experience* (1958); James A. Henretta and Gregory H. Nobles, *Evolution and Revolution: American Society, 1600–1820* (1987); Howard Mumford Jones, *O Strange New World* (1967); Alvin M. Josephy, Jr., *The Indian Heritage of America* (1968); Lawrence H. Leder, *America, 1603–1789* (1972); Paul R. Lucas, *American Odyssey, 1607–1789* (1984); Gary B. Nash, *Red, White, and Black: The Peoples of Early America*, 2d. ed. (1982); Jerome R. Reich, *Colonial America* (1984); Richard C. Simmons, *The American Colonies: From Settlement to Independence* (1976); Clarence L. Ver Steeg, *The Formative Years, 1607–1763* (1964); and Wilcomb E. Washburn, *The Indian in America* (1975).

THE FIRST DISCOVERY OF AMERICA

James Axtell, *The European and the Indian* (1981), and *The Invasion Within: The Contest of Culture in Colonial North America* (1981); Henry W. Bowden, *American Indians and Christian Missions: Studies in Cultural Conflict* (1981); William Cronon, *Changes in the Land: Indians, Colonists, and the Ecology of New England* (1983); Alfred W. Crosby, *The Columbian Exchange: Biological and Cultural Consequences of 1492* (1972); William N. Denevan, ed., *The Native Population of the Americas in 1492* (1976); Henry F. Dobyns, *Their Numbers Became Thinned: Native American Population Dynamics in Eastern North America* (1983); Harold E. Driver, *The Indians of North America*, 2d. ed. (1969); Brian M. Fagan, *The Great Journey: The Peopling of Ancient America* (1987); John S. Henderson, *The World of the Ancient Maya* (1981); Francis Jennings, *The Invasion of America: Indians, Colonialism, and the Cant of Conquest* (1975), and *The Ambiguous Iroquois Empire* (1984); Yasuhide Kawashima, *Puritan Justice and the Indian* (1986); Shepard Krech, III, ed., *Indians, Animals, and the Fur Trade* (1981); Calvin Martin, *Keepers of the Game: Indian-Animal Relationships and the Fur Trade* (1978), and ed., *The American Indian and the Problem of History* (1987); Neal Salisbury, *Manitou and Providence: Indians, Europeans, and New England, 1500–1643*

(1982); Bernard Sheehan, *Savagism and Civility: Indians and Englishmen in Colonial Virginia* (1980); Alden T. Vaughan, *The New England Frontier: Puritans and Indians, 1620–1675*, rev. ed. (1979); Carl Waldman and Molly Braun, *Atlas of the North American Indian* (1985); and J. Leitch Wright, Jr., *The Only Land They Knew: American Indians of the Old South* (1981).

PREPARING EUROPE FOR WESTWARD EXPANSION

Paul H. Chapman, *The Norse Discovery of America* (1981); Carlo M. Cipolla, *Guns, Sails, and Empires: Technological Innovation and the Early Phases of European Expansion, 1400–1700* (1966); Alfred W. Crosby, *Ecological Imperialism: The Biological Expansion of Europe, 900–1900* (1986); E. L. Jones, *The European Miracle: Environments, Economics, and Geopolitics in the History of Europe and Asia* (1981); William H. McNeill, *The Rise of the West* (1963), and *Plagues and Peoples* (1976); Frederick J. Pohl, *The Viking Settlements of North America* (1972); and Robert R. Reynolds, *Europe Emerges: Transition Toward an Industrial World-Wide Society, 600–1750* (1961).

EXPLORERS, CONQUERORS, AND THE MAKING OF NEW SPAIN

Charles R. Boxer, *The Portuguese Seaborne Empire* (1969); David Carrasco, *Quetzalcoatl and the Irony of Empire* (1982); Nigel Davies, *The Aztecs* (1973); J. H. Elliott, *Imperial Spain, 1469–1716* (1963), and *The Old World and the New, 1492–1650* (1970); Charles Gibson, *The Aztecs under Spanish Rule* (1964), and *Spain in America* (1966); Clarence H. Haring, *The Spanish Empire in America* (1947); James Lockhart and Stuart B. Schwartz, *Early Latin America: Colonial Spanish America and Brazil* (1983); Alfred Metraux, *The History of the Incas* (1969); Samuel E. Morison, *Christopher Columbus, Mariner* (1956), and *The European Discovery of America: The Southern Voyages, A.D. 1492–1616* (1974); J. H. Parry, *The Age of Reconaissance* (1963), *The Spanish Seaborne Empire* (1966); and *The Discovery of South America* (1974); G. V. Scammell, *The World Encompassed: The First European Maritime Empires* (1981); Tzvetan Todorov, *The Conquest of America* (1984); Nathan Wachtel, *The Vision of the Vanquished* (1977); and Silvio Zavala, *New Viewpoints on the Spanish Colonization of America* (1968).

CHALLENGERS FOR NORTH AMERICA: FRANCE AND ENGLAND

Roland H. Bainton, *Here I Stand: Martin Luther* (1950), and *The Reformation of the Sixteenth Century* (1963); William J. Bouwsma, *John Calvin* (1987); Carl Bridenbaugh, *Vexed and Troubled Englishmen, 1590–1642* (1968); Mildred Campbell, *The English Yeoman under Elizabeth and the Early Stuarts* (1942); Patrick Collinson, *The Elizabethan Puritan Movement* (1967); G. R. Elton, *England under the Tudors,* 2d. ed. (1974); C. H. and Katherine George, *The Protestant Mind of the English Reformation* (1961); Peter Laslett, *The World We Have Lost,* 3d. ed. (1984); Samuel E. Morison, *The European Discovery of America: The Northern Voyages,* A.D. *500–1600* (1971); Wallace Notestein, *The English People on the Eve of Colonization, 1603–1630* (1954); Theodore K. Rabb, *Enterprise and Empire: Merchant Gentry Investment in the Expansion of England, 1575–1630* (1967); Lawrence Stone, *The Crisis of the Aristocracy, 1558–1641* (1965); Michael Walzer, *The Revolution of the Saints* (1968); and Keith Wrightson, *English Society, 1580–1680* (1982).

JOINING IN THE INVASION OF AMERICA

Charles R. Boxer, *The Dutch Seaborne Empire* (1965); Carl Bridenbaugh, *Jamestown, 1544–1699* (1980); Nicholas P. Canny, *The Elizabethan Conquest of Ireland* (1976); Ralph Davis, *The Rise of the Atlantic Economies* (1973); W. J. Eccles, *The Canadian Frontier, 1534–1760,* rev. ed. (1974), and *France in America* (1972); Alice P. Kenney, *Stubborn for Liberty: The Dutch in New York* (1973); Karen O. Kupperman, *Settling with the Indians: English and Indian Cultures in America, 1580–1640* (1980), and *Roanoke: The Abandoned Colony* (1984); James Lang, *Conquest and Commerce: Spain and England in the Americas* (1975); Samuel E. Morison, *Samuel de Champlain* (1972); David B. Quinn, *The Elizabethans and the Irish* (1966), and *North America from Earliest Discovery to First Settlements* (1977); A. L. Rowse, *The Expansion of Elizabethan England* (1955), and *The Elizabethans and America* (1959); George L. Smith, *Religion and Trade in New Netherland* (1973); Allen W. Trelease, *Indian Affairs in Colonial New York* (1960); and Alden T. Vaughan, *American Genesis: Captain John Smith and Virginia* (1975).

CHAPTER 2

Plantations and Cities
Upon a Hill, 1620–1700

NOVA BRITANNIA.

OFFERING MOST

Excellent fruites by Planting in
VIRGINIA.

Exciting all such as be well affected
to further the same.

LONDON
Printed for SAMVEL MACHAM, and are to be sold at
his Shop in Pauls Church-yard, at the
Signe of the Bul-head.
1609.

FIG. II.

PLANTATION

Charleston, July 24th, 1769.

O BE SOLD,

On Thursday the third Day

A CARGO

NINETY-FOUR

PRIME HEALTHY

EGROES,

CONSISTING OF

ty-nine Men, Fifteen Boys,

wenty-four Women, and

xteen Girls.

JUST ARRIVED,

e Brigantine DEMBIA, Fran-

Bare, Master, from SIERRA-

ON, by

DAVID & JOHN DEAS.

Indigo

94.

M

3

F

*J*ohn Punch wanted his freedom. He was a black indentured servant who joined two white indentured servants and tried to flee Virginia in 1640, only to be caught by local residents. Brought before the Governor's council, the colony's highest court, the judges ordered the flogging of each runaway—thirty lashes well-laid-on. Then in a telling ruling, these officials also revealed their thinking about the future status of blacks in England's North American colonies. The two whites had their terms of service extended by one year, but the judges ordered John Punch to "serve his said master . . . for the time of his natural life here or elsewhere."

Persons of African heritage were first transported to Virginia in 1619. In August of that year, a Dutch vessel sailed north from the West Indies, where it had been trading or, more likely, stealing slaves from the Spanish. The Dutch ship entered Chesapeake Bay and sold some twenty "Negars," as John Rolfe described the human cargo, to settlers caught up in the early tobacco boom.

Virginia's first white settlers did not automatically assume that transplanted Africans were permanently unfree. They treated some blacks as indentured servants, a status that conveyed the prospect of personal freedom after four or five years of laboring for someone else. After all, English law did not recognize human slavery. The key phrase was *in favorem libertatis* (in favor of liberty), and the central tenet, wrote a contemporary legal authority, held that no person should ever "make or keep his brother in Christ, servile, bond, and underling forever unto him, as a beast rather than as a man."

During the 1630s, some black Virginians, like John Philip who "qualified as a free man and Christian to give testimony" in court, did gain their personal freedom. Others, like Anthony Johnson, not only owned land but held servants of African origin as well, proof that permanent, inheritable slavery for blacks was a concept not yet fully developed in the Chesapeake Bay region.

By the 1640s, however, blacks faced a deteriorating legal status, ultimately leaving them outside the bounds of English liberty. In 1639 the new colony of Maryland guaranteed "all . . . Christians (slaves excepted)" the same "rights, liberties, . . . and free customs" as enjoyed by "any natural born subject of England." Worried about sporadic Indian raids, the Virginia assembly in 1640 ordered planters to arm themselves and "all those of their families which be capable of [bearing] arms . . . (excepting Negroes)." In 1643 the same assembly decreed that black women, like all adult males, would henceforth be "tithables"—those counted for local taxes because they worked in the fields. Black female servants planted, tended, and harvested tobacco crops while white female servants performed household work—further evidence of discrimination based on skin color.

Local laws may well have been catching up with the growing reality of lifetime slavery for blacks, as compared to temporary service for whites. In 1640 the Virginia council heard other runaway cases, besides that of John Punch. One of these involved a black man named Emmanuel, who ran away with several whites. The judges handed out severe penalties, including whippings and extended terms of service for the whites. The leader of the group endured branding with an "R" on his face and had one of his legs shackled in irons for a year. Emmanuel received the same penalty, but no mention was made of an extension of service. Emmanuel apparently was a slave for life already.

Between 1640 and 1670 the distinction between short-term servitude for whites and permanent, inheritable slavery for blacks became firmly fixed. In appearance and by cultural and religious tradition, Africans were not like the English. As with the "wild" Irish and Indian "savages," noticeable differences translated into assumptions of inferiority, and blacks became "beastly heathens," not quite human.

Such thinking helped justify interchanging words like "black" and "slave," so that by the 1690s slavery in the English colonies had emerged as a caste status for blacks only. Now fully excluded from the tradition of English liberty, local law defined Africans as chattels (movable property), and their masters had complete legal control over their lives.

John Punch and Emmanuel were among the first blacks in the Chesapeake Bay area who

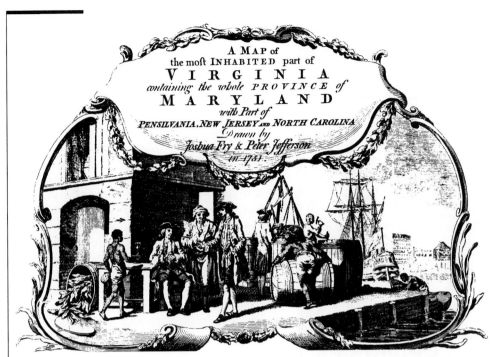

Many of the first blacks in Virginia were not slaves but indentured servants who came from the West Indies.

felt the stinging transition from servitude to slavery. They were also among the thousands of Europeans and Africans who helped settle England's North American colonies between 1620 and 1700. The societies and life-styles of these migrants had many differences, as comparisons between the founding of the northern and southern colonies will demonstrate. There were, however, common points for all migrants regardless of status or condition; they faced a titanic struggle to survive in an alien land. Although thousands died, some 250,000 settlers inhabited England's mainland colonies by 1700, and resulted in the formation of another powerful European empire in the Americas.

FROM SETTLEMENTS TO SOCIETIES IN THE SOUTH

Smoking or chewing tobacco, wrote King James I, was "loathsome to the eye, hateful to the nose, harmful to the brain, and dangerous to the lungs." Despite the king's admonition, John Rolfe's experiments saved the Virginia Company—at least temporarily—by providing the colony with an economic base. Early settlers grew tobacco with enthusiasm. The first exports occurred in 1617. By the mid-1630s, Virginians were selling a million pounds a year; and by the mid-1660s annual tobacco crops for export reached 15 million pounds.

Company directors did not initially encourage the tobacco boom. Wanting a diversified economy, they sent out workers knowledgeable in the production of such commodities as silk, wine, glass, and iron, but all these efforts failed. Virginia's climate and soil were ideal for raising tobacco. Also, new land for cultivation was plentiful, since the "stinking weed" quickly depleted the soil of its minerals. Accepting reality, the London investors soon hailed tobacco as the savior of their venture. Other difficulties, however, cost the directors their charter, but not before company activities laid the basis for England's first enduring colony.

The rise of the tobacco industry in the colonies spurred tobacco consumption in England.

Searching for Laborers

Life in Virginia presented constant hardships, including death at an early age. Migrants quickly succumbed to diseases like malaria, typhoid fever, and dysentery. Survival, it seemed, depended upon "seasoning," or getting used to an inhospitable climate. Bad relations with Powhatan's Indians also caused mayhem and death, and the English and Native Americans fought in many isolated clashes. All told, the company convinced nearly 14,000 individuals to attempt life in America, and only about 1150 were still alive and residing in the James River area in 1624, the year the company lost its charter.

Trying to overcome "a slaughter house" reputation, company leaders pursued various policies to keep the venture going. Sir Thomas Smith, a wealthy London merchant, used his boundless energy to keep the venture alive. He fervently tied company fortunes to England's potential for national greatness, and his influence at court resulted in more generous charter rights in 1609 and 1612, which expanded company boundaries to include the island of Bermuda—soon a source of profitable cash crops. Also under Smith's guidance, the company secured a steady supply of laborers, and it managed affairs in Virginia with an iron hand while attempting to improve Indian relations. Each activity was crucial to long-term development.

To encourage prospective laborers, company directors mounted publicity campaigns. These efforts, at best, neutralized Virginia's reputation as a deathtrap. More successful in securing workers was the development of the system of indentured servitude, modeled along the lines of contractual farm service. During early Stuart times, between a fourth and a third of England's families had servants. Many young men and women, having no access to land, made agreements to work for a year or more as farm laborers in return for food, lodging, and modest wages. They had few other prospects for employment, and virtually no chance of gaining title to their own freehold farms.

In theory, Virginia held out the opportunity of potential economic independence for landless farm servants and the urban poor. As early as 1609, the mayor of London asked the company "to ease the city and suburbs of a swarm of unnecessary inmates." Besides redeeming "many a wretch from . . . the hands of the executioner," another official wrote, Virginia would "wash your doors from idle persons . . . and employ them." The problem was to get these struggling poor to America. Individuals without money needed only to sign bonded contracts, or indentures, in which they legally exchanged four or five years of labor for passage costs. After completing their terms of service, their masters owed them "freedom dues," including clothing, farm tools, and in some cases land to begin anew as free persons.

The system of indentured servitude slowly took form after 1609. At first, the company offered free passage along with shares of stock to those who signed up for seven years of labor. When terms were up, workers were to gain title to one hundred acres of land as well as any stock dividends. The bait was eventual economic freedom, but even with high numbers of unemployed, few persons applied. Getting by marginally or facing a hangman's noose remained more attractive than an early—and often brutal—death in America.

Some venturesome souls, mostly young, unattached males, signed on as company-managed laborers. To make sure these servants would take orders and work, Sir Thomas Smith and his advisors gave dictatorial powers to their governors in Virginia. Lord De La Warr, who arrived in 1610, organized the colony along military lines. He ruled by martial law, as did his immediate successors, Sir Thomas Gates and Sir Thomas Dale. Their *Lawes Divine, Moral, and Martiall* (1612) provided harsh penalties for even the smallest offense.

Company servants were an undisciplined lot, less interested in work than in "bowling in the streets" of Jamestown, as an observer described workers' attitudes. When caught loafing, they paid with bloodied backs from public floggings, and when some laborers stole boats and tried to escape in 1612, Governor Gates showed no mercy. Their sentences included death by firing squad, hanging, or breaking upon the wheel, all as a warning to others with ideas of violating company contracts.

English Subjects at Home

Stories of brutal treatment and high mortality rates undercut company efforts to secure a steady flow of laborers. Changes had to be made, and a reform-minded faction led by Sir Edwin Sandys prepared new instructions, known as the "great charter" of 1618.

The overriding goal was to frame incentives that would make risking settlement more attractive. Key provisions included an end to martial rule and a declaration assuring Virginians government "by those free laws which his Majesty's subjects live under in England." The charter promised a local representative assembly, which came to be known as the House of Burgesses. Its first meeting took place in late July 1619, a cornerstone gathering pointing toward governments with a popular voice in England's North American colonies.

The first English legislative assembly, the House of Burgesses, met in 1619 at the church in Jamestown. They accepted several bills, including those regulating attendance at divine services and morals.

Besides guaranteeing political rights, the charter spoke of economic incentives, including the notion of "private plantations" and "headrights." Heretofore, the company controlled all acreage, but now potential settlers could purchase land without first serving as company laborers. Fifty acres per person would be given to those who migrated or those who paid for the passage of others to Virginia. Headrights would permit English families with funds to relocate and get title to enough property to grow tobacco and, perhaps, prosper. After all, Virginia had land in abundance but very few laborers, while England had a shortage of land and an oversupply of workers.

Even with these reforms, Virginia's unhealthful reputation kept families from migrating. English merchants and sea captains, however, developed a booming trade in indentured servants. They made handsome profits from delivering servants to labor-hungry planters and from headright patents, which they accumulated and sold to others with enough capital to purchase large tracts of land before migrating. In a few cases buying up headrights resulted in the establishment of large plantations; still, three-fourths of all English settlers entering seventeenth-century Virginia were indentured servants.

The vast bulk of these migrants were single males under the age of twenty-five with no employment prospects in England. The unbalanced sex ratio concerned company officials. Wanting to give Virginia a "more settled" feeling, they contracted with ninety "uncorrupt" young women in 1619 to go to Jamestown and be auctioned as wives. The plan worked well, but because of other problems the company only sent over one more shipment of women. Stable family life was not a characteristic of the rough-and-tumble society of early Virginia.

Crushing Powhatan's Confederacy

Bickering, bloodshed, and death characterized relations with Powhatan's Indians as the English planted tobacco farms along the James River. John Rolfe's marriage to Powhatan's daughter, Pocahontas, in 1614, which implied a political alliance of sorts, eased tensions—but only briefly. Rolfe soon took Pocahontas to England, where she became an instant celebrity, and both of them encouraged settlement in Virginia. Unfortunately, while preparing to return home in 1616, Pocahontas contracted smallpox and died.

Two years later, Powhatan also died, leaving his more militant half-brother Opechancanough in charge of the Confederacy. Watching the growing English presence with misgivings, Opechancanough decided that slaughtering the intruders was the only means left to save his people. On Good Friday, March 22, 1622, his warriors struck everywhere. Before the massacre was over, the Indians killed 347 settlers, about one-third of the English colonists, including John Rolfe. Opechancanough, however, had failed to exterminate the enemy, and in many ways the massacre of 1622 was the beginning of the end for Virginia's coastal natives. White settlers, now more convinced than ever that Indians were savages, took vengeance whenever they could.

Retreating inland, Opechancanough waited twenty-two years before striking again. The attack came in April 1644, and another 300 or more colonists died. The 1644 massacre was a last desperate gasp by Virginia's natives. The numbers of whites now were too overwhelming for total destruction. As for Opechancanough, the settlers took him prisoner and, even though he was crippled by old age, a white guard shot him to death for no apparent reason in 1646. That same year, Confederacy chiefs signed a treaty and submitted to English rule. The survivors of Powhatan's once-mighty league eventually accepted life on a reservation, as so many other remnant Indian tribes would be forced to do in the face of Europeans sweeping westward across the North American continent.

A Model for Royal Colonies

The massacre of 1622 was also a fatal blow to the Virginia Company. James I had begun to dream of huge sums flowing into his treasury from taxes on the tobacco trade. Using the massacre as one pretext, Crown officials moved in court against the company and brought about its dissolution in 1624. James then declared Virginia a royal colony and sent out his own governor. He did not promise basic political rights to the settlers and canceled the privilege of a local assembly. In a virtual throwback to the days of martial law, the king authorized his officials to rule absolutely.

Neither James nor his son Charles I (1625–1649) were advocates of popular rights or representative forms of government. They adhered to divine right theories of kingship, which meant that monarchs were literally God's political stewards on earth. Virginians, Charles insisted, would have to accept a government which "shall immediately depend upon ourself."

The planters, however, would not be denied a voice in government, and the royal governors shrewdly called upon locally-prominent men to serve as advisory councilors. The governors also began authorizing assemblies, conveniently referred to as conventions, to deal with local problems. Still, relations between royal governors and colonists were turbulent. In 1634 one governor, Sir John Harvey, known as a "choleric and impatient" man, got into a fist fight with one of his councilors. He punched out his opponent's teeth and threatened to hang the other councilors. In response, the councilors had Harvey arrested and sent him back to England in chains.

Finally in 1639, King Charles, facing dissent at home because of his high-handed rule, relieved some of the pressure by granting Virginians a representative assembly, thereby assuring some local participation in colony-related decision making. Unlike the Spanish and French, English settlers had refused to accept total political control by a far-off parent state. They would share in decision making affecting their lives as colonists in America.

Proprietary Maryland and the Carolinas

Charles's concession suggests the expediency with which the Stuart kings viewed colonization. Assuring basic rights did attract more settlers, which in turn meant larger tobacco crops, more tax revenues for the Crown, and the development of additional colonies, which also enhanced England's stature among the nations

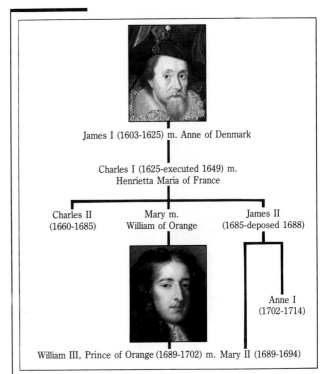

Figure 2.1
The Stuart Monarchy of England

of Europe. Also, some settlements could be used as dumping grounds for troublesome groups in England, such as the Puritans, and vast stretches of territory could be granted to court favorites. The Stuarts had the power to make men wealthier by awarding them huge estates in America, which fostered loyalty among powerful gentlemen at court who might otherwise choose to turn against the Crown.

Sir George Calvert, described as a "forward and knowing person," was one such favored courtier. Serving as James I's secretary of state, he took charge of dissolving the Virginia Company. A year later he converted to Roman Catholicism and had to leave the government. To reward his loyal service, however, the king named Calvert the first Lord Baltimore and granted him permission to colonize Newfoundland, an effort that failed. Then in 1632 Charles I awarded Calvert title to 10 million acres surrounding the northern end of Chesapeake Bay. The king called the grant "Maryland" after his own Catholic wife, Henrietta Maria; and he named Calvert lord proprietor over these lands.

When Calvert died, his son Cecilius, the second Lord Baltimore, took charge of the venture and sent out the first settlement parties.

Sir George Calvert

The idea was for Maryland to function as a haven for persecuted Roman Catholics. Those Catholics who migrated received substantial personal estates in return for annual quitrents, or land taxes, paid to Lord Baltimore. Many more Protestants than Catholics took up land patents, also with quitrents, and Maryland soon took on an appearance similar to its Chesapeake neighbor Virginia, as a tobacco-producing colony.

The Maryland charter granted the Baltimore proprietors absolute political authority, but in 1635 Cecilius Calvert, hoping to induce further settlements, granted a representative assembly. As the colony grew, Catholics and Protestants fought bitterly over control of local politics. In an attempt to protect the minority Catholics, Calvert approved an Act of Religious Toleration in 1649, which guaranteed all adult males voting or officeholding rights as long as they subscribed to the doctrine of the Trinity. While only a form of toleration, this act represented a step toward liberty of conscience; yet the political bickering among Maryland's settlers continued for years to come.

While colonists in Maryland gained some religious freedom, religious warfare convulsed England. During the 1640s, civil war turned English subjects against one another. Puritan "Roundheads" rose up against the "Cavalier" supporters of Charles I, who had refused to let Parliament meet for several years. In 1649 the victorious Puritans showed willful contempt for divine right theories of kingship by beheading Charles. Oliver Cromwell, leader of Puritan mili-

tary forces, then took political control of England as Lord Protector. After his death, Parliament invited the exiled son of Charles I to reestablish the Stuart monarchy—in exchange for promises to call Parliament regularly and support the Anglican church.

The restoration of Charles II (1660–1685) left the new king with many political debts, and in 1663 he paid off eight powerful gentlemen by awarding them title to all lands lying south of Virginia and north of Spanish Florida. The region was already known as Carolus, the Latin equivalent of Charles. The new proprietors quickly set about the task of finding settlers, which proved difficult because of a dramatic new boom in England's economy—and consequent decrease in unemployment.

Trying to assist the settlement process, one of the proprietors, Sir Anthony Ashley Cooper, assisted by his brilliant secretary, political philosopher John Locke, produced the "Fundamental Constitutions for Carolina" (1669). This

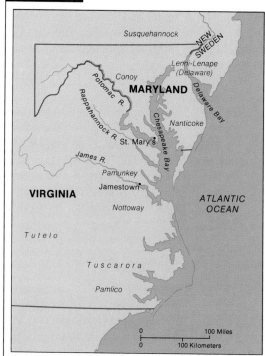

Chesapeake Settlements, 1650

Charleston (spelled Charles Town until the Revolution) was a focal point of early settlement in the Carolinas and became the major port town in the southern colonies during the eighteenth century.

document spelled out unworkable plans for a complex social order in which "landgraves" and "caciques" held vast estates, functioned as an American nobility, but shared the responsibilities of local government with smaller landholders. More important, the proprietors offered attractive headright provisions of up to 150 acres per person, guarantees of a representative assembly and religious toleration, and a fateful promise that free persons "shall have absolute power and authority over . . . negro slaves."

Even with generous terms, the Carolinas grew slowly. The Albemarle region of northeastern North Carolina developed as settlers spilled over from Virginia. William Byrd II, a prominent Virginia planter of the early eighteenth century, described the Albemarle inhabitants as having "a thorough aversion to labor" and a "disposition to laziness for their whole lives." Most inhabitants subsisted marginally by exporting tobacco and various timber-derived products like pitch, tar, and potash.

The proprietors focused on settling South Carolina. They made contact with small-scale English farmers on the island of Barbados who were selling out to well-capitalized gentlemen building large sugar plantations. In 1670 a group of these Barbadians founded Charleston, and a steady trade in deerskins and horsehides soon developed with interior natives. A few greedy migrants even dealt in humans by getting local Indians to capture tribal enemies, who were then sold off as slaves to the West Indies.

Picking up on the promise of the proprietors, Barbadian migrants owning slaves brought their chattels with them. Unlike the Chesapeake area, then, slavery existed from the outset in South Carolina and took even firmer hold when rice production became the mainstay of economic activity after 1690. Thus by the end of the seventeenth century, English colonists in the southern colonies had constructed their lives around the exportation of cash crops, supported increasingly by black slave labor. And with time, the institution of slavery gave white southerners a common identity—with serious long-term consequences.

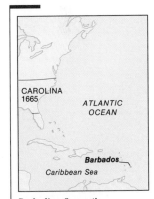

Barbadian Connection

RELIGIOUS DISSENTERS COLONIZE NEW ENGLAND

English men and women migrated to America for many reasons. Certainly the hope of economic betterment was a prime motivating factor, but in New England the initial emphasis reflected more directly on a communal desire to provide a hospitable environment for Calvinist religious ideas. Beginning in the 1620s, New England emerged as a haven for English religious dissenters of two main groups: Separatists and Puritans.

Separatists believed the Church of England to be so corrupt that it could not be salvaged.

The Pilgrims hated the elaborate ritual of church services like this one at St. Paul's Cathedral, London. They believed true church membership was not a matter of state decision, and as a result they fled elsewhere.

So as not to compromise their beliefs, their only course was to sever all ties to the Anglican church and establish their own religious communities of like-minded worshipers.

The intrepid band known as the Pilgrims were separatists from Scrooby Manor, a village in eastern England. Facing official harassment, they fled to Holland in 1607 but found it difficult to make decent livings there. Furthermore, they worried about their children losing their sense of English identity. As a result, they sought a patent to settle in North America, where they could set up their own community and worship as they pleased.

The first party of Pilgrims sailed west in 1620. Before landing at Plymouth, they drew up the Mayflower Compact, which guaranteed decision making by elected officials and a representative assembly. The compact, however, only gave voting rights to adult males who were church members. The Pilgrims would tolerate "strangers" in their community and encourage them to seek God's grace—the basis of church membership—as long as they showed "due submission and obedience" to the authority of the congregation of church members. In this sense, the compact was not an advanced statement of popular government; its purpose was to assure the Pilgrims full political control in Plymouth Colony.

Disaffection and Repression at Home

Far more numerous in England than the Separatists were those who wanted to "purify" the Church of England from within. The Puritans, as these dissenters were known, have often been characterized as prudish, ignorant bigots who hated the thought of anyone having a good time. Modern historical research, however, has shattered this stereotype. The Puritans were reformers who, as recipients of John Calvin's legacy, took biblical matters seriously. They believed that God's word should order the steps of every person's life. What troubled them most about the Protestant Reformation in England was that it did not go far enough. They viewed the Church of England as "corrupt" in organization and filled with unscriptural doctrine; they

Forty-one Pilgrims signed the Mayflower Compact—which provided government in Plymouth Colony—just before arriving in America.

longed for far-reaching institutional change that would rid the Anglican church of its imperfections. When church and state leaders harassed them, they responded in various ways, including the planting of a model utopian community in New England.

By the early 1600s, the Puritans numbered in the hundreds of thousands. Their emphasis upon reading scripture particularly appealed to literate members of the middle classes and lesser gentry—merchants, skilled craft workers, professionals, and freehold farmers. The Puritans prided themselves on hard work and the pursuit of one's "calling" as a way to glorify the Almighty. They also searched for signs of having earned God's saving grace, which all Puritans sought through a personal conversion experience. They testified in their prayer groups to these experiences—and hoped that others would agree they had joined God's "visible saints" on earth. To be a visible saint meant that a person was fit for church membership.

By comparison, the Church of England, as a state-supported church, claimed all citizens, regardless of their spiritual nature, as church members. Besides this problem, the Anglican church, from the Puritan perspective, put too much emphasis on ritual. Its elaborate hierarchy of church officials did not include enough educated ministers who understood the Bible, let alone the need to teach parishioners to seek God's grace; rather Anglican clergymen were the friends and relatives of the well-connected. They were like "Mr. Atkins, curate of Romford, thrice presented for a drunkard," "Mr. Goldringe, parson of Laingdon Hills, . . . convicted of fornication," and "Mr. Cuckson, vicar of Linsell, . . . a pilferer, of scandalous life."

In his youth as king of Scotland, James Stuart, now King James I, had regular dealings with John Knox and his Presbyterian followers, and he developed a decided distaste for religious dissenters. "I will harry them out of the land," he boldly proclaimed after becoming king of

England, "or else do worse." But like Queen Elizabeth before him, James quietly endured the Puritans. He never felt secure enough in his authority to test his will against their expanding influence.

During King James's reign, the Puritans moved aggressively toward their goal. They built a political base from which to demand reform by winning elections for seats in Parliament. James put up with their protests, but his son, Charles I, confronted the Puritans more boldly. He named William Laud, whom the Puritans considered a Roman Catholic in Anglican garb, as archbishop of the Church of England. Laud was particularly adept at persecuting his opponents. In response, the Puritans pushed a bill through Parliament denouncing "popish" practices in church and state. Finally, Charles used his prerogatives to disband Parliament and tried to rule by himself between 1629 and 1640, thus abetting the advent of the civil war.

In the late 1620s the Puritans were not yet ready for war, but some in their numbers had decided upon an "errand into the wilderness." In 1629 they secured a joint-stock charter for the Massachusetts Bay Colony. Investors knew that they were underwriting the peopling of an utopian religious community in America. As for King Charles, the prospect of ridding the realm of some Puritans was incentive enough to give royal approval to the Bay Company charter.

Mission to New England

The Puritans organized their venture carefully. They placed their settlement effort under John Winthrop, a prominent lawyer and landholder. In 1630 some 700 Puritans crowded onto eleven ships and joined Winthrop in sailing to Massachusetts. They were the vanguard of what became the *Great Migration,* or the movement of an estimated 20,000 persons to New England by 1642. These men and women did not cross the Atlantic as indentured servants but as families leaving behind the religious repression and worsening economic conditions of Charles I's England.

More than any other person, John Winthrop worked tirelessly to promote the Puritan errand. Aboard the flagship *Arbella* before landing in Massachusetts Bay, he delivered a sermon, known as "A Model of Christian Charity," in which he asserted: "We must consider that we shall be as a city upon a hill; the eyes of all people are upon us." The Puritan mission

John Winthrop (1588–1649) led the Puritans to New England and served several terms as the governor of Massachusetts Bay Colony.

Edward Winslow (1595–1655), dedicated to building a colony unfettered by a state church, was a principal leader of the first Pilgrims.

John Endecott (c. 1589–1665) led a band of Puritans to New England in 1628 and settled the community of Salem.

was to order human existence in the Bay Colony according to God's word. Such an example, Winthrop and other company leaders hoped, would inspire England and the rest of Europe, thereby causing the full realization of the Protestant Reformation.

Curious events back in England facilitated attempts to build a model society in the wilderness. For some reason, perhaps because of a well-placed bribe, the Bay Company charter did not specify a location for stockholder (General Court) meetings. Seizing the opportunity, John Winthrop and others drafted the Cambridge Agreement in August 1629; they decided to carry the charter with them and hold all stockholder meetings in New England—3000 miles from the meddlesome king's officials. Since only a few stockholders, all of whom were Puritans, migrated, this meant that decision making for the colony would be controlled in General Court sessions by a handful of men fully committed to the Puritan mission.

Winthrop and other stockholders, once in Massachusetts, soon faced challenges to their all-inclusive authority. Typical was a protest in 1632 from settlers who refused to pay taxes under the "bondage" of no voice in government. The solution was to create a category of citizenship known as "freeman." Freemen would be similar to stockholders; they could participate in government. Like the Pilgrims, however, only male church members received such status; the leaders assumed that these visible saints would not subvert the colony's purpose.

The government of Massachusetts developed out of this agreement. As the colony grew, the General Court became an elective assembly with freemen from each town sending delegates to Boston to represent local concerns. The governorship, too, was elective on an annual basis, with John Winthrop dominating the office until his death in 1649. Town ministers were not eligible for political offices, so the government was not technically a theocracy. Clergymen, however, met in synods and offered written advice to Winthrop and other leaders regarding religious issues; and their observations did affect political decision making.

Initially, Winthrop wanted to keep all settlers in or near Boston, but with migrants pour-

The Bay Colony Charter served as the basis for government in Massachusetts until 1684, when the Crown retracted it because citizens were too independent of England's authority.

ing into the colony, that proved impossible. The General Court started to issue town charters, and settlements spread in semi-circular fashion out from Boston and into the interior.

Designated proprietors guided the establishment of Puritan towns, emphasizing community control over individual lives. A 1635 law—later repealed—stated that inhabitants had to live within a half mile of the town church. Each family received a house lot near the village green, farmland away from the center of the town, and access to pasture land and woodlots. Some towns perpetuated the European open field system. Families received title to strips of land in several fields and worked in common with other townspeople to bring in yearly crops. In other towns, families had all their farmland concentrated in one area.

These property arrangements reflected on English patterns of land distribution as well as the desire to promote godly behavior, especially since some first-generation settlers were not Puritans. Village life was not totally restrictive, as long as families viewed the Bay Colony, in the words of the Reverend John Cotton, as "the setting forth of God's house, which is His church," rather than as a place to do whatever struck one's fancy.

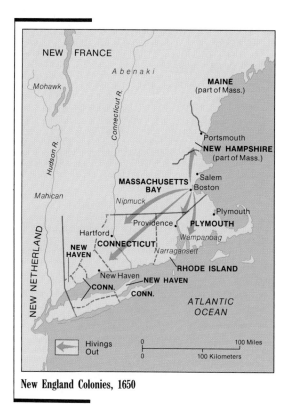

New England Colonies, 1650

Town leaders promoted harmonious living conditions. They set off lots for taverns, schools, and meeting houses. Taverns served as community centers in which people socialized and cheerfully drank alcohol, which they believed was essential to good health. School lots satisfied concerns about education. Puritans advocated literacy so that everyone could "understand the principles of religion and . . . laws of the country." Beginning in the 1640s, the General Court ordered each town to tax inhabitants to pay for formal schooling in reading and writing for all children. (The desire to have a learned clergy led to the founding of Harvard College in 1636.) The meeting house promoted social unity and was the gathering place for town meetings and church services. It was the duty of church members to encourage non-Puritans in their midst to study the Bible, pray fervently, and seek God's grace so that they might also enjoy political and religious rights as well as eternal salvation.

Testing the Limits of Toleration

The first generation of Puritans worked hard and prospered. Farming was the primary means of gaining a livelihood, although some coastal inhabitants took to shipbuilding, fishing, and mercantile activity. Prosperity, however, did not prevent serious controversies. These disagreements suggested how the Puritan system functioned on behalf of orthodoxy—and against diverse opinions—to assure adherence to the wilderness errand.

No Puritan was purer than Roger Williams. When this well-educated clergyman arrived in Boston in 1631 and announced that "Bishop Laud pursued me out of the land," John Winthrop graciously welcomed him. Soon Williams received an offer to teach in the Boston church, but he refused because of rules requiring mandatory worship. To hold services with the unconverted in attendance was to be no purer than the Church of England. It "stinks in God's nostrils," Williams proclaimed.

So off Williams went, first to Salem and then to Plymouth Colony, where Governor William Bradford and the Pilgrims embraced him. Only the visible saints attended church services in Plymouth. The Pilgrims soon dismissed him for "strange opinions" having to do with questions of land ownership. Williams had become friendly with local Indians and had concluded that any Crown-based land patent was fraudulent—and that Puritans and Pilgrims alike were thieves because they had not purchased their land from the natives. Moving back to Salem, Williams next denounced government leaders who meddled in church affairs. So long as churches were subject to state control, they would be as corrupt as the Church of England.

John Winthrop remained Williams's friend and kept advising him to temper his opinions, but other Puritan leaders had had enough. Orthodox adherence to the Puritan mission meant that this contentious young minister, no matter how well-educated, could not be tolerated. With Winthrop's reluctant approval, the General Court banished him in October 1635. To avoid being sent back to England, Williams fled to the Narragansett Indians, with whom he spent the

In a typical seventeenth-century meetinghouse, town meetings and government activities occurred on the main floor, with the second floor reserved for church services.

winter and from whom he eventually purchased land for a new community—Providence, Rhode Island.

Because of Roger Williams's influence, the colony of Rhode Island took form as a center of religious toleration. Settlers there welcomed all faiths, including Judaism, and the government stayed out of matters of personal conscience. As for Williams, he became so pure in his later years that he would not worship with anyone except his wife. Personal conscience was truly sacred, he thought, which made him an advance agent for notions like religious freedom and separation of church and state.

In the meantime, others like Anne Hutchinson tested the limits of orthodoxy. She was a woman of powerful mind and presence who frightened leaders like John Winthrop. Hutchinson, the mother of thirteen children, moved with her family to Boston in 1634, where she served as a midwife. She spoke openly about her religious views, which had a strong mystical element. Once humans experienced saving grace, she believed, the "Holy Spirit illumines the heart," and God would offer direct revelation, meaning that his true saints no longer needed the church or the state to help order their daily existence.

Hutchinson's ideas earned the label "Antinomian," which Puritans defined as being against the laws of human governance. To Winthrop, who thought that God's revelation ended with scripture, Hutchinson was an advocate of social anarchy. She was threatening to ruin the Puritan mission, since there would be no purpose to human institutions of any kind, except to control the unregenerate. He viewed the Antinomian crisis as far more serious than the purist musings of Roger Williams, since the movement came to involve large numbers of people.

With Antinomianism spreading so rapidly, orthodox Puritans readied themselves for battle. In 1637 Bay Colony clergymen assembled in a synod and denounced Antinomianism as "blasphemous." They also insisted that Hutchinson's brother-in-law, the Reverend John Wheelwright, recant his views, including the tenet of Antinomians regarding the inability of human beings to prepare themselves for salvation. Wheelwright held his ground, and he was banished. He and his followers went off to

Anne Hutchinson was tried before the General Court for her religious views. When the court could not get her to retract her ideas, she was banished from the Bay Colony.

found Exeter, New Hampshire. Now the target was Hutchinson. Ordered to appear before the General Court, she masterfully defended herself for two days, only to be declared guilty of sedition for dishonoring her spiritual parents, Winthrop and the other magistrates. As "a woman not fit for our society," she too was banished, and in the spring of 1638 she migrated to Rhode Island where she helped to establish Portsmouth.

"Hivings Out" Provoke Bloody Indian Relations

For those who accepted orthodoxy, Massachusetts was paradise compared to England's repressive atmosphere, but for dissidents like the Antinomians, Bay Colony leaders seemed just as intolerant as Charles I or Archbishop Laud. As a result, they had no choice but to locate elsewhere, and that is how Rhode Island began. Eventually settlers there pulled themselves together into a confederaton and, thanks to Roger Williams, gained a separate patent in 1644. Then in 1663 King Charles II granted a more generous charter. Local political offices, including the governorship, were to be elective, and the Crown also declared that no person should ever be "molested, . . . [or] punished for any differences of opinion in matters of religion." This clause made Rhode Island a unique haven for religious freedom in Puritan New England.

Even before John Wheelwright's exodus to New Hampshire, a few hardy settlers had located in that region. Other venturesome souls established themselves along the coast of Maine. Massachusetts tried unsuccessfully to maintain control of both areas, but in 1681 New Hampshire became a separate royal colony. The Bay Colony did sustain its authority over Maine by purchasing the land patents of rival claimants, and this territory remained a thinly-settled appendage of Massachusetts until the granting of statehood in 1820.

Connecticut also started to emerge as a Puritan colony during the 1630s. The Reverend Thomas Hooker, who viewed John Winthrop as too dictatorial, led 100 settlers into the Connecticut River valley in May 1636. By year's end, another 700 Puritans had followed Hooker's path, resulting in the founding of towns like Hartford, Wethersfield, and Windsor. John Davenport guided a party of London Puritans to Boston in 1637 but after a few months decided that Winthrop was not exercising enough power. He led his flock to the mouth of the Quinnipiac River, where they established New Haven. Eventually, the various Connecticut settlements came together politically and gained a Crown charter (1662) as generous as Rhode Island's. Connecticut Puritans, however, had little interest in promoting religious diversity; as in Massachusetts, the Congregational church dominated spiritual life.

These "hivings out," as Winthrop called them, adversely affected relations with the native populace. A devastating smallpox epidemic in 1633 temporarily delayed Indian resistance. But when Hooker's followers moved into the Connecticut River valley, they settled on land claimed by the Pequots, who decided to resist and struck at Wethersfield in April 1637, killing several people. A force of Puritans and Narragansett Indians, who hated the Pequots, retaliated a month later by surrounding and setting fire to the main Pequot village on the Mystic River. Some 400 men, women, and children died in the flames. "Horrible was the stink and scent therof," wrote one Puritan, but destroying the Pequots "seemed a sweet sacrifice" to assure the peace and safety of those seeking to plant themselves on fertile Connecticut lands.

The Puritans were no worse than Virginians or Carolinians in their treatment of Native Americans. In some ways, they tried to be better. The Bay Colony charter mandated that Indians be brought "to the knowledge . . . of the only true God and . . . the Christian faith." Most Puritans ignored this charge, but the Reverend John Eliot devoted his ministry to converting the natives. Besides translating the Bible into an Algonquian tongue, he established four towns for "praying Indians," which by 1650 held a population of over 1000. But most of these natives did not seek conversion. They were remnant members of once vital tribes, who were trying to survive while retaining as much of their cultural heritage as possible in the face of an irreversible European invasion.

John Eliot (1604–1690) was known as the Puritan Apostle to the Indians. The title page from the Bible translated into Algonquian tongue is shown here also.

SURVIVING IN EARLY AMERICA

Just as Opechancanough tried to wipe out the Virginians, Metacomet, better known to the Puritans as King Philip, attempted to do the same in New England. The son of Massasoit, a Wampanoag chieftain who, like Squanto, had aided the early Pilgrims, Metacomet felt threatened by the spread of white settlements. In 1671 the Pilgrims hauled him into court on the grounds of plotting against their colony and exacted a statement of submission to English authority. Thoroughly humiliated, Metacomet swore revenge.

The life and death struggle known as King Philip's War began during the summer of 1675 when various Indian tribes joined Metacomet's warriors in raiding towns along the Massachusetts-Connecticut frontier. Taking advantage of the settlers' habits, the Indians often struck during Sunday church meetings. By early 1676, all of New England was in chaos; and

Metacomet's forces even attacked towns within twenty miles of Boston. But there were too many Puritans (around 50,000) and not enough Indians (fewer than 12,000) to annihilate the whites, and when a "praying" Indian shot and killed Metacomet, King Philip's War rapidly lost its momentum.

Metacomet's warriors had leveled or done substantial damage to several towns, and almost 2000 Puritan settlers died in the war. Roughly twice as many Indians lost their lives in what proved to be a futile effort to contain the ever-expanding English. Still, this was not the Indians' last gasp. A few years later, remnant native groups began getting support from the French in Canada and once again started attacking New England's frontier towns.

King Philip's War was bloody, but surviving in New England was less difficult than surviving in the Chesapeake region, where local Indians had been crushed by the mid-1640s. While having its dangerous moments, life in early New England was far more secure than in the South, as comparative experiences reveal so graphically.

Life and Death, North and South

During the seventeenth century, New England's population grew steadily by natural increase. Most of the 25,000 migrants crossed the ocean before the outbreak of England's civil war in the 1640s, yet by the end of the century some 93,000 colonists inhabited New England. In the Chesapeake, by comparison, as many as 100,000 persons attempted settlement, but only about 85,000 were living in Virginia and Maryland in 1700. If it had not been for the constant influx of new migrants, these two colonies might have ceased to exist altogether.

The Chesapeake colonists experienced shorter, less healthy lives than their New England counterparts and were survived by fewer children. In 1640, for instance, Chesapeake migrants had no more than a fifty percent chance of surviving their first year in America. Hot, steamy summers fostered repeated outbreaks of malaria and typhoid fever, and dysentery and poisoning from brackish drinking water killed

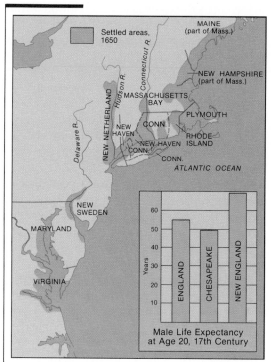

Population Comparison of New England and Chesapeake, Mid-1600s

younger. Marriages lasted an average of twenty-five years before one or the other spouse died. Longevity resulted in large families, averaging seven to eight children per household. In some locales, nine out of ten children survived infant diseases and grew to adulthood knowing not only parents but grandparents as well. Families with living grandparents were a unique characteristic of Puritan New England and reflected lifespans more typical of modern America than early modern Europe.

From a demographic perspective, then, New England families were far more stable and secure than those of the Chesapeake. Because Puritans crossed the Atlantic in family units, the ratio of women to men was more evenly balanced than in Virginia or Maryland, where most migrants were not married. Planters seeking laborers for their tobacco fields preferred young males, which skewed the sex ratio against women and hindered the development of family life. Before 1640, only one woman migrated to the Chesapeake for every six men;

thousands. New England's drinking water was safer, although Puritans generally preferred home-brewed beer, and the harsher winter climate helped kill deadly germs. As a result, the Puritans enjoyed longer, healthier lives.

In New England, twenty percent of all Puritan males surviving infancy lived into their seventies. Even with the hazards of childbirth, Puritan women lived almost as long. In Virginia and Maryland, men who survived into their early twenties had reached middle-age; on the average, they would not live beyond their mid-forties. For women in their early twenties, there was little likelihood of surviving beyond their late thirties. Given an average life expectancy of fifty to fifty-five years back in England, the Chesapeake region deserved its reputation as a human graveyard. In comparison, early New England represented an utopian health environment.

Longer life meant longer marriages and more children. Men in New England were usually in their mid-twenties when they married, and their wives were only two to three years

A unique characteristic of Puritan New England was families with living grandparents, as illustrated in this portrait of Abigail Gerrish and her grandmother.

and as late as 1700, males still outnumbered females by a ratio of more than three to two.

Indentured servitude also affected population patterns. Servants could not marry until they had completed their terms. Typically, women were in their mid-twenties before they first wed, which combined with short adult life expectancies curbed the number of children they could bear. Seventeenth-century Chesapeake families averaged only two or three children, and a quarter of them did not survive to the age of one. Marriages lasted an average of seven years before one or the other spouse died. Two-thirds of all surviving children lost one parent by the age of eighteen, and one-third lost both. Rarely did children know grandparents. Death was as much a daily reality as life for Chesapeake families, at least until the early eighteenth century when disease stopped wreaking such havoc.

Roles for Men, Women, and Children

The early Puritans looked at their mission as a family undertaking, and they referred to families as "little commonwealths." Not only were families to "be fruitful and multiply," but they also were to serve as agencies of education and religious instruction, as well as centers of vocational training and social welfare. Families cared for the destitute and elderly; they took in orphans; and they housed servants and apprentices—all under one roof and subject to the authority of the father.

The Puritans carried *patriarchal* values across the Atlantic and planted them in America. New England law, reflecting its English base, subscribed to the doctrine of *coverture,* which subordinated the legal status of women to the authority of their husbands, who were the undisputed heads of households. Unless there were prenuptial agreements, all property brought to marriages by women belonged to their mates. Husbands, who by custom and law directed their families in prayer and scripture reading, were responsible for assuring decency and good order in family life. They also represented their families in all community political, economic, and religious activities.

Wives also had major family responsibili-

Colonial women had many responsibilities including taking care of the children, cooking, spinning, sewing, and protecting her family from danger or harm.

ties. "For though the husband be the head of the wife," the Reverend Samuel Willard explained, "yet she is the head of the family." It was the particular calling of mothers to nurture their children in godly living, as well as perform many other tasks—tending gardens, brewing beer, raising chickens, cooking, spinning, and sewing—when not helping in the planting and harvesting of crops.

Most Puritan marriages functioned in at least outward harmony. If serious problems arose, local churches and courts intervened to end the turmoil. Puritan law, again reflecting English precedent, made divorce quite difficult. The process required the petitioning of assemblies for bills of separation, and the only legal grounds were bigamy, desertion, and adultery. A handful of women, most likely battered or abandoned wives, effected their own divorces by setting up separate residences. At times, the courts brought unruly husbands under control, such as a Maine husband who brutally clubbed his wife for refusing to feed the family pig. There were times when wives defied patriar-

CHILDBIRTH IN EARLY AMERICA

When the Mayflower left Plymouth, England, September 16, 1620, on its historic voyage to the New World, three of its 102 passengers were pregnant. Elizabeth Hopkins and Susanna White were each in their seventh month of pregnancy. Mary Norris Allerton was in her second or third month.

Their pregnancies must have been excruciatingly difficult. After a few days of clear weather, the Mayflower ran into "fierce storms" that lasted for six of the voyage's nine-and-one-half weeks. For days on end, passengers were confined to the low spaces between decks, while torrential winds blew away clothing and supplies and the ship tossed and rolled on the heavy seas.

While the ship was still at sea, Elizabeth Hopkins gave birth to a baby boy named Oceanus after his birthplace. Two weeks later, while the Mayflower was anchored off Cape Cod, Susanna White also had

a baby boy. He was christened Peregrine, a name that means "pilgrim." Peregrine White lived into his eighties, but Oceanus Hopkins died during the Pilgrim's first winter in Plymouth. In the spring of 1621, Mary Norris Allerton died in childbirth; her baby was stillborn.

Childbirth in colonial America was a difficult and sometimes dangerous experience for women. During the seventeenth and eighteenth centuries, between one and one-and-one-half percent of all births ended in the mother's death—as a result of exhaustion, dehydration, infection, hemorrhage, or convulsions. Since the typical mother gave birth to between five and eight children, her lifetime chances of dying in childbirth ran as high as one in eight. This meant that if a woman had eight female friends, it was likely that one might die in childbirth.

Understandably, many colonial women regarded pregnancy with dread. In their letters, women often referred to childbirth as "the Dreaded apperation," "the greatest of earthly miserys," or "that evel hour I look forward to with dread." Many, like New England poet Anne Bradstreet, approached childbirth with a fear of impending death. In a poem entitled "Before the Birth of One of Her Children," Bradstreet wrote,

> How soon, my Dear, death may my steps attend,
> How soon't may be thy lot to lose thy friend.

In addition to her anxieties about pregnancy, an expectant mother was filled with apprehensions about the survival of her newborn child. The death of a child in infancy was far more common than it is today. In the healthiest seventeenth century communities, one infant in ten died before the age of five. In less healthy environments, three children in ten died before their fifth birthday. Puritan minister Cotton Mather saw eight of his fifteen children die before reaching the age of two. "We have our children taken from us," Mather cried out, "the Desire of our Eyes taken away with a stroke."

Given the high risk of birth complications and infant death, it is not surprising to learn that pregnancy was surrounded by superstitions. It was widely believed that if a mother looked upon a "horrible spectre" or was startled by a loud noise her child would be disfigured. If a hare jumped in front of her, her child was in danger of suffering a harelip. There was also fear that if the mother looked at the moon, her child might become a lunatic or sleepwalker. A mother's ungratified longings, it was thought, could cause an abortion or leave a mark imprinted on her child's body. At the same time, however, women were expected to continue to perform work until the onset of labor, since hard work supposedly made for an easier labor. Pregnant women regularly spun thread, wove clothing on looms, performed heavy lifting and carrying, milked cows, and slaughtered and salted down meat.

Today, most women give birth in hospitals under close medical supervision. If they wish, women can take anesthetics to relieve labor pains. During the seventeenth and eighteenth centuries, the process of childbirth was almost wholly different. In colonial America, the typical woman gave birth to her children at home, while female kin and neighbors clustered at her bedside to offer support and encouragement. When the daughter of Samuel Sewall, a Puritan magistrate, gave birth to her first child on the last day of January 1701, at least eight other women were present at her bedside, including her mother, her mother-in-law, a midwife, a nurse, and at least four other neighbors.

Most women were assisted in childbirth not by a doctor but by a midwife. Most midwives were older women who relied on practical experience in delivering children. One midwife, Martha Ballard, who practiced in Augusta, Maine, delivered 996 women with only four recorded fatalities. Skilled midwives were highly valued. Communities tried to attract experienced midwives by offering a salary or a house rent-free. In addition to assisting in childbirth, midwives helped deliver the offspring of animals, attended the baptisms and

burials of infants, and testified in court in cases of bastardy.

During labor, midwives administered no painkillers, except for alcohol. Pain in childbirth was considered God's punishment for Eve's sin of eating the forbidden fruit in the Garden of Eden. Women were merely advised to "arm themselves with patience" and prayer and to try, during labor, to restrain "those dreadful groans and cries which do so much to discourage their friends and relations that are near them."

After delivery, new mothers were often treated to a banquet. At one such event, visitors feasted on "boil'd pork, beef, fowls, very good roast beef, turkey-pye, [and] tarts." Women from well-to-do families were then expected to spend three to four weeks in bed convalescing. Their attendants kept the fireplace burning and wrapped them in a heavy blanket in order to help them sweat out "poisons." Women from poorer families were generally back at work in one or two days.

During the second half of the eighteenth century, customs of childbirth began to change. One early sign of change was the growing insistence among women from well-to-do urban families that their children be delivered by male midwives and doctors. Many upperclass families assumed that in a difficult birth trained physicians would make childbirth safer and less painful. In order to justify their presence, physicians tended to take an active role in the birth process. They were much more likely than midwives to intervene in labor with forceps and drugs.

Another important change was the introduction in 1847 of two drugs—ether and chloroform—to

relieve pain in childbirth. By the 1920s, the use of anesthesia in childbirth was almost universal. The practice of putting women to sleep during labor contributed to a shift from having children at home to having children in hospitals. In 1900, over ninety percent of all births occurred in the mother's home. By 1940, over half took place in hospitals, and by 1950, the figure had reached ninety percent.

The substitution of doctors for midwives and of hospital delivery for home delivery did little in themselves to reduce mortality rates for mothers. It was not until around 1935, when antibiotics and transfusions were introduced that a sharp reduction in the maternal mortality rate occurred. In 1900, maternal mortality was about sixty-five times higher than it is today, and not much lower than it had been in the mid-nineteenth century. By World War II, however, death in childbirth had been cut to its present low level.

In recent years, a reaction has occurred against the sterile impersonality of modern hospital delivery. Beginning in the 1960s, a growing number of women elected to bear their children without anesthetics, so that they could be fully conscious during childbirth. Many women also chose to have their husbands or a relative or a friend present during labor and delivery and to bear their children in special "birthing rooms" that provide a home-like environment. In these ways, many contemporary women have sought to recapture the broader support network that characterized childbearing in the colonial past, without sacrificing the tremendous advances that have been made in maternal and infant health.

chalism. One case involved a Massachusetts woman who faced community censure for beating her husband and even "egging her children to help her, bidding them knock him in the head."

Family friction arose from other sources as well, stemming from the absolute control fathers exercised over property and inheritances. If sons wanted to marry and establish separate households, they had to conform to the will of their fathers, who controlled the land. Family patriarchs normally delayed the passing of property until sons had reached their mid-twenties and selected mates acceptable to parents. Delayed inheritances help explain why so many New Englanders did not marry until several years after puberty. Since parents also bestowed dowries on daughters as their contributions to new family units, romantic love had less to do with mate selection than parental desires to unite particular family names and estates.

Puritans expected brides and grooms to learn to love one another as they went about their duty of conceiving and raising the next generation of children. In most cases, spouses did develop lasting affection for one another, as captured by the gifted Puritan poetess Anne Bradstreet in 1666 when she wrote to her "Dear and loving Husband":

> If ever two were one, then surely we.
> If ever man were lov'd by wife, then thee;
> If ever wife was happy in a man,
> Compare with me the women if you can.

Young adults who defied patriarchal authority were rare. If they did, they could expect to hear what one angry Bay Colony father told his unwanted son-in-law: "As you married her without my consent, you shall keep her without my help." Also unusual were instances of illegitimate children, despite the lengthy gap between puberty and marriage. As measured by illegitimate births, premarital sex could not have been that common in early New England— not a surprising find among people living in closely-controlled communities who sought to honor the Almighty by reforming human society.

The experiences of seventeenth-century Chesapeake colonists were very different. The

Many indentured servants risked an early death in Chesapeake Bay in return for the prospect of gaining economic freedom as an independent landholder.

system of indentured servitude was open to abuse. Free planters ruled as patriarchs but with no sense of nurturing the next generation; rather, they presumed that they were dealing with "lazy, simple people," as one commentator stated, who "professed idleness and will rather beg than work." The goal was to get as much labor as possible out of servants, since forty percent died before completing their contracts. Disease was the major killer, but hard-driving planters also contributed to early deaths.

Servants responded to cruel treatment in various ways. A few committed suicide, while others, like John Punch, ran away. Some slaughtered farm animals, set buildings on fire, or broke tools. Local laws, as drafted by freeholding planters, specified harsh penalties. Besides floggings and brandings, resisting servants faced extensions of service, as one unfortunate man learned after he killed three pigs belonging to his master. The court added six years to his term of service.

Indentured servitude also inhibited family life. Since servants could not marry, the likelihood of illicit sexual activity increased. Quite frequently, females became the unwilling sexual partners of lustful masters or male servants. Margerie Goold, for example, warded off attempted rape by her master in 1663, but another servant, Elizabeth Wild, was less successful. The planter, however, helped her induce an abortion. One-fifth of Maryland's indentured females faced charges of "bastardy," reflecting both a shortage of women and a labor system giving masters much leeway in managing their servants. Finally in 1692, Virginia officials tried to improve the situation by adopting a statute that mandated harsh penalties for "dissolute masters" getting "their maids with child."

Still, the fate of female and male servants was not always abuse or death. Many survived, gained title to land, and enjoyed, however briefly, personal freedom in America. A few women, usually widows, gained influence. Margaret Brent, for example, controlled over 1000 acres in Maryland and even served as the executor of Governor Leonard Calvert's estate in 1647. Brent was daring enough to demand the right to vote, a plea that male legislators dismissed as a subversive attempt to undermine the natural order of human relationships.

Brent's case suggests that high death rates in combination with an unbalanced sex ratio may have, at least temporarily, enhanced the status of some Chesapeake women. English and colonial law recognized the status of *femes sole,* or permitting single, adult women and widows to own and manage property and households for themselves. Chesapeake women who outlived two or three husbands could acquire significant holdings through inheritances and then maintain control by requiring prenuptial contracts of future spouses. Once married, however, any property not so protected fell to new husbands because of *coverture.*

Since widowed mothers could not presume that they would outlive new husbands, most prenuptial contracts protected property for their children by previous marriages. Indeed, few children grew to adulthood without burying one or both parents, and there were extreme cases like that of Agatha Vause, a Virginia child whose father, two stepfathers, mother, and guardian uncle all died before she was eleven years old.

The fragility of life resulted in complex family genealogies with some households containing children from three or four marriages. In some instances, local Orphans' Courts had to take charge because all adult relatives had died. Because parents did not live that long, children quite often received their inheritances by their late teens, much earlier than in New England. This advantage only meant that economic independence, like death, came earlier in life.

COMMERCIAL VALUES AND THE RISE OF CHATTEL SLAVERY

By 1650, there were signs that the Puritan mission was in trouble. From the outset, many non-Puritan settlers, including merchants in Boston, had shunned the religious values of the Bay Colony's founders. By the 1660s, children and grandchildren of the migrating generation displayed less zeal about seeking and earning God's grace; they were becoming more like southern settlers in their eagerness to get ahead economically. By 1700, their search for worldly prosperity even brought some New Englanders into the international slave trade.

Declension in New England

"Declension," or movement away from the ideals of the Bay Colony's founding fathers, resulted in tensions between settlers adhering to the original mission and those attracted to rising commercial values. When clergymen proposed a major compromise known as the "Half-Way Covenant" in 1662, more secular-minded settlers cheered while traditionalists jeered. The covenant recognized that many children were not preparing for salvation, a necessary condition for full church membership, as their parents had done. The question was how to keep them—and their offspring—aspiring toward a spiritual life. The solution was half-way membership, which permitted the baptism of the children and grandchildren of professing saints. If still in the church, ministers and full members could continue to urge these children to focus their lives on seeking God's eternal rewards.

Many communities disdained the Half-Way Covenant because of what it suggested about changing values. As one minister wrote, it was "as if the Lord had no further work for his people to do but every bird to feather his own nest." With time, most accepted the covenant to help preserve some semblance of a godly society in New England.

Spreading commercial values took hold for many reasons, including the natural abundance of the New England environment and an inability to sustain fervency of purpose among American-born offspring who had not personally felt the religious repression of early Stuart England. Also, Puritans still in England, after overthrowing Charles I, generally ignored the model society in America; this left the impression that the errand had been futile, and no one back in Europe really cared.

The transition in values occurred gradually, as shown in various towns where families bought and sold common field strips so that all their landholdings were in one place. The next step was to build homes on these sites and become "outlivers," certainly a more efficient way to practice agriculture yet also a statement that making one's living was more important than village life—with its emphasis on laboring together in God's love. In Boston and other port towns, such as Salem, merchants gained increasing community stature because of their wealth. By the early eighteenth century, some of them were earning profits from the African slave trade. Their new-found status was symbolized by retinues of household servants, or more properly slaves taken from Africa.

Clergymen strongly disapproved of these trends. Their sermons took on the tone of "jeremiads," modeled on the prophet Jeremiah who kept urging Israel to return to the path of godliness. In Calvinist fashion, they warned of divine retribution or "afflictions" from the Almighty, and they pointed to events like King Philip's War as proof that Jehovah was punishing New England. In 1679 the ministers met in another synod and listed several problems,

everything from working on the sabbath to swearing and sleeping during sermons. Human competitiveness and contention, they sadly concluded, were in ascendance. Worse yet, the populace, in its rush to garner wordly riches, showed little concern that Winthrop's "city upon a hill" had become the home of the acquisitive Yankee trader.

Stabilizing Life in the Chesapeake

By 1675, there were some indications that life in Maryland and Virginia could be something more than brief and unkind. The death rate dropped; more children survived; the sex ratio started to balance out; and life expectancy figures rose. By the early 1700s, Chesapeake residents lived well into their fifties. This was comparable to England but still ten to fifteen years shorter than in New England. These patterns suggested greater family stability, as shown by longer marriages and more children—the average union now produced seven to eight offspring with five to six children surviving into adulthood.

Not only did life become more stable, but an elite group of families, controlling significant property and wealth, had appeared. By 1700, the great tidewater families—the Byrds, Carters, Fitzhughs, Lees, and Randolphs among others—were making their presence felt and had started to dominate social and political affairs in the Chesapeake area. These gentlemen-planters copied the lifestyle of England's rural gentry class. They constructed lavish manor houses from which they ruled over their plantation estates and dispensed hospitality and wisdom as the most important local leaders of their tobacco-producing society.

One such person was William Byrd II, who inherited 26,000 fertile acres along the James River in 1705. He built the magnificent Westover plantation, raised a large family, served on the governor's council, and assumed, as he wrote to an English correspondent, that he was "one of the patriarchs" of Virginia society. By the time of his death in 1744, Byrd had holdings of 180,000 acres, and he owned at least 200 slaves.

Lavish estates like Westover, built by William Byrd II, illustrate the wealth and dominance of aristocratic planters in Virginia.

Educated in England, Byrd read widely, put together an impressive personal library, and wrote extensively on any subject that interested him. His "secret" diaries describe how he treated others, including his wife, Lucy Parke Byrd. When they argued, Byrd on occasion demonstrated his presumed masculine superiority with sexual bravado. In 1710 "a little quarrell" was "reconciled with a flourish . . . performed on the billiard table." This was part of his assertive, self-confident manner. He was the master of everything on his plantation and a patriarch of the realm of Virginia.

For every great planter, there were dozens of small farmers who lacked the wealth to obtain land, slaves, and high status in society. Most eked out bare livings, yet they dreamed of the day when they, or their children, might live in the style of William Byrd. Meantime, they deferred to their "betters" among the planter elite, who in turn "treated" them to large quantities of alcohol on election days and expressed gentlemanly concern about the welfare of their families. All of this was part of an ongoing bonding ritual among white inhabitants who, no matter how high or low in status, considered themselves superior to black slaves—whose numbers were now growing rapidly on the bottom rung of Maryland and Virginia society.

The Beginnings of American Slavery

Slavery, which had existed from earliest recorded history, was dying out in much of Europe by the fifteenth century. Then the Portuguese mariners of Prince Henry started coasting along sub-Saharan Africa, making contact with various cultures and peoples, some of whom were willing to barter in human flesh as well as in gold and ivory. The first Portuguese expeditions represented the small beginnings of a trade that forcibly relocated nearly 10,000,000 Africans in the Americas during the next 350 years.

Africa had a population of about 50,000,000 at the time of Columbus. There was great geographic diversity with vast deserts, grassy plains, and tropical rainforests. Mighty kingdoms like Ghana had flourished in West Africa but had been overrun by Muslims from the north in the eleventh century, resulting in the empire of Mali and its magnificent trading and learning center, Timbuktu. Farther to the south in Guinea were smaller kingdoms like Benin in which the populace farmed or worked at such crafts as pottery making, weaving, and metalworking. These cultures placed a primacy on

West African Kingdoms, Late 1400s

family life and were mostly matrilineal in the organization of kinship networks, and they had well-developed political systems and legal codes.

These kingdoms also had elaborate regional trading networks which the Portuguese and other Europeans, offering guns and various iron products, easily tapped into. In time, Europeans came to identify certain coastal areas with particular commodities. Upper Guinea contained the rice and grain coasts, and Lower Guinea the ivory, gold, and slave coasts.

Early Portuguese traders found that Africans held slaves—mainly individuals captured in tribal wars—who generally had the status of family members. The Portuguese initiated the slave trade when they learned that coastal chiefs would trade for European weapons to use in attacking interior states, with the goal of capturing enemies who could then be sold into slavery for yet more European goods.

Once this vicious trading cycle began, there did not seem to be any way to stop it. Decade after decade, thousands of Africans experienced the agony of being shackled in collars and ankle chains, marched in gangs or *coffles* to the coast, thrown into *barracoons* or slave pens, and then packed aboard ships destined for ports-of-call in the Americas. One slave, Olaudah Equiano, who made the voyage during the eighteenth century, recalled the "loathsomeness of the stench" from overcrowded conditions, which made him "so sick and low" that he neither was "able to eat, nor had . . . the desire to taste anything."

Some refused to eat and died, but the Europeans made tools that would break jaws, pry open mouths, and jam food down unwilling throats. Other Africans jumped overboard and drowned, but the Europeans soon placed large nets on the sides of their vessels. About fifteen percent of those forced onto slave ships did not survive. For those who did, there was the frightening realization of having lost everything familiar in their lives.

Slave decks on many of the ships arriving in America were overcrowded and cramped. As indicated in this picture, slaves became emaciated from inadequate food during the crossing.

During the sixteenth century, the Spanish and Portuguese started transporting Africans into their colonies. These slaves were not thought of as family members, but rather as disposable beings whose energy was to be used, as long as it lasted, in mining or agricultural operations. High mortality rates among the migrants did not seem to bother their European masters because more slave ships always appeared on the horizon. As a result, areas like Brazil and the West Indian sugar islands soon earned deserved reputations as centers of human exploitation and death.

Shifting to Slavery in Maryland and Virginia

The English North American colonies existed at the outer edge of the African slave trade until the very end of the seventeenth century. In 1650 the population of Virginia approached 15,000 settlers, including only 500 persons of African descent. By comparison, the English

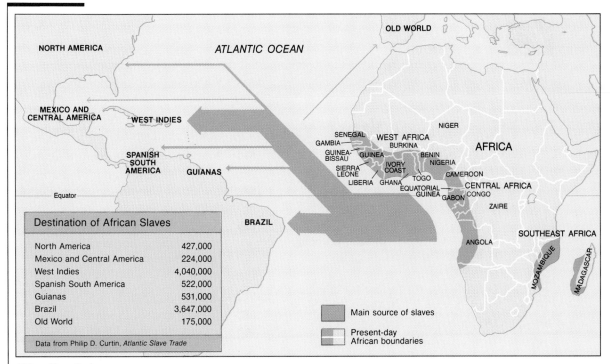

African Slave Trade

The destinations of slaves traded between 1520 and 1810 shows the heaviest concentration in Central and South America.

Destination of African Slaves	
North America	427,000
Mexico and Central America	224,000
West Indies	4,040,000
Spanish South America	522,000
Guianas	531,000
Brazil	3,647,000
Old World	175,000
Data from Philip D. Curtin, *Atlantic Slave Trade*	

sugar colony of Barbados already held 10,000 slaves, a majority of the population. English Barbadians had started to model their economy on that of other Caribbean sugar islands whereas Virginians, with a steady supply of indentured servants, had not yet made a full transition to slave labor.

Factors supporting a shift, however, were present by the 1640s, as evidenced by laws discriminating against Africans and court cases involving blacks like John Punch and Emmanuel. In the same decade, a few Chesapeake planters started to invest in Africans; Governor Leonard Calvert of Maryland, for example, asked "John Skinner mariner" to ship him "fourteen negro-men-slaves and three women-slaves." Planters like Calvert were ahead of their time because slaves cost significantly more to purchase than indentured servants. Yet for those planters who invested, they owned their laborers for life and did not have to pay freedom dues. Further, they soon discovered that Africans, having built up immunities to

tropical diseases like malaria and typhoid fever, generally lived longer than white servants. Resistance to such diseases made Africans a better long-term investment, at least for well-capitalized planters.

Then in the 1660s two additional factors encouraged the shift to slave labor. First, Virginia legislators in 1662 decreed that slavery was an inheritable status, "according to the condition of the mother." The law made yet unborn generations subject to slavery, a powerful incentive for risking an initial investment in human chattels. If slaves kept reproducing, planters would control a never-ending supply of laborers. Second, the availability of indentured servants began to drop as economic conditions improved in England. With more opportunity for work, poorer citizens were less willing to risk life and limb for a chance at economic independence in America.

Also abetting the shift was the chartering of the Royal African Company in 1672 to develop England's role in the slave trade. Royal

1609–1618 System of indentured servitude developed

1611–1614 Rolfe cultivates mild-tasting tobacco

1617 First tobacco shipments sent to England

1619 First blacks sold in Virginia; delegates meet at Jamestown in first elected assembly

1622 Opechancanough's Indians fail in attempt to massacre all Virginia Company settlers

1624 Virginia Company dissolved

1625 Charles I becomes king of England

1629 English Crown issues Massachusetts Bay Company charter to Puritans

1630 Winthrop leads Puritan settlers to Massachusetts Bay

1632 Crown grants Maryland proprietary patent to Calvert family

1635–1636 Williams banished from Massachusetts, then settles in Rhode Island

1637 Puritans exterminate the Pequots in Connecticut

1638 Hutchinson banished from Massachusetts

1643–1649 Puritan Civil War rages against Charles I in England

1644 Second attempted massacre of Virginia settlers fails

1646 Powhatan's Confederacy accepts English rule

1649 Puritans behead Charles I; Cromwell takes control of England's government; Maryland adopts Acts of Religious Toleration

1660 Charles II restored to English throne

1662–1663 Crown grants royal corporate charter to Connecticut and Rhode Island, and rewards eight court favorites with a proprietary charter to the Carolinas

1670 Barbadians settle with slaves in South Carolina

1675–1676 King Philip's (Metacomet's) War devastates New England

1681 New Hampshire becomes a royal colony

1680–1700 Slavery takes firm hold in Virginia and Maryland

1739 Stono slave uprising occurs in South Carolina

African vessels soon made regular visits to Chesapeake Bay; and as the supply of slaves increased, asking prices began to decline—at the very time that the cost of buying indentured servants began to climb. In 1698 the company lost its monopoly, and New England merchants vigorously entered the slave trade. Yankee merchants now had something in common with Chesapeake planters, besides English roots and language. Both were profiting from the international traffic in human flesh.

Population figures tell the rest. In 1670 Virginia contained about 40,000 settlers, which included an estimated 6000 white servants and 2000 black slaves. By 1700, the number of slaves had grown to 16,000, and by 1750 white Virginians owned 120,000 slaves—about forty percent of the total population. The same general pattern characterized Maryland, where by 1750 there were 40,000 slaves—some thirty percent of the populace. In the Chesapeake area, indentured servitude was by then a lifeless institution. White planters, great and small, now measured their wealth and status in terms of plantations owned and slaves managed.

The World the Slaves Made

Historians once argued that slavery in English North America was harsher than the Spanish-American version. They pointed to the moderating influence of the Roman Catholic church, which mandated legal recognition of slave marriages as a sacramental right; and ancient legal precedents influencing Spanish law, which meant that slaves could earn wages for their labor in off hours and buy their freedom. Although Spanish laws may have been more humane, daily working and living conditions were not. Most slaves destined for Caribbean and South American settlements did not survive long enough to marry or enjoy other legal rights, but in North America, where early deaths were not so pervasive among migrants, slaves more easily reconstructed meaningful lives for themselves.

About ten percent of those Africans coming to the colonies entered port towns in the North like Boston and became domestic servants, craft workers, or in rare cases, farmhands out in the countryside. The rest labored in the South, mostly on small plantations where field work dominated their existence. There was little chance for family life, at least in the early years, because planters purchased an average of three males for every female. In addition, southern law did not recognize slave marriages—in case masters wanted to sell off some of their chattels. Anglican church leaders accepted the situation. In New England, by comparison, the Congregational church insisted that slave marriages be recognized and respected by masters.

Facing a loss of personal freedom and pervasive racism, southern slaves made separate lives for themselves, particularly on larger plantations where their numbers were large enough to form their own communities in the slave quarters. Here they maintained African cultural traditions and developed distinctive forms of music. In South Carolina's sea island region, slaves continued to give their children African names, and they worked out a distinct dialect,

Old Plantation shows that slaves made separate lives for themselves but always had to deal with the reality that their masters had legal control.

known as Gullah, to communicate with one another in a unique combination of African and English sounds. In many places, female slaves managed slave quarter life, thus maintaining the matrilineal nature of African kinship ties.

Most slaves did not engage in casual sexual liaisons; rather, they selected partners and had large families, even if slave quarter marriages had no standing in law. As a consequence, the ratio of men to women balanced itself out over time, which in turn sped up natural population increase. Large families became a source of slave community pride. Natural increase also undercut the need to continue heavy importations of chattels. As a result, only five percent— 399,000 persons—of all imported Africans ended up in English North America.

Such comparisons are relative. Nowhere in the Americas did slavery operate in an uplifting fashion. And while blacks on large southern plantations carried on traditional cultural practices, they still had to face masters or overseers who might whip them; sell off their children; or maim or kill them, if they tried to run away. Always present was the realization that whites considered them to be a subhuman species of property, which left scant room for human dignity in life beyond the slave quarters.

Despite the oppression, Africans did contribute to that life. In South Carolina, for example, many early migrants were expert at raising and herding animals, and they helped make possible a thriving trade in cattle. Others who came from the rice coast region of Africa used their agricultural skills in fostering South Carolina's development as a major producer of rice. These and many other contributions went unrecognized in the rush for profits in the maturing commercial world of English North America, except in the ironic sense of creating further demand among white settlers for additional black laborers.

CONCLUSION

While most blacks adapted to slavery, some remained defiant. They stole food, broke farm tools, or in few cases, poisoned their masters. In rare instances, they resorted to rebellion. In September 1739, twenty slaves in the Stono River area of South Carolina rose up, seized some weapons, killed a few whites, and started marching toward Spanish Florida. Within a few days frightened planters rallied together and crushed the Stono uprising by shooting or hanging the rebels.

The South Carolina legislature soon approved a more repressive slave code, which all but restricted the movement of blacks to their home plantations. No legislator gave thought to the other possibility, which was to abandon the institution of slavery. While long in developing, slavery now supported southern plantation agriculture and the production of cash crops like tobacco and rice.

Just as the southern colonies had made a fateful shift from servitude to slavery, New Englanders experienced another kind of transition. Slowly but surely, they had forsaken their utopian, religiously-oriented errand into the wilderness, and service to mammon had replaced loyalty to God and community. The religious side would remain, but the fervor of a higher spiritual mission was in rapid decline by 1700. Material gain was now a quality shared in common by white English colonists in America—North and South.

Prosperity, which had come after so much travail and death, promoted a sense of unlimited opportunity in profiting from the abundance of the American environment. Other realities, however, were also taking shape. The colonists learned that Crown officials now expected them to conform to new rules governing the emerging English empire. And because of these imperial laws, much turmoil lay ahead for the people inhabiting English North America.

REVIEW SUMMARY

English men and women came to North America for many different reasons. Some sought wealth, others a religious haven, and still others a chance to establish ideal communities. These factors, along with climate and geography, shaped the different colonies.

- Englishmen traveled to Virginia in search of gold but discovered a fortune in tobacco
- Puritans voyaged to New England charged with a keen sense of mission
- North and South experienced very different demographic patterns and developed distinctly different social institutions
- slavery emerged in the South
- free labor dominated the North

But in one way North and South were similar. In both sections, English settlers relentlessly attacked Native Americans.

SUGGESTIONS FOR FURTHER READING

OVERVIEWS AND SURVEYS

Sydney E. Ahlstrom, *A Religious History of the American People* (1972); Bernard Bailyn, *Education in the Forming of American Society* (1960); Thomas Bender, *Community and Social Change in America* (1978); Carol R. Berkin, *Within the Conjurer's Circle: Women in Colonial America* (1974); Rowland Berthoff, *An Unsettled People* (1971); Richard D. Brown, *Modernization: The Transformation of American Life, 1600–1865* (1976); David Brion Davis, *The Problem of Slavery in Western Culture* (1966); John Hope Franklin and Alfred A. Moss, Jr., *From Slavery to Freedom*, 6th ed. (1987); Philip Greven, *The Protestant Temperament* (1977); Nathan I. Huggins, *Black Odyssey: The Afro-American Ordeal in Slavery* (1977); Steven Mintz and Susan Kellogg, *Domestic Revolutions: A Social History of American Family Life* (1988); Edwin J. Perkins, *The Economy of Colonial America* (1980); John E. Pomfret and Floyd M. Shumway, *Founding the American Colonies, 1583–1660* (1970); and Robert V. Wells, *The Population of the British Colonies in America before 1776* (1975).

FROM SETTLEMENTS TO SOCIETIES IN THE SOUTH

Carl Bridenbaugh, *Myths and Realities: Societies of the Colonial South* (1952); Paul G. E. Clemens, *The Atlantic Economy and Colonial Maryland's Eastern Shore* (1980); Converse D. Clowse, *Economic Beginnings of Colonial South Carolina, 1670–1730* (1971); Wesley Frank Craven, *The Southern Colonies in the Seventeenth Century* (1949); David Galenson, *White Servitude in Colonial America* (1981); David W. Jordan, *Foundations of Representative Government in Maryland, 1632–1715* (1988); Aubrey C. Land, et al., eds., *Law, Society, and Politics in Early Maryland* (1977); Richard L. Morton, *Colonial Virginia*, 2 vols. (1960); David B. Quinn, ed., *Early Maryland in a Wider World* (1982); M. Eugene Sirmans, *Colonial South Carolina, 1663–1763* (1966); Abbot E. Smith, *Colonists in Bondage: White Servitude and Convict Labor, 1607–1776* (1947); and Clarence L. Ver Steeg, *Origins of a Southern Mosaic* (1975).

RELIGIOUS DISSENTERS COLONIZE NEW ENGLAND

David Grayson Allen, *In English Ways: The Movement of Societies and the Transferal of English Local Law and Custom to Massachusetts Bay* (1981); Bernard Bailyn, *The New England Merchants in the Seventeenth Century* (1955); Francis J. Bremer, *The Puritan Experiment* (1976); Charles E. Clark, *The Eastern Frontier: The Settlement of Northern New England, 1610–1763* (1970); Charles L. Cohen, *God's Caress: The Psychology of Puritan Religious Experience* (1986); Kai T. Erikson, *Wayward Puritans* (1966); Stephen Foster, *Their Solitary Way: The Puritan Social Ethic* (1971); David D. Hall, *The Faithful Shepherd: A History of the New England Ministry* (1972); Charles E. Hambrick-Stowe, *The Practice of Piety: Puritan Devotional Disciplines* (1982); James Holstun, *A Rational Millennium: Puritan Utopias* (1987); Sydney V. James, *Colonial Rhode Island* (1975); Mary J. A. Jones, *Congregational Commonwealth: Connecticut, 1636–1662* (1968); Lyle Koehler, *A Search for Power: The 'Weaker Sex' in New England* (1980); David Konig, *Law and Society in Puritan Massachusetts, 1629–1692* (1979); George D. Langdon, Jr., *Pilgrim Colony, 1620–1691* (1966); Perry Miller, *Orthodoxy in Massachusetts, 1630–1650* (1933), *The New England Mind: The Seventeenth Century* (1939), and *The New England Mind: From Colony to Province* (1953); Edmund S. Morgan, *The Puritan Dilemma: John Winthrop* (1958), and *Visible Saints: The History of a Puritan Idea* (1963); Robert G. Pope, *The Half-Way Covenant* (1969); Darrett B. Rutman, *American Puritanism: Faith and Practice* (1970); Harry S. Stout, *The New England Soul: Preaching and Religious Culture* (1986); Laurel Thatcher Ulrich, *Good Wives: Image and Reality in the Lives of Women in Northern New England, 1650–1750* (1982); William K. B. Stoever, *A Faire and Easy Way to Heaven: Covenant Theology and Antinomianism* (1978); David E. Van Deventer, *The Emergence of Provincial New Hampshire, 1623–1741* (1976); and Robert E. Wall, Jr., *Massachusetts Bay: The Crucial Decade, 1640–1650* (1972).

SURVIVING IN EARLY AMERICA

Wesley Frank Craven, *White, Red, and Black: The Seventeenth Century Virginian* (1971); John Demos, *A Little Commonwealth: Family Life in Plymouth Colony* (1970); Carville Earle, *The Evolution of a Tidewater Settlement System* (1978); Richard P. Gildrie, *Salem, Massachusetts* (1975); Philip J. Greven, Jr., *Four Generations: Colonial Andover, Massachusetts* (1970); Stephen Innes, *Labor in a New Land: Economy and Society in Springfield* (1983); Douglas E. Leach, *Flintlock and Tomahawk: King Philip's War* (1958); Kenneth A. Lockridge, *A New England Town: Dedham, Massachusetts, 1636–1736*, rev. ed. (1985); Paul R. Lucas, *Valley of Discord: Church and Society Along the Connecticut River, 1636–1725* (1976); Gloria L. Main, *Tobacco Colony: Life in Early Maryland, 1650–1720* (1983); Edmund S. Morgan, *The Puritan Family*, rev. ed. (1966), and *American Slavery, American Freedom: The Ordeal of Colonial Virginia* (1975); Darrett B. Rutman, *Winthrop's Boston, 1630–1649* (1965), and with Anita H. Rutman, *A Place in Time: Middlesex County, Virginia, 1650–1750*, 2 vols. (1984); David E. Stannard, *The Puritan Way of Death* (1977); Thad W. Tate and David L. Ammerman, eds., *The Chesapeake in the Seventeenth Century* (1979); Roger Thompson, *Sex in Middlesex: Popular Mores in a Massachusetts County, 1649–1699* (1986); and Robert V. Wells, *Revolutions in Americans' Lives: A Demographic Perspective* (1982).

COMMERCIAL VALUES AND THE RISE OF SLAVERY

Timothy H. Breen and Stephen Innes, *"Myne Owne Ground": Race and Freedom on Virginia's Eastern Shore, 1640–1676* (1980); Jay Coughtry, *The Notorious Triangle: Rhode Island and the Atlantic Slave Trade, 1700–1807* (1981); Basil Davidson, *The African Genius* (1969); Richard S. Dunn, *Sugar and Slaves: The Rise of the Planter Class in the English West Indies, 1624–1713* (1972); Winthrop D. Jordan, *White Over Black, 1550–1812* (1968); Herbert S. Klein, *Slavery in the Americas: Virginia and Cuba* (1967), and *The Middle Passage* (1978); Allan Kulikoff, *Tobacco and Slaves: Southern Cultures in the Chesapeake, 1680–1800* (1986); Kenneth A. Lockridge, *The Diary, and Life, of William Byrd II of Virginia, 1674–1744* (1987); Edgar J. McManus, *Black Bondage in the North* (1973); Daniel C. Littlefield, *Rice and Slaves: Ethnicity and the Slave Trade in Colonial South Carolina* (1981); Gerald W. Mullin, *Flight and Rebellion: Slave Resistance in Virginia* (1972); Richard Olaniyan, *African History and Culture* (1982); James Rawley, *The Transatlantic Slave Trade* (1981); Daniel Blake Smith, *Inside the Great House: Planter Family Life in Chesapeake Society* (1980); and Peter H. Wood, *Black Majority: Negroes in Colonial South Carolina through the Stono Rebellion* (1974).

A TOBACCO PLANTATION

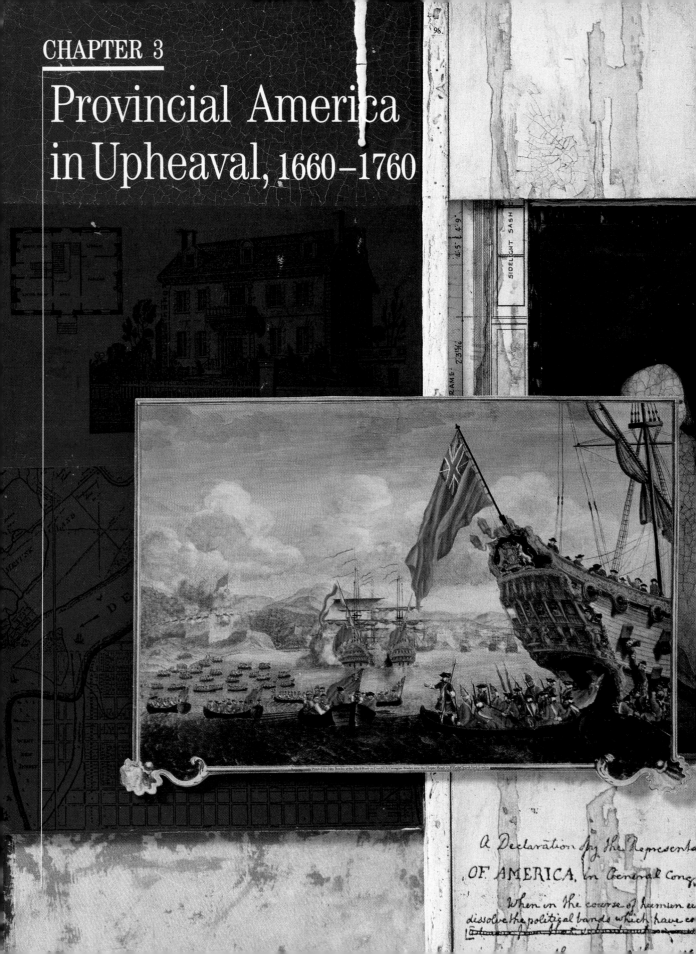

CHAPTER 3

Provincial America in Upheaval, 1660–1760

A Declaration by the Representa

OF AMERICA, in General Cong

When in the course of human e

dissolve the political bands which have c

Hannah Dustan (1657–1736) and Eliza Lucas (1722–1793) never knew one another. Dustan lived in the town of Haverhill on the Massachusetts frontier, and Lucas spent her adult years in the vicinity of Charleston, South Carolina. Even though of different generations, both were inhabitants of England's developing North American empire. Like so many other colonists, perpetual imperial warfare affected their lives as England, France, and Spain repeatedly battled for supremacy in Europe and America between 1689 and 1763.

During the 1690s, as part of a war involving England and France, frontier New Englanders experienced devastating raids by Indian parties from French Canada. On the morning of March 15, 1697, a band of Abenakis struck Haverhill. Hannah Dustan's husband and seven of her children saved themselves by racing for the community's blockhouse. Hannah, who had just given birth a few days before, was not so lucky. The Abenakis captured her, as well as her baby and midwife Mary Neff.

After some discussion, the Indians "dashed out the brains of the infant against a tree," as the well-known Puritan minister, the Reverend Cotton Mather, later wrote, but decided to spare Hannah and Mary along with a few other captives. The plan was to march these residents to the principal Abenaki village in Canada where they would "be stripped and scourged and [made to] run the gauntlet through the whole army of Indians." If they survived, they would be adopted into the tribe, literally to become white Indians.

The Abenakis split up their captives. Two male warriors, three women, and seven children escorted Hannah, Mary, and a young boy named Samuel Lenorson. Hannah, although in a virtual state of shock, maintained her composure as the party walked northward day after day. She prayed fervently, noted Mather, for some means of escape. Just before dawn one morning, she awoke to find all her captors sound asleep. Seizing the moment, she roused Mary and Samuel, handed them hatchets, and told them to crush as many skulls as possible. Suddenly the Indians were dying, and only two, a badly wounded woman and a child, escaped.

Hannah then led the way by taking a scalping knife and finishing the bloody work. When Hannah and the other captives got back to Haverhill they had ten scalps, for which the Massachusetts General Court awarded them a bounty of £50 in local currency. New Englanders hailed Hannah Dustan as a true heroine—a woman whose courage overcame the French and Indian enemies of England's empire in America.

Cotton Mather spread Dustan's story far and wide, hoping to rekindle the faith of New England's founders. If citizens would just "humble" themselves before God, he argued, the Almighty would stop afflicting society with the horrors of war and provide for the "quick extirpation" of all "bloody and crafty" enemies. Mather's jeremiad, however, had little effect. The war soon ended, and New Englanders devoted themselves more than ever before to acquiring personal wealth.

After a long and full life, Hannah Dustan died in 1736. Two years later, George Lucas, a prosperous Antigua planter who was also an officer in the British army, moved to South Carolina, where he owned three rice plantations. He wanted to get his family away from the Caribbean region, since hostilities were brewing with Spain.

When war did come a year later, Lucas returned to Antigua to resume his military duties. Leaving an ailing wife, he placed his seventeen-year-old daughter Eliza in charge of his Carolina properties. The responsibility did not faze her; she wrote regularly to her "Dear Papa" for advice, and the plantations prospered. The war, however, disrupted rice trading routes into the West Indies, and planters needed other cash crops to be sold elsewhere. George Lucas was aware of the problem and sent Eliza seeds for indigo plants, the source of a valued deep-blue dye, to see whether indigo could be grown profitably in South Carolina.

With the help of knowledgeable slaves, Eliza conducted successful experiments. In 1744 a major dye broker in England tested her indigo "against some of the best French" indigo and rated it "in his opinion . . . as good." Just twenty-two years old, Eliza had pioneered a crop that brought additional wealth to Caro-

Because of the experiments of young Eliza Lucas, South Carolina became a major center of indigo production in the British empire.

lina's planters and became a major trading staple of the British empire.

Had Eliza chosen to marry before this time, she could have lost the legal independence to conduct her experiments; but she favored no suitor until she met and wed Charles Pinckney, a widower of great wealth and high social standing. In later life, she took pride in the success of her children. Charles Cotesworth Pinckney (b. 1746) was a powerful voice in the Constitutional Convention of 1787, and Thomas Pinckney (b. 1750) represented President Washington during 1795 in negotiating an agreement called Pinckney's Treaty, which resolved western boundary questions with Spain.

A heralded woman of her generation, Eliza Lucas Pinckney died at the end of the Revolutionary era, nearly 140 years after the birth of Hannah Dustan. Dustan's life paralleled the years in which England laid the foundations for a mighty empire in America. Between 1660 and 1700, the colonists offered resistance but had to adjust to new imperial rules governing their lives. Then a series of wars with France and Spain caused more turbulence. Even with so much upheaval, the colonies grew and prospered, and after 1760 Americans were in a position to question their subordinate relationship with Britain. The coming of the American Revolution cannot be appreciated without looking at the development of the English empire in America—and how that experience affected the lives of passing generations of colonists like Hannah Dustan and Eliza Lucas Pinckney.

DESIGNING ENGLAND'S NORTH AMERICAN EMPIRE

During the 1760s, Benjamin Franklin tried to explain why relations between England and the colonies had turned sour. He blamed British trade policies designed to control American commerce. "Most of the statutes, or acts, . . . of parliaments, . . . for regulating, directing, or restraining of trade," Franklin declared, "have been . . . political blunders, . . . for private advantage, under pretense of public good." The trade system, he concluded, had become both oppressive and corrupt.

Little more than a hundred years before, the colonists had traded as they pleased. After 1650, however, Oliver Cromwell and then the restored Stuart monarch Charles II (1660–1685) worked closely with Parliament to design trade policies that exerted greater control over the activities of the American colonists.

To Benefit the Parent State

Certain key ideas underlay the new, more restrictive policies. Most important was the concept of *mercantilism*, a term not invented until the late eighteenth century but which describes what England's leaders set out to accomplish. Their goal was national greatness and, as one courtier told Charles II, the challenge was to develop "trade and commerce" so that it "draws [a] store of wealth" into England.

Mercantilist thinkers believed the world's supply of wealth was not infinite but fixed in quantity. Any nation that gained wealth automatically did so at the expense of another. In economic dealings, then, the most powerful nations always maintained a favorable balance of trade by exporting a greater value of goods than they imported. To square accounts, hard money in the form of gold and silver would flow into creditor nations. Governments controlling the most precious metals would be the most self-sufficient and could use such wealth to stimulate internal economic development as well as strengthen military forces. This assured not only national survival but ascendancy over other countries.

Mercantilist theory also demonstrated how colonies could best serve their parent states. Gold and silver extracted from Central and South America had underwritten Spain's rise to national glory in the sixteenth century. Al-

Mercantilist policies stimulated England's economy in the late 1600s and led to a boom in the shipbuilding industry in areas like Broad Quay, Bristol.

though such easy wealth did not exist in eastern North America, the colonies could contribute to a favorable trade balance for England by producing staple crops like tobacco, rice, and sugar, thus ending any need to import these goods from other countries.

The American provinces, in addition, could supply valuable raw materials—for example, timber products. England had plundered its own forests to provide winter fuel and construct a strong naval fleet, making it necessary to import wood from the Baltic region. Now the colonies could help fill timber demands, again reducing foreign imports while supplying a commodity vital to national security. Stands of American timber could also be fashioned into fine furniture and sold back to the colonists. Ideally, England's overseas colonies would serve as a source of raw materials and staple crops as well as a marketplace for manufactured goods.

Mercantilist reasoning affirmed the principle that the colonies existed to benefit and strengthen the parent state. As such, provincial economic and political activities had to be closely managed. To effect these goals, Parliament passed a series of Navigation Acts (1651, 1660, 1663, and 1673), which formed the cornerstone of England's commercial relations with the colonies and the rest of the world. The acts banned foreign merchants and vessels from participating in the colonial trade; proclaimed that certain "enumerated" goods could only be shipped to England or other colonies (the first list included dyewoods, indigo, sugar, and tobacco, with furs, molasses, rice, and wood products such as masts, pitch, and tar being added later); and specified that European goods destined for America had to pass through England.

Through the Navigation System, England became the central trading hub of the empire, which resulted in a great economic boom at home. Before 1660, for example, the Dutch operated the largest merchant fleet in Europe and dominated the colonial tobacco trade. They went to war with England over the first Navigation Act (1651), but this short-lived contest (1652–1654) proved futile. After 1660, key industries like shipbuilding began to prosper as

This ship's carpenter was typical of those employed in a booming colonial industry—one-fourth or more of all English-registered vessels were produced in the colonies.

never before. By the late 1690s, the English merchant fleet had outdistanced all competitors, including the Dutch, which seemed to bear out mercantilist ideas regarding one nation's strength coming at another's expense.

In the colonies the Navigation Acts had mixed effects. New Englanders, taking advantage of nearby timber supplies, strengthened their economy by heavy involvement in shipbuilding. By the early 1700s, Americans were constructing one-fourth or more of all English merchant vessels. In the Chesapeake Bay region, however, the enumeration of tobacco resulted in economic difficulties. By the 1660s, planters were producing too much tobacco for consumption in the British Isles alone, and because of the costs of merchandising the crop through England the price became too high to support large sales in Europe. Consequently, the glut of tobacco in England caused prices to decline, resulting in hard times and much anger among Chesapeake planters.

Seizing Dutch New Netherland

Charles II learned from his father's mistakes. He never claimed divine authority in decision making, and so as not to appear too power-hungry, he passed himself off at court as a sensuous, lazy, vulgar man whose major objectives were to attend horse races, tell bawdy jokes, and seduce women. His mistresses like Nell Gwynn became national celebrities, and they bore him at least fourteen illegitimate children. When asked about his lustful ways, he replied, as if mocking the Puritans who had beheaded his father, "God will not damn a man for taking a little unregular pleasure by the way."

Charles II

Charles often played the foppish fool, but he was an intelligent person with a vision for England's greatness. He began his reign determined "to improve the general traffic and trade of the kingdom," as one courtier observed. Besides urging Parliament to legislate the Navigation System, Charles pursued other plans for enhancing England's imperial status. None was more important than challenging Dutch supremacy over the Hudson and Delaware river valleys.

The precedent for attacking territory claimed by England's imperial rivals came in 1654 when Oliver Cromwell launched a fleet with 8000 troops to strike at the heart of New Spain. Cromwell's "Western Design" expedition failed to conquer the primary targets of Puerto Rico, Hispaniola, or Cartagena (modern-day Columbia). The fleet, however, seized the island of Jamaica, which in time became a center for illegal commerce with New Spain, as well as a major slave trade marketing center.

Charles hated everything about Cromwell and proved it by having the Lord Protector's corpse exhumed and hanged in public before a cheering crowd. Still, he borrowed freely from Cromwell's precedents, and New Netherland, a colony having the geographic misfortune of lying between New England and the Southern colonies, was an obvious target, especially since Dutch sea captains used it as a base for conducting illegal trade with English settlers. To enforce the Navigation Acts, reasoned Charles and his advisors, the colony had to be conquered.

New Netherland was the handiwork of the Dutch West India Company, a joint stock venture chartered in 1621. The company soon sent out a governor and employees to the Hudson River area to develop the fur trade with local Indians, particularly the Five Nations of Iroquois inhabiting upper New York west of Fort Orange (Albany).

Iroquois Nations

At the outset, the company showed little interest in settlement, but leaders had to reckon with food shortages. To encourage local agricultural production, the company announced in 1629 that vast landed estates, or *patroonships,* would be made available to men of wealth who transported at least fifty families to New Netherland. The migrants would become tenant farmers for their patroons, who hoped to live like medieval lords on manorial estates. Since the Dutch home economy was booming, few subjects accepted these less-than-generous terms; and only Rensselaerwyck, surrounding Fort Orange, was much of a success.

The New Netherland colony was also internally weak and unstable. The governors were a sorry lot, typified by Wouter van Twiller (1633–1638), a vain, crude man who was pleasant, claimed a contemporary, only "as long as there is any wine." In 1643 his successor, William Kieft, started a war with Indians around New Amsterdam (New York City), which devastated the colony's settlers. Facing bankruptcy in 1647, company directors asked Peter Stuyvesant to save the venture. However, he became embroiled in bitter disputes with the settlers, whom he repeatedly infuriated with his high-handed policies.

Still, New Netherland's population pushed toward 8000 by 1660, counting Puritans who had settled on Long Island. New Amsterdam held people from all over Europe, as well as many African slaves. The unpopularity of Stuyvesant, the absence of any voice in government, and the denial of freedom of worship separate from the Dutch Reformed church all weakened feelings of loyalty and favored an English take-over.

In the early days of his monarchy, Charles II strengthened his political base at home by making generous land grants in America, such as rewarding eight loyal court favorites with the Carolinas patent (see pp. 44–45). In 1664 the king gave his brother, James, the Duke of York, title to all Dutch lands in North America, on the obvious condition that they be conquered. James quickly hired Colonel Richard Nicolls to organize a small invasion fleet. When the flotilla appeared before New Amsterdam in August 1664, Governor Stuyvesant failed to rally the populace. With hardly an exchange of shots, New Netherland became the Duke of York's province of New York.

Proprietary Difficulties in New York and New Jersey

Unlike his older brother, James was an inflexible man. Although hard-working, he was a humorless autocrat. He even treated his mistresses coldly, as if they were "given him by priests for penance," wrote one court wag. Nor was James sensitive to the political trends of his time. He hated Parliament for having executed his father and was intolerant of representative government. As he once explained, popular assemblies of any kind often "prove destructive to, or very often disturb, the peace of the government wherein they are allowed."

James's proprietary charter had no clause mandating an assembly for his colony, and he instructed Colonel Nicolls to make no concessions. As a shrewd administrator, Nicolls got around the problem by granting other rights. In his Articles of Capitulation, he confirmed all inhabitants, including the Dutch, in their land

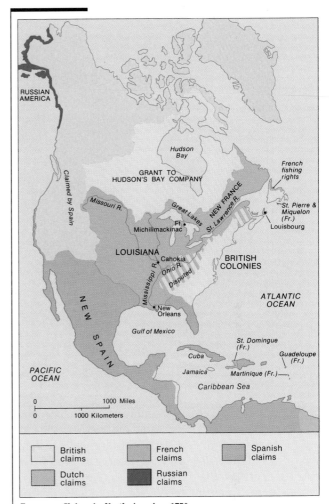

European Claims in North America, 1750

titles. Next he announced the Duke's Laws, which provided for local government and guaranteed basic liberties like trials by jury and religious toleration, as long as settlers belonged to and supported some church.

The Long Island Puritans, however, kept demanding a representative assembly, and they refused to pay local taxes, arguing that they were "enslaved under an arbitrary power." The absence of a popularly-based assembly for New York's colonists continued to be a source of friction. Finally, in the early 1680s James conceded the point; but after becoming king in 1685 he broke his promise, which was one reason for a local rebellion in 1689 (see p. 82).

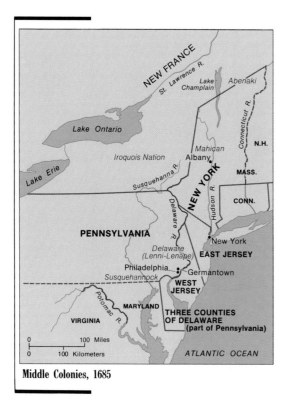

Middle Colonies, 1685

To make matters more confusing, in 1664, James turned over all his proprietary lands between the Hudson and Delaware rivers to John, Lord Berkeley, and Sir George Carteret, two court favorites who were also Carolina proprietors. Unfortunately, Colonel Nicolls did not learn of this grant until after he had offered some Puritans land patents in the eastern portion of what became the colony of New Jersey, named after Carteret's childhood home, the Isle of Jersey off the coast of England.

Until the end of the century, questions regarding proprietary ownership of New Jersey plagued the colony's development. Settlement proceeded slowly, with the population moving toward 15,000 by 1700. Most colonists engaged in commercial farming and raised a variety of grain crops, which they marketed through New York City and Philadelphia, the two port towns that would dominate the region. Because of ongoing confusion over land titles, as well as proprietary political authority, the Crown decided in 1702 that New Jersey would henceforth be a royal province.

Planting Penn's "Holy Experiment"

During the English Civil War of the 1640s, a number of radical religious sects—Ranters, Seekers, and Quakers among them—began to appear in England. Each represented a small band of fervent believers determined to recast human society in the mold of a particular religious vision. George Fox founded the Society of Friends, and his followers came to be called "Quakers," because Fox, who went to jail many times, warned one judge to "tremble at the word of the lord."

The Quakers adhered to many controversial ideas. They believed that all persons had a divine spark, or "inner light," which, when fully nurtured, allowed them to commune directly with God. Like Anne Hutchinson before them, they saw little need for human institutions. They had no ministers and downplayed the importance of the Bible, since they could order their lives according to revelation received directly from God.

In addition, the Quakers held a unique social vision. All humans, they argued, were equal in the sight of God. Thus they wore unadorned black clothing and refused to remove their broad-brimmed hats when social superiors passed by them. Women had full access to leadership positions and could serve as preachers and missionaries. Members of the sect also refused to take legal oaths, which they considered a form of swearing, and they were pacifists, believing that warfare would never solve human problems. In time, Quakers became antislavery advocates, arguing that God did not hold some persons inferior because of skin color.

Early English Quakers were intensely fervent, and during the 1650s and 1660s they sent many witnesses of their faith to America. These individuals, about half of them women, fared poorly in the colonies. Puritan magistrates told them of their "free liberty to keep away from us" and threw them out. Two Quaker males were so persistent in coming back to Boston that officials finally hanged them in 1659, and they gave a third witness, Mary Dyer, a gallows reprieve. Dyer, however, returned the next

Quakers used their plain dress as a way to protest the worldliness of the upper class in England. Clothing did not make the person, rather, one's relations with God did.

year, was hanged, and became a martyr to her vision of a more harmonious world.

William Penn first became a Quaker in the early 1660s while a college student at Oxford. Hoping to cure his son's radicalism, Penn's father, who had received estates in Ireland for his part in leading Cromwell's 1654 expedition against New Spain, sent William on a tour of the Continent. Penn returned in a more worldly frame of mind, but he soon adopted Quaker beliefs again. He was so outspoken that he even spent time in jail, but his father's high standing at court—the elder Penn supported the Stuart restoration—gave Penn access to Charles II.

During the 1670s, George Fox traveled to America, hoping to find a haven for his followers. He also encouraged Penn to use his family connections to obtain a land grant. King Charles acceded to Penn's request for a proprietary charter in 1681, stating that his purpose was to "enlarge our British empire" and pay off a £16,000 debt long since due the estate of Penn's father. Years later, Penn claimed that Charles's real motivation was "to be rid of" the Quakers "at so cheap a rate" by conveying to him title to "a desert three thousand miles off."

Pennsylvania, meaning Penn's woods, was hardly a desert. It was a bountiful tract, and Penn wanted to make the most of it, both as a sanctuary for oppressed religious groups and as a source of personal income from quitrents. He laid his plans carefully, making large grants to English Quakers, and he drew up plans for a commercial center—Philadelphia, or the City of Brotherly Love. He sent agents to Europe in search of settlers, offering generous land packages with low annual quitrents. He also wrote his First Frame of Government (1682), which guaranteed a legislative assembly and full freedom of religion.

Like the Puritans before him, Penn had an utopian vision, in this case captured by the phrase "holy experiment." Unlike the Puritans, Penn wanted to mold a society in which peoples of diverse backgrounds and religious beliefs lived together harmoniously—a bold idea in an era not known for its toleration.

Determined to succeed, Penn sailed to America in 1682, landing first in the area known as the Three Lower Counties, which later became Delaware. He had purchased this strip of land from the Duke of York to assure an easy exit for commerce flowing out of Philadelphia to Atlantic trade routes. Until 1701, Delaware existed as an appendage of Pennsylvania, but then Penn granted it a separate assembly. Until the Revolution, however, the proprietary governors of Pennsylvania also headed Delaware's government.

Next Penn journeyed upriver to lay out Philadelphia. Some settlers were already present, and during the next few years others migrated not only from England but also from Wales, Scotland, Ireland, Holland, Germany, and Switzerland. Typical were Germans from the Rhineland who followed their religious leader, Daniel Francis Pastorius, and founded Germantown to the north of Philadelphia. From the very outset, Pennsylvania developed along pluralist lines, an early sign of what later charac-

In Penn's treaty with the Indians, he sought to treat Native Americans fairly in negotiating land rights. However, Pennsylvania colonists and Penn's own officials wanted to push the native populace westward as rapidly as possible.

terized the cultural ideal of the United States as a whole.

Penn envisioned a "peaceable kingdom" and sought cordial relations with local Indians. Before leaving England, he wrote to the Delawares, the dominant tribe in the region, explaining that the king of England "hath given me a great province." He asked that "we may always live together as neighbors and friends." True to his word, Penn met with the Delawares and told them that he would not take land from them unless agreed to by tribal chieftains. What emerged was the "walking purchase" system in which the natives sold land based on the distance that a person could travel on foot in a day. Even though the system was open to abuse, Penn's goal was honest dealing, which had rarely been the case in other colonies.

Completing these and other tasks, Penn returned to England in 1684 to encourage fur-

ther settlement. That was no problem. Pennsylvania was very attractive, particularly with dissenter religious groups. By the early 1700s, the population exceeded 20,000. Colonists poured through the booming port of Philadelphia and then fanned out into the fertile countryside. There they set up family farms, raising livestock and growing abundant grain crops, which they marketed to the West Indies and Europe. The settlers prospered, and Pennsylvania gained a reputation as "one of the best poor man's countries in the world."

Still not all was perfect in the peaceable kingdom. Religious sects segregated themselves, wanting little to do with one another. To Penn's dismay, life in Philadelphia was more raucous than pious. Drinking establishments and brothels sprang up in large numbers, and endless bickering characterized local politics. Quakers dominated the government but fought endlessly over the prerogatives of power. Penn thought these "brutish, . . . scurvy quarrels" were a "disgrace" to the colony, but his pleas for harmony went unheard. Equally disturbing from his point of view, settlers refused to pay quitrents "to supply me with bread," yet he kept funding the colony's development.

Hoping to solve such problems, Penn returned in 1699. His presence had a moderating influence—but only as long as he stayed. Before leaving for the last time, he announced a new Charter of Liberties (1701), which placed all legislative authority in the assembly's lower house, to be checked only by a proprietary governor with the advice of a council of well-to-do local gentlemen. This document served as the basis of Pennsylvania's unicameral government until the Revolution.

Peace, prosperity, pluralism, and religious toleration were the hallmarks of Penn's utopian vision. In his old age, however, he considered the holy experiment a failure. He concluded that peaceable kingdoms on earth were beyond human reach, and having even endured prison for debts contracted on behalf of his colony, Penn died an embittered man in 1718. By seeking a better life for all peoples, he had infused a sense of high social purpose into the American experience.

Characteristic of Quaker farms in Pennsylvania, David Twining's homestead emphasizes harmonious and peaceful relations.

DEFYING THE IMPERIAL WILL: PROVINCIAL CONVULSIONS AND REBELLIONS

Establishing the Middle colonies was an integral part of England's imperial expansion within the framework of mercantilist thinking. Certainly the Dutch understood this, and they fought two additional wars with England (1664–1667 and 1672–1674), hoping to recoup their losses. In the last war, they even recaptured New York only to renounce all claims in the peace settlement. After that time, the Dutch focused their activities on other parts of the world, even if some of their mariners continued to trade illegally with the colonists.

Besides standing up to the Dutch, Charles and his advisors worked to tighten up the empire in other ways. They sent the first customs officers to America to collect duties on enumerated goods being traded between colonies—and then to foreign ports. Crown officials also crossed the Atlantic to determine whether the colonists were cooperating with the Navigation System. The Americans increasingly felt England's constraining hand, which in some locales helped to bring on violence.

Bacon's Bloody Rebellion in Virginia

With tobacco glutting the market in England, Virginia's economy went into a tailspin during the 1660s. The planters blamed the Navigation Acts, which stopped them from dealing directly with such foreign merchants as the Dutch; and it did not improve the planters' mood when, in 1667, Dutch war vessels captured nearly the whole English merchant fleet hauling that year's crop out of Chesapeake Bay, resulting in the total loss of a year's worth of work.

Besides economic woes, there were other problems. Some Virginians thought that their longtime royal governor, Sir William Berkeley, had become a tyrant. Berkeley handed out patronage jobs to a few favored planters, known as the "Green Spring" faction (named after Berkeley's plantation). Such favors allowed the governor to dominate the assembly and lay heavy taxes at a time when settlers were suffering economically. As a consequence, some planters lost their property, and young males just completing terms of indentured service saw few prospects for ever gaining title to land and achieving economic independence. In 1670 Berkeley and the assembly approved a fifty-acre property holding requirement for voting privileges. This action fed suspicions that the governor and his cronies were out to gain all power for themselves.

In 1674 young Nathaniel Bacon jumped into the simmering pot. From a wealthy English family and educated at Cambridge, he had squandered his inheritance before reaching his mid-twenties. Bacon's despairing father sent him to Virginia with a stipend to start a plantation, hoping that the experience would force his son to grow up. When Bacon arrived, Berkeley greeted him warmly, stating that "gentlemen of your quality come very rarely into this country."

Bacon was ambitious, and he sought acceptance among Berkeley's favored friends, who controlled the lucrative Indian trade. He asked the governor for a trading license, but Berkeley denied the request, feeling that the young man had not yet proven his worth. Incensed by his rejection, Bacon started opposing Berkeley at every turn. He organized other substantial planters—also not favored by Berkeley—into his own "Castle" faction (after his plantation), and he also appealed to Virginia's growing numbers of propertyless poor for support.

Stirrings among Indian tribes made matters worse. Far to the north in New York, the Five Nations of Iroquois had become more aggressive in their quest for furs. They started pushing other tribes southward toward Virginia, and some spilled onto frontier plantations, resulting in a few killings.

Bacon demanded reprisals, but Berkeley urged caution, noting that a war would only add to Virginia's tax burdens. Bacon asked for a military commission, stating that he would organize an army of volunteers. The governor refused, at which point Bacon charged his adversary with being more interested in protecting profits from his Indian trading monopoly than in saving settlers' lives. Bacon pulled together a force of over 1000 men, described as "the scum of the country" by Berkeley's supporters, and indiscriminately started killing local Indians.

In response, Berkeley declared Bacon "the greatest rebel that ever was in Virginia" and sent out militiamen to corral the volunteers, but Bacon's force eluded them. The governor also called a new assembly, which met at Jamestown in June 1676. Among reforms designed to pacify the "mutineers," the burgesses restored voting rights to all freemen. Events had gone too far, however, and a shooting war broke out. Before it ended, Bacon's force burned Jamestown to the ground, and Berkeley fled across Chesapeake Bay. What finally ended the struggle was Bacon's death from dysentery in October 1676.

When Charles II learned of the uprising, he considered it an affront to royal authority and a threat to his tax revenues on tobacco. The colonists had to be disciplined, so he authorized a flotilla of eleven ships and 1000 troops to cross the Atlantic and restore order. By the time the troops arrived, Berkeley was back in control. Royal advisors with the king's army, however, removed the aging governor from office on the grounds that his policies had helped to stir up trouble. Governors who placed self-interest above imperial need—to the detriment of stability and prosperity—would no longer be tolerated.

After 1676, the Crown started sending governors to Virginia

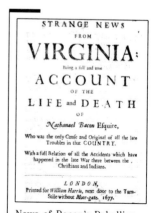

News of Bacon's Rebellion

with detailed instructions on managing the colony as an imperial enterprise. Some of the new governors were former military officers, and they acted as if they were running a garrison outpost of empire. In response, Virginia's leading gentlemen, previously divided into pro- and anti-Berkeley factions, settled their differences in the face of this new threat to local autonomy. They rallied the people to their side, got themselves elected regularly to the House of Burgesses, and worked to preserve the colony's interests against meddling imperial officials.

This fundamental recasting of political lines was an important development. No more would rising planter elite leaders fight to the death among themselves. They would stand united in defense of local rights and privileges, making it clear that the Crown could only push so far in demanding compliance.

The Glorious Revolution Spills Into America

The king's reactions to Bacon's Rebellion fit a larger pattern of asserting more authority over America. New England, with its independent ways, was an obvious target. Back in the mid-1660s, royal commissioners had visited Massachusetts and seen Dutch merchant vessels trading openly in Boston harbor in violation of the Navigation Acts. Puritan leaders were surly about the matter, stating that "the laws of England . . . do not reach [to] America." Once home, the angry commissioners urged the Crown to take over the colony, but nothing happened—at least not for a few years.

Then in 1675 King Charles, seeking more effective control over the colonies, designated certain Privy Council members to serve as the Lords of Trade and Plantations. The Lords, in turn, sent agents and customs officials to America. The most notorious was Edward Randolph, a grim, dedicated bureaucrat who never met a Puritan he liked. Soon he was bombarding the Lords of Trade with negative reports. In the face of Randolph's commentary, the Lords proceeded to have the Bay Colony charter revoked in 1684.

Randolph, however, was not solely responsible for voiding the charter. The Lords had developed plans for setting up two or three large administrative territories in North America. New England made a natural unit, based on geographic cohesion and forms of economic production. King Charles thought the scheme too radical, but when James became king in 1685, the Lords gained permission to set up the Dominion of New England, which stretched from Nova Scotia to the Delaware River.

James II liked the Dominion concept because it favored the Church of England, even though other faiths would be tolerated. Also, local representative assemblies would cease to exist, and all political decisions would be in the hands of a governor and a large advisory council made up of Crown appointees. James wrote the New Yorkers with pleasure and informed them that their pleas for an assembly had been superseded by the Dominion. As for Connecticut and Rhode Island, the Lords were already trying to void their charters in court.

From the outset, the Dominion was a bad idea, perhaps made worse by naming as governor Sir Edmund Andros, a man of aristocratic bearing with impressive military credentials. Among his councilors was the despised Edward Randolph. Images of tyranny floated through Puritan minds when Andros debarked in Boston in late 1686 and demanded that a building be found for holding Anglican church services. It all smacked of garrison government in which the highest ranking military officer had complete authority, with no popular checks whatsoever.

Andros expected the Puritans to conform to the imperial will. He announced plans to rewrite all land deeds, none of which the General Court had awarded in the king's name and, then, to impose quitrents, which New Englanders had never paid. He announced import taxes to underwrite the expenses of his government, and he started prosecuting violaters of the Navigation Acts.

Meanwhile, in England, James II had created an uproar by pushing his authority too far. In defiance of England's Protestant tradition, he flaunted his Roman Catholic beliefs in public and declared that his newborn son, now next in line for the throne, would be raised a Catholic. The thought of yet more turbulence over religion was too much for influential English leaders to bear. In December 1688, they drove James from the realm and offered the throne to his Protestant daughter, Mary, and her husband, the Dutch prince, William of Orange, as joint monarchs. As part of the Glorious Revolution, Parliament also placed strict limitations on royal prerogatives by adopting the Declaration of Rights (1689), which at long last assured Parliament an equal, if not dominant, voice in Britain's political affairs.

When news of the Glorious Revolution reached Boston, local Puritan leaders went into action, urged on by rumors that James, who had fled to France, was conspiring with Andros, French Canadians, and Indians to seize New England and turn it into a bastion of Roman Catholicism. Denouncing Andros and his followers as "bloody devotees of Rome," they seized the governor on April 18, 1689, threw him in jail, and then shipped him back to England. They did so, they insisted, to end Andros's arbitrary rule, and they asked William and Mary to restore their original corporate charter.

The coup in Massachusetts helped spark a rebellion in New York, where a volatile mix of ethnic and class tensions resulted in a violent upheaval. Francis Nicholson served in New York City as the Dominion's lieutenant governor. Wealthy Dutch and English landholders and merchants cooperated with his rule, which bred resentment among poorer Dutch and English settlers, like the Puritans on Long Island. Jacob Leisler, a combative local merchant of German origin, also hated the favored families. They had snubbed him socially, despite his marriage to a wealthy Dutch widow. Even worse, from his point of view, they cared little about securing popular political rights.

When reports of the rumored "popish" plot and the Massachusetts coup reached New York, Leisler exhorted the anti-Nicholson settlers to rise up and defend themselves. He organized 500 of them into a military force, and on May 31 they captured Fort James guarding New York harbor. Within a few days, Nicholson fled to England amid cries that all Dominion "popish dogs and devils" must be jailed. Leisler then set up an interim government and waited for advice from England, hoping that the new monarchs would grant a popularly-based assembly. In addition, Leisler allowed mobs to harass and rob wealthy families.

The third colony jolted by a revolt in 1689 was Maryland, where quarrels between Catholics and Protestants remained a perpetual source of tension. The proprietary governor, William Joseph, tried to contain the popish conspiracy rumors, but John Coode, a nervous local planter, organized the Protestant Association to defend Marylanders from the impending slaughter. Rumormongers soon were whispering that the Catholic proprietor and his local governor were in on the plot. That was all Coode needed. He led 250 followers to St. Mary's, where in July 1689 they removed Joseph from office, called their own assembly, and then sent representatives to England to plead for royal government.

In a chain reaction, three uprisings had occurred in the American colonies during a span of four months. Although each had its own local character, the common issue, besides the rumored popish conspiracy, was the question of how extensive colonial rights would be in the face of tightening imperial administration. All the colonists could do now was wait to hear from the new monarchs—and hope for the best.

New England's Witchcraft Hysteria

William and Mary, at first, had little time to deal with the provincial rebellions. Warfare had broken out in Europe (the War of the League of Augsburg, 1689–1697). Spilling over into America, the contest caused havoc in the lives of frontier settlers like Hannah Dustan. French and Indian raiding parties made orphans of many children, including a few who ended up in Salem Village (now Danvers), Massachusetts, the center of the 1692 witchcraft episode.

Puritans, like most Europeans and colonists elsewhere, believed in witchcraft. They thought that the devil could materialize in various shapes and forms, damaging lives at will. Satan's agents included witches and wizards, women and men possessed by his evil spirits. Some 100 New Englanders had faced accusations of practicing witchcraft before 1692, numbers that were insignificant in comparison to

As the witchcraft trials proceeded, many young girls became more strident in their accusations. They fell into fits and shouted that the accused had cast some sort of spell over them.

accused witches hunted down and executed in Europe.

Reasons abound for the outbreak of the witchcraft hysteria. By the early 1690s, New Englanders had lost their charter, lived under the Dominion, rebelled against Edmund Andros, and engaged in war with the hated French. These unsettled conditions may have made the populace overly suspicious and anxious about evil influences in their midst.

In addition, special tensions affected the Salem area. Salem Town, the port, was caught up in New England's commercial life while outlying settlers around Salem Village remained quite traditional in seeking God's grace before material wealth. Resentment by the villagers was growing, expressed even before 1690 as "uncharitable expressions and uncomely reflections tossed to and fro." These tensions came out in the pattern of accusations when in early 1692 a few adolescent girls, among them some of the war orphans from Maine, started having their "fits."

Before the hysteria ended, the "afflicted" girls made hundreds of accusations before a special court to root the devil out of Massachusetts. With increasing frequency they pointed to prosperous citizens like those of Salem Town. The penalty for practicing witchcraft was death, and twenty men and women were executed (nineteen by hanging and one by the crushing weight of stones). But by the end of the year the craze was over, probably because too many citizens of rank and influence, including the new governor's wife, had been accused of doing the devil's work.

In time, most participants in the Salem witchcraft trials admitted to being deluded. And if the episode accomplished nothing else, it supported New England's transition to a commercial society by making traditional beliefs—and those who espoused them—appear foolish.

Settling Anglo-American Differences

During 1691, William and Mary began to address colonial issues. As constitutional monarchs, they were not afraid of popularly-based assemblies. In the case of Massachusetts, they approved a royal charter in which the Crown named royal governors and stated that all male property holders, not just church members, had the right to vote. On the other hand, the monarchs did not tamper with the established Congregational church, thereby reassuring old-line Puritans that conforming to the Church of England was not necessary as long as Bay Colony residents supported England's imperial aspirations.

New York also became a royal colony in 1691, complete with a local representative assembly. Henry Sloughter, the royal governor, delivered the news, but Jacob Leisler hesitated to step aside, fearing that Sloughter might be an agent of King James. Leisler's obstinacy led to his arrest and hasty trial for treason. His enemies gave all the testimony that the court needed to sentence him to a ghastly death—by hanging, disemboweling, drawing and quartering and, if that were not enough, decapitation. It was little solace to Leisler's followers that Parliament, in reviewing the case, later declared him innocent of treason.

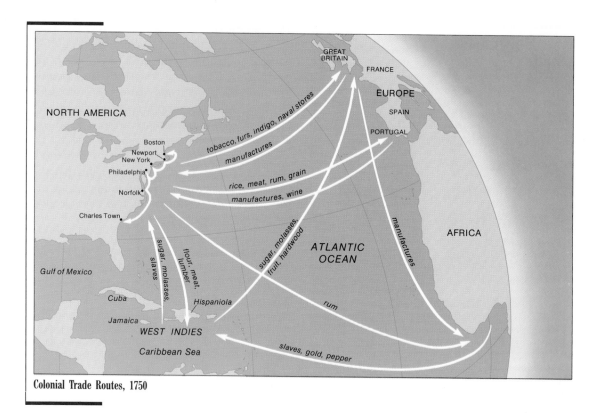

Colonial Trade Routes, 1750

In the case of Maryland, the Calverts lost political control in 1692 in favor of royal government, although they still held title to the land and could collect quitrents. Shortly thereafter, a Protestant assembly banned Roman Catholics from political office. Not until 1715 did the Calverts regain political control. By then they had converted to Anglicanism and were no longer a threat to Protestant sensibilities.

The transformation revealed a movement toward the royal model of government in which the colonies established legislative assemblies to express and defend their local concerns. Crown-appointed governors, in turn, pledged themselves to enforce the Navigation Acts and other imperial laws. As long as the colonists cooperated, they would not face autocratic forms of government. Nor would the Crown permit the kind of loose freedom of early colonial days, because in gaining basic rights, the Americans also accepted responsibility for conducting their daily affairs within the imperial framework. The Glorious Revolution—and its reverberations in America—had made this compromise possible.

Maintaining the delicate balance between imperial intrusiveness and local autonomy was the major challenge of the eighteenth century. Until the 1760s, both sides tried to make the compromise work. The Crown demonstrated its resolve through the Navigation Act of 1696, which set up the Board of Trade and Plantations as a permanent administrative body to advise England's leaders on colonial matters. This act also mandated the establishment of vice-admiralty courts in America to punish smugglers and others who violated the rules of trade. The Board of Trade operated to promote efficiency, not officiousness, yet colonists who cheated and got caught faced stiff penalties from vice-admiralty court judges.

The Board of Trade generally acted with discretion, even in recommending a few acts to restrain colonial manufactures competing with home industries. Parliament in 1699 adopted legislation that outlawed any exportation of woolen products from America, or from colony to colony. The intent was to get the colonists to buy finished woolens from manufacturers in England rather than develop their own industry. In 1732 there was a similar act involving beaver hats, and in 1750 Parliament passed the Iron Act, which forbade the colonists from producing finished iron or steel products. They could, however, prepare raw iron for final manufacturing in England. As a whole, these acts had few adverse effects on the provincial economy. They simply reinforced fundamental mercantile notions regarding colonies as sources of raw materials and as markets for finished goods.

Occasionally, imperial administrators went too far, such as with the Molasses Act of 1733. In support of a thriving rum industry based mostly in New England, colonial merchants roamed the Caribbean for molasses which cost less on French and Dutch West Indian islands. To placate British West Indian planters, Parliament tried to redirect the trade with a heavy duty (6 pence per gallon) on foreign molasses brought into the colonies. Enforcing the trade duty could have ruined the North American rum industry, but customs officers wisely did not attempt to collect the duty, a sensible solution to a potentially inflammatory issue.

As the eighteenth century progressed, imperial officials tried not to be overbearing. In certain instances, they actually stimulated provincial economic activity by offering large cash bounties for growing export crops like indigo; it seems that Eliza Lucas's efforts had the potential to challenge France's dominant position in the production of that valued dye. Caught up as the empire was in warfare with France and Spain, home leaders did not want to tamper with a system that, by and large, worked. The colonists, for their part, gladly accepted what many have referred to as the "era of salutary neglect."

MATURING COLONIAL SOCIETIES IN UNSETTLED TIMES

Besides the maintenance of stable relations with the parent state, other factors stimulated the maturing of the American provinces after 1700. Certainly the expanding population base, which saw a doubling of numbers nearly every twenty years, strengthened the colonies, as did the pattern of widespread economic prosperity, even if not shared evenly among the populace. In times of internal social turmoil, such as the religious upheaval known as the Great Awakening (see pp. 93–94), the colonists disagreed but did not lose sight of their joint need to keep building their communities. Finally, their participation in a series of imperial wars, in which they made valuable contributions to Britain's military triumphs, instilled a vital sense of confidence. By the 1760s, the colonists took pride in what they had accomplished together as subjects inhabiting the British empire in North America.

An Exploding Population Base

Between 1700 and 1760, the colonial population mushroomed from 250,000 to 1.6 million persons—and to 2.5 million by 1775. "People multiply faster here than in Europe," noted one foreign visitor at mid-century. "As soon as a person is old enough he may marry without any fear of poverty," he claimed, because "a newly married man can, without difficulty, get a spot of ground where he may comfortably subsist with his wife and children."

Natural population increase, predicated upon abundant land, early marriages, and high

Table 3.1

Colonial Population Growth, 1660–1760

Year	White	Black	Total
1660	70,200	2900	73,100*
1680	138,100	7000	145,100
1700	223,100	27,800	250,900
1720	397,300	68,900	466,200
1740	755,500	150,000	905,500
1760	1,267,800	325,800	1,593,600
1780	2,111,100	566,700	2,677,800

Note: All estimates rounded to the nearest hundred.
* Includes the population of New Netherland.
From *The American Colonies: From Settlement to Independence* by R.C. Simmons. Copyright © 1976 by R.C. Simmons. Reprinted by permission of Harold Matson, Inc.

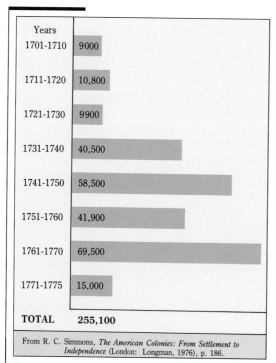

Years	
1701-1710	9000
1711-1720	10,800
1721-1730	9900
1731-1740	40,500
1741-1750	58,500
1751-1760	41,900
1761-1770	69,500
1771-1775	15,000
TOTAL	**255,100**

From R. C. Simmons, *The American Colonies: From Settlement to Independence* (London: Longman, 1976), p. 186.

Figure 3.1

Slave Importation Estimates, 1701–1775

From *The American Colonies: From Settlement to Independence*, by R. C. Simmons. Copyright © 1976 by R. C. Simmons. Reprinted by permission of Harold Matson Company, Inc.

only to face discrimination themselves when a new Parliamentary law, the Test Act of 1704, stripped non-Anglicans of political rights. During the next several years, they also endured crop failures and huge rent increases from their English landlords.

In a series of waves between 1725 and 1775, over 100,000 Scots-Irish descended upon North America, lured by reports of "a rich, fine soil before them, laying as loose . . . as the best bed in the garden." Philadelphia was their main port of entry, and they moved out into the backcountry where they squatted on open land and earned reputations as bloodthirsty Indian fighters. In time, the Scots-Irish took the Great Wagon Road through the Shenandoah Valley and started filling in the Southern backcountry.

Even before the first Scots-Irish wave, Germans from the area of the upper Rhine River began streaming into the Middle colonies. Some, like Amish, Moravian, and Mennonite sectarians, were fleeing religious persecution; others were escaping crushing economic circumstances caused by overpopulation, crop failures, and heavy local taxes. So many Germans came through Philadelphia that Benjamin

fertility rates, was only one source of the population explosion. Equally significant was the introduction of non-English peoples. Between 1700 and 1775, for example the British North American slave trade reached its peak, resulting in the involuntary entry of an estimated 250,000 Africans into the colonies. The black population grew from 28,000 in 1700 to over 500,000 in 1775, with most living as chattel slaves in the South. At least forty to fifty percent of the Afro-American population increase was attributable to the booming slave trade.

Among European groups, the Scots-Irish and Germans predominated, although a smattering of French Huguenot, Swiss, Scottish, Irish, and Jewish migrants joined the westward stream. The Scots-Irish had endured many privations. Originally Presbyterian lowlanders from Scotland, they had migrated to Ulster (northern Ireland) in the seventeenth century at the invitation of the Crown. Once there, they harassed the Catholic Irish with a vengeance,

By 1775, some 100,000 Germans had migrated to Pennsylvania where they became known as Pennsylvania Dutch—a corruption of the word Deutch, meaning German.

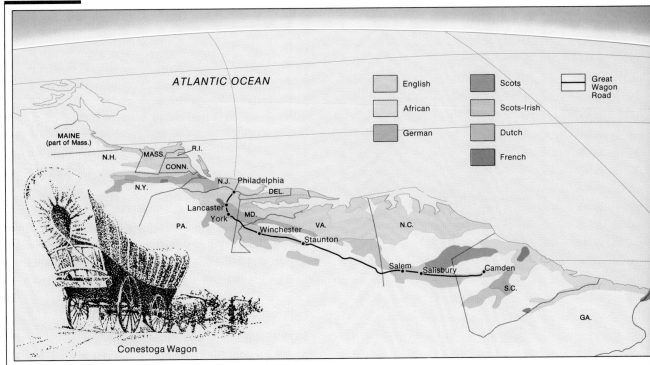

ATLANTIC OCEAN

English   Scots

African   Scots-Irish

German   Dutch

French

Great Wagon Road

MAINE (part of Mass.)

N.H.   R.I.

MASS.

CONN.

N.Y.   N.J.   Philadelphia

DEL.

Lancaster   MD.

York

PA.   Winchester   VA.   N.C.

Staunton

Salem   Salisbury   Camden

S.C.

GA.

Conestoga Wagon

Distribution of Immigrant Groups and the Great Wagon Road, Mid-1700s
The Conestoga wagon was important to the settlement and movement of the colonies.

Franklin questioned whether "Pennsylvania, founded by the English, [will] become a colony of aliens, who will shortly be so numerous as to Germanize us, instead of our Anglifying them?" But Franklin's fears could not stop the German migrants, whose population exceeded 100,000 by 1775.

Many destitute Germans crossed the Atlantic as "redemptioners." This system was similar to indentured servitude, except families migrated together and shippers promised heads of households a few days' time, upon arrival in America, to find some person or group to pay costs of passage. If they failed, then ship captains auctioned them off at market, making tidy profits by selling their labor for terms of three to six years. The redemptioner system was full of abuses, such as packing passengers on ships like cattle and serving them worm-infested food; and hundreds died before seeing America. For those who survived, the dream of prospering someday as free colonists remained viable.

One reason for such optimism was that more settlers were enjoying longer life spans, as reflected in higher birth and lower death rates. Estimates indicate that post-1700 Americans were dying at an average of 20 to 25 per 1000 annually, but births numbered 45 to 50 per 1000 settlers. By comparison, the rates in England between 1700 and 1750 were 34 births per 1000 for every 33 deaths.

Longer lives reflected better health and agricultural abundance. Colonists had plentiful supplies of food. Nutritious diets led to improved overall health, making it easier for Americans to fight virulent diseases. Even the poorest person, claimed a New England doctor, had regular meals of "salt pork and beans, with bread of Indian corn meal," as well as ample supplies of home-brewed beer and distilled spirits. In the same period, food supplies in Europe were dangerously thin. Thousands of western Europeans starved to death between 1740 and 1743 due to widespread crop failures.

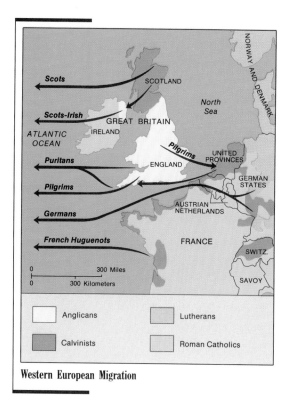

Western European Migration

The "Europeanizing" of America

Compared to Europe, America was a land of boundless prosperity. However, there were wide disparities in wealth, rank, and privilege, which the colonists accepted as part of the natural order of life. They did so because of the pervasive influence of European values, such as the need for hierarchy and deference in social and political relations. The eighteenth century was still an era in which individuals believed in three distinct social orders—the monarchy, the aristocracy, and the "democracy" of common citizens. All persons had an identifiable place in society, fixed at birth; and to try to improve one's lot was to risk instability in the established rhythms of the universe.

These notions, dating back to Aristotle and other ancient thinkers, served as justifications for the highly stratified world of early modern Europe, featuring monarchical families like the Tudors and Stuarts and blood-line aristocrats who passed hereditary titles from one generation to the next. Among those threatening

Europe's established social order were ambitious commoners who had acquired great wealth in commerce. They too craved high status, and they tried to earn a place for themselves at the top of the social pyramid by copying the manners and customs of those born into privileged social stations.

The same could be said for wealthy elite families that had emerged in America by the eighteenth century. In Virginia names like Byrd, Carter, and Lee were of the first rank; the Pinckneys and Rutledges dominated South Carolina; in New York the Schuylers and Livingstons were among the favored with great estates along the Hudson River, modelled after Dutch patroonships; and in Massachusetts those of major consequence included merchant families like the Hutchinsons and Olivers.

Elite families set themselves apart from the rest of colonial society by imitating English aristocratic lifestyles. Wealthy Southern gentlemen employed gangs of slaves to produce the staple crops that generated the income to construct lavish manor houses with elaborate formal gardens. Northern merchants built residences of Georgian design and filled them with fashionable Heppelwhite or Chippendale furniture. Together, they thought of themselves as the "better sort," and they expected deference from the "lower sort" (also described as the "common herd" or "rabble") in social and political matters.

One characteristic, then, of the "Europeanizing" of colonial society was growing economic stratification, with extremes of wealth and poverty becoming more visible. In Chester County, Pennsylvania, where commercial farming predominated, the wealthiest ten percent of the people owned twenty-four percent of the taxable property in the 1690s, which jumped to thirty-four percent by 1760. Their gain came at the expense of the bottom thirty percent, who held seventeen percent in the 1690s but only six percent in 1760. The pattern was even more striking in urban areas like Boston and Philadelphia. By 1760, the top ten percent owned over sixty percent of the available wealth; the bottom thirty percent held less than two percent.

Nevertheless there was a large middle class, and it was still possible to get ahead in

Once the early hardships of settlement had been overcome, Virginia's planter gentry began to copy the life-style of England's country gentry.

colonial America. Over ninety percent of the population lived in the countryside and made their livings from some form of agricultural production. By European standards, the ownership of property was widespead, yet there were also many instances of extreme poverty. Some of the worst cases were among urban dwellers, many of whom eked out the barest of livelihoods as unskilled day laborers or merchant seamen. These individuals at least enjoyed some personal freedom, which placed them above black slaves, who formed twenty percent of the population but enjoyed none of its prosperity or political rights.

With colonial wealth concentrated in fewer and fewer hands, a second "Europeanizing" trend was toward hardened class lines. Elite families increasingly intermarried among themselves, and they spoke openly of an assumed right to serve as political stewards for the people. As one Virginia gentleman proclaimed in the 1760s, "men of *birth* and *fortune*, in every government that is free, should be invested with power, and enjoy higher honors than the people. If it were otherwise, their privileges

A room from the Samuel Powel house in Philadelphia depicts the gracious life-style of wealthy urban merchants.

COLONIAL PASTIMES

For much of the past three hundred years, Puritans have been the subject of considerable bad press. Novelists and historians have pictured them as dour, sour individuals, dressed in black with faces cast in a permanently disapproving expression. H. L. Mencken, the twentieth-century opponent of what he saw as the Puritan legacy in America, defined Puritanism as "the haunting fear that some one, some where, may be happy." Thomas Babington Macaulay, the nineteenth-century English writer, perhaps best set the tone for Mencken. "The Puritan," Macaulay noted, "hated bear-baiting, not because it gave pain to the bear, but because it gave pleasure to the spectators."

Is there any truth to such broad-brushed stereotyping? What was the Puritans' attitude toward games, sports, and amusements? And how did their attitudes differ from southern Americans? The answers to such questions indicate the differences between Americans North and South.

Commenting on Puritan religious leaders Increase and Cotton Mather, one historian observed, "Though father and son walked the streets of Boston at noonday, they were only twilight figures, communing with ghosts, building with shadows." Certainly, as the quote suggests, the Puritan clergy were sober figures. They looked askance at frivolous behavior. Into this category they lumped sports, games, and amusements played for

the pure joy of play. In 1647 the Massachusetts Bay Colony outlawed shuffleboard. A ban against bowling followed in 1650. Football and other sports were similarly treated.

Puritan leaders were opposed to any Sabbath amusements. Sunday was a day for worship—not work, and certainly not play. Remaining true to the teachings of the Prophet Isaiah, Cotton Mather condemned those who tried to justify Sabbath sports: "Never did anything sound more sorrowfully or odious since the day the World was first bless'd with such a day." Those who broke the Sabbath were punished. They were denied food, publicly whipped, or placed in stocks.

Nor did Puritans condone pit sports which matched animal against animal. Before the eighteenth century, pit sports (or blood sports) were popular and commonplace in Europe and the American South. People would travel long distances to watch dogs fight bulls, bears, badgers, or other dogs. Cockfighting was equally popular. Were these spectators cruel? Perhaps not. The "bloodied animals," noted a historian of humanitarianism, "were probably not victims of cruelty. Cruelty implies a desire to inflict pain and thus presupposes an empathic appreciation of the suffering of the object of cruelty. Empathy, however, seems not to have been a highly developed trait in premodern Europe."

Unlike Europeans and Southerners, Puritans condemned such activity. They did empathize with the animals. "What Christen [sic] heart," wrote Puritan Philip Stubbes, "can take pleasure to see one poor beast to rent, teare, and kill another, and all for his foolish pleasure?"

Although Puritans outlawed pit sports and insisted on the strict observance of the Sabbath, they did not oppose all sports and games. They supported such activities as walking, archery, running, wrestling, fencing, hunting, fishing, and hawking—as long as they were engaged in at a proper time and in a proper manner. Moderate recreation devoid of gambling, drunkenness, idleness, and frivolousness could refresh the body and spirit and thus serve the greater glory of God. This last point was the most important for the Puritans. Recreations had to help men and women better serve God; they were never to be ends in themselves.

Different attitudes towards sports and games emerged in the southern colonies. Almost from the time of settlement, Southerners exhibited an interest—oftentimes bordering on a passion—for various sports. They were particularly attracted to sports that involved opportunities for betting and demonstrations of physical prowess.

Cock fights attracted Southerners from every class. The matches were advertised in newspapers and eagerly anticipated; and at important events thousands of dollars in bets would change hands. For Northern observers the entire affair attracted only scorn and disgust. Elkanah Watson, who traveled to the South in the mid-1800s, was upset to see "men of character and intelligence giving their countenance to an amusement so frivolous and scandalous, so abhorrent to every feeling of humanity, and so injurious in its moral influence."

Horse racing even surpassed cockfighting as a favorite southern pastime. Wealthy Southerners liked to trace their ancestry to the English aristocracy, and they viewed horse racing and horse breeding as aristocratic occupations. In fact, by the eighteenth century the ownership of horses had taken on a cultural significance. As one student of the subject explained, "By the turn of the century possession of . . . these animals had become a social necessity. Without a horse, a planter felt despised, an object of ridicule. Owning even a slow footed saddle horse made the common planter more of a man in his own eyes as well as those of his neighbors. . . ."

Horse races matched owner against owner, planter against planter, in contests where large sums of money and sense of per-

sonal worth often rode on the outcome. In most races planters rode their own horses, making the outcome even more important. Intensely competitive men, planters sometimes cheated to win, and many races ended in legal courts rather than on the racetrack.

If planters willingly battled each other on the racetrack, they did not ride against their social inferiors. When James Bullocke, a tailor, challenged Mr. Mathew Slader to a race in 1674, the county court informed the tailor that it was "contrary to Law for a Labourer to make a race being a Sport for Gentlemen." For his efforts, the court fined Bullocke two hundred pounds of tobacco and cask. Although laborers and slaves watched the contests, and even bet among each other, they did not mix socially with the gentry.

Unlike the Puritans who believed sports should serve God, Southerners participated in sports as an outlet for their very secular materialistic, individualistic, and competitive urges. But neither North nor South had a modern concept of sports. Colonial Americans seldom kept records, respected equality of competition, established sports bureaucracies, standardized rules, or quantified results—all hallmarks of modern sports. Yet each section engaged in leisure activities which reflected their social and religious outlooks.

would be less, and they would not enjoy an equal degree of liberty with the people."

Here was a classic statement of deferential thinking. Although widespread property holding allowed great numbers of free white males to vote, they most often chose among members of the elite to represent them in elective offices, particularly colonial assemblies. Once elected, these stewards did constant battle with Crown-appointed governors and councilors in upper houses over the prerogatives of decision making. In colony after colony during the eighteenth century, elite leaders chipped away at royal authority, arguing that the assemblies were "little parliaments" with the same legislative rights in their respective territorial spheres as Parliament had over all British subjects.

More often than not, governors had only feeble backing from the home government and lost these disputes. As a result, the assemblies gained many prerogatives, including the right to initiate all money and taxation bills. Because governors depended on the assemblies for their salaries, they often approved local legislation not in the best interests of the Crown in exchange for bills appropriating their annual salaries. By the 1760s, the colonial assemblies had thus emerged as powerful agencies of government.

As self-conscious, assertive elite leaders, colonial gentlemen also read widely and kept themselves informed about European political activities. They were particularly attracted to the writings of a band of "radical" whig pamphleteers in England who repeatedly warned of ministerial officials who would use every corrupting device to grab all power and authority as potential tyrants at home. The radical whigs spoke of the delicate fabric of liberty; and provincial leaders, viewing themselves as the protectors of American rights, were increasingly on guard, in case the Crown became too oppressive, as it had been during the 1680s in demanding conformity to the imperial will.

Since gentlemen of birth and fortune lived each day knowing that home government leaders viewed them as second-class citizens, they took challenges to their local autonomy seriously. At least some in their number were ready to mobilize and lead the populace in resisting any new wave of perceived imperial tyranny,

should a time come when the parent state attempted to return to arbitrary government.

Intellectual and Religious Awakening

Besides politics, colonial leaders were fascinated by Europe's dawning Age of Reason, also called the Enlightenment. The approach to learning was secular, based on scientific inquiry and the systematic collection of information. A major goal was to unlock the physical laws of nature, as the great English physicist Sir Isaac Newton, often considered the father of the Enlightenment, had done in explaining mathematically how the force of gravity held the universe together (*Principia Mathematica,* 1687).

Europe's leading intellectuals, likewise heavily influenced by English political thinker John Locke, tried to identify laws governing human behavior. In his *Essay Concerning Human Understanding* (1690), Locke described the human mind as a blank sheet (*tabula rasa*) at birth waiting to be influenced by the experiences of life. If people followed the insights of reason, social ills could somehow be reduced or eliminated from the human environment, and each person, as well as society as a whole, could advance toward greater harmony and perfection.

The key watchword of the Enlightenment was *rationalism,* meaning a firm trust in the ability of the human mind to solve earthly problems—and much less faith in the centrality of God as an active, judgmental force in the universe. Whereas John Winthrop believed that earthquakes were signs of God's wrath, his great-great grandson, John Winthrop IV, who became the Hollis Professor of Mathematics and Natural Philosophy at Harvard College in the mid-1730s, argued that movements in the earth's surface had natural causes, which he explained in scientific terms.

Like their counterparts in Europe, learned colonists pursued all forms of knowledge. Naturalists John Bartram of Philadelphia and Dr. Alexander Garden of Charleston systematically collected and classified American plants. Benjamin Franklin became the best known provincial student of science. In the 1740s he helped found the American Philosophical Society, devoted to disseminating new knowledge, and in the 1750s he laid plans for the College of Philadelphia (founded 1755, later called the University of Pennsylvania), to train young men in the methods of scientific inquiry. After publishing his *Experiments and Observations on Electricity* (1751), Franklin's fame spread throughout the western world for having unveiled the mysteries of electrical energy.

A few clergymen, such as Boston's Cotton Mather, also dabbled in science but without forsaking strongly-held religious convictions. During a terrible New England smallpox epidemic in 1720 and 1721, Mather was outspokenly in favor of inoculation, which involved purposely inducing slight infections. Many thought that inoculations would only spread the disease, but Mather proved its preventive effects by collecting statistics. Whereas fifteen percent of uninoculated smallpox victims did not survive, just three percent died from inoculations. Still, it would be years before most colonists accepted inoculation as a sensible medical procedure for controlling this terrible disease.

Unlike Mather, many ministers viewed Enlightenment rationalism with distaste, because it seemed to undermine orthodox religious values by reducing God to a prime mover who had set the universe in motion only to leave humans to chart their own destiny. (This system of thought was known as Deism.) Others worried about the loss of religious faith emphasizing the need for repentance, conversion, and God's saving grace. They felt that the populace, rushing to get ahead economically, had become too complacent, as if their wealth and good works guaranteed eternal salvation. For some clergymen, then, the time was right for a new emphasis on vital religious faith.

During the 1720s and 1730s in Europe and America, many ministers started holding revivals. The first colonial outpouring occurred in the mid-1720s in New Jersey, where Dutch Reformed Theodorus Frelinghuysen and Presbyterian Gilbert Tennent attacked what the latter called the "presumptuous security" of his parishioners.

During 1734, Jonathan Edwards, a Congregational minister in Northampton, Massachusetts, began a series of revival "harvests" among

Benjamin Franklin (1706-1790) typified colonial men of science and the Enlightenment in his search to unlock the mysterious laws of the universe.

the youth in his community. Edwards was a learned student of the Enlightenment who argued that experiencing God's grace was essential to the comprehension of the universe and its laws. Thus he joyously preached about the need for salvation, noting that the inhabitants of Northampton, both young and old, were now "full of the presence of God." In 1741 he delivered his best known sermon, "Sinners in the Hands of an Angry God," in which he dangled his audience over "the abyss of *hell*" as a vivid plea to place God at the center of human existence. Appealing to the senses more than to rational inquiry, Edwards felt, was the surest means to uplift individual lives and improve society as a whole.

These local revivals soon turned into the Great Awakening after the dynamic English preacher, George Whitefield, appeared in America. Just twenty-four years old in 1740, Whitefield made a total of seven tours to the colonies, traveling thousands of miles, delivering hundreds of sermons, and speaking to gath-

George Whitefield (1714-1770) was heavily influenced by the Methodist movement among Anglicans in England and fired the Great Awakening in the colonies.

erings as large as 30,000. With a booming, melodious voice, he preached the essentials of gaining God's "free gift" of grace. Even Benjamin Franklin, a confirmed skeptic, felt moved when Whitefield appeared in Philadelphia. He went to the meeting "resolved to give nothing" but in the end, as he confessed, "I emptied my pocket wholly into the collector's dish, gold and all."

The Great Awakening had several important effects. The movement split America's religious community into "new" and "old" light camps. When in 1740 Gilbert Tennent preached his widely-read sermon, "The Danger of an Unconverted Ministry," he represented many revivalists in advising their listeners to shun clergymen who, while well-educated, showed no visible signs of God's grace. Thousands paid attention, and they started breaking away from congregations where ministers were suspect. In response, clergymen facing separatist movements denounced the Awakening as an anti-intellectual fraud being perpetrated by unlettered fools of no theological training. In many

locales, the contention became so heated that friends and neighbors, when not arguing, stopped speaking.

All of the turmoil, however, had a positive side. Those feeling a new relationship with God were less willing to submit to established authority and more willing to speak out on behalf of basic liberties. Typical were Baptists in New England, who under the leadership of Isaac Backus demanded the right to separate completely from the Congregational establishment and support their own ministers and churches. Baptists in Virginia, displaying anything but deferential behavior, started attacking the mores of the planter elite by calling for the "entire banishment of *dancing, gaming,* and sabbath-day diversions." Sometimes, those in authority became vicious. For example, a Virginia sheriff "violently jerked" a Baptist speaker off a platform and "beat his head against the ground" before administering "twenty lashes with his horse whip." The victim responded by returning to the stage and preaching even more vigorously "with a great deal of liberty."

Liberty became a watchword of the Awakening movement, as did a concern with the proper training of clergymen. Prior to the 1740s, there were only three colonial colleges, Harvard (1636), William and Mary (1693), and Yale (1701). In demanding toleration for diverse ideas, Presbyterian revivalists set up the College of New Jersey (1747, later Princeton), to train New Light clergymen; Baptists founded the College of Rhode Island (1764, later Brown); and the Dutch Reformed established Queen's College (1766, later Rutgers). In 1769 a New Light Congregational minister, Eleazar Wheelock, received a charter for Dartmouth College to carry the new birth message to Native Americans. Of the remaining colonial institutions, only King's College (1757, later Columbia), founded by Anglicans, and the College of Philadelphia had no interest in New Light theology, but in recognizing religious pluralism, they admitted students on a non-sectarian basis.

The Great Awakening questioned established authority at every turn and provoked movement toward a clearer definition of fundamental human rights as well as toleration of divergent ideas. This gave the revivalists something in common with Enlightenment rationalists—faith that human progress was possible. That this sentiment could prevail, despite many instances of repression, was a sign of colonial maturity and self-confidence.

International Wars Beset America

Participation in a series of wars involving Britain and its two North American rivals, France and Spain, also contributed to America's growing self-confidence. During the seventeenth century, Spain maintained its grip on Florida as well as the Gulf coast. French Canadians, operating from bases in Montreal and Quebec, explored throughout the Great Lakes region and then down into the Mississippi Valley. In 1682 an expedition headed by Robert Cavelier de La Salle reached the mouth of the Mississippi River. La Salle, who dreamed of a mighty French empire west of the Appalachian Mountains, claimed the whole region for his monarch, Louis XIV. Except for some fur trading posts, however, little came of La Salle's grand vision.

One reason was that the French monarchy, consumed by European affairs, did not actively encourage settlement in New France. As late as 1760, no more than 75,000 French subjects lived in all of Canada and the Mississippi Valley. Some were farmers or fisherman, and most others were fur traders. On the whole, they treated Native Americans with respect, and because the French population was so small, the Indians did not worry about losing ancient tribal lands. Positive relations with the Indians certainly paid off, once European warfare spilled over into America. The advantage of having thousands of potential allies willing to join in combat against British settlers made the French Canadians a very dangerous enemy, as events proved during the imperial wars between 1689 and 1763.

Each of the four wars had a European as well as an American name. The first, the War of the League of Augsburg (1689–1697), known in the colonies as King William's War, was a limited conflict with no major battles in America.

René-Robert Cavelier, Sieur de La Salle claimed the whole of the Mississippi Valley for France. His dream of empire inspired other French leaders with the idea of an empire encircling the British North American colonies.

What made this war so frightening were bloody border incidents involving Indians and colonists—typical was the attack on Hannah Dustan's Haverhill—which resulted in some 650 deaths among the English colonists. The Treaty of Ryswick, which ended the contest, did not upset the balance of international power because there were no major exchanges of territory.

Five years later the next war erupted after Louis XIV succeeded in placing his grandson Philip on the Spanish throne. Other nations feared that Louis intended to run Spain himself, a threat to the established balance of power among European countries. What ensued was the War of the Spanish Succession (1702–1713), which the colonists called Queen Anne's War—named after the new English monarch Anne (1702–1714), another Protestant daughter of James II. This time, the Anglo-Americans found themselves dueling with Spain as well as France. Sporadic fighting resulted in fewer than 500 colonial deaths in twelve years.

The Treaty of Utrecht, which ended the conflict, was a virtual declaration of Britain's growing imperial might. British armed forces had won major territorial gains, including Hudson Bay, Newfoundland, and Nova Scotia in

Canada. In addition, the British secured from Spain the strategically vital Rock of Gibraltar, guarding the entrance to the Mediterranean Sea, as well as the *Asiento*—a trading pact allowing the English to sell 4800 slaves annually in New Spain.

The scope of Britain's triumph, coming at the expense of its two major European rivals, deterred additional warfare for twenty-five years, but further conflict seemed inevitable. In 1721 the Board of Trade urged the "enlarging and extending of the British settlements" in North America as "the most effectual means to prevent the growing power . . . of the French in those parts." Ten years later, board members called for the creation of a military colony in the buffer zone between South Carolina and Florida, and they talked of sending over convicted felons and other desperate persons to act as soldier/settlers.

General James Oglethorpe, a wealthy member of Parliament, heard of these discussions and pursued the idea. A true philanthropist as well as imperialist, he hoped to roll back Spanish influence in the area while improving the lot of England's struggling poor. In 1732 King George II (1727–1760) issued a charter for Georgia, granting twenty-one trustees all the land between the Savannah and Altamaha rivers for twenty-one years to develop the region, after which the colony would revert to the Crown and function under royal authority.

Oglethorpe played on anti-Spanish sentiment, and large monetary donations poured in to underwrite the first settlements. Colonists were hard to find, largely because of the rules devised by Oglethorpe and the other trustees. To assure good order, they outlawed liquor. To promote personal industry and hard work, as well as spread out settlements in an effective defensive line, they limited individual grants to 500 acres, and they banned slavery. To guard against breaches in the settlement line, property could only be passed from father to son. If there were no male heirs, it then reverted to the trustees.

Those who did migrate to Georgia complained endlessly. Some wanted slaves; others, referring to Oglethorpe as "our perpetual dictator," called for a popular assembly; and they all demanded alcohol. As a social experiment to

Table 3.2

The Imperial Wars, 1689–1763			
European Name	*American Name*	*Dates*	*Peace Treaty*
War of the League of Augsburg	King William's War	1689–1697	Ryswick
War of the Spanish Succession	Queen Anne's War	1702–1713	Utrecht
War of Jenkins' Ear	King George's War	1739–1748	
War of the Austrian Succession		1744–1748	Aix-la-Chapelle
Seven Years' War	French and Indian War*	1756–1763	Paris

*This term came into vogue when nineteenth-century historians first employed the phrase "French and Indian War." The colonists most often referred to this contest as "the war."

uplift the poor, the colony failed. The trustees acknowledged this failure by turning Georgia back over to the Crown in 1752, a year ahead of schedule. By that time, they had already conceded on the issues of slavery and strong drink. Thereafter, Georgia looked more and more like South Carolina, with large rice and indigo plantations underpinning the local economy. By 1770, the colony's populace was pushing toward 25,000, nearly half of whom were slaves.

The founding of Georgia angered the Spanish, as did England's cheating on the *Asiento* agreement, especially in reference to the clause allowing just one English vessel a year to sell goods in the Caribbean. The one turned into shiploads, involving smugglers like Captain Robert Jenkins, whom the Spanish caught in 1731. As a warning to others, his captors cut off his ear. Seven years later Jenkins appeared before Parliament and held up his severed ear as an affirmation of Spanish barbarity. When asked to describe his feelings when facing mutilation, he boldly replied: "I commended my soul to God, and my cause to my country!"

Such testimony was part of a campaign by England's merchants to provoke anti-Spanish sentiment, with the hope of using cries for war to gain more trading rights in New Spain. In 1739 the War of Jenkins' Ear resulted. Then a dispute over who belonged on the Austrian throne brought England and France to formal blows in the War of the Austrian Succession, which the colonists called King George's War (1744–1748).

This international conflict saw James Oglethorpe lead an unsuccessful expedition against Florida in 1740. In 1741 a combined British-colonial force tried to capture Cartagena. It was a disaster, with three-fourths of the 3000 American troops dying from disease. Finally, a New England army achieved success when, in 1745, it captured the mighty French fortress of Louisbourg, the so-called "Gibraltar of the New World" guarding the entrance to the St. Lawrence River.

The war cost as many as 5000 American lives, and the victory at Louisbourg symbolized that sacrifice. In 1748 when Britain signed the Treaty of Aix-la-Chapelle, however, it gave back Louisbourg to regain territory lost in India, which was worth much more in the minds of

In 1745 William Pepperrell led 90 vessels and 4000 soldiers in an attack to claim the French fortress at Louisbourg. Forty days later the siege ended and the New England army won control.

the king's negotiators than a huge, non-income-producing fortress. The colonists resented this action, but they were powerless to do anything given their subordinate status in the empire

Showdown: The Great War for the Empire

The Treaty of Aix-la-Chapelle really settled nothing. The three combatants were on a showdown course, after France's decision to push into western Pennsylvania and the Ohio Valley with the intent of taking complete control of the fur trade in that area. As a center for that commerce, French-Canadian officials selected a site (modern-day Pittsburgh) where the Monongahela and Allegheny rivers join to form the Ohio River.

By 1753, the British ministry knew of these plans and ordered colonial governors to challenge the French advance and "repel force by force" if necessary. A group of Virginians, among them Governor Robert Dinwiddie, had recently formed the Ohio Company for the purpose of gaining title to half a million acres in that region. French control would have ended their land speculating designs, so Dinwiddie and the Virginia council, after receiving the ministry's statement, sent a young major of militia, twenty-one-year-old George Washington, to northwestern Pennsylvania with a warning to the French to get out. Politely, the French declined.

In the spring of 1754 Washington led 200 Virginia militiamen toward the forks of the Ohio River and learned that the French were already there constructing Fort Duquesne. Foolishly, he skirmished with a French party, killing ten and capturing twenty. Washington hastily retreated and constructed Fort Necessity, but the French overran this position in July, send-

ing Washington and his comrades home as prisoners-of-war. Out of these circumstances erupted a war that cost Spain valued territory and France the whole of its North American empire.

At the very time (June 1754) that Washington was preparing to defend Fort Necessity, delegates from seven colonies had gathered in Albany, New York, to discuss common plans for defense and how to secure the neutrality of powerful Indian groups like the Iroquois, should war come. Delegates Benjamin Franklin and Thomas Hutchinson proposed an intercolonial plan of government, but it received no support from the provincial assemblies. The significance of the Albany Conference lay in its attempt to effect cooperation among the colonies against a common enemy—an important precedent in later years. Meantime, as Franklin stated, "everyone cries, union is necessary, but when they come to the . . . form of the union, their weak noodles are perfectly distracted."

Home government officials ignored the Albany Plan of Union, but the Fort Necessity debacle resulted in a fateful decision to send Major General Edward Braddock to Virginia with regular troops and orders to raise regiments in America. He arrived in February 1755 and then trudged overland—Washington came along as a volunteer officer—toward Fort Duquesne. On July 9, about eight miles from the French fort, a much smaller French and Indian force, attacking from all sides, nearly destroyed the British column, leaving two-thirds of Braddock's soldiers dead or wounded. Washington, appalled by one of the worst defeats in British military history, spoke of being "most scandalously beaten by a trifling body of men." The General himself fell mortally wounded during the battle.

Braddock's defeat was an international embarrassment, yet King George II and his advisors hesitated to plunge into full-scale war. They knew, as proved to be the case, that the financial burden would be immense. Finally, a formal declaration of war did come in May 1756.

The Seven Years' War (1756–1763), later referred to in America as the French and Indian War, more accurately should be called "the great war for the empire." Certainly William Pitt, the king's new chief minister, viewed the

French and Indian War, 1756-1763

CHRONOLOGY
OF KEY EVENTS

1651–	Parliament approves the Navigation
1673	Acts
1660	Charles II restored to English throne
1664	Charles authorizes the Duke of York to seize New Netherland; New York and New Jersey founded
1676	Bacon's Rebellion breaks out in Virginia
1681	Penn granted proprietary charter for Pennsylvania
1685	James II becomes king of England, and approves Dominion of New England
1688–	Glorious Revolution in England forces
1689	James II into exile; William and Mary accede to throne
1689	Puritans in Massachusetts overthrow Sir Edmund Andros; Jacob Leisler's Rebellion occurs in New York; John Coode's Protestant Association rebels against proprietary authority in Maryland
1689–	Colonists engage in King William's
1697	War against France, settled by Treaty of Ryswick
1692	New England faces witchcraft hysteria

1696	Parliament establishes the Board of Trade and approves vice-admiralty courts for America
1702	Anne becomes queen of England
1702–	Colonists fight against France and
1713	Spain in Queen Anne's War, settled by Treaty of Utrecht
1714	George I of the House of Hanover becomes king of England
1727	George II becomes king of England
1732	Colony of Georgia founded under auspices of Oglethorpe
1733	Parliament legislates the Molasses Act
1739	War of Jenkins' Ear breaks out against Spain
1740	Whitefield begins preaching tours, turning local revivals into the Great Awakening
1744–	War of Jenkins' Ear broadens into King
1748	George's War against France and Spain, settled by Treaty of Aix-la-Chapelle
1751	Franklin publishes his *Experiments and Observations on Electricity*
1754	Washington defends Fort Necessity and helps to bring on Seven Years' War
1759	Quebec conquered by British forces under General James Wolfe
1763	Treaty of Paris ends Seven Years' War

contest this way, arguing that America was "where England and Europe are to be fought for." Not a modest man, Pitt stated categorically that he alone could "save England and no one else can."

Pitt's strategic plan was simple enough. He let King Frederick the Great of Prussia, Britain's ally, bear the brunt of warfare in Europe, and he placed the bulk of England's military resources in America with the intent of strangling New France. He also advanced a young group of dynamic officers, like General James Wolfe, over the heads of less capable men. It all paid off in a series of carefully orchestrated military advances that saw Quebec fall in September 1759 to the forces of General Wolfe. In September 1760 Montreal surrendered to the army of General Jeffrey Amherst, with hardly an exchange of musket shots. The British empire was triumphant.

CONCLUSION

The fall of the French empire in North America took place in the face of mounting hostility between British military leaders and the colonists. Americans joined provincial regiments and fought beside British redcoats, but most did not care for the experience. They found the king's regulars to be rough, crude, and morally delinquent. They viewed the king's officers as needlessly overbearing and aristocratic. They resented being treated as inferiors, "sufficient" only, as one British colonel wrote, "to . . . drive our wagons . . . fell our trees, and do the works that in inhabited countries are performed by peasants."

Young George Washington explained how Virginia's recruits "behaved like men, and died like soldiers" during Braddock's defeat, as compared to the British regulars, who "behaved with more cowardice than it is possible to conceive." On the other hand, General James Wolfe later described provincial troops as "the dirtiest most comtemptible dogs that you can conceive." The Americans, concluded another British officer, were a "naturally obstinate and ungovernable people, . . . utterly unacquainted with the nature of subordination in general."

The Americans were proud of their contributions to the triumphant British empire. They hoped that the Crown would treat them with greater respect in the days ahead. But the king's ministers thought more like British military officers in America. They believed that the colonists had done more to serve themselves than the British empire during the Seven Years' War. Because of many problems related to the war, the Crown decided to crack down on the obstinate American colonists.

Apparently the king's ministers had not learned very much from the previous hundred years of Anglo-American history. Before 1690, when the rules by which the empire would operate had become too restrictive, serious colonial resistance ensued. After 1690, an accommodation of differences assured the Americans basic rights and some local autonomy, as long as they supported the empire's economic and political goals. Now more self-confident than ever before, provincial Americans would again resist plans to make them fully subordinate—and this time would break the bonds of empire.

REVIEW SUMMARY

After the Restoration of Charles II in 1660, England attempted to tighten its imperial control over North America. At the same time, the English fought a series of wars with its foremost rivals France and Spain.

> the rise of mercantilism, monopolism, and materialism
>
> provincial reactions to new British policies and the Glorious Revolution in America
>
> the notion and practice of salutary neglect
>
> and the great wars for the empire

By 1760 Britain had gained a mastery over North America but had yet to master their own colonists.

SUGGESTIONS FOR FURTHER READING

OVERVIEWS AND SURVEYS

Wesley Frank Craven, *The Colonies in Transition, 1660–1713* (1968); Lawrence A. Cremin, *American Education, 1607–1783* (1970); John E. Ferling, *A Wilderness of Miseries: War and Warriors in Early America* (1980); Lawrence H. Gipson, *The British Empire Before the American Revolution,* 15 vols. (1936–1970); Jack P. Greene and J. R. Pole, eds., *Colonial British America* (1984), and Greene, *Peripheries and Centers: Constitutional Development in the British Empire and the United States, 1607–1788* (1986); Richard Hofstadter, *America at 1750* (1971); Douglas E. Leach, *Arms for Empire: A Military History of the Colonies, 1607–1763* (1973); David S. Lovejoy, *Religious Enthusiasm in the New World* (1985); John J. McCusker and Russell R. Menard, *The Economy of British America, 1607–1789* (1985); Alison G. Olson, *Anglo-American Politics, 1660–1775* (1973); Richard Slotkin, *Regeneration Through Violence: The Mythology of the American Frontier, 1600–1860* (1973); and Gary M. Walton and James F. Shephard, *The Economic Rise of Early America* (1979).

DESIGNING ENGLAND'S NORTH AMERICAN EMPIRE

Joyce O. Appleby, *Economic-Thought and Ideology in Seventeenth-Century England* (1978); Edwin B. Bronner, *William Penn's "Holy Experiment," 1681–1701* (1962); Thomas J. Condon, *New York Beginnings: The Commercial Origins of New Netherland* (1968); Wesley Frank Craven,

New Jersey and the English Colonization of North America (1964); Mary Maples Dunn, *William Penn: Politics and Conscience* (1967); J. William Frost, *The Quaker Family in Colonial America* (1972); Lawrence A. Harper, *The English Navigation Laws* (1939); Joseph E. Illick, *Colonial Pennsylvania: A History* (1976); Michael Kammen, *Empire and Interest: The American Colonies and the Politics of Mercantilism* (1970); James T. Lemon, *The Best Poor Man's Country: A Geographical Study of Pennsylvania* (1972); Gary B. Nash, *Quakers and Politics: Pennyslvania, 1681–1726* (1968); Robert C. Ritchie, *The Duke's Province: Politics and Society in New York, 1660–1691* (1977); Sharon V. Salinger, *"To Serve Well and Faithfully": Labor and Indentured Servants in Pennsylvania, 1682–1800* (1987); Jack M. Sosin, *English America and the Restoration Monarchy of Charles II* (1980); Frederick B. Tolles, *Quakers and Atlantic Culture* (1960); Stephen S. Webb, *The Governors-General: The English Army and the Definition of Empire, 1569–1681* (1979); Stephanie G. Wolf, *Urban Village: Germantown, Pennsylvania, 1683–1800* (1976); and Arthur J. Worrall, *Quakers in the Colonial Northeast* (1980).

DEFYING THE IMPERIAL WILL: PROVINCIAL CONVULSIONS AND REBELLIONS

Thomas J. Archdeacon, *New York City, 1664–1710: Conquest and Change* (1976); Paul Boyer and Stephen Nissenbaum, *Salem Possessed: The Social Origins of Witchcraft* (1974); Lois Green Carr and David W. Jordan, *Maryland's Revolution of Government, 1689–1692* (1974); John Putnam Demos, *Entertaining Satan: Witchcraft and the Culture of Early New England* (1982); Phillip S. Haffenden, *New England in the English Nation, 1689–1713* (1974); Michael G. Hall, *Edward Randolph and the American Colonies* (1960); Chadwick Hansen, *Witchcraft at Salem* (1969); Richard R. Johnson, *Adjustment to Empire: The New England Colonies, 1675–1715* (1981); Carol F. Karlsen, *The Devil in the Shape of a Woman: Witchcraft in New England* (1987); Lawrence H. Leder, *Robert Livingston, 1654–1728, and the Politics of Colonial New York* (1961); David S. Lovejoy, *The Glorious Revolution in America* (1972); Jerome R. Reich, *Leisler's Rebellion, 1664–1720* (1953); William L. Shea, *The Virginia Militia in the Seventeenth Century* (1983); Ian K. Steele, *The English Atlantic, 1675–1740: Communication and Community* (1986); Jack M. Sosin, *English America and the Revolution of 1688* (1982); Wilcomb E. Washburn, *The Governor and the Rebel: A History of Bacon's Rebellion* (1957); and Stephen S. Webb, *1676: The End of American Independence* (1984).

MATURING COLONIAL SOCIETIES IN UNSETTLED TIMES

Fred Anderson, *A People's Army: Massachusetts in the Seven Years' War* (1984); Bernard Bailyn, *The Origins of American Politics* (1968), *The Peopling of British North America* (1986), and *Voyagers to the West* (1986); J. M. Bumsted and John E. Van De Wetering, *What Must I Do To Be Saved? The Great Awakening* (1976); Patricia U. Bonomi, *A Factious People: Politics and Society in Colonial New York* (1971), and *Under the Cope of Heaven: Religion, Society, and Politics in Colonial America* (1986); Richard L. Bushman, *From Puritan to Yankee; Character and the Social Order of Connecticut, 1690–1765* (1967), and *King and People in Provincial Massachusetts* (1985); Kenneth Coleman, *Colonial Georgia: A History* (1976); Bruce C. Daniels, ed., *Power and Status: Officeholding in Colonial America* (1986); Robert J. Dinkin, *Voting in Provincial America, 1689–1776* (1977); A. Roger Ekirch, *Bound for America: The Transportation of British Convicts to the Colonies, 1718–1775* (1987); Edwin S. Gaustad, *The Great Awakening in New England* (1957); Jack P. Greene, *The Quest for Power: The Lower Houses of Assembly in the Southern Colonies, 1689–1776* (1961); Nathan O. Hatch and Harry S. Stout, eds., *Jonathan Edwards and the American Experience* (1987); Alan Heimert, *Religion and the American Mind: From the Great Awakening to the Revolution* (1966); James A. Henretta, *"Salutary Neglect": Colonial Administration under the Duke of Newcastle* (1972); Rhys Isaac, *The Transformation of Virgina, 1740–1790* (1982); Christopher M. Jedrey, *The World of John Cleaveland: Family and Community in New England* (1979); Francis Jennings, *Empire of Fortune: Crown, Colonies, and Tribes in the Seven Years' War* (1988); Stanley N. Katz, *Newcastle's New York, 1732–1753* (1968); Sung Bok Kim, *Landlord and Tenant in Colonial New York, 1664–1775* (1978); Douglas E. Leach, *Roots of Conflict: British Armed Forces and Colonial Americans, 1677–1763* (1986); William G. McLoughlin, *Isaac Backus and the American Pietistic Tradition* (1966); Henry F. May, *The Enlightenment in America* (1976); Richard L. Merritt, *Symbols of American Community, 1735–1775* (1966); Edmund S. Morgan, *Inventing the People: The Rise of Popular Sovereignty in England and America* (1988); Robert E. Newbold, *The Albany Congress* (1955); William Pencak, *War, Politics, and Revolution in Massachusetts* (1981); Howard H. Peckham, *The Colonial Wars, 1689–1762* (1964); J. R. Pole, *The Gift of Government: Political Responsibility from the Restoration to Independence* (1986); Thomas L. Purvis, *Proprietors, Patronage, and Money: New Jersey, 1703–1776* (1986); Alan Rogers, *Empire and Liberty: American Resistance to British Authority, 1755–1763* (1974); Patricia J. Tracy, *Jonathan Edwards, Pastor* (1980); Allan Tully, *William Penn's Legacy: Pennsylvania, 1726–1775* (1977); and Michael Zuckerman, *Peaceable Kingdoms: New England Towns in the Eighteenth Century* (1970).

CHAPTER 4

Breaking the Bonds of Empire, 1760 – 1775

Boston was a tension-filled community in early 1770. Since the autumn of 1768, British redcoats had mustered daily and patrolled the streets, determined to restore order among troublesome colonists who had repeatedly resisted a whole new wave of imperial legislation. Boston's common day laborers, semiskilled workers, and apprentices particularly resented the redcoats' presence. The king's troops competed for scarce jobs because, when not on duty, they could work for extra wages on a piecemeal basis. Thus these redcoats were making times harder for ordinary citizens in a community suffering from a prolonged economic depression.

Throughout 1769 troop baiting by Boston's workingmen and women had resulted in fist-fights and bloodied faces. Bad feelings continued to mount as winter snows covered the ground. Then on March 2, 1770, an ugly confrontation took place. A young, off-duty soldier, Patrick Walker, entered John Gray's ropemaking establishment and asked for work. Seizing the opportunity to be insulting, one of Gray's workers snorted: "Well, then go and clean my shithouse." Taken aback, the soldier snapped in response: "Empty it yourself." Upset and angry, Walker fled amidst threats and a few punches from other laborers.

Walker soon told his story to comrades like Mathew Kilroy and William Warren in the 29th regiment, and he convinced several of them to join him in teaching these workers a lesson. Feeling strength in numbers, the soldiers headed back to Gray's. A general melee ensued as the off-duty redcoats swung their clubs and the workers fought back with their rope-making tools. After some time the soldiers retreated. This fight would have been lost to history, had it not been an important precursor of the so-called "Boston Massacre" three days later.

Monday, March 5, was bitterly cold, but heated emotions among workers and soldiers could have melted the deep piles of snow in the streets. Although a number of isolated fights occurred over the weekend, an eerie calm pervaded on Monday. Boston's working people had drawn the line. They had decided to challenge the redcoats' continued presence in their town. Small groups of day laborers, apprentices, and merchant seamen began milling about early in the evening. Slowly, but without an appearance of overall direction, these groups moved toward King Street, the site of the Customs House. Here a small party of soldiers from the 29th regiment, including Privates Kilroy and Warren, were on guard duty.

As the crowd grew, it began to envelop the troops. Suddenly, angry citizens began pelting the soldiers with mud, snowballs, rocks—indeed anything that could be thrown. Captain Thomas Preston tried to steady his detachment, but one of his men, fearing for his life, panicked. He leveled his musket and a shot rang out. Ignoring Preston's orders to stop, other soldiers also fired their weapons. Before the shooting ceased, a number of civilians lay wounded and dying.

All told, five men lost their lives, including Samuel Gray, a relative of John Gray and a participant in the March 2 brawl; seventeen-year-old Samuel Maverick, brother-in-law of shoemaker Ebenezer Mackintosh, Boston's notorious crowd leader during the Stamp Act riots of 1765; and Crispus Attucks, an unemployed mulatto merchant seaman. Bostonians hailed these men as martyred heroes in their struggle to defend American liberties.

On the Death of Five young Men who was Murthered, *March* 5th 1770. By the 29th Regiment.

Popular leaders of Boston used handbills such as this to keep the populace stirred up against local British officials.

Certainly the Boston Massacre was a tragic incident. Captain Preston and his troops were tried for murder. The court found all but two of the redcoats innocent on the grounds of having been forced into a life-threatening situation by an enraged crowd of citizens. The court declared Private Kilroy and another soldier guilty on reduced charges of manslaughter, and pleading benefit of clergy, these two men had their thumbs seared with a hot branding iron before regaining their freedom.

Long before these verdicts, royal officials had removed the hated redcoats from Boston. In this important sense, the working citizens of Boston had won at the cost of five lives. They had freed their community of British regulars and unwanted economic competition. Within another four years, however, redcoats would once again appear in the troublesome port city of Boston.

On a most basic level, economic competition was the spark that ignited the Massacre, but the people of Boston understood that other issues were involved. When the redcoats had first disembarked in October 1768, a deeply concerned local minister, Andrew Eliot, proclaimed: "Good God! What can be worse to a people who have tasted the sweets of liberty! Things have come to an unhappy crisis, . . . and the moment there is any bloodshed all affection will cease." Ordinary Bostonians perceived the presence of British military regiments during peacetime as a sure sign that the colonists were falling into a condition of political slavery.

The presence of the king's troops in Boston also indicated that, since the end of the French and Indian War, serious internal problems had beset the British empire. Home government leaders were annoyed with the American colonists, and the colonists resented what they thought of as Britain's constraining hand. Communications started to break down, so much so that a permanent rupture of political affections was taking place. The coming of the American Revolution may be traced directly to the year 1763 when British ministers began to tighten the imperial reins. They had many reasons for their actions, but they had no idea that the developing crisis was serious enough to turn the American colonists toward open rebellion.

PROVOKING AN IMPERIAL CRISIS

In 1763 British subjects everywhere toasted the Treaty of Paris that ended the worldwide Seven Years' War. The empire had gained territorial jurisdiction over French Canada and the whole of the Mississippi Valley, except for a tiny strip of territory around New Orleans that France deeded to Spain. The Spanish, in turn, had to cede the Floridas to Britain to regain the Philippines and Cuba, the latter having fallen to a combined Anglo-American force in 1762. Brit-

Effective propaganda such as Paul Revere's engravings of the Boston Massacre helped increase outrage over the event. It appears the British soldiers are firing without provocation into an innocent-looking crowd of citizens.

ain likewise made substantial gains in India. Most important from the colonists' perspective, the French and Spanish "menaces" had been removed from their backs, which should have signaled a new era of imperial harmony. That was not to be the case.

A Legacy of Colonial Problems

For the chief ministers in Great Britain under the youthful and vigorous monarch George III, who was twenty-five years old in 1763, the most pressing concern was Britain's national debt. During the Seven Years' War it had skyrocketed from £75 million to £137 million sterling. Annual interest payments on the debt amounted to £5 million alone. Advisors to the Crown struggled with ways to get the debt under control, a most difficult task considering the newly-

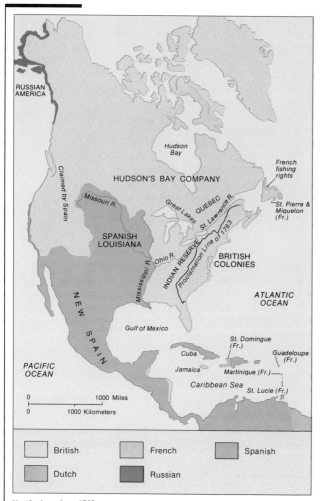

North America, 1763
With the signing of the Peace of Paris, Great Britain received almost all of the French holdings.

merchants and seamen carried more trade goods than prisoners, and the products that they exchanged helped sustain the French and Spanish war efforts.

When the chief war minister William Pitt, normally a supporter of American interests, learned in 1760 that one hundred or more colonial vessels flying British flags were in the Spanish port of Montecristi, he sputtered with anger and ordered customs officers in North America to search inbound provincial vessels with greater rigor. The ministry was furious about such quasi-treasonous activity and was ready in 1763 to tighten controls on American commerce.

A host of issues relating to newly-won territories to the north and west of the Anglo-American settlements also concerned the king's ministers. Most important was their dread of prolonged warfare on the frontier, and the financial costs associated with it, should land-hungry whites push into Indian hunting grounds too quickly. With French authority gone, Native Americans were on guard. They had few reasons to trust British traders and settlers. To prove the case, western Indians found that in the absence of French competition, trade goods had suddenly become more expensive. Futhermore, British officials hesitated to deal in guns and ammunition; and some tribes correctly suspected that royal military officials had given them infectious blankets, taken from soldiers who had died of smallpox, during recent wartime parleys seeking their neutrality.

The vacuum caused by the collapse of French authority and fears that British officials would ignore the encroachment of white settlers on tribal lands inspired Pontiac, an Ottawa war chief, to build an alliance of several western Indian tribes, including the Chippewas, Delawares, Hurons, Mingoes, Potawatomis, and Shawnees. Pontiac's first targets were former French forts which the British now occupied and for which they refused to pay rents—as the French had regularly done in recognition of tribal ownership of the land.

Beginning in May 1763, Pontiac's warriors struck with a vengeance at these posts, putting the major fortress at Detroit under heavy siege and attacking white settlements running in a

won territories that the home government now had to govern.

Closely linked to the debt issue was the matter of American smuggling activity. Many colonial merchants, eager for profits of any kind, had traded illegally with the enemy during the war. Even though the Royal Navy had blockaded French and Spanish ports in the Caribbean, traders from New England and elsewhere used various pretexts to effect business deals. Some claimed to sail on missions of benevolence and exchanged prisoners-of-war to cover up illegal trading operations. These wily

Protest Takes a Violent Turn

Adams did not participate directly in crowd actions himself—nor did the informal patriot governing body, known as the Loyal Nine. (Adams and Otis were not members of this group but were the principal guides in directing the politics of defiance.) The Loyal Nine communicated specific protest plans to men like Ebenezer Mackintosh, a shoemaker living in the South End of town, and Samuel Swift, a cobbler from the North End. Prior to 1765, these two craftsmen were leaders of "leather apron" gangs (workers' associations) from their respective districts. The North End and South End gangs, as the better sort of citizens thought of them, were in reality fraternal organizations providing fellowship for artisans, apprentices, and common day laborers.

Each year these leather apron workers looked forward to November 5, known as Pope's Day. This referred to an alleged seventeenth-century plot by a Roman Catholic, Guy Fawkes, to blow up Parliament. November 5 was an established anti-Catholic holiday during which street leaders like Mackintosh and Swift led separate parades of North and South End workers marching through the streets, holding high crude effigies of the devil and the Pope. These working people not only vented their anti-Catholic feelings and their fears of Satanic influences as they marched, but they also prepared for the annual fistfight between North Enders and South Enders, which traditionally took place after the two groups had converged on the center of Boston. The fighting was so vicious in 1764 that at least one person died.

During the summer of 1765, Samuel Adams and the Loyal Nine convinced the North and South End associators to stop fighting among themselves and unite in defense of essential political liberties. This juncture proved a critical step in ending any attempted administration of the Stamp Act in Massachusetts.

On the morning of August 14, 1765, the local populace awoke to find an effigy of Andrew Oliver (and a boot, representing Lord Bute, Grenville's predecessor) hanging in an elm tree—later labeled the Liberty Tree—on the South End. An appalled Governor Bernard

In celebration of the anti-Catholic holiday, this Pope's Day Parade engraving shows the devil standing behind the pope.

Crowds protesting imperial policies, in this case burning stamped documents and newspapers, were normally made up of ordinary citizens, particularly the working poor.

demanded that the figures be removed, but no one touched them, knowing that they were under the protection of the Sons of Liberty. That evening a crowd numbering in the thousands gathered around the tree to watch Ebenezer Mackintosh, known as the "Captain General of Liberty Tree," solemnly remove the effigies and exhort everyone present to join in a march through the streets. Holding the effigies high on a staff, Mackintosh and Swift led what was an orderly procession. As they marched, the people shouted: "Liberty, Property, and No Stamps."

The crowd worked its way to the local dockyards, where the Sons of Liberty ripped apart a building recently constructed by Andrew Oliver. Rumor had it that Oliver intended to store his quota of stamped paper there. Next, the crowd moved toward Oliver's stately home. Some of the Sons tore up the fence, ransacked the first floor (the Oliver family had fled), and imbibed from the well-stocked wine cellar. Others gathered on a hill behind the Oliver residence. Materials from Oliver's building as well as the wooden fence provided kindling for a huge bonfire that ultimately consumed the effigies as the working men and women of Boston cheered. By midnight, this crucial crowd action was over.

Early the next morning, as Thomas Hutchinson later wrote, the thoroughly intimidated Oliver "despairing of protection, and finding his family in terror and distress, . . . came to the sudden resolution to resign his office before another night." Mackintosh's crowd, rather than Crown officials, were now in control of Boston. After this crowd action, no one thought at all about taking Oliver's stamp distributorship. Intimidating threats and selective property destruction had preserved the interests of the community over those of the Crown.

Had Boston's Sons of Liberty and their leaders been solely concerned with undermining the Stamp Act, they would have ceased their rioting after Oliver's resignation. They had, however, other accounts to settle. A misleading rumor began to circulate through the streets claiming that Thomas Hutchinson was very much in favor of the Stamp Act, indeed had even helped to write the tax plan. As a result, the Sons came out again on the evening of August 26. After visiting a few others, the crowd descended upon Hutchinson's palatial home, one of the most magnificent in the province. They ripped it apart. As the lieutenant governor later portrayed the scene, "they continued their possession until daylight; de-

stroyed, carried away, or cast into the street, everything that was in the house; demolished every part of it, except for walls, as lay in their power."

Who started the rumor remains a moot point, but Hutchinson's political enemies were well known. Further, some people may have vented their frustrations with the depressed local economy by ransacking the property of a person with imperial connections who was prospering during difficult times. Whatever the explanation, royal authority in Massachusetts had suffered another serious blow. The mere threat of crowd violence gave Samuel Adams and his popular rights faction a powerful weapon that Hutchinson and other royalist officials never overcame.

Resistance Spreads Across the Landscape

By rendering the office of stamp distributor powerless, Boston had set a pattern for resistance, and the other provinces were quick to act. Before the end of August, Augustus Johnston, Rhode Island's distributor-designate, had been cowed into submission. In September, Maryland's distributor, Zachariah Hood, not only resigned but fled the province after a crowd destroyed his home. Jared Ingersoll was the victim in Connecticut. While he was on the road to Hartford, the local Sons surrounded him and demanded his resignation. They then rode with him to Hartford where the staid Ingersoll renounced the office in public and cheered for liberty—to the delight of a menacing crowd. By November 1, there was virtually no one foolish or bold enough to distribute stamps in America. Only colonists in Georgia experienced a short-lived implementation of the despised tax.

While the colonists employed intimidation and violence, they also petitioned King and Parliament. Assembly after assembly prepared remonstrances stating that taxation without representation was a fundamental violation of the rights of Englishmen. Patrick Henry, a young and aggressive backcountry Virginia lawyer, had a profound influence on these official petitions. Henry first appeared in the Virginia House of Burgesses (lower house of the Assem-

Patrick Henry first entered the Virginia House of Burgesses in May 1765 and presented a series of resolutions repudiating the Stamp Act.

bly) in mid-May 1765. The session, meeting in Williamsburg, was coming to a close. Only a handful of burgesses were still present when Henry presented seven resolutions. They endorsed the first four, which reiterated the no taxation without representation theme, but they rejected the other three as being too militant in tone.

Newspapers throughout the provinces reprinted all seven of Henry's resolutions. The fifth stated that the Virginia Assembly held "the only exclusive right and power to lay taxes and impositions upon the inhabitants of this colony." The sixth asserted that Virginians were "not bound to yield obedience to any law" not approved by their Assembly. The seventh indicated that anyone thinking otherwise would "be deemed an enemy by His Majesty's colony."

These three resolutions read as if the Virginia burgesses had denied King and Parliament all legislative authority over the American provinces. They seemed to be advocating some form of dual sovereignty in which the American assemblies held final authority over legislative matters in America—comparable in scope to Parliament's authority over the British Isles. This was a radical concept, in fact too radical for most of the Virginia burgesses. Yet the reprinting of all seven of the Virginia Resolutions, as they came to be known, encouraged other assemblies to prepare strongly worded petitions during the summer and fall of 1765.

An important sign of intercolonial unity, also related to the petitioning process, was the Stamp Act Congress, held in New York City during October 1765. At the urging of James Otis, Jr., the Massachusetts General Court wrote the other provincial assemblies and called for an intercolonial congress to draft a full statement of grievances. Nine colonies responded, and twenty-seven delegates appeared.

Generally speaking, cautious gentlemen of the upper ranks dominated the Stamp Act Congress, and their "Declarations" on behalf of American rights had a far more conciliatory tone than the Virginia Resolutions. For instance, the delegates attested to "all due subordination to that august body, the Parliament of Great Britain." Since it was not feasible for Americans "from their local circumstances" to be represented in Parliament, the only way to protect "all the inherent rights and liberties" of the colonists was for Parliament to concede its right of taxation to the provincial assemblies. With these words, the Stamp Act Congress disbanded, having shown that leaders from different colonies could meet together and agree on common principles. The Congress also suggested that unified resistance might be possible, should events ever make that necessary.

Another, more telling blow to the Stamp Act was an intercolonial economic boycott. Merchants in New York City were the first to act. On October 31, they pledged not to order "goods or merchandise of any nature, kind, or quality whatsoever, usually imported from Great Britain, . . . unless the Stamp Act be repealed." Within a month merchants in the other principal port towns, including Boston and Philadelphia, drafted similar agreements. A trade boycott of British goods, particularly with the remnants of economic depression still plaguing the empire, was bound to win support for repeal among merchants and manufacturers in Britain.

On November 1, 1765, commerce in the colonies came to a halt, and trading vessels remained in ports because no stamped clearance papers could be obtained. Courts ceased functioning, since so many legal documents required stamps. Newspapers stopped publication, at least temporarily. For all of their bravado, the Americans really did not want to defy the law. As November gave way to December, however, popular leaders began to apply various forms of pressure on more timid citizens. By the beginning of 1766, colonial business and legal activity started returning to normal, and newspaper editors commenced printing again—all without the use of stamps.

George Grenville had grossly miscalculated. Not willing to be treated as errant children, the colonists, in defending their liberties, sent petitions to Parliament, intimidated and harassed royal officials, destroyed property, cut off the importation of British goods and, finally, openly defied the law. Americans hoped for a return to the old days of salutary neglect, but they also wondered whether the king's ministers would understand and back down in the face of such determined resistance.

Parliament Retreats

Instability in the British cabinet, as much as American protest, helped to bring about repeal of the Stamp Act. George III had never liked George Grenville. In July 1765, the king asked him to step aside in favor of the Marquis of Rockingham, who was more sympathetic toward the Americans. Rockingham's political coalition, however, was brittle, and his term as chief minister lasted just long enough to effect repeal.

Looking for political allies, Rockingham took advantage of pressure from English traders and manufacturers who were extremely worried about the American boycott. He also

This mournful group of government members carries the dead Stamp Act to its grave after its repeal in 1766.

linked arms with William Pitt, England's most influential politician. Pitt was eloquent in the repeal debates before Parliament. He exhorted his fellow M.P.s to recognize the colonists as "subjects of this kingdom equally entitled . . . to all the natural rights of mankind and peculiar privileges of Englishmen." The M.P.s listened and in March 1766 rescinded the Stamp Act.

Home government leaders, however, had by no means accepted colonial arguments. They insisted upon a statement designed to make it clear that King and Parliament were the supreme legislative voices of empire. As companion legislation to the repeal bill, then, the M.P.s approved the Declaratory Act, which specifically denied the claims of American assemblies to "the sole and exclusive right of imposing duties and taxes . . . in the colonies." The Declaratory Act forcefully asserted that Parliament had "full power and authority to make laws and statutes . . . *in all cases whatsoever.*" Having repealed the Stamp Act for the sake of imperial harmony, Parliament still had the right to tax all British subjects anytime it chose. The M.P.s had stated their position—and in terms irreconcilable with the stance taken by the Americans.

A SECOND CRISIS: THE TOWNSHEND DUTIES

What was needed in 1766 was an extended cooling-off period, but that was not to happen. The Rockingham ministry, which would have been willing to leave the colonists alone, collapsed. King George III called for a new cabinet in the summer of 1766. He wanted William Pitt to be in charge of the government. In poor health, Pitt agreed to organize a ministry in return for peerage status as the Earl of Chatham. No longer the "Great Commoner," Pitt retired to the House of Lords, letting others provide for legislation in the House of Commons. One man in particular, Chancellor of the Exchequer Charles Townshend, rushed forward to fill the void in leadership. To the amazement of many, Townshend proclaimed that he knew how to tax the colonists. The result was the ill-advised Townshend Duties of 1767, which renewed tension between Britain and America.

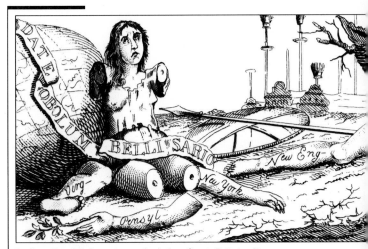

In Ben Franklin's cartoon, depicting Great Britain dismembered of her four limbs, he was hoping to preserve the empire by satirically dismembering it.

Formulating a New Taxation Scheme

Benjamin Franklin, who was in England serving as an agent for various colonies, inadvertently helped formulate Townshend's plan. In a lengthy interview before Parliament during the repeal debates, Franklin, who was out of touch with American sentiment, stated emphatically that the colonists only objected to direct or "internal" taxes, such as those embodied in the Stamp Act. They did not object, he claimed, to indirect or "external" taxes, which may be defined as duties placed on trade goods for the purpose of gaining imperial revenue. Pointing out that Franklin was the most respected colonist of the era, Charles Townshend seized upon this distinction and came up with his ill-advised taxation scheme.

Townshend believed that the Americans had to be taxed, if for no other reason than to prove the complete, indivisible sovereignty of Parliament. In June 1767, Parliament agreed with him by authorizing the Townshend Duties, which were nothing more than import duties on a short list of trade items: British-manufactured glass, paper and lead products, painters' colors, and a three-pence-a-pound duty on tea. Townshend proclaimed that his plan would net the

Crown £35 to £40 thousand per year. In time, once the colonists got used to the idea, the list of taxable products could be lengthened. Meantime, the revenue would go toward the administration of royal governments in America.

At first, it seemed that Townshend knew what he was doing. The plan was subtle and generated very little colonial opposition. Attempts by popular leaders to stir up the populace against the duties failed in the autumn of 1767. Except for tea, the duties were on luxury items, rarely used by the majority of colonists. Moreover, the tea tax could be evaded by opening illicit trading connections with Dutch tea merchants—and Americans were still quite adept at the art of smuggling.

Mustering Further American Resistance

Late in the year, John Dickinson, a landholder and lawyer residing in the area of Philadelphia, began publishing a series of newspaper essays, later printed as a pamphlet entitled *Letters from a Farmer in Pennsylvania.* Dickinson assailed Townshend's logic. Americans, he pointed out, had not distinguished between internal and external taxes. Certainly they had long accepted duties designed "to regulate trade" and facilitate the flow of imperial commerce. They now faced trade duties "for the single purpose" of raising revenue. Taxes disguised as trade duties, warned a most suspicious Dickinson, were "a most dangerous innovation" with the potential for turning the colonists into "abject slaves." Yet Dickinson, a man of considerable wealth who feared the destructive potential of crowds, urged caution in resistance; he called for the colonial assemblies merely to petition Parliament, hoping its members would listen to reason.

In February 1768, the Massachusetts General Court, at the prompting of Samuel Adams, sent a Circular Letter to the other assemblies with arguments predicated upon Dickinson's widely-reprinted pamphlet. Mild in tone, the Circular Letter reiterated Dickinson's call for petitions. If the British ministry had ignored the Massachusetts document, nothing of consequence might have happened. However, Lord

Hillsborough, who had recently taken the new cabinet post of Secretary for American Affairs, overreacted and provoked needless conflict.

Hillsborough believed the Circular Letter was insubordinate. He quickly fired off orders to Governor Bernard to confront the General Court and demand an apology. If the delegates refused (they did overwhelmingly), Bernard was to dissolve the assembly and call for new elections. In addition, Hillsborough sent his own circular letter to the other colonial governors, insisting that they not allow their assemblies "to receive or give any countenance to this seditious paper" from Massachusetts. If they did, such assemblies were also to be dissolved. The result of Hillsborough's actions actually strengthened the colonists' resolve when new elections swelled the ranks of delegates firmly committed to standing up to any kind of Parliamentary taxation.

Just as the Circular Letter angered Hillsborough, so did the rough treatment experienced by royal customs collectors, particularly in Boston where the Crown had recently located a new five-man Board of Customs Commissioners. When members of the Board, which was to coordinate all customs collections in America, arrived at the end of 1767, jeering crowds greeted them at the docks. The commissioners found it virtually impossible to walk the streets or carry out their official duties without harassment.

More serious trouble erupted in June 1768 when a crowd attacked local customs collectors who had seized John Hancock's sloop *Liberty* on charges of smuggling in a cargo of Madeira wine. (Hancock was notorious for illegal trading.) The new commissioners fled to Fort Castle William in Boston harbor for personal safety. Even before the *Liberty* riots, they had sent reports to Hillsborough about the unruly behavior of Bostonians, and they had asked for military protection.

In the wake of the August 1765 Stamp Act riots, members of the royalist political faction had likewise talked in private about calling for military support. Governor Bernard demurred, thinking that the presence of redcoats might provoke even greater turmoil in the streets. Hillsborough, in turn, was not going to tolerate

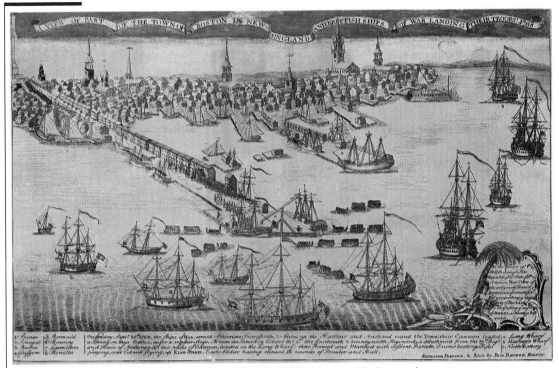

Two British regiments landed at Boston's Long Wharf in 1768 to try to settle increased unrest among the colonists.

such abusive behavior from the Bostonians, even in the absence of a formal gubernatorial request for troops. Just before the *Liberty* riots took place, he issued orders for four regiments to proceed to Boston. The troops were "to give every legal assistance to the civil magistrate in the preservation of the public peace; and to the officers of the revenue in the execution of the laws of trade and revenue."

When the first redcoats arrived in the fall of 1768 without serious incident, members of the royalist political faction breathed more easily and went about their duties with new courage. It appeared as if crowd rule, civil anarchy, and open harassment were tactics of the past. Samuel Adams and the popular faction, however, kept demanding more resistance, and on August 1, 1768, they convinced an enthusiastic town meeting to accept a non-importation agreement regarding British goods. New Yorkers signed a similar document a few days later. Philadelphians refused at first to go along with

Table 4.1

Estimated Population of Colonial Port Towns Compared to London, England (1775)

London, the capital of the British empire, had an enormous population base by the standards of the largest cities in the colonies. The king's ministers were aware of this striking discrepancy, and they regarded American port towns like Boston as minor trading outposts in which a few well-trained redcoats could easily restore order among protesting colonists. Lord Hillsborough certainly believed so, but events proved him wrong.

London	700,000
Philadelphia	28,000
New York City	23,000
Boston	16,000
Charleston	12,000
Newport	11,000
Baltimore	10,000

their two northern neighbors, bowing to the pressure of influential merchants. They hoped that a petition from the Pennsylvania Assembly would change Parliament's mind. Somewhat reluctantly, they finally joined the trade boycott in February 1769. Pressure from popular leader Christopher Gadsden, backed by threats of crowd action, forced the merchants of Charleston into line during August 1769. It had taken a year, but now all the major port towns had endorsed yet another trade boycott in defense of political liberties.

The colonists did more than boycott. In some of the port towns there was talk of producing their own manufactured goods, such as woolen cloth, in direct defiance of imperial restrictions. With the boycott in full force, wealthier citizens could no longer get the most fashionable fabrics from London, and popular leaders encouraged them to join poorer colonists in wearing homespun cloth—a sign of personal sacrifice for the cause. Some leaders urged all "genteel ladies" to master the skills of spinning and weaving. The *Boston Gazette* asked "Daughters of Liberty" everywhere to

First then throw aside your high top
   knots of pride
Wear none but your own country linen
Of economy boast. Let your pride be
   the most
To show clothes of your make and
   spinning.

Upper-class women, by and large, were not persuaded. They did not like the itchy feeling of homespun, and they considered spinning and weaving to be beneath their station in society. For poorer women, particularly those in the port towns, the trade boycott generated extra piecemeal work in the production of homespun cloth. This meant some extra income, but it really had no long-term effect in improving the lot of the poor in America. Homespun was abundant, and the market price remained quite low. While wealthier women itched, complained, and worried about losing their status, poorer women were donating their labor to the defense of American rights. For them the term sacrifice held a special meaning.

Parliament Backs Down Again

The trade boycott seriously hurt merchants and manufacturers in the British Isles. By the beginning of 1770, the Townshend program had netted only about £20 thousand in revenue, a paltry sum when compared to the loss in American trade, estimated to be as high as £7 million. Once again, the colonists had found the means to force Parliament to re-evaluate its position.

It may have been fortunate for Charles Townshend that he died unexpectedly in 1768 at the age of forty-one. He did not have to listen to the abuse that his infamous duties took in debates before Parliament in early 1770. By that time the Pitt ministry had collapsed. In January 1770 George III asked amiable Lord Frederick North to form a new cabinet and give some direction to drifting governmental affairs. North, listening to the wrath of powerful merchants and manufacturers, moved quickly to settle differences with America. He went before

The House of Commons, which enacted such legislature as the Stamp Act, Townshend Duties, and Tea Act, faced more and more resistance from the colonies as trade boycotts continued.

Parliament on March 5, 1770 (ironically the same day as the Boston Massacre), and called for repeal of the Townshend Duties, except for the tax on tea, which was to stand as a symbolic reminder of Parliament's right to tax and legislate in all cases whatsoever.

Like the Stamp Act confrontation, the colonial trade boycott of 1768–1770 had a telling effect. King and Parliament had backed off again, but it was going to be the last time.

THE RUPTURING OF IMPERIAL RELATIONS

Lord North was a sensible leader who wanted to avoid taxation schemes and other forms of legislation that could provoke more trouble. He knew that imperial relations had been strained almost to a breaking point by too many restrictive policies thrown at the colonists in too short a time after so many years of salutary neglect. North carefully avoided challenging the Americans between 1770 and 1773. In turn, the colonial resistance movement clearly waned. For a brief period, then, there were no new issues to stir further conflict—only old problems needing resolution.

When Parliament stepped away from the Townshend Duties, for instance, most colonists wanted to discontinue the boycott and return to normal trade, despite the irritating tax on tea. They knew well that the duty could be avoided by more smuggling of Dutch tea. Slowly, economic relations with the British Isles improved, and British subjects in England and America enjoyed a brief period of mutually supportive economic prosperity.

The Necessity of Vigilance

Political relations were not so resilient. Many colonists had become very suspicious of the intentions of home government officials. Provincial leaders tried to explain what had happened since 1763 by drawing on the thoughts of England's "radical" Whig opposition writers of the early eighteenth century. Men such as John Trenchard and Thomas Gordon, who had penned an extended series of essays known as

Cato's Letters (1720–1723), had repeatedly warned about corruption in government caused by high ministerial officials lusting after power. If not somehow checked, citizens like the colonists would find themselves stripped of all liberties and living in a state of tyranny (often described as "political slavery").

Indeed, what took firm hold during the 1760s was an American world view, or ideology, that saw liberties under attack by such grasping, power-hungry leaders as George Grenville and Charles Townshend in England and their royalist puppets in America, as personified by such officials as Thomas Hutchinson and Andrew Oliver. In attempting to explain what had happened, the evidence of a conspiracy seemed overwhelming. There were His Majesty's regular troops along the frontier and in Boston, and there were ships of the Royal Navy patrolling in American waters, all during peacetime. The colonists had been cut off from frontier lands, and perhaps worst of all, there had been two willful attempts to tax them, literally to deprive them of property without any voice in the matter.

As never before, great numbers of colonists doubted the good will of the home government. Even if Lord North was behaving himself and keeping Parliament in check, many suspected that ministerial inaction was only a ploy, nothing more than a trick designed to lull Americans into a false sense of security while conspiring royal officials devised new and even more insidious plans to strip away all political rights.

Popular leaders exhorted the citizenry to be vigilant at all times. They employed various devices to ensure that the defense of liberties was not forgotten. In Boston, for example, Samuel Adams and his political lieutenants declared March 5 to be an annual commemorative holiday to honor the five fallen martyrs of the massacre. Each year there was a large public meeting and grand oration to stir memories and remind the populace of the possible dangers of a new ministerial assault.

At the 1772 observance, Dr. Joseph Warren, a committed radical and close associate of Samuel Adams, gave an impassioned speech. He vividly recalled *"that dreadful night . . . when our streets were stained with the blood of our brethren; . . . and our eyes were tormented*

O MURD'RER! RICHARDSON! *with their latest breath*
Millions will curse you when you sleep in death!
Infernal horrors sure will shake your soul
When o'er your head the awful thunders roll.
Earth cannot hide you, always will the cry
Of Murder! Murder! haunt you 'till you die!
To yonder grave! with trembling joints repair,
Remember, SEIDER'S *corps lies mould'ring there;*

THOSE HATED CUSTOMS INFORMERS

Benedict Arnold, who later became famous for turning against the American cause of liberty, was a prospering merchant in New Haven, Connecticut, prior to the Revolution. One of Arnold's trading vessels returned from the West Indies in January 1766 and managed to unload its cargo of rum and molasses without paying the required trade duties. Like hundreds of other colonial merchants, Arnold thought nothing of evading imperial customs collectors in American port towns. The economy was bad, and many merchants were struggling to avoid bankruptcy. In addition, many argued that not paying duties at a time when the colonists were demanding repeal of the Stamp Act was a justifiable form of protest against the willfulness of the home government.

In attempting to counter colonial smuggling, British customs officials were in regular contact with informers, or local inhabitants who listened for rumors in the streets and secretly provided evidence about merchants evading the law. Informers expected cash payments for their services, and if Vice-Admiralty courts ruled against an offending merchant, informers sometimes shared in profits gained from the sale of confiscated cargoes. To be an informer could be lucrative, but it also assured the wrath of other local citizens, should colonists caught smuggling find out who had broken the street code of noncooperation with custom officials.

Peter Boles was a seaman working for Benedict Arnold who had helped to unload the smuggled cargo. Late in January he approached his employer and asked for extra wages, implying that the money would help keep him quiet. Arnold responded tersely that he did not hand out bribes. Boles went straight to the New Haven customs office. The chief collector was not there, so the informer announced that he would return later with important information.

When Arnold learned of Boles's action, he sought out the mariner, "gave him a little chastisement," and told him to get out of New Haven permanently. Boles agreed to leave, but two days later he was still in town drinking at a local tavern. Arnold, now backed by a number of seamen, confronted Boles a second time and forced him to sign a prepared confession. "Being instigated by the devil," Boles admitted, under some duress, that "I justly deserve a halter for my malicious and cruel intentions." He also promised "never to enter the same [town] again."

Four hours later, at 11 P.M., Boles was still tippling at the tavern. This time Arnold returned with yet more followers. The party grabbed Boles and, with Arnold in the lead, dragged the informer to the town's whipping post, where he "received forty lashes with a small cord, and was conducted out of town." Peter Boles was not heard from again.

More law-abiding community leaders were outraged when they heard about of Boles's punishment. They had Arnold and a few members of his crowd arrested for disturbing the peace, which ultimately cost each a small fine. In response, Arnold organized a demonstration and parade. Dozens of citizens participated in this evening spectacle, which saw effigies of the local magistrates who had issued the arrest warrants carried through the streets on pretended gallows and then consumed in a huge bonfire. As Arnold wrote later, these magistrates had acted as if they wanted to "vindicate, protect, and caress an informer," rather than stand up for American rights when colonial trade "is nearly ruined by the . . . detestable Stamp and other oppressive acts." Vigilante justice for "infamous informers" like Boles, he maintained, was an effective way to loosen the stranglehold of imperial restrictions on provincial commerce and, at the same time, defend basic rights.

The whipping and banishment of Boles was a relatively mild punishment. Angry crowds often covered informers with tar and feathers before strapping them onto wooden rails and "riding" them out of town. In some instances, informers nearly lost their lives, which happened to Ebenezer Richardson of Boston. A combative person and occasional employee of the customs office, Richardson provided damaging information about a prominent local merchant in 1766, for which this informer was "frequently abused by the people." Then in early 1770 Richardson gained the community's wrath by defying citizens enforcing Boston's nonimportation agreement protesting the Townshend Duties. Events got out of hand, and he became the greatest "monster of the times."

Since August 1768, when Bostonians accepted Samuel Adams's call for nonimportation, an informal group known as "the Body" managed the harassment of violators. Merchants who kept importing British goods endured much abuse as "Importers." Roving bands of citizens struck at night, break-ing windows and defacing their property, which included coating walls with a combination of mud and feces known as "Hillsborough treat." During the day, crowds moved from location to location, posting large wooden hands pointing toward the shops of offending merchants. As customers came and went, they received verbal abuse while dodging handfuls of Hillsborough treat being flung at them.

On February 22, 1770, a crowd visited a shop in Boston's North End, unfortunately across the street from Richardson's residence. The ever belligerent informer suddenly appeared and, in the face of verbal taunts and flying debris, tried to remove the hand. Soon he retreated to his house with the crowd, including a large number of boys, following close behind. "Come out, you damn son of a bitch," they shouted, and they started to break the windows. Inside Richardson and another man loaded their muskets, and when the crowd threatened to enter the house, the informer first warned his assailants and then fired. He severely wounded an eleven-year-old boy, Christopher Seider, who died several hours later. Only the intervention of well-known patriot gentlemen saved Richardson from being lynched.

Samuel Adams and other popular leaders in Boston took full advantage of this ugly incident. They planned an elaborate funeral in which some 2500 mourners solemnly marched in front and back of Seider's coffin from Liberty Tree to the burial ground. Hundreds more lined the streets as the procession passed by. John Adams considered Seider a martyr to the cause of liberty. Lieutenant Governor Thomas Hutchinson, the leader of the royalist faction, was less charitable.

Christopher Seider's death and emotional funeral were signs of the tension boiling in the streets of Boston over imperial policies like the Townshend Duties. That British redcoats were present to help enforce imperial law and keep the populace under control only made matters worse. In the week following Seider's funeral, there was a dramatic increase in incidents of troop baiting, all of which culminated in the Boston Massacre.

As for Ebenezer Richardson, he soon stood trial on the charge of willfully murdering Seider. His argument was self-defense. His wife and two daughters were in the house and had been struck by eggs, stones, and various forms of Hillsborough treat. The Superior Court judges realized that manslaughter was the proper charge, not "damn him—hang him—murder no manslaughter," the phrase enraged Bostonians shouted at the jurors as they left the courtroom to deliberate.

The jury did return a verdict of guilty of murder; however, the court, headed by Thomas Hutchinson, initiated a series of legal maneuvers that in 1772 secured Richardson's freedom by the king's pardon. Now an outcast, Boston's most notorious informer tried to find work, only to be reviled and sent on his way. Finally, he secured employment with the customs office in Philadelphia, but more than once he disappeared to avoid a coat of tar and feathers because everywhere colonists knew him as the "execrable villain, . . . as yet unchanged" customs informer who had shot down young Christopher Seider.

Tension increased between Great Britain and America when Rhode Islanders burned the *Gaspée*, a royal naval vessel which patrolled for smugglers in the area.

with the sight of the mangled bodies of the dead." Then he turned to future prospects, reminding hundreds in attendance that it might happen again—and in more destructive terms. Warren's "imagination" conjured up "our houses wrapped in flames, our children subjected to the barbarous caprice of a raging soldiery; our beauteous virgins exposed to all the insolence of unbridled passion." The message of constant vigilance to preserve liberties could not be missed.

Local confrontations, too, kept emotions stirred up. One such incident occurred in June 1772 and involved a Royal Naval vessel, the *Gaspée*, which patrolled for smugglers in the waters of Rhode Island. The ship's crew and its captain, William Dudingston, were particularly efficient. Finally, Rhode Islanders had had enough. One day they sent out a sloop that purposely flaunted itself before the *Gaspée*. Suspecting illicit trading activity, Dudingston gave chase but ran aground as the smaller vessel swept close to shore. That evening, a crowd, disguised as Indians, descended upon the stranded ship and burned it. One "Indian" deliv-

ered the supreme insult by firing a load of buckshot into Dudingston's buttocks.

Crown officials were furious about the *Gaspée*'s destruction. They set up a royal commission of inquiry but never obtained any useful information concerning the perpetrators of this crowd action. Curiously, popular leaders, ignoring the reasons why the *Gaspée* was in American waters in the first place, set up a hue and cry about the royal commission. They were fearful that its intent was to send suspects to England for trial. As a result, several provincial assemblies established committees of correspondence to communicate with each other, should home government leaders appear to threaten liberties of any kind, in this case trials of citizens outside districts where alleged crimes had been committed. These committees were soon writing back and forth regarding serious problems over tea.

The Tea Crisis of 1773

The third and final assault on American rights, as the colonists perceived matters, grew out of a rather inconspicuous piece of legislation, known as the Tea Act of 1773. When Lord North proposed this bill, he had no idea that it would precipitate a disastrous sequence of events; in fact, he was hardly even thinking about the American provinces. His prime concern was the East India Company, a joint-stock trading venture dating back to the early seventeenth century whose officials ruled over British interests in India.

Having prospered for years, the company was in desperate economic straits in the early 1770s. One reason was that the recent colonial boycott had cost the company its place in the American tea market. With tea warehouses bulging, company directors sought marketing concessions from Parliament in 1773 (they also requested a £1.5 million loan to refinance company operations). They asked to have the authority to ship tea directly from India to America. As matters then stood, company tea had to be sent through England, adding significantly to the final market price. In May 1773, King and Parliament acceded to these various requests and, in turn, forced the company to give up some of its political authority in India.

To reduce costs even more, the company proceeded to name its own tea agents in the major American ports. They were to function as local distributors for six percent commissions. The net effect of these changes was to make company tea much more competitive with, if not cheaper than, smuggled Dutch blends—a fact that pleased Lord North very much.

He was even more pleased to have found a way, he thought, to get the Americans to accept the tea tax—and symbolically, at least, recognize Parliament's sovereignty. How could they refuse cheaper tea, even with the Townshend duty added to the price? He could not imagine that the colonists would stand on principle and keep purchasing more expensive Dutch tea just to avoid the three pence a pound trade duty. Lord North should have listened to the M.P. who warned him during the debates on the Tea Act that "if we don't take off the duty they won't take the tea."

In September 1773, the company dipped into its warehouses and readied its first American consignments of 600,000 pounds of tea worth £60 thousand. Vigilant Americans were waiting. Conditioned by years of warding off undesirable imperial legislation, they were looking for signs of further conspiratorial acts. A small economic saving meant nothing in the face of what appeared to be another, more insidious plot to reduce the colonists to a state of political slavery. Although such a world view may seem far-fetched today, popular leaders and the general populace were thinking in confrontational terms. East India Company tea had to be resisted.

Once again, the port town of Boston became the focal point of significant protest. In early November a crowd took to the streets and tried to intimidate the tea agents (among them Thomas and Elisha Hutchinson, sons of Thomas

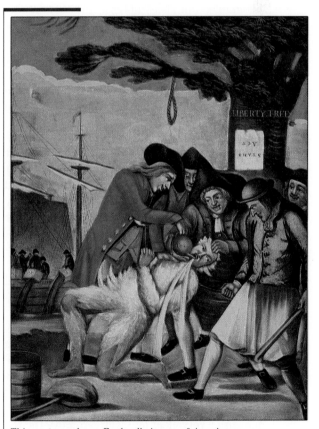

This cartoon shows England's image of America as a bunch of colonial hoodlums defying imperial authority by tarring and feathering the local tax collector.

who was now the royal governor) into resigning. The merchant agents, who had not received official commissions as yet, refused to submit; the crowd did not press the matter and waited for a more timely moment to force resignations. On November 27 the first tea ship, the *Dartmouth*, arrived. The local customs collectors fled to Castle William, and the local committee of correspondence, headed by Samuel Adams and his associates, put guards on the *Dartmouth* and two other tea ships entering the port within the next few days. The popular faction repeatedly insisted that the three tea ships be sent back to England, but Governor Thomas Hutchinson refused. Instead, he called upon Royal Naval vessels in the vicinity to block the port's entrance.

No person in Massachusetts had been more maligned by Adams and his popular party following. This native-son royal governor could be fair-minded but also stubborn, and this time he decided that a showdown was necessary. The popular rights group had gotten its way by threats and intimidation for far too long. After all, the crowd had backed off in early November, and the governor mistakenly viewed this as a sign of popular indifference about the tea issue.

By imperial law, unclaimed cargo had to be unloaded after twenty days in port and sold at public auction. Since the tea ships could not escape the harbor, Hutchinson fully expected to have them unloaded after the twenty-day waiting period. Once the tea had been sold, the Townshend duty would be paid from the revenues obtained, and the governor would have upheld the law of King and Parliament. Hutchinson's plan to stand firm on behalf of imperial authority—and against his troublesome, long-time enemies—turned out very poorly.

The waiting period for the *Dartmouth* was over on December 16. That day a mass meeting of local citizens took place at Old South Church. Samuel Adams and his faction made one last attempt to communicate the gravity of the situation to Hutchinson. They sent a messenger to him with a very clear message—remove the tea ships, or else. Hutchinson refused again. Late in the day, Adams appeared before the huge gathering and reportedly shouted: "This meeting can do no more to save the country." The moment for crowd action had been proclaimed. Several dozen artisans, apprentices, and day laborers, led by Ebenezer Mackintosh, went to the docks disguised as Indians. They climbed aboard the tea ships and dumped 342 chests of tea valued at £10,000 into the harbor. It took nearly three hours to complete the work of the Boston Tea Party.

Tea confrontations occurred later in other ports, but none so destructively as in Boston. Philadelphians used the threat of tar and feathers to convince local officials to send back the first tea ships to arrive there. The governor of South Carolina outmaneuvered the local populace and managed to get the tea landed, but the company product lay rotting in a warehouse and was never sold. New Yorkers had to wait until the spring of 1774 for tea ships to appear in their port. They jeered loudly at the docks, and an intelligent sea captain raised anchor and fled for the high seas. Once again, Bostonians stood out for their bold defiance of imperial law.

Parliament Adopts the Coercive Acts

The Boston Tea Party shocked Lord North and other British officials. North decided that the "rebellious" Bostonians simply had to be taught a lesson, and Parliament adopted a series of legislative bills, collectively known as the *Coercive Acts*. Although King and Parliament aimed these laws against Massachusetts, the Coercive Acts held implications for colonists elsewhere who believed the parent state was only using the Tea Party as a pretext for the final destruction of American liberties.

King George III signed the first act, known as the Boston Port Bill, into law at the end of March 1774. This bill literally closed the port of Boston, making trade illegal until such time as local citizens paid for the tea. In May Parliament passed the Massachusetts Government Act and the Administration of Justice Act. The first vastly expanded the powers of the royal governor, abolished the elective council (upper house of the General Court), and replaced it with appointed councilors of the Crown's choosing. Town meetings were prohibited without the governor's permission, except for annual spring election gatherings.

As matters turned out, Governor Hutchinson never exercised this vastly expanded authority. Dismayed by the Tea Party, he asked for a leave of absence, and the Crown replaced him with General Thomas Gage, Britain's North American military commander, who held the governorship until the final disruption of royal government in the Bay Colony.

The Administration of Justice Act provided greater protection for customs collectors and other imperial officials in Massachusetts. If they injured or killed anyone while carrying out their duties, the governor had the right to move trials to some other colony or to England. The assumption was that local juries were too biased to render fair judgments.

Finally, in early June 1774 Parliament sanctioned the fourth coercive bill, which was an amendment to the Quartering Act of 1765. The earlier law had outlined procedures relating to the provision of housing for redcoats and had specifically excluded the use of private dwellings of any kind. The 1774 amendment gave General Gage the power to billet his troops anywhere, including unoccupied private homes, as long as the army paid fair rental rates. Parliament passed this law because Gage was bringing several hundred troops to Boston with him.

Quebec Act of 1774

The Quebec Act, approved in June 1774, was seen by the colonists as another piece of coercive legislation. Actually, this bill, mainly concerned with the territorial administration of Canada, provided for a royal governor and a large appointed advisory council, but no popularly elected assembly. Roman Catholicism was to remain the established religious faith for the French-speaking populace. In addition, the Ohio River was to become the new southwestern boundary of Quebec.

Ever vigilant colonial leaders viewed the Quebec Act as confirming all the worst tendencies of imperial legislation over the past decade. Parliament had denied local representative government; it had ratified the establishment of a branch of the Christian faith that was repugnant to militantly Protestant Americans, especially New Englanders; and it had cut into western lands that well-placed provincial speculators, among them Benjamin Franklin and George Washington, had fixed upon for future population expansion. The Quebec Act, thousands of Americans concluded, smacked of abject political slavery.

Even without the Quebec Act, Lord North had made a tactical error by encouraging Parliament to pass so much legislation. The port bill punishing Boston was one thing; some Americans felt that the Bostonians had gone too far and deserved some chastisement. But the sum total of the Coercive Acts caused widespread concern because they seemed to violate the sanctity of local political institutions, to distort normal judicial procedures, and to favor military over civil authority. For most colonists, the Coercive Acts produced feelings of solidarity with (rather than separateness from) the Bostonians, which was critical to mounting yet higher levels of unified resistance.

Hurling Back the Challenge: The First Continental Congress

News of the full array of Coercive Acts provoked a frenzied wave of intercolonial activity, the most important expression of which was the calling of the first Continental Congress. This body assembled in Philadelphia on September 5, 1774, and gentlemen of all political persuasions were there (Georgia was the only colony not represented). Among the more radical delegates were Samuel Adams and his younger cousin John, as well as Patrick Henry. George Washington was present, mostly silent in debates but firmly committed to protecting fundamental rights. More conservative dele-

As the largest American city and a central geographic point, Philadelphia was a logical choice for the delegates of the First Continental Congress to gather in 1774.

gates were also in attendance, such as Joseph Galloway of Pennsylvania and John Jay of New York. The central question facing all the delegates was how belligerent the Congress should be. The more cautious delegates wanted to find some means to settle differences with Britain, but the radicals believed that well-organized resistance could get King and Parliament to back down a third time.

Indeed, political maneuvering for dominance of the Congress began even before the sessions got under way. More conservative delegates favored meeting in the Pennsylvania State House, a building symbolizing ties with British rule. The radicals argued in favor of Carpenter's Hall, a gathering place for Philadelphia's laborers. The latter building was chosen. The delegates thus seemed to identify with the people and their desire to preserve political liberties rather than with the suspect hand of British authority. Then the radicals insisted upon naming Charles Thomson, a popular leader in

Philadelphia, secretary for the Congress. He gained the post and was able to manipulate the minutes so that the actions of the radicals dominated the official record.

These signs foreshadowed what was to come. Accounts of the work of the first Continental Congress clearly indicate that Samuel Adams, Patrick Henry, and others of their more radical persuasion had a field day. Although they went along with the preparation of an elaborate petition to Parliament, which came to be known as "The Declaration of Colonial Rights and Grievances," these experienced molders of the colonial resistance movement demanded much more. They drew upon the old arsenal of weapons that had caused Parliament to retreat before, and they added a new weapon. Just in case there was no way to get the Coercive Acts repealed, they insisted that Americans should begin to prepare for war.

To assure that Congress moved in the right direction, Samuel Adams and his allies back in

Massachusetts had done some careful planning. This came to light on September 9, 1774, when a convention of citizens in Suffolk County (Boston and environs) adopted a series of resolutions written by Dr. Joseph Warren. Once approved, Paul Revere, talented silversmith and active member of Adams's popular rights faction, mounted his horse and rode hard for Philadelphia. Revere arrived in mid-September and laid the Suffolk Resolves before Congress. Not only did these statements strongly profess American rights, but they also called for a full-blown economic boycott and the rigorous training of local militia companies, just in case it became necessary to defend lives, liberty, and property against the redcoats of Thomas Gage.

Congress approved the Suffolk Resolves—and with them the initial step in organization for possible civil war. The delegates also committed themselves to a plan of economic boycott, which came to be called the Continental Association. It amounted to a comprehensive plan of non-importation and non-consumption of British goods, to be phased in over the next few months, as well as non-exportation of American products if Parliament had not retreated within a year.

The Association also called upon every American community to establish a local committee of observation charged with having all citizens subscribe to the boycott. In reality, the Association was a loyalty test. Citizens who refused to sign were about to become outcasts from the cause of liberty. The term of derision applied to them was *tory;* however, they thought of themselves as loyalists—maintaining their allegiance to the Crown.

The only countercharge of any consequence during the first Congress came from Joseph Galloway, a wealthy Philadelphia lawyer who had long served as Pennsylvania's speaker of the house. Galloway desperately wanted to maintain imperial ties because he feared what the "common sort" of citizens might do if those ties were irrevocably lost. He could imagine nothing but rioting, dissipation, and the confiscation of the property of economically successful colonists. For him, the continuation of any kind of political and social order in America

In the Society of Patriotic Ladies, a satirical British cartoon, babbling women are capable of resisting the Crown but incapable of controlling their own children.

depended on the stabilizing influence of British rule.

Galloway drew on the Albany Plan of Union of 1754 (see p. 98) and proposed a central government in America that would be superior to the provincial assemblies. It would consist of a "grand council" to be elected by colonial assemblymen and a "president general" to be appointed by the Crown. Just as grand council legislation would have to meet Parliament's approval, imperial acts from King and Parliament would have to gain the assent of the grand council and president.

Galloway's Plan of Union, as it came to be known, represented a structural alternative allowing Americans a greater voice in imperial decision making affecting the colonies, and it foreshadowed the future commonwealth organization of the British empire. But the more

CHRONOLOGY OF KEY EVENTS

1760 George III becomes king of England

1763 Pontiac's Indian uprising results in bloodshed along the American frontier (May–August); Grenville named chief minister of government (July); Privy Council approves the Orders-in-Council and Proclamation of 1763 (October)

1764 Parliament adopts the Revenue (Sugar) Act (April)

1765 Parliament passes the Stamp Act (March); Rockingham replaces Grenville as chief minister (July); Americans turn to crowd violence to protest the stamp tax (August–October); Stamp Act Congress convenes in New York City (October)

1766 Parliament repeals the Stamp Act but claims complete legislative authority over America in Declaratory Act (March); George III asks Pitt to form a new government (July)

1767 Parliament passes the Townshend Duties (June); Dickinson denounces the duties in his *Letters from a Farmer in Pennsylvania* (November 1767–January 1768)

1768 Hillsborough named Secretary for American Affairs (January); Massachusetts adopts a controversial Circular Letter against the Townshend Duties (February); Hillsborough orders British troops to restore order in Boston (June)

1769 Colonists mount boycott against British goods in protesting continuation of the Townshend Duties

1770 North forms a new cabinet (January) and calls for repeal of the Townshend Duties, except the tax on tea (March); Boston Massacre results in the death of five colonists (March)

1772 Rhode Islanders burn the British naval vessel *Gaspée* (June); Bostonians establish a committee of correspondence to communicate with all towns in the colony (November)

1773 Provincial assemblies set up intercolonial committees of correspondence (March–July); Parliament approves the Tea Act (May); Bostonians dump East India Company tea into harbor (December)

1774 Parliament adopts the Coercive Acts (March–June) and the Quebec Act (June); First Continental Congress meets in Philadelphia, approves the Continental Association trade boycott but rejects Galloway's Plan of Union (September–October)

radical delegates called the proposal impractical and dismissed it as an idea that would divert everyone from the task of the moment, which was to get Parliament to rescind the Coercive Acts. In a close vote Galloway's Plan went down to defeat.

Later, at the urging of the radicals, Secretary Thomson expunged all references to Galloway's Plan from the official minutes of Congress on the grounds of demonstrating American unity to King and Parliament. As for Galloway, he faced growing harassment as a loyalist in the months ahead and eventually fled to the British army for protection.

When the first Continental Congress ended its deliberations in late October 1774, its program was one of continued defiance, certainly not conciliation or submission. The delegates understood the course they had chosen. One of their last acts was to mandate a second Continental Congress, to convene in Philadelphia on May 10, 1775, "unless the redress of grievances, which we have desired, be obtained before that time."

As the fall of 1774 gave way to another cold winter, Americans awaited the verdict of King and Parliament. Would the Coercive Acts be withdrawn, or would there be further steps pointing toward war? Local committees of observation were busily at work encouraging—and in some cases coercing—the populace to boycott British goods, and militia companies were out vigorously training, while in Britain, King George III and Lord North quickly dismissed the work of the first Continental Congress. They had decided the parent state could not retreat a third time.

CONCLUSION

In September 1774, Lord North observed: "The die is now cast, the colonies must either submit or triumph." Hitherto harmonious relations between Britain and America had become increasingly discordant between 1763 and the end of 1774. The colonists refused to accept undesirable imperial acts, and they successfully resisted such taxation plans as the Stamp Act and the Townshend Duties. In the process they came to believe firmly that ministerial leaders in England were involved in a deep-seated plot to deprive them of their fundamental liberties. When something as inconsequential as the Townshend duty on tea precipitated yet another crisis, neither side was willing to disengage. By early 1775 both were determined to show their resolve.

A small incident that well illustrates the deteriorating situation occurred in Boston during March 1774. At the state funeral of Andrew Oliver, the Bay Colony's most recent lieutenant governor and former stamp distributor-designate, a large gathering of ordinary citizens came out to watch the solemn procession. As Oliver's coffin was slowly lowered into the ground, these Bostonians, many of them veterans of the American resistance movement, suddenly burst into loud cheers.

Such an open expression of hatred and contempt epitomized the deep strain in British-American relations. It was almost as if the cheers were for the burial of imperial authority in America. Certainly these colonists demonstrated no pride in their British citizenship that day. Such striking changes in attitudes, over just a few years, pointed toward the fateful clash of arms known as the War for American Independence.

REVIEW SUMMARY

The American Revolution resulted from misunderstanding on both sides of the Atlantic. Great Britain emphasized its sovereign rights; Americans jealously protected their traditional liberties. Between 1763 and 1775 the two sides repeatedly clashed over a series of issues.

> Imperial problems—debts, Indians, and smuggling
> imperial taxation and colonial responses
> American aristocrats and American mobs battle for power
> and the movement from economic boycott and crowd actions to outright defiance and open rebellion

This dramatic clash of wills and beliefs led to the American Revolution.

SUGGESTIONS FOR FURTHER READING

OVERVIEWS AND SURVEYS

Richard Maxwell Brown, *Strain of Violence: Historical Studies of American Violence and Vigilantism* (1975); Robert M. Calhoon, *Revolutionary America: An Interpretive Overview* (1976); Marc Egnal, *A Mighty Empire: The Origins of the Revolution* (1988); Lawrence Henry Gipson, *The Coming of the Revolution, 1763–1775* (1954); Merrill Jensen, *The Founding of a Nation, 1763–1776* (1968); Stephen G. Kurtz and James H. Hutson, eds., *Essays on the American Revolution* (1973); James Kirby Martin, *In the Course of Human Events: An Interpretive Exploration of the Revolution* (1979); Robert Middlekauff, *The Glorious Cause, 1763–1783* (1982); Edmund S. Morgan, *The Birth of the Republic, 1763–1789*, rev. ed. (1977); and Esmond Wright, *Fabric of Freedom, 1763–1800*, rev. ed. (1978).

PROVOKING AN IMPERIAL CRISIS

Thomas C. Barrow, *Trade and Empire: The British Customs Service in America, 1660–1775* (1967); Robert A. Becker, *Revolution, Reform, and the Politics of American Taxation, 1763–1783* (1980); Colin Bonwick, *English Radicals and the American Revolution* (1977); John Brewer, *Party Ideology and Popular Politics at the Accession of George III* (1976); John Brooke, *King George III* (1974); John L. Bullion, *A Great and Necessary Measure: George Grenville and the Genesis of the Stamp Act, 1763–1765* (1981); Ian R. Christie, *Crisis of Empire, 1754–1783* (1966), and with Benjamin W. Labaree, *Empire or Independence, 1760–1776* (1976); John Derry, *English Politics and the American Revolution* (1976); Joseph A. Ernst, *Money and Politics in America, 1755–1775* (1973); Michael Kammen, *A Rope of Sand: Colonial Agents, British Politics, and the Revolution* (1968); James L. McKelvey, *George III and Lord Bute* (1973); Lewis B. Namier, *England in the Age of the American Revolution*, rev. ed. (1961), and *The Structure of Politics at the Accession of George III*, rev. ed. (1957); Howard H. Peckham, *Pontiac and the Indian Uprising* (1947); Francis Philbrick, *The Rise of the West, 1754–1830* (1965); John Shy, *Toward Lexington: The Role of the British Army in the Coming of the Revolution* (1965); Jack M. Sosin, *Whitehall and the Wilderness: The Middle West in British Colonial Policy, 1760–1775* (1961), and *The Revolutionary Frontier, 1763–1783* (1967); Neil R. Stout, *The Royal Navy in America, 1760–1775* (1973); Robert W. Tucker and David C. Hendrickson, *The Fall of the First British Empire* (1982); Carl Ubbelohde, *The Vice-Admiralty Courts and the American Revolution* (1960); Franklin B. Wickwire, *British Subministers and Colonial America, 1763–1783* (1966); and Esmond Wright, *Franklin of Philadelphia* (1986).

"LIBERTY, PROPERTY, AND NO STAMPS" AND A SECOND CRISIS: THE TOWNSHEND DUTIES

Richard R. Beeman, *Patrick Henry* (1974); John H. Cary, *Joseph Warren* (1961); Paul Gilje, *Road to Mobocracy: Popular Disorder in New York City, 1763–1834* (1987); E. Stanly Godbold, Jr., and Robert W. Woody, *Christopher Gadsden* (1982); Dirk Hoerder, *Crowd Action in Revolutionary Massachusetts, 1765–1780* (1977); Pauline R. Maier, *From Resistance to Revolution: Colonial Radicals and the Development of Opposition to Britain, 1765–1775* (1972), and *The Old Revolutionaries: Political Lives in the Age of Samuel Adams* (1980); Edmund S. and Helen M. Morgan, *The Stamp Act Crisis*, rev. ed. (1962); Lewis B. Namier and John Brooke, *Charles Townshend* (1964); Gary B. Nash, *The Urban Crucible: Social Change, Political Consciousness, and the Origins of the Revolution* (1979); Charles S. Olton, *Artisans for Independence: Philadelphia Mechanics and the Revolution* (1975); Peter Shaw, *The Character of John Adams* (1976), and *American Patriots and the Rituals of Revolution* (1981); Peter D. G. Thomas, *British Politics and the Stamp Act Crisis* (1975), and *The Townshend Duties Crisis: The Second Phase of the Revolution, 1767–1773* (1987); John W. Tyler, *Smugglers and Patriots: Boston Merchants and the Advent of the Revolution* (1986); John J. Waters, Jr., *The Otis Family in Provincial and Revolutionary Massachusetts* (1968); and Hiller B. Zobel, *The Boston Massacre* (1970).

THE RUPTURING OF IMPERIAL RELATIONS

David Ammerman, *In the Common Cause: American Response to the Coercive Acts of 1774* (1974); Bernard Bailyn, *The Ideological Origins of the American Revolution* (1967), *The Origins of American Politics* (1968), and *The Ordeal of Thomas Hutchinson* (1974); Richard R. Beeman, *The Evolution of the Southern Backcountry: A Case Study of Lunenburg Country, Virginia, 1746–1832* (1984); Richard D. Brown, *Revolutionary Politics in Massachusetts: The Boston Committee of Correspondence, 1772–1774* (1970); Edwin G. Burrows and Michael Wallace, "The Ideology and Psychology of National Liberation," *Perspectives in American History*, 6 (1972), pp. 167–302; H. Trevor Colbourn, *The Lamp of Experience: Whig History and the Intellectual Origins of the Revolution* (1965); Jere R. Daniell, *Experiment in Republicanism: New Hampshire Politics and the Revolution, 1741–1794* (1970); Bernard Donoughue, *British Politics and the American Revolution: The Path to War, 1773–1775* (1964); A. Roger Ekirch, *"Poor Carolina": Politics and Society in North Carolina, 1729–1776* (1981); Jay Fliegelman, *Prodigals and Pilgrims: The American Revolution Against Patriarchal Authority, 1750–1800* (1982); Larry R. Gerlach, *Prologue to Independence: New Jersey in the Coming of the Revolution* (1976); Ronald Hoffman, *A*

Spirit of Dissension: Economics, Politics, and the Revolution in Maryland (1973); Benjamin W. Labaree, *The Boston Tea Party* (1964); David S. Lovejoy, *Rhode Island Politics and the Revolution, 1760–1776* (1958); Stephen E. Lucas, *Portents of Rebellion: Rhetoric and Revolution in Philadelphia, 1765–1776* (1976); Bernard Mason, *The Road to Independence: The Revolutionary Movement in New York, 1773–1777* (1966); John A. Neuenschwander, *The Middle Colonies and the Coming of the American Revolution* (1973); Gregory H. Nobles, *Divisions Throughout the Whole: Politics and Society in Hampshire County, Massachusetts, 1740–1775* (1983); J. G. A. Pocock, *The Machiavellian Moment: Florentine Political Thought and the Atlantic Republican Tradition* (1975); Caroline Robbins, *The Eighteenth-Century Commonwealthman* (1959); Clinton Rossiter, *Seedtime of the Republic: The Origin of the American Tradition of Political Liberty* (1953); Richard A. Ryerson, *The Revolution Is Now Begun: The Radical Committees of Philadelphia, 1765–1776* (1978); and David Curtis Skaggs, *Roots of Maryland Democracy, 1753–1776.*

CHAPTER 5

The Times That Tried Many Souls, 1775 – 1783

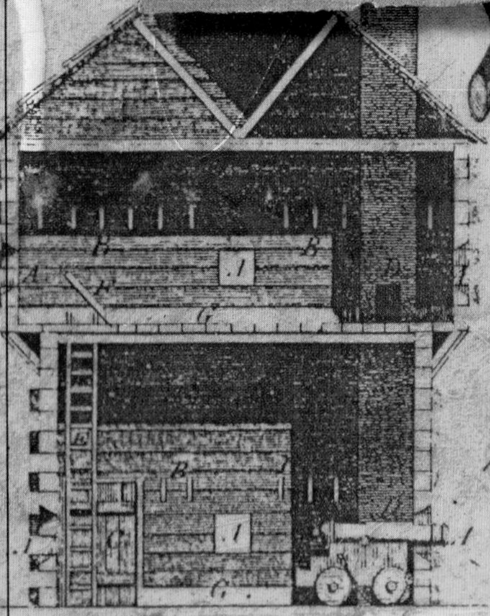

A TOBACCO PLANTATION

FIG. II.

76.

FIG. V.

*J*oseph Plumb Martin was a dedicated patriot soldier, one of 11,000 men and women who formed the backbone of General George Washington's Continental forces. When that army entered its Valley Forge winter campsite in December 1777, Martin recorded despondently that the soldiers' trail could "be tracked by their blood upon the rough frozen ground." The Continentals were "now in a truly forlorn condition—no clothing, no provisions, and as disheartened as need be." They had fought hard against Hessians and British regulars that summer and autumn but had not prevented the forces of General Sir William Howe from taking Philadelphia, the rebel capital. Washington had chosen Valley Forge as a winter encampment because, as a hilly area, it represented an easily defensible position some twenty miles northwest of Philadelphia, should Howe's soldiers venture forth from their comfortable quarters.

General Washington himself was very worried about the conditions facing his troops. If something was not done, and soon, the commander in chief stated, "this army must inevitably . . . starve, dissolve, or disperse." Private Martin thought the same: "Had there fallen deep snows (and it was the time of year to expect them) or even heavy and long rainstorms, the whole army must inevitably have perished." The weather was bitterly cold, but the soldiers, using what energy they had left, constructed "little shanties that are scarcely gaier than dungeon cells," as the Marquis de Lafayette described their housing.

Making matters more difficult was the lack of food and clothing. Martin claimed that, upon first entering Valley Forge, he went a full day and two nights without anything to eat, "save half a small pumpkin, which I cooked by placing it upon a rock, the skin side uppermost, and making fire upon it." His comrades fared no better. Within two days of moving into Valley Forge, a common grumble could be heard everywhere: "No Meat! No Meat!" By the first of January the words had become more ominous: "No bread, no soldier!"

Thus began a tragic winter of desperation for George Washington's Continentals. Some 2500 soldiers, or nearly one-fourth of the army, perished before the army broke camp in June 1778. They died from exposure to the elements, malnutrition, and virulent diseases like typhus and smallpox. Indeed, it was not uncommon for soldiers to return to their huts and find comrades, too weak to drill or go on food hunting expeditions, frozen stiff in their beds. To add to the woes of the camp, more than 500 of the army's horses starved to death. It was impossible to dispose of their carcasses in the frozen ground, which only made worse the deplorable sanitation conditions and the consequent spread of disease.

Under such desolate circumstances, hundreds of soldiers deserted. If Washington had not let his troops leave camp to requisition food in the countryside or if there had not been an unusually early shad run in the Schuylkill River, which flowed behind the encampment, the army might have perished.

The extreme suffering at Valley Forge has usually been attributed to the severe weather and a complete breakdown of the army's supply system. In fact, weather conditions were no worse than in other years. (The most miserable winter encampment in terms of frigid temperatures and deep piles of snow came two years later when the Continentals settled into Jockey Hollow near Morristown, New Jersey.) The major reason for the deprivation at Valley Forge was widespread indifference toward an army made up of the poor, the expendable, and the unfree in American society. In addition, civilian leaders did not move quickly to correct obvious supply problems.

Joseph Plumb Martin clearly thought this was the case. He was a young man from Connecticut, without material resources, who had first enlisted during 1776 at the very height of patriot enthusiasm for the war—sometimes called the *rage militaire*. He soon learned that there were few glories in soldiering. Camp life was dull but also dangerous, given the many killer diseases that ravaged armies of the era. Battle was a frightening experience. Before 1776 was over, Martin had faced the hurtling musket balls and bloodied bayonets of British soldiers in the Continental army's vain attempt to defend New York City and vicinity. He did not renew his enlistment and returned home.

George Washington led a bedraggled, half-starved army of 11,000 men and a few women into Valley Forge in December 1777.

For a poor, landless person, economic prospects at home were not much better than serving for promises of regular pay in the Continental army. In 1777 Martin stepped forth again and agreed to enlist as a substitute for some local gentlemen being threatened by an attempted draft. For a specified sum of money ("I forgot the sum"), he became their substitute. As Martin later wrote, "they were now freed from further trouble, at least for the present, and I had become the scapegoat for them."

The experiences of Martin typified those of so many others who performed long-term Continental service on behalf of the cause of liberty. After an initial rush to arms in defiance of British authority in 1775, the harsh realities of camp life and pitched battles dampened patriot enthusiasm to the point that by December 1776 the Continental army all but ceased to exist. Washington's major task became that of securing enough troop strength and material support to shape an army capable of standing up time after time to British forces.

The commander in chief found his long-term soldiers among the poor and deprived groups of Revolutionary America. In addition, major European nations like France, Spain, and Holland also came to the rescue with additional troops, supplies, and vital financial support. Working together, even in the face of so much popular indifference, these allies-in-arms outlasted the mighty land and sea forces of Great Britain, making possible a generous peace settlement that guaranteed independence for the group of former British colonies that now called themselves the thirteen United States.

RECONCILIATION OR INDEPENDENCE

Crown officials in England gave scant attention to the acts of the First Continental Congress because they believed that the time had come to teach the American provincials a military lesson. George III explained why. The colonists, he asserted, "have boldly thrown off the mask and avowed nothing less than a total independence of the British legislature will satisfy them." This was an inaccurate perception, but it lay behind the decision to turn the most powerful military machine in the western world, based on its record in recent wars, against the troublemakers in America and to break resistance to British authority once and for all.

The Shooting War Starts

During the winter of 1774–75, the king's ministers prepared for what they thought would be nothing more than a brief demonstration of military force. General Gage received "secret" orders to employ the redcoats under his command "to arrest and imprison the principal actors and abettors" of rebellion; however, if the likes of Samuel Adams, John Hancock, and Joseph Warren could not be captured, then Gage was to challenge in any way he deemed appropriate "this rude *rabble* without plan, without concert, and without conduct . . . unprepared to encounter with a regular force." Above all else, he was to strike hard with a decisive blow.

In a series of related showdown decisions, King and Parliament also authorized funds for a larger force of regular troops in America and named three high ranking generals—William Howe, Henry Clinton, and "Gentleman" Johnny Burgoyne—to sail to Boston and join Gage. They declared Massachusetts to be in a state of rebellion, which permitted redcoats to shoot down suspected rebels on sight, should the need arise. Eventually this act would be applied to all thirteen provinces.

General Gage received the ministry's secret orders in mid-April 1775. Being on the scene, he was not quite as convinced as his superiors about American martial weakness. Gage had repeatedly urged caution in his reports to home officials, but now there was no choice; he had to act. Because the rebel leaders had already gotten word of the orders and fled into the countryside, Gage decided upon a reconnaissance in force mission. He would send a column of redcoats to Concord, a town some twenty miles

British troops marched to Concord to destroy patriot stores of gunpowder and military supplies. This painting was based on an eye-witness sketch.
Photograph courtesy Concord Museum, Concord, MA

northwest of Boston known to be a storage point for patriot gunpowder and military supplies. Once there, the troops were to seize or destroy as much weaponry and ammunition as possible. Gage hoped this maneuver could be effected without bloodshed, fearing a full-scale war would follow if patriot lives were lost.

After dark on April 18 some 700 British regulars under Lieutenant Colonel Francis Smith moved out across Boston's back bay. Popular leaders monitored this activity, and soon Paul Revere and William Dawes were riding through the countryside alerting the populace to what was happening. In Lexington, five miles east of Concord and on the road that the king's troops had taken, seventy militiamen, trained to respond at a moment's notice, gathered at the tavern with their captain, John Parker. Samuel Adams and John Hancock were also there. Obviously outnumbered, the Minutemen debated what course of action to take, and they decided to respond to the redcoats' provocative incursion into the countryside by acting as an army of observation.

Parker and his men lined up across the village green as the British column bore down on them at dawn (Adams and Hancock, as known enemies, fled into the woods). The Minutemen were not there to exchange shots but to warn the regulars against trespassing on the property of free-born British subjects. As the redcoats came closer, Parker tried to shout out words to this effect. He was never heard. A shot rang out just as the Minutemen, having made their protest, turned to leave the green. The shot caused troops at the front of the British column to level their arms and fire. Before order was restored, several of Parker's men lay wounded, mostly shot in the back. Eight of them died in what was the opening volley of the War for American Independence.

The redcoats regrouped and continued their march to Concord, as if nothing much had happened. Once there, a party moved out of town to cross the Old North Bridge in search of weapons and gunpowder, but rallying militiamen repulsed them. Falling back to the center of town, they left behind three dead comrades. Now blood had been spilled on both sides.

Lieutenant Colonel Smith began to fear that his column might be cut off by onrushing

Paul Revere, a talented silversmith, warned the citizens between Boston and Concord that the British soldiers were out in force.

citizen-soldiers, so he ordered a retreat. The rest of the day turned into a rout as an aroused citizenry fired away at the British from behind trees and stone fences. Only a relief column of some 1100, which Gage had the foresight to send out, saved Smith's troops. Final casualty figures showed 273 redcoats dead or wounded, as compared to 95 colonists. Lexington and Concord were clear blows to the notion of the invincibility of British arms and suggested that American citizens, when defending their own property, could hold their own against better-trained British soldiers.

As word of the bloodshed spread, New Englanders rallied to the patriot banner. Within days thousands of people poured into hastily assembled military camps surrounding Boston. Thomas Gage and his soldiers were now trapped, and they could only hope that promised reinforcements would soon reach them. The *rage militaire* was on, and it seemed that everyone wanted to be a soldier—and take a pot shot at a redcoat or two before returning home again.

Most colonists believed that it would only be a matter of weeks before the ministry regained its senses and restored all American rights. They did not realize that the Crown was unwaveringly committed to putting down all resistance among the citizenry, or that the conflict would become a long and grueling full-scale war in which the ability to endure would determine the eventual winner.

Moderates Versus Radicals in Congress

The shadow of Lexington and Concord loomed heavily as the second Continental Congress convened in Philadelphia in May 1775. Despite the recent bloodshed, few delegates were firm advocates of independence. New Englanders like Samuel and John Adams were leaning that way, but the vast majority held out hope for a reconciliation of differences. By the early summer of 1775, two factions had emerged in Congress: the one led by New Englanders, favoring a formal declaration of independence; and the opposing moderate faction, whose strength lay in the middle colonies and whose most influential leader was John Dickinson of Pennsylvania. The two factions debated issues with regard to possible effects on the subject of independence. The moderates remained the dominant faction into the spring of 1776, but then the weight of the spreading rebellion swung the pendulum decisively toward independence.

Early Congressional wrangling centered on the organization of the Continental army. In mid-June 1775, the delegates, at the urging of the New Englanders, voted to adopt the patriot forces around Boston as a Continental military establishment. They asked the other colonies to supply additional troops and unanimously named wealthy Virginia planter George Washington, who had been appearing in Congress in his military uniform, to serve as commander in chief. Washington did have qualifications for the job. He had extensive military experience, gained during the French and Indian War. Also, he was a Southerner. His presence at the head of the army was a way to involve the other colonies, at least symbolically, in what was still a localized war fought by New Englanders.

While the delegates agreed on the need for central military planning and coordination, the moderates worried about how British officials

LEXINGTON AND CONCORD: The Shot Heard Round the World

After the bloody skirmish at Lexington, Lieutenant Colonel Francis Smith's redcoats marched toward their intended target, the village of Concord, which served as a central storage point for patriot powder and arms. Smith's troops were to "seize and destroy" these military goods.

Just east of Concord, Smith's column found the road blocked by 250 Minutemen under Major John Buttrick. Choosing not to fight, Buttrick ordered his citizen-soldiers to retreat. They did so in disciplined fashion, marching into Concord just ahead of the redcoats and then to higher ground a mile north of the village across Old North Bridge.

Colonel Smith soon had his troops out hunting for supplies. He sent six companies up to North Bridge to seize any powder and weapons stored at farms in that area. Once there, Captain Lawrence Parsons led three companies across the bridge, right past the patriot militia. Captain Walter Laurie secured the bridge with the remaining companies.

At this juncture, just a little before 10 A.M., Buttrick's Minutemen saw a cloud of smoke rising from the village. The British were burning Concord's liberty tree, along with some gun carriages. A worried patriot officer shouted, "Would you let them burn down our town?" Angered by this prospect, Buttrick's troops advanced and engaged Laurie's redcoats, firing at each other across the bridge. Sustaining several casualties, the British fell back to Concord in the face of these shots "heard 'round the world."

By late morning, Smith knew that the local patriots, fearing an incursion, had earlier that week moved most of the military supplies to other locales. The redcoat mission was a failure. Worse yet, hundreds of militiamen, enraged by news of events at Lexington, were gathering behind trees and stone fences, just waiting for Smith's retreat.

Had General Gage not sent out a relief force under Hugh, Lord Percy, Smith's redcoats might have been exterminated. The two British columns linked up just east of Lexington. By sundown, they had reached Charlestown Peninsula, just north of Boston, having barely survived the opening round of the War for American Independence.

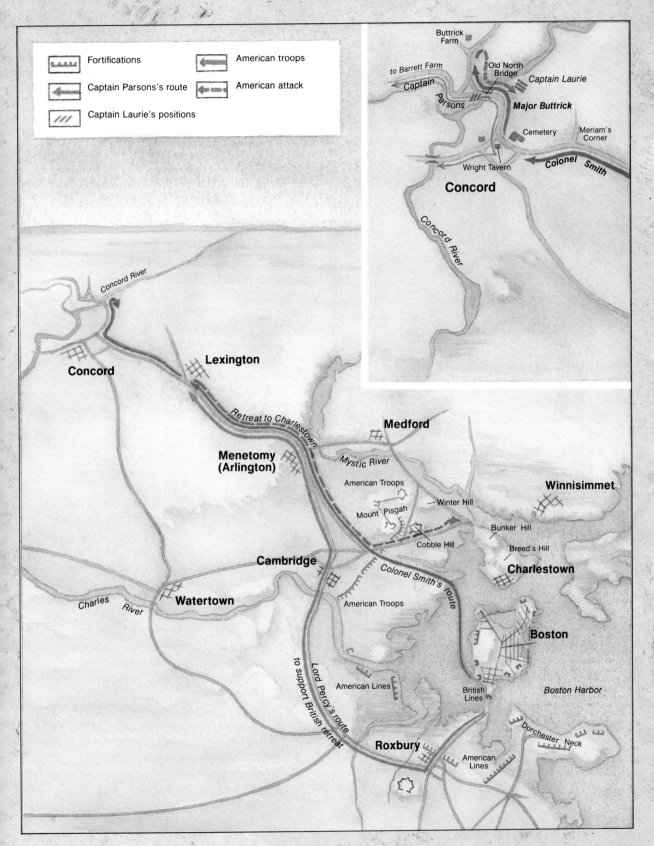

Fortifications

Captain Parsons's route

Captain Laurie's positions

American troops

American attack

Buttrick Farm

to Barrett Farm

Old North Bridge

Captain Laurie

Captain Parsons

Major Buttrick

Cemetery

Meriam's Corner

Wright Tavern

Colonel Smith

Concord

Concord River

Concord River

Lexington

Concord

Retreat to Charlestown

Medford

Mystic River

Menetomy (Arlington)

American Troops

Winter Hill

Winnisimmet

Mount Pisgah

Bunker Hill

Cobble Hill

Breed's Hill

Cambridge

Colonel Smith's route

Charlestown

Watertown

Charles River

American Troops

Boston

Lord Percy's route to support British retreat

American Lines

British Lines

Boston Harbor

Roxbury

American Lines

Dorchester Neck

141

George Washington, who regularly appeared in Congress in military uniform, was a natural choice to serve as the Continental army's commander in chief.

would view the formation of an independent American army. At the urging of John Dickinson, they wanted Congress to prepare a formal statement explaining this bold action. In early July the delegates approved the "Declaration of the Causes and Necessity for Taking up Arms," which they promptly sent to England. The Declaration stressed that the purpose of a Continental force was not "to dissolve that union which has so long and so happily subsisted between us." Rather, the army had been formed to assure the defense of American lives, liberty, and property until "hostilities shall cease on the part of the aggressors, and all danger of their being renewed shall be removed, and not before." Obviously, given home government attitudes about American intentions, this document received scant ministerial attention.

The moderates were individuals in a bind. Concerned about American rights, they also feared independence. Like many other colonists of substantial wealth, they envisioned internal chaos without the stabilizing influence of British rule. Moreover, they doubted whether a weak, independent American nation could long survive among aggressive European powers.

The moderates thus tried to keep open the channels of communication with the British government. Characteristic of such attempts was John Dickinson's "Olive Branch" petition, approved by Congress just a few days after the Declaration. This document stated that "our breasts retain too tender a regard for the kingdom from which we derive our origin" to want independence. It implored George III to intercede with Parliament and find some means to preserve English liberties in America. Like other petitions before it, the Olive Branch had no impact on home government officials. Indeed, by the fall of 1775 King and Parliament were already planning full military mobilization. This was one form of a response to the Olive Branch. The other was a public declaration that all the colonies were now in open rebellion.

The Deepening Martial Conflict

No matter what they tried, Congressional moderates accomplished little, except as an obstacle to independence. The war kept spreading, making a formal renunciation of British allegiance seem almost anticlimactic. On May 10, 1775, for example, citizen soldiers under Vermont's Ethan Allen and Connecticut's Benedict Arnold seized the once-mighty fortress of Ticonderoga at the southern end of Lake Champlain. This action netted the Americans several dozen serviceable cannons which would eventually be deployed to help drive British forces from Boston.

Taking Ticonderoga raised the question of luring Canada into the rebellion. Many hoped that Quebec would become the fourteenth colony, so much so that Congress approved a two-pronged invasion in the late summer of 1775. One column under General Richard Montgomery traveled down Lake Champlain and seized Montreal. The second column under Colonel Benedict Arnold proceeded on a harrowing march through the woods of Maine and finally emerged before the walls of Quebec City. Early on the morning of January 31, 1775, combined forces under these two commanders boldly tried to take the city but were repulsed. Montgomery lost his life, Arnold was seriously wounded, and great numbers of rebel troops were killed or captured. The patriot attempt to seize Canada had failed. This effort, however, made it increasingly difficult to argue that Americans were only interested in defending their homes and families until political differences were resolved.

Meanwhile, back in Boston, Generals Howe, Clinton, and Burgoyne arrived in May 1775 and urged General Gage to resume the offensive against the New Englanders. That opportunity came on June 17 just after patriot forces moved onto Charlestown peninsula north of Boston's back bay. The rebels planned to dig in on Bunker Hill but constructed the most extended portions of their line on Breed's Hill closer to Boston. After lengthy debate the British generals decided upon a frontal assault by 2500 troops under William Howe to show the rebels the awesome power of concentrated British arms.

That afternoon, as citizens in Boston watched the Battle of Bunker Hill from rooftops, Howe's detachment made three separate charges, finally dislodging the patriots, who were running out of ammunition. It was the bloodiest battle of the whole war. The British suffered 1054 casualties—forty percent of the redcoats engaged. American casualties amounted to 411, or thirty percent. Among those slain was Samual Adams's political associate, Dr. Joseph Warren, mourned by patriots everywhere.

The realization that patriot soldiers had been driven from the field undermined the euphoria that followed the rout of the redcoats at Lexington and Concord. Still, the British gained little advantage because they had failed to pursue the fleeing rebels. They remained trapped in Boston, surrounded by thousands of armed and angry colonists. Henry Clinton summarized

To make it easier to outflank the rebels, the British launched artillery at Charlestown— where rebels had taken cover—with the intent of burning it to the ground.

THE BATTLE OF BUNKER HILL

Early on Friday evening, June 16, 1775, rebel military leaders held an urgent meeting in Cambridge, Massachusetts. Intelligence had just reached them that redcoats under Lieutenant General Thomas Gage would soon attempt to break out of Boston. The British plan was to cross the body of water south of Boston, take Dorchester Heights, then sweep north through Cambridge, the patriot army command base, and send the patriot army, now numbering well over 10,000 volunteers, reeling back into the countryside. The target date for this operation was Sunday, June 18.

Those assembled in Cambridge decided to divert the British from their plans by moving rebel lines yet closer to Boston. They gave orders to Colonel William Prescott to fortify Bunker Hill on Charlestown peninsula, just to the north of Boston. The patriots now would control terrain from which they could cannonade the city, if necessary. And if the British decided to dislodge the patriots, they would have to storm a hill rising 130 feet from sea level.

Before midnight on the 16th, Prescott, leading more than 1000 rebel soldiers, reached Bunker Hill. At this point, he called together the other officers, including Colonel Richard Gridley, an experienced military engineer, to discuss the location of earthworks. As they studied the terrain around them, they could see another hill some 600 yards closer to Boston, which rose sharply to 75 feet above sea level. Gridley recommended a line of trenches and a redoubt on that site. Bunker Hill, the group concluded, would serve as a secondary line of defense.

Moving forward as quietly as possible, the Americans dug in rapidly on Breed's Hill, knowing that daylight would expose their activity. At dawn on Saturday, June 17, sailors on board a British war vessel in the harbor spied the new rebel position and opened up with cannon fire. The cannonade awoke everyone in the vicinity, including General Gage, who soon met in a council of war with three other generals, William Howe, Henry Clinton, and John Burgoyne, all of whom had recently arrived in Boston.

General Gage, despite his superior rank as commander of British military forces in North America, deferred to the three major generals in his presence. Since Gage had repeatedly urged caution in handling the rebels, many home leaders had begun to ask whether he was too timid for the task at hand. The appearance of Howe, Clinton, and Burgoyne, he knew, was hardly a vote of confidence.

During the imperial wars, British military officers had repeatedly characterized the colonists as faint-hearted fighters. Reflecting this attitude, the three generals could not fathom how Gage had gotten his troops trapped by untrained, disorganized, and ill-disciplined rebels. The generals, not surprisingly, demanded an immediate offensive against Prescott's force. They hoped for so crushing a victory that rebel resistance would disintegrate completely.

Then they debated tactics. Henry Clinton wanted to seize control of the narrow neck of land behind Bunker Hill connecting Charlestown peninsula to the mainland. That maneuver would trap Prescott's force, which then could be defeated and captured at leisure. Howe and Burgoyne favored a direct frontal assault. The rebels would wither and run, they argued, in the face of concentrated, disciplined British arms, firepower, and bayonets. Reluctantly, Gage, not wanting to risk the exposure of his troops to armed provincials on both sides of Charlestown Neck, agreed to a frontal assault. He hoped that the other generals were right, that the Americans would flee rather than fight, but deep inside he expected heavy casualties.

British regulars were well-trained soldiers. They would rather stand up to furious enemy fire than the wrath of their officers and the brutal military penalties for insubordination of any kind. Insolence toward an officer or attempted desertion resulted in punishments of up to 1000 lashes well-laid-on, which few persons could survive.

New soldiers received rigorous training in the basics of combat. When deployed in front of the enemy, they moved easily from column formations into three battle lines. After troops in the first line fired their smoothbore muskets, affectionately known as the "Brown Bess," they reloaded as their comrades in the next two lines stepped in front of them and fired their muskets in turn.

Smoothbore muskets were inaccurate weapons with an effective range of less than eighty yards. Experienced soldiers going through the steps of ramming powder and ball down the barrel could rarely get off more than two shots a minute. Thus most casualties came from bayonet wounds when competing armies, once having fired three or four rounds at very close range, charged forward and en-

gaged in hand-to-hand combat. The bayonet, strapped to the end of the musket, was the major killing weapon of eighteenth-century European-style warfare, and the proficient soldier more often stabbed his opponent to death.

Knowing all of this, General Howe, whom Gage placed in charge of the assault, envisioned a crushing victory over a motley band of rebels. By 3 P.M., more than 2000 redcoats had been ferried across the bay and were ready to advance. Howe sent forward troops on his left under General Robert Pigot directly at Breed's Hill to divert the Americans. In turn, he led columns along the shore to break through a patriot line behind a rail fence. He expected to sweep these defenders aside in a classic flanking maneuver, then swing sharply to the left and cut Prescott's soldiers off from retreat as they dueled with Pigot's redcoats on their front. Bayonets would finish the assignment.

Galling fire ruined the first British assault. The patriots held off shooting until the last possible moment, then unleashed a furious series of blasts. The redcoats staggered and fell back. Wrote one British officer with Howe, we "were served up in companies against the grass fence, without being able to penetrate . . . . Most of our grenadiers and light infantry, in presenting themselves, lost three-fourths, and many nine-tenths, of their men." Far to the left Pigot's soldiers also ran back from the blistering volleys of musket balls coming from Prescott's defenders in the redoubt and line of trenches.

Retreating on all fronts, the British regrouped and then tried

to execute Howe's plan a second time. "It was surprising," wrote an observer, to watch the redcoats "step over . . . dead bodies, as though they had been logs of wood." Once again, exclaimed one British officer, "an incessant stream of fire" forced them back. From his vantage point in Boston, General Burgoyne described what was happening as "a complication of horror . . . more dreadfully terrible" than anything he had ever seen. He wondered whether "defeat" would bring on "a final loss to the British empire in America."

At this critical juncture, Howe, reinforced by 400 fresh troops, decided to throw everything against the redoubt, where, unknown to him, Prescott's troops were running out of ammunition. Now the British, with regimental pride at stake, shouted "push on, push on." Within minutes they overran the Americans, most of whom lacked bayonets to defend themselves. Prescott's coolness under heavy fire resulted in an orderly retreat, but most of the rebel casualties occurred when defenders did not evacuate in time.

The misnamed Battle of Bunker Hill was over within little more than an hour. Most of the patriots did escape, having no way of knowing that they had participated in the bloodiest fight of the Revolutionary War. The figure of 1465 combined casualties shocked everyone in what General Clinton called "a dear bought victory." Yet the British had really gained nothing of consequence because the Americans still controlled the countryside surrounding Boston and Charlestown peninsula.

it best when he called Bunker Hill "a dear bought victory," adding dryly that "another such would have ruined us."

New England and Canada did not long remain the only theaters of war. Before the end of 1775 fighting erupted in the South. In Virginia the protagonist was John Murray, better known as Lord Dunmore, the last royal governor of the Old Dominion. In May 1774, Dunmore had dissolved the Assembly because the burgesses had called for a day of fasting and prayer in support of the Bostonians. Incensed at Dunmore's arbitrary action, Virginia's gentlemen planters started meeting in provincial conventions, acting as if royal authority no longer existed.

Dunmore resented such impudence. In June 1775, he left Williamsburg and announced that British subjects still loyal to the Crown should join him in bringing the planter elite to its senses. Very few citizens came forward. By autumn Dunmore, headquartered on a naval vessel in Chesapeake Bay, had concluded that planter resistance could only be broken by turning Virginia's slaves against their masters. In early November he issued an emancipation proclamation. It read in part: "And I do hereby further declare all indentured servants, Negroes, or others . . . free, that are able and willing to bear arms."

Dunmore hoped that Virginia's slaves would break their chains and join with him in teaching their former masters that talk of liberty was a two-edged sword. The plan backfired. Irate planters suppressed copies of the Proclamation and spread the rumor of a royal hoax designed to lure blacks into Dunmore's camp so that he could sell them to the owners of West Indian sugar plantations, where inhuman working conditions and very high mortality rates prevailed. Despite these tactics, as many as 2000 slaves did take their chances and escape to the royal standard.

Those blacks who first fled became a part of Dunmore's "Ethiopian" regiment, which made the mistake of engaging Virginia militiamen in a battle at Great Bridge in December 1775. Having had no time for even the fundamentals of military training, they took a beating. This battle ended any semblance of royal authority in Virginia. Dunmore and his following soon retreated to a flotilla of vessels in the Bay. During the next few months the numbers of his adherents kept growing, but then smallpox struck hard, killing hundreds. In the summer of 1776 Dunmore sailed away, leaving behind a planter class that closely guarded its human property while demanding independence from those whom it denounced as tyrants.

Resolving the Independence Question

Lord Dunmore's experiences highlighted the collapse of British political authority. Beginning in the summer of 1775, colony after colony witnessed an end to royal government. To fill the void, the patriots elected *ad hoc* provincial congresses. These bodies functioned as substitute legislatures and dealt with pressing local issues, and they took particular interest in suppressing suspected loyalists.

During that same summer, Massachusetts moved one step farther by asking the Continental Congress for permission to create a more enduring government based on a written constitution. After ousting its royal governor, New Hampshire followed suit. These requests forced Congress to act. It did so in early November, stating that Massachusetts, New Hampshire, and any others might adopt "such a form of government, as . . . will best produce the happiness of the people," yet only if written constitutions specified that these governments would exist until "the present dispute between Great Britain and the colonies" comes to an end. The moderates realized that new state governments, as much if not more than a separate army, had the appearance of *de facto* independence, and they did everything in their power to prevent a total rejection of British political authority in America.

John Dickinson led the campaign in Congress to restrain discussion of a declaration of independence by getting the Pennsylvania Assembly to instruct its delegates to "dissent from, and utterly reject, any propositions . . . that may cause or lead to a separation from our mother country." New York, Delaware, Maryland, and South Carolina soon followed suit. Thus there was to be no resolution of the independence question in 1775.

Events outside of Congress were about to overwhelm the moderates. In January 1776 Thomas Paine, a recent migrant from England who had once been a corsetmaker's apprentice, published a pamphlet entitled *Common Sense.* It became an instant best seller, running through 25 editions and 120,000 copies over the next three months. *Common Sense* electrified the populace with its dynamic, forceful language. It communicated a sense of urgency about moving toward independence, and it attacked Congressional moderates as not being bold enough to break with the past.

Paine likewise denounced the British monarchy. He wrote: "The folly of hereditary right in Kings, is that nature disapproves it . . . by giving mankind *an ass for a lion.*" He encouraged Americans to adopt republican forms of government, since "every spot of the old world is overrun with oppression." The fate of all humans everywhere, he concluded, hung in the balance. *Common Sense* put severe pressure on the moderates, but they held on doggedly, hoping against hope that Great Britain would turn from its belligerent course and begin serious negotiations with Congress.

At the end of February 1776, another significant incident took place in the form of a short, bloody battle between loyalists and patriot militia at Moore's Creek Bridge in North Carolina. This fight resulted in more than a rout of local tories. Now facing a shooting war, North Carolina's provincial congress reversed orders to its Congressional delegates and allowed them to discuss independence and vote on a plan of national government. Soon after, the Virginians, furious about Lord Dunmore's activities, issued similar instructions. Then leaders in Rhode Island, impatient with everyone else, boldly declared their own independence in May. The moderates were rapidly losing their ability to block resolution of the independence question.

On June 7, 1776, Richard Henry Lee, speaking on behalf of the Virginia provincial convention, presented formal resolutions to Congress. Lee urged separation and called for the creation of a national government and the formation of alliances with foreign nations in support of the war effort. Within a few days the delegates

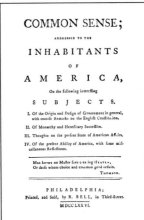

Thomas Paine's *Common Sense,* first published in January 1776, urged the colonists to independence and a bold new world of political freedom.

named two committees, one headed by John Dickinson to produce a plan of central government and another to prepare a statement on independence. Thomas Jefferson, a tall, red-haired Virginian, agreed to write a draft text, which came before Congress on July 1. With slight modifications, including the deletion of a statement blaming the slave trade on the king, the delegates formally and unanimously accepted Jefferson's draft and declared the colonies forever free of Great Britain on July 4, 1776.

The Declaration of Independence proclaimed to the world that Americans had been terribly mistreated by the parent state. Indeed, much of the text reads as a summary list of grievances, ranging from misuse of a standing army of redcoats in the colonies and the abuse of the rightful powers of popularly elected colonial assemblies to the ultimate crime, starting an unjustified war against loyal subjects. The Declaration blamed George III for the pattern of tyranny. He had failed to control his ministers, thereby abandoning his role as servant of the people.

The Declaration, moreover, represented much more than a succinct interpretation of issues and events culminating in civil war. Thomas Jefferson believed that if the American

The Declaration of Independence was presented to Congress on July 1, 1776 and unanimously accepted on July 4.

Revolution was to succeed, it must be founded on a clear and noble purpose. Since "all men are created equal" and have "certain unalienable rights," which Jefferson defined as "life, liberty, and the pursuit of happiness," Americans needed to dedicate themselves to the establishment of a whole new set of political relationships guaranteeing all citizens fundamental liberties. The great task facing the Revolutionary generation would be to institute republican forms of government, predicated upon the rule of law and human reason. Governments had "to effect" the "safety and happiness" of all citizens in the name of human decency, and all citizens would be obligated to work for the greater good of the whole community.

Through the Declaration of Independence, then, the Revolutionaries dedicated themselves to uplifting humanity in a world overrun by greed and petty human ambition. None of these

ideals was going to be realized, however, unless the means could be found to defeat the huge British military force arriving in America at the very time that Congress was debating and approving the Declaration.

WITHOUT VISIBLE ALLIES: THE WAR IN THE NORTH

British officials had made a great blunder in 1775. Thinking of the colonists as "a set of upstart vagabonds, the dregs and scorn of the human species," the British had woefully underestimated their opponent. Lexington and Concord drove home this reality. And although cabinet leaders and generals continued to presume their superiority, they became far more serious about planning for the war. It was now clear that snuffing out the rebellion would be a complex military assignment, given the sheer geographic size of the colonies and the absence of a strategically vital center, such as a national capital, which, if captured, would end the war. It was also clear that the use of an invading army was not the easiest way to regain the political allegiance of a people who placed less and less value on being British subjects.

Britain's Massive Military Buildup

Directing the imperial war effort were King George, Lord North, and Lord George Germain, who became the American Secretary in 1775. Germain, who had once been court-martialed for cowardice and thrown out of the British army, was a surprisingly effective administrator adept at working within England's complicated and inefficient military bureaucracy. His skills came through in planning for the campaign of 1776—the largest land and sea offensive executed by any western nation until the Allied invasion of North Africa in 1942.

Step by step, Germain pulled the elements together. Of utmost importance was overall campaign strategy. It involved concentrating as many troops as possible on the port of New York City, where great numbers of loyalists lived, then subduing the surrounding countryside as a food and supply base. Loyalists would be used to reinstitute royal government, and the king's forces would engage and destroy the rebel army. Germain believed that the American will to resist had to be shattered, and he hoped that it would take only one campaign season. The longer the rebels lasted, he thought, the greater would be their prospects for success.

Next came the matter of assembling the military forces. It was not the practice in Britain, or anywhere in Europe for that matter, to draw upon all able-bodied males. By and large, the middle classes were exempt from service because they were considered productive members of society. This meant that the rank and file would come from two sources. First, there were poorer, less productive citizens in the British Isles who would be recruited or dragooned into service. Since life in European armies was often brutal, it was not always possi-

Because the "more productive" middle class did not fight in the war, British troops were generally made up of poorer sorts.

ble to convince or coerce even the most destitute of subjects to sign enlistment papers. To assure adequate numbers, then, George III and his advisors turned to Germany. Over the course of the war, six German principalities offered up 30,000 soldiers. Some 17,000 came from Hesse-Cassel, where the local head of state forced many of his subjects into service. In return, he received direct cash payments from the British Crown for each soldier that he supplied. Hessians and downtrodden Britons, including some Irish, thus made up the king's army.

As important as troop recruitment was the problem of military leadership. The ministry felt that General Gage was too timid and too respectful of Americans. They recalled him in October 1775, naming William Howe overall commander in chief, and they placed his brother Richard, Admiral Lord Howe, in charge of the naval flotilla to carry royal troops to America. The Howe brothers, however, would not be hard-hitting commanders. Politically, they identified with whig leaders in England who believed the Americans had some legitimate grievances.

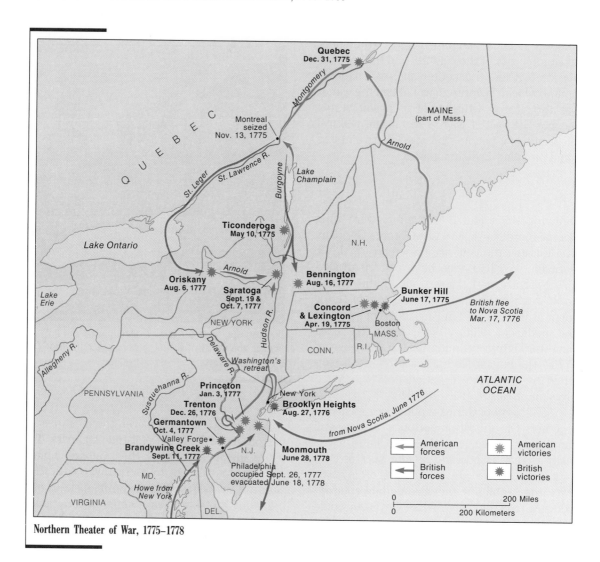

Northern Theater of War, 1775–1778

Even though Lord Germain expected the Howe brothers to use their combined land-naval forces to smash and bayonet the rebels into submission, they intended to move slowly, using the presence of the king's troops to persuade Americans to sign loyalty oaths and renounce the rebellion. Undermining the strategic goal of wiping out rebel resistance in only one campaign season, these less than bold actions of the Howes helped to save the patriot cause.

The Campaign for New York

Not yet aware of the scale of British mobilization, New Englanders cheered loudly in mid-March 1776 when General Howe took redcoats and loyalists in tow and fled by sea to Halifax, Nova Scotia. British control of Boston had become untenable because General Washington placed cannons captured at Ticonderoga on Dorchester Heights overlooking the city. Howe's choice was to flee or be bombarded into submission. Washington, however, did not relax. For months he had predicted that the British would strike at New York City. He was absolutely right.

The king's army soon converged on Staten Island, across the bay from Manhattan. William Howe, sailing from Halifax, arrived with 10,000 soldiers at the end of June. During July, as Americans excitedly read their Declaration of

Independence, more and more redcoats appeared, another 20,000 by mid-August. They came in some 400 transports escorted by 70 naval vessels and 13,000 sailors under Admiral Lord Howe's supervision. All told, the Howe brothers had 43,000 well-supplied, well-trained, and well-armed combatants. By comparison, George Washington had 28,000 troops on his muster rolls, but only 19,000 were present and fit for duty. To make matters worse, the bulk of the rebel force lacked good weapons or supplies and were deficient in training and discipline.

The decision to defend New York, which the Continental Congress insisted upon and to which Washington acceded, was one of the great blunders of the war. Completely outnumbered, the American commander unwisely divided his soldiers between Manhattan and Brooklyn Heights, separated by the East River. The Howe brothers responded on August 22 by landing troops at Gravesend, Long Island, putting them in an excellent position to trap Washington's force in Brooklyn. For some inexplicable reason, however, Lord Howe chose not to move his naval vessels into the East River, which would have sealed off Washington's escape route. The rebel army took a severe beating from the redcoats and Hessians, but they escaped back across the East River. Washington had been lucky, and he learned from his error. He never again allowed his troops to be placed in such a potentially disastrous position.

The Howe brothers bumbled along through the rest of the campaign season. Every time they had the advantage, they failed to destroy the rebel army. They drove Washington's forces northward out of Manhattan, then wheeled about and captured some 2000 rebels defending Fort Washington, located high on a bluff overlooking the Hudson River. Two days later a British column under Charles, Lord Cornwallis,

While Washington's officers urged that New York be burned to keep the enemy from using it as a base, Congress vetoed the proposal. However, a fire broke out in the city on September 20, 1776, and both sides accused the other of starting it.

crossed the Hudson and nearly caught another sizable patriot contingent at Fort Lee in New Jersey, across from Fort Washington. One of Washington's most able field commanders, Nathanael Greene of Rhode Island, managed to extricate his force just in time.

Washington had already moved into New Jersey. He took charge and ordered a retreat, hoping that he could get his soldiers across the Delaware River and into Pennsylvania before the onrushing Cornwallis, who was far more aggressive than the Howes, caught up with the dispirited rebel band. By early December what remained of Washington's army had made it into Pennsylvania.

Saving the Cause at Trenton

As the half-starving, battle-wearied patriot troops fled, hundreds of them also deserted. They had learned that British muskets and bayonets could maim and kill. Others, ravaged by disease or wounded in battle, were left behind along the way with the hope of receiving decent treatment from their pursuers. The American army was all but extinct. As Washington wrote in mid-December, "I think the game is pretty near up. . . . No man, I believe, ever had a greater choice of difficulties and less means to extricate himself from them." Having virtually destroyed his prey, William Howe ordered his troops into winter camps and returned to New York City. He ignored his charge to end the rebellion in one campaign season, fully satisfied that mopping up operations could be easily conducted in the spring of 1777.

At this juncture George Washington established his credentials as an innovative commander. He assessed his desperate position and decided upon a bold counterstroke. Success might save his army; defeat would surely ruin it. With muster rolls showing only 6000 troops, he divided his soldiers into three groups and tried to recross the icy Delaware River on Christmas evening. Their targets were British outposts in New Jersey. Only Washington's near-frozen band of 2400 accomplished this daring maneuver.

At dawn they reached Trenton, where Colonel Johann Rall's unsuspecting Hessians were still groggy with liquor from their Christmas celebration. The fight was over in a moment. Four hundred men got away, but the Continentals captured almost 1000 Hessians. Within another few days the elated Americans again outdueled British units at Princeton. Stunned by this flurry of rebel activity, Howe redeployed his New Jersey outposts in a semicircle much closer to New York.

Washington had done much more than just regain lost ground. He had saved the Continental army from extinction. Never again during the war would the British come so close to total victory—and all because of a failure to annihilate Washington's shattered forces when the opportunity was there. William Howe never seemed to understand this mistake. He relaxed in his winter quarters in New York and gloried in the knighthood awarded him for his victory at Brooklyn Heights.

Also of importance was Howe's decision to pull in his outposts. As the British army had marched across New Jersey, it lured thousands of neutrals and loyalists to its banner. These individuals had signed loyalty oaths, thus identifying themselves publicly as enemies of the Revolution. As the British army drew back, it left the tories exposed to the fury of local patriots, who had anything but warm feelings for neighbors whose true allegiance had been revealed.

England refused to believe that the "children" were growing up and tried to keep a tight rein on the colonies.

Time and again throughout the war, British military commanders committed the error of not sustaining support for the king's friends in America. They rarely took advantage of the reservoir of loyal subjects—some twenty percent of the populace—who stood ready to fight the rebels and do anything else within reason to assure a continuation of British rule. After all, the official attitude seemed to be that they were just colonists, a part of the rude American rabble. Such haughtiness represented a major blindspot, when an essential military task involved regaining the allegiance of enough citizens to effect a complete revival of imperial political authority in America.

On the rebel side, the Trenton and Princeton victories did not result in a new outpouring of popular support for Washington's army. When the Continentals had been in flight across New Jersey, Thomas Paine stepped forth with his first *Crisis* paper. He begged the populace to rally at this moment of deep despair. "These are the times that try men's souls," Paine stated forcefully. "The summer soldier and the sunshine patriot will, in this crisis, shrink from the service of his country; but he that stands it now, deserves the love and thanks of man and woman." Many read Paine's words, but the massive British campaign effort of 1776 had snuffed out the *rage militaire.*

The Real Continentals

One of the greatest problems facing Washington and the Continental Congress after 1776 was sustaining the rebel army's troop strength. The commander in chief only had 10,000 soldiers (7363 present and fit for duty) in May 1777. This number increased substantially during the summer and fall, but only an estimated 11,000 Continentals entered Valley Forge. For the remainder of the war, Washington's core of regulars rarely was more sizable. At times, as few as 5000 soldiers stood with him.

Certainly after his experiences in 1776, Washington understood that he must maintain "a respectable army" in the field and wear down the enemy, hoping ultimately to break Britain's will to continue the fight. He needed soldiers who would commit themselves to long-term

Diversity of dress among colonial army soldiers was common, but more common was the fact that few soldiers ever had the prescribed wear.

service (three years or the duration), submit to rigorous training and discipline, and accept privation in the field. These were hardly glamorous prospects, especially when service often entailed death or permanent dismemberment. Still, Washington, Congress, and the states could promise cash bounties for enlisting, as well as regular pay, decent clothing, adequate food, and even land at war's end. For people who had nothing to lose, long-term service in the Continental army was worth considering.

After 1776, then, the rank and file of the Continental army came to be made up of economically hard pressed and unfree citizens. Private Joseph Plumb Martin was probably better off than most who enlisted—or were forced into service. The bulk of Washington's long-term Continentals were young (generally ranging in age from their early teens to mid-twenties), landless, unskilled, poverty-stricken men whose families were also quite poor. Also well represented were indentured servants and slaves who stood as substitutes for their masters in return for guarantees of personal freedom.

In 1777 Massachusetts became the first state to authorize the enlistment of blacks—both slaves and freemen. Rhode Island soon followed suit by raising two black regiments. Southern states were far more reluctant to allow slaves to substitute for their masters, but Virginia and Maryland ultimately did so, which caused one patriot general to query why so many "sons of freedom" seemed so anxious "to trust their all to be defended by slaves." Add to these groups captured British soldiers and deserters, particularly Hessians and Irishmen, as well as tories and criminals who were often given a choice between military service or the gallows, and a composite portrait of the real Continental army begins to emerge.

The title page of a first edition of a history of black fighters.

Eighteenth-century armies also accepted women in the ranks. Like their male counterparts, they were invariably living on the margins of society. These women "on the ration" (more literally half rations) must be differentiated from so-called "camp followers," or those who marched along with their husbands or were prostitutes. Women in service performed various functions, ranging from caring for the sick and wounded, cooking, and mending clothes, to scavenging battlefields for clothes and equipment and burying the dead. Occasionally, these same women became directly involved in battle, as personified in the mythical heroine Molly Pitcher, who allegedly first supplied water and then ended up firing a cannon at the Battle of Monmouth Court House in 1778. The British army allowed one woman in the ranks for every ten men; the Continental ratio was closer to one in fifteen.

Deborah Sampson served in the army under the name of Timothy Thayer.

Whether male or female, a unifying characteristic of Washington's post-1776 Continentals was poverty and, in many cases, lack of personal freedom. In their social profile, they looked very much like their counterparts in the British army. As a group, they repeatedly risked their lives in return for promises: food, clothing, pay, and even land on which to make a decent living after the war. Their dreams of future prosperity depended upon the success of the rebellion, and that is one reason why they willingly endured, even though the far more prosperous civilian populace ignored their privation at such places as Valley Forge.

RESCUING THE PATRIOTS: TOWARD GLOBAL CONFLICT

The struggles of the American rebels did not go unobserved in European diplomatic circles. France and Spain, in particular, hoped that the rebellion would succeed. Their concerns, however, were not wholly altruistic. Territorial losses sustained during the Seven Years' War had swung the European balance of power decisively in Britain's favor. From the perspective of the Duc de Choiseul, France's foreign minister, post-1763 disagreements between Britain and America represented an opportunity to cut the puffed-up British lion down to size. Losing the colonies would weaken Britain immeasurably. France, concluded Choiseul, could only benefit by Americans gaining their independence.

Neither Choiseul nor his successor, the Comte de Vergennes, who became France's foreign minister in 1774, were beacons of the Age of Enlightenment. They supported monarchism, not republicanism, and they had little interest in fostering political liberties. Rather, they were hardened and cynical diplomatic veterans who hoped to take advantage of this new set of circumstances. And if they could shape events properly, they would advance France's future while exacting revenge on an old and despised enemy.

France Offers Covert Assistance

Before 1775, the French sent spies to America to report on events, and when possible to help stir up ill-will toward Britain. Once the war started, Vergennes adopted the shrewd posture of providing secret aid to the rebels while maintaining a public stance of disinterested neutrality. He did not want France to get caught between the colonies and England, should the Americans falter on the battlefield or suddenly reconcile differences. But if the rebels demonstrated their long-term resolve and proved worthy in combat, then France would enter the war and help crush the British.

Vergennes was a master manipulator in the court of Louis XVI. In 1775, for instance, one of his diplomatic agents, the Caron de Beaumarchais, perhaps best known for writing the librettos of the *Marriage of Figaro* and the *Barber of Seville,* made contacts with prominent Americans in London. These discussions resulted in the formation of a trading company, Roderigue Hortalez & Cie., the sole purpose of which was to funnel war matériel (paid for by the French government) to the rebels. Although some of the merchandise was obsolete, the bulk of it proved crucial to the rebel cause. Shipments made in 1777, in fact, went to the Continental army's Northern Department in upstate New York and would be used in defeating General John Burgoyne's British army at Saratoga. Secret French aid, not only in the form of war goods but also cash loans and subsidies, strengthened the rebels immeasurably

and eventually allowed Vergennes and the French government to come out into the open against Britain.

In public, Vergennes quite often treated the American commissioners to France—Benjamin Franklin, Arthur Lee, and Connecticut merchant Silas Deane—with virtual disdain. Franklin, well-known before his arrival in Paris (he had been admitted to the French Academy of Sciences during 1772 in recognition of his electrical experiments), dominated the American delegation, whose task was to seek a formal alliance. The aging Philadelphian became a celebrity in France. With his simple dress, witty personality, worldly charm, and shrewd mind, he embodied the ideals of republicanism. But it was not just Franklin's skillfulness as a diplomat that resulted in an alliance. Vergennes had the French government primed and ready to enter the war, once conditions in America were right. Britain's military failures during 1777 soon prompted formal French intervention.

The British Seize Philadelphia

Sir William Howe was the focal point of Britain's problems. He may have been a good tactician in battle, but he had little appreciation of strategy, which Lord George Germain kept attempting to explain to him. The home government's plan for 1777 was to send an army under Burgoyne south from Canada through the Lake Champlain corridor. In turn, Howe was to move troops up the Hudson River, eventually linking with Burgoyne at Albany. Called the Hudson Highlands strategy, the goal was to cut off New England from the rest of the colonies before sweeping eastward in reconquering the very region that had been the seedbed of rebellion.

Sir William, however, favored going after and destroying the main Continental army. During May and June 1777, he tried to lure Washington into a major battle, but the American commander refused the bait and held to a very defensible position in New Jersey's Watchung Mountains. At this juncture Howe made a decision that may have cost Britain the war. All but abandoning the primary campaign goal of joining up with Burgoyne, he resolved to seize Philadelphia, hoping at the same time to catch and crush Washington's Continentals as

Washington's plan for the battle at Germantown was too complex, and American columns, attacking from different directions, became confused and started firing at one another.

they moved into eastern Pennsylvania to protect the rebel capital. Howe loaded 15,000 soldiers onto vessels in New York harbor—he left behind a reserve force under General Henry Clinton—and sailed out to sea in the middle of the campaign season.

Howe's flotilla came up through Chesapeake Bay in August, landing at Head of Elk in Maryland. On September 11, the British mauled the Continentals at Brandywine Creek, southwest of Philadelphia, but the engagement did not destroy the rebel army. Within another two weeks Sir William proudly led his troops into Philadelphia; except for the establishment of comfortable winter quarters, Howe had taken nothing of consequence. The Continental Congress had already moved westward to York, Pennsylvania. Howe's presence cheered local loyalists (they did not know they were to be abandoned in the spring of 1778), and all British proponents felt relief when Washington's attack on British troops at Germantown failed in early October. Then the realization began to

dawn that chasing after the main rebel army and seizing the enemy's capital had been a hollow quest—and had cost the British dearly.

Capturing Burgoyne's Army at Saratoga

The 1777 British descent from Canada had been planned carefully, at least on paper. One of its many aspects involved the use of Indian allies as auxiliary troops. At first, both sides asked the tribes of the North, particularly the powerful Six Nations of Iroquois, to remain neutral in what the Continental Congress called a "family quarrel." The combatants, however, trying to gain every possible advantage, could not long resist tapping into Indian manpower. Guy Johnson, British superintendent of northern Indian affairs, asked various tribes to fight under the king's banner. Similarly, American commissioners requested direct assistance, but the British had the advantage of the arguments. After all, colonial settlers were the obvious culprits in seizing tribal lands, whereas British officials had tried to stop these encroachments by insisting that territory west of the Appalachians was a permanent Indian reserve.

General Burgoyne's army, strengthened by hundreds of Indians now on the warpath, moved out in mid-June. The main column of nearly 8000 pushed into Lake Champlain and drove the rebels from Fort Ticonderoga in early July. A second column of 1700 under Colonel Barry St. Leger moved up the St. Lawrence River and into Lake Ontario, before sweeping south toward Fort Schuyler (formerly Fort Stanwix) at the western end of the Mohawk Valley. St. Leger's troops were to act as a diversionary force. Soon they had 750 desperate rebel defenders of Fort Schuyler under siege. Seemingly nothing could stop these two columns, which were to come together again in Albany.

After seizing Ticonderoga, Burgoyne became less aggressive about his southward movement. Like William Howe in 1776, he did not take his opponent seriously enough, and under the leadership of General Philip Schuyler, the Continental army's Northern Department had started to rally. The rebels blocked Burgoyne's path by cutting down trees, ripping up bridges, and moving boulders into fording points on streams. Soon the British advance had been slowed to less than a mile a day. Then Congress replaced Schuyler—New Englanders did not like him because of his supposed aristocratic airs—with Horatio Gates.

Word of Gates's elevation was a factor in getting New England militiamen to come out and support the Continentals. Another was Burgoyne's lack of control of his Indians. A few of them murdered and scalped a young woman, Jane McCrea, who was betrothed to one of his loyalist officers. Burgoyne refused to punish the culprits, fearing he might drive off all of his Indian allies. In so doing, he conveyed a message of barbarism that impelled more militiamen, determined to save their families from scalping knives, to take gun in hand.

In addition, St. Leger's diversionary force ran into trouble. Militiamen in the Mohawk Valley under General Nicholas Herkimer, in alliance with Oneidas and Tuscaroras of the Six Nations, tried to break through to Fort Schuyler. On August 6, they clashed with St. Leger's loyalists and Indians, among them Mohawks, Cayugas, and Senecas also of the Six Nations, at the Battle of Oriskany. Herkimer and half of his column were killed or wounded that day, one of the bloodiest of the war.

Oriskany was the beginning of the end for the once mighty Iroquois nation, whose tribes were now hopelessly divided and consuming each other in combat. When war chieftain Joseph Brant (Thayendanegea) of the Mohawks led numerous bloody frontier raids for the British, a Continental army expedition under General John Sullivan marched into central New York during 1779 and destroyed every Iroquois village it came upon. After the war was over, the more aggressive Iroquois moved west into the Ohio country, where they kept fighting white frontiersmen; others, less militant, moved quietly onto reservations in western New York.

St. Leger's victory was temporary. Continentals under Benedict Arnold rushed west and drove off St. Leger without a second major fight. Arnold sent a dim-witted local loyalist into St. Leger's camp with fabricated news of thousands of rebel soldiers moving rapidly toward Fort Schuyler. The Indians, satiated with the bloodshed at Oriskany, quickly broke camp and fled, leaving the British colonel no alternative but to retreat back into Canada.

The British met with various Indian tribes to convince them to fight against the Continentals.

Joseph Brant believed the Iroquois could not remain neutral and that their only chance was to side with the British.

Burgoyne had now lost his diversionary force. He suffered yet another major setback in mid-August when New Hampshire militiamen under General John Stark overwhelmed some 900 Hessians who were out raiding for supplies near Bennington in the Vermont territory. With little prospect of relief from New York City, Burgoyne's army was now all but entrapped some thirty miles north of Albany at Saratoga along the Hudson River. In two desperate battles (September 19 and October 7) the British force tried to find a way around the well-entrenched rebels, but brilliant field generalship by Benedict Arnold inspired the Americans to victory. It was all over for Burgoyne, and he surrendered his army to Horatio Gates on October 17, 1777.

According to one British soldier on the Saratoga surrender field, "we marched out, . . . with drums beating and the honors of war, but the drums seemed to have lost their former inspiring sounds, . . . as if almost ashamed to be heard on such an occasion." Losing an army at Saratoga was an unnecessary disaster for Britain, caused primarily by William Howe's unwillingness to work in concert with Burgoyne and

carry through on the Hudson Highlands strategy. It was a great triumph for the Americans. This victory convinced Vergennes that it was now safe for France to commit to the rebel cause publicly.

In early February 1778, the French government signed two treaties with the American commissioners. One recognized American independence, and the other encouraged trade between the two allies. On March 20, Louis XVI formally greeted the American commissioners at court and announced that the new nation had gained France's diplomatic recognition. In June 1778, a naval battle in the English Channel between British and French warships resulted in formal declarations of war by both powers. The drum beat for British rule over the thirteen states had taken on the cadence of a death march.

THE WORLD TURNED UPSIDE DOWN

When George Washington learned about the French alliance, he declared a holiday for "rejoicing throughout the whole army." On that spring day in 1778, the Continentals at Valley Forge enjoyed themselves immensely. There was much to celebrate. They had survived the winter, and they had also benefited from the rigorous field training of colorful Baron Friedrich von Steuben, a pretended Prussian nobleman who had volunteered to teach the soldiery how to fight in more disciplined fashion. Equally important, the announcement of open, direct aid from France, which included land troops and naval reinforcements, improved prospects for actually beating the British. Washington, so elated by this turn in events, winked at the issuance of "more than the common quantity of liquor" to his soldiers, which he knew would result in "some little drunkenness among them."

Revamping British Strategy

The alliance with France changed the fundamental character of the American rebellion. British officials realized that they were no longer contending with upstart rebels seeking independence through civil war. They were now involved in a world war. France, with its well-trained army and highly mobile navy, had the ability to strike British territories anytime and anywhere it chose. In fact, the French started to put together a powerful land-naval expedition with the purpose of invading England. Bad weather and poor organization in the French high command, however, undercut this effort.

In addition, the French, while renouncing any desire to retake Canada, had designs on the valuable British sugar islands in the Caribbean. They built up troop strength in the French West Indies and soon had a four-to-one advantage. When the Spanish (with their fixation on regaining Gibraltar) and the Dutch also joined the war in 1779 and 1780 respectively, the British found themselves in a most precarious position, threatened with major territorial losses across the globe.

This new reality resulted in a redesigned British war plan—the southern strategy—during the late spring of 1778. Troops could no longer be massed against the Americans; instead, they would have to be dispersed to threatened points, such as the West Indies, and later Gibraltar. The first step came in May 1778, when Sir Henry Clinton, who had taken over as North American commander from a shamed William Howe, received orders to evacuate Philadelphia. In June he retreated to New York City, narrowly averting a disastrous defeat by Washington's pursuing Continentals at Monmouth in central New Jersey.

Clinton was to hang on as best he could at the main British base, but he would have to accept a reduction in troops for campaigning elsewhere, a process which started during the fall of 1778. He was to avoid major engagements with Washington's army in the North while he implemented Britain's southern strategy.

Lord George Germain and other Crown officials mistakenly assumed that loyalists existed in far greater numbers in the South. In what was a slight modification of the 1776 campaign strategy, then, the idea was to direct the king's friends, primarily as substitutes for depleted British forces, in partisan (guerrilla) war. Bands of armed loyalists would operate in conjunction with a main redcoat army to subdue all rebels, beginning in Georgia and then moving in carefully planned steps northward. When any previously rebel-dominated region had been fully secured, royal government would be reintroduced. Ultimately through attrition the whole South would be brought back into the British fold, opening the way for eventual subjugation of the North. This strategy required patience as well as careful nurturing of loyalist sentiment. Both seemed very possible when a detachment of 3500 redcoats sailed south from New York in November 1778, and quickly reconquered Georgia.

Until the French alliance, the South was a secondary theater of war, although there had been sporadic fighting between loyalists and rebel militia. White-Indian relations were more bloody. As in the North, both sides maneuvered for the favor of the most powerful Indian nations, the Cherokees, Creeks, Choctaws, and Chickasaws. These four nations had 10,000 warriors among them, compared to an estimated 2000 among all the northern Iroquois.

Britain's southern Indian superintendent, John Stuart, had a network of agents working among the tribes. Late in 1775 he focused on winning over the Cherokees and Creeks, who had the most warriors, urging them to fight in concert with loyalists. Stuart was particularly successful with the Overhill Cherokees led by Dragging Canoe. In the summer of 1776 they attacked frontier settlements from Virginia to South Carolina, butchering families who had unwisely moved onto traditional tribal hunting grounds.

Dragging Canoe's raids had two major effects. First, in September 1776 hundreds of Virginia and North Carolina frontiersmen came together as militia and wreaked mayhem on the most easterly Cherokee towns. During October the Virginians proceeded farther west to the Overhill Cherokee villages. Dragging Canoe and his warriors retreated, agreeing to forswear further assistance to the British. This took the Cherokees out of the war. Second, the other major tribes, seeing what had happened, snubbed John Stuart's agents and backed off from the "family quarrel." By 1777, then, the southern Indians had been neutralized. Although a band of Creeks under Alexander McGillivray did work with the British after their invasion of Georgia, Native Americans did not figure prominently in Britain's post-1778 strategy.

Sir Henry Clinton, who was probably less decisive than William Howe, took his time in expanding on the redcoats' success in Georgia. Finally in late 1779, he sailed with 7600 troops toward his target—Charleston, South Carolina. There General Benjamin Lincoln, with just 3000 Continental regulars and a smattering of militia, found himself completely outnumbered and trapped when part of Clinton's force moved inland and cut off escape routes. Facing prospects of extermination, Lincoln surrendered without much of a fight in May 1780. This was the only time during the war that the British captured an American army.

Clinton's victory at Charleston was a second major advance in the southern strategy. The British commander sailed back to New York in high spirits, leaving behind Lord Cornwallis to secure all of South Carolina. Clinton had ordered Cornwallis to move forward with care, making sure that loyalist partisans always had firm control of territory behind his advancing army. Ironically, Cornwallis was one of the few aggressive British generals in America, and his desire to rush ahead and get on with the fight helped undermine the southern strategy.

At first, Cornwallis's boldness reaped dividends. After learning about the fall of Charleston, the Continental Congress ordered Horatio Gates, now known as the "hero of Saratoga," to proceed south, pull together a new army, and check Cornwallis. Gates botched the job completely. He gathered troops, mostly raw militiamen, in Virginia and North Carolina, then rushed his soldiers into the British lair.

Early on the morning of August 16, 1780, Cornwallis's force intercepted Gates's column near Camden, South Carolina. Not only did the American troops lack training, but bad provisions had made them ill. The evening before the Battle of Camden they had supped on "a hasty meal of quick baked bread and fresh beef, with a dessert of molasses, mixed with mush or dumplings," which, according to one of Gates's officers, "operated so cathartically as to dis-

order many of the men" just before the fight. Cornwallis's army devastated the rebels in yet another crushing defeat in the South.

The Tide of War Turns at Last

During 1780 everything seemed to go wrong for the American cause. Besides major setbacks in the South, officers and soldiers directly under Washington's command were increasingly restive about long overdue wages and inadequate supplies. In July 1780 the officers threatened mass resignations unless Congress did something—and quickly. In September a frustrated Benedict Arnold switched his allegiance back to the British. By the end of the year, Continental army troop strength fell below 6000. Then, as the New Year dawned, Washington faced successive mutinies among his hardened veterans in the Pennsylvania and New Jersey lines. The Continental army appeared to be disintegrating, so much so that the commander in chief put aside plans for a possible strike against New York City. Even though French troops under the Comte de Rochambeau were now in the vicinity, Washington's own numbers were too slight to pursue such an elaborate venture.

Quite simply, it looked as if the British were winning the endurance of wills. As one despondent Continental officer wrote: "It really gives me great pain to think of our public affairs; where is the public spirit of the year 1775? Where are those flaming *patriots* who were ready to sacrifice their lives, their fortunes, their all, for the public?" At no time during the war, except for those dark days just before Washington's raid at Trenton, had the rebel cause appeared more bleak.

But British successes in the South moved the redcoats toward a far greater failure. General Cornwallis's army overreached itself. After Camden, Cornwallis started pushing toward North Carolina. His left wing under Major Patrick Ferguson, whose soldiers were mostly loyalists, was soon under the eye of growing numbers of "over-the-mountain" frontiersmen. They were grimly determined to protect their homesteads and families from Ferguson's loyalists, who repeatedly shot down or hanged patri-

Popular Protest in Early America

When it was discovered that students at a medical college were robbing corpses from a nearby graveyard, an angry mob stormed the college. Alexander Hamilton tried to dissuade them.

Bacon's Rebellion (1676) in Virginia is one illustration of colonial attempts to overthrow imperial authority. When Governor Berkeley refused to sign the commission appointing Nathaniel Bacon commander in chief of an army to put down Indian uprisings, the insurgents became more hostile (right). Fearing an attack from Berkeley and his forces, Bacon's followers burned Jamestown to the ground (below), and Berkeley fled across Chesapeake Bay.

Prior to the Civil War, there were three peak periods of popular protest. The first occurred between 1670 and 1700 and primarily involved resistance to England's assertion of imperial authority over its developing North American colonies. The second period, the years between 1760 and 1790, coincided with the era of the American Revolution and witnessed a striking upsurge in protest directed against the acts of King and Parliament. The third turbulent period began during Andrew Jackson's presidency and lasted until the Civil War. The years between 1830 and 1860 saw Americans protesting and clashing among themselves over a host of divisive matters, especially those relating to the increasingly pluralistic character of nineteenth-century American society.

Political protest, much of it aimed at new imperial restrictions, was commonplace in the late seventeenth century. During the whole of the colonial period, there were eighteen insurgent uprisings in Britain's North American colonies. Thirteen of these erupted in the 1670–1700 period. Citizens gathered in armed groups and employed the force of numbers in attempts to overthrow this or that high-handed imperial official. Generally, their goal was the preservation of local rights against what they viewed as some abuse of power. Two-thirds of the eighteen uprisings did not involve the loss of lives, but when they did, as with Bacon's Rebellion in Virginia (1676), they could be bloody affairs, indeed.

Up through the American Revolution, popular protest reflected upon a corporate ideal in society. Crowds and rioters were not just perpetrating mindless mayhem. Rather, they believed they were protecting the community's interest when problems could not be solved through legal means. During the late seventeenth century, for example, Virginians produced far too much tobacco to be absorbed by waiting overseas markets. At various times, the House of Burgesses debated whether crop-planting restrictions should be imposed as a way to raise collapsing prices. In 1682, when the Burgesses failed to act, some local planters formed into bands and went about the countryside cutting down tobacco plants. Four leaders were arrested, and the government executed two of them for organizing this extralegal action.

Protesting crowds, by and large, focused on the destruction of property rather than lives as the best means to uphold the community's interest. When leaders in Massachusetts authorized the construction of a smallpox hospital on an island near Marblehead in the early 1770s, the decision angered local citizens, who were fearful of that dreaded disease being spread among them by the patients. Community pressure led to the hospital's closing, but then an outbreak of smallpox took place. To make sure the facility would never reopen, a crowd of citizens put on disguises, went out to the building, and burned it to the ground, which from their point of view was an admittedly extralegal but fully justified action.

Crowds did more than destroy property. They also used threats and intimidation to effect their purposes. Particularly galling to citizens of colonial port towns was the Royal Navy's practice of impressment, or forcing unwilling inhabitants to join the crews of naval vessels. British law allowed impressment because of the ongoing need for sailors, a reflection of the harshness of naval discipline. When naval vessels docked in port towns, sailors regularly took flight, resulting in constant manpower shortages. Typical of impressment turmoil were crowd actions in Boston during November 1747 when Rear

Pro Patria

The first Man that either distributes or makes use of Stampt Paper, let him take Care of his House, Person, & Effects.

Vox Populi;

We Dare

The destruction of property often served as warnings to those who might be threatening the community's best interest. The threatening handbill (left) was distributed around New York the night after a ship bearing stamps arrived. The Boston Tea Party (below) involved several dozen "Indians," who dumped 342 chests of tea into the harbor.

Admiral Charles Knowles ordered out press gangs. After three days of rioting, which saw the royal governor flee the city and crowds along the waterfront free numbers of persons seized by Knowles's crews, the Admiral conceded the point and sailed away, but not before threatening to fire on the town. Sustained intimidation thus worked to preserve the personal liberty of the common seamen of Boston.

As with instances of stopping press gangs, popular protest often had a strong moral dimension. During April 1788 citizens in New York City ransacked a medical college because students and doctors at the school had robbed graves to secure cadavers for dissection. It all started when a young lad accidentally saw his mother's lifeless body at the college. The mob believed it was acting in everyone's best interest because of the assumption that proper burials helped assure life in heaven. Five years later, in October 1793, citi-

zens tore down Mother Carey's bawdyhouse. Like many brothel owners in New York City, Mother Carey rented rooms to secretive lovers. The crowd attacked this particular establishment because a young woman had been raped there by a customer but had failed to gain justice in the courts.

On the whole, inhabitants of colonial and Revolutionary America were careful not to be too destructive in their use of protest and violence, but it would be misleading

John Malcomb, a minor customs official, was treated roughly when he tried to collect trade duties in Boston. Forced to drink large quantities of tea, he was tarred and feathered and threatened with hanging.

to conclude that all crowds were sensitive to human life. In certain situations, particularly those involving Indians and black colonists, protesting white settlers could be merciless. Late in 1763 inhabitants of frontier Pennsylvania's Paxton Township near the Susquehanna River, angry over the government's failure to offer funds for defense during the Seven Years' War and Pontiac's Uprising, butchered twenty Christian Indians in their vicinity. Then the "Paxton Boys" marched on Philadelphia, causing virtual panic in the city, but shrewd negotiators, including Benjamin Franklin, turned them away. In 1712 and 1741 New York City faced incipient black uprisings. Some twenty slaves started a number of fires and killed several whites in the first instance. Even though there may have been no "conspiracy" in the second case, a rash of fires caused panic among white New Yorkers. As with the Stono Uprising of 1739, white reprisals were brutal, and angry crowds stirred the courts to pass out extremely harsh death penalities, including burning at the stake.

Such incidents actually pointed toward the future. In the third period of heightened popular protest, the years 1830–1860, racial fears played an important role, as did anti-immigrant feelings, directed mostly at the Irish. Jacksonian America represented an era of expanding political privileges for white males, with a growing emphasis on individualism. As the United States became more of a pluralistic society, fears of losing one's standing in society stirred particularly violent popular protest.

Groups outside the white mainstream endured repeated harassment. Perhaps because of economic competition, but certainly with deeply embedded racist feelings, white inhabitants in Cincinnati raided, burned, and destroyed prop-

During the second period of protest, resistance to imperial authority continued. In 1781 thirteen hundred veteran troops from Pennsylvania started a march on Congress to demand overdue pay and their discharge from service (above).

Even though Thomas Hutchinson had not been appointed a stamp distributor and he was opposed to the Stamp Act, this 1774 cartoon (left) from *The Massachusetts Calendar* expresses the hatred many felt toward Hutchinson for his Loyalist standing.

Many groups outside the white mainstream suffered during the third period of protest. Between 1832 and 1839, Mormon settlements in Missouri were repeatedly under attack (right), while propaganda from abolitionists portrayed the South as a land where dueling, cock-fighting, brawling, and the inhumane treatment of slaves were everyday occurances (below). In 1838 the new building of the Abolition Society was burned to the ground in Pennsylvania (bottom, right).

erty in the city's black district in 1829, which had the effect of driving away half the black population—an estimated 1300 persons. Such racial disturbances became a common urban phenomenon, as were assaults on white abolitionists who spoke out against slavery. When Pennsylvania's Anti-Slavery Society completed a new headquarters building in Philadelphia during 1838, many whites became upset when black citizens were allowed to attend lectures. Within a few days of the hall's opening, a crowd of 3000 attacked the building, ransacked it, and then burned it to the ground.

Intolerance helps to explain Jacksonian era protest. The lynch mob that murdered Mormon prophet Joseph Smith and his brother Hyrum in 1844 in Nauvoo, Illinois, remains a most striking example of violent popular protest over differing religious beliefs, in this case having to do with the issue of polygamy. To establish their right to worship as they pleased, the Mormons were forced to move several hundred miles west to Utah.

By the Jacksonian era, popular protest had become something less than corporate in intent. Too often, it was now a matter of prejudiced citizens attacking any person or group whose appearance, beliefs, and ethnic or racial characteristics threatened them. The United States had a long way to go in adjusting to pluralism, and that is one reason why Abraham Lincoln, writing in 1837, worried whether the republic could survive in the face of so much popular protest, which he called "something of an ill omen amongst us."

The Know-Nothings often blamed the problems of the country on immigrants, as illustrated in this 1856 cartoon entitled "Americans Shall Rule America" (right). In 1851 vigilantes hanged a notorious member of the Sydney Ducks (an Australian gang) accused of robbery and murder (below).

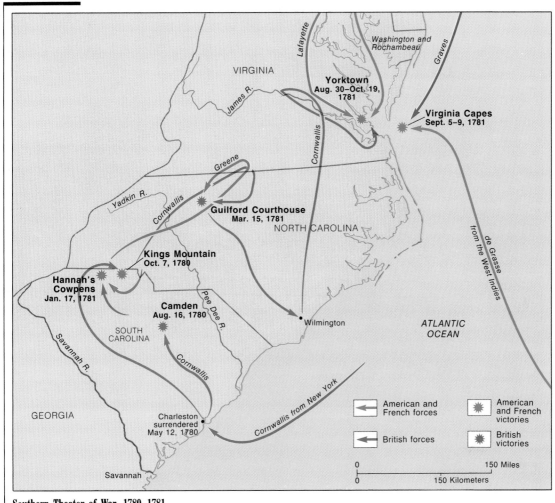

Southern Theater of War, 1780–1781

ots who fell in their path. Feeling their presence, Ferguson began retreating. When he spied Kings Mountain rising up from the rolling Piedmont landscape of northern South Carolina, he calculated that he and his 1100 followers could withstand any assault from atop the mountain. On October 7, 1780, the frontiersmen attacked from all sides. Ferguson fell mortally wounded in the thick of the battle; the rest of his column was killed, wounded, or captured; and the mountain men hanged nine of Ferguson's loyalists as a warning to others who might fight for the king.

The Battle of Kings Mountain destroyed the left wing of Cornwallis's army. Compound-

ing the damage, the main British force had not really secured South Carolina. Whenever Cornwallis moved his troops to a new locale, rebel guerrilla bands under such leaders as "Swamp Fox" Francis Marion emerged from their hiding places and wreaked vengeance on tories who had aided the British force or threatened rebels. Once again, the British had not effectively protected citizens favorably disposed toward them, which in combination with the debacle at Kings Mountain cut deeply into the loyalist support available to Cornwallis.

Despite these reverses, the British general seemed unconcerned. Like his fellow officers, Cornwallis held Americans in contempt, believ-

Rebel resistance was kept alive by guerilla leaders like Francis Marion. Here he leads his troops across the Pee Dee River to attack the British in South Carolina.

ing that it was only a matter of time until superior British arms would destroy the rebels. Cornwallis, however, did not bargain on facing the likes of Nathanael Greene, whom George Washington insisted should replace Gates as the Southern Department commander. Greene arrived in North Carolina during December 1780. Not surprisingly, there were very few troops available for duty and, as Greene stated despondently, the "appearance" of those in camp "was wretched beyond description."

Greene was a military genius. Violating the military maxim of concentrating troop strength as much as possible, he decided to divide his soldiers into three groups, one of which would work with partisan rebel bands. The idea was to let Cornwallis chase after the other two columns of just over 1100 each, until the redcoats were worn out. At that point, Greene would fight.

Cornwallis took the bait. He went after Greene and sent a detached force after the other rebel column headed by shrewd, capable General Daniel Morgan of Virginia. Morgan's troops lured the onrushing British into a trap at Hannah's Cowpens in western South Carolina on January 17, 1781. Only 140 of the 1100 British soldiers escaped being killed, captured, or wounded. Meanwhile, Cornwallis relentlessly pursued Greene, who kept retreating before him. Finally, on March 15, 1781, the rebels squared off for battle at Guilford Courthouse in central North Carolina. The combatants fought throughout the afternoon, until the Americans abandoned the field. Greene's force had inflicted 506 casualties, as compared to 264 of their own. Cornwallis had gained a technical victory, but his troops were exhausted from Greene's game of "fox and hare," and the rebels were still very much in the field.

With combined Franco-American forces, General Washington put Yorktown under siege and entrapped General Cornwallis's army.

Franco-American Triumph at Yorktown

Cornwallis retreated to the seacoast to rest his army, then decided to take over British raiding operations in Virginia, which had begun in January 1781 under turncoat Benedict Arnold. In storming northward, Cornwallis totally abandoned the southern strategy. Nathanael Greene was now free to reassert full rebel authority in the states south of Virginia.

Back in New York, Sir Henry Clinton fumed. He wanted to discipline his subordinate but lacked the courage. Instead, he sent Cornwallis orders in July to establish a defensive base and to refrain from conducting any offensive maneuvers. His army was to function only as a garrison force, until Clinton issued further orders. A most reluctant Cornwallis selected Yorktown, with easy access to Chesapeake Bay.

At this juncture, everything fell into place for the Americans. George Washington learned from General Rochambeau that a French naval fleet would be making its way north from the West Indies. If that fleet could seal off the entrance to the Bay and Washington could surround Cornwallis's army on land, a major victory was in the making.

The rebel commander seized the opportunity. In concert with Rochambeau, he started marching soldiers south, leaving only enough troops behind to keep Clinton guessing that combined Franco-American forces might strike at New York City. In early September the French fleet, after dueling with British warships, took control of Chesapeake Bay. As the month came to a close, some 7800 French troops and 9000 Continentals and militiamen surrounded the British army of 8500 at Yorktown. Cornwallis wrote Clinton: "If you cannot relieve me very soon you must expect to hear the worst." His army was trapped.

Using traditional siege tactics, Washington and Rochambeau squeezed Cornwallis into submission. It did not take long. On October 17 a lone British drummer marched toward the Franco-American lines with a white flag showing. Two days later, on a bright, sunny autumn afternoon, the army of Charles, Lord Cornwallis, marched out from its lines in solemn procession and laid down its arms. As these troops did so, their musicians played an appropriate song, "The World Turned Upside Down." The surrender at Yorktown was an emotional scene. A second British army had been captured in America, and the question now was whether Great Britain still felt strong enough to continue the war.

A Most Generous Peace Settlement

It was not the great Franco-American victory at Yorktown alone that brought the British to the peace table. It was the accumulated total of wounds being inflicted by the Americans and their European allies, with Yorktown being the most damaging, that forced the home ministers into negotiations.

As early as 1778, Britain had felt the effects of world war. Daring seaman John Paul Jones, known as the "father of the American navy," had conducted raids along the English and Scottish coasts during that year. In 1779, while

sailing in the North Sea, Jones lost his own vessel, the *Bon Homme Richard,* but captured the British war frigate *Serapis* in a dramatic naval engagement, all in the sight of England.

By 1781, French and Spanish warships attacked British vessels at will in the English channel, and French warships threatened British possessions in the West Indies. France and Spain

John Paul Jones

were about to launch an expedition against Gibraltar. In the spring of 1781 a Spanish force under Bernardo de Gálvez captured a sizable British garrison at Pensacola, Florida, and the British soon experienced setbacks as far away as India. The allies had demonstrated that they could carry the war anywhere, even to the shores of England, suggesting the prospect of disastrous consequences for the British empire.

Keenly aware of these many threats, Lord North received the news of Yorktown "as he would have taken a [musket] ball in the breast." In March 1782, North's ministry collapsed, and a new cabinet opened negotiations with designated American peace commissioners—Benjamin Franklin, John Adams, and John Jay—in France. On November 30, 1782, the representatives agreed to preliminary peace terms, pending final ratification by both governments. The other belligerents also started coming to terms, largely because the naval war had turned against France and Spain, and British troops had saved Gibraltar. All parties signed the final peace accords at Paris on September 3, 1783.

The major European powers now recognized the United States as a separate nation, capable of carving out its own existence in the western world. Further, the peace accords established the Mississippi River as the western boundary line of the new nation and 31 degrees of north latitude as the southern boundary. Britain returned the lands south of this line, constituting Florida, to Spain. Although the American commissioners failed to gain Canada, which they tried to get, they had obtained title to the vast reserve of Indian territory lying between the Appalachian Mountains and the Mississippi River. The treaty was silent about the rights of Indians, whose interests the British ignored, despite repeated promises during the war to protect the lands of Native Americans who joined the king's cause. All told, then, effective bargaining by the peace commissioners gave the former colonists a huge geographic base on which to build the new American republic.

The peace settlement also contained other significant provisions. Britain recognized American fishing rights off the coast of Eastern Canada, thus sustaining a major New England in-

CHRONOLOGY OF KEY EVENTS

1775 War breaks out at Lexington and Concord (April); Second Continental Congress convenes in Philadelphia (May); British soldiers prevail at Bunker Hill (June); Lord Dunmore issues proclamation freeing Virginia's slaves November); Americans fail to conquer Quebec (December)

1776 Paine publishes *Common Sense* (January); Congress declares independence (July); Howe attacks Long Island and launches New York campaign (August); Southerners retaliate against the Overhill Cherokees (September–October); Washington directs stunning victory at Trenton (December)

1777 Washington loses battles at Brandywine Creek and Germantown, Howe captures Philadelphia, and Burgoyne surrenders his army at Saratoga (September–October)

1778 France signs an alliance with the Americans (February) and goes to war with Britain (June); Jones raids along England's coast (April–May); British forces evacuate Philadelphia and suffer defeat at Monmouth (June); British recapture Georgia (December)

1779 Spain enters war against Britain (June); Sullivan conducts raid against Iroquois Indians (August–September); Jones captures British war frigate *Serapis* (September)

1780 British capture Charleston (May), defeat the rebels at Camden (August), but lose at Kings Mountain (October); Arnold renounces the rebel cause (September); Britain declares war on the Dutch (December)

1781 Rebels defeat British troops at the Cowpens (January), and fight Cornwallis to a draw at Guilford Courthouse (March); Gálvez captures Pensacola (May); Cornwallis surrenders to Franco-American force at Yorktown (October)

1782 Lord North's ministry falls from power (March); peace commissioners sign preliminary treaty between Britain and America (November)

1783 Belligerents approve final peace terms at Paris (September); last British troops evacuate the United States (November)

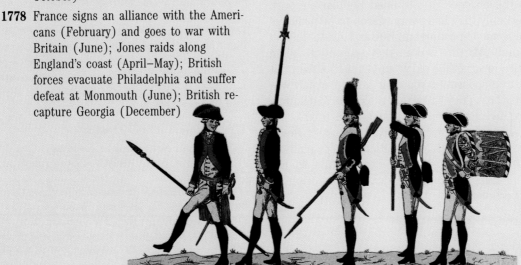

dustry, and the British promised not to carry away slaves when evacuating their troops (which they did anyway). At the same time, they demanded that prewar debts be paid to British merchants (few actually were) and insisted upon full restoration of the rights and property of loyalists. The American commissioners agreed to have Congress make such a recommendation to the states (which they generally ignored). The peace treaty, then, both established American independence and laid the groundwork for future conflict.

CONCLUSION

The Americans came out remarkably well in 1783. They emerged not only victorious in war but at the peace table as well. The young republic had outlasted Great Britain and, with invaluable assistance from foreign allies, particularly France, had earned its freedom from European monarchism and imperialism. It was far from certain, however, that the United States could remain independent or have much of a future as a nation, given the quarrels among the thirteen sovereign states.

One group that did not cheer lustily at the prospects of peace were the officers and soldiers of the Continental army. They believed they had made the greatest sacrifices, too often in the absence of sustained popular support. Certainly they had every reason to be proud of their accomplishments. But as Private Joseph Plumb Martin wrote, they resented being "turned adrift like old worn-out horses" without just compensation for their services. Such was their fate. They knew that their pain and suffering had sustained the vision of a bright and glorious future for America, but only if Revolutionary Americans settled their political differences—especially those relating to the implanting of republican ideals in institutions of government.

REVIEW SUMMARY

The American Revolution was more than a matter of declaring independence. Also crucial was winning

the military contest known as the War for American Independence.

> the debate over independence
> the poor, unprivileged, and unfree confronted the British troops
> the Battle of Saratoga resulted in formal French intervention on behalf of the patriots
> the American war encompassed the globe
> the Battle of Yorktown convinced British officials to seek peace and grant independence

Although the Revolution led to American independence, it did not solve all the social issues raised by the Declaration of Independence.

SUGGESTIONS FOR FURTHER READING

OVERVIEWS AND SURVEYS

John R. Alden, *The American Revolution, 1775–1783* (1954); Marcus Cunliffe, *George Washington: Man and Monument*, rev. ed. (1982); R. Ernest Dupuy, et al., *The American Revolution: A Global War* (1977); Don Higginbotham, *The War of American Independence, 1763–1789* (1971), ed., *Reconsiderations on the Revolutionary War* (1978), and *George Washington and the American Military Tradition* (1985); Ronald Hoffman and Peter J. Albert, eds., *Arms and Independence: The Military Character of the American Revolution* (1984); Piers Mackesy, *The War for America, 1775–1783* (1965); James Kirby Martin and Mark Edward Lender, *A Respectable Army: The Military Origins of the Republic, 1763–1789* (1982); Dave R. Palmer, *The Way of the Fox: American Strategy in the War for America, 1775–1783* (1975); Eric Robson, *The American Revolution in Its Political and Military Aspects, 1763–1783* (1955); Charles Royster, *A Revolutionary People at War: The Continental Army and American Character, 1775–1783* (1979); John Shy, *A People Numerous and Armed: Reflections on the Military Struggle for American Independence* (1976); and Robert K. Wright, Jr., *The Continental Army* (1983).

RECONCILIATION OR INDEPENDENCE

Joseph L. Davis, *Sectionalism in American Politics, 1774–1787* (1977); H. James Henderson, *Party Politics in the Continental Congress* (1974); Merrill Jensen, *The Articles of Confederation: An Interpretation of the Social-Constitutional History of the American Revolution, 1774–1781* (1940); Jackson Turner Main, *The Sovereign States, 1775–1783* (1973); Jerrilyn Greene Marston, *King and Congress: The Transfer of Political Legitimacy, 1774–1776* (1987); and Jack N. Rakove, *The Beginnings of National Politics: An Interpretive History of the Continental Congress* (1979).

WITHOUT VISIBLE ALLIES: THE WAR IN THE NORTH

Rodney Atwood, *The Hessians* (1980); George A. Billias, ed., *George Washington's Generals* (1964), and ed., *George Washington's Opponents* (1969); Richard Buel, Jr., *Dear Liberty: Connecticut's Mobilization for the Revolutionary War* (1980); John C. Dann, ed., *The Revolution Remembered: Eyewitness Accounts of the War for Independence* (1980); Linda Grant DePauw, "Women in Combat: The Revolutionary War Experience," *Armed Forces and Society*, 7 (1981), pp. 209–26; Sylvia R. Frey, *The British Soldier in America* (1981); Don R. Gerlach, *Proud Patriot: Philip Schuyler and the War of Independence, 1775–1783* (1987); Barbara Graymont, *The Iroquois in the American Revolution* (1972); Robert A. Gross, *The Minutemen and Their World* (1976); Don Higginbotham, *Daniel Morgan* (1961); Ira D. Gruber, *The Howe Brothers and the American Revolution* (1972); Richard J. Hargrove, Jr., *General John Burgoyne* (1983); Richard M. Ketchum, *The Winter Soldiers* (1973); Joseph Plumb Martin, *Private Yankee Doodle: Being a Narrative . . . of a Revolutionary Soldier,* ed. George F. Scheer (1962); Paul David Nelson, *General Horatio Gates* (1976), and *Anthony Wayne: Soldier of the Early Republic* (1985); John S. Pancake, *1777: The Year of the Hangman* (1977); Gary Alexander Puckrein, *The Black Regiment in the American Revolution* (1978); Jonathan Gregory Rossie, *The Politics of Command in the American Revolution* (1975); Paul H. Smith, *Loyalists and Redcoats: A Study in British Revolutionary Policy* (1964); and Willard M. Wallace, *Traitorous Hero: The Life and Fortunes of Benedict Arnold* (1954).

RESCUING THE PATRIOTS: TOWARD GLOBAL CONFLICT

Samuel F. Bemis, *The Diplomacy of the American Revolution,* rev. ed. (1957); Jonathan R. Dull, *A Diplomatic History of the American Revolution* (1985); Louis R. Gottschalk, *Lafayette Joins the American Army* (1937); Ronald Hoffman and Peter J. Albert, eds., *Diplomacy and Revolution: The Franco-American Alliance of 1778* (1981); Reginald Horsman, *The Diplomacy of the New Republic, 1776–1815* (1985); James H. Hutson, *John Adams and the Diplomacy of the American Revolution* (1980); Lawrence S. Kaplan, ed., *The American Revolution and "A Candid World"* (1977); Richard B. Morris, *The Peacemakers: The Great Powers and American Independence* (1965); Orville T. Murphy, *Charles Gravier, Comte de Vergennes* (1982); Louis W. Potts, *Arthur Lee: A Virtuous Revolutionary* (1981); Charles R. Ritcheson, *British Politics and the American Revolution* (1954); William C. Stinchcombe, *The American Revolution and the French Alliance* (1969); Gerald Stourzh, *Benjamin Franklin and American Foreign Policy* (1969); Richard W. Van Alstyne, *Empire and Independence: The International History of the American Revolution* (1965); and Paul A. Varg, *Foreign Policies of the Founding Fathers* (1963).

THE WORLD TURNED UPSIDE DOWN

R. Arthur Bowler, *Logistics and the Failure of the British Army in America, 1775–1783* (1975); E. Wayne Carp, *To Starve the Army at Pleasure: Continental Army Administration and American Political Culture, 1775–1783* (1984); Jeffrey J. Crow and Larry E. Tise, eds., *The Southern Experience in the American Revolution* (1978); John Morgan Dederer, *Making Bricks Without Straw: Nathanael Greene's Southern Campaign and Mao Tse-Tung's Mobile War* (1983); Jonathan R. Dull, *The French Navy and American Independence, 1774–1787* (1975); William M. Fowler, Jr., *Rebels Under Sail: The American Navy During the Revolution* (1976); W. Robert Higgins, ed., *The Revolutionary War in the South* (1979); Ronald Hoffman, Thad W. Tate, and Peter J. Albert, eds., *An Uncivil War: The Southern Backcountry During the American Revolution* (1985); Lee Kennett, *The French Forces in America, 1780–1783* (1977); Henry Lumpkin, *From Savannah to Yorktown* (1981); George S. McCowen, Jr., *The British Occupation of Charleston, 1780–82* (1972); Samuel Eliot Morison, *John Paul Jones* (1959); James H. O'Donnell, III, *Southern Indians in the American Revolution* (1973); John S. Pancake, *The Destructive War, 1780–1782* (1985); Hugh F. Rankin, *Francis Marion: The Swamp Fox* (1973); David Syrett, *Shipping and the American War, 1775–83: A Study of British Transport Organization* (1970); John A. Tilley, *The British Navy and the American Revolution* (1987); Russell F. Weigley, *The Partisan War: The South Carolina Campaign of 1780–1782* (1970); Franklin B. and Mary Wickwire, *Cornwallis: The American Adventure* (1970); and William B. Willcox, *Portrait of a General: Sir Henry Clinton in the War of Independence* (1964).

FIG. II.

TOBACCO PLANTATION

94.

CHAPTER 6

Securing the Republic and Its Ideals, 1776–1789

DESCRIPTION OF A SLAVE SHIP.

PLATE 33

A Declaration by the Representatives of the UNITED STATES
F AMERICA, in General Congress assembled.

When in the course of human events it becomes necessary for one people to
dissolve the political bands which have connected them with another, and to
separate and equal

Nancy Shippen was a product of Philadelphia's best lineage. Although she was born in 1763, the political turmoil leading to rebellion did not affect her early life. As a privileged daughter in an upper-class family, it was her duty to blossom into a charming woman, admired for her beauty and social graces, rather than develop her intellect. Her education consisted of the refinement of skills that would please and entertain—dancing, cultivating her voice, playing musical instruments, painting on delicate china, and producing pieces of decorative needlework.

Had Nancy shown any interest in politics, an exclusively masculine preserve, she would have shocked everyone, including her father, William Shippen. Shippen was a noted local physician who espoused independence in 1776. That was his prerogative as paterfamilias; where he led, according to the customs of the time, his family followed. Indeed, he was a proud father in 1777 when, at his urging, Nancy displayed her patriotic virtue by sewing shirt ruffles for General Washington.

Three hundred miles away in Boston, another woman by the name of Phillis Wheatley was also reckoning with the American Revolution. Her life had been very different from that of Nancy Shippen. Born on Africa's West Coast in the early 1750s, slave catchers had snatched her from her parents. At the Boston slave market, Mrs. John Wheatley, looking for a young female slave to train in domestic service, noticed her. In Phillis the Wheatley family got much more; their new slave yearned to express her thoughts and feelings through poetry.

Conventional wisdom dictated that slaves should not be educated. Exposure to reading and writing might make them resentful, perhaps even rebellious. Sensing Phillis's talents, the Wheatley family defied convention. She mastered English and Latin, even preparing translations of ancient writings. By 1770 some of her poems had been published, followed in 1773 by a collection entitled *Poems on Various Subjects, Religious and Moral.* In one verse addressed to Lord Dartmouth, Britain's Secretary for American Affairs, she queried:

I young in life, by seeming cruel fate
Was snatch'd from Afric's fancy'd seat:
Such was my case. And can I then but
  pray
Others may never feel tyrannic sway?

Experiencing the tyranny of slavery influenced Phillis's feelings about the presence of redcoats in Boston. Late in 1775 she sent a flattering poem to George Washington. He responded gratefully and called her words "striking proof of your great poetical talents."

Little as Phillis Wheatley and Nancy Shippen had in common, they lived in an era in which men thought of all women, regardless of their rank in society, as second-class human beings. In the case of Phillis, she carried the additional burden of being black in an unabashedly racist society. Like other women in Revolutionary America, they could only hope that the ideals of human liberty might someday apply to them.

For Nancy Shippen, there were two male tyrants in her life. The first was her father William, who in 1781 forced her into marriage with Henry Beekman Livingston, a son of one of New York's most powerful and wealthy families. The man she truly loved had only "honorable expectations" of a respectable income. So her father insisted that she wed Livingston. The rejected suitor wanted to know "for what reason in this *free* country a lady . . . must be married in a hurry and given up to a man whom she dislikes." None of the Shippens responded. In truth, the answer was that Nancy legally belonged to her father until she became the property of the second tyrant in her life—her husband Henry.

The marriage was a disaster, most likely because Henry was a known philanderer. Nancy took her baby daughter and moved back to her family. She wanted full custody of the child, who by law was the property of her husband. Henry made it clear that he would never give up his legal rights to his daughter, should Nancy embarrass him in public by seeking a bill of divorcement. Even if she had defied him, divorce bills were very hard to get because they involved proving adultery or desertion.

Although they were from diverse cultures, Phillis Wheatley and Nancy Shippen were considered second-class citizens because they were women.

To keep actual custody of her daughter, then, Nancy accepted her entrapment. Several years later Henry relented and arranged for a divorce, but by that time Nancy's spirit was broken. This former belle of Philadelphia society lived on unhappily in hermit-like fashion until her death in 1841. Having been so favored at birth, her adult years were a personal tragedy, primarily because of her legal dependence on the will of men.

Phillis Wheatley, by comparison, enjoyed some personal freedom before her untimely death in 1784. Mr. and Mrs. Wheatley died during the war period, and their will provided for Phillis's emancipation. She married John Peters, a free black man, and bore him three children. But John Peters was poor, and there was scant time for poetry. It was very difficult for free blacks to get decent jobs, and Phillis struggled each day to help her family avoid destitution. She lived long enough to see slavery being challenged in the North; but she died knowing that blacks, even when free, invariably faced discrimination based on race, forcing families like hers to exist on the margins of Revolutionary society.

The experiences of Phillis Wheatley and Nancy Shippen raise basic questions about the character of the Revolution. Did the cause of liberty really change the lives of Americans? If it was truly a movement to end tyranny, secure human rights, and ensure equality of opportunity, then why did individuals like Wheatley and Shippen benefit so little? A major reason was that white, adult males of property and community standing put greater emphasis on setting up an independent nation between 1776 and 1789 than on securing human rights. The ideology of liberty could not be denied, however. Primarily, the Revolutionary era saw the creation of a new nation and the articulation of fundamental ideals regarding human freedom and dignity—ideals that shaped the course of American historical development.

ESTABLISHING NEW REPUBLICAN GOVERNMENTS

Winning the war and working out a favorable peace settlement represented two of three crucial elements that made the rebellion successful. The third element centered on the formation of stable governments, certainly a challenging task because it involved the careful definition of how governments should function to support life, liberty, and property (or happiness, as Jefferson framed the triad). Everyone agreed that a monarchical system, indeed any form capable of producing political tyranny, was unacceptable. A second point of consensus was that governments should be republican in character. Sovereignty, or ultimate political authority, previously residing with King and Parliament, should be vested in the people. After all, political institutions presumably existed to serve them. As such, citizens should be governed by laws, not by power-hungry officials, and laws should be the product of collective deliberations of representatives elected by the citizenry.

Defining the core ideals of republicanism—popular sovereignty, rule by law, and legislation by elected representatives—was not a source of disagreement. Yet revolutionary leaders argued passionately about the organization and powers of new governments, both state and national, as well as the extent to which basic political rights should be put into practice. At the heart of the argument was the concept of *public virtue:* whether citizens were capable of subordinating their self-interest to the greater good of the whole community. While some leaders answered in the affirmative, others did not. Their trust or distrust of the people directly affected how far they were willing to go in implementing republican ideals.

Leaders who believed that citizens could govern themselves and not abuse public privileges for private advantage were in the vanguard of political thinking in the western world. As such, they may be called radicals. They were willing to establish "the most democratical forms" of government, as Samuel Adams so aptly capsulized their thinking.

More cautious, elitist Revolutionary leaders feared what the masses might do without the restraining hand of central political authority. As one of them wrote: "No one loves liberty more than I do, but of all tyranny I most dread that of the multitude." These leaders remained attached to traditional notions of hierarchy and deference in social and political relationships. They still thought that the "better sort" of citizens—men of education, wealth, and proven ability, whom they now defined as "natural aristocrats"—should be the stewards who guided the people. For such leaders the success of the Revolution depended upon a transfer of power from the despoilers of liberty in Britain to "enlightened" gentlemen like themselves in America. As a precaution against a citizenry abusing its liberty, they wanted a strong central government to replace King and Parliament, a government controlled by more cautious Revolutionaries in the interests of national political stability.

People Victorious: The New State Governments

In the wake of collapsing British authority during 1775 and 1776, radical and cautious Revolutionaries squared off in constitutional conventions. Their heated debates produced ten new state constitutions by the end of 1777, plus a plan of national government written by the Continental Congress. Connecticut and Rhode Island kept their liberal colonial charters, which had provided for the popular election of executive officials, and simply deleted all references to British sovereignty; Massachusetts ratified a new state constitution in 1780.

Looking at this first constitutional settlement of the Revolution, leaders who had firm faith in the people prevailed because of the emergence of three essential characteristics. First, there was general agreement that governments derive their authority from the consent of the governed. From that day to this, there has been no retreat from the principle of popular sovereignty. Second, although the state constitution-makers varied in their commitment, free, white, adult male citizens (about twenty percent of the total population) gained expanded voting and office-holding rights. The movement clearly was toward greater popular participation in governmental decision making. Third, the central government would not have the power to inhibit the state governments and the people in the management of the republic's political affairs.

Pennsylvanians produced the most democratic of the first state constitutions. Decision-making authority resided in an annually elected one-chamber, or unicameral assembly. All white male citizens, with or without property, could now vote for legislators. By comparison, Maryland constitution-framers were much less trusting. They maintained a three-tiered structure of government, reminiscent of the king and two houses of Parliament. Potential voters had to meet modest property holding requirements (at least £30 in local currency). Those elected to the lower house had to own at least a fifty-acre freehold while those chosen for the upper house needed to be worth £1000 in local currency. For the governor, the property requirement was £5000. In Pennsylvania, ordinary citizens could control their own political destiny, but in Maryland wealthier citizens were to act as stewards for the people, hence continuing the tradition of deferential politics.

The other state constitutions varied between these two extremes. Those of New Hampshire, North Carolina, and Georgia were more like Pennsylvania. New York, Virginia, and South Carolina resembled the Maryland plan more closely. Delaware and New Jersey were in the middle.

Only New Jersey defined the electorate without regard to gender. Its 1776 constitution gave the vote to "all free inhabitants" meeting minimal property qualifications. This permitted some women to vote. Since all property in marriage belonged to husbands, New Jersey had technically extended franchise rights only to widows and spinsters (very few divorced women were to be found anywhere in America). Nonetheless, great numbers of married women went to the polls regularly. Not until 1807 did New Jersey disenfranchise females, and it happened on the alleged grounds that they were more easily manipulated by self-serving political candidates. For a brief time,

New Jersey extended the right to vote to all free inhabitants until 1807, when women were disenfranchised.

then, at least one state regarded women, not just free, white, adult males, as a legitimate voice in government. Although the experiment worked, this concept proved too radical for the male-dominated political culture of Revolutionary America.

Because of the first state constitutions, male citizens with more ordinary backgrounds, less personal wealth, and a greater diversity of occupations began to hold higher political offices after the Revolution started. As an excited citizen noted, elected delegates to the new Virginia Assembly were more "plain and of consequence, less disguised, but I believe to be full[y] as honest, less intriguing, more sincere." Not "so politely educated, nor so highly born" as in the past, these delegates were "the people's men (and the people in general are right)." Radical leaders throughout the states heartily endorsed these sentiments.

The Articles of Confederation

In June 1776 the Continental Congress called for a plan of national government. John Dickinson, the well-known reluctant Revolutionary, took the lead. Concerned about losing the stabilizing influence of British authority, Dickinson proposed a strong central government in the constitution his committee drafted for Congress. The Confederacy was to be called "THE UNITED STATES OF AMERICA," and it would exist "for their common defense, the security of their liberties, and their mutual and general welfare." Not surprisingly, the states would have little authority. Each would retain only "as much of its present laws, rights and customs, as it may think fit . . . in all matters that shall not interfere with the Articles of this Confederation."

The exigencies of war kept interrupting Congressional debate on Dickinson's draft. Furthermore, the radical Revolutionaries who dominated Congress in late 1776 and 1777 did not like this plan. They feared power too far removed from the people. After all, they had rebelled against a distant government which they had perceived as tyrannical. When they finally completed revisions in November 1777, they had turned Dickinson's draft inside out. The Articles now stated: "Each state retains its sovereignty, freedom, and independence, and every power, jurisdiction and right, which is not . . . expressly delegated to the United States, in Congress assembled." At most, then, the central government could coordinate activities among the states. It could manage the war, but it did not even have taxation authority to support that effort. If Congress needed money (it obviously did), it could "requisition" the states. The states, however, could decide for themselves whether or not they would send funds to Congress.

Fundamentally penniless and powerless, the Confederation government represented the optimistic view that a virtuous citizenry did not require the constraining hand of central authority. This bold vision—fully in line with the rejection of King and Parliament as a far distant, autocratic government—pleased radicals like Samuel Adams, Thomas Paine, and Thomas Jefferson. Jefferson wrote glowingly of the "ease" with which the people "had deposited the monarchical and taken up . . . republican government," as easily as "throwing off an old and putting on a new suit of clothes." But cautious Revolutionaries still harbored grave doubts, and

events over the next few years convinced them that the first constitutional settlement was folly.

CRISES OF THE CONFEDERATION

Internal difficulties soon beset the young republic. In the minds of the cautious Revolutionaries, the delicate fabric of the new nation seemed to be unraveling. They viewed the years between 1776 and 1787 as a "critical period" because of problems encountered with the sovereign states and the people. These included ratifying the Articles of Confederation, establishing a national domain west of the Appalachians, finding some means to pay for the war, achieving stable diplomatic relations with foreign powers, and guarding against domestic insurrections. Over time, those who advocated a strong central government formed an informal political group, known as the *nationalists*. With each passing year, the nationalists became more and more frustrated by the Confederation. Finally, in 1787 they overwhelmed their opposition by pressing for and getting a new national government.

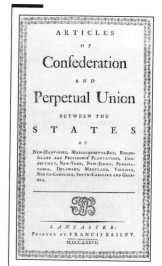

The Articles of Confederation

Struggle to Ratify the Articles

Given the wartime need for national unity in the face of a common enemy, Congress asked each state to approve the Articles of Confederation quickly. Overcoming much indifference, twelve states had finally ratified by January 1779—but Maryland still held out.

Those propertied gentlemen who controlled Maryland's Revolutionary government objected to one specific provision in the Articles. Although Dickinson's draft had designated

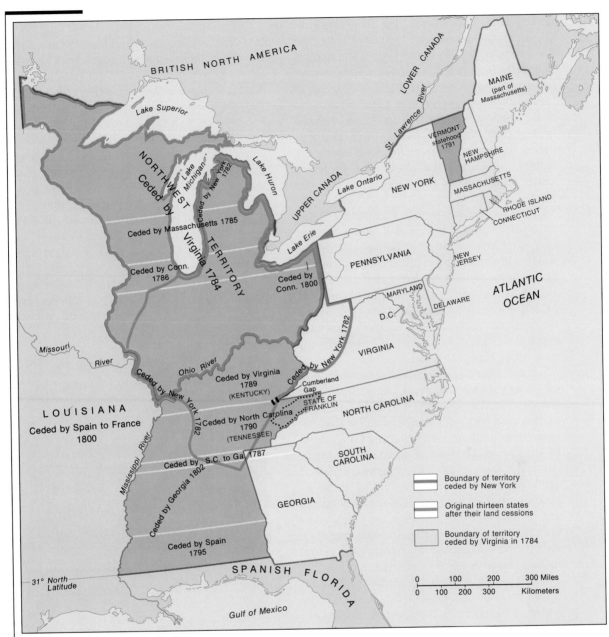

Western Land Claims Ceded by the States
The battle over conflicting states' claims to western lands was a major issue facing the Continental Congress.

all lands west of the Appalachian Mountains as a national domain, belonging to all of the people for future settlement, the final version left these lands in the hands of states having sea-to-sea clauses in their colonial charters. This was a logical extension of the principle of state sovereignty. Maryland, having a fixed western boundary, had no such western claim. Nor did Rhode Island, New Jersey, Pennsylvania, or Delaware.

Maryland's leaders simply refused to be cut off from western development. In public, they talked in terms of high principle. Citizens from "landless" states should have as much right to resettle in the West as inhabitants of "landed" states. But that was not the only issue. Many

Maryland leaders had invested in pre-Revolutionary land companies trying to get title to large chunks of western territory. They had done so by appealing to the Crown and making purchases from individual Indians, who without tribal approval were willing to "sell" rights in return for alcohol and other "gifts." Wanting to avoid needless warfare, the Crown had refused to recognize any such titles. After independence, there was new hope for these land speculators, but only if the Continental Congress rather than some of the states controlled the West.

The Maryland Assembly adamantly refused ratification unless the landed states turned over their charter titles to Congress. Virginia, which had the largest claim, including the vast region north of the Ohio River that came to be known as the "Old Northwest," faced the most pressure. Forsaking local land speculators for the national interest, the Virginia assembly broke the deadlock in January 1781 by agreeing to cede its claims to Congress.

If self-interest had not been involved, ratification would have followed quickly. But greedy Maryland leaders continued to hold out. They pronounced Virginia's grant unacceptable because of a condition not permitting Congress to award lands on the basis of Indian deeds. Fortunately for the republic, the war intervened. It suddenly appeared that Maryland might be invaded by the British, and leaders in Congress urged ratification in exchange for promises of Continental military support. Now cornered, the Maryland Assembly reluctantly gave in and ratified the Articles of Confederation.

March 1, 1781, the day formal ratification ceremonies finally took place, elicited only muted celebrations. Some cheered "the union," at long last "indissolubly cemented," as an optimist wrote. Certainly, too, the creation of a national domain for a rapidly expanding population pleased many citizens. The nationalists, on the other hand, believed that Maryland's behavior showed how self-interest could be masked as public virtue. With so many problems needing solutions, they wondered how long the republic could endure when any sovereign state had the ability to thwart the will of the other twelve.

Contention Over Financing the War

From the very first, many problems plagued the new government. Under the Articles, Congress had no power of taxation; it repeatedly asked the states to pay a fair proportion of war costs. The states, also hard pressed for funds, rarely sent in more than fifty percent of their requisitions. In the meantime, soldiers like Joseph Plumb Martin endured shortages of food, clothing, camp equipment, and pay. With each passing month, the army grew increasingly angry with its role as a creditor to the republic.

The lack of tax revenues forced Congress to resort to various expedients to meet war costs. Between 1775 and 1780, it issued some $220 million in paper money. Lacking any financial backing, these "Continentals" became so worthless by 1779 that irate army officers complained how "four months' pay of a private [sol-

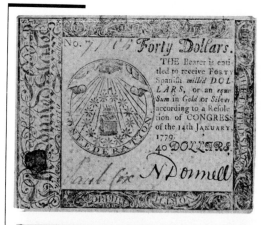

While the Continental Congress issued its currency, the states also put money in the marketplace to facilitate commerce.

dier] will not procure his wretched wife and children a single bushel of wheat." In addition, largely to get military supplies, Congress issued interest-bearing certificates of indebtedness. Without any means to pay interest, these notes, which also circulated as money, rapidly lost value. In 1780 there was an attempt to refinance Continental dollars at a 40 to 1 ratio, but the plan failed. If it had not been for grants and loans from allies like France and the Netherlands (Spain offered little financial support), the war effort might well have collapsed.

Deeply disturbed by these conditions, many nationalists in the Continental Congress acted forcefully to institute financial reform. Their leader was the wealthy Philadelphia merchant, Robert Morris, sometimes called the "financier of the Revolution," who became Congress's Superintendent of Finance in 1781. His assistant superintendent, Gouverneur Morris (no relation), a wealthy New Yorker then practicing law in Philadelphia, was also vital to shaping the events that lay ahead, as were Alexander Hamilton of New York and James Madison of Virginia. Hamilton summarized their feelings this way: "The Confederation . . . gives the power of the purse too entirely to the state legislatures. . . . That power, which holds the purse strings absolutely, must rule."

At the urging of the nationalists, Congressional delegates approved the Impost Plan of 1781. It called for import duties of five percent on all foreign trade goods entering the United States, the revenues to belong to Congress. These funds could be used to pay the army, to back a stable national currency and, ultimately, to meet foreign loan obligations. Because the plan involved giving Congress taxation authority, the delegates recommended it in the form of an amendment to the Articles. Amendments required the approval of all thirteen states.

Reluctant as they were to share taxation powers with the central government, many state leaders agreed with Robert Morris, who had warned: "The political existence of America depends on the accomplishment of this [Impost] plan." By the fall of 1782, twelve states had ratified. But Rhode Island hesitated, reasoning that, with little land to tax, its war debt could be most easily funded through state im-

Robert Morris and Gouverneur Morris were key figures in the institution of financial reform.

port duties. If there had to be a choice, state interests would come first. The Assembly voted against ratification. Once again, the tyranny of the minority had prevailed; one state had blocked the will of the other twelve.

In this crucial matter the nationalists had allies. Most prominent were disgruntled officers in the Continental army. Rarely had the soldiers been paid, and in 1780 Congress promised the officers half-pay postwar pensions as their price for staying in the service. Without a fixed source of revenue, Congress lacked the ability to meet these obligations.

After a group of high-ranking officers learned about Rhode Island's decision, they sent a menacing petition to Congress in December 1782. It stated: "We have borne all that men can bear—our property is expended—our private resources are at an end." With no likelihood of pensions being funded, they insisted upon five years of full pay when mustering out of the service. Even with British troops still on American soil, the angry officers warned Congress: "Any further experiments on their patience may have fatal effects."

Threatened Military Coup: The Newburgh Conspiracy

For years, officers and soldiers alike had been complaining about the ungenerous, downright stingy treatment they received from Revolutionary leaders and civilians. Convinced that the general populace had lived well at home while the army endured privation, sickness, and death in the field, they spoke with impassioned feelings about the absence of citizen virtue. As one officer bluntly wrote: "I hate my countrymen." Personal sacrifice for the good of the whole community, it seemed to the Continentals, had been exacted only from those with the fortitude to fulfill the obligation of long-term military service.

After the surrender at Yorktown, Washington moved 11,000 troops north to Newburgh, New York. From this campsite on the Hudson River, the Continental army waited for peace terms and kept its eye on British forces in New York City. As peace negotiations dragged on during 1782, officers and soldiers feared they would be disbanded without back pay and promised pensions. When Rhode Island refused to ratify the Impost Plan, their worst fears seemed to be realized.

Curiously, when the Congressional nationalists received the officers' hotly worded petition, they were more pleased than worried. They soon devised a plan to use these threats to extort taxation authority from the states. If need be, they would encourage the army to go back into the field and threaten the civilian populace with a military uprising. The danger, of course, was that the army might get out of control, seize the reins of government, and push the Revolution toward some form of military dictatorship.

Making no headway with the states, which refused to be bullied, the nationalists turned to George Washington in February 1783. As Alexander Hamilton wrote to him, the critical issue was "the establishment of general funds. . . . In this the influence of the army, properly directed, may cooperate." But Washington refused any help; perhaps better than anyone in Revolutionary America, he understood that military power had to remain subordinate to civil-

ian authority, or the republic would never be free. At this juncture, Robert Morris and other Congressional nationalists began "conspiring" with General Horatio Gates, second in command at Newburgh, who had often dreamed of replacing Washington at the head of the army.

Gates made his move in early March. He authorized two Newburgh Addresses, prepared by members of his staff. They warned the officers to "suspect the man [Washington] who would advise to more moderation and forbearance." If peace comes, let nothing separate you "from your arms but death," not until the army had realized financial justice. The first Address instructed the officers to attend a meeting to vent grievances—and take action. Dismayed, Washington called this proposal "disorderly," but he nevertheless approved a meeting for March 15. He would not attend, he stated, but would let Gates be in charge.

Despite his promise, Washington appeared at this showdown meeting and pleaded with the officers to temper their rage and not go back into the field. That would destroy everything the army had accomplished during eight long years of war. The officers appeared unmoved as he spoke. Then preparing to read a letter, Washington reached into his pocket, pulled out spectacles, and put them on. The officers, never having seen him wear eyeglasses before, started to murmur. Sensing a possible mood shift, the commander calmly stated: "Gentlemen, you must pardon me. I have grown gray in your service and now find myself growing blind." These heartfelt words caught the angry officers off guard. They recalled that they, too, had offered their lives for a cause larger than any of them. They were the true, virtuous republicans of Revolutionary America, and many openly wept. In that instant, the threat of a possible mutiny, or worse, a military coup directed against the states and the people, came to an end.

Washington promised that he would do everything in his power to secure "complete and ample justice" for the army. He did send a circular letter to the states and begged them to give more power to Congress. And even though the British were still in New York, he also started to furlough soldiers, so that further troublesome incidents would not occur. The nationalists in Congress came up with another Impost Plan in 1783, but this one, too, failed to win unanimous ratification. The Plan was still languishing in late 1786, but by that time the nationalists were pursuing other avenues of change.

Drifting Toward Disunion

Despite the Paris settlement and the final removal of British troops, most citizens engaged in another battle beginning in late 1783—this one against a hard-hitting economic depression. It had many sources. In the South, planters had lost 60,000 slaves, many of whom the British had carried off. In addition, crop yields for 1784 and 1785 were small, largely because of bad weather. In New England, farmers reeled from the effects of new British trade regulations. The Orders-in-Council of 1783 prohibited the sale of many American farm products in the British West Indies, formerly a key market for New England goods, and required other products to be shipped to and from the islands in British vessels. This was a blow to New England's carrying trade and shipbuilding industry.

Making matters even worse, American merchants in all the states rushed to re-establish old trading connections with their British counterparts. The Americans bought far too many goods on easy credit terms, which hard-pressed citizens could not afford. Many of these merchants faced total ruin by 1785.

The central government could do little. It did send John Adams to Britain in 1785 as the first minister from the United States. Adams, however, made no headway in getting British officials to back off from the Orders-in-Council. He glumly reported that "they rely upon our disunion" to avoid negotiations.

To add to these economic woes, significant postwar trading ties did not develop with France. In fact, American exports to France far exceeded the value of imports (roughly $2,000,000 a year during the 1780s). The same held true with the Dutch. And even though some merchants sent a trading vessel to China in 1784, all the new activity was insignificant in comparison to the renewed American dependency on British manufactured goods. The former colonists stayed glued to the old imperial trading network, and it was years before they gained full economic independence.

Some merchants, primarily from the Middle Atlantic states, were anxious to break free of Britain's economic hold. An opportunity presented itself in 1784 after Congress named John Jay, one of the Paris peace commissioners, to be its secretary of foreign affairs. Jay soon started negotiations with Don Diego de Gardoqui, Spain's first minister to the United States. Gardoqui talked about his government's concern that Americans, now streaming into the trans-Appalachian west, would in time covet Spanish territory beyond the Mississippi River. To stem the tide, Gardoqui informed Congress that Spain would not allow the Mississippi to serve as an outlet for western agricultural goods. In an attempt to assuage bad feelings, however, Gardoqui offered an advantageous commercial treaty.

John Jay

Jay and a number of powerful merchants from the Middle Atlantic states saw merit in the Spanish proposal. They viewed a developing west—settlements were sprouting in Kentucky and Tennessee—as a potential threat to eastern economic dominance. Meanwhile, Gardoqui had Spanish agents circulating through the west. They encouraged American settlers to become Spanish subjects in return for trade access to the Mississippi River. Gardoqui's idea was to build a wall of settlers in the trans-Appalachian west to protect Spanish holdings beyond the Mississippi. Basically, his agents did little more than stir up resentment, both toward Spain and leaders like Jay, who appeared to be selling out western interests for a commercial treaty of undetermined value.

When Jay reported on his discussions to Congress in the summer of 1786, tempers flared. The southern states voted as a bloc against any such treaty, which ended the Jay-Gardoqui negotiations. Southerners and westerners still suspected that Jay and his eastern merchant allies would not hesitate to abandon them altogether for petty commercial gains. Some leaders in Congress, as one delegate explained, started speaking "lightly of a separation and dissolution of the Confederation." Such talk helped galvanize the nationalists into dramatic action, as did a rebellion that now convulsed Massachusetts.

Daniel Shays's Rebellion

Postwar economic conditions were so bad in several states that citizens began demanding tax relief from their governments. In western Massachusetts, desperate farmers, caught between high taxes (to pay off the state's war debt) and depressed economic circumstances, rose up in resistance during the fall of 1786.

Men like Daniel Shays, a Revolutionary War veteran, were losing their freehold farms—and in some cases being thrown into debtors' prison. Viewing their plight as political tyranny, they believed that they had the right to break the chains of oppression, just as they had done in rising up against the British a few years before.

The farmers of western Massachusetts tried to resist in orderly fashion. They first met in impromptu conventions and sent petitions to the state assembly. Getting no relief, they turned to crowd actions. In late August 1786, more than a thousand farmers poured into Northampton and shut down the county court. This was the first of many closures. By popular mandate, citizens would no longer permit judges to seize property or condemn people to debtors' prison as the penalty for not paying taxes.

State leaders in Boston started to panic, fearing the "rebels" would soon descend upon them. Desperately, they resorted to a public

Shays's Rebellion convinced many citizens throughout the republic that a strong national government was needed, if for no other reason than to control domestic insurrections.

appeal for funds. Frightened Bostonians opened their purses. They subscribed £5000 to pay for an eastern Massachusetts army headed by former Continental general Benjamin Lincoln. Lincoln's assignment was to march into western parts of the state and subdue the Shaysites.

The insurrection soon fizzled out. Lacking weapons and suffering in bitter cold weather, Daniel Shays and his followers were desperate. In January 1787 they attacked the federal arsenal at Springfield. A few well-placed cannon shots, resulting in four casualties, drove them off. In mid-February the eastern Massachusetts army fell upon Shays's followers at Petersham, routing the farmers, who lacked guns to defend themselves. The Petersham engagement, along with tax relief from the assembly and amnesty for leaders of the uprising, ended the dispute.

Shays's Rebellion, however, held broader significance. The confrontation galvanized the nationalists into action. Wrote George Washington: "Good God! . . . There are combustibles in every state, which a spark might set fire to." Only a national government of "energy" could save the republic from sinking "into the lowest state of humiliation and contempt." The nationalists thus intensified their campaign for a new constitutional settlement, one designed to bring the self-serving sovereign states and the people under control.

HUMAN RIGHTS AND SOCIAL CHANGE

The years between 1776 and 1787 were not just a time of mounting political confrontation between nationalists and localists. The period also witnessed the establishment of many fundamental human rights. When Thomas Jefferson penned his famous words, "all men are created equal," he informed George III that kings were not superior to the people by some artificial right of birth. Jefferson went on to say that all human beings had "certain inalienable rights," or rights beyond governmental control. Republican governments had the responsibility to respect and guarantee these rights, including "life, liberty, and the pursuit of happiness," for all citizens.

At the same time, Americans had waged civil war against Britain to preserve property rights. Tyrannical governments, for example, threatened property through taxation without representation. In trying to protect property rights while expanding human rights, however, Revolutionary leaders learned that the two could clash. They found it much easier to guarantee human rights when property rights, such as those related to the ownership of slaves, were not also at stake. Thus there were some striking contradictions in efforts to enshrine greater freedom for all inhabitants in Revolutionary America.

In Pursuit of Religious Conscience

Since the Great Awakening, dissenter groups had expressed opposition to established churches in the colonies. The Baptists were particularly outspoken. They wanted official toleration and an end to taxes used exclusively for state-supported churches. A major breakthrough came in 1776, thanks to George Washington's close friend George Mason, who wrote the Virginia Declaration of Rights, a document appended to the new state constitution. It guaranteed all citizens equal entitlement "to the free exercise of religion, according to the dictates of conscience." This statement provided for official toleration of dissenter sects but did not halt taxes going exclusively to the established Anglican church.

Three years later, Thomas Jefferson, with the support of Baptists from the backcountry, took up the cause. He presented a bill calling for the complete separation of church and state. On and off for seven years, the assembly debated this legislation. In 1786 the will of those who argued for complete freedom of conscience, including the right to believe nothing and support no church, prevailed. In later years, Jefferson would be labeled an atheist for his part in guaranteeing religious freedom. But to him the Statute of Religious Freedom was just as important as the Declaration of Independence, and he had these sentiments engraved on his tombstone.

Disestablishment quickly followed in other states, particularly in the South where the An-

YELLOW FEVER IN PHILADELPHIA: PILLS AND POLITICS

Death stalked the streets of Philadelphia in 1793 in the form of a yellow fever epidemic. The first case appeared in August, and by the time the epidemic disappeared in November, yellow fever had killed ten percent of the city's population, while another forty-five percent had fled in terror. At the height of the epidemic, Philadelphia was a city under siege; with city services interrupted; communications impaired; the port closed; the economy in shambles; and people locked in their homes, afraid to venture beyond their doorsteps. To make matters worse, the city's leaders—unable to reach agreement on what caused the disease or what should be

done to combat it—attacked each other in endless debates. The result was that Philadelphia, America's premiere city, all but shut down.

Philadelphia's plight is not hard to explain, for yellow fever is a pulverizing, terrifying disease. Caused by a virus, the disease is spread by the female mosquito. Yellow fever's early symptoms are nearly identical to those of malaria: the victim feels flush and then develops chills, followed by a sizzling fever, accompanied by a severe headache or backache. The fever lasts for two or three days, and then the patient usually enjoys a remission.

Mild cases of yellow fever stop here. For the less fortunate, however, remission soon gives way to jaundice (hence "yellow" fever), and the victim starts to hallucinate. Massive internal hemorrhaging follows, and the patient starts vomiting huge quantities of black blood. Next, the victim goes into convulsions and then lapses into a coma. A lucky few emerge from the coma to escape death, but the vast majority die from internal bleeding.

If any American city seemed well equipped to handle a medical crisis, it was Philadelphia. It was the nation's leading center of medicine, home to the prestigious College of Physicians, America's first medical school (1765), and to America's most famous physician, Dr. Benjamin Rush, a founder of the Pennsylvania Society for Promoting the Abolition of Slavery and a signer of the Declaration of Independence. The City of Brotherly Love could also point with pride to Franklin's Pennsylvania Hospital (1752), the first hospital in America and a model facility for the worthy poor.

Yet for all of its luster, Philadelphia's medical community was no match for yellow fever. The basic problem was that doctors in 1793 could not agree on what caused the disease, how it spread, or how to treat it. Many physicians, including Dr. Rush, cited local factors. They blamed the disease on the decaying vegetation and rotting filth that littered Philadelphia's streets and docks, producing an atmospheric "miasma" that was carried by the wind, infecting anyone who breathed its noxious fumes. Rejecting local causes, other physicians argued that yellow fever was a contagious disease. It had been imported to Philadelphia, they insisted, by the two thousand French refugees who had fled the revolution (and a yellow fever epidemic!) in Haiti to seek political asylum in the United States.

Physicians in 1793 had no way of settling the dispute. Those who blamed the epidemic on dirty streets sounded just as believable as those who pointed an accusing finger at sickly foreigners. What made the controversy truly remarkable, however, was the extent to which it became embroiled in politics, for what began as a purely medical debate quickly degenerated into a raging political battle.

With very few exceptions, the doctors who insisted that yellow fever was contagious were Federalists, while the anticontagionists were almost all Jeffersonian Republicans. Taught by the French Revolution to be wary of free-thinking political ideas, Federalist doctors regarded yellow fever as just another unwanted French import. Ablaze with pro-French sympathies, anticontagionist Republicans saw the French refugees as honored friends who brought virtue rather than death. The source of the epidemic, they insisted, lay with the unvirtuous filth at their doorsteps.

Partisan leaders tried desperately to bend this medical debate to their political advantage. To Federalists, the doctrine of importation demanded that the United States protect itself from the French menace. Therefore, trade with French West Indian islands should be suspended; French refu-

gees who had gained entry to the United States should be quarantined; and future refugees excluded. Republicans, by contrast, denounced these demands as a federal plot to ruin profitable trade with the West Indies and to infect Americans with a new disease—hatred of all things French. Nor was their concern unfounded, for public hysteria was definitely building. At one point, amid persistent rumors that the French had poisoned the public drinking wells in preparation for a full-scale invasion, Philadelphians threatened violence against the innocent refugees.

At the height of the turmoil, politics even influenced how physicians treated the victims of yellow fever. At the beginning of the epidemic, doctors were pretty evenly divided, without regard to politics, into two schools. One prescribed stimulants—quinine bark, wine, and cold baths; while the other recommended bleeding—drawing off huge quantities of the patient's blood. (Dr. Rush had long been an advocate of the bleeding treatment. He recommended removing about four-fifths of the patient's blood supply, more than enough to kill all but the unkillable!)

Alexander Hamilton was personally responsible for converting this medical squabbling into a political issue. After managing to survive an attack of yellow fever, he published a ringing testimonial to the life-saving properties of the bark and wine cure. The treatment had been prescribed, he declared, by Dr. Edward Stevens of Philadelphia, a longtime friend of Hamilton. Dr. Stevens was the only physician in the City of

Brotherly Love who was a publicly confessed Federalist.

A few days after his testimonial appeared, Hamilton published a second article in which he ridiculed Dr. Rush's "new treatment." Hamilton's attack was immediately echoed by Federalist editors across the country, and in the wake of their articles, the public came to regard "bark" as the Federalist cure and "bleeding" as the Republican cure.

The controversy over yellow fever raged until the epidemic ended in the fall. Philadelphia's struggle against yellow fever was one of the many times that Americans would infuse their discussions of health problems with nonmedical concerns. In future epidemics, notions of class, race, individual virtue, and even gender would color public discussions of health, just as surely as politics enlivened the medical debate over yellow fever in Philadelphia in 1793 when the republic was young.

glican church (soon to become the Protestant Episcopal Church of America) had been dominant. In New England, only Rhode Islanders, following in the tradition of Roger Williams, had enjoyed full latitude in worship. With the Revolution, however, the cause of religious freedom started to move forward in other New England states. Lawmakers began letting citizens decide which local church to support with their taxes. This development represented a partial victory for individuals who preferred worshipping as Presbyterians or Baptists. These and other dissenters still had to accept Congregationalism as the established state church, continuing a pattern of official favoritism dating back to Puritan times. Complete separation of church and state, including the right not to support any church or to deny all religious creeds, did not occur in New England until the early nineteenth century.

Freedom of religion was one among a number of fundamental rights to make headway during the Revolutionary era. Several of the states adopted bills of rights similar to Virginia's, guaranteeing freedom of speech, assembly, and the press, as well as trials by jury. Other states started revising their legal codes, making them less harsh. There was a sense that criminals could become useful citizens, which after the 1790s resulted in prisons oriented toward rehabilitation. Fewer crimes would now carry the death penalty. In Virginia, Thomas Jefferson revised the state legal code. His work put an end to such feudal practices as primogeniture and entail (passing and committing property only to eldest sons through the generations). Running through all these acts was the republican assumption that citizens should have the opportunity to lead productive lives, uninhibited by laws violating personal conscience or denying the opportunity to acquire property.

The Propertyless Poor and the West

For many Revolutionary Americans, gaining property remained only a dream. At least twenty percent of the population lived at the poverty level or below, eking out precarious existences as unskilled laborers. Indeed, wealth was more unevenly distributed in 1800 than it had been in 1750. For the poor, then, there were many missed opportunities, unless one counts the striking increase in almshouses and other relief organizations, evidence in itself that poverty was spreading.

One missed opportunity related to the property of an estimated 500,000 loyalists, of whom one-fifth fled permanently to such places as England, Canada, the Bahamas, and various West Indian islands. State governments seized their land and other forms of property worth millions, which could have been redistributed to poorer citizens. Instead, the states quickly sold off confiscated property to the highest bidders as a source of wartime revenues. This practice favored men of wealth with investment capital and worked against any substantial redistribution of property.

Another opportunity lay with the enormous trans-Appalachian frontier awaiting development. Washington's Continental soldiers, who ranked among the poorest members of Revolutionary society, had been promised western lands for long-term service. When they mustered out in 1783, they received land warrant certificates. In order to survive, most veterans soon exchanged these certificates for the bare necessities of life. As a result, very few were ever able to begin anew in the Ohio country once military tracts had been set aside and surveyed.

Still, western lands remained a source of hope for economically downtrodden soldiers and civilians alike. In 1775 explorer Daniel Boone blazed the "Wilderness Road" to Kentucky. Others, like rugged Simon Kenton, scouted down the Ohio River from Pittsburgh. Where these frontiersmen went, thousands of land-hungry easterners soon followed. By 1790, Kentucky had a population of 74,000, and Tennessee held 36,000. These settlers paid dearly for their invasion of Indian lands. The Shawnees, Cherokees, and Chickasaws fought back in innumerable bloody clashes. The white death toll reached 1500. Besides losing ancient tribal lands, Indian deaths were also extensive.

White settlements in Kentucky and Tennessee created pressures to open territory north of the Ohio River. After ceding the Old Northwest to the United States in 1783, however, the British did not abandon their military

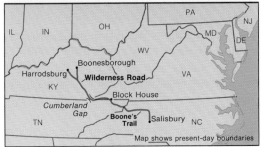

One of the most famous frontiersmen of his day, Daniel Boone blazed the Wilderness Road to Kentucky in 1775.

acres each with proceeds from the sale of the sixteenth section to be used to finance public education. The Northwest Ordinance of 1787 refined governmental arrangements, gave a bill of rights to prospective settlers, and proclaimed slavery forever banned north of the Ohio River— a prohibition Thomas Jefferson had wanted but failed to get included in the 1784 Ordinance. In establishing these ground rules, the land ordinances may have been the most significant legislation of the Confederation period.

The ordinances were not fully enlightened, since Congress, in its desperate search for revenue, viewed the Old Northwest as a source of long-term income. The smallest purchase individual settlers could make was 640 acres, priced at $1.00 per acre, and there were to be no purchases on credit. Families of modest means, let alone poor ones, could not meet such terms. Consequently, Congress dealt mainly

posts there. To maintain the lucrative fur trade with the Indians, they bolstered the Miamis, Shawnees, Delawares, and remnant groups of the Iroquois nations with a steady supply of firearms. Whites foolish enough to venture north of the Ohio River rarely survived, and the region remained closed to large numbers of westward-moving settlers well into the 1790s.

Despite the British and Indians, Congress was eager to open the Ohio country. With this goal in mind, the delegates approved three land ordinances. The 1784 Ordinance provided for territorial government and guaranteed settlers that they would not remain in permanent colonial status. When enough people (later specified at 60,000) had moved in, a constitution could be written, state boundaries set, and admission to the union as a full partner would follow. The 1785 Ordinance called for orderly surveying of the region. Townships of six miles square were to be laid out in grid-like fashion— each township to contain 36 sections of 640

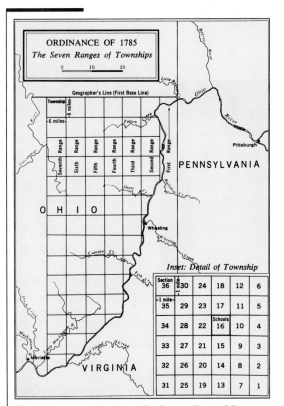

The first survey of national lands was directed by Thomas Hutchins, a native of New Jersey.

with well-to-do land speculators—and even extended them deeds to millions of acres on credit! All of these actions cut off the poorest citizens from the West, unless they were willing to squat on uninhabited land until driven off. And that is what many did to survive.

Women Appeal For Fundamental Liberties

Like the poor, women experienced little success in gaining basic rights for themselves in Revolutionary America. Among their advocates was Abigail Adams. In the spring of 1776, she wrote her husband John, then in Philadelphia arguing for independence, and admonished him to "remember the ladies, and be more generous and favorable, to them than your ancestors." "Remember all men would be tyrants if they could," she boldly concluded, and then she warned: "If particular care and attention is not paid to the ladies, we are determined to foment a rebellion, and will not hold ourselves bound by any laws in which we have no voice, or representation."

Abigail Adams

Joking with his wife, John Adams replied by asking whether American women were now in league with the British ministry. Should political independence come, he wrote, "we know better than to repeal our masculine system," claiming that men "have only the name of masters." But Adams's banter was just that. He knew very well by law and social practice, women were legally dependent on men, as the case of Nancy Shippen so vividly illustrated. Women gained no significant political rights during the Revolutionary period, except briefly in New Jersey.

Still, women contributed enthusiastically to the cause. Some, like "The Association" headed by Esther DeBerdt Reed of Philadelphia, called themselves "daughters of liberty" and met regularly to make clothing for the Continental army. Others, like Mary Hays of Lancaster County, Pennsylvania, were not as well off economically. Making her living as a domestic servant, she accompanied her husband to war. A tough-talking, daring person, Mary helped fire a cannon at the Battle of Monmouth in June 1778 and was almost hit by a flying British cannon ball when it passed between her legs. To this she replied: "It was lucky it did not pass a little higher, for in that case it might have carried away something else." Later generations, worried lest America's youth be corrupted by Mary's earthy manner, redefined her role as a water bearer to troops and turned her into the far more feminine "Molly Pitcher," a role that would have made Mary laugh. After the war she lived in penury as a charwoman, although she did obtain a small war pension just before her death.

What held the greatest potential for women, at least for those of middling and affluent status, was the ideology of republicanism, which directly influenced family life by giving broader scope to the role of mothers. Patriot leaders repeatedly asserted that the republic would founder without virtuous citizens. Hence it became a special trust for mothers to implant strong moral character and civic virtue in their children, especially their sons, so that they would uphold the obligations of disinterested citizenship for the good of the nation.

The concept of "republican motherhood" had potentially liberating qualities. It became the calling of republican mothers to manage the domestic sphere of family life, just as husbands were to take responsibility for the family's economic welfare. This duty reduced traditional male dominance in all family concerns. Elevating the role of women in family life may also have affected the nature of courtship by putting more emphasis upon affection than parental control in the making of marriages. However, the importance of this emerging tendency should not be exaggerated, as Nancy Shippen's experiences indicate.

If women were to be responsible for instilling proper values in future generations, they needed more and better schooling. During the

1780s and 1790s, some states started taxing citizens for the support of elementary education. Massachusetts broke new ground in 1789 by requiring its citizens to pay for female as well as male elementary education. In addition, these two decades saw the opening of many new private schools, such as the Young Ladies Academy of Philadelphia (founded in 1787). The academies offered more advanced education to daughters of well-to-do families in subjects traditionally reserved for males, such as mathematics, science, and history. This was a major breakthrough because popular lore held that too much exposure to "masculine" subjects would destroy the minds of young women. The female academies quickly demonstrated otherwise.

Still, the emphasis in expanding opportunities for middle- and upper-class women was upon service to the family and the republic, not on individual development and self-fulfillment. That is what bothered Judith Sargent Murray of Massachusetts, who wrote extensively about the need for comparable educational experiences for men and women. Murray argued that women could exist independently of men and lead satisfying lives, but she was very much ahead of her time. Most men in Revolutionary America resisted further change for women. As a Marylander insisted in 1790, pursuing the principle that "all mankind are born equal" was being "taken in too extensive a sense" concerning females, and would undermine "those charms which it is the peculiar lot of the fair sex to excel in." Thus while republican motherhood offered higher status, most men still thought of women as a form of property whose existence should be devoted to masculine welfare and happiness.

The Question of Race

Revolutionary ideology placed a premium on such terms as liberty and equality. Almost everyone recognized that it was inconsistent to use such terms and hold 500,000 Afro-Americans (one-fifth of the population in 1776) in perpetual bondage. It was this incongruity that Phillis Wheatley addressed in her poem to Lord Dartmouth. Lord Dunmore also pointed it out

As a republican mother, Mrs. Noah Smith nurtured and raised her children, especially the boys, to be selfless citizens of the republic.

In order for women to instill their children with proper republican values, a growing emphasis was placed on education for women. This painting depicts a ceremony at a Young Ladies' Seminary.

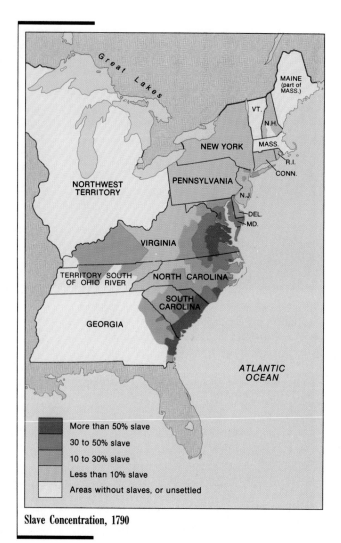

Slave Concentration, 1790

Legend:
- More than 50% slave
- 30 to 50% slave
- 10 to 30% slave
- Less than 10% slave
- Areas without slaves, or unsettled

These leaders did something else; they went into action. In 1774 Philadelphians, among them Benjamin Franklin, organized an abolition society. Pressure from this group and from anti-slavery Quakers resulted in Pennsylvania becoming the first state (1780) to declare human bondage illegal. (Actually, Vermont, an unorganized territory, did so in 1777 in a proposed state constitution.) Soon other states followed, and by 1790 slavery was a dying institution in the North.

Slaves themselves were also very active in challenging human bondage. Quok Walker of Massachusetts ran away from his master in April 1781 and sought refuge with a friendly neighbor. His master located Walker a few days later and accosted him with a whip. Beaten severely, Walker stood his ground. He sued for his freedom, pointing out that the new state constitution had proclaimed that "all men are born free and equal." The State Superior Court upheld Walker in 1783, which signaled the beginning of the end of slavery in Massachusetts.

Many Revolutionary leaders hoped that the drive to abolish slavery would also extend into the South. During the 1780s, there were some positive signs. Only South Carolina and Georgia were still involved in the international slave trade after 1783. States such as Maryland, Delaware, and Virginia passed laws making it easier for planters to free individual slaves. George Washington was one among a few wealthy planters who took advantage of Virginia's manumission law. He referred to slavery as a "misfortune" that sullied Revolutionary ideals, and in his will he provided for the emancipation of his slaves.

Washington, as in most other ways, was unusual. Far more typical was Thomas Jefferson. In his *Notes on the State of Virginia* (1785), he called slavery "a perpetual exercise" in "the most unremitting despotism." Fearing the worst should human bondage continue, he wrote: "I tremble for my country when I reflect that God is just." Such thinking led him to propose in Congress during 1784 that slavery never be allowed to spread north of the Ohio River. Jefferson, however, could not bring himself to free his own slaves. His chattels formed

dramatically in November 1775 when he offered emancipation to Virginia's slaves (see p. 146) in return for bearing arms against their rebellious masters.

For generations, colonial Americans had taken slavery for granted, as if it were part of the natural order of life. All of the talk during the 1760s and 1770s about impending political slavery undermined this unquestioned attitude, so much so that even slaveholding patriots like Patrick Henry asked whether the institution was not "repugnant to humanity . . . and destructive to liberty?" Some Revolutionary leaders decisively answered "yes."

the economic base of his way of life. Their labor gave him the time he needed for politics and, ironically, the time to work so persuasively on behalf of human liberty.

Support for his lifestyle was not the only reason Jefferson held back. He was representative of his times in believing blacks to be inherently inferior to whites. In the *Notes*, he made a number of comparisons of ability detrimental to blacks, such as in the category of reasoning power. To prove his point, Jefferson scoffed at the poems of Phillis Wheatley, which he described as "below the dignity of criticism." Jefferson thought, too, that the emancipation of all blacks would result in racial war and "the extermination of the one or the other race." Thus a man who labored so diligently for human rights in his own lifetime remained in bondage to the racist concepts of his era.

Negative racial attitudes were the norm in Revolutionary America, as the growing number of freed blacks learned again and again. Because of the general abolition and individual manumission movements, the free black population approached 60,000 by 1790 and 108,000 by 1800 (eleven percent of the total Afro-American population). Like the some 5000 black Continental army veterans, Phillis Wheatley, and George Washington's former slaves, these individuals repeatedly had to struggle to survive in a hostile society.

Not only did they survive, but they made worthy lives for themselves. Many free blacks moved to the large northern port towns, where slavery was no longer a threat. They lived in their own neighborhoods, and skilled workers opened shops to serve one another. Some, including both males and females, performed domestic service for well-to-do white families, but they did so as free persons. They also established their own churches and schools. By 1790, free blacks in Philadelphia and Baltimore had set up congregations that became the basis for the African Methodist Episcopal church. African Baptist and African Presbyterian denominations also developed, and these churches provided opportunities for formal education, since black children were rarely welcome in white schools.

Under the leadership of Absalom Jones (top), St. Thomas's African Episcopal Church was established, while Richard Allen founded the African Methodist Church (bottom).

Whether in the North or the South, the reality more often than not was open discrimination. As a group, free blacks responded by providing for one another and believing in a better day when Revolutionary ideals regarding human freedom and liberty had full meaning in their lives. In this sense, they still had much in common with their brethren in slavery.

SECOND NEW BEGINNING, NEW NATIONAL GOVERNMENT

In 1787 many Revolutionary leaders were more concerned about internal political stability than securing human rights. With all the talk of breaking up the Confederation, with Shays's Rebellion not yet completely quelled, and with the states arguing endlessly about almost everything, political leaders believed that matters of government should take primacy, or the republican experiment might be forever lost. Certainly the nationalists felt this way, and they were pushing hard for a new constitutional settlement.

In September 1786, representatives from five states met briefly in Annapolis, Maryland, to discuss pressing interstate commercial problems. Those present included strong nationalists like Alexander Hamilton, John Dickinson, and James Madison. Since so few states were represented, the delegates abandoned their agenda in favor of an urgent plea asking all the states to send delegates to a special constitutional convention "for the . . . sole purpose of . . . digesting a plan supplying such defects as exist" in the Articles of Confederation.

This time the states responded, largely because of the specter of civil turmoil associated with Shays's Rebellion. Twelve states—Rhode Island refused to participate—named seventy-four delegates, fifty-five of whom would attend the Constitutional Convention in Philadelphia. As the Continental Congress instructed the delegates in February 1787, their purpose was to revise the Articles of Confederation, making them "adequate to the exigencies . . . of the union." Some nationalists, however, had other ideas. They wanted a whole new plan of national government. Their ideas would dominate the proceedings from beginning to end, and their determination produced the Constitution of 1787.

The Framers of the Constitution

The men who gathered in Philadelphia were successful lawyers, planters, and merchants of education, wealth, and wide-ranging accomplishments, not ordinary citizens. They represented particular states, but most of them thought in national terms, based on experiences like serving in the Continental Congress and the Continental army. They feared for the future of the republic, unless someone did something—and soon—to strengthen the weak national government as a means of containing the selfishness of particular states. Having for years been frustrated by the Revolution's initial constitutional settlement, they seized the opportunity for change and made the most of it.

Among those present during the lengthy proceedings, which stretched from May 25 to September 17, was the revered George Washington, who served as the Convention's president. Other notable leaders included James Madison, Alexander Hamilton, Gouverneur and Robert Morris, and John Dickinson. Benjamin Franklin, at eighty-one, was the oldest delegate. He offered his finely tuned diplomatic tact in working out compromises that kept the proceedings moving forward.

Although the delegates disagreed vehemently, they never let differences over particular issues deflect them from their purpose—to find the constitutional means for an enduring republic. The Constitution was not perfect, as Benjamin Franklin stated on the last day of the Convention, but it did bring stability and energy to national government—and it has endured.

A Document Full of Compromises

If the nationalists had been doctrinaire, their deliberations would have collapsed. They held fast to their purpose—providing for a strong central government—but were flexible about ways to achieve that goal. Thus they were able to compromise on key issues. The first great point of difference dealt with the structure of government, and the eventual compromise required the abandonment of the Articles of Confederation.

Slight of build and reserved, James Madison of Virginia has been called the "father of the Constitution." A diligent student of history and politics, he worked out a proposed plan of national government, then arranged to have it presented by Governor Edmund Randolph, a

James Madison

more outgoing, forceful Virginian, at the outset of the Convention. This strategy worked, and the delegates gave the "Virginia Plan" their full attention. It outlined a three-tiered structure: with an executive branch and two houses of Congress.

Delegates from the less populous, smaller states objected. Under the Virginia Plan, representatives to the two chambers of Congress would be apportioned to the states according to population, whereas under the Articles, each state, regardless of population, had an equal voice in national government. For delegates like lawyer William Paterson of New Jersey, the latter practice ensured that the interests of the smaller states would not be sacrificed to those of the more populous, larger states. Thus Paterson countered with his "New Jersey Plan" on June 15. It retained equal voting in a unicameral national legislature, and it also vested far greater authority, including the powers of taxation and regulation of interstate and foreign commerce, in the central government. Paterson's plan was more consistent with the Convention's original charge—a point in its favor.

For a time it seemed that the delegates had reached an impasse, and some threatened to leave. By mid-July, however, they had hammered out an agreement. The "Great Compromise" proposed a three-tiered structure (Presidency, Senate, and House of Representatives) with a significant increase in specified powers to be distributed among these branches. Central to the compromise was proportional representation in the lower house, and two senators for each state, whether large or small, in the upper house. Although senators could vote separately, they could also operate in tandem to protect state interests.

Having passed the crucial structural hurdle, the Convention turned to other issues, not the least of which was slavery. Delegates from the Deep South wanted guarantees that would prevent any national tampering with their chattels. Some Northerners, however, including those who had supported abolition in their states, preferred constitutional restrictions on slavery.

For a while, it appeared that there would be no compromise. In the heat of debate, South Carolinian Pierce Butler blurted out that the North and the South were "as different as . . . Russia and Turkey." Later on, Gouverneur Morris suggested that it was impossible "to blend incompatible things," and he urged everyone to "take a friendly leave of each other" and go home. Finally, both sides made concessions for the sake of union. What they produced was the first major national compromise on slavery (to be followed by others, such as the Compromises of 1820 and 1850).

In the 1787 North-South compromise, the delegates left matters purposely vague. By mutual agreement, the Constitution neither endorsed nor condemned slavery. It did guarantee southerners that slaves would count as "three-fifths" of white persons for purposes of determining representation in the lower house. Even though this meant more Congressional seats for the South, direct taxes would also be based on population, including "three-fifths of all other persons." Thus the South would also pay more in taxes. The delegates also agreed that there would be no national ruling against importing slaves from abroad until 1808.

George Washington (on the podium) presides at the Constitutional Convention on May 25, 1787.

Although these clauses gave implicit recognition to slavery, it should be noted that the 1787 Land Ordinance, adopted by the Continental Congress in New York at the same time, forever barred slavery from the Northwest Territory. The timing has led some historians to conclude that inhibiting the spread of slavery was also part of the compromise, representing a major concession to northern interests.

The North-South Compromise kept the Convention and the republic together by temporarily mollifying most delegates on an extremely divisive issue. Still, chattel slavery was so inconsistent with the ideals of human liberty that the problem could not be sidestepped forever.

A third set of issues provoking compromise had to do with the office of president. Nobody seemed sure what range of authority the national executive should have, how long the term of office should be, or how the president should be elected. By early September, the delegates, fatigued by endless debates and extremely hot weather during three months of meetings, set-tled these questions quickly. The president could veto Congressional legislation; yet Congress could impeach the executive if presidential powers were abused. Four years seemed like a reasonable term-of-office, and reelection would be possible.

To make the president less susceptible to manipulation by public opinion, the delegates made the office indirectly elective through the device of the electoral college. Each state would have the same number of electors as representatives and senators. If the states so chose, citizens could vote for electors, who would assemble in turn as a national body to name the president. The candidate with a majority would become president. The person with the second highest total would become vice-president. Should the electors fail to decide (this happened in the elections of 1800 and 1824), the matter would be turned over to the House of Representatives, where each state would have one vote in choosing a president.

The subject of the presidency might have been more contentious had no person of

George Washington's universally acclaimed stature been on the scene. Washington was the one authentic popular hero and symbol of national unity to emerge from the Revolution, and the delegates were already thinking of him as the first president. Since he was so fully trusted as a firm apostle of republican principles who had disdained the mantle of a military dictator, defining the mode of election and powers of the national executive were not insurmountable tasks.

The Ratification Struggle

On September 17, 1787, thirty-nine delegates affixed their signatures to the proposed Constitution. Benjamin Franklin hoped that more of the delegates would sign, and he echoed the thoughts of those who did so by indicating that "there are several parts of this Constitution which I do not at present approve. . . . It therefore astonishes me, Sir," he stated, "to find this system approaching so near to perfection as it does." Pointing toward a seal with a carving of the sun on the president's chair, Franklin concluded: "At length I have the happiness to know that it is a rising and not a setting sun."

The delegates who signed the Constitution of 1787 knew there would be significant opposition because their plan cut so heavily into state authority. Before finishing their deliberations, they made the shrewd move of agreeing that only nine states needed to ratify the Constitution—through special state conventions rather than through state legislatures—to allow the new government to commence operations. The nationalists were not going to let one or two states destroy months of work—and what they viewed as the best last hope for a languishing republic.

In another astute move, the nationalists started referring to themselves as *Federalists,* and they disarmed their opponents by calling them *Antifederalists.* Actually, the Antifederalists were the real federalists; they wanted to continue the confederation of sovereign states. This confusion in terminology may have gotten some local Federalist candidates elected to state ratifying conventions, thus helping to secure victory for the Constitution.

The nationalists were also very effective in explaining the Convention's work. The essence of their argumentation appeared in *The Federalist Papers,* a series of eighty-five remarkably cogent newspaper essays written by James Madison, Alexander Hamilton, and John Jay on behalf of ratification in New York. Under the name "Publius," they discussed various aspects of the Constitution and tried to demonstrate how the document would ensure political stability and provide enlightened legislation.

The new government, they asserted, had been designed to protect the rights of all citizens. No one self-serving faction ("a landed interest, a manufacturing interest, a mercantile interest, a monied interest"), whether representing a minority or majority of citizens, could take power completely and deprive others of their liberties and property. The Constitution would check and balance these interest groups because basic powers (executive, legislative, judicial) would be divided among the various branches of government. The system was truly federal, they also argued, because some authority remained with the states as a further protection against power-hungry, self-serving factional interest groups.

Beyond these advantages, the Constitution embodied the principle of representative republicanism, as Madison explained in his famous *Federalist No. 10* essay. Large election districts for the House of Representatives would make it more difficult for particular interest groups to manipulate elections and send "unworthy candidates" to Congress. Citizens of true merit, of "the most diffusive and established characters," could rise up, emerge triumphant, and then enact laws beneficial to everyone.

The nationalists admitted that they were overturning the first con-

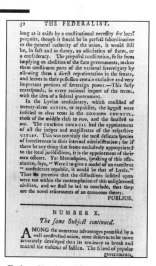

Federalist No. 10, written by James Madison

1775 Boone crosses the Appalachian barrier and lays out Wilderness Road to Kentucky

1776 Congress encourages the colonies to establish republican governments (May), and authorizes committee to draft Articles of Confederation (June); Virginia adopts Mason's Declaration of Rights (June)

1777 Congress approves revised draft of Articles of Confederation and calls for ratification (November)

1779 Murray composes an essay, "On the Equality of Sexes," later published in 1790

1780 Pennsylvania becomes first state to declare chattel slavery illegal

1781 Articles of Confederation finally ratified by all states (March); Walker flees his master (April), resulting in court decision ending slavery in Massachusetts

1782 Rhode Island refuses to approve Impost Plan of 1781, precipitating a crisis with the Continental army

1783 Washington urges moderation at Newburgh and ends threat of a military coup (March)

1785 First edition of Jefferson's *Notes on the State of Virginia* published (May); Jay begins negotiations with Spain's foreign minister Gardoqui (August)

1786 Virginia adopts Jefferson's Statute of Religious Freedom (January); Annapolis Convention calls for a national constitutional convention (September)

1787 Shays's Rebellion reaches climax with Springfield and Petersham engagements (January–February); delegates meet in Philadelphia to draft a new constitution (May–September); Congress adopts Northwest Land Ordinance, forever barring slavery north of the Ohio River (July)

1788 Hamilton, Madison, and Jay write the *Federalist Papers*, and key states ratify the Constitution

1789 New national government convenes in New York City (April)

stitutional settlement. The emphasis would now be on a national government whose acts would be "the supreme law of the land." Federal leaders would be drawn from citizens of learning and wealth, many like those nationalists who had never fully trusted the people. From their perspective, the people had failed the test of public virtue. They had shown more interest in their individual welfare, for instance, than in making material or personal sacrifices to support the Continental war effort. They had formed into troublesome factions like the Maryland land speculators and the Massachusetts rebel followers of Daniel Shays, all to the detriment of the republic's political stability.

The nationalists, now expecting to function as the new nation's political stewards, did not repudiate the concept of popular sovereignty. Rather, they enshrined it in such notions as representative republicanism. The people were to have a political voice, in the abstract at least, and they were to remain the constituent authority of American government. Their stewards, supposedly detached from selfish concerns, could now more easily check narrow interests inhibiting stable national development.

The Antifederalists understood, and they viewed this new settlement with alarm. One writer, "Centinel," stated that the Constitution would support "in practice a *permanent* ARISTOCRACY." Another, calling himself "Philadelphiensis," saw in it "a conspiracy against the liberties of his country, concerted by a few *tyrants*, whose views are to lord it over the rest of their fellow citizens." These arguments, reminiscent of those orginally stirring up Revolutionary fervor in the 1760s and 1770s, did not deflect nationalist momentum.

There would be close calls in some ratifying conventions, as in Massachusetts, New York, and Virginia (see Table 6.1). The nationalists were always ready to counter Antifederalist objections. When there were complaints about the absence of a national bill of rights, they promised that the first Congress would prepare one. When there were cries for a second convention, they argued that the new government should first be given a chance. If it did not work, they would support another convention. The new plan of government did work, as George Washington's presidential administration demonstrated—though not quite in the fashion the nationalists had planned.

Table 6.1

Ratification of the Constitution of 1787

State	Date	Vote Yes	Vote No
Delaware	December 8, 1787	30	0
Pennsylvania	December 12, 1787	46	23
New Jersey	December 18, 1787	38	0
Georgia	January 2, 1788	26	0
Connecticut	January 9, 1788	128	40
Massachusetts	February 16, 1788	187	168
Maryland	April 26, 1788	63	11
South Carolina	May 23, 1788	149	73
New Hampshire	June 21, 1788	57	47
Virginia	June 25, 1788	89	79
New York	July 26, 1788	30	27
North Carolina*	November 21, 1789	194	77
Rhode Island**	May 29, 1790	34	32

*On July 21, 1788, the first ratifying convention in North Carolina voted 184 to 84 not to consider approval of the Constitution. The vote recorded in the chart is that of the second convention.

**Rhode Island not only refused to participate in the Philadelphia Constitutional Convention but also decided not to call a state ratifying convention. Only after the United States Senate threatened to sever commercial ties with Rhode Island did the state government agreee to a convention that reluctantly approved the Constitution.

CONCLUSION

In 1776 those radical Revolutionaries who believed in a virtuous citizenry had sought to expand popular participation in government. By and large they succeeded. This first constitutional settlement proved to be unsatisfactory, however, largely because the weak central government under the Articles of Confederation lacked the authority to support even the minimal needs of the new nation. Blaming the states and the people, the nationalist leaders produced a second constitutional settlement in 1787 by drafting a plan for a powerful central government. It was to be above the people and the states, strong enough to establish and preserve national unity and stability.

The new national government began meeting in 1789. But no sooner had Madison's "diffusive and established" gentlemen started to govern than they fell to fighting among themselves over a host of controversial issues. To gain allies, they turned back to the people. Against the wishes of many nationalists, some leaders started to organize political parties and urged the citizenry to support their candidates as a means of stopping the opposition. By the mid-1790s, the people were becoming a true constituent voice in national politics. Concepts of deference and stewardship were now in retreat; common citizens at last emerged as the backbone of what would one day be a system of political democracy.

The years between 1776 and 1789 thus secured the republic and republican ideals. Yet notions regarding each person's right to enjoy life, liberty, happiness, and property in an equalitarian society fell far short of full implementation. Women remained second-class citizens, and the shackles of slavery still manacled most Afro-Americans. Even with the opening of the trans-Appalachian West, which came at the expense of thousands of Native Americans, poorer citizens found it difficult to gain access to farmland on which to enjoy personal prosperity. Although future generations would fight, even to the point of civil war, over the full realization of republican ideals, there was no escaping their presence. In this sense, the years before 1789 had witnessed a revolution in human expectations.

REVIEW SUMMARY

Independence did not guarantee long-term national survival. Fearful of a strong, centralized government, Americans framed the Articles of Confederation, which created a decentralized government. During the Confederation period the nation was plagued by internal and external problems.

> Continental army almost revolted
> postwar depression caused widespread suffering
> European nations regarded the young republic with contempt
> Shays's Rebellion raised the specter of renewed revolution
> women, blacks, and poor persons made little headway in gaining basic rights

As a result of these problems, nationalists wrote the Constitution of 1787, which they hoped would save the republic.

SUGGESTIONS FOR FURTHER READING

OVERVIEWS AND SURVEYS

Richard R. Beeman, Stephen Botein, and Edward C. Carter, II, eds., *Beyond Confederation: Origins of the Constitution and American National Identity* (1987); Edward Countryman, *The American Revolution* (1985); Staughton Lynd, *Class Conflict, Slavery, and the United States Constitution* (1967); Merrill Jensen, *The New Nation, 1781–1789* (1950); Forrest McDonald, *E Pluribus Unum: The Formation of the American Republic, 1776–1790* (1965); Gordon S. Wood, *The Creation of the American Republic, 1776–1787* (1969); and Alfred F. Young, ed., *The American Revolution: Explorations in the History of American Radicalism* (1976).

ESTABLISHING NEW REPUBLICAN GOVERNMENTS

Willi Paul Adams, *The First American Constitutions* (1980); Christopher Collier, *Roger Sherman's Connecticut: Yankee Politics and the Revolution* (1971); Edward Countryman, *A People in Revolution: Political Society in New York, 1760–1790* (1981); Robert J. Dinkin, *Voting in Revolutionary America* (1982); Jackson Turner Main, *The Upper House in Revolutionary America, 1763–1788* (1967), and *Political Parties Before the Constitution* (1973); James Kirby Martin, *Men in Rebellion: Higher Governmental Leaders and the Coming of the Revolution* (1973); Jerome J. Nadelhaft, *The Disorders of War: The Revolution in South Carolina* (1981); Stephen E. Patterson, *Political Parties in Revolutionary Massachusetts* (1973); and J. R. Pole, *Political Representation in England and the Origins of the American Republic* (1966).

CRISES OF THE CONFEDERATION

Roger J. Champagne, *Alexander McDougall* (1976); Jacob E. Cooke, *Alexander Hamilton* (1982); Lawrence Delbert Cress, *Citizens in Arms: The Army and the Military to the War of 1812* (1982); Thomas Doerflinger, *A Vigorous Spirit of Enterprise: Merchants and Economic Development in Revolutionary Philadelphia* (1986); E. James Ferguson, *The Power of the Purse: American Public Finance, 1776–1790* (1961); Dale W. Forsythe, *Taxation and Political Change in the Young Nation, 1781–1833* (1977); Van Beck Hall, *Politics Without Parties: Massachusetts, 1780–1791* (1972); Ronald Hoffman and Peter J. Albert, eds., *Sovereign States in an Age of Uncertainty* (1981); Richard H. Kohn, *Eagle and Sword: The Federalists and Military Establishment in America, 1783–1802* (1975); Peter S. Onuf, *The Origins of the Federal Republic: Jurisdictional Controversies in the United States, 1775–1787* (1983), and *Statehood and Union: The Northwest Ordinance* (1987); Irwin H. Polishook, *Rhode Island and the Union, 1774–1795* (1969); Norman K. Risjord, *Chesapeake Politics, 1781–1801* (1978); Charles R. Ritcheson, *Aftermath of Revolution: British Policy, 1783–1805* (1969); Malcolm Rohrbough, *The Trans-Appalachian Frontier, 1775–1850* (1979); C. Edward Skeen, *John Armstrong, Jr., 1758–1843* (1981); Reginald C. Stuart, *War and American Thought: To the Monroe Doctrine* (1982); David Szatmary, *Shays' Rebellion* (1980); Robert J. Taylor, *Western Massachusetts in the Revolution* (1954); Clarence L. Ver Steeg, *Robert Morris* (1954); and Alfred F. Young, *The Democratic-Republicans of New York, 1763–1797* (1967).

HUMAN RIGHTS AND SOCIAL CHANGE

John K. Alexander, *Render Them Submissive: Responses to Poverty in Philadelphia, 1760–1800* (1980); Ira Berlin and Ronald Hoffman, eds., *Slavery and Freedom in the Age of the American Revolution* (1983); Fawn Brodie, *Thomas Jefferson* (1974); Wallace Brown, *The Good Americans* (1969); Joy Day Buel and Richard Buel, Jr., *The Way of Duty: A Woman and Her Family in Revolutionary America* (1984); Robert McCluer Calhoon, *The Loyalists in Revolutionary America, 1760–1781* (1973); David Brion Davis, *The Problem of Slavery in the Age of Revolution, 1770–1823* (1975); Linda Grant DePauw and Conover Hunt, *"Remember the Ladies": Women in America, 1750–1815* (1976); Eric Foner, *Tom Paine and Revolutionary America* (1976); Philip S. Foner, *Labor and the American Revolution* (1977); Adele Hast, *Loyalism in Revolutionary Virginia* (1982); J. Franklin Jameson, *The American Revolution Considered as a Social Movement* (1925); Linda Kerber, *Women of the Republic: Intellect and Ideology in Revolutionary America* (1980); Elizabeth P. McCaughey, *From Loyalist to Founding Father: William Samuel Johnson* (1980); Duncan J. Macleod, *Slavery, Race, and the American Revolution* (1974); Jackson Turner Main, *The Social Structure of Revolutionary America* (1965); Gary B. Nash, *Forging Freedom: Philadelphia's Black Community, 1720–1840* (1988); William H. Nelson, *The American Tory* (1961); Mary Beth Norton, *The British-Americans: The Loyalist Exiles in England, 1774–1789* (1972), and *Liberty's Daughters: The Revolutionary Experience of American Women, 1750–1800* (1980); Merrill D. Peterson, *Thomas Jefferson and the New Nation* (1970); Theda Perdue, *Slavery and the Evolution of Cherokee Society, 1540–1866* (1979); Janie Potter, *The Liberty We Seek: Loyalist Ideology in New York and Massachusetts* (1983); Benjamin Quarles, *The Negro in the American Revolution* (1961); Donald L. Robinson, *Slavery in the Structure of American Politics, 1765–1820* (1971); Marylynn Salmon, *Women and the Law of Property in Early America* (1986); Catherine M. Scholten, *Childbearing in American Society, 1650–1850* (1985); Gregory A. Stiverson, *Poverty in a Land of Plenty: Tenancy in Eighteenth-Century Maryland* (1978); James W. St. G. Walker, *The Black Loyalists: The Search for a Promised Land in Nova Scotia and Sierra Leone, 1783–1870* (1976); John Todd White, "The Truth About Molly Pitcher," in James Kirby Martin and Karen R. Stubaus, eds., *The American Revolution: Whose Revolution?*, rev. ed. (1981), pp. 99–105; Lynne Withey, *Dearest Friend: A Life of Abigail Adams* (1980); Arthur Zilversmit, *The First Emancipation: The Abolition of Slavery in the North* (1967); and Judith Walzer Leavitt and Ronald L. Numbers, *Sickness and Health in America: Readings in the History of Medicine and Public Health* (1978).

SECOND NEW BEGINNING, NEW NATIONAL GOVERNMENT

Charles A. Beard, *An Economic Interpretation of the Constitution of the United States* (1913); George A. Billias, *Elbridge Gerry* (1976); Stephen R. Boyd, *The Politics of Opposition: Anti-federalists and the Acceptance of the Constitution* (1979); Christopher Collier and James L. Collier, *Decision in Philadelphia* (1987); Linda Grant DePauw, *The Eleventh Pillar: New York State and the Federal Constitution* (1966); Michael Kammen, *A Machine That Would Go By Itself: The Constitution in American Culture* (1986); Jackson Turner Main, *The Anti-Federalists: Critics of the Constitution, 1781–1788* (1961); Frederick W. Marks, III, *Independence on Trial: Foreign Affairs and the Constitution* (1973); Forrest McDonald, *We the People: The Economic Origins of the Constitution* (1958), and *Novus Ordo Seclorum: The Intellectual Origins of the Constitution* (1985); Clinton Rossiter, *1787: The Grand Convention* (1973); Robert A. Rutland, *The Ordeal of the Constitution: The Antifederalists and the Ratification Struggle of 1787–88* (1966); and Garry Wills, *Explaining America: The Federalist* (1981).

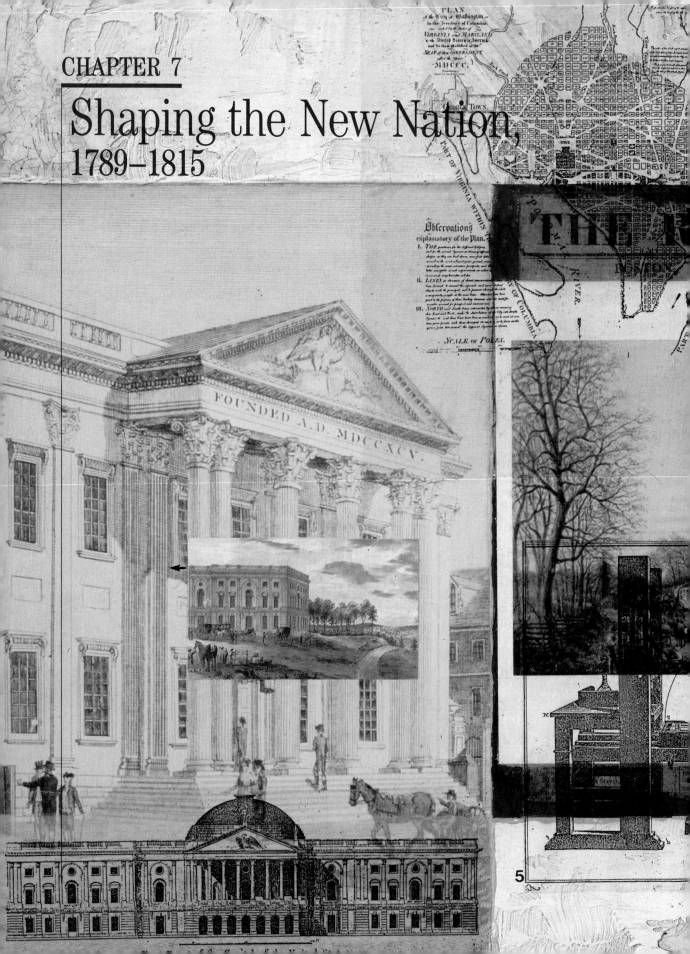

CHAPTER 7

Shaping the New Nation,
1789–1815

FOUNDED A.D. MDCCXCV.

5

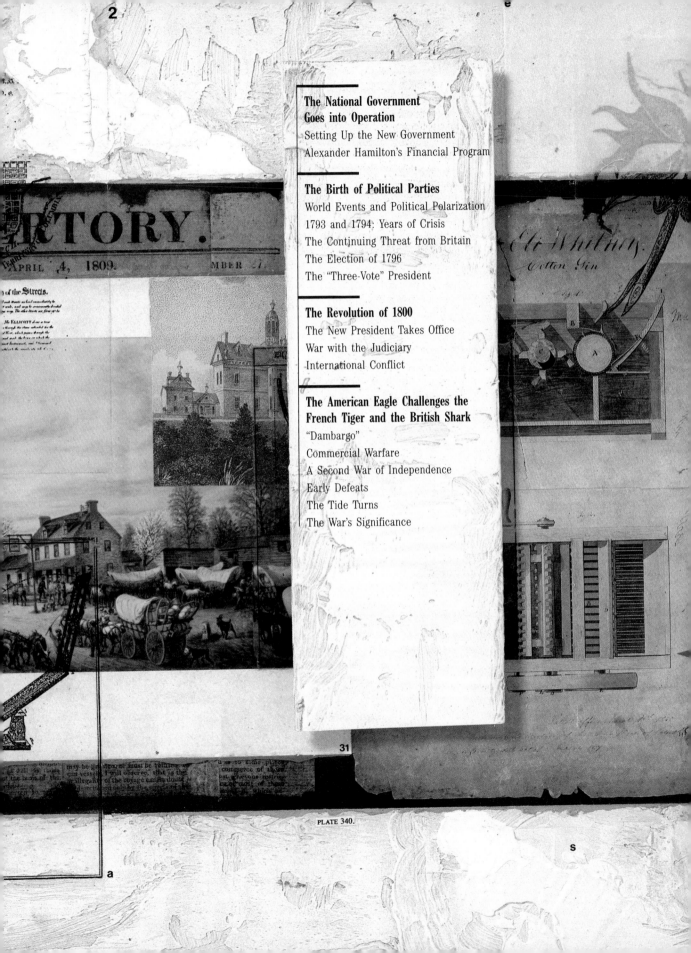

During the last years of the eighteenth century, defeat, disease, and death seemed the lot of Ohio's Indians. In 1794, an armed American expedition led by Major General "Mad" Anthony Wayne crushed an Indian army at the Battle of Fallen Timbers, near present-day Toledo, Ohio, and forced the Indians to give up 25,000 square miles of land north of the Ohio River.

Forty-five thousand white settlers poured into Ohio over the next six years, bringing epidemics of influenza, measles, and smallpox in their wake. Indian villages were ravaged and hundreds of Indians died. Whites encroached on Indian hunting grounds, killing the wild game that provided the Indians with food. Deprived of their ancestral homelands, faced with serious food shortages, and suffering a severe loss of population, the fabric of Indian life began to unwind. Tribal unity eroded, villages broke apart, and violent disputes became widespread. To escape their problems, many Indians turned to alcohol and the numbing relief it provided.

One of the Indians who suffered from the breakdown of Indian society was a Shawnee youth named Lalawethika. Several months before he was born in 1774, Lalawethika's father, a Shawnee chief, was killed by white frontiersmen who had crossed onto Indian land in violation of a treaty. Shortly thereafter, his mother, a Creek, deserted her children. As a young man, Lalawethika became a dissolute, drunken idler. In 1805, however, during a frightening epidemic, he underwent a powerful religious experience that altered the course of his life. Overcome with a sense of his own wickedness, Lalawethika fell into a trance during which he met the Indian Master of Life. On the basis of this mystical experience, he decided that it was his duty "to reclaim the Indians from bad habits" and convince them to return to their ancestral way of life. He adopted the name Tenskwatawa and called upon his tribesmen to reject all aspects of white civilization (especially drinking), cease tribal warfare, and unify in order to resist white encroachment on their land. White Americans called him the Shawnee Prophet.

Tenskwatawa's religious teachings quickly attracted converts across the Old Northwest.

When Indiana's territorial governor, William Henry Harrison, heard of Tenskwatawa's growing influence, he tried to undermine the Prophet's support. He challenged the Prophet to "cause the sun to stand still, the moon to change its course." Harrison's challenge backfired when the Prophet successfully predicted a total eclipse of the sun. Indians from as far away as Saskatchewan soon flocked to the new religion.

In an effort to halt the advance of white settlers, Tenskwatawa and his older brother, the renowned warrior Tecumseh, attempted to organize a great Indian confederation including tribes from as far north as Wisconsin, as far west as Arkansas, and as far south as Florida. Alarmed by the brothers' success at organizing an Indian confederation, Harrison decided that the time had come to end the Indian threat. In November, 1811, while Tecumseh was traveling across the South trying to rally support from southern Indian tribes, Harrison succeeded in drawing Tenskwatawa into a battle along the Tippecanoe River in Indiana. While the battle raged, Tenskwatawa called upon the Master of Life to protect his warriors and cause the white soldiers to flee. The Prophet's magic failed. Harrison's thousand troops forced the Indians to retreat and then burned their village, forever destroying the Prophet's prestige. Tenskwatawa's defeat at the Battle of Tip-

Tenskwatawa and his brother, Tecumseh, attempted to forge an Indian confederation to resist further encroachment by white settlers.

The Picture Exhibition.

UNION:
OR, THE TWELVE
Federal Pillars.

In early 1790, two states, North Carolina and Rhode Island, continued to support the Articles of Confederation, and residents of Vermont threatened to join Canada.

pecanoe marked the beginning of the end of effective Indian resistance in the Old Northwest, and it shattered his dream of a great Indian confederation.

For Tenskwatawa and the Indians of the Ohio Valley, the opening years of the nineteenth century were a period of rapid depopulation, land loss, and demoralization. For the young United States, in contrast, these were years of rapid economic and territorial expansion, growing political maturity, and deepening national identity. It was during this dramatic period that the United States established a strong and vigorous national government.

THE NATIONAL GOVERNMENT GOES INTO OPERATION

The United States was the first modern nation to achieve independence through a successful revolution against colonial rule. It set an example that was followed in the nineteenth century by the Spanish colonies of Central and South America and in the twentieth century by the African and Asian colonies of other European empires. In one crucial respect, the United States differs from other nations that have broken free from colonial rule. While most former colonies remained underdeveloped economically and unstable politically, the United States succeeded in establishing a growing economy, a stable political system, and a strong sense of national unity. The achievement of a viable nationhood did not occur without struggle. The first two decades under the Constitution of 1787 were years of conflict, violence, and even threats of disunion and civil war. During the 1790s and early 1800s, the young republic confronted many of the same problems that face the newly independent nations of Africa and Asia today. Like other new nations born in anticolonial revolutions, the United States faced the challenge of building a sound economy, preserving national independence, and creating a stable, representative political system which provided a legitimate place for opposition.

In 1790, it was not at all obvious that the United States would be able to create a strong national government, a prosperous economy, or a stable two-party political system. For one thing, it was still unclear whether the new government would be able to consolidate support among the American people. Only about five percent of adult males in the United States had voted to ratify the new Constitution and two states, North Carolina and Rhode Island, continued to support the Articles of Confederation. Citizens of Vermont threatened to join Canada.

The new nation also faced severe economic and foreign policy problems. A huge debt remained from the Revolutionary War and paper money issued during the war was virtually worthless. Along with these pressing economic problems were foreign threats to the new nation's independence. In violation of the peace treaty of 1783 ending the Revolutionary War, Britain continued to occupy forts in the Old Northwest. Spain refused to recognize the new nation's southern and western boundaries.

Finally, it was still uncertain in 1790 what place there would be in the new nation for a formal political opposition. At the beginning of the decade, there was little acceptance of the idea of a legitimate political opposition organized into a formal party. During the 1790s, many groups, ranging from Western frontiersmen to New England Federalists, threatened to secede from the Union. Commitment to civil liberties and freedom of the press was limited. There were recurrent attempts, during the 1790s, to prevent duly elected presidents from taking office as well as to pass laws giving the party in power the right to persecute political opponents and curb newspaper criticism.

One question haunted the new nation in 1790: could it successfully create a stable, democratic society?

Setting Up the New Government

The Constitution of 1787 created a general framework of government. But ratification of the new Constitution only marked the beginning of the process of nation building. Serious problems still remained; the most immediate problem facing the new nation was the lack of the machinery of government. No examples of colonies which had won their independence existed. America was on uncharted ground.

The new government consisted of nothing more than seventy-five post offices, a large debt, a small number of unpaid clerks, and an army consisting of just 672 soldiers. There was no federal court system, no navy, and no system for collecting taxes. Conditions were so bad that George Washington, the new president, had to borrow $3000 just to move to the new capital, which was then located in New York City.

It fell to Congress to take the initial steps toward putting the new national government

This depiction of an early courthouse in 1804 was done by Lewis Miller.

into operation. While the Senate devoted three weeks to debating how the president should be addressed (one committee proposed "His Highness the President of the United States and Protector of the Rights of the Same"), the House of Representatives, under the leadership of James Madison considered far more pressing problems. To raise revenue, Madison skillfully convinced Congress to pass an import tariff. To encourage American shipping, Congress imposed discriminatory duties upon foreign ships entering American ports. To provide a structure for the executive branch of government, Congress created the departments of state, treasury, and war. Congress also organized a federal judicial system consisting of a Supreme Court with six justices, a district court in each state, and federal courts of appeal, each comprised of two Supreme Court justices sitting with a district judge.

Finally, in order to strengthen popular support for the new government, Congress adopted and proposed to the states a Bill of Rights. Congress considered 210 amendments to the Constitution proposed by state ratifying conventions, including proposals to restrict the federal government's power to tax, to prohibit a standing army in peacetime, and to curtail the power of the federal courts. The House approved seventeen of these, of which the Senate agreed to twelve. The states subsequently ratified ten amendments. These first ten amendments guaranteed individual liberties, including freedom of speech and religion, the right to peaceably assemble, and the right to petition government. They also ensured that the national government could not infringe on such rights as freedom of the press and trial by jury. In an effort to reassure Antifederalists that the powers of the new government were limited, the tenth amendment "reserved to the States respectively, or to the people" all powers not specified in the Constitution.

While Congress was fleshing out the new government, George Washington organized the executive branch. He fully realized the importance of the task before him. "I walk on untrodden ground," he observed. "There is scarcely any part of my conduct that may not hereafter be drawn into precedent." Instead of governing through his vice-president, he decided to conduct presidential business through a cabinet system modeled somewhat after Britain's. Washington consulted his cabinet officers and listened to them carefully, but he made the final decisions, just as he had done while serving as commander in chief.

He asked Henry Knox, an old military comrade, to be secretary of war. As postmaster general, he named Samuel Osgood, who carried out his tasks in a single room with the help of two clerks. He tapped fellow Virginian Edmund Randolph as attorney general. As secretary of state, he named another Virginian, Thomas Jefferson. And he named his former aide-de-camp, Alexander Hamilton, to head the Treasury Department.

Alexander Hamilton's Financial Program

Early in 1790, leadership shifted from the legislative branch of government to the executive branch, away from James Madison to Alexander Hamilton, the first secretary of the treasury. Hamilton brought to his post a clearly defined political philosophy. The fiscal ineptitude of the government under the Articles of Confederation convinced him that the nation's future stability depended upon an alliance between citizens of wealth and influence and the federal government. No society could succeed, he maintained, "which did not unite the interest and credit of rich individuals with those of the state."

Along with his conviction that only an economic and political elite could foster stability, Hamilton expressed deep doubt in the capacity of the common people to govern themselves. "All communities," he maintained, "divide themselves into the few and the many. The first are rich and well-born, the other the mass of the people. . . . The people are turbulent and changing; they seldom judge or determine right."

To keep the masses in check, Hamilton also favored a strong national government. Born in the British West Indies of an illegitimate union in 1757, Hamilton never developed the intense loyalty to a state that was common among many Americans of the time. Instead, he was a staunch nationalist who wanted the United States to become a powerful, unified nation. During the Constitutional Convention, Hamilton had proposed to extinguish the states or reduce them to a smaller scale, and he remained an advocate of a powerful national government. His ideal was the Britain of George III: "I have no scruple in declaring . . . that the British government is the best in the world, and I doubt much whether anything short of it will do in America."

Ten days after Hamilton took office, Congress asked him to report on ways to solve the nation's financial problems. He immediately realized that he had an opportunity to create a financial program that would embody his political philosophy. His fiscal proposals sought to strengthen the federal government at the expense of the states and "make it in the immediate interest of the moneyed men to cooperate with government in its support."

The paramount problem facing Hamilton was the huge Revolutionary War debt. In 1789, the national debt stood at over $50 million. The federal treasury was so poor that the United States was unable to pay the interest on French and Dutch loans or to pay the ransoms of American sailors held by North African pirates or even to pay its diplomatic staff abroad.

Hamilton argued that it was vital that the nation fund these debts in order to establish the credit of the federal government. "States, like individuals, who observe their engagements are respected and trusted," he wrote. As a step toward restoring the nation's credit, Hamilton proposed in his *Report on the Public Credit* (1790) that the government fund the national debt by borrowing money and issuing new bonds, and assume all state debts from the Revolutionary War.

Controversy immediately erupted. States like Georgia, Maryland, and North Carolina, which had already paid off their war debts, opposed assumption of state debts. Many Southern states objected that the proposal benefited Northern interests at the expense of the South, since four-fifths of the debt was owed to Northern investors. James Madison begged his colleagues to vote down the proposal, arguing that it would award unconscionably large profits to speculators who had bought the bonds of soldiers, widows, and orphans for as little as ten or fifteen cents on the dollar.

For six months, Congress remained deadlocked. As the debate raged, sectional animosities between the North and South mounted. Several New England Congressmen threatened secession. Senator Richard Henry Lee of Virginia responded by declaring that he preferred disunion "to the rule of a fixed insolent northern majority." The nation's future seemed in jeopardy. Then, in early June 1790, fearful for the nation's survival, Alexander Hamilton, James Madison, and Thomas Jefferson met and achieved a compromise that secured passage of Hamilton's plan. In exchange for Southern votes in Congress, Hamilton promised his support for locating the future national capital on the banks of the Potomac River.

Hamilton's debt program successfully established the credit of the United States at home and abroad. By funding the debt, he succeeded in creating an alliance between men of wealth and property, who had purchased much of the Revolutionary War debt, and the national government. His financial scheme put more than $50 million into the hands of men who, he believed, were best qualified to use it for constructive national purposes. Repayment of the war debt also firmly established the United States as a good credit risk. European investment capital started pouring into the new nation in large amounts.

As a second step toward strengthening the national government and cementing the link between the government and the business community, Hamilton proposed the creation of a national bank, modeled after the Bank of England, to issue currency, collect taxes, hold government funds, regulate the nation's financial system, and make loans to the government and private borrowers.

In 1791, Congress passed a bill creating a national bank for a term of twenty years. Thomas Jefferson urged Washington to veto it on the grounds that Hamilton was abusing the Constitution. The Constitution, he argued, did not specifically give Congress the power to create a bank. Trying to stay above the controversy, Washington asked Hamilton for a formal reply. Hamilton responded by developing the doctrine of implied powers. This doctrine stated that the government could do anything "necessary and proper" to carry out its Constitutional functions (in this case its fiscal duties).

The first Bank of the United States was remarkably successful. It helped regulate the currency of private banks. It provided a reserve of capital on which the government and private investors drew, and it helped attract foreign investment to the credit-short new nation. In 1811, however, the jealousy of private commercial banks, chartered by individual states, convinced Congress to allow the bank to expire.

The final plank in Hamilton's plan to strengthen the nation's economic base was a proposal that the national government aid the nation's infant industries. In his *Report on Manufactures* (1791), Hamilton argued that the nation's longterm interests "will be advanced, rather than injured, by the due encouragement of manufactures." Through high tariffs designed to protect American industry from foreign competition, government bounties and subsidies, and internal improvements of transportation, he hoped to break Britain's manufacturing hold on America.

Jefferson and Madison attacked Hamilton's proposal. Hamilton's industrial vision of America's future directly challenged Jefferson's ideal of a nation of freehold farmers, tilling the fields, communing with nature, and maintaining personal freedom by virtue of land ownership. Manufacturing, Jefferson believed, should be left to Europe, since it bred cities, cesspools of human corruption. Like slaves, factory workers would be manipulated by their masters, who not only would deny them satisfying lives but also make it impossible for them to think and act as independent citizens.

Unfortunately for Hamilton, whose farsighted ideas foreshadowed the nation's future, Jefferson's vision was more in line with the republic's pre-industrial, agrarian character. Although Congress provided limited assistance to a number of depressed industries, notably fisheries, it rejected most of Hamilton's proposals. Clearly, America's founding fathers were divided on their notion of how best to build a strong nation.

THE BIRTH OF POLITICAL PARTIES

When George Washington assembled his first cabinet, there were no national political parties in the United States. In selecting cabinet members, he paid no attention to partisan labels and simply chose the individuals he believed were best qualified to run the new nation. In the new Congress, there were no party divisions. In all the states except Pennsylvania, politics were not waged between parties, but, rather, between impermanent factions built around leading families, political managers, ethnic groups, or such interest groups as debtors and creditors.

When Washington retired from the presidency in 1797, the nature of the American political system had radically changed. The first president complained bitterly about "the baneful effects of the Spirit of Party," which, he

George Washington's first cabinet consisted of Secretary of War Henry Knox, Secretary of the Treasury Alexander Hamilton, Secretary of State Thomas Jefferson, and Attorney General Edmund Randolph.

feared, had come to dominate American politics. Local and state factions had given way to two competing national parties, known as the Federalists and Jeffersonian Republicans. They nominated political candidates, managed electoral campaigns, and generated distinctive outlooks or ideologies. By 1796, the United States had produced the first modern party system in world history. These political parties breathed dynamic new life into the concept of popular sovereignty by making the people the ultimate arbiters in American political life.

The process of party formation did not take place smoothly. The framers of the Constitution had not prepared their plan of government with political parties in mind. They hoped that the "better sort of citizens," rising above popular self-interest, would be able to debate key issues and reach harmonious consensus regarding how best to legislate for the nation's future. Thomas Jefferson reflected widespread sentiments when he declared in 1789, "If I could not go to heaven but with a party, I would not go there at all."

Despite a belief that parties were evil and that they posed a threat to enlightened government, leaders in Washington's first administration created the world's first modern political parties. Divisons first emerged in 1791 over Hamilton's proposals to forge a bond between merchant, shipping, and financial interests and a strong federal government committed to creating an industrial economy. Hamilton's opponents struck back. On the grounds that Hamilton's fiscal plans threatened his vision of the republic, James Madison organized congressional opposition and retained the poet Philip Freneau to edit a newspaper, the *National Gazette,* as an instrument to warn the populace about Hamilton's designs. Madison and his ally Thomas Jefferson saw in Hamilton's program an effort to establish the kind of corrupt patronage society that existed in Britain, with a huge public debt, a standing army, high taxes, and government-subsidized monopolies. Hamilton's aim, declared Jefferson, was to assimilate "the American government to the form and spirit of the British monarchy."

Hamilton responded in kind, by creating another national party—the Federalists. He secured John Fenno to publish the *Gazette of the United States,* and, claiming that his opponents wanted to return the national government to its weak condition under the Articles of Confederation, he organized a loyal following. He built a national political faction linking supporters in George Washington's cabinet, sympathetic members of Congress, and state and local leaders. By 1794, his faction had evolved into the first national political party in history capable of nominating candidates, coordinating votes in Congress, staging public meetings, organizing petition campaigns, and disseminating propaganda.

World Events and Political Polarization

World events intensified partisan divisions. On July 14, 1789, 20,000 French men and women stormed the Bastille, a hated royal fortress, marking the beginning of the French Revolu-

Twenty thousand angry Parisians stormed the royal prison, the Bastille, on July 14, 1789, marking the beginning of the French Revolution.

tion. For three years France experimented with a constitutional monarchy. Then in 1792, the revolution took a fateful turn. In August, Austrian and Prussian troops invaded France to put an end to the revolution. French revolutionaries responded by officially deposing King Louis XVI and placing him on trial. He was found guilty, and in January, 1793, beheaded. France declared itself a republic and launched a reign of terror against counterrevolutionary elements in the population. Three hundred thousand suspects were arrested; 17,000 were executed. A general war erupted in Europe pitting revolutionary France against a coalition of European monarchies, led by Britain. With two brief interruptions, this war lasted twenty-three years.

Many Americans reacted enthusiastically to the overthrow of the French king and the creation of a French republic. The French people, they believed, had joined America in a historic struggle against royal absolutism and aristocratic privilege. Thomas Jefferson expressed the attitude of staunch defenders of the French Revolution when he said that he was willing to see "half the earth desolated" if this were necessary to secure human liberty and freedom.

More cautious gentlemen expressed horror at the cataclysm sweeping France. The French Revolution, they feared, was not merely a rebellion against royal authority, but a mass assault against property and Christianity. Conservatives urged President Washington to support England in its war against France. "Gallomen" asked him to support France.

Washington believed that involvement in the European war would weaken the new nation before it had firmly established its independence. He proposed to keep the country "free from political connections with every other country, to see them independent of all, and under the influence of none." The president, however, faced a problem. During the War for American Independence, the United States had signed an alliance with France (see p. 158). Washington asked his cabinet whether the alliance was still in force. Jefferson argued the alliance was still valid. Hamilton said that it was not, because the alliance had been made with the deposed government of King Louis XVI. Washington followed Hamilton's advice that the

United States could disregard the alliance, and issued a proclamation of neutrality on April 22, 1793. Jefferson subsequently resigned his post as secretary of state.

1793 and 1794: Years of Crisis

During 1793 and 1794 a series of explosive new controversies further divided the followers of Hamilton and Jefferson. Along with the growing opposition to Hamilton's fiscal program, Washington's administration confronted a French effort to entangle America in its war with England, armed rebellion in western Pennsylvania, Indian uprisings, and the threat of war with Britain. These controversies intensified party spirit and in Congress promoted an increase in voting along party lines.

Controversy first arose early in 1793 over the actions of "Citizen" Charles Genêt. In April, Genêt, minister of the French Republic, disembarked at Charleston, South Carolina. As he pompously proceeded up the coast, passing out military commissions and privateering letters authorizing Americans to attack British commercial vessels, crowds gathered and cheered. Washington was not impressed. He did not think Genêt had any right to involve American citizens in European disputes. Not only did he refuse to meet Genêt, he issued a neutrality proclamation stating that the conduct of the United States would be "friendly and impartial toward the belligerent powers."

Genêt quickly faded from the scene (in fact he became the first foreigner to be granted political asylum because his political faction was overturned by one yet more radical). His brief flurry intensified party feeling. In fact, some citizens, in states from Vermont to South Carolina, started organizing Democratic-Republican clubs to celebrate the triumphs of the French Revolution. Hamilton suspected that these societies really existed to stir up grass-roots opposition to the Washington administration. Jefferson hotly denied these accusations.

Political polarization was further intensified by the outbreak of popular protests in western Pennsylvania known as the Whiskey Rebellion against Hamilton's financial program. To help fund the nation's war debt, Hamilton convinced Congress in 1791 to pass a whiskey excise tax. Frontier farmers objected to the tax on whiskey as unfair. On the frontier, the only practical way to sell surplus corn was to distill it into whiskey, and frontier farmers regarded a tax on whiskey the same way American colonists had regarded Britain's stamp tax.

By 1794, western Pennsylvanians had had enough. Like the Shaysites of 1786, they rose up in defense of their property and the fundamental right to earn a decent living unfettered by oppressive taxes. Tax collectors were met with muskets and tarred and feathered. Frontiersmen organized a march on Pittsburgh, and 7000 westerners participated in this demonstration of unity. With that, the Whiskey "rebels" dispersed, having shown that they could stop collection of the tax.

Before the march on Pittsburgh took place, Washington ordered Pennsylvania and surrounding states to send 15,000 militiamen to Harrisburg, where, dressed in full military regalia, he greeted them. They were ordered to disperse the rebels, but by the time the army crossed the mountains, the uprising was over. The army did round up a few leaders, but the president later pardoned the two men convicted of treason. The new government had proved to the nation that it would enforce laws enacted by Congress.

Thomas Jefferson viewed the Whiskey Rebellion from quite a different perspective. He saw the fiendish hand of Hamilton in what he called a rebellion that "could never be found." Hamilton had "pronounced and proclaimed and armed against" the people for the sheer pleasure of suppressing liberties. And further, Jefferson claimed, Hamilton had done so because westerners no longer supported Washington's administration. He had used the army to stifle legitimate opposition to unfair government policies.

President Washington reviewed some of his troops at Fort Cumberland, Maryland, before they were sent to disperse the Whiskey rebels.

The Continuing Threat from Britain

The Whiskey Rebellion coincided with the eruption of a crisis in America's relations with Britain. For a decade, a major source of tension between the two nations had been Britain's refusal to evacuate forts in the old Northwest, which it had agreed to do in the treaty ending the Revolution. Control of those forts impeded white settlement of the Great Lakes region and allowed the British to monopolize the fur trade. Frontiersmen believed that British officials at those posts sold firearms to Indians and incited uprisings against white settlers. American resentment grew when the British governor-general of Canada told a delegation of western Indians that Britain would soon join them in a war against the United States.

War appeared imminent when British warships stopped 300 American ships carrying food supplies to France and seized their cargoes. The British also took seamen suspected of desertion and pressed them into the British navy.

Washington acted decisively to end the sources of friction. First, he moved to end the Indian threat. In 1790 and again in 1791 he sent armies to clear the Ohio country of Indians. Both forces met bloody defeat at the hands of Little Turtle's Miami Confederacy. Thoroughly frustrated, Washington called upon Anthony Wayne, an outstanding Revolutionary War general, to organize yet another army. Wayne took his time, trained his soldiers well, and overwhelmed the resisting Indians at the Battle of Fallen Timbers in northwestern Ohio on August 20, 1794. During the summer of 1795, Wayne met with representatives of the Miami Confederacy and persuaded them to cede much of the present state of Ohio in return for cash, presents, and a promise that the federal government would treat Indian nations fairly in land dealings.

The president's next move was to send Chief Justice John Jay to London to negotiate a treaty with the British government. The United States' strongest negotiating tool was a threat to join an alliance of European trading nations to resist British trade restrictions. Alexander

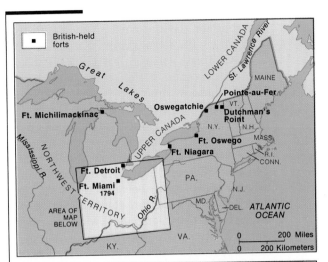

British Posts and Indian Battles

Hamilton undercut the American position by secretly informing the British minister that Washington would not join the alliance.

Having lost his best bargaining chip, Jay had to secure the best agreement he could. Britain promised to evacuate its forts on American soil and pay damages for ships it had seized. The British further agreed not to harass American shipping, provided the ships did not carry contraband to Britain's enemies. The treaty also permitted the United States to trade with India and carry on restricted trade with the British West Indies. In exchange, Britain received permission to continue the fur trade. The treaty said nothing at all about searching

American ships for British deserters or compensation for slaves carried off by the British army during the Revolution.

Jay's Treaty solidified party lines. Publication of the terms of the treaty unleashed a storm of protest from the emerging Jeffersonian Republicans. Republican newspapers and pamphlets denounced the treaty as craven submission to British imperial power and as a sop to wealthy commercial, shipping, and trading interests. Southerners were particularly vocal in their disapproval, because the treaty required them to repay pre-Revolutionary debts owed to British merchants, while Northern shipping interests collected damages for ships and cargoes that had been seized. Republicans in Philadelphia carried an effigy of the Chief Justice through the streets, guillotined it, and blew it up with gunpowder. In the same city, a crowd broke windows at the British embassy in Philadelphia, and in New York a mob pelted Alexander Hamilton with stones. Washington declared that public unrest was greater "than it has been at any period since the Revolution."

Angry Republicans denounced John Jay's treaty as inadequate, and hanged his effigy in Charleston, South Carolina.

Washington called a special session of the Senate to study the treaty. By exactly the two-thirds majority required by the Constitution, the Federalist-controlled Senate approved the treaty, with the exception of a section restricting trade with the British West Indies.

Undecided whether to sign the treaty, Washington learned that the British had captured French diplomatic messages that indicated that Secretary of State John Randolph had divulged state secrets to the French. At a cabinet meeting, Washington forced Randolph to read the dispatches and provide an explanation of his conduct. The embarrassed Randolph denied any guilt, but resigned. Washington, fearful that the French government was trying to transform the United States into a French satellite, signed the treaty.

Washington never anticipated the wave of outrage that greeted his decision. Republicans accused him of forming an Anglo-American alliance, and they made his last years in office miserable by attacking him for conducting himself like a "tyrant." Benjamin Franklin's grandson called the president a dictator: "If ever a nation was debauched by a man, the American Nation has been debauched by Washington. . . . If ever a nation has been deceived by a man, the American Nation has been deceived by Washington." It was even suggested that he should be impeached because he had overdrawn his $25,000 salary. Privately, Washington complained that he was being compared to the Roman emperor Nero and to a "common pickpocket."

Republicans sought to kill the treaty in the House of Representatives by refusing to appropriate the funds necessary to carry out the treaty's terms unless the president submitted all documents relating to the treaty negotiations. Washington refused to comply with the House's request for information, thereby establishing the principle of executive privilege. This precedent gave the chief executive authority to withhold information from Congress on grounds of national security. In the end, fear that rejection of the Jay Treaty would result in disunion or war convinced the House to approve the needed appropriations.

Washington's popularity returned within a few months when he announced a treaty had been negotiated with Spain opening up the Mississippi River to American trade. Spain, fearing joint British and American action against her American colonies, recognized the Mississippi River as the new nation's western boundary and the 31st parallel (the northern border of Florida) as America's southern boundary. The Treaty of San Lorenzo also granted Americans the right to navigate the Mississippi River as well as the right to export goods, duty free, through New Orleans.

President Washington was now in a position to retire gracefully. He had avoided war, crushed the Indians, and pushed the British out of western forts. He had established trade with the West Indies and Asia and opened the Northwest Territories to settlement. He had even reached agreement with North African pirates to release American prisoners and leave American ships alone.

In a farewell address, published in a Philadelphia newspaper in September, 1796, Washington announced his retirement and offered his countrymen "the disinterested warnings of a parting friend." Disturbed by what he saw as the growth of partisan divisions within the country, he warned against "the baneful effects of the spirit of party" and called on Americans to cherish the Union. Referring to France's barefaced attempts to interfere with American domestic politics, he warned against "the insidious wiles of foreign influence." He urged the country not to align itself with either France or Britain, fearing that this would involve the country in needless wars. Declaring the "primary interests" of America and Europe to be fundamentally different, he argued that "it is our true policy to steer clear of permanent alliance with any portion of the foreign world."

The Election of 1796

Washington's announcement of 1796 that he would not seek a third term set the stage for one of the most critical presidential elections in American history. The contest was the first in which voters chose between two established, competing political parties. It was also the first test of whether the country could transfer power through a contested election.

The Federalists chose John Adams, the first vice-president, as their presidential candidate, and the Republicans selected Thomas Jefferson. In an effort to attract Southern support, the Federalists selected Thomas Pinckney of South Carolina as Adams's running mate. The Republicans, hoping to attract votes in New York and New England, named Aaron Burr of New York as their vice-presidential nominee.

John Adams built up the country's armed forces and headed off war with France.

Both parties turned directly to the people for support. Republicans printed thousands of posters and handbills that portrayed their candidate as "a firm Republican" while they depicted his opponent as "the champion of rank, titles, and hereditary distinctions." Federalists countered by organizing meetings and rallies at which they condemned Jefferson as the leader of a "French faction" intent on undermining religion and morality.

For the first time in American history, common people became directly involved in a presidential election—a development illustrated by an incident that took place in New York City in early November, 1795. A prominent Federalist alderman ordered two Irish boatmen to take him across the East River from Brooklyn to Manhattan. When the boatmen refused, the alderman had the "impudent rascals" arrested, locked in a local jail, and tried without a jury and without being allowed to testify in their own behalf. They were found guilty of "insulting a magistrate" and sentenced to two months at hard labor.

Jeffersonians quickly seized upon this incident as a way of generating support among the laboring classes in the election of 1796. New York Republicans demanded that the state legislature remove the alderman from office for oppressing the "innocent poor." When the legislature refused to act, a Republican attorney named William Keteltas attacked the Federalist-controlled legislature for "the most flagrant abuse of rights." The legislature found the Republican attorney guilty of contempt and jailed him for more than a month when he refused to apologize. To protest the legislature's actions, the Republican party assembled the largest crowd ever gathered in New York City— 2000 people. When Keteltas was finally released from prison, another large Republican crowd that included many poor craftsmen drove him through the city's streets in a carriage decorated with a French flag and an American flag, a picture of a man being whipped, and a banner stating ironically: "What you rascal, insult your superiors." Such events dramatized the differences between the two parties and actively involved large numbers of common people in the election.

In the popular voting, Federalists drew much of their support from New England; from commercial, shipping, manufacturing, and banking interests; from Congregational and Episcopalian clergy; and from professionals and farmers who produced for markets. Republicans attracted votes from the South; from smaller planters; from backcountry Baptists, Methodists, and Roman Catholics; and from small merchants, tradesmen, craftsmen, and subsistence farmers.

The vote in the electoral college was complicated by a split within the Federalist party. Alexander Hamilton disliked Adams and wanted a president he could control. He developed a complicated scheme to elect Thomas Pinckney, the Federalist candidate for vice-president. According to Hamilton's plan, Southern electors would drop Adams's name from their ballots, while still voting for Pinckney. Thus Pinckney would receive more votes than Adams and be elected president. When New Englanders learned of this plan, they dropped Pinckney from their ballots, ensuring that Adams would win the election. When the final votes were tallied, Adams received seventy-one votes, only three more than Jefferson. Under the electoral system then in use, Jefferson was elected vice-president.

The "Three-Vote" President

Sixty-one years old at the time of his election, Adams was already famous as one of the nation's founders. As a delegate to the Continental Congress, he had been a member of the committee assigned to write the Declaration of Independence; as a diplomat, he took a leading role in the negotiations ending the Revolutionary War.

As president, Adams successfully guided the country through serious troubles at home and abroad. Faced by dissension in his own party and the bitter opposition of the Republicans, he built up the nation's army and navy and avoided outright war with France. In order to preserve peace, however, he had to defy his own party, which destroyed his political career.

The collapse of America's alliance with France shaped Adams's four years in office. Since 1795, the French, resentful of what they considered America's pro-British foreign policy, had launched an aggressive campaign against American shipping, particularly in the West Indies, capturing hundreds of vessels carrying the United States flag. They also refused to recognize the American diplomats sent to them. Meanwhile, Britain, in spite of the Jay Treaty, continued to search American vessels, seize cargoes, and impress American sailors.

Adams, like Washington, was grimly determined to keep the United States neutral. One of his first acts as president was to call a special session of Congress to consider ways to keep peace. Declaring that the United States would not permit itself to be "humiliated under a colonial spirit of fear and a sense of inferiority," he called upon Congress to arm American merchant ships, purchase new naval vessels, erect harbor defenses, expand the artillery and cavalry, and give the president authority to recruit a larger army. To pay for the increased defense spending, Adams called on Congress to enact a land tax, a tax on houses (popularly known as the "window tax"), a stamp tax, and a tax on slaves. Finally, the president told Congress that the best way for the country to protect its neutral rights was to threaten to join with other neutral states in a defensive naval alliance. By a

When President Adams sent a mission to France in 1797 to negotiate an end to French seizures of American merchant ships, agents of the French government demanded a bribe. In this 1798 cartoon, a five-headed Frenchman demands money from the American negotiators.

single vote, a bitterly divided House of Representatives authorized the president to arm American merchant ships, but it postponed consideration of other defense measures.

At the same time that Adams asked Congress to build up the nation's defenses, he announced the appointment of a commission to attempt negotiations with France. Three agents of the French government, referred to simply as X, Y, and Z, demanded a bribe of $250,000 as well as an American loan of several million dollars to France before the American envoys could see the Foreign Minister Talleyrand. Insulted, the Americans broke off the negotiations and returned home. This incident, known as the XYZ affair, provoked the popular slogan: "Millions for defense, but not one cent for tribute."

Congress moved swiftly to prepare the country for war. While Adams had called for only 3000 additional troops to form a standing army and authority to recruit 20,000 troops for a reserve army, the Federalist majority in Congress voted to raise the standing army to 20,000 and the reserve army to 30,000. Adams selected George Washington as commanding general of the United States army, and, at Washington's insistence, appointed Alexander Hamilton second in command. From 1798 to 1800, the United States waged an undeclared naval war with France.

The Federalist-controlled Congress also sought to suppress political opposition and stamp out sympathy for revolutionary France by enacting the Alien and Sedition laws in 1798. These laws gave the government the power to

BIRTH CONTROL IN THE EARLY REPUBLIC

One of the most hotly debated philosophical questions in late eighteenth-century America and Europe was whether human beings were capable of improvement. Famous writers of the Enlightenment argued that people were naturally good and that all of society's problems could be solved by the application of reason. English philospher, William Godwin, described the future in particularly glowing terms. He wrote that in the future "there would no longer be a handful of rich and a multitude of poor . . . There will be no war, no crime, no administration of justice, as it is called, and no government. Beside this, there will be no disease, anguish, melancholy, or resentment."

On the other side of the debate on human perfectability was a young Anglican clergyman, Thomas Robert Malthus. Parson Malthus argued that human perfection was unattainable because human population growth would inevitably ex-

ceed the growth of the world's food supply. He asserted—on the basis of figures collected by Benjamin Franklin—that population tends to increase geometrically (1, 2, 4, 8) while subsistence only grows arithmetically (1, 2, 3, 4). Ultimately population would be held in check by famine, war, and disease.

Malthus's gloomy vision of the future failed to come true because large numbers of people began to limit the number of children through the use of birth control. Nowhere was the limitation of births more striking than in the United States. In 1800, the American birthrate was higher than the birthrate in any European nation. The typical American woman bore an average of seven children. She had her first child around the age of twenty-three and bore children at two-year intervals until her early forties. Had the American birthrate remained at this level, the nation's population would have reached 2 billion by 1990.

Late in the eighteenth century, however, Americans began to have fewer children. Between 1800 and 1900 the birthrate fell forty percent, most sharply among the middle and upper-middle class. Where the typical American mother bore seven children in 1800, the average number of children she bore had fallen to three-and-one-half in 1900. Instead of giving birth to her last child at the age of forty or later, by 1900 the typical American woman bore her last child at the age of thirty-three. The decline of the birthrate is such an important historical breakthrough that it has its own name: the demographic transition.

The sharp decline in birthrates is a phenomenon easier to describe than to explain. The drop in fertility was not because contraceptive devices were suddenly discovered. The basic birth control techniques used before the Civil War—coitus interruptus (withdrawal), douching, and condoms—were known since ancient times. Ancient Egyptian papyri and the Old Testament describe cervical caps and spermicides, while ancient Greek physicians were aware of the contraceptive effects of douching. Rather, contraception was simply used haphazardly and ineffectively. Nor was the decline in birthrates a result of urbanization. Although fertility fell earliest and most rapidly in the urban Northeast, the decline in fertility occurred in *all* parts of the country, in rural as well as urban areas and in the South and West as well as the Northeast.

What accounted for the declining birthrate? In part, the reduction in fertility reflected the growing realization among parents that in an increasingly commercial and industrial society children were no longer economic assets who could be productively employed in household industries or bound out as apprentices or servants. Instead, children required significant investment in the form of education to prepare them for respectable careers and marriages. The emergence of a self-conscious middle class concerned about social mobility and maintaining an acceptable standard of living also encouraged new limits on family size.

The shrinking size of families also reflected a growing desire among women to assert control over their lives. Much of the impetus behind birth control came from women who were weary of an unending cycle of pregnancy, birth, nursing, and new pregnancy. A letter written by a sister of Harriet Beecher Stowe suggests the desperation felt by many women who were singlehandedly responsible for bearing and rearing a family's children. "Harriet," her sister observed, "has one baby put out for the winter, the other at home, and number three will be here the middle of January. Poor thing, she bears up wonderfully well . . . She says she shall not have any more children, she knows for certain for a while."

How did Americans limit births? Periodic abstinence—or what is now known as the rhythm method—was the most widely advocated method of birth control. Unfortunately, knowledge about women's ovulation cycle, menstruation, and conception was largely inaccurate and most advice writers suggested that the "safe period" was the ten days halfway between menstrual periods—which is in fact the time when a woman is most likely to conceive.

Other principal methods of contraception included coitus interruptus—withdrawal prior to ejaculation—and douching the vagina after intercourse. Less common was the insertion of a sponge soaked in a spermicidal fluid into the vagina. None of these methods, however, were especially effective in preventing conception. Other popular forms of birth control were heavily influenced by superstition. These included ingestion of teas concocted out of fruitless plants; having a woman engage in violent movements immediately after intercourse; and having intercourse on an inclined plane in order to prevent the sperm from reaching the egg or to prevent the egg from leaving the ovary.

One discovery in 1839, the vulcanization of rubber, did advance the mass production of an inexpensive and effective birth control device for males: the condom. But during the nineteenth century condoms were mainly used for protection against venereal disease, not for birth control.

Given the ineffectuality of other methods of contraception, it is not surprising to learn that abortion was a major method of population control. By 1860, according to one estimate, twenty percent of pregnancies were terminated by abortion, compared to thirty percent today. Popular practices used to induce abortion included taking hot baths, jumping off tables, doing heavy exercises, drinking nauseating concoctions, and poking sharp instruments into the uterus.

Why was abortion so widespread during the Victorian age? In part, it reflected the general ignorance of the reproductive process. It was not until 1827 that the existence of the human egg was established. Before that time it was believed by many scientists that the human sperm constituted a miniature person which grew into a baby in the mother's womb. Thus there was no notion of a moment of conception when egg and sperm unite.

Furthermore, for most of the nineteenth century it was difficult to determine whether a woman was pregnant or simply suffering menstrual irregularity. A mother only knew she was pregnant for sure when she could feel the child stir within her. This occurs around the fourth or fifth month of pregnancy and in most jurisdictions abortions prior to this time were not considered crimes. It would not be until the late nineteenth century that most jurisdictions in the United States declared abortions to be criminal offenses.

The decline in birthrates carried far-reaching consequences for family life. First of all, motherhood and the strain of pregnancy ended earlier for women. They had an increasing number of years when young children were no longer their primary responsibility. It also meant that parents were free to invest more time, energy, and financial resources in each individual child.

imprison or deport any foreigner believed to be dangerous to the United States; lengthened the period necessary before immigrants could receive citizenship; and made it a crime to attack the government with "false, scandalous, or malicious" statements or writings. Adams, unhappy with the "spirit of falsehood and malignity" that threatened to undermine loyalty to the government, signed the measures.

During the winter and spring of 1798–99, the United States seemed perilously close to civil war. Partisan Federalist prosecutors and judges used the Sedition Act to secure indictments against twenty-five persons, most of them Republican editors and printers. Ten were eventually convicted; one was a congressman from Vermont. The most notorious attempt to use the law to suppress dissent took place in July 1798, when Luther Baldwin, the pilot of a garbage scow, was arrested in a Newark, New Jersey, tavern for criminal sedition. While cannons roared through Newark's streets to celebrate a presidential visit to the city, Baldwin was overheard saying "that he did not care if they fired through [the president's] arse." For his drunken remark, Baldwin was arrested, locked up for two months, and fined.

Republicans accused the Federalists of conspiring to subvert fundamental liberties. The state legislatures of Kentucky and Virginia adopted resolutions written by Thomas Jefferson and James Madison denouncing the Alien and Sedition Acts as a severe infringement on freedom of expression. The Virginia and Kentucky Resolutions advanced the idea that the states have the right to declare federal laws null and void, and they helped to establish the theory of "states' rights."

With the Union in danger, violence erupted. In the spring of 1799, resentment against the window tax provoked German settlers in eastern Pennsylvania to defy federal tax collectors. President Adams called out federal troops to suppress the so-called Fries Rebellion. The leader of the rebellion, an auctioneer named John Fries, was captured, convicted of treason, and sentenced to be hanged. Adams followed Washington's example in the Whiskey Rebellion and pardoned Fries, but Republicans feared

that the Federalists were prepared to use the nation's army to suppress dissent.

Adams moved decisively to solve the chief source of dissension within the country: America's tangled relations with France. Early in 1799, in a last-ditch effort to avert full-scale war, he attempted to reestablish diplomatic relations. When Federalist senators refused to go along with the plan, Adams threatened to resign and leave the presidency in the hands of Vice-President Jefferson. In 1800, after seven months of wearisome negotiations, the American negotiators worked out an agreement known as the Convention of 1800. The agreement freed the United States from the alliance with France; in exchange, America forgave $20 million in damages caused by the illegal seizure of American merchant ships during the 1790s.

Adams kept the peace, but at the cost of a second term as president. Federalists who had wanted war with France reacted furiously. Hamilton vowed to destroy Adams: "If we must have an enemy at the head of Government, let it be one whom we can oppose, and for whom we are not responsible."

THE REVOLUTION OF 1800

In 1800, the young republic faced another critical test. Could national leadership pass peacefully from one political party to another? Once again, the nation had a choice between John Adams and Thomas Jefferson. This election was more than a contest between two men; it was also the first real party contest for control of the national government. Partisan feelings ran deep. Federalists feared that Jefferson would reverse all the accomplishments of the preceding twelve years. A Republican president, they thought would overthrow the Constitution by returning power to the states, dismantle the army and navy, and overturn Hamilton's financial system.

The Republicans charged that the Federalists, by creating a large standing army, imposing heavy taxes, and using federal troops and the federal courts to suppress dissent, were conspiring to subvert personal liberties. They worried that the Federalists' ultimate goal was to centralize power in the national government and involve the United States in the European war on the side of Britain.

The contest was one of the most vicious in American history. Jefferson's Federalist opponents called him an "atheist in religion, and a fanatic in politics." They claimed he was a drunkard, an enemy of religion, and the father of numerous mulatto children. Timothy Dwight, the president of Yale, predicted that a Jefferson administration would see "our wives and daughters the victims of legal prostitution; soberly dishonored; speciously polluted." The *Connecticut Courant* warned that "there is scarcely a possibility that we shall escape a Civil War. Murder, robbery, rape, adultery, and incest will be openly taught and practiced."

Jefferson's supporters responded by charging that President Adams was a warmonger, a spendthrift, and a monarchist who longed to reunite Britain with its former colonies. Republicans even claimed that the president had sent General Thomas Pinckney to England to procure four mistresses, two for himself and two for Adams. Adams's response: "I do declare if this be true, General Pinckney has kept them all for himself and cheated me out of my two."

The election was extremely close. The Federalists won all of New England's electoral votes, while the Republicans dominated the South and West. The final outcome hinged on the results in New York. Rural New York supported the Federalists, and Republican fortunes therefore depended on the voting in New York City. There, Jefferson's running mate, Aaron Burr, created the most successful political machine the country had yet seen. Burr organized rallies, established ward committees, and promoted loyal supporters for public office. Burr's efforts paid off; New York's twelve electoral votes went

Aaron Burr

Table 7.1

Election of 1800		
Candidate	*Party*	*Electoral Vote*
Jefferson	Republican	73
J. Adams	Federalist	65

to the Republicans. Declared one Republican: the election "has been conducted . . . in so miraculous a manner that I cannot account for it but from the intervention of a Supreme Power and our friend Burr the agent."

Jefferson appeared to have won by a margin of eight electoral votes. But a complication soon arose. The Constitution allowed each elector to vote twice, with the candidate receiving the most votes becoming president and the candidate who finished second becoming vice-president. Because each Republican elector had cast one ballot for Jefferson and one for Burr, the two men received exactly the same number of electoral votes.

Under the Constitution, the election was now thrown into the Federalist-controlled House of Representatives. Burr refused to declare that he would not accept the presidency, and so the Federalists faced a choice. They could help elect Jefferson—"a brandy-soaked defamer of churches," "a contemptible hypocrite"—or they could throw their support to Burr—"a profligate," "a voluptuary." Hamilton came out against Burr, whose "public principles have no other spring or aim than his own aggrandizement," but most Federalists supported the New Yorker.

As the stalemate persisted, Virginia and Pennsylvania mobilized their state militias. Recognizing "the certainty that a legislative usur-

Thomas Jefferson

Republicans celebrated Thomas Jefferson's win in the election of 1800 with a victory flag inscribed: "T. Jefferson President . . . John Adams no more."

pation would be resisted by arms," as Jefferson noted, the Federalists finally backed down. On February 17, 1801, after six days of balloting and thirty-six ballots, the House of Representatives finally elected Thomas Jefferson the third President of the United States. As a result of the election, Congress adopted the twelfth amendment to the Constitution, which gives each elector in the Electoral College one vote for president and one for vice-president.

The New President Takes Office

At noon, March 4, 1801, Thomas Jefferson, clad in clothes of plain cloth, road on horseback from a nearby boarding house to the new United States Capitol in Washington. Without help, he dismounted, hitched his horse to a railing, entered the Senate chamber, and took the presidential oath of office. Then, in a weak voice, he delivered his inaugural address—a classic statement of democratic principles.

His first concern was to urge conciliation and to allay fear that he planned a new revolution. "We are all Republicans," he said, "we are all Federalists." Echoing George Washington's Farewell Address, he asked his listeners to set aside partisan and sectional differences and remember that "every difference of opinion is not a difference of principle." Only a proper respect for principles of majority rule and minority rights, he declared, would allow the new nation to thrive.

In the remainder of his address he laid out the principles which would guide his administration: a frugal, limited government; reduction of the public debt; states' rights; encouragement of agriculture; and a limited role for government in peoples' lives. To reassure Federalists who feared that he would refuse to repay the national debt, he committed his administration to the "sacred preservation of the public faith." And to critics who worried that he would align the United States with France, he promised to continue John Adams's policy of neutrality. "Peace, commerce and honest friendship with all nations," was his goal, he declared, "entangling alliances with none."

Jefferson called his election "the revolution of 1800." It was, he said, "as real a revolution in the principles of our government as that of 1776 was in its form." Once in office, Jefferson moved quickly to return the nation to Republican principles and reverse Federalist policies which tended toward centralization of power, heavy taxes and a permanent national debt, suppression of civil liberties, and involvement in European wars.

He tried to eliminate the formality of official and social occasions in Washington. He associated formality with aristocracy and informality with republicanism, and he began the practice of having guests shake hands with the president instead of bowing. He also placed dinner guests at a round table, so that no individual would have to sit in a more important place than any other.

Jefferson initially renounced the president's patronage powers. Of the first 600 political appointees named to federal office by Presidents Washington and Adams, all but six were Federalists. The new president promised to remove as few of these officeholders as possible. He said he would only remove "midnight" appointees who had been appointed to office by President Adams during his last days in office, or officials guilty of misconduct. Nothing more should be asked of government officeholders, Jefferson declared, than that they be honest, able, and loyal to the Constitution.

Republicans in Congress attempted to implement Jefferson's policies. They repealed all internal taxes, including Hamilton's tax on whiskey and Adams's taxes on houses and slaves, leaving only the federal tariff on imported goods. They fired all tax inspectors. They cut government expenditures and reduced the size of the army (to 3000 soldiers and 172 officers), the navy (to six frigates), and foreign embassies (to three, in Britain, France, and Spain). They trimmed the national debt in seven years from $83 million to $50 million. They carried out their pledge to eliminate the Federalist's restrictive laws by reducing the fourteen-year residency requirement for citizenship to five years; allowing the Alien and Sedition laws to lapse; and pardoning and remitting the fines of persons convicted under the Sedition Act. They cut the price of public lands and extended credit to purchasers in order to encourage landownership and rapid western settlement.

In one area, Jefferson felt his hands tied. He considered the Bank of the United States "the most deadly" institution to republican government. But Hamilton's bank had been legally chartered for twenty years and Jefferson's secretary of the treasury, Albert Gallatin, said that the bank was needed to provide credit for the nation's growing economy. So Jefferson allowed the bank to continue to operate, but he weakened its influence by distributing the federal government's patronage among twenty-one state banks and ordered it to establish branches in Washington and New Orleans to better serve the federal government. "What is practicable," Jefferson commented, "must often control pure theory."

Contemporaries were astonished by the sight of a president who had renounced all the practical tools of government: an army, a navy, taxes, and political patronage. Jefferson's actions promised, said a British observer, "a sort of Millennium in government." Jefferson's goal was, indeed, to create a new kind of government, wholly unlike the centralized, corrupt, patronage-ridden one against which Americans had rebelled in 1776.

War with the Judiciary

When Thomas Jefferson took office, not a single Republican served as a federal judge. In Jefferson's view, the Federalist party had prostituted the federal judiciary into a branch of their political party and intended to use the courts to frustrate Republican plans. "From that battery," said Jefferson, "all the works of republicanism are to be beaten down and erased."

The first major political battle of Jefferson's presidency involved his effort to weaken the Federalist party's control of the federal judiciary. Three weeks before Jefferson became president, the lame-duck Federalist-controlled Congress had passed a new judiciary law. This act created sixteen new federal judgeships—along with nearly 200 marshals, attorneys, bailiffs, and messengers—and President Adams had filled all the newly created positions with Federalists. Worse yet from a Republican perspective, the act also extended the jurisdiction of the federal courts over issues such as bankruptcy and land disputes, previously the exclusive domain of state courts, thereby strengthening the power of the central government at the expense of the states. Finally, the act reduced the number of Supreme Court justices effective with the next vacancy, delaying Jefferson's opportunity to name a new Supreme Court justice.

Jefferson's supporters in Congress demanded that the judiciary act be repealed. Federalists declared that the act could not be revoked, since the Constitution stated that federal judges could not be removed except by impeachment. Republicans replied that since the Constitution gave Congress the right to create federal courts and to determine their jurisdiction, it gave Congress the power to eliminate judgeships as well. The repeal passed, but just barely. In the Senate, Vice-President Aaron Burr cast the decisive vote for repeal, and the

House of Representatives went along by a margin of twenty-seven votes.

While Congress debated repeal of the Judiciary Act of 1801, another skirmish erupted in the war over the federal courts. One of Adams's "midnight appointments" was William Marbury, a loyal Federalist. Although approved by the Senate and signed by the president, Marbury never received his letter of appointment. When Jefferson became president, Marbury demanded that Secretary of State James Madison issue the commission. Madison refused and Marbury sued, claiming that under Section 13 of the Judiciary Act of 1789, the Supreme Court had the power to issue a court order which would compel Madison to give him his judgeship.

The case threatened to provoke a direct confrontation between the judiciary and the executive and legislative branches of the federal government. If the Supreme Court ordered Madison to give Marbury his judgeship, the secretary of state was likely to ignore the court. Even worse, Jeffersonians in Congress might act to limit the high court's power. This is precisely what had happened in 1793 when the Supreme Court had ruled that a state might be sued in federal court by non-residents. Congress had retaliated by initiating the Eleventh Amendment, which restricted such suits.

John Marshall

John Marshall, the new Chief Justice of the Supreme Court, was well aware of the Court's delicate position. When Marshall became the nation's fourth Chief Justice in 1801, the Supreme Court lacked prestige and public respect. Presidents found it difficult to get people to serve as justices. The Court was considered so insignificant that it held its sessions in a clerk's office in the basement of the Capitol and only met six weeks a year.

In his opinion in *Marbury* v. *Madison*, the Chief Justice ingeniously expanded the Court's power without directly provoking the Jeffersonians. Marshall conceded that Marbury had a right to his appointment, but ruled the Court had no authority to order the secretary of state to act, since the section of the Judiciary Act that gave the Court the power to issue an order was unconstitutional. This was the first time that the Supreme Court had declared an act of Congress unconstitutional.

Marbury v. *Madison* established the power of the federal courts to review the constitutionality of federal laws and invalidate acts of Congress when they were determined to be unconstitutional. This power, known as *judicial review*, provided the basis for the important place that the Supreme Court occupies in American life today.

Marshall's decision in *Marbury* v. *Madison* intensified Republican party hatred of the courts. Jefferson complained that Marshall's opinion threatened to "make the judiciary a despotic branch" and turn the Constitution into "a mere thing of wax" which the court could shape any way it pleased.

Republicans next moved to use the impeachment process to rid the federal courts of judges whom they considered unfit or overly partisan. "We shall see who is master of the ship," declared one Jeffersonian. "Whether men appointed for life or the immediate representatives of the people . . . are to give laws to the community." In Jefferson's eyes, impeachment was the only effective way to make the federal courts responsive to the public will. Federalists responded by accusing the administration of endangering the independence of the federal judiciary.

In February, 1803, three weeks before the Court handed down its decision in *Marbury* v. *Madison*, Republicans in Congress launched impeachment proceedings against Federal District Judge John Pickering of New Hampshire. Alcoholic and possibly insane, Pickering was convicted and removed from office.

On the same day that Pickering was convicted, the House of Representatives voted to impeach Supreme Court Justice Samuel Chase, a staunch Federalist and a signer of the Declaration of Independence. There was no doubt that Chase was guilty of unrestrained partisanship and injudicious statements. From the bench, he had openly denounced equal rights and universal suffrage and accused the Jeffersonians of atheism and power-hunger. After the repeal of the Judiciary Act of 1801, Justice Chase had assailed the "mobocracy," which was undermining the U.S. Constitution. An irate President Jefferson called for Chase's impeachment. "Ought this seditious and official attack on the principles of the Constitution . . . to go unpunished?" he asked Republicans in Congress. The Constitution specified, however, that a judge could only be removed from office for "treason, bribery, or other high crimes," and Chase was only accused of judicial misconduct. While a majority of the Senate found Chase guilty, seven Republicans broke ranks and the Jeffersonians could not muster the two-thirds majority needed to convict. "Impeachment is a farce which will not be tried again," Jefferson wrote.

Chase's acquital had important consequences for the future. If the Jeffersonians had succeeded in removing Chase, it is likely that they would have removed other Federalist judges from the federal bench. Since the day Chase was acquited, there have been no further attempts to remove federal judges solely on the grounds of misconduct or partisanship and no further efforts to reshape the federal courts through impeachment. Despite the Republicans' active hostility toward an independent judiciary, during Jefferson's presidency the Supreme Court established the principles of judicial supremacy and judicial review. The ultimate effect of these actions was to establish the federal courts as a vigorous and equal third branch of government.

International Conflict

In his inaugural address, Thomas Jefferson declared that his fondest wish was for peace. "Peace is my passion," he repeatedly insisted. As president, however, Jefferson was unable to realize his wish. His presidency occurred during a time of grave international tensions, and Jefferson, like Presidents Washington and Adams, faced the difficult task of trying to preserve American independence and neutrality in a world torn by war and revolution.

The new president's first major foreign policy crisis came from the "Barbary pirates" who preyed on American shipping off the coast of North Africa. The conflict had first erupted in the year 1785, when Algerian pirates boarded an American merchant schooner sailing off the coast of Portugal, took its twenty-one member crew to Algeria, and enslaved them for twelve years. After eight years, a hundred more American hostages seized from captured American ships joined the captives. Finally, in 1795, Congress approved the immense ransom of $1 million for release of the hostages. By 1800, one-fifth of all federal revenues were being paid to the North African states as tribute.

Barbary States

Jefferson refused to pay tribute. Instead, he sent eight ships to the Mediterranean to enforce a blockade of Tripoli. One of the ships, the *Philadelphia*, was captured and its crew imprisoned. On the night of February 16, 1804, Lieutenant Stephen Decatur, slipped into Tripoli harbor, boarded the captured ship, and set it on fire. A year later, a small force of American marines marched 600 miles across the desert from Egypt, attacked the city Derna in Tripoli from the rear, and captured it. Tripoli agreed to make peace. The phrase "To the shores of Tripoli" in the Marine Corps hymn refers to the military conflict that took place between these "state-sponsored" pirates and American military forces.

At the same time that conflict raged with the Barbary pirates, a more serious crisis loomed on the Mississippi River. In 1795, a treaty with Spain had given western farmers the right to ship their produce down the Mississippi River and load cargoes of corn, whiskey, and pork in New Orleans aboard ships bound for the east coast and foreign ports. In 1800, Spain secretly ceded the Louisiana territory to

France, and farmers lost the right to reload cargo in New Orleans. Westerners exploded with anger. Many demanded war.

The prospect of France controlling the Mississippi deeply troubled Jefferson. Spain held only a weak and tenuous grip on the Mississippi, but France was a much stronger power. It raised the specter of a French colonial empire in North America, blocking American expansion. The transfer of Louisiana to Spain, stated Jefferson, "reverses all the political relations of the United States. . . . The day France takes possession of New Orleans . . . we must marry ourselves to the British fleet and nation." The United States appeared to have only two options: diplomacy or war.

The president sent James Monroe to join Robert Livingston, the American minister to France, with instructions to purchase New Or-

leans and as much of the Gulf Coast as they could for $2 million. If these proposals were to fail, Jefferson instructed Monroe to begin talks with Britain to form a military alliance against France.

Circumstances played into the Americans' hands when France failed in its efforts to suppress a slave rebellion in Haiti. A hundred thousand slaves, inspired by the example of the French Revolution, had revolted, destroying 1200 coffee and 200 sugar plantations. In 1800, French troops sent to crush the slave insurrection and reconquer Haiti met a determined resistance led by a former slave named Toussaint L'Ouverture, and then they were wiped out by mosquitoes carrying yellow fever. "Damn sugar, damn coffee, damn colonies," declared Napoleon. Without Haiti, Napoleon had little interest in keeping Louisiana.

Two days after Monroe's arrival, the French finance minister unexpectedly announced that France was willing to sell not just New Orleans, but all of Louisiana Province, a territory extending from Canada to the Gulf of Mexico and westward as far as the Rocky Mountains. The American negotiators agreed on a price of $15 million, or about 4 cents an acre.

The Constitution did not give the president specific authorization to purchase land, and Jefferson considered asking for a constitutional amendment empowering the government to acquire territory. In Congress, Federalists bitterly denounced the purchase. They noted that it would take a stack of silver dollars fifty miles high to pay for Louisiana. Jefferson himself said that the purchase made a "blank paper of the Constitution." In the end, Jefferson, fearing that Napoleon might change his mind, simply sent the agreement to the Senate, which ratified it. "The less said about any constitutional difficulty, the better," he stated. In a single stroke, Jefferson had doubled the size of the country.

The acquisition of Louisiana terrified many Federalists, who knew that the creation of new western states would dilute their political influence. "Adopt this Western World into the Union," warned one Federalist, "and you destroy at once the weight and importance of the Eastern States." In the winter of 1803–1804, a group of Federalist congressmen devised a plan

The American flag was raised over New Orleans in 1803 after the Louisiana Purchase.

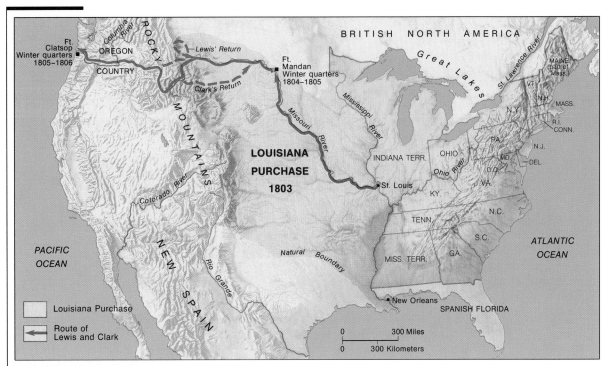

The Louisiana Purchase and Route of Lewis and Clark
No one realized how much territory Jefferson acquired through the Louisiana Purchase until Lewis and Clark explored the far West.

for "a new confederacy, exempt from the corrupt and corrupting influence and oppression of the aristocratic Democrats of the South." This "Northern Confederacy," which would consist of New Jersey, New York, New England, and Canada, was to be established with the backing of Britain.

Alexander Hamilton repudiated this scheme, and the conspirators next turned to Vice-President Aaron Burr. In return for Federalist support in a campaign for the governorship of New York, Burr was to swing New York into the Northern Confederacy. Burr carried New York City, largely with Federalist votes, but was badly beaten upstate, in part by Hamilton's opposition. Incensed and irate, Burr challenged Hamilton to a duel. On July 11, 1804, at Weehawken, New Jersey, the two men faced each other with pistols, and Burr killed Hamilton. When a New Jersey grand jury indicted Burr for murder, he fled the region.

Burr was a ruined politician and a fugitive from the law. The Republican party stripped his control over political patronage in New York and dropped him from Jefferson's presidential ticket. In debt, on the edge of bankruptcy, his fortunes at their lowest point, the desperate Burr became involved in a conspiracy for which he would be put on trial for treason.

During the spring of 1805, Burr travelled to the West, where he and an old friend, James Wilkinson, commander of United States forces in the Southwest and military governor of Louisiana, hatched an adventurous scheme. It is still uncertain what their goal was, since Burr, in his efforts to lure support, told different stories to different people. At various times Burr said that he planned to colonize land in the Mississippi Valley; to seize Spanish territory in Texas, California, and New Mexico; and even to separate the states and territories west of the Appalachians from the rest of the Union and create an empire with himself as its head. Burr tried unsuccessfully to get British naval and financial support for his plan.

In the fall of 1806, Burr and some sixty schemers travelled down the Ohio River, toward New Orleans, where they hoped to incite disgruntled French settlers to revolt. Wilkinson, recognizing that the scheme was doomed to failure, decided to betray Burr. He wrote a letter to Jefferson describing a "deep, dark, wicked, and widespread conspiracy."

Burr was tried for treason in 1807 at a trial presided over by Supreme Court Chief Justice John Marshall. To President Jefferson's disgust, the Senate acquitted Burr, despite evidence showing that he had planned treason, because Chief Justice Marshall set a very strict definition of treason that required each act of treason to be attested to by two witnesses.

THE AMERICAN EAGLE CHALLENGES THE FRENCH TIGER AND THE BRITISH SHARK

In 1804, Jefferson was easily reelected, with 162 electoral votes to only 14 for his Federalist opponent, Charles C. Pinckney. His second term began, he later wrote, "without a cloud on the horizon." But storm clouds soon gathered, as a result of renewed war in Europe. Jefferson faced the difficult challenge of keeping the United States out of the European war and defending the nation's rights as a neutral.

In May, 1803, just two weeks after Napoleon sold Louisiana to the United States, France declared war on Britain. For the next twelve years the conflict engulfed Europe. French armies quickly conquered much of the European continent and Napoleon massed his troops and assembled a fleet of flat boats in preparation for an invasion of England. In 1805, the British under Admiral Horatio Nelson sank eighteen French and Spanish ships off Spain's Cape Trafalgar and captured 14,000 men. Victory at the battle of Trafalgar ended Napoleon's hope of invading England and established British naval supremacy for the next century. Britain was master of the seas; but France remained supreme on the land.

In the election of 1804, Thomas Jefferson dropped Aaron Burr from the Republican ticket and replaced him with another New Yorker, George Clinton.

The early years of the war were a source of immense profits for American shipowners and merchants, who, as John Adams put it, lined their pockets while Europeans slit each others' throats. As citizens of a neutral nation, the Americans were able to trade with both France and Britain, but this encouraged retaliation from Britain and France. Opportunities for quick profits evaporated in 1805, when an English court ruled (in the *Essex* case) that United States ships could not carry cargo from French colonies to France. Britain then began to blockade American ports, intercept American ships, and confiscate cargoes bound for France.

France and Britain sought to starve each other by imposing blockades. In 1806 and 1807, Napoleon tried to ruin England's economy by cutting off its trade with the continent of Europe. His "Continental System" ordered the seizure of any neutral ship that visited a British port, paid British duties, or allowed itself to be searched by a British vessel. Britain retaliated by issuing a series of orders in council which forbade trade with French ports and other ports in Europe under French control. United States shipping was caught in the crossfire. By 1807, France had seized 500 ships and Britain nearly a thousand.

Americans were also angered by the British practice of impressment. The British navy, desperately in need of sailors, claimed the right to stop neutral ships on the high seas, remove seamen alleged to be British subjects, and impress them into the British navy. By 1811, nearly 10,000 American sailors had been forced into the British navy.

Outrage over impressment reached a fever pitch in 1807, when the British man-of-war *Leopard* fired three broadsides at the American naval frigate *Chesapeake,* which had refused to stop at the order of the *Leopard's* commander. The blasts killed three American sailors and wounded eighteen more. British authorities then boarded the American ship and removed four sailors, only one of whom was a British subject.

The country clamored for war. Even Federalists joined in the anti-British outcry. Said one, "Without substantial reparation for the crying offense against our honor, rights and independence, we must go to war." "Never, since the battle of Lexington," observed Jefferson, "have I seen this country in such a state of exasperation."

"Dambargo"

The president, fearful that the young nation was not ready for war, tried to find a peaceful way to persuade Britain and France to respect American neutrality. He believed that the best course was to close American markets to them, on the assumption that American trade was so vital that European industry would collapse without it. As Jefferson knew, Americans consumed a third of all British manufacturing. In late 1807, at the president's urging, Congress adopted an embargo which closed American ports to foreign ships and prohibited American trade with foreign countries.

The embargo was an unpopular and costly failure. It hurt the United States economy even more than it did Britain or France. Exports fell from $108 million in 1807 to just $22 million in 1808. Agricultural prices declined sharply, particularly in the South, and nearly 30,000 seamen were left jobless while their ships stood idle. The embargo breathed new life into the Federalist party, which regained power in several New England states and made substantial gains in the Congressional elections of 1808. "Would to God," said one American, "that the embargo had done as little evil to ourselves as it has done to foreign nations!"

Jefferson had believed that Americans would cooperate with the embargo out of a sense of patriotism. Instead, evasions of the embargo were widespread and smuggling flourished, particularly through Canada. To enforce the embargo, Jefferson took steps that infringed on his most cherished principles: individual liberties and opposition to a strong central government. He had to mobilize the army and navy to enforce the blockade, and in April, 1808, he declared the Lake Champlain region of New York, along the Canadian border, in a state of insurrection.

Across New England, Federalists demanded that the president abandon the embargo. Soon, their outcries were joined by many disillusioned New England Republicans. In effect for fifteen months, the embargo exacted no political concessions from either France or Britain, but it had produced economic hardship, evasion of the law, and political dissension at home. Just three days before Jefferson left office, the embargo was repealed. Upset by the failure of the embargo, the sixty-five-year-old Jefferson looked forward to his retirement:

To obtain sailors for its ships, Britain seized naturalized American citizens from American ships and forced them into the British navy.

"Never did a prisoner, released from his chains, feel such relief as I shall on shaking off the shackles of power."

The task of defending America's neutral rights now fell to Jefferson's successor, James Madison. Small in stature and frail in health, Madison was one of the towering figures who had won the nation's independence and guided it through its difficult early years. At the Constitutional Convention, Madison played a leading role in formulating the principles of federalism and separation of powers that underlie the American system of government. As a member of Congress, he sponsored the Bill of Rights and founded the Republican party. As secretary of state to Thomas Jefferson, he kept the United States out of the European war. When he became president, Madison sought to continue Jefferson's policy of using economic coercion to force Britain and France to respect American neutrality.

Commercial Warfare

To replace the embargo, Congress adopted the Non-Intercourse Act in March 1809, which reopened trade with all countries except Britain and France. Non-Intercourse was no more successful than the embargo in convincing the two belligerents to stop their attacks on American shipping. Congress replaced it in 1810 with a new measure, Macon's Bill No. 2, which reopened trade with France and Britain. It also stipulated that if either Britain or France respected America's neutral rights, the United States would stop trade with the other nation, unless it too agreed to halt its interference with American shipping.

Napoleon saw an opportunity to involve the United States in his war with Britain. In November, 1810, the wily French emperor announced that France would repeal its restrictions on American trade. In fact, France continued to seize American ships and cargoes, but Madison snapped at the bait. In early 1811, Madison announced that the United States would continue to trade with France, but would prohibit all trade with Britain. When negotiations with Britain failed, he urged Congress to prepare the nation for war.

A Second War of Independence

A growing number of Americans had come to believe that only war could preserve America's neutral rights and national honor. Even Jefferson admitted that the policy of "peaceable coercion" had failed to stop the seizure of American ships and impressment of American sailors. War, said the peace-loving former president, would be "the second weaning from British principles, British attachments, British manners and manufactures."

The growth of pro-war feeling was visibly apparent in the elections of 1810, when 63 of 142 Congressmen were swept out of the House of Representatives. The young Republicans who replaced them were called "War Hawks" because of their intense pro-war stance. Led by Henry Clay of Kentucky and John C. Calhoun of South Carolina, the War Hawks favored the conquest of Canada and Spanish-held Florida.

Further contributing to war fever was belief that the British were responsible for increasing Indian hostilities on the frontier. Westerners accused Britain of inciting Indian attacks and supplying them with arms and ammunition. Frontier anger peaked in November, 1811, when the Shawnee Prophet attacked General William Henry Harrison's frontier army at Tippecanoe Creek in Indiana, killing more than sixty Ameircan soldiers and wounding 100. Since British guns were found on the battlefields, westerners concluded that the British were responsible for the incident.

By the summer of 1812, Madison himself believed that war with England was inevitable. In his war message to Congress, he listed America's grievances against Britain: interference with American trade; impressment of thousands of American citizens; the blockade of the American coast; and British-incited attacks by Indians, who "spare neither age nor sex." A divided House and Senate responded by voting to declare war on Britain. The vote (79–49 in the House and 19–13 in the Senate) was close, with proponents of war concentrated in the South and West.

Ironically, the United States declared war at precisely the time its policy of economic coercion had achieved success. In May, England's

Prime Minister Spencer Perceval had decided to repeal his country's trade restrictions, but he was assassinated before he had actually revoked the orders. Finally, on June 16, just two days before war was declared, the British government repealed the orders in council. Hopeful that the United States would reconsider its declaration of war, Britain refrained from hostilities at sea until November 1812.

Early Defeats

The United States was woefully unprepared for war. The army consisted of fewer than 7000 soldiers; the navy of less than 20 vessels. There were very few trained officers. Most were, in Madison's words, "survivors of the revolutionary band . . . disqualified by age or infirmities."

The American strategy called for a three-pronged invasion of Canada, to force a change in British trade policies, while the American navy harassed British shipping. The attack on Canada was a disastrous failure. At Detroit,

2000 American troops were forced to surrender to a much smaller British and Indian force. An attack across the Niagara River, near Buffalo, resulted in 900 American prisoners of war, when the New York State militia refused to provide support. Along Lake Champlain, a third army retreated into American territory after failing to cut undefended British supply lines. By the end of 1813, British forces controlled key forts in the old Northwest, including Detroit and Fort Dearborn, the site of Chicago. The only consolation for the Americans was a string of naval victories in single ship encounters.

Repeated military defeats took a toll on Madison's popularity. In the presidential election of 1812, he narrowly defeated the Federalist candidate DeWitt Clinton. The switch of one state would have thrown the election to the Federalists.

In 1813 America confronted new problems with a disheartening lack of success. American armies continued to suffer defeat in the swamps west of Lake Erie. In January, an Amer-

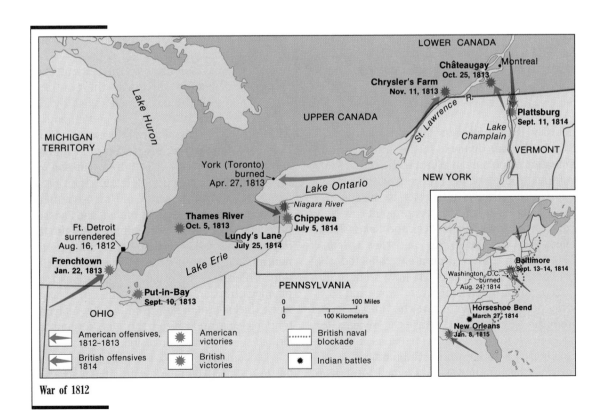

War of 1812

ican army advancing toward Detroit was defeated and captured at Frenchtown on the Raisin River. After the battle, Indians massacred wounded American prisoners. In April, Americans staged a raid across Lake Ontario to York (Toronto) in Canada. American soldiers set fire to the two houses of the provincial parliament, an act which would bring retaliation in the form of the British burning of Washington, D.C. An abortive attempt to capture Montreal in the fall of 1813 ended without an attack.

Only a series of unexpected victories at the end of the year raised American spirits. On September 10, 1813, America won a major naval victory at the Battle of Put-in-Bay at the western end of Lake Erie. There, Master-Commandant Oliver Hazard Perry blockaded a British fleet of six ships. Though Perry's flagship, the *Lawrence*, was disabled in the fighting, he went on to capture the British fleet. He reported his victory in the famous words, "We have met the enemy and they are ours." American control of Lake Erie forced a British retreat into Canada. On October 5, 1813, General William Henry Harrison overtook the retreating British army and their Indian allies at the Thames River and won a decisive victory, in which the Indian leader Tecumseh was killed, ending the fighting strength of the Northwestern Indians.

The Tide Turns

In early 1814, prospects for an American victory in the war dimmed. In the spring, Britain defeated Napoleon in Europe, freeing 18,000 veteran troops for an invasion of the United States. The British plan was to invade the United States at three separate points: at New York across the Niagara River and Lake Champlain, the Chesapeake Bay, and New Orleans. The London *Times* accurately reflected the confident English mood: "Oh, may no false liberality, no mistaken leniency, no weak and cowardly policy interpose to save the United States from the blow! Strike! Chastise the savages, for such they are . . . Our demands may be couched in a single word—Submission!"

At Niagara, however, a small American army stopped the British advance at hard-fought battles at Chippewa and Lundy's Landing. Then, American naval forces commanded

by Thomas Macdonough defeated a British fleet at Plattsburgh Bay, forcing 11,000 British troops to retreat back into Canada.

In a second attempt to invade the United States, Britain landed a force on the Chesapeake Bay coast, defeated the Americans at the Battle of Bladensburg, and marched to Washington, D.C. On August 24, 1814, the British captured and burned Washington, humiliating the nation. For seventy-two hours, President Madison was forced to hide in the Virginia and Maryland countryside. The British next moved on Baltimore.

On September 13, 1814, the British attacked Baltimore. All through the night the British fleet bombarded Fort McHenry, which guarded the city. In the light of the "rockets' red glare, the bombs bursting in air," Francis Scott Key, a young lawyer, saw the American flag waving over the fort. At dawn on September 14, he beheld the flag still waving. The Americans had repulsed the British attack. Key was moved to write on the back of an old envelope a poem entitled "The Star-Spangled Banner." Soon, the words of the poem were sung to an old English tune, "To Anacreon in Heaven." The song was destined to become the young nation's national anthem.

Americans had little to sing about. The country faced grave threats in the South. In 1813, the Creek Indians, encouraged by the British, had attacked American settlements in what are now Alabama and Mississippi. Frontiersmen from Georgia, Mississippi, and Tennessee, led by Major General Andrew Jackson, retaliated and succeeded in defeating the Creeks in March, 1814, at the battle of Horseshoe Bend in Alabama. The Creek War ended, and Jackson proceeded to cut British supply lines in the South. Jackson knew that Spain, supposedly neutral, had allowed Britain to use the Florida port of Pensacola as a base of operations for a planned invasion of New Orleans. In a single week, Jackson marched from Mobile, Alabama, to Pensacola and seized the city, forcing the British to delay their invasion.

On January 8, 1815, the British fleet and a battle-tested 10,000-man army finally attacked New Orleans in an attempt to seize control of the mouth of the Mississippi River. Jackson assembled a ragtag army, including French pi-

On August 24, 1814, British troops avenged an American attack on York, Ontario, by marching into Washington, D.C., and setting fire to the Capitol and the White House.

rates, Choctaw Indians, Western militia, and freed slaves, to defend the city. Although British forces outnumbered Americans by more than two to one, American artillery and sharpshooters stopped the invasion. American losses totaled only 8 dead and 13 wounded, while British casualties were 2036, including their commanding officer. Ironically, Jackson's astonishing victory at the battle of New Orleans took place two weeks after the signing of a peace treaty ending the War of 1812.

Negotiations to end the war had commenced in Ghent, Belgium, in August 1814. The British called for retention of forts on United States soil, cessions of territory in Maine and New York, and a permanent reservation for Indians in the American Northwest. American negotiators rejected these demands and instead asked for a return to the situation as it was before the war. Britain, exhausted by twelve years of war with France and convinced that the American war was so difficult and costly that it would never be won, accepted the American proposal. On December 24, 1814, a peace treaty was signed. None of the issues that Americans had fought the war over— impressment, naval blockades, or the British orders in council—were mentioned in the peace treaty.

The War's Significance

The war of 1812 is often treated as unimportant, a minor footnote to the bloody European War between France and Britain. Actually, the war was crucial for the future of the United States. First of all, the war effectively destroyed the Indians' ability to resist American expansion. Native Americans were crushed in the

1789 First session of Congress meets; Washington inaugurated as first president; Federal Judiciary Act establishes a federal court system

1790 Treasury Secretary Alexander Hamilton recommends that Congress fund the federal debt, assume state debts incurred during the Revolution, and establish a national bank

1791 Controversy over Hamilton's fiscal program leads to a political schism between Federalists and Republicans

1792 George Washington reelected president The Bill of Rights becomes part of the Constitution

1793 French King Louis XVI beheaded; President Washington issues a neutrality proclamation in response to news that revolutionary France had declared war on Britain; Citizen Genêt Affair; Thomas Jefferson resigns as Secretary of State

1794 Whiskey Rebellion; General Anthony Wayne defeats Indians at the battle of Fallen Timbers

1795 Jay's Treaty

1796 George Washington's "Farewell Address"; John Adams elected president

1797 The XYZ Affair

1798 Undeclared naval war with France begins; Alien and Sedition Acts; The Kentucky and Virginia resolutions are drafted by Thomas Jefferson and James Madison

1800 Washington, D.C., becomes the national capital

1801 War with the Barbary pirates; John Marshall becomes Chief Justice of the Supreme Court; Electoral ballot count results in a tie between Thomas Jefferson and Aaron Burr

1803 *Marbury* v. *Madison*; Louisiana Purchase; Lewis and Clark expedition begins

1804 Impeachment of Federal District Judge John Pickering and Supreme Court Associate Justice Samuel Chase; Alexander Hamilton killed in a duel with Aaron Burr; Thomas Jefferson reelected president

1806 Aaron Burr charged with treason

1807 United States frigate *Chesapeake* attacked by the British frigate *Leopard*; Embargo Act prohibits most trade with foreign nations

1808 James Madison elected president; Non-Intercourse Act repeals the embargo but prohibits trade with Britain and France

1810 Macon's Bill No. 2 reopens trade with Britain and France

1811 Congressional elections won by the War Hawks; The Battle of Tippecanoe; Congress allows charter of the Bank of the United States to lapse

1812 Congress declares war against England; Madison reelected president

1813 West Florida seized by the United States; Battle of Lake Erie; Battle of the Thames

1814 Battle of Horseshoe Bend; The British burn Washington, D.C.;Commander Thomas Macdonough defeats British fleet at Lake Champlain; Hartford Convention convenes; Treaty of Ghent ends War of 1812

1815 The Battle of New Orleans

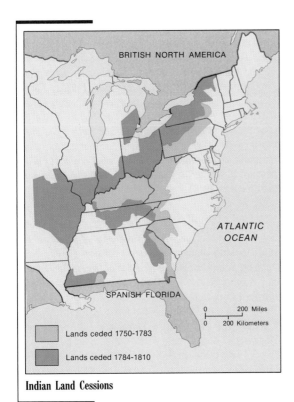

Lands ceded 1750-1783

Lands ceded 1784-1810

Indian Land Cessions

North by General William Henry Harrison and in the South by General Andrew Jackson. Abandoned by their British allies, the Indians were forced to make treaties as best they could. Reluctantly, they conceded most of their lands north of the Ohio River and in south and west Alabama.

Second, the war allowed the United States to rewrite its boundaries with Spain and solidify control over the lower Mississippi River and the Gulf of Mexico. Although the United States did not conquer Canada or defeat the British empire, it had fought the world's strongest power to a draw. Spain recognized the significance of this fact, and in 1818 abandoned Florida. In 1819 they agreed to an American boundary running clear to the Pacific Ocean.

Third, the war ended America's brief experiment with a two party political system. Many Federalists believed that the real reason for the War of 1812 was to help Napoleon in his struggle against Britain, and they opposed the war by refusing to pay taxes, boycotting war loans, and refusing to furnish troops. In December 1814, delegates from Connecticut, Massa-chusetts, and Rhode Island, and several counties in New Hampshire and Vermont gathered in Hartford, Connecticut, and recommended a series of constitutional amendments to restrict the power of Congress to make war, regulate commerce, and admit new states. The convention also wanted to make presidents ineligible for reelection (in order to break the grip of Virginians on the presidency) and to abolish the three-fifths compromise (which increased the political clout of the South).

Unfortunately for the Federalists, the Hartford Convention took place at the same time that news arrived about the Treaty of Ghent and the Battle of New Orleans. Branded as traitors, the Federalists never recovered.

CONCLUSION

Early in the evening of February 11, 1815, the British sloop *Favorite,* flying a flag of truce, entered New York harbor bearing copies of the peace treaty ending the War of 1812. By 8:30 P.M., the news had spread throughout the city. Bells pealed and cannons boomed. Cheering crowds congregated in the streets, carrying candles. Despite bungling, incompetence, and threats of disunion, the new nation had fought Britain to a draw and affirmed its independence. *Niles' Register* summed up the prevailing mood: "Who would not be an American? Long live the Republic! All hail! Last asylum of oppressed humanity."

In 1789, it was an open question whether the Constitution was a workable plan of government. It was still unclear whether the new nation could establish a strong and vigorous national government or win the respect of nations overseas. For a quarter century, the new nation battled threats to its existence. It faced insurrections in the West, plots to dismember the country, repeated schemes to manipulate presidential elections, threats of secession and civil war, foreign interference with American shipping and commerce, and finally war with the world's strongest power. The nation overcame all of these problems.

By any standard, the new nation's achievements were impressive. During the first quarter century under the Constitution, the country adopted a bill of rights, protecting the rights of the individual against the power of the central government; enacted a financial program that secured the government's credit and stimulated the economy; and created the first political parties in history which directly involved large segments of the population in national politics. Confronted by war and revolution, the new nation acquired Louisiana and much of the Gulf Coast, doubling the size of the nation; defeated powerful Indian confederations in the Northwest and South, opening new lands for settlement; evicted British troops from American soil; and won international respect in the fight for American independence. A nation, strong and viable, had emerged from its baptism by fire.

REVIEW SUMMARY

Major economic and political challenges faced the new nation following the ratification of the Constitution:

> organizing a new government
> paying off the Revolutionary War debt
> building a prosperous economy
> creating a stable political system

During the first quarter century under the Constitution, the nation solved these problems by

> adopting a bill of rights protecting individual liberties
> enacting a financial program that secured the nation's credit and stimulated the economy
> creating the first political parties in history
> purchasing Louisiana, doubling the nation's size
> winning international respect for American independence

SUGGESTIONS FOR FURTHER READING

OVERVIEWS AND SURVEYS

Jacob E. Cooke, "The Federalist Age: A Reappraisal," in George A. Billias and Gerald N. Grob, eds., *American History: Retrospect and Prospect* (1971); John R. Howe, *From the Revolution Through the Age of Jackson* (1973); Seymour M. Lipset, *The First New Nation: The United States in Perspective* (1963); John Mayfield, *The New Nation, 1800–1845* (1982); John C. Miller, *The Federalist Era, 1789–1801* (1960); Marshall Smelser, *The Democratic Republic, 1801–1815* (1968).

THE NATIONAL GOVERNMENT GOES INTO OPERATION

Richard R. Beeman, *The Old Dominion and the New Nation, 1788–1801* (1972); Richard H. Kohn, *Eagle and Sword: The Federalists and the Creation of the Military Establishment in America, 1783–1802* (1975); Forrest McDonald, *The Presidency of George Washington* (1967); Carl Prince, *The Federalists and the Origins of the U.S. Civil Service* (1978); R. A. Rutland, *The Birth of the Bill of Rights, 1776–1791* (1955); Gerald Stourzh, *Alexander Hamilton and the Idea of Republican Government* (1970); Leonard D. White, *The Federalists: A Study in Administrative History* (1948).

THE BIRTH OF POLITICAL PARTIES

Ralph Brown Adams, *The Presidency of John Adams* (1975); Harry Ammon, *The Genêt Mission* (1973); Joyce Appleby, *Capitalism and a New Social Order: The Republican Vision of the 1790s* (1984); James M. Banner, *To the Hartford Convention: The Federalists and the Origins of Party Politics in Massachusetts, 1789–1815* (1970); Lance Banning, *The Jeffersonian Persuasion* (1978); Samuel Flagg Bemis, *Jay's Treaty* (1923); S. F. Bemis, *Pinckney's Treaty* (1926); Steven R. Boyd, ed., *The Whiskey Rebellion* (1985); Richard Buel, Jr., *Securing the Revolution: Ideology in American Politics, 1789–1815* (1972); William N. Chambers, *Political Parties in a New Nation* (1963); Joseph Charles, *The Origins of the American Party System* (1956); Jerald A. Combs, *The Jay Treaty* (1970); Noble E. Cunningham, Jr., *The Jeffersonian Republicans: The Formation of Party Organization, 1789–1801* (1957); Manning J. Dauer, *The Adams Federalists* (1953); Alexander De Conde, *Entangling Alliance: Politics and Diplomacy Under George Washington* (1958); A. De Conde, *The Quasi-War: Politics and Diplomacy of the Undeclared War with France, 1797–1801* (1966); Felix Gilbert, *To the Farewell Address* (1961); Paul Goodman, *The Democratic Republicans of Massachusetts* (1964); Sanford W. Higgenbotham, *The Keystone in the Democratic Arch: Pennsylvania Politics, 1800–1816* (1952); Richard Hofstadter, *The Idea of a Party System: The Rise of Legitimate Opposition in the United States, 1740–1840* (1969); John R. Howe, *The Changing Political Thought of John Adams* (1966); Lawrence S. Kaplan, *Colonies into Nation: American Diplomacy, 1763–1801* (1972); Kaplan, *Jefferson and France: An Essay on Politics and Political Ideas* (1967); Stephen G. Kurtz, *The Presidency of John Adams: The Collapse of Federalism, 1795–1800* (1957); Leonard W. Levy, *Legacy of Suppression: Freedom of Speech and Press in Early American History* (1960); Eugene P. Link, *Democratic Republican Societies, 1790–1800* (1942); Gilbert L. Lycan, *Alexander Hamilton and American Foreign Policy: A Design for Greatness* (1970); John C. Miller, *Crisis in Freedom: The Alien and Sedition Acts* (1951); Bradford Perkins, *The First Rapprochment: England and the United States, 1795–1805* (1955); Carl E. Prince, *New Jersey's Jeffersonian*

Republicans (1967); Norman Risjord, *Chesapeake Politics, 1781–1800* (1978); Arthur M. Schlesinger, Jr., ed., *History of United States Political Parties, Volume I: 1798–1860: From Factions to Parties* (1973); A. M. Schlesinger, Jr., and Fred L. Israel, eds., *History of American Presidential Elections, 1789–1968* (1971); Bernard Schwartz, *The Great Rights of Mankind* (1977); Louis M. Sears, *George Washington and the French Revolution* (1960); Peter Show, *The Character of John Adams* (1976); William Sinchcombe, *The XYZ Affair* (1980); James Morton Smith, *Freedom's Fetters: The Alien and Sedition Laws and American Civil Liberties* (1956); Paul A. Varg, *The Foreign Policy of the Founding Fathers* (1963); Patricia Watlington, *The Partisan Spirit* (1972); Alfred F. Young, *The Democratic Republicans of New York* (1967); John Zvesper, *Political Philosophy and Rhetoric: A Study of the Origins of American Party Politics* (1977).

THE REVOLUTION OF 1800

Henry Adams, *History of the United States During the Administrations of Thomas Jefferson [and] of James Madison (1889–1891); James H. Broussard, The Southern Federalists, 1800–1816* (1979); Edward S. Corwin, *The "Higher Law" Background of American Constitutional Law* (1955); Noble E. Cunningham, Jr., *The Jeffersonian Republicans in Power: Party Operations, 1801–1809* (1963); N. Cunningham, Jr., *The Process of Government Under Jefferson* (1979); Alexander De Conde, *The Affair of Louisiana* (1976); D. O. Dewey, *Marshall Versus Jefferson: The Political Background of Marbury v. Madison* (1970); Richard E. Ellis, *The Jeffersonian Crisis: Courts and Politics in the Young Republic* (1971); David Hackett Fischer, *The Revolution of American Conservatism: The Federalist Party in the Era of Jeffersonian Democracy* (1965); Charles G. Haines, *The American Doctrine of Judicial Supremacy* (1932); George Lee Haskins and Herbert A. Johnson, *History of the Supreme Court of the United States, vol. 2, Foundations of Power: John Marshall, 1801–15* (1981); C. William Hill, *The Political Theory of John Taylor* (1977); Daniel Walker Howe, "European Sources of Political Ideas in Jeffersonian America," in *Reviews in American History*, 10 (1982), 28–44; R. W. Irwin, *Diplomatic Relations of the United States and the Barbary Powers* (1931); Robert M. Johnstone, Jr., *Jefferson and the Presidency: Leadership in the Young Republic* (1979); Linda K. Kerber, *Federalists in Dissent* (1970); Ralph Ketcham, *Presidents Above Party: The First American Presidency, 1789–1829* (1984); Shaw Livermore, *The Twilight of Federalism* (1962); Drew McCoy, *The Elusive Republic: Political Economy in Jeffersonian America* (1980); Forrest McDonald, *The Presidency of Thomas Jefferson* (1976); Howard B. Rock, *Artisans of the New Republic: The Tradesmen of New York City in the Age of Jefferson* (1979); Robert E. Shalhope, *John Taylor of Caroline: Pastoral Republican* (1980); Daniel Sisson, *The American Revolution of 1800* (1974); Marshall Smelser, *The Democratic Republic, 1801–1815* (1968); Charles G. Steffen, *The Mechanics of Baltimore: Workers and Politics in the Age of Revolution* (1984); Leonard D. White, *The Jeffersonians: A Study in Administrative History, 1801–1829* (1951); James S. Young, *The Washington Community, 1800–1828* (1966).

THE AMERICAN EAGLE CHALLENGES THE FRENCH TIGER AND BRITISH SHARK

Samuel Flagg Bemis, *John Quincy Adams and the Foundations of American Foreign Policy* (1949); Roger H. Brown, *The Republic in Peril: 1812* (1964); H. S. Halbert and T. H. Ball, *The Creek War of 1813 and 1814* (1970); Reginald Horsman, *The Causes of the War of 1812* (1962); Bradford Perkins, *Castlereagh and Adams: England and the United States, 1812–1823* (1964); B. Perkins, *Prologue to War: England and the United States, 1805–1812* (1961); Burton Spivak, *Jefferson's English Crisis: Commerce, Embargo, and the Republican Revolution* (1979); J.C.A. Stagg, *Mr. Madison's War: Politics, Diplomacy, and Warfare in the Early American Republic, 1783–1830* (1983). Charles Akers, *Abigail Adams: An American Woman* (1979); Alexander Balinky, *Albert Gallatin: Fiscal Theories and Policy* (1958); Irving Brant, *James Madison*, 6 vols. (1941–1961); Fawn M. Brodie, *Thomas Jefferson: An Intimate Biography* (1974); Jacob Ernest Cooke, *Alexander Hamilton* (1982); Marcus Cunliffe, *George Washington: Man and Monument* (1958); R. David Edmunds, *Shawnee Prophet* (1983) and *Tecumseh and the Quest for Indian Leadership* (1984); Thomas Flexner, *George Washington* (1965–1969); Douglas Southall Freeman, *George Washington: A Biography* (1948–1957); Ralph Ketcham, *James Madison* (1971); Phyllis Lee Levin, *Abigail Adams* (1987); Milton Lomask, *Aaron Burr* (1979–1982); Dumas Malone, *Jefferson and His Time*, 5 vols. (1948–1974); John C. Miller, *Alexander Hamilton* (1959); Broadus Mitchell, *Alexander Hamilton* (1957–1962); Merrill Peterson, *The Jefferson Image in the American Mind* (1960); M. Peterson, *Thomas Jefferson and the New Nation* (1970); Ernest Spaulding, *His Excellency George Clinton* (1964); Raymond Walters, Jr., *Albert Gallatin: Jeffersonian Financier and Diplomat* (1957); Lynne Withey, *Dearest Friend: A Life of Abigail Adams* (1981).

The Growth of American Nationalism

The Era of Good Feelings

Neo-Hamiltonianism

Strengthening American Finances

Protecting American Industry

Conquering Space

Judicial Nationalism

Defending American Interests in Foreign
Affairs

The Roots of American Economic Growth

Accelerating Transportation

Speeding Communications

Resistance to Technological Innovation

Transforming American Law

Early Industrialization and Urbanization

The Growth of Political Factionalism
and Sectionalism

The Panic of 1819

The Missouri Crisis

CHAPTER 8

Nationalism, Economic Growth, and the Roots of Sectional Conflict, 1815–1824

As 1810 began, Francis Cabot Lowell, a thirty-six-year-old Boston importer, was bitterly discouraged. His health was failing and his importing business was in ruins as a result of the war between Britain and France. Uncertain about which way to turn, he decided to travel abroad. While overseas he discovered his true calling. In Britain, he was deeply impressed by the textile factories at Manchester and by the enormous wealth generated by the British cotton industry. Although it was illegal to export textile machinery or plans, Lowell carefully studied the power looms and at great personal risk secretly made sketches of the designs. Upon his return to Boston in 1813, Lowell constructed textile machinery superior to any he had seen in England and proceeded to organize the Boston Manufacturing Company. In Waltham, Massachusetts the next year, the new company erected the world's first factory able to convert raw cotton into cloth by power machinery under one roof.

To staff the machinery in his new textile mill, Lowell chose a labor force different from that found in any previous factory. Determined not to duplicate the misery and squalor of England's textile mills, Lowell decided to recruit his labor force not from the families of the poor or from young children, but from among the virtuous daughters of New England farmers, who agreed to work in Lowell's mill for two or three years as a way of earning a dowry or an independent income. Because spinning and weaving had long been performed by women in the home, and because young women were willing to work for half or one-third the wages of young men, they seemed to offer a perfect solution to the factory's labor needs.

To break down the prejudice that factory work was degrading and immoral, the company announced that it would employ only women of good moral character, and it threatened to fire any employee guilty of smoking, drinking, lying, swearing, or any other immoral conduct. To keep a close watch over employees' moral character, the company required employees to attend church and provided boarding houses, where mill girls lived under the careful supervision of housekeepers of impeccable character.

Within a few years, the new factory was overwhelmed with job applicants and was "more puzzled to get rid of hands than to employ them."

The opening of the Boston Manufacturing Company's textile mill in 1814 marked a symbolic beginning to a new era in the nation's history. Throughout the Western world, the conclusion of the Napoleonic Wars brought an end to a period of global war and revolution and the start of a new period of nationalism and economic growth. For Americans, the end of the War of 1812 unleashed a new spirit of nationalism, the rapid growth of cities and industry, and a torrent of expansion westward.

In the War of 1812, the United States had fought the greatest power on earth to a draw. Andrew Jackson's smashing victory at the Battle of New Orleans had restored a sense of national pride and national unity. In the immediate aftermath of the war, a new spirit of nationalism and patriotic fervor swept aside bitter political and sectional divisions. The growing nationalism of the era was apparent in the adoption of economic programs to promote national economic growth; a series of Supreme Court decisions which established the supremacy of the federal government and expanded the powers of Congress; and the proud assertion of American interest and power in foreign policy.

The years following the War of 1812 were also a period of dramatic territorial and economic expansion, reflected in the rapid growth of cities, the beginnings of a revolution in transportation, the expansion of the cotton kingdom into the old Southwest, and the rise of industry in New England. It was during these crucial years that Americans laid the foundation for the nation's future economic and territorial growth and expansion.

Paradoxically, it was during these years of nationalism and expansion, known to contemporaries as "The Era of Good Feelings," that the roots of future sectional and political conflicts were planted. Westward expansion, the rapid growth of industry in the North, and the strengthening of the federal government created problems that would dominate American political life for the next forty years.

Lowell, Massachusetts, along the Merrimack River, was one of the first American mill towns.

THE GROWTH OF AMERICAN NATIONALISM

At noon on March 4, 1817, a crowd of 8000, the largest to have ever gathered in Washington, D.C., assembled across from the burned out U.S. Capitol to witness the inauguration of the nation's fifth president. James Monroe, the new president, was already well-known to the American people. The last Revolutionary War leader to reach the White House, Monroe had joined the Revolutionary army in 1776, spent the terrible winter of 1777 at Valley Forge, served in the Virginia assembly and Confederation Congress, became minister to France and Great Britain and governor of Virginia, and did duty simultaneously as secretary of state and secretary of war during the War of 1812. With the Federalist party in a state of collapse, Monroe had swept to an easy 183 to 34 electoral victory over Senator Rufus King of New York, carrying all but three states.

In his inaugural address, Monroe expressed his hope of ending partisan strife in the country. The war, he declared, had renewed and reinvigorated a sense of national unity. The passions of party which had divided the country had dissipated and American society had become "one great family with a common interest."

The Era of Good Feelings

Early in the summer of 1817, as a conciliatory gesture toward the Federalists who had opposed the War of 1812, Monroe embarked on a goodwill tour through the Northeast and Midwest. Everywhere Monroe went, citizens greeted him warmly, holding parades and banquets in his honor. In Federalist Boston, a crowd of 40,000 welcomed the Republican president. In Washington, John Quincy Adams expressed amazement at the acclaim with which the president had been greeted. "Party spirit has indeed subsided throughout the Union to a degree that I should have thought scarcely possible." A Federalist newspaper, reflecting on the end of party warfare and the renewal of national unity, called the times the "Era of Good Feeling."

The phrase "the era of good feelings" is often used to describe the period encompassing the two administrations of James Monroe. The Federalist party had collapsed, and a single

President Monroe was the last president to dress in the fashions of the eighteenth century, powdering his hair and wearing a cocked hat, knee-length pants, and white-topped boots.

party, the Jeffersonian Republicans, dominated national politics. The Republican party accepted the nationalistic principles of the Federalist party and Congress enacted a nationalist economic program involving a second national bank, a protective tariff, and improvements in transportation. Landmark Supreme Court decisions established national supremacy over the states and a series of foreign policy triumphs extended the nation's boundaries and protected its shipping and commerce. The new spirit of national political unity reached its climax in the presidential election of 1820. When Monroe ran for reelection, he was unopposed and won the electoral vote 231 to 1. To all outward appearances, Americans had exterminated the "baneful weed of party strife" and united the country under Republican principles.

To the American people, James Monroe was the popular symbol of the era of good feel-

ings. In appearance and outlook, he epitomized the values of the age of George Washington and the founding fathers. A dignified and formal man, nearly six feet in height, Monroe was the last president to wear the fashions of the eighteenth century. He wore his hair in a powdered wig tied in a queue and dressed himself in a cocked hat, a black broadcloth tailcoat, knee breeches, long white stockings, and buckled shoes.

His political values, too, were those of an earlier day. Like George Washington, he hoped for a country without political parties, governed by leaders chosen on their merits. As president, he sought to eliminate party and sectional rivalry, which he regarded as destructive of republican government. Anxious to unite all sections of the country, he tried to appoint a representative of each section to his cabinet and appointed John Quincy Adams, a former Federalist and son of a Federalist president, secretary of state. A new era of national unity appeared to have dawned.

Neo-Hamiltonianism

Traditionally, the Republican party had stood for limited government, states' rights, and a strict interpretation of the Constitution. By 1815, however, the party had moved toward adopting former Federalist positions on a national bank, protective tariffs, a standing army, and national roads. At the same time, many Federalists had embraced the old Republican ideal of states' rights. Former President John Adams commented: "Our two great parties have crossed over the valley and taken possession of each other's mountain."

In a series of policy recommendations submitted to Congress along with the peace treaty ending the War of 1812, Madison revealed the extent to which the Republicans had adopted policies they had previously criticized. To restore a stable and uniform currency, he advocated creation of the second Bank of the United States to succeed the first bank which had been allowed to lapse in 1811. To provide for the nation's defense, he called for a permanent 20,000 man army and a strong navy. To facilitate transportation and communications, he recommended a far-reaching program of internal improvements. To encourage industry, he endorsed a protective tariff. In subsequent messages to Congress, Madison called for an extensive system of roads and canals, new military academies, and the establishment of a national university in Washington—proposals, an opponent commented caustically, which "out-Federalized the Federalists." John Randolph, an old-style Republican who continued to cling to the older Jeffersonian principle of limited government, dismissed Madison's proposals as nothing but "old Federalism, vamped up into something bearing the superficial appearance of Republicanism."

In Congress, Madison's nationalistic program found strong support among a group of young politicians who had risen to national prominence at the time of the War of 1812. The generation of leaders that had steered the country through the Revolutionary era and early national period was passing from the scene and was succeeded by a new generation, eager to use federal government to promote national economic development. Convinced that inadequate roads, the lack of a national bank, and dependence on foreign imports had nearly permitted a British victory in the war, these young leaders were enthusiastic proponents of a national bank to provide a stable financial system, a protective tariff to promote industry, and government aid for transportation.

The leader of this young group of politicians was Henry Clay, a Republican from Kentucky, who represented the opinion of many Westerners. First elected to the House in 1811, Clay was one of the War Hawks who had urged President Madison to defend national honor and wage war against Britain. Named Speaker on his first day in the House of Representatives, Clay sought to use his new position to advance an economic program that he would later call the "American System." According to this plan, the government would use revenue from a protective tariff to finance internal improvements of roads and canals to aid expansion in the West. The protective tariff, in turn, would stimulate industry and expand the market for western farmers.

Eager to use the federal government to promote economic development, young politicians like Henry Clay of Kentucky and John C. Calhoun of South Carolina supported a protective tariff to stimulate industry, a national bank to promote economic growth, and federally funded aid for transportation.

Another leader of postwar nationalism was John C. Calhoun, a Republican from South Carolina, who also entered Congress in 1811 and quickly became the outstanding representative of the Southern states. Later in his political career Calhoun became the nation's leading exponent of states' rights, but at this point in his life he seemed to John Quincy Adams, "above all sectional and factious prejudices more than any other statesman of this Union with whom I have ever acted."

The other dominant political figure of the era was Daniel Webster, a Federalist from Massachusetts, who was the leading representative of the Northeast. Elected to Congress in 1812, the man nicknamed "Black Dan" for his dark hair and eyebrows opposed the War of 1812, the creation of a second national bank, and a protectionist tariff. Later in his career, after industrial interests replaced shipping and importing interests in the Northeast, Webster became a staunch defender of the national bank and a high tariff.

Strengthening American Finances

The War of 1812 had revealed the need for a new national bank. The charter of the first Bank of the United States had expired just before the war leaving the nation's banking system in the hands of approximately three hundred private state-chartered banks. There was no national currency in circulation. Payment for goods and services was either made in specie—gold or silver—or in the notes of private commercial banks, which greatly fluctuated in value.

To finance the war effort, the government borrowed from private banks at high interest rates. As demand for credit rose, the private banks issued notes greatly exceeding the amount of gold or silver that they held. One Rhode Island bank issued $580,000 in notes, backed up by only $86.48 in specie. The result was a wave of inflation. Prices jumped forty percent in two years. As the number of bank notes multiplied, their value decreased, until notes issued by Baltimore and Washington banks were worth about a quarter less than their face value. To make matters still worse, in 1814, after the British burned the nation's Capi-

tol, most banks outside of New England stopped redeeming their notes in gold or silver.

The federal government found itself unable to redeem millions of dollars deposited in banks. Soldiers, army contractors, and government securities holders went unpaid and the Treasury temporarily went bankrupt. After the war was over, many banks still refused to resume payments in gold or silver.

Supporters of a second Bank of the United States argued that a national bank would promote monetary stability and provide a safe place to deposit government funds. A national bank strengthened the banking system by refusing to accept the notes issued by overspeculative private banks and ensuring that bank notes were readily exchangeable for gold or silver. Critics denounced the proposed bank as unconstitutional.

By a narrow margin, Congress voted in 1816 to charter a second Bank of the United States for twenty years and give it the privilege of holding government funds without paying interest for their use. In return, it required the bank to pay a bonus of $1.5 million to the federal government and let the president name five of the bank's twenty-five directors.

Protecting American Industry

The War of 1812 provided tremendous stimulus to American manufacturing. The war encouraged manufacturers to produce many goods previously imported from overseas. By 1816, one hundred thousand factory workers, two-thirds of them women and children, produced more than $40 million worth of goods a year. Capital investment in textile manufacturing, sugar refining, and other industries totaled $100 million.

One of the results of peace, however, was a flood of cheap British imports which threatened to overwhelm the nation's infant industries. In 1815, $83 million worth of British goods reached American shores and the next year imports climbed to $155 million. In Parliament, a British minister defended the practice of dumping goods at prices below their actual cost on grounds that outraged American opinion. "It is well worth while," the minister declared, "to

In many of the new textile mills, the daughters of farmers made up the bulk of the employees.

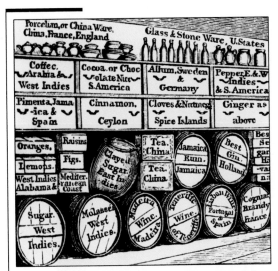

Porcelian, or China Ware, China, France, England		Glass & Stone Ware, U.States	
Coffee. Arabia & West Indies	Cocoa, or Chocolate Nut, S. America	Allum, Sweden & Germany	Pepper E. & W. Indies & S. America
Pimenta, Jamaica & Spain	Cinnamon, Ceylon	Cloves & Nutmegs Spice Islands	Ginger as above

At the end of the War of 1812, America's infant industries were threatened by a deluge of cheap foreign imports.

incur a loss upon the first exportation, in order, by a glut, to stifle in the cradle those rising manufactures in the United States which the war had forced into existence." So severe was the perceived threat to the nation's economic independence that Thomas Jefferson, who had once denounced manufacturing as a menace to the nation's republican values, spoke out in favor of protecting manufacturing industries: "We must now place the manufacturer by the side of the agriculturalist."

By imposing a duty on imported goods, supporters of a tariff hoped to make American goods more competitive. Critics opposed the tariff on the grounds that it would make foreign goods more expensive to buy and would provoke foreign retaliation. Daniel Webster feared that a tariff would harm New England shipping interests, and John Randolph of Virginia argued that a tariff was discriminatory because it benefited certain privileged business interests at the expense of consumers. He asked rhetorically, "On whom bears the duty on coarse woollens and linens, and blankets, upon salt and all the necessities of life?" His answer: "On poor men and slaveholders."

Proponents of the tariff prevailed, perpetuating protective duties set during the War of

1812. With import duties ranging from fifteen to thirty percent on cotton, textiles, leather, paper, pig iron, wool, and other goods, the tariff promised to protect America's growing industries from low cost competition.

Conquering Space

The end of the War of 1812, unleashed a mad rush of pioneers seeking land in Indiana, Illinois, Ohio, northern Georgia, western North Carolina, Alabama, Mississippi, and Tennessee. Pioneers demanded cheaper land and clamored for better transportation to move goods to Eastern markets.

In 1800, the American people were still nestled along the Atlantic coastline. More than two-thirds of the new nation's population still lived within fifty miles of the Atlantic seaboard and the center of population rested within eighteen miles of Baltimore. Only two roads cut across the Allegheny Mountains, and no more than half a million pioneers had moved as far west as Kentucky, Tennessee, or the western portion of Pennsylvania. Cincinnati was a town of 15,000 people; Buffalo and Rochester, New York, did not yet exist. Kickapoo, Miami, and Wyandotte Indians populated the areas that became the states of Illinois, Indiana, Michigan, and Wisconsin, while the Cherokee, Chicasaw, Choctaw, and Creek Indians considered the future states of Alabama, Mississippi, and western Georgia their domain.

At first, westward expansion occurred slowly. Between 1802, when Ohio was admitted to the Union, and the beginning of the War of 1812 not a single new state was carved out of the West. Thomas Jefferson estimated in 1803 that it would be a thousand years before settlers occupied the region east of the Mississippi. Following the War of 1812, settlers rapidly swept into the Ohio and Mississippi valleys. Four states quickly joined the union: Louisiana in 1812, Mississippi in 1817, Illinois in 1818, and Alabama in 1819.

Many farmers demanded that Congress revise the nation's land policies. Initially, Congress viewed federal lands as a source of revenue and public land policies reflected that view. Under a policy adopted in 1796, the federal gov-

The Conestoga wagon carried people and goods in the push for westward expansion. Settlers moved west and north along the Ohio and Mississippi rivers before moving to open farmlands further inland.

ernment only sold land in blocks of at least 640 acres. In practice, this policy tended to retard land sales and concentrate land ownership in the hands of a few large land companies and wealthy land speculators rich enough to afford to purchase large landholdings. In 1820, Congress sought to make it easier for farmers to purchase homesteads in the West by selling land in small lots suitable for operation by a family. Congress reduced the minimum allotment offered for sale from 640 acres to 80 acres. The minimum price per acre fell from $2 to $1.25. In 1796, a pioneer farmer purchasing a western farm had to pay $1280. In 1820, land could be purchased for just $100. The second Bank of the United States encouraged land purchases by liberally extending credit. The result was a boom in land sales. For a decade, the government sold about one million acres of land annually.

As the nation expanded westward, many Americans demanded that the federal government build a system of roads and canals to bind the nation together. In 1808, Albert Gallatin, Thomas Jefferson's secretary of the treasury, had proposed a $20 million scheme to construct turnpikes and canals. As a result of state and sectional jealousies and constitutional doubts, the federal government funded only a single turnpike, the National Road, stretching westward from Baltimore through Ohio and Indiana to Vandalia, Illinois.

In 1816, John C. Calhoun introduced a new proposal for federal aid for road and canal construction. Failure to link the nation together with an adequate system of transportation would, Calhoun warned, lead "to the greatest of calamities—disunion." "Let us," he exclaimed, "bind the republic together with a perfect system of roads and canals. Let us conquer space." Narrowly, Calhoun's proposal passed. But on the day before he left office, Madison vetoed the bill on constitutional grounds and recommended adoption of a constitutional amendment giving the federal government the power to build and maintain roads. Congress abandoned further proposals for internal improvements at federal expense.

Despite the failure to adopt a program of federally financed internal improvements, Congress had adopted major parts of the nationalist neo-Hamiltonian economic program. It had established a second Bank of the United States to provide a stable means of issuing money and a safe depository for federal funds. It had enacted a tariff to raise duties on foreign imports and guard American industries from low-cost competition, and it had instituted a new public land policy to encourage western settlement. In short, Congress had translated the spirit of national pride and unity that the nation felt after the War of 1812 into a legislative program that placed the national interest above narrow sectional interests.

Judicial Nationalism

The exuberant nationalism of the postwar period was also apparent in the decisions of the Supreme Court under Chief Justice John Marshall. Since his appointment to the Court in the last days of John Adams's administration in 1801, Chief Justice Marshall had succeeded in establishing the prestige and protecting the independence of the federal judiciary. When Marshall took office, the Court met in the basement of the Capitol and was rarely in session longer than six weeks a year. Since its creation in 1789, the Court had only decided one hundred cases, and the Supreme Court justices, including the chief justice, also served in the federal circuit courts.

As chief justice, Marshall greatly expanded the Court's authority. In the landmark 1803 decision in the case of *Marbury* v. *Madison*, he established the Supreme Court as the final arbiter of the Constitution and set the precedent that the Court had the power to declare acts of Congress unconstitutional. In the 1810 case of *Fletcher* v. *Peck*, he established the principle that the Court had the power to declare state laws void, and in 1816, in *Martin* v. *Hunter's Lessee*, the Court ruled that the Supreme Court had the power to review legal decisions by state courts.

After the War of 1812, Marshall wrote a series of decisions that strengthened the powers of the national government and opened the way for economic expansion. In *McCullough* v. *Maryland* (1819), the Court dealt with the constitutionality of the Bank of the United States. In a direct attack on the second Bank of the United States, the state of Maryland had placed a tax on the bank notes of all banks not chartered by the state, including the Baltimore branch of the national bank. In his decision, Marshall dealt with two fundamental questions. The first was whether the federal government had the power to incorporate a bank. The answer to this question, the Court ruled, was yes, because the Constitution granted Congress implied powers to do whatever was "necessary and proper" to carry out its powers. "Let the end be legitimate," Marshall wrote, "let it be within the scope of the Constitution, and all means which are appropriate, which are plainly adapted to that end, which are not prohibited, but consistent with the letter and spirit of the constitution, are constitutional."

The second question raised in *McCullough* v. *Maryland* was whether a state had the power to tax a branch of the Bank of the United States. In answer to this question, the Court said no. The Constitution, the Court asserted, created a new government with sovereign power over the states. "The power to tax involves the power to destroy," the Court declared, and the states did not have the right to exert an independent check on the authority of the federal government.

The Supreme Court under John Marshall played an important role in encouraging economic competition and development. In the case of *Dartmouth* v. *Woodward* (1819), the Supreme Court encouraged business growth by ruling that states could not unilaterally control private corporations. The case involved the efforts of the New Hampshire legislature to alter the charter of Dartmouth College, which had been granted by George III in 1769. The Court held that a charter was a valid contract protected by the Constitution and that states do not have the power to alter or impair contracts by unilateral action.

Five years later, in *Gibbons* v. *Ogden* (1824), the Court broadened the federal government's power to regulate interstate commerce and struck down state limitation on interstate transportation. The Court overturned a New York law that had awarded a monopoly

John Marshall and the six other members of the Supreme Court appear on the podium in this 1822 painting of the House of Representatives by Samuel F. B. Morse.

over steamboat traffic on the Hudson River, ruling that the Constitution had specifically given Congress the power to regulate commerce.

Under John Marshall, the Supreme Court established a distribution of constitutional powers that the country still follows. The Supreme Court became the final arbiter of the constitutionality of federal and state laws, and the federal government exercised sovereign power over the states. As a result of these decisions, it became increasingly difficult to argue that the union was a creation of the states, that states could exert an independent check on federal government authority, or that Congress's powers were limited to those specifically conferred by the Constitution.

Defending American Interests in Foreign Affairs

The War of 1812 stirred a new nationalistic spirit in foreign affairs. The decision in 1815 to put an end to raids by the Barbary pirates on American commercial shipping in the Mediterranean signaled a change in foreign policy. For seventeen years the United States had paid tribute to the ruler of Algiers. Taking advantage of the War of 1812, the Algerian leader had declared the United States owed him another $27,000, dismissed the American ambassador, seized American ships, and enslaved American citizens. Congress responded in March, 1815, by sending Captain Stephen Decatur and a fleet of ten ships into the Mediterranean where he captured two Algerian gun boats, towed the ships into the Algiers harbor, and threatened to bombard the city. As a result, all the North African states agreed to treaties releasing American prisoners without ransom, ending all demands for American tribute, guaranteeing American commerce would not be interfered with, and providing compensation for American vessels that had been seized.

Having successfully defended American interests in North Africa, Monroe turned his attention to grievances with Britain left over from the War of 1812. The countries left a host of issues unresolved in the peace treaty ending the war, including disputes over boundaries, trading and fishing rights, and rival claims to the Oregon region. The two governments moved quickly to settle these issues. The Rush-Bagot Agreement, signed with Great Britain in 1817, removed military ships from the Great Lakes. In 1818, Britain granted American fishermen the rights to fish in eastern Canadian waters, agreed to the 49th parallel as the boundary between the United States and Canada from Minnesota to the Rocky Mountains, and consented to joint occupation of the Oregon region.

The critical foreign policy issue facing the United States after the War of 1812 was the fate of Spain's New World empire. In 1808, Napoleon deposed the Spanish king, and Spain's New World colonies took advantage of the situation to fight for their independence. These revolutions aroused enormous sympathy in the United States, but unrest in Spain's New World colonies also raised the specter of European intervention. Suspicion grew that such European powers as Austria, France, Prussia, and Russia might use military force to suppress the New World revolutions and restore Spain's colonial empire. These powers had agreed to "put an end to the system of representative government, in whatever country it may exist in Eu-

rope," and they subdued uprisings in Italy in 1820 and Spain in 1822. Americans feared that the European powers might seek to put down revolutionary movements and restore monarchical order in the New World.

Monroe's initial concern was to secure the nation's southern and southwestern borders. A source of particular concern was Florida, which was still under Spanish control. Pirates, runaway slaves, and marauding Indians used Florida as a sanctuary and a jumping off point for raids on settlements in Georgia. To put an end to these incursions, in December, 1817, Monroe authorized General Andrew Jackson to lead a punitive expedition against the Seminole Indians in Florida. Jackson proceeded to crush the Seminoles, destroy their villages, and overthrow the Spanish governor. He also court-martialed and executed two British citizens whom he accused of inciting the Seminoles to commit atrocities against Americans.

Jackson's actions provoked a furor in Washington. Spain protested Jackson's acts and demanded that he be punished. Secretary of War John C. Calhoun and other members of Monroe's cabinet urged the president to reprimand Jackson for acting without specific authorization. In Congress, Henry Clay called for Jackson's censure. Secretary of State Adams, however, saw in Jackson's actions an opportunity to wrest Florida from Spain.

Instead of apologizing for Jackson's conduct, Adams declared that the raid into Florida was a legitimate act of self-defense justified by a 1795 treaty in which Spain had promised to check hostile incursions into American territory. Adams informed the Spanish government that either it would have to police Florida effectively or give it to the United States. Convinced that American annexation was inevitable, Spain ceded Florida to the United States in the Adams-Onis Treaty of 1819, and the United States agreed to honor $5 million in damage claims by Americans against Spain. Under the treaty, Spain relinquished its claims to Oregon, and the United States temporarily renounced its claims to Texas.

Meanwhile, the United States feared European intervention in two areas—the Pacific Northwest and Latin America. In 1821, Russia

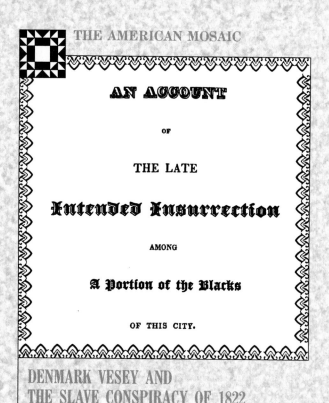

AN ACCOUNT

OF

THE LATE

Intended Insurrection

AMONG

A Portion of the Blacks

OF THIS CITY.

DENMARK VESEY AND THE SLAVE CONSPIRACY OF 1822

"Do not open your lips! Die silent, as you shall see me do." Speaking from the gallows, Peter Poyas soon met his death with stoic dignity— as did five others on the second day of July in 1822. Among the five was Denmark Vesey, whose quiet composure at death reflected the steely courage with which he had led blacks in and around Charleston, South Carolina, in plotting insurrection. As their trials revealed, for over a year Vesey and his lieutenants had planned, recruited, and hoarded the provisions for the fight. Only betrayal by a few slaves had prevented what could well have become the bloodiest slave revolt in America's history.

Many whites were surprised at the revelation of Vesey's leader-

ship. In their eyes he seemed to have few grievances. Born in the late 1760s in either Africa or the Caribbean, he served as a slave to Captain Joseph Vesey, a Bermuda slave trader who settled in Charleston in 1783 as a slave broker and ship merchandiser. In 1800 Denmark Vesey won $1500 in the East Bay Lottery. He then purchased his freedom for $600 and opened a carpentry shop; by 1817 he had amassed savings of several thousand dollars. He was literate and well-traveled. He had once been offered the opportunity to return to Africa as a free man and rejected it. "What did he have to be upset about?" many whites must have asked. Well, for one thing, his wife and several of his

children were still in bondage. He also deeply resented white interference in the lives of free blacks as well as slaves.

Vesey was a proud man and frequently rebuked friends who acquiesed to such traditional displays of deference as bowing to whites on the street. One remembered Vesey telling him "all men were born equal, and that he was surprised that anyone would degrade himself by such conduct; that he would never cringe to whites, nor ought any who had the feelings of a man."

As in cities throughout the nation, blacks in Charleston were meeting oppression by forging their own institutions and creating self-affirming communities. A key part of this process was religious independence. At the close of the War of 1812 black Methodists in Charleston outnumbered white ones ten to one. After an unsuccessful attempt by blacks to control their destinies within the white church, Morris Brown went to Philadelphia and was ordained by the African Methodist Episcopal church. In 1818, following a dispute over a burial ground, more than three-fourths of the 6000 black Methodists of Charleston withdrew from the white-led churches. Morris Brown was appointed bishop, and the African Church of Charleston was established.

White authorities quickly saw the danger of such independent churches as possible seedbeds of radicalism. Thus they harassed church meetings and jailed church leaders. Beginning in 1820 legislation was passed to reduce the free black population of South Carolina. Finally in 1821 the city of Charleston closed the Hampstead

Church, which had been the leader of the independent church movement—and which included Denmark Vesey among its members. That closing became the spark that ignited Vesey to action. He began holding meetings, often in his own home, with other members of the congregation, such as Rolla Bennett, "Gullah Jack" Pritchard, Monday Gell, and Ned and Peter Poyas. They became the nucleus of what came to be called the Vesey Conspiracy.

Later testimony indicates that Vesey was well aware of several recent events that convinced him that the tide of history was changing. Foremost was the successful slave rebellion in Haiti that began in 1791. Vesey "was in the habit of reading to me all the passages in the newspapers that related to St. Domingo, and apparently every pamphlet he could lay his hands on that had any connection with slavery," one rebel testified. Vesey was also knowledgeable about the Missouri debates; the same rebel reported, "He one day brought me a speech which he told me had been delivered in congress by a Mr. [Rufus] King on the subject of slavery; he told me this Mr. King was the black man's friend, that he, Mr. King, had declared . . . that slavery was a great disgrace to the country."

Vesey used religion as a potent force to spur blacks to join him in armed rebellion. At almost every meeting he "read to us from the Bible, how the children of Israel were delivered out of Egypt from bondage." He also frequently used the passage: "Behold the day of the Lord cometh, and thy spoil shall be divided in the midst of thee. For I shall gather all nations against Jerusalem to battle; and

the city shall be taken." In addition "Gullah Jack," born in Africa, was known as a powerful conjurer, and many were convinced his power could protect them from harm.

There was a distinctly Pan-African cast to the conspiracy. A number of the leaders had lived in either Africa or the Caribbean. One of them, Monday Gell, had apparently corresponded with the president of Haiti. Charleston blacks were told that "Santo Domingo and Africa will assist us to get our liberty, if we will only make the motion first." The motion they planned was bold indeed. They were to attack the city at seven different points, capture weapons at the arsenal, set fire to the city, and kill all whites they encountered.

The plan was bold but not rashly undertaken. They prepared for a deadline in the second week of July 1822. Large numbers were needed and available. Blacks outnumbered whites ten to one in the area surrounding Charleston, and recruiting extended to plantations as far away as eighty miles. The big problem was a shortage of arms until the arsenal was taken. So blacksmiths began making bayonets and spikes. Anything that could be used as a weapon was hoarded, along with gun powder. Draymen, caters, and butchers were recruited to supply horses. Hundreds of blacks from all classes and occupations were contacted, but the nucleus remained skilled artisans, free and slave, from Charleston.

The dangers of advance planning and a widespread network were leaks and betrayal. For months luck held, but in late May 1822 a slave reported an attempt

to recruit him to the insurrection. As authorities began to investigate, the betrayals escalated, and the authorities deployed military force to quash the rebellion before it had a chance to get started. Ten slaves were arrested on June 17-18, and the court began hearings. On June 22 Vesey was captured and stood trial the next day, while "Gullah Jack," the only major leader still free, tried to continue the revolt. Three days after the July 2 executions "Gullah Jack" was arrested. By August 9 more than thirty blacks had been hanged and many more deported.

White retaliation was swift and sure. So was white hysteria. The executions were public, and blacks were forbidden to dress in black or wear black crepe to mourn the dead. Examples were also made of the informers, who were freed and granted life-time annuities. Finally, whites responded to Vesey's conspiracy with further antiblack legislation.

On the surface little good came from Denmark Vesey's bold plan. Its chances of success were meagre at best. During Vesey's sentencing, the presiding magistrate told him, "It is difficult to imagine what *infatuation* could have prompted you to attempt an enterprise so wild and visionary. You were a free man; were comparatively wealthy; and enjoyed every comfort, compatible with your situation. You had therefore, much to risk and little to gain. From your age and experience you *ought* to have known, that success was impracticable." Nevertheless Vesey took his indomitable stand. While recruiting for the Union army, the great black abolitionist Frederick Douglass called upon blacks "to remember Denmark Vesey."

claimed control of the entire Pacific coast from Alaska to Oregon and closed the area to foreign shipping. At the same time, rumors spread throughout Europe that France was about to help Spain crush the rebellions in Spain's Latin American colonies.

European intervention threatened British as well as American interests. Not only did Britain have a flourishing trade with Latin America, which would decline if Spain regained its New World colonies, but it also had claims to the Oregon region. In 1823, British Foreign Minister George Canning proposed that the United States and Britain jointly express their opposition to further European intervention in the Americas.

Monroe initially regarded the British proposal favorably. He sought the advice of former presidents Thomas Jefferson and James Madison, who counseled acceptance. With Great Britain "on our side," wrote Jefferson, "we need not fear the whole world." Secretary of State Adams opposed a joint Anglo-American declaration, fearing that it would make the United States "a cock-boat in the wake of the British man-of-war." Convinced that the British would use their sea power to prevent European intervention whether or not the United States agreed to be their partner, Adams urged the president to issue an independent declaration of American policy. Monroe decided to follow Adams's advice.

In his annual message to Congress in 1823, Monroe outlined the principles that have become known as the Monroe Doctrine. He announced that the Western Hemisphere was henceforth closed to any further European colonization, and he declared that the United States would regard any attempt by European nations "to extend their system to any portion of this hemisphere as dangerous to our peace and safety." He also said that the United States would not interfere in internal European affairs.

For the American people, the Monroe Doctrine was the proud symbol of American hegemony in the Western Hemisphere. Unilaterally, the United States had defined its rights and interests in the New World. It is true that during the first half of the nineteenth century the United States lacked the military power to enforce the Monroe Doctrine and depended upon the British navy to deter European intervention in the Americas. But the nation had clearly warned the European powers that any threat to American security would provoke American retaliation.

The era of good feelings marked one of the most successful periods in American diplomacy. Apart from ending the attacks of the Barbary pirates on American shipping, the United States settled many of its disagreements with Britain, acquired Florida from Spain, defined its western and southwestern boundaries, convinced Spain and Russia to relinquish their claims to the Oregon region, and delivered a strong warning that European powers were not to interfere in the Western Hemisphere.

THE ROOTS OF AMERICAN ECONOMIC GROWTH

The years following the War of 1812 was a period of explosive economic growth. At the beginning of the nineteenth century, the United States was an overwhelmingly rural and agricultural nation. Ninety percent of the population in the Northeast and ninety-five percent of the people of the South lived on farms or in villages with fewer than 2500 inhabitants. The nation's population was small and scattered over a vast geographical area—just 5.3 million in 1800, compared to Britain's 15 million and France's 27 million.

Transportation and communication had changed little over the previous half century. A coach ride between Boston and New York took three days; from New York to Philadelphia, another two days. South of the Mason-Dixon line, the situation was far worse. Except for a single stage coach which traveled between Charleston and Savannah, no public transportation of any kind could be found in the Southern states. It took twenty days to deliver a letter between Maine and Georgia.

American houses, clothing, and agricultural methods were surprisingly primitive. Fifty miles inland, half the houses were log cabins, lacking even glass windows. Farmers planted their crops in much the same way as their parents and grandparents. Few farmers practiced crop rotation, used fertilizers, or drained fields. They made plows out of wood, allowed their swine to run loose, and left their cattle outside except on the coldest nights.

Manufacturing was still quite backward. In rural areas, farm families grew their own food, produced their own soap and candles, wove their own blankets, and constructed their own furniture. The leading manufacturing industries—iron-making, textiles, and clothes-making—employed only about 15,000 people in mills or factories.

At the beginning of the nineteenth century, the nation's future economic prospects seemed bleak. In the space of just three decades, however, the United States became a world leader in industry. The era stretching from the end of the War of 1812 to the mid-1830s was a critical period for the nation's future economic growth. During these years the United States overcame a series of serious obstacles that stood in the way of sustained economic expansion. The development of steamboats, canals, and ultimately railroads reduced transportation costs and speeded communications. The rapid growth of cities created expanding markets for industrial goods. Improvements in farming dramatically increased agricultural productivity, stimulated industrialization by paying for imports of machinery and manufactured goods, and freed many children of farmers to work in industry and commerce. A series of technological innovations, highlighted by the development of the "American System" of mass production and interchangeable parts, stimulated productivity. By the early 1830s, the United States had already become an industrial power second only to Great Britain.

Accelerating Transportation

At the outset of the nineteenth century, the lack of reliable, low cost transportation was a major barrier to American industrial development. Slow and cumbersome, the stage coach was the major form of transportation. Twelve passengers, crowded along with their bags and parcels, traveled at just four miles an hour. In Connecticut and Massachusetts, Sunday travel was still forbidden by law.

The major form of public transportation in the early nineteenth century was the stage coach. Unprotected from the weather, twelve passengers traveled with baggage between their knees at only four miles per hour.

Wretched roads plagued travelers. Larger towns had roads paved with cobblestones; potholes in major highways were filled with stones. Most roads were simply dirt paths. Rain left these roads muddy and rutted. The presence of tree stumps in the middle of many roads posed a serious obstacle to carriages. Charles Dickens aptly described American roads as a "series of alternate swamps and gravel pits."

The cost of transporting goods overland was prohibitive. It cost as much to transport a ton of freight three hundred miles over land as it did to ship it from Philadelphia to Europe. Worse yet, tolls on "post roads" were extremely high. In New Jersey, a one-horse cart was charged three cents a mile.

Builders inaugurated a new era in transportation in 1791 with the construction of a sixty-six-mile-long turnpike between Philadelphia and Lancaster, Pennsylvania, which stimulated a craze for toll road construction. By 1811, 135 private companies in New York had invested $7.5 million in 1500 miles of road. By 1838, Pennsylvania had invested $37 million to build 2200 miles of turnpikes.

Robert Fulton's *Clermont*, the first commercially successful steamboat, was 150 feet long, 18 feet wide, weighed 100 tons, and sailed 5 miles per hour.

In spite of the construction of turnpikes, the cost of transporting freight over land remained high, at least fifteen cents to move a ton of goods a mile. Water transportation was cheaper, and farmers often shipped their farm produce down the Mississippi, Potomac, or Hudson rivers by flatboat or raft. Unfortunately, water transportation was slow and few vessels were capable of going very far upstream. The trip downstream from Pittsburgh to New Orleans took a month; the trip upstream against the current took four months. Steam power offered the obvious solution, and inventors built at least sixteen steamships before Robert Fulton successfully demonstrated the practicality of steam navigation in 1807 by sailing a 160-ton side-wheeler, the *Clermont*, 150 miles from New York City to Albany in only 32 hours. "Fulton's folly," as critics mockingly referred to it, opened a new era of faster and cheaper water transportation.

The construction of canals connecting major waterways further improved water transportation. Prior to the War of 1812, construction companies built scarcely a hundred miles of canals because of heavy costs which ran $25,000 to $80,000 a mile. The spectacular success of the Erie Canal, however, touched off an enormous wave of canal construction.

On Wednesday, October 25, 1825, the state of New York opened the Erie Canal, which connected the Great Lakes to the Atlantic Ocean. To celebrate the opening, New Yorkers fired cannons, placed at eight-mile intervals along the 364-mile length of the canal. The canal was a stupendous engineering achievement. Three thousand workers, using hand labor, toiled for eight years to build the canal. They had cut through forests, dug through rock, and built over swamps. They built eighty-four locks, each fifteen feet wide and ninety feet long, to raise or lower barges ten feet at a time. They even raised a river nine feet with a 900-foot dam and built eighteen aqueducts, one over 800-feet long, over rivers and valleys.

The "big ditch" sparked an economic revolution. Before the canal was built, it cost $100 and took twenty days to transport a ton of freight from Buffalo to New York City. After the canal was opened, the cost fell to $5 a ton and transit time was reduced to six days. By 1827, as a result of the canal, wheat from central New York state could be bought for less in Savannah, Georgia, than wheat grown in Georgia itself.

The success of the Erie Canal led other states to embark on expensive programs of canal building. Pennsylvanians, aware that it cost more to transport goods 150 miles within

The greatest engineering feat of the Erie Canal took place at the town of Lockport, where seven locks, each capable of raising or lowering a barge ten feet, were constructed.

their state than it did for New Yorkers to ship goods 750 miles between New York City and Ohio, spent $10 million to build a canal between Philadelphia and Pittsburgh. The states of Illinois, Indiana, and Ohio launched expensive projects to connect the Ohio and Mississippi rivers to the Great Lakes. By 1840, 3326 miles of canals had been dug at a cost of $125 million.

Cities like Baltimore and Boston which were unable to reach the west with canals experimented with the railroad, a novel form of transportation. At first, a railroad was simply a highway lined with a double track of wood rails, which allowed a horse or mule to pull a stage coach or wagon. In 1829 the Delaware and Hudson Canal Company imported two English steam locomotives, but found the engines too heavy for American rails and trestles. In 1830 the first American-built locomotives were put into regular operation on the Baltimore and Ohio, Charleston and Hamburg, and Mohawk and Hudson railroads.

These early railroads suffered from nagging engineering problems and vociferous opposition. The first rails were simply wooden beams with a metal strip nailed to the surface. The strips frequently curled up, cutting through the train's floor. Brakes were wholly inadequate, consisting of wooden blocks operated by a foot pedal. Boilers exploded so frequently that passengers had to be protected by bales of cotton. Engine sparks set fire to fields and burned unprotected passengers. One English traveler counted thirteen holes burned in her dress after a short ride.

Prejudice against railroads was widespread. Vested interests, including turnpike and bridge

The earliest railroad locomotives, patterned after horse-drawn stage coaches, were simply boilers mounted on wheels.

companies, stage coaches, ferries, and canals, sought laws to prohibit trains from carrying freight. A group of Boston doctors warned that bumps produced by trains traveling at fifteen or twenty miles an hour would lead to cases of "concussion of the brain." An Ohio school board declared that "such things as railroads . . . are impossibilities and rank infidelity."

In spite of such objections, it quickly became clear after 1830 that railroads were destined to become the nation's chief means of moving freight. During the 1830s, construction companies laid down 3328 miles of track, roughly equal to all the miles of canals in the country. With an average speed of ten miles an hour, railroads were faster than stage coaches, canals, and steamboats, and unlike water-going vessels, could travel in any season.

The transportation revolution sharply reduced the cost of shipping goods to market and stimulated agriculture and industry. New roads, canals, and railroads speeded the pace of commerce and strengthened ties between the East and West.

Speeding Communications

An inadequate transportation system was not the only obstacle standing in the way of economic development. Poor communication was another important problem. During the 1790s, it took three weeks for a letter to travel from New York to Cincinnati or Detroit and four weeks to arrive in New Orleans. In 1799 it took a week for news of George Washington's death to reach New York City. A decade and a half later, it still took forty-nine days for word of the peace treaty ending the War of 1812 to reach New York.

By the early 1830s, a decade before Samuel F. B. Morse invented the telegraph, improvements in transportation had already speeded the transmission of information. In 1831 it took just fifteen and a half hours for the text of Andrew Jackson's State of the Union address to travel from Washington to New York—eight times faster than in 1799. By 1841 a letter traveled between New York and New Orleans in nine days and between New York and Cincinnati in five days—three times faster than in 1815.

Not only had communications become faster and more reliable, the amount of information transmitted also increased markedly. In 1790 there were just 92 newspapers in the United States, with a total annual circulation of less than 4 million. By 1820 the number of papers published had jumped to 512, with an annual circulation of 50 million, and by 1835 there were 1258 newspapers in the United States with a circulation of over 90 million. When Alexis de Tocqueville, a French observer, visited the United States in 1831, he was shocked at the amount of information available even in frontier regions: "I do not think that in the most enlightened rural districts of France there is an intellectual movement either so rapid or on such a scale as in this wilderness."

Resistance to Technological Innovation

At the beginning of the nineteenth century, the United States lagged far behind Europe in the practical application of science and technology. There was probably just one steam engine in regular operation in the United States in 1800, one hundred years after simple engines had been first used in Europe. Only eight cotton mills operated in the United States, ten years after the first cotton mill's construction. Inventors, like Oliver Evans, designer of an early locomotive, and John Fitch, creator of the first steamboat, failed because they were unable to finance their projects or persuade the public to use their inventions.

The lack of skilled machinists presented a particularly severe barrier to innovation. In 1805, when Robert Fulton wanted to build a torpedo, he could find only one mechanic in New York who could follow his plans, a Frenchman who spoke virtually no English. Two years later, when he needed an engine to propel the *Clermont* up the Hudson River, he had to import a steam engine from England, since American craftsmen could not construct such a complicated machine.

Another serious impediment to the application of science and technology to the growth of industry was an inadequate system of higher education. Harvard, the nation's most famous college, graduated just thirty-nine men a year, no more than it had graduated in 1720. Harvard's entire undergraduate faculty consisted of the college president, a professor of theology, a professor of mathematics, a professor of Hebrew, and four tutors. All the nation's libraries put together contained barely 50,000 volumes. Noah Webster, author of the nation's first dictionary, admitted grudgingly: "Our learning is superficial in shameful degree . . . our colleges are disgracefully destitute of books and philosophical apparatus."

Even in educated circles, resistance to technological change was widespread. Jedidiah Morse, a graduate of Yale College and pastor of a church near Boston, gave pointed expression to the widespread hostility toward change. "Let us guard against the insidious encroachments of innovation," he wrote, "the evil and beguiling spirit which is now stalking to and fro through the earth, seeking how he may destroy."

Transforming American Law

The growth of an industrial economy in the United States required something more than the construction of roads, canals, and railroads, improved communications, or even a more positive outlook on technological innovation. It also required a decisive shift in American law. At the beginning of the nineteenth century, the nation's legal system reflected the values of a slowly-changing agricultural society. The law presumed that goods and services had a just price, independent of supply and demand. Courts forbade many forms of competition and innovation in the name of a stable society. Courts and judges legally protected monopolies and prevented lenders from charging "usurous" rates of interest. The law allowed property owners to sue for damages if a mill was built upstream and it flooded their land or impeded their water supply. After 1815, however, the American legal system favored economic growth, profit, and entrepreneurial enterprise. Courts increasingly viewed risk and profit as beneficial.

In the 1810s and 1820s American law made the decisive shift from a pre-market to a market economy. By the 1820s, courts, particularly in the Northeast, had begun to abandon many traditional legal doctrines which stood in the way of a competitive market economy. Courts dropped older legal doctrines which assumed that goods and services had an objective price, independent of supply and demand. Courts rejected many usury laws, which limited interest rates, and struck down legal rules that prevented tenants from making alterations on a piece of land, including the addition of a building or clearing of trees. Courts increasingly held that only the market could determine interest rates or prices or the equity of a contract.

To promote rapid economic growth, courts and state legislatures gave new powers and privileges to private firms. They gave companies building roads, bridges, canals, and other public works the power to appropriate land and allowed private firms to avoid legal penalties for fires, floods, or noise they caused on the grounds that the companies served a public purpose. Courts also reduced the liability of companies for injuries to their own employees, ruling that an injured party had to prove negligence or carelessness on the part of an employer in order to collect damages. The legal barriers to economic expansion had been struck down.

Early Industrialization and Urbanization

By the late 1820s, transportation costs had been cut, communication accelerated, and popular resistance to technological innovation largely overcome. Manufacturers began to adopt labor-saving machinery which allowed workers to produce more goods at lower costs. At the same time, urban manufacturing centers began to grow at a rapid pace. New urban and industrial patterns had become an increasingly important aspect of American life.

When Friedrich List, a German traveler, visited the United States in the 1820s, he was astonished by the amount of public interest in technology. "Everything new is quickly introduced here," List wrote. "There is no clinging to old ways; the moment an American hears the word 'invention' he pricks up his ears." By the 1820s and 1830s, no nation in the world had gone so far toward adopting production methods emphasizing mechanization, standardization, and mass production. So impressed were foreigners with these methods of manufacture that they called them the "American system of production."

The single most important figure in the development of the American system was Eli Whitney, the inventor of the cotton gin. In 1798, Whitney persuaded the U.S. government to award him a contract for ten thousand muskets to be delivered within two years. At the time Whitney made his offer, the federal arsenal at Springfield, Massachusetts, was capable of producing only 245 muskets in two years. Since Whitney had no factory and no experience making guns, his offer seemed preposterous.

Whitney proposed manufacturing muskets according to a "new principle" which would enable an unskilled worker to produce muskets faster than those made by a gunsmith. Until then, rifles had been manufactured by skilled craftsmen, who made individual parts by hand and then carefully fitted the pieces together. Whitney's idea was to develop precision machinery to make parts which would be interchangeable from one gun to another. For months, Whitney struggled to develop drill presses, lathes, cutters, and grinders that would allow a worker with little manual skill to manufacture identical gun parts. The first year he produced 500 muskets.

In 1801, Whitney demonstrated his new system of interchangeable parts to John Adams and Thomas Jefferson. He disassembled ten muskets and put ten new muskets together out of the individual pieces. His system was a success.

Other industries soon applied Whitney's "American system of manufacturing." In 1815 manufacturers of wooden clocks began to use interchangeable parts. Makers of sewing machines used mass production techniques as early as 1846, and the next year, manufacturers mechanized the production of farm machinery.

Innovation was not confined to manufacturing. During the years following the War of 1812, American agriculture underwent a transformation nearly as profound and far-reaching as the revolution taking place in industry.

In 1793 Charles Newbold, a New Jersey farmer, spent his entire fortune of $30,000 developing an efficient cast iron plow. Farmers

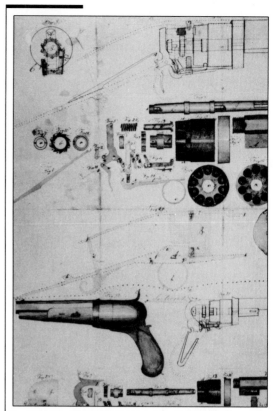

In 1835, Samuel Colt filed his first patent for a revolver made out of interchangeable parts.

refused to use it, fearing that iron would poison the soil and cause weeds to grow. Twenty years later, a Scipio, New York, farmer named Jethro Wood patented an improved iron plow made out of interchangeable parts. Unlike wooden plows, which required two men and four oxen to plow an acre in a day, Wood's cast iron plow allowed one man and one yoke of oxen to plow the same area. Demand was so great that manufacturers infringed on Wood's patents and produced thousands of copies of this new plow each year.

During the early decades of the nineteenth century, American agriculture underwent a revolution. Machines increased farmers' productivity and commercial agriculture, in which farmers specialized in a money crop and bought most of their supplies with the proceeds, replaced subsistence farming.

During the eighteenth century, most farm families were largely self-sufficient. They raised their own food, made their own clothes and shoes, and built their own furniture. Cut off from markets by the high cost of transportation, farmers sold only a few items, like whiskey, corn, and hogs, in exchange for such necessities as salt and iron goods. Farming methods were primitive. With the exception of plowing and furrowing, most farmwork was performed by hand. European travelers deplored the backwardness of American farmers, their ignorance of the principles of scientific farming, their lack of labor-saving machinery, and their wastefulness of natural resources. Few farmers applied manure to their fields as fertilizer or practiced crop rotation, and as a result soil erosion and soil exhaustion were commonplace. Commented one observer, "Agriculture in the South does not consist so much in cultivating land as in killing it."

Beginning in the last decade of the eighteenth century, agriculture underwent profound changes. Farmers began to grow larger crop surpluses and specialize in cash crops. A growing demand for cotton for England's textile mills led to the introduction of long-staple cotton into the islands and lowlands of Georgia and South Carolina. Eli Whitney's invention of the cotton gin in 1793—which permitted an individual to clean 50 pounds of cotton in a single day, 50 times more than could be cleaned by hand—made it practical to produce short-staple cotton in the South. Other cash crops raised by Southern farmers included rice, flax, hemp, and sugar. In the Northeast, the growth of mill towns and urban centers created a growing demand for hogs, cattle, sheep, corn, wheat, wool, butter, milk, cheese, fruit, vegetables, and hay to feed horses.

A shortage of farm labor encouraged many farmers to adopt labor-saving machinery. Prior to the introduction in 1803 of the cradle scythe—a rake used to gather up grain and deposit it in even piles—a farmer could not harvest more than half an acre a day. The horse rake—a device introduced in 1820 to mow hay—allowed a single farmer to perform the work of eight to ten men. The invention in 1836 of a mechanical thresher, used to separate the

With Eli Whitney's cotton gin, the amount of cotton fiber that a slave could separate from seed increased from one pound a day to fifty pounds.

wheat from the chaff, helped to cut in half the man-hours required to produce an acre of wheat.

By 1830 the roots of America's future industrial growth had been firmly planted. Back in 1807, the nation had just fifteen or twenty cotton mills, containing approximately eight thousand spindles. By 1831 the number of spindles in use totaled nearly a million and a quarter. By 1830 Pittsburgh produced 100 steam engines a year; Cincinnati, 150. Factory production had made obsolete household manufacture of shoes, clothing, textiles, and farm implements. The United States had become the world's second leading industrial nation, trailing only Great Britain.

At the beginning of the nineteenth century, the United States was a nation of farms and rural villages. The nation's four largest cities together contained only 180,000 persons and were the country's only cities with more than 10,000 inhabitants. Boston, which in 1800 contained just 25,000 inhabitants, looked much as it had prior to the Revolution. Its streets were still paved with cobblestones and were unlighted at night. Older gentlemen could still be seen dressed in three-cornered hats, knee breeches, white-topped boots, ruffled shirts, and powdered wigs. New York was so small that Wall Street was considered to be uptown and Broadway was a country drive. New York's entire police force, which only patrolled the city at night, consisted of two captains, two deputies, and seventy-two assistants.

During the 1820s and 1830s, the nation's cities grew at an extraordinary rate. The urban population increased at a rate of sixty percent a decade, five times as fast as that of the country as a whole. In 1810, New York City's population was less than 100,000. Two decades later it was more than 200,000. Over the same span, Pittsburgh's population climbed from 4768 to 15,369; Richmond from 9735 to 16,060; and Louisville from 1357 to 10,341.

The chief cause of this urban growth was the migration of people away from farms and villages. The growth of commerce drew thousands of the sons of farmers to work as bookkeepers, clerks, and salesmen. The expansion of factory enterprise demanded thousands of laborers, mechanics, teamsters, and factory operatives. The need of rural areas for services available only in urban areas also promoted the growth of cities. Frontier farmers needed nails, horseshoes, glass, and farm implements, and to meet this demand iron foundries, blacksmith shops, and glass factories arose in Pittsburgh. Farmers needed their grain milled and their livestock butchered, and a grain processing and meatpacking industry sprouted up in "Porkopolis," Cincinnati. Manufacturers in Lexington produced hemp sacks and rope for Kentucky farmers, and Louisville businesses cured and marketed tobacco.

Already by the 1820s, the rapid growth of the nation's cities had created a vast array of urban problems. These ranged from a lack of clean drinking water to inadequate sewage facilities to a pressing need for public transportation. Sanitation was the most serious problem. Most city-dwellers used outdoor privies, which emptied into vaults and cesspools, sometimes leaking into the soil and contaminating the water supply. Kitchen wastes were thrown into ditches and refuse was thrown into trash piles by the side of the streets. Every horse in a city deposited as much as twenty pounds of manure and urine on the streets each day. To help remove the garbage and refuse, many cities allowed packs of dogs, goats, pigs, or cattle to scavenge freely. The editor of one New York

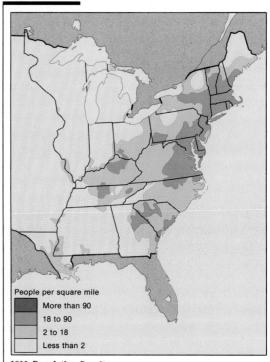

People per square mile

More than 90

18 to 90

2 to 18

Less than 2

1810 Population Density

newspaper described the filth that plagued that city's streets in vivid terms: "The offal and filth, of which there are loads thrown from the houses in defiance of an ordinance which is never enforced, is scraped up with the usual deposits of mud and manure into big heaps and left for weeks together on the sides of the streets." The absence of adequate sanitation contributed to a heavy urban mortality rate and to recurrent outbreaks of such epidemic diseases as typhoid, dysentery, typhus, cholera, and yellow fever.

Following the War of 1812, however, some steps were taken to promote a more comfortable existence for the nation's growing urban population. In about 1815 primitive toilets, called water closets, began to appear in the homes of the well-to-do. Around the same time, coal-burning iron ranges began to replace open fireplaces for cooking and iron stoves appeared to heat houses during the winter. To provide light after darkness fell, Boston in 1822 introduced the first gas-fueled street lights, and in-

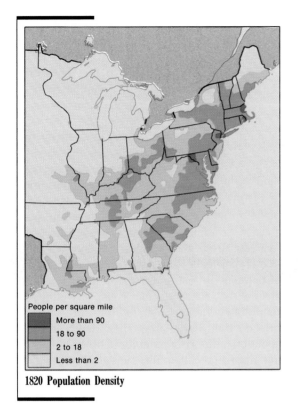

1820 Population Density

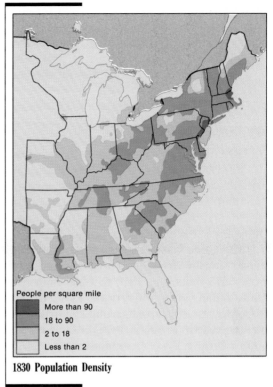

1830 Population Density

dividual households relied upon new kinds of lamps burning whale oil or turpentine. A public bus system made its first appearance in New York City in 1828. The 1830s witnessed the formation of the first full-time professional police forces in the United States.

Unfortunately, many of the improvements in urban life were only enjoyed by the well-to-do. Slums began to appear on New York's lower east side as early as 1815 and by the 1840s over 18,000 men, women, and children were crowded into damp, unlighted, ill-ventilated cellars with six to twenty persons living in a single room. In Boston's slums, a Committee on Internal Health reported in 1849, there lived men, women, and children "huddled together like brutes without regard to sex, age or a sense of decency, grown men and women sleeping together in the same apartment, and sometimes wife, brothers, and sisters in the same bed." Problems of slums and urban poverty were left for later generations of Americans to try to solve.

THE GROWTH OF POLITICAL FACTIONALISM AND SECTIONALISM

The "Era of Good Feelings" began with a burst of nationalistic fervor. The economic program adopted by Congress, including a national bank and a protective tariff, reflected the growth of a feeling of national unity. The Supreme Court promoted the spirit of nationalism by establishing the principle of federal supremacy. Industrialization and improvements in transportation also added to the sense of national unity by contributing to the nation's economic strength and independence and linking the West and the East together.

This same period also witnessed the emergence of growing factional divisions in politics and a deepening sectional split between the North and South. A severe economic depression between 1819 and 1822 provoked bitter division over questions of banking and tariffs.

Geographic expansion exposed latent tensions over the morality of slavery and the balance of economic power. It was during the "Era of Good Feelings" that the political issues arose that would dominate American politics for the next forty years.

The Panic of 1819

In 1819 financial panic struck the country. Banks failed, mortgages were foreclosed, and agricultural prices fell by half. Unemployment mounted, investment in western lands collapsed, and the trade expansion that followed the War of 1812 came to an abrupt halt.

The panic was terrifying in its scope and impact. In New York State, property values fell from $315 million in 1818 to $265 million in 1820. In Richmond, property values fell by half. In Pennsylvania, land values plunged from $150 an acre in 1815 to $35 in 1819. In Philadelphia, 1808 individuals were committed to debtors' prison. In Boston, the figure was 3500.

For the first time in American history, the problem of urban poverty commanded public attention. In New York in 1819, the Society for the Prevention of Pauperism counted 8000 paupers, out of a population of 120,000. The next year, the figure climbed to 13,000. Fifty thousand people were unemployed or irregularly employed in New York, Philadelphia, and Baltimore, and one foreign observer estimated that half a million people were jobless nationwide. To address the problem of destitution, newspapers appealed for old clothes and shoes for the poor and churches and municipal governments distributed soup. Baltimore set up twelve soup kitchens in 1820 to give food to the poor.

The downswing spread like a plague across the country. In Cincinnati, bankruptcy sales occurred almost daily. In Lexington, Kentucky, factories worth half a million dollars were idle. Matthew Carey, a Philadelphia economist, estimated that three million people, one-third of the nation's population, were adversely affected by the panic. In 1820 John C. Calhoun commented: "There has been within these two years an immense revolution of fortunes in every part of the Union; enormous numbers of persons utterly ruined; multitudes in deep distress."

There was no one cause for the panic. Rather it was the result of a combination of causes. A catastrophic drop in cotton prices in 1818 cut the income of many southern farmers. A sharp curtailment of credit in 1818 by the second Bank of the United States, intended to curb inflation, resulted in banks suspending payment in gold or silver. A Congressional order in 1817 mandating the resumption of land payments in hard currency forced many land purchasers to default. An influx of cheap European manufactured goods closed many factories.

The ordeal of the panic unleashed a storm of popular protest and a spate of proposals to ensure that the economic collapse would not recur. Many debtors agitated for "stay laws" to provide them relief from their debts and the abolition of imprisonment for debt. Manufacturing interests called for increased protection from foreign imports, but a growing number of Southerners believed that the root of their troubles lay in high protective tariffs which raised the cost of imported goods and reduced the flow of international trade. Many people clamored for a reduction in the cost of government and pressed for sharp reductions in federal and state budgets. Many Americans, particularly in the South and West, blamed the panic on the nation's banks and particularly the tight money policies of the Bank of the United States.

By 1823 the panic was over. However, the depression left a lasting imprint upon American politics. It stirred widespread discontent and led to vocal demands for radical changes in the administration of government. Financial distress led groups throughout the country to demand the democratization of state constitutions and the elimination of property requirements for voting and officeholding. The panic also heightened hostility toward banks and other "privileged" corporations and monopolies that profited on the basis of political favoritism.

Another result of the panic was to accelerate the split within the Republican party into a number of loose factions. Sectional tensions also increased by leading northern manufactur-

CHRONOLOGY OF KEY EVENTS

1785 Oliver Evans invents first automatic flour mill

1786 John Fitch invents first steamboat

1793 Samuel Slater erects the first American textile mill at Pawtucket, Rhode Island

1797 Charles Newbold patents the first cast-iron plow

1807 Robert Fulton's steamboat *Clermont* makes its first run across the Hudson River; In Connecticut, Seth Thomas and Eli Terry begin to manufacture clocks with interchangeable parts

1816 Congress declares war on Algiers; Second Bank of the United States chartered by Congress; James Monroe elected president

1817 Bonus Bill establishing fund for building roads and canals vetoed by President Madison; The New York legislature authorizes building of the Erie Canal; Rush-Bagot Agreement; Seminole War

1818 Convention of 1818, signed with Britain, fixes the northern boundary of Louisiana territory

1819 Financial panic; Adams-Onis Treaty; *Dartmouth* v. *Woodward* decision by Supreme Court; *McCullough* v. *Maryland* decision

1820 Missouri Compromise; James Monroe re-elected president

1823 Monroe Doctrine

1824 *Gibbons* v. *Ogden* decision

1825 Erie Canal officially opens

1827 First railroad in the United States is built in Quincy, Massachusetts

1831 Practical reaper invented by Cyrus McCormick

ing interests to press for higher tariffs and a growing number of Southerners, who had previously supported a nationalistic economic program, to turn against protective tariffs, internal improvements, and a national bank.

The Missouri Crisis

In the midst of the panic of 1819, a crisis over slavery erupted with stunning suddenness—as Thomas Jefferson wrote, like "a fireball in the night." The crisis was ignited by Missouri's application for statehood, and it involved the status of slavery west of the Mississippi River.

East of the Mississippi, the Mason-Dixon line and the Ohio River formed a natural boundary between the North and South. States south of this line were slave states; states north of this line had either abolished slavery or adopted gradual emancipation plans. West of the Mississippi, however, there was no clear line to demarcate between free and slave states.

Controversy arose in February, 1819, when James Tallmadge, a New York Republican, introduced an amendment to the bill authorizing Missouri to form a state government. The amendment prohibited the further introduction of slaves into Missouri and provided for emancipation of all children of slaves at the age of twenty-five. Voting along ominously sectional lines, the House approved the Tallmadge amendment. The amendment was defeated in the Senate, where senators from the South received support from northern allies.

Southern politicians responded to the Tallmadge proposal with fury. John Randolph declared that "God has given us Missouri and the devil shall not take it from us." Southern leaders denounced Tallmadge's amendment as part of a Federalist plot to regain power. They declared the United States to be a union of equals and that Congress had no power to place special restrictions upon a state. Talk of disunion and civil war was rife. Senator Freeman Walker of Georgia envisioned "civil wars . . . a brother's sword crimsoned with a brother's blood."

Northern politicians responded with equal vehemence. Said Representative Tallmadge, "If blood is necessary to extinguish any fire which I have assisted to kindle, I can assure you gentlemen, while I regret the necessity, I shall not forbear to contribute my mite." Northern leaders argued that national policy, enshrined in the Northwest Ordinance, committed the government to halt the expansion of the institution of slavery. They warned that the extension of slavery into the West would inevitably increase the pressures to reopen the African slave trade.

This was not the first occasion in which Congress vigorously debated slavery and sectional power. In 1790, a bitter dispute arose over whether Congress should accept antislavery petitions. In 1798, a furor erupted over a proposal to extend the Northwest Ordinance prohibition on slavery to Mississippi. In 1804, a new uproar broke out over a proposal to bar new slaves from Louisiana. In 1801 and again in 1819, Federalists had protested the three-fifths compromise, which included three-fifths of the slave population in apportioning representation in the House of Representatives.

Never before had passions been so heated or sectional antagonisms so overt. In the Northeast, for the first time, philanthropists like Elias Boudinot of Burlington, New Jersey, succeeded in mobilizing public opinion against the west-

ward expansion of slavery. Mass meetings convened throughout the North. The vehemence of public feeling was apparent in an editorial that appeared in the New York *Advertiser*:

> THIS QUESTION INVOLVES NOT ONLY THE FUTURE CHARACTER OF OUR NATION, BUT THE FUTURE WEIGHT AND INFLUENCE OF THE FREE STATES. IF NOW LOST—IT IS LOST FOREVER.

Compromise resolved the crisis of 1819. The Senate voted to allow Missouri to enter the Union without restrictions on slavery, and to preserve the sectional balance, it voted to admit Maine, which had previously been a part of Massachusetts, as a free state. Senator Jesse Burgess Thomas of Illinois then added an amendment which prohibited slavery from the rest of the Louisiana Purchase north of 36°30' latitude. Henry Clay then skillfully steered the compromise through the House, where a handful of antislavery representatives and senators, fearful of the threat to the Union, threw their support behind the proposals. Narrowly, the compromise measures passed.

A new crisis erupted when the Missouri constitutional convention directed the state legislature to forbid migration of free blacks and mulattoes into the state. This crisis, too, was resolved by compromise. Congress required Missourians to promise that they would not abridge the constitutional rights of United States citizens.

What made compromise possible in 1819 and 1820 was the fact that most Northerners were apathetic toward the Tallmadge amendment, and opponents of slavery were disunited. Public attention was focused on the panic of 1819 and the resulting depression. Leadership of the drive to restrict slavery in Missouri had been assumed by the Presbyterian and Congregationalist churchmen, provoking widespread hostility from an anti-clerical and anti-Federalist opposition.

Southerners won a victory in 1820, but they paid a high price. While the area north of the compromise line would be organized into many states, the southern portion would form only a single state. If the South was to defend its political power against an antislavery majority, it

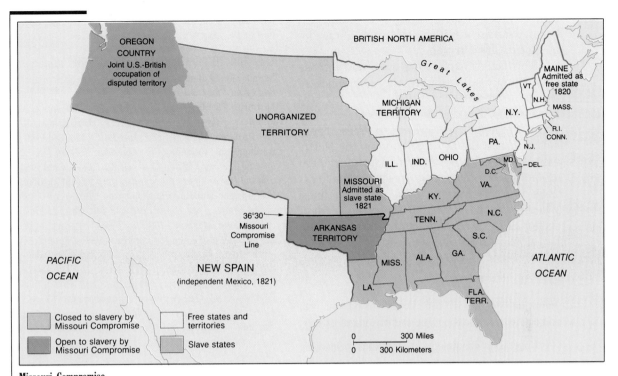

Missouri Compromise
The agreement reached in the Missouri Compromise temporarily settled the argument over slavery in the territories.

had only two options in the future. It would either have to forge new political alliances with the North and West or it would have to acquire new territory in the Southwest, which would inevitably reignite northern opposition to the expansion of slavery.

The Era of Good Feelings ended on a note of foreboding. Although compromise had been achieved, it was clear that sectional conflict had not been resolved, only postponed. Sectional antagonism, Jefferson wrote, "is hushed, indeed, for the moment. But this is a reprieve only, not a final sentence. A geographical line, coinciding with a marked principle, moral and political, once conceived and held up to the angry passions of men, will never be obliterated; and every new irritation will mark it deeper and deeper." John Quincy Adams agreed. The Missouri crisis, he wrote, is only the "title page to a great tragic volume."

CONCLUSION

The "Era of Good Feelings" came to a formal close on March 4, 1825, the day that John Quincy Adams was inaugurated as the nation's sixth president. Adams, who had served eight years as his predecessor's secretary of state, believed that James Monroe's term in office would be regarded by future generations of Americans as a "golden age." In his inaugural address, he spoke with pride of the nation's achievements since the War of 1812. A strong spirit of nationalism pervaded the nation and the country stood united under a single political party, the Republicans. The nation had settled its most serious disputes with England and Spain and had extended its boundaries to the Pacific. It had asserted its diplomatic independence and encouraged the wars for national independence in Latin America. It had developed a strong manufacturing system and had begun to create a system of transportation adequate to a great nation.

This era of explosive growth and intense nationalism also witnessed the emergence of new political divisions as well as growing sectional animosities. The period following the War of 1812 brought rapid growth to cities, manufacturing, and the factory system in the North, while the South's economy remained oriented around slavery and cotton. These two great sections were developing along diverging lines. Whether the spirit of nationalism or the spirit of sectionalism would triumph was the great question dominating American politics.

REVIEW SUMMARY

Following War of 1812 a new spirit of nationalism, and patriotic fervor swept the country, manifested by

> Congress's enactment of programs promoting national economic growth
>
> Supreme Court decisions establishing the supremacy of the federal government and expanding the powers of Congress
>
> The proud assertion of national power in foreign policy

Industrialization and improvements in transportation and communications also contributed to the nation's strength.

A serious economic depression in 1819 and a bitter controversy over the admission of Missouri as a slave state produced growing factional divisions in politics and a deeping sectional split between the North and the South.

SUGGESTIONS FOR FURTHER READING

OVERVIEWS AND SURVEYS

W. Elliot Brownlee, *Dynamics of Ascent: A History of the American Economy* (1974); Stuart Bruchey, *The Roots of American Economic Growth, 1607–1815* (1968); George Dangerfield, *The Awakening of American Nationalism* (1965); G. Dangerfield, *The Era of Good Feelings* (1952); Robert Heilbroner, *The Economic Transformation of America* (1977); John R. Howe, *From the Revolution Through the Age of Jackson* (1973); John Mayfield, *The New Nation, 1800–1845* (1982); Douglas C. North, *The Economic Growth of the United States, 1790–1860* (1961); Sid-

ney Ratner, James H. Soltow, and Richard Sylla, *The Evolution of the American Economy* (1979).

THE GROWTH OF AMERICAN NATIONALISM

Samuel Flagg Bemis, ed., *The American Secretaries of State and Their Diplomacy*, vol. 4 (1927–1967); Edward M. Burns, *The American Idea of Mission: Concepts of National Purpose and Destiny* (1957); Robert K. Faulkner, *The Jurisprudence of John Marshall* (1968); Lloyd C. Gardner et al., *Creation of the American Empire: U.S. Diplomatic History* (1973); C. C. Griffin, *The United States and the Disruption of the Spanish Empire* (1937); George Lee Haskins and Herbert A. Johnson, *History of the Supreme Court of the United States, vol. 2, Foundations of Power: John Marshall, 1801–15* (1981); Ernest R. May, *The Making of the Monroe Doctrine* (1975); Frederick W. Merk, *Manifest Destiny and Mission in American History: A Reinterpretation* (1963); F. W. Merk, *The Monroe Doctrine and American Expansionism, 1843–1849* (1966); Paul C. Nagel, *One National Indivisible: The Union in American Thought, 1776–1861* (1964); Dexter Perkins, *The Monroe Doctrine* (1927); J. H. Powell, *Richard Rush: Republican Diplomat* (1942).

THE ROOTS OF AMERICAN ECONOMIC GROWTH

Richard A. Bartlett, *The New Country: A Social History of the American Frontier, 1796–1890* (1974); Alfred D. Chandler, Jr., *The Railroads: The Nation's First Big Business* (1965); A. D. Chandler, *The Visible Hand* (1977); Howard Chudacoff, *The Evolution of American Urban Society* (1975); Victor S. Clark, *History of Manufactures in the United States, 1607–1860* (1916); Thomas C. Cochran, *Frontiers of Change: Early Industrialization in America* (1981); Clarence H. Danhof, *Change in Agriculture: The Northern United States, 1820–1870* (1969); Paul David, *Technical Choice, Innovation and Economic Growth* (1975); Lance Davis et al., *American Economic Growth: An Economist's History of the United States* (1972); Everett Dick, *The Lure of the Land: A Social History of the Public Lands* (1970); Joseph A. Durrenberger, *Turnpikes: A Study of the Toll Road Movement* (1968); John Faragher, *Sugar Creek* (1986); Albert Fishlow, *American Railroads and the Transformation of the Antebellum Economy* (1965); Paul W. Gates, *The Farmer's Age: Agriculture, 1815–1860* (1960); Siegfried Giedion, *Mechanization Takes Command* (1948); Carter Goodrich, ed., *Canals and American Economic Development* (1961); C. Goodrich, *Government Promotion of American Canals and Railroads, 1800–1890* (1960); Eric F. Haites, James Mak, and Gary M. Walton, *Western River Transportation: The Era of Early Internal Development, 1810–1860* (1975); Oscar and Mary Handlin, *Commonwealth: A Study of the Role of Government in the American Economy* (1969); Louis Hartz, *Economic Policy and Democratic Thought* (1954); Morton Horwitz, *The Transformation of American Law,*

1780–1860 (1977); David A. Hounshell, *From the American System to Mass Production* (1984); Louis C. Hunter, *Steamboats on the Western Rivers* (1949); James Williard Hurst, *Law and the Conditions of Freedom in the Nineteenth-Century United States* (1967); J. W. Hurst, *The Legitimacy of the Business Corporation in the Law of the United States, 1780–1970* (1970); David J. Jeremy, *Transatlantic Industrial Revolution: The Diffusion of Textile Technology Between Britain and America, 1790–1800* (1981); Arthur M. Johnson and Barry Supple, *Capitalists and Western Railroads: A Study in the Nineteenth Century Investment Process* (1967); John F. Kasson, *Civilizing the Machine: Technology and Republican Values in America, 1776–1900* (1976); Darwin P. Kelsey, ed., *Farming in the New Nation* (1972); Susan Previant Lee and Peter Passell, *A New Economic View of American History* (1979); Leonard W. Levy, *The Law of the Commonwealth and Chief Justice Shaw* (1957); Blake McKelvey, *American Urbanization: A Comparative History* (1973); Nathan Miller, *The Enterprise of a Free People: Aspects of Economic Development in New York State During the Canal Period, 1792–1838* (1962); Zane Miller, *The Urbanization of America* (1973); William Nelson, *The Americanization of the Common Law: The Impact of Legal Change on Massachusetts Society, 1760–1830* (1975); James D. Norris, *R.G. Dun and Co., 1841–1900* (1978); Douglas C. North, *Growth and Welfare in the American Past* (1974); F. S. Philbrick, *The Rise of the West, 1754–1830* (1965); Glenn Porter and Harold C. Livesay, *Merchants and Manufacturers: Studies in the Changing Structure of Nineteenth-Century Marketing* (1971); J. Potter, "The Growth of Population in America, 1700–1860" in D. V. Glass and D. E. C. Eversley, eds., *Population and History* (1965); Alan R. Pred, *Urban Growth and the Circulation of Information* (1973); Malcolm J. Rohrbough, *The Land Office Business* (1960); M. J. Rohrbough, *The Trans-Appalachian Frontier* (1979); Nathan Rosenberg, *Technology and American Economic Growth* (1972); Harry Scheiber, *Ohio Canal Era: A Case Study of Government and the Economy, 1820–1861* (1969); Leo F. Schnore, ed., *The New Urban History: Quantitative Explorations by American Historians* (1975); Robert E. Shaw, *Erie Water West: A History of the Erie Canal, 1792–1854* (1966); Carl Siracusa, *A Mechanical People: Perceptions of the Industrial Order in Massachusetts, 1815–1880* (1979); Merritt Roe Smith, *Harpers Ferry Armory and the New Technology* (1978); John F. Stover, *Iron Road to the West: American Railroads in the 1850s* (1978); J. F. Stover, *The Life and Decline of the American Railroad* (1970); George Rogers Taylor, *The Transportation Revolution* (1951); Jon C. Teaford, *The Municipal Revolution in America: Origins of Modern Urban Government, 1650–1825* (1975); Peter Temin, *Causal Factors in American Economic Growth in the Nineteenth Century* (1975); P. Temin, *Iron and Steel in Nineteenth Century America* (1964); Stephan Thernstrom and Richard Sennett. eds., *Nineteenth-Century Cities: Essays in the New Urban History* (1969); Robert L. Thompson, *Wiring a Continent: The History of the Telegraph Industry in the United States, 1832–1866* (1947); Dale Van Every, *The Final Challenge: The American Frontier, 1804–1845* (1964); Richard C. Wade, *The Urban Frontier* (1959); Caroline F. Ware, *The Early New England Cotton Manufacture* (1931); Sam Bass Warner, Jr., *The Private City: Philadelphia in Three Periods of Its Growth* (1968); S. B. Warner, Jr., *The Urban Wilderness* (1972); James W. Whitaker, ed., *Farming in the Midwest, 1840–1900* (1974).

THE GROWTH OF POLITICAL FACTIONALISM AND SECTIONALISM

David Brion Davis, *The Problem of Slavery in the Age of Revolution, 1770–1823* (1975); Don E. Fehrenbacher, *The South and Three Sectional Crises* (1980); Staughton Lynd, *Class Conflict, Slavery and the United States Constitution* (1967); Duncan J. MacLeod, *Slavery, Race, and the American Revolution* (1974); Glover Moore, *The Missouri Controversy* (1953); D. L. Robinson, *Slavery in the Structure of American Politics, 1765–1820* (1971); Murray N. Rothbard, *The Panic of 1819: Reactions and Policies* (1962). Harry Ammon, *James Monroe: The Quest for National Identity* (1971); Leonard Baker, *John Marshall: A Life in Law* (1974); Samuel Flagg Bemis, *John Quincy Adams and the Foundations of American Foreign Policy* (1949); S. F. Bemis, *John Quincy Adams and the Union* (1956); Richard Current, *Daniel Webster and the Rise of National Conservatism* (1968); Gerald T. Dunne, *Justice Joseph Story and the Rise of the Supreme Court* (1970); Clement Eaton, *Henry Clay and the Art of American Politics* (1957); Mary W. M. Hargreaves, *The Presidency of John Quincy Adams* (1975); John Horton, *James Kent: A Study in Conservatism* (1939); George A. Lipsky, *John Quincy Adams: His Theory and Ideas* (1950); F. N. Stites, *John Marshall: Defender of the Constitution* (1981); Barbara M. Tucker, *Samuel Slater and the Origins of the American Textile Industry, 1790–1860* (1984); Glyndon G. Van Deusen, *The Life of Henry Clay* (1937); Charles M. Wiltse, *John C. Calhoun: Nationalist, 1782–1828* (1944).

FOUNDED A.D. MDCCXCV.

of the Capitol of the United States

CHAPTER 9
Power and Politics in Jackson's America

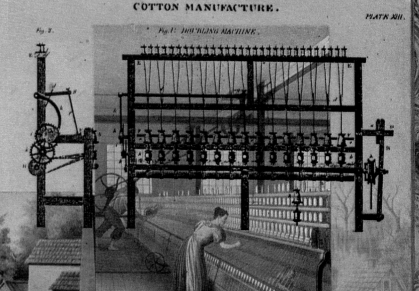

COTTON MANUFACTURE.

PLATE 340.

*T*t was, without a doubt, the most exciting, colorful, and dirty presidential campaign in American history. In 1840, William Henry Harrison, a military hero best known for defeating an Indian alliance at the Battle of Tippecanoe in 1811, challenged the Democratic incumbent, Martin Van Buren, for the presidency.

Harrison's campaign began at 9:30 A.M., Monday, May 4, 1840. A huge procession, made up of an estimated 75,000 people, marched through the streets of Baltimore to celebrate Harrison's nomination by the Whig party convention. Although Harrison was college-educated and brought up on a plantation with a work force of some 200 slaves, his Democratic opponents had already tried to belittle him as the "log cabin" candidate, who was happiest on his backwoods farm sipping hard cider. Harrison's supporters enthusiastically seized on this image and promoted it in a number of colorful ways. They distributed barrels of hard cider, passed out campaign hats and placards, and mounted eight log cabins on floats.

Harrison's campaign brought many innovations to the art of electioneering. For the first time, a presidential candidate spoke out on his own behalf. On the morning of Saturday, June 6, 1840, before a Columbus, Ohio, crowd of 25,000, Harrison gave the first campaign speech ever delivered by a candidate. Harrison's backers also coined the first campaign slogans: "Tippecanoe and Tyler Too," "Van, Van is a used up man," and "Matty's policy, 12-1/2 cts. a day and french soup, Our policy, 2 Dolls. a day and Roast Beef." They staged log cabin raisings, including the erection of a 50-by-100-foot cabin on Broadway in New York City. They sponsored barbeques, including one in Wheeling, West Virginia, where a crowd devoured 360 hams, 26 sheep, 20 calves, 1500 pounds of beef, 8000 pounds of bread, 1000 pounds of cheese, and 4500 pies. Harrison's campaign managers even distributed whiskey bottles in the shape of log cabins, manufactured by the E. C. Booz Distillery of Philadelphia, thereby adding the word "booze" to the American vocabulary.

While defending their man as a "peoples'" candidate, Harrison's backers heaped an unprecedented avalanche of personal abuse on his Democratic opponent. The Whigs accused President Van Buren of eating off golden plates and lace tablecloths, drinking French wines, perfuming his whiskers, and wearing a corset. Whigs in Congress denied Van Buren an appropriation of $3665 to repair the White House lest he turn the executive mansion into a "palace as splendid as that of the Caesars." The object of this rough and colorful kind of campaigning was to show that the Democratic candidate harbored aristocratic leanings, while Harrison truly represented the people.

The Harrison campaign provided a number of effective lessons for future politicians, most notably an emphasis on symbols and imagery over ideas and substance. Fearful of alienating voters and dividing the Whig party, the political convention that nominated Harrison agreed to adopt no party platform. Harrison himself said not a single word during the campaign about his principles or proposals. He closely followed the suggestion of one of his advisors that he "rely entirely on the past" (that is, his reputation as a general and victor over the Indians), and offer no indication "about what he thinks now, or what he will do hereafter."

The new campaign techniques worked exceedingly well. In 1840, voter turnout was the highest it had ever been in a presidential election: nearly eighty percent of eligible voters cast ballots. The log cabin candidate for president won fifty-three percent of the popular vote and a landslide victory in the Electoral College.

POLITICAL DEMOCRATIZATION

The two decades between 1820 and 1840 marked a notable advance of democracy in American politics. Property requirements for voting and office holding were abolished. Direct methods of selecting presidential electors, county officials, state judges, and governors replaced indirect methods. Voter participation skyrocketed, particularly in federal elections. Other political innovations included the spread of the secret ballot, the first appearance of national presidential nominating conventions, and

In 1840 the Whig party tried to mobilize voter support for William Henry Harrison by distributing gaily-colored handkerchiefs and whiskey bottles shaped like log cabins.

the emergence of two new political parties, the Democrats and Whigs, engaged in nationwide political struggle.

The Expansion of Voting Rights

The most dramatic political innovation of the early nineteenth century was the repeal of property qualifications for voting and office holding. New York State was one of many states to eliminate property restrictions on voting. In 1821, New York debated the wisdom of extending voting rights to all men over the age of twenty-one. Conservatives led by Federalist James Kent argued that universal suffrage was a bad idea since men who owned no property had no stake in the well-being of society. Agricultural interests feared that universal manhood suffrage would allow merchants and manufacturers to dominate state politics by controlling their employees' votes. Proponents of universal manhood suffrage replied that "we are not a government of the people" as long as restrictions upon voting continued to exist.

In 1821 fewer than two adult males in five in New York could legally vote for senator or governor. Under the new constitution adopted in 1821, all adult white males were allowed to vote, as long as they paid taxes or had served in the militia. Five years later, an amendment to the state's constitution eliminated the taxpaying and militia qualifications and established universal white manhood suffrage.

At the time of the Revolution, every American colony imposed formal restrictions on the right to vote and hold public office. Following the English principle that voters had to have a stake in the community, the colonies generally required citizens to own a certain minimum amount of land in order to qualify. Aspirants for public office were required to meet higher property qualifications. In North Carolina, a senator was required to own at least three hundred acres of land and in South Carolina, a representative had to own at least five hundred acres and ten slaves. A number of the colonists also imposed a religious test. In Connecticut, New Hampshire, New Jersey, and Vermont no atheist, Jew, or Roman Catholic could hold a public office.

In practice, restrictions on voting were not particularly burdensome. By European standards, a relatively large proportion of the population was qualified to vote because ownership of land was widespread. Moreover, curbs on voting were loosely enforced and easily evaded and men who did not meet property requirements were sometimes allowed to vote on grounds of "good character." Nevertheless, the laws barred a significant and growing segment of the adult white male population from voting.

During the early nineteenth century, virtually every state repealed the remaining property restrictions on voting. By 1840, only three states—Louisiana, Rhode Island, and Virginia—still restricted the suffrage to white male property owners and taxpayers.

In most states, the transition from property qualifications to universal white manhood suffrage occurred gradually, without violence and with surprisingly little dissension. In Rhode Island, however, the question of political democratization provoked an episode known as the "Dorr War." In 1841 Rhode Island still operated

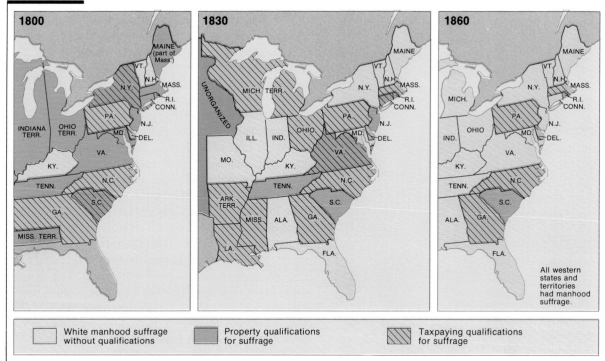

White manhood suffrage without qualifications

Property qualifications for suffrage

Taxpaying qualifications for suffrage

Extension of Manhood Suffrage

Some states and territories reserved the suffrage to property holders and taxpayers, while others permitted an alternative such as period of residence.

under a Royal Charter granted in 1663, which restricted suffrage to landowners and their eldest sons. The charter lacked a bill of rights and grossly underrepresented growing industrial cities, such as Providence, in the state legislature. As Rhode Island grew increasingly urban and industrial, the state's landless population increased and fewer residents were eligible to vote. By 1841 just 11,239 out of 26,000 adult males were qualified to vote. In that year, Thomas W. Dorr, a Harvard-educated attorney, organized an extralegal convention to frame a new state constitution and abolish voting restrictions. The state's governor declared Dorr and his supporters guilty of insurrection, proclaimed a state of emergency, and called out the state militia. Dorr tried unsuccessfully to capture the state arsenal at Providence. He was arrested and found guilty of high treason, and sentenced to life imprisonment at hard labor. To appease popular resentment, the governor

pardoned Dorr the next year, and the state adopted a new constitution with liberal suffrage provisions in 1843.

While universal white manhood suffrage was becoming a reality, restrictions on voting by blacks and women remained intact. Only one state, New Jersey, had given unmarried women property holders the right to vote following the Revolution, but the state rescinded this right at the time it extended suffrage to all adult white men. Most states also explicitly denied free blacks the right to vote. By 1858 free blacks were eligible to vote in just four Northern states: New Hampshire, Maine, Massachusetts, and Vermont.

In contrast, immigrants were often permitted to vote if they had declared their intention to become citizens. During the nineteenth century, twenty-two states and territories permitted immigrants who were not yet naturalized citizens to vote.

In addition to removing property and tax qualifications for voting and office holding during the five decades preceding the Civil War, state after state reduced residency requirements for voting and substituted direct election of government officials for indirect methods. Prior to 1820, state legislatures in most states chose presidential electors, governors, and county officials. Four years later, only six of the nation's twenty-four states still chose presidential electors in the state legislature, and eight years later the only state to still do so was South Carolina. In order to encourage popular participation in politics, most states also instituted statewide nominating conventions, opened polling places in more convenient locations, extended the hours that polls were open, and adopted the secret ballot.

Popular Attacks on Privilege

Political innovations of the early nineteenth century were all part of a democratic impulse that was sweeping the country. In all parts of the nation, Americans waged popular struggles against a vast array of social institutions that smacked of special privilege and aristocratic pretension. Established churches, the bench, and the legal and medical professions all saw their elitist status stripped away.

To make the judiciary more responsive to public opinion, most states made the local judicial office an elected position. To open up the legal profession, many states allowed any individual to practice law without formal training. Some states stripped local medical societies of the power to license physicians, allowing unorthodox doctors, including many women, who prescribed medications based on herbs, roots, or alcohol, to compete freely with established doctors.

In upstate New York the surge of democratic sentiment took the form of violent protests, known as the "anti-rent wars," against an old system of land tenure, under which landlords and land companies collected a yearly tribute from farmers as well as a share of the proceeds from the sale of a farm. From 1839 to 1843, tenant farmers, disguised as Indians, tarred and feathered sheriffs and deputies and successfully agitated for a new state constitution that prohibited feudal land tenure.

This new spirit of democracy had enormous political impact. Prior to the nineteenth century, American politics were dominated by deference. Voters generally followed the leadership of local leading families. During the first quarter of the nineteenth century, however, this system of deference politics disintegrated and the influence of local elites declined sharply.

In their place arose a new breed of professional politicians. In the 1820s, political innovators such as Martin Van Buren, the son of a tavern keeper, and Thurlow Weed, a newspaper editor in Albany, New York, devised new campaign tools, featuring such things as organized torchlight parades, subsidized partisan newspapers, and nominating conventions. These political bosses and manipulators soon discovered the technique most successful in arousing popular interest in politics was to attack a privileged group or institution which had used political influence to attain power or profit.

The "Anti-Masonic party" was the first political movement to win a widespread popular following by attacking a special interest. In the mid-1820s, a growing number of people in New York and surrounding states had come to believe that members of the Fraternal Order of Freemasons monopolized many of the region's most prestigious political offices and business positions and had used their connections to enrich themselves. They noted, for instance, that Masons held twenty-two of the nation's twenty-four governorships.

In 1826, in the small town of Batavia, New York, William Morgan, a former Mason, disappeared. Morgan had written an exposé of the organization in violation of the order's vow of silence, and rumor soon spread that he had been tied up with heavy cables and dumped into the Niagara River. When no indictments were brought against the alleged perpetrators of Morgan's kidnapping and murder, many upstate New Yorkers accused local constables, justices of the peace, and judges, who were members of the Masons, with obstruction of justice.

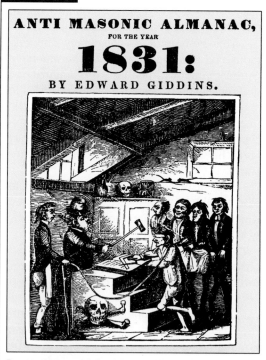

By attacking special privilege and demanding equality of opportunity for all citizens, the Anti-Masonic party won broad support in New York and other northern states.

By 1830, Anti-Masons had captured half the vote in New York and had gained substantial support throughout New England. Clearly, the new democratized forms of politics worked effectively to mobilize voters.

THE RISE OF PARTIES

The framers of the Constitution saw no place for organized political parties in the new nation that they created. They associated political parties with the aristocratic alliances based on patronage that dominated politics in England during the eighteenth century. Organized political parties, it was feared, would divide the nation, and partisan spirit would detract from a sense of the public good.

Despite widespread opposition to the idea of parties, the first years of the new republic did give rise to two competing political parties, the Federalists and the Republicans (see pp. 205–206). The first party system, however, differed in two important respects from the kinds of political parties Americans are familiar with today. First, the Federalists and Republicans tended to have a strong sectional character, with the Federalists dominant in New England and the Republicans dominant elsewhere. Furthermore, the two parties denied the legitimacy of parties and never accepted the principle of a loyal political opposition.

After the War of 1812, a time in which the Federalists were stigmatized as disloyal, the nation reverted to a period of one-party government in national politics. The death of the Federalist party created the illusion of national political unity, but appearances were deceptive. Without the discipline imposed by competition with a strong opposition party, the Republican party began to fragment into cliques and factions.

During James Monroe's presidency, the Republican party disintegrated as a stable national organization. Following his overwhelming election in 1816, Monroe sought to promote the ideal expressed by George Washington in his Farewell Address: a nation free of partisan divisions. Hostile to the very idea of parties, Monroe called them "the curse of the country," asserting that they were "not necessary for free government." As president, Monroe, like Washington, aspired for a status above party. Like Washington, too, he appointed rival factional leaders such as John Quincy Adams and John C. Calhoun to his cabinet. He refused to use federal patronage to strengthen the Republican party and he took the position that Congress, not the president, was the best representative of the public will, and it should define public policy, except in the area of foreign affairs. Lacking a strong leader, the Republican party began to break apart. Factional and sectional rivalries grew increasingly bitter, and party machinery fell into disuse.

Birth of the Second Party System

Over time, local and personal factions began to coalesce into a new political party system. Three critical developments contributed to its creation. The first was the financial panic of 1819 and subsequent depression (see p. 258). Factories closed and laborers were left jobless. Banks called in their loans. Currency in circulation fell from $100 million in 1817 to just $45 million in 1819. Production of staple crops fell by half and land values declined by fifty to seventy percent. "Such is the depreciation of the value of property," said one western newspaper, "that the accumulated labor of years is not now sufficient to pay a trifling debt, and property some years since which could have sold for eight to ten thousand dollars will scarcely, at this time, pay a debt of five hundred."

Farmers, particularly in the South and West, demanded enactment of stay laws to postpone repayment of debts. In the state of Mississippi, debtors asked the state to print paper money, which could be used to pay off creditors. Ardent nationalists called for higher tariffs to protect infant industries and government-financed transportation improvements to reduce the cost of trade.

Many artisans and farmers blamed banks for causing the panic by printing excessive numbers of worthless paper money and demanded that banknotes be replaced by hard money, gold and silver coinage. In Congress, Senator Thomas Hart Benton of Missouri gave voice to the growing antibank sentiment. "I know towns, yea cities," the senator declared, "where this bank already appears as an engrossing proprietor. All the flourishing cities of the West are mortgaged to this money power. . . . They are in the jaws of the monster!" During the 1820s, the Republican party in such states as Alabama, Georgia, Kentucky, New Hampshire, North Carolina, Ohio, Pennsylvania, and Tennessee divided over questions of debt relief, bank regulation, and state support for internal improvements.

A second source of political division was southern alarm over the slavery debates in Congress in 1819 and 1820 (see pp. 259–261). At his home in Monticello, Thomas Jefferson worried that the debates might be the "[death] knell of the Union." Many southern leaders feared that the Missouri Crisis might spark a realignment of national politics along sectional lines. Such a development, John Quincy Adams wrote, was "terrible to the South—threatening in its progress the emancipation of all their slaves, threatening in its immediate effect that southern domination which has swayed the Union for the last twenty years."

Sectional animosities spurred many Southerners to forge poltical alliances with the North. As early as 1821, Old Republicans in the South—those who opposed high tariffs, a national bank, and federally-funded internal improvements—had begun to form a loose alliance with Senator Martin Van Buren of New York and the Republican party faction he commanded, the Albany Regency.

The third major source of political division was presidential sucession. The "Virginia Dynasty" of presidents, a chain that had begun with George Washington and included Thomas Jefferson, James Madison, and James Monroe, was at its end by 1824.

Traditionally, selection of the party's candidate was left to a caucus of the Republican party's members of Congress. Early in 1824, the caucus met in closed session and chose William Crawford, Monroe's secretary of the treasury, as the party's choice. But this did not end the issue of succession. Only one-quarter of the Republican senators and representatives bothered to attend the Congressional caucus and Republican members of Congress from eight states showed their disapproval of this nominating method by refusing to participate. Explained John Quincy Adams: "A majority of the whole people of the United States and a majority of the States [are] utterly adverse to the nomination by Congressional caucus, thinking it adverse to the spirit of the Constitution and tending to corruption."

The early favorite, Crawford, who had the support of Thomas Jefferson, suffered a stroke and was left partially disabled. Four other candidates emerged: Secretary of State John Quincy Adams, the son of the nation's second president and the only candidate from the North; John C. Calhoun, Monroe's secretary of war, but with little support outside his native South Carolina, he decided to settle for the vice-presidency; Henry Clay, the Speaker of the House, a staunch advocate of a national bank, a protective tariff to aid manufacturing, and gov-

In this 1824 cartoon Andrew Jackson is being attacked by a pack of dogs, who represent defenders of the Congressional party caucus.

ernment support of internal improvements in transportation; and General Andrew Jackson, the hero of the Battle of New Orleans and victor over the Creek and Seminole Indians. About the last-named, Thomas Jefferson commented dryly, one might as well try "to make a soldier of a goose as a President of Andrew Jackson."

In the election of 1824, Jackson received the greatest number of votes both at the polls and in the electoral college, followed by Adams, Crawford, and then Clay. But he failed to receive a constitutional majority, and under Article II of the Constitution, the election was thrown into the House of Representatives,

Table 9.1

Election of 1824			
Candidate	Party	Popular Vote	Electoral Vote
J. Q. Adams	no	113,122	84
Jackson	party	151,271	99
Clay	designations	47,531	37
Crawford		40,856	41

which was required to choose from among the top three vote-getters. There, Henry Clay persuaded his supporters to vote for Adams, commenting acidly that he did not believe "that killing two thousand five hundred Englishmen at New Orleans" was a proper qualification for the presidency. Adams was elected on the first ballot.

The Philadelphia *Observor* charged that Adams had made a secret deal to obtain Clay's support. Five days later, Adams appointed Clay secretary of state, seeming to confirm the charges of a "corrupt bargain." Jackson was outraged, since he could legitimately argue that he was the popular favorite. The general exclaimed, "The Judas of the West has closed the contract and will receive the thirty pieces of silver."

The Presidency of John Quincy Adams

John Quincy Adams was one of the most brilliant and well-qualified men to serve in the White House. He had served as a diplomat, a Harvard professor, a United States senator, and was one of the nation's ablest secretaries of state. During the early stages of his career, he negotiated the treaty that ended the War of 1812, acquired the Floridas, and conceived the Monroe Doctrine. But like his father, Adams lacked the personal warmth and the political skills necessary to generate a loyal following or put through his programs. He said that his adversaries regarded him as "a man of reserved, cold, austere and forbidding manners," "a gloomy misanthrope," and "an unsocial savage."

Opposition to Adams appeared almost immediately. Jackson and his supporters accused the new president of "corruptions and intrigues" to gain Henry Clay's support. Only a heavy snowfall prevented a pro-Jackson crowd from disrupting the inaugural festivities by burning Adams in effigy.

Adams's inaugural address created even more opposition from states' rights advocates. In his address, he advocated an active role for the federal government, announcing his support for a high federal tariff to protect industry, a federal program of transportation improvements, federal support for the arts and sciences, and establishment of a national university. Adams's proposals infuriated many Republicans who still believed in traditional Jeffersonian principles of limited government, strict construction of the Constitution, and states' rights. Jefferson himself condemned Adams's proposals, declaring in a stinging statement that they would create "an aristocracy . . . riding and ruling over the plundered ploughman and beggared yeomanry." The address also upset defenders of slavery who opposed any expansion of federal authority, fearing that this might set a precedent for interference with slavery.

Adams's ability to govern was further undermined by his unwillingness to adapt to the practical demands of politics. He disapproved of the very idea of partisanship, made no effort to use the patronage powers to build support for his proposals, and refused to fire federal officeholders who openly opposed his policies. He even considered naming Andrew Jackson to his cabinet.

Adams's policies on Indian removal cost him still more support. Although he, like his predecessor Monroe, wanted to remove southern Indians to the trans-Mississippi West, he believed that the state and federal governments had a duty to abide by Indian treaties and to purchase, not merely annex, Indian lands. Adams's decision to repudiate and renegotiate a fraudulent treaty that stripped the Georgia Creek Indians of their land outraged land-hungry Southerners and Westerners.

Even in the realm of foreign policy, his strong suit prior to the presidency, Adams met with frustration. His attempts to peacefully acquire Texas from Mexico failed as did his efforts to persuade Britain to permit American trade with the British West Indies.

The major political issue of Adams's presidency involved raising the federal tariffs on imported goods. Textile producers proposed higher taxes on imports to protect their industry from foreign competition. Southern cotton planters opposed an increase because it would raise the cost of manufactured goods.

Andrew Jackson's supporters in Congress sought to exploit the tariff question in order to

John Quincy Adams won the election of 1824 in the House of Representatives even though Andrew Jackson received the most popular votes.

embarrass President Adams and help Jackson win the presidency in 1828. They framed a bill, soon known as the Tariff of Abominations, designed to win support for Jackson in Kentucky, Missouri, New York, Ohio, and Pennsylvania while weakening the Adams administration in New England. The bill raised duties on iron, hemp, and flax, and lowered the tariff on woolen goods. John Randolph of Virginia accurately described the object of the bill as an effort to encourage "manufactures of no sort or kind, except the manufacture of a President of the United States."

The Tariff of Abominations provoked a furor in the South. The legislatures of Georgia, Mississippi, South Carolina, and Virginia denounced the tariff as unconstitutional and oppressive. On an even more ominous note for the future, Vice-President John C. Calhoun anonymously published an essay that advanced the principle of "nullification." A single state, Calhoun maintained, might overrule or "nullify" a federal law within its own territory, until three-quarters of the states had upheld the law as constitutional. But rather than implement this doctrine, the state of South Carolina waited to see what attitude the next president would adopt toward the tariff.

The Election of 1828

"J. Q. Adams who can write" squared off against "Andy Jackson who can fight" in the election of 1828, one of the most bitter campaigns in American history. Jackson's followers repeated the charge that Adams was an "aristocrat" who had obtained office as a result of a "corrupt bargain." The Jackson forces also alleged that the president had used public funds to buy personal luxuries, installed gaming tables in the White House, and served as a pimp for the Czar while serving as minister to Russia. They even charged that Mrs. Adams had been born out of wedlock.

Adams's supporters countered by digging up an old story that Jackson had begun living with his wife before she was legally divorced from her first husband. They called the general a slave trader, a gambler, and a backwoods buffoon who could not spell correctly more than one word out of four. One Philadelphia editor published a handbill picturing the coffins of twelve men allegedly murdered by Jackson.

The Jackson campaign in 1828 was the first to directly appeal for voter support through a professional political organization. Skilled political organizers, like Martin Van Buren of New York, Amos Kendall of Kentucky, and Thomas Ritchie of Virginia created a vast network of pro-Jackson newspapers, which pictured the general as the "candidate of the people" and Adams as a Federalist in Republican clothing who believed that the "few should govern the many." Jackson supporters set up an extensive network of campaign committees and subcommittees to organize mass rallies, parades, barbeques, and erect hickory poles, Jackson's symbol, "in every village as well as upon the corners of many city streets." Together, these political techniques succeeded in transforming a broad heterogeneous political combination including former Federalists, Republicans, and supporters and opponents of banks, protective tariffs, and internal improvements, into a successful political movement.

For the first time in American history, a presidential election was the focus of public attention. Twice as many voters cast ballots in the election of 1828 as in 1824, four times as many as in 1820. As in most previous elections, the vote divided along sectional lines. Jackson swept every state in the South and West and Adams won the electoral votes of every state in the North except Pennsylvania and part of the electoral vote of New York.

Contemporaries interpreted Jackson's election as a triumph for political democracy. Jackson supporters called the vote a victory for the "farmers and mechanics of the country" over the "rich and well born." Even Jackson's opponents agreed that the election marked a watershed in the nation's political history, signaling the beginning of a new democratic age. One Adams supporter said bluntly, "a great revolution has taken place."

ANDREW JACKSON: THE POLITICS OF THE COMMON PERSON

Supporters of Adams regarded Jackson's victory with deep pessimism. A justice of the Supreme Court declared, "The reign of King 'Mob' seems triumphant." John Randolph of Virginia feared that "the country is ruined past redemption." But enthusiasts greeted Jackson's victory as a great triumph for the people. At the inaug-

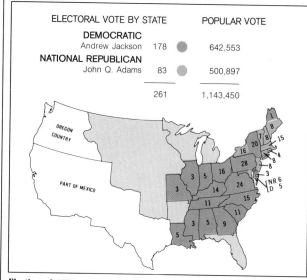

ELECTORAL VOTE BY STATE		POPULAR VOTE
DEMOCRATIC		
Andrew Jackson	178	642,553
NATIONAL REPUBLICAN		
John Q. Adams	83	500,897
	261	1,143,450

Election of 1828

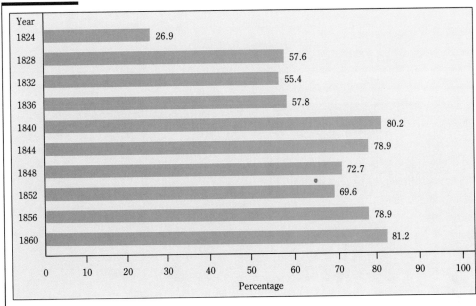

Figure 9.1
Voter Population

ural, a cable, stretched in front of the east portico of the Capitol to keep back the throngs, snapped under the pressure of the surging crowd. As many as 20,000 well-wishers attended a White House reception to honor the new president, muddying rugs, breaking furniture, and damaging china and glassware. "It was a proud day for the people," commented one Kentucky newspaperman. "General Jackson is their own President."

To the public, the new president was primarily known as a military hero, who had volunteered to serve in the Revolutionary War at the age of thirteen, defeated the British at the Battle of New Orleans, crushed the Creek Indians, and in 1819 led a punitive expedition against the Seminole Indians and helped to drive the Spanish out of Florida.

But Jackson's career was a good bit more complicated than that. Born in 1767 in a frontier region along the North and South Carolina border known as the Waxhaws, he was the first president to be born in a log cabin or west of the Appalachian Mountains. His parents were a poor farm couple from Northern Ireland. His father died two weeks before his birth, and his mother and only two brothers died during the American Revolution. At the age of thirteen

Jackson joined the mounted militia of South Carolina. He was taken prisoner and a British officer severely slashed Jackson's hand and head when the boy refused to shine the officer's shoes.

After the Revolution, Jackson began to study for the law in Salisbury, North Carolina, and was admitted to the bar in 1787. A year later he was named public prosecutor for the Western district of North Carolina, an area that included what would become the state of Tennessee. Subsequently, Jackson became Tennessee's first U.S. congressman, a senator, and judge of the Tennessee Supreme Court.

Although Jackson later gained a reputation as the champion of the common people, in Tennessee he was allied by marriage, business, and political ties to the state's "beaver-hat" conservatives and against the "beaver-skinner" yeomanry. As a land speculator, cotton planter, and attorney, he accumulated a large personal fortune and acquired over 100 slaves. His candidacy for the presidency was initially promoted by speculators, creditors, and elite leaders in Tennessee who hoped to exploit Jackson's popularity in order to combat antibanking sentiment and fend off challenges to their dominance of state politics.

Twenty thousand people attended a reception for President Jackson at the White House, trampling rugs, breaking furniture, and stealing china.

Few presidents have aroused as much controversy as Andrew Jackson. To his admirers, he was a firm leader who strengthened the powers of the presidency. To his opponents, he was a ruthless tyrant whose policies only served to weaken the American economy and bring about the financial panic of 1837. He has been admired as a champion of working men and women and praised as an opponent of special privilege, and villified as an Indian killer. His economic policies have been interpreted as an anticapitalist attack on banks and other powerful business corporations but also as a procapitalist attempt to open the doors of economic opportunity to new men on the rise. However one evaluates his presidency, there can be no doubt that he left an indelible stamp on the nation's highest office; indeed, on a whole epoch in American history.

Expanding the Powers of the Presidency

In office, Jackson greatly expanded the power and prestige of the presidency. He was the first president to fire a cabinet officer, the first to use federal troops to put down a labor strike, the first to open diplomatic relations with the Far East, and the first to declare that the president, and not Congress, was the best representative of the people. Jackson was also the first president to declare that the Union would not be peacefully dissolved. In the name of opposing special privilege, he declared war on the national bank, vetoed federal aid for internal improvements, paid off the national debt, and lowered the federal tariff. Few presidents ever aroused deeper passions than Andrew Jackson.

As president, Jackson articulated a political ideology that convinced many Americans that their votes mattered. Central to the Jacksonian ideology was a belief in the dignity and worth of common folk. Among the principles espoused by Jackson and his followers was the "principle of democratic republicanism": "an abiding confidence in the virtue, intelligence, and full capacity for self-government of the great mass of our people," and a deep-rooted disdain for the "better classes" who claim a "more enlightened wisdom" than common men and women.

Jackson and his supporters also endorsed the view that there was a fundamental conflict in American society between "the hard working members of society"—the honest mechanic, farmer, and capitalist—and the "non-producing" classes, who grew rich on the basis of monopoly, favoritism, and special privileges. Inequalities of wealth and power were the direct result of government intervention in the economy, which had made "the rich richer and the powerful more potent." Only free competition in a open marketplace would ensure that wealth would be distributed in accordance with each person's "industry, economy, enterprise, and prudence." The goal of the Jacksonians was to remove all impediments that prevented farmers, artisans, and small shopkeepers from getting a greater share of the nation's wealth.

Nowhere was the Jacksonian ideal of openness made more concrete than in Jackson's theory of rotation in office or the spoils system. In his first annual message to Congress, Jackson defended the principle that public offices should be rotated among party supporters on the grounds that it would help the nation achieve its Republican ideals. Performance in public office, Jackson maintained, required no special intelligence or training, and rotation in office would insure that the federal government did not develop a class of corrupt civil servants set apart from the people. In the United States, Jackson noted, "Where offices are created solely for the benefit of the people . . . no one has any more intrinsic right to official station than another." His supporters spoke in less lofty terms, viewing the system as a way to reward political party loyalists and build a stronger party organization. As Jacksonian Senator William Marcy of New York proclaimed, "To the victor belongs the spoils."

Actually, Jackson replaced fewer than 1000 of the nation's 10,000 civil servants on political grounds during his first eighteen months in office, and fewer than twenty percent of federal officeholders were removed during his administration. Moreover, many of the men Jackson appointed to office had backgrounds of wealth and social eminence. Nor was Jackson the originator of the spoils system. By the time Jackson took office, a number of states, including New York and Pennsylvania, practiced political patronage.

During the Jacksonian era, land, tariff, and banking policies dominated national politics. In the heated political battles swirling around these questions two competing national political parties emerged. Compared to the issues that dominated British politics during the same years—slave emancipation, factory regulation, and assistance to the poor—the questions

To solidify popular support, the Jacksonians openly defended the principle that public offices should be given to loyal party supporters.

Americans fought over might seem trivial. Nevertheless, vital interests were at stake, relating to such fateful questions as equality to opportunity, the distribution of wealth, the balance of sectional power, and the proper role of government in the economy.

Clearing the Land of Indians

The first political controversy of Jackson's presidency to raise these momentous questions involved Indian policy. At the time Jackson took office, 125,000 Native Americans still lived east of the Mississippi River. Cherokee, Choctaw, Chickasaw, and Creek Indians—60,000 strong—held millions of acres in what would become the southern cotton kingdom stretching across Georgia, Alabama, and Mississippi. The political question was whether Indians would be permitted to stand in the way of white expansion. By 1840, Jackson and his successor, Martin Van Buren, had answered this question. All Indians east of the Mississippi had been uprooted from their homelands and moved westward, with the exception of rebellious Seminoles in Florida and small numbers of Indians living on isolated reservations in Michigan, North Carolina, and New York.

Since the presidency of Thomas Jefferson, the federal government had been committed to two conflicting Indian policies. The assimilation policy encouraged Indians to adopt white American customs and economic practices. The government provided financial assistance to missionaries in order to Christianize and educate Native Americans and convince them to adopt single family farms. According to the American Board of Commissioners for Foreign Missions, "There is no place on earth to which they can migrate, and live in the savage and hunter state. The Indian tribes must, therefore, be progressively civilized, or successively perish." By the 1820s, the Cherokee had demonstrated the ability of Native Americans to adapt to changing conditions while maintaining their tribal heritage. These people had developed a written alphabet, opened schools, established churches, built roads, operated printing presses, and even adopted a constitution.

The other policy, removal, was first suggested by Thomas Jefferson as the only way to ensure the survival of Indian cultures. The goal of this policy was to encourage the voluntary migration of Indians westward to tracts of land where they could live free from white harassment. As early as 1817, James Monroe declared that the nation's security depended upon rapid settlement along the southern coast and that it was in the best interests of Native Americans to move westward. In 1825 he set before Congress a plan to resettle all eastern Indians upon tracts in the West where whites would not be allowed to live.

Andrew Jackson's Indian policy was to promise remuneration to tribes that would move westward, while offering small plots of land to individual Indians who would operate family farms. Jackson received an opportunity to put this policy into effect early in his presidency when a controversy erupted between the Cherokee nation and the state of Georgia. The Cherokee people had adopted a constitution asserting sovereignty over their land, and the state of Georgia responded by claiming that the Cherokee fell under its jurisdiction. The discovery of gold on Cherokee land triggered a land

In 1809 a Cherokee named Sequoyah began to devise an alphabet, consisting of letters based on English, Greek, and Hebrew. The Cherokee nation's weekly newspaper, the *Cherokee Phoenix,* was printed with this alphabet.

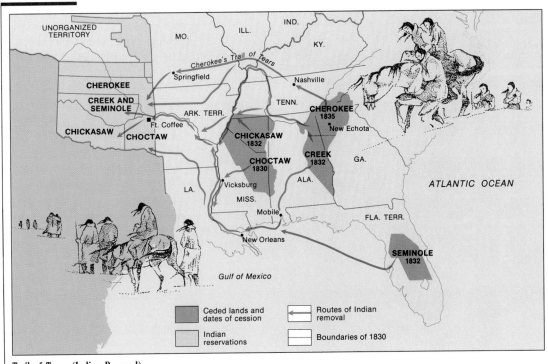

Trail of Tears (Indian Removal)

rush, and the Cherokee nation sued to keep white settlers from encroaching upon their territory. In two important cases, *Cherokee Nation* v. *Georgia* in 1831 and *Worcester* v. *Georgia* in 1832, the Supreme Court denied Georgia's right to extend state laws over the Cherokee people, but also ruled that the Cherokee were not entitled under the Constitution to sue in federal courts. The Court did hold, however, that under treaties with the Cherokee, the federal government had a responsibility to exclude intruders from Indian lands. Angered, Jackson supposedly exclaimed: "John Marshall has made his decision; now let him enforce it."

Under Jackson, the primary thrust of federal policy was to encourage Indian tribes to sell all tribal lands in exchange for new lands in Oklahoma and Arkansas. Such a policy, the president maintained, would open new farm land to whites while offering Indians a haven where they would be free to develop at their own pace. "There," he wrote, "your white broth-

ers will not trouble you, they will have no claims to the land, and you can live upon it, you and all your children, as long as the grass grows or the water runs, in peace and plenty."

Pushmataha, a Choctaw chieftain, called on his people to reject Jackson's offer. Far from being a "country of tall trees, many water courses, rich lands and high grass abounding in games of all kinds," the promised preserve in the West was simply a barren desert. Jackson warned that if the Choctaw refused to move west, he would destroy their nation.

During the winter of 1831, the Choctaw became the first tribe to walk the Trail of Tears westward. Promised government assistance failed to arrive and malnutrition, exposure, and an epidemic of cholera killed many members of the nation. In 1836, the Creek suffered the hardships of removal. About 3500 of the tribe's 15,000 members died along the westward trek. Those who resisted removal were chained and marched in double file.

THE CHOLERA EPIDEMIC OF 1832: SINNERS AND SAINTS

In the spring of 1832, Americans braced themselves for an attack by cholera—what one historian has called "the classic epidemic disease of the nineteenth century." They knew it was coming. Throughout the preceding year, newspapers had reported with alarm the disease's escape from its Asiatic homeland and its westward march across Europe. The press had turned shrill when cholera crossed the Atlantic Ocean—the last great barrier that shielded the Americas from this horrible plague—and struck Canada in June 1832. Despite the certainty that the disease would soon reach the United States, however, nei-

ther the federal, state, nor local governments did much to prevent or even prepare for an epidemic.

Nothing in their inventory of illnesses, not even the ravages of smallpox or malaria, had prepared Americans for the terror that seized them when cholera finally appeared. Their fear is easily understood: cholera killed approximately half of those who contracted it, and it struck with unbelievable rapidity. A New Yorker who survived the 1832 epidemic testified that he was walking down the street when he suddenly fell forward on his face "as if knocked down with an axe."

Cholera's symptoms, which mimic those of severe arsenic poisoning, are indeed spectacular. The onset of the disease is marked by acute diarrhea, uncontrollable vomiting, and violent abdominal cramps. Within hours, this sudden and massive loss of fluids causes dehydration, and the victim's extremities feel cold, the face turns blue, and the feet and hands appear dark and swollen. Unless proper medical treatment is provided, death can follow within a few hours after the first symptoms appear, or, at most, within a few days. Even more than its devastating symptoms, it was the disease's ability to kill so swiftly that terrorized the public. "To see individuals well in the morning & buried before night, retiring apparently well & dead in the morning is something which is appalling to the boldest heart," exclaimed another survivor of America's first cholera epidemic.

The cause of cholera was not discovered until 1883 when Robert Koch, the famous scientist, led a commission to Egypt that isolated *Vibrio comma*, the guilty bacterium. These deadly germs settle in the intestines of their victims, following a journey along any one of several pathways that lead to the human digestive tract. Although dirty hands or raw fruits and vegetables often transmit the disease, most cholera epidemics are spread by polluted drinking water from sewage-contaminated water systems.

Unfortunately, America's cities in 1832 harbored more than enough filth to nurture an epidemic. New York was especially dirty. Residents were required by law to pile their garbage in the gutter in front of their homes for removal by the city, but it seldom got collected. (With their characteristic sense of humor, New Yorkers dubbed these piles of stinking, decomposing garbage "corporation pie.") The only effective "sanitary engineers" in New York were the thousands of swine that roamed the streets gorging themselves on the refuse.

Thanks to this filth, cholera unleashed a great plague of death when it reached New York. Thousands died in the epidemic, producing so many bodies that the undertakers could not keep up with the volume and had to stack corpses in warehouses and public buildings to await burial. In short, cholera hit New York with the same force with which yellow fever had knocked Philadelphia to its knees in 1793.

In the midst of their suffering, New Yorkers could not help but wonder why some people contracted the disease while others escaped it. To answer this question, America's physicians espoused a doctrine of predisposing causes. People who kept God's laws, they explained, had nothing to fear, but the intemperate and the filthy stood at great risk. In fact, physicians elaborated their warnings about "predisposing" or "exciting" causes into a jeremiad against sin. Impiety, imprudence, idleness, drunkenness, gluttony, and sexual excess all left their devotees weakened and "artificially stimulated," their bodies to be vulnerable to cholera.

Because the disease was "decidedly vulgar," physicians predicted that it would confine itself largely to the lower classes—specifically, to blacks and to the Irish, who were thought by upper-class indi-

viduals to be the most intemperate and debauched members of society. Here, then, was a classic example of how the medical profession appropriated social attitudes regarding class and race to blame the victims of disease for their suffering.

Again, the doctors appeared to be right, but for the wrong reasons. Cholera was indeed a "poor man's plague"; sin, however, was not the explanation. The upper classes suffered less because they fled the cities and dispersed to country homes and lodges where pure water and low population density prevented infection. The poor, by contrast, could not afford to leave: they had to remain and take their chances.

Typically, most of New York's lower classes lived in tiny, unvented apartments where entire families (and perhaps a boarder or two) occupied a single room, while the most wretched hoveled in unfurnished cellars whose walls glistened with sewage and slime every time it rained. Instead of pure water imported in hogsheads from fresh water springs in the countryside (the only water the wealthy would touch), poor people drew their drinking water from the river or from contaminated shallow wells. Though New Yorkers had long joked that their water was an excellent purgative, they might as well have called it "liquid death" when cholera swept the land.

Once cholera struck, physicians found that none of the traditional remedies of heroic medicine worked. In addition to bloodletting, they treated their patients with laudanum (the main ingredient of which was opium), tobacco smoke enemas, and huge doses of calomel, a chalky mercury com-

pound employed as a cathartic. In desperation, one of New York's leading physicians (a practical thinker) even recommended plugging the patient's rectum with beeswax to halt the diarrhea.

Many Americans turned to quacks or treated themselves with home remedies. It made no difference. Those who survived the epidemic did so in spite of the medical care they received, not because of it.

Cholera receded from the land almost as quickly as it had come. By the fall of 1832 the epidemic had spent its fury, and by the winter it was gone. When it struck again in 1866, Americans had learned how to battle the disease. They no longer talked about cholera in moral terms as God's vengeance on the poor and the wicked. Instead, they approached it as a social problem amenable to human intervention. They imposed quarantines, opened emergency hospitals, increased the powers of health authorities, removed the trash and garbage from city streets, and cleaned up municipal water supplies. The contrast between 1832 and 1866 could not have been more complete.

Within the span of two generations, the public changed the way it viewed disease. American physicians became more scientific in handling and treating the sick— eloquent testimony to the medical advances in a modernizing society.

The Cherokee, emboldened by the Supreme Court decisions that declared that Georgia law had no force on Indian territory, resisted removal. Fifteen thousand Cherokee joined in a protest against Jackson's policy: "Little did [we] anticipate that when taught to think and feel as the American citizen . . . [we] were to be despoiled by [our] guardian, to become strangers and wanderers in the land of [our] fathers, forced to return to the savage life, and to seek a new home in the wilds of the far west, and that without [our] consent." The federal government bribed a faction of the tribe to leave the land in exchange for transportation costs and $5 million, but the majority of the people held out until 1838, when the army evicted them from their land. All totaled, 4000 Cherokee died along the trail to Oklahoma.

A number of tribes organized resistance against removal. In the Old Northwest, the Sauk and Fox Indians fought the Black Hawk War to recover ceded tribal lands in Illinois and Wisconsin. The United States Army and the Illinois state militia ended resistance by wantonly killing nearly 500 Sauk and Fox men, women, and children who were trying to retreat across the Mississippi River. In Florida, the military put down Seminole resistance at a cost of $20 million and 1500 troops, and even then only after the treacherous act of seizing the Seminole leader Osceola during peace talks.

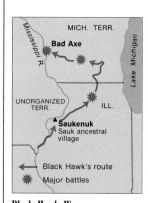

Black Hawk War

By twentieth-century standards, Jackson's Indian policy was both callous and brutal. Despite the semblance of legality—ninety-four treaties were signed with Indians during Jackson's presidency—Indian migrations to the West usually occurred under the threat of government coercion. Even before Jackson's death in 1845, it was obvious that tribal lands in the West were no more secure than Indian lands had been in the East. In 1851 Congress passed the Indian Appropriations Act, which sought to concentrate the western Native American population upon reservations.

Why were such morally indefensible policies adopted? The answer is that many white Americans regarded Indian control of land and other natural resources as a serious obstacle to their desire for expansion and as a potential threat to the nation's security. Even had the federal government wanted to, it probably lacked the resources or military means to protect eastern Indians from the encroaching white farmers, squatters, traders, and speculators. By the 1830s, a growing number of missionaries and humanitarians agreed with Jackson that Indians needed to be resettled westward for their own protection. Given the nation's commitment to limited government and its lack of experience with social welfare programs, the removal program was doomed from the start. Contracts for food, clothing, and transportation were let to the lowest bidders, many of whom failed to fulfill their contractual responsibilities. Indians were resettled on arid lands, unsuited for intensive farming. The tragic outcome was readily foreseeable.

The problem of preserving native cultures in the face of an expanding nation was not confined to the United States. Jackson's removal policy can only be properly understood when it is seen as part of a broader process: the political and economic incorporation of frontier regions into expanding nation states. During the early decades of the nineteenth century, European nations were penetrating into many frontier areas, from the steppes of Russia to the plains of Argentina, the veldt of South Africa, the outback of Australia, and the American West. In each of these regions, national expansion was justified on the grounds of strategic interest (to preempt settlement by other powers) or in the name of opening valuable land to settlement and development. In each case, expansion was accompanied by the removal or wholesale killing of native peoples.

Sectional Disputes over Public Lands and Nullification

Bitter sectional disputes erupted during Jackson's presidency. Differences first arose in a debate over the disposal of public lands. After

After signing an agreement to leave Florida and move west, most of the Seminole refused to go and tried to resist the army's efforts to drive them from Florida.

the Revolutionary War, the federal government possessed one-quarter billion acres of public land; the Louisiana Purchase added another half billion acres to the public domain. These public lands constituted the federal government's single greatest resource. Early in the new nation's history, the sale of public land served as the primary source of public revenue. By 1820 the idea of using the proceeds of the sale of public land to pay off government expenses gave way to a new view that land should be sold as rapidly and cheaply as possible in order to promote the establishment of farms.

To encourage the rapid sale of public land, Congress in 1820 reduced the minimum land purchase to just 80 acres, at a price of $1.25 per acre. A variety of groups pressed Congress to ease access to land still further. Squatters, who violated federal laws that forbade settlement prior to the completion of public surveys, pressured Congress to adopt preemption acts which would permit them to buy the land at the minimum price of $1.25 when it came up for sale. Urban workingmen—agitating under the slogan "Vote Yourself a Farm"—demanded free

homesteads for any American who would settle the public domain. Transportation companies, which built roads, canals, and later railroads, called for public land grants to help fund their projects.

Westerners, led by Senator Thomas Hart Benton of Missouri, proposed that Congress gradually reduce the price of government land that remained unsold. This proposal, known as "graduation," provoked a contest between southern and eastern members of Congress for western support.

Southern politicians hoped to use the dispute over public land policy to gain western support in their drive to reduce the federal tariff. Senator Robert Hayne of South Carolina called on the South and West to unite in affirming the principle of states' rights and John C. Calhoun's doctrine of nullification against attempts by the Northeast to strengthen the powers of the federal government (on nullification, see p. 273). Senator Daniel Webster of Massachusetts answered Hayne in one of the most celebrated orations in American history. The United States, Webster proclaimed, was not

Daniel Webster made his famous reply to Hayne in front of forty-seven senators and the vice-president.

simply a creation of the states. It was a creation of the people, who had invested the Constitution and the national government with ultimate sovereignty. If a state disagreed with an action of the federal government, it had a right to sue in federal courts or seek to amend the Constitution, but it had no right to nullify a federal law. It was delusion and folly to think that Americans could have "Liberty first and Union afterwards," Webster declared. "Liberty and Union, now and forever, one and inseparable."

Jackson had not revealed where he stood on the questions of state sovereignty and the principle of nullification until April 13, 1830, at a Jefferson Day dinner, when he made his position clear. He stood up, fixed his eyes on Vice-President John C. Calhoun, and offered a toast that expressed his sentiments in ringing terms: "Our Union: It must be preserved." Calhoun, who first advanced the nullification argument, responded to Jackson's challenge and offered the next toast: "The Union, next to our liberty, most dear. May we always remember that it can only be preserved by distributing equally the benefits and burdens of the Union."

Relations between Jackson and Calhoun were becoming increasingly strained. Jackson learned that Calhoun, while secretary of war under Monroe, had called for Jackson's court-martial for his conduct of the Seminole War in Florida. Jackson was also angry because Mrs. Calhoun had snubbed the wife of Secretary of War John H. Eaton, because she was the daughter of a tavern keeper. Jackson's own late wife Rachel had been snubbed by society (partly because she smoked a pipe and partly because she married Jackson before a divorce from her first husband was final), and the president had empathy for Peggy Eaton. In 1831, Jackson reorganized his cabinet and forced Calhoun's supporters out. The next year, Calhoun became the first vice-president to resign his office.

To conciliate the South, Jackson recommended in his message to Congress in 1831 that the federal tariff be reduced. Revenue from the existing tariff was so high that the federal debt was quickly being paid off; in fact on January 1, 1835, the U.S. Treasury had a balance of $440,000, not a penny of which was owed to anyone. The new tariff adopted in 1832 was

In 1831 the Peggy Eaton affair provoked a political break between President Andrew Jackson and his vice-president, John C. Calhoun.

somewhat lower than the tariff of 1828 but maintained the principle of protection. South Carolina's fiery "states' righters" responded aggressively. In November, 1832, a state convention in South Carolina declared the tariffs of 1828 and 1832 void within the state.

Jackson acted decisively during the nullification crisis. In a "Proclamation to the People of South Carolina," Jackson became the first president to declare the Union indissoluble. If the crisis went on, he declared, "our country will be like a bag of meal with both ends open. Pick it up in the middle or endwise, and it will run out. I must tie the bag and save the country." He announced that nullification was illegal, and then asked Congress to give him the power to use force to execute federal law—a Force Act—which Congress promptly enacted. Privately, Jackson threatened to "hang every leader . . . of that infatuated people, sir, by martial law, irrespective of his name, or political or social position." At the same time, in an effort to reduce South Carolina's sense of grievance, he persuaded Congress to enact a compromise tariff, with lower levels of protection.

South Carolinians regarded Jackson's actions as "the mad rages of a driveling dotard," but they backed down, rescinding the ordinance nullifying the federal tariff. As a final gesture of defiance, however, the state adopted an ordinance nullifying the Force Act.

No other Southern state yet shared South Carolina's fear of federal power or its militant desire to assert the doctrine of states' rights. South Carolina's anxiety had many sources. By 1831 declining cotton prices (from 31 cents a pound in 1818 to 8 cents a pound), a protracted depression, and growing concern about the future of slavery had turned the state from a staunch supporter of economic nationalism into the nation's most aggressive advocate of states' rights. Increasingly, economic grievances fused with anxieties over slavery. In 1832, the Palmetto State was one of just two states whose population was made up of a majority of slaves, and by that year the state was desperately uneasy about the future of slavery. In 1831 and 1832 militant abolitionism had erupted in the North, slave insurrections had occurred in Southampton County, Virginia, and Jamaica, and Britain was moving to emancipate all slaves in the British Caribbean.

In their grievance about the federal tariff, South Carolinians found an ideal way of debating the question of state sovereignty without debating the morality of slavery. Following the Missouri Compromise (see pp. 259–261), a slave insurrection led by Denmark Vesey had been uncovered in Charleston in 1822. In 1832 South Carolinians did not want to stage debates in Congress that might bring the explosive slavery issue to the fore and possibly incite a slave revolt.

The Bank War

Jackson's war against the second Bank of the United States was the major political issue of his presidency. To understand what was at stake in the battle, it is necessary to know that at the time Jackson assumed the presidency the national banking system was completely different than it is today. Since Congress coined only a limited supply of money, the American people relied upon bank notes issued by private commercial banks, of which there were 329 in 1829. These private banks supplied the credit necessary to finance land purchases, business operations, and economic growth. The notes they issued were promises to pay gold or silver, but they were backed by a limited amount of precious metal and they fluctuated greatly in value.

The federal government formed the second bank of the United States in 1816 in order to regulate the notes issued by private banks. By demanding payment in gold or silver, the bank could discipline overspeculative private banks. The federal government owned twenty percent of the bank's stock and named five of its twenty directors.

The panic of 1819 had aroused widespread antibank sentiment, especially among Southerners and Westerners whose mortgages were foreclosed by the second bank. Wage earners and small businessmen blamed the bank for economic fluctuations. Frontier settlers in new states like Mississippi criticized the bank for restricting the availability of loans. Opposition came from commercial banks in New York and Philadelphia, who coveted the bank's privileged

position, and from old-line Jeffersonians who continued to regard the bank as unconstitutional, despite the Supreme Court's decision in *McCullough* v. *Maryland.* The bank's political influence also inspired animosity. Senator Daniel Webster, for example, was the bank's chief lobbyist and a director of the bank's Boston branch. But the bank's most serious opponent was Jackson, who had questioned the bank's constitutionality and ability to produce a sound currency in his first annual message in 1829.

In 1832 Congress, at the urging of Henry Clay, Daniel Webster, and other Jackson opponents, passed a bill rechartering the bank. The charter of the bank was not due to expire until 1836, but Webster and Clay hoped to use it as an issue in the 1832 presidential election. Jackson had frequently attacked the bank as an agency through which speculators, monopolists, and other seekers of economic privilege cheated honest farmers and mechanics. Now, his adversaries wanted to force him either to sign the bill for recharter, alienating voters hostile to the bank, or veto it, alienating conservative voters who favored a sound banking system.

Jackson vetoed the bill in a forceful message that condemned the bank as a privileged "monopoly" created to make "rich men . . . richer by act of Congress." In the presidential campaign of 1832, Henry Clay tried to make an issue of Jackson's bank veto, but Jackson swept to an easy second term victory, defeating Clay 219 electoral votes to 49.

Jackson interpreted his victory as a vindication of his bank veto, and in September, 1833, took a further step to undermine the bank's political and economic power. He ordered his treasury secretary to remove federal revenues from the Bank of the United States and deposit them in selected state banks, which came to be known as "pet" banks. The secretary of the treasury and his successor resigned rather than carry out the president's order, and it was only after Jackson appointed a new secretary that the deposits were finally removed.

The bank president, Nicholas Biddle, responded to this move by reducing loans and calling in debts. "This worthy President," said Biddle, "thinks that because he has scalped Indians and imprisoned Judges he is to have his

As this anti-Jackson cartoon illustrates, defenders of the second Bank of the United States regarded Jackson's bank war as a threat to destroy the nation's economic health.

way with the Bank. He is mistaken." Jackson retorted: "The Bank . . . is trying to kill me, but I will kill it." Jackson's decision to remove federal deposits from the national bank prompted his adversaries in the Senate to formally censure the president's actions as arbitrary and unconstitutional.

Jackson's decision to withdraw funds from the bank drew strong support from many conservative businessmen who believed that the bank's destruction would increase the availability of credit and open up new business opportunities. Jackson, however, hated all banks. Having crippled the Bank of the United States, he promptly launched a crusade to replace all bank notes with hard money. Jackson believed that the only sound currency was gold and silver, and between 1833 and 1836 he took a series of actions designed to eliminate bank notes from circulation. Denouncing "the power which the moneyed interest derives from a paper currency," the president prohibited banks receiving federal deposits from issuing bills valued at

less than $5. Then, in the Specie Circular of 1836, Jackson prohibited payment for public lands in anything but gold or silver.

To Jackson's supporters, the presidential veto was a principled assault upon a bastion of wealth and special privilege. His efforts to curtail the circulation of bank notes was an effort to rid the country of a tool used by commercial interests to exploit farmers and working men and women. To his critics, the bank veto was an act of economic ignorance that destroyed a valuable institution which promoted monetary stability, eased the long distance transfer of funds, provided a reserve of capital on which other banks drew, and helped regulate the bank notes issued by private banks. The effort to limit the circulation of bank notes was a misguided act by a "backward-looking" president who failed to understand the role of a banking system in a modern economy.

Debate still rages over the effects of Jackson's banking policies. Land sales and canal construction boomed following Jackson's deci-

The opposition Whig party blamed the panic of 1837 on Andrew Jackson's banking policies and his Specie Circular. They attacked his hand-picked successor, Martin Van Buren, for rejecting federal aid to business.

sion to remove federal funds from the bank. Prices climbed twenty-eight percent in just three years and the quantity of money in circulation rose sixty-four percent. Then in 1837, just after Jackson had been succeeded as president by Democrat Martin Van Buren, a deep financial depression struck the nation, known as the panic of 1837.

Cotton prices fell by half. In New York City, fifty thousand people were thrown out of work and two hundred thousand lacked adequate means of support. From across the country came "rumor after rumor of riot, insurrection, and tumult." "Hard Times! is the cry from Madawaska to Galena," declared a New York newspaper. Mobs in New York broke into the city's flour warehouse. Orestes Brownson, one of the nation's most prominent thinkers, announced that revolution was only waiting for the "signal to rush to the terrible encounter, if the battle have not already begun."

Historians no longer place primary blame on Andrew Jackson for the inflation and subse-

quent depression that followed the bank war. It now appears that heavy investment by British investors in American roads and canals, followed by the decision of the British government in 1836 to raise interest rates, were the chief causes of the panic of 1837.

If Jackson's policies did not cause the panic, they did reduce the ability of the government to help the country climb out of the depression. Jackson's handpicked successor as president, Martin Van Buren, responded to the economic depression in an extremely rigid way. A firm believer in the Jeffersonian principle of limited government, Van Buren refused to provide government aid to business. "The less government interferes," Van Buren said, "the better for general prosperity."

Fearful that the federal government might lose funds it had deposited in private banks, Van Buren convinced Congress in 1840 to adopt an independent treasury system, under which federal funds were locked up in insulated subtreasuries, totally divorced from the banking system. This plan deprived the banking system of the funds that might have aided recovery. The country did not fully pull out of the depression until the mid-1840s.

The Jacksonian Court

Presidents' judicial appointments represent one of their most enduring legacies. In his two terms as president, Andrew Jackson appointed five justices to a court then composed of just seven justices. The death of John Marshall in 1835 not only allowed Jackson to name the Chief Justice, but meant that he had named a majority of the members of the Court. The man Jackson tapped as Chief Justice was his attorney general, Roger B. Taney, the co-author of the bank veto. He led the court for nearly three decades.

Taney was the first Chief Justice to wear trousers instead of knee breeches and in many other ways he broke with tradition and led the Court in new directions. As Chief Justice his Court issued a series of landmark rulings intended to promote national economic growth by encouraging enterprise and competition by freeing entrepreneurs from traditional restrictions imposed by the common law. Under Taney, the Supreme Court upheld the doctrine of limited liability for corporations, provided legal sanction to state subsidies for canals, turnpikes, and railroads, and reduced the liability of employers for injuries caused by their operations. Taken together, the decisions of the Taney Court played a vital role in the emergence of the American system of free enterprise.

Shortly after his confirmation as Chief Justice, Taney was faced by a case which raised an issue vital to the nation's future economic growth. The case was *Charles River Bridge* v. *Warren Bridge,* and the question the case raised was whether monopolies granted by states in the past would be allowed to block competition from new enterprises. In 1828, the state of Massachusetts chartered a company to build a bridge connecting Boston and neighboring Charlestown. The owners of an existing bridge sued on the grounds that under a charter granted to them in 1785 they had an implied right to have no competition. In its decision the

Court ensured that monopolistic privileges granted in the past would not be allowed to harm the public welfare. The Court held that contracts conferred no rights except those explicitly stated in the contract and that any ambiguity in wording should be construed in the public interest. In three respects the Court's decision epitomized the ideals of Jacksonian democracy. In its goal of eliminating artificial barriers to opportunity, its commitment to progress, enterprise, and economic growth, and its emphasis upon free competition in an open marketplace, the Court in the Charles River Bridge case sought to extend Jacksonian principles to the legal system.

Jackson's Legacy

Andrew Jackson was one of the nation's most resourceful and effective presidents. Over the opposition of hostile majorities in Congress, he succeeded in carrying out his most important policies, affecting banking, internal improvements, Indians, and tariffs. Jackson used the veto power more often than all earlier presidents had together over the preceding forty years, and he used it in such a way that he succeeded in representing himself as the champion of the people against special interests in Congress. His skillful use of patronage and party organization and his successful manipulation of public symbols helped him create the nation's first modern political party with national appeal.

Despite his popular appeal, Jackson's legacy is the object of great dispute among historians. His Indian policies, under which 45,000 Native Americans were uprooted from their tribal homelands and relocated west of the Mississippi, continue to arouse passionate criticism. Although Jackson has often been viewed as the president of the common man, his economic policies did little to help yeoman farmers, artisans, and the working man, and actually weakened the ability of the federal government to regulate the nation's economy. Indeed, many historians now believe that slaveholders, not small farmers or workingmen, gained most from Jackson's policies. His Indian policy helped to open new lands for slaveholders and his view of limited government forestalled federal interference with slavery.

RISE OF A POLITICAL OPPOSITION

During the thirty-two years following Andrew Jackson's election to the presidency in 1828, the Democratic Party controlled the White House for all but eight years. Twice the opposition candidate won the election, only to die soon after taking office. It would be a mistake, however, to assume that the Jacksonians faced no effective opposition. Although it took a number of years for Jackson's opponents to coalesce into an effective national political organization, by the mid-1830s the Whig party, as the opposition came to be known, was able to battle the Democratic party on almost equal terms throughout the country. By 1840, the Whigs were strong enough to oust Democratic president Martin Van Buren, from the White House.

The party was formed in 1834 as a coalition of National Republicans, Anti-Masons, and disgruntled Democrats, who were united by their hatred of "King Andrew" Jackson and his "usurpations" of Congressional and judicial authority. The party took its name from the seventeenth-century British Whigs who had defended English liberties against the usurpations of pro-Catholic Stuart kings.

In 1836 the Whigs mounted their first presidential campaign. The party ran three regional candidates against Martin Van Buren: Daniel Webster, the senator from Massachusetts and ardent defender of the Bank of the United States who had substantial appeal in New England; Hugh Lawson White, who had appeal in the South; and William Henry Harrison, who had defeated the Shawnee Prophet at the Battle of Tippecanoe and appealed to the West and to Anti-Masons in Pennsylvania and Vermont. The party strategy was to throw the election into the House of Representatives, where the Whigs would unite behind a single candidate. Van Buren easily defeated all his Whig opponents, winning 170 electoral votes to just 73 for his closest rival.

The emergence of Martin Van Buren as Jackson's successor as president precipitated a major realignment of party support. Unlike the southern slave-owning Jackson, Van Buren was a "Yankee" from New York, disliked by many Southerners who feared that he could not be trusted to protect slavery. In 1836 many Southern Democrats defected to the Whigs and the party carried Georgia, Kentucky, Maryland, and Tennessee.

Ironically, as president, Van Buren supported a Congressional rule—known as the Gag Rule—which quashed all debate over slavery in the Senate and House of Representatives. His independent treasury scheme combined with his staunch opposition to any federal interference in the economy lured Calhoun and the southern nullifiers back to the Democratic party. Conversely, his attacks on paper money and his scheme to remove federal funds from the private banking system alienated many conservative Democrats who threw their support to the Whigs.

Following his strong showing in the election of 1836, William Henry Harrison received the united support of the Whig party in 1840. Benefiting from the panic of 1837 and from a host of colorful campaign innovations, Harrison easily defeated Van Buren 234 to 60 in the electoral vote.

John Tyler's Tumultuous Presidency

Unfortunately, Harrison caught cold while delivering a two-hour inaugural address in the freezing rain. Barely a month later he died of pneumonia, the first president to die in office. His successor was John Tyler of Virginia, an ardent defender of slavery, a staunch advocate of states' rights, and a former Democrat, whom the Whigs nominated in order to attract Democratic support to the Whig ticket.

A firm believer in the principle that the federal government should exercise no powers other than those expressly enumerated in the Constitution, Tyler rejected the entire Whig legislative program, which called for reestablishment of a national bank, an increased tariff, and federally-funded internal improvements. "He is," commented John Quincy Adams, "a political sectarian of the slave-driving, Virginian,

John Tyler's opponents mocked him as "His Accidency" because he was the first vice-president to take office as president upon the death of his predecessor.

Jeffersonian school, principled against all improvement, with all the interests and passions and vices of slavery rooted in his moral and political constitution."

The Whig party was furious. An angry mob gathered at the White House, threw rocks through the windows, and burned the president in effigy. To protest Tyler's rejection of the Whig political agenda, all members of the cabinet but one resigned. Tyler had become a president without a party.

"His Accidency" vetoed nine bills during his four years in office, more than any previous one-term president, frustrating not only the Whig plan to recharter the national bank, but also dashing the party's hopes of raising the tariff while simultaneously distributing proceeds of land sales to the states. In 1843 Whigs in the House of Representatives made Tyler the subject of the first serious impeachment attempt. On January 10, 1843, Whigs introduced resolutions of impeachment charging Tyler with gross usurpation of power. The resolutions were defeated by a vote of 127 to 83.

Ironically, it was during John Tyler's tumultuous presidency that the nation's new two-party system achieved full maturity. Prior to Tyler's ascension to office, the Whig party had been a loose conglomeration of diverse political factions unable to agree on a party platform. During Tyler's presidency, Senator Henry Clay of Kentucky succeeded in uniting the Whig party behind a specific political agenda. On important issues, four-fifths of all Whig members of Congress regularly voted together. At the same time, the Whigs created an elaborate party organization and network of party newspapers in all parts of the country. Never before had party identity been so high or partisan sentiment so strong.

Who Were the Whigs?

The Jacksonians made a great effort to persuade voters to identify their cause with Thomas Jefferson and their Whig opponents with Alexander Hamilton. A radical Jacksonian Democrat put the point bluntly. "The enemies of the people go by different names—Tory, Federalist, National Republican, Whig." In spite of Democratic charges to the contrary, however, the Whigs were not simply a continuation of the Federalist party. Like the Democrats, the Whigs drew support from all parts of the nation. Indeed, the Whigs often predominated among the southern representatives in Congress. Like the Democrats, the Whigs were a coalition of sectional interests, class and economic interests, and ethnic and religious interests.

The Democrats tended to draw support from among small farmers who were less engaged in commercial agriculture, from more isolated and less prosperous towns, and from among the Scots-Irish, and later the Irish-Catholic. The Whig party attracted the overwhelming majority of free blacks, British and German Protestant immigrants, business-oriented farmers, educators and professionals, manufacturers, upwardly aspiring manual laborers, and active members of Presbyterian, Unitarian, and Congregational churches.

1819 Financial panic

1820 The Missouri Compromise passed; The Land Act of 1820; James Monroe re-elected

1821 New York Constitutional Convention reduces qualifications for voting

1824 John Quincy Adams elected president by the House of Representatives

1825 President James Monroe calls for voluntary removal of eastern Indians to lands west of the Mississippi

1826 Anti-Masonic movement arises in New York state following the disappearance and apparent murder of William Morgan

1828 Congress passes "Tariff of Abominations"; Vice-President John C. Calhoun's anonymous *South Carolina Exposition and Protest* asserts the right of states to nullify federal laws; Andrew Jackson elected president

1830 Congress passes bill authorizing Indian removal; Webster-Hayne debate on land policy and the nature of the federal Union; Anti-Masonic party holds the first national party convention

1831 President Jackson reorganizes cabinet, removing pro-Calhoun faction and strengthening position of Secretary of State Martin Van Buren

1832 Beginning of Jackson's war against the Bank of the United States; Special convention in South Carolina nullifies the federal tariff acts of 1828 and 1832; Jackson reelected president; John C. Calhoun becomes the first vice-president to resign

1833 Compromise Tariff gradually lowers tariffs; Force Act, passed the same day, authorizes President Jackson to enforce federal revenue laws by force if necessary; Emergence of Whig party

1835 For the only time in its history the United States government is free from debt; Jackson calls for suppression of abolitionist propaganda; War against Seminole Indians and runaway slaves begins in Florida; Roger B. Taney succeeds John Marshall as Chief Justice of the Supreme Court

1836 Jackson's Specie Circular; Congress adopts the Gag Rule; Martin Van Buren elected president

1837 Financial panic; *Charles River Bridge* v. *Warren Bridge* decision

1840 Congress passes Van Buren's Independent Treasury Act; William H. Harrison, a Whig, elected president

1841 Harrison's death thirty days after taking office makes John Tyler president; Congress passes general preemption

1842 Dorr War

The Whig coalition included supporters of Henry Clay's "American System" of high tariffs and internal improvements, John C. Calhoun and his ardent states' rights followers, Quakers and Methodists alienated by Jackson's Indian removal policies, and bankers and businessmen frightened by the antibusiness rhetoric of state Democratic candidates and Jackson's reallocation of bank deposits and emphasis upon hard money.

Although the Whigs played an important role in national politics for only two decades, they were as successful as the Democrats in articulating a social philosophy that would influence later American political ideas. In contrast to the class conflict theories upheld by the Democrats, the Whigs emphasized the essential harmony of interests in America between capital and labor. In Europe, exclaimed Daniel Webster, there "was a clear and well defined line, between capital and labor," but in America "we have no such visible and broad distinction." The amount of upward mobility available to American workers softened class distinctions. The Whigs idealized the "self-made man," who starts "from an humble origin, and from small beginnings rise[s] gradually in the world, as a result of merit and industry . . . ." In America, the path to wealth is open to all; "the wheel of fortune is in constant operation, and the poor in one generation furnish the rich of the next."

More than Democrats, Whigs attached heavy emphasis to humanitarian reform, which they believed was necessary to contain the new social and economic forces unleashed in American life. The extension of political democracy, the growth of cities and industry, and a rapid increase in wealth would be dangerous unless coupled with "growing intelligence, uprightness, self-respect [and] trust in God." Accordingly, leadership in a democratic society should be invested in men of talent, knowledge, and character.

Finally, the Whigs tended to celebrate technology and factory enterprise as forces which would increase national wealth and improve the condition of life for Americans. Unlike many Democrats, most Whigs saw no essential conflict between American democracy and the forces of industrialism, such as banks, tariffs, internal improvements, corporations, and factories.

In 1848 and 1852 the Whigs tried to repeat their successful 1840 log cabin presidential campaign by nominating national military heroes for the presidency. The party won the 1848 election with General Zachary Taylor, an Indian fighter and hero of the Mexican War, who had boasted that he had never cast a vote in a presidential election. Like Harrison, Taylor confined his campaign speeches to uncontroversial platitudes. "Old Rough and Ready," as he was known, died after just 1 year and 127 days in office. In 1852, the Whigs nominated another Indian fighter and Mexican War hero, General Winfield Scott, who carried just four states for his dying party. "Old Fuss and Feathers," as he was called, was the last Whig presidential nominee to play an important role in a presidential election.

CONCLUSION

When James Monroe began his second term as president in 1821, he rejoiced at the idea that the country was no longer divided by political parties. Political parties, he believed, were "the curse of the country" and the worst of all evils in a republic, breeding disunity, demagoguery, and corruption. Even before Monroe's second term had ended, new political divisions had already begun to evolve, creating a new and increasingly democratic system of politics.

When Monroe's second term began, American politics were still largely dominated by deference. Competing political parties were nonexistent and voters generally deferred to the leadership of local elites or leading families. Political campaigns tended to be relatively staid affairs. Direct appeals by candidates for support were considered in poor taste. Election procedures were also very different. Most states imposed property and taxpaying requirements on suffrage, and conducted voting by voice. Presidential electors were generally chosen by state legislatures. Given the fact that citizens had only the most indirect say in the election of the president, it is not surprising that voting participation was extremely low, amounting to less than thirty percent of eligible voters.

Between 1820 and 1840, a revolution took place in American politics. Property requirements for voting and officeholding were abolished and the secret ballot became the practice. Voters gained the right to directly choose presidential electors. Party nominating conventions arose. By the mid-1830s, two new national political parties—the Democrats and Whigs— were competing in virtually every state in the Union. Professional party managers used partisan newspapers, speeches, parades, rallies, and political barbeques to mobilize popular support. By 1840 voting participation had reached unprecedented levels. Nearly eighty percent of the eligible voters went to the polls. Our modern political system had been born.

Andrew Jackson, the nation's seventh president, was the dominant political figure during the 1820s and 1830s. As president, he spelled out the new democratic approach to politics. In the name of eliminating special influence and privilege and promoting equality of opportunity, he helped institute the national political nominating convention, defended the spoils system, destroyed the second Bank of the United States, and opened millions of acres of Indian lands to white settlement. A strong and determined leader, Jackson greatly expanded the power and prestige of both the presidency and the federal government. When South Carolina asserted the right of a state to nullify the federal tariff, Jackson made it clear that he would not tolerate their defiance of federal authority.

By the mid-1830s, Jackson's opponents had joined together to form the Whig party. Like Jackson's Democratic party, the Whigs were a new party coalition that drew support throughout the country. In 1840 the Whigs succeeded in electing William Henry Harrison to the presidency. Unfortunately, Harrison died a month after taking office and his successor, John Tyler, opposed Congressional Whigs' program of a new national bank and federal support for internal improvements.

REVIEW SUMMARY

Between 1820 and 1840, American politics underwent far-reaching changes, including

- abolition of property qualifications for voting and office holding
- decline of deference
- expansion of the electorate
- rise of the two-party system

The dominant political figure of the era was Andrew Jackson. As president he

- strengthened the power and prestige of the presidency
- defended the spoils system
- relocated Indians west of the Mississippi River
- opposed South Carolina's nullifiers
- "killed" the second Bank of the United States

SUGGESTIONS FOR FURTHER READING

OVERVIEWS AND SURVEYS

Edward Pessen, *Jacksonian America: Society, Personality, and Politics* (1978); Robert V. Remini, *The Revolutionary Age of Andrew Jackson* (1985); Arthur M. Schlesinger, *The Age of Jackson* (1945).

POLITICAL DEMOCRATIZATION

Lee Benson, *The Concept of Jacksonian Democracy: New York as a Test Case* (1961); J. S. Change, *Emergence of the Presidential Nominating Convention, 1789–1832* (1973); Henry Christman, *Tin Horns and Calico: A Decisive Episode in the Emergence of Democracy* (1945); Donald B. Cole, *Jacksonian Democracy in New Hampshire. 1800–1851* (1970); Ronald Formisano, *The Birth of Mass Political Parties: Michigan, 1827–1861* (1971); R. Formsano, *Transformation of Political Culture: Massachusetts Parties, 1790s–1840s* (1983); Marvin E. Gettleman, *The Dorr Rebellion: A Study in American Radicalism, 1833–1849* (1973); M. J. Heale, *The Presidential Quest: Candidates and Images in American Political Culture, 1787–1852* (1982); Richard Hofstadter, *The Idea of a Party System: The Rise of a Legitimate Opposition in the United States, 1780–1840* (1969); Robert Kelley, *The Cultural Pattern in American Politics: The First Century* (1979); Peter D. Levine, *The Behavior of State Legislative Parties in the Jacksonian Era, New Jersey, 1829–1844* (1977); Shaw Livermore, *The Twilight of Federalism: The Disintegration of the Federalist Party, 1815–1830* (1962); Richard P. McCormick, *The Second American Party System* (1966); R. P. McCormick, *The Presidential Game: The Origins of American Presidential Politics* (1982); Edward Pessen, *Riches, Class, and Power*

Before the Civil War (1973); Merrill Peterson, ed., *Democracy, Liberty and Property: The State Constitutional Conventions of the 1820s* (1966); Loman Ratner, *Anti-Masonry: The Crusade and the Party* (1969); Robert V. Remini, *The Election of Andrew Jackson* (1963); R.V. Remini, *Martin Van Buren and the Making of the Democratic Party* (1959); Arthur M. Schlesinger, Jr., ed., *History of U.S. Political Parties, 1789–1860: From Factions to Parties* (1973); A. M. Schlesinger, Jr. and Fred L. Israel, eds., *History of American Presidential Elections, 1789–1968* (1971); J. Mills Thornton, III, *Politics and Power in a Slave Society: Alabama, 1800–1860* (1978); W. P. Vaughn, *The Antimasonic Party in the United States, 1826–1843* (1983); Harry L. Watson, *Jacksonian Politics and Community Conflict: The Emergence of the Second Party System in Cumberland County, North Carolina* (1982); Chilton Williamson, *American Suffrage from Property to Democracy, 1760–1860* (1960); Charles Rosenberg, *The Cholera Years: The United States in 1832, 1849, and 1866* (1962).

ANDREW JACKSON: THE POLITICS OF THE COMMON PERSON

John Ashworth, *"Agrarians" and "Aristocrats": Party Political Ideology in the United States, 1837–1846* (1983); Jean H. Baker, *Affairs of Party: The Political Culture of Northern Democrats in the Mid-Nineteenth Century* (1983); Amy Bridges, *A City in the Republic: Antebellum New York and the Origins of Machine Politics* (1984); Matthew A. Crenson, *The Federal Machine: Beginnings of Bureaucracy in Jacksonian America* (1975); James C. Curtis, *Andrew Jackson and the Search for Vindication* (1976); A. H. DeRosier, Jr., *The Removal of the Choctaw Indians* (1970); B. W. Dippie, *The Vanishing American: White Attitudes and U.S. Indian Policy* (1982); Cecil Eby, *"That Disgraceful Affair": The Black Hawk War* (1973); Daniel Feller, *Public Lands in Jacksonian Politics* (1984); William W. Freehling, *Prelude to Civil War: The Nullification Controversy in South Carolina, 1816–1836* (1966); M. D. Green, *The Politics of Indian Removal: Creek Government and Society in Crisis* (1982); Charles G. Haines and Foster H. Sherwood, *The Role of the Supreme Court in American Government and Politics, 1835–1864* (1957); Bray Hammond, *Banks and Politics in America: From the Revolution to the Civil War* (1957); Stanley I. Kutler, *Privilege and Creative Destruction: The Charles River Bridge Case* (1971); Richard Latner, *The Presidency of Andrew Jackson: White House Politics, 1829–1837* (1979); John M. McFaul, *The Politics of Jacksonian Finance* (1972); R. C. McGrane, *The Panic of 1837* (1924); Marvin Meyers, *The Jacksonian Persuasion* (1957); M. D. Peterson, *Olive Branch and Sword: The Compromise of 1833* (1982); F. P. Prucha, *American Indian Policy in the Formative Years* (1962); Fritz Redlich, *The Molding of American Banking: Men and Ideas* (1968); Hugh Rockoff, *The Free Banking Era* (1975); Ronald K. Satz, *American Indian Policy in the*

Jacksonian Era (1975); Bernard Schwartz, *From Confederation to Nation: The American Constitution, 1835–1877* (1973); W. G. Shade, *Banks or No Banks: The Money Issue in Western Politics, 1832–1865* (1972); J. R. Sharp, *The Jacksonians versus the Banks* (1970); W. B. Smith and A. H. Cole, *Fluctuations in American Business, 1790–1860* (1935); Paul Studenski and Herman E. Krooss, *Financial History of the United States* (1963); Peter Temin, *The Jacksonian Economy* (1969); Richard H. Timberlake, Jr., *The Origins of Central Banking in the United States* (1978); J. Van Fenstermaker, *The Development of American Commercial Banking, 1782–1837* (1965); Herman J. Viola, *Thomas L. McKenney: Architect of America's Early Indian Policy* (1974); John William Ward, *Andrew Jackson: Symbol for an Age* (1955); Leonard D. White, *The Jacksonians: A Study in Administrative History, 1829–1861* (1954); Jean Alexander Wilburn, *Biddle's Bank: The Crucial Years* (1967).

RISE OF A POLITICAL OPPOSITION

Thomas Brown, *Politics and Statesmanship: Essays on the American Whig Party* (1985); Daniel Walker Howe, *The Political Culture of the American Whigs* (1979); Thomas H. O'Connor, *Lords of the Loom: The Cotton Whigs and the Coming of the Civil War* (1968). Irving H. Bartlett, *Daniel Webster* (1978); Maurice G. Baxter, *One and Inseparable: Daniel Webster and the Union* (1984); Norman D. Brown, *Daniel Webster and the Politics of Availability* (1969); Alfred A. Cave, *An American Conservative in the Age of Jackson: The Political and Social Thought of Calvin Colton* (1969); William N. Chambers, *Old Bullion Benton: Senator from the New West* (1956); Oliver Perry Chitwood, *John Tyler: Champion of the Old South* (1964); Freeman Cleaves, *Old Tippecanoe: William Henry Harrison and His Times* (1939); Donald B. Cole, *Martin Van Buren and the American Political System* (1984); Richard N. Current, *Daniel Webster and the Rise of National Conservatism* (1955) and *John C. Calhoun* (1966); James C. Curtis, *The Fox at Bay: Martin Van Buren and the Presidency, 1837–1841* (1970); Robert F. Dalzell, Jr., *Daniel Webster and the Trial of American Nationalism, 1843–1852* (1973); Martin Duberman, *Charles Francis Adams, 1807–1886* (1961); Robert G. Gunderson, *The Log Cabin Campaign* (1959); Richard Hofstadter, *The American Political Tradition* (1948); Robert J. Morgan, *A Whig Embattled: The Presidency Under John Tyler* (1954); Sydney Nathans, *Daniel Webster and Jacksonian Democracy* (1973); John Niven, *Martin Van Buren and the Romantic Age of American Politics* (1983); Robert V. Remini, *Andrew Jackson and the Course of American Empire, 1767–1821* (1977), *Andrew Jackson and the Course of American Freedom, 1822–1832* (1981) and *Andrew Jackson and the Course of American Democracy, 1833–1845* (1984); R. V. Remini, *Martin Van Buren and the Making of the Democratic Party (1959);* G. G. Van Deusen, *The Life of Henry Clay* (1937).

CHAPTER 10

The Ferment of Reform

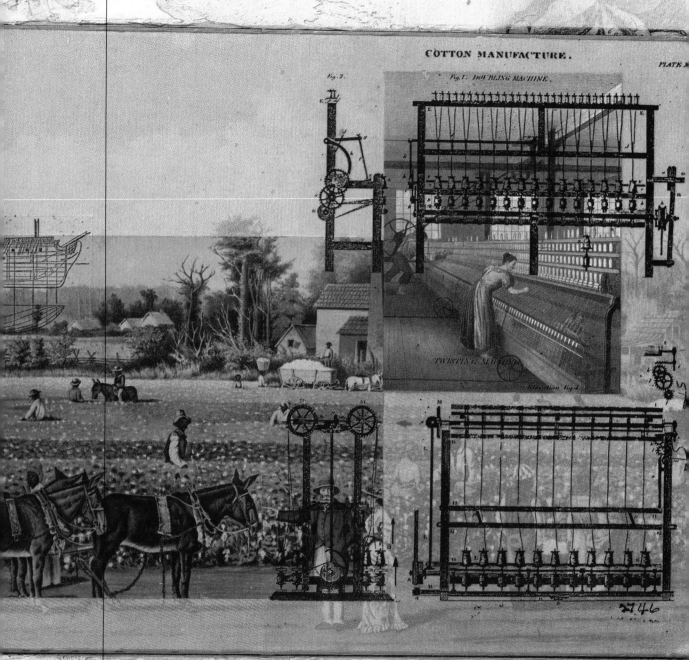

COTTON MANUFACTURE.

PLATE 340.

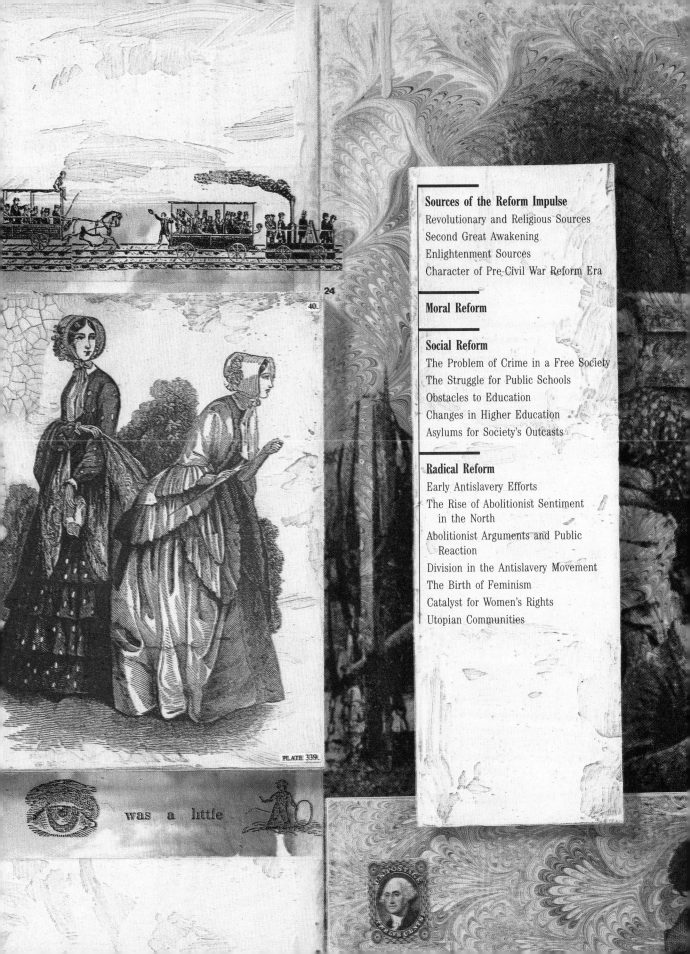

On July 4, 1835, the citizens of Vicksburg, Mississippi decided to rid their fair city of professional gamblers and prostitutes. Following a Fourth of July barbeque, a group of vigilantes abducted, whipped, tarred and feathered, and banished a gambler who insulted a respectable citizen. The townspeople, fearful of retaliation, launched a series of raids on the gaming houses and brothels. After one townsperson was killed during a raid, the citizens promptly lynched five gamblers.

During the decades before the Civil War, newspapers were filled with such reports of crime, vice, and violence in the growing cities of the North, in the slave South, and on the frontier. New York's chief of police told unsettling tales of thieving young rowdies, stealing from the city's piers, junk shops, and warehouses, and of young girls, vulnerable to sexual exploitation, trying to support themselves by selling toothpicks. One report estimated that 10,000 prostitutes plied their trade in that city in 1850. Rumors spread about "free love" being practiced by certain religious sects and utopian communities, about depraved slave masters abusing slave women, and about alleged immoral behavior behind convent walls.

Duelling—a form of deadly combat—was a commonly used resolution to a quarrel in the slave states and southwestern territories. In one 1818 duel between two cousins, the combatants faced off with shotguns at four paces! Lynchings, too, were widely reported, and were not confined to the South. Lynchings were customarily directed against whites, not blacks, as would be the case after the Civil War—though in one instance, in May 1835, a white mob burned two blacks to death for allegedly murdering two children. It was in Carthage, Illinois, in 1844, that a mob dragged Joseph Smith, Jr., the founder of the Mormon church, from a jail cell and shot him to death. Newspapers, like the nationally respected *Niles' Weekly Register*, defended the custom of lynching as democracy in action. "As law, in every country, emanates from the people," the newspaper editorialized, ". . . the unanimous agreement, among the people, to put a man to death . . . rended the act legal to all intents and purposes."

Incidents of mob violence in which reformers, dissenters, and alleged wrong-doers were dragged through the streets behind galloping horses, seemed to confirm criticism by Europeans that democracy inevitably led to anarchy. A nation in which the vice-president had to carry a gun while presiding over the Senate—lest the senators attack each other with knives or pistols—brought forth questions about how a free society could maintain stability and moral order. Americans sought to answer these questions through the avenues of religion, education, and increasingly after 1800, social reform.

SOURCES OF THE REFORM IMPULSE

The first half of the nineteenth century saw a great surge in collective efforts to improve society through reform. Reformers in the United States and Britain launched unprecedented campaigns to assist the handicapped, reform criminals and prostitutes, outlaw alcohol, guarantee women's rights, achieve world peace, and abolish slavery. Our modern systems of free, public schools, prisons, and hospitals for the infirm and the mentally ill are all legacies of this first generation of American reform.

What were the sources of the reform impulse? Why was the "demon of reform," as Ralph Waldo Emerson called it, unleashed with such vigor in pre-Civil War America?

Revolutionary and Religious Sources

One source of inspiration for reformers was the example of those patriots of the Revolution who had risked their lives and honor to overcome tyranny and injustice. Pre-Civil War reformers pictured their own efforts as an attempt to realize the republican ideals, enshrined in the Declaration of Independence, which had ushered in a new age of liberty and equality. Proponents of women's rights, world peace, temperance, and abolition all drafted Declarations of Sentiments modeled on the wording of the Declaration of Independence. The theory of natural rights embodied in the

Declaration led abolitionists like William Lloyd Garrison to challenge the justice of the institution of slavery and feminists like Elizabeth Cady Stanton to call for equal rights for women. The principles of liberty and equality set forth in the Declaration encouraged educational reformers like Horace Mann to work to improve the nation's educational system and humanitarians like Dorothea Dix to reform the treatment of the mentally ill. Early nineteenth-century reformers saw their own crusades as the fulfillment of the political struggles begun during the Revolution.

Religion further strengthened reformers' zeal. Almost all the leading reformers were devoutly religious men and women, who wanted to deepen the nation's commitment to Christian principles. Two significantly different trends in Protestant thought stimulated the rise of reform activity: religious liberalism and evangelical revivalism. The first was an emerging humanitarian form of religion that rejected the harsh Calvinist doctrines of original sin and predestination. Its preachers stressed the basic goodness of human nature and each individual's capacity to follow the example of Christ.

William Ellery Channing (1780–1842) was America's leading exponent of religious liberalism. Born in Boston, he was educated at Harvard and served as a tutor to a slaveholding Virginia family before becoming the minister of Boston's Federal Street Church. In 1815 the quiet and dignified young minister became involved in a conflict within New England Congregationalism which pitted traditionalists, who believed that people were born with original sin, against liberals, who maintained that humankind was basically good.

William Ellery Channing

In Baltimore in 1819, Channing delivered a sermon entitled "Unitarian Christianity," which proclaimed the principles of his faith and be-

From the end of the Revolution to shortly after the Civil War, dueling flourished in the United States, particularly in the South and West.

came the intellectual foundation for American Unitarianism. The new religious denomination stressed individual freedom of belief, a united world under a single God, and the mortal nature of Jesus Christ, whom individuals should strive to emulate. Wits defined Unitarianism as a religion dedicated to "the fatherhood of God, the brotherhood of man, and neighborhood of Boston." Channing's belief that the sole purpose of Christianity was "the perfection of human nature, the elevation of men into nobler beings" stimulated many reformers to work toward improving the conditions of the physically handicapped, the criminal, the pauper, and the enslaved. Religious liberals, such as Unitarians and Quakers, joined reform movements in far higher numbers than their percentage in the population would suggest.

Second Great Awakening

The religious source of the reform impulse can also be found in the enthusiastic revivals that swept the nation in the early nineteenth cen-

Many people attended revival meetings lasting all night or for several days in a row, and the assembled crowd made "almost constant cries of 'Amen! Amen!' 'Jesus! Jesus!' 'Glory! Glory!'"

tury. These revivals sought to awaken Americans to their need for religious rebirth and redemption. Highly emotional meetings were held by preachers in all sections of the country to revitalize religious feelings. This great religious fervor came to be called the Second Great Awakening.

On August 6, 1801, some 25,000 men, women, and children poured into the small frontier community of Cane Ridge, Kentucky, in search of religious salvation. Twenty-five thousand was a fantastic number of people at a time when the population of the whole state of Kentucky was a quarter million, and the state's largest city, Lexington, had only 1795 residents. The Cane Ridge camp meeting went on for a week. Baptists, Methodists, and ministers of other denominations joined together to preach to the vast throng. Within three years, similar

revivals had swept across Kentucky, Tennessee, and Ohio.

The revivalists appealed to their followers to repent their sins—and sin was not a metaphysical abstraction to them. Drinking and dueling were capital sins. Luxury, high living, indifference to religion, preoccupation with worldly and commercial matters—all these were denounced as sinful. Preachers exhorted their audiences to save America from the corrosive effects of selfishness and materialism. Leaders of the revivals believed that the nation as a whole could only be redeemed if individuals truly repented their sins and accepted Jesus Christ as their personal savior. If men and women did not seek God through Christ, the nation would face divine retribution.

What explains the rapid rise of revivalism? The growing separation of church and state that followed the Revolution was now complete. At the same time state governments deprived established churches of the colonial era of state support (Virginia ended state support for churches in 1786, Connecticut in 1818, and Massachusetts in 1833), the number of denominations expanded. Revivals provided a vehicle for dramatically increasing church membership and ensuring that America would remain a God-fearing nation.

By the 1830s three-quarters of the American people were members of a church. The religious revivals also influenced the political rhetoric of pre-Civil War America. The evangelical themes of sin, sacrifice, repentance, rebirth, and national mission shaped political discourse. Above all, the revivals inspired a widespread sense that the nation was standing close to the millennium, a thousand years of peace and brotherhood, when sin, war, and tyranny would vanish from the earth. The evangelical revivals helped reinforce the conviction that Americans had been chosen by God to lead the world toward "a millennium of republicanism."

Charles Grandison Finney (1792–1875), the "father of modern revivalism," grew up and studied law in western New York. In 1821 he underwent a violent conversion experience. The story of his conversion became as familiar to many American Protestants as the Scriptural account of Paul's conversion on the road to

Damascus. On a Sabbath evening Finney, then a prosperous young lawyer, thumbed through the pages of a Bible as part of his research on a court case. He soon began to read the text more closely, overwhelmed by questions he had never before considered. "What are you waiting for?" a voice seemed to be saying. "Are you leading a righteous life?" Gripped by fear, Finney worried his heart was dead to God. Then it seemed as if he "met the Lord Jesus Christ face to face." The Holy Spirit seemed to be speaking to him, asking him, "Will you doubt?" Finney cried out, "No I will not doubt; I cannot doubt." Suddenly , his sense of guilt and sinfulness was gone. He had been born again.

Finney believed that he had "a retainer from the Lord Jesus Christ to plead his cause," and despite his rejection of formal theology training, he began to convert souls to Christ in the small towns of upstate New York. He introduced a series of "new measures" to win converts. He prayed for sinners by name; he held "protracted meetings" which lasted night after night for a week or more; he set up an "anxious bench" at the front of the meeting, where the almost-saved could receive special prayers; and he encouraged women to actively participate in revivals.

In Wilmington, Delaware; Rochester, New York; Reading and Lancaster, Pennsylvania; and in New York City, Finney led revivals. His message was that anyone could experience a redemptive change of heart and a resurgence of religious feeling. If only enough people converted to Christ, Finney told his listeners, the millennium would arrive within three years.

Revival meetings attracted both frontier settlers and city folk, slaves and masters, farmers and shopkeepers. The revivals had their greatest appeal among isolated farming families on the Western and Southern frontier and upwardly mobile merchants, shopkeepers, artisans, and skilled laborers in the expanding commercial and industrial towns of the North. They drew support from social conservatives who feared that America would disintegrate into a state of anarchy without the influence of evangelical religion, and also enlisted followers among poorer whites and slaves in the South. Above all, revivals attracted large numbers of young women, who took an active role organizing meetings, establishing church organizations, and editing religious publications.

Enlightenment Sources

The roots of reform could also be found in the philosophy of the Enlightenment and the early triumphs of science and technology, which bred a widespread faith in the capacity of human beings to improve society through the use of reason. During the mid and late eighteenth century, French *philosophes*, Scottish moral philosophers, and such American thinkers as Benjamin Franklin and Thomas Jefferson developed a set of principles of enormous importance for reform. One principle was that human beings were not innately sinful, but were basically good. Given a favorable environment, people's moral character would improve. A second principle was that poverty, disease, crime, and ignorance were not inevitable, but could be overcome by reform. By reshaping the environment, humankind could eliminate human misery. The development of the steam engine, gas-fueled lamps, pot-bellied stoves, and interchangeable parts were all dramatic examples of humankind's expanding ability to make life better.

Perhaps most importantly, Enlightenment thinkers believed that there were higher laws within nature that should govern human institutions, and that these principles, like the laws of science, could be discovered through the power of reason. Among these natural laws were the inalienable rights to liberty and equality.

Character of Pre-Civil War Reform Era

During the first decades of the nineteenth century, America's revolutionary heritage, religious liberalism and revivalism, and Enlightenment philosophy all played their parts in producing a spirit of optimism, a sensitivity to human suffering, and a boundless faith in humankind's capacity to improve social institutions. This faith in human perfectability inspired early nineteenth-century efforts at reform and allowed different kinds of reformers to work together.

Church leaders encouraged their flocks to engage in works of "practical benevolence"—to save the nation from gambling, drinking, horse-racing, atheism, and anarchy. Many middle class women, particularly in the Northeast, took active public roles in temperance and antislavery movements, and led campaigns against the moral depravity found in saloons, houses of prostitution, and other centers of "lewd and lascivious" segregated male entertainment. Many members of the growing urban working class campaigned for public schools, penal reform, and abolition of imprisonment for debt. Each of these groups sought to demonstrate the ability of an enlightened public to influence politics and perfect human institutions.

Reformers varied widely in their motives. Some people turned to reform as a way of enforcing order in society. Others were motivated by a religious vision of creating a godly society on Earth. Still others viewed reform as a way of instilling the values associated with the Protestant Ethic: sobriety, punctuality, self-discipline, and personal responsibility.

Over time, the character of reform shifted. During the 1820s and 1830s, the primary tool of reform was the voluntary society, which sought to accomplish its goals through moral force. Reform societies sought to persuade Americans to abstain from alcohol and recognize the sinfulness of slavery. Increasingly, however, reformers came to believe that to be successful their programs needed the help of state and local governments. Establishment of public school systems, prisons that rehabilitated rather than punished, asylums for the mentally ill that used the most advanced medical principles—all of these reforms required government action. By the 1840s, more and more temperance advocates called for legislation to prohibit the sale and manufacture of liquor, and a growing number of antislavery proponents believed that the abolition of slavery could only be achieved through political action.

MORAL REFORM

The drive to uplift the nation's moral and spiritual values generated a number of interdenominational groups. Various associations sprang up to battle profanity and Sabbath-breaking, to place a Bible in every American home, to provide religious education for the children of the poor, and to curb the widespread heavy use of hard liquor. Discouraging drinking, gambling, and vulgar entertainments (such as bear baiting and cock fighting), while encouraging observance of the Sabbath, would "restore the government of God" said Reverend Lyman Beecher, an influential Presbyterian minister.

Perhaps the most dramatic attempts to purify the nation's morals were staged by numerous Magdalen (referring to reformed prostitutes) societies which strove in the 1830s and 1840s to rehabilitate "fallen women" and provide them with educational and employment opportunities. The New York Moral Reform Society had 15,000 members in 1837, and three years later had doubled the number of branches in New England and upstate New York. Members walked into brothels and prayed for the prostitutes, publicized in the newspapers the names of men who patronized prostitutes, visited prostitutes in jails, and lobbied for state laws that would make male solicitation of prostitutes a crime.

The largest movement for moral reform during the early nineteenth century was the anti-drinking crusade. Heavy drinking of hard liquor was an integral part of American life at that time. Many people believed that downing a glass of whiskey before breakfast was conducive to good health. Instead of taking coffee breaks, people took a dram of liquor at eleven and again at four o'clock, as well as drinks after meals "to aid digestion," and a nightcap before going to sleep. Campaigning politicians offered voters generous amounts of liquor, and on the frontier, one evangelist noted, "a house could not be raised, a field of wheat cut down, nor could there be a log rolling, a husking, a quilting, a wedding, or a funeral without the aid of alcohol."

By 1820 the typical adult American consumed more than seven gallons of absolute alcohol a year (compared to 2.8 gallons now). Consumption had risen markedly in two decades, fueled by the growing amounts of corn distilled by farmers into cheap whiskey. In the 1820s, a gallon of whiskey cost just a quarter.

Temperance propaganda often suggested that just a social drink with a friend could lead to being a confirmed drunkard and death by suicide.

By the first decades of the nineteenth century, a growing number of observers believed that drinking posed a serious threat to the health and morals of the republic. Religious denominations such as the Presbyterians, Quakers, and Methodists claimed that drinking distilled liquor was ungodly. Physicians, led by Philadelphian Benjamin Rush, a signer of the Declaration of Independence, warned that distilled spirits could destroy a person's health and even cause death. Many middle-class women blamed alcohol for the abuse of wives and children and the squandering of family resources. Still others identified drinking with crime, poverty, and inefficient and unproductive labor. The stage was set for the appearance of an organized movement against liquor. In 1826 the nation's first formal national temperance organization was born: the American Society for the Promotion of Temperance. Led by socially prominent clergy and laymen, the new organization called for total abstinence from distilled liquor. Within three years, 222 state and local antiliquor groups labored to spread this message.

By 1835 membership in temperance organizations had climbed to 1.5 million, and an estimated 2 million Americans had taken the "pledge" to abstain from hard liquor. Temperance reform drew support from many Southerners and Westerners who were otherwise indifferent or hostile to reform. Temperance reformers did not rid the nation of the demon rum, but they helped reduce annual per capita consumption of alcohol from seven gallons in 1830 to just three gallons a decade later, forcing four thousand distilleries to close. Fewer employers provided workers with eleven o'clock or four o'clock drams, and some businesses began to fire employees who drank on the job.

The sudden arrival of hundreds of thousands of immigrants from "heavy drinking" cultures heightened the concerns of temperance reformers. Between 1830 and 1860, nearly two million Irish arrived in the United States along with an additional 893,000 Germans. In Ireland land was in such short supply that many young men were unable to support a family by farming. The only solution was to delay marriage and socialize with other young men in "bachelor groups," a ritual that often involved heavy drinking. These immigrants probably drank no more than most native-born Americans prior to the 1830s, but the heavy drinking of immigrants was regarded as a sign of their supposed moral degeneracy.

The 1840s saw two new approaches to the temperance movement. The first was the Washingtonian movement, in which reformed alcoholics sought to reform other drinkers. As many as 600,000 drinkers took the Washingtonian pledge of total abstinence. The new reform group evoked ambivalent emotions among old-guard temperance advocates, many of whom refused to provide financial support to the ex-alcoholics.

The second was a move away from a reliance on moral suasion toward efforts to place legal restrictions on the sale and manufacture of alcohol. The belief grew among temperance advocates that drinkers were unable to voluntarily resist the enticements of alcohol. Argued one minister: "You might almost as well persuade the chained maniac to leave off howling, as to persuade him to leave off drinking." At first, many temperance reformers called for tavern closings, but increasingly they sought restrictions on the sale and manufacture of liq-

uor. In 1851, after much political wheeling and dealing, Maine passed the nation's first effective statewide prohibition law. The Maine law became a national model, and for a brief time many other states followed Maine's example.

SOCIAL REFORM

The goal of the nation's first reformers was to uplift the nation's morals and spread Christian values by establishing interdenominational voluntary societies to distribute Bibles and religious tracts, promote observance of the Sabbath, and curb drinking. Beginning in the 1820s a new phase of reform—social reform—spread across the country. Social reformers sought to solve such social problems as crime, illiteracy, poverty, and disease by erecting prisons, public schools, and asylums for the deaf, the blind, and the mentally ill.

In lower Manhattan, just a one minute walk from Broadway, stood Five Points, a slum area of liquor stores and noxious tenements, of

As early as the 1820s, urban slums like New York City's Five Points began to appear. These areas of poverty, prostitution, filth, and violence attracted beggars, pimps, prostitutes, and hoodlums.

pimps and prostitutes, beggars and drunkards. Here, members of the Ladies Home Missionary Society of the Methodist Episcopal Church found neglected children by the score, "born in sin, nurtured in crime; the young mind sullied in its first bloom, the young heart crushed before its tiny call for affection has met one answering response."

As early as the 1820s, Americans discovered that gangs of juveniles lived beyond the reach of moral influence. The nation's growing cities teemed with delinquents who had gone through "infancy and childhood without a mother's care or a father's protection." In response, they called for the creation of substitute families in the form of public schools, houses of refuge, and penitentiaries.

The Problem of Crime in a Free Society

During the pre-Civil War decades reformers began to look upon crime as essentially a social problem, not the result of original sin or human depravity but of environment, faulty emotional growth, and parental neglect. They regarded even the worst criminal as a misguided brother. Instead of whipping or punishing criminals in stocks, it was the duty of a humane society to remove the underlying causes of crime, to sympathize and show patience toward criminals, and try to reform them—rather than simply punish them. By the 1840s, there was a growing conviction that crime could best be combated by a combination of expanded education and improved houses of correction, where punishment would be tailored to the circumstances and character of the individual offender and where offenders could be shielded from the corrupting influence of a depraved environment.

Prior to the American Revolution, punishment for crimes generally involved some form of corporal punishment, ranging from the death penalty for serious crimes to public whipping, confinement in stocks, and branding for lesser offenses. Jails were used for temporary confinement for criminal defendants awaiting trial or punishment, and prisoners were sometimes chained with leg rings, handcuffs, and iron bands around the waist. Conditions in these early jails were abominable. Debtors were confined with prisoners, and offenders of both sexes and all ages were confined in large groups in cramped cells. Prisoners were customarily charged for expenses of food and lodging.

In the early nineteenth century, a new moral revulsion over the spectacle of public punishment led to the rapid construction of penal institutions in which the "disease" of crime could be quarantined and inmates could be gradually rehabilitated in a carefully controlled environment. Two rival prison systems competed for public support. After constructing Auburn Prison, New York State authorities adopted a system in which inmates worked in large workshops during the day and slept in separate cells at night. Convicts had to march in lockstep and refrain from speaking or even looking at each other. In Pennsylvania's Eastern State Penitentiary, constructed in 1829, authorities placed even greater stress on the physical isolation of prisoners. Every prison cell had its own exercise yard, work space, and toilet facilities. Under the Pennsylvania plan, prisoners

Rigid discipline and extensive rules restricting the inmates' movements and speech were thought to be important elements in criminal reform.

lived and worked in complete isolation from each other. Called *penitentiaries* or *reformatories,* these new prisons reflected the belief that hard physical labor and solitary confinement might encourage introspection and instill habits of discipline that would rehabilitate criminals.

Other innovations of the early nineteenth century related to crime and law enforcement included the first use of insanity as a legal defense and the first efforts to outlaw capital punishment and abolish imprisonment for debt.

The principle of criminal law that a criminal act should only be legally punished if the offender was fully capable of distinguishing between right and wrong opened the way to the development of one of the most controversial aspects of American jurisprudence, the insanity defense. The question arose dramatically in 1835, when a deranged Englishman named Richard Lawrence walked up to President Andrew Jackson and fired two pistols at him at a distance of six feet. Incredibly, both guns misfired, and Jackson was unhurt. Lawrence believed that Jackson's attack on the second Bank of the United States had prevented him from

obtaining money that would have enabled him to claim the English throne. The court, ruling that Lawrence was clearly suffering from a mental delusion, found him insane and not subject to criminal prosecution.

Another major innovation of the criminal justice system in the pre-Civil War decades was the drive to outlaw capital punishment. Prior to the 1830s, most states reduced the number of crimes punishable by death and began to perform executions outside of public view, lest the public be stimulated to acts of violence by the spectacle of hangings. In 1847 Michigan became the first modern jurisdiction to outlaw the death penalty and was soon followed by Rhode Island and Wisconsin.

By the early nineteenth century, imprisonment for debt also spurred demands for reform. As late as 1816, an average of 600 residents of New York City were in prison at any one time for failure to pay debts. More than half owed less than $50, and more than one-third owed less than $25. New York's debtor prisons provided no food, furniture, or fuel for their inmates, who would have starved without the assistance of relatives or the charity of humane societies. In a Vermont case, state courts imprisoned a man for a debt of just 54 cents, and in Boston a woman was taken from her three children as a result of a $3 debt.

Imprisoned debtors, were, of course, unable to pay off their debts. Reformers regarded imprisonment as irrational and beginning with New York State in 1817, states eliminated the practice of jailing people for trifling debts. Subsequently other states forbade the jailing of women for debt.

The Struggle for Public Schools

Of all the ideas advanced by antebellum reformers, none was more radical than the principle that all American children, regardless of class, should be educated to their fullest capacity at public expense. Educational reformers left the nation with a lasting legacy—a faith that schools provided the single best approach to the nation's future. Education was the key to individual opportunity and advancement. It would produce an enlightened and responsible

The first presidential assassination attempt in history occurred when Richard Lawrence tried to kill Andrew Jackson.

citizenry, prevent the hardening of class divisions, and prepare children for a changing society by teaching not only science and literature, but also the values of cooperation, punctuality, good citizenship, patience, and self-discipline.

From the early days of settlement, Americans have attached special importance to education. During the seventeenth century, the New England Puritans, who believed that all people should be able to read the Bible, required every town to establish a public school supported by fees from all but the poorest families. In the late eighteenth century, Thomas Jefferson popularized the idea that a democratic republic required an enlightened and educated citizenry and that government had a duty to assist in the education of a meritocracy based on talent and ability. Early nineteenth-century educational reformers extended these ideas and struggled to make universal public education a reality.

As a result of their efforts, the United States became, after Denmark, the first country in the world to establish a system of tax supported, tuition-free public schools. Support for public schools was widespread: it came from working people as well as wealthier individuals, and it was largely the result of local efforts around the country. The struggle for public schools made the greatest gains in the Northeast and then the Midwest.

Prior to the 1840s apprenticeship had been a major form of education, and formal schooling was largely limited to those who could afford to pay. Even "free" schools often required the payment of tuition, and primary schools often required entering students to already be literate, barring students who had not been taught to read by their parents. Many schools admitted pupils regardless of age, mixing young children with young adults in their twenties, and classrooms could contain as many as eighty pupils. Few textbooks were available and most learning amounted to monotonous repetition of facts. School buildings were generally unpainted, overcrowded, and lacked blackboards or windows.

During the 1820s and 1830s the urban population grew at a rate of over sixty percent a decade, and then exploded in the 1840s, in-

During the early nineteenth century, many young women flocked to schools. This painting shows young women attending an evening school.

creasing ninety-two percent. The astounding growth of eastern cities made middle-class citizens suddenly aware of gangs of juvenile delinquents, vagrant children, and illiteracy and degradation among the urban poor. At first, many social conservatives championed Sunday Schools as a way "to reclaim the vicious, to instruct the ignorant, to secure the observance of the Sabbath . . . and to raise the standard of morals among the lower classes of society." By the mid-1820s, increasing immigration heightened the pressures for public schooling. Educator Calvin Stowe, the husband of novelist Harriet Beecher Stowe of *Uncle Tom's Cabin* fame, warned that "unless we educate our immigrants they will be our ruin. It is no longer a mere question of benevolence, of duty, or of enlightened self-interest . . . we are prompted to it by the instinct of self-preservation."

Horace Mann (1796–1859) of Massachusetts was the nation's leading educational reformer. As a child he had wrestled with intense fears of sin and damnation. He turned away from his strict Calvinist upbringing, however, converted to Unitarianism, and came to believe that teachers could mold children to the de-

Horace Mann

sired state of near perfection. As a lawyer and Massachusetts state legislator, Mann took the lead in establishing a state board of education, and then resigned his seat as a state senator to become secretary of the board in 1837.

In his twelve years as board secretary, Mann waged successful campaigns against formidable opposition to tax private property in order to pay for public schools and keep formal religious instruction outside of schools and confined to churches. His other notable achievements included a doubling of state expenditures on education, state support for teacher training, an improved curriculum in schools, grading of pupils by age and ability, and a lengthened school year. He was also partially successful in curtailing the use of the rod in student discipline. In 1852, three years after Mann left office to take a seat in the United States Congress, Massachusetts adopted the first compulsory school attendence law in American history. By 1860 there were three hundred high schools in the United States; almost one hundred of them were located in Massachusetts.

Demands for schools were not confined to the conservatives who sought social discipline. There was also widespread demand for schooling from the urban workers. Many artisans, mechanics, and skilled laborers called for schools that would mix wealthy children with the children of the working class. Members of the working class supported public education even though it meant they would be deprived of the wages of their children under the age of fifteen, who often earned as much as one-fifth of the family's income. Some viewed schooling as a way to limit competition from child apprentices. These youths increasingly, were being substituted for skilled adult labor, because they could be paid much lower wages.

Obstacles to Education

Prior to the Civil War, educational opportunities for women and non-whites were severely restricted. Most cities specifically excluded blacks from the public schools; cities like New York and Boston consigned black children to inferior segregated schools. Not until 1855 did Massachusetts become the first state to admit students to public schools irrespective of "race, color, or religious opinions."

In 1832, Prudence Crandell, a Quaker schoolteacher in Canterbury, Connecticut, sparked a major controversy by admitting Sarah Harris, the daughter of a free black farmer, into her school. After white parents withdrew their students from the school, the young schoolteacher tried to turn her school into an institution for the education of free blacks. Hostile neighbors broke the school's windows, contaminated its well with manure, and denied students seats on stagecoaches and pews in church. In 1833, after the state adopted a law making it a crime to teach black students who were not residents of Connecticut, state authorities arrested Crandall. She was tried twice, convicted, and jailed. After

Prudence Crandall

her release, a local mob attacked Crandall's school building with crowbars and attempted to burn the structure. It never opened again.

Education of women beyond the level of handicrafts and basic reading and writing was largely confined to separate female academies and seminaries for the affluent. Emma Hart Willard opened one of the first academies offering an advanced education to women in Philadelphia in 1814. Later, in the Troy Female Seminary, which opened in Troy, New York, in 1821, Mrs. Willard offered instruction in mathematics, history, geography, and physics to women preparing to become teachers.

Catholics, too, suffered discrimination in the public schools. Many teachers showed an anti-Catholic bias by using texts that portrayed the Catholic church as a threat to republican values and reading biblical passages from the Protestant version of the Scriptures. Beginning in New York City in 1840, Catholics decided to establish a separate system of parochial schools in which children would receive a religious education as well as training in the arts and sciences.

Changes in Higher Education

Educational reform was not limited to improvements in elementary education. At the beginning of the nineteenth century, most colleges offered their students, who usually enrolled at the ages of twelve to fifteen, only a narrow training in the classics designed to prepare them for the ministry. During the 1820s and 1830s, in an effort to adjust to the "spirits and wants of the age," colleges broadened their curricula to include the study of history, literature, geography, modern languages, and the sciences. The entrance age and requirements demanded of students also were raised.

The number of colleges began to grow. Many of the new colleges, particularly in the South and West, were church-affiliated, but several states, including Georgia, Tennessee, Virginia, and Michigan established state universities. Prior to the Civil War, sixteen states provided some financial support to higher education, and in New York City by the 1850s, an education, from elementary school to college, was available tuition-free.

A few institutions of higher education opened their doors to blacks and women prior to the Civil War. In 1833 Oberlin College became the nation's first coeducational college, and four years later, Mary Lyon established the first women's college, Mount Holyoke, to train teachers and missionaries. A number of western state universities also admitted women. In addition, three colleges for blacks were founded before the Civil War, and a few other colleges, including Oberlin, Harvard, Bowdoin, and Dartmouth admitted small numbers of black students.

Asylums for Society's Outcasts

A number of reformers devoted their attention to the special problems of the mentally ill, the deaf, and the blind. In 1841, Dorothea Dix (1802–1877), a thirty-nine-year-old former schoolteacher, volunteered to give religious instruction to women incarcerated in the East Cambridge, Massachusetts, House of Correction. Inside the House of Correction, she was horrified to find mentally ill inmates dressed in rags and confined to a single dreary room without any source of heat. Shocked by what she saw, she embarked on a lifelong crusade to reform the treatment of the mentally ill.

After a two-year secret investigation of every jail and almshouse in Massachusetts, Dix issued a report to the Massachusetts state legislature. The mentally ill, she found, were mixed indiscriminantly with paupers and hardened criminals. Many were confined "in cages, closets, cellars, stalls, pens! Chained, naked, beaten with rods and lashed into obedience." When keepers of institutions questioned the report's credibility, accusing Dix of "sensational and slanderous lies," Dix enlisted the support of influential men such as Horace Mann, who en-

One early treatment for mental illness was the "circulating swing," which was supposed to help individuals suffering from depression.

couraged the state to construct a large addition to the state hospital for the insane.

Following her successes in Massachusetts, Dix carried her campaign for state-supported asylums nationwide, traveling 30,000 miles in ten years and persuading more than a dozen state legislatures to improve institutional care for the insane. Congress approved her proposal for a federal system of hospitals for the mentally ill, but President Franklin Pierce vetoed it on the grounds that it was unwise for the federal government to assume responsibility for the nation's poor.

The pre-Civil War era saw repeated attempts to assist the dependent and vulnerable. Thomas Hopkins Gallaudet (1787–1851), moved by the plight of a deaf-mute named Alice Cogswell, established in 1817 the nation's first school, in Hartford, Connecticut, to teach deaf-mutes to read and write, read lips, and communicate through hand signals. Samuel Gridley Howe (1801–1876) accomplished for the blind what Gallaudet achieved for the deaf. He established the country's first school for the blind in Boston and produced printed materials with raised type. He aroused national attention by his successful instruction of Laura Bridgman, a blind deaf-mute.

RADICAL REFORM

The initial thrust of reform—moral reform— was to strengthen the Christian character of the United States and to rescue the nation from infidelity and intemperance. A second line of reform, social or humanitarian reform, sought to alleviate such sources of human misery as crime, cruelty, disease, and ignorance. The goal of a third line of reform, radical reform, was to regenerate the nation's social order by eliminating the underlying sources of inequality. Radical reformers sought to perfect society by eradicating slavery, solving the problems of racial and sexual discrimination, and constructing model communities.

Early Antislavery Efforts

Dramatic growth in antislavery sentiment sparked the most influential of the radical reform movements. The struggle against slavery

represented a great change in moral values. As late as the 1750s, no church had discouraged its members from owning or trading in slaves. The governments of Britain, France, Denmark, Holland, Portugal, and Spain openly participated in the slave trade. Slaves could be found in each of the thirteen American colonies, and prior to the American Revolution only one colony, Georgia, had sought to prohibit slavery.

Within half a century, however, protests against the institution of slavery had become widespread. By 1804 nine states north of Maryland and Delaware had either emancipated their slaves or adopted gradual emancipation schemes. Both the United States and Britain outlawed the African slave trade in 1807. In 1833 Britain emancipated 780,000 slaves in the British West Indies, and in 1848 France and Denmark freed slaves in their New World colonies.

When Congress prohibited the African slave trade, there were grounds for believing that slavery was a dying institution. In 1787 Congress had barred slavery from the Old Northwest, the region north of the Ohio River. The number of slaves freed by their masters had risen dramatically in the Upper South during the 1780s and 1790s, and more antislavery societies had been formed in the South than in the North. At the present rate of progress, predicted one religious leader in 1791, within fifty years it will "be as shameful for a man to hold a Negro slave, as to be guilty of common robbery or theft."

When William Lloyd Garrison initiated a call for an immediate end to slavery in 1831, however, the grounds for optimism had evaporated. Despite the cutting off of the legal slave trade, the slave population had continued to grow, climbing from 1.5 million in 1820 to over 2 million a decade later. A new cotton kingdom had emerged in the lower South and Southwest, and free blacks were subject to increasingly harsh discrimination in the North.

A major impediment to emancipation was the widespread belief that blacks and whites could not coexist equally in the United States and that any plan for emancipation required separation of the races. The result was a spate of proposals for gradual emancipation and deportation of black Americans. In 1816 a group of prominent ministers and politicians formed the American Colonization Society to resettle free blacks in West Africa, encourage planters to voluntarily emancipate their slaves, and create a group of black missionaries who would spread Christianity in Africa. Various plans for African colonization gained the support of the nation's major political figures, including Thomas Jefferson, James Madison, James Monroe, and John Marshall, and during the 1820s Congress helped fund the cost of transporting free blacks to Liberia (a colony and later a country established in West Africa in 1820 by eighty-eight free blacks). In the face of this widespread consensus in favor of colonization, many staunch opponents of slavery confined their efforts to lobbying for state emancipation acts and measures to prevent the kidnapping and sale of free blacks.

A few blacks supported African colonization in the belief that it provided the only alternative to continued degradation and discrimination. Paul Cuffe (1759–1817), a Quaker sea captain who was the son of a former slave and an Indian woman, led the first experiment in colonization. In 1815 he transported thirty-eight free blacks to Sierra Leone, on the western coast of Africa, and devoted thousands of his own dollars to the cause of colonization. By the 1820s, however, it was apparent that colonization was a wholly impractical solution to the nation's slavery problem. Each year the nation's slave population rose by roughly 50,000, but in 1830 the American Colonization Society succeeded in persuading just 259 free blacks to migrate to Liberia, bringing the total number of blacks colonized in Africa to just 1400.

The Rise of Abolitionist Sentiment in the North

Free blacks took the lead in condemning colonization and discriminatory "black laws" in the North. As early as 1817, over 3000 members of Philadelphia's black community staged a protest against colonization, where they denounced the policy as "little more merciful than death." In 1829 David Walker (1785–1830), a free black owner of a second-hand clothing store, issued from Boston the militant *Appeal to the Colored Citizens of the World* threaten-

ing insurrection and violence if calls for the abolition of slavery and improved conditions for free blacks were not realized. The next year, some forty black delegates from eight states held the first of a series of annual conventions that denounced slavery and called for an end to discriminatory laws in the northern states.

In 1829 a twenty-five-year-old white Bostonian named William Lloyd Garrison (1805–1879) added his voice to the outcry against colonization and other gradualist approaches to the problem of slavery. He denounced colonization as a cruel hoax designed to promote the racial purity of the Northern population while doing nothing to end slavery in the South. Colonization, Garrison insisted, was "a libel upon republicanism—a libel upon the Declaration of Independence—a libel upon Christianity." Instead, he called for "immediate emancipation." By this, he meant the immediate and unconditional release of slaves from bondage without compensation to slave owners.

On the first day of January, 1831, he began publishing *The Liberator,* a militant abolitionist newspaper, which was the country's first publication to demand an immediate end to slavery. On the front page of the first issue, he defiantly declared: "I will not equivocate—I will not excuse—I will not retreat a single inch—AND I WILL BE HEARD." Upset by Garrison's plea, the state of Georgia offered a $5000 reward to anyone who brought him to the state for trial.

Within four years, 200 antislavery societies had sprouted up in the North, and had mounted a massive propaganda campaign to proclaim the sinfulness of slavery. These societies distributed a million pieces of abolitionist literature and sent 20,000 tracts directly to the South.

The initial weapon abolitionists used against slavery was moral suasion. Many abolitionists had labored in earlier movements for moral reform—movements to spread Christian tracts; enforce observance of the Sabbath; suppress vice, intemperance, and lotteries; and educate the poor. They believed that direct appeals to conscience would convince slaveholders that slavery was a moral evil. Abolitionists sought "the destruction of error by the potency of truth—the overthrow of prejudice by the power of love—and the abolition of slavery

A REGULAR ROW IN THE BACKWOODS.

GOUGING FIGHTS AND BACKCOUNTRY HONOR

Nobody ever called them pretty. Eastern and European travelers to the American southern backcountry employed many descriptive and emotive adjectives—disgusting, brutal, savage, uncivilized, disgraceful, barbaric, unsightly—but never once pretty. And, indeed, backcountry fights, whether called "gouging" matches, "rough-and-tumble" contests, or "no holds barred" battles, were not attractive affairs. Men fought all out, using fists, hands, feet, elbows, knees, teeth, and whatever other part of their anatomy promised to do bodily damage to their opponents. Capturing the temper of these battles, Anglican minister Charles Woodmason counseled, "I would advise you when You do fight Not to act like Tygers and Bears as these Virginians do—Biting one anothers Lips and Noses off, and *gouging* one another—that is, thrusting out one anothers Eyes,

and kicking one another on the Cods, to the Great damage of many a Poor Woman."

The goal of a gouging match was the disfigurement of one's opponent. This could be accomplished in any number of ways, but the most popular was eye gouging. Fighters manicured their fingernails hard and sharp so that they could use them as a fulcrum to pry out their adversary's eye. On seeing a renowned fighter badly mauled, a passerby remarked, "'You have come off badly this time, I doubt?' 'Have I,' says he triumphantly, showing from his pocket at the same time an eye, which he had extracted during the combat, and preserved as a trophy."

Reading descriptions of these sanguinary contests provokes a series of questions. Who would engage in such activities? And why? Were the contests considered sports or manifestations of blood feuds? And what of the spectators

and the law—did they enjoy and allow and condone such barbarities? Finally, what do the contests tell us about the society in which they flourished?

Gouging centered in the region of rivers and largely untamed backcountry south of the Ohio River. It was a land of dangers and violence and early deaths. Organized Indian tribes threatened settlers. Wild animals roamed the heavily wooded forests. Outlaws practiced their professions almost unchecked by the law. High infant mortality rates, short life expectancies, dangerous occupations, and random violence stood as grim reminders that life in this region of nature was, as philosopher Thomas Hobbes once noted, "solitary, poor, nasty, brutish, and short."

The men who disfigured each other in gouging matches had been hardened by their environment and their occupations. Many worked on the rivers as roust-abouts, rivermen, or gamblers. Others were hunters, herders, or subsistence farmers. No planta-tions dotted their world; no landed aristocrats dominated them. As Elliott J. Gorn, a leading historian of the subject, commented, "the upland folk lived in an intensely local, kin-based society. Rural hamlets, impassible roads, and provincial isolations—not growing towns, internal improvements, or international commerce—characterized the backcountry."

The work these men performed was physically demanding and dan-gerous. Working on a Mississippi barge or trapping game in the backcountry exposed men to all the forces of nature and did not foster a gentle view of life. Death and pain were everywhere to be seen. Mark Twain remembered such men from his boyhood expe-riences in a raw river town: "Rude, uneducated, brave, suffer-ing terrific hardships with sailor-like stoicism; heavy drinkers, coarse frolickers . . . , heavy fight-ers, reckless fellows, every one, elephantinely jolly, foul witted, profane, prodigal of their money, bankrupt at the end of the trip, fond of barbaric finery, prodigious braggarts . . . ." They were not Jacksonian men on the make or respectable churchgoers. Rather they were men who worked hard, played hard, and drank hard.

Since they spent most of their lives in the company of other men, much of their sense of self-worth came from how their companions viewed them. They did not use money or piety as yardsticks for measuring the worth of a man. Bravery, strength, conviviality, and a jealous sense of personal honor determined the cut of a man. The

ability to drink, boast, and fight with equal ability marked a back-country Renaissance man.

Question a man's honor and you questioned in the most pro-found sense his manhood. If aris-tocratic Southerners dueled over such slights, backcountry laborers gouged over them. Northerners found this touchy sense of honor perplexing. Philip Vickers Fithian, a New Jerseyite who traveled to the South in the 1770s, com-mented about the reason for one fight, "I suppose either that they are lovers, and one has in Jest or reality some way supplanted the other; or has in a merry hour called him a *Lubber* or a *Thick-Skull,* or a *Buckskin,* or a *Scots-man,* or perhaps one has mislaid the other's hat, or knocked a peach out of his Hand, or offered him a dram without wiping the mouth of the Bottle . . . ." Any ex-cuse, thought Fithian, could lead to mortal combat. But he misread the situation. In truth, any insult, no matter how slight, could be judged serious enough to provoke violence.

Once men exchanged angry words and angrier challenges, their combat provided entertain-ment for their companions. At the fights, drinking and boasting con-tinued, and the line between par-ticipant and spectator was hazy. One fight often led to another and general melees were not uncom-mon. Were such contests sports? Probably not, but it was not a question that anyone would have posed. Just as there was little dis-tinction between participant and spectator, there was little differ-ence between sport and battery.

Gouging matches were certainly not civilized affairs, and as civil-ized behavior and culture pene-trated the backcountry men ceased to settle their differences

in such brutal contests. This is not to say that they stopped fighting. Rather they "defended their honor" in more "civilized" ways. Bowie knives, swords, and pistols re-placed honed thumbnails and filed teeth as the weapons of choice. And these "affairs of honor" were held before a few solemn wit-nesses rather than a host of cheering friends. During an earlier time, it was considered an un-manly sign of fear for a person to carry a weapon. But more refined sensibilities reversed this notion. By the mid-nineteenth century weapon carrying had become an indication of manliness. "Thus," as Gorn observed, "progress . . . slowly circumscribed rough-and-tumble fighting, only to substitute a deadlier option. Violence grew neater and more lethal as men checked their savagery to murder each other."

But if gouging became a relic of another age, it remained a par-ticularly telling relic. It provides an important clue to the values of the Southern backcountry. How men fought—just as how they worked or played—indicates much about their lives. The men who gouged led strenuous, often violent lives. They were not the sort of men to turn pale at the sight of blood or even at the sight of an eyeless eye socket. They admired toughness, fearlessness, and even meanness—not piety, gentleness, and sensitivity. As Gorn so aptly noted, "Violent sports, heavy drink-ing, and impulsive pleasure seek-ing were appropriate for men who lives were hard, whose futures were unpredictable, and whose opportunities were limited. Goug-ing champions were group leaders because they embodied the basic values of their peers."

313

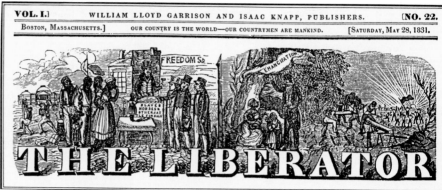

The symbol of radical abolitionism, Garrison sought immediate freedom for slaves without compensation to their owners.

by the spirit of repentance." To spread their ideas, they organized antislavery societies, distributed newspapers and tracts, and circulated petitions. They avoided concrete proposals for emancipation, fearing to become embroiled in debates over the details of specific plans.

Abolitionist Arguments and Public Reaction

Arguments against slavery advanced by the abolitionists focused on the illegality, immorality, and economic backwardness of the institution. Slavery was illegal because it violated the principles of natural rights to life and liberty embodied in the Declaration of Independence. Justice, said Garrison, required that the nation "secure to the colored population . . . all the rights and privileges that belong to them as men and as Americans." Slavery was sinful because slaveholders, in the words of abolitionist Theodore Weld, had usurped "the prerogative of God." Masters reduced a "God-like being" to a manipulable "THING." Slavery also encouraged sexual immorality and undermined the institutions of marriage and the family. Not only did slave masters sexually abuse and exploit slave women, abolitionists charged, but in some older southern states, such as Virginia and Maryland, they bred slaves for sale to the more recently settled parts of the Deep South. Slav-

ery was economically retrogressive because slaves, motivated only by fear, did not exert themselves willingly. By depriving their labor force of any incentive for performing careful and diligent work and by barring slaves from acquiring and developing productive skills, planters hindered improvement in crop and soil management. Abolitionists also charged that slavery impeded the development of towns, canals, railroads, and schools.

The growth of antislavery agitation provoked a harsh public reaction. Mobs led by "gentlemen of property and standing" attacked the homes and businesses of abolitionist merchants, destroyed abolitionist printing presses, disrupted antislavery meetings, and attacked black neighborhoods. Crowds pelted abolitionist reformers with eggs and even stones. During anti-abolitionist rioting in Philadelphia in October, 1834, a white mob destroyed forty-five homes in the city's black community. A year later, a Boston mob dragged Garrison through the streets and almost lynched him before authorities took him to a city jail for his own safety. That same year, the citizens of East Feliciana, Louisiana, offered a $50,000 reward for the capture, dead or alive, of Arthur Tappan, president of the American Anti-Slavery Society. States in both the North and South debated "gag" laws to suppress antislavery agitation, and the postmaster general refused to deliver antislavery tracts to the South. In each session of Congress between 1836 and 1844 the House of Representatives adopted gag rules allowing that body to automatically table resolutions or petitions concerning the abolition of slavery.

On November 7, 1837, the abolitionist movement suffered its first martyr. The Reverend Elijah P. Lovejoy was editor of a militant antislavery newspaper in Alton, Illinois, a town located across the Mississippi river from slaveholding St. Louis, Missouri. Three times, mobs destroyed Lovejoy's printing presses and attacked his house. When a fourth printing press arrived, Lovejoy armed himself and guarded the new press at the warehouse. The anti-abolitionist mob set the warehouse on fire and shot Lovejoy as he fled the building. The following day, opponents of the abolitionists lined the streets and cheered as the mutilated corpse was dragged through the town.

Abolitionists never expected such a reaction. "When we first unfurled the banner of *The Liberator*," Garrison wrote, "we did not anticipate that . . . the free states would voluntarily trample under foot all order, law and government, or brand the advocates of universal liberty as incendiaries." This violent response produced division and fragmentation within the antislavery movement.

Division in the Antislavery Movement

By the late 1830s, abolitionists faced a terrible dilemma. Moral suasion had not only failed, it had produced a violent counterreaction against abolitionism. In the face of vicious attacks, opponents of slavery grew increasingly divided over questions of strategy and tactics.

At the 1840 annual meeting of the American Anti-Slavery Society in New York, abolitionists split over such questions as women's right to participate in the administration of the organization and the advisability of nominating abolitionists as independent political candidates outside the major parties. Garrison won control of the organization and his opponents promptly walked out. From this point on, no single organization could speak for abolitionism.

Among the members of the Executive Committee of the Pennsylvania Anti-Slavery Society was Lucretia Mott, seated in the front row second from the right.

One group of abolitionists looked to politics as the most promising way to end slavery. Limited political activities such as circulating petitions and asking political candidates about their stands on slavery had proven inadequate, and a growing number of abolitionists proposed the creation of an independent political party dedicated to the elimination of slavery.

The Liberty party, founded in 1840 under the leadership of Arthur and Lewis Tappan, wealthy New York City businessmen, and James G. Birney of Alabama, a former slaveholder, called upon Congress to abolish slavery in the District of Columbia, end the interstate slave trade, and cease admitting new slave states to the Union. The party also sought the repeal of local and state "black laws" which discriminated against free blacks. The Liberty party nominated Birney for president in 1840 and again in 1844. Although he gathered less than 7100 votes in his first campaign, he received 62,000 votes four years later and captured enough votes in Michigan and New York to deny Henry Clay the presidency.

In 1848 antislavery Democrats (known in New York State as Barnburners, because of their willingness to burn down the Democratic "barn" in order to rid undesirable persons from

The Barnburners were New York Democrats who opposed the expansion of slavery. Their opponents charged that they were willing to burn down the Democratic "barn" to get rid of undesirable party members and policies.

the party) and Conscience Whigs (in contrast to Cotton Whigs) merged with the Liberty party to form the Free Soil party. Unlike the Liberty party, which was dedicated to the abolition of slavery and equal rights for blacks, the Free Soil party narrowed its demands to the abolition of slavery in the District of Columbia and exclusion of slavery from the federal territories. The Free Soilers also wanted a homestead law to provide free land for western settlers, high tariffs to protect American industry, and federally sponsored internal improvements. Campaigning under the slogan "free soil, free labor, free men," the new party polled 300,000 votes in the presidential election of 1848 and helped to elect the Whig, Zachary Taylor.

Another group of abolitionists, led by William Lloyd Garrison, turned in a more radical direction. The radicals began to question whether the Bible represented the word of God, withdrew from membership in established churches that condoned slavery, demanded equal rights for women, and called for the voluntary dissolution of the Union. Taking the position that "it is the duty of the followers of Christ to suffer themselves to be defrauded . . . and barbarously treated, without resort to ei-

ther their own physical energies, or the force of human law," Garrison and his supporters established the New England Non-Resistance Society in 1838. Members refused to vote, hold public office, or bring suits in court. In 1854 Garrison attracted noteriety by publicly burning a copy of the Constitution, which he called "a covenant with death and an agreement with Hell." From a single-minded focus on the immorality of slavery, the radical Garrisonians expanded their commitment to universal emancipation into a wider-reaching attack on all forms of inequality and violence, and sought to link antislavery to such reforms as women's rights, world government, and international peace.

Throughout the North, black abolitionists played a vital role in the struggle against slavery and discrimination. They staged protests against segregated seating in "Negro-pews" in churches and on public transportation. They circulated petitions, organized boycotts, and brought court suits in an effort to make segregated schools illegal. Free blacks in New York and Pennsylvania launched petition drives for equal voting rights. Northern blacks also had a pivotal role in the "underground railroad" which provided escape routes for southern slaves to the northern states and into Canada. Black churches offered sanctuary to runaways and black "vigilance" groups in cities like New York and Detroit offered physical resistance to slave catchers.

During the 1840s, fugitive slaves such as William Wells Brown, Henry Bibb, and Harriet Tubman helped to arouse northern sympathy for the slaves' plight. Their first-hand tales of whippings and separation from spouses and children erased the notion that slaves were content under slavery and undermined beliefs in racial inferiority. Tubman risked her life by making nineteen trips into slave territory in order to free as many as 300 slaves. Slaveholders posted a reward of $40,000 for the capture of the "Black Moses."

Frederick Douglass was the most famous fugitive slave and black abolitionist. His early life epitomized many of the cruelties of slavery. He was born in 1818, the son of a Maryland slave woman and an unknown white father. At the age of six, he was sold away from his mother to work on a plantation of one of the largest slaveholders on Maryland's eastern shore. At the age of fifteen, he was sold again, and then he was rented out to a local farmer known as a "Negro breaker." After repeated beatings and whippings at the hand of this cruel farmer, Douglass fought back and defeated him in a fist fight. After this, he was no longer punished. In 1838, at the age of twenty, he escaped from slavery by borrowing the papers of a free black sailor.

In the North, Douglass became the first runaway slave to speak out on behalf of the antislavery cause. When many Northerners refused to believe that this eloquent orator could possibly have been a slave, he responded by writing an autobiography that identified his previous owners by name. Although he initially allied himself with William Lloyd Garrison, Douglass later started his own newspaper, *The North Star,* and supported political action against slavery.

By the 1850s, a growing number of black abolitionists felt a deep sense of pessimism about their cause. Colonizationist sentiment appeared again among blacks. In a period of fifteen months after passage of the Federal Fugitive Slave Law in 1850, some 13,000 free blacks fled the North for Canada. In 1854, Martin Delany (1812–1885), a Pittsburgh doctor who had studied medicine at Harvard, organized a National Emigration Convention to investigate possible sites for black colonization in Haiti, Central America, and West Africa. Other black abolitionists responded to their sense of hopelessness by reassessing their faith in nonviolence. Black abolitionists in Ohio adopted resolutions encouraging slaves to escape and called on their fellow citizens to violate any law that "conflicts with reason, liberty and justice, North or South." A meeting of fugitive slaves in Cazenovia, New York, declared that "the State motto of Virginia, 'Death to Tyrants,' is as well the black man's as the white man's motto." By the late 1850s, a growing number of free blacks had concluded that it was just as legitimate to use violence to secure the freedom of the slaves as it had been to establish the independence of the American colonies.

Harriet Tubman, a fugitive slave who led 19 raids into slave territory, and Sojourner Truth, who was born a slave in New York state in 1797, were leading proponents of abolitionism. In 1841 Frederick Douglass gained public notice by giving a powerful speech against slavery. He not only opposed slavery, but all forms of racial discrimination.

Over the long run, the fragmentation of the antislavery movement worked to the advantage of the cause. Henceforth, Northerners could support whichever form of antislavery best reflected their views. Moderates could vote for political candidates with abolitionist sentiments without being accused of radical Garrisonian views or of advocating violence for redress of grievances.

The Birth of Feminism

The women's rights movement was another major legacy of radical reform in the early nineteenth century. At the beginning of the century, women were prohibited from voting or holding office in every state; they had no access to higher education and were excluded from professional occupations. American law was guided by the principle that a wife had no legal identity apart from her husband. She could not be sued, neither could she bring a legal suit, make a contract, or own property. She was not permitted to control her own wages or gain custody of her children in case of separation or divorce, and under many circumstances she was even deemed incapable of committing crimes.

The decades stretching from the late eighteenth century to the Civil War witnessed a dramatic transformation of women's economic and social position. In some respects the status and opportunities of women clearly improved. Instead of bearing children at two-year intervals after marriage, as was the case throughout the colonial era, early nineteenth-century women bore fewer children and ceased childbearing at younger ages. During these decades the first women's college was established and the first men's college opened its doors to women students. More women were postponing marriage or not marrying at all; unmarried women gained new employment opportunities as "mill girls" and elementary schoolteachers; and a growing number of women achieved eminence as novelists, editors, teachers, and leaders of church and philanthropic societies.

Compared to men, however, women lost political and economic status. As voting rights were extended to greater and greater numbers of white males, including large groups of recent immigrants, the gap in political power between women and men widened. Even though women made up a core of supporters for many reform movements, men excluded them from positions of decision making and relegated them to separate female auxiliaries. Women also lost status as economic production shifted away from the household to the factory and workshop. During the late eighteenth century, the need for a cash income led women and older children to engage in a variety of household industries, including weaving and spinning. Increasingly, however, these tasks were performed in factories and mills.

These shifts in women's status were part of a broader process of economic change involving the spread of a market-oriented economy and increased economic productivity and specialization. The expansion of a market economy separated work from the home, and gradually extinguished the domestic industries which had employed all family members. The effect of such far-reaching changes was to increasingly isolate middle-class women along with their small children in a separate "sphere of domesticity." This concept of a separate female sphere carried important implications for reform. Since women were believed to be uncontaminated by the competitive struggle for wealth and power, a growing number of women argued that they had a duty—and the capacity—to exert an uplifting moral influence upon American society.

Two such women were Catherine Beecher (1800–1874) and Sarah Josepha Hale (1788–1879). Beecher, the eldest sister of Harriet Beecher Stowe, was one of the nation's most prominent educators before the Civil War. A woman of many talents and strong leadership, she wrote a highly regarded book on domestic science and spearheaded the campaign to convince school boards that women were suited to serve as schoolteachers. Hale edited the nation's most popular women's magazines, the *Ladies Magazine* and *Godey's Ladies Book*. She led a successful campaign to make Thanksgiving a national holiday, and she also composed the famous nursery rhyme "Mary Had a Little Lamb."

Both Beecher and Hale worked tirelessly for women's education (Hale helped organize Vassar College) and gave voice to the grievances of women—the abysmally low wages paid to women in the needle trades (twelve-and-a-half cents a day for a fourteen-hour workday), the physical hardships endured by female operatives in the nation's shops and mills (where women workers were awakened at five, required to work fourteen hours a day by lamplight, standing all the while, breathing particles thrown off by the spindles and looms), and the enfeebling of women's intellectual aspirations. Even though both women rejected equal rights, they were important transitional figures in the emergence of feminism. Each significantly broadened society's definition of "women's sphere" and assigned women vital social responsibilities: to shape the character of children, to morally uplift husbands, and to promote causes of "practical benevolence," including Sunday Schools, playgrounds, and seamen's aid societies (which aided not sailors but abandoned wives, widows, and orphans).

Suddenly, other women were breaking down old barriers and forging new opportunities in a more dramatic fashion. Frances Wright (1795–1852), a Scottish-born reformer and lecturer, received the nickname "The Great Red Harlot of Infidelity" because of her radical ideas about birth control, liberalized divorce laws, and legal rights for married women. In 1849 Elizabeth Blackwell (1821–1910) became the first American woman to receive a degree in medicine. A number of women became active as revivalists. Perhaps the most notable was Phoebe Palmer (1807–1874), a Methodist preacher who ignited religious fervor among thousands of Americans and Canadians.

Catalyst for Women's Rights

The direct cause of feminist agitation was a public debate over women's proper place, occasioned by female participation in the abolitionist movement. By 1838 more than one hundred female antislavery societies had been created, and women abolitionists were circulating petitions, editing abolitionist tracts, and organizing antislavery conventions. A key question was

In 1868 Elizabeth Blackwell founded the Women's Medical College in New York City, so that women physicians could receive an education of the highest caliber.

whether women abolitionists would be permitted to lecture to "mixed" audiences of men and women. In 1837 a national women's antislavery convention resolved that women should overcome this taboo: "The time has come for women to move in that sphere which providence has assigned her, and no longer remain satisfied with the circumscribed limits which corrupt custom and a perverted application of Scripture have encircled her."

The women who first broke the bonds of propriety and widened the women's sphere were Angelina Grimke (1805–1879) and her sister Sarah (1792–1873). Born in Charleston, South Carolina, to a wealthy slaveholding family, the two sisters moved to Philadelphia, joined the Society of Friends (Quakers), and became active in the abolitionist cause. In 1837 Angelina gained national notoriety by lecturing against slavery to audiences that included men as well as women. Shocked by this breach of the separate sexual spheres ordained by God, ministers in Massachusetts called on their fellow clergy to forbid women the right to speak from church pulpits. Sarah Grimke responded with a pamphlet entitled *Letters on the Condition of Women and the Equality of the Sexes,* one of the first modern statements of feminist principles. She denounced the injustice of lower pay and denial of equal educational opportunities for women. Her pamphlet expressed outrage that women were "regarded by men, as pretty toys or as mere instruments of pleasure" and taught to believe that marriage is "the *sine qua non* [indispensable element] of human happiness and human existence." Men and women, she concluded, should not be treated differently since both were endowed with inherent natural rights.

In 1840, after the American Anti-Slavery Society split over the issue of women's rights, the organization proceeded to name three female delegates to a World's Anti-Slavery Convention to be held in London later that year. In London these women were denied the right to take part in the convention on the grounds that their participation would offend British public opinion. The convention relegated them to seats in a balcony.

Eight years later, Lucretia Mott, who had been denied the right to serve as a delegate in the World's Anti-Slavery Convention, and Elizabeth Cady Stanton organized the first women's rights convention in history. The convention was held in July, 1848, at Seneca Falls, New York. They drew up a Declaration of Sentiments, modeled on the Declaration of Independence, specifying fifteen specific inequities under which women suffered. After detailing "a history of repeated injuries and usurpations on the part of men toward woman," it concluded that "he has endeavored, in every way that he could, to destroy her confidence in her own powers, to lessen her self-respect, and to make her willing to lead a dependent and abject life."

Among the resolutions adopted by the convention, only one was not ratified unanimously— that women be granted the right to vote. Of the sixty-six women and thirty-four men who signed the Declaration of Sentiments at the convention (including black abolitionist Frederick Douglass), only two lived to see the ratification of the women's suffrage amendment to the Constitution seventy years later.

By mid-century women's rights conventions had been held in every northern state.

A Quaker leader, abolitionist, feminist, and the mother of six children, Lucretia Mott was an ardent opponent of slavery and often met with angry and violent mobs.

Despite ridicule from the public press—the *Worcester (Massachusetts) Telegraph* denounced women's rights advocates as "Amazons"—female reformers contributed to important, if limited, advances against discrimination. They succeeded in gaining adoption of Married Women's Property Laws in a number of states, granting married women full control over their income and property. A New York law passed in 1860 gave women joint custody over children and the right to sue and be sued, and in several states women's rights reformers secured adoption of permissive divorce laws that granted divorce for any "misconduct" that "permanently destroys the happiness of the petitioner and defeats the purposes of the marriage relationship."

Utopian Communities

Another aspect of radical reform emerged in the founding of ideal communities. During the early days of the republic, when the outlook for the future was bleakest, Tom Paine wrote

The Changing American Landscape

PART ONE

Twilight in the Wilderness (1860) by Frederic E. Church.

At the end of F. Scott Fitzgerald's *The Great Gatsby*, a leading character muses about what Long Island must have looked like to the first Dutch sailors: "Its vanished trees, the trees that made way for Gatsby's house, had once pandered in whispers to the last and greatest of human dreams; for a transitory enchanted moment man must have held his breath in the presence of this continent, compelled into an aesthetic contemplation he neither understood nor desired, face to face for the last time in history with something commensurate to his capacity for wonder." Fitzgerald's eloquent sentence raises an interesting question: What was America like before white settlers started to recreate the New World in the image of the Old? It was a wild, heavily forested land, where woods grew thick to the margins of coves and rivers. Forests stretched seemingly forever, for one thousand miles north to south and well westward. It was said that a squirrel could travel from the Ohio River to Lake Erie by simply jumping from tree to tree. The same could be said from the Hudson River to Niagara Falls or from Harpers Ferry to Muscle Shoals.

The trees were immense, many thirty to forty feet around. Decayed, hollowed-out sycamores could house a pioneer family overnight, and one in Ross County, Ohio, was converted into a two-horse stable. Records of grapevines sixteen feet around at the base give substance to the Henry Wadsworth Longfellow line, "This is the forest primeval."

Other areas were covered with lush grasses—wild rye, blue grass, and clover. And over the land roamed buffalo, deer, elk, antelope, and bear. Beavers lived in the rivers, and the now extinct passenger pigeon and Carolina parrot

Schroon Mountain, Adirondacks (1838). Thomas Cole's landscapes "carried the eye over scenes of wild grandeur peculiar to our country, over our aerial mountain tops with their mighty growth of forest . . . along the banks of streams never deformed by culture." Bighorn sheep, the American blue crab, the Carolina parakeet, and flowering trees (top, left to right) were all indigenous to America at the time.

soared above the forests and grasslands. America was, in short, a land that inspired wonder—and perhaps fear and anxiety.

Western Europeans regarded the wild, rugged land as a hostile environment, a place where evil as well as trees flourished. For them, America was the wilderness, a region of wild beasts unchecked by civilization. Their prejudices against wilderness had deep roots. In classical mythology Pan, the god of the woods, had the legs, ears, and tail of a goat; the body of a man; and a sensual, uncontrolled nature. In the wilderness lived wood-spirits and Trolls, man-eating ogres and werewolves. In the Anglo-Saxon epic *Beowulf*, the tribal hero battles gigantic, blood-drinking fiends "in an unvisited land among wolf-haunted hills, wind-swept crags, and perilous fen-tracks."

Even the Judeo-Christian tradition preached against the wilderness. The term occurs 245 times in the Old Testament (Revised Standard Version) and thirty-five times in the New. Always it was a cursed land, a lawless land. As Puritan ministers knew and often reminded their congregations, Adam and Eve were forced out of the garden to the wilderness (a "cursed" land full of "thorns and thistles"); after leaving Egypt the Israelites wandered in the "howling waste of the wilderness" before entering Canaan, and Christ "was led up by the Spirit into the wilderness to be tempted by the devil."

For Puritans and other European colonists, then, the wilderness was a place to be tamed. No sooner did colonists arrive in America than they set about trying to reproduce the "civilized" world they left. Far from wanting to create something new, the first colonists wanted to preserve something old and familiar. As architectural historian Lewis Mumford noted, "In the villages of the New World there flickered up the last dying embers of the medieval order."

A log cabin on the road near York, Pennsylvania (1788).

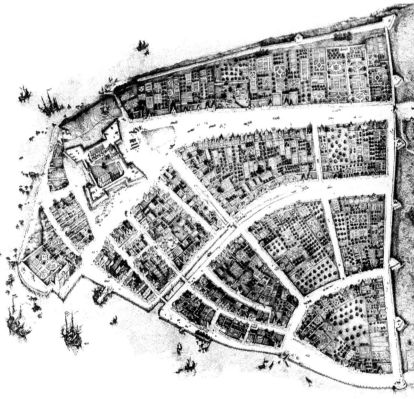

New Amsterdam as shown in the Castello Plan of 1660.

The Hope Estate Plantation near Baton Rouge, Louisiana.

The military plaza in San Antonio, Texas (1857).

The common in New Haven, Connecticut (1780).

words that have continued to inspire future generations of Americans: "We have it within our power to begin the world anew." This fervent belief in the attainability of a just social and political order has long been a cornerstone of the American creed. But at no time was this spirit stronger than during the 1820s, '30s, and '40s, when literally hundreds of utopian communities were created in Massachusetts, in the Old Northwest of upstate New York, Ohio, and Indiana, and in Tennessee and Texas. These experimental communal societies were called "utopian communities" because they provided blueprints for a perfectionist vision of an ideal society.

The thousands who flocked to these communities were inspired by a belief that human beings were capable of perfectability in moral character and rationality, and that all social evils and weaknesses of human nature could be eliminated. If people were not perfect, it was solely because the existing society and its institutions were irreparably flawed. Utopians believed that a competitive economy encouraged people's acquisitiveness; that the institutions of marriage and the family distracted individuals from their obligations to humanity as a whole; and that organized religions spread prejudice. Liberated from oppressive customs and institutions, individuals would at last be rational and virtuous.

The specific characteristics of these communities differed greatly. Some were rooted in religious teachings, others were the product of the Enlightenment's faith in reason. Some condemned sexuality, others rejected marriage and advocated "free love." Many called for establishment of communal ownership of property and cooperative production. Some of these communities were explicitly designed to serve as models for the surrounding society, others were inspired by a desire to withdraw from a corrupt world and establish a community based on love instead of coercion. All of these communities are important, however, because they epitomize the spirit of reform and the belief in limitless possibilities characteristic of pre-Civil War America.

The early models for utopian communities were Mother Ann Lee's Shaker communities and Robert Owen's New Harmony. Ann Lee was born in Manchester, England, in 1736, the daughter of an English blacksmith. After joining a small sect known as the Shakers in 1758, she began to preach that the millennium was at hand and that the time had come for people to totally renounce sin. God, she believed, had both male and female aspects. She also believed that sexual intercourse was the basic cause of human sin.

In 1774 she arrived in New York City, and two years later she established the first Shaker settlement northwest of Albany, New York. By 1800, there were twelve Shaker colonies. These communities placed Shaker men and women on a level of sexual equality and both sexes served as elders and deacons. Aspiring to live like the early Christians, the Shakers adopted communal ownership of property and a way of life emphasizing simplicity. Dress was kept simple and uniform. Shaker architecture and furniture were devoid of ornament—no curtains on windows, carpets, or pictures. on the wall—but pure and elegant in form.

The two most striking characteristics of the Shaker communities were their Shaker dances and abstinence from sexual relations. The Shakers believed that religious fervor should be expressed through the head, heart, and the mind, and their ritual religious practices included shaking, shouting, and dancing. The Shakers also adopted strict rules concerning celibacy. They replenished their membership by admitting volunteers and taking in orphans.

Robert Owen's experimental community at New Harmony presented a striking contrast to the Shaker colonies. Owen was a paternalistic Scottish industrialist who was deeply troubled by the social consequences of the industrial revolution. Inspired by the philosophy of the Enlightenment, especially the idea that people are shaped by their environment, Owen purchased a site in Indiana where he sought to establish common ownership of property and abolish religion. At New Harmony the marriage ceremony was reduced to a single sentence and children were raised outside of their natural parents' homes. The community lasted just three years, from 1825 to 1828.

Some forty utopian communities were inspired by the French theorist Charles Fourier, who hoped to eliminate poverty and dignify

Officially named "The United Society of Believers in Christ's Second Appearing," the Shakers received their popular name from the contortions they made during religious dances.

manual labor through the establishment of scientifically organized cooperative communities called *phalanxes*. Each phalanx was to be set up as a "joint stock company" in which profits were divided according to the amount of money members had invested, their skill, and their labor. Fourier coined the term *feminism*, and in the phalanxes, women members received equal job opportunities and equal pay, equal participation in decision making, and the right to speak in public assemblies. Although one Fourier community lasted for eighteen years, most quickly fell apart.

Most well-known of all utopian experiments was Brook Farm, a cooperative community located in West Roxbury, Massachusetts, nine miles from Boston. Brook Farm was an attempt to apply the ideas of American transcendentalism to everyday life. Transcendentalism was the philosophy associated with Ralph Waldo Emerson, the greatest American thinker of his generation. The Boston-born, Harvard-trained Emerson (1803–1882) was ordained as

a Unitarian minister but resigned his pulpit in 1832 because he believed that Unitarianism, in rejecting the harsh Calvinist doctrines of original sin and divine omnipotence and substituting a faith in reason and human goodness, had grown more concerned with people's material well-being than their spiritual condition. As a lecturer, essayist, and poet, the "Seer of Concord" rejected the supernatural basis of Christianity and declared instead that all individuals had within themselves the seeds of divinity. Emerson believed that each individual had a capacity to transcend ordinary understanding and commune with the spiritual force in the universe.

In 1841, George Ripley, who had also been a Unitarian clergyman, founded Brook Farm in an effort to realize Emerson's ideal of "self-reliance" and provide Christianity with new inspiration and new vision. His community's goal was "to substitute brotherly cooperation for selfish competition; to prevent anxiety in men by competent supplying in them of necessary wants." "Our ulterior aim is nothing less than Heaven on Earth," declared one community member. Brook Farm's residents, who never numbered more than 200, supported themselves through farming, teaching, and the manufacture of clothing. The most famous member of the community was Nathaniel Hawthorne, who based his 1852 novel *The Blithedale Romance* on his experiences.

In his letters, he recorded his experiences playing "chambermaid to a group of cows" and working in the "gold mine," as he called the community's manure pile. After three years, the community's members converted Brook Farm into a Fourier phalanx. In 1847 the community's central structure, the phalanstery, burned down, and the community was abandoned soon afterward.

The currents of radical antislavery thought inspired Frances Wright, a fervent Scottish abolitionist, to found Nashoba Colony in 1826, near Memphis, Tennessee, as an experiment in interracial living. She established a racially integrated cooperative community in which slaves were to receive an education and earn enough money to purchase their own freedom. Unfortunately, publicity about Fanny Wright's desire to abolish the nuclear family, religion, private property, and slavery created a furor and the community dissolved after only four years.

Perhaps the most notorious and successful experimental colony was John Humphrey Noyes's Oneida Community. Noyes began his career as a lawyer, was converted in one of Charles Finney's revivals, and proceeded to study theology for three years at Andover Theological Seminary and Yale. Convinced that the second coming of Christ had taken place in 70 A.D., Noyes believed that the final millennium would only occur when people strove to be-

Among the famous writers and reformers associated with Brook Farm were Nathaniel Hawthorne and Margaret Fuller.

CHRONOLOGY OF KEY EVENTS

1801 Cane Ridge religious revival in Kentucky

1808 Congress outlaws the African slave trade

1810 American Board of Commissioners for Foreign Missions formed

1816 American Bible Society founded

1817 American Tract Society founded

1819 Unitarian Church founded by William Ellery Channing

1821 Massachusetts establishes first public high school; Emma Hart Willard opens the Troy Female Seminary; The Kentucky legislature abolishes imprisonment for debt

1825 Beginning of Charles G. Finney's religious revivals in New York State Founding of New Harmony

1826 Founding of American Society for the Promotion of Temperance

1830 First Annual Convention of free blacks in Philadelphia

1831 William Lloyd Garrison founds *The Liberator*

1833 American Anti-Slavery Society formed

1836 Abolitionists begin to deluge Congress with antislavery petitions

1837 Angelina and Sarah Grimke lecture to mixed audiences of men and women; Abolitionist Elijah P. Lovejoy murdered in Alton, Illinois; Massachusetts creates first state board of education and appoints Horace Mann secretary

1840 Sarah Grimke's *Letters on the Equality of the Sexes and the Condition of Women* Frederick Douglass escapes from slavery

1840 Conflict between Catholics and Protestants over religious instruction in New York State public schools; Conservative abolitionists withdraw from American Anti-Slavery Society; Washingtonian temperance movement appears; James G. Birney runs for president as Liberty party candidate

1841 Dorothea Dix begins crusade on behalf of the mentally ill; Brook Farm founded

1848 First women's rights convention

1852 Massachusetts adopts first compulsory school attendance law

1855 Massachusetts desegregates its public schools

come perfect through an "immediate and total cessation from sin."

In Putney, Vermont, in 1835 and in Oneida, New York, in 1848, he established perfectionist communities that practiced communal ownership of property and "complex marriage." Complex marriage meant that every member of the community was married to every member of the opposite sex. Exclusive emotional or sexual attachments were forbidden and sexual relations were to be arranged through an intermediary in order to protect a woman's individuality. Men were required to practice *coitus interruptus* (withdrawal) as a method of birth control, and, after the Civil War, the community conducted experiments in eugenics—the selective control of mating in order to improve the hereditary qualities of children. Other notable features of the community were mutual criticism sessions and communal childrearing. Oneida flourished in its original form until 1880.

John Humphrey Noyes, founder of Oneida, believed all work was equally honorable, and men and women alike participated in "bag bees" during which traveling bags were produced for export.

CONCLUSION

The pre-Civil War reform era came to a symbolic end in 1865 when William Lloyd Garrison, the abolitionist, closed down his militant newspaper *The Liberator* and called upon the American Anti-Slavery Society to disband.

The first half of the nineteenth century witnessed the rise of the first secular movements in history which sought to educate the deaf and blind, care for the mentally ill, extend equal rights to women, and abolish slavery. Inspired by the revolutionary ideals of the Declaration of Independence and the Bill of Rights, the Enlightenment faith in reason, and liberal and evangelical religious principles, educational reformers created a system of free public education; prison reformers constructed specialized institutions to reform criminals; temperance reformers sought to end the drinking of liquor; and utopian socialists established ideal communities to serve as models of a better world.

The Civil War largely brought an end to the era of optimistic, perfectionist reform. The grim violence of the war shattered the pre-Civil War reformers' confidence in the "perfectability of man" and sparked a reaction against the emotionalism and utopian idealism of pre-Civil War reform. Although a large number of abolitionists continued to fight for black equality and many feminists moved from women's rights to the fight for women's suffrage, a period of retrenchment set in during the 1870s and 1880s, when counter-reformers reversed many of the accomplishments of prewar reformers by restoring capital punishment and making divorce laws more stringent. This new generation also made uninhibited use of the power of the state to enforce purity and morality by reenacting blue laws, forbidding the sale of goods on Sundays, censoring art, and blocking the distribution of contraceptive information.

Still, many of the goals of the antebellum reformers would live on. The pre-Civil War reformers' spirit of hope and their willingness to question established customs and institutions would survive as a source of inspiration for later proponents of penal reform, women's rights, labor unions, and racial justice.

REVIEW SUMMARY

Inspired by the Declaration of Independence, liberal religion, revivalism, and the Enlightenment's faith in reason, many nineteenth-century Americans joined reform movements dedicated to improving society. The major groups were:

> temperance reformers, who condemned the drinking of hard liquor
>
> educational reformers, who created a system of free public schooling
>
> prison reformers, who constructed institutions to raise the moral level of criminals
>
> abolitionists, who attempted to end slavery
>
> feminists, who sought equal rights for women
>
> utopian socialists, who established ideal communities

SUGGESTIONS FOR FURTHER READING

OVERVIEWS AND SURVEYS

Whitney R. Cross, *The Burned Over District* (1950); David Brion Davis, ed., *Antebellum Reform* (1967); Clyde S. Griffin, *The Ferment of Reform, 1830–1860* (1968); Alice Felt Tyler, *Freedom's Ferment: Phases of American Social History to 1860* (1944); Ronald G. Walters, *American Reformers, 1815–1860* (1978).

SOURCES OF THE REFORM IMPULSE

Edwin S. Gaustad, ed., *The Rise of Adventism: Religion and Society in Mid-Nineteenth America* (1974); Sydney V. James, *A People Among Peoples: Quaker Benevolence in Eighteenth-Century America* (1963); Paul Johnson, *A Shopkeeper's Millennium: Society and Revivals in Rochester, New York, 1815–1837* (1979); William G. McLoughlon, *Modern Revivalism* (1959); Perry Miller, *The Life of the Mind in America from the Revolution to the Civil War* (1965); H. Richard Niebuhr, *The Kingdom of God in America* (1937); Timothy L. Smith, *Revivalism and Social Reform in Mid-19th Century America* (1957).

MORAL REFORM

John R. Bodo, *The Protestant Clergy and Public Issues, 1812–1848* (1954); Charles C. Cole, Jr., *The Social Ideas of the Northern Evangelists* (1954); Joel Dannenbaum, *Drink and Disorder: Temperance Reform in Cincinnati* (1984); Charles I. Foster, *An Errand of Mercy: The Evangelical United Front, 1790–1837* (1960); Clifford S. Griffin, *Their Brothers' Keepers: Moral Stewardship in the United States, 1800–1865* (1960); Joseph R. Gusfield, *Symbolic Crusade: Status Politics and the American Temperance Movement* (1963); Robert L. Hampel, *Temperance and Prohibition in Massachusetts* (1982); Mark Lender and James Kirby Martin, *Drinking in America* (1987); John R. McKivigan, *The War Against Proslavery Religion: Abolitionism and the Northern Churches* (1984); W. J. Rorabaugh, *The Alcoholic Republic: An American Tradition* (1979); Ian R. Tyrell, *Sobering Up: From Temperance to Prohibition in Antebellum America* (1979).

SOCIAL REFORM

David Allmeindinger, *Paupers and Scholars: The Transformation of Student Life in Nineteenth-Century New England* (1975); Robert H. Bremner, *From the Depths: The Discovery of Poverty in the United States* (1956); Marianna C. Brown, *The Sunday School Movement in America* (1961); Peter J. Coleman, *Debtors and Creditors in America: Insolvency, Imprisonment for Debt, and Bankruptcy* (1974); Lawrence Cremin, *American Education: The National Experience* (1980); Norman Dane, *Concepts of Insanity in the United States* (1964); Allen F. Davis and Mark H. Haller, eds., *The Peoples of Philadelphia: A History of Ethnic Groups and Lower-Class Life, 1790–1940* (1973); David Brion Davis, *Homicide in American Fiction, 1798–1860* (1957); Albert Deutsch, *The Mentally Ill in America* (1949); Ruth Elson, *Guardians of Tradition: American Schoolbooks of the Nineteenth Century* (1964); Michael Feldberg, *The Turbulent Era: Riot and Disorder in Jacksonian America* (1980); Edmund Fuller, *Prudence Crandell* (1971); Gerald Grob, *The State and the Mentally Ill* (1973); Joseph M. Hawes, *Children in Urban Society: Juvenile Delinquency in Nineteenth-Century America* (1971); Willard A. Heaps, *Riots, U.S.A., 1765–1970* (1970); W. Eugene Hollon, *Frontier Violence: Another Look* (1974); Joel T. Headley, *Great Riots of New York, 1712–1873* (1970); Sidney L. Jackson, *America's Struggle for Free Schools* (1965); Michael B. Katz, *The Irony of Early School Reform* (1970); Carl F. Kaestle, *The Evolution of an Urban School System: New York City, 1750–1850* (1973); C. F. Kaestle, *Pillars of the Republic: Common Schools and American Society, 1780–1860* (1983); C. F. Kaestle and Maris A. Vinovskis, *Education and Social Change in Nineteenth-Century Massachusetts* (1980); Vincent P. Lannie, *Public Money and Parochial Education* (1968); Robert M. Mennel, *Thorns and Thistles: Juvenile Delinquency in the U.S., 1825–1840* (1973); Donald H. Meyer, *The Instructed Conscience: The Shaping of the American National Ethic* (1972); Raymond L. Moll, *Poverty in New York, 1783–1825* (1971); Roger Lane, *Policing the City, Boston, 1822–1855* (1967); R. Lane, *Violent Death in the City: Suicide, Accident and Murder in Nineteenth Century Philadelphia* (1979); W. David Lewis, *From Newgate to Dannemora: The Rise of the Penitentiary in New York, 1790–1845* (1965); Robert S. Pickett, *House of Refuge: Origins of Juvenile Reform in New York State, 1815–1847* (1969); Leonard D. Richards, *"Gentlemen of Property and Standing": Anti-Abolitionist Mobs in Jacksonian America* (1970); James F. Richardson, *The New York Police: Colonial Times to 1901* (1970); J. F. Richardson, *Urban Police in the United States* (1974); David Rothman, *The Discovery of the*

Asylum (1971); Lee Soltow and Edward Stevens, *The Rise of Literacy and the Common School in the United States* (1981); David B. Tyack, *The One Best System: A History of American Urban Education* (1974); Paul O. Weinbaum, *Mobs and Demagogues: The New York Response to Collective Violence in the Early Nineteenth Century* (1979); Rush Welter, *Popular Education and Democratic Thought in America* (1962); Thomas A. Woody, *A History of Women's Education in the United States* (1929).

RADICAL REFORM

Howard Bell, *A Survey of the Negro Convention Movement, 1830–1861* (1969); Barbara J. Berg, *The Remembered Gate: Origins of American Feminism, The Woman and the City, 1800–1860* (1978); Arthur E. Bestor, Jr., *Backwoods Utopias: The Sectarian and Owenite Phases of Communitarian Socialism in America, 1663–1829* (1950); R. J. M. Blackett, *Building an Antislavery Wall: Black Americans in the Atlantic Abolitionist Movement* (1983); Frederick J. Blue, *Free Soilers: Third Party Politics, 1848–1854* (1973); Maren Lockwood Carden, *Oneida: Utopian Community to Modern Corporation* (1969); Nancy F. Cott, *The Bonds of Womanhood: "Woman's Sphere" in New England, 1780–1835* (1977); David Brion Davis, *The Problem of Slavery in the Age of Revolution, 1770–1823* (1975); D. B. Davis, *Slavery and Human Progress* (1984); Carl N. Degler, *At Odds: Women and the Family from the Revolution to the Present* (1981); Ann Douglas, *The Feminization of American Culture* (1977); Donald Egbert and Stow Persons, eds., *Socialism in American Life* (1952); Barbara Leslie Epstein, *The Politics of Domesticity: Women, Evangelism, and Temperance in Nineteenth-Century America* (1981); Michael Fellman, *The Unbounded Frame: Freedom and Community in Nineteenth-Century American Utopianism* (1973); Lawrence Foster, *Religion and Sexuality: Three American Communal Experiments of the Nineteenth Century* (1981); George Fredrickson, *The Black Image in the White Mind* (1971); Larry Gara, *Liberty Line: The Legend of the Underground Railroad* (1961); J. F. C. Harrison, *Quest for a New Moral World: Owen and the Owenites in Britain and America* (1969); Blanche Hersh, *The Slavery of Sex: Feminist Abolitionists in Nineteenth Century America* (1978); Nancy Hewitt, *Women's Activism and Social Change* (1984); Mark Holloway, *Heavens on Earth: Utopian Communities in America* (1966); Rosabeth Moss Kanter, *Commitment and Community: Communes and Utopias in Sociological Perspective* (1972); Louis J. Kern *An Ordered Love: Sex Roles and Sexuality in Victorian Utopias* (1981); Aileen Kraditor, *Means and Ends in American Abolitionism* (1969); Alma Lutz, *Crusade for Freedom: Women of the Antislavery Movement* (1968); Carleton Mabee, *Black Freedom* (1970); Keith Melder, *Beginnings of Sisterhood, 1800–1850* (1977); Raymond L. Muncy, *Sex and Marriage in Utopian Communities* (1973); Charles Nordhoff, *The Communistic Societies of the United States* (1965); John Humphrey Noyes, *History of*

American Socialisms (1870); Jane H. and William H. Pease, *They Who Would Be Free: Blacks' Search For Freedom, 1831–1861* (1974); W. H. Pease, *Black Utopia: Negro Communal Experiment in America* (1963); Lewis Perry and Michael Fellman, eds., *Antislavery Reconsidered* (1979); Benjamin Quarles, *Black Abolitionists* (1968); Nicholas V. Riasanovsky, *The Teachings of Charles Fourier* (1969); C. Duncan Rice, *The Rise and Fall of Black Slavery* (1975); Mary P. Ryan, *Cradle of the Middle Class: The Family in Oneida County, New York, 1790–1865* (1981); M. P. Ryan, *Womanhood in America* (1983); Richard H. Sewell, *Ballots for Freedom* (1976); Gerald Sorin, *Abolitionism: A New Perspective* (1972); Phillip J. Staudenraus, *The African Colonization Movement* (1961); James Brewer Stewart, *Holy Warriors: The Abolitionists and American Society* (1976); Frederick B. Tolles, ed., *Slavery and "The Woman Question"* (1952); William Wilson, *The Angel and the Serpent* (1964); Nancy Woloch, *Women and the American Experience* (1984); Arthur Zilbersmit, *The First Emancipation: The Abolition of Slavery in the North* (1967); Lois Banner, *Elizabeth Cady Stanton* (1980); Frank L. Byrne, *Prophet of Prohibition: Neal Dow and His Crusade* (1961); Charles Crowe, *George Ripley: Transcendentalist and Utopian Socialist* (1969); Merton Dillon, *Elijah Lovejoy, Abolitionist Editor* (1961); Isabelle Webb Entrekin, *Sarah Josepha Hale and Godey's Lady's Book* (1946); Edward Farrison, *William Wells Brown: Author and Reformer* (1969); Betty Fladeland, *James Gilespie Birney: Slaveholder to Abolitionist* (1955); Frank O. Gatell, *John Gorham Palfrey and the New England Conscience* (1963); Cyril Griffith, *African Dream: Martin Delany and the Emergence of Pan-African Thought* (1975); Ralph Volney Harlow, *Gerrit Smith, Philanthropist and Reformer* (1939); Gerda Lerner, *The Grimke Sisters from South Carolina: Pioneers for Women's Rights and Abolition* (1967); Katherine Du Pre Lumpkin, *The Emancipation of Angelina Grimke* (1974); Helen E. Marshall, *Dorothea Dix: Forgotten Samaritan* (1937); Waldo E. Martin, Jr., *The Mind of Frederick Douglass* (1984); Milton Meltzer, *Tongue of Flame: The Life of Lydia Maria Child* (1965); Walter M. Merrill, *Against Wind and Tide: A Biography of William Lloyd Garrison* (1963); Jonathan Messerli, *Horace Mann: A Biography* (1972); Jane H. and William Pease, *Bound With Them in Chains: A Biographical History of the Antislavery Movement* (1972); Benjamin Quarles, *Frederick Douglass* (1948); Richard H. Sewall, *John P. Hale and the Politics of Abolition* (1965); Katherine Kish Sklar, *Catharine Beecher: A Study in American Domesticity* (1973); James Brewer Stewart, *Joshua Giddings and the Tactics of Radical Politics* (1970); John L. Thomas, *The Liberator, William Lloyd Garrison* (1963); and *Theodore Weld, Crusader for Freedom* (1950); Robert David Thomas, *The Man Who Would Be Perfect* (1977); Nancy Tomes, *A Generous Confidence: Thomas Story Kirkbride and the Art of Asylum-Keeping* (1984); Bertram Wyatt-Brown, *Lewis Tappan and the Evangelical War against Slavery* (1969).

The Divided North, The Divided South

COTTON MANUFACTURE.

Fig. 1. DOUBLING MACHINE.

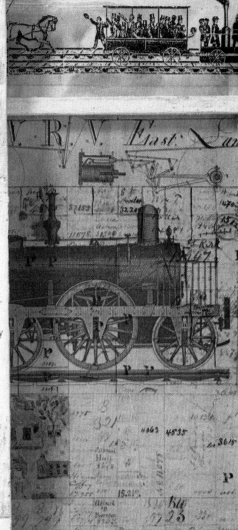

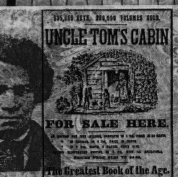

When was a little

In the early 1790s, slavery appeared to be a dying institution. Slave imports into the New World were declining and slave prices were falling because the crops (tobacco, rice, and indigo) grown by slaves did not generate enough wealth to pay for their upkeep. In Maryland and Virginia, planters were replacing tobacco, a crop that used a slave labor force, with wheat and corn, which did not. At the same time, leading Southerners, including Thomas Jefferson, denounced slavery as a source of debt, economic stagnation, and moral dissipation. A French traveler reported that people throughout the South "are constantly talking of abolishing slavery, of contriving some other means of cultivating their estates."

Then a mechanical wizard from Massachusetts gave slavery a new lease on life. The young man's name was Eli Whitney. Even as a teenager, Whitney was well known for his mechanical genius. At the age of twelve, he produced a violin that "made tolerable good musick." At fifteen he took over his father's workshop in Westborough, Massachusetts, and began manufacturing nails. By the time he was eighteen, he had begun to produce other items that were in demand, including hat pins and walking sticks. Young Whitney hoped to become something more than a clever mechanic, and at the age of twenty-three he abandoned his father's workshop and entered college at Yale.

In 1792, just after his graduation, Whitney made a fateful decision. He accepted a tutoring job on a South Carolina plantation. His journey south was filled with disasters. During the boat trip, he became sea sick. Before he could recover, his boat ran aground on rocks near New York City. Then, while seeking another boat, he contracted smallpox. The only good thing to happen during his journey was that he was befriended by a charming southern widow named Catharine Greene, whose late husband, General Nathanael Greene, had been one of George Washington's leading generals during the American Revolution. When he arrived in the South, Whitney discovered that his promised salary as a tutor had been cut in half. He quit the job and decided to accept Mrs. Greene's invitation to visit her plantation near Savannah while he considered his future plans.

During Whitney's visit, a group of planters visited the Greene plantation and bemoaned the sorry state of southern agriculture. They said that they desperately needed a money crop to pay off their debts. Cotton was the obvious choice, because England's expanding textile mills devoured every bit of the crop they could purchase. However, the kind of cotton that grew best in Georgia—green seed, short-staple crop—was useless because it took ten hours for a person to separate one pound of lint from the small tough seeds. "Gentlemen," said Mrs. Greene, "tell your troubles to Mr. Whitney, he can make anything."

In just ten days Whitney devised an ingenious contraption for removing seeds from the cotton boll. Within a month, Whitney's cotton engine (gin for short) could separate fiber from seeds faster than fifty men working by hand.

Eli Whitney

Historians continue to debate whether Whitney himself invented the cotton gin or whether he got the original idea from someone else, perhaps a slave. There can be no doubt, however, that Whitney's cotton gin revitalized southern slavery. Between 1792, when Whitney arrived on the Greene plantation, and 1794 the price of slaves doubled. By 1825 field hands, who brought $500 apiece in 1794, were worth $1500. As the price of slaves grew, so, too, did the number of slaves. During the first decade of the nineteenth century, the number of slaves in the United States increased by thirty-three percent; during the following decade, the slave population grew another twenty-nine percent.

At the same time that the institution of slavery expanded in the South, it declined in the North. In 1780 Pennsylvania adopted the first emancipation law in the New World. Judicial decision freed slaves in Massachusetts and New Hampshire, and other northern states adopted gradual emancipation acts. By the beginning of the nineteenth century, the new republic was fatefully divided into a slave section and a free section.

A DIVIDED CULTURE

By 1860 most Americans believed that the Mason-Dixon line divided the nation into two distinct civilizations. Each region had its own "manners, habits, customs, principles, and ways of thinking."

A belief that the cultures of the North and South were fundamentally different was not a new idea on the eve of the Civil War. During the bitter political battles of the 1790s, New England Federalists pictured the South as a backward, economically stagnant society in which manual labor was degraded and wealth was dissipated in personal luxury. Many Southern Republicans countered by denouncing the corrupt, grasping, materialistic society of the North.

Despite obvious differences, the pre-Civil War North and South were in certain respects strikingly similar. Both sections were predominantly rural. Both had booming economies and were engaged in speculation and trade. Both were rapidly expanding westward. Both enacted democratic political reforms and voted for the same national political parties.

Despite these similarities, most Americans thought of their nation as divided into two halves, a commercial civilization and an agrarian civilization, each operating according to entirely different sets of values. Many factors contributed to this sense of sectional difference. Diction, work habits, diet, and labor systems distinguished the two sections. One section included slave-based agriculture; the other emphasized commercial agriculture based on family farms and a developing industrial sector resting upon wage labor.

In the North, the population was more than fifty percent greater than in the South, urbanization was far more advanced, European immigrants arrived in far greater numbers, and

In 1812, Rochester, New York, did not exist. Two decades later, as a result of the construction of the Erie Canal, Rochester was the fastest growing city in the United States.

commerce, finance, manufacturing, and transportation were more developed. In the South, commercial and financial institutions were less developed, transportation facilities were more primitive, and cities were smaller and fewer in number. Most important of all, a third of the South's population lived in slavery.

THE EMERGENCE OF A NEW INDUSTRIAL ORDER IN THE NORTH

To all outward appearances, life in the North in 1790 was not much different than it had been in 1740. The vast majority of the people—over ninety percent—still lived and worked on farms or in small rural villages. Not one Northerner in thirteen worked in either trade or manufacturing.

Conditions of life remained primitive. In 1790, as in 1740, the typical house—a single-

When hay had to be gathered or quilts assembled or apples picked or corn husked, farm families from miles around gathered together to assist one another. This "haying bee" took place in 1825 in Southbridge, Massachusetts.

story one or two room log or wood frame structure—was small, sparsely furnished, and afforded little personal privacy. Sleeping, eating, and work spaces were not sharply differentiated, and mirrors, curtains, upholstered or padded chairs, carpets, desks, and book cases were luxuries enjoyed only by wealthy families.

Even prosperous farming or merchant families lived simply. Many families ate meals out of a common pot or bowl—just as their ancestors had in the seventeenth century. Standards of cleanliness remained exceedingly low. Bed bugs were constant sleeping companions and people seldom bathed or washed their clothes.

Daily life was physically demanding. Most families made their own cloth, clothing, and soap. Because they lacked matches, they lit fires by striking a flint again and again until a spark ignited some tinder. Lacking indoor plumbing, chamber pots had to be emptied and even dishes were rarely washed. Homes were typically heated by a single open fireplace and illuminated by candles. Housewives hand-carried water from a pump, well, or stream and threw dirty water or slops out the window or

carried them outside. Family members hauled grain to a local grist mill or milled it by hand. They cut, split, and gathered wood, and fed it into a fireplace.

In 1860, as in 1790, the North remained predominantly a rural agricultural society, but profound and far-reaching changes had taken place. Subsistence agriculture had declined and been replaced by commercial agriculture. Household production had been supplanted by centralized manufacturing outside the home, and nonagricultural employment had begun to overtake agricultural employment. By 1860 nearly half of the North's population made a living outside of agriculture.

These economic transformations are all aspects of the Industrial Revolution—a revolution which reverberated through every aspect of life. It raised living standards, transformed the work process, and relocated hundreds of thousands of people across oceans and from rural farms and villages into fast-growing industrial cities.

The most obvious consequence of this revolution was an impressive increase in wealth, per capita income, and commercial, middle-class job opportunities. Between 1800 and 1860, output increased twelvefold and purchasing power doubled. New middle-class occupational opportunities proliferated. Increasing numbers of men found work as agents, bankers, brokers, retail and sales clerks, merchants, professionals, and traders.

Living standards rose sharply, at least for the rapidly expanding middle class. Instead of making cloth at home, families began to buy it. Instead of hand milling grains or making clothing, an increasing number of families began to buy processed grains and ready-made clothes. Kerosene lamps replaced candles as a source of light; coal replaced wood as fuel; friction matches replaced crude flints. Even poorer families had begun to cook their food on cast-iron cookstoves and heat their rooms with individual room heaters. The advent of railroads and the first canned foods brought variety to the northern diet year round.

Physical comfort increased markedly. Padded seats, spring mattresses, and pillows became more common. By 1860 many urban middle-class families had central heating, indoor plumbing, and wall-to-wall carpeting.

Houses became larger and more affordable. The invention, in the 1830s, of the balloon frame—a lightweight house frame made up of boards nailed together—as well as prefabricated doors, window frames, shutters and sashes, resulted in larger and more affordable houses. The cost of building a house fell by forty percent, and two-story houses, with four or five rooms, became increasingly common.

A revolution in values and sensibility accompanied the changes that took place in standards of living. Standards of cleanliness and personal hygiene rose sharply. People bathed more frequently, washed their clothes more often, and dusted, swept, and scrubbed their houses more regularly. Standards of propriety also rose. The respectable classes blew their noses into handkerchiefs, instead of wiping them with their sleeves, and disposed of their spittle in spitoons.

Pre-Civil War Northerners regarded all of these changes as signs of progress. A host of northern political leaders, mainly Whigs and

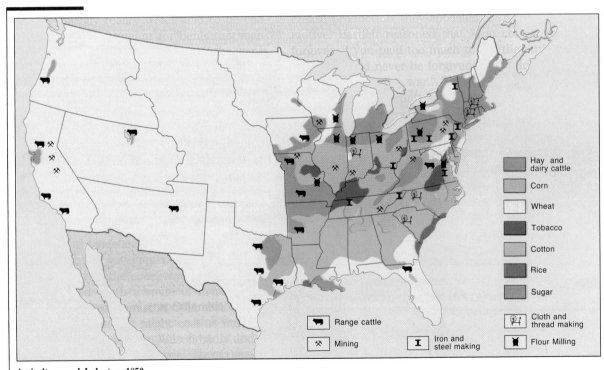

Agriculture and Industry, 1850

Legend:
- Hay and dairy cattle
- Corn
- Wheat
- Tobacco
- Cotton
- Rice
- Sugar
- Range cattle
- Mining
- Iron and steel making
- Cloth and thread making
- Flour Milling

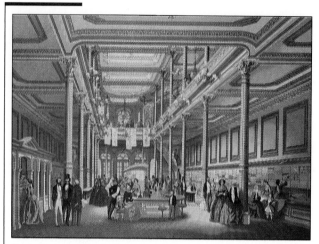

Opulent shops like L. J. Levy and Company's Dry Goods Store appeared in northern cities in increasing numbers during the 1850s.

later Republicans, celebrated the North as a region of bustling cities, factories, railroads, and prosperous farms and independent craftsmen—a stark contrast to an impoverished, backward, slave South, suffering from soil exhaustion and economic and social decline.

Although the industrial revolution brought many material benefits, critics decried its negative consequences. Radical labor leaders deplored the bitter suffering of factory and sweatshop workers, the breakdown of craft skills, the vulnerability of urban workers to layoffs and economic crises, and the maldistribution of wealth and property. Conservatives lamented the disintegration of an older household-centered economy, in which husbands, wives, and children had labored together. Southern slaveowners, like George Fitzhugh, argued that the North's growing class of free laborers were slaves of the marketplace, suffering even more insecurity than the South's chattel slaves, who were provided for in sickness and old age.

The Eve of the Industrial Revolution

In 1790 most farm families in the rural North produced little more than they needed for themselves. Except for a few necessities such as iron goods, rum, salt, and sugar, farm families, often with the assistance of neighbors, pro-

duced most of what they needed to live. Instead of using money to purchase necessities, farm families entered into complex exchange relationships with relatives and neighbors and used barter to acquire the goods they needed.

Skilled craftsmen, assisted by an apprentice or two and an occasional journeyman, produced specialized and luxury goods. Such crafts as blacksmithing, bootmaking, carriage-building, leather-working, paper-making, and woodworking were performed by hand in a small shop or a home. The North's few industries were tiny. Iron foundries produced just 30,000 tons of iron a year. All the North's shoemakers produced barely 80,000 pairs of shoes annually.

By the 1820s a new pattern had begun to emerge. Farm families raised cash crops for sale and used the proceeds to buy goods produced by others. Independent craftsmen gave way to an increasingly industrial economy of wage laborers and salaried employees. As late as 1800, less than ten percent of the labor force was composed of "employees" who worked for wages. By 1820 the number of wage earning employees had quadrupled.

The Transformation of the Rural Countryside

In 1828 Dexter Whittemore, the owner of a small country store in rural Fitzwilliam, New Hampshire, seized on an opportunity to make money. Braided hats were the rage, and the New Hampshire shopkeeper knew that he could sell as many hats as he could get his hands on. He arranged for local farm families to pick up split palm leaves from his store, braid the leaves into hats, and return them to the store, in exchange for credits on the store's ledgers. By the early 1830s Whittemore was marketing about 23,000 hats annually, and by the 1850s the figure had climbed to 80,000.

For cash-poor farm families, the opportunity to earn a cash income was a godsend. Roxanna Bowker Stowell, one of Whittemore's hatmakers, pleaded with the storekeeper for a chance to work. "Money is so very scarce and we must have some," she told him. Each month she earned a dollar by braiding five hats—money that could be used to pay off debts, fi-

As late as the 1820s, most manufacturing took place by hand in small shops or mills. By the 1840s and 1850s, large-scale factory production had grown increasingly common.

nance farm improvements, purchase household goods, or send a child to school.

Beginning in the late eighteenth century, household industries provided work for thousands of men, women, and children in rural areas. Shopkeepers or master craftsmen supplied farm families with raw materials, paid piece rates, and marketed the product. Among the goods produced by farm families for sale were towels, sheets, table linens, jeans, coverlets, socks, gloves, carpets, thread, nails, and farm utensils. The quantity of goods produced by farm families was incredible. In New Hampshire forty families produced 13,000 pounds of maple sugar annually. In 1809 farm families near Philadelphia produced more than 230,000 yards of cloth for sale, four times the amount of cloth produced by the area's textile factories. In Massachusetts, farm households produced more than 100,000 pairs of shoes a year. As early as 1792, Alexander Hamilton reported that the rural areas surrounding America's cities had become "a vast scene of household manufacturing . . . in many instances to an extent not only sufficient for the supply of the families in which they are made, but for sale, and even for export."

Commercial agriculture replaced subsistence farming. Farm families found that they could raise their standard of living by producing for sale and using the earnings to buy goods like candles, medicines, and soap previously made by farm wives. In New Hampshire farmers raised sheep for wool; in western Massachusetts they began to fatten cattle and pigs for sale to Boston; in eastern Pennsylvania, they specialized in dairying.

After 1820, the household industries that had employed thousands of women and children began to disappear. Manufacturing increasingly moved into shops and factories in cities. New England farm families began to buy their shoes, furniture, cloth, and sometimes even their clothes, ready-made. Small rural factories closed their doors and village artisans who produced for local markets found themselves unable to compete against cheaper city-made goods. As local opportunities declined, many long-settled farm areas suffered a sharp loss of population. Convinced that "agriculture is not the road to wealth, nor honor, nor to happiness," thousands of young people left farm fields for cities.

The Disruption of the Artisan System of Labor

As late as the 1820s, skilled craftsmen, known as *artisans* or *mechanics*, performed most manufacturing in small towns and larger cities. They made shoes and men's clothing, built houses, and set type. These craftsmen manufactured goods in traditional ways—by hand in their own home or in a small shop located nearby—and marketed the goods they produced. Mathew Carey, a Philadelphia newspaperman, personified the early nineteenth-century artisan-craftsman. He not only composed articles and editorials that appeared in his newspaper, he also set the paper's type, operated the printing press, and hawked the newspaper.

The artisan class was divided into three subgroups. At the highest level were self-employed master craftsmen. They were assisted by skilled journeymen, who owned their own tools but lacked the capital to set up their own shops, and by apprentices, teenaged boys who typically served a three year term in exchange for training in a craft.

Urban artisans did not draw a sharp separation between home and work. A master shoemaker made shoes in a ten-foot square shed located behind his house. A printer bound books or printed newspapers in a room below his family's living quarters. Typically, a master

craftsman lived in the same house with his assistants. The household of Everard Peck, a Rochester, New York, publisher, was not unusual. It included his wife, his children, his brother, his business partner, a day laborer, and four journeyman printers and bookbinders.

Nor did urban artisans draw a sharp division between work and leisure. Work patterns tended to be irregular and were frequently interrupted by breaks during which masters and journeymen would drink whiskey or other alcoholic beverages. During slow periods or periodic layoffs, workingmen enjoyed fishing trips and sleigh rides, cockfights and bear-baiting, as well as drinking and gambling at local taverns. Artisans often took unscheduled time off to attend boxing matches, horse races, and exhibitions by traveling musicians and acrobats.

Between 1790 and the Civil War, new patterns of work emerged that undermined the older way of life. Skilled tasks, previously performed by skilled craftsmen, were divided and subcontracted out to less expensive unskilled laborers. Small shops were replaced by large

Although boxing was illegal in most parts of the country, it remained a popular form of entertainment.

"machineless" factories, which made the relationship between employer and employee increasingly impersonal. Many masters abandoned their supervisory role to foremen and contractors and substituted unskilled teenaged boys for journeymen. New words, descriptive of the new relationships—like employer, employee, boss, and foreman—suddenly entered the language.

During the early nineteenth century, the work process, especially in the building trades, printing, and the rapidly expanding consumer manufacturing industries such as tailoring and shoemaking, was radically reorganized. The changes that took place in the shoemaking industry in Rochester, New York, during the 1820s and 1830s illustrate this process. Instead of making an entire shoe himself, a master would fit a customer, rough-cut the leather uppers, and then send the uppers and soles to a boarding house, where a journeyman would shape the leather. The journeyman would then send the pieces to a binder, a woman who worked in her own home, who would sew the shoes together. Finally, she would send the shoe to a store, where it would be sold to a customer. Tremendous gains in productivity sprang from the division and specialization of labor.

By 1850, the older household-based economy, in which assistants lived in the homes of their employers, had disappeared. Young men moved out of rooms in their master's home into hotels and boarding houses in distinct working-class neighborhoods. The older view that each workman should be attached to a particular master, who would supervise his behavior and assume responsibility for his welfare, declined. The older paternalistic view was replaced by a new conception of labor as a commodity, like cotton, that could be acquired or disposed of according to the laws of supply and demand.

The Introduction of the Factory System

In 1789 the Pennsylvania legislature placed an advertisement in English newspapers offering a cash bounty to any English textile worker who would migrate to the state. Samuel Slater, who

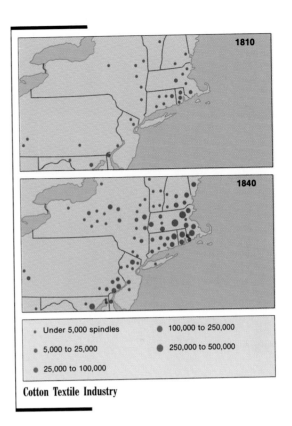

Cotton Textile Industry

Key:
- Under 5,000 spindles
- 5,000 to 25,000
- 25,000 to 100,000
- 100,000 to 250,000
- 250,000 to 500,000

was just finishing an apprenticeship in a Derbyshire textile mill, read the ad. He went to London, booked passage to America, and landed in Philadelphia. There he learned that Moses Brown, a Quaker merchant, had just completed a mill in Pawtucket, Rhode Island, and needed a manager. Slater applied for the job and received it, along with a promise that if he made the factory a success he would receive all the business's profits, less the cost and interest on the machinery.

On December 21, 1790, the mill opened. Seven boys and two girls, between the ages of seven and twelve, operated the factory's seventy-two spindles. Slater soon discovered that these children, "constantly employed under the immediate inspection of a [supervisor], " could produce three times as much as whole families working in their homes. To keep the children awake and alert, Slater whipped them with a leather strap or sprinkled them with water. On Sundays the children attended a special school Slater founded for their education.

Samuel Slater's textile mill, which opened in Pawtucket, Rhode Island, in 1790, was the first successful factory in the United States.

The opening of Slater's mill marked the beginning of a widespread movement to consolidate manufacturing operations under a single roof. During the last years of the eighteenth century, merchants and master craftsmen, discontented about the inefficiency of their workforce, created the nation's first modern factories. Within these centralized workshops, employers closely supervised employees, synchronized work to the clock, and punished infractions of rules with heavy fines or dismissal. In 1820 just 350,000 Americans worked in factories or mills. Four decades later, on the eve of the Civil War, the number soared to 2 million.

Child labor offered one solution to the problem of acquiring an inexpensive and reliable factory labor force. During the early phases of industrialization, textile mills and factories producing agricultural tools, metal goods, nails, and rubber had a ravenous appetite for cheap teenage laborers. In many mechanized industries, from one-quarter to over half of the workforce was made up of young men or women under the age of twenty.

The unmarried daughters of farmers provided a particularly important workforce in the first stages of industrialization. During the first half of the nineteenth century, unmarried women made up a majority of the workforce in cotton textile mills and a substantial minority of workers in factories manufacturing ready-made clothing, furs, hats, shoes, and umbrellas. Women workers were also employed in significant numbers in the manufacture of buttons, furniture, gloves, gunpowder, shovels, and tobacco.

Many women found the new work opportunities available in factories exhilarating. Eleven-year-old Lucy Larcom went off to the Lowell textile mill enthusiastically: "The novelty of it made it seem easy, and it really was not hard, just to change the bobbins on the spinning-frames every three quarters of an hour or so. . . . The intervals were spent frolicking around among the spinning-frames, teasing and talking to the older girls, or entertaining ourselves with games and stories in a corner."

Unlike farm work or domestic service, employment in a mill offered female companionship and an independent income. Wages were twice what a woman could make as a seamstress, tailoress, or schoolteacher. Furthermore, most mill girls viewed the work as only a temporary measure. Most worked in the mills less than four years, and frequently interrupted their stints in the mill for several months at a time with trips back home.

By the 1830s, as competition in the textile industry increased, conditions within the mills deteriorated. Employers cut wages, lengthened the workday, and required mill workers to tend four looms instead of just two. Hannah Borden, a Fall River, Massachusetts, textile worker, was required to have her loom running at 5 A.M. She was given an hour for breakfast and half an hour for lunch. Her workday ended at 7:30 P.M., fourteen-and-a-half hours after her workday had begun. For a six-day work week, she received between $2.50 and $3.50.

The mill girls militantly protested the wage cuts. In 1834 and again in 1836, the mill girls went out on strike. An open letter spelled out the workers' complaints: "sixteen females [crowded] into the same hot, ill-ventilated attic"; a workday "two or three hours longer a day than is done in Europe"; and workers compelled to "stand so long at the machinery . . . that varicose veins, dropsical swelling of the feet and limbs, and prolapsus uter[us], diseases that end only with life, are not rare but common occurrences."

During the 1840s, fewer and fewer native-born women were willing to work in the mills. "Slavers," which were long, black wagons that criss-crossed the Vermont and New Hampshire countryside in search of mill hands, arrived in Rhode Island and Massachusetts mill towns empty. Increasingly, employers replaced the native-born millgirls with a new class of permanent factory operatives: immigrant women from Ireland.

Labor Protests

In 1806 journeymen shoemakers in New York City organized one of the nation's first labor strikes. The workers' chief demands were not higher wages and shorter hours. Instead, they protested the changing conditions of work. They staged a "turn-out" or "stand-out," as a strike was then called, to protest the use of cheap unskilled and apprentice labor and the subdivision and subcontracting of work. To ensure that journeymen did not resume work, a "tramping committee" patrolled the shops. The strike ended when the city's largest shoe employers asked municipal authorities to criminally prosecute the shoemakers for conspiracy to obstruct trade. A court found the journeymen shoemakers guilty and fined them one dollar plus court costs.

By the 1820s, a growing number of journeymen were protesting the practices of employers, which, they charged, were undermining the independence of workingmen, reducing them to the status of "a humiliating servile dependency, incompatible with the inherent natural equality of men." Unlike their counterparts in Britain, American journeymen did not protest against the introduction of machinery into the workplace. Instead, they protested wage reductions, declining standards of workmanship, and the increased use of unskilled and semiskilled workers. Journeymen charged that manufacturers had reduced "them to degradation and the loss of that self-respect which had made the

In the 1840s, young immigrant women, mainly from Ireland, began to replace Yankee farm girls in the early textile mills.

mechanics and laborers the pride of the world." They insisted that they were the true producers of wealth, and that manufacturers, who did not engage in manual labor, were unjust expropriators of wealth.

In an attempt to raise wages, restrict hours, and reduce competition from unskilled workers, skilled journeymen formed the nation's first labor unions. In larger eastern cities like Boston, New York, and Philadelphia, as well as smaller western cities like Cincinnati, Louisville, and Pittsburgh, they formed local trade unions and city trades' assemblies. House carpenters, handloom weavers, comb makers, shoemakers, and printers formed national societies to uphold uniform wage standards. In 1834 journeymen established the National Trades' Union, the first organization of American wageearners on a national scale. By 1836 union membership had climbed to 300,000.

These early unions faced bitter hostility. To counter the influence of the newly formed unions, employers banded together in employers' associations, which claimed that unions' methods were "most obnoxious, coercive, and detrimental to the peace, prosperity and best interests of the community."

During the 1830s, rapid inflation and mounting competition for jobs encouraged the growth of unions. By the late 1830s, an estimated 300,000 American workers were union members.

Employers also requested prosecution of unions as criminal combinations. In 1806, in a case involving Philadelphia shoemakers, a Pennsylvania court established an important precedent by ruling that a labor union was guilty of criminal conspiracy if workers struck to obtain wages higher than those set by custom. Other court decisions declared unions to be illegal constraints on trade. In 1842, in the landmark case *Commonwealth* v. *Hunt*, the Massachusetts Supreme Court established a new precedent by recognizing the right of unions to exist and restricting the use of the criminal conspiracy doctrine.

In addition to establishing the nation's first labor unions, journeymen during the 1830s also formed political organizations, known as Working Men's parties, as well as mutual benefit societies, libraries, educational institutions, and producers' and consumers' cooperatives. Working men and women published at least sixty-eight labor papers, and they agitated for free public education, reduction of the work day, and abolition of capital punishment, state mili-

tias, and imprisonment for debt. Following the panic of 1837, land reform was one of labor's chief demands. One hundred sixty acres of free public land for those who would actually settle the land was the demand, and "Vote Yourself a Farm" became the popular slogan.

The Movement for a Ten-Hour Day

The greatest success of pre-Civil War working men and women was the establishment of a ten-hour day in all the major cities of the Northeast except Boston. In 1835 carpenters, masons, and stonecutters in Boston staged a seven month strike in favor of a ten-hour day. The strikers demanded that employers reduce excessively long hours worked in the summer and spread them throughout the year. Quickly, the movement for a ten-hour workday spread to Philadelphia, where carpenters, bricklayers, plasterers, masons, leather dressers, and blacksmiths went on strike. Parades and bands marched through the city carrying banners which read "From 6 to 6." Textile workers in Paterson, New Jersey, were the first factory operatives to strike for a reduction in work hours. Soon, women textile operatives in Lowell added their voices to the call for a ten-hour day, contending that such a law would "lengthen the lives of those employed, by giving them a greater opportunity to breathe the pure air of heaven" as well as provide "more time for mental and moral cultivation."

In 1840 the federal government introduced a ten-hour workday on public works projects. In 1847 New Hampshire became the first state to adopt a ten-hour day law. It was followed by Pennsylvania in 1848. Both states' laws, however, included a clause that allowed workers to voluntarily agree to work more than a ten-hour day. Despite the limitations of these state laws, agitation for a ten-hour day did result in a reduction in the average number of hours worked, to approximately 11.5 by 1850.

The Laboring Poor

In January of 1850, police arrested John McFeaing in Newburyport, Massachusetts, for stealing wood from the wharves. McFeaing pleaded necessity and a public investigation was conducted. Investigators found McFeaing's wife and four children living "in the extremity of misery. The children were all scantily supplied with clothing and not one had a shoe to his feet. There was not a stick of firewood or scarcely a morsel of food in the house, and everything betokened the most abject want and misery."

The quickening pace of trade and finance during the early nineteenth century not only increased the demand for middle-class clerks and shopkeepers, it also dramatically increased demand for unskilled workers, such as cartmen, coal heavers, day laborers, deliverymen, dockworkers, draymen, longshoremen, packers, and porters. Two facts shaped the lives of these unskilled workers. One was that their families earned incomes that hovered near what contemporaries defined as the poverty line. The other was that even this meager income depended on the contributions of more than one family breadwinner.

In 1851 Horace Greeley, editor of the New York *Tribune*, estimated the minimum weekly budget needed to support a family of five. Essential expenditures for rent, food, fuel, and clothing amounted to $10.37. In that year, a shoemaker or a printer earned just $4 to $6 a week, a male textile operative $6.50 a week, and an unskilled laborer just $1 a week. The only manual laborers able to earn Greeley's weekly budget were blacksmiths and machinists.

To make matters worse, blue collar workers suffered frequent periods of unemployment. In Massachusetts upward of forty percent of all workers were out of a job for part of a year, usually for four months or more. Fluctuations in demand, inclement weather, interruptions in transportation, technological displacement, fire, injury, and illness all could leave workers jobless.

Typically, a male laborer earned just two-thirds of his family's income. The other third was earned by wives and children. Many married women performed work that could take place in the home, such as making embroideries and artificial flowers, tailoring garments, or doing laundry. The wages of children were critical for a family's standard of living. Children under the age of fifteen contributed twenty percent of the income of many working-class families. These children worked, not because their parents were heartless, but because children's earnings were absolutely essential to the family's survival.

To provide protection against temporary unemployment, many working-class families scrimped and saved in order to buy a house or a garden. In Newburyport, Massachusetts, many workingmen bought farm property on the edge of town. On New York City's East Side, many families kept goats and pigs. Ownership of a house was a particularly valuable source of security, since a family could always obtain an extra income by taking in boarders and lodgers.

Immigrants: The New Working Class

During the summer of 1845, a "blight of unusual character" devastated Ireland's potato crop, the basic staple in the Irish diet. A few days after potatoes were dug from the ground, they began to turn into a slimy, decaying, blackish "mass of rottenness." Expert panels, convened to investigate the blight's cause, suggested that it was a result of "static electricity" or the smoke that billowed from railroad locomotives or "mortiferous vapours" rising from underground volcanoes. In fact, the cause was a fungus that had traveled from America to Ireland.

"Famine fever"—dysentery, typhus, and infestations of lice—soon spread through the Irish countryside. Observers reported seeing children crying with pain and looking "like skeletons, their features sharpened with hunger and their limbs wasted, so that there was little left but bones, their hands and arms." Masses of bodies were buried without coffins, a few inches below the soil.

Over the next ten years, three-quarters of a million Irish died and another two million left their homeland for Great Britain, Canada, and the United States. Freighters, which carried American and Canadian timber to Europe, offered fares as low as $17 to $20 between Liverpool and Boston—fares subsidized by English landlords eager to be rid of the starving peasants. As many as ten percent of the emigrants perished while still at sea. In 1847, 40,000 or twenty percent of those who set out from Ireland, died along the way. "If crosses and tombs

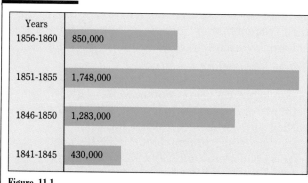

Figure 11.1
Total Immigration, 1840-1860

vests all across Europe failed, and reached 2,600,000 in the 1850s. Most of these immigrants came from Germany, Ireland, and Scandinavia, pushed from their homelands by famine, eviction from farm lands by landlords, and the destruction of traditional handicrafts by factory enterprises. Attracted to the United States by the prospects of economic opportunity and political and religious freedom, many of the European dispossessed braved the voyage across the Atlantic.

By the 1850s, the Irish comprised half the population of Boston and New York, and German immigrants made up a significant proportion of the population in Cincinnati, Milwaukee, and St. Louis. The new immigrants found employment in construction work, domestic service, factories, foundries, and mining. As early as 1855, German and Irish immigrants constituted ninety-six percent of New York City's shoemakers and tailors.

The Divided North

During the decades preceding the Civil War, it was an article of faith among Northerners that

could be erected on water," wrote the United States commissioner for emigration, "the whole route of the emigrant vessels from Europe to America would long since have assumed the appearance of a crowded cemetery."

At the beginning of the nineteenth century, only about 5000 immigrants arrived in the United States per year. During the 1830s, however, immigration climbed sharply as 600,000 immigrants poured into the country. This figure jumped to 1,700,000 in the 1840s, when har-

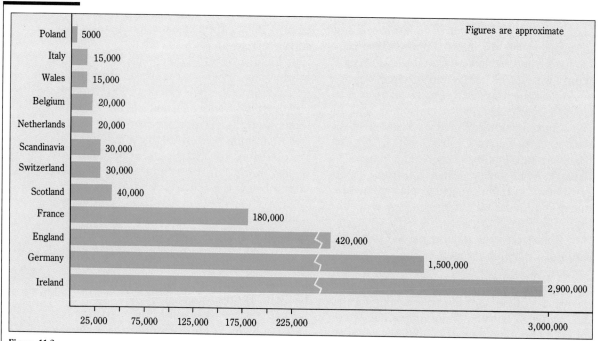

Figure 11.2
Immigration by Country of Origin, 1840-1860

theirs was a society of unprecedented economic equality and opportunity, free of rigid class divisions and glaring extremes of wealth and poverty. It was a land where even a "humble mechanic" had "every means of winning independence which are extended only to rich monopolists in England." How accurate is this picture of the pre-Civil War North as a land of opportunity, where material success was available to all?

In fact, the fraction of wealth held by those at the top of the economic hierarchy appears to have increased substantially before the Civil War. While the proportion of wealth controlled by the richest ten percent of families rose from fifty percent in the 1770s to seventy percent in 1860, the real wages of unskilled northern workers stagnated or, at best, rose at a modest rate. By 1860 half of all free whites held less than one percent of the North's real and personal property, while the richest one percent owned twenty-seven percent of the region's wealth—a level of inequality comparable to that found in early nineteenth-century Europe and greater than that found in the United States today. In towns as different as Stonington, Connecticut, and Chicago, Illinois, between two-thirds and three-quarters of all households owned no property.

The first stages of industrialization and urbanization in the North, far from diminishing social inequality, actually widened class distinctions and intensified social stratification. At the top of the social and economic hierarchy was an elite class of families—linked by intermarriage, membership in exclusive social clubs, and residence in exclusive neighborhoods—as rich as the wealthiest families of Europe. At the bottom were the working poor—immigrants, casual laborers, free blacks, widows, and orphans—who might be thrown out of work at any time. These poor, propertyless, unskilled laborers comprised a vast floating population, which trekked from city to city in search of work. They congregated in urban slums like Boston's Ann Street and New York's Five Points, where starving children begged for pennies and haggard prostitutes plied their trade.

In between these two extremes were family farmers and a rapidly expanding urban middle class of northern workingmen, shopkeepers,

The North's growing cities were characterized by sharp contrasts of wealth and squalor. Only a few blocks separated spacious, well-furnished New York City homes from damp, unlighted cellars where 18,000 slum dwellers resided.

merchants, bankers, agents, and brokers. This was a highly mixed lot of people who ranged from prosperous entrepreneurs and professionals to hardpressed journeymen, who found their craft skills increasingly obsolete.

Does this mean that the pre-Civil War North was not the fluid, "egalitarian" society that Jacksonians claimed? The answer is a qualified "no." In the first place, the North's richest individuals, unlike Europe's aristocracy, were not ostentatiously rich; they were a working class, engaged in commerce, insurance, finance, shipbuilding, manufacturing, landholding, real estate, and the professions. Even more importantly, wealthy Northerners publicly rejected the older Hamiltonian notion that the rich and well-born were superior to the masses of people. During the early decades of the nineteenth century, wealthy Northerners shed the wigs, knee breeches, ruffled shirts, and white-topped boots that had symbolized high social status in

POLICING THE 1830s CITY

During the mid-1830s, a wave of rioting without parallel in earlier American history swept the nation's cities. In April 1834, in New York City, three days of rioting pitting pro-Democrat against pro-Whig gangs erupted during municipal elections. The violence was so intense that the state militia had to be called out to restore order. In July, another New York mob stormed the house of a prominent abolitionist, carried the furniture into the street, and set it on fire. Over the next two days, a mob gutted New York's Episcopal African Church and attacked the homes of many of the city's free blacks. Once again, the state militia had to be called out to quell the disturbances.

Rioting was not confined to New York City. On August 11, 1834, a mob sacked and burned a convent in Charleston, Massachu-setts, near the site of Bunker Hill, followed by a series of impassioned anti-Catholic sermons by the Reverend Lyman Beecher, the father of novelist Harriet Beecher Stowe. Two months later, a pro-slavery riot swept Philadelphia, destroying forty-five homes in the city's black community.

Altogether there were at least 115 incidents of mob violence during the 1830s, compared to just 7 incidents in the 1810s and 21 incidents in the 1820s. *Niles' Register,* a respected newspaper of the time, reported that a "spirit of riot or a disposition to 'take the law into their own hands' prevails in every quarter." Abraham Lincoln, then a young Springfield, Illinois, attorney, echoed these sentiments. "Outrages committed by mobs," he lamented, had become "the every-day news of the times."

Mob violence during the 1830s had a variety of sources. A rate of urban growth faster than any previous decade was one major contributor to social turbulence during the 1830s. Urban populations grew by sixty percent, and the sharp upsurge in foreign immigration heightened religious and ethnic tensions. The number of immigrants entering the country jumped from just 5000 a year at the beginning of the century to over 50,000 annually during the 1830s.

Another source of violence was abolitionism, which emerged at the beginning of the decade and produced a violent reaction. The belief that abolitionists favored miscegenation—interracial marriages of blacks and whites—enflamed anti-Negro sentiment. The mobs that attacked black homes and churches, that burned white abolitionists' homes and businesses, and disrupted antislavery meetings, were often led by "gentlemen of property and standing." These old-stock merchants and bankers feared that abolitionist appeals to the middle class and especially to women and children threatened their patriarchal position in local communities and even in their own families.

The birth of a new two-party political system also contributed to a growing climate of violence. Mob violence frequently broke out on election days as rival Democratic and Whig gangs tried to steal ballot boxes and keep the opposition's voters from reaching local polling places.

Traditional methods of preserving public order proved totally inadequate by the 1830s. The nation's cities were "policed" by a handful of unpaid, untrained, uniformed, and unarmed sheriffs, aldermen, marshals, constables, and nightwatchmen. In New England towns, tithingmen armed with long black sticks tipped with brass patrolled streets searching for drunkards, disorderly children, and wayward servants.

These law officers were not a particularly effective deterrent to crime. Nightwatchmen generally held other jobs during the day and sometimes slept at their posts at night. Sheriffs, aldermen, marshals, and constables made a living not by investigating crime or patrolling city streets but by collecting debts, foreclosing on mortgages, and serving court orders. Victims of crime had to offer a reward if they wanted these unpaid law officers to investigate a case.

This early system of maintaining public order worked in earlier decades when the rates of serious crime were extremely low and cities had informal mechanisms that helped maintain order. Most cities

were small and compact and lacked any distinct working class ghettos. Shopkeepers usually lived at or near their place of business and apprentices, journeymen, and laborers tended to live in or near the house of their master. By the mid-1830s, however, this older pattern of social organization had clearly broken down. The poor and the working class were increasingly segregated by neighborhoods. Youth gangs, organized along ethnic and neighborhood lines, proliferated. Older mechanisms of social control had weakened.

After 1830, drunken brawls, robberies, beatings, and murders all increased in number. Fear of crime led city leaders to look for new ways of preserving public order. Many municipal leaders regarded the new professional police force established in London in 1829 by the British Parliament as a model. London's police, nicknamed "bobbies" after Prime Minister Robert Peel, were trained, full-time professionals. They wore distinctive uniforms to make them visible to the public, patrolled regular beats, and lived in the neighborhoods they patrolled.

Initially, resistance to the establishment of professional police forces in American cities was intense. Taxpayers feared the cost of a police force. Local political machines feared the loss of the night watch as a source of political patronage. By the mid-1840s, however, continued rising crime rates overcame opposition to the establishment of a professional police force.

In New York City, the turning point came following the unsolved murder of Mary Rogers, who worked in a tobacco shop. On July

25, 1841, she disappeared. Three days later, the body of the "beautiful cigar girl" was found in a river. The coroner said she had died not from drowning, but from being abused and murdered by a gang of ruffians. The case aroused intense passion in New York City, prompting vocal demands for an end to waterfront gangs. But the city's constables said that they would only investigate the murder if they were promised a substantial reward. Public opinion was outraged. In 1844 the New York state legislature authorized the establishment of a professional police force to investigate crimes and patrol streets in New York City. Boston appointed its first police officers in 1838 and Philadelphia established a modern police department in 1854.

The life of a mid-nineteenth century police officer was exceptionally dangerous. In many cities, members of gangs, like New York's Bowery B'hoys, Baltimore's Rip Raps, and Philadelphia's Schuylkill Rangers, actually outnumbered police officers and regularly harassed them. Many officers resisted wearing uniforms on the grounds that any distinctive dress made them readily identifiable targets for street gangs. In New York City, four officers were killed in the line of duty in a single year.

After 1850, in large part as a result of more efficient policing, the number of street disorders and homicides in American cities began to drop. Despite the introduction of the Colt revolver and other easily concealed and relatively inexpensive handguns during the middle years of the century, the nation's cities had become far less violent and more orderly places than they had been two decades before.

colonial America and began to dress like other men, signaling their acceptance of an ideal of social equality. One wealthy Northerner succinctly summarized the new ideal: "These phrases, the higher orders, and lower orders, are of European origin, and have no place in our Yankee dialect."

Above all, it was the North's relatively high rates of economic and social mobility that gave substance to a widespread belief in equality of opportunity. Although few rich men were truly "self-made" men who had climbed from "rags to riches," there were many dramatic examples of upward mobility and countless instances of more modest climbs up the ladder of success. Industrialization rapidly increased the number of nonmanual jobs in commerce, industry, and the professions. There were new opportunities for lawyers, bookkeepers, business managers, brokers, and clerks. Giving additional reinforcement to the belief in opportunity was a remarkable rate of physical mobility. Each decade, half the residents of northern communities moved to a new town.

Even at the bottom of the economic hierarchy, prospects for advancement increased markedly after 1850. During the 1830s and 1840s, less than one unskilled worker in ten managed in the course of a decade to advance to a white collar job. After 1850, the percentage moving up doubled. The sons of unskilled laborers were even more likely to advance to skilled or white collar employment. Even the poorest unskilled laborers often were able to acquire a house and a savings account.

It was the reality of physical and economic mobility that convinced the overwhelming majority of Northerners that they lived in a uniquely open society, in which differences in wealth or status were the result of industry and ambition.

SOUTHERN DISTINCTIVENESS

In 1785 Thomas Jefferson jotted down a brief list of differences that distinguished the North and South:

In the North they are
cool
sober
laborious
independent
jealous of their own liberties and just to those of others,
interested
chicaning
superstitious and hypocritical in their religion.
In the South they are
fiery
voluptuary
indolent
unsteady
zealous for their own liberties, but trampling on those of others,
generous
candid
without attachment or pretensions to any religion but that of the heart.

Pre-Civil War Americans regarded Southerners as distinct people, who possessed their own unique set of values and way of life. It was widely though mistakenly believed that the North and South had originally been settled by two distinct groups of immigrants, each with its own ethos. Northerners were said to be the descendants of seventeenth-century English Puritans and Southerners were the descendants of England's country gentry. In the eyes of many pre-Civil War Americans this historical background had contributed to two distinct kinds of Americans: the aggressive, individualistic, money-grubbing Yankee and the southern cavalier. According to the popular stereotype, the cavalier, unlike the Yankee, was violently sensitive to insult, indifferent to money, and preoccupied with honor.

The Plantation Legend

During the three decades before the Civil War, writers from both the North and South created a popular image of the South now known as the "plantation legend"—a stereotype well known to anyone who has ever seen the film *Gone With the Wind.* Authors such as Virginia congressman George Tucker, Baltimore lawyer

This idyllic painting of a cotton plantation was the stereotype of the southern half of America. In actuality, smaller farms outnumbered large slave-worked holdings.

John Pendleton Kennedy, New Yorker James Kirk Paulding, and William Gilmore Simms of South Carolina pictured Southerners in terms of a small number of stereotypes: aristocratic masters; beautiful southern belles leading lives of leisure; faithful black household servants; superstitious field hands; and surly poor white trash. According to the popular stereotype, the South was a land in economic decline, and white southern society was rigidly divided into two classes: slaveholders and poor whites.

This image of the South as "a land of cotton" where "old times" are "not forgotten" receive its most popular expression in 1859 in a song called "Dixie," written by a Northerner named Dan D. Emmett to enliven shows given by a troupe of black-faced minstrels on the New York stage. In the eyes of many Northerners, uneasy with their increasingly urban, individualistic commercial society, the culture of the South seemed to have many things disappearing from the North—a leisurely pace of life, a clear social hierarchy, and an indifference to money.

The Old South: Images and Realities

The realities of Southern life were far more complicated than the plantation legend suggested. The South was much more than a land of cotton plantations. Unlike the slave societies of the Caribbean, which produced crops exclusively for export, the South devoted much of its energy to raising food stocks and livestock.

In addition, large parts of the South were unsuited to plantation life. In the mountainous regions of eastern Tennessee and western Virginia few plantations and few slaves were found. The pre-Civil War South embraced a wide variety of regions, varying in their geographic, economic, and social characteristics. It included such geographical areas as the Piedmont, Tidewater, coastal plain, piney woods, Delta, Appalachian Mountains, upcountry, and a fertile "black belt"—regions that clashed repeatedly over such political questions as debt relief, taxes, apportionment of representation, and internal improvements.

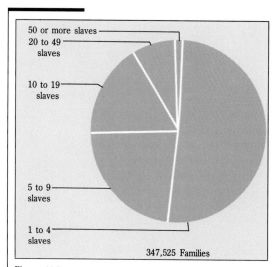

Figure 11.3
Slave-Owning Population, 1850

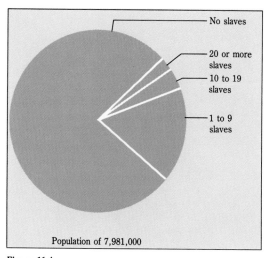

Figure 11.4
Southern White Population, 1860

The social structure of the white South was much more intricate than the two-class picture of proud aristocrats disdainful of honest work and ignorant, vicious, exploited poor whites. Actually, large slaveholders were an extreme rarity. In 1860 just 11,000 Southerners—three-quarters of one percent of the white population—owned more than 50 slaves; just 2358 owned as many as 100 slaves. Although large slaveholders were few in number, they owned most of the South's slaves. Over half of all slaves lived on plantations with 20 or more slaves and a quarter lived on plantations with more than 50 slaves.

Slave ownership was not confined to a small elite. In the first half of the nineteenth century, one-third of all southern white families owned slaves, and a majority of white southern families either owned slaves, had owned them, or expected to own them. These slaveowners were a diverse lot. A few were black, mulatto, or Indian; a tenth were women; and more than one in ten worked as artisans, businessmen, or merchants rather than as farmers or planters. Few led lives of leisure or refinement. The average slaveowner lived in a log cabin rather than a mansion and was a farmer rather than a planter. The average holding varied between four and six slaves, and most slaveholders possessed no more than five.

The lives of southern women similarly did not conform to traditional stereotypes. The popular image of southern womanhood was of a hoop-skirted southern belle. In reality, Southern women suffered under heavier household burdens than their northern counterparts. They married earlier, bore more children, and were more likely to die young. They lived in greater isolation, had less access to the company of other women, and lacked the satisfactions of voluntary associations and reform movements. Their education was briefer and much less likely to result in opportunities for independent careers.

The plantation legend was misleading in still other respects. Slavery was not unprofitable nor was it a dying institution. In 1860 the South was richer than any country in Europe except England, and it had achieved a level of wealth unmatched by Italy or Spain until the eve of World War II. Instead of stagnating, per capita income was growing thirty percent more rapidly in the South than in the North between 1840 and 1860 and exceeded the income of the states in the West by fourteen percent. Personal income of Southerners lagged well behind the Northerner's, in spite of the rapid growth rate. Per capita income in the South in 1860 was twenty-five percent lower than in the North.

The southern economy generated enormous wealth, both for individuals and the nation as a whole. Well over half of the richest one percent of Americans in 1860 lived in the South. Even more importantly, southern agriculture helped finance early nineteenth-century American economic growth. Cotton exports paid for the commodities and technology America needed to begin its industrial revolution and created the conditions necessary to attract foreign capital and labor. Southern agriculture also stimulated the growth of northern business. A huge textile industry arose in New England to process the South's cotton. And since the South, like other slave societies, did not develop its own financial and commercial facilities, northern bankers, insurance agents, and cotton brokers developed substantial businesses.

Impact of Slavery on the Southern Economy

Although it is clear that slavery was highly profitable, it is also apparent that slavery impeded the development of industry and cities in the South and contributed to high debts, soil exhaustion, and a lack of technological innovation. Philosopher and poet, Ralph Waldo Emerson, said that "slavery is no scholar, no improver; it does not love the whistle of the railroad; it does not love the newspaper, the mail-bag, a college, a book or a preacher who has the absurd whim of saying what he thinks; it does not increase the white population; it does not improve the soil; everything goes to decay." There appeared to be a large element of truth in Emerson's observation.

Despite its profitability, slavery had a number of deleterious economic effects on southern society. In the first place, the South, like other slave societies, did not produce urban centers for commerce, finance, and industry on a scale equal to those found in the North. Virginia's largest city, Richmond, had a population of just 15,274 in 1850. That same year, Wilmington, North Carolina's largest city, had just 7264 inhabitants, while Natchez and Vicksburg, the two largest cities in Mississippi, had less than 3000 white inhabitants.

Southern cities were small because they failed to develop diversified economies. Unlike the cities of the North, southern cities rarely became processing or finishing centers and southern ports rarely engaged in international trade. Their primary functions were to market and transport cotton or other agricultural crops, supply local planters and farmers with such necessities as agricultural implements, and produce the small number of manufactured goods needed by farmers, such as cotton gins.

An overemphasis on slave-based agriculture led Southerners to neglect industry and transportation improvements, and as a result manufacturing and the southern transportation system lagged far behind the North's. In 1860 the North had approximately 1.3 million industrial workers compared to the South's 110,000, and northern factories manufactured nine-tenths of the industrial goods produced in the United States. The North produced seventeen times as much cotton and woolen goods as the South, thirty times as many boots and shoes, twenty times as much pig iron, and twenty-four times as many locomotive engines.

The South's transportation network was primitive by northern standards. Traveling the 1460 miles from Baltimore to New Orleans in 1850 meant riding five different railroads, two stage coaches and two steamboats. Most southern railroads served primarily to transport cotton to southern ports where the crop could be shipped on northern vessels to northern or British factories for processing.

Because of high rates of personal debt, southern states kept taxation and government spending at much lower levels than in the North. As a result, Southerners lagged far behind Northerners in their support for public education. Illiteracy was widespread. In 1850, twenty percent of all southern white adults could not read or write. In contrast, the national figure for illiteracy was eight percent and .42 percent in New England. At mid-century, southern pupils attended thirty-six fewer days in class each year, spent fewer years in school, and were half again as likely to be truant as northern pupils. Southern states established few orphanages, hospitals, or asylums for the mentally ill.

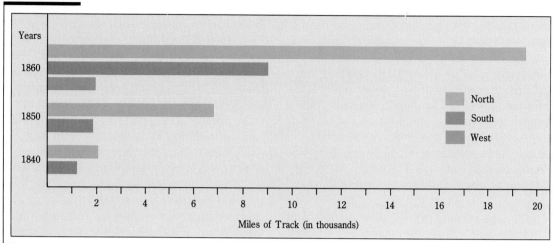

Figure 11.5
Railroad Growth, 1840-1860

Because large slaveholders owned most of the region's slaves, wealth was even more stratified in the South than in the North. In the deep South, the middle class held a relatively small proportion of the region's property, but wealthy planters owned a very significant portion of the productive lands and slave labor. In 1850, seventeen percent of the farming population held two-thirds of all acres in the rich cotton growing regions of the South.

There were indications that during the last decade before the Civil War slave ownership was becoming concentrated in fewer and fewer hands. As soil erosion and exhaustion diminished the availability of cotton land, scarcity and heavy demand forced up the price of land and slaves beyond the reach of most, and in newer cotton regions yeomen farmers were pushed off the land as planters expanded their holdings. In cotton growing regions of Louisiana, for example, nearly half of all rural white families owned no land. During the 1850s, the percentage of the total white population owning slaves declined significantly. By 1860, the proportion of whites holding slaves had fallen from about one-third to one-fourth. As slave and land ownership grew more concentrated, a growing number of whites were forced by economic pressure to leave the land and move to urban centers.

Growth of a Distinctive Southern Identity

Beginning in the 1830s, a new and aggressive sense of southern "nationalism" appeared in the South. The South began to conceive of itself more and more as the true custodian of America's revolutionary heritage. Southern travelers who ventured into the North, regarded it as a "strange and distant land" and expressed disgust about its vice-ridden cities and its grasping materialism.

At the same time, southern intellectuals began to defend slavery not as a necessary evil but as a positive good, arguing that it created a hierarchical society in the South superior to the leveling democracy of the North. By the late 1840s, a new more explicitly racist rationale for slavery emerged.

With the emergence of militant abolitionism in the North, sharpened by slave uprisings in Jamaica and Southampton County, Virginia, the South began to see itself ringed by enemies. Southern leaders responded aggressively. On the floor of the Senate in 1837, John C. Calhoun pronounced slavery "a good—a positive good" and set the tone for future southern pro-slavery arguments. Prior to the 1830s, southern statements on slavery had been defensive; afterwards, they were defiant.

In the 1840s, a growing number of southern ministers, journalists, and politicians began to denounce the North's form of capitalism as "wage slavery." The condition of free labor, they argued, was actually "worse than slavery," because slaveholders, unlike greedy northern employers, provide for their employees "when most needed, when sickness or old age has overtaken [them]." Northern workers, they declared, were simply "slaves without masters."

Writers like George Fitzhugh argued that slavery was a beneficent institution, which permitted the development of an upper class devoted to high intellectual pursuits. The champions of slavery maintained that the South's hierarchical, organic society was superior to the individualistic, materialistic civilization of the North, in which abolitionism, feminism, and labor unrest indicated that the social order was disintegrating.

During the 1840s, a growing number of Southerners defended slavery on explicitly racial grounds. In doing so, they were able to draw upon new pseudo-scientific theories of permanent racial inferiority. Some of these theories came from Europe, which was seeking justification of imperial expansion over non-white people in Africa and Asia. Other racist ideas were drawn from northern scientists, who developed an elaborate theory of "polygenesis" that claimed that blacks and whites were separate species.

The Decline of Antislavery Sentiment in the South

During the eighteenth century, the South was unique among slave societies in its openness to antislavery ideas. In Maryland and North Carolina, Quakers freed more than 1500 slaves and sent them out of state. Scattered Presbyterian, Baptist, and Methodist ministers and advisory committees condemned slavery as a sin "contrary to the word of God." As late as 1827, the number of antislavery organizations in the South actually outnumbered those in the free states by at least four to one.

By the mid-1830s, however, agitation against slavery had largely ended in the South.

Southern religious sects that had expressed opposition to slavery in the late eighteenth century modified their antislavery beliefs. Quakers and Unitarians who were strongly antagonistic to slavery emigrated. By the second decade of the century, antislavery sentiment was confined to Kentucky, the Piedmont counties of North Carolina, and the mountains in eastern Tennessee.

Authorities stifled public debate. Southern state legislatures adopted a series of laws suppressing criticism of the institution. In 1830 Louisiana made it a crime to make any statement that might produce discontent or insubordination among free blacks. Six years later, Virginia made it a felony for any member of an abolition society to come into the state and for any citizen to deny the legality of slavery.

The silent pressure of public opinion limited public discussion of the slavery question. College presidents or professors suspected of sympathy with abolitionists lost their jobs. Mobs attacked editors who dared to print articles critical of slavery. One Richmond, Virginia, editor fought eight duels in two years. In Parkville, Missouri, and Lexington, Kentucky, crowds dismantled printing presses of antislavery newspapers. An "iron curtain" against the invasion of antislavery propaganda was erected.

Only once, in the wake of Nat Turner's famous slave insurrection in 1831, did a southern state openly debate the possibility of ending slavery. These debates in the Virginia legislature in January and February, 1832, ended with the defeat of proposals to abolish slavery.

James G. Birney was one of many Southerners to discover that it was hopeless to work for slave emancipation in the South. Birney was born into a wealthy Kentucky slaveholding family, and, like many members of the South's slave-owning elite, educated at Princeton. After graduation, he moved to Huntsville, Alabama, where he practiced law and operated a cotton plantation. In Huntsville, he developed qualms about slavery and began to work as an agent for the American Colonization Society. Soon, his doubts about slavery had grown into an active hatred for the institution. He returned to Kentucky, emancipated his slaves, and in 1835 organized the Kentucky Anti-Slavery Society.

In Kentucky, Birney quickly discovered that public opinion vehemently opposed antislavery. A committee of leading citizens in Danville informed him that they would not permit him to establish an antislavery newspaper in the city. When Birney announced that he would go through with his plans anyway, the committee bought out the paper's printer and the town's postmaster announced that he would refuse to deliver the newspaper. In a final effort to publish his paper, Birney moved across the Ohio River into Cincinnati, but a mob destroyed his press while the city's mayor looked on.

After 1830 the South's desire to defend the institution of slavery against outside attack led to a growing hostility toward virtually all forms of social reform. Declared one southern newspaper editor, the South "has uniformly rejected the isms which infest Europe and the Eastern and Western states of this country." Many Southerners spoke proudly of the rejection of the reforms that flourished in the North. The South, said one South Carolina scientist, was "the breakwater which is to stay that furious tide of social and political heresies now setting toward us from the shores of the old world." Only the temperance movement made headway in the South.

"Reforming" Slavery from Within

Many white Southerners felt genuine moral doubts about slavery. For the most part, however, these doubts were directed into efforts to reform the institution, ameliorate the position of slaves, and make slavery conform to the ideal depicted in the Old Testament.

During the early eighteenth century, ministers from such denominations as the Quakers, Moravians, and Anglicans launched the first concerted campaigns to convert slaves in the American colonies to Christianity. Missionaries established schools and taught several thousand slaves to read and recite scripture. They stressed that Christian slaves would make more loyal and productive workers, less likely to stage insurrections. The Great Awakening of the 1730s and '40s stimulated renewed efforts

to promote Christianization, but it was not until the early nineteenth century that most slaveowners expressed concern for converting their slaves to Christianity.

There were also early nineteenth-century efforts to revise slave codes. The slave codes of the eighteenth century were exceedingly harsh. They permitted owners to punish slaves by castration and amputation. Slaveholders had no specific obligations for housing, food, or clothing, and many observers reported seeing slaves half-clothed or naked. Few eighteenth-century masters showed any concern for marriages, families, or religion among slaves.

During the early nineteenth century, the southern states enacted new codes regulating the punishment of slaves and setting down minimum standards for maintenance. State legislatures defined killing a slave with malice as murder, and made dismemberment and some other cruel punishments illegal. Three states forbade the sale of young slave children from their parents, and four states permitted slaves to be taught to read and write.

Many of the new laws went unenforced, but they suggested that a new code of values and behavior was emerging under slavery. Paternalism was the defining characteristic of this new code. According to this new ideal, slaveholding was "a duty and a burden" carrying strict moral obligations. A humane master of a plantation was supposed to show concern for the spiritual and physical well-being of his slaves.

These limited efforts to provide certain minimal protections for slaves were accompanied by tighter restrictions on other aspects of slave life. Private manumissions were made illegal. Southern states instituted the death penalty for any slaves involved in plotting a rebellion. Most states prohibited slaves from owning firearms, horses, or drums (which might be used during an insurrection), placed tight restrictions on slave funerals, and barred black preachers from conducting religious services unless a white person was present. In order to restrict contact between free blacks and slaves, a number of southern states required manumitted slaves to leave the state. Other restrictive laws quarantined vessels containing black sailors and imprisoned black sailors who stepped on shore.

Southern Economic, Literary, Religious, and Educational Movements

By the 1830s, a growing number of Southerners wanted to free the South from economic, religious, and cultural dependence upon the North. These southern "nationalists" sought to preserve the cultural and intellectual distinctiveness of the South and insulate the southern economy from the corrupting commercial and industrial values of the North.

Beginning in 1837, southern leaders attempted to increase the South's economic self-sufficiency by promoting commerce and industry and holding a series of commercial conventions. Economic self-sufficiency was necessary, they argued, if the South were to hold an equal place in the nation. Manufacturing, wrote a Mobile, Alabama, editor, was "the only safe and effectual remedy against Northern oppression."

The objective of these conventions was to diversify the southern economy and rescue the South from northern "pecuniary and commercial supremacy." Efforts to develop the southern economy were surprisingly successful. Southern railroad mileage quadrupled between 1850 and 1860—although southern track mileage still trailed the free states by 14,000. By 1860 Richmond manufactured more tobacco than any other American city and exported more goods to South America than any other United States port, including New York.

Other southern nationalists strove to create southern-oriented educational institutions and develop a distinctive southern literature. As early as the 1820s, influential southern leaders argued that the South had to create its own institutions of higher learning in order to protect the young from, in Jefferson's words, "imbibing opinions and principles in discord" with those of the South. School books, declared one southern magazine, "have slurs and innuendoes at slavery; the geographies are more particular in stating the resources of the Northern States; the histories almost ignore the South; the arithmetics contain in their examples reflections upon the Southern states."

The struggle for independent southern colleges achieved considerable success. By 1860 Virginia had twenty-three colleges and Georgia

thirty-two, while New York had seventeen colleges and Massachusetts just eight. In 1856 the University of Virginia had 558 students, compared to just 361 at Harvard.

In religion as in education, there were growing calls for regional independence. Between 1835 and 1845, the slavery question had been raised at national meetings of the Baptist and Methodist churches, which included three-fourths of the southern population. A growing number of Southerners began to believe that the northern churches were "mixed up with the whole machinery of abolition and antislavery agitation and invasion." In 1844 southern delegates to the Methodist General Conference set up the Methodist Episcopal Church South to free themselves "from the oppressive jurisdiction of the majority in the North. The next year, Southern Baptists established a separate Southern Baptist Convention.

At the same time that educators and churchmen denounced "Northern domination in Our Schools and Pulpits," southern sectionalists called for a distinctive and peculiarly southern literature. More than thirty periodicals were founded with the word "Southern" in their title, all intended to "breathe a Southern spirit, and sustain a strictly Southern character." Authors like Nathaniel Beverly Tucker and William Gilmore Simms called on the South to write on southern themes and overcome the taunts of "Englishmen and Northernmen" that they were intellectually inferior.

Southern Radicalism

By the early 1850s, a growing number of aggressive Southerners had moved beyond earlier calls for separate southern factories, colleges, and churches. Militant nationalists called for the annexation of Latin American and Caribbean territory and demanded that the international slave trade be reopened to increase the supply of slaves and broaden slave ownership.

In a bid to acquire new lands for slavery, a filibustering expedition was launched from New Orleans in 1851 to secure Cuba for the South. After this failed, many extreme southern nationalists supported the efforts of William Walker, "the gray-eyed boy of destiny," to extend slave labor into Latin America. In 1853, with considerable southern support, Walker raised a private army and unsuccessfully invaded Mexico. Two years later, he launched the first of three invasions of Nicaragua. On his final foray in 1860, he was taken prisoner by a British officer, handed over to Honduran authorities, and, at the age of thirty-six executed by a firing squad. In the late 1850s, another group of ardent southern expansionists, the Knights of the Golden Circle, developed plans to create an independent slave empire stretching from Maryland and Texas to northern South America and the West Indies. The only practical effect of these schemes was to enflame northern opinion against an aggressive southern slaveocracy.

SLAVERY

The primary distinguishing characteristic of the South was dependence on slave labor. During the decades before the Civil War, four million black Americans, one-third of the South's population, labored as slaves.

Two unrelated incidents suggest the complexity of the institution of slavery. The first took place in 1811. Lilburne and Isham Lewis, two nephews of Thomas Jefferson, ordered Lilburne's slaves to lash a slave named George to the kitchen floor of their southwest Kentucky farm. The seventeen-year-old slave had run away, returned, and then broken a treasured pitcher. Enraged and probably drunk, Lilburne seized an axe and nearly decapitated the young slave. Then the brothers had their terrorized slaves dismember the victim and throw the pieces on the fire.

The second picture of slavery is from 1825. In that year, Joseph Davis, a Mississippi planter, met Robert Owen, a Scottish industrialist and utopian reformer. Inspired by Owen's vision of society operating according to the principles of voluntary cooperation, Davis attempted to reorganize his plantation at Davis Bend, thirty miles south of Vicksburg. Davis provided slave families with two-room cabins and supplied food freely. His most famous innovation was a form of self-government for the slave community. No slave of the more than 300 on his plantation could be punished without being tried and convicted by a jury of his peers. Later Joseph's younger brother, Jefferson Davis, the future president of the Confederacy, put a similar system into practice on his plantation.

During the early nineteenth century, abolitionists developed a devastating moral indictment of slavery. They attacked slaveowners for breaking marriages, selling children from parents, dividing families, systematically breeding slaves for sale, and taking slave mistresses as concubines. They attacked masters for working slaves to death and inadequately feeding them. Slavery was "the sum of all villainies," they declared, because it encouraged every other sin.

Slavery's apologists responded to these charges, maintaining that, on the whole, masters were decent, slaves were content, and slaves' living conditions were superior to those of many free workers in the North. Ardent proslavery writers asserted that planter paternalism and public opinion protected slaves from abuse, but several questions remained. How repressive was slavery in the United States? What conditions did slaves live under?

In general, slaves were overworked, poorly clad, inadequately housed, and received the minimum of medical care. Debt, the death of a master, or merely the prospect of economic gain frequently tore slave husbands from wives and slave parents from children. However, as brutal and destructive as the institution of slavery was, slaves were not defenseless or emasculated victims. Slaves were able to sustain ties to their African past and maintain a separate life. Through religion, folklore, music, and family life as well as more direct forms of resistance, slaves were able to sustain a vital culture supportive of human dignity.

The Legal Status of Slaves

Every southern state enacted a slave code which defined the slaves' status and the slaveowners' power. To a considerable degree, these codes treated slaves like a piece of property. Like a domestic animal, a slave could be bought, sold, and leased. A master also had the right to compel a slave to work. The codes prohibited slaves from owning property, testifying against whites in court, or from making contracts. Slave

The primary objective of the slave codes was to enforce discipline. Under the slave codes, slaves were forbidden from striking whites or using insulting language toward white people, holding a meeting without a white person present, visiting whites or free blacks, or leaving plantations without permission. The laws prohibited whites and free blacks from teaching slaves to read and write, gambling with slaves, or supplying them with liquor, guns, or poisonous drugs. Most of the time, authorities loosely enforced these legal restrictions, but whenever fears of slave uprisings spread, enforcement tightened.

Slave Labor

Simon Gray was a slave. He was also the captain of a Mississippi River flatboat and the builder and operator of a number of sawmills. Emanuel Quivers was a slave. He worked at the Tredegar Iron Works of Richmond, Virginia. Andrew Dirt was also a slave. He was a black overseer.

Slaves performed all kinds of work. During the 1850s, half a million slaves lived in southern towns and cities, where they were hired out by their owners to work in ironworks, textile mills, tobacco factories, laundries, shipyards, and mechanics' homes. Other slaves labored as lumberjacks, as deckhands and firemen on river boats, and in sawmills, gristmills, and quarries. Many other slaves were engaged in construction of roads and railroads. Most slaves, to be sure, were field hands, raising cotton, hemp, rice, tobacco, and sugar cane. Even on plantations not all slaves were menial laborers. Some worked as skilled craftsmen or artisans such as blacksmiths, shoemakers, or carpenters; others held domestic posts such as coachmen or house servants; and still others held managerial posts. At least two-thirds of the slaves worked under the supervision of black foremen, called drivers. Not infrequently they managed the whole plantation in the absence of their masters.

For most slaves, slavery meant back-breaking field work on small farms or larger plantations. On the typical plantation, slaves worked "from day clean to first dark." Solomon Northrup, a free black who was kidnapped and enslaved for twelve years on a Louisiana cotton

Despite the physical harshness of life under slavery, slaves were able to sustain a sense of dignity and self-worth through their religious and cultural traditions.

marriages were not recognized by the law. Under the slave codes, slavery was lifelong and hereditary, and any child born to a slave woman was the property of her master.

The slave codes did give slaves limited legal rights. In order to refute abolitionist contentions that slavery was unjust and inhumane, southern legislators adopted statutes regulating slaves' hours of labor and establishing certain minimal standards for slave upkeep. Most states defined the wanton killing of a slave as murder, prohibited cruel and unusual punishments, and extended to slaves accused of capital offenses the right to trial by jury and legal counsel. Whipping was not regarded by southern legislatures as a cruel punishment, and slaves were prohibited from bringing suit to seek legal redress for violations of their rights.

Slave quarters were often small, run-down cabins, housing six or more slaves.

Although most slaves labored as field hands, many worked as skilled craftsmen or as household servants.

Hardworking slaves on a Virginia plantation pick and carry cotton while white overseers look on.

plantation, wrote a graphic description of the work regimen imposed on slaves: "The hands are required to be in the cotton field as soon as it is light in the morning, and, with the exception of ten or fifteen minutes, which is given them at noon to swallow their allowance of cold bacon, they are not permitted to be a moment idle until it is too dark to see, and when the moon is full, they often times labor till the middle of the night." Even then, the slaves' work was not over; it was still necessary to feed swine and mules, cut wood, and pack the cotton. At planting or harvest time, work was even more exacting, as planters required slaves to stay in the fields fifteen or sixteen hours a day.

To maximize productivity, slaveowners assigned each hand a specific set of tasks throughout the year. During the winter, field slaves ginned and pressed cotton, cut wood, repaired buildings and fences, and cleared fields. In the spring and summer, field hands plowed and hoed fields, killed weeds, and planted and cultivated crops. In the fall, slaves picked, ginned and packed cotton, shucked corn, and gathered peas. Elderly slaves cared for children, made clothes, and prepared food.

Labor on large plantations was as rigidly organized as in a factory. Under the gang system, which was widely used on cotton plantations, field hands were divided into plow gangs and hoe gangs, each commanded by a driver. Under the task system, mainly used on rice plantations, each hand was given a specific daily work assignment.

Because slaves had little direct incentive to work hard, slaveowners combined a variety of harsh penalties with positive incentives. Some masters denied passes to disobedient slaves or forced them to work on Sundays or holidays. Other planters confined disobedient hands to private or public jails, and one Maryland planter required a slave to eat the worms he had failed to pick off tobacco plants. Chains and shackles were widely used to control runaways. Whipping was a key part of the system of discipline and motivation. On one Louisiana plantation, a slave was lashed every four-and-a-half days. In his diary, Bennet H. Barrow, a Louisiana planter, recorded flogging "every hand in the field," breaking his sword on the head of one slave, shooting another slave in the thigh, and cutting another with a club "in 3 places very bad."

But physical pain alone was not enough to elicit hard work. To stimulate productivity, some masters gave slaves small garden plots and permitted them to sell their produce. Others distributed gifts of food or money at the end of the year. Still other planters awarded prizes, holidays, and year-end bonuses to particularly productive slaves. One Alabama master permitted his slaves to share in the profits of the cotton, peanut, and pea crops.

Material Conditions of Slave Life

Deprivation and physical hardship were the hallmarks of life under slavery. It now seems clear that the material conditions of slave life approximated those of the poorest, most downtrodden free laborers in the North and Europe. Although the material conditions for slaves improved greatly in the nineteenth century, slaves remained much more likely than southern whites to die prematurely, suffer malnutrition or dietary deficiencies, or lose a child in infancy.

A slave's life expectancy under slavery was short—just twenty-eight to thirty-six years, or as much as twelve years less than that of American whites. The infant mortality rate among slaves was twice as high as among white newborns.

The slaves' diet was monotonous and unvaried, consisting largely of corn meal and salt pork and bacon. Only rarely did slaves drink milk or eat fresh meat and vegetables. This diet provided enough bulk calories to ensure that slaves had sufficient strength and energy to work as productive field hands. It did not provide adequate nutrition, and as a result slaves suffered from vitamin and protein deficiencies and such ailments as beriberi, kwashiorkor, and pellagra.

The physical conditions in which slaves lived were truly miserable. Lacking privies and any sanitary disposal of garbage, slaves had to urinate and defecate in the cover of nearby bushes and live surrounded by decaying food.

Chickens, dogs, and pigs lived next to the slave quarters, and in consequence, animal feces contaminated the area. Such squalor contributed to high rates of dysentery, typhus, diarrhea, hepatitis, typhoid fever, and intestinal worms.

Slave quarters were cramped and crowded. The typical cabin—a single, windowless room, with a chimney constructed of clay and twigs and a floor made up of dirt or planks resting on the ground—ranged in size from 10×10 feet to 21×21 feet. These small cabins were often quite crowded, containing five, six, or more occupants. On some plantations, slaves lived in single-family cabins; on others, two or more shared the same room. On the largest plantations, unmarried men and women were sometimes lodged together in barracks-like structures. Josiah Henson, the Kentucky slave who served as the model for Harriet Beecher Stowe's Uncle Tom, described his plantation's cabins this way:

> We lodged in log huts. . . . Wooden floors were an unknown luxury. In a single room were huddled, like cattle, ten or a dozen persons, men, women, and children. . . . There were neither bedsteads nor furniture. . . . Our beds were collections of straw and old rags. . . . The wind whistled and the rain and snow blew in through the cracks, and the damp earth soaked in the moisture till the floor was muddy as a pig sty.

Slave Family Life

In 1858, after being sold away from his family, a Georgia slave named Abream Scriven wrote the following words to his wife: "Give my love to my dear father and mother and tell them good bye for me. . . . My dear wife for you and all my children my pen cannot express the grief I feel to be parted from you. I remain your true husband until death."

According to antebellum critics of slavery, the greatest evil inflicted by the "peculiar institution" was the havoc it inflicted on the slave family. In truth, slavery exacted a terrible toll on black family life. Slave sales often broke up slave families. Severe constraints limited the authority of slave parents. Slave women were vulnerable to sexual exploitation from masters and overseers. Deliberate and systematic efforts to breed slaves were not unknown.

Despite the constant threat of sale and family breakup, Afro-Americans managed to forge strong family ties and personal relationships. Despite the fact that southern law provided no legal sanction for slave marriages, most slaves established de facto arrangements which were often stable over long periods of time. In spite of frequent family disruption, a majority of slaves grew up in families headed by a father and a mother. Nuclear family ties stretched outward to an involved network of extended kin. In large measure because of the strength and flexibility of their kin ties, black Americans were able to resist the psychologically debilitating effects of slavery.

Individual slave families existed under conditions of intense strain. Husbands were frequently sold away from their wives. During the Civil War, nearly twenty percent of ex-slaves reported that an earlier marriage had been terminated by "force." The sale of children from parents was even more common. Over the course of a thirty-five-year lifetime, the average slave had a fifty-fifty chance of being sold at least once and was likely to witness the sale of several members of his or her immediate family.

Even in instances in which marriages were not broken by sale, slave husbands and wives often resided on separate farms or plantations and were owned by different individuals. On large plantations, one slave father in three had a different owner than his wife and could visit his family only at his master's discretion. On smaller holdings, divided ownership occurred even more frequently. The typical farm and plantation were so small that it was difficult for many slaves to find a spouse at all. As one ex-slave put it, men "had a hell of a time getting a wife during slavery."

Other obstacles stood in the way of an independent family life. Many slaves had to share their single room cabins with relatives and other unrelated slaves. On larger plantations, food was cooked in a common kitchen and children were cared for in a communal nursery while their parents worked in the fields. Even on model plantations, children between the ages of seven and ten were taken from their parents and sent to live in separate cabins.

Slavery imposed rigid limits on the authority of slave parents. Nearly every slave child went through an experience similar to one recalled by a young South Carolina slave named Jacob Stoyer. Jacob was being trained as a jockey. His trainer beat him regularly, for no apparent reason. Jacob appealed to his father for help, but his father simply said to work harder, "for I cannot do anything for you." When Jacob's mother argued with the trainer, she was whipped for her efforts. From this episode, Jacob learned a critical lesson: that the ability of slave parents to help their own children was sharply limited.

Of all the evils associated with slavery, abolitionists most bitterly denounced the sexual abuse suffered by slave women. Abolitionists claimed that slaveholders adopted deliberate policies to breed slaves for sale in the lower South—"like oxen for the shambles"—and kept "black harems" and sexually exploited slave women. Some masters did indeed take slave mistresses and concubines. One slave, Henry Bibb, said that a slave trader forced his own wife to become a prostitute.

Planters also sought to increase slave birthrates through a variety of economic incentives. Many slaveholders gave bounties in the form of cash or household goods to mothers who bore healthy children and increased rations and lightened the workload of pregnant and nursing women.

Contrary to what early nineteenth-century abolitionists charged, the sexual life of slaves was not casual or promiscuous nor did slave women become mothers at a particularly early age. Some slave mothers, like some white mothers, engaged in premarital intercourse and bore children outside of marriage. Most slave women settled into a long-lasting monogamous relationship in their early twenties, which lasted, unless broken by sale, until she or her husband died.

Slave Cultural Expression

Despite the harshness and misery of life under slavery, it did not destroy the slaves' ability to develop a distinctive life and culture. Even under the weight of slavery, blacks developed a vital religion, music, and folklore. Through their

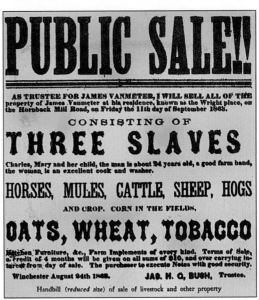

Slavery's worst evil was that it reduced human beings to the status of property. Under slavery, slaves could be bought, sold, leased, and traded—apart from spouses, parents, and children.

This sketch of a slave dance in Lynchburg, Virginia, illustrates how slaves used their precious leisure time and hints at the rich folk culture they tried to perpetuate.

families, their religion, and their cultural traditions, slaves were able to fashion an autonomous culture and community, beyond the direct control of their masters.

During the late eighteenth and early nineteenth centuries, slaves embraced Christianity, but they molded and transformed it to meet their own needs. Slaves' religious beliefs were a mixture of African traditions and Christianity. From their African heritage, slaves brought a hopeful and optimistic view of life, which contrasted sharply with evangelical Protestantism's emphasis on human sinfulness. In Protestant Christianity the slaves found an emphasis on love and the spiritual equality of all men that strengthened their ties to other blacks. Many slaves fused the concepts of Moses, who led his people to freedom, and Jesus, who suffered on behalf of all humankind, into a promise of deliverance in this world.

A major form of black religious expression was the spiritual. Slave spirituals, like "Go Down Moses" with its refrain "let my people go," indicated that slaves identified with the history of the Hebrew people, who had been oppressed and enslaved, but achieved eventual deliverance. In addition to the spiritual, another major form of slave cultural expression was folklore. Folktales were much more than amusing stories; slaves used them to comment on the whites around them and to convey everyday lessons for living. Among the most popular slave folktales were animal trickster stories, like the Brer Rabbit tales, derived from similar African stories, which told of powerless creatures who achieve their will through wit and guile rather than power and authority. These tales taught children how they had to function in a white dominated world and held out the promise that the powerless would eventually triumph over the strong.

Slave Resistance

It was a basic tenet of the pro-slavery argument that slaves were docile, content, faithful, and loyal. "Our slave population is not only a happy one," said a Virginia legislator, "but it is a contented, peaceful, and harmless one."

In fact, there is no evidence that the majority of slaves were content. One scholar has identified more than 200 instances of attempted insurrection or rumors of slave resistance between the seventeenth century and the Civil War. Many slaves who did not directly rebel made their masters' lives miserable through a variety of indirect protests against slavery, including sabotage, stealing, malingering, murder, arson, and infanticide.

Four times during the first thirty-one years of the nineteenth century, slaves attempted major insurrections. In 1800, a twenty-four-year-old Virginia slave named Gabriel Prosser, who was a blacksmith, led a march of perhaps fifty armed slaves on Richmond. The plot failed when a storm washed out the road to Richmond, giving the Virginia militia time to arrest the rebels. White authorities executed Prosser and twenty-five other conspirators.

In 1811 in southern Louisiana, between 180 and 500 slaves, led by Charles Deslondes, a free mulatto from Haiti, marched on New Orleans, armed with axes and other weapons. Slave-owners retaliated by killing eighty-two blacks, and placing the heads of sixteen leaders on pikes.

Denmark Vesey was a former West Indian slave who had been born in Africa, bought his freedom, and moved to Charleston, South Carolina. In 1822 he devised a conspiracy to take over the city on a summer Sunday when many whites would be vacationing outside the city. (See Chapter 8 Special Feature, pp. 246–247.) Before the revolt could take place, however, a domestic slave of a prominent Charlestonian informed his master. The authorities proceeded to arrest 131 blacks and hang 37.

The most famous slave revolt took place nine years later in Southampton County in southern Virginia. On August 22, 1831, Nat Turner, a trusted Baptist preacher, led a small group of fellow slaves into the home of his master Joseph Travis and killed the entire Travis household. By August 23, Turner's force had increased to between sixty and eighty slaves and had killed more than fifty whites. The local militia counterattacked and killed about 100 blacks. Twenty more slaves, including Turner, were later executed. Turner's revolt sparked a panic which spread as far south as Alabama and Louisiana. One Virginian worried that "a Nat Turner might be in any family."

Slave uprisings were much less frequent and less extensive in the American South than in the West Indies or Brazil. Outright revolts did not occur more often because the prospects of success were bleak and the consequences of defeat catastrophic. As one Missouri slave put it, "I've seen Marse Newton and Marse John Ramsey shoot too often to believe they can't kill" a slave.

The conditions that favored revolts elsewhere were absent in the South. In Jamaica, blacks outnumbered whites ten to one, whereas in the South whites were a majority in every state except Mississippi and South Carolina. In addition, slaveholding units in the South were much smaller than in other slave societies in the Western Hemisphere. Half of all slaves in the United States worked on units of twenty or less; in contrast, many sugar plantations in Jamaica had more than 500 slaves.

The unity of the white population in defense of slavery made the prospects for rebellion bleak. In Virginia in 1830, 100,000 of the state's 700,000 whites were members of the state militia. Finally, southern slaves had few havens to which to escape. The major exception was the swamp country in Florida, where black "maroons" joined with Seminole Indians in resisting the United States Army.

Recognizing that open resistance would be futile or even counterproductive, most plantation slaves expressed their opposition to slavery in a variety of subtle ways. Most day to day resistance to slavery took the form of breaking tools, feigning illness, doing shoddy work, stealing, and running away. These acts of resistance most commonly occurred when a master or overseer overstepped customary bounds. Through these acts, slaves established a right to proper treatment.

Free Blacks

In 1860, 250,000 black Americans were not slaves. After the American Revolution, slaveowners freed thousands of slaves, and countless others emancipated themselves by running away. In Louisiana, a large free black creole population had emerged under Spanish and French rule, and in South Carolina a creole population had arrived from Barbados. The number of free blacks in the Deep South increased rapidly with the arrival of thousands of light colored refugees from the black revolt in Haiti.

Free blacks varied profoundly in status. Most lived in poverty, but in a few cities such as New Orleans, Baltimore, and Charleston, free blacks worked as skilled carpenters, shoemakers, tailors, and millwrights. In the lower South, a few free blacks achieved high occupational status and actually bought slaves. One of the wealthiest free blacks was William Ellison, the son of a slave mother and a white planter. As a slave apprenticed to a skilled artisan, Ellison had learned how to make cotton gins, and at the age of twenty-six bought his freedom with his overtime earnings. At the time of his death in 1861, he had acquired the home of a former South Carolina governor, a shop, lands, and

While many free blacks lived in poverty, some worked as skilled carpenters, tailors, millwrights, or sawyers.

sixty-three slaves worth more than $100,000.

Free people of color occupied an uneasy middle ground between the dominant whites and the masses of slaves. Legally, courts denied them the right to serve on juries or to testify against whites. Some, like William Ellison, distanced themselves from those black people who remained in slavery and even bought and sold slaves. Others identified with slaves and poor free Negroes and took the lead in establishing separate black churches.

In addition to the 150,000 free blacks who lived in the South, another 100,000 free blacks lived in the North. Although free blacks comprised no more than 3.8 percent of the population of any northern state, they faced intense legal, economic, and social discrimination. They were prohibited from marrying whites and were forced into the lowest paying jobs. Whites denied them equal access to education, relegated them to segregated jails, cemeteries, asylums, and schools, forbid them from testifying against

whites in court, and, in all but four states—New Hampshire, Maine, Massachusetts, and Vermont—denied them the right to vote.

Free blacks in the North typically lived in tenements, sheds, and stables. An 1847 visitor described the typical black dwelling in Philadelphia as "a desolate pen," six feet square, without windows, beds, or furniture, possessing a leaky roof and a floor so low in the ground "that more or less water comes in on them from the yard in rainy weather." According to the *New York Express*, the principal residence of free blacks in that city was a house with eight or ten rooms, "and in these are crowded not infrequently two or three hundred souls."

During the 1830s or even earlier, free blacks in both the North and South began to suffer from heightened discrimination and competition from white immigrants in the skilled trades and even in such traditional occupations as domestic service. In the late 1850s, the plight of free blacks worsened in states like South Carolina and Maryland. White mechanics and artisans, bitter over the competition they faced from free people of color, demanded that the states legislate the reenslavement of free blacks. During the winter of 1859, politicians introduced twenty bills restricting the freedom of free blacks in the South Carolina legislature. None of them passed. The next summer, Charleston officials moved house to house, demanding that free people of color provide documentary proof of their freedom and threatening to reenslave those who lacked evidence. A panic followed, and hundreds of free blacks emigrated to the North. Some 780 emigrated from South Carolina before secession; another 2000 more left during the first month and a half of 1861.

CONCLUSION

In 1857 Hinton Rowan Helper, the son of a western North Carolina farmer, published one of the most politically influential books ever written by an American. Entitled *The Impending Crisis of the South*, the book argued that slavery was incompatible with economic progress. Using statistics drawn from the 1850 cen-

CHRONOLOGY OF KEY EVENTS

1793	Cotton gin invented
1801	Gabriel plot to overthrow slavery uncovered
1806	Philadelphia cordwainers prosecuted as an illegal conspiracy
1822	Denmark Vesey's conspiracy to lead a slave uprising in South Carolina exposed
1828	Workingmen's parties appear in eastern cities
1829	David Walker's *Appeal to the Colored Citizens of the World*
1831	Nat Turner's slave insurrection; Virginia convention debates the issue of slavery

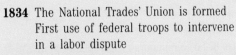

1834	The National Trades' Union is formed First use of federal troops to intervene in a labor dispute
1836	Anti-Catholic tract *Awful Disclosures of Maria Monk, as Exhibited in a Narrative of Her Suffering During a Residence of Five Years as a Novice, and Two Years as a Black Nun, in the Hotel Dieu Nunnery at Montreal* is published
1840	Ten-hour day established for federal employees
1842	*Commonwealth* v. *Hunt* decision
1844	Slavery issue splits Methodist Episcopal Church into northern and southern camps
1845	Baptist Church splits over the slavery issue; Failure of Irish potato crop
1857	Hinton Helper's *Impending Crisis of the South*

sus, Helper maintained that by every possible measure, the North was growing far faster than the South and that slavery was the cause of the South's economic backwardness.

Helper's thesis was that southern slavery was inefficient and wasteful, inferior in all respects to the North's free labor system, that it impoverished the region, degraded labor, inhibited urbanization, thwarted industrialization, and stifled progress. A rabid racist, Helper accompanied a call for the abolition of slavery with a demand for black colonization overseas. He concluded his book with a call for the South's nonslaveholders to overthrow the region's planter elite.

Helper's book produced a nationwide furor. *The New York Tribune* distributed 500 copies a day, viewing the book as the most effective propaganda against slavery ever written. Many Southerners burned it, fearful that it would divide the white population and undermine the institution of slavery.

By 1857, when Helper's book appeared, the North and South had become in the eyes of many Americans two distinct civilizations, with their own distinct set of values and ideals: one increasingly urban and industrial, the other committed to slave labor. Although the two sections shared many of the same ideals, ambitions, and prejudices, they had developed along diverging lines. In increasing numbers, Northerners identified their society with progress and believed that slavery was an intolerable obstacle to innovation, self-improvement, and commercial and economic growth. A growing number of Southerners, in turn, regarded their rural and agricultural society as the true embodiment of republican values. The great question before the nation was whether it could continue to exist half slave, half free.

REVIEW SUMMARY

During the decades before the Civil War, the Northern and Southern economies developed along diverging lines. The North was characterized by

rapid growth of commerce, finance, and manufacturing

entry of large numbers of European immigrants

By contrast, the South claimed

smaller and fewer cities

less-developed commercial establishments, financial institutions, and transportation facilities

a slave-based economy

SUGGESTIONS FOR FURTHER READING

OVERVIEWS AND SURVEYS

Daniel Boorstin, *The Americans: The National Experience* (1965); Russel B. Nye, *Society and Culture in America, 1830–1860* (1974); Edward Pessen, *Jacksonian America: Society, Personality, and Politics* (rev. ed., 1978).

THE EMERGENCE OF A NEW INDUSTRIAL ORDER IN THE NORTH

Hal S. Barron, *Those Who Stayed Behind: Rural Society in Nineteenth-Century New England* (1984); Stuart Blumin, *The Urban Threshold* (1975); Dennis Clark, *The Irish in Philadelphia* (1973); Allen F. Davis and Mark H. Haller, eds., *The Peoples of Philadelphia* (1973); Kathleen N. Conzen, *Immigrant Milwaukee, 1836–1860* (1977); Alan Dawley, *Class and Community: The Industrial Revolution in Lynn* (1976); Robert Doherty, *Society and Power: Five New England Towns, 1800–1860* (1977); Thomas Dublin, *Women at Work: The Transformation of Work and Community in Lowell, Massachusetts, 1826–1860* (1979); John Faragher, *Sugar Creek* (1986); Robert Ernst, *Immigrant Life in New York City, 1825–1863* (1949); Michael Frisch, *Town into City: Springfield, Massachusetts and the Meaning of Community, 1840–1880* (1972); Howard M. Gitelman, *Workingmen of Waltham* (1974); Steven Hahn and Jonathan Prude, eds., *The Countryside in the Age of Capitalist Transformation* (1985); Oscar Handlin, *Boston's Immigrants* (1959); Marcus L. Hansen, *The Atlantic Migration, 1607–1860* (1940); Susan Hirsch, *Roots of the American Working Class: The Industrialization of Crafts in Newark, 1800–1860* (1978); Joan M. Jensen, *Loosening the Bonds: Mid-Atlantic Farm Women, 1750–1850* (1986); Maldwyn A. Jones, *American Immigration* (1960); Alice Kessler-Harris, *Out to Work: A History of Wage-Earning Women in the United States* (1982); Alexander Keyssar, *Out of Work: The First Century of Unemployment in Massachusetts* (1986); Peter R. Knights, *The Plain People of Boston, 1830–1860* (1971); Bruce Laurie, *Working People of Philadelphia* (1980); Kerby A. Miller, *Emigrants and Exiles: Ireland and the Irish Exodus to North America* (1985); Edward Pessen, *Most Uncommon Jacksonians: Radical Leaders of the Early Labor Movement* (1967); E. Pessen, *Riches, Class and Power Before the Civil War* (1973); Jonathan Prude, *The Coming of Industrial Order: Town and Factory Life in Rural Massachusetts, 1810–1860* (1983); W. J. Rorabaugh, *The Craft Apprentice* (1986); Lee Soltow, *Men and Wealth in the United States, 1850–1870* (1975); Christine Stansell, *City of Women: The Female Laboring Poor in New York, 1785–1860* (1987); Philip Taylor, *The Distant Magnet: European Immigration to the United States of America* (1971); Stephan Thernstrom, *Poverty and Progress, Social Mobility in a Nineteenth Century City* (1964); S. Thernstrom, *The Other Bostonians* (1973); Anthony F. C. Wallace, *Rockdale: The Growth of an American Village in the Early Industrial Revolution* (1978); Norman Ware, *The Industrial Worker, 1840–1860* (1978); Sean Wilentz, *Chants Democratic: New York City and the Rise of the American Working Class, 1788–1850* (1984).

SOUTHERN DISTINCTIVENESS

Edward L. Ayers, *Vengeance and Justice: Crime and Punishment in the Nineteenth-Century American South* (1984); Fred Bateman and Thomas Weiss, *A Deplorable Scarcity: The Failure of Industrialization in the Slave Economy* (1981); John B. Boles and Evelyn Thomas Nolen, *Interpreting Southern History* (1987); Blaine A. Brownell and David R. Goldfield, eds., *The City in Southern History* (1977); Dickson D. Bruce, Jr., *Violence and Culture in the Antebellum South* (1979); Orville Vernon Burton and Robert C. McMath, Jr., eds., *Class, Conflict and Consensus: Antebellum Southern Community Studies* (1982); Randolph B. Campbell, *A Southern Community in Crisis: Harrison County, Texas, 1850–1880* (1983); R. B. Campbell and Richard G. Lowe, *Wealth and Power in Antebellum Texas* (1977); Jane Turner Censer, *North Carolina Planters and Their Children, 1800–1860* (1984); Catherine Clinton, *The Plantation Mistress: Woman's World in the Old South* (1982); Carl N. Degler, *The Other South: Southern Dissenters in the Nineteenth Century* (1974); Clement Eaton, *The Freedom-Of-Thought Struggle in the Old South* (1940); Drew Gilpin Faust, *The Sacred Circle: The Dilemma of the Intellectual in the Old South* (1977); D. G. Faust, *The Ideology of Slavery, 1830–1860* (1981); D. G. Faust, *James Henry Hammond and the Old South* (1982); James D. Foust, *The Yeoman Farmer and Westward Expansion of U.S. Cotton Production* (1975); Alison Goodyear Freehling, *Drift Toward Dissolution: The Virginia Slavery Debate of 1831–1832* (1982); Jean E. Friedman, *The Enclosed Garden: Women and Community in the Evangelical South, 1830–1900* (1985); Eugene D. Genovese, *The Political Economy of Slavery* (1965); E. D. Genovese, *The World the Slaveholders Made* (1969); David R. Goldfield, *Cotton Fields and Skyscrapers: Southern City and Region, 1607–1980* (1982); George D. Green, *Finance and Economic Development in the Old South* (1972); J. William Harris, *Plain Folk and Gentry in a Slave Society* (1985); Michael S. Hindus, *Prison and Plantation: Crime, Justice, and Authority in Massachusetts and South Carolina, 1767–1878* (1980); Suzanne Lebsock, *The Free Women of Petersburg, 1784–1860* (1984); Raimondo Luraghi, *The Rise and Fall of the Plantation South* (1978); John McCardell, *The Idea of a Southern Nation* (1979); Edward Magdol and Jon L. Wakelyn, eds., *The Southern Common People* (1980); Robert E. May, *The Southern Dream of a Caribbean Empire, 1854–1861* (1973); James Oakes, *The Ruling Race* (1982); Anne Firor Scott, *The Southern Lady: From Pedestal to Politics, 1830–1930* (1970); Steven M. Stowe, *Intimacy and Power in the Old South* (1987); Ronald T. Takaki, *A Pro-Slavery Crusade: The Agitation to Reopen the African Slave Trade* (1971); William R. Taylor, *Cavalier and Yankee: The Old South and the American National Character* (1961); Jack K. Williams, *Dueling in the Old South* (1980); Harold D. Woodman, *King Cotton and His Retainers: Financing and Marketing the Cotton Crop of the South, 1800–1825* (1968); Ralph A. Wooster, *The People in Power: Courthouse and Statehouse in the Lower South, 1850–1860* (1969); R. A. Wooster, *Politicians, Planters, and Plain Folk: Courthouse and Statehouse in the Upper South, 1850–1860* (1975); Gavin Wright, *The Political Economy of the Cotton South* (1978); Bertram Wyatt-Brown, *Southern Honor: Ethics and Behavior in the Old South* (1982).

SLAVERY

Ira Berlin, *Slaves Without Masters: The Free Negro in the Antebellum South* (1974); Eugene H. Berwanger, *The Frontier Against Slavery: Western Anti-Negro Prejudice and the Slavery Extension Controversy* (1967); John B. Boles, *Black Southerners, 1619–1869* (1983); John W. Blassingame, *The Slave Community: Plantation Life in the Ante-Bellum South* (1979); J. W. Blassingame, *Slave Testimony: Two Centuries of Letters, Speeches, Interviews, and Autobiographies* (1977); John H. Bracey, Jr., August Meier, and Elliott Rudwick, eds., *American Slavery: The Question of Resistance* (1971); James O. Breeden, ed., *Advice Among Masters: The Ideal in Slave Management in the Old South* (1980); Michael Craton, ed., *Roots and Branches: Current Directions in Slave Studies* (1979); Daniel J. Crowley, *African Folklore in the New World* (1977); Leonard P. Curry, *The Free Black in Urban America, 1800–1850* (1981); Paul A. David et al., eds., *Reckoning With Slavery* (1976); Charles B. Dew, "The Slavery Experience," in *Interpreting Southern History*, John B. Boles and Evelyn Thomas Nolen, eds. (1987); Dena J. Epstein, *Sinful Tunes and Spirituals: Black Folk Music to the Civil War* (1977); Paul D. Escott, *Slavery Remembered* (1979); Eugene D. Genovese, *From Rebellion to Revolution: Afro-American Slave Revolts in the Making of the Modern World* (1979); E. D. Genovese, *Roll, Jordan, Roll: The World the Slaves Made* (1974); Claudia D. Goldin, *Urban Slavery in the American South, 1820–1860* (1976); Herbert G. Gutman, *The Black Family in Slavery and Freedom, 1750–1925* (1976); H. G. Gutman, *Slavery and the Numbers Game* (1975); Janet Sharp Hermann, *The Pursuit of a Dream* (1981); Michael P. Johnson and James L. Roark, eds., *Black Masters: A Free Family of Color in the Old South* (1984); M. P. Johnson and J. L. Roark, *No Chariot Let Down: Charleston's Free People of Color on the Eve of the Civil War* (1984); James Hugo Johnston, *Race Relations in Virginia and Miscegenation in the South, 1776–1860* (1970); Jacqueline Jones, *Labor of Love, Labor of Sorrow* (1985); Charles Joyner, *Down by the Riverside: A South Carolina Slave Community* (1984); Kenneth F. Kiple and Virginia Himmelsteib King, *Another Dimension to the Black Diaspora: Diet, Disease, and Racism* (1981); Lawrence Levine, *Black Culture and Black Consciousness* (1977); Ronald L. Lewis, *Coal, Iron, and Slaves* (1979); Leon Litwack, *North of Slavery: The Negro in the Free States* (1961); Donald G. Mathews, *Religion in the Old South* (1977); Gary B. Mills, *The Forgotten People: Cane River's Creoles of Color* (1977); Michael Mullin, *American Negro Slavery* (1976); Stephen B. Oates, *The Fires of Jubilee: Nat Turner's Fierce Rebellion* (1975); Leslie Howard Owens, *This Species of Property: Slave Life and Culture in the Old South* (1976); Richard Price, ed., *Maroon Societies: Rebel Slave Communities in the Americas* (1973); Albert J. Raboteau, *Slave Religion: The "Invisible Institution" in the Antebellum South* (1978); George P. Rawick, *From Sundown to Sunup: The Making of the Black Community* (1972); Willie Lee Rose, *A Documentary History of Slavery in North America* (1976); W. L. Rose, *Slavery and Freedom* (1982); Todd L. Savitt, *Medicine and Slavery* (1978); William K. Scarborough, *The Overseer: Plantation Management in the Old South* (1966); Kenneth M. Stampp, *The Peculiar Institution: Slavery in the Antebellum South* (1956); Robert S. Starobin, *Denmark Vesey: The Slave Conspiracy of 1822* (1970); R. S. Starobin, *Industrial Slavery in the Old South* (1970); Dorothy Sterling, ed., *We Are Your Sisters: Black Women in the Nineteenth Century* (1984); Sterling Stuckey, *Slave Culture* (1987); Mark Tushnet, *The American Law of Slavery, 1810–1860* (1981); William L. Van Deburg, *The Slave Drivers* (1979); Michael Vlach, *The Afro-American Tradition in Decorative Arts* (1978); Richard C. Wade, *Slavery in the Cities: The South, 1820–1860* (1964); Thomas L. Webber, *Deep Like the Rivers: Education in the Slave Quarter Community, 1831–1865* (1978); Deborah Gray White, *Ar'n't I a Woman: Female Slaves in the Plantation South* (1985); Joel Williamson, *New People: Miscegenation and Mulattoes in the United States* (1980).

CHAPTER 12

Surge to the Pacific

*E*arly in April 1846, eighty-seven pioneers led by George Donner, a well-to-do sixty-two-year-old farmer, set out from Springfield, Illinois, for California. As this group of pioneers headed westward, they never imagined the hardship and tragedy they would encounter. Like many emigrants, they were ill-prepared for the dangerous trek. The pioneers' twenty-seven wagons were loaded not only with necessities but with fancy foods and liquor and such luxuries as built-in beds and stoves. George Donner's wife Tamsen had sewn $10,000 into a quilt and packed a wagon full of paints and schoolbooks for a young ladies' academy she planned to establish in California.

On July 20, at Fort Bridger, Wyoming, the party decided to take a shortcut. Lansford W. Hastings, an explorer, wagon train guide, and California booster, had suggested in a guidebook that pioneers could save 400 miles by cutting south of the Great Salt Lake. Hastings himself had never taken his own shortcut. He was trying to overthrow California's weak Mexican government and hoped to bring in enough emigrants to start a revolution. His misleading advice was designed to attract settlers to California.

At first, the trail was "all that could be desired." But soon huge boulders, arid desert, and dangerous mountain passes, slowed the expedition to a crawl. During one stretch, the party traveled only thirty-six miles in twenty-one days. A desert crossing that Hastings said would take two days actually took six days and nights, and forced the party to bury many of their valuables in the sand.

Twelve weeks after leaving Fort Bridger, the Donner party reached the eastern Sierra Nevada and prepared to cross Truckee Pass, the last remaining obstacle before they arrived in California's Sacramento Valley. On October 31, they climbed the high Sierra ridges in an attempt to cross the pass, but early snows and five-foot-high drifts blocked their path. "The snow came on so suddenly," Leanna Donner wrote, "that we had barely time to pitch our tent, and put up a brush shed, as it were, one side of which was open."

Trapped by the early snow, the party built crude tents and tepees, covered with clothing, blankets, and animal hides, which were soon buried under fourteen feet of snow. The pioneers intended to slaughter their livestock for food, but many of the animals perished in forty foot snow drifts. To survive, the Donner party was forced to eat mice, their rugs, and even their shoes. In the end, surviving members of the party escaped starvation only by eating the flesh of those who died.

Finally in mid-December, a group of twelve men and five women made a last-ditch effort to cross the pass to find help. They took only a six day supply of rations, consisting of finger-sized pieces of dried beef—two pieces per person per day. During a severe storm, two of the group died. The surviving members of the party "stripped the flesh from their bones, roasted and ate it, averting their eyes from each other, and weeping," More than a month passed before seven frost-bitten survivors reached an American settlement. By then, two other men had died and two Indian guides had been shot and eaten.

Relief teams immediately sought to rescue the pioneers still trapped near Truckee Pass. During the winter, four successive rescue parties broke through and brought out the survivors. The situation that the rescuers found was

Margaret Reed was one of only forty-seven survivors of the original party of eighty-one pioneers to reach California.

unspeakably gruesome. Thirteen were dead. Surviving members of the Donner party were delirious from hunger and over-exposure. One survivor was found in a small cabin next to the cannibalized body of a young boy. Of the original eighty-seven members of the party, only forty-seven survived.

It took a century and a half for Americans to expand as far west as the Appalachian Mountains, a few hundred miles from the Atlantic Coast. It took another fifty years to push the frontier to the Mississippi River. By 1830 fewer than 20,000 pioneers had crossed the Mississippi.

A small number of explorers, fur trappers, traders, and missionaries had ventured far beyond the Mississippi River. These trailblazers drew a picture of the American West as a land of promise, a paradise of plenty, filled with fertile valleys and rich land. During the 1840s, tens of thousands of American families chalked "GTT" (Gone to Texas) on their gates or painted "California or Bust" on their wagons, and joined the trek westward. By 1850, pioneers had pushed the edge of settlement all the way to Texas, the Rocky Mountains, and the Pacific Ocean.

OPENING THE WEST

Before the nineteenth century began, mystery shrouded the Far West. Mapmakers knew very little about the shape, size, or topography of the land west of the Mississippi River. British, French, and Spanish trappers, traders, and missionaries had traveled the Upper and Lower Missouri River and the Pacific Coast. But most of western North America was unknown to Americans.

The popular conception of the West was largely a mixture of legend and guesswork. Educated people, like Thomas Jefferson, believed that the West was populated by primeval beasts and that a "Northwest Passage" connected the Missouri River with the Columbia River and the Pacific Ocean. They had only a primitive conception of the Rocky Mountains. They believed that only a single ridge of moun-

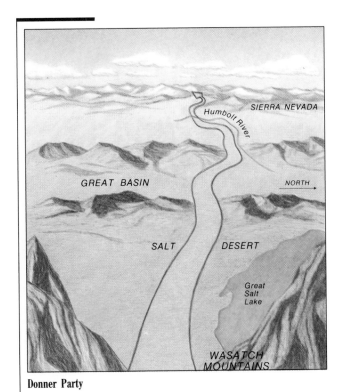

Donner Party

tains, known as the "Shining Mountains" or "Stony Mountains" needed to be crossed before one could see the Pacific Ocean.

Pathfinders

Beginning in 1803, explorers, hunters, soldiers, naturalists, trappers, and traders accumulated an enormous body of geographical information about the West. The first wave of exploration was touched off July 5, 1803, when President Thomas Jefferson dispatched his personal secretary, Meriwether Lewis, and William Clark to explore along the Missouri and Columbia rivers as far as the Pacific. As a politician interested in the rapid settlement and commercial development of the West, Jefferson wanted Lewis and Clark to establish American claims to the region west of the Rocky Mountains, gather information about furs and minerals in the region, and identify sites for trading posts and settlements. As a scientist, the president also instructed the expedition to collect information covering the diversity of life in the West, ranging from cli-

Meriwether Lewis, assisted by army captain William Clark, 34 soldiers, 10 civilians, and an Indian woman guide named Sacajawea, led an expedition up the Missouri River, across the northern Rocky Mountains, and along the tributaries of the Columbia River to the Pacific Ocean.

mate, geology, and plant growth to fossils of extinct animals and Indian religions, laws, and customs.

In 1806, the year that Lewis and Clark returned from their 8000-mile expedition, a young army lieutenant named Zebulon Montgomery Pike left St. Louis to explore the southern border of the Louisiana Territory, just as Lewis and Clark had explored the territory's northern portion. Traveling along the Arkansas River, Pike saw the towering peak that now bears his name. Pike and his party then traveled into Spanish territory along the Rio Grande and Red River. Pike's description of the wealth of Spanish towns in the Southwest brought many American traders to the region.

Pike's report of his expedition, which was published in 1810, helped to create one of the most influential myths about the American West: that it was nothing more than a "Great American Desert," a treeless and waterless land

of dust storms and starvation. "Here," wrote Pike, is "barren soil, parched and dried up for eight months of the year . . . [without] a speck of vegetation." This image of the West as a region of savages, wild beasts, and deserts received added support from another government-sponsored expedition—one led by Major Stephen H. Long in 1820 in search of the source of the Red River. Long's report described the West as "wholly unfit for cultivation, and . . . uninhabitable by a people depending upon agriculture for their subsistence." This report helped implant the image of the Great American Desert deeply in the American mind, retarding western settlement for a generation.

The view of the West as a dry, barren wasteland was not fully offset until the 1840s when another government-sponsored explorer, John C. Fremont, who was nicknamed "The Pathfinder," mapped much of the territory between the Mississippi Valley and the Pacific Ocean. His glowing descriptions of the West as a paradise of plenty captivated the imagination of many midwestern families who, by the 1840s, were eager for new lands to settle.

Mountain Men

More important than government explorers in opening the Far West to settlement were traders and trappers who caught beaver and bartered with the Indians for pelts. These were the men who blazed the great westward trails through the Rockies and Sierra Nevada and who stirred the popular imagination with stories of redwood forests, geysers, and fertile valleys in California, Oregon, and other areas west of the Rocky Mountains. These men also undermined the ability of the Blackfoot and other western Indians to resist American expansion by encouraging inter-tribal warfare, making Indians dependent on American manufactured goods, killing the animals that provided the basis for their hunting economy, introducing alcohol, and spreading disease.

Soon after Lewis and Clark completed their expedition, fur traders and trappers began to follow in their footsteps. Lewis and Clark brought back reports of rivers and streams in the northern Rockies teeming with beaver and

Each year at midsummer, Indians and mountain men met at the Trapper's Rendezvous, where they received their pay, picked up supplies, and drank and gambled.

otter. Beginning in 1807, keel boats ferried fur trappers up the Missouri River. Called "mountain men," these trappers brought $3,750,000 worth of furs to St. Louis between 1815 and 1830. By the mid-1830s, these trappers had marked the overland trails that would lead pioneers to Oregon and California.

The central figures in the story of the western fur trade were two businessmen, William Henry Ashley and Andrew Henry, who established the Rocky Mountain Fur Company in 1822. Instead of buying skins from Indians, Ashley and Henry placed ads in St. Louis newspapers asking for white trappers willing to go to the wilderness. Among the adventurous trappers who answered the ads were Jedediah Strong Smith (the first American to enter California from the east) and James Bridger (discoverer of the Great Salt Lake), whose exploits were legendary even in their own time. In 1822 Ashley and Henry sent one hundred trappers out along the upper Missouri River. Three years later, Ashley and Henry introduced the "rendezvous" system, under which trappers met once a year at an agreed-upon meeting place to barter pelts for supplies. "The rendezvous," wrote one participant, "is one continued scene of drunkenness, gambling, and brawling and fighting, as long as the money and the credit of the trappers last."

The life of the mountain men was difficult and dangerous. Novelist Washington Irving said that they lived "a life of more continued exertion, peril, and excitement" than any other Americans of their time. Threatened by dangerous animals and confronted by floods, blizzards, and exposure, trappers also faced competition from British Hudson's Bay Company, which in 1824 had established a fort on the banks of the Columbia River in Oregon and sent brigades of traders into the northern Rocky Mountains to search for pelts. One trapper in five died on the trails.

At the same time that mountain men searched for beaver in the Rockies and along the Columbia River, other groups of trappers, led by Jedediah Smith and James Pattie, began to trap furs in the Southwest, then part of Mex-

In 1826 Jedediah Smith led a party of trappers through Utah, across the Colorado River, then across the Mojave Desert and the San Bernadino Mountains to the Pacific.

ico. In the summer of 1826, Smith and a party of fifteen trappers became the first Americans to go overland through the Southwest. The next year, after nearly dying of thirst, they discovered a westward route to California, across the burning Mojave Desert and the San Bernardino Mountains to the Pacific Coast. Jim Beckwourth, a black mountain man who was the son of a Virginia slave, discovered a pass through the Sierra Nevada that became part of the overland trail to California.

By 1840, when the last annual rendezvous was held, the romantic era of the mountain men, dressed in fringed buckskin suits, had come to an end. Fur bearing animals had been trapped almost to extinction, and profits from trading, which amounted to as much as 2000 percent during the early years, fell steeply. Instead of hunting furs, some trappers became scouts for the army or pilots for the wagon trains that were just beginning to carry pioneers on the overland trails to Oregon and California.

Trailblazing

On September 1, 1821, William Becknell, an American trader, left Arrow Rock, Missouri, with a band of men and $300 worth of goods on pack animals. Two months and nearly 800 miles later—after he had been forced to cut the ear off a mule and drink the blood in order to survive and had drunk the contents of a buffalo's stomach because he could find no water—his caravan arrived in Santa Fe. A year later, Becknell took the first wagons across the same crude trail. Over the next twenty-five years, 80 wagons and 150 traders used the Santa Fe Trail each year. Mexican settlers of Santa Fe purchased cloth, hardware, glass, books, and the region's first printing press. Many goods were shipped on into northern Mexico and California. On their return, American traders carried Mexican blankets, beaver pelts, wool, mules, and Mexican silver coins. By the 1850s and 1860s, more than 5000 wagons a year took the trail across long stretches of desert, dangerous

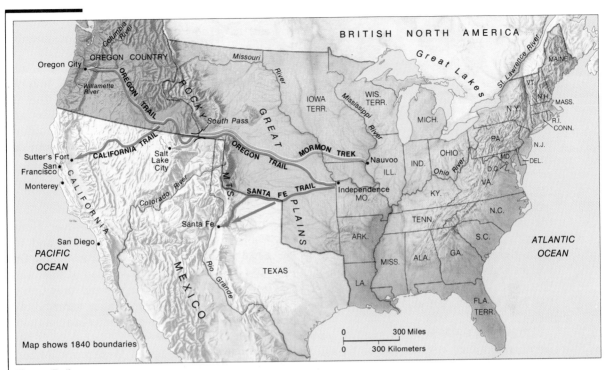

Western Trails

For as many as eight months, pioneers traveled fifteen or twenty miles a day, sixteen hours a day, in wagon trains made up of 50, 100, or 150 covered wagons.

water crossings, and treacherous mountain passes.

From its beginnings, the Santa Fe Trail stirred the imaginations of Americans. Before Becknell blazed the Santa Fe Trail, few Americans had entered the Spanish Southwest. Santa Fe had served as the northern capital of Spain's vast American empire for 212 years, but Spain had severely restricted the town's contact with Americans. Then, just weeks before Becknell arrived, Mexico proclaimed independence from Spain and Americans began to trade with the area. By the 1830s, traders had extended the trail into California, with branches reaching Los Angeles and San Diego. The Santa Fe Trail made the Spanish Southwest increasingly economically dependent on the United States and hastened American expansion into the areas that became Arizona, California, and New Mexico.

The Santa Fe Trail was primarily a road for merchants, unlike the Oregon and California trails, which carried pioneer settlers into the Far West. In 1811 and 1812, fur trappers marked out the Oregon Trail, the longest and most famous pioneer route in American history. This trail crossed about 2000 miles from Independence, Missouri, to the Columbia River country of Oregon. During the 1840s, 12,000 pioneers traveled the trail's whole distance to Oregon. In 1846 and 1847, Mormons, fleeing persecution in Illinois because of their religious beliefs, followed another route, known as the Mormon Trail, to the valley of the Great Salt Lake in Utah. After gold was discovered in California in 1848, thousands of gold seekers took an offshoot of the Oregon Trail through the Sierra Nevada to the California gold fields. In the summer of 1850, the peak year of pioneering, 55,000 gold seekers followed the trail to California.

Travel on the Oregon Trail was a tremendous test of human endurance. The journey by wagon train took six months. Settlers encountered prairie fires, sudden blizzards, and impassable mountains. Cholera and other diseases were common, and food, water, and wood were scarce. Only the stalwart dared brave the physical hardship of the westward trek.

SPANISH AND INDIAN AMERICA

When Americans ventured westward, they did not enter virgin land. Large parts of the Far West were already occupied by Indians and Mexicans, who had lived in the region for hundreds of years and established their own distinctive ways of life.

Spanish America

In 1528 a storm shipwrecked Alvar Nuñez Cabeza de Vaca, a landed aristocrat, and 100 Spanish explorers on the coast of Texas. One after another, the explorers died of starvation, disease, and exposure. In the end, only Cabeza de Vaca and three companions survived. For eight years, the four men wandered relentlessly through the frontier wilderness that would later be known as Texas, New Mexico, and Arizona.

During their trek, they heard Indians tell of Seven Cities of Cibola, seven cities with golden rooftops. On his return to Mexico City in 1536, Cabeza de Vaca repeated this story to Antonio de Mendoza, Mexico's first viceroy. Early in 1539, the viceroy sent a Franciscan friar named Marcos de Niza to investigate the story. The friar returned saying that he had seen, in the distance, cities whose rooftops glistened in the sunlight. Convinced that he had found the seven cities of gold, in late 1539 Mendoza dispatched an expedition under Francisco Vásquez de Coronado to conquer the territory. All Coronado found were seven Zuni Indian villages built of adobe and stone. There was no gold to be found.

Half a century before the first English colonists arrived at Jamestown, Spain had already established permanent settlements in the Far West. Because of a fear that other European nations would claim territory too close to Mexico, Spain in the late sixteenth century planted a colony in New Mexico and a century later built the first settlements in Arizona and Texas. In the late eighteenth century, fearful that Britain and Russia might occupy the Pacific Coast, Spain established outposts in California. By

1800 New Spain, Spain's northernmost American province, extended from present-day Montana to Mexico and from the Pacific Ocean to the Mississippi River.

The Mission System

Roman Catholic priests from Spain played an important role in the settlement of the Spanish Southwest. Jesuit and Franciscan missionaries established missions to teach Christianity to the Indians. They brought Indians in from their villages and forced them to live in mission communities, where they were taught such trades as weaving, blacksmithing, candlemaking, and leather-working, and were forced to work in workshops, orchards, and fields for long hours.

New Mexico was the first center of mission activity in the Southwest. In 1598 Don Juan de Oñate, son of the governor of Mexico, led the first successful effort to colonize the region. Oñate imposed the Spanish *encomienda* system (see pp. 19–20), which bound the Indians to the land as serfs and brought in priests to convert the Indians to Catholicism. In 1610 a permanent capital was set up in Santa Fe, which was the first seat of government in the present-day United States.

By 1630 Spain had established twenty-five missions in New Mexico and claimed to have converted 60,000 Pueblo Indians to Christianity. The missionaries' attempts to suppress Indian tribal ceremonies and force them to adopt Spanish ways led to repeated clashes between Spaniards and the Indians which culminated in 1680 in an Indian revolt. In that year, Popé, an Indian priest from the San Juan Pueblo, led the revolt that destroyed Spanish churches and ranches, sacked the city of Santa Fe, and drove the Spanish out of New Mexico. Indians killed more than 400 Spaniards as they tried to destroy all traces of the Roman Catholic church. By 1696, however, Spain had successfully reconquered New Mexico and had broken the power of the Pueblo Indians.

Catholic missionaries had less success in what is now Arizona. During the late 1600s, the Catholic church sent priests into Arizona to establish missions. After 1690 Father Eusebio

Between 1769 and 1823, Spain built twenty-one missions between San Diego and San Francisco. Here Indians perform a native dance at a San Francisco mission in 1816.

Francisco Kino founded twenty-four Jesuit missions. The Yuma and Apache Indians, however, refused to accept Christianity and Spanish control and forced the Spanish to abandon all but two of their missions.

Although the Catholic church tried to establish missions in central, east, and southwest Texas after 1690, its efforts were largely unsuccessful. Apache and Comanche bitterly resisted the missionaries' efforts to introduce Christianity and farming. By the early 1800s, only 4000 Spanish settlers resided in Texas.

Mission life reached its peak of development in California. However, Spain did not colonize California, despite its closeness to Mexico, until 1769. In the mideighteenth century, Spain learned that Russian seal hunters and traders were moving south from Alaska into California. Determined to halt the Russian ad-

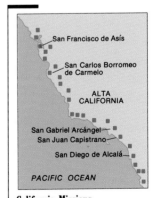

California Missions

vance down the Pacific Coast, Spanish authorities dispatched Captain Gaspar de Portola to explore and settle the region. On his expedition, de Portola discovered San Francisco Bay and established presidios (military forts) at San Diego and Monterey, California. Accompanying de Portola's expedition was a Franciscan father Junipero Serra, who established the first Californian mission, San Diego de Alacala, near the present-day site of San Diego. Between 1769 and 1823, Spain established twenty-one missions in California, extending from San Diego northward to Sonoma. By 1830, 30,000 of California's 300,000 Indians worked on missions, where they harvested grain and herded 400,000 cattle, horses, goats, hogs, and sheep.

Impact of the Mexican Revolution

In 1810 Miguel Hidalgo y Costilla, a Mexican priest, led a revolt against Spanish rule. This uprising was put down, but it started Mexico's struggle for independence. On September 21, 1821, Mexico finally won its independence from Spain.

The Mexican Revolution marked the beginning of a period of far-reaching change in the Southwest. In New Mexico and Arizona, the collapse of Spanish authority allowed American traders to bring American goods into the area and trappers to search the region for beaver furs. In Texas, Mexican independence convinced many Americans that the province was theirs for the taking. American adventurers staged a series of filibuster expeditions into Texas, and in 1820 Moses Austin of Missouri successfully petitioned Spanish officials in San Antonio to allow Americans to colonize the sparsely populated province. Under Mexican rule, California was also opened up to American commerce and settlement. By 1848 Americans made up about half of California's non-Indian population.

Mexican independence also led to the demise of the mission system in California. After the revolution, many Mexicans in California wanted the missions to be "secularized"—

After it won independence from Spain, Mexico secularized the missions and divided the land into ranchos. This painting shows a master of a rancho in the Mexican Southwest.

broken up and their property divided among Indians or sold or given away to private citizens. In 1833–34 the Mexican government confiscated California mission properties and exiled the Franciscan friars. Some of the land was given to the Indians, who were inexperienced in property ownership and quickly lost control of their holdings. The Mexican government also issued grants of mission land to private citizens. By 1846 missions' lands and cattle had largely passed into the hands of 800 private landowners called rancheros, who controlled 8 million acres of land in units (ranchos) ranging in size from 4500 acres to 50,000 acres. The ranchos were run like feudal estates, and the Indians who worked on the estates had a status similar to that of slaves. Indeed, the death rate of Indians who worked on ranchos was twice as high as the rate among southern slaves, and by 1848 one-fifth of California's Indian population had died.

Western Indians

Americans sometimes mistakenly think of the West as a virgin territory that was largely unpopulated prior to the coming of the pioneers. It was not. In 1840, before large numbers of pioneers and farmers crossed the Mississippi, at least 300,000 Indians lived in the Southwest, on the Great Plains, in California, and on the Northwest Pacific Coast.

The Native American peoples of the West were not a single people. More than 200 different tribes lived west of the Mississippi River in the early nineteenth century, each with its own language, religious beliefs, kinship practices, and system of government.

Best-known of the western Indians were the twenty-three Indian tribes—including the Cheyenne and Sioux—who lived on the Great Plains and hunted buffalo. For many present-day Americans, the Plains Indians, riding on horseback, wearing a warbonnet, and living in a tepee, are regarded as the typical American Indians. In fact, the Plains Indians only began to acquire horses from the Spanish and guns from British and French fur traders in the sixteenth century. Not until the middle of the eighteenth century did all the Indian tribes have horses and guns.

On the eastern Plains, Indians combined farming and hunting. For half the year, these Indians lived in permanent villages in earthen lodges, raising corn, beans, squashes, and tobacco. After they harvested their crops, these tribes traveled west to hunt buffalo. Indians of the western Plains, like the Blackfoot, Crow, and Comanche, did not farm; they lived throughout the year in portable tepees and hunted buffalo, antelope, deer, and elk for subsistence.

South and west of the Plains, in the huge arid region that is now Arizona and New Mexico, sophisticated farmers, like the Hopi and Zuni, coexisted with nomadic hunters and gatherers, like the Apache and Navajo. In the Great Basin, the harsh barren region between the Sierra Nevada and the Rocky Mountains that extends across Utah, Nevada, arid eastern California, and northwestern Arizona, food was so scarce that peoples like the Paiutes and the Gosiutes subsisted upon berries, pine nuts, and roots as well as insects, rabbits, reptiles, and mice. Conditions were so harsh that the people of the Great Basin often lived in bands consisting of a single family.

In California, Indians occupied small villages during the winter, but moved during the rest of the year gathering wild plants and seeds, hunting small game, and fishing in the rivers. More than 100,000 Indians still lived in California when the area was acquired by the United States in 1848.

Along the northwest Pacific Coast, the heavily wooded area that extends from northern California to southern Alaska, lived a great number of tribes which developed an elaborate social hierarchy based on wealth and descent. The Indians who lived on the northwest coast found an abundant food supply in the sea, coastal rivers, and forests. They took salmon, seal, whale, and otter from the coastal waters and hunted deer, moose, and elk in the forests.

Indians of the western Plains, like the Blackfoot, lived in portable tepees and hunted game for subsistence.

The Impact of European and American Contact

Even before the Civil War, contact with white traders, trappers, and settlers had produced profound changes in Native American societies. The most obvious change was a sharp decline in the size of the Indian population. In California disease and deliberate campaigns of extermination killed 70,000 Indians between 1849 and 1859. Many Indian women were forced into concubinage and many men into virtual slavery. One Indian hater expressed widespread sentiments: "We must kill them big and little, nits will be lice." In the Great Basin, impoverished Gosiutes and Paiutes were shot by trappers for sport. In Texas, the Karankawas and many of the other original tribes of the area largely disappeared. Further west, Comanche, Kiowa, and Apache warriors bitterly resisted white encroachment on their land. White settlers accused these warriors of impaling women on fenceposts, staking men under the sun with their eyelids removed, and heaping burning coals on their genitals. Tribes in the Pacific Northwest and the northern Plains struggled desperately to slow the arrival of whites along the Oregon Trail. The Nez Percé and Flathead Indians expelled American missionaries from their tribal lands, and the Snake, Cheyenne, Shasta, and Rogue River Indians tried futilely to cut emigrant routes.

To protect the emigrants, the federal government mounted a series of punitive attacks against the western Indians and established army posts throughout the West. The government also signed a succession of treaties with western Indian tribes placing tribal lands into federal hands. Between 1853 and 1857 alone, Indian tribes ceded 174 million acres of their land.

SETTLING THE FAR WEST

In 1841, a party of sixty-nine pioneers left Missouri for California, led by an Ohio schoolteacher named John Bidwell. The members of the party knew little about western travel: "We only knew that California lay to the west." The hardships the party endured were nearly unbearable. They were forced to abandon their wagons and eat their pack animals, "half roasted, dripping with blood." American pioneering of the Far West had begun. The next year another 200 pioneers went west. Within two years, more than one thousand pioneers had crossed the Plains into California and Oregon. Who were these pioneers? What forces drove them to abandon civilization for the wilderness?

The Staging Grounds

Most of the pioneers who migrated to the Far West came from the states that border the Mississippi River: Missouri, Arkansas, Louisiana, and Illinois. These states had themselves recently left frontier status behind them. Louisiana had only become a state in 1811; Illinois in 1818; Missouri in 1821; and Arkansas in 1836.

The rugged life of the pioneer was not a new experience for many of these people. Either they or their parents had already moved several times before reaching the Mississippi Valley. They also had a temperament well-suited to pioneering. During the early nineteenth century, the Mississippi Valley seemed to many observers to be a region of restless energy, violence, and boisterous tall talk. It was a land where yeomen farmers and respectable tradesmen lived alongside lawless gamblers, rivermen, and roustabouts.

Contemporary observers were shocked by the brutal pastimes of the inhabitants of the Mississippi Valley, which included "rough-and-tumble" bare-fisted fighting, in which combatants tried to gouge out an opponent's eyes and tear off his testicles. Mark Twain vividly described the kinds of men he had seen while growing up in Hannibal, Missouri: "Rude, uneducated, brave, suffering terrific hardships with sailor-like stoicism; heavy drinkers . . . heavy fighters, reckless fellows, every one, elephantinely jolly, foul witted, profane; profligal of their money . . . yet in the main, honest, trustworthy, faithful to promises and duty, and often picaresquely magnanimous."

The Mississippi Valley was filled with restless men and women, thirsty for adventure and eager to better themselves. In 1833, when Iowa was cleared of Indians and opened to settlement, thousands of families pulled up stakes and poured into the area.

Iowa Fever

In 1854 Horace Greeley, a newspaper editor, gave Josiah B. Grinnell, a New Yorker, a famous piece of advice. "Go West, young man, and grow up with the country," said Greeley. Grinnell took Greeley's advice, moved west, and later founded Grinnell, Iowa.

Before 1830 Iowa was Indian land, occupied by the Sauk, Fox, Missouri, Pottowatomi, and other Indian tribes. The defeat of the Sauk and Fox Indians in the Black Hawk War in 1832 opened the first strip of Iowa to settlement. Even before Iowa became a territory in 1838, settlers raced across the Mississippi and established farms and founded such cities as Davenport, Dubuque, and Iowa City. By 1840 Iowa's population had risen to 40,000.

Because no government land office was established in Iowa until 1838, many early settlers were squatters who set up farms on land that they did not own. Because they had cleared the land and built houses, they believed that the federal government would give them the right to purchase the land at minimum prices when it came up for sale. Unfortunately, many real estate speculators, known as "claim-jumpers," tried to take the squatters' land away by out-bidding them when public auctions were held. Squatters formed more than 100 land-claim associations—extra-legal associations of local settlers—to eliminate competitive bidding and protect their holdings when the lands were offered for sale. In 1841 Congress recognized squatters' rights. The Preemption Bill of 1841 stated that squatters who lived on surveyed government land and made improvements on the land could buy up to 160 acres for $1.25 an acre.

At the same time that settlers poured into Iowa, other emigrants migrated to Michigan, Minnesota, and Wisconsin. Lumberjacks and miners were the first to arrive. Soon they were followed by farmers and tradesmen. Even before this northern tier of states was filled, people in the Mississippi Valley were pushing across the Great Plains into the Far West.

Curiously, these pioneers did not settle on the Plains first. It was not until the 1870s and 1880s that pioneers settled on the prairies of Nebraska, Montana, and the Dakotas. Earlier advances into the West had been more or less gradual. In the 1840s, however, emigrants leap-frogged treeless prairies, deserts, and mountains for the west coast. The reason was simple. The Plains were held by hostile Indians, and furthermore, the pioneers erroneously believed that the Plains had little land fit for cultivation. Pioneers moved instead westward along the overland trails to Oregon and California or south to Texas.

Life on the Trail

Each spring, pioneers gathered at Independence and St. Joseph, Missouri, and Council Bluffs, Iowa, to begin a 2000-mile journey westward. For many families, the great spur for emigration was economic: the financial depression of the late thirties, accompanied by floods and epidemics in the Mississippi Valley. Said one woman: "We had nothing to lose, and we might gain a fortune." Between 1841 and 1867, more than 350,000 trekked along the overland trails.

With the exception of the fortune hunters seeking gold in California, most pioneers traveled with their families and relatives. Even single men attached themselves to family groups. In virtually every recorded case, it was the husband, and not the wife, who made the decision to set out on the overland trail. Said one woman, "the thought of becoming a pioneer's wife never entered my mind."

At first, pioneers tried to maintain the rigid sexual division of labor that characterized early nineteenth-century America. Men drove the wagons and livestock, stood guard duty, and hunted buffalo and antelope for extra meat. Women got up at four in the morning, collected wood and "buffalo chips" (animal dung used for fuel), hauled water, kindled campfires, kneaded

Life along the westward trails was a tremendous test of human endurance. Pioneers encountered arid desert, difficult mountain passes, dangerous rivers, and quicksand. At least 20,000 pioneers died along the overland trails.

dough, and milked cows. At the end of the day, men expected women to fix dinner, make the beds, air out the wagons to prevent mildew, wash the clothes, and tend the children. As necessity arose, however, women also took on men's work. They drove wagons, yoked cattle, and loaded wagons.

Accidents, disease, and sudden disaster were ever-present dangers. Children fell out of wagons, oxen hauling wagons became exhausted and died, and diseases such as typhoid, dysentery, and mountain fever killed many pioneers. Emigrant parties also suffered devastation from buffalo stampedes, prairie fires, and floods. Pioneers buried at least 20,000 emigrants along the Oregon Trail.

Still, despite the hardships and tragedies on the trail, few emigrants ever regretted the decision to move. As one pioneer put it: "Those who crossed the plains . . . never forgot the ungratified thirst, the intense heat and bitter cold, the craving hunger and utter physical exhus-

tion of the trail. . . . But there was another side. True they had suffered, but the satisfaction of deeds accomplished and difficulties overcome more than compensated and made the overland passage a thing never to be forgotten."

MANIFEST DESTINY

In 1844 John L. O'Sullivan, editor of the *Democratic Review,* referred in his magazine to America's "Manifest Destiny to overspread the continent allotted by Providence for the free development of our yearly expanding millions." One of the most influential slogans ever coined, *manifest destiny* expressed the emotion that led Americans to risk their lives to settle the Far West.

The idea that America had a special destiny and divine mission encouraged men and women to dream big dreams. "We Americans," wrote Herman Melville, one of this country's greatest novelists, "are the peculiar, chosen people—the Israel of our time." Manifest destiny inspired a twenty-nine-year-old named Stephen F. Austin to talk grandly of colonizing the Mexican province of Texas with "North American population, enterprise and intelligence." It led land-hungry Westerners, flocking to the Pacific Northwest, to declare "54° 40′ or fight!" Aggressive nationalists invoked the idea to justify Indian removal, war with Mexico, and American expansion into Cuba and Central America. More positively, the idea of manifest destiny inspired missionaries, farmers, and pioneers who dreamed only of transforming empty plains and fertile valleys into farms and small towns.

Gone to Texas

In 1822, when the first caravan of American traders traversed the Santa Fe Trail and the first hundred fur trappers searched the Rocky Mountains for beaver, a small number of Americans blazed a trail to another frontier, Texas.

In the summer of 1820 Moses Austin, a bankrupt fifty-nine-year-old Missourian, asked Spanish authorities for a large Texas land tract which he would promote and sell to American pioneers. On the face of it, Austin's request was preposterous. Austin had been a Philadelphia dry goods merchant, a Virginia mine operator, a Louisiana judge, and a Missouri banker. But early in 1821 the Spanish government gave him permission to settle 300 families in Texas. Spain welcomed the Americans for two reasons: to provide a buffer against hostile Indian tribes and to develop the land, since only 3500 native Mexicans had settled in Texas. Moses Austin did not live to see his dream realized. On a return trip from Mexico City, he died of exhaustion and exposure.

Before he died, he made his son Stephen promise to carry out his dream of colonizing Texas. In 1822 Stephen led the first group of 150 settlers to Texas. By the end of 1824, young Austin had attracted 272 colonists to Texas and had persuaded the newly independent Mexican government that encouragement of American immigration was the best way to develop Texas. To attract colonists, Mexico in 1825 gave each new settler 4428 acres of land. The Mexican government also agreed to give land agents (called empresarios) 67,000 acres of land for every 200 families they brought to Texas. Mexico imposed two conditions on land ownership: settlers had to become Mexican citizens and they had to convert to Roman Catholicism. By 1830 there were 16,000 Americans in Texas, four times the Mexican population.

As the Anglo population swelled, Mexican authorities grew increasingly suspicious of the growing American presence in Texas. Mexico feared that the United States planned to use the Texas colonists to acquire the province by revolution. In 1827 the Mexican government sent General Manuel de Mier y Terán to investigate the situation.

In his report, Terán warned that unless the Mexican government took timely measures, American settlers in Texas were certain to rebel. Differences in language and culture, Terán believed, had produced bitter enmity between the colonists and native Mexicans. The colonists, he noted, refused to learn the Spanish language, maintained their own separate schools, and conducted most of their trade with

This 1879 painting by John Gast depicts the spirit of manifest destiny leading pioneers, farmers, railroads, and telegraphs across the continent.

the United States. They complained bitterly that they had to travel more than 500 miles to reach a Mexican court and resented the efforts of Mexican authorities to deprive them of the right to vote.

To reassert its authority over Texas, the Mexican government abolished slavery in the province, authorized the establishment of a chain of military posts manned by convict soldiers, levied customs duties, restricted trade with the United States, and decreed an end to further American immigration. These actions might have provoked Texans into a revolution, but in 1832, General Antonio López de Santa Anna, a Mexican politician and soldier, became Mexico's president; and colonists hoped that he would make Texas a self-governing state within the Mexican republic. Once in power, however, Santa Anna proved to be less liberal than many Americans had believed. In 1834, he overthrew Mexico's constitutional government and made

Stephen Austin

Santa Anna

wandering about the country as a near-derelict, returned to live with the Cherokee. During his stay with the tribe, Houston was instrumental in forging peace treaties among several warring Indian nations. In 1832 Houston traveled to Washington to demand that President Jackson live up to the terms of the removal treaty. Jackson did not meet Houston's demands, but instead sent him unofficially to Texas to keep an eye on the American settlers and the growing anti-Mexican sentiment.

In the middle of 1835, scattered local outbursts erupted against Mexican rule. A group of settlers led by the famous frontiersman Jim Bowie ousted a Mexican garrison from Nacogdoches. Another group of Texas rebels rescued a hot-tempered Southerner named William Travis when he was held prisoner at a Mexican garrison at Anahuac. Then, a small band of Texas riflemen captured Mexico's military headquarters in San Antonio. Revolution was underway.

himself dictator. When Stephen Austin went to Mexico City to try to settle the Texans' grievances, Santa Anna had him arrested and held prisoner in a Mexican jail for two years.

The situation in Texas grew increasingly tense. To tighten his grip on the province, Santa Anna established a series of military garrisons in Texas. Moving in a different direction on November 3, 1835, American colonists adopted a constitution and organized a temporary government, but voted overwhelmingly against declaring independence. A majority of colonists hoped to attract the support of Mexican liberals in a joint effort to depose Santa Anna.

While holding out the possibility of compromise, the Texans prepared for war by electing Sam Houston commander of whatever military forces he could muster. Houston, one of the larger than life figures who won Texas independence, had a remarkable background. At the age of fifteen, he had run away from home and lived for three years with the Cherokee Indians in eastern Tennessee. During the War of 1812, he had fought in the Creek War under Andrew Jackson. At thirty he was elected to the House of Representatives and at thirty-four he was elected governor of Tennessee. Many Americans regarded him as the heir apparent to Andrew Jackson.

Then, suddenly, in 1829 scandal struck. Houston married a woman seventeen years his junior. Within three months, the marriage was mysteriously annulled. Depressed and humiliated, Houston resigned as governor, and after

One of the most colorful leaders of the struggle for Texas independence, Sam Houston lived for a time with the Cherokee Indians, became a popular hero of the Creek War, and became a congressman and later governor of Tennessee.

Texas Revolution

Soon, the ominous news reached Texas that Santa Anna himself was marching north with 7000 soldiers to crush the revolt—an army filled with raw recruits with little or no training, including many Indian troops who spoke and understood little Spanish. Santa Anna's initial goal was to recapture San Antonio. Sam Houston ordered San Antonio abandoned, but 150 Texas rebels decided to defend the city and make their stand at an abandoned Spanish mission, the Alamo. The Texans were led by William Travis and included frontier heroes Davy Crockett and Jim Bowie.

For twelve days, Mexican forces lay siege to the Alamo. Travis issued an appeal for reinforcements, but only thirty-two men were able to cross Mexican lines. Legend has it that on the evening of March 5, Travis, realizing that defense of the Alamo was futile, drew a line in the dirt with his sword. Only those willing to die for Texas independence, Travis announced to the garrison, should step across the line and defend the Alamo. All but one man did. Jim Bowie, too sick to move from his cot, called over some friends and had them carry him across Travis's line.

At 5 A.M., March 6, Mexican troops scaled the mission's walls. By 8 A.M., the fighting was over. One hundred eighty-three defenders lay dead—including several Mexican defenders who had fought for Texas independence. (Seven defenders surrendered, and about fifteen persons survived, including an American woman and her child.) Mexican forces soaked the defenders' bodies in oil, stacked them like cordwood outside the mission, and set them ablaze. If the Alamo was a defeat, it was also a psychological victory. Santa Anna's troops suffered 1550 casualties—eight Mexican soldiers

By 8 A. M. on March 6, the fight at the Alamo was over. One hundred eighty-three defenders were dead and eight Mexican soldiers had died for each defender.

TEJANOS AT THE ALAMO

General Antonio López de Santa Anna, backed by some 2400 Mexican troops, put the Alamo under siege on February 23, 1836. On that day he ordered the hoisting of a red flag, meaning "no quarter," which only hardened the resolve of the Alamo's small contingent of defenders, including the legendary Jim Bowie, Davy Crockett, and William Barret Travis. Also inside the Alamo were men like Juan Seguin and Gregorio Esparza. They represented a handful of Tejano defenders. As native residents of Texas, they despised Santa Anna for having so recently overthrown the Mexican Constitution of 1824 in favor of dictatorship.

San Antonio was a center of the Tejano population of Texas. Juan Seguin's father, Don Erasmo, was a wealthy local rancher who in earlier years had encouraged the opening of the Mexican province of Coahuila y Tejas to nonnative Anglos from the United States. Most of the Anglos settled far to the east of San Antonio, but those who traveled to the Tejano settlements knew Don Erasmo as a generous host who entertained lavishly at his *hacienda,* "Casa Blanca." His son Juan was also locally prominent and had helped immeasurably in driving Mexican troops under General Martin Perfecto de Cós, Santa Anna's brother-in-law, out of San Antonio late in 1835. His reward was a commission as a captain of Texas cavalry.

Much less is known about Gregorio Esparza. He lived with his wife and four children in San Antonio, and Juan Seguin had recruited him for his cavalry company. When Santa Anna's advance troops appeared on February 23, Esparza quickly gathered up his family and rushed for protection behind the thick walls of the old Spanish mission known locally as the Alamo.

The Alamo defenders were in an all-but-impossible position, and each day Santa Anna kept tightening his siege lines. Inside the Alamo, the defenders looked to Jim Bowie for leadership, but he was seriously ill with pnuemonia. So they accepted orders from William Barret Travis. With 1000 troops, Travis had argued, the Alamo would never fall. His numbers, however, barely approached 200. As a result, Travis regularly sent out couriers with urgent messages for relief. His words were direct. He would never "surrender or retreat." He would "die like a soldier who never forgets what is due to his own honor and that of his country." For those at the Alamo, the alternatives were now "VICTORY OR DEATH."

Late in February, Travis prepared yet another appeal, this time addressed to Sam Houston, commander in chief of the Texas army. Time was running out, Travis wrote. "If they overpower us," he explained, "we hope posterity and our country will do our memory justice. Give me help, oh my country!" Travis handed the message to Juan Seguin, who borrowed Jim Bowie's horse and rode off with his aide, Antonio Cruz, under the cover of a driving rainstorm. They eventually found Houston, far to the east, but there was nothing anyone could do now to save those defenders still with Travis.

Early on the morning of March 6, 1836, the Alamo fell to 1800 attacking Mexican soldiers. The fighting was so brutal that 600 of Santa Anna's troops lay dead or wounded before the last of the 183 defenders faced mutilation from countless musket balls and bayonet thrusts. Gregorio Esparza was torn to shreds as the Mexicans reached the church inside the courtyard. Only women, children, and one Tejano, who claimed that he was a prisoner, survived. Later that day Mrs. Esparza received permission to bury her husband with Christian rites. Santa Anna issued orders to have the bodies of all other defenders heaped into piles and set on fire.

During the next several weeks Santa Anna's troops pushed steadily eastward with the goal of destroying another Texas army being hastily assembled by Sam Houston. The Seguins, father and son, played key parts in providing resistance. Don Erasmo worked furiously to collect needed food supplies, and Juan led troops in harassing and delaying the Mexican column, all of which aided in the staging of Houston's stunning victory over Santa Anna at the Battle of San Jacinto on April 21, 1836—the day the Republic gained its independence.

As the Texas uprising gained momentum in late 1835 and early 1836, Tejanos had to choose which side to support. Some hoped that uniting with the Anglos would force Santa Anna to renounce his dictatorship in favor of the liberal 1824 constitution. Few actually favored independence because they knew that Anglos held them in contempt, which caused men like Gregorio Esparza's brother to join Santa Anna's army and fight against the Alamo defenders. He

suspected that heavy-handed rule under the Mexican dictator could not be worse and might well be better than living under culturally and racially intolerant Anglos from the United States.

From the very outset, Anglos entering Texas spoke of Tejanos and Mexicans as debased human beings, comparable in many ways to Indian "savages" blocking the advancement of white European civilization. In 1831 colonizer Stephen F. Austin wrote: "My object, the sole and only desire of my ambitions since I first saw Texas, was to . . . settle it with an intelligent, honorable, and enterprising people." Four years later, Austin still wanted to see Texas "Americanized, that is settled by a population that will harmonize with their neighbors on the *East*, in language, political principles, common origin, sympathy, and even interest." The success of the Texas Revolution, from Austin's point of view, would assure that Anglo-Americans pouring into the region would not be ruled by what he considered the inferior native populace.

Increasingly before and after 1836, Anglo migrants employed terms of racial and cultural derision to describe the native Tejanos. They were the most "lazy, indolent, poor, starved set of people as ever the sun shined upon"; they were "slaves of popish superstitions and despotism"; and they spent "days in gambling to gain a few bits than to make a living by honest industry." With their mixture of Spanish, Indian, and black parents, they were a "mongrel" race, a "swarthy looking people much resembling . . . mulattoes."

Worse yet, they behaved at times like depraved, violent, less-

than-human creatures as personified by Santa Anna at the Alamo and later at Goliad, where 300 captured rebels were systematically shot to death. Wrote one Anglo veteran of the Texas Revolution late in life: "I thought that I could kill Mexicans as easily as I could deer and turkeys." He apparently did so while shouting: "Remember the Alamo! Remember Goliad!"

Yet this veteran, like so many others looking back at the days of the Texas Revolution, only recalled selected portions of the Alamo story. They talked of the bravery of Bowie, Crockett, and Travis but ignored the courage of Tejanos like Don Carlos and Juan Seguin and Gregorio Esparza. Nor did they remember that Juan Seguin received an honorable military discharge before serving as mayor of San Antonio until 1842 when Anglo rumor-mongers accused him of supporting an attempted military invasion from Mexico.

To save himself, Seguin fled across the border but eventually returned to his native Texas and lived out his days quietly far removed from the public limelight. No doubt Seguin wondered whether he had made the right decision in not joining the side of Santa Anna, especially as he experienced the racial and cultural hatred directed against Mexican-Americans as the United States surged toward the Pacific. Although those thoughts are not known, it is fortunate that his story and those of other Tejano resisters have not been forgotten. Surely they too deserve remembrance as heroes of the Alamo and the Texas Revolution.

died for every defender. "Remember the Alamo" became the battle cry of the Texas war of independence.

One disaster after another followed the Alamo. Three weeks after defeat at the Alamo, James Fannin and his men surrendered to Mexican forces at Goliad with the understanding that they would be treated as prisoners of war. Santa Anna set aside the agreement and ordered the 330 Texans marched out of town and shot. Then, another Texas detachment at San Patricio was overwhelmed. But the defeats had an unexpected side-effect. They gave Sam Houston time to raise and train an army. Volunteers from the American South flocked to his banner. On April 21, his army of less than 800 men surprised Santa Anna's army as it camped out on the San Jacinto River, east of present-day Houston. The Texas rebels, who suffered nine dead and thirty wounded, killed 630 of the enemy and captured 730. The next day, Houston's army captured Santa Anna himself and forced him to sign a treaty granting Texas its independence.

For many Mexican settlers in Texas, defeat meant that they would be relegated to a second-class social, political, and economic position. The new Texas constitution denied citizenship and property rights to those who failed to support the revolution. Consequently, many Mexican landowners fled the region.

Texas grew rapidly following independence. In 1836, 5000 immigrants arrived in Texas, boosting its population to 30,000. By 1847, its population had reached 140,000. The region also grew economically. Although cotton farming dominated the Texas economy, cattle were becoming an increasingly important industry. Mexican landowners abandoned thousands of cattle after the revolution, and by the 1840s, 300,000 wild cattle roamed the range. By 1850 the first American cowboys were driving 60,000 cattle a year to New Orleans, Chicago, and California.

These cowboys borrowed the clothing, customs, and even the songs of earlier Mexican cow hands, known as *vaqueros*. Like the vaqueros, the cowboy used a rope, known as a lariat (reata), to corral cattle and utilized a special saddle (now known as a "western" saddle) with a horn. The cowboys also borrowed the vaque-

ros' clothing, including the wide brimmed hat, the high heel pointed toe boots, and leather leggings, known as chaps (short for chaparrerjos), that protected the cowboy's legs. Their nickname, wrangler, came from a Spanish word, *catallerango*. Many cowboy songs, like "The Streets of Laredo," were actually translations of Mexican ballads.

The Texas Question

Texas had barely won its independence before it decided to become a part of the United States. A referendum held soon after the Battle of San Jacinto showed Texans favored annexation by a vote of 3277 to 93. Despite this vote, it was a decade before Texas joined the Union.

The annexation question was one of the most controversial issues in American politics in the late 1830s and early 1840s. The issue was not Texas but slavery. The admission of Texas to the Union would upset the sectional balance of power in the United States Senate. President Andrew Jackson, acutely conscious of the opposition to admitting Texas as a slave state, agreed only to recognize Texas independence. In 1838 John Quincy Adams, a member of the House of Representatives, staged a twenty-two day filibuster which successfully blocked annexation. It appeared that Congress had settled the Texas question. For the time, Texas remained an independent republic.

It was at this point that proslavery Southerners began to popularize a conspiracy theory that would eventually bring Texas into the Union as a slave state. In 1841 John Tyler, an ardent defender of slavery as a positive good, became president following the death of William Henry Harrison. Tyler and his secretary of state, John C. Calhoun, argued that Great Britain was scheming to annex Texas and transform it into a haven for runaway slaves. According to this theory, British slave emancipation in the West Indies had been a total economic disaster and the British hoped to undermine slavery in the American South by turning Texas into a British satellite state. (In fact, British abolitionists, but not the British government, were working to convince Texas to outlaw slavery in exchange for British foreign aid.) Sam Houston played along with this ploy by conducting highly visible negotiations with the British government. If the United States would not annex Texas, Houston warned, Texas would seek the support of "some other friend."

The Texas question was the major political issue in the presidential campaign of 1844. James Polk, the Democratic candidate, ardently supported annexation. His victory encouraged Tyler to submit a resolution to Congress calling for annexation. Congress, fearing British intentions, narrowly approved the resolution in 1845.

Oregon

The first halting steps toward settlement of the Pacific Northwest took place in 1810 when John Jacob Astor, who had made a fortune in the Great Lakes fur trade, decided to plant a trading post at the mouth of the Columbia River. He hoped Astoria would gain a monopoly over the western fur trade and then ship the furs to eager customers in China.

Astor sent two expeditions to the Far West: one by land and one by sea. Both met with disaster. The sea expedition ran aground on a sandbar at the entrance of the Columbia River, killing eight men. Then, after dropping several passengers off at Astoria, the ship proceeded northward, where Indians destroyed it and massacred the crew. The land expedition was nearly as unlucky. After setting out from St. Louis in 1811, the expedition tried to navigate the rapids of the Snake River and cross the Utah desert on foot. By the time the weary survivors reached Astoria, they found that the British already controlled the fur trade. When the War of 1812 began, the British navy made it impossible to supply Astoria, and Astor sold the post to Canadian traders.

For nearly two decades, Britain dominated the Pacific Northwest. The British Hudson's Bay Company established a powerful fort at the mouth of the Columbia River with a dock for ocean-going ships. It scattered smaller forts and trading posts throughout the Pacific Northwest. To ensure that the region was self-sufficient in food, the company set up farms, orchards, and ranches.

As British fur traders expanded their activities in the Pacific Northwest, American politicians grew alarmed that Britain, and not the

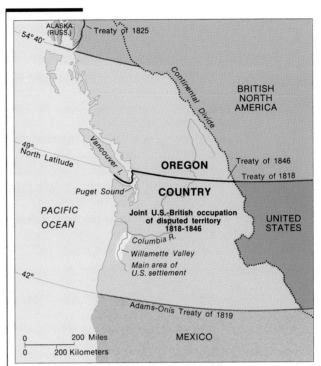

Oregon Country, Pacific Northwest Boundary Dispute
The United States and Great Britain nearly came to blows over the disputed boundary in Oregon.

United States, would gain sovereignty over the region. American diplomats moved quickly to try to solidify American claims to Oregon. Spain, Russia, Britain, and the United States all claimed the Pacific Northwest. In 1818 British and American negotiators agreed that nationals of both countries could trade in the region, and this agreement was renewed in 1827. In 1819 the United States persuaded Spain to cede its claims to Oregon to the United States, and two years later Secretary of State John Quincy Adams warned Russia that the United States would oppose any Russian attempts to occupy the territory.

Attempts by politicians, merchants, and fur traders to promote American settlement of Oregon fell on deaf ears. In the end, it was neither commerce nor politics but religion that led to American settlement of Oregon. In 1831 three chiefs of the Nez Percé tribe and another from the Flathead nation arrived in St. Louis. There the Indians said that the reason they had come eastward was to learn "the true mode of worshipping the great Spirit." This episode led to an explosion of interest in missionary activity in the Pacific Northwest. The *Christian Advocate*, a leading religious newspaper, declared: "Let the Church awake from her slumbers and go forth in her strength to the salvation of those wandering of our native forests."

The first missionaries arrived in Oregon in 1834. In the spring of that year, the Reverend Jason Lee and his nephew Daniel joined a fur trading expedition and trekked to Oregon. There, the Hudson's Bay Company, fearful that missionaries would upset the profitable fur trade with the Indians, convinced the Lees to found their mission in the fertile Willamette Valley, near present-day Salem, where few Indians lived.

Other missionaries soon followed. The most famous western missionaries were Marcus Whitman, a young doctor, and his wife Narcissa Prentiss Whitman, who were sent west in 1836 by the Methodists. The couple founded a mission at Waiilatpu, near present-day Walla Walla, Washington, where they taught the Cayuse Indians how to till fields and irrigate their crops and how to build mills to grind their corn and wheat. A fellow missionary described their goal: "We point them with one hand to the Lamb of God, with the other to the hoe as the means of saving their famishing bodies." The Whitmans persisted in their efforts to convert the Indians to Christianity until 1847, when a severe epidemic of measles broke out in the area. Many Indians blamed the epidemic on the white missionaries, and the Whitmans and twelve others were murdered.

Before his death, Marcus Whitman made an epic 3000 mile journey to Boston, during which he publicized the attractions of the Pacific Northwest and warned easterners of the need to offset British influence in the region. Upon his return to Oregon in 1843, Whitman guided nearly 900 immigrants along the Oregon Trail. The "great western migration," as this journey was known, generated enormous national interest and convinced hundreds of families that it was safe to travel over the Oregon Trail. "The Oregon fever," reported *Niles' Weekly Register,* "is raging in almost every part of the Union." By the mid-1840s, 6000 Americans had moved to Oregon.

The rapid influx of a large number of land-hungry Americans into Oregon in the mid-1840s forced Britain and the United States to finally decide whether Oregon would be British or American. In the presidential election of 1844, the Democratic party demanded the "reoccupation" of Oregon and annexation of the entire Pacific Northwest coast up to the edge of Russian-held Alaska, which was fixed at 54° 40′. The slogan "fifty-four forty or fight" helped Democratic candidate James Polk win the presidency in 1844.

In truth, Polk had little desire to go to war with Britain. As an ardent proslavery Southerner, he did not want to add new free states in the Pacific Northwest. Furthermore, he believed that the northern-most portions of Oregon country were unsuitable for agriculture. Therefore in 1846 he readily accepted compromise on the boundary dispute. Britain agreed to extend the United States–Canadian boundary along the forty-ninth parallel from the Rocky Mountains to the Pacific Ocean.

The Mormon Frontier

Pioneers migrated to the west for a wide variety of reasons. Some were driven westward by the hope of economic and social betterment, others by a restless curiosity and an urge for adventure. The Mormons moved west for an entirely different reason: to escape religious persecution.

In the history of religion, few stories are more dramatic than that of the Mormons. It is a story with the haunting Biblical overtones of divine revelations and visitations, of persecution and martyrdom, of an exodus two-thirds of the way across a continent, and of ultimate success in establishing a religious society in an uninhabited desert. This story, however, did not take place in a foreign land and in the distant past. It took place in the United States during the nineteenth century.

The Mormon church had its beginnings in upstate New York, which, during the early nineteenth century was a hotbed of religious fervor. Methodist, Baptist, Presbyterian, Universalist, and Campbellite preachers all eagerly sought out converts and tried to bring them into their sects. A fourteen-year-old named Joseph Smith,

Jr., the son of a farmer, listened closely to these preachers, but he was left uncertain which way to turn. "So great were the confusion and strife among the different denominations," Smith later recalled, "that it was impossible for a person, young as I was . . . to come to any certain conclusion who was right and who was wrong."

In the spring of 1820, Smith went into the woods near Palmyra, New York, to seek divine guidance. Suddenly, he was "seized upon by some power that entirely overcame me." According to his account, a brilliant light revealed to him "two personages," who announced that they were God the Father and Christ the Savior. They told him that all existing churches were false and that the true church of God was about to be reestablished on earth.

Three years later, young Smith underwent another supernatural experience. On the evening of September 21, 1823, "a personage" visited his bedroom and said "that God had work for" him to do. The spectral visitor told him of the existence of a set of buried golden plates which contained a lost section from the Bible describing a tribe of Israelites that had lived in America. The next morning, Smith said, he made his way to nearby Hill Cumorah and unearthed the golden plates which were deposited in a stone box. He was forbidden to remove them or reveal their existence for four years. Finally, in 1827 Smith acquired the plates and with the aid of magic stones, translated them into English. In 1830, the messages on the plates were published as the *Book of Mormon.*

For Mormons, the visions and revelations received by Joseph Smith, Jr., beginning in 1820, marked the dawn of a new age in human history. They signaled the end of "the Great Apostasy" of 1400 years during which Catholic and Protestant churches had deluded the world. On April 6, 1830, Smith formally founded the Church of Christ, later renamed the Church of Jesus Christ of Latter-Day Saints, and he committed the church to establishing the kingdom of God on earth.

At first, members of the church were mainly relatives and neighbors. Soon Smith attracted several thousand followers largely from isolated rural parts of New England, New York, and Pennsylvania, and the frontier Midwest. The converts to Mormonism were usually small farmers, mechanics, and tradesmen who had been displaced by the growing commercial economy and who were repelled by the rising tide of liberal religion and individualism in early nineteenth-century America.

Because Joseph Smith said that he conversed with angels and received direct revelations from the Lord, local authorities threatened to indict him for blasphemy. He and his followers responded by moving to Kirtland, Ohio, near Cleveland, where they built their first temple. It was in Kirtland that the Mormons first experimented with an economy planned and controlled by the church. Church trustees controlled the property of church members and put members to work building a temple and other community structures.

From Kirtland, the Mormons moved to Independence, Missouri, and then to a town called Far West, in northern Missouri. Disputes almost immediately broke out between Mormons and "gentiles," as non-Mormons were called. Beginning in 1832, proslavery mobs attacked the Mormons, accusing them of inciting slave insurrection. They burned several Mormon settlements and seized Mormon farms and houses. At the massacre at Haun's Hill, eighteen Mormon men and a boy were killed. Joseph Smith, Jr., was arrested for treason and sentenced to be shot, but he managed to escape several months later. Fifteen thousand Mormons fled from Missouri to Illinois after Governor L. W. Boggs proclaimed them enemies who "had to be exterminated, or driven from the state."

After years of warfare in Missouri, in 1839 communities of Mormons, including many converts from Britain and northern Europe, resettled along the east bank of the Mississippi River in the town of Commerce, Illinois. They changed the name of the town to Nauvoo, and it soon grew into the largest city in the state. Both Illinois Whigs and Democrats eagerly sought support among the Mormons. In exchange for their votes, the state legislature awarded Nauvoo a special charter that made the town an autonomous city-state, complete with its own 2000-man militia, with guns provided by the state.

Trouble arose again. A group of anti-Mormons led by a young lawyer named Thomas

C. Sharp accused the Mormons of sending secret diplomatic missions to France, Russia, and the Republic of Texas; practicing polygamy; and instituting theocratic rule by setting up a secret Council of Fifty. These accusations divided the Mormon church, and on June 7, 1844, a dissident group within the church published a newspaper denouncing the practice of polygamy and attacking Joseph Smith for trying to become "king or lawgiver to the church."

On Smith's orders, the city marshal and Mormon legionnaires destroyed the dissidents' printing press. Authorities charged Smith with treason, but the Illinois governor gave Smith his pledge of protection. Smith and his brother were then confined to a Carthage, Illinois, jail cell. Late in the afternoon of June 27, 1844, a mob of prominent citizens, aided by jail guards, broke into Smith's cell, shot him and his brother, and threw their bodies out of a second story window. The Mormon prophet was dead.

Why did the Mormons seem so menacing? Why did many western settlers agree with the Reverend Finis Ewing when he said that "the 'Mormons' are the common enemies of mankind and ought to be destroyed"? Today, it is hard to believe that Mormons could ever have been regarded as subversive, since they are known for their abstinence from tobacco and alcohol

Although only ten to twenty percent of Mormon families were polygamous, Mormons were often accused of corrupting moral values.

and their stress on family and communal responsibility. Why were they subjected to continuing persecution?

Anti-Mormonism was rooted in a struggle for economic and political power between individualistic frontiersmen and Mormons, who voted as their elders told them to do and who manipulated real estate as a bloc. Many early nineteenth-century Americans were suspicious of any combination for political or economic advantage, and feared that the Mormons had an unfair advantage in the struggle for wealth and power.

Mormonism was also denounced as a threat to fundamental social values. Protestant ministers railed against Mormonism as a threat to Christianity, since Mormons rejected the legitimacy of established churches and insisted that the *Book of Mormon* was Holy Scripture, equal in importance to the Bible. They attacked Mormonism as a preposterous hoax which played upon the credulity of naive and superstitious minds. The Mormons were also accused of corrupting moral values, especially after rumors about the practice of polygamy began to spread after 1842. Mormons practiced polygamy for half a century before it was outlawed in 1890. It was justified theologically as an effort to reestablish the patriarchal Old Testament family. Polygamy also served an important social function, by absorbing single or widowed women into Mormon communities. Critics denounced polygamy as "a slavery which debases and degrades womanhood, motherhood and family," but contrary to popular belief it was not widely practiced. Altogether, only ten to twenty percent of Mormon families were polygamous and nearly two-thirds involved a man and two wives.

After the murder of Joseph Smith, the Mormons decided to migrate across a thousand miles of unsettled prairie and arid desert to a new refuge outside the boundaries of the United States. They finished their temple in Nauvoo (which the poet John Greenleaf Whittier called "the most splendid and imposing architectural monument in the new world") and conducted religious rituals before beginning their exodus to the Far West.

The Mormon church was on the verge of splintering. A new leader, Brigham Young, emerged, and he led the Mormons to a new Zion where they might live in safety. Young had begun his career as an uneducated carpenter, printer, and glazier, but he had found in Mormonism the inspiration that would transform him into the leader whose efforts allowed the church to survive. In February of 1846 the first Mormon wagons left Nauvoo and by fall 15,000 Mormons had reached the west bank of the Missouri River. There they learned that an Illinois mob had burned their temple to the ground.

Early in April, the first wagons began to move again. On July 23, Young looked out upon the Great Salt Lake and said, "This is the right place." More than 85,000 Mormon migrants followed in the steps of Young's trek. By the time of his death in 1877, 125,000 Mormons lived in Utah.

As governor of the Mormon state of Deseret and later as governor of Utah, Young oversaw the building of Salt Lake City and 186 other Mormon communities, developed church-owned businesses, and established the first cooperative irrigation projects. He also publicly preached polygamy in 1852 and had twenty-seven wives and fifty-six children. In 1857 public outrage over polygamy led President James Buchanan to replace Young with a non-Mormon governor and send an army force of 2500 to force the Mormons to obey federal law. Young responded by mobilizing a Mormon militia and blocking the route of advancing United States troops. This episode, known as the Mormon War or "Buchanan's Blunder," ended in 1858, when the Mormons accepted the new governor and Buchanan issued a general pardon.

Today, the Mormon church is the fastest growing religious group in the United States and its members are known for their industriousness, sobriety, and thrift. A century ago, anti-Mormons regarded the church quite differently—as a fundamental threat to American values. Early nineteenth-century American society attached enormous importance to individualism, secularism, monogamous marriage, and private property, and the Mormons were believed to threaten each of these values. In a larger sense, the Mormons' aspirations were truly American. They sought nothing less than the establishment of the kingdom of God on earth—a dream that was, of course, not new in this country. In seeking to build God's kingdom, the Mormons were carrying on a quest that had been begun by their Puritan ancestors two centuries before.

THE MEXICAN WAR

When Brigham Young led the Mormons on their odyssey to their western Zion, he was seeking a homeland outside the boundaries of the United States. When he arrived at the Great Salt Lake during the summer of 1847, Utah as well as California, Nevada, and parts of Arizona, Colorado, New Mexico, and Wyoming, had all become United States territory as a result of an American war with Mexico.

Why War?

Early in March 1846, President James K. Polk ordered Brigadier General Zachary Taylor to march 3000 troops southwest from Corpus Christi, Texas, to "defend the Rio Grande." On March 28 Taylor's men completed the 150 mile march and set up camp along the Rio Grande, directly across from the Mexican city of Matamoros. Taylor's forces stood on a stretch of land claimed by both Mexico and the United States.

Taylor's forces proceeded to build a makeshift fort, with walls nine feet high and fifteen feet thick. On April 25, a Mexican cavalry force crossed the Rio Grande and clashed with a small American squadron, forcing the Americans to surrender after the loss of several lives. "Hostilities may be considered to have commenced," Taylor wrote to President Polk. "American blood has been spilled."

On May 8, the day before he had received word of the skirmish, Polk and his cabinet decided to press for war with Mexico. On May 11, after he received word of the border clash, Polk asked Congress to acknowledge that a state of war already existed "by the act of Mexico herself . . . notwithstanding all our efforts to avoid it." "Mexico," the president announced, "has passed the boundary of the United States, has invaded our territory and shed American blood on American soil." Congress responded by declaring war on Mexico.

The Mexican War was the nation's first war to be reported in newspapers as it actually happened.

Fifteen years before the United States was plunged into Civil War, it fought a war against Mexico that added half a million square miles of territory to the United States. It was the first American war fought almost entirely outside the United States. It was also the first American war to be reported, while it happened, by daily newspapers. It was a controversial war that bitterly divided American public opinion. It was also the war that gave young officers named Ulysses S. Grant, Robert E. Lee, Thomas "Stonewall" Jackson, William Tecumseh Sherman, and George McClellan their first experience in a major conflict.

The underlying cause of the Mexican War was the inexorable movement of American pioneers into the Far West. As Americans marched westward, they moved into land claimed by Mexico, and inevitably Mexican and American interests clashed.

The immediate cause of the conflict was the annexation of Texas in 1845. After the defeat at San Jacinto in 1836, Mexico made one

abortive attempt to reconquer Texas in 1842. Even after this defeat, Mexico refused to recognize Texas independence and warned the United States that annexation of Texas would be tantamount to a declaration of war. In early 1845, when Congress voted to annex Texas, Mexico expelled the American ambassador and cut diplomatic relations, but it did not declare war.

Polk told his commanders to prepare for the possibility of war. He ordered American naval vessels in the Gulf of Mexico to position themselves outside Mexican ports; he dispatched United States forces in the Southwest under the command of Zachary Taylor to Corpus Christi; and secretly, he warned the Pacific fleet to prepare to seize ports along the California coast in the event of war.

Peaceful settlement of the two countries' grievances still seemed possible. In the fall of 1845, the president sent John Slidell as "envoy extraordinary and minister plenipotentiary" to Mexico City with a proposal to peacefully resolve the two countries' differences, which included a dispute over Texas's boundary and the Mexican government's failure to compensate Americans citizens for losses suffered through revolution and theft. Slidell was authorized to cancel the damage claims and pay $5 million if the Mexicans agreed to recognize the Rio Grande as the southwestern boundary of Texas. (Earlier, the Spanish government had defined the Texas boundary as the Nueces River, 130 miles north and east of the Rio Grande.)

Polk had larger objectives in mind than simply settling the boundary and claims disputes. He also wanted to persuade Mexico to sell its two northwestern provinces to the United States. He directed Slidell to offer up to $5 million for the province of New Mexico—which included Nevada and Utah and parts of four other states—and up to $25 million for California.

Polk was anxious to acquire California, because in mid-October 1845 he had learned falsely that Britain was on the verge of making California a British protectorate. Rumors flourished that the British were paying Mexican troops to reassert authority in the province. Giving credence to Polk's fears was the fact that in 1839 Britain and France had taken military action against Mexico to force it to meet its debt obligations. It was widely believed that Mexico had agreed to cede California to Britain as payment.

Immediate preventative actions seemed necessary, and so Polk instructed his consul in Monterey to agitate among Californians for annexation by the United States. He also dispatched a young Marine Corps lieutenant, Archibald H. Gillespie, along the overland trail to California, apparently to foment revolt against Mexican authority.

The Mexican government, already incensed over the annexation of Texas, refused to negotiate. Mexico's new President José Herrera refused to receive Slidell and ordered his leading commander, General Mariano Paredes y Arrillaga, to assemble an army and reconquer Texas. Paredes proceeded to topple Herrera's government and declare himself president. He also refused to receive Slidell. The failure of Slidell's mission led Polk to order Zachary Taylor's men to advance to the Rio Grande. A clash between a band of Mexican troops and an American squadron of dragoons led Congress to declare war on Mexico on May 13, 1846.

Heated debate followed the declaration of war. Supporters of the war claimed that Mexico was responsible for the hostilities because it had severed relations with the United States, threatened war, refused to receive an American emissary or to pay the damage claims of American citizens, and "invaded our territory and shed American blood on American soil." Others supported the war because they believed it was America's destiny "to cover the whole northern, if not the southern continent" and bring the blessing of democracy to a benighted and oppressed people.

The war's critics denounced the conflict as an immoral land grab by an expansionistic power against a weak neighbor that had been independent barely two decades. They claimed that Polk deliberately provoked Mexico into war by ordering American troops into disputed territory. A Delaware senator declared that ordering Taylor to the Rio Grande was "as much an act of aggression on our part as is a man's pointing a pistol at another's breast."

Many opponents of the war argued that responsibility lay with an aggressive southern slaveocracy intent upon getting more land for cotton cultivation and more slave states to balance northern free states in the Senate. "Bigger pens to cram with slaves," was the way poet James Russell Lowell put it. Others blamed the war on expansion-minded westerners who were hungry for land and on eastern trading interests who dreamed of establishing "an American Boston or New York" in San Francisco to increase trade with Asia. Mexicans denounced the war as a brazen attempt by the United States to seize Mexican territory.

"From the Halls of Montezuma"

The American battle plan called for a three-pronged attack. Colonel Stephen Kearny had the task of securing New Mexico and occupying California, while naval forces under Commodore John D. Sloat blockaded the California coast and General Zachary Taylor invaded Mexico, to force a Mexican surrender. Kearny easily accomplished his mission. In less than two months, he marched his 1700 man army more than one thousand miles, and on August 16, 1846, occupied Santa Fe and declared New Mexico's 80,000 inhabitants American citizens.

Meanwhile, American settlers in California's Sacramento Valley, fearful that Mexican authorities were about to expel them from the region, revolted. At dawn on June 10, 1846, a small group of buckskin-clad Americans led by frontiersman Ezekiel Merritt seized Sonoma, Spain's northernmost settlement in California, proclaimed an independent Republic of California, and raised a flag showing a grizzly bear facing a red star. As a result, the revolt was known as the Bear Flag Rebellion.

In early July, the Bear Flag was replaced by the stars and stripes. On July 7, 1846, United States naval forces under Commodore John D. Sloat captured the California town of Monterey and proclaimed California a part of the United States. In January 1847 United States troops under Stephen Kearny and Commodore Robert F. Stockton won the Battle of San Gabriel near Los Angeles, completing the American conquest of California.

The American invasion of northern Mexico proved to be a disappointment because it did

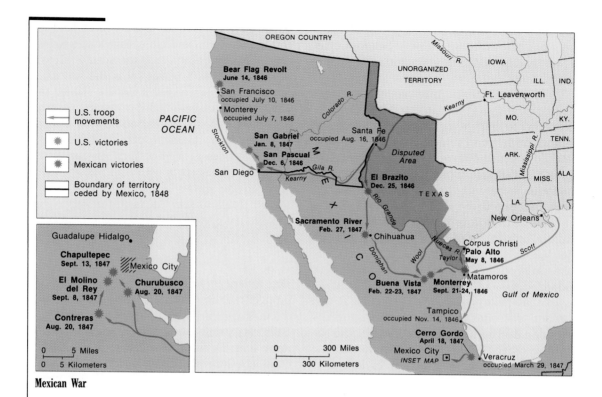

Mexican War

Chapultepec castle was the last major obstacle before American troops reached Mexico City. After two days of bombarding the castle, two storming parties charged and scaled the castle walls.

not lead Mexico to sue for peace, as Polk had hoped. In December 1846 Colonel A. W. Doniphan led 856 Missouri cavalry volunteers 3000 miles across mountains and desert into the northern Mexican province of Chihuahua. He occupied El Paso and then captured the capital city of Chihuahua. Meanwhile, 6000 volunteers under the command of Zachary Taylor defeated a Mexican force of 15,000 at the battle of Buena Vista on February 22 and 23, 1847.

Despite the unbroken string of American victories, Mexico refused to negotiate an end to the war. In disgust, Polk ordered General Winfield Scott to invade central Mexico from the sea, march inland, and capture Mexico City. On March 9, 1847, the Mexicans allowed Scott and a force of 10,000 men to land unopposed at the Gulf of Mexico garrison of Veracruz. As American soldiers encircled the fortress, ships and land-based mortars lobbed shells into the seaport. Three weeks later the garrison surrendered. Scott's losses totaled thirteen dead and fifty-five wounded.

Scott's forces then began to march on the Mexican capital. On April 18, at a mountain pass near Jalapa, a 9000-man American force met 13,000 Mexican troops and in bitter hand-to-hand fighting, forced the Mexicans to flee. As Scott's army pushed on toward Mexico City, it stormed a Mexican fortress at Contreras and then routed a Mexican force of 30,000 at Churubusco on August 19 and 20. For two weeks, from August 24 to September 7, Scott observed an armistice to allow the Mexicans to consider peace proposals. When the negotiations failed, Scott's 6000 remaining men attacked El Molino del Rey—the King's Mill—and stormed Chapultepec, a fortified castle guarding Mexico City's gates, on September 13, 1847. A day later, the Americans entered the Mexican capital. At 7 A.M., September 14, 1847, the American flag was raised over Mexico City—an event memorialized in the Marine Corps hymn with the line "from the halls of Montezuma."

Despite the capture of their capital, the Mexicans refused to surrender. Hostile crowds staged demonstrations in the streets and snipers fired shots and hurled stones and broken bottles from the tops of flat-roofed Mexican houses. To quell the protests, General Scott ordered the streets "swept with grape and canister" and artillery "turned upon the houses whence the fire proceeded." Outside the capital, belligerent civilians attacked army supply wagons, and guerrilla fighters harassed American troops. Senator Daniel Webster of Massachusetts expressed the prevailing sentiment: "Mexico is an ugly enemy. She will not fight—and will not retreat."

War Fever and Antiwar Protests

During the first few weeks following the declaration of war a frenzy of prowar hysteria swept the country. Two hundred thousand men responded to a call for 50,000 volunteers. Novelist Herman Melville observed that in his hometown of Lansingburgh, New York, "a military ardor pervades all ranks. . . . Nothing is talked about but the halls of the Montezumas." In New York, placards bore the slogan "Mexico or Death." Many newspapers, especially in the North, declared that the war would benefit the Mexican people by bringing them the blessings of democracy and liberty. The *Boston Times* said that an American victory "must necessarily be a great blessing," because it would bring "peace into a land where the sword has always been the sole arbiter between factions" and would introduce "the reign of law where license has existed for a generation."

In Philadelphia, 20,000 turned out for a prowar rally, and in Cincinnati, 12,000 celebrated Zachary Taylor's victories with cannon salutes, parades, and speeches. In Tennessee, 30,000 men volunteered for 3000 positions as soldiers, prompting one applicant to complain that it was "difficult even to purchase a place in the ranks." Poet Walt Whitman, then editor of the *Brooklyn Eagle*, echoed the prevailing mood: "Yes, Mexico must be chastized." The war was particularly popular in the West. Of the 69,540 men who volunteered for service in the war, more than 40,000 enlisted in the western states.

From the war's very beginning a small but highly visible group of intellectuals, clergymen, pacifists, abolitionists, and Whig and Democratic politicians denounced the war as brutal aggression against a "poor, feeble, distracted country." Literary and reform circles were particularly vocal in their opposition to the war. Congregationalist minister Theodore Parker declared that if the "war be right then Christianity is wrong, a falsehood, a lie." Abolitionist William Lloyd Garrison's militant newspaper the *Liberator* expressed open support for the Mexican people: "Every lover of Freedom and humanity throughout the world must wish them the most triumphant success."

Most Whigs supported the war—in part, because the two leading American generals, Taylor and Scott, were Whigs and in part because they remembered that opposition to the War of 1812 had destroyed the Federalist party. A small number of prominent Whigs, from the South as well as the North, openly opposed the war. Thomas Corwin of Ohio denounced the war as merely the latest example of American injustice to Mexico: "If I were a Mexican I would tell you, 'Have you not room enough in your own country to bury your dead.' " A freshman congressman from Illinois named Abraham Lincoln lashed out against the war, calling it immoral, proslavery, and a threat to the nation's republican values. One of his constituents branded him "the Benedict Arnold of our district," and he was denied renomination by his own party.

As newspapers informed their readers about the hardships and savagery of life on the front, public enthusiasm for the war waned. The war did not turn out to be the romantic exploit that Americans envisioned. Troops complained that their food was "green with slime" and "acted as an instantaneous emetic." Their meat, they said, would stick "if thrown against a smooth plank." Diarrhea, amoebic dysentery, measles, and yellow fever ravaged American soldiers. Seven times as many Americans died of disease and exposure as died of battlefield injuries. Of the 90,000 Americans who served in the war, only 1721 died in action. Another 11,155 died from disease and exposure to the elements.

Public support for the war was further eroded by reports of brutality against Mexican civilians. Newspaper reporters claimed that the chapparal was "strewn with the skeletons of Mexicans sacrificed by" American troops. After one of their members was murdered, the Arkansas volunteer cavalry surrounded a group of Mexican peasants and began an "indiscriminate and bloody massacre of the poor creatures." A

young lieutenant named George G. Meade reported that volunteers in Matamoros robbed the citizens, stole their cattle, and killed innocent civilians "for no other object than their own amusement." If only one-tenth of the horror stories were true, General Winfield Scott wrote, it was enough "to make Heaven weep, and every American of Christian morals blush for his country."

Usually, the political party in power benefits from a war, but the Democrats actually lost support. In the congressional election of 1846, which took place six months after the outbreak of war, the Democrats lost control of the House of Representatives to the Whigs.

Dissent even made its way to the battlefield. A group of enlisted Irish-Catholic Americans, shocked by the desecration of Catholic churches, deserted to the Mexican side, formed the San Patricio Battalion, and fought against the American army. At Churubusco, sixty-five members of the battalion were captured. Fifty were executed and eleven others were punished with fifty lashes apiece and the letter "D" (for "deserter") branded on their cheeks.

A young essayist and poet named Henry David Thoreau staged the most important act of protest against the Mexican War. On July 4, 1845, the twenty-eight-year-old poet, convinced that "the mass of men live lives of quiet desperation," walked into the woods near Concord, Massachusetts, to live alone. He put up a cabin near Walden Pond as an experiment: to see if it was possible for a person to live truly free. "I went into the woods," he wrote, "because I wished to live deliberately, to front only the essential facts of life, and see if I could not learn what it had to teach, and not, when I came to die, discover that I had not lived." The most significant incident during his twenty-six-month stay at Walden Pond took place on July 23, 1846, when he was jailed for failing to pay his one dollar poll tax, his protest against his country's involvement in the Mexican War. He spent just one night in jail because his tax was paid, much to his disgust, by one of his relatives.

It was in response to his arrest that Thoreau wrote an essay that was a source of inspiration for Leo Tolstoi, Mahatma Gandhi, and Martin Luther King. Thoreau entitled his essay

"Civil Disobedience." In it he declared the duty of every individual was to protest a government law, even though it had been enacted with the consent of the majority, when it conflicted with moral law. "Any man more right than his neighbor," he wrote, "constitutes a majority of one." So how should an individual protest a moral wrong? Here Thoreau was at his most creative. He described a type of disobedience that disrupted the everyday workings of society and dramatized the moral issues at stake, without resort to violence. Individual acts of protest, he argued, would awaken the conscience of those people whose consciences could still be stirred.

Out of Thoreau's jailing grew a legend. Ralph Waldo Emerson, America's greatest philosopher, visited Thoreau in jail. Emerson asked, "Henry, why are you here?" Thoreau replied, "Why are you not here?"

Negotiating the Peace

Difficult negotiations followed the war. After American troops entered the Mexican capital, Santa Anna, again the Mexican president, resigned and the Mexican Congress was forced to retreat to a provincial capital to try to reorganize. Not until mid-November 1847, was a new civilian government able to gain control over the country and name a peace negotiator.

As Americans waited impatiently for a final peace settlement, they grew increasingly divided over their war aims. Ultra-expansionists, who drew support from such cities as Baltimore, New York, and Philadelphia as well as from the West, wanted the United States to annex all of Mexico. Many Southerners, led by John C. Calhoun, called for a unilateral withdrawal to the Rio Grande. They opposed annexation of Mexico because they did not want to extend American citizenship to Mexicans. Most Democratic party leaders, however, wanted at least the third of Mexico south and west of the Rio Grande.

Suddenly on February 22, 1848, word reached Washington that a peace treaty had been signed. On February 2, 1848, Nicholas Trist, a Spanish-speaking State Department official, signed the Treaty of Guadalupe Hidalgo, ending the Mexican War. Trist had actually been ordered home two months earlier by Polk, but he had continued negotiating anyway, fearing that his recall would be "deadly to the cause of peace."

The treaty gave the United States only those parts of Mexico that Polk had originally sought to purchase. It ceded California, Nevada, Utah, New Mexico, and parts of Arizona, Colorado, Kansas, and Wyoming to the United States for $15 million and the assumption of $3.25 million in debts owed to Americans by Mexico. The treaty also settled the Texas border dispute in favor of the United States, placing the Texas-Mexico boundary at the Rio Grande.

Ultra-expansionists called on Polk to toss the treaty into the wastepaper basket. William Tecumseh Sherman called the treaty "just such a one as Mexico might have imposed on us had she been the conqueror." But a war-weary public wanted peace. Polk quickly submitted the treaty to the Senate, which ratified it overwhelmingly. The war was over.

The War's Significance

The story of America's conflict with Mexico tends to be overshadowed by the story of the Civil War, which began only a decade and a half later. In fact, the conflict had far-reaching consequences for the nation's future. It increased the nation's size by one-third, but it also created deep political divisions that threatened the country's future.

The most significant result of the Mexican War was to reignite the question of slavery in the western territories—the very question that had divided the country in 1819. Even before the war had begun, philosopher and writer Ralph Waldo Emerson had predicted that the United States would "conquer Mexico, but it will be as the man who swallows the arsenic which will bring him down in turn. Mexico will poison us." The war convinced a growing number of Northerners that southern slaveowners had precipitated the war in order to open new lands to slavery and acquire new slave states. Most significant of all, the war weakened the party system and made it increasingly difficult for congressional leaders to prevent the issue of slavery from dominating congressional activity.

Political Crisis of the 1840s

Prior to the Mexican War, the major political issues that divided Americans were questions of tariffs, banking, internal improvements, and land. Political positions on these issues largely divided along party lines. After the outbreak of war with Mexico, a new issue began to dominate American politics—the extension of slavery in the western territories—and public opinion began to polarize and party cohesion began to break down. Party factions and sectional divisions began to grow more important than traditional party coalitions.

The question of slavery burst into the public spotlight one summer evening in 1846. Congressman David Wilmot, a Pennsylvania Democrat, introduced an amendment to a war appropriations bill, known as the Wilmot Proviso, which forbade slavery in any territory acquired from Mexico. The states of New York, Massachusetts, Michigan, and Vermont adopted resolutions endorsing the Wilmot Proviso.

Throughout the North, thousands of working-men, mechanics, and farmers feared that free workers would be unable to successfully compete against slave labor. "If slavery is not excluded by law," said one northern congressman, "the presence of the slave will exclude the laboring white man."

Southerners denounced the Wilmot Proviso as "treason to the Constitution." The state Democratic party in Alabama denied that Congress had authority to limit slavery in the territories and declared that the state would secede if the Wilmot Proviso were enacted into law. Polk tried to quiet the debate between "Southern agitators and Northern fanatics" by assuring moderate Northerners that slavery could never take root in the arid southwest—but to no avail. With the strong support of Westerners, the amendment passed the House of Representatives twice but was defeated in the Senate.

Although the Wilmot Proviso did not become law, the issue it raised—the extension of slavery in the western territories—continued

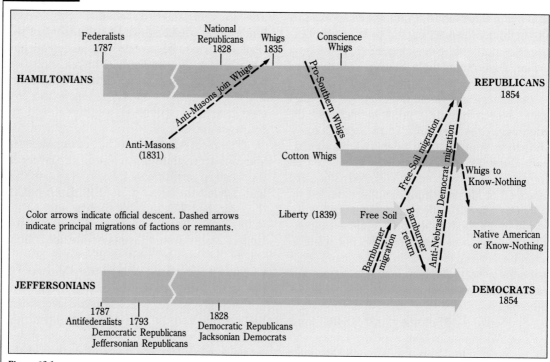

Figure 12.1
Chronological Development of American Political Parties to 1854

to contribute to the growth of political factionalism. In 1848, the Free Soil party was founded to oppose the westward expansion of slavery, favoring free land for western homesteaders. Its supporters consisted of dissident New England Whigs (known as "conscience" Whigs because of their opposition to slavery), antislavery New York Democrats (known as "Barnburners"), and former members of the Liberty party. Under the slogan "free soil, free speech, free labor, and free men," the party nominated ex-President Martin Van Buren as presidential nominee in 1848 and polled 291,000 votes, enough to split the Democratic vote and throw the election to Whig candidate Zachary Taylor.

Up until the last month of 1848, much of the debate over slavery in the Mexican cession seemed academic. Most Americans thought of the newly acquired territory as simply "waste" filled with "broken mountains and dreary desert." William Tecumseh Sherman summed up prevailing sentiment when he said he would not trade two eastern counties for all the Far West. Then in December in his farewell address Polk electrified Congress with the news that gold had been discovered in California—and suddenly the question of slavery was inescapable.

The California gold fields attracted prospectors from a wide variety of countries. Approximately 23,000 of the 85,000 people who flocked to California in 1849 were not United States citizens.

The Gold Rush

On January 24, 1848, less than ten days before the signing of the peace treaty ending the Mexican War, James W. Marshall, a thirty-six-year-old carpenter and handyman, noticed several bright bits of yellow mineral near a sawmill that he was building for his employer, John A. Sutter, a Swiss-born immigrant who owned one of the great ranches that dotted California's Sacramento Valley. Marshall thought that the mineral was either "fools' gold," which shatters when struck by a hammer, or gold, which is malleable. "I then tried it between two rocks," Marshall wrote, "and found that it could be beaten into a different shape but not broken." He told the men working with him: "Boys, by God, I believe I have found a gold mine."

On March 15, a San Francisco newspaper, the *Californian,* published the first printed account that gold had been found. Within two weeks, the paper had lost its staff and was forced to shut down its printing press. In its last edition it told its readers: "The whole country, from San Francisco to Los Angeles . . . resounds with the sordid cry of Gold! Gold! Gold! while the field is left half-planted, the house half-built, and everything neglected but the manufacture of picks and shovels."

In 1849, 85,000 men arrived in California—half overland and half by ship around Cape Horn or across the Isthmus of Panama. Only half were Americans; the rest came from Britain, Australia, Germany, France, Latin America, and China. Platoons of soldiers deserted; sailors jumped ship; husbands left wives; apprentices ran away from their masters; farmers and businessmen deserted their livelihoods. In July, 1850, sailors abandoned 500 ships in San Francisco Bay. Within a year, California's population had swollen from 14,000 to 100,000. The popu-

1803 Louisiana Purchase; Lewis and Clark expedition

1807 Fur trappers and traders penetrate into the region of the Missouri and Yellowstone rivers

1818 United States and Britain agree to jointly occupy Oregon region

1820 Spain gives Moses Austin the right to settle 300 families in Texas; Expedition led by Major Stephen H. Long originates myth of the "Great American Desert"

1821 Santa Fe Trail opens

1824 James Bridger discovers the Great Salt Lake

1825 William H. Ashley organizes the Trappers' Rendezvous

1826 Jedediah Smith explores California and the Pacific Northwest

1827 United States and Britain extend joint occupation of Oregon

1830 Joseph Smith, Jr., publishes the *Book of Mormon*; First covered wagons make it to the foot of the Rocky Mountains

1831 Mormons migrate from New York State to Ohio

1834 Reverend Jason Lee explores the Willamette Valley

1836 Texas proclaims independence from Mexico; Three thousand Mexican troops under Santa Anna storm the Alamo

1838 John Quincy Adams's filibuster defeats move to annex Texas

1839 Mormons establish Nauvoo, Illinois

1841 First wagon train arrives in California

1843 First overland caravans to Oregon

1844 Joseph Smith, Jr., assassinated at Carthage, Illinois; James Polk, campaigning on the slogan "54° 40' or fight," asserts America's claim to "all Oregon"

1845 Texas annexed by joint resolution of Congress; John Slidell's unsuccessfully negotiates to purchase New Mexico and California from Mexico

1846 Mexican War begins; United States–British settle dispute over Oregon by dividing the region along the 49th parallel; Wilmot Proviso proposed; California conquered by the United States

1847 General Winfield Scott captures Vera Cruz and Mexico City; Mormons arrive in the Great Salt Lake Valley

1848 Treaty of Guadalupe Hidalgo; Secret attempts to purchase Cuba from Spain; Gold rush begins

1853 Gadsden Purchase

lation of San Francisco, which stood at 459 in the summer of 1847, reached 20,000 within a few months.

During the early years of the gold rush, men traveled to California without women. Few women arrived during the early years—only 700 in 1849. In 1850, women made up only eight percent of California's population. In mining areas, they made up less than two percent.

The gold rush transformed California from a sleepy society into one that was wild, unruly, ethnically-diverse, and violent. Philosopher Josiah Royce, whose family arrived in the midst of the gold rush, declared that the Californian was "morally and socially tried as no other American ever has been tried." In San Francisco alone there were more than 500 bars and 1000 gambling dens. In the span of eighteen months, the city burned to the ground six times. There were a thousand murders in San Francisco during the early '50s, but only one conviction. Forty-niners, who had come to California seeking gold, slaughtered Indians for sport, drove Mexicans from the mines on penalty of death, and sought to restrict the immigration of foreigners, especially Chinese immigrants. The military government was incapable of keeping order, and leading merchants formed vigilance committees, which attempted to rule by lynch law and establishment of "popular" courts.

The rapid influx of miners into California led to a frenzy of price gouging. A bottle of molasses or a pint-and-a-half of vinegar sold for a dollar. Pork was $5 a pound. Eggs went for as much as $4 a dozen. Toothpicks were sold for 50 cents apiece. The value of real estate exploded. A lot in San Francisco purchased in 1847 for $16.50 sold for $6000 in the spring of 1848 and was later resold for $48,000.

The gold rush era in California lasted less than a decade. By the mid-1850s, the lone miner who prospected for gold with a pick, a shovel, and a wash pan was already an anachronism. Mining companies using heavy machinery replaced the individual prospector. Systems of dams exposed whole river bottoms. Drilling machines drove shafts 700 feet into the earth. Hydraulic mining machines blasted streams of water against mountainsides. The romantic era of California gold mining had come to a close.

CONCLUSION

By 1860, the gold rush was over. Prospectors had found more than $350 million worth of gold. Certainly, some fortunes were made—one prostitute claimed to have made $50,000 after a year's work—but few struck it rich.

Ironically, the two men most responsible for the gold rush died penniless. James W. Marshall, who discovered the first gold bits, eventually became a blacksmith in Kelsey, California, and died in poverty. John A. Sutter, on whose ranch gold was discovered, was left bankrupt as a result of the gold rush. His workmen deserted to hunt gold, and his crops rotted in the fields. Forty-niners trespassed on his land and stole his cattle. He died in 1880 in Pennsylvania while lobbying congressmen to reimburse him for the losses he had suffered because of the discovery.

By 1850 the American flag flew over an area that stretched from sea to sea. In the span of just five years, the United States had increased in size by one-third and acquired an area that included the states of Arizona, California, Colorado, Idaho, Nevada, New Mexico, Oregon, Texas, Utah, Washington, and Wyoming.

The first to carry the American flag into the Far West were a small coterie of government explorers, fur trappers, traders, and missionaries. These were the people who found the fertile valleys and great forests of the West, marked trails, and stirred the imagination of many midwesterners eager for adventure. Ranchers, farmers, and tradesmen followed, taking the overland trails across treeless plains, dangerous mountains, and arid deserts, into Texas, Oregon, and California. The United States acquired Texas through annexation. Negotiations with Britain gave the United States half of the Oregon country. California and the great Southwest became part of the United States as a result of war with Mexico.

The exploration and settlement of the Far West is one of the great epics of nineteenth-century history. America's dramatic territorial expansion also created severe problems. In addition to providing the United States with its richest mines, greatest forests, and most fertile farm land, the Far West intensified the sectional conflict between the North and South and

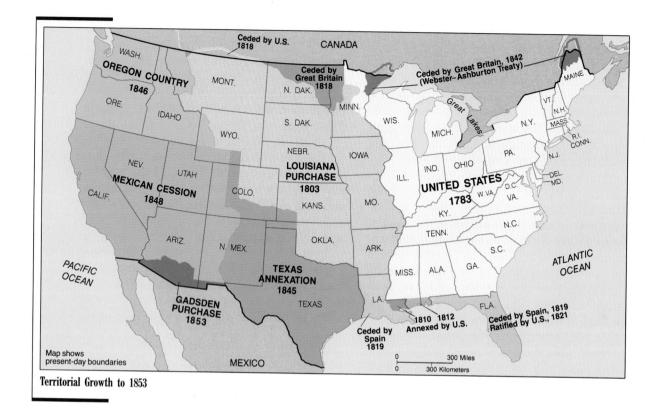

Territorial Growth to 1853

raised the fateful question of whether slavery would be permitted in the western territories. Could democratic political institutions resolve the question of slavery in the western territories? That question would dominate American politics in the 1850s.

REVIEW SUMMARY

Between 1830 and 1850, the nation expanded its boundaries to include Arizona, California, Colorado, Idaho, Nevada, New Mexico, Oregon, Texas, Utah, Washington, and Wyoming. The first Americans to venture into this area were

> government-commissioned explorers
> commercially-motivated trappers and traders
> Protestant missionaries

The political events behind this expansion included

> annexation of Texas in 1845
> partition of Oregon country in 1846 following negotiations with Britain
> wresting California and the great Southwest from Mexico in 1848, after the Mexican War

SUGGESTIONS FOR FURTHER READING
OVERVIEWS AND SURVEYS

Ray A. Billington, *The Far Western Frontier, 1830–1860* (1956); R. A. Billington, *Westward Expansion* (1974); Thomas R. Hietala, *Manifest Design: Anxious Aggrandizement in Late Jacksonian America* (1985); Reginald Horsman, *Race and Manifest Destiny: The Origins of American Racial Anglo-Saxonism* (1981); Howard R. Lamar, *Reader's Encyclopedia of the American West* (1977); Frederick Merk, *History of the Westward Movement* (1978); Martin Ridge and R. A. Billington, *America's Frontier Story* (1969); Bernard DeVoto, *The Year of Decision: 1846* (1943) and *Across the Wide Missouri* (1947); Albert K. Weinberg, *Manifest Destiny* (1935).

OPENING THE WEST

Gloria G. Cline, *Exploring the Great Basin* (1963); R. L. Duffus, *The Santa Fe Trail* (1930); William H. Goetzmann, *Army Exploration in the American West, 1803–1863* (1959); W. H. Goetzmann, *Exploration and Empire: Explorer and Scientist in the Winning of the West* (1966); Michael P. Malone, ed., *Historians and the American West* (1983); Dale L. Morgan, *Jedediah Smith and the Opening of the West* (1953); Francis Parkman, *The Oregon Trail* (1849); Gerald Rawling, *The Pathfinders* (1964); Richard Slotkin, *The Fatal Environment: The Myth of the Frontier in the Age of Industrialization* (1985); David J. Wishart, *The Fur Trade of the American West* (1979).

SPANISH AND INDIAN AMERICA

Rodofo Acuna, *Occupied America: A History of Chicanos* (1981); Robert F. Berkhofer, Jr., *The White Man's Indian: Images of the American Indian from Columbus to the Present* (1978); Albert Camarillo, *Chicanos in California* (1984); Arnoldo De Leon, *The Tejano Community, 1836–1900* (1982); A. De Leon, *They Called Them Greasers: Anglo Attitudes Toward Mexicans in Texas, 1821–1900* (1983); Edward P. Dozier, *The Pueblo Indians of North America* (1970); Harold E. Driver, *Indians of North America* (1969); Fred Eggan, *The American Indian* (1966); Jack Forbes, *Native Americans of California and Nevada* (1968); John Garcia, *The Lost Land* (1984); Robert F. Heizer and Alan Almquist, *The Other Californians* (1971); R. F. Heizer and M. A. Whipple, eds. *California Indians* (1971); Alice Kehoe, *North American Indians: A Comprehensive Account* (1981); Robert H. Lowie, *Indians of the Plains* (1963); Cecil Robinson, *Mexico and the Hispanic Southwest in America Literature* (1977); Robert Rosenbaum, *Mexicano Resistance in the Southwest* (1982); Robert F. Spencer and Jesse D. Spencer, *The Native Americans: Ethnology and Backgrounds of the North American Indians* (1977); W. R. Swagerty, ed., *Scholars and the Indian Experience: Critical Reviews of Recent Writings in the Social Sciences* (1984); Wilcomb Washburn, *The Indian in America* (1975); David J. Weber, *The Mexican Frontier, 1821–1846: The American Southwest Under Mexico* (1982).

SETTLING THE FAR WEST

John Mack Faragher, *Women and Men on the Overland Trail* (1979); Julie Roy Jeffrey, *Frontier Women: The Transmississippi West, 1840–1880* (1979); Sandra L. Myres, *Westering Women and the Frontier Experience, 1800–1915* (1982); Lillian Schlissel, *Women's Diaries of the Westward Journey* (1982); Joanna Stratton, *Pioneer Women* (1982); John Unruh, *The Plains Across: The Overland Emigrants and the Trans-Mississippi West* (1979).

MANIFEST DESTINY

Leonard J. Arrington, *Brigham Young: American Moses* (1984); L. J. Arrington, *Great Basin Kingdom* (1958); William C. Binkley, *The Texas Revolution* (1952); Richard L. Bushman, *Joseph Smith and the Beginnings of Mormonism* (1984); Malcolm Clark, Jr., *Eden Seekers: The Settlement of Oregon, 1812–1862* (1981); Robert B. Flanders, *Nauvoo: Kingdom on the Mississippi* (1965); Norman F. Furniss, *The Mormon Conflict, 1850–1859* (1960); Robert Gottlieb and Peter Wiley, *America's Saints: The Rise of Mormon Power* (1984); Norman A. Graebner, *Empire on the Pacific* (1967); Klaus Hansen, *Quest for Empire: The Political Kingdom of God and the Council of Fifty in Mormon History* (1967); Marvin S. Hill and James B. Allen, eds., *Mormonism and American Culture* (1972); Frederick Merk, *Fruits of Propaganda in the Tyler Administration* (1971); F. Merk, *The Oregon Question: Essays in Anglo-American Diplomacy and Politics* (1967); F. Merk, *Slavery and the Annexation of Texas* (1972); William Mulder and A. Russell Mortensen, eds., *Among the Mormons: Historic Accounts by Contemporary Observors* (1973); David M. Pletcher, *The Diplomacy of Annexation: Texas, Oregon, and the Mexican War* (1973); Earl Pomeroy, *The Pacific Slope: A History* (1965); Jan Shipps, *Mormonism: The Story of a New Religious Tradition* (1984); Wallace Stegner, *The Gathering of Zion: The Story of the Mormon Trail* (1964); Philip Taylor, *Expectations Westward: The Mormons and the Emigration of their British Converts in the Nineteenth Century* (1966).

THE MEXICAN WAR

K. Jack Bauer, *Cotton Versus Conscience: Massachusetts Whig Politics and Southern Expansion, 1843–1848* (1967); K. J. Bauer, *The Mexican War, 1846–1848* (1974); K. J. Bauer, *Zachary Taylor* (1985); Walton Bean, *California: An Interpretive History* (1978); Warren A. Beck and David A. Williams, *California: A History of the Golden State* (1972); Gene M. Brack, *Mexico Views Manifest Destiny, 1821–1846: An Essay on the Origins of the Mexican War* (1976); S. V. Conner and O. B. Faulk, *North America Divided: The Mexican War, 1846–1848* (1971); Eric Foner, "The Wilmot Proviso Revisited" *Journal of American History,* 56 (1969); Paul W. Gates, ed., *California Ranchos and Farms, 1846–1862* (1967); Neal Harlow, *California Conquered: War and Peace on the Pacific, 1846–1850* (1982); J. S. Holliday, *The World Rushed In* (1981); Robert Johannsen, *To The Halls of the Montezumas: The Mexican War in the American Imagination* (1985); Rudolph M. Lap, *Blacks in Gold Rush California* (1977); Frederick Merk, "Dissent in the Mexican War," in *Dissent in Three American Wars,* ed. Samuel E. Morison et al. (1970); C.W. Morrison, *Democratic Politics and Sectionalism: The Wilmot Proviso Controversy* (1967); Rodman W. Paul, *California Gold: The Beginning of Mining in the Far West* (1947); R. W. Paul, *Mining Frontiers of the Far West, 1848–1880* (1963); R. H. Peterson, *Manifest Destiny in the Mines: A Cultural Interpretation of Anti-Mexican Nativism in California, 1848–1853* (1975); Andrew F. Rolle, *California: A History* (1969); John H. Schroeder, *Mr. Polk's War: American Opposition and Dissent* (1973); Alexander Saxton, *The Indispensable Enemy: Labor and the Anti-Chinese Movement in California* (1975); Kevin Starr, *Americans and the California Dream, 1850–1915* (1973); John E. Weems, *To Conquer a Peace: The War Between the United States and Mexico* (1974).

CHAPTER 13

The House Divided, 1850–1859

Early in 1864, a New York economist named John Smith Dye published a book entitled *The Adder's Den or Secrets of the Great Conspiracy to Overthrow Liberty in America.* In his volume, Dye set out to prove that for over thirty years a ruthless southern "slave power" had engaged in a deliberate, systematic plan to subvert civil liberties, pervert the Constitution, and extend slavery into the western territories.

In Dye's eyes, the entire history of the United States was the record of repeated southern plots to expand slavery. An arrogant and aggressive "slave power," he maintained, had entrenched slavery in the Constitution, caused financial panics to sabotage the northern economy, dispossessed Indians from their native lands, and incited revolution in Texas and war with Mexico in order to expand the South's slave empire. Most important of all, he insisted, the southern slaveocracy had secretly assassinated two presidents by poison and unsuccessfully attempted to murder three others.

According to Dye, this campaign of political assassination began in 1835, when John C. Calhoun, outraged by Andrew Jackson's opposition to states' rights and nullification, encouraged a deranged man named Richard Lawrence to kill Jackson. This plot failed when Lawrence's pistols misfired. Six years later, in 1841, Dye argued, a successful attempt was made on a president's life. William Henry Harrison had refused to cooperate in a southern scheme to annex Texas, and, as a result, he died of symptoms resembling arsenic poisoning just thirty days after taking office, leaving John Tyler, a strong defender of slavery, in the White House.

The next president to die at the hands of the slave power, Dye claimed, was Zachary Taylor. A Louisiana slaveowner who had commanded American troops in the Mexican War, Taylor had shocked Southerners by opposing the extension of slavery into California. Just sixteen months after taking office, Taylor was stricken by acute gastroenteritis, caused, claimed Dye, by arsenic poisoning. Taylor was succeeded by Vice-President Millard Fillmore, who was more sympathetic to the southern cause. Just three years later, Dye maintained, another attempt was made on a president's life.

The slave power considered Franklin Pierce, a New Hampshire Democrat, unreliable. On the way to his inauguration, Pierce's railroad car derailed and rolled down an embankment. The president and his wife escaped injury, but their twelve-year-old son was killed before their eyes. In the future, Pierce toed the southern line.

In 1857 yet another attempt was made to kill a president. On February 23, 1857, President-elect James Buchanan, a Pennsylvania Democrat, dined at Washington's National Hotel. Buchanan had won the Democratic presidential nomination in the face of fierce Southern opposition, and, in Dye's view, the slaveocracy wanted to remind Buchanan who was in charge. Southern agents sprinkled arsenic on the lump sugar used by Northerners to sweeten their tea. Because Southerners drank coffee and used granulated sugar, no Southerners were injured. According to Dye, sixty Northerners were poisoned, including the president, and thirty-eight died. Frightened by his brush with death, Buchanan proved to be a reliable tool of the slave power.

John Smith Dye's book was only the most extreme example of conspiratorial charges that had been made by abolitionists since the late 1830s. By the 1850s, a growing number of Northerners had come to believe that an aggressive southern slave power had seized control of the federal government and threatened to subvert republican ideals of liberty, equality, and self-rule. At the same time, an increasing number of Southerners had begun to believe that antislavery radicals dominated northern politics and would "rejoice" in the ultimate consequences of abolition: race war, racial amalgamation, and, as one militant southern leader put it, "the Africanization of the South." Sectional animosities were becoming increasingly ideological and inflamed, moving the torn nation closer to secession and war.

During the 1850s, the American political system became incapable of containing the sectional disputes between the North and South that had smoldered for more than half a century. One major political party, the Whigs, collapsed. Another, the Democrats, split into northern and southern factions. With the break-

In 1864 New York economist John Smith Dye argued that the Slave Power had secretly poisoned two presidents—William Henry Harrison and Zachary Taylor—and had conspired to murder three others.

slave labor, and on July 29 they held a mass meeting and resolved "that no slave or Negro should own claims or even work in the mines." They ordered the Texans out of the gold fields within twenty-four hours.

Three days later, the white miners elected a delegate to a California convention that had been called to frame a state constitution and apply for admission to the Union. At the convention, the miners' delegate proposed that "neither slavery nor involuntary servitude" should ever "be tolerated" in California. The convention adopted his proposal unanimously.

California's application for admission to the Union as a free state in September of 1849 raised the question that would dominate American politics during the 1850s: would slavery be allowed to expand into the West or would the West remain free soil? It was the issue of slave expansion—and not the morality of slavery—which made political antislavery respectable in the North, polarized public opinion, and initiated the chain of events that led the United States to civil war.

down of the party system, it was no longer possible to contain the explosive issues raised by slavery. The bonds that had bound the country for more than seven decades began to unravel.

THE CRISIS OF 1850

On a hot July day in 1849 an expedition of Texas slaveowners and their slaves arrived in the California gold fields. As curious prospectors looked on, the Texans staked out claims and put their slaves to work panning for gold. White miners were outraged. They considered it unfair that they should have to compete with

In California white miners refused "to swing a pick by side with the Negro." Their delegate to the California constitutional convention of 1849 proposed that "neither slavery nor involuntary servitude . . . shall ever be tolerated in this state."

California's decision to prohibit slavery exacerbated a sectional conflict that had been raging in Congress since the beginning of 1849. In January of that year, antislavery Congressmen demanded an end to the slave trade in the District of Columbia. Proslavery Southerners countered by calling for a new and more effective law to apprehend runaway slaves and by claiming that Texas, a slave state, actually owned a huge chunk of New Mexico territory. The crisis deepened when southern Democrats called for a southern convention to be held in Nashville in June 1850 to propose ways of protecting the South's interests. California's application for statehood in September 1849, made sectional crisis inescapable.

Southerners expressed outrage at the idea of admitting a free state to the Union without also admitting a slave state. In the past, Congress had always paired the admission of a free state and a slave state. In 1836 and 1837, Congress had admitted Arkansas as a slave state and Michigan as a free state. In 1845 Florida and Texas had joined the Union as slave states, but Congress restored the sectional balance by admitting Iowa as a free state in 1846 and Wisconsin in 1848. If California was admitted as a free state, there would be sixteen free states and only fifteen slave states. The sectional balance of power in the Senate would be upset, and the South feared that it would lose its ability to shape political events.

Prospects for a peaceful resolution of the sectional conflict seemed bleak. When the Thirty-first Congress convened in December, 1849, neither the Democrats nor the Whigs had a stable majority. Southern Whigs were deserting their party in droves, and northern and southern Democrats were badly split. Election of a Speaker of the House took three weeks and sixty-three ballots.

In the North, opponents of the westward expansion of slavery made striking gains, particularly within the Democratic party. Coalitions of Democrats and Free Soilers in Connecticut, Illinois, Indiana, Massachusetts, New York, Ohio, Vermont, and Wisconsin elected congressmen determined to prevent southern expansion. The Massachusetts Democratic Convention adopted a party platform that declared: "we are opposed to slavery in every form and color, and in favor of freedom and free soil wherever man lives." Every northern state legislature except Iowa's asserted that Congress had the power and duty to exclude slavery from the territories.

Southern hotspurs talked openly of secession. Robert Toombs of Georgia declared that if the North deprived the South of the right to take slaves into California and New Mexico, "I am for disunion." Albert Gallatin Brown of Mississippi echoed these sentiments in ringing terms, announcing that he too favored disunion to "social and sectional degradation." Such bold talk inched the nation closer to secession.

The South's Dilemma

Why were the South's political leaders so worried about whether slavery would be permitted in the West when geography and climate made it unlikely that slavery would ever prosper in the area? The answer lies in the South's growing consciousness of its minority position within the Union. If slavery were prohibited from the Mexican cession, declared one southern politician, then the section would become "the inferior, the Bondsman in fact, of the North." A Virginia Democrat echoed these sentiments with bold words. The Wilmot Proviso, he said, "says in effect to the Southern man, Avaunt! you are not my equal, and hence are to be excluded as carrying a moral taint with you." For more and more Southerners, the region's future depended upon whether the West was opened or closed to slavery.

During the first half of the nineteenth century, slavery in the Western Hemisphere was confined to a small and ever decreasing number of areas. During the early years of the nineteenth century, Spain's newly independent New World colonies abolished slavery. Then in 1833, Britain emancipated its slaves in Jamaica, Trinidad, Guiana, Saint Vincent, Saint Lucia, Tobago, Grenada, Montserrat, and other possessions in the Caribbean. A decade and a half later, France abolished slavery in its Caribbean colonies. By 1850, New World slavery was confined to Brazil, Cuba, Puerto Rico, a small number of Dutch colonies, and the American South.

British slave emancipation in the Caribbean was followed by an intensified campaign to

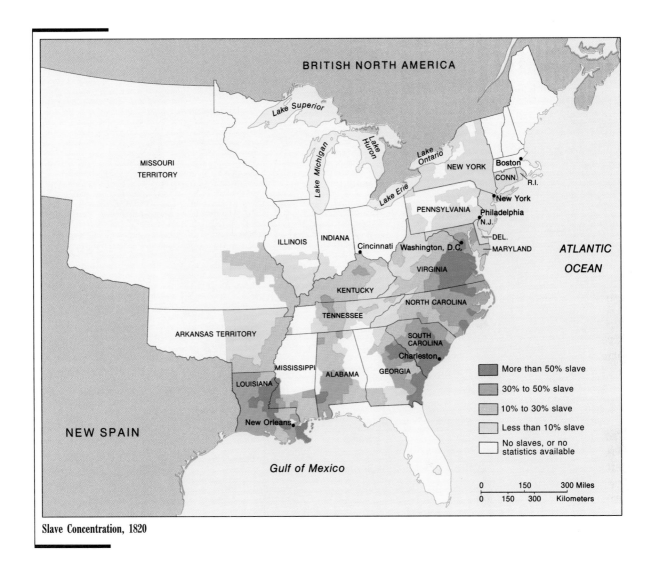

Slave Concentration, 1820

eradicate the international slave trade. In areas like Brazil and Cuba, slavery could not long survive once the slave trade was cut off, because these countries slave populations were unable to naturally reproduce their numbers. Only in the American South could slavery survive without the Atlantic slave trade.

Exacerbating southern fears about slavery's future was a sharp decline in slavery in the upper South. Between 1830 and 1860, the proportion of slaves in Missouri's population fell from eighteen percent to ten percent; in Kentucky it fell from twenty-four percent to nineteen percent; and in Maryland it fell from twenty-three percent to thirteen percent. Many leaders in the South feared that in the future

the upper South would soon become a region of free labor.

By the middle of the nineteenth century, Southern slaveowners faced a dilemma. Slave labor was becoming an exception in the world. Within the South itself, slave ownership was becoming concentrated in fewer and fewer hands. Abolitionists were stigmatizing the South as out of step with the times. Many of the South's leading politicians feared that these criticisms of slavery would weaken lower-class white support for slavery.

The desire to ensure lower-class white support for slavery led some Southerners to agitate for reopening of the African slave trade. For most southern leaders, the best way to demon-

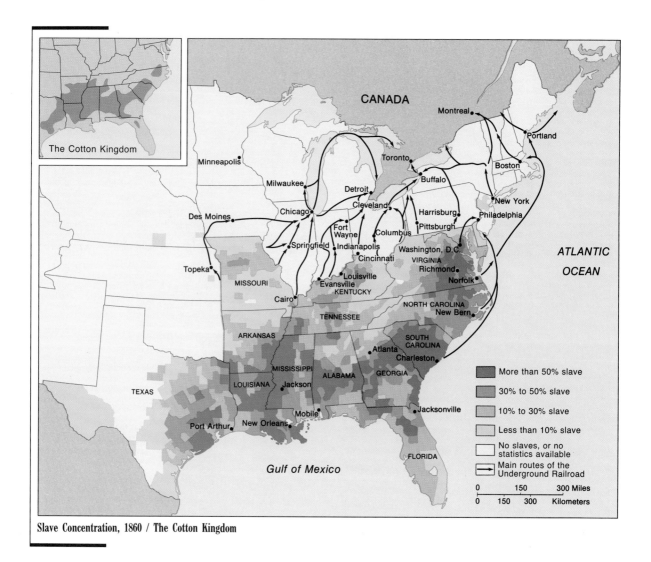

The Cotton Kingdom

More than 50% slave

30% to 50% slave

10% to 30% slave

Less than 10% slave

No slaves, or no
statistics available

Main routes of the
Underground Railroad

| 0 | 150 | 300 Miles |

| 0 | 150 | 300 | Kilometers |

Slave Concentration, 1860 / The Cotton Kingdom

strate that slavery was a "progressive" institution was to ensure that Congress not infringe on the right of the South to take slaves into the western territories. Without such a guarantee, declared an Alabama politician, "THIS UNION CANNOT STAND."

The Compromise of 1850: The Illusion of Sectional Peace

Early on the evening of January 21, 1850, Senator Henry Clay of Kentucky trudged through knee-deep snowdrifts to visit Senator Daniel Webster of Massachusetts. Clay, seventy-three years old, was a sick man, wracked by a severe

cough, but he braved the snowstorm because he feared for the Union's future.

For four years Congress had bitterly and futilely debated the question of slave expansion. Ever since David Wilmot had proposed that slavery be prohibited from any territory acquired from Mexico, opponents of slavery had argued that Congress possessed the power to regulate slavery in the western territories and to exclude slavery from the lands won from Mexico. Ardent proslavery Southerners responded by denying that Congress had any right to exclude slavery from a territory.

Politicians had repeatedly but unsuccessfully tried to work out a compromise. One compromise proposal had been simply to extend the Missouri Compromise line to the Pacific Ocean. Slavery would be forbidden north of 36° 30′, but permitted south of that line. This proposal attracted the support of moderate Southerners but generated little support outside the region. The other compromise proposal, supported by two key Democratic senators, Lewis Cass of Michigan and Stephen Douglas of Illinois, was known as "squatter sovereignty" or "popular sovereignty." It declared that the people actually living in a territory should decide whether or not to allow slavery.

Unfortunately, neither of these formulas offered an acceptable solution to the whole range of issues dividing the North and South. It was up to Henry Clay, who had just returned to Congress after a seven years' absence, to discover a formula that would allow the sections to compromise their differences.

For an hour on the evening of January 21, Clay outlined his plan to save the Union. Clay told Daniel Webster that a compromise could only be effective if it addressed all the issues that divided the North and South. He proposed that California be admitted as a free state; that territorial governments be established in New Mexico and Utah without any restrictions on slavery; that Texas relinquish its claim to land in New Mexico in exchange for federal assumption of Texas's unpaid debts; that Congress enact a stringent and enforceable fugitive slave law but declare that it had no power to deal with the interstate slave trade; and that slavery be permitted in the District of Columbia, but the slave trade be abolished.

A week later, Clay stood before the Senate and offered his proposal to resolve the conflict peacefully. Drawing upon his reputation as the "Great Compromiser" who had fashioned the Missouri Compromise and the Compromise Tariff of 1833, which resolved the nullification controversy, Clay appealed to Northerners and Southerners for "mutual forebearance" and asked them to place patriotism ahead of sectional loyalties.

For eight months debate raged through Congress over the question of slavery expansion. On March 4, John C. Calhoun, the "Sentinel of the South," offered his response to Clay's

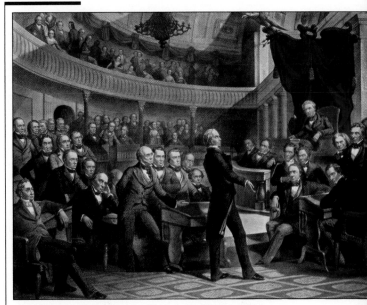

Seventy-three-year-old Henry Clay pleads his case for sectional compromise. The Senate chamber was so crowded when he made his speech that the temperature reached 100 degrees.

compromise proposal. Calhoun was dying of tuberculosis and was too ill to speak publicly, so his speech was read by a colleague, Senator J. M. Mason of Virginia, while the South Carolinian grimly looked on. He warned the North that the only way to save the Union was to "cease the agitation of the slave question," concede "to the South an equal right" to the western territories, return runaway slaves, and accept a constitutional amendment which would protect the South against northern violations of its rights. In the absence of such concessions, Calhoun argued, the South's only option was to secede.

Three days later, Daniel Webster, the North's most spellbinding orator, abandoned his previous opposition to the expansion of slavery into the western territories and threw his support behind Clay's compromise. "Mr. President," he began, "I wish to speak today not as a Massachusetts man, nor as Northern man, but as an American . . . I speak today for the preservation of the Union. Hear me for my cause." The sixty-eight-year-old

Massachusetts Whig called on both sides to compromise their differences in the name of patriotism. The North, he insisted, could afford to be generous because climate and geography ensured that slavery would never be profitable in the western territories. He concluded by warning his listeners that "there can be no such thing as a peaceable secession. . . . Secession! Peaceable secession! Sir, your eyes and mine are never destined to see that miracle. The dismemberment of this vast country without convulsion! . . . Who is so foolish . . . as to expect to see any such thing?"

Webster's speech provoked a storm of outrage from opponents of compromise. Senator William H. Seward of New York called Webster a "traitor to the cause of freedom." The Reverend Theodore Parker declared that "no living man has done so much to debauch the conscience of the nation . . . I know of no deed in American history done by a son of New England to which I can compare this, but the act of Benedict Arnold." Webster's speech did have one important effect. It reassured moderate Southerners that powerful interests in the North were committed to compromise.

Still, opposition to compromise continued to come from many quarters. Whig President Zachary Taylor argued that California, New Mexico, Oregon, Utah, and Minnesota should all be admitted to statehood before the question of slavery was addressed—a proposal which would have given the North a ten vote majority in the Senate. William H. Seward, speaking for abolitionists and other opponents of slave expansion, denounced the compromise proposal for conceding too much to the South and proclaimed that there was a "higher law" than the Constitution, a law which demanded opposition to slavery. At the same time, many southern extremists bridled at the idea of admitting California as a free state. In July, northern and southern senators opposed to the very idea of compromise joined ranks to defeat a bill that would have admitted California to the Union and organized New Mexico and Utah without reference to slavery.

Compromise appeared to be dead. A bitterly disappointed and exhausted Henry Clay dejectedly left the Capitol, his efforts apparently for nought. Then with unexpected suddenness the outlook abruptly changed. On the evening of July 9, 1850, President Taylor died of gastroenteritis, five days after taking part in a Fourth of July celebration held to celebrate the building of the still unfinished Washington Monument. He was succeeded by Millard Fillmore, a fifty-year-old New Yorker and ardent supporter of compromise.

In Congress, leadership in the fight for a compromise passed to Stephen Douglas, a Democratic senator from Illinois. An arrogant and dynamic leader, five feet, four inches in height, with stubby legs, a massive head, bushy eyebrows, and a booming voice, Douglas was known as the "Little Giant." Douglas abandoned Clay's strategy of gathering all issues dividing the sections into a single "omnibus" bill and instead introduced Clay's proposals one at a time. In this way, he was able to gather support from

Just over five feet tall, Stephen A. Douglas, the senator from Illinois, was known as the "Little Giant" and a "steam engine in britches" for his powerful voice and his legislative skill.

varying coalitions of Whigs and Democrats and Northerners and Southerners. At the same time, banking and business interests and speculators in Texas bonds lobbied and even bribed congressmen to support compromise. Despite these manipulations, the compromise proposals never succeeded in gathering solid congressional support. In the end, only four senators and twenty-eight representatives voted for all the compromise measures. Nevertheless, the compromise measures passed.

As finally approved, the compromise admitted California as a free state, allowed the territorial legislatures of New Mexico and Utah to settle the question of slavery in those areas, set up a stringent federal law for the return of runaway slaves, abolished the slave trade in the District of Columbia, and gave Texas $10 million to abandon its claims to territory in New Mexico.

The compromise created the illusion that the territorial issue had been resolved once and for all. "There is rejoicing over the land," wrote one Northerner, "the bone of contention is removed; disunion, fanaticism, violence, insurrection are defeated." Sectional hostility had been defused; calm had returned. But, as one southern editor correctly noted, it was "the calm of preparation, and not of peace."

The Fugitive Slave Law

The Fugitive Slave Law was the most divisive element in the Compromise of 1850. In 1842 the Supreme Court had ruled in the case of *Prigg* v. *Pennsylvania* that state authorities could not be compelled to return fugitive slaves to their Southern owners. Massachusetts, Pennsylvania, Rhode Island, and Vermont proceeded to enact personal liberty laws which forbade state officials from assisting in the return of runaways and prohibited fugitives from being imprisoned in state jails.

In order to prevent runaways from finding sanctuary in the North, the Fugitive Slave Law stripped accused runaways of the right to trial by jury and the right to testify in their own defense. The law stipulated that accused runaways stand trial in front of special commissioners, not a judge or a jury, and that the commissioner could send a runaway to the South solely on the basis of an affidavit sworn by anyone who claimed to be the slave's owner. Thus, there was no way to stop a slaveholder from identifying free blacks as fugitives and forcing them into slavery.

In addition, the law provided a payment of $10 to a commissioner if a fugitive was returned to slavery but only $5 if the fugitive was freed—a provision that outraged many Northerners, who regarded it as a bribe to ensure that any black accused of being a runaway would be found guilty. Finally, the law required all United States citizens to assist in the apprehension of runaway slaves. Anyone who refused to aid in the capture of a fugitive or interfered with the arrest of a slave or tried to free a slave already in custody was subject to a heavy fine and imprisonment.

The Fugitive Slave Law provoked outrage in the North. Within two months, thousands of Northerners were converted to the free-soil doctrine that slavery should be barred from the western territories. "We went to bed one night old-fashioned, conservative, compromise, Union Whigs," wrote a Massachusetts factory owner, "and waked up stark mad Abolitionists." An Ohio congressman charged that the bill was part of a southern plot to extend slavery throughout the West, and the New York *Tribune* went even further and said that the Southern slaveocracy wanted to extend slavery not only into the West but into the North as well.

Attempts to enforce the new law aroused wholesale opposition. In Congress, a Free Soiler declared that it would be the same as "murder" to return a fugitive to slavery. Eight Northern states attempted to invalidate the law by enacting "personal liberty" laws which forbade state officials from assisting in the return of runaways and extended the right of jury trial to fugitives. Southerners regarded these attempts to obstruct the return of runaways as a violation of the Constitution and federal law.

The free black communities of the North responded defiantly to the 1850 law. Northern blacks provided about 1500 fugitive slaves with sanctuary along the underground railroad to freedom. Others established vigilance committees to protect blacks from hired kidnappers who were searching the North for runaways. Fifteen thousand free blacks, convinced that

PHYSICIANS AND PLANTERS, PRESCRIPTION FOR SLAVE MEDICAL CARE

"So perverse and stubbornly foolish are these people," one slaveholder wrote of his bondsmen, "they are either running into the hospital without cause or braving such a disease as cholera, by concealing the symptoms." Maintenance of slaves' health presented masters with diverse dilemmas. In the continual battle of wills between slaves and their owners over the amount and type of work to be performed, pretending to be sick became a form of "striking" for some slaves. Due to the state of medicine at the time, however, other slaves feared the cure more than the disease. Determining who really was sick was a tricky but crucial matter. Complicating the task were issues of profits, humanitarianism, and racism. Sick slaves could produce few profits; dead slaves none. At the same time, to

provide healthy living conditions and constant medical care cost money, which cut into profits. Most masters liked to see themselves as paternalists who took good care of their "slave children." Planters and physicians consequently spent much time trying to determine appropriate responses to slave illnesses.

Feigning illness was an art that some slaves learned through trial and error. Some complaints worked better than others, as the Virginia slave James L. Smith discovered. He detested shooing crows from the cornfield but knew that if he acted sick "they will give me something that will physic me to death." That something was frequently ipecac, which induced vomiting. In response to an earlier stomach complaint Smith's mis-

tress had "made me drunk with whiskey"—a state he had not enjoyed. So he finally decided to claim to have injured his leg and stayed in his room, eating less, to give his claim credibility. Two weeks later, after the crows had deserted the cornfield for the cherry orchard, Smith "began to grow better very fast."

For the same reason that Smith avoided certain imaginary complaints, a number of slaves concealed symptoms of real diseases. Most masters called in the doctor only after the failure of home remedies—many of which had unpleasant and occasionally fatal side effects. Treatment by a physician was not always better. Eighteenth-century medical science was still primitive and had cures for only a handful of conditions. Otherwise doctors resorted to the use of excessive drugs and diuretics, leeching and blood-letting, purging and sweating, all of which caused discomfort and often weakened the body's ability to fight the disease. Many slaves therefore preferred to treat themselves with herbal cures that had been quietly passed down through the generations. Some home remedies in the slaves' quarters were superior to white ones and were occasionally reported in medical journals. Others, however, were based on superstition, and conjurers sometimes caused treatable diseases to progress to irreversible states. For some blacks the decision to conceal an illness was an act of independence. Even though an unannounced illness meant they had to continue to work while sick, some slaves preferred that to surrendering their bodies to the care of white owners and physicians.

Once planters had overcome the hurdle of determining which

slaves were ill, they then had to decide upon a course of action. Here humanitarian and profit concerns frequently intersected. Slaveowners were concerned about blacks' health for essentially three reasons: protecting their financial investment in their slaves, preventing the spread of illness to themselves and their families, and concern for the slaves as human beings. The decision of when to call in a doctor was difficult even for those with the best intentions. To his overseer Thomas Jefferson specified certain illnesses for which physicians should be summoned as they could provide "certain relief," but insisted that "in most other cases they oftener do harm than good."

For many reasons home care was the first resort of most planters in all cases except those where the value of professional care was obvious. Treatments for some illnesses were fairly standardized, well-known, and easily performed by laymen. Many planters questioned the need to pay a doctor to treat such maladies. Through various suppliers, they obtained such commonly used drugs as calomel, castor oil, ipecac, laudanum, opium, camphor, and quinine. They consulted various household medical guides about proper dosages. Frequently the home cures worked as well or better than professional services. Often, however, planters misdiagnosed. Even if the improper treatment made the condition no worse, it prolonged the course of the illness until too late for effective treatment.

Some slaveholders consciously waited until everything else had failed to call in a doctor. Planter Robert Carter of Virginia sent a dying patient to a physician with a note: "I do not wish to continue practice any longer on Peter—and now I deliver him to you." Such actions infuriated doctors, who were then blamed for their low cure rates. On some plantations where the doctor was not summoned until death was at hand, slaves superstitiously began to link the doctor's arrival with life's departure, giving them another reason to conceal their symptoms.

There were limits to paternalism. The growing knowledge of the impact of environment on health did not induce many planters to improve substantially the living quarters or diets of their bondsmen. That cut into profits too drastically for the perceived benefits. Hence inadequate diets, clothing, and shelter dramatically decreased slaves' health. Economic and humane considerations were offset by a racism that placed less value on black life. Landon Carter administered rattlesnake powder to his slaves during an attack of "bilious fever." It seemed to help but produced unpleasant side effects. "I wish my own fears did not prevent my giving it to my Children," Carter wrote in his diary—displaying a willingness to "experiment" on blacks that was not uncommon for physicians or planters. Slaves had no authority to refuse any kind of treatment.

Blacks were sometimes treated differently from whites because of perceived physiological differences. A number of the perceptions were accurate assessments distilled from experience. Physicians could not help but note variations in the susceptibility to specific diseases or in the responses to treatment between the two groups. Modern researchers have found physiological bases for some of their observations, such as the effect of the sickle-cell trait in the blood of many blacks on some malarial viruses. At the time, however, those differences were often used and exaggerated as justification for both slavery and inadequate black health care. Some asserted that black bodies were uniquely suited for hard labor as well as slavery— a proposal not supported by mortality statistics.

Samuel W. Cartwright of Louisiana was a leading medical apologist for slavery. He argued that blacks were intellectually inferior because dark pigmentation was more than skin deep. "Even the negro's brain and nerves," he wrote, "are tinctured with a shade of pervading darkness." To support his claims of black bodies and minds being built for slavery, Cartwright explained all "unslavelike" behavior as diseases peculiar to blacks. Careless habits were a symptom of what he called *Dysaetesia Aethiopica*. Slaves who ran away were affected with *Drapetomania*. He could not accept that either could be rational forms of resistance to slavery.

The health care of slaves illustrates the interplay of medicine and public values. Physicians became apologists for slavery and built lucrative careers on treating "negro illnesses." Although slaves often sought to control their medical destinies through secret self-treatment, ultimate authority over their bodies rested in the property rights of their owners. Those owners most frequently acted on the basis of self-interest, which sometimes, but not always, coincided with benevolence. Few valued black life as highly as white. Medical care, like most other life and death matters, was controlled by the white establishment.

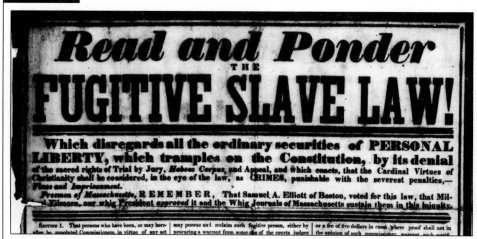

No part of the Compromise of 1850 drew more outrage from Northerners than the Fugitive Slave Law. An Ohio congressman defiantly stated: "Let the President drench our land of freedom in blood; but he will never make us obey that law."

blacks could never achieve equality in America, emigrated to Canada, Haiti, the British Caribbean, and Africa after the adoption of the 1850 federal law.

The South's demand for an effective fugitive slave law was a major source of sectional tension. Efforts to enforce the law resulted in abuses that repelled many northern moderates. In one instance, a free black named James Hamlet was seized in New York and sent into slavery. Riots directed against the law broke out in many cities. In Christiana, Pennsylvania, in 1851, a gun battle broke out between abolitionists and slave catchers, and in Wisconsin, an abolitionist editor named Sherman M. Booth freed Joshua Glover, a fugitive slave, from a local jail. In Boston, federal marshals and twenty-two companies of state troops were needed to prevent a crowd from storming a court house to free a fugitive named Anthony Burns.

One northern moderate who was repelled by the fugitive slave law was a forty-one-year-old mother of six from Maine named Harriet Beecher Stowe. In 1851 she wrote *Uncle Tom's Cabin*, the single most powerful attack on slavery ever written. Stowe had learned about slavery while living in Cincinnati, Ohio, across from slaveholding Kentucky, and in her book she

succeeded in personalizing the abstract horrors of slavery. Characters like Eliza Harris, the mother forcibly separated from her husband; Simon Legree, the wicked overseer; and Uncle Tom, the slave who sacrificed his life to prevent the whipping of a slave woman, awakened millions of Northerners to the moral evil of slavery. Southerners denounced Stowe as a "wretch in petticoats" and copies of the book were burned in Alabama, but in the North the book sold an unprecedented number of copies—50,000 in eight weeks, 300,000 copies in a year, one million copies in sixteen months. "No book ever had such sudden and universal success," wrote one contemporary. "It is bought as fast as it can be printed."

No novel has ever exerted a stronger influence on American public opinion. Legend has it that when President Lincoln met Mrs. Stowe during the Civil War, he said, "So this is the little woman who made this big war."

DISINTEGRATION OF THE PARTY SYSTEM

As late as 1850, the two party system was, to all outward appearances, still healthy. Every state, except South Carolina, had two effective politi-

Apologists for slavery denounced *Uncle Tom's Cabin* as inaccurate. Harriet Beecher Stowe responded by writing *The Key to Uncle Tom's Cabin*, which provided documentary proof of the abuses she described in her novel.

cal parties. Both the Democratic party and the Whigs were able to attract support in every section and in every state in the country. Voter participation was at extremely high levels and neither party was able to gain more than fifty-three percent of the national vote. Then, in the space of just five years, the two party system began to disintegrate in response to two issues: massive foreign immigration and the reemergence of the issue of the expansion of slavery.

The first sign of the breakdown of the party system occurred during the debates over the Compromise of 1850. Whigs in the Deep South felt their party was unreliable on the slavery question and joined the Democratic party in large numbers. The political system was further fragmented by the sudden rise of the Know Nothings, an anti-immigrant, anti-Catholic third party, to power in many states. By 1856 the Whig party had collapsed and been replaced by a new sectional party, the Republicans.

The Know Nothings

Four times in American history the emergence of a small, vigorous third party has led to a major realignment of the American political system. In the 1830s, the rise of the Anti-Masonic party opened the way to the creation of a party system dominated by the Democratic and Whig parties. In the 1890s, the emergence of the Populist party among southern and midwestern farmers generated a shift in voting among the Democratic and Republican parties. Finally, in 1968 George Wallace's American Independent party led to a massive shift of voters away from the Democratic party into the Republican party.

The most momentous shift in party sentiment in American history, however, took place in the early 1850s following the rise of a party viciously opposed to immigrants and Catholics. This party, which was known as the American party or Know Nothing party, crippled the Whig party, weakened the Democratic party, and made the political system incapable of resolving the growing crisis over slavery.

Hostility toward immigrants and Catholics had deep roots in American culture. The Protestant religious revivals of the 1820s and 1830s

After Philadelphia's Catholic bishop convinced the city's board of education in 1844 to use both the Catholic and Protestant versions of the Bible in schools, a vicious anti-Catholic riot erupted.

stimulated a "No Popery" movement. Prominent northern clergymen, mostly Whigs in politics, accused the Catholic church of conspiring to overthrow democracy and subject the United States to Catholic despotism. Popular fiction offered graphic descriptions of priests seducing women during confession and nuns cutting unborn infants from their mothers' wombs and throwing them to dogs. A popular children's game was called "break the Pope's neck." Anti-Catholic sentiment culminated in mob rioting and church and convent burning. In 1844 a Philadelphia mob rampaged Irish neighborhoods, burning churches and houses.

The advent of massive immigration from Ireland and Germany after 1845 led to a renewed outburst of antiforeign and anti-Catholic sentiment. Between 1846 and 1855, over three million foreigners arrived in America. In cities such as Chicago, Milwaukee, New York, and St. Louis, immigrants actually outnumbered native-born American citizens. Nativists—ardent opponents of immigration—claimed that immigrants posed a serious threat to the nation's republican values. Catholics, they charged, were responsible for a sharp increase in poverty, crime, and drunkenness and were subservient to a foreign leader, the Pope. Thousands of native-born Americans responded with

outrage when Catholic Archbishop John Hughes of New York declared, "Everyone should know that we have for our mission to convert the world—including the inhabitants of the United States—the people of the cities and the people of the country, the officers of the navy and the marines, commanders of the army, the legislatures, the Senate, the Cabinet, the President, and all!"

To native-born Protestant workers, the new immigrants posed a tangible economic threat. The late 1840s and early 1850s were a period of disruptive economic change. Rapid inflation followed the discovery of gold in California. The growth of railroads disrupted local markets and eliminated jobs in river and canal transportation. Economic slumps in 1851 and 1854 resulted in severe unemployment and wage cuts, and native workers blamed Irish and German immigrants for the plight. Complained one resentful New Yorker: "Are American mechanics to be borne down, crushed, or driven to western wilds?" In addition to presenting an economic threat, the immigrants posed a palpable political threat. Concentrated in the large cities of the eastern seaboard, Irish and German immigrants voted as blocs and quickly built up strong political organizations.

In 1849 a New Yorker named Charles Allen responded to the increase in foreign immigration by forming a secret fraternal society made up of native-born Protestant workingmen. Allen called this secret society "The Order of the Star Spangled Banner," and it soon formed the nucleus of a new political party known as the Know Nothing or the American party. The party received its name from the fact that when members were asked about the workings of the party, they were supposed to reply, "I know nothing."

By 1855 the Know Nothings had captured control of all New England except Vermont and Maine and were the dominant opposition party to the Democrats in New York, Pennsylvania, Maryland, Virginia, Tennessee, Georgia, Alabama, Mississippi, and Louisiana. In the presidential election of 1856, the party supported Millard Fillmore and won more than twenty-one percent of the popular vote and eight electoral

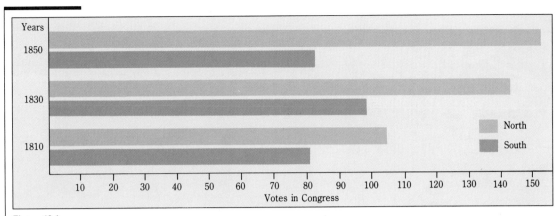

Figure 13.1
Number of Votes in Congress, North versus South

votes. In Congress, the party had five senators and forty-three representatives. Between 1853 and 1855, the Know Nothings replaced the Whigs as the nation's second largest party.

By 1856, however, the Know Nothing party was already in decline. Many Know Nothing officeholders were relatively unknown men with little political experience. In office, the Know Nothings proved unable to enact their legislative program, which included a twenty-one-year residency period before immigrants could become citizens and vote, a limitation on political officeholding to native-born Americans, and restrictions on the sale of liquor.

Respectable public opinion spoke out vehemently against the dangers posed by the party. In 1855 an Illinois Whig politician named Abraham Lincoln denounced the Know Nothings in eloquent terms.

> I am not a Know-Nothing. How could I be? How can any one who abhors the oppression of Negroes be in favor of degrading classes of white people? Our progress in degeneracy appears to me pretty rapid. As a nation we began by declaring "all men are created equal." We now practically read it, "all men are created equal, except Negroes." When the Know-Nothings get control, it will read "all men are created equal, except Negroes, and foreigners, and Catholics." When it comes to this I should prefer emigrating to some

country where they make no pretense of loving liberty—to Russia, for example, where despotism can be taken pure and without the base alloy of hypocrisy.

After 1855 the Know Nothing party was supplanted in the North by a new and explosive sectional party, the Republicans. By 1856 northern workers felt more threatened by the southern slave power than by the Pope and Catholic immigrants. At the same time, fewer and fewer Southerners were willing to support a party that ignored the question of slave expansion. As a result the Know Nothing party rapidly dissolved.

Nevertheless, the Know Nothings left an indelible mark on American politics. The Know Nothing movement eroded loyalty to the national political parties, helped destroy the Whig party, and undermined the capacity of the political system to contain the issue of slavery.

Young America

For nearly four years following the Compromise of 1850, agitation over the question of slavery expansion abated. Most Americans were sick of the continuing controversy over slavery and turned their attention away from politics and focused instead on railroads, cotton, and trade. The early 1850s were heady years for Ameri-

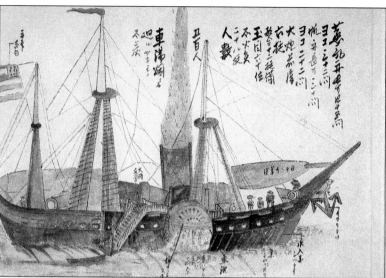

Commodore Matthew Perry's display of armor and technology led Japan to accept the Treaty of Kanagawa, opening Japanese ports to American trade. These drawings were done by artists dispatched by Japanese officials to keep a visual record of Perry's activities.

cans, as dreams of expansion into Asia, the Caribbean, and Central America swept the country. Majestic clipper ships raced from New York to China in as little as 104 days. Steamship and railroad promoters launched ambitious schemes to build transit routes across Central America to link California and the Atlantic Coast. Expansionists sponsored filibustering expeditions into Cuba, Mexico, and Nicaragua.

The whole world was opening up to American influence. In 1853 Commodore Matthew Perry sailed into Tokyo Harbor with three steam frigates and five warships and ended Japan's era of isolation from the western world. The next year, Perry forced the Japanese to accept the Treaty of Kanagawa which opened Japanese ports to American trade, established low import duties, and permitted the United States to open a consulate in Japan.

When Franklin Pierce, a New Hampshire Democrat, was inaugurated as the nation's fourteenth president in March 1853, he gave voice to the popular feeling that a new era of sectional peace had begun. "I fervently hope," declared the new president, "that the question is at rest, and that no sectional or ambitious or fanatical excitement may again threaten the durability of our institutions or obscure the light of our prosperity."

The appearance of sectional calm was deceptive. Both the Democratic and Whig parties were deeply divided. In the presidential election of 1852, six different candidates had run. Although Pierce scored an impressive electoral college victory, 254 to 42, his margin in the popular vote was just 44,000 votes. He actually received 14,000 fewer votes than his opponents in the North.

In office, Pierce tried to unite the country around an aggressive program of foreign expansion called "Young America." As president, he sought to annex Hawaii, expand American influence in Honduras and Nicaragua, and acquire new territory from Mexico and Spain. He announced that his administration would not be deterred from his plans "by any timid forebodings of evil" raised by the slavery question. However, each attempt to expand the nation's boundaries merely reignited sectional disputes over slavery.

Pierce was the first "doughface" president. He was, in the popular phrase, "a Northern man with Southern principles." Many Northerners suspected that Pierce's real goal was to acquire new territory for slavery. This suspicion was first raised in 1853, when the president instructed James Gadsden, his minister to Mexico, to purchase a large area south of the Rio Grande to provide a route for a southern railroad to California. Antislavery senators forced Pierce to reduce the size of the Gadsden Purchase, but they were unable to prevent the deal from being completed.

Cuba was the next object of Pierce's ambitions. Southern slaveholders coveted Cuba's 300,000 slaves, and other Americans wanted to free Cuba's white population from Spanish rule. In 1853 Pierce instructed his ambassador to Spain to offer $130 million for Cuba, but Spain refused the offer. The next year, three of Pierce's diplomatic ministers, meeting in Ostend, Belgium, sent a dispatch, later titled the Ostend Manifesto, to the secretary of state urging the military seizure of Cuba if Spain contin-ued to refuse to sell the island. The Ostend Manifesto outraged Northerners, who regarded the manifesto as a brazen attempt to expand slavery in defiance of Spain's sovereign rights.

The Kansas-Nebraska Act

In 1854, less than four years after the adoption of the Compromise of 1850, a piece of legislation was introduced in Congress which revived the issue of slave expansion, shattered all illusions of sectional peace, destroyed the Whig party, divided the Democratic party, and resulted in the creation of the Republican party. Ironically, the author of this piece of legislation was Senator Stephen A. Douglas, the very man who had pushed the compromise through Congress—and a man who had sworn after the passage of the Compromise of 1850 that he would never make a speech on the slavery question again.

In January 1854 Douglas, the chairman of the Senate Committee on Territories, proposed that the area west of Iowa and Missouri—which

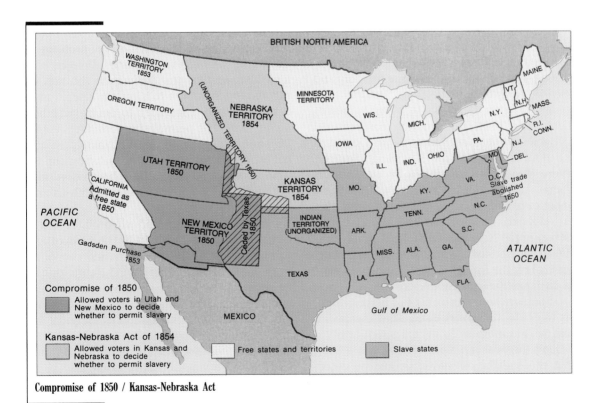

Compromise of 1850 / Kansas-Nebraska Act

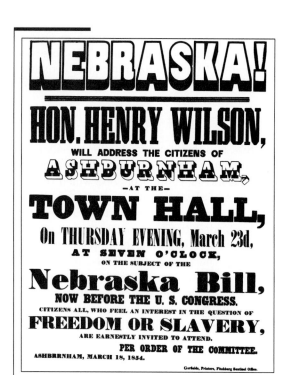

Stephen Douglas's proposal to organize Kansas and Nebraska and repeal the Missouri Compromise produced a furious reaction in the North.

had been set aside as a permanent Indian reservation—be organized as Nebraska territory and opened to white settlement. Douglas had sought to open Nebraska territory to settlement since 1844, but southern congressmen had objected because Nebraska was located in the northern half of the Louisiana Purchase where slavery was prohibited by the Missouri Compromise. In order to forestall southern opposition, Douglas's original bill ignored both the Missouri Compromise and the status of slavery in the Nebraska territory. It simply provided that Nebraska, when admitted as a state, could enter the Union "with or without slavery," as its "constitution may prescribe."

Southern senators would not permit Douglas to evade the slavery issue. They demanded that he add a clause to his bill specifically repealing the Missouri Compromise and stating that the question of slavery would be determined on the basis of popular sovereignty. For reasons still in dispute, Douglas relented to southern pressure. "By God, Sir," Douglas said,

"you are right. I will incorporate it in my bill, though I know it will raise a hell of a storm." In its final form, Douglas's bill created two territories, Kansas and Nebraska, and declared that the Missouri Compromise was "inoperative and void" because it was "inconsistent with the principles of nonintervention by Congress with slavery in the States and Territories, as recognized by the legislation of 1850." With solid support from southern Whigs and southern Democrats and half the votes of northern Democratic congressmen, the measure passed. On May 30, 1854, President Pierce signed the measure into law.

Why did Douglas risk reviving the slavery question? His critics accused him of yielding to the Southern pressure because of his presidential ambitions and a desire to enhance the value of his holdings in Chicago real estate and western lands. They charged that the Illinois senator's chief interest in opening up Kansas and Nebraska was to secure a right of way for a transcontinental railroad that would make Chicago the transportation center of mid-America.

Douglas's supporters, on the other hand, pictured him as a statesman laboring for western development and a sincere believer in popular sovereignty as a solution to the problem of slavery in the western territories. Douglas had long insisted that the democratic solution to the slavery issue was to allow the people who actually settled a territory to decide whether slavery would be permitted or forbidden. Popular sovereignty, he believed, would allow the nation to "avoid the slavery agitation for all time to come." Moreover, he believed that slavery could never be extended into Kansas and Nebraska anyway.

In order to understand why Douglas introduced the Kansas-Nebraska Act, it is important to realize that by 1854 political and economic pressure to organize Kansas and Nebraska had become overwhelming. Midwestern farmers agitated for new land. Railroad promoters viewed territorial organization as essential for construction of a transcontinental railroad. Missouri slaveholders, already bordered on two sides by free states, believed that slavery in their state was doomed if they were surrounded by free territory. All wanted to see the region opened to settlement.

Revival of the Slavery Issue

Neither Douglas nor the southern leaders who supported the Kansas-Nebraska Act anticipated the explosion of fury that the act raised throughout the North. Opponents of the act denounced it as "a gross violation of a sacred pledge; as a criminal betrayal of precious rights" and part of a secret plot "to exclude from a vast unoccupied region, immigrants from the Old World and free laborers from our own States, and convert it into a dreary region of despotism, inhabited by masters and slaves." Abraham Lincoln said that when he read the provisions of the bill in the newspaper, he was "thunderstruck and stunned" and was aroused "as he had never been aroused before." Opponents burned so many figures of Douglas from trees, the Illinois senator joked, "I could travel from Boston to Chicago by the light of my own effigy."

Douglas predicted that the "storm will soon spend its fury," but it did not subside. Northern Free Soilers regarded the Missouri Compromise line as a "sacred compact" which had forever excluded slavery from the northern half of the Louisiana Purchase. Now, they feared that under the guise of popular sovereignty, the Southern slave power threatened to spread slavery across the entire western frontier. Five northern state legislatures adopted resolutions condemning the act, and in the fall elections of 1854, forty-four of the fifty-one northern Democratic congressmen who voted for the act were defeated.

No single piece of legislation ever passed by Congress had more far-reaching political consequences than the Kansas-Nebraska Act. Its passage radically realigned party support. In both the South and North, conservative Whigs moved into the Democratic party. At the same time, free-soil Whigs and Democrats deserted their parties in droves. Anti-Nebraska groups, uniting dissident Democrats, Free Soilers, Whigs, and Know Nothings, sprouted up across the North and swept the Democrats out of office. In the midterm elections of 1854, the Democrats lost every free state except California and New Hampshire. The number of northern Democratic congressmen fell from ninety-three to twenty-seven.

At the same time that the Kansas-Nebraska Act killed the Whig party and divided the Democrats, it brought a new political party into existence. In almost every northern state, groups arose to protest the repeal of the Missouri Compromise. On February 28, 1854, in Ripon, Wisconsin, a leading Whig named Alvan E. Bovay headed a protest meeting which proposed that anti-Nebraska groups join together and adopt the name "Republican." They took this name not only because it was the label used by Thomas Jefferson and his followers but because the new party wanted to place the national interest above sectional interests. In Washington, a caucus of thirty antislavery Whig and Democratic congressmen endorsed the proposal for formation of a new party opposed to the expansion of slavery.

On July 13, 1854, the anniversary of the Northwest Ordinance which had outlawed slavery in the Old Northwest, Republican conventions were held in Indiana, Ohio, and Vermont. In the fall of 1854, the new party contested congressional elections for the first time and won 108 seats in the House of Representatives, compared to just 83 seats for the Democrats and 43 seats for the Know Nothings.

The new party was a combination of diverse elements. It contained antislavery radicals, moderate and conservative Free Soilers, old line Whigs, former Jacksonian Democrats, nativists, and antislavery immigrants. It included a number of men and women, like William H. Seward of New York, who believed that blacks should receive civil rights including the right to vote. The new party also attracted many individuals, like Salmon P. Chase and Abraham Lincoln, who favored colonization as the only workable solution to slavery. Despite their differences, however, all of these groups shared a conviction that the western territories should be saved for free labor and free white men. "Free labor, free soil, free men," was their slogan.

THE GATHERING STORM

Because the Kansas-Nebraska Act stated that the future status of slavery in the territories was to be decided by popular vote, both anti-

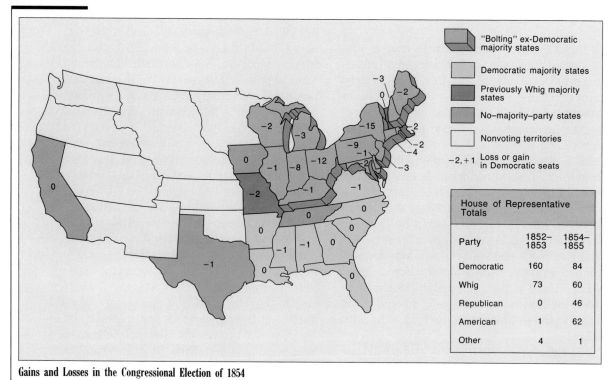

Gains and Losses in the Congressional Election of 1854
The sectional rift grew even sharper after the Kansas-Nebraska Act.

slavery Northerners and proslavery Southerners competed to win the region for their section. Since Nebraska was too far north to attract slaveowners, Kansas became the arena of sectional conflict. For six years, proslavery and antislavery factions fought in Kansas as popular sovereignty degenerated into violence.

"Bleeding Kansas": Rehearsal for Civil War

Across the drought-stricken Ohio and Mississippi valleys, thousands of land-hungry farmers crowded onto river boats and covered wagons to stake a claim to part of Kansas's 126,000 square miles of territory. Along with these pioneers came a small contingent of settlers whose express purpose was to keep Kansas free soil. Even before the 1854 act had been passed, Eli Thayer, a businessman and educator from Worcester, Massachusetts, had organized the New England Emigrant Aid Company to promote the emigration of antislavery New Englanders to Kansas to "vote to make it free." By the summer of 1855, over 9000 pioneers—mainly midwestern free soilers—had settled in Kansas.

Slaveholders from Missouri expressed alarm at rumors that the Emigrant Aid Society had raised $5 million to move abolitionists to Kansas. They feared that this "vast monied corporation" wanted to convert Kansas into a haven for runaway slaves. In response, slaveowners formed "Blue Lodges," "Social Bands," and "Sons of the South" to "repel the wave of fanaticism which threatens to break upon our border." One Missouri lawyer told a cheering crowd that he would hang any "free soil" emigrant who came into Kansas.

Competition between proslavery and antislavery factions in Kansas reached a climax on May 30, 1855, when Kansas held territorial elections. Although only 1500 men were registered to vote, 6000 ballots were cast, many of them by proslavery "border ruffians" from Missouri. As a result, a proslavery legislature was selected, which passed laws stipulating that only proslavery men could hold office or serve on juries. Other statutes called for the death penalty for anyone inciting a slave insurrection and five years imprisonment for anyone questioning the legality of slavery in Kansas.

Free Soilers called the election a fraud and held their own "Free State" convention in Topeka in the fall of 1855. At this convention, delegates drew up a constitution which not only prohibited slavery in Kansas, but also barred free Negroes from the territory. Like the Free Soilers who settled California and Oregon, Northerners in Kansas wanted the territory to be free and white. They submitted the Topeka constitution to the territory's voters December 15. Voters approved the document by an overwhelming majority of 1731 to 46. The Topeka government then asked Congress to admit Kansas as a free state.

When Congress convened in January, 1856, it was confronted by two rival governments in Kansas—one officially authorized but fraudulently elected, the other unauthorized but claiming majority support. President Franklin Pierce threw his support behind the proslavery legislature and asked Congress to admit Kansas to the Union as a slave state. The Topeka government, he declared, was "of revolutionary character," and he warned Free Soilers that any organized resistance to Kansas's proslavery government would be regarded as "treasonable insurrection."

Violent confrontations soon broke out between Northern and Southern settlers over rival land claims, town sites, and railroad routes—and, most dangerous of all, the question of slavery. In January 1856 a leader of Kansas Free Soilers was attacked in Leavenworth, hacked with knives and hatchets, and left to die outside his cabin. Next, an assassin shot a proslavery

Between May and September 1856, terrorism and guerilla warfare swept across Kansas, leaving 200 dead and $2 million in property damage. In one incident, Kansas Free Soilers fired on a proslavery settlement at the Battle of Hickory Point.

sheriff after he and a posse arrested six free-state citizens for "contempt of court."

Angry threats added to the violent atmosphere. Proslavery newspapers called on Southerners to annihilate the Free Soilers: "Let us purge ourselves of all abolition emissaries . . . and give distinct notice that all who do not leave immediately for the East, will leave for eternity!" The North's most renowned minister, Henry Ward Beecher, responded to these threats by urging that Free Soilers be sent heavily armed, since "one Sharps rifle will have more moral influence upon slaveholders than a hundred bibles." A young Free Soiler declared that if the slave power continued "its aggressive acts . . . the war cry heard upon our plains will reverate not only through the hemp and tobacco fields of Missouri but through the 'Rice Swamps,' the cotton and sugar plantations of the Sunny South."

In May 1856 the storm broke. A proslavery grand jury indicted several members of the Free Soil Topeka government for high treason. On May 21, 1856, 800 proslavery men, many from Missouri, marched into Lawrence, Kansas, to arrest the leaders of the antislavery government. The posse burned the Free Soil Hotel, looted a number of houses, destroyed two antislavery printing presses, and killed one man.

KANSAS TERRITORY

MISSOURI

Missouri R.

Kansas R.

Topeka
Lawrence

Kansas City

Osawatomie

Pottawatomie Creek

Marais des Cygnes

Attacks by free-state forces

Attacks by pro-slavery forces

Bleeding Kansas

One member of the posse declared: "Gentlemen, this is the happiest day of my life. I was determined to make the fanatics bow before me in the dust and kiss the territorial laws. I have done it, by God."

"Bleeding Sumner"

On May 19, 1856—two days before the "sack of Lawrence"—Senator Charles Sumner of Massachusetts delivered a two-day speech in which he denounced "The Crime Against Kansas." In his speech, Sumner charged that there was a Southern conspiracy to make Kansas a slave state. This was, he shouted, a crime "which is without example in the records of the past. . . . It is the rape of a virgin territory, compelling it to the hateful embrace of slavery." The Massachusetts senator proceeded to argue that a number of southern senators, including Senator Andrew Butler of South Carolina, stood behind this conspiracy. Launching into a bitter personal diatribe, Sumner accused Senator Butler of taking "the harlot, Slavery," for his "mistress" and then made fun of a medical disorder Senator Butler had. At the rear of the Senate chamber, Stephen Douglas muttered: "That damn fool will get himself killed by some other damned fool."

On May 21, Senator Butler's nephew, Congressman Preston Brooks of South Carolina,

entered a nearly empty Senate chamber. Brooks was convinced that he had a duty to "avenge the insult to my State." Sighting Sumner at his desk, Brooks charged at him and struck the Massachusetts senator over the head with his cane. He swung so hard that the cane broke into pieces. Brooks caned Sumner, rather than challenge him to a duel, because he regarded the senator as his social inferior—and wanted to use the same method slaveholders used to chastize slaves. Brooks then quietly left the Senate chamber, leaving Sumner "as senseless as a corpse for several minutes, his head bleeding copiously from the frightful wounds, and the blood saturating his clothes." It took Sumner three years to recover from his injuries and return to his Senate seat.

In the South, Brooks became an instant hero. Merchants in Charleston, South Carolina, bought Brooks a new cane inscribed, "Hit him again." Students at the University of Virginia sent him a cane with "a heavy gold head . . . [shaped like a] human head, badly cracked and broken." A vote to expel Brooks from the House of Representatives failed because every southern representative but one voted against expulsion. Instead, Brooks was censured. He resigned his seat and was immediately reelected to Congress.

In the North, Sumner was regarded as a martyr to the cause of freedom. Rallies to protest the assault were held in Albany, Cleveland, Detroit, New Haven, New York, Providence, and Rochester. One million copies of Sumner's "Crime Against Kansas" speech were distributed. A young Massachusetts woman summed up popular feeling in the North, condemning Brooks's assault with these words: "If I had been there I would have torn his eyes out and so I would now if I could."

A War of Revenge

Early Friday morning, May 23, 1856, John Brown, a fifty-six-year-old Vermont native and an ardent abolitionist, received word that Senator Sumner had been assaulted. Upon hearing the news, Brown, a "strange, resolute, repulsive, iron-willed, inexorable old man," said "something must be done to show these barbarians that we, too, have rights." A devout Bible-quot-

Clutching a pen in one hand and a copy of his "Crime Against Kansas" speech in the other, Senator Charles Sumner attempts to defend himself against an attack by South Carolina Congressman Preston Brooks.

ing Calvinist who believed that he had a personal responsibility to overthrow slavery, Brown announced that the time had come "to fight fire with fire" and "strike terror in the hearts of proslavery men." The next day, in reprisal for the "sack of Lawrence" and the assault on Sumner, Brown and six companions dragged five proslavery men and boys from their beds at Pottawatomie Creek, split open their skulls with an axe, cut off their hands, and laid out their entrails.

A war of revenge erupted in Kansas. A proslavery newspaper declared: "If murder and assassination is the program of the day, we are in favor of filling the bill." Columns of proslavery Southerners ransacked free farms and took "horses and cattle and everything else they can lay hold of" while they searched for Brown and the other "Pottawatomie killers." Armed bands looted enemy stores and farms. At Osawatomie, proslavery forces attacked John Brown's headquarters, leaving a dozen men dead. At Black Jack, John Brown's men killed four Missourians, and proslavery forces retaliated by blockading the free towns of Topeka and Lawrence. Free Soilers raided proslavery settlements at Fort Saunders, Fort Titus, Franklin, New Georgia, and Treadwell. Guerrilla warfare in southeastern Kansas left 200 dead.

The Election of 1856

The presidential election of 1856 took place in the midst of Kansas's civil war. President Pierce hoped to be renominated for a second term in office, but northern indignation over the Kansas-Nebraska Act led the Democrats to choose a less controversial candidate. On the seventeenth ballot, northern and western Democrats succeeded in winning the nomination for James Buchanan, a sixty-five-year-old Pennsylvania bachelor, who had been minister to Great Britain when the struggle over the Kansas-Nebraska bill was taking place. The dying Whig party and the southern wing of the Know Nothing party nominated former President Millard Fillmore.

The Republican party held its first national convention in Philadelphia in June and adopted a platform denying the authority of Congress and of territorial legislatures "to give legal ex-

Titled "The Right Man for the Right Place," this 1856 Know Nothing political cartoon depicts Millard Fillmore as a peacemaker, standing between Republican John C. Fremont, armed with a rifle, and Democrat James Buchanan, armed with a knife.

istence to slavery" in the territories. The convention nominated the dashing young explorer and soldier John C. Fremont for president as young Republicans chanted, "Free Speech, Free Soil and Fremont." Fremont was a romantic figure who had led more than a dozen major explorations of the Rocky Mountains and Far West and won the nickname "the Pathfinder." After accepting the Republican nomination, he declared that Kansas should be admitted to the Union as a free state. This was his only public utterance during the entire campaign. A few weeks later, the northern wing of the Know Nothing party threw its support behind Fremont.

The election was one of the most bitter in American history and the first one in which voting divided along rigid sectional lines. The Democratic strategy was to picture the Republican party as a hotbed of radicalism. Said Buchanan: "The Black Republicans must be, and can with justice be, boldly assailed as disunionists, and this charge must be reiterated again and again."

Democrats called the Republicans the party of disunion and described Fremont as a Catholic, a drunkard, a bastard, and a "black abolitionist" who would destroy the union, "a man whose only merit, so far as history records it, is in the fact that he was born in South Carolina, crossed the Rocky Mountains, subsisted on frogs, lizards, snakes and grasshoppers, and captured a woolly horse."

Across the North, Republicans responded to the Democratic charges by openly declaring their opposition to slavery. Local Republican clubs sent petitions to Congress demanding "the speedy, peaceful and equitable dissolution of the existing union." An Ohio congressman declared: "I look forward to the day when there shall be a servile insurrection in the South; when the black man . . . shall assert his freedom and wage a war of extermination against his master."

Buchanan, the Democrat, won only a minority of the popular vote—forty-five percent to thirty-three percent for Fremont and twenty-two percent for Fillmore. Because of the presence of Millard Fillmore, the Whig and Know Nothing nominee, Buchanan narrowly carried five northern states and triumphed in the Electoral College, by 174 votes to 114 for Fremont and 8 for Fillmore.

The election results revealed how polarized the nation had become. The South, except for Maryland, voted solidly Democratic. Fremont did not receive a single vote south of the Mason-Dixon line. At the same time, the Northernmost states were solidly Republican. Virtually every county north of New York City, Cleveland, and Chicago, voted Republican.

In their first presidential campaign, the Republicans had made an extremely impressive showing. Eleven free states voted for Fremont. If only two more states had voted in his favor, the Republican would have won the election.

The Supreme Court Speaks

In his inaugural address, Buchanan declared that "the great object of my administration will be to arrest . . . the agitation of the slavery question in the North." He then predicted that a forthcoming Supreme Court decision would once and for all settle the controversy over slavery in the western territories. Two days after Buchanan's inauguration, the high court handed down its decision.

On March 6, 1857, in a small room in the Capitol basement, the Supreme Court finally decided a question that Congress had evaded for decades: whether Congress had the power to prohibit slavery in the territories. Repeatedly, Congress had declared that this was a constitutional question that the Supreme Court should settle. Now, for the first time, the Supreme Court offered its answer.

The case originated in 1846, the year that the Wilmot Proviso had attempted to bar slavery from territory acquired from Mexico. A Missouri slave, Dred Scott, sued to gain his freedom. Scott's argument was that while he had been the slave of an army surgeon, he had lived for four years in Illinois, a free state, and Wisconsin, a free territory, and that his residence on free soil had erased his slave status despite his return to Missouri, a slave state. In 1850 a Missouri court gave Scott his freedom, but two years later, the Missouri Supreme Court reversed this decision and returned Scott to slavery. Scott then appealed to the federal courts for his freedom.

The case proceeded through the federal courts for five years. It was argued before the Supreme Court in 1856, at precisely the time that Senator Charles Sumner was delivering his bitter attack on the slave power.

For over a year, the Court withheld its decision. Many thought that the Court delayed its ruling to ensure a Democratic victory in the 1856 elections. Finally, in March, 1857, Chief Justice Roger B. Taney announced the Court's decision. By a 7–2 margin, the Court ruled that Dred Scott had no right to sue in federal court, that the Missouri Compromise was unconstitutional, and that Congress had no right to exclude slavery from the territories.

All nine justices rendered separate opinions, but the Chief Justice delivered the opinion that expressed the position of the Court's majority. His opinion represented a judicial defense of the most extreme proslavery position.

Chief Justice Taney made two sweeping rulings. The first was that Dred Scott had no right to sue in federal court because neither slaves nor free blacks were citizens of the United States. At the time the Constitution was adopted, the Chief Justice wrote, Negroes had been "regarded as beings of an inferior order" with "no rights which the white man was bound to respect."

Second, Taney declared that Congress had no right to exclude slavery from the federal territories since any law excluding slave property from the territories was a violation of the Fifth Amendment. For the first time since *Marbury* v. *Madison* in 1803, the Court declared an act of Congress unconstitutional. The Missouri Compromise was unconstitutional, the Court declared, because it prohibited slavery north of 36° 30'. Newspaper headlines summarized the Court's rulings: "SLAVERY ALONE NATIONAL—THE MISSOURI COMPROMISE UNCONSTITUTIONAL—NEGROES CANNOT BE CITIZENS—THE TRIUMPH OF SLAVERY COMPLETE."

In a single decision, the Court sought to resolve all the major constitutional questions raised by slavery. It declared that the Declaration of Independence and the Bill of Rights were not intended to apply to black Americans. It stated that the Republican party platform—barring slavery from the western territories—as well as Stephen Douglas's doctrine of "popular sovereignty"—which stated that territorial governments had the power to prohibit slavery—were both unconstitutional.

Republicans reacted with scorn. The decision, said the New York *Tribune,* carried as much moral weight as "the judgment of a majority of those congregated in any Washington barroom." Radical abolitionists called for secession. Many Republicans—including an Illinois politician named Abraham Lincoln—regarded the decision as part of a slave power conspiracy to legalize slavery throughout the United States.

The Dred Scott decision was a major political miscalculation. In its ruling, the Supreme Court sought to solve the slavery controversy once and for all. Instead the Court intensified sectional strife, undercut possible compromise solutions to the divisive issue of slave expansion, and weakened the moral authority of the judiciary.

Dred Scott

Chief Justice Roger Taney

The Lecompton Constitution: "A Swindle and a Fraud"

Late in 1857, President Buchanan faced a major test of his ability to suppress the controversy over slavery. In September proslavery forces in Kansas met in Lecompton, the territorial capital, to draft a constitution that would bring Kansas into the Union as a slave state. Recognizing that a proslavery constitution would be defeated in a free, fair election, proslavery delegates withheld the new state charter from the territory's voters. Instead, the people of Kansas were allowed to vote only on the question of whether they preferred "The constitution with slavery" or "The constitution without slavery." In either case, however, the new constitution guaranteed slave ownership as a sacred right. A Free Soiler described the proslavery proposal this way: "Vote to take this arsenic with bread and butter, or without bread and butter." Free Soilers boycotted the election and, as a result, "The constitution with slavery" was approved by a 6000 vote margin.

President Buchanan, fearful that the South would secede if Kansas were not admitted to the Union as a slave state, accepted the proslavery Lecompton constitution as a satisfactory application of the principle of popular sovereignty. He then demanded that Congress admit Kansas as the sixteenth slave state and declared that Kansas was "already a slave state as much as Georgia or South Carolina."

Stephen Douglas was aghast. "A small minority" of proslavery men in Kansas, he declared, had "attempted to cheat and defraud the majority by trickery and juggling." Appalled by this travesty of the principle of popular sovereignty, Douglas broke with the Buchanan administration. "If this constitution is to be forced down our throats," he exclaimed, "in violation of the fundamental principle of free government, under a mode of submission that is a mockery and an insult, I will resist it to the last." In retaliation, southern Democrats stripped Douglas of his chairmanship of the Senate Committee on Territories.

After a rancorous debate, the Senate passed a bill that admitted Kansas as a slave state under the Lecompton constitution. The House of Representatives rejected this measure and instead substituted a compromise, known as the English bill, which allowed Kansans to vote on the proslavery constitution. As a thinly veiled bribe to encourage Kansans to ratify the document, the English bill offered Kansas a huge grant of public land if it approved the Lecompton constitution. While federal troops guarded the polls, Kansas voters overwhelmingly rejected the proslavery constitution.

The bloody battle for Kansas had come to an end. Free Soilers took control of the territorial legislature and repealed Kansas's territorial slave code. Stripped of any legal safeguards for their slave property, most Kansas slaveowners quickly left the territory. When the federal census was taken in 1860, just two slaves remained in Kansas.

The nation would never be the same. To antislavery Northerners, the Lecompton controversy showed that the slave power was willing to undermine democratic processes in an attempt to force slavery upon a free people. In Kansas, they charged, proslavery forces had used violence, fraud, and intimidation to expand the territory open to slavery. To the more extreme opponents of slavery in the North, the lesson was clear. The only way to preserve freedom and democratic procedures was to destroy slavery and the slave power through force of arms.

CRISIS OF THE UNION

In 1858, Senator William H. Seward of New York examined the sources of the conflicts between the North and the South. Some people, said Seward, thought the sectional conflict was "accidental, unnecessary, the work of interested or fanatical agitators, and therefore ephemeral." Seward believed that these people were wrong. The roots of the conflict went far deeper. "It is an irrepressible conflict," Seward said, "between opposing and enduring forces."

By 1858, a growing number of Northerners believed that two fundamentally different and antagonistic civilizations had developed within the United States. They were convinced that an aggressive southern slave power had seized control of the federal government and imperiled the liberties of free men. They saw two societies—one dedicated to freedom, one to slavery—locked in a life and death struggle. Declared the New York *Tribune*: "We are not one people. We are two peoples. We are a people for Freedom and a people for Slavery. Between the two, conflict is inevitable."

At the same time, an increasing number of Southerners expressed alarm at the growth of antislavery and antisouthern sentiment in the North. They feared that Republicans would never be satisfied with halting the expansion of slavery into the western territories. Eventually, the "Black Republicans" would try to undermine slavery in the states where it already existed. As the decade closed, the dominant question of American political life was whether the nation's leaders could find a peaceful way to resolve the differences separating the North and South.

The Lincoln-Douglas Debates

The critical issues dividing the nation—slavery versus free labor, popular sovereignty, and the legal and political status of black Americans—

were brought into sharp focus in a series of dramatic forensic duels during the 1858 election campaign for United States senator from Illinois. The campaign pitted a little-known lawyer from Springfield named Abraham Lincoln against Senator Stephen A. Douglas, the front runner for the Democratic presidential nomination in 1860.

The contest received intense national publicity. The New York *Tribune* thought that "no local contest in this country ever excited so general or so profound an interest as that now waging in Illinois." One reason for the amount of public attention was that the political future of Stephen Douglas was at stake. Douglas had openly broken with the Buchanan administration over the proslavery Lecompton constitution and had joined with Republicans to defeat the admission of Kansas to the Union as a slave state. Now, many wondered, would Douglas assume the leadership of the free soil movement? Might he capture the leadership of the Republican party, as some party leaders hoped? These questions would be answered during Douglas's fateful encounter with Abraham Lincoln.

The public knew little about the man the Republicans selected to run against Douglas. Lincoln had been born on February 12, 1809, in a log cabin near Hodgenville, Kentucky, and he grew up on the wild Kentucky and Indiana frontier. At the age of twenty-one, he moved to Illinois, where he worked as a clerk in a country store, volunteered to fight Indians in the Black Hawk War, became a local postmaster and a lawyer, and served four terms in the lower house of the Illinois General Assembly. A Whig in politics, Lincoln was elected in 1846 to the United States House of Representatives but his stand against the Mexican War had made him too unpopular to win reelection. After the passage of the Kansas-Nebraska Act in 1854, Lincoln reentered politics and in 1858 the Republican party nominated him to run against Douglas for the Senate.

Lincoln accepted the nomination with the famous words: "'A house divided against itself cannot stand.' I believe this Government cannot endure permanently half-slave and half-free." He did not believe the Union would fall, but he did predict that it would cease to be divided. Lincoln proceeded to argue that Stephen Douglas's Kansas-Nebraska Act and the Supreme Court's Dred Scott decision were part of a conspiracy to make slavery lawful "in all the States, old as well as new—North as well as South."

Lincoln followed Douglas across the state, attended his speeches, and offered rebuttals the next day. Then on July 24, 1858, the Republican candidate formally challenged Douglas to a series of debates. Over the next four months Lincoln and Douglas crisscrossed Illinois, traveling nearly 10,000 miles and participating in seven face-to-face debates before crowds of up to 15,000.

Douglas's strategy in the debates was to picture Lincoln as a fanatical "Black Republican" and "amalgamationist" whose goal was to foment civil war and emancipate the slaves and make them the social and political equals of whites. Lincoln denied that he was a radical. He said that he supported the fugitive slave law and opposed any interference with slavery in the states where it already existed. He also said that he was not in favor "of bringing about in any way the social and political equality of the white and black races."

Lincoln's debate strategy was to argue that Stephen Douglas's indifference to the moral evil of slavery disqualified him from leadership of the antislavery cause. Douglas, Lincoln pointed out, did not care if slavery was voted up or down in the territories. Lincoln's own position was clear. "If slavery is not wrong, nothing is wrong," he declared.

During the course of the debates, Lincoln and Douglas presented two sharply contrasting views of the problem of slavery. Douglas argued that slavery was a dying institution that had reached its natural limits and could not thrive where climate and soil were inhospitable. He asserted that the problem of slavery could best be resolved if it were treated as essentially a local problem. Lincoln, on the other hand, regarded slavery as a dynamic, expansionistic institution, hungry for new territory. He argued that if Northerners allowed slavery to spread unchecked, slaveowners would make slavery a national institution and would reduce all laborers, white as well as black, to a state of virtual slavery.

The sharpest difference between the two candidates involved the issue of black Americans' legal rights. Douglas was unable to conceive of blacks as anything but inferior to whites and he was unalterably opposed to Negro citizenship. "I want citizenship for whites only," he declared. Lincoln said that he, too, was opposed to granting free blacks full legal rights. But he insisted that black Americans were equal to Douglas and "every living man" in their right to life, liberty, and the fruits of their own labor.

The debates reached a climax on a damp chilly August 27. At Freeport, Illinois, Lincoln asked Douglas to reconcile the Supreme Court's Dred Scott decision, which had denied Congress the power to exclude slavery from a territory, along with popular sovereignty. Could the residents of a territory "in any lawful way" exclude slavery prior to statehood? Douglas replied by stating that the residents of a territory could exclude slavery by refusing to pass laws protecting slaveholders' property rights. "Slavery cannot exist a day or an hour anywhere," he declared, "unless it is supported by local police regulations."

Lincoln had maneuvered Douglas into a trap. Any way he answered, Douglas was certain to alienate northern Free Soilers or proslavery Southerners. The Dred Scott decision had given slaveowners the right to take their slaves into any western territories. Now Douglas said that territorial settlers could exclude slavery, despite what the Court had ruled. Douglas won reelection, but his statements fatally antagonized both Southerners and northern Free Soilers. Southerners—already repelled by Douglas's opposition to the proslavery Lecompton constitution—were further alienated by his "Freeport Heresy," and Free Soilers were repulsed by Douglas's refusal to speak out against the moral wrongness of slavery.

In the final balloting, the Republicans actually outpolled the Democrats. The Democrats, however, had gerrymandered the voting districts so skillfully that they kept control of the state legislature, which then elected United States senators. By a vote of fifty-four to forty-six, the Illinois legislature reelected the Little Giant to the Senate.

Although Lincoln failed to win a Senate seat, his battle with Stephen Douglas had catapulted him into the national spotlight and made him a serious presidential possibility in 1860. As Lincoln himself noted, his defeat was "a slip and not a fall."

Harpers Ferry

On August 19, 1859, John Brown, the Kansas abolitionist, and Frederick Douglass, the celebrated black abolitionist and former slave, met in an abandoned stone quarry near Chambersburg, Pennsylvania. For three days, the two men discussed whether violence could be legitimately used to free the nation's slaves. The Kansas guerrilla leader asked Douglass if he would join a band of raiders who would seize a federal arsenal and spark a mass uprising of slaves. "When I strike," Brown said, "the bees will begin to swarm, and I shall need you to help hive them."

"No," Douglass answered. Brown's plan, he knew, was suicidal. Brown had earlier proposed a somewhat more realistic plan. According to that scheme, Brown would have launched guerrilla activity in the Virginia mountains, providing a haven for slaves and an escape route into the North. That scheme had a chance of working. Brown's new plan was hopeless.

Up until the Kansas-Nebraska Act, abolitionists had been averse to the use of violence. Opponents of slavery had hoped to use moral suasion and other peaceful means to eliminate slavery. By the mid-1850s, the abolitionists' aversion to violence was beginning to fade. In 1858 William Lloyd Garrison complained that his followers were "growing more and more warlike." They spoke of "cleaving tyrants down from the crown to the groin." On the night of October 16, 1859, violence came and John Brown was its instrument.

As early as 1857, John Brown had begun to raise money and recruit men for an invasion of the South. He gained financial support from six prominent abolitionists and philanthropists—Dr. Samuel Gridley Howe, the Reverend Thomas Wentworth Higginson, the Reverend

CHRONOLOGY OF KEY EVENTS

1850 Compromise of 1850; Millard Fillmore becomes president following the death of Zachary Taylor; Nashville convention denies Congress's right to exclude slavery from the western territories

1852 Harriet Beecher Stowe's *Uncle Tom's Cabin* is published; Franklin Pierce elected president

1853 Emergence of a nativist political party, the Know Nothings

1854 Kansas-Nebraska Act; Republican party appears; Commodore Perry opens Japan to American trade; Ostend Manifesto

1855 "Bleeding Kansas" begins

1856 John Brown's raid at Pottawatomie, Kansas; Congressman Brooks's attack on Senator Charles Sumner; James Buchanan elected president

1857 Dred Scott decision; Lecompton constitution ratified

1858 Lecompton constitution overwhelmingly rejected in a Kansas referendum; Stephen Douglas joins Republicans in opposing acceptance of the Lecompton constitution; Lincoln-Douglas debates

1859 A Southern convention in Vicksburg calls for reopening the African slave trade; Kansas voters ratify a constitution prohibiting slavery; John Brown's raid on Harpers Ferry

Theodore Parker, Franklin B. Sanborn, Gerrit Smith, and George L. Stearns. These men were later known as the "Secret Six." He told his backers that only through insurrection could this "slave-cursed Republic be restored to the principles of the Declaration of Independence."

In the summer of 1859, Brown rented a Maryland farmhouse. His plan was to capture the federal arsenal at Harpers Ferry, Virginia (now West Virginia), and arm slaves from the surrounding countryside. His long range goal was to drive southward into Tennessee and Alabama, raiding federal arsenals and inciting slave insurrections. Failing that, he hoped to ignite a sectional crisis which would destroy slavery.

At eight o'clock Sunday evening, October 16, John Brown led a raiding party of eighteen men toward Harpers Ferry. Brown drove a rickety old wagon, loaded with 200 rifles, 200 revolvers, and other weapons, while his men walked behind, rifles on their shoulders. At the covered bridge that led into Harpers Ferry they captured the lone night watchman and cut the town's telegraph lines. Encountering no resistance, Brown's raiders seized the federal arsenal, an armory, and a rifle works along with several million dollars worth of arms and muni-

As Robert E. Lee's marines break through the brick walls of John Brown's stronghold at Harpers Ferry, he "felt the pulse of his dying son with one hand and held his rifle with the other, and commanded his men with the utmost composure . . . ."

tions. Brown then sent out several detachments to round up hostages and liberate slaves.

During the night, a church bell began to toll, warning neighboring farmers and militiamen from the surrounding countryside that a slave insurrection was under way. Local townspeople awakened from their beds and gathered in the streets, armed with axes, knives, and squirrel rifles. Within hours, militia companies from villages within a thirty mile radius of Harpers Ferry cut off Brown's escape routes and trapped Brown's men in the armory. Twice, Brown sent men carrying flags of truce to negotiate. On both occasions, drunken mobs, yelling "Kill them, Kill them," gunned the men down.

John Brown's assault against slavery lasted less than two days. Early Tuesday morning, October 18, United States Marines, commanded by Colonel Robert E. Lee and Lieutenant J. E. B. Stuart, arrived in Harpers Ferry. Brown and his men took refuge in a fire station and shot through holes battered in the building's brick wall. A hostage later described the climactic scene: "With one son dead by his side and an-

other shot through, he felt the pulse of his dying son with one hand and held his rifle with the other and commanded his men . . . encouraging them to fire and sell their lives as dearly as they could."

Later that morning, Colonel Lee's marines stormed the station and battered down its doors. Brown and his men continued firing until the leader of the storming party cornered Brown and knocked him unconscious with a sword. Five of Brown's party escaped, ten were killed, and seven, including Brown himself, were taken prisoner.

One week later, John Brown was put on trial in a Virginia court, even though his attack had occurred on federal property. The proceedings lasted six days. Brown refused to plead insanity as a defense, and he was found guilty of treason, conspiracy, and murder and was sentenced to die on the gallows.

The trial's high point came at the very end when Brown was allowed to make a five minute speech, which helped convince thousands of Northerners that this grizzled man of fifty-nine, with his "piercing eyes" and "resolute countenance," was a martyr to the cause of freedom. Brown denied that he had come to Virginia to commit violence. His only goal, he said, was to liberate the slaves. "If it is deemed necessary," he told the Virginia court, "that I should forfeit my life for the furtherance of the ends of justice and mingle my blood with the blood of millions in this slave country whose rights are disregarded by wicked, cruel, and unjust enactments, I say let it be done."

December 2 was Brown's execution date. Before he went to the gallows, Brown wrote out one last message: "I . . . am now quite certain that the crimes of this guilty land will never be purged away but with blood." At 11 A.M., he was led to the execution site, a halter was placed around his neck, and a sheriff led him over a trap door. The sheriff cut the rope and the trap door opened. As the old man's body convulsed on the gallows, a Virginia officer cried out: "So perish all enemies of Virginia!"

Across the North, church bells tolled, flags flew at half-mast, and buildings were draped in black bunting. Ralph Waldo Emerson compared Brown to Jesus Christ and declared that his death had made "the gallows as glorious as the cross." Poet Henry Wadsworth Longfellow predicted that Brown's execution "will be a great day in our history; the date of a new Revolution,—quite as needed as the old one." William Lloyd Garrison, previously the strongest exponent of nonviolent opposition to slavery, announced that Brown's death had convinced him of "the need for violence" to destroy slavery. He told a Boston meeting that "every slaveholder has forfeited his right to live," if he opposed immediate emancipation.

Prominent northern Democrats and Republicans, including Stephen Douglas and Abraham Lincoln, spoke out against Brown's raid and his tactics. Lincoln expressed the views of the Republican leadership when he denounced Brown's raid as an act of "violence, bloodshed, and treason," which deserved to be punished by death. Southern whites refused to believe that politicians like Lincoln and Douglas expressed the opinions of most Northerners. These men condemned Brown's "invasion," observed a Virginia senator, "only because it failed."

CONCLUSION

The northern reaction to John Brown's raid convinced many white Southerners that a majority of Northerners wanted to free the slaves and incite full-scale race war. Southern extremists, known as "fire-eaters," told large crowds that John Brown's attack on Harpers Ferry was "the first act in the grand tragedy of emancipation, and the subjugation of the South in bloody treason." As a result of Brown's raid and the northern public's reaction, a growing number of Southern whites began to regard secession and the establishment of a separate slaveholding confederacy as the South's only option. A Virginia newspaper noted that there were "thousands of men in our midst who, a month ago, scoffed at the idea of a dissolution of the Union as a madman's dream, but who now hold the opinion that its days are numbered."

Between 1819 and 1860, the critical issue that divided the North and South was the extension of slavery into the western territories. The Compromise of 1820 had settled this issue for nearly thirty years by drawing a dividing line across the Louisiana Purchase, which prohibited slavery north of latitude 36° 30′, but permitted slavery south of that line.

The seizure of vast new territories from Mexico reignited the issue of slavery expansion. The Compromise of 1850 attempted to settle the problem by admitting California as a free state but allowing slavery in the rest of the Mexican cession. Enactment of the Fugitive Slave Law as part of the compromise exacerbated sectional tensions.

The question of slavery in the territories exploded once again in 1854, when Senator Stephen A. Douglas proposed that Kansas and Nebraska territories be opened to white settlement and that the status of slavery be decided according to the principle of popular sovereignty. The Kansas-Nebraska Act convinced many Northerners that the South wanted to open all federal territories to slavery and brought into existence a new sectional party, the Republicans, committed to excluding slavery from the territories.

Sectional conflict was intensified by the Supreme Court's Dred Scott decision, which declared that Congress could not exclude slavery from the western territories, and by John Brown's raid on Harpers Ferry. The final bonds that had held the Union together had come unraveled.

REVIEW SUMMARY

The addition of new land from Mexico raised the question that dominated American politics during the 1850s: whether slavery would be permitted in the western territories. Key points in the decade-long conflict were

- the Compromise of 1850 which attempted to settle the issue by admitting California as a free state but allowing slavery in the rest of the Mexican cession
- the 1854 decision to open the Kansas and Nebraska territories to white settlement, and resolve the slavery question according to the principle of "popular sovereignty"

Sectional conflict was further intensified by

- collapse of the Whig party
- rise of the strongly regional Republican party
- the Supreme Court's *Dred Scott* decision, which forbade Congress from excluding slavery in the territories
- John Brown's raid on Harpers Ferry

SUGGESTIONS FOR FURTHER READING

OVERVIEWS AND SURVEYS

David Brion Davis, *The Slave Power Conspiracy and the Paranoid Style* (1970); Michael Holt, *The Political Crisis of the 1850s* (1978); James M. McPherson, *Ordeal by Fire* (1981); Allan Nevins, *The Ordeal of the Union* (1947) and *The Emergence of Lincoln* (1950); David Potter, *The Impending Crisis, 1848–1861* (1976); Joel H. Sibley, *The Partisan Imperative: The Dynamics of American Politics Before the Civil War* (1985); Kenneth Stampp, *The Imperiled Union* (1980).

THE CRISIS OF 1850

William L. Barney, *The Road to Secession: A New Perspective on the Old South* (1972); John Barrywell, *Love of Order: South Carolina's First Secession Crisis* (1982);

W. Stanley Campbell, *The Slave Catchers: Enforcement of the Fugitive Slave Law, 1850–1860* (1968); William J. Cooper, *Liberty and Slavery* (1983); W. J. Cooper, *The South and the Politics of Slavery, 1828–1856* (1978); Barbara J. Fields, *Slavery and Freedom on the Middle Ground* (1985); Holman Hamilton, *Prologue to Conflict: The Crisis and Compromise of 1850* (1964); Joseph G. Rayback, *Free Soil: The Election of 1848* (1970).

DISINTEGRATION OF THE PARTY SYSTEM

Thomas Alexander, *Sectional Stress and Party Strength* (1967); Carleton Beales, *Brass Knuckles Crusade: The Great Know-Nothing Conspiracy* (1960); Ray Allen Billington, *The Protestant Crusade, 1800–1860* (1938); Paul W. Gates, *Fifty Million Acres: Conflicts over Kansas Land Policy, 1854–1890* (1954); Charles G. Hamilton, *Lincoln and the Know-Nothing Movement* (1954); Michael F. Holt, *Forging a Majority: The Formation of the Republican Party in Pittsburgh, 1848–1860* (1969); James C. Malin, *The Nebraska Question, 1852–1854* (1953); Stuart C. Miller, *The Unwelcome Immigrant* (1969); Alice Nichols, *Bleeding Kansas* (1954); Roy F. Nichols, "The Kansas-Nebraska Act: A Century of Historiography," *Mississippi Valley Historical Review*, 43 (1956); W. Darrell Overdyke, *The Know-Nothing Party in the South* (1950); William E. Parrish, *David Rice Atchison of Missouri* (1961); James A. Rawley, *Race and Politics: "Bleeding Kansas" and the Coming of the Civil War* (1969); Joel H. Silbey, *The Shrine of Party: Congressional Voting Behavior, 1841–1852* (1967); J. H. Silbey, *The Transformation of American Politics, 1840–1860* (1967).

THE GATHERING STORM

Dale Baum, *The Civil War Party System: The Case of Massachusetts, 1848–1876* (1984); Robert M. Cover, *Justice Accused* (1975); Don E. Fehrenbacher, *The Dred Scott Case: Its Significance in American Law and Politics* (1978); Eric Foner, *Free Soil, Free Labor, Free Men: The Ideology of the Republican Party before the Civil War* (1970); Paul Finkelman, *An Imperfect Union: Slavery, Federalism and Comity* (1981); A. Leon Higginbotham, Jr., *In the Matter of Color: Race and the American Legal Process* (1978); Michael F. Holt, *Forging a Majority: The Formation of the Republican Party in Pittsburgh, 1848–1860* (1969); Stanley I. Kutler, *The Dred Scott Decision* (1967); Stephen E. Maizlish, *The Triumph of Sectionalism: The Transformation of Ohio Politics* (1983); Thomas D. Morris, *Free Men All: The Personal Liberty Laws of the North* (1974); Arthur M. Schlesinger, Jr. and Fred L. Israel, eds., *History of U.S. Political Parties* (1973); Hans L. Treffouse, *The Radical Republicans* (1969).

CRISIS OF THE UNION

Jules Abels, *Man on Fire: John Brown and the Cause of Liberty* (1971); R. O. Boyer, *The Legend of John Brown* (1973); Robert W. Johannsen, *Stephen A. Douglas* (1973); Don E. Fehrenbacher, *Prelude to Greatness: Lincoln in the 1850s* (1962); Henry V. Jaffa, *Crisis of the House Divided: An Interpretation of the Issues in the Lincoln-Douglas Debates* (1959); Truman Nelson, *The Old Man: John Brown at Harpers Ferry* (1973); Stephen B. Oates, *To Purge This Land with Blood: A Biography of John Brown* (1970); S. B. Oates, *With Malice Toward None: The Life of Abraham Lincoln* (1977); Benjamin Quarles, *Allies for Freedom: Blacks and John Brown* (1974); B. Quarles, *Blacks on John Brown* (1972); Jeffrey Rossbach, *Ambivalent Conspirators: John Brown, the Secret Six, and a Theory of Slave Violence* (1983); Louis Ruchames, ed., *John Brown: The Making of a Revolutionary* (1969).

CHAPTER 14

A Nation Shattered by Civil War, 1860–1865

PLATE 3

No. 62

ooking eastward from Sharpsburg into the mountains of western Maryland, General Robert E. Lee uttered the fateful words: "We will make our stand." Behind him was the Potomac River, and to his front was Antietam Creek. Having invaded Union territory in early September 1862, Lee dispersed his Army of Northern Virginia, some 50,000 strong, across the countryside to capture strategic points like Harpers Ferry and to rally the citizens of this border, slaveholding state behind the Confederate cause. Now he issued orders for his troops to regather with all haste at Sharpsburg. A major battle was in the making. General George B. McClellan's Army of the Potomac, numbering nearly 100,000 soldiers, was rapidly descending upon Lee's position.

Early on the morning of September 17, the great battle began. As the day progressed, Union forces attacked in five uncoordinated waves, which allowed Lee to maneuver his heavily-outnumbered troops from point to point in warding off federal assaults. As usual, Lee calculated his opponent's temperament correctly. McClellan was too timid to throw everything into the battle at once. As darkness fell, the Confederates still held their lines, but Lee knew that if McClellan attacked again the next morning, the southern army might well be annihilated.

Among those rebel troops who marched into Maryland was twenty-five-year-old Thomas Jefferson Rushin. He had grown up secure in his social station as the second son of Joel Rushin, a prospering west Georgia cotton planter who owned twenty-one slaves. Young Thomas was anxious to show those far-off "Black Republican" Yankees that southern gentlemen would never shrink from battle in defense of their way of life. He enlisted in Company K of the Twelfth Georgia Volunteers in June 1861. At 5:30 A.M. on September 17, 1862, Sergeant Rushin waited restlessly north of Sharpsburg—where the first Union assault occurred.

As dawn beckoned, Rushin and his comrades first heard skirmish fire, then the booming of cannons. Out in an open field, they soon engaged Yankee troops appearing at the edge of a nearby woods. The Twelfth Georgia Volunteers stood their ground until pulled back at 6:45 A.M. When that order came, sixty-two of the Georgians lay dead or wounded, among them the lifeless remains of Thomas Jefferson Rushin.

To the south of Sharpsburg, the battle soon heated up. At 9:00 A.M., General Ambrose E. Burnside's Union soldiers prepared to cross a stone bridge over Antietam Creek. On the other side was sharply rising ground, on top of which troops in gray waited, ready to shoot at any person bold enough to venture onto what became known as Burnside Bridge.

The Eleventh Connecticut Volunteers were among those poised for the advance. Included in their number was eighteen-year-old Private Alvin Flint, Jr., who had enlisted a few months before in Company D. He was from Hartford where his father, Alvin, Sr., worked in a papermaking factory. Flint's departure from home was sorrowful because his mother had just died of consumption. A few weeks later, he received word that his younger sister had succumbed to the same disease.

Flint's own sense of foreboding must have been overwhelming as he charged toward the bridge. In an instant, he became part of the human carnage, as minié balls poured down from across the bridge. Bleeding from a mortal wound, he died before stretcher-bearers from the Ambulance Corps could reach him.

Flint never knew that his father and younger brother had recently joined another Connecticut regiment, affording Alvin, Sr., the chance to visit the battlefield a month later in search of his son's remains. Grieving deeply, his father wrote the *Hartford Courant* and decried the loss of "my boy" who "was brutally murdered" because of this "hellish, wicked rebellion." "Oh how dreadful was that place to me," he wrote in agony, where his son "had been buried like a beast of the field!"

Fifty-three-year-old Alvin Flint, Sr., gave up, returned to his regiment, and marched toward Fredericksburg, Virginia, where another major battle took place in December 1862. A month later, the two remaining Flints died of typhoid fever which was raging through the Union army.

Thomas Jefferson Rushin   Alvin Flint, Jr.

As the human toll mounted higher and higher, Civil War battlefields became hallowed ground. Southerners named these sites after towns while Northerners named them for nearby landmarks like rivers and streams. In the South, the Battle of Sharpsburg symbolized a valiant stand against overwhelming odds, and in the North the Battle of Antietam represented a turning point in the war because Union troops had, at last, held the field after Lee, astonished that McClellan did not continue the fight, ordered a retreat back into Virginia on that same evening of September 17.

Different names could not change the results. With 23,000 dead and wounded soldiers, Antietam turned out to be the bloodiest one-day action of the Civil War. And before the slaughter ended in 1865, total casualties reached 1.2 million people, including 620,000 dead—more than the total number of United States troops who lost their lives in World War I and II combined. Back in April 1861, when the Confederates fired on Fort Sumter, no one foresaw such carnage. No one imagined bodies as "thick as human leaves" decaying in fields around Sharpsburg, or how "horrible" looking would be "the faces of the dead."

The coming of the Civil War could be compared to a time bomb ready to explode. The fundamental issue was slavery, or, more specifically, whether the "peculiar institution" would be allowed to spread across the American landscape. Southerners also feared that northern

leaders would use federal authority to declare slavery null and void throughout the land. They made their stand behind states' rights and voted to secede. The North, in response, went to war to save the Union, but always lurking in the background was the issue of permitting the continued existence of slavery. The carnage of the war settled the matter. A few days after Antietam, President Abraham Lincoln announced the Emancipation Proclamation, which transformed the Civil War into a struggle to end slavery—and the way of life it supported—as a means of destroying Confederate resistance and preserving the federal Union.

FROM SECESSION TO FULL-SCALE WAR

On April 23, 1860, the Democratic party gathered in Charleston, South Carolina, to select a presidential candidate. No nominating convention faced a more difficult task. The delegates argued bitterly among themselves, and in a rehearsal of what was to come, many southern delegates left the convention. The break up of the Democratic party cleared the way for Lincoln's election, which in turn provoked the secession of seven southern states by February 1861. As the Union came apart, all Americans watched closely to see how "Honest Abe," the "Railsplitter" from Illinois, would handle the secession crisis.

Electing a New President

Even before the Democratic convention met, there was evidence that the party was crumbling. Early in 1860, Jefferson Davis of Mississippi introduced a series of resolutions in the Senate calling for federal protection of slavery in all western territories. More extreme "Fire-eaters," such as William L. Yancey of Alabama, not only embraced Davis's proposal but announced that he and others would leave the convention if the party did not defend their inalienable right to hold slaves and nominate a Southerner for president. Playing to cheering galleries in Charleston, the center of secessionist sentiment, delegates from eight southern states walked out after the convention rejected an extreme proslavery platform.

Those who remained tried to nominate a candidate, but after dozens of ballots no one received a two-thirds majority. So the delegates gave up and agreed to reconvene in Baltimore in another six weeks. But that convention also failed to produce a consensus. Finally, in two separate meetings, northern delegates named Stephen A. Douglas as their candidate while southern delegates chose John C. Breckinridge of Kentucky.

To confuse matters further, a short-lived party, the Constitutional Unionists, emerged. This coalition of former Whigs, Know Nothings, and Unionist Democrats adopted a platform advocating "no political principle other than the Constitution of the country, the union of the states, and the enforcement of the laws." They nominated John Bell of Tennessee, and he enjoyed some support in the border states, drawing votes away from both Douglas and Breckinridge and making it easier for the sectional Republican party to carry the election.

When the Republicans met in Chicago during mid-May, they were very optimistic, especially with the Democrats hopelessly divided. Delegates constructed a platform with many promises, including high tariffs in an appeal to gain the support of northern manufacturers

and a homestead law in a bid to win the backing of citizens wanting free farmland. On the slave expansion issue, there was no compromise with the South. "The normal condition of all the territory of the United States is that of freedom," the platform read, and no federal, state, or local legislative body could ever "give legal existence to slavery in any territory."

To ensure victory, Republican party regulars sought a candidate, as one of them stated, "of popular origin, . . . who had no record to defend and no radicalism of an offensive character." This left out Senator William H. Seward, the front-runner, who was widely-known as a strong antislavery advocate. Seward fell short of a majority on the first ballot. Then the skilled floor managers of Abraham Lincoln, the local favorite from Illinois—a state that the Republican party had failed to carry in 1856—started what became a landslide for their candidate.

The 1860 presidential campaign took place in a lightning-charged atmosphere of threats and fears bordering on hysteria. Rumors of slave revolts, town burnings, and the murder of women and children swept the South. Newspapers reported the imminence of John Brown-style invasions and of slaves stockpiling strychnine to poison water supplies. In one Alabama town, a mob hanged a stranger, thinking him to be an abolitionist. Across the South, militia companies armed themselves and started to drill just in case that "black-hearted abolitionist fanatic" Lincoln won the election.

According to custom, Lincoln stayed at home and let others speak for him. His supporters inflamed sectional tensions by bragging that slavery would never survive their candidate's presidency. Stephen Douglas, desperately trying "to save the Union," announced that "I will go South" and embarked on the first nationwide speaking tour of a presidential nominee. When he did, southern Democrats asked him to withdraw in favor of Breckinridge, whom they thought had the best chance to beat Lincoln; but Douglas refused, maintaining a public posture that only he could defeat the Republican candidate.

On election day, November 6, 1860, Lincoln won only 39.9 percent of the popular vote, but he received 180 electoral college votes, 57 more

This 1860 campaign cartoon shows Abraham Lincoln, "the fittest of all candidates," outdistancing his opponents.

than the combined total of his opponents. The vote was purely sectional; Lincoln's name did not appear on the ballots of ten southern states. Even when totaling all the popular votes against him, Lincoln still would have won in the electoral college by seventeen votes because he carried the most populous states—all in the North. His election dramatically demonstrated to Southerners their minority status.

Secession Disrupts the Union

Lincoln told one friend during the campaign that Southerners "have too much good sense, and good temper, to attempt the ruin of the government." He explained to others that he would support a constitutional amendment protecting slavery where it already existed, but Southerners believed otherwise. Northerners, especially abolitionists, stated a Georgian, were "a troublesome . . . set of meddlers." The choice for the South, as the Mississippi secession convention framed the alternatives, was either to "submit to degradation, and to the loss of [slave] property worth four billions," or to leave the Union. No matter what, "the South will never submit," was the common statement. Secession, then, meant liberation from the oppression of Black Republicans.

South Carolina led the way when its legislature, in the wake of Lincoln's victory, unanimously called for a secession convention. On December 20, 1860, the delegates voted 169 to 0 to leave the Union. The rationale had long since been developed by John C. Calhoun. State authority was superior to that of the nation, and as sovereign entities, states could leave as freely as they had joined the Union. South Carolina, as the delegates announced, had "resumed her position among the nations of the world."

By early February 1861, the Deep South states of Georgia, Florida, Alabama, Mississippi, Louisiana, and Texas had also voted for secession. Representatives from the seven states first met in Montgomery, Alabama, on February 8 and proclaimed a new nation, the Confederate States of America. They elected Jefferson Davis provisional president and wrote a plan of government, which they modeled on the federal Constitution, except for its emphasis on states'

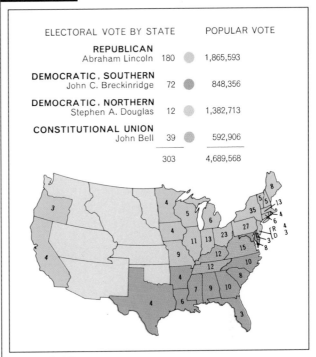

Election of 1860

rights. The southern government would consist of an executive branch headed by a president, a two-house Congress, and a Supreme Court. The Confederate constitution limited the president to a single six-year term; required a two-thirds vote of Congress to admit new states or enact appropriations bills; and forbade protective tariffs and government funding of internal improvements.

For some Northerners, such as newspaper editor Horace Greeley of the New York *Tribune*, the wise course was to let the "wayward sisters" of the South "depart in peace." A more conciliatory approach, suggested by Senator John J. Crittenden of Kentucky, was to enshrine the old Missouri Compromise line of 36° 30′ in a constitutional amendment that would also promise no future restrictions on slavery where it existed. Neither alternative appealed to Lincoln. Secession was unconstitutional, he maintained, and appeasement, especially any plan endorsing the spread of slavery, was unacceptable. "On the territorial question," he stated, "I

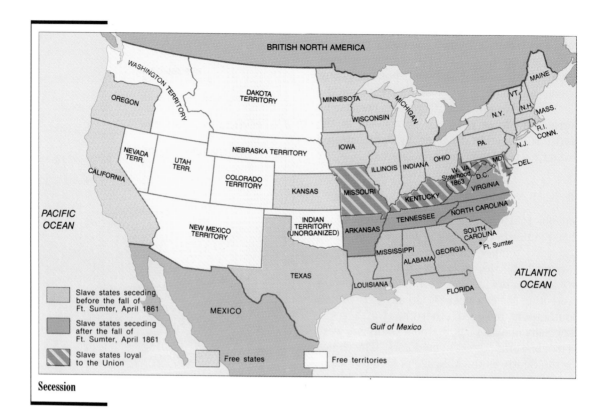

Secession

am inflexible." These words killed the Crittenden Compromise.

President-elect Lincoln, enduring pressure from all sides to do something, decided instead to do nothing until after his inauguration. He continued to hope that pro-Unionist sentiment in the South would win out over secessionist feelings. Also, eight slave states remained in the Union, and controversial statements might have pushed some or all of them into the Confederate camp. Lincoln made his moves carefully, so carefully that some leading Republicans misread him as a bumbling, inept fool. William Seward, his future secretary of state, even politely offered to run the presidency on his behalf.

Lincoln Takes Command

On February 11, 1861, Lincoln left his beloved home of Springfield, Illinois, for the last time. All the way to the nation's capital, as his special train stopped in town after town, the president-elect spoke in vague, conciliatory terms. Between stops, he worked on his inaugural address, which embodied his plan.

On March 4 Lincoln raised his hand and swore to uphold the Constitution as the nation's sixteenth president. Then he read his inaugural address, with its powerful but simple message. The Union was "perpetual," and secession was illegal. To resist federal authority was both "insurrectionary" and "revolutionary." As president, he would support the Union by maintaining possession of federal properties in the South. Then Lincoln appealed to the southern people: "We are not enemies, but friends." But he warned: "In your hands, my dissatisfied countrymen, and not in mine, is the momentous issue of civil war. . . . You can have no conflict without yourselves being the aggressors."

Even as he spoke, Lincoln knew that the seceding states had taken possession of all federal installations within their borders—with the exception of Fort Sumter, guarding the entrance to Charleston harbor, and Fort Pickens along the Florida coast at Pensacola. The next day Lincoln received an ominous report. Major Robert Anderson, in charge of Fort Sumter, was running out of provisions and would have to abandon his position within six weeks unless resupplied.

Lincoln had a month to back off or decide upon a showdown. He consulted his cabinet, only to get sharply conflicting advice. Finally, he sent an emissary to South Carolina to gather facts. At the end of March, he received a distressing report. South Carolinians, the agent informed him, had "no attachment to the Union" and were anxious for war. Now Lincoln realized how grossly he had overestimated the extent of pro-Union feeling in the South. He would stand firm.

Knowing full well the implications of his actions, Lincoln ordered the navy to take provisions to Fort Sumter. Just before the expedition left, he sent a message to South Carolina's governor, notifying him that "if such attempt be not resisted, no effort to throw in men, arms, or ammunition, will be made." It was up to the rebels, from Lincoln's point of view, to decide whether they wanted war.

Before the supply expedition arrived, Confederate General P. G. T. Beauregard presented Major Anderson with a demand that he and his troops withdraw from Fort Sumter. Anderson replied that he would do so, if not resupplied. Knowing that help was on the way, Confederate officials ordered the cannonading of Fort Sumter. The firing commenced at 4:30 A.M. on April 12, 1861. Thirty-four hours later, Major Anderson surrendered. On April 15 Lincoln announced that an "insurrection" existed and called for 75,000 volunteers to put down the southern rebellion. The Civil War had begun.

An Accounting of Resources

The firing on Fort Sumter caused both jubilation and consternation. Most citizens thought that a battle or two would quickly end the conflict, so they rushed to enlist, not wanting to miss the action. The emotional outburst was particularly strong in the South where up to 200,000 enthusiasts tried to join the fledgling Confederate military machine. Several thou-

During the thirty-four-hour bombardment of Fort Sumter, citizens of Charleston watched from waterfront rooftops.

sand had to be sent home because it was impossible to muster them into the service in so short a time with even the bare essentials of war—weapons, camp equipment, uniforms, and food.

Professional military men like Lieutenant Colonel Robert E. Lee, who had experienced combat in the Mexican War, were less enthusiastic. "I see only that a fearful calamity is upon us," he wrote. Lee was anxious "for the preservation of the Union," but he felt compelled to defend the "honor" of Virginia, should state leaders opt for secession. If that happened, he would resign his military commission and "go back in sorrow to my people and share the misery of my native state."

Virginians seceded (April 17) in direct response to Lincoln's war declaration. By late May, North Carolina, Tennessee, and Arkansas had also voted to leave the Union, meaning that eleven states containing a population of nearly 9 million people, including 3.5 million slaves, ultimately proclaimed their independence. On

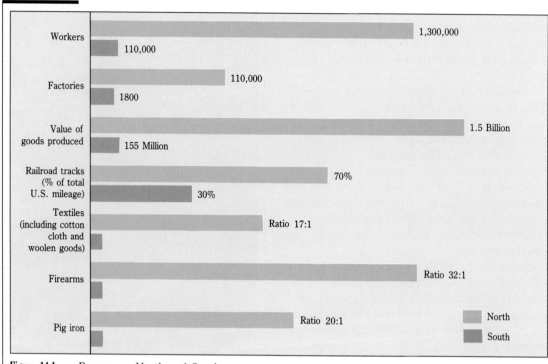

Figure 14.1   Resources, North and South

the other hand, four slaveholding states bordering the North—Delaware, Maryland, Kentucky, and Missouri—equivocated about secession. Lincoln understood that sustaining the loyalty of the border states was critical. Besides making it more difficult for the Confederates to carry the war into the North, their presence gave the Union, with 23 million people, a decisive population edge, a major asset should there be a prolonged war.

Set in this frame, Robert E. Lee's gloom reflected more than a personal dilemma about conflicting loyalties; it also related to a realistic appraisal of what were overwhelming northern advantages going into the war. The value of northern property was twice that of the South; the banking capital advantage was ten to one, and it was eight to one in investment capital. The North could easily underwrite the production of war goods, whereas the South would have to struggle, given its scarce capital resources and an industrial capacity far below that of the North. In 1861 there were just 18,000 Confederate manufacturing establishments employing 110,000 workers. By compari-

son, the North had 110,000 establishments utilizing the labor of 1.3 million workers.

By other crucial resource measures, such as railroad mileage, representing the capacity to move armies and supplies easily, the Union was way ahead of the Confederacy. The North had 22,000 miles of track, compared to 9000 for the South. In 1860 United States manufacturers produced 470 locomotives, only 17 of which were built in the South. That same year the North produced 20 times as much pig iron, 17 times the clothing, and 32 times as many firearms. Indeed, over 95 percent of all firearms came out of northern factories, a major reason why the Confederacy could not absorb all those who wanted to enlist in the spring of 1861. The South went to war with a serious weapons shortage.

With this imbalance, it is incredible that the South did so well in the early going, coming so close to securing independence, and that the North did so badly. Among the southern assets, at least in 1861, was sheer geographic size. As long as the Confederacy retained a defensive posture, the North would have to demonstrate an ability to win more than an occasional battle. It would have to conquer a massive region, and this factor alone emboldened southern leaders. In analogies alluding to the American Revolution, they discussed how the British, with superior resources, had failed to reconquer the colonies. If Southerners maintained their resolve, something likely to happen when soldiers were defending homes and families, nothing, it appeared, could extinguish desires for national independence.

In addition, the South held an initial advantage in generalship. When secession occurred, regular army officers, some of them trained at West Point, had to decide which side to serve. Most, like Robert E. Lee, stood with their states. There were about 300 available West Pointers, and some 120 joined the Confederate army. Of those senior in age, the South did better with the talents of Lee (fifty-four), Joseph E. Johnston (fifty-four), and Albert Sidney Johnston (fifty-eight), as compared to the North's draw of Joseph Hooker (forty-seven), Henry W. Halleck (forty-six), and George G. Meade (forty-seven).

As mature senior commanders, men like the two Johnstons and Lee immediately gravitated to the top of the new Confederate command structure. The Union structure, however, was already in place, with the aging hero of the Mexican War, "Old Fuss and Feathers" Winfield Scott (seventy-four), serving as general-in-chief in April 1861. Younger West Pointers, such as Ulysses S. Grant (thirty-nine), William Tecumseh Sherman (forty-one), and George B. McClellan (thirty-four), were not even in the service. Grant had developed a drinking problem after the Mexican War and was running a general store in Illinois; Sherman had fared poorly as a banker in San Francisco and was heading a military academy in Louisiana; and McClellan was in the railroad business. Even with West Point credentials, it took Grant and Sherman time to work through the pack of lackluster military professionals ahead of them.

Then there was the matter of civilian leadership. At the outset, the South appeared to have the advantage. Jefferson Davis, elected by popular mandate against no opposition to head the Confederacy, possessed superb qualifications. Besides being a wealthy slaveholder, he

Despite valiant southern efforts to produce war goods, the advantage of material resources in the North took its toll. This photograph shows the equipment used by General Grant during his campaigns in the South.

had a West Point education, had fought in the Mexican War, had served in Congress, and had been Franklin Pierce's secretary of war (1853–1857). Further, he looked like a president. "He bears the marks of greatness," wrote an admirer in 1862, because "above all, the gentleman is apparent, the *thorough, high-bred,* polished gentleman."

Appearances, however, were deceptive. Davis was a hard-working but ineffective administrator. He would not delegate authority and became tangled up in details; he surrounded himself with weak assistants; he held strong opinions on all subjects; and he was invariably rude with those who disagreed

Jefferson Davis

with him. Perhaps worst of all, he was not an inspirational leader, something the South desperately needed after war weariness set in. A close associate aptly described Davis in 1865; "Few men could be more chillingly, freezingly cold."

Abraham Lincoln, by comparison, lacked the outward demeanor of a cultured gentleman. Republican campaign literature of 1860 stated: "We know Old Abe does not look very handsome, but if all the ugly men in the U.S. vote for him, he will surely be elected." Worse yet, his credentials were unimpressive. He had no formal schooling; he spent his childhood in poverty before succeeding as a country lawyer; he had served only one term in Congress; and he had virtually no military experience, except for brief duty as a militia captain during the Black Hawk War (1832). As Lincoln liked to joke, he "fought, bled, and came away" barely alive—not because of contact with "fighting Indians" but because of "many bloody struggles with the mosquitoes."

Many Northerners shook their heads as Lincoln entered the White House. With his tall, thin frame and long legs, he stumbled as he walked, half hunched over in baggy clothes. When he listened, he appeared to be daydreaming; yet he did listen, and when he spoke in return, stated one newspaper reporter, "the dull, listless features dropped like a mask." Citizens soon found that Lincoln viewed himself as a man of the people, eager to do everything necessary to save the Union. They saw him bear up under unbelievable levels of criticism, yet those who disagreed with him came to admire his ability to reflect and think through the implications of proposed actions—then move forward decisively. As "Old Abe" or "Father Abraham," he emerged as an inspirational leader in the North's drive for victory.

"FORWARD TO RICHMOND!" AND "ON TO WASHINGTON!"

War hysteria was pervasive after Fort Sumter, and Southerners exuded confidence. As a Virginian wrote, "all of us are . . . ripe and ready. . . . I go for taking Boston and Cincinnati. I go

for wiping them out." Another, having sent forth five sons, offered his daughter who "desires me to say . . . that if you will furnish her with *suitable arms* she will undertake deeds of daring that will astonish many of the sterner sex." Northerners were equally delirious with war fever. In New York, a woman reported on "the terrible excitement" of a city full of "excited crowds" reveling in "the incessant movement and music of marching regiments." It was a bittersweet time with loved ones parting, she said in describing a "young wife . . . packing a regulation valise for her husband"; the courageous wife "doesn't let him see her cry."

The populace clearly wanted a fight. Throughout the North, the war cry was "Forward to Richmond!" referring to the Virginia city that had been selected as the permanent capital of the Confederacy. Throughout the South, anyone shouting "On to Washington!" could expect to hear cheering voices in return. The land between the two capitals soon became a major combat zone, and the bloodshed began after President Lincoln, bowing in mid-July to pressure for a demonstration of Union superiority-in-arms, ordered General Irvin McDowell and 30,000 half-trained "Billy Yanks" to engage General P. G. T. Beauregard and his "Johnny Rebs," who were gathering at sleepy Manassas Junction, lying near a creek called Bull Run twenty-five miles southwest of the federal capital.

The Battle of Bull Run (First Manassas) occurred on Sunday, July 21. Citizens of Washington packed picnic lunches and went out to observe the action. Because the battlefield soon became shrouded in smoke, they saw little except Union soldiers finally breaking off and fleeing past them in absolute panic. Bull Run had its glorious moments, such as when Virginians under Thomas J. Jackson held onto a key hill, despite a crushing federal assault. This earned Jackson his nickname, "Stonewall," and he became the South's first authentic war hero. There were no heroes for the North. As Union troops straggled back into Washington, they "looked pretty well whipped." Bull Run, with 2700 Union and 2000 Confederate casualties, proved to Lincoln that the nation was in for a long-term struggle.

The departure of the Seventh Regiment conveys the sense of early enthusiasm everyone had before the war.

Planning the Union Offensive

Bull Run showed the deficiencies of both sides. Union troops had not been trained well enough to stand the heat of battle. The Confederates were so disorganized after sweeping their adversaries from the field that they could not take advantage of the rout and strike a mortal blow at Washington. Lincoln now realized, too, that he had to devise a comprehensive strategy—a detailed war plan—to break the southern will of resistance. Also, he needed to find young, energetic generals who could organize Union forces and guide them to victory. Devising a war strategy proved to be much easier than locating military leaders with the capacity to execute those plans.

Well before Bull Run, Lincoln turned to Winfield Scott for an overall strategic design, and the general came up with the Anaconda Plan—which like the snake, was capable of squeezing the resolve out of the Confederacy. The three essential coils included a full naval blockade of the South's coastline to cut off shipments of war goods and other supplies from Europe; a campaign to gain control of the Mississippi River, thereby splitting the Confederacy into two parts; and a placement of armies at key points to ensure that Southerners could not wiggle free of the squeeze. Once accomplished, Scott predicted, pro-Unionists would rise up, discredit secessionist hotheads, and lead the South back into the Union, all in a year's time.

Lincoln liked certain features. He ordered the blockade, a seemingly impossible assignment, given a southern coastline stretching for 3550 miles and containing 189 harbors and navigable rivers. In early 1861 the United States Navy had only 7600 seamen and 90 warships,

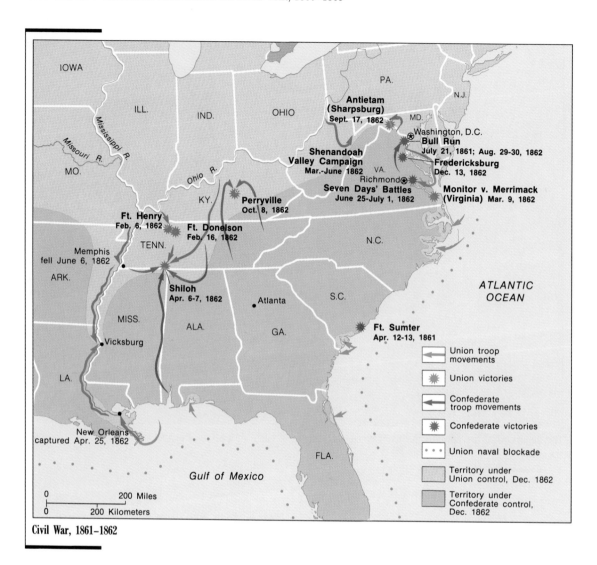

Civil War, 1861–1862

21 of which were unusable. With a burst of energy under Secretary Gideon Welles, the navy expanded to 20,000 sailors and 264 ships by late 1861 and continued building to 650 vessels and 100,000 sailors thereafter. Lincoln's "paper blockade," as detractors called it, became more effective with each passing month, and it also was a political success. Neutral powers generally respected the blockade, which seriously hampered southern efforts to gain essential war supplies from abroad.

Lincoln also concluded that splitting the Confederacy was critical. He ordered General Henry W. Halleck, headquartered in St. Louis, and General Don Carlos Buell, based in Louis-

ville, to build great armies for the western theater, and he worked with the Navy Department to devise the means to gain ascendancy on the Mississippi. The latter effort resulted in the risky campaign of Captain David G. Farragut, whose fleet of twenty-four wooden ships and nineteen mortar vessels captured New Orleans in late April 1862. Farragut's triumph was a major first step in cutting the South apart and crippling dreams of independence.

The third part of the Anaconda Plan, Lincoln thought, was naive. Fort Sumter convinced him that the slaveholding elite had too powerful a grip on the southern populace to expect any significant rallying of pro-Unionists. Nor should armies sit on the sidelines, or train endlessly and wait for a decisive battle. After all, Bull Run had accomplished little except to embarrass Lincoln. By July 1861, the president was talking about huge, muscular armies, mightier than anything the South, with its limited resources, could ever muster. After Bull Run, he got Congress to authorize the enlistment of 500,000 additional volunteer troops, far beyond the number recommended by Scott.

For a man with no formal training in military strategy, Lincoln was way ahead of the generals immediately surrounding him. As he explained to one of them, "we have the *greater* numbers," and if "superior forces" could strike "at *different* points at the *same* time," breakthroughs would occur, and then the South could be disemboweled from the inside. His approach pointed toward unrestrained total war, implying the complete destruction of the South, if need be, to save the Union. What the former militia captain needed were generals of like mind.

Lincoln hoped that he found such a person in George B. McClellan, whom he brought to Washington to replace McDowell. McClellan happened to be in the public eye because he had just directed a small force in saving the territory of western Virginia from Confederate raiders. (West Virginia joined the Union as a separate state in 1863.) McClellan turned out to be one of Lincoln's mistakes.

Yankee Reverses and Rebel Victories in the East

George McClellan was a man of great bravado who had finished second in his West Point class and authored a book on the art of war. He could organize and train troops like no one else, as evidenced by his work with the Army of the Potomac. He was also an inspiring leader, adored by his troops. As he told Lincoln with his usual brashness, "I can do it all." Unfortunately, he was incapable of using effectively what he had built.

In 1864 David G. Farragut organized and led the naval assault on Mobile Bay, one of the last bastions of southern defense in the Gulf Coast region.

President Lincoln put great stock in General McClellan by naming him commander of the Army of the Potomac and general-in-chief of Union forces.

Lincoln gave McClellan everything necessary to do the job. Not only did the president name him commander of the Army of the Potomac, which at peak strength numbered 150,000 troops, but he made him general-in-chief after Winfield Scott retired in the fall of 1861. The problem was McClellan's unwillingness to move his showcase force into combat. When Lincoln called for action, McClellan demanded more

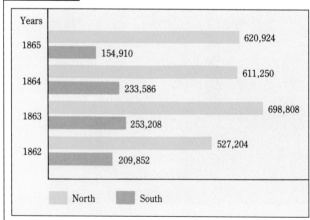

Figure 14.2
Comparative Troop Strength, North and South

troops. The rebels, he claimed from spy reports, had 220,000 soldiers at Manassas Junction. In reality the actual number of soldiers was closer to 36,000. To counter them, McClellan wanted at least 273,000 men before entering the field.

To give McClellan his due, his approach to the war was different from Lincoln's. McClellan intended to maneuver his army but avoid large battles. He wanted to save soldiers' lives, not expend them, and he thought that he could threaten Southerners into submission by getting them to realize the futility of standing up to so superior a force—and so brilliant a general in command. In time, he would catch the rebels off guard and seize Richmond. Then, he believed, the game would be over.

For Lincoln, now convinced that only crushing victories orchestrated along several fronts could break the Confederate will, McClellan had contracted a bad case of "the slows." In January 1862 the angry president laughed and told a friend, "I am thinking of taking the field myself." By March, he no longer covered his feelings. So that McClellan would concentrate on campaigning, Lincoln removed him as general-in-chief and ordered him to use the Army of the Potomac.

What ensued was McClellan's Peninsula campaign. He transported his army down through Chesapeake Bay, landing between the York and James rivers, about seventy-five miles southeast of Richmond. In May his army moved forward at a snail's pace, which allowed the Confederates to mass 70,000 troops before him. By the end of the month, his advance units were approaching the outskirts of Richmond. Rebel forces under Joseph E. Johnston struck the main Union army near the Chickahominy River on May 31 and June 1. The Battle of Seven Pines cost a total of 10,000 casualties, among them a seriously wounded General Johnston.

Johnston's misfortune opened the way for Robert E. Lee, then advising President Davis on military matters, to assume command of the Army of Northern Virginia. Evaluating his opponent, Lee called in "Stonewall" Jackson's corps from the Shenandoah Valley and went after the Union army aggressively. McClellan all but panicked. Insisting that his army now faced 200,000

Robert E. Lee

rebels (the number was 90,000), he retreated after two inconclusive fights north of the Chickahominy. What ensued was the Battle of the Seven Days (June 25– July 1), in which combined casualties reached 30,000, two-thirds sustained by the Confederates, but Lee's offensive punches prevailed— and saved Richmond. McClellan soon boarded his troops and returned to Washington.

In the meantime, Lee sensed other opportunities. In defending Richmond, the rebels had abandoned their advanced post at Manassas Junction, and a Union force numbering 45,000 under General John Pope had moved into position there. Having just come in from the western theater, Pope was as blind to danger as McClellan was cautious. He thought the enemy a trifle and kept exhorting his officers to "study the probable lines of retreat of our opponents." What he did not factor in was the brilliance of Lee, who, once sure of McClellan's decision to retreat, wheeled about and rushed northward straight toward Pope.

Lee broke all the rules by dividing his force and sending Jackson's corps in a wide, looping arc around Pope. On August 29, Jackson began a battle known as Second Bull Run (Second Manassas). When Pope turned to face Jackson, Lee hit him from the other side. The battle raged for another day and ended with Union troops fleeing toward Washington. Combined casualties were 19,000 (10,000 for the North).

In spite of another monstrous body count, the Army of the Potomac had gained nothing in over a year's campaigning. A tired, frustrated Lincoln said: "We might as well stop fighting." Somehow, he knew, he had to get the war off dead center; he was already working on plans to that effect, including an emancipation proclamation. Lee gave Lincoln the opportunity to use that document when he led his army into Maryland in early September, moving toward Antietam and a rendezvous with McClellan.

Federal Breakthrough in the West

The two Union western commanders, Halleck and Buell, also suffered from "the slows." Neither responded to Lincoln's pleas for action. Halleck, however, was not afraid to let his subordinates take chances. Brigadier General Ulysses S. Grant had a good idea about how to break through 50,000 Confederate troops—under the overall command of General Albert Sidney Johnston—spread thinly along a 150-mile line running westward from Bowling Green, Kentucky, to the Mississippi River. The weak points were the two rebel forts, Henry and Donelson, guarding the Tennessee and Cumberland rivers in far northern Tennessee.

Grant sensed that a combined land and river offensive might reduce these forts, thereby cutting through the rebel defensive line and opening states like Tennessee to full-scale invasion. Working with Flag Officer Andrew H. Foote, who commanded the Union gunboats, the Federals reduced both forts in February 1862. Grant even earned the nickname "Unconditional Surrender" when

Ulysses S. Grant

he told the commander of Fort Donelson to choose between capitulation or annihilation, which netted the Union cause 15,000 rebel prisoners.

After breaking the Confederate line, Grant's army of 40,000 poured into Tennessee, following after Johnston, who retreated all the way to Corinth in northern Mississippi. Cautioned by Halleck "to strike no blow until we are strong enough to admit no doubt of the result," Grant settled his army in at Pittsburg Landing, twenty-five miles north of Corinth along the Tennessee River—with advanced lines around a humble log church bearing the name Shiloh. There he waited for reinforcements coming south under General Buell. Flushed with confidence, Grant did not bother to order a careful posting of picket guards.

When Johnston received additional troops under General Beauregard, he decided to attack. At dawn on April 6, 40,000 rebels overran Grant's outer lines, and for two days the battle raged before the Federals drove off the Confederates. The Battle of Shiloh (Pittsburg Landing) cost 20,000 combined casualties. General Johnston died the first day from a severe leg wound, which cost the South a valued commander. Grant, so recently hailed as a war hero, now faced severe criticism for not having secured his lines. Some even claimed that he was dead drunk when the rebels first struck, undercutting—at least for the moment—thoughts of elevating him to higher command.

With other Union victories along the Mississippi corridor, and with Farragut's capture of New Orleans, the Union western offensive was making headway. The only portion of the Mississippi River yet to be conquered was a 110-mile stretch running north from Port Hudson, Louisiana, to Vicksburg, Mississippi; but with powerful rebel gun batteries trained on the river, Union gunboats could not pass through this strategic zone and cut the Confederacy in half. General Grant would redeem his reputation at Vicksburg in 1863.

TO AND FROM EMANCIPATION: THE WAR ON THE HOME FRONT

Rarely a man of humor, Jefferson Davis laughed when he read a letter from a young woman demanding that her soldiering boyfriend be sent home to wed her. Even though "I is willin'" to marry him, she wrote, the problem was "Jeem's capt'in," who "ain't willin'" to let him leave the front. She begged President Davis to intervene, promising that "I'll make him go straight back when he's done got married and fight just as hard as ever." Thinking it good for morale, Davis ordered the leave, and true to his bride's word, "Jeem" did return to his unit in one of thousands of incidents involving ordinary citizens trying to maintain the normal rhythms of life in the midst of a terrible war.

Keeping up morale—and the will to endure at all costs—was a major challenge for both sides, once citizens at home accepted the reality of a long and bloody conflict. Issues threatening to erode popular resolve were different in the North and the South. How civilian leaders handled these problems had a direct bearing on the outcome of the conflict; and northern leaders, drawing upon greater resources, proved more adept at finding solutions designed to keep up morale while breaking the southern will to continue the war.

An Abundance of Confederate Shortages

With their society lacking an industrial base, southern leaders understood the need for securing material aid from Europe, just as the American colonists had received foreign support to sustain their rebellion against Britain. Secession enthusiasts thought that Europe's dependence on cotton would assure them unofficial assistance, if not diplomatic recognition as an independent nation. "Cotton," predicted the Charleston *Mercury*, "would bring England to her knees." It did not. There was already a glut in the European marketplace, and textile manufacturers after 1861 turned to Egypt, India, and Brazil for new cotton supplies.

The British decided to stay out of the conflict, and Queen Victoria declared their neutrality in May 1861. Despite concerted diplomatic efforts, other European nations followed Britain's lead and officially ignored the Confederacy. What secessionist enthusiasts had not fully considered was that European countries were just as dependent upon northern grain crops to help feed their populace. In addition, nations like Britain, having long since abandoned slavery, had serious moral qualms about publicly recognizing a slave power.

The Confederacy, however, received small amounts of secret aid from Europe. By 1865, blockade runners brought an estimated 600,000 European-produced weapons into southern ports, and in 1862 English shipyards built two commerce raiders, the *Florida* and *Alabama*, before protests from Washington ended such activity. The Richmond government also received about $710 million in foreign loans, secured by promises to deliver cotton; but the tightening Union naval blockade made the shipping of cotton difficult, discouraging further

Although neither the *Monitor* (foreground) nor the *Merrimack* won a decisive victory when they met, they helped introduce a new era in naval warfare by demonstrating the superior capacity of ironclads over wooden vessels.

European loans because of the mounting risk of never being paid back.

From the very outset, Union naval superiority was a critical factor in isolating the South. There was a moment of hope in March 1862 when a scuttled United States naval vessel, the *Merrimack,* now covered with iron plates, given a huge ram, and renamed the C.S.S. *Virginia,* steamed out into Norfolk Bay and battered a fleet of wooden Union blockade vessels. Losing engine power, the *Merrimack* retreated, then returned the next day to discover a new adversary, the *Monitor,* also clad in iron and ready to fight. The *Merrimack* held its own in the ensuing battle but finally backed away, as if admitting that whatever the South tried, the North could counter it effectively. The Confederacy simply lacked the funds to build a fleet of any consequence, which allowed the Union navy to dominate the sea lanes.

The effects of cutting the South off from external support were profound. By the spring of 1862, citizens at home were experiencing many shortages—and getting mad about it. Common items like salt, sugar, and coffee had all but disappeared, and shoes and clothing were at a premium. In 1863 bread riots broke out in several southern cities, including Richmond, where citizens demanded basic food because, as they shouted, "we are starving." Shortages abetted rapid inflation, as did the overprinting of Confederate dollars. The central government put a total of $1.5 billion into circulation to help pay for the war. Between 1861 and 1865, prices spiraled upward on the average of 7000 percent.

Once it was obvious that cotton would not bring significant foreign support, Jefferson Davis tried to turn adversity to advantage by urging citizens to raise less cotton and grow more food. Farm women, thrown into new roles as heads of households with husbands and older sons off at war, did so, but then Richmond-based tax collectors appeared and started seizing portions of these crops—wheat, corn, and peas—to feed the armies. For struggling wives, this was too much. Many wrote their husbands and begged them to come home; and some did, which only aggravated an increasing desertion problem.

Most Southerners, in trying to comprehend so many difficulties, blamed their central government. When the Confederate Congress, for example, enacted a conscription act in April

Table 14.1

Previous Occupations of Sampled White Union and Confederate Soldiers

Civil War soldiers came rather evenly from all occupational categories, an indication that fighting the war did not fall disproportionately on any one economic group. Confederate claims to the contrary, Union armies were not made up heavily of the foreign born. While 31 percent of all white northern males of military age were foreign born, only 26 percent of white Union soldiers were non-natives. By comparison, some 10 percent of all southern troops were foreign born, even though only 7.5 percent of Confederate males of military age were non-natives. The South, then, drew more heavily on its supply of foreign-born residents than did the North, just as the Confederacy called upon a far greater proportion of its eligible population (90 percent as compared to 40 percent for the Union) to fight the war. Running out of troops by late 1864, the only source left for the South was the slave population.

Occupational Categories	Union Troops	Total Male Population North (1860 Census)	Confederate Troops	Total Male Population South (1860 Census)
		(all numbers are in percentages)		
Farmers and farm laborers (includes southern planters)	47.5	42.9	61.5	57.5
Skilled laborers	25.1	24.9	14.1	15.7
Unskilled laborers	15.9	16.7	8.5	12.7
White collar and commercial	5.1	10.0	7.0	8.3
Professional	3.2	3.5	5.2	5.0
Miscellaneous and unknown	3.2	2.0	3.7	.8

Source: *Ordeal by Fire: The Civil War and Reconstruction* By James M. McPherson. Copyright © 1982 by Alfred A. Knopf, Inc. Reprinted by permission.

1862—the first draft law in United States history—because of rapidly declining enlistments, a North Carolina soldier wrote: "I would like to know what has been done to the main principle for which we are now fighting—*States' Rights!*—Where is it? . . . When we hear men comparing the despotism of the *Confederacy* with that of the Lincoln government—*something must be wrong.*" The fault lay with power-hungry leaders like Davis, many argued, not with a political philosophy inherently at odds with the need for effective, centralized military planning to defeat the northern war machine.

In the months that followed, charges of political high-handedness in Richmond could be heard everywhere. The draft law, for example, allowed individuals to purchase substitutes, and with rapid inflation, avoiding service became a wealthy man's prerogative—the right of those "whose relatives are conspicuous in society," as a Mississippian complained to President Davis. When the central government in October 1862 exempted from the draft all those managing twenty or more slaves, ordinary citizens

were furious with their planter leaders. Some started referring to the contest as "a rich man's war and a poor man's fight."

These were serious problems, indeed. The great planters, as a means of protecting their slave property, had shouted states' rights to rally their more humble neighbors on behalf of independence. With all the shortages and sacrifices, however, disaffection with these same planters was on the rise because they violated the tenets of states' rights and wrote laws favoring their class. Working in combination with a dawning realization that the North had overpowering resources and numbers, some Southerners concluded, even before the end of 1862, that "the enemy is superior to us in everything but courage." Courage, especially when leaders in Richmond appeared to be so self-serving, could only be sustained for so long.

Directing the Northern War Effort

Although Abraham Lincoln focused most of his energies on military matters, he did not neglect other vital areas, including diplomatic relations with foreign powers and domestic legislation. His diplomatic objective was to keep European nations from supporting the Confederacy, and his domestic goal was to maintain high levels of popular support for the war effort. Lincoln was successful on both counts, but he took many risks, the most dramatic being his announcement of an Emancipation Proclamation.

Unlike Jefferson Davis, Lincoln delegated authority whenever he could. In foreign affairs, he relied heavily on Secretary of State William Seward, whom European leaders came to regard as hotheaded but effective. Early in the war, for example, Lord John Russell, Britain's foreign secretary, met briefly—and unofficially—with fire-eating William L. Yancey, who was in London to seek diplomatic recognition for the Confederacy. When informed of the meeting, Seward drafted a strong letter, all but threatening the British with war. Russell never saw the text, but he learned about it and decided not to meet again with commissioners of the Confederacy. "For God's sakes," Russell stated, "let us if possible, keep out of it," as if intimidated by Seward's bluster.

There were other tense moments, as in November 1861 when the United States warship *San Jacinto* intercepted a British packet vessel, the *Trent*, and seized two Confederate envoys, James M. Mason and John Slidell, who were on their way to the courts of Europe. England vehemently protested such an overt violation of maritime law—stopping and searching neutral vessels on the high seas. The often bellicose Seward took these threats seriously, and he and Lincoln, with the skillful help of United States Ambassador to England Charles Francis Adams (the son and grandson of two presidents), smoothed over differences by apologizing for the *Trent* affair and releasing the envoys from jail.

Then a few months later, Seward received reports that English shipyards were completing two ironclad ram vessels, similar to the *Merrimack*. This time the United States threatened serious repercussions, and British officials confiscated the ironclads, thus averting another crisis. All in all, Seward, with Lincoln's backing, convinced the major European powers that they could "commit no graver error than to mix . . . in our affairs." With Europe held at bay, the North could fully concentrate its energies on defeating the South.

Also helping the Yankee cause was wartime prosperity, which Lincoln and a Republican-dominated Congress tried to enhance. In 1862 Congress passed the Homestead Act, which granted 160 acres free to individuals who agreed to farm that land for at least five years; the Morrill Land Grant Act, which offered each state huge parcels of public land if they would establish agricultural colleges; and the Pacific Railway Act, which laid the basis for constructing a transcontinental railroad after the war. Under the leadership of Lincoln's treasury secretary, Salmon P. Chase, Congress approved National Banking acts in 1863 and 1864, which clamped down on irresponsible financial practices and provided for a uniform national currency. Also, the Republican Congress, to protect the North's manufacturing interests from foreign competition, approved tariff acts that raised import duties nearly fifty percent.

Under the watchful eye of Secretary Chase, the government likewise resorted to various expedients to finance the war effort. In 1861 Congress approved a modest income tax, with rates that only fell on the wealthy. The government also taxed the states, borrowed heavily (around $2.2 billion), and issued "greenbacks," a fiat currency which, like Confederate dollars, had no backing but held its value better because of growing confidence that the Union would win the war. At no time did the Lincoln administration need to confiscate farm goods, a morale booster in and of itself.

Historians have debated whether the economic boom in the North generated by the Civil War sped up the process of industrialization in the United States. By some measures, such as the average annual growth in the real value of manufactures, the war in its rapid consumption of goods caused a downturn from 7.8 percent (1840–1860) to 2.3 percent (1860s). On the other hand, some business entrepreneurs, John D. Rockefeller and Andrew Carnegie among them, made monumental profits from war contracts, and their capital and ideas about large-scale business organization certainly accelerated movement toward a full-scale industrial economy in post–Civil War America.

The intense level of governmental activity resulted in charges that Lincoln's true purpose was to become a dictator. These accusations started soon after Fort Sumter when the new president, acting by himself since Congress was not then in session, declared an insurrection and began a military build-up. Shortly thereafter, secessionist-minded Marylanders attacked Yankee troops moving through Baltimore to the federal capital. To quell such turbulence, Lincoln suspended the writ of habeas corpus in Maryland and ordered the arrest and jailing of leading advocates of secession, including Baltimore's mayor and several local legislators.

Whether the president had the power to violate fundamental civil rights, even in the face of war, quickly produced a response from the southern-dominated Supreme Court headed by Roger B. Taney, a Marylander himself. In *Ex Parte Merryman* (1861), the Court proclaimed Lincoln's action unconstitutional, but in actual fact John Merryman, one of those arrested, remained in jail with no trial date on charges of little substance except encouraging Maryland's secession.

During the war, Lincoln authorized the arrest of some 14,000 dissidents and had them jailed without any prospect for a trial. He was careful, however, not to go after his political opponents, particularly leading members of the Democratic party. The president worked to have open and fair elections, operating on a distinction between legitimate dissent in support of the nation and willful attempts to subvert the Union. Most agree that Lincoln, given the tense wartime climate, showed sensitivity toward basic civil rights. At the same time, he clearly tested the limits of presidential powers.

Some of his political opponents, mostly Peace Democrats who favored negotiating an end to the war and letting the South leave the Union, regularly described Lincoln as a doer of all evil. These "Copperheads," as their detractors called them, had some support in the Midwest, and they rallied around individuals like Congressman Clement L. Vallandigham of Ohio. In 1863 Union military officials arrested him on nonspecific charges, but Lincoln ordered him set free and banished to the South. Vallandigham then moved to Canada where he conducted a vigorous election campaign to become governor of Ohio, which he decisively lost. Lincoln wisely ignored the matter, hoping that Vallandigham and other Peace Democrats, who regularly bewailed the Emancipation Proclamation, could not muster enough popular support to undermine the Union cause.

Issuing the Emancipation Proclamation

Abraham Lincoln believed fervently in the ideals of the Declaration of Independence, which gave Americans "the right to rise" out of poverty, as he described his own experience, and "get through the world respectably." He also admired the Declaration's emphasis on human liberty, which made chattel slavery inconsistent with the ideals of the Revolution. Slavery, he wrote as early as 1837, was "founded both on injustice and bad policy."

After becoming president, Lincoln promised not to interfere with slavery in established southern states, and when the war erupted, he moved slowly toward emancipation. His only war aim, he claimed well into the spring of 1862, was to save the Union, and when in August 1861, General John C. Fremont, then heading federal military operations in Missouri, declared an end to slavery in that state, the president not only rescinded the proclamation but rebuked Fremont publicly by removing him from command in Missouri.

For a man who despised slavery, Lincoln held back in resolving the emancipation question for many reasons. First, he did not want to drive slaveholding border states like Missouri into the Confederacy. Second, he worried about pervasive racism; white Northerners had willingly taken up arms to save the Union, but he wondered whether they would keep fighting to liberate the black population. Third, if he moved too fast, he reasoned, he might lose everything, including the Union itself, if northern peace advocates seized upon popular fears of emancipation and created an overwhelming demand to stop the fighting in favor of southern independence. Fourth, he had personal doubts as to whether blacks and whites could ever live together in freedom.

For all these reasons, Lincoln proceeded cautiously, allowing people and events to decide the issue. He did not seek close identity with radical Republicans in Congress, led by Charles Sumner and Benjamin Wade in the Senate and Thaddeus Stevens in the House, men who built a strong coalition in favor of ending slavery. When these same radicals scoffed at his proposals for compensated emancipation at $500 a head or for colonization in Central America or Liberia, he stated, "I can only go just as fast as I can see how to go." Lincoln did support a series of radical-sponsored bills adopted by Congress in the spring and early summer of 1862. One such act ended slaveholding in western territories and the nation's capital; and a second bill, the Confiscation Act, freed all slaves belonging to masters fighting against the Union.

By the summer of 1862, Lincoln had finally made up his mind. The death toll, he now reasoned, had become too great; all the maiming and killing had to have some larger purpose, transcending the primary war aim of preserving the Union. For Lincoln, the contest had become a test to see whether the republic, at long last, had the capacity to live up to its Revolutionary ideals, which could only be determined by announcing the Emancipation Proclamation.

Lincoln knew he was gambling with northern morale at a time when Union victories were all but nonexistent, when enlistments were in decline, and when war weariness had set in. He was aware that racists, such as the person who wrote and called him a "god-damned black nigger," would spread their poison far and wide. Lincoln therefore waited for the right moment, such as after an important battlefield triumph, to quiet his critics who would surely say the emancipation was a desperate measure designed to cover up presidential mismanagement of the war.

As a shrewd politician, Lincoln began to prepare white northerners for what was coming. He explained to readers of the New York *Tribune* in late August: "If I could save the Union without freeing any slaves, I would do it; and if could save it by freeing all the slaves, I would do it." He would not speak of high ideals

Individuals who participated in Civil War battles could not believe the carnage. Antietam proved to be the bloodiest day of the war, with combined casualties of 23,000.

in public, but would treat his assault on slavery as an act to bring about total military victory.

On September 22, 1862, five days after the Battle of Antietam, Lincoln announced his preliminary Emancipation Proclamation, which called upon Southerners to lay down their arms and return to the Union by year's end, or to accept the abolition of slavery. Getting no formal response, on January 1, 1863, he declared all slaves in the Confederacy "forever free." The final document called emancipation "an act of justice, warranted by the Constitution upon military necessity." Out of necessity, too, slavery could continue to exist in the four Union border states—to assure a united front against the rebels.

In private Lincoln referred to the horrible carnage at Antietam as "an indication of Divine will" that had forever "decided the question" of emancipation "in favor of the slaves." He did not see how slavery, even in the loyal border states, could long outlast the war, and he happily envisioned a republic now moving forward toward the realization of its ideals.

Lincoln did something else in the wake of Antietam, which hardly was a great military victory. He fired George McClellan for not using his superior troop strength to destroy Lee's army when the opportunity had so clearly presented itself. In trying to save soldiers' lives, Lincoln reasoned, McClellan's timidity would actually cost thousands more in the days ahead; he was right. The president kept searching for a commander with the capacity to bring down the Confederacy in a war now dedicated to abolishing slavery as a means to preserve the Union.

Emancipation Tests Northern Resolve

Reaction to the preliminary proclamation varied widely. With Democrats in Congress calling for impeachment, some cabinet members urged Lincoln to reconsider. They also feared repercussions in the upcoming November elections. The Republicans did lose seats, but they still controlled Congress, despite the efforts of many Democrats to smear "Black Republican"

ANTIETAM: "We Will Make Our Stand"

As George B. McClellan moved his Army of the Potomac into Maryland during September 1862, chasing after Robert E. Lee's Army of Northern Virginia, a Union soldier stumbled upon cigars lying in a field wrapped in a piece of paper. The paper was a copy of Lee's orders regarding his invasion of Maryland. The Confederate general had divided his force to strike at such vulnerable federal posts as Harpers Ferry.

McClellan now had the opportunity to destroy separate components of Lee's army. The Union general did speed up his advance but not at a fast enough pace to take advantage of circumstances.

Learning of McClellan's discovery, Lee issued urgent orders for his units to reassemble at Sharpsburg. Most critical were "Stonewall" Jackson's soldiers, who easily captured Harpers Ferry and a Union garrison of 12,000 on September 15. Had McClellan attacked Lee on the 16th before Jackson's troops covered the fifteen miles from Harpers Ferry to Sharpsburg, he might have crushed his opponent. As usual, McClellan hesitated, preferring to refine his battle plan for the 17th.

There was nothing wrong with the plan. The idea was to throw the weight of Union troops against Lee's left flank, north of Sharpsburg. Meantime, General Ambrose E. Burnside was to create a diversion by crossing the stone bridge over Antietam Creek southeast of town, thereby pinning down rebels that could be shifted to support Lee's left flank.

The Union army, however, never got its punches coordinated. Three assaults on Lee's left from dawn until late morning proved futile. Then the battle shifted toward the center, where soldiers fought along a sunken farm road, since known as Bloody Lane. In the early afternoon, Burnside finally got his troops across the bridge, and they threatened to crush Lee's right flank before a column of Confederates rushing north from Harpers Ferry cut off this thrust.

Antietam was the bloodiest day of the war. Once again, President Lincoln was furious with McClellan's unaggressive generalship, and he soon removed him from command. More important, the appearance of a Union victory, based on Lee's retreat back into Virginia, gave Lincoln what he needed, the opening to announce his Emancipation Proclamation.

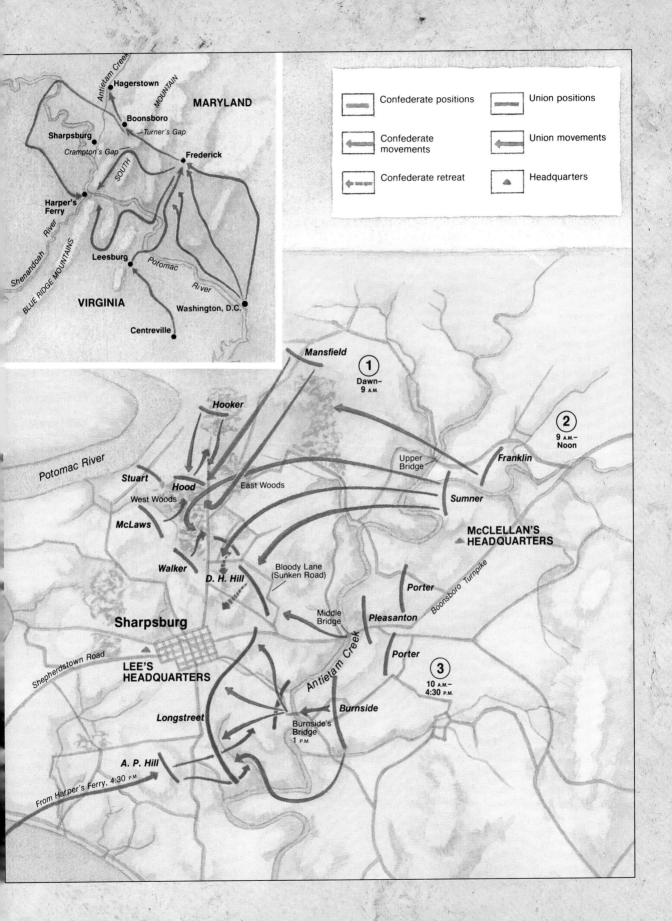

MARYLAND

Hagerstown

Antietam Creek

MOUNTAIN

Boonsboro

Turner's Gap

Sharpsburg

Crampton's Gap

Frederick

SOUTH

Harper's Ferry

Shenandoah River

BLUE RIDGE MOUNTAINS

Leesburg

Potomac River

VIRGINIA

Washington, D.C.

Centreville

	Confederate positions		Union positions
	Confederate movements		Union movements
	Confederate retreat		Headquarters

Mansfield

① Dawn– 9 A.M.

② 9 A.M.– Noon

Hooker

Franklin

Potomac River

Upper Bridge

Stuart

Hood

East Woods

West Woods

Sumner

McLaws

McCLELLAN'S HEADQUARTERS

Walker

D. H. Hill

Bloody Lane (Sunken Road)

Porter

Boonsboro Turnpike

Sharpsburg

Middle Bridge

Pleasanton

Porter

③ 10 A.M.– 4:30 P.M.

Shepherdstown Road

LEE'S HEADQUARTERS

Antietam Creek

Burnside

Longstreet

Burnside's Bridge 1 P.M.

A. P. Hill

From Harper's Ferry, 4:30 P.M.

The announcement of Lincoln's intent to emancipate the slaves throughout the Confederate states brought joy, tempered by caution, to black Americans.

candidates. Certainly, too, frustration with so many battlefield reverses, as much as news of the proclamation, hurt the Republicans at the polls.

At the other end of the spectrum, many criticized Lincoln for not going far enough. Abolitionists chided him for only offering half a loaf, and female activists like Susan B. Anthony and Elizabeth Cady Stanton formed the Woman's Loyal National League dedicated to the eradication of slavery in all the states. Foreign opinion generally applauded Lincoln, although a few commentators made caustic remarks about a curious new "principle" that no American would henceforth be allowed to own slaves "unless he is loyal to the United States."

In the Confederacy, the planter elite played on traditional racist themes and used the proclamation to rally citizens wavering in their resolve. Here was proof, shouted planter leaders, that every indignity the South had suffered was part of a never ending abolitionist plot to stir up

slave rebellions and "convert the quiet, ignorant black son of toil into a savage incendiary and brutal murderer."

Back in the North, blacks were jubilant. Frederick Douglass stated: "We shout for joy that we live to record this righteous decree." Standing outside the White House on New Year's Day, 1863, a group of blacks sang praises to the president, shouting that "they would hug him to death" if he would "come out of that palace" and greet them. For black Americans, the Civil War, at last, meant liberation.

Until this point, blacks had found the war frustrating. Federal officials barred their attempts to enlist. Not wanting to stir up racial violence, Lincoln avoided the issue, and most early black enlistments were in the navy. Finally in 1862, Secretary of War Edwin M. Stanton, with the president's backing, called for the enlistment of blacks—North and South. In a model program, Colonel Thomas W. Higginson of Massachusetts worked with former slaves in the Sea Island region of South Carolina, an area under Union control, to mold them into a well-trained regiment. They fought effectively in the coastal region running south to Florida, demonstrating that black Americans were fully capable of earning distinction in combat.

The success of Higginson's regiment helped break down racial stereotypes. Still, the War Department kept black and white troops in separate units and always named white officers to command black regiments. Before the war ended, 186,000 blacks served in the Union army (ten percent of the total), and another 29,000 were in the navy (twenty-five percent of the total). Some 135,000 were former slaves, delighted to be free at last of their masters, and 40,000 died fighting to save the Union and defending the prize of freedom for black Americans.

Having gained their freedom, they now could "march through . . . fine thoroughfares," wrote one black observer, as "Negro soldiers!—with banners flying." Still, as they marched, they received lower pay until protests ended such discrimination in 1864, and they more often drew menial work assignments, such as

digging latrines and burying the dead after battle. Emancipation, black Americans soon realized, was just the beginning of a great struggle that lay ahead to overcome the prejudice and hatred that had locked them in slavery for so many years.

BREAKING CONFEDERATE RESISTANCE, 1863–1865

During the spring of 1863, Union war sentiment sagged to a new low point. Generals kept demanding more troops, yet with the exception of black enlistees there were few new recruits. Congress faced up to reality in March and passed a Conscription Act, which provided for the drafting of males between the ages of twenty and forty-five. Draftees could buy exemptions for $300.00—an average wage for half a year—or hire substitutes. All told, federal conscription produced 166,000 soldiers, roughly three-fourths of whom were substitutes.

Conscription infuriated many Northerners, particularly day laborers who lacked the in-

Despite an excellent record in combat, black soldiers often found themselves the victims of discrimination. Black regiments were kept separate from white units and were commanded by white officers.

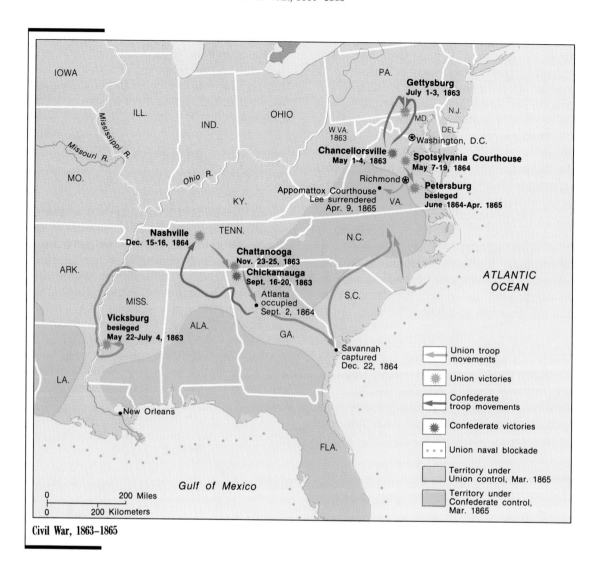

Civil War, 1863–1865

come to buy their way out of the service. Riots took place in several cities, and the worst were in New York where Irish workers, sensing a plot to force them into the Union army so that newly-freed slaves would get their jobs, vented their rage in mid-July 1863. The rampaging started when workers assaulted a building in which a draft lottery was taking place. For a week the streets were not safe, particularly for blacks, who in a few cases were beaten to death or hanged by roaming mobs. Only the intervention of federal troops ended the mayhem, but not before 100 or more persons died.

Moderate Republicans wondered whether the northern war effort could outlast such seri-ous turmoil on the home front, but Lincoln would not back down on emancipation. As a Senate leader said of him, "he is stubborn as a mule when he gets his back up," and Lincoln approached the war the same way, continuing his search for a commanding general with the capacity and the tenacity to achieve total mili-tary victory.

The Tide Turns: Gettysburg and Vicksburg

Even before he relieved McClellan of command, Lincoln had named a new general-in-chief,

Henry W. Halleck. "Old Brains," as the soldiers called him because of his West Point education and voluminous writings on strategy, moved to Washington from the western theater in the summer of 1862. Life in the field was one thing; life in the nation's capital was another. The pressures of office caused Halleck to have a nervous breakdown.

Lincoln did not replace Halleck but functioned as his own general-in-chief until the spring of 1864. His greatest frustration was with commanders of the Army of the Potomac, which the masterful Robert E. Lee continued to subject to embarrassing defeats. After dismissing McClellan, Lincoln named General Ambrose E. Burnside, famous for his huge sideburns, to head the eastern army. Burnside did not have the slows. He rushed south and, on December 13, 1862, foolishly engaged Lee in a frontal assault at Fredericksburg, Virginia. His force outnumbered Lee's by a ratio of 3 to 2, and his casualties that day were nearly 11,000, compared to under 5000 for the Army of Northern Virginia.

Shattered by the defeat, Burnside asked to be relieved, and Lincoln replaced him with "Fighting Joe" Hooker, who liked to swear and brag a lot but, like the proverbial bully, proved to be a weakling after receiving a good punch. Moving south in late April 1863, Hooker crossed the Rappahannock River and quickly squared off with Confederates in what became a slugfest known as the Battle of Chancellorsville. The intense action resulted in a combined casualty count of 21,000 before Hooker retreated back across the Rappahannock on the evening of May 5. "Stonewall" Jackson, shot accidentally by his own pickets, died a few days later, costing General Lee and the South an authentic military genius. As for Hooker, Chancellorsville ended his command.

At this juncture, with the war taking a toll on the Virginia countryside, Lee asked Jefferson Davis for permission to lead his troops northward into Pennsylvania, where they could disrupt rail traffic, live off the land, intimidate civilians, and, most important, try to win a battle so overwhelming that Lincoln would be forced to accept peace terms favorable to the Confederacy. During June, Lee executed his plan, and the Army of the Potomac tagged along far to the east, keeping an eye fixed on the Confederate offensive maneuver. Late in the month, Lincoln asked George G. Meade, a colorless but competent general, to assume command. The two armies squared off against each other early on July 1, just west of a small Pennsylvania town called Gettysburg.

The Battle of Gettysburg, lasting three days, was the bloodiest engagement of the war, with combined casualties of over 50,000. On the third day, hoping that he could split and rout his adversary, Lee massed soldiers under General George Pickett for an assault on the center of the Union line. Pickett's Charge, sometimes called "the hightide of the Confederacy," sent some 13,000 rebels hurtling across a mile of open, gradually rising fields. For the Union soldiers, it was a turkey shoot, costing Lee nearly 8000 soldiers. Late the next day, Lee retreated, his army battered but not yet broken. Rather than boldly pursuing, the Union force followed along at a safe distance, causing Lincoln to accuse Meade of acting like "an old woman trying to shoo her geese across the creek."

Yet Gettysburg was a decisive battle. Never again would Lee have the troop strength to carry the war into enemy territory. Furthermore, the timing of the engagement was important because the federal siege of Vicksburg on the Mississippi River was just ending successfully.

Early in 1863, General Grant had secured permission to attempt the reduction of that city. Through a series of intricate maneuvers, he moved 75,000 troops south through eastern Arkansas well past his target, then swept east across the Mississippi and slowly turned west in a wide arc, securing his lines against rebel marauders along the way. By late May, Grant had Vicksburg under siege, and his artillery bombarded that city and its defenders for six weeks. Reduced to living in caves and eating rats, troops under General John C. Pemberton and local citizens held on valiantly until they could take no more, and on July 4, the day after Pickett's Charge, Grant accepted their surrender. A few days later, after rebel defenders capitulated at Port Hudson, Union forces had finally cut the Confederacy in two.

At the Battle of Fredericksburg, General Ambrose Burnside ordered an assault on well-entrenched Confederate soldiers. The Confederates mowed down the Union soldiers as they marched forward.

With these triumphs, the war turned against the South. However, the combat was far from over, as Lincoln knew only too well as he rode a train to Gettysburg to dedicate a national memorial cemetery before a large crowd in November 1863. In Gettysburg he urged all citizens to "resolve that these dead shall not have died in vain; . . . and that this government of the people, by the people, for the people, shall not perish from the earth."

Crushing Blows from Grant and Sherman

Vicksburg revived Grant's tarnished reputation, and after Union forces suffered an embarrassing defeat at the Battle of Chickamauga in northwestern Georgia on September 19–20, 1863, Lincoln named him overall commander of western forces. Once in the vicinity, Grant quickly restored federal fortunes in the campaign for Chattanooga, Tennessee (November 1863). Now it was possible to plunge an army into Georgia and cut away at the heart of the Confederacy.

Early in 1864, Lincoln decided to name Grant general-in-chief, despite critics who said that the western commander was a dirty, uncouth little man who drank too much whiskey—to which Lincoln reputedly said that if he could get the brand name he would send abundant supplies to his other generals. Grant arrived in Washington during March, and he soon unveiled his war plan. Promising to limit "the carnage . . . to a single year," he wanted Union armies to advance on "a common center" inside the Confederacy. They were to pursue the enemy relentlessly: "Get at him as soon as you can. Strike at him as hard as you can, and keep moving on." Further, in a virtual declaration of total war, he wanted to destroy all property that could be used to support the rebel armies.

Grant, for his part, decided to travel with General Meade, still in command of the Army of the Potomac, so that there would be no faint-hearted maneuvers. Their target was not Richmond but Lee's army, which Grant intended to grind into dust. The general-in-chief called upon his old ally, General William Tecumseh Sherman, now commanding western forces, to march to Atlanta and destroy key southern railheads there. As Sherman proceeded, he was to challenge the Confederate Army of Tennessee under General Joseph E. Johnston, now recovered from wounds suffered in defending Richmond in the spring of 1862.

Grant and Sherman began operations in May 1864, and the spectacle made for blood-soaked newspaper headlines. Grant moved across the Rappahannock River and engaged Lee in the Battle of the Wilderness (May 5–6). Union forces took a beating, but now something

was different. They did not retreat but rolled southeastward in what became the month-long campaign for Virginia. Again and again the soldiers clashed at such places as Spotsylvania Court House (May 7–19) and Cold Harbor (June 1–3), within a few miles of Richmond. Finally, the two exhausted armies settled along siege lines at Petersburg, southeast of the Confederate capital, with Grant waiting for Lee's army to disintegrate.

There had been nothing quite like the Virginia campaign before. Grant started with 120,000 soldiers, and half of them were casualties by early June. To preserve his army, Lee lived up to one of his nicknames, "King of Spades," by repeatedly ordering his troops to dig up earth, indeed anything, to provide cover from the relentless fury of federal minié balls flying at them. By the time Lee reached the Petersburg trenches in mid-June, his army had been reduced by more than one-third to 40,000 soldiers.

Both Grant and Sherman advocated total war—ripping the Confederacy apart from the inside to break southern morale. Here Sherman's troops are destroying rail track so that supplies could no longer be shipped to rebel armies.

PICKETT'S CHARGE AT GETTYSBURG

For two days the death toll mounted, but nothing conclusive had yet happened in the Battle of Gettysburg. Late on the evening of July 2, 1863, General Robert E. Lee made the fateful decision. The next afternoon, on the third day of fighting, 13,000 troops under the command of Major General George E. Pickett would attack the center of the Union line, which stretched for three miles south of Gettysburg along Cemetery Ridge, a mile to the east of Lee's five-mile line along Seminary Ridge. His soldiers, Lee believed with pride, could do anything. The question was whether, in the face of concentrated enemy fire, they could drive their adversaries from the field and achieve a victory so crushing, that it would result in southern independence.

Late on the morning of July 3, Pickett's officers and men started to assemble for their assignment under the cover of woods along Seminary Ridge. The fear of death lurked among them, but they spoke of courage and the need "to force manhood to the front." In numerous engagements they had seen their comrades die in ghastly

ways from metal hurled by Yankee weapons. They suppressed thoughts of death as best they could and prayed for God's help in girding themselves up for battle.

Like their commanders, these "Johnny Rebs," as battle-tested veterans, knew what to expect as they prepared to march across the open fields toward Cemetery Hill. At first, solid shot from enemy artillery, fired mostly from cannons called Napoleons, would fly at them from up to a mile away. As they moved closer, within 400 yards or so, enemy cannon would unleash canister, or large tin cans filled with lethal cast iron pellets. Once in flight, the cans fell away, and the pellets ripped human beings to shreds. Within 200 yards, if not before, "Billy Yanks" would start firing their rifled muskets, the basic infantry weapon of the Civil War. With grooves inside the barrel, the rifled musket shot the minié ball, really an elongated bullet, up to 400 yards or more with accuracy.

To reduce enemy firepower, Lee ordered a heavy cannonade to weaken the Union center. He hoped to knock out enemy artillery units and cause mayhem among the massed infantry on

Cemetery Hill. The bombardment began at 1:00 P.M. and lasted for over an hour-and-a-half. Federal cannons quickly responded in what proved to be the greatest artillery barrage of the Civil War. One officer compared the noise to "that from the falls of Niagara." Another stated "that the earth shook as if in fright." When southern officers spotted Union cannoneers pulling their artillery pieces back to greater cover, they concluded that much damage had been done. They were wrong. Sensing that so great a cannonade would be followed by an infantry attack, Brigadier General Henry J. Hunt, artillery chief for the Army of the Potomac, ordered his units to regroup and reload with canister shot.

As the battlefield fell silent, another drama played itself out. Lieutenant General James Longstreet, Lee's valuable deputy, was adamantly opposed to the plan, believing that the charge would only produce a senseless slaughter. Yet it was his responsibility, as Pickett's corps commander, to order the charge. A little after 2:30 P.M., Pickett rode up to Longstreet and said: "General, shall we advance?" Longstreet looked away and made no reply. The handsomely-dressed Pickett, described by one officer as a "desperate-looking character" with long, flowing locks of hair, saluted and stated grandly: "I am going to lead my division forward, sir."

Soon Pickett was riding among the assembled regiments and shouting: "Up men and to your posts! Don't forget today that you are from old Virginia." The afternoon was excruciatingly hot, and the soldiers had been lying down to protect themselves from the Union cannonade. Now with officers urging them into line, the men were soon ready to leave the woods and press forward with red battle flags unfurled before them. Even before the advance, a few soldiers fell to the ground, suffering from "seeming sunstroke," but more likely from fear. As for the rest, wrote a rebel lieutenant, they formed a "beautiful line of battle."

From the Union vantage point on Cemetery Hill, officers and soldiers whispered back and forth that "the enemy is advancing." The waiting Yankees "grew pale" as they crouched behind stone fences and hastily-constructed earthworks. Pickett's front stretched for half a mile, and the rebels moved forward in three battle lines, "man touching man, rank pressing rank, and line supporting line." At first, Union artillery fire was sporadic, cutting only occasional holes in Pickett's proud lines. When soldiers fell, torn to bits by cannon balls, those beside them closed ranks, as if nothing had happened.

While the Confederates advanced, Union infantry troops held their fire, reported Major General Winfield S. Hancock, whose corps took the brunt of Pickett's Charge.

Then when Pickett's front line neared 300 yards, Union officers gave the command to fire. Hunt's artillery belched forth with canister shot, and minié balls flew through the air. Rebel officers suddenly realized how little damage Lee's cannon barrage had done. They had been deceived by Hunt's decision to pull back his cannon. There was no weakness in the Union line.

Still the Confederates came on, now at double quick step, determined to break through or to die honorably in the attempt. Rebel soldiers leveled their muskets, yet few got off shots before being struck down. Only 5000 made it to the stone wall where they temporarily breached the Union line. Those who made it were shot, stabbed by bayonets, captured, or driven back in hand-to-hand combat. In little more than twenty minutes Pickett's Charge was all over. Wrote General Hancock afterward, the Confederates "were repulsed . . . and sought safety in flight or by throwing themselves on the ground to escape our fire. Their battle flags were ours and the victory was won."

Retreating as best they could, fewer than half of the rebels made it back to Seminary Ridge. Pickett, a survivor among the officers, rode up to Lee in tears and shouted that his division had been massacred. Lee replied softly: "Never mind, general; all this has been *my* fault. It is *I* who have lost this fight, and you must help me out of it in the best way you can." Then Lee rode among the broken soldiers, soothing them by saying over and over again: "All this will come right in the end. . . . All good men must rally."

Gettysburg was the high mark of human carnage during the Civil War. Combined Union and Confederate casualties of 50,000 or more after three days of battle were greater than total British and American casualties in eight years of fighting during the War for American Independence (1775–1783). The huge increase in human carnage reflected many changes in the conduct of war over the past eighty years. Significant technological improvements in weaponry, as represented in the expanded range and accuracy of the rifled musket over its smoothbore predecessor, turned Civil War battlefields into deadly killing zones.

Soldiers of Robert E. Lee's generation had been trained in the advantages of offensive tactical maneuvers. The massed charge of infantry troops during the Mexican War of 1846–48, in which Lee and many other high-ranking Civil War officers fought, had worked in storming positions without great loss of life. But this was before the development of the rifled musket, which occurred during the 1850s.

After Gettysburg, Lee never attempted another massed charge of soldiers. His army fought purely on the defensive until its surrender in April 1865. And as Union troops buried slain rebels after Lee's retreat on July 4, they spoke of how the Confederates had "advanced magnificently, unshaken by shot and shell" into the jaws of death. Certainly, too, more than one Yankee wondered at the irony of a sign hanging from a tree on Cemetery Hill: "All persons found using firearms in these grounds will be prosecuted with the utmost rigor of the law."

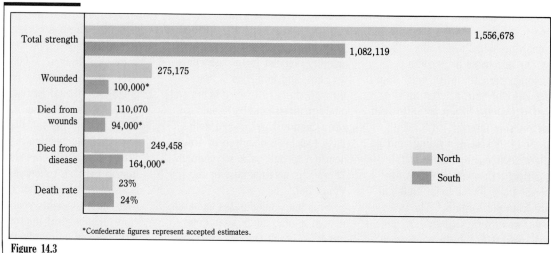

Figure 14.3
The Human Cost of War

In the North, Peace Democrats called Grant a "butcher," but the general-in-chief, with Lincoln's backing, held tight to the war plan. Winning was now only a matter of time, since the president, as the manager of the Union's superior resources, could supply more troops and keep waging a war of attrition. The South, however, had no manpower left to give. Of an estimated 1.2 million white males between the ages of sixteen and fifty, some ninety percent had already seen Confederate military service; the comparable figure for the North was forty percent.

In late 1864 Jefferson Davis admitted the South's need for new manpower when he called for the conscription of slaves. Furious planters, however, apparently blind to reality, screamed about states' rights and once again denounced their president as a tyrant. One leader proclaimed: "The day that the Army of [Northern] Virginia allows a Negro regiment to enter their lines as soldiers they will be degraded, ruined, and disgraced." Finally, the Richmond government in March 1865 called for the enlistment of 300,000 slaves, but by that time it was too late for Southerners "to gain our independence," as a Georgian noted with irony, "by the valor of our slaves." The war was over before black regiments could be organized.

If the Confederacy had any hope for survival in the fall of 1864, it centered on the upcoming presidential election. The Republicans,

calling themselves the National Union party, renominated Lincoln in June with a new vice-presidential running mate, Andrew Johnson, a Democrat who had served as Tennessee's Union war governor after Grant's invasion of that state in early 1862. The Democrats nominated George B. McClellan, who ran on a platform promising a negotiated end to the war, even if that meant independence for the Confederacy—a position that McClellan thought too extreme to support. A despairing Lincoln, looking at the horrible casualty figures in Virginia, feared repudiation at the polls by a populace too sickened by the carnage to let him finish the fight.

Lincoln's pessimism proved groundless. He had not counted on General Sherman, who was moving slowly toward Atlanta in the face of stout rebel resistance. In early September Sherman wired the president: "Atlanta is ours, and fairly won." News of the capture of a major Confederate railroad and manufacturing center thrilled Northerners. It was obvious that the South was in serious trouble, and voters gave Lincoln a resounding victory. On November 8, 1864, he received 55 percent of the popular vote and 212 electoral college votes, compared to just 21 for McClellan. Lincoln's reelection pleased Union soldiers in the field. One of Sherman's corporals wrote excitedly that his comrades now marched forward "with our Hartes contented nowing that we have a president that will not declare peace on no other terms then an Uncondishnell Surrender."

Total War Forces Surrender

In the eighteenth century, warfare never affected the whole populace. Armies were small, and combat could be conducted in war zones away from population centers. The Civil War, however, touched nearly every American life. Families gave fathers and sons to the armed services; and women assumed the management of farms or moved to the cities and took jobs to keep factories going in the production of war goods. Hundreds of women, more rigidly segregated from combat than had been the case at the time of the War for American Independence, became nurses, and they fought to save thousands of lives.

Serving the fallen was grim work at best. Too often hospitals were centers of filth and death. Women like Dorothea Dix, superintendent of Union army nurses, and Clara Barton, who later founded the American Red Cross (1881), put up with enormous personal privation to comfort those in pain. Still, they could hardly relieve the suffering. Medicine was too primitive to cope with the killer diseases, such as typhoid fever and malaria, that swept

Sally Tompkins first opened a private hospital in Richmond to care for wounded Confederate soldiers after the first Battle of Bull Run.

Table 14.2		
Incidence of Disease Among Union Soldiers		
Sickness was a chronic problem in both the Union and Confederate armies. White federal troops were ill on the average of $2\frac{1}{2}$ times a year, and black soldiers were ill on the average $3\frac{1}{4}$ times a year. Black soldiers also died at a more rapid rate from their illnesses, and there is no satisfactory explanation for these higher rates.		
	Whites	*Blacks*
Average Annual Number of Sick Cases per 1000 Troops	2435	3229
Average Annual Number of Deaths from Sickness per 1000 Troops	53.4	143.4
Source: From *The Life of Billy Yank: The Common Soldier of the Union* by Bell Irvin Wiley. Copyright 1952 by Bell I. Wiley. Reprinted by permission of Louisiana State University Press.		

through camps and cut down thousands of soldiers like Alvin Flint, Sr. In fact, fewer Union troops died in battle than from bouts of diarrhea and dysentery.

Because doctors had no sense of the importance of sterilization, germs spread rapidly as surgeons cut off arms and legs to save wounded soldiers from gangrene poisoning. Troops on both sides would have agreed with the Alabama private who wrote in 1862: "I beleave the doctors kills more than they cure." For those who survived the crude surgery of the times, only a small portion recovered in the type of clean, well-managed hospital run by Sally L. Tompkins in Richmond. Indeed, Confederate leaders did not officially permit the use of female nurses until the autumn of 1862; once they did, they found that death rates were lower than in hospitals employing only male nurses.

In forcing an end to all the suffering and killing, General Sherman, after taking Atlanta,

1860 Democratic party splits up in Charleston (April); Lincoln nominated by Republican party in Chicago (May); Lincoln wins the election (November) over Douglas (northern Democrat), Breckinridge (southern Democrat), and Bell (Constitional Union); South Carolina secedes from the Union (December)

1861 Ten additional southern states secede (January-June); Confederacy formed in Montgomery, Alabama (February); Lincoln inaugurated as sixteenth president (March); Fort Sumter falls to Confederate artillery (April); Lincoln declares an "insurrection," calls for troops, and announces a naval blockade (April); Southerners win at Bull Run (July)

1862 Grant and Foote capture Forts Henry and Donelson (February); *Monitor* duels with *Merrimack* (March); Grant prevails at Shiloh (April); Confederacy adopts conscription (April); Farragut captures New Orleans (April); McClellan mounts unsuccessful Peninsula campaign (March-July); Union troops defeated at second Bull Run (August); McClellan fights Lee at Antietam, and Lincoln issues preliminary Emancipation Proclamation (September); Lee overwhelms Union army at Fredericksburg (December)

1863 Lincoln proclaims emancipation (January); Congress passes Conscription Act (March); Lee defeats Federals at Chancellorsville but loses "Stonewall" Jackson (May); North wins at Gettysburg and Vicksburg (July); Draft riots occur in New York City (July); Union army beaten at Chickamauga (September); Grant assumes overall western command and defeats Confederates at Chattanooga (November)

1864 Lincoln names Grant general-in-chief (March); Union and Confederate armies fight in campaign for Virginia (May-June); Sherman takes Atlanta (September), and marches through Georgia (November-December); Lincoln outpolls McClellan in presidential election (November); Davis suggests using slaves as Confederate soldiers (November)

1865 Sherman marches through the Carolinas (January-April); Lee retreats from Petersburg trenches and surrenders at Appomattox (April); Union flag raised again over Fort Sumter (April); Lincoln assassinated by Booth (April); Confederate forces surrender throughout the South (April-June)

proposed to march his troops eastward to Savannah, Georgia, then north toward Grant's army in Virginia. He intended to "demonstrate the vulnerability of the South," he wrote, "and make its inhabitants feel that war and individual ruin are synonymous terms." Before year's end, his soldiers cut a swath through Georgia sixty miles wide, and in January 1865 they entered South Carolina, which they considered "the birth place of Dark Treason" against the Union. "South Carolina cried out the first for war," wrote an Iowa soldier, "and she shall have it to her hearts content." In systematic fashion, Sherman's army broke the southern capacity to keep fighting by burning and leveling everything in sight.

As word of Sherman's devastating march reached Lee's troops in the Petersburg trenches, they deserted in droves, wanting to get back home to protect their loved ones. By late March, Lee's Army of Northern Virginia had fewer than 35,000 troops, compared to Grant's total of 115,000. The situation was all but hopeless, so the Confederate commander ordered a retreat to the west, and Richmond fell on April 3. Grant's soldiers moved quickly to encircle the disintegrating rebel army, and they soon had their prey entrapped.

On April 9, Lee met with Grant and surrendered at Appomattox. The two generals reminisced for a few moments about serving in the Mexican War, and then said good-bye, but not before Grant graciously allowed the Confederates to keep their horses—they had to give up their weapons—so that they could make their way home more easily. Lee's surrender served as a signal to other Confederate commanders to lay down their arms and accept military defeat. The Civil War, at long last, had ended.

CONCLUSION

At noon on Good Friday, April 14, 1865, a crowd gathered to watch Major General Robert Anderson raise over Fort Sumter the very same flag that he had surrendered four years before. A genuinely moved Anderson said: "I thank God that I have lived to see this day." Then he hoisted up the "weather-beaten, frayed, and shell-torn old flag" as naval vessels out in Charleston harbor fired their cannons in salute. Citizens at the fort wept and cheered, realizing that the national tragedy was finally over—a tragedy that had forever sealed the fate of secession. The states, while far from reunited, would continue together as a nation.

Just a few hours later, another shot rang out in Washington, D.C. John Wilkes Booth, a racist fanatic who hated Abraham Lincoln for emancipating black Americans, gained access to the presidential box at Ford's Theater and shot the president at point blank range. The next morning at 7:22 A.M., four years to the day after he had declared an insurrection and called up federal troops, Lincoln died quietly.

In his last days, Lincoln felt the elation of knowing that a war begun to preserve the Union had achieved its objective. Further, in recognition of the horrible price in lives maimed and destroyed, he took pride in the elimination of slavery from the American landscape, which he called the "act" that would put "my name . . . into history." Lincoln had also started to speak openly of citizenship for blacks as part of his reconstruction plans. And as the populace mourned his passing, they too turned to the difficult task of how best to bring the South—defeated, destroyed, but still with a streak of defiance—back into the nation.

REVIEW SUMMARY

The Civil War was the great national tragedy in American history, destroying lives and property. What started as a conflict over the constitutional issue of secession in time also became a victorious crusade to abolish slavery.

> Lincoln refused to allow the Southern states to leave the Union
> the North slowly began to produce generals and an army to defeat the South
> the Emancipation Proclamation ended the South's hope of finding foreign allies
> both sides experienced the hardships of total war
> by 1865 the North's great advantages in population, industrial capacity, and political leadership had worn out the South

As a result, the Civil War preserved the Union and brought slavery to a virtual end.

SUGGESTIONS FOR FURTHER READING

OVERVIEWS AND SURVEYS

William L. Barney, *Flawed Victory* (1975); Bruce Catton, *The Centennial History of the Civil War*, 3 vols. (1961–1965); Henry S. Commager, ed., *The Blue and the Gray*, 2 vols., rev. ed. (1973); David Donald, ed., *Why the North Won the Civil War* (1960), and *Liberty and Union* (1978); Shelby Foote, *The Civil War*, 3 vols., (1958–1974); James M. McPherson, *Ordeal by Fire* (1982), and *Battle Cry of Freedom* (1988); Allan Nevins, *The War for the Union*, 4 vols. (1959–1971); Peter J. Parish, *The American Civil War* (1975); and Emory M. Thomas, *The Confederate Nation, 1861–1865* (1979).

FROM SECESSION TO FULL-SCALE WAR

Michael C. C. Adams, *Our Masters the Rebels* (1978); Bern Anderson, *By Sea and By River* (1962); William L. Barney, *The Road to Secession* (1972), and *The Secessionist Impulse: Alabama and Mississippi in 1860* (1974); Steven A. Channing, *Crisis of Fear: Secession in South Carolina* (1970); Richard N. Current, *Lincoln and the First Shot* (1963); Michael P. Johnson, *Toward a Patriarchal Republic: The Secession of Georgia* (1977); Albert J. Kirwain, *John J. Crittenden* (1962); Charles R. Lee, *The Confederate Constitutions* (1963); David M. Potter, *Lincoln and His Party in the Secession Crisis*, 2nd ed. (1962); Donald E. Reynolds, *Editors Make War: Southern Newspapers in the Secession Crisis* (1970); Kenneth M. Stampp, *And the War Came: The Secession Crisis, 1860–1861* (1950); Emory M. Thomas, *The Confederacy as a Revolutionary Experience* (1971); Bell I. Wiley, *The Road to Appomattox* (1956); and Ralph A. Wooster, *The Secession Conventions of the South* (1962).

"FORWARD TO RICHMOND!" AND "ON TO WASHINGTON!"

Michael Barton, *Good Men: The Character of Civil War Soldiers* (1981); Thomas L. Connelly, *The Marble Man: Robert E. Lee* (1973), and with Archer Jones, *The Politics of Command: Factions and Ideas in Confederate Strategy* (1973); Paul D. Escott, *After Secession: Jefferson Davis* (1978); Douglas S. Freeman, *R. E. Lee: A Biography*, 4 vols. (1934–1935); William A. Frassanito, *America's Bloodiest Day: Antietam* (1978); Earl J. Hess, *Liberty, Virtue, and Progress: Northerners and Their War for the Union* (1988); Gerald F. Linderman, *Embattled Courage: Combat in the Civil War* (1987); Alan T. Nolan, *The Iron Brigade* (1961); Stephen B. Oates, *With Malice Toward None: Abraham Lincoln* (1979), and *Abraham Lincoln: The Man Behind the Myths* (1984); James I. Robertson, *The Stonewall Brigade* (1963); Benjamin P. Thomas, *Abraham Lincoln* (1954); Frank E. Vandiver, *Rebel Brass: The Confederate Command System* (1956), and *Jefferson Davis and the Confederate States* (1964); Ezra J. Warner, *Generals in Gray* (1959); Bell I. Wiley, *The Life of Johnny Reb* (1943), and *The Life of Billy Yank* (1952); T. Harry Williams, *Lincoln and His Generals* (1952), and *McClellan, Sherman, and Grant* (1962); and Le Grand J. Wilson, *The Confederate Soldier* (1980).

TO AND FROM EMANCIPATION: THE WAR ON THE HOME FRONT

Thomas B. Alexander and Richard E. Beringer, *The Anatomy of the Confederate Congress* (1972); Curtis A. Amlund, *Federalism in the Southern Confederacy* (1966); Dale Baum, *The Civil War Party System* (1984); Herman Belz, *A New Birth of Freedom: The Republican Party and Freedmen's Rights* (1976); Stuart L. Bernath, *Squall Across the Atlantic: Civil War Prize Cases* (1970); Allan G. Bogue, *The Earnest Men: Republicans of the Civil War Senate* (1981); Dudley Cornish, *The Sable Arm: Negro Troops in the Union Army*, 2nd. ed. (1987); LaWanda Cox, *Lincoln and Black Freedom* (1981); Beth G. Crabtree and James M. Patton, eds., *"Journal of a Secesh Lady"* (1979); David P. Crook, *The North, the South, and the Powers, 1861–1865* (1974), and *Diplomacy During the American Civil War* (1975); David Donald, *Lincoln Reconsidered* (1956); Martin Duberman, *Charles Francis Adams* (1961); Eric Foner, *Politics and Ideology in the Age of the Civil War* (1980); Norman B. Ferris, *The Trent Affair* (1977); John Hope Franklin, *The Emancipation Proclamation* (1963); George M. Fredrickson, *The Inner Civil War* (1965); Louis Gerteis, *From Contraband to Freedman: Federal Policy Toward Southern Blacks, 1861–1865* (1973); Brian Jenkins, *Britain and the War for the Union* (1974); Jacqueline Jones, *Labor of Love, Labor of Sorrow* (1985); Frank L. Klement, *The Copperheads of the Middle West* (1960); Leon F. Litwack, *Been in the Storm So Long* (1979); James M. McPherson, *The Struggle for Equality* (1964), and ed., *The Negro's Civil War* (1965); Mary E. Massey, *Refugee Life in the Confederacy* (1964), and *Bonnet Brigades* (1966); Robert M. Myers, ed., *The Children of Pride: Georgia and the Civil War* (1972); Frank L. and Harriet Owsley, *King Cotton Diplomacy*, rev. ed. (1959); Benjamin Quarles, *The Negro in the Civil War* (1953); James A. Rawley, *The Politics of Union* (1974); Willie Lee Rose, *Rehearsal for Reconstruction: The Port Royal Experiment* (1964); Joel H. Sibley, *A Respectable Minority: The Democratic Party in the Civil War Era* (1977); Dean Sprague, *Freedom Under Lincoln* (1965); Richard C. Todd, *Confederate Finance* (1954); Hans L. Trefousse, *The Radical Republicans* (1969); V. Jacque Voegeli, *Free But Not Equal: The Midwest and the Negro* (1967); Gordon H. Warren, *Fountain of Discontent: The Trent Affair* (1981); Bell I. Wiley, *The Plain People of the Confederacy* (1943), and *Confederate Women* (1975); T. Harry Williams, *Lincoln and the Radicals* (1941); Forrest G. Wood, *Black*

Scare: Racist Response to the Civil War and Reconstruction (1968); C. Vann Woodward, ed., *Mary Chesnut's Civil War* (1981), and with Elisabeth Muhlenfeld, eds., *The Private Mary Chesnut* (1984); and Wilfred B. Yearns, *The Confederate Congress* (1960).

BREAKING CONFEDERATE RESISTANCE, 1863–1865

Adrian Cook, *Armies of the Streets: The New York Draft Riots* (1974); Richard E. Beringer, Herman Hattaway, Archer Jones, and William N. Still, Jr., *Why the South Lost the Civil War* (1986); Robert F. Durden, *The Gray and the Black* (1972); William A. Frassanito, *Gettysburg* (1975), and *Grant and Lee* (1983); Joseph T. Glatthaar, *The March to the Sea and Beyond* (1985); U. S. Grant, *Personal Memoirs*, 2 vols. (1885–1888); Herman Hattaway and Archer Jones, *How the North Won* (1983); Lawrence L. Hewitt, *Port Hudson: Confederate Bastion* (1987); Harold M. Hyman, *A More Perfect Union: The Impact of the Civil War and Reconstruction on the Constitution* (1973); Jay Luvaas, *The Military Legacy of the Civil War* (1959); William S. McFeely, *Grant: A Biography* (1981); Grady McWhiney and Perry D. Jamieson, *Attack and Die: Civil War Military Tactics and the Southern Heritage* (1982); James M. Merrill, *William Tecumseh Sherman* (1971); Philip S. Paludan, *A Covenant with Death: Equality in the Civil War Era* (1975); James L. Roark, *Masters Without Slaves* (1977); and John B. Walters, *Merchant of Terror: General Sherman and Total War* (1973).

Reconstruction: North, South, and West, 1865–1877

Fig.4

& Co.

4

2

*Washington City, D.C.
April 15, 1865.—*

Sir:
Abraham Lincoln, President
United States, was shot by an as-
sassin this evening, at Ford's Theatre
City and died at the hour of 22...
About the same time at which
President was shot, an Assassin
the ... chamber of the Hon. Wm. H.
Secretary of State, and stabbed him
several places, in the throat, neck,
face, ... and mortally wounded

e

G

As Thomas Pinckney approached El Dorado, his plantation on the Santee River in South Carolina, he felt a quiver of apprehension. Pinckney, a captain in the defeated Confederate army, had stayed the night with neighbors before going to reclaim his land. "Your negroes sacked your house," they reported, "stripped it of furniture, bric-a-brac, heirlooms, and divided these among themselves. They got it in their heads that the property of whites belongs to them." Pinckney remembered the days when his return home had been greeted with slaves' chants of "Howdy do, Marster! Howdy do, Boss!" Now he was welcomed with an eerie silence, and he did not even see any of his former slaves until he went into the house. There, a single servant seemed genuinely glad to see him, but she pleaded ignorance as to the whereabouts of the other freedmen. He lingered about the house until after the dinner hour; still no one appeared, so he informed the servant that he would return in the morning and expected to see all his former slaves.

On his ride back the next day, Pinckney nostalgically recalled his days as a small boy when the slaves had seemed happy to see him as he accompanied his mother on her Saturday afternoon rounds. He could not believe he had any reason to fear his "own people" whom he "could only remember as respectful, happy and affectionate." Yet he was armed this time, and after summoning his slaves, he quickly noticed that they too were armed. Their sullen faces reflected their defiant spirits.

Pinckney told them, "Men, I know you are free. I do not wish to interfere with your freedom. But I want my old hands to work my lands for me. I will pay wages." The blacks remained silent as he gave further reassurances. Finally one responded, "0 yes, we gwi wuk! We gwi wuk fuh ourse'ves. We ain' gwi wuk fuh no white man." Confused Pinckney asked how they expected to support themselves and where they would go. They quickly informed him that they intended to stay and work "right here on de lan' whar we wuz bo'n an' whar belongs tuh us." One former slave, dressed in a Union army uniform, stood beside his cabin, brought his rifle down with a crash, and declared, "I'd like tuh see any man put me outer dis house."

After giving his former bondsmen time to reconsider, Pinckney joined with his neighbors in an appeal to the Union commander at Charleston, who sent a company of troops and addressed the blacks himself. Since they still refused to work for him, Pinckney decided to "starve" them into submission. Soon his head plowman begged food for his hungry family, claiming he wanted to work, "But de other niggers dee won' let me wuk." Pinckney held firm, and the man returned several days later saying, "Cap'n, I come tuh ax you tuh lemme wuk fuh you, suh." Pinckney pointed him to the plow and let him draw his rations. Slowly, his other former slaves drifted back to work. "They had suffered," he later recalled, "and their ex-master had suffered with them."

All over the South this scenario was acted out with variations, as former masters and former slaves sought to define their new relationships. Frequently Union officials were called upon to arbitrate; the North had a stake in the final outcome. At the same time the other sections of the nation faced similar problems of determining the status of heterogeneous populations whose interests were sometimes in conflict with the majority. The war had reaped a costly harvest of death and hostility, but at the same time it accelerated the modernization of the economy and society. Western expansion forced Americans to deal with the often hostile presence of the Plains Indians; the resumption of large-scale immigration raised issues of how to adapt to an increasingly pluralistic society made up of many different ethnic and religious groups. More and more the resolution of conflicting interests became necessary: farmer versus industrialist, whites versus blacks, Republicans versus Democrats, Indians versus settlers, North versus South, management versus labor, immigrant versus native born, men versus women, one branch of government versus another. Complicating these issues were unresolved questions about federal authority, widespread racial prejudice in both North and South, and strongly held beliefs in the sanctity of property.

Reconstruction offered an opportunity to balance conflicting interests with justice and fairness. In the end, however, the government was unwilling to establish ongoing programs

Although freedmen hoped that emancipation would release them from supervised gang labor in cotton fields, many were forced to sign yearly labor contracts and work under conditions similar to slavery.

and permanent mechanisms to protect the rights of minorities. As on Pinckney's plantation, economic power usually became the determining factor in establishing relationships. Authorities sacrificed the interests of both Afro-Americans and the Indians of the West to the goals of national unity and economic growth. In 1865 a planter predicted the outcome, using a reference to the black Shakespearian character Othello. "Where shall Otello go? Poor elk—poor bufaloe— poor Indian—poor Nigger—this is indeed a white man country." Yet in the ashes of failure were left two cornerstones on which the future could be built—the Fourteenth and Fifteenth amendments to the Constitution.

POSTWAR CONDITIONS AND ISSUES

General William T. Sherman proclaimed, "War is all hell." Undoubtedly it was for most soldiers and civilians caught up in the actual throes of battle and for the families of the 360,000 Union and 258,000 Confederate soldiers who would never return home. The costs of war, however, were not borne equally. Many segments of the northern economy were stimulated by wartime demands, and with the once powerful planters no longer there, Congress enacted programs to aid industrial growth. Virtually exempt from the devastation of the battlefield, the North built railroads and industries and increased agricultural production at the same time that torn-up southern rails were twisted around trees, southern factories were put to the torch, and southern farmland lay choked with weeds.

In 1865 Southerners were still reeling from the bitter legacy of total war. General Philip Sheridan announced that after his troops had finished in the Shenandoah Valley even a crow would have to carry rations to fly over the area. One year after the war, Carl Schurz noted that along the path of Sherman's march the countryside still "looked for many miles like a broad black streak of ruin and desolation." Southern cities suffered the most. A northern reporter described Columbia, South Carolina, as a "wilderness of ruins . . . blackened chimneys and crumbling walls." Atlanta, Richmond, and Charleston shared the same fate. Much of what was not destroyed was confiscated, and emancipation divested Southerners of another $2 bil-

Viewing the devastation of Richmond, Virginia, and other southern cities convinced many white Southerners that they had already paid a high enough price for secession.

lion to $4 billion in assets. The decline of southern wealth has been estimated at more than forty percent during the four years of war.

The War's Impact on Individuals

Returning soldiers and their wives had to reconstruct relationships disrupted by separation—and the assumption of control by the women on farms and plantations. War widows envied them that adjustment. While the homeless wandered, one plantation mistress moaned, "I have not one human being in the wide world to whom I can say 'do this for me.'" Another noted, "I have never even so much as washed out a pocket handkerchief with my own hands, and now I have to do all my work." Southerners worried about how to meet their obligations; Confederate currency and bonds were worthless except as collectors' items—and even as collectors' items, they were too plentiful to have much value. One planter remarked drily that his new son "promises to suit the times, haveing remarkably large hands as if he might one day be able to hold plough handles." Many white Southerners, rich and poor, imagined the end of slavery would bring a nightmare of black revenge, rape, and pillage unless whites retained social control.

For four million former slaves, emancipation had come piecemeal, following the course of the northern armies, and it was not finalized until the ratification of the Thirteenth Amendment in December 1865. By then most border states had voluntarily adopted emancipation, but the amendment destroyed the remnants of slavery in Delaware and Kentucky. Most blacks waited patiently for the day of freedom, continuing to work the plantations but speaking up more boldly. Sometimes the Yankees came, proclaimed them free, and then left them to the mercy of their masters. Most, therefore, reacted cautiously to test the limits of their new freedom.

Many blacks had to leave their plantations, at least for a short time, to feel liberated. A few were confused as to the meaning of freedom and thought they would never have to work again. Soon most learned they had gained everything—and nothing. As Frederick Douglass, the famous black abolitionist, noted, the freedman "was free from the individual master but a slave of society. He had neither money, property, nor friends. He was free from the old plantation, but he had nothing but the dusty road under his feet. He was free from the old quarter that once gave him shelter, but slave to the rains of summer and the frosts of winter. He was turned loose, naked, hungry, and destitute to the open sky."

The wartime plight of homeless and hungry blacks as well as whites impelled Congress to take unprecedented action, establishing on March 3, 1865, the Bureau of Refugees, Freedmen, and Abandoned Lands within the War Department. The bureau was to provide "such issues of provisions, clothing, and fuel" as were needed to relieve "destitute and suffering refugees and their wives and children." Never before had the national government assumed responsibility for relief. Feeding and clothing the population had not been deemed its proper function. Considered drastic action, warranted only by civil war, the bureau was supposed to operate for just a year.

Under Commissioner Oliver O. Howard, the bureau had its own courts to deal with land and

POSTWAR CONDITIONS AND ISSUES

labor disputes. Agents in every state provided rations and medical supplies and helped to negotiate labor contracts between freedmen and landowners. The quality of the service rendered to blacks depended on the ability and motivation of the individual agents. Some courageously championed the freedmen's cause; others sided with the former masters. One of the most lasting benefits of the Freedmen's Bureau was the schools it established, frequently in cooperation with such northern agencies as the American Missionary Association. During and after the war, blacks of all ages flocked to these schools to taste the forbidden fruit of education. The freedmen shrewdly recognized the keys to the planters' power—land, literacy, and the vote. The white South legally denied all three to blacks in slavery, and many freedmen were determined to have them all.

Some former bondsmen had a firmer grasp of reality than their "liberators." Southern whites had long claimed to "know our Negroes" better than outsiders could. Ironically, this was proven false, but the reverse *was* true. Slaves knew their ex-masters very well. One freedman pleaded, "Gib us our own land and we can take care ourselves; but widout land, de ole massas can hire us or starve us, as dey please."

Later generations have laughed at the widespread rumor among freedmen that they were to receive "forty acres and a mule" from the government, but the rumor did have some basis. During the war, General Sherman was plagued with swarms of freedmen following his army, and in January 1865 he issued Special Field Order 15 setting aside a strip of abandoned coastal lands from Charleston, South Carolina, to Jacksonville, Florida, for the exclusive use of freedmen. Blacks were to be given "possessory titles" to forty acre lots. Three months later the bill establishing the Freedmen's Bureau gave the agency control of thousands of acres of abandoned and confiscated lands to be rented to "loyal refugees and freedmen" in forty acre plots for three year periods with an option to buy at a later date. By June 1865, forty thousand blacks were cultivating land they believed would be theirs to keep. Al-

Freedmen realized that education was one key to real freedom and flocked to schools opened by the Freedmen's Bureau, the American Missionary Association, and various religious and rights groups.

though a few congressmen continued to advocate land confiscation and redistribution, the dream of "forty acres and a mule" was a casualty of the battle for control of Reconstruction.

Unresolved Issues

At war's end some issues had been settled, but at a terrible cost. As historian David Potter noted, "slavery was dead, secession was dead, and six hundred thousand men were dead." There still remained a host of problems arising from the nature of civil war and the results of that war, complicated further by the usual postwar dislocations. Reconstruction was shaped by the unresolved issues.

The first of these concerned the status of the freedmen. They were indeed free, but were they citizens? The Dred Scott decision (1857) had denied citizenship to all blacks. Even if it were decided that they were citizens, what rights were conferred by that citizenship? Would they be segregated as free blacks in the antebellum North had often been? Also, citizenship did not automatically confer suffrage; women were proof of that. Were the freedmen to be given the ballot? These were weighty matters complicated by racial prejudice and constitutional and partisan questions.

The Constitution had been severely tested by civil war, and many felt it had been twisted by the desire to save the Union. Once the emergency was over, how were constitutional balance and limits to be restored? Except during the terms of a few strong presidents, Congress had been the most powerful branch of government during the nation's first seventy years. Lincoln had assumed unprecedented powers, and Congress was determined to regain its ascendency. The ensuing battle directly influenced Reconstruction policies and their implementation.

Secession was dead, but what about states' rights? Almost everyone agreed that a division of power between the national and state governments was crucial to the maintenance of freedom. The fear of centralized tyranny remained strong. There was reluctance to enlarge federal power into areas traditionally controlled by the states, even though action in some of those areas was essential to craft the kind of peace many desired. Hesitation to reduce states' rights, however, led to timid and compromised solutions to issues such as suffrage. Also troubling many was federal action in the realm of social welfare—an idea so new that it failed to win lasting acceptance by that generation.

Another constitutional question concerned the status of the former Confederate states and how they were to be readmitted to the Union. There was no constitutional provision for failed secession, and many people questioned whether the South had actually left the Union or not. The query reflected self-interest rather than an intellectual inquiry. Ironically, Southerners and their Democratic sympathizers now argued that the states had never legally separated from the rest of the nation, thus denying validity to the Confederacy in order to quickly regain their place in the Union. Extremists on the other side—Radical Republicans—insisted that the South had reverted to the status of conquered territory, forfeiting all rights as states. Under territorial governments, Representative Thaddeus Stevens declared, Southerners could "learn the principles of freedom and eat the fruit of foul rebellion." Others, including Lincoln, believed that the Confederate states had remained in the Union but had forfeited their rights. This constitutional hair-splitting grew out of the power struggle between the executive

Thaddeus Stevens

and legislative branches to determine which had the power to readmit the states and on what terms. It also reflected the hostility of some Northerners toward the "traitorous rebels" and the unwillingness of some Southerners to accept the consequences of defeat.

Lingering over all these questions were partisan politics. Although not provided for in the Constitution, political parties had played a major role in the evolving American government. The road to war had disrupted the existing party structure—killing the Whig party, dividing the Democratic party, and creating the Republican party. The first truly sectional party, the Republican party had very few adherents in the South. Its continued existence was dubious in the face of the probable reunion of the northern and southern wings of the Democratic party. Paradoxically, the political power of the South, and in turn the Democratic party, was increased by the abolition of slavery. As freedmen, all blacks would be counted for representation; as slaves only three-fifths of them had been counted. Thus the Republican party's preceived need to make itself a national party in order to survive also colored the course of Reconstruction.

PRESIDENTIAL RECONSTRUCTION

Early in the conflict, questions regarding the reconstruction of the nation were secondary to winning the war—without victory there would be no nation to reconstruct. Nonetheless, Lincoln had to take some action as Union forces pushed into the South. Authority had to be imposed in the reclaimed territory, so the president named military governors for Tennessee, Arkansas, and Louisiana in 1862 after federal armies occupied most of those states. He also began formulating plans for civilian government for those states and future Confederate areas as they came under the control of Union forces. The result was a Proclamation of Amnesty and Reconstruction issued in December of 1863 on the constitutional basis of the president's power to pardon.

Lincoln's Plan

Called the ten percent plan, Lincoln's provisions were incredibly lenient. With a few exceptions, mainly Confederate military and civilian officials, all rebels could receive pardon by merely swearing their allegiance to the Union and their acceptance of the end of slavery. In other words, former Confederates were not required to say they were sorry—only to promise they would be good in the future. Moreover after only ten percent of the number who had voted in 1860 had taken the oath, a state could form a civilian government. When such states produced a constitution outlawing slavery, Lincoln promised to recognize them as reconstructed.

Tennessee, Arkansas, and Louisiana met Lincoln's requirements and soon learned they had only cleared the first barrier in what became a long obstacle course. Radical Republicans, such as Representative Thaddeus Stevens of Pennsylvania and Senator Charles Sumner of Massachusetts, were outraged by the president's generosity. They thought the provisions did not adequately punish Confederate treason, restructure southern society, protect the rights of blacks, or aid the Republican party. The Radicals were in a minority, but many moderate Republicans were also dismayed by Lincoln's leniency and shared the Radical view that Reconstruction was a congressional, not a presidential, function. As a result Congress recognized neither the three states' elected congressmen nor their electoral votes in the 1864 election.

After denying the president's right to reconstruct the nation, Congress drew up a plan for reconstruction: the Wade-Davis Bill. Its terms were much more stringent, yet not unreasonable. A majority, rather than ten percent, of each states' voters had to declare their allegiance in order to form a government. Only those taking "ironclad" oaths of their past Union loyalty were allowed to participate in the making of new state constitutions. Barely a handful of high-ranking Confederates, however, were to be permanently barred from political participation. The only additional requirement imposed by Congress was the repudiation of the Confederate debt; Northerners did not want Confederate bondholders to benefit from their investment at a cost to loyal taxpayers. Congress would determine when a state had met these requirements.

Constitutional collision was postponed by Lincoln's pocket veto of the bill and his assassination on April 12, 1865. While most of the nation mourned, some Radicals rejoiced at the results of John Wilkes Booth's action. Lincoln

had been a formidable opponent and had articulated his position on the South in his second
inaugural address. Calling for "malice toward
none" and "charity for all," he proposed to
"bind the nation's wounds" and achieve "a just
and lasting peace." His successor, Andrew
Johnson, on the other hand, had announced,
"Treason is a crime, and crime must be punished." A southern Democrat who supported
the Union war effort and was placed on the
1864 ticket as a gesture of unity, Johnson's political affiliation was less than clear, but some
considered him a weaker opponent than Lincoln. Radical Senator Benjamin Wade proclaimed, "By the gods there will be no trouble
now in running this government."

Radicals also found comfort in, but miscalculated, Johnson's hatred of the planters. He
hated them for their aristocratic domination of
the South, not for their slaveholding. Born of
humble origins in Raleigh, North Carolina, and
illiterate until adulthood, Johnson entered politics in Tennessee as a successful tailor who
championed the cause of the yeomanry. He did
not share the desire for black legal equality of
some of the Radicals and advocated strict adherence to the Constitution. Instead of reversing Lincoln's course, Johnson pursued it,
strengthening a little the proclaimed requirements but in the end accepting less than complete adherence.

Johnson's Plan

Congress was not in session when Johnson became president so he had about eight months
to pursue policies without congressional hin-
drance. He issued his own proclamation of amnesty in May 1865 which barred everyone with
taxable property worth more than $20,000.
Closing one door, he opened another by providing for personal presidential pardons for excluded individuals. By year's end he had issued
about 13,000 pardons. The most important aspect of the pardons was Johnson's claim that
they restored all rights, including property
rights. Thus many freedmen with crops in the
ground suddenly found their masters back in
charge—a disillusioning first taste of freedom
which foreclosed further attempts at widespread land redistribution.

Andrew Johnson served as a state legislator and governor before going to the Senate in 1857 and being
selected as Lincoln's running mate in 1864.

Johnson's amnesty proclamation did not
immediately end the Radicals' honeymoon period with him, but his other proclamation the
same day caused deep concern. In it he announced plans for the reconstruction of North
Carolina, which would become the pattern for
all states. A native Unionist was named provisional governor with the power to call a constitutional convention elected by loyal voters.
Omitting Lincoln's ten percent provision, Johnson did eventually require ratification of the
Thirteenth Amendment, repudiation of Confederate debts, and state constitutional provisions
abolishing slavery and renouncing secession.
He also recommended limited black suffrage,
primarily to stave off congressional attempts to
give the vote to all black males.

The presidential plan fell short of the Radicals' hopes, but many moderates might have
accepted it if the South had complied with the
letter and the spirit of Johnson's proposals. Instead, Southerners seemed determined to ignore their defeat, even to make light of it. The

Johnson (left) and Stevens sharply differed on Reconstruction policy. This *Harper's Weekly* cartoon depicts them as drivers of colliding trains.

Black Codes in the South

At the very least, Northerners expected adherence to the abolition of slavery, and the South was blatantly forging new forms of bondage. Blacks were to be technically free, but whites expected them to work and live as they had before emancipation. To accomplish this, the new state governments enacted a series of laws known as the Black Codes. This legislation granted certain rights denied to slaves. Freedmen had the right to marry, own property, sue and be sued, and testify in court. Complex legalisms, however, often took away what was apparently given. All states prohibited racial intermarriage, some forbade freemen to own certain types of property, such as alcoholic beverages and firearms. Most so tightly restricted black legal rights that they were practically nonexistent. Laws imposed curfews on blacks, segregated them, and outlawed their right to congregate in large groups.

The Black Codes did more than merely provide means of racial control; they also sought to fashion a labor system as close to slavery as possible. Some required special licenses for any

state governments, for the most part, met the minimum requirements (Mississippi and South Carolina refused to repudiate the debt and Mississippi declined to ratify the Thirteenth Amendment), but their apparent acceptance grew out of a belief that very little had actually changed, and Southerners proceeded to show almost total disregard for northern sensibilities. Presenting themselves, like prodigal sons, for admission to Congress were four Confederate generals, six Confederate cabinet officials, and as the crowning indignity, Confederate Vice-President Alexander H. Stephens. Most Northerners were not exceedingly vindictive. Although Union soldiers had sung, "We'll hang Jeff Davis in a sour apple tree," he, and only he, served more than a few months in prison, and the only execution was not for treason but for alleged war crimes at the Confederate prison camp in Andersonville, Georgia. Still the North did expect some sign of change and hoped for some indication of repentence by the former rebels.

The freedom of ex-slaves was sharply curtailed through black codes and vagrancy laws. This sketch shows the provost guard in New Orleans rounding up vagrant blacks in 1864.

DAY OF JUBILO:
SLAVES CONFRONT EMANCIPATION

Rooted in Africa, the oral tradition became one of the tools slaves used to maintain a sense of self-worth. Each generation heard the same stories, and story-telling did not die with slavery. The day that slaves first learned of their emancipation remained vivid in their own minds and later in those of their descendents. The great-grandchildren of a strong willed woman named Caddy relished the family account of her first taste of freedom:

> Caddy threw down that hoe, she marched herself up to the big house, then she looked around and found the mistress. She went over to the mistress, she flipped up her dress and told the white woman to do something. She said it mean and ugly. This is what she said: *Kiss my ass!*

Caddy's reaction was not typical. There was no typical response. Reminiscences of what was called the "Day of Jubilo" formed a tapestry as varied as the range of personality. Some, however, seem to have occurred more frequently than others. Many freedmen echoed one man's description of his and his mother's action when their master announced their emancipation: "Jes like tarpins or turtles after 'mancipation. Jes stick our heads out to see how the land lays."

Caution was a shrewd and realistic response. One of the survival lessons in slavery had been not to trust whites too much. This had been reinforced during the war when Union troops moved through regions proclaiming emancipation only to depart, leaving blacks at the mercy of local whites. One elderly slave described the aftermath to a Union correspondent. "Why, the day after you left, they jist had us all out in a row and told us they was going to shoot us, and they did hang two of us; and Mr. Pierce, the overseer, knocked one with a fence rail and he died the next day. Oh, Master! we seen stars in de day time."

Environment played a role in slaves' reactions to the Day of Jubilo. Urban slaves frequently enjoyed more freedom than plantation slaves. Even before emancipation such black social institutions as schools and churches emerged in many cities. When those cities were liberated, organized celebrations occurred quickly. In Charleston 4000 black men and women paraded before some 10,000 spectators. Two black women sat in one mule-drawn cart while a mock auctioneer shouted, "How much am I offered?" In the next cart a black-draped coffin was inscribed with the words "Slavery is Dead." Four days after the fall of Richmond blacks there held a mass rally of some 1500 people in the First African Church.

Knowledge of their freedom came in many forms to the slaves. Rural slaves were less likely to enjoy the benefits of freedom as early as urban slaves. Many heard of the Emancipation Proclamation through the slave grapevine or from Union soldiers long before its words became reality for them. Masters sometimes took advantage of the isolation of their plantations to keep their slaves in ignorance or to make freedom seem vague and frightening. Their ploys usually failed, but learned patterns of deference made some freedmen unwilling to challenge their masters. Months after emancipation one North Carolina slave continued to work without compensation, explaining to a northern correspondent, "No, sir; my mistress never said anything to me that I was to have wages, nor yet that I was free; nor I never said anything to her. Ye see I left it to her honor to talk to me about it, because I was afraid she'd say I was insultin' to her and presumin', so I wouldn't speak first. She ha'n't spoke yet." There were, however, limits to his patience; he intended to ask her for wages at Christmas.

Numerous freedmen described the exuberance they felt. One elderly Virginia black went to the barn, jumped from one stack of straw to another, and "screamed and screamed!" A Texas man remembered, "We all felt like horses" and "everybody went wild." Other blacks recalled how slave songs and spirituals were updated, and "purty soon ev'ybody fo' miles around was singin' freedom songs."

Quite a few slaves learned of freedom when a Union officer or Freedmen's Bureau agent read them the Emancipation Proclamation—often over the objections of the master. "Dat one time," Sarah Ford declared, "Massa Charley can't open he mouth, 'cause de captain tell him to shut up, dat he'd do the talkin'.'" Some masters, however, still sought to have the last word. A Louisiana planter's wife announced immediately after the Union officer departed, "Ten years from today I'll have you all back 'gain."

Fear did not leave all slaves as soon as their bondage was lifted. Jenny Proctor of Alabama recalled that her fellow slaves were stunned by the news. "We didn' hardly know what he means. We jes' sort of huddle 'round together like scared rabbits, but after we knowed what he mean, didn' many of us go, 'cause we didn' know where to of went." James Lucas, a former slave of Jefferson Davis, explained, "folks dat ain' never been free don' rightly know de *feel* of bein' free. Dey don' know de meanin' of it."

Freedmen quickly learned that one could not eat or wear freedom. "Dis livin' on liberty," one declared, "is lak young folks livin' on love after they gits married. It just don't work." They searched for the real meaning of liberty in numerous ways. Some followed the advice of a black Florida preacher, "You ain't none 'o you, gwinter feel rale free till you shakes de dus ob de Ole Plantashun offen you feet," and moved. Others declared their independence by legalizing their marriages and taking new names or publicly using surnames they had secretly adopted while in slavery. "We had a real sho' nuff weddin' wid a preacher," one recalled. "Dat cost a dollar." When encouraged to take his old master's surname, a black man declared, "Him's nothing to me now. I don't belong to he no longer, an' I don't see no use in being called for him." Education was the key for others. "If I nebber does do nothing more while I live," a Mississippi freedman vowed, "I shall give my children a chance to go to school, for I considers education next best ting to liberty."

Most came to a good understanding of the benefits and limits of their new status. One explained, "Why, sar, all I made before was Miss Pinckney's, but all I make now is my own." Another noted, "You could change places and work for different men." One newly freed slave wrote his brother, "I's mightly well pleased tu git my eatin' by de 'sweat o' my face, an all I ax o' ole masser's tu jes' keep he hands off o' de Lawd Almighty's property, fur *dat's me.*" A new sense of dignity was cherished by many. An elderly South Carolina freedman rejoiced, "Don't hab me feelins hurt now. Used to hab me feelins hurt all de times. But don't hab em hurt now, no more." Charlie Barbour exulted over the fact "dat I won't wake up some mornin' fer fin' dat my mammy or some ob de rest of my family am done sold." Most agreed with Margrett Millin's answer when she was asked decades later whether she had liked slavery or freedom better. "Well, it's dis way. In slavery I owns nothin'. In freedom I's own de home and raise de family. All dat cause me worryment and in slavery I has no worryment, but I takes de freedom."

Southern whites frequently vented their frustrations on blacks. In the New Orleans riot of July 30, 1866, thirty-seven blacks and three white sympathizers were killed after a Radical Republican meeting.

job except agricultural labor or domestic service. Most mandated the signing of yearly labor contracts, which sometimes required blacks to call the landowner "master" and allowed withholding wages for minor infractions. To accomplish the same objective Mississippi prohibited black ownership or even rental of land. Mandatory apprenticeship programs took children away from their parents, and vagrancy laws allowed authorities to arrest blacks "wandering or strolling about in idleness" and use them on chaingangs or rent them out to planters for as long as a year.

When laws failed, some southern whites resorted to violence. In Memphis whites resented the presence of black troops at nearby Fort Pickering. A local paper asserted "the negro can do the country more good in the cotton field than in the camp" and chastised "the dirty, fanatical, nigger-loving Radicals of this city." In May 1866 a street brawl erupted between white policemen and recently discharged black soldiers. That night, after the soldiers had returned to the fort, white mobs attacked the black section of the city—with the encouragement of the police and local officials, one of whom urged the mob to "go ahead and kill the last damned one of the nigger race." The reign of terror lasted over forty hours and left forty-six blacks and two whites dead. This and other outbreaks of violence disgusted northern voters.

Most Northerners would not have insisted on black equality or suffrage, but the South had regressed too far. Some black codes were even identical to the old slave codes, with the word "negro" substituted for "slave." At the same time, reports of white violence against blacks filtered back to Washington. It is no wonder that upon finally reconvening in December 1865, Congress refused to seat the representatives and senators from the former Confederate states and instead proceeded to investigate conditions in the South.

CONGRESSIONAL RECONSTRUCTION

To discover what was really happening in the South, Congress established the Joint Committee on Reconstruction, which conducted inquiries and interviews that provided graphic examples of white repression and brutality toward blacks. Prior to the committee's final report, even moderates were convinced that action was necessary. In 1866 Congress passed a moderate civil rights bill and an act extending the life of the Freedmen's Bureau and granting it new powers to protect black rights. Even though the South had ignored much of Johnson's advice, such as granting limited suffrage to blacks, he stubbornly held to his conviction that reconstruction was complete and vetoed both bills, arguing that they were unconstitutional and labeling his congressional opponents as "traitors."

His language did not create a climate of cooperation, and eventually Congress overrode both vetoes. To protect its handiwork and establish an alternate program of reconstruction, Congress then drafted the Fourteenth Amendment. Undoubtedly the most significant legacy of Reconstruction, the first article of the amendment defined citizenship and the basic rights of citizenship. Every person born in the United States and subject to its jurisdiction is declared a citizen. It also forbids any state from abridging "the privileges and immunities" of citizenship, from depriving any person of "due process of law," and from denying citizens the "equal protection of the laws." Although one hundred years passed before its provisions were enforced as intended, the amendment has been interpreted to mean that states as well as the federal government are bound by the Bill of Rights—an important constitutional change that paved the way for the civil rights decisions and laws of the twentieth century.

The remaining four sections of the amendment spelled out Congress's minimum demands for postwar change and was the South's last chance for a lenient peace. A creation of the congressional moderates, the amendment did not require black suffrage but reduced the "basis of representation" proportionately for those states not allowing it. Former Confederate leaders were also barred from holding office

Table 15.1

Reconstruction Amendments, 1865–1870			
Amendment	*Main Provisions*	*Congressional Passage* (⅔ majority in each house required)	*Ratification Process* (¾ of all states including ex-Confederate states required)
13	Slavery prohibited in United States	January 1865	December 1865 (twenty-seven states, including eight southern states)
14	1. National citizenship 2. State representation in Congress reduced proportionally to number of voters disfranchised 3. Former Confederates denied right to hold office	June 1866	Rejected by twelve southern and border states, February 1867 Radicals make readmission of southern states hinge on ratification Ratified July 1868
15	Denial of franchise because of race, color, or past servitude explicitly prohibited	February 1869	Ratification required for readmission of Virginia, Texas, Mississippi, Georgia Ratified March 1870

"THERE ARE VERY FEW MEN WHO HAVE BEEN ABANDONED BY THE PEOPLE UNLESS THEY HAVE DESERTED THEM FIRST" (THAT'S SO)

In the autumn of 1866 President Johnson made his famous "swing around the circle" to several northern and western cities, campaigning against Radicals running for re-election.

unless pardoned by Congress—not the president. Finally, neither Confederate war debts nor compensation to former slaveholders were ever to be paid. The amendment passed Congress in June 1866 and was sent to the states for ratification.

President Johnson bridled at this assault on his perceived powers and urged the southern states not to ratify the amendment. All but Tennessee decided to take his advice and wait for further congressional action. They and Johnson miscalculated; both hoped that the public would repudiate the amendment in the 1866 congressional elections. Johnson hit the campaign trail, urging people to oust the Radicals. His "swing around the circle" was met by hecklers and humiliation. The campaign was vicious, characterized by appeals to racial prejudice by the Democrats and charges of Democratic treason by the Republicans. Although few elections

are referenda on any single issue, the Republicans won overwhelming victories, which they interpreted as a mandate for congressional reconstruction.

"Radical" Reconstruction Initiatives

The election results along with southern intransigence finally gave the Radicals an upper hand. In 1867 Congress passed the Military Reconstruction Act that raised the price of readmission. The act declared all existing "Johnson governments," except Tennessee's, void and divided the South into five military districts headed by military governors granted broad powers to govern. Delegates to new constitutional conventions were to be elected by all qualified voters—a group that by congressional stipulation included black males. Following the ratification of a new state constitution providing for black suffrage, elections were to be held and the state would be readmitted after it had ratified the Fourteenth Amendment.

Obviously, Johnson was not pleased with the congressional plan; he vetoed every part of it, only to see his vetoes overridden. Nevertheless, as commander in chief he reluctantly appointed military governors, and by the end of 1867 elections were held in every state but Texas. Many white Southerners boycotted the elections, and the South came under the control of Republicans supported by Union forces. In a way, however, Southerners had brought more radical measures upon themselves by their inflexibility. As the *Nation* declared in 1867,

> Six years ago, the North would have rejoiced to accept any mild restrictions upon the spread of slavery as a final settlement. Four years ago, it would have accepted peace on the basis of gradual emancipation. Two years ago, it would have been content with emancipation and equal civil rights for the colored people without the extension of suffrage. One year ago, a slight extension of the suffrage would have satisfied it.

Congress realized the plan it had enacted was unprecedented and subject to challenge by

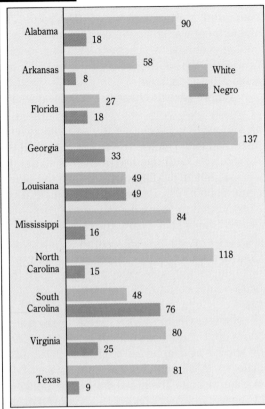

Alabama	90	White
	18	Negro
Arkansas	58	
	8	
Florida	27	
	18	
Georgia	137	
	33	
Louisiana	49	
	49	
Mississippi	84	
	16	
North Carolina	118	
	15	
South Carolina	48	
	76	
Virginia	80	
	25	
Texas	81	
	9	

Figure 15.1
Composition of State Constitutional Conventions under Congressional Reconstruction

the other two branches of government. To check Johnson's power to disrupt, Congress took two other actions on the same day it passed the Military Reconstruction Act. The Command of the Army Act limited presidential military power. The Tenure of Office Act required Senate consent for the removal of any official whose appointment had required the Senate's confirmation. It was meant in part to protect Secretary of War Edwin M. Stanton, who supported the Radicals.

The Supreme Court had also shown its willingness to challenge Reconstruction actions in two important cases of 1866. In *Ex parte Milligan* the justices struck down the conviction of a civilian by a military tribunal in an area where civil courts were operating. Another decision ruled as void a state law barring ex-

Confederates from certain professions on the basis that the act was *ex post facto*. Nevertheless, other decisions reflected a hesitation to tackle some of the thornier issues of Reconstruction. Important cases were pending, and Congress acted in March 1868 to limit the court's power to review cases. Because the congressional action was clearly constitutional, the Supreme Court acquiesed and in *Texas* v. *White* (1869) even acknowledged congressional power to reframe state governments.

President Johnson was not so accommodating. He sought to sabotage military reconstruction by continuing to pardon former Confederates, removing military commanders who were Radical sympathizers, and naming former Confederates to federal positions. Congress was angry but could not find adequate grounds for impeachment. In August 1867 Johnson finally came to the Radicals' aid in their quest to remove him; he deliberately violated the Tenure of Office Act to test its constitutionality. Of course, his choice for the test case was Stanton. After some complex maneuvering, which saw Stanton briefly returned to and removed again from office, the House voted impeachment on February 24, 1868.

The Senate was given eleven articles of impeachment for its trial of the president. Eight related to the violation of the Tenure of Office Act and another to violation of the Army Act. Only the last two reflected the real reasons for congressional action. Johnson was accused of "inflammatory and scandalous harangues" against Congress and of "unlawfully devising and contriving" to obstruct congressional will. The heated and bitter trial lasted from March 5 to May 26. During its course, a good legal case was made that Johnson had not technically

Johnson's defense centered on the legitimate uses of his executive powers.

violated the Tenure of Office Act. Radical prosecutors continued to argue that Johnson had committed "high crimes and misdemeanors," but they also asserted that a president could be removed for political reasons, even without being found legally guilty of crimes.

The vote for conviction fell one short of the required two-thirds majority, setting the precedent that a president must be guilty of serious misdeeds to be removed from office. The outcome was a political blow to the Radicals, costing them some support. The action, however, did make Johnson more cooperative for the last months of his presidency.

Black Suffrage

In the 1868 presidential election, the Republicans won with Ulysses S. Grant, whose Civil War victories made his name a household word. He ran on a platform that endorsed congressional reconstruction, urged repayment of the national debt, and defended black suffrage in the South as necessary but supported the right of each northern state to restrict the vote. His slogan, "Let us have peace," was appealing, but his election was less than a ringing endorsement for Radical policies. The military hero who had seemed invincible barely won the popular vote in several key states.

While Charles Sumner and a few other Radicals had long favored national black suffrage, only after the Republicans' electoral close call in 1868 did the bulk of the party begin to consider a suffrage amendment. Many were undoubtedly swayed by the political certainty that the black vote would be theirs and might give them the margin of victory in future close elections. Others were embarrassed by the hypocrisy of forcing black suffrage on the South while only seven percent of northern blacks could vote. Still others believed that granting blacks the right to vote would relieve whites of any further responsibility to protect black rights.

Suffrage supporters faced many objections to an amendment. One was based on the lack of popular support. At that time only seven northern states granted blacks the right to vote, and since 1865 referendum proposals for black suffrage in eight states had been voted down. In fact only in Iowa and Minnesota (both containing miniscule black populations) had voters supported the extension of the vote. The amendment was so unpopular that, ironically, it could never have won adoption without its ratification by the southern states, where black suffrage already existed.

A more serious challenge was the question of whether Congress could legislate suffrage at all. Before Reconstruction the national government had never taken any action regarding the right to vote; suffrage had been considered not a right, but a privilege which only the states could confer. The Radical answer was that the Constitution expressly declared that "the United States shall guarantee to every State in this Union a republican form of government." Charles Sumner further asserted that "anything for human rights is constitutional" and that black rights could only be protected by black votes.

Senator George Vickers sarcastically asked, "does not the doctrine of human rights asserted by the senator apply as well to females as to males? " Although he was "no advocate for woman suffrage," he noted that "if the Congress of the United States had been composed exclusively of women we should have had no civil war. We might have had a war of words, but that would have been all." When one senator did propose female suffrage, a colleague informed him that "to extend the right of suffrage to negroes in this country I think is necessary for their protection; but to extend the right of suffrage to women is not necessary."

Some women, such as Elizabeth Cady Stanton and Susan B. Anthony, did not want to rely upon their fathers, brothers, or husbands to protect their rights. As leaders of the Women's Loyal League both had worked hard for the adoption of the Thirteenth Amendment, only to be rewarded by inclusion of the word "male" in the Fourteenth Amendment of the Constitution—the first time that word appears. Some women, such as Lucy Stone of the American Woman's Suffrage Association, accepted the plea of long-time woman suffrage supporter Frederick Douglass that it was the "Negro's hour," and worked for ratification. Anthony, however, vowed to "cut off this right arm of mine before I will ever work for or demand the ballot for the Negro and not the woman." Such

Susan B. Anthony (left) moved from Temperance work to join with Elizabeth Cady Stanton in 1869 to form the National Woman Suffrage Association.

differences played a role in splitting the women's movement in 1869 between those working for a national suffrage amendment and those who concentrated their efforts on the state level. Anthony and Stanton founded the National Woman Suffrage Association to battle for a constitutional amendment and other feminist reforms. Others became disillusioned with that approach and established the American Woman Suffrage Association, which focused on obtaining suffrage on a state-by-state basis.

Actually, women did not lose much by not being included in the Fifteenth Amendment. To meet the various objections, compromise was necessary, and the resulting amendment did not grant the vote to anyone. It merely stated that the vote could not be denied "on account of race, color, or previous condition of servitude." Suffrage was still essentially to be controlled by the states, and other bases of exclusion were not deemed unconstitutional. These loopholes would eventually allow white Southerners to make a mockery of equal rights.

Although congressional reconstruction was labeled "Radical," compromise had instead produced another essentially moderate plan. What Congress did *not* do is as important as what it did. It did not even guarantee the right to vote. There was only one execution for war crimes and only Jefferson Davis was imprisoned for more than a few months. For all but a handful, ex-Confederates were not permanently barred from voting or holding office. By 1872 only about 200 were still denied the right to hold office. Most local southern governments were undisturbed. Land as well as rights were restored to former rebels, eliminating the possibility of extensive land redistribution. Most areas that had traditionally been the states' domain remained so, free from federal meddling. For example, no requirements were placed on the states to provide any education to freedmen. The only attempt by the national government to meet the basic needs of its citizens was the temporary Freedmen's Bureau—justified only as an emergency measure. The limited nature of Reconstruction doomed it as an opportunity to provide means for the protection of minority rights.

Such congressional moderation reflected the spirit of the age. Enduring beliefs in the need for strict construction of the Constitution and in states' rights presented formidable barriers to truly radical changes. Property rights were considered sacrosanct—even for "traitors." Cherished ideals of self-reliance and the conviction that a person determined his or her own destiny led many to support Horace Greeley's so-called root, hog, or die approach to the Negro problem. By ending the threat of slavery, he argued, "we may soon break up our Freedmen's Bureaus and all manner of coddling devices and let the negroes take care of themselves." Few agreed with Charles Sterns who argued that even a hog could not root without a snout—that there could be no equality of opportunity where one group had long been allowed an unfair advantage. Many instead sided with an editorialist for the New York *Herald* commenting on the bill to extend the life of the Freedmen's Bureau: "The bill ought to be called an act to support the negroes in idleness by the honest labor of white people, or an act to establish a gigantic and corrupt political machine for the benefit of the radical faction and a swarm of officeholders." Clearly the idea of affirmative action had even less support then than it did one hundred years later.

Tainting every action was the widespread conviction that blacks were not equal to whites. Many Northerners were more concerned with keeping blacks in the South than with abstract black rights. New York Senator Roscoe Conkling catered to the northern fear of black immigration while calling for support of the Fourteenth Amendment in 1866:

> Four years ago mobs were raised, passions were aroused, votes were given, upon the idea that emancipated negroes were to burst in hordes upon the North. We then said, give them liberty and rights in the South, and they will stay there and never come into a cold climate. We say so still, and we want them let alone, and that is one thing that this part of the amendment is for.

Even Radical Representative George Julian admitted to his Indiana constituents, "the real trouble is that *we hate the negro*. It is not his ignorance that offends us, but his color."

The plan for Reconstruction evolved fitfully, buffeted first one way and then another by the force of the many unresolved issues at war's end. If permanent changes were very limited, nonetheless precedents had been set for later action and for a brief time congressional reconstruction brought about the most democratic governments the South had ever seen—or would see for another hundred years.

RECONSTRUCTION IN THE SOUTH

Regardless of the specific details hammered out in Washington, any dictated peace would probably have been unpalatable to southern whites. They were especially leery of any action that seemed to threaten white supremacy—whether or not that was the intended result. Even before the war, suspicion greeted every northern move. Southerners continued to see a radical abolitionist behind every bush.

The Freedmen's Bureau established during the last year of the war operated for five years in the South. Most Southerners criticized and condemned the bureau from its first day to its last. Many believed its agents were partial to blacks. As one Mississippi planter declared, "The negro is a sacred animal. The Yankees are about negroes like the Egyptians were about cats." Actually there was a great diversity in the background and goals of bureau agents. Some were idealistic young New Englanders who, like the Yankee schoolmarms, came south to aid blacks in the transition to freedom. Others were army officers whose first priority was to maintain order—often by siding with the landowners. All were overworked, underpaid, and under pressure.

The results of bureau actions were mixed in regard to conditions for blacks. The agents helped to negotiate labor contracts which blacks were forced to sign to obtain rations. Frequently the wages were well below the rate at which slaves had been hired before the war. While it should be remembered that money was scarce at the time, these contracts helped to keep blacks on the farm—someone else's farm. On the other hand, between 1865 and 1869 the bureau issued over 21 million rations, of which about 5 million went to whites. Thus it showed that the government could establish and administer a massive relief program, as it would again be called upon to do during the Depression of the 1930s. The bureau also operated more than forty hospitals, opened hundreds of schools, and accomplished the herculean task of resettling some thirty thousand people displaced by the war.

Carpetbaggers, Scalawags, and Black Republicans

Until the passage of the Reconstruction Acts in 1867, southern governments were much the same as they had been before the war. Afterwards, however, Republican officeholders joined bureau agents in directing the course of Reconstruction. Despised by many whites, these men, depending on their origins, were derisively labeled "carpetbaggers," "scalawags," and "nigrahs." Opponents considered all three groups despicable creatures whose "black and tan" governments were tyrannizing native whites while engaged in an orgy of corruption. These myths lingered long after the restoration of Democratic party rule.

Northerners who came to the South during or after the war and became engaged in politics were called carpetbaggers. They supposedly arrived with a few meager belongings in their carpetbags, which would expand to hold ill-gotten gains from looting an already devastated South. Probably what most infuriated whites was the carpetbaggers' willingness to cooperate with blacks. Calling them "a kind of political dry-nurse for the negro population," native whites accused the carpetbaggers of cynically exploiting blacks for their own gain. Many agreed with the charge that the carpetbaggers were standing "right in the public eye, stealing and plundering, many of them with both arms around negroes, and their hands in their rear pockets, seeing if they cannot pick a paltry dollar out of them."

White Southerners who voted for Republicans were labeled scalawags. The term, said to be derived from Scalloway, "a district in the Shetland Islands where small, runty cattle and horses were bred," had been used previously as a "synonym for scamp, loafer, or rascal." Thus southern white Republicans were depicted as people "paying no taxes, riding poor horses, wearing dirty shirts, and having no use for soap." Such men were said to have "sold themselves for office" and become a "subservient tool and accomplice" of the carpetbaggers.

Most detested by white Southerners were the black Republicans. Having long characterized blacks as inferior creatures dependent on white management for survival, Southerners loathed the prospect of blacks in authority. They feared that blacks would exact payment for their years of bondage. Democrats also knew that racism was their best rallying cry to regain power. Thus Reconstruction governments were denounced for "Ethiopian minstrelsy, Ham radicalism in all its glory." Whites claimed ignorant blacks, incapable of managing their own affairs, were allowed to run the affairs of state with disastrous results. A

This cartoon shows Grant and Union soldiers propping up carpetbag rule with bayonets while the "Solid South" staggers under the weight.

former governor of South Carolina observed, "All society stands now like a cone on its Apex, with base up."

Such legends persisted for a long time, despite contrary facts. Southern whites had determined even before Reconstruction began that it would be "the most galling tyranny and most stupendous system of organized robbery that is to be met with in history." The truth was, as W. E. B. DuBois later wrote, "There is one thing that the white South feared more than negro dishonesty, ignorance, and incompetency, and that was negro honesty, knowledge, and efficiency." To a surprising degree they got what they most feared.

Black voters were generally as fit to vote as the millions of illiterate whites enfranchised by Jacksonian democracy. Black officials as a group were as qualified as their white counterparts. In South Carolina two-thirds of them were literate, and in all states most of the acknowledged leaders were well educated and

In an historic first, seven blacks were elected to the 41st and 42nd Congresses. Between 1869 and 1901 two blacks became senators and twenty blacks served in the House.

articulate. They usually had been members of the northern or southern free black elite or part of the slave aristocracy of skilled artisans and household slaves. Hiram Revels, a United States senator from Mississippi, was the son of free blacks who had sent him to college in the North. James Walker Hood, the presiding officer of the North Carolina constitutional convention of 1867, was a black carpetbagger from Pennsylvania who came to the state as an African Methodist Episcopal Zion missionary. Some, such as Francis Cardoza of South Carolina, were the privileged mulatto sons of white planters. Cardoza had been educated in Scottish and English universities. During Reconstruction fourteen such men served in the United States House of Representatives and two in the Senate.

Even if black Republicans had been incompetent, they could hardly be held responsible for the perceived abuses of so-called black reconstruction. Only in South Carolina did blacks have a majority of the delegates to the constitutional convention provided for by the Reconstruction Acts. Neither did they dominate the new governments; only for a two-year period in South Carolina did blacks control both houses of the legislature. None were elected governor, although P. B. S. Pinchback, the lieutenant governor of Louisiana, did serve as acting governor

for a short time. When the vote was restored to ex-Confederates, blacks comprised only one-third of the voters of the South, and only in two states did they have a majority.

Actually, carpetbaggers dominated most Republican governments. They accounted for less than one percent of the party's voters, but constituted about sixty percent of the congressmen sent to Washington. Although some carpetbaggers did resemble the southern stereotypes of them, most did not. Many had come south before black enfranchisement and could not have predicted political futures based on black votes. Most were Union veterans whose wartime exposure to the region convinced them that they could make a good living there without having to shovel snow. Some brought with them much needed capital for investment in their new home. A few came with a sense of mission to educate blacks and reform southern society.

Obviously, if blacks constituted only one-third of the population and carpetbaggers less than one percent, those two groups had to depend on the votes of a sizable number of native white Southerners to obtain office in some regions of the South. Those men came from diverse backgrounds. Some scalawags were members of the old elite of bankers, merchants, industrialists, and even some planters who, as former Whigs, favored the "Whiggish" economic policies of the Republican party and hoped to control and use the black vote for their own purposes. Upon discovering their inability to dominate the Republican governments, most of these soon drifted into alliance with the Democrats. The majority of southern white Republican voters, who had resented planter domination and had opposed secession, were yeoman farmers and poor whites from areas where slavery had been unimportant.

To win their vote the Republicans appealed to class interests. In Georgia they proclaimed, "Poor White men of Georgia: Be a Man! Let the Slave-holding aristocracy no longer rule you. Vote for a constitution which educates your children free of charge; relieves the poor debtor from his rich creditor; allows a liberal homestead for your families; and more than all, places you on a level with those who used to

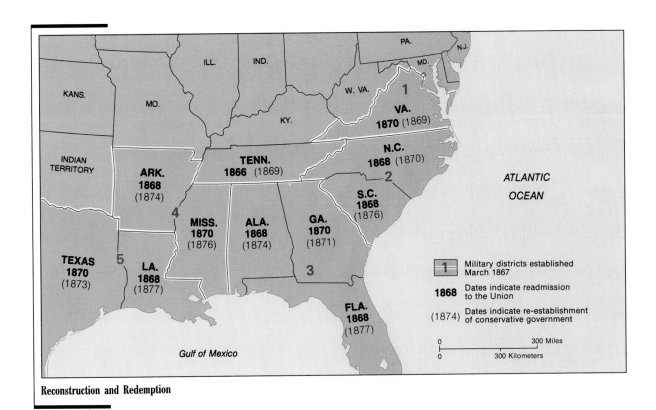

Reconstruction and Redemption

Map labels:
- VA. **1870** (1869)
- N.C. **1868** (1870)
- TENN. **1866** (1869)
- ARK. **1868** (1874)
- S.C. **1868** (1876)
- MISS. **1870** (1876)
- ALA. **1868** (1874)
- GA. **1870** (1871)
- TEXAS **1870** (1873)
- LA. **1868** (1877)
- FLA. **1868** (1877)
- ATLANTIC OCEAN
- Gulf of Mexico

Legend:
- **1** Military districts established March 1867
- **1868** Dates indicate readmission to the Union
- (1874) Dates indicate re-establishment of conservative government

0 — 300 Miles
0 — 300 Kilometers

boast that for every slave they were entitled to three-fifths of a vote in congressional representation." Many accepted such arguments and joined blacks to put Republicans into office. The coalition, however, was always shaky, given the racism of poor whites. The scalawags actually represented a swing vote which finally swung toward the Democratic party of white supremacy later in the 1870s.

Character of Republican Rule

While the coalition lasted, the Republican governments became the most democratic that the South had ever had. More people could vote for more offices, all remaining property requirements for voting and office holding were dropped, representation was made fairer through reapportionment, and more offices became elective rather than appointive. Salaries for public officials made it possible to serve without being wealthy. Most important, universal male suffrage was enacted with the support of black legislators. Ironically, by refusing to deny southern whites what had been denied to them—the vote—blacks sowed the seeds of their own destruction.

The Republican state constitutions brought the South firmly into the mainstream of national reform and often remained in effect years after the end of Reconstruction. Legislatures abolished automatic imprisonment for debt and reduced exercise of the death penalty. More institutions for the care of the indigent, orphans, mentally ill, deaf, and blind were established. Tax structures were overhauled, reducing head taxes and increasing property taxes to relieve somewhat poorer taxpayers. At the same time, the southern railroads, harbors, and bridges were rebuilt.

Reforms also affected the status of women, increasing their rights in the possession of property and divorce. Although giving women legal control of their property was mainly intended to protect the families of their debt-ridden husbands, blacks in particular pushed for more radical changes. When William Whip-

Blacks eagerly participated in politics when allowed. In this 1867 election in the nation's capital they served as polling place judges and lined up as early as 2 A.M. to vote.

public schools below the Mason-Dixon line were meager to nonexistent. In every state blacks were among the main proponents of state supported schools, but most accepted segregated facilities as necessary compromises. Some blacks did not even desire integration; they believed their children could not flourish in environments tainted by white supremacy. By 1877 some 600,000 blacks were in schools, but only the University of South Carolina and the public schools of New Orleans were integrated.

As desirable as many of the new social services were, they required money, which was scarce. The war had destroyed not only railroads and bridges but also much of the southern tax base. The necessary tax increases were bound to be unpopular, as were soaring state debts. Both were blamed on corruption, with some justification. Louisiana governor Henry C. Warmouth netted some $100,000 dollars in a year in which his salary was $8000. A drunken South Carolina governor signed an issue of state bonds for a woman in a burlesque show. One black man was paid $9000 to repair a bridge with an original cost of only $500. Contracts for rebuilding and expanding railroads, subsidies to industries, and bureaucracies for administering social services offered generous opportunities for graft and bribery. When these occurred, southern whites loudly proclaimed that they knew it would happen if shifty former slaves were given the keys to the till.

Actually, although blacks received a large share of the blame, they received little of the profit. A smaller percentage of blacks than whites were involved in the scandals. Also the corruption that the Democrats denounced at every turn was rather meager compared to the shenanigans of contemporary northern Democratic regimes such as the Boss Tweed Ring of New York. There seemed to be an orgy of national corruption that infected both parties. Indeed, in the South a Democratic state treasurer who came to office after Reconstruction deserves the dubious distinction of being the largest embezzler of the era.

The "tyranny" that so distressed southern whites did not include wholesale disfranchisement or confiscation of their lands. In fact, the

per's motion to give South Carolina women the vote did not receive a second, he persevered and declared:

> However frivolous you may think it, I know the time will come when every man and woman in this country will have the right to vote. I acknowledge the superiority of woman. There are large numbers of the sex who have an intelligence more than equal to our own. Is it right or just to deprive these intelligent beings of the priviledges which we enjoy? The time will come when you will have to meet this question. It will continue to be agitated until it must ultimately triumph. However derisively we may treat these noble women, we shall yet see them successful in the assertion of their rights.

One area where black legislators had the most success was the laying of foundations for public education. Antebellum provisions for

William Marcy Tweed came to dominate New York politics and is estimated to have looted between $30 and $200 million before being jailed.

demands of most blacks were quite reasonable and moderate. Their goals were expressed by the declarations of the many postwar black conventions, such as a Virginia one in 1865 that declared, "All we ask is an *equal chance* with the white *traitors* varnished and japanned with the oath of amnesty."

Black and White Economic and Social Adaptation

Just as the ex-slaves on Thomas Pinckney's plantation had learned, freedmen everywhere soon realized that the economic power of whites had diminished little. If anything, land became more concentrated in the hands of a

few. In one Alabama county, the richest ten percent of landowners increased their share of landed wealth from fifty-five percent to sixty-three percent between 1860 and 1870. Some blacks, usually through hard work and incredible sacrifice, were able to obtain land. The percentage of blacks owning property increased from less than one percent to twenty percent. Indeed, blacks seemed to fare better than poor whites. One observer noted, "The negro, bad as his condition is, seems to me, on the whole, to accommodate himself more easily than the white to the change of situation." The truth of his assertion is reflected in the fact that the percentage of whites owning land dropped from eighty to sixty-seven percent. Increasingly, poor blacks and whites became agricultural laborers on someone else's land.

The black landless farmers, like the slaves before them, were not mere pawns. If they could not control their destinies, at least they could shape them. As one northern observer wrote, "They have a mine of strategy to which the planter sooner or later yields." Through strikes and work slow-downs, blacks resisted contract and wage labor, because working in gangs under white supervision smacked too much of slavery. When they could not own land, they preferred to rent it, but the few who had the cash to do so found few southern whites would risk the wrath of their neighbors by breaking the taboo against renting to blacks.

Sharecropping emerged both as a result of black desire for autonomy and whites' lack of cash. Landowners gave blacks as well as poor whites a plot of land to work in return for a share of the crops. Freedom from white supervision was so desirable to blacks that they sometimes hitched mule teams to their old slave cabins and carried them off to their assigned acres. To put distance between themselves and slavery, many black men would not allow their wives and children to work in the fields.

Sharecropping at first seemed to be a good bargain for blacks as they frequently negotiated their way to a half share of the crops. Their portion of the profits from southern agriculture, including all provisions, rose from twenty-two percent under slavery to fifty-six percent by the end of Reconstruction. Moreover, they were making more for working less. Fewer family members worked and black men labored shorter hours; as a group blacks worked one-third fewer hours than under slavery. Per capita black income increased quickly after the war to about one-half that of whites but then stagnated.

Sharecropping later proved to be disastrous for most blacks and poor whites. They needed more than land to farm; they also required seeds, fertilizers, and provisions to live on until they harvested their crops. To obtain these they often borrowed against their share of the crops. Falling crop prices, high credit rates, and sometimes unscrupulous cheating by creditors left many to harvest a growing burden of debt with each crop. In many states when the Democrats regained power, laws favoring creditors were passed, leading to debt peonage.

If most freedmen did not win economic freedom, they benefited from freedom in other ways. It was no longer illegal to learn to read and write, and blacks pursued education with much zeal. Many even paid as much as ten per-

Blacks obtained a little more freedom to control working conditions under the sharecropping system, but their poverty limited their access to machinery and many relied on "human power" for plowing.

cent of their limited incomes for tuition. They began to learn the fundamentals, and a growing number also sought higher education. Between 1860 and 1880 over 1000 blacks earned college degrees. Some went north to college, but most went to one of the thirteen southern colleges established by the American Missionary Association and black and white churches with the assistance of the Freedmen's Bureau. A permanent legacy of Reconstruction were such schools as Howard and Fisk.

Blacks were also able to enjoy and expand their rich cultural heritage. Religion was a central focus for most, just as it had been in slavery. Withdrawing from white congregations with segregated pews and self-serving sermons on the duty of servants to their masters, freedmen everywhere established separate black churches. The membership in such antebellum denominations as the African Methodist Episcopal soared. In essence, blacks declared their religious independence, and their churches became centers of political and social activities as well as religious ones. As one carpetbagger noted, "The colored preachers are *the great power* in controlling and uniting the colored vote." The churches also functioned as vehicles for self-help and sources of entertainment.

Most blacks desired racial intermingling no more than whites. Many could not feel free until they had removed themselves and their children as far as possible from white arrogance. They created separate congregations and acquiesced to segregated schooling. Nevertheless, they did not want to be publicly humiliated by such measures as separate railroad cars. They frequently used their limited political power to protect civil rights through clauses in state constitutions and legislation, as well as by appeals for the enforcement of national laws. Consequently blacks did enjoy the use of public facilities to a greater degree than they would during the following seventy-five years.

The very changes that gave blacks hope during Reconstruction distressed poor whites. Black political equality rankled them, but much more serious was their own declining economic status. As their landownership declined, more whites became dependent on sharecropping and low wage jobs, primarily in the textile industry. Even these meager opportunities were eagerly greeted; as one North Carolina preacher proclaimed, "Next to God, what this town needs is a cotton mill." Economic competition between poor whites and blacks was keen, but, their common plight also favored cooperation based on class interest. The economic pressures applied by the white elite frequently hurt both groups as well as middle-class yeoman farmers, and for brief periods during Reconstruction they warily united in politics. Invariably, however, these attempts were shattered by upper-class appeals to white supremacy and racial unity.

Ironically, while poor whites were perceived by nearly everyone as the group most hostile to blacks, they shared many aspects of a rich southern cultural heritage. Aesthetic expression was based on utility and reflected their need to use wisely what little they had. Quilts were not merely functional but often quite beautiful. In camp meetings and revivals, poor whites practiced a highly emotional religion, just as many blacks did. Both groups spun yarns and sang songs that reflected the perils of their existence and provided folk heroes. They also shared many superstitions as well as useful folk remedies. Race, however, was a potent wedge between the groups that upper class whites frequently exploited for their own political and economic goals.

Planters no longer dominated the white elite; sharecropping turned them and others into absentee landlords. The sons of the old privileged families joined the growing ranks of lawyers, railroad entrepreneurs, bankers, industrialists, and merchants. In some ways the upper and middle classes began to merge, but in many places the old elite and their sons still enjoyed a degree of deference and political leadership. Their hostility toward blacks was not as intense, largely because they possessed means of control. When their control slipped, however, they also became ranting racists.

So strongly were southern whites of all classes imbued with a belief in white superiority that most could not imagine total black equality. A Freedmen's Bureau agent reported in 1866 that "a very respectable old citizen . . . swore that, if he could not thrash a negro who insulted him, he would leave the country." Whites' attitudes towards blacks were as irra-

The Ku Klux Klan and other white terrorist groups sought through violence to eliminate black gains. This 1874 cartoon and others like it helped arouse the public to demand action against the Klan.

tional as they were generalized. Most whites exempted the blacks they knew from such generalizations. As an Alabama planter declared in 1865, "If all were like some of mine I wouldn't say anything. They're as intelligent and well behaved as anybody. But I can't stand free niggers anyhow!"

Violent White Resistance

Large numbers of whites engaged in massive resistance to Reconstruction. Unlike the resistance of southern blacks one hundred years later, however, this brand of resistance was not passive but very aggressive. In 1866, some bored young men in Pulaski, Tennessee, organized a social club with all the trappings of fraternal orders—secret rituals, costumes, and practical jokes. They soon learned that their antics intimidated blacks; thenceforth the Ku Klux Klan grew into a terrorist organization, copied all over the South under various names. A historian of the Klan asserts that it "whipped, shot, hanged, robbed, raped, and otherwise outraged Negroes and Republicans across the South in the name of preserving white civilization." A major goal of the Klan was to intimidate Republican voters and restore Democrats to office. In South Carolina, when blacks working for a scalawag began to vote, Klansmen visited the plantation and "whipped every nigger man they could lay their hands on." The group's increasing lawlessness alarmed many people and led to congressional action. The Klan was broken up by three Enforcement Acts (1870–71) which gave the president the right to suspend habeas corpus against "armed combinations" interfering with any citizen's right to vote. In 1871 Grant did so in nine South Carolina counties. Disbanding the Klan, however, did little to decrease southern violence or the activities of similar terrorist groups.

Some blacks were probably never allowed to vote freely. At the peak of Reconstruction there were less than 30,000 federal troops stationed in the entire South—hardly enough to protect the rights of 4.5 million blacks. In addition to economic intimidation, violence against freedmen escalated in most states as the Democrats increased their political power with appeals to white supremacy and charges of Republican corruption. When victory seemed close, Democrats justified any means to the desired end that they called redemption. A South Carolina Democratic campaign plan in 1876 urged, "Never threaten a man individually. If he deserves to be threatened, the necessities of the times require that he should die. A dead Radical is very harmless." One Democratic candidate for governor in Louisiana proclaimed, "We shall carry the next election if we have to ride saddle-deep in blood to do it." In six heavily black counties in Mississippi such tactics proved highly successful—reducing Republican votes from more than 14,000 in 1873 to only 723 in 1876. Beginning with Virginia and Tennessee in 1869, by 1876 all but three states—Louisiana, Florida, and South Carolina—had Democratic "Redeemer" governments. The final collapse of Reconstruction became official during the following year with the withdrawal of federal troops from the three unredeemed states.

RETREAT FROM RECONSTRUCTION

In the end, the South could be said to have lost the war but won the peace. After 1877 southern whites found little resistance to their efforts to forge new institutions to replace both the economic benefits and racial control of slavery. By 1910 they had devised a system of legalized repression that gave whites many of the benefits of slavery without all the responsibilities. Surely this was not what the North had envisioned after Appomattox. How did it happen?

Northern Shifts in Attitudes

The basic cause can be seen in an 1874 conversation between two Republicans during which one declared that the people were "tired out with this wornout cry of 'Southern Outrages!!!' Hard times and heavy taxes make them wish the . . . 'everlasting nigger' were in [hell] or Africa. . . . It is amazing the change that has taken place in the last two years in the public sentiment." A shifting political climate, economic hard times, increasing preoccupation with other issues, and continued racism combined to make most Northerners wash their hands of the responsibility for the protection of black rights.

Republican awareness of the party's vulnerability after the election of 1868 had provided additional incentive for promoting black suffrage with the Fifteenth Amendment. In the 1872 presidential election the Republican party was split; a number, calling themselves Liberal Republicans, formed a separate party and supported their own candidate, *New York Tribune* editor Horace Greeley, rather than Grant. Among Greeley's campaign pledges was a more moderate southern policy. Even with the Democrats also nominating Greeley, Grant easily won reelection, but the fear of disgruntled Republicans merging with Democrats remained. By 1874 Republicans were becoming aware that the black vote would not save them. That year the Democrats captured the House and gained in the Senate—a victory spurred by revelations of Republican corruption and by an economic depression.

Grant had undoubtedly been a great general, but military prowess does not automatically guarantee the leadership qualities needed for an effective presidency. Too easily flattered by men of wealth, he made some dismal appointments and remained loyal to individuals who did not merit his trust. The result was a series of scandals; Grant was not personally involved, but his close association with the perpetrators blemished both his and his party's image. The first major scandal involved Credit Mobiliér, a dummy construction company used to milk money from railroad investors in order to line the pockets of a few insiders, including Vice-President Schuyler Colfax and a number of other prominent Republicans. Later, bribes and kickback schemes surfaced that involved Indian trading posts, post office contracts, and commissions for tax collection. Such revelations as well as the corruption in some southern Republican governments did little to enhance the public image of the party, and Democrats were quick to make corruption a major issue—both in the North and the South.

At least as detrimental to Republican political fortunes was the depression that followed the panic of 1873, which was caused by overinvestment in railroads and risky financial deals. Lasting six years, it was the most serious economic downturn the nation had yet experienced. Whatever their cause, depressions usually result in "voting the rascals out." Democratic fortunes were bound to rise as the people's fell. Yet economic distress had an even wider impact on Reconstruction. People's attention became focused on their pocketbooks rather than on abstract ideals of equality and justice. Economic scrutiny brought such issues as currency and tariffs to the forefront. As the depression deepened, many questioned Republican support for "sound money" backed by gold and the retirement of the legal tender "greenback" paper money that had been issued during the war. The money supply was not keeping pace with the economy. The resulting deflation favored creditors over debtors, and most farmers were debtors.

Actually, the panic of 1873 merely brought into clearer focus the vast changes occurring in the North during Reconstruction. The South had never had the undivided attention of the rest of the nation. Such events as the completion of the first transcontinental railroad in 1869 often overshadowed reports of "southern outrages." The United States was experiencing the growing pains of economic modernization and western expansion. The Republican platform of 1860 had called for legislation favoring both of these as well as stopping the expansion of slavery. Comprised of diverse interest groups, the party went through a battle for its soul during Reconstruction. For a while the small abolitionist faction had gained some ascendancy due to postwar developments. By the late 1870s, however, the Republican party had foresaken its reformist past to become a protector of privilege rather than a guarantor of basic rights. In effect, Republicans and Democrats joined hands in conservative support of railroad and industrial interests.

Racism and American Indians

The major reason for the decline of Reconstruction was the pervasive belief in white supremacy. There could be little determination to secure equal rights for those who were considered unequal in all other respects. Reconstruction became a failed opportunity to resolve justly the status of one minority, and the climate of racism almost ensured failure for others as well. Western expansion not only diverted attention from Reconstruction but also raised the question of what was to be done about the Plains Indians. They, too, were considered inferior to whites. William H. Seward, who later became secretary of state, spoke for most white Americans when in 1860 he described the Negro as "a foreign and feeble element like the Indians, incapable of assimilation." Indeed, while Reconstruction offered hope to Afro-Americans, for the American Indian hope was fading.

In the end, blacks were oppressed; Native Americans were exterminated. From the white viewpoint the reason was obvious. As a so-called scientific treatise of the 1850s explained, "The *Barbarous* races of America . . . although

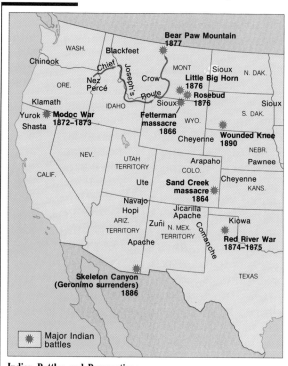

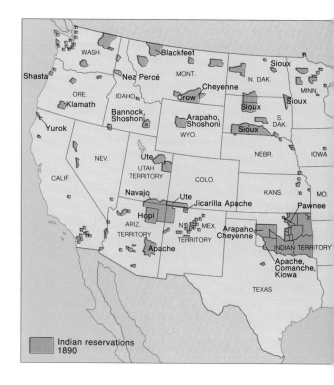

Indian Battles and Reservations

Chief Joseph

nearly as low in intellect as the Negro races, are essentially untameable. Not merely have all attempts to civilize them failed, but also every endeavor to enslave them. Our Indian tribes submit to extermination, rather than wear the yoke under which our negro slaves fatten and multiply." Because most Africans, like Europeans, depended on agriculture rather than hunting, they adapted more easily to agricultural slavery. Black labor was valuable, if controlled; Indians were merely barriers to expansion.

Most Plains Indians relied upon the buffalo for practically all their needs—from food and clothing to shelter and fuel. Nomadically following the herds, many had no concept of private property. Chief Joseph of the Nez Perce eloquently expressed the Indians' perspective. "The earth

was created by the assistance of the sun, and it should be left as it was. . . . The country was made without lines of demarcation, and it is no man's business to divide it." Their cultures were not monolithic, but most shared a world view that stressed the unity of life and the sacredness of their relationship with nature. As Chief Joseph proclaimed, "The earth and myself are of one mind."

Tribal organization differed greatly from American government; tribes were loosely structured and chiefs had more ceremonial than political power. Thus Indians did not always accept treaties made by chiefs. From the white viewpoint the most significant characteristic of many of the Plains Indian tribes, such as the Cheyenne, Sioux, and Arapaho, was their ability as mounted warriors. Using horses introduced by the Spanish, about 250,000 Indians had resisted white encroachment for two centuries. Most had no desire for assimilation; they merely wanted to be left alone. "If the Indians had tried to make the whites live like them," one Sioux declared, "the whites would have resisted, and it was the same way with the Indians."

Although some tribes could coexist peacefully with settlers, many others had a way of life incompatible with white culture. Only one could prevail, and as Theodore Roosevelt later noted, few whites would accept the idea that "this continent could have been kept as nothing but a game reserve for squalid savages." Thus United States Indian policy focused on getting more territory for white settlement. Prior to Reconstruction this was done by signing treaties that divided land between Indians and settlers and restricted the movement of each on the lands of the other. Frequently Indian consent was fraudulently obtained, and white respect for Indian land depended on how desirable it was for settlement. As the removal of the civilized Southern Cherokees to Oklahoma had shown in the 1830s, compatability of cultures did not protect Native Americans from the greed of whites.

During the Civil War, Sioux, Cheyenne, and Arapaho braves rejected the land cessions made by their chiefs. Violence against settlers erupted as frontier troop strength was reduced to fight the Confederacy. The war also provided an excuse to nullify previous treaties and pledges with the tribes resettled in Oklahoma by Andrew Jackson's Indian removal. Some did support the Confederacy, but all suffered the consequences of Confederate defeat. Settlers moved into the most desirable land, pushing the Indians farther south and west.

By the close of the Civil War, Indian hostility had escalated, especially after an 1864 massacre. The territorial governor of Colorado persuaded most of the warring Cheyennes and Arapahoes to come to Fort Lyon on Sand Creek, promising them protection. Colonel J. M. Chivington's militia, however, attacked an Indian camp flying a white flag and the American flag and killed 450 Indian men, women, and children. The following year Congress established a committee to investigate the causes of conflict. Its final report in 1867 led to the creation of an Indian Peace Commission charged with negotiating settlements. At two conferences in 1867 and 1868 Indian chiefs were asked to restrict their tribes to reservations in the undesirable lands of Oklahoma and the Black Hills of the Dakotas in return for supplies and assistance from the government.

Although buffaloes were crucial to American Indian culture, many Americans killed them for sport. Here buffalo heads adorn the offices of the Kansas Pacific Railway.

Most Indians did not consider the offer very generous. Some acquiesced and others resisted, but in the end federal authorities subdued or killed them all. Several factors made their resistance unsuccessful. Railroads had penetrated the West, bringing in both settlers and federal troops more rapidly. The use of repeating firearms beginning in the 1870s destroyed the effectiveness of Indian mounted warriors. The most important factor, however, was the destruction of the buffalo herds upon which the Indians were as dependent as modern Americans are upon electricity. In 1872 the Indian commissioner accurately forecasted that in a few years the "most powerful and hostile bands of today" would be "reduced to the condition of supplicants for charity."

In 1876, the final year of Reconstruction, Colonel George A. Custer's defeat at Little Big Horn called attention to the "Indian problem." The stage was set for this confrontation with Chief Sitting Bull's Sioux warriors and their Cheyenne allies two years earlier when gold was discovered in the Black Hills. The territory suddenly became tempting, and miners began

In this 1898 watercolor, an Indian participant in the Battle of Little Big Horn depicts its aftermath. As Sitting Bull and others stand watching, Sioux and Cheyenne warriors ride horseback over the corpses of Custer (left center) and his men.

pouring into the lands guaranteed to the Indians only five years before. "The white man is in the Black Hills just like maggots," one Indian lamented.

Despite Sitting Bull's victory, the die had been cast during Reconstruction. All that remained were "mopping up" exercises. Federal authorities solved the Indian problem by reducing the number of Indians to a level that posed no threat. Still, white Americans would not leave the Indians alone. The exact nature of the Indians' status, like that of Afro-Americans, would be determined after Reconstruction was over. The treatment of both, as well as of immigrants, would be justified by the increasingly virulent racism of whites, which was given "scientific" support by the scholars of the late nineteenth century. One thing was clear in 1876: Northerners who believed that the only good Indian was a dead Indian could hardly condemn southern whites for their treatment of blacks. The patriotism engendered by the 1876 centennial of the Declaration of Independence also fostered a desire for unity among white Americans—at the expense of non-whites.

Final Retreat

By 1876 fewer Americans championed black rights. Some of the old abolitionist Radicals had grown tired of what had become a protracted and complex problem and therefore justified their withdrawal from the fight by the failures of some southern Reconstruction governments. Those least likely to do so, such as Thaddeus Stevens and Charles Sumner, were dead. Until his death in 1874, Sumner had struggled to get Congress to pass a civil rights act that would spell out more specifically the guarantees of the Fourteenth Amendment. He proposed that segregation of all public facilities, including schools, be declared illegal and the right of blacks to serve on juries specified. After his death, in part as a tribute to him but mostly as one provision of a larger political bargain, Congress enacted the Civil Rights Act of 1875. The act did not include Sumner's clause on schools and did not provide any means of enforcement. For blacks it was a paper victory that marked an end of national action on their behalf. Never effectively enforced, the act was rendered totally impotent by Supreme Court decisions of the late nineteenth century.

By 1876 all the elements were present for a national retreat on Reconstruction: the distraction of economic distress, a deep desire for unity among whites, the respectability of racism, a frustrated weariness with black problems by former allies, a growing conservatism on economic and social issues, a changing political climate featuring a resurgence of the Democratic party, and finally a general public disgust with the failure of Reconstruction. The presidential election of that year sealed the fate of Reconstruction and brought about an official end to it.

Corruption was a major issue in the election and the Democrats chose Samuel J. Tilden, a New Yorker whose claim to fame was breaking up the notorious Boss Tweed Ring. The Republicans nominated Rutherford B. Hayes, a man who had offended few—largely by doing little. Increasing Democratic strength was reflected by Tilden's winning the popular vote and leading Hayes in the electoral vote 184 to 165, but 185 votes were needed for election, and 20 votes were disputed—19 of them from Louisiana, Florida, and South Carolina. They were the only southern states still under Republican rule with the backing of federal troops. There was flagrant fraud on both sides, but Tilden clearly deserved at least one vote—all he needed for election.

With no constitutional provision for such an occurrence, Congress established a special commission to decide which returns were valid. The commission was composed of seven Republicans, seven Democrats, and one independent, but when the independent could not serve, another Republican was named. The vote to give all 20 electoral votes and thus the presidency to Hayes was 8 to 7, following strict party lines. Democrats were outraged, and a constitutional crisis seemed in the making if a united Democratic front in Congress rejected the commission's findings.

A series of agreements between Hayes's advisors and southern Democratic congressmen averted the crisis. In what came to be called the "Compromise of 1877," Hayes agreed to support federal aid for southern internal improvements, especially a transcontinental

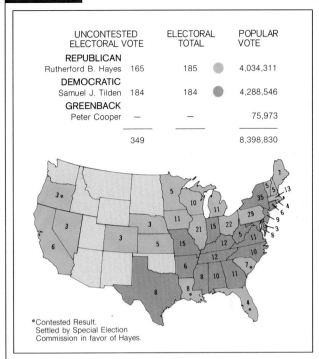

UNCONTESTED ELECTORAL VOTE	ELECTORAL TOTAL	POPULAR VOTE
REPUBLICAN		
Rutherford B. Hayes 165	185	4,034,311
DEMOCRATIC		
Samuel J. Tilden 184	184	4,288,546
GREENBACK		
Peter Cooper —	—	75,973
349		8,398,830

*Contested Result.
Settled by Special Election
Commission in favor of Hayes.

Election of 1876

railroad. He also promised to appoint a southern Democrat to his cabinet and to allow southern Democrats a say in the allocation of federal offices in their region. Most important, however, was his pledge to remove the remaining federal troops from the South. In return, the Democrats supported the findings of the electoral commission, and Hayes became president.

Scholars once considered the Compromise of 1877 an important factor in the end of Reconstruction. Actually, its role was more symbolic than real; it merely buried the corpse. The battle for the Republican party's soul had been lost by its abolitionist faction well before the election of 1876. The Democratic party had never sought to extend or protect blacks' rights. The Supreme Court began to interpret the Fourteenth and Fifteenth amendments very narrowly—stripping them of their strength. Thus black Americans were left with a small number of allies, and one by one many of their rights were lost during the next four decades.

CHRONOLOGY OF KEY EVENTS

1863 Emancipation Proclamation issued; Lincoln's Proclamation of Amnesty and Reconstruction

1865 Freedmen's Bureau established; Wade-Davis Bill passed and vetoed; Lee surrenders at Appomattox; Lincoln assassinated; Johnson's Proclamation of Amnesty begins presidential reconstruction; Black Codes enacted; Ratification of the Thirteenth Amendment ends slavery

1866 Ku Klux Klan founded; American Equal Rights Association started

1867 First Reconstruction Acts begin congressional reconstruction

1868 Conviction of Johnson falls short by one vote; Indian Peace Commission conference that leads to establishing reservations in Oklahoma and the Black Hills; Ratification of the Fourteenth Amendment

1870 Ratification of the Fifteenth Amendment

1872 Sioux Wars

1875 Civil Rights Act Passed

1876 Custer defeated at Little Big Horn; Disputed election between Tilden and Hayes

1877 Hayes removes remaining troops from the South

CONCLUSION

As the Civil War closed, many unresolved issues remained. The most crucial two involved the status of the freedmen and of the former Confederate states. The destinies of both were inextricably intertwined. Anything affecting the status of either influenced the fate of the other. Quick readmission of the states with little change would doom black rights. Enforced equality of blacks under the law would create turbulence and drastic change in the South. This difficult problem was further complicated by constitutional, economic, and political considerations, ensuring that the course of Reconstruction would be chaotic and contradictory.

Presidential Reconstruction under both Lincoln and Johnson favored rapid reunification and white unity more than changes in the racial structure of the South. The South, however, refused to accept even the end of slavery, as was blatantly demonstrated by the Black Codes. Congressional desire to reestablish legislative supremacy and the Republican need to build a national party combined with this southern intransigence to unite Radical and moderate Republicans on the need to protect black rights and to restructure the South. What emerged from congressional reconstruction were Republican governments that expanded democracy and enacted needed reforms, but were deeply resented by many southern whites. At the core of that resentment was not disgust over incompetence or corruption, but hostility to black political power in any form.

Given the pervasiveness of racial prejudice, what is remarkable is not that the Freedmen's Bureau, the constitutional amendments, and the civil rights legislation did not produce permanent change, but that these actions were taken at all. Cherished ideas of property rights, limited government, and self-reliance as well as an almost universal belief in black inferiority almost guaranteed that the experiment would fail. The first national attempt to resolve fairly and justly the question of minority rights in a pluralistic society was abandoned in less than a decade. Indians, blacks, and women saw the truth of the Alabama planter's words of 1865: "Poor elk—poor buffaloe—poor Indian—poor

Nigger—this is indeed a white man country." Nevertheless, less than a century later seeds planted by the amendments would finally germinate, flower, and be harvested.

REVIEW SUMMARY

The issue of racial equity was the main arena in the struggle to control the South's postwar destiny. Both Lincoln and Johnson offered the white South rather lenient terms for readmittance to the Union, but Southerners resisted all changes. This led Congress to enact stronger measures to protect the basic rights of blacks and to ensure loyal governments in the South.

- ratification of the Fourteenth and Fifteenth Amendments
- passage of the Reconstruction Acts
- supporting reform-minded Republican governments in the southern states

This mood did not last long. Preoccupied with economic development and western expansion, white Americans lost interest in Reconstruction issues, and the prevalence of racism caused the rights of blacks to be ignored or trampled.

SUGGESTIONS FOR FURTHER READING

POSTWAR CONDITIONS AND ISSUES

W. E. B. DuBois, *Black Reconstruction* (1935); Eric Foner, *Politics and Ideology in the Age of the Civil War* (1980); John Hope Franklin, *Reconstruction After the Civil War* (1961); Peter Kolchin, *First Freedom* (1974); Morgan Kousser and James McPherson, ed., *Region, Race, and Reconstruction* (1982); Leon Litwack, *Been in the Storm So Long* (1980); James M. McPherson, *Ordeal by Fire* (1982); Rembert W. Patrick, *Reconstruction and the Nation* (1967); James G. Randall and David Donald, *Civil War and Reconstruction* (1969); James Roark, *Masters Without Slaves* (1977); Willie Lee Rose, *Rehearsal for Reconstruction* (1964); Kenneth Stampp, *The Era of Reconstruction* (1965).

PRESIDENTIAL RECONSTRUCTION

William R. Brock, *An American Crisis* (1963); LaWanda Cox, *Lincoln and Black Freedom* (1981); John H. and Lawanda Cox, *Politics, Principles, and Prejudice* (1963); David Donald, *The Politics of Reconstruction* (1965); William B. Hesseltine, *Lincoln's Plan of Reconstruction*

(1960); Peyton McCrary, *Abraham Lincoln and Reconstruction* (1978); Eric McKitrick, *Andrew Johnson and Reconstruction* (1960); Patrick W. Riddleburger, *1866: The Critical Year Revisited* (1979); James Sefton, *The United States Army and Reconstruction* (1967).

CONGRESSIONAL RECONSTRUCTION

Herman Belz, *Reconstructing the Union* (1960); Michael L. Benedict, *A Compromise of Principle* (1974) and *The Impeachment of Andrew Johnson* (1973); Fawn M. Brodie, *Thaddeus Stevens* (1959); David Donald, *Charles Sumner and the Rights of Man* (1970); Ellen DuBois, *Feminism and Suffrage* (1978); Stanley I. Kutler, *The Judicial Power and Reconstruction Politics* (1968); Hans L. Trefousse, *Impeachment of a President* (1975) and *The Radical Republicans* (1969).

RECONSTRUCTION IN THE SOUTH

Stephen J. DeCanio, *Agriculture in the Postbellum South* (1974); Paul D. Escott, *Many Excellent People* (1985); Eric Foner, *Nothing But Freedom* (1983); Herbert G. Gutman, *The Black Family in Slavery and Freedom* (1976); Stephen Hahn, *The Roots of Southern Populism* (1983); William C. Harris, *The Day of the Carpetbagger* (1979); Thomas Holt, *Black Over White* (1977); Jay R. Mandle, *The Roots of Black Poverty* (1978); Robert C. Morris, *Reading, 'Riting, and Reconstruction* (1981); Otto H. Olson, ed., *Reconstruction and Redemption in the South* (1980); Howard Rabinowitz, *Race Relations in the Urban South* (1978); Roger L. Ransom and Richard Sutch, *One Kind of Freedom: The Economic Consequences of Emancipation* (1977); Joe Gray Taylor, *Louisiana Reconstructed* (1975); Allen Trelease, *White Terror* (1971); Ted Tunnell, *Crucible of Reconstruction* (1981); Sarah Woolfolk Wiggins, *The Scalawag in Alabama Politics* (1977).

RETREAT FROM RECONSTRUCTION

Ralph K. Andrist, *The Long Death: The Last Days of the Plains Indians* (1964); Robert F. Berkhofer, *The White Man's Indian* (1978); Eugene H. Berwanger, *The West and Reconstruction* (1981); Charles Fairman, *Reconstruction and Reunion* (1971); William Gillette, *Retreat from Reconstruction* (1979) and *The Right to Vote* (1969); Norris Handley, Jr., ed., *The American Indian* (1974); Eric S. Lunde, *Horace Greeley* (1980); William McFeeley, *Grant: A Biography* (1981); John G. Neihardt, *Black Elk Speaks* (1932); Keith Ian Polakoff, *The Politics of Inertia* (1973); Nell Irvin Painter, *The Exodusters* (1978); Francis Paul Prucha, *American Indian Policy in Crisis* (1976); Ronald T. Takaki, *Iron Cages* (1979); Mark W. Summers, *Railroads, Reconstruction and the Gospel of Prosperity* (1984); Wilcomb E. Washburn, *The Indian in North America* (1975) and *Red Man's Land/White Man's Law* (1971); C. Vann Woodward, *Reunion and Reaction* (1951).

Sitting Bull

GLIDDEN'S PATENT
STEEL BARB FENCE WIRE

GALVANIZED or JAPANNED

On a cold winter's night in December 1900, seventy-five of the richest, most influential American businessmen gathered at the New York University Club. They met for a testimonial dinner in honor of Charles Schwab, president of Carnegie Steel Company. Seated to the honoree's right was J. P. Morgan, the powerful investment banker and consolidator of industry. He had been placed there so that he would not miss a word of Schwab's speech. When Schwab finally rose, he delivered a verbal bombshell lobbed with feigned innocence at the entire structure of the steel industry. In his speech he rhapsodized over low prices and stability for steel. This future was to be ushered in by a scientifically integrated firm which would supplant numerous companies—many of which produced more stock certificates than steel.

Morgan did not miss the point. For several years he and others had been busily creating trusts among the producers of such finished steel products as tubes and wire. Through trusts, they hoped to unite or eliminate competitors in order to raise prices. Andrew Carnegie's company was the largest supplier of raw steel to such companies, and he hated trusts. Thus when American Tin Plate Company threatened to cancel its orders with Carnegie unless he refused to sell to its competitors, he decided to beat them at their own game. He joined several informal arrangements to fix prices, known as "pools," only to sabotage them from within. Morgan and his cohorts soon realized that depending on Carnegie for raw steel would doom their consolidation schemes. Consequently, in July 1900 National Tube, American Steel and Wire, and American Hoop canceled all their contracts with Carnegie. They were going to produce their own steel or buy it from others—and put Carnegie out of business.

Rather than surrender, Carnegie telegraphed instructions to his company's officers: "Crisis has arrived, only one policy open; start at once hoop, wire, nail mills . . . Extend coal and coke roads, announce these; also tubes . . . Have no fear as to result, victory certain. Spend freely for finishing mills, railroads, boat lines." By continuing his policy of spending money to make money, Carnegie knew he could produce superior products at cheaper prices. After Schwab assured him that they could manufacture tubes at a price $10 a ton cheaper than National Tube, he decided to pay no dividends on common stock and began plans to build a $12 million tube plant.

The overcapitalized, antiquated, and scattered plants of his competitors would have been no match for Carnegie's new ones. Panicked promoters scurried to J. P. Morgan in the weeks before the testimonial dinner. Few doubted Federal Steel president Elbert Gary's assertion that Carnegie could "have driven entirely out of business every steel company in the United States." Carnegie, however, wanted to retire, and Schwab's speech was aimed at producing a bargain, not a war. After the dinner Morgan fired dozens of questions at Schwab. Later they held an all-night session at Morgan's house. In the early hours of the next day Morgan finally said, "Well, if Andy wants to sell, I'll buy. Go find his price."

Schwab approached Carnegie on the golf course, where he might be more inclined to cooperate. Carnegie listened and asked Schwab to return the next day for an answer. At that time Carnegie handed him a slip of paper with his asking price of $480,000,000 written in pencil. When Schwab gave Morgan the offer, he glanced at it and replied, "I accept the price." A few days later Morgan stopped by Carnegie's office, shook hands on the deal and stated, "Mr. Carnegie, I want to congratulate you on being the richest man in the world."

Two of the best had locked in combat, and both were victors. Carnegie had his millions to endow libraries, and anything else that struck his fancy. Morgan founded United States Steel Corporation. A colossus even among the existing giants of American industry, it was capitalized at $1.4 billion, a figure three times larger than the annual budget of the United States. The fates of Carnegie and Morgan reflected the momentous changes after the Civil War. Moving from the ranks of second-rate industrial powers, by 1900 the nation was the leader—with a manufacturing output exceeding the combined total of Great Britain, France, and Germany. The speed with which this happened seems more suited to fairy tales than reality. As Andrew Carnegie exclaimed in 1886, "The old nations of the earth creep on at a snail's pace; the Republic thunders past with the rush of an express."

Many yardsticks supported his assertion. Between 1870 and 1914 railroad mileage increased from 53,000 to 250,000 miles—more than the combined mileage of the rest of the world. Almost every sector of the economy grew in multiples of two or more from the 1860s to 1900. Land under agricultural production doubled; the Gross National Product was six times larger; the amount of manufactured goods per person tripled.

This phenomenal growth resulted from the foundations laid by antebellum industrial development, the abundance of the land and its people, technological breakthroughs, and a favorable business climate—ideologically, financially, legally, and politically. The rapidity of change produced chaotic conditions, which led to new managerial styles and finally to economic consolidation and the rise of such supercorporations as United States Steel.

The forces of economic modernization swept through all sections and all segments of the economy. The results were profound alterations of the social order that touched virtually every aspect of life. Much of what is now commonplace—electric lights, petroleum, the telephone, the skyscraper, the camera, the typewriter—was largely unknown prior to the Civil War. The natures of work and marketing were drastically transformed, affecting all social relationships. The new order produced a few big winners such as Carnegie and Morgan, but there were losers, too.

AMERICA: LAND OF PLENTY

In 1847 Walt Whitman boasted, "Yankeedoodledom is going ahead with the resistless energy of a sixty-five-hundred-horse-power steam engine. . . . Let the Old World wag on under its cumbrous load of form and conservatism; we are of a newer, fresher race and land. And all we have to say is, to point to fifty years hence and say, Let those laugh who win." By 1897 Ameri-

Lavish displays of wealth were common in the business world, as in this 1901 dinner meeting of officials of the Carnegie Steel Company to celebrate the formation of U.S. Steel.

cans were laughing. Their victory was facilitated by the abundance of the nation's new land, new people, and new ideas.

Mineral and Geographic Possibilities

Explorers and early settlers in North America were disappointed not to find an abundance of gold and silver such as had enriched their Spanish neighbors to the south. Only in the nineteenth century did Americans begin to realize the vast wealth that their expansionism had brought. Most spectacular was the discovery of gold in California in the 1840s. It sparked frenzied prospecting all through the West. Each new discovery led to "rushes," creating mining towns almost overnight. Between 1850 and the 1880s thousands of men and women of almost every ethnic background helped create makeshift social institutions whenever and wherever strikes were made in California, Nevada, Montana, Idaho, Colorado, and the Black Hills of the Dakotas.

Wherever it moved, the mining frontier tended to follow the same pattern. Adventurous optimists searched for the elusive glint of precious metals. After living weeks or months at subsistence level, many went home poorer. A few, however, did strike it rich—usually as discoverers rather than miners. Inexpensive and inefficient placer mining (washing loose ore from gravel) quickly exhausted the easily obtainable supplies of precious metals. Extracting ore beneath the ground and in veins of quartz was expensive. It required large capital investments best raised by mining syndicates, which were frequently financed by eastern and European investors. Prospectors usually sold their claims to these companies for a fraction of their value.

As mining became an organized business, its focus moved to less exotic but more useful minerals such as copper, lead, talc, zinc, quartz, and oil. These fed the growing demands of the industrializing East. By the 1880s mining no longer represented easy riches for pioneering individuals; it had become an integrated part of the modernizing, industrial economy of the nation.

The extraction of the nation's mineral resources played an important role in the rise of basic industry. Prior to the Civil War, manufacturing centered mainly on such consumer goods as textiles, paper, and flour, which were processed from farm or forest materials. Emerging basic industries such as steel, petroleum, and electric power depended upon large supplies of various minerals, which seemed to become available as needed. Sometimes new deposits were found; other times new uses for minerals spurred the mining of known deposits.

Iron working was extensive prior to the war, and major deposits were found from 1850 onward in Michigan and Minnesota. Wrought iron could be forged into plows and other implements. It was limited, however, by its lack of durability and could be used successfully only on farms and in small businesses. Then Andrew Carnegie and others employed technological breakthroughs to produce large quantities of relatively cheap and durable steel. The availability of steel opened new manufacturing vistas, and between 1870 and 1900 the output of

steel grew from 850,000 tons to over 10.5 million tons.

The same pattern developed in the mining of other minerals. Copper had been found in Michigan prior to the war and in Arizona in the 1870s. A much richer copper deposit was discovered in Butte, Montana, in 1881. At first mainly used for household products, copper became a key ingredient in such new fields as oil refining, electrical generation and conduction, and telephone communications. Most went into the miles and miles of wiring that electrified the cities. The new uses for copper modernized America and increased demand for the mineral. Its output grew from 8000 tons in 1860 to 800,000 tons in 1914, and by 1900 the annual value of copper production almost equaled that of gold and silver combined.

Coal mining had also been a minor enterprise before 1850, but its production grew from about a half million tons in 1860 to 270 million tons in 1900. Its spectacular rise was generated by the increased use of coal-burning steam engines to power machinery and locomotives. In 1876 visitors to the Philadelphia Centennial Exhibition were awed by the massive Corliss reciprocating machine with its thirty-foot fly

At the Philadelphia Centennial Exhibition of 1876, visitors gaped at the gigantic Corliss reciprocating steam engine. With a fly wheel thirty feet in diameter, it powered all the equipment in Machinery Hall.

wheel. Its size was no more impressive than the change it symbolized. As late as 1869 almost half of all power used in manufacturing came from water wheels; by 1900 coal-burning steam engines supplied eighty percent of such power. Earlier dependence on water supplies had forced manufacturers to locate along rivers—often in rather sparsely populated rural areas. The steam engine, and later the gasoline and electric engines, allowed new freedom in selecting plant sites, and manufacturing began to move to the cities that supplied both workers and transportation connections.

Even more dramatic was the rise of petroleum. Many people were aware of large reserves in Pennsylvania, which seeped into streams and springs, but demand was mainly limited to such uses as patent medicines of dubious value. In 1855 Pennsylvania businessman George Bissell decided to explore other possible uses. He sent a sample to a Yale professor who hailed its potential use as both a lighting source and lubricating oil. Encouraged by that report, Bissell funded drilling efforts, and in 1859 his employee, Edwin L. Drake, tapped the first oil well in Titusville, Pennsylvania. Commonly labeled "Drake's folly," it marked the beginning of another growing industry. Oil was needed to lubricate the increasing number of machine parts, and in the 1870s about 20 million barrels were being produced annually. After John D. Rockefeller and others began refining oil into kerosene, it also provided a popular form of illumination, displacing candles before being replaced by electricity.

An officer in Rockefeller's Standard Oil Company is reputed to have volunteered to drink all oil ever found outside of Pennsylvania. He was fortunate that no one held him to his word. Although for the rest of the century most of the nation's oil continued to come from the Appalachian area and the Midwest, growing demand led to the search for "liquid gold" in the Southwest. In 1901 a well shot a 160-foot stream of oil into the air at Spindletop, Texas. New sources were thus available for the development of the gasoline engine in the twentieth century. Abundant natural resources and technology often interacted—each shaping the evolution of the other.

Called Drake's Folly, the first oil well was drilled in Titusville, Pennsylvania, in 1859. Edwin Drake (in top hat) got his inspiration from watching salt-well drilling operations.

Technological Change

Seldom has a single generation experienced such rapid change as in the late nineteenth century. Technology dramatically transformed much of their lives. Bewildering as the changes sometimes were, the public generally welcomed new inventions with wide-eyed awe. Some of the most important public events were like mass rituals to the new god of technology. Completion of the first transcontinental railway at Promontory Point, Utah, on May 10, 1869, was greeted with parades and thanksgiving services as well as the ringing of the Liberty Bell. Awed sightseers crammed expositions celebrating "progress." At the Philadelphia Centennial Exposition, visitors confronted for the first time not only the Corliss engine but also Alexander Graham Bell's telephone, bicycles, the type-

The Columbian Exposition of 1893 in Chicago celebrated the enormous technological progress of the late nineteenth century. In the Palace of Electricity many visitors saw their first electric lamp.

writer, the elevator, and even the "floor covering of the future"—linoleum. By the time of the World's Columbian Exposition at Chicago in 1893, the Corliss engine was obsolete, and many of the miracles of 1876 were commonplace "necessities." At the exposition everything was powered by electricity, including 5000 arc lamps and 100,000 incandescent bulbs.

These mass rituals reflected a nationalistic pride, voiced by the Commissioner of Patents in 1892: "America has become known the world around as the home of invention." The patent record definitely supported his contention. Whereas only 276 inventions had been recorded during the Patent Office's first decade in the 1790s, during the single year of the Columbian Exposition 22,000 patents were issued.

The impact of new inventions was enormous. In 1889 an economist wrote that to catalog "what the world did not have half a century ago is almost equivalent to enumerating all those things which the world now regards as constituting the dividing lines between civiliza-

tion and barbarism." Technological change affected the lives of individuals far more than any political or philosophical development of the era. Even a select list of late nineteenth-century inventions would fill numerous pages. Offices became mechanized with the invention of the typewriter in 1867 and the development of a practical adding machine in 1888. As clerical work became more needed as well as requiring less skill, it was classed as women's work with lower pay scales. Numerous inventions such as George Westinghouse's air brake, which made longer, faster trains possible, revolutionized railroad transportation. Later, electric streetcars profoundly changed the character of urban development by enhancing the rise of suburbs.

Along with transportation changes, communication innovations welded a unified nation from a collection of island communities. Links with the rest of the world also increased when an Atlantic telegraphic cable was completed in 1866. New inventions in the field of printing made popular newspapers with wide circulations a reality—along with mass advertising. Photographic advances culminated in George Eastman's Kodak hand-held camera in 1888. However, few, if any, inventions rivaled the importance of Bell's 1876 "toy." Telephones rapidly became necessities—over one and one-half million were installed by 1900.

Increasingly, new inventions such as the telephone relied upon cheap and efficient sources of electricity. Here the name of Thomas Edison stands above the rest. Beginning his career at an early age by peddling candy and newspapers on trains, he soon became a telegrapher and discovered various improvements. The success of his ideas convinced him to go into the "invention business." Establishing a research lab at Menlo Park, New Jersey, in 1876, he promised to produce "a minor invention every ten days and a big thing every six months or so." He pretty much kept his promise, inventing the phonograph in 1877 and the incandescent light bulb in 1879, as well as hundreds of other devices such as a better telephone, the dictaphone, the mimeograph, the dynamo, motion pictures, and electric transmission. With backing from banker J. P. Morgan, he created the first electric company in 1882 in New York City and formed the Edison General Electric Company in 1888 to produce light bulbs.

In his Menlo Park, New Jersey, laboratory, Thomas Edison aimed at practicality in his inventions and obtained over 1000 patents. Here he is listening to his phonograph in 1888.

As in all research, Edison followed a number of blind alleys, but his only serious mistake was the choice of direct electrical current. This limited the range of transmission to a radius of about two miles. Westinghouse's development of an alternating current system in 1886 soon supplanted direct current, forcing even Edison's companies to make the switch. Westinghouse also acquired and improved an electric motor that had been invented by a Croatian immigrant named Nikola Tesla in 1888.

While a handful of inventors struck it rich, more often inventions paved the way to vast fortunes for such entrepreneurs as Carnegie. The success of most of the captains of industry came from their effective exploitation of new technology. Carnegie invented no new product but utilized such advances in steel production as the Bessemer and open-hearth processes to produce cheap and plentiful steel. In like manners, Rockefeller built his industrial empire on new refining methods, and Gustavus Swift's meat packing operation depended on the invention of the refrigerated railroad car. Eventually machine-made, interchangeable parts revolutionized every industry with the increased use of mass production.

The course of United States industrialism was profoundly influenced by the relative abundance of natural resources and scarcity of manpower. In the beginning Americans burned wood extravagantly. Later, seemingly inexhaustible supplies of coal and metal ores continued the bias toward labor-saving and material-consuming technology. Thus while population only tripled, industrial output grew nine times larger between 1860 and 1914. Population changes and growth, however, played an important role in the expanding economy.

Population Patterns and the New Industrial Workforce

Technology produced machines that displaced many skilled craftsmen and farmers, but paid employment also increased. For example, by the 1890s mechanization allowed one farmer to harvest eighteen times as much wheat as he had done by hand in 1830. Nevertheless, the needs of a rapidly expanding population created so many new markets that the agricultural workforce still grew by fifty percent. At the same time nonagricultural employment rose 300 percent. As early as 1880 the number of people employed in manufacturing, transportation, and construction grew to 5 million from only 1.5 a generation earlier. During the next decade, farmers became a minority for the first time, and by 1900 six out of every ten Americans made their living outside of agriculture.

Those not engaged in farming increasingly concentrated in the cities. Between 1860 and 1900 urban residents increased from 6 million to 24 million. This clustering of population was essential to the expansion of industry—both feeding it and being fed by it. Some economic historians contend that of all the factors spurring growth none was more important than the rise of an American mass market. Both the urban population boom and the transportation revolution created markets unparalleled in vastness and accessibility.

Mass markets would not have inevitably led to mass production and mass marketing without the public's acceptance of standardized goods. Several factors made Americans more receptive than Europeans to such goods. Class

Many people were lured to the cities with the promise of excitement, modern conveniences, and better, higher-paying jobs.

distinctions, though not absent, were more blurred and became increasingly so with the rise of ready-made clothing. Also, physical mobility broke down many of the local loyalties so prevalent in Europe. Such forces created opportunities that modern mass advertising exploited. Nowhere were changes greater than in the food industry. Food processors originally produced limited quantities for nearby markets. As transportation advances widened distribution areas, producers first relied on wholesale merchants and agents to sell their goods to the public. Then the marketing of consumer goods underwent a remarkable transformation. The communication revolution allowed manufacturers to peddle their wares directly to the consumer. Rather than selling nonperishable foods by the barrel to wholesalers, they now packaged them in smaller containers of standard size and weight. By 1900, $90 million was being spent annually to convince Americans of the advantages of specific brand names; modern advertising had embarked on its persistent quest to shape the tastes of the public.

Advertising increased demand for many products, creating more industrial jobs for urban consumers. The dramatic expansion of this industrial workforce was fed mainly by massive migration to the cities. Although more people were being born than were dying in American cities, the natural increase of the urban population accounted for no more than one-fifth of its growth. This was true for several reasons. A declining fertility rate reduced the number of children produced by the average woman from over 7 in 1800 to 3.6 in 1900, and this decline was most pronounced in the cities, where more women worked outside the home and had access to birth control information. Also, infectious disease led to higher death rates in the cities; an 1890 report revealed that twenty-four percent of the babies born in cities died in their first year.

The migration accounting for four-fifths of urban population growth came from two sources: internal migration and foreign immigration. Some eight or nine million of the eighteen million new urban residents were probably migrants from rural America. They moved for a variety of reasons. One was an increasing surplus of young men and women in the countryside. Rural birth rates remained high while mechanization decreased the number of hands needed to produce a crop. Such surpluses naturally "pushed" people from rural areas, but the cities also "pulled" them with the promise of more excitement, variety, and modern conveniences. Urban jobs also paid more; in 1890 clerical workers earned almost four times as much as farm laborers. While the average agricultural laborer earned $244 a year, clerical workers averaged $848.

Internal migration, however, did little to meet the five-fold increase in demand for industrial labor. Even before the Civil War native-born Americans could no longer be lured in sufficient numbers to the factories. Rural white Americans more frequently joined the growing ranks of white-collar workers. Rural black Americans would have gladly taken even the lowest factory job but were passed over in favor of foreign workers. Thus in 1890 only seven percent of black males worked in industry, and as late as 1900 about ninety percent of black Americans remained in the South—the least urbanized section of the nation.

Unlike industrializing European nations, therefore, the United States did not rely primarily on its own population to produce its industrial workforce. The "pull" of these job opportunities and factors "pushing" Europeans out of their native countries produced a virtual flood of immigration. Some European villages lost half their residents as 14 million people came to the United States. The large numbers fostered industrialization but eventually produced a backlash from native-born Americans (see Chapter 17).

America's "newer, fresher race and land" provided the material basis for economic expansion. The "Land of Plenty" produced resources, people, and machinery in seemingly inexhaustible amounts. Nevertheless, even such wealth does not adequately explain the phenomenal mushrooming of American industry or the rise of large corporations. Less tangible developments nurtured the fantastic growth rate.

A FAVORABLE CLIMATE: THE ROLE OF IDEOLOGY, POLITICS, AND FINANCE

People, materials, and machinery were the "seeds" of industrialization. For a good harvest, however, good soil, favorable climatic conditions, and adequate fertilization were required. The bountiful economic harvest of the late nineteenth century depended on the "good soil" of popular support fostered by intellectual and cultural justifications. Favorable governmental policies created a desirable climate, while legal and financial developments provided the needed "fertilizer." The combination produced not only more industries but also larger industries. In 1870 shops and factories had an average of eight employees. Thirty years later the average workforce was four times as large, and approximately 1450 factories employed 500 or more workers.

Social Darwinism and the Gospel of Wealth

Expanding economic opportunities fostered cut-throat competition from which fewer and fewer winners emerged. The road to wealth by the new captains of industry was strewn with ruined competitors and broken labor movements. Ruthlessness not only became increasingly necessary, it was also transformed into a virtue by the twin ideologies of Social Darwinism and the Gospel of Wealth.

For such men as Andrew Carnegie the works of Social Darwinists Herbert Spencer and William Graham Sumner helped to relieve any unwelcome guilt. "I remember that light came as in a flood and all was clear," Carnegie later recalled about his reaction to Spencer's writings. Spencer and his followers applied the biological concepts of Charles Darwin to the workings of society. Just as competition for survival insured that the fittest of a species would live longer and produce more offspring, a similar process of natural selection in society was said to cause the fittest individuals to survive and flourish in the marketplace. Survival of the fit-

This portrait of the family of William Astor illustrates that the rich lived lavishly. Parties of the wealthy were especially ostentatious; at one guests smoked cigarettes rolled in hundred dollar bills after coffee.

test not only enriched the winners but also society as a whole. Human evolution would produce what Spencer called "the ultimate and inevitable development of the ideal man" through a culling process. "If [individuals] are sufficiently complete to live, they do live," he wrote, "and it is well that they should live. If they are not sufficiently complete to live, they die and it is best they should die."

According to the Social Darwinists, poverty and slums were as inevitable as the concentration of wealth in the hands of the "fittest." Spencer pleaded that "there should not be a forcible burdening of the superior for the support of the inferior." His disciple Sumner declared, "If we do not like the survival of the fittest, we have only one possible alternative, and that is the survival of the unfittest." In other words, governmental or charitable intervention to improve the conditions of the poor interfered with the functioning of natural law and prolonged the life of "defective gene pools" to the detriment of society as a whole.

The so-called fittest naturally greeted "scientific" endorsement of their elite positions with eagerness. Rockefeller told his Baptist Sunday school class, "The growth of large business is merely the survival of the fittest. This is not an evil tendency in Business. It is merely the working out of a law of nature and a law of God." His statement illustrates that the captains of industry did not rely solely on science for justification; they also looked to religion. Indeed, although some businessmen used the jargon of Darwinism, Andrew Carnegie was one of the few actually to read and understand the dense, obtuse writings of Spencer.

Few business leaders were intellectuals, and some who understood Darwinist principles found the ruthlessness of the theory an unpalatable justification for their ruthless actions. They sought their solace in religious rationales for the accumulation of great wealth. Since colonial times, the Protestant work ethic had denounced idleness and viewed success as evidence of being among the "elect"—God's chosen people. Building upon this base, apologists constructed the "Gospel of Wealth." Some simply and boldly declared God's sanction of their wealth; Rockefeller asserted, "God gave me my riches." Not surprisingly, Carnegie was the one to produce a written, logically argued rationale. "Not evil, but good, has come to the race," he wrote, "from the accumulation of wealth by those who have the ability and energy that produces it." The masses would waste extra income "on the indulgence of appetite." On the other hand, "Wealth, passing through the hands of the few," Carnegie declared, "can be a much more potent force for the elevation of our race than if it had been distributed in small sums to the people themselves." In other words, the "fittest" at the top could decide for people what they needed better than they could decide for themselves. In Carnegie's case, he took that responsibility seriously with the distribution of his vast wealth to such philanthropic causes as founding libraries.

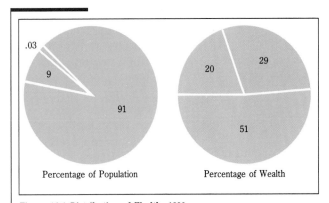

Figure 16.1 Distribution of Wealth, 1890
The bulk of the wealth was concentrated in less than 10 percent of the population, while 0.03 percent controlled 20 percent of the wealth.
George K. Holmes, "The Concentration of Wealth," *Political Science Quarterly,* vol. 8, no. 4, December 1893, p. 593.

As this illustration of the "Ladder of Fortune" (1875) shows, the American people were constantly assured that riches, success, and the favor of God were the rewards for morality and hard work.

Among the most effective apologists for the wealthy, however, were religious leaders of the era. In 1901 Bishop William Lawrence proclaimed, "Godliness is in league with riches." Not only did the elite deserve their riches, but the poor also were responsible for their status. The eminent preacher Henry Ward Beecher argued that "no man suffers from poverty unless it be more than his fault—unless it be his *sin.*" Perhaps the most popular evangelist for the Gospel of Wealth was Russell Conwell, who delivered his celebrated speech "Acres of Diamonds" approximately 6000 times between 1861 and 1925. In it he declared that anyone could get rich and asserted, "I say that you ought to get rich, and it is your duty to get rich." To those preaching sacrifice and vows of poverty, Conwell proclaimed, "It is a mistake of these pious people to think you must be awfully poor in order to be pious." Instead he asserted,

> Money is power, and you ought to be reasonably ambitious to have it. You ought because you can do more good with it than you could without it. Money printed your Bible, money builds your churches, money sends your missionaries, and money pays your preachers. . . . The man who gets the largest salary can do the most good with the power that is furnished to him.

Thus the maldistribution of wealth was not only inevitable but also desirable according to

Horatio Alger stories

both scientific and religious thought. Probably more important was the support provided by popular culture. *McGuffey Readers* continued to stress the virtue of hard work and its inevitable rewards in poems such as "Try, Try Again." Novelist Horatio Alger penned numerous stories whose heroes rose from poverty to comfortable middle class membership through diligence and good fortune. Both reinforced the idea that success always came to those who deserved it and the image of America as a land of opportunity. Finally, economic theory also lent respectability to greed and to the idea that government should not intervene in the economy.

Laissez-faire in Theory and Practice

In 1776 Adam Smith's *The Wealth of Nations* presented arguments that would long be used to explain the workings of a free economy and to prescribe government's role in that economy. Smith asserted that the market was directed and controlled by an "invisible hand" comprised of a multitude of individual choices. If government did not meddle, competition engendered by an unregulated market naturally led to the production of desired goods and services at reasonable prices. Short supply of a good in demand increased the price of that good, thereby encouraging more people to produce it in order to reap large profits. This increased production eventually caused the price to fall as supply equaled or even exceeded demand. In short, if everyone were left free to act according to self-interest, the result would be an economy best suited to meet the needs of general society.

Acceptance of the "invisible hand" of supply and demand economic theory naturally led to a policy called "laissez-faire." Government's proper role was to leave the economy alone. Apologists maintained that any governmental interference inevitably disrupted the operation of the natural forces that ordered the economy—thus producing a disorderly, inefficient market. Businessmen naturally endorsed the theory's rejection of governmental regulation. At the same time, however, they saw no contradiction in asking for government aid and subsidies to foster industrialization. To a large extent the industrialists got what they wanted—a laissez-faire policy that left them alone, except to help. Ironically, this distortion of theory helped to produce an economy where business consolidation wreaked havoc upon the very competition needed for natural regulation of the economy.

Absolute free enterprise never really existed. There was plenty of governmental activity—just not in the area of regulation. Indeed the freedom of action given to businessmen following the Civil War boggles the modern mind. No laws protected the consumer from adulterated foods, spurious claims for ineffective or even dangerous patent medicines, the sale of stock in nonexistent companies, or unsafe and overpriced transportation services. No regulating agency existed prior to the establishment of the Interstate Commerce Commission in 1887. The proclamation "Let the buyer beware" asked people to make decisions and choices without adequate access to the information needed to protect their interests.

Fraudulent claims for patent medicines

While denying support and protection to consumers or workers, government at all levels aided businessmen. Alexander Hamilton's vision of an industrializing nation fostered by favorable governmental action never entirely died and was rejuvenated by the rise of the

Republican party. Among the party's many promises in 1860 were pledges to enact higher tariffs, to subsidize the completion of a transcontinental railroad, and to establish a stable national banking system. The victory of Republican ideology undoubtedly helped to create a favorable environment for rapid industrialization. There was no sharp break with the past, however; nor was there a great victory by business over agriculture. The pattern of governmental aid to business was, as one historian has noted, "like certain kinds of embroidery . . . boldly visible but not of simple design." No form of aid was without antebellum precedents. Many concessions to business had wide public support that crossed party lines, often because other groups also benefited. Both the motives behind many actions and their results were mixed. In addition, the gains from some probusiness legislation were larger on paper than in practice. At the same time, agriculture was far from unrepresented and powerless, as can be seen by the passage of the Homestead and Morrill Land Grant Acts, which provided free land to settlers and financed agricultural education.

Tariffs had a long history. Two days before Lincoln took office, Democratic President Buchanan signed the Morrill Tariff, marking the first increase in the tariff since 1842. That inaugurated an upward, practically uninterrupted, rise in tariff rates for the rest of the century. As the average rate approached fifty percent, the duties on some commodities exceeded eighty percent of foreign manufacturers' prices. Many businessmen received what consumers considered a lavish gift. For example, the duty on steel rails was $28 a ton, allowing American manufacturers to charge $67 a ton even though the English could produce rails at $36 a ton. In 1870 when that tariff was enacted, however, Americans were unable to produce rails at competitive prices. Without protection the rise of the American steel industry would have undoubtedly been hampered. Yet even after Carnegie and others were able to greatly reduce the cost of steel production, the tariff remained— allowing higher profits at the expense of consumers. Such bonanzas should not, however, obscure the fact that tariffs were widely viewed

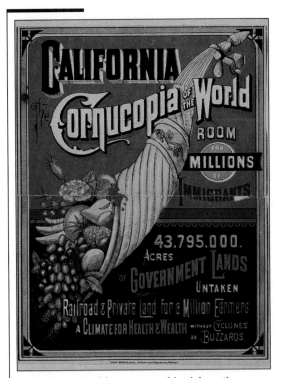

Railroads received huge tracts of land from the government to finance construction. This poster advertised over 43 million acres of land for sale in California.

as serving the national interest by fostering economic independence from the British and others.

Other forms of subsidy were also meant to serve the public good. Dwarfing all others were the land grants to railroads. In 1862 and 1864 Congress granted twenty square miles of public land in alternating sections for each mile of track laid by the Union Pacific and Central Pacific railroads in order to speed the completion of a transcontinental route. Only the scale of these grants was new; prior to the war railroads had already received nearly 20 million acres of federal land. By the time the grants ended, a total of 130 million acres of federal land went to various railroads, along with some 51 million acres of state land. Congress gave all those acres to a handful of people—creating some of America's wealthiest families. Nevertheless, as the 1869 celebrations of the completion of the first transcontinental line reflected, the public was not outraged. After all, even that incredible number of acres constituted less than seven percent of the national domain in the West. In return the government paid only half fare to move troops and supplies. In addition, the value of the remaining land increased, and the uniting of the East and West spurred the entire economy. Only a decade after the grants' end were they denounced.

Business also benefited from favorable labor and financial legislation as well as low interest loans. Individuals exploited these policies for personal gain, and the results were not uniformly positive. Aid to business, however, was never unlimited or unrestricted, and it enjoyed wide public support at first. Indeed nationalism infused the process of industrialization. Many Americans took pride in the nation's growing economic power. When John D. Rockefeller explained his business activities by saying, "I wanted to participate in the work of making our country great," his words fell on sympathetic ears. Only after the problems of industrialization became more apparent did the public begin to cry "foul."

Corporations and Capital Formation

Why the government aided business was not as important as the results of that aid. In the same manner, legal and financial developments were largely ignored until they began to bear bitter fruit for some people. One such occurrence was the rise of the corporation and decline of individual ownership and partnerships.

Corporations were certainly not new; they had long been used to finance ventures too expensive or too risky for a single individual to undertake—such as the English colonization of the New World. There were many advantages to incorporation for large-scale enterprises. By selling "shares" to a multitude of individual investors, the great sums of capital needed by modern industry could be amassed. Corporations did not risk the disruption of operation due to death of a partner or arguments between partners. Individuals could also hedge their bets. Rather than using all one's capital to buy a single ship, for example, one could buy a ten percent interest in ten ships. Thus a hurricane

or pirates could not wipe out one's investment with a bout of bad luck.

Despite the long history of corporations, changes dating from the Jacksonian period paved the way for their postwar domination of the economy. The first of these changes was the shift from the old practice of states issuing individual charters to each corporation. New standard corporation laws allowed businessmen to incorporate on their own, provided they met the requirements of the laws. Following the Civil War, courts also began to affirm the principle of "limited liability." Previously, bankruptcy could bring not only the loss of one's investment but also seizure of personal property by creditors. A corporation's liability finally became limited to its assets—making investment a safer and more desirable venture. One knew just how much could be lost.

One favorable court decision, *Santa Clara County* v. *The Southern Pacific Railroad* (1883), was a perversion of the Fourteenth Amendment. The Court ruled that a corporation was a legal "person" and therefore entitled to all the protections granted by the amendment. States could not deny corporations "equal protection of the law" or deprive them of their rights or property without "due process" of the law. In other words, all regulations had to apply equally to flesh-and-blood persons and to corporations. Corporations were eventually granted the "right" to "reasonable" profits—to be determined by the courts, not the state.

Instead of receiving "equal protection," corporations actually became privileged members of society. Real people whose rights were protected by the Constitution were also held personally responsible for illegal activities. There were no handcuffs or jail cells large enough for "corporate persons." Punishing individuals for corporate crimes was also difficult, because corporate directors acted merely as employees of the company. A popular saying noted that a corporation had neither a soul to be damned nor a body to be kicked. Such advantages helped to spur the growth of corporations; by 1904 almost seventy percent of all manufacturing employees worked for corporations.

Perhaps the greatest advantage of corporations remained the ability to raise large

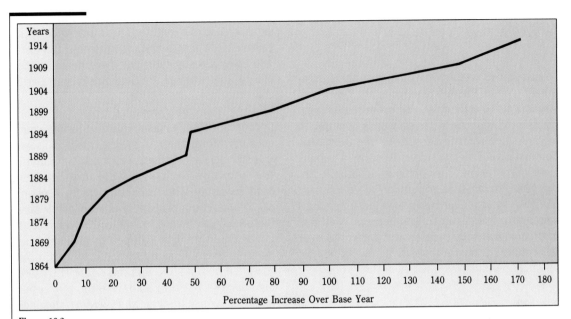

Figure 16.2
Index of Manufacturing Production, 1864–1914

amounts of capital. The expansion of industry in the late nineteenth century required big infusions of money. Every sector of the economy demanded capital: farmers needed new machinery to increase productivity, manufacturers needed new plants to utilize the latest technology, cities needed new construction to service the needs of the urban population.

From where was all this money to come? Some, of course, was generated by the rising Gross National Product, which grew from $225 per person in 1870 to nearly $500 in 1900. Technologically increased productivity put more money into the hands of people—"extra money" not needed to meet physical needs. Their collective decision on its use laid the foundations for the modern American economy. Many chose to use their "extra money," or capital, to make more money by investment. The result was "capital deepening." An increasing share of the national income was invested rather than spent for personal consumption. Indeed the proportion of income going to capital formation almost doubled from fifteen percent at the time of the war to twenty-nine percent in the 1880s.

Increasing amounts of this capital were in-

vested in manufacturing. One reason was the role of investment bankers such as J. P. Morgan, who marketed corporate stocks and bonds. Foreign investment was also important; by 1900 Europeans had $3.4 billion invested in the United States, which represented approximately one-third of the almost $10 billion invested in manufacturing. This was rich fertilizer indeed for growth.

The net result of the favorable conditions of the late nineteenth century was industrial supremacy. Americans reveled in their nation's transformation to a colossus outproducing the entire world. Vast mineral wealth, technological breakthroughs, population changes, popular support, beneficial government policies, liberal corporation laws, and the availability of capital fostered this transformation. Many of these factors not only influenced the speed and size of the industrial "harvest" but also the nature of the fruit. At first the favorable conditions worked like overfertilized land—producing too many plants for the available space and resources. In this overgrown industrial garden competition created chaos until such people as Andrew Carnegie found ways to prune away their rivals.

ECONOMIC GROWTH AND CONSOLIDATION

"You might as well endeavor to stay the formation of clouds, the falling of rains, the flowing of streams, as to attempt . . . to prevent the organization of industry." These words of John D. Rockefeller's attorney described the inevitable domination of entire industries by a single, large corporation. That point is debatable, but the fact remains that in industry after industry men like Rockefeller and Carnegie eliminated competitors and controlled markets. Methods of domination were refined and perfected over the course of time. A look at the evolution of a few major industries illustrates the process.

Railroads

Americans developed a love/hate relationship with the railroads. The same locomotive that inspired Walt Whitman's rhapsody to its "fierce-throated beauty" was described by Frank Norris in 1901 as "the leviathan, with tentacles of steel clutching into the soil, the soulless Force, the iron-hearted Power, the Master, the Colos-

sus, the Octopus." There might be differing visions, but no one doubted the importance of the railroads. "The generation between 1865 and 1895 was already mortgaged to the railroads," Henry Adams wrote, "and no one knew it better than the generation itself."

The railroads provoked strong emotions because of their crucial role in forging a new society. More than anything else, railroads transformed a continent of isolated communities into a unified nation with an interdependent economy. Their rails brought raw materials to population centers, making possible large factories which mass produced goods. Those goods could then be shipped to national mass markets over the same rails. Not only did railroadmen help lay the foundation for the rise of big business, but they also were the pioneers of business consolidation and modern management styles. The trails they blazed became well worn by the turn of the century.

The early railroads were strictly local affairs. By 1865 there were already 35,000 miles of rails but few linked up in any rational way. Eleven different gauges of rail caused both goods and passengers to be unloaded from one set of cars and reloaded on another set— sometimes at a depot on the opposite side of town. Between New York and Chicago, cargo had to be unloaded and reloaded as many as six times. In some cases the inefficiency was intentional. Many small antebellum roads purposely adopted different gauges and conflicting schedules to prevent being swallowed up by larger, powerful competitors.

Unlike many European rail systems, American railroads grew with little advance planning or regulation by government. Their development was far from orderly, and they sprouted like weeds in populous areas where immediate profits could be made. Especially in the antebellum South too many small lines serviced the same places. Four hundred companies sprang up—each with an average track length of a mere forty miles. Twenty lines provided service between Atlanta and St. Louis. The inevitable result was rate wars that prevented any southern railroad from being financially secure.

Such glutting of markets produced chaos and cut-throat competition in the emerging

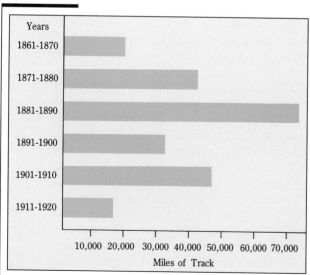

Figure 16.3
Railroad Construction, 1861–1920
U.S. Bureau of the Census, 1975.

After a period of intense competition in the railroad industry, a few rail barons consolidated lines by often ruthless methods, seemingly carving up the nation at will.

basic industries. As the first really big businesses, railroads first confronted the problem. Consolidation of competing railroads may have served the public interest in the long run, but the methods used were frequently less than pure. Some rival railroads sought to establish "pools" to divide traffic and raise rates. Such cooperation between competitors, however, was not legally enforceable. Greed doomed many such agreements.

Most consolidation came from eliminating competition rather than cooperation. The former shipping magnate Cornelius Vanderbilt gained control of the New York Central Railroad in 1867 by buying two key lines that connected with it. He then refused to accept any rail cars going to or from the Central. His embargo worked but was much criticized. Vanderbilt's response was, "Can't I do what I want with my own?" He proceeded to acquire more lines to connect New York with Chicago and beyond. The net result of his ruthlessness was a personal fortune and an efficient, well-constructed railway system.

The battle for control of the railroads in the East was not always so flamboyant, but the results were the same. When the dust settled, there were four main trunklines in the Northeast and five in the Southeast. The average track length of a railroad grew from a mere 100 miles in 1865 to over 1000 in two decades. Seven major groups controlled over two-thirds of the nation's railroad mileage.

One reason for the consolidation movement was the huge amount of capital required for construction. Competition needed to be limited to ensure an adequate return on the investment. Railroads' capital needs also hastened the rise of the corporation. Few individuals had $50 million to build the Erie Railroad. Without corporations a united rail network would have been a long time coming. Sometimes, however, the sale of stock became a business of its own. Without any regulations on the sale of securities, stock did not have to be backed with assets. Daniel Drew dabbled in cattle as well as railroads and was reputed to have fed his herds salt to make them drink lots of water, thereby increasing their weight at sale by as much as fifty pounds. The sale of stock not backed by assets became known as "watering stock." One-third of the stock issued in 1885 probably exceeded the value of assets held by the companies issuing the stock.

The construction of the railroads of the East required large amounts of capital, but a return on the investment came quickly. This was not true in the West. There railroads often preceded settlement and, therefore, traffic for their lines. Because of the need for transcontinental routes, land grants became the solution. Contemporary and later analysts have questioned the size of those grants, but they undoubtedly had the desired effect. By the turn of the century there were five transcontinental routes.

Unlike factories, railroad operations could not be centralized at a single location. Their activities covered hundreds of miles and employed thousands of workers. Safety and market conditions also required the entire system to operate as a single unit under a tight schedule. These conditions caused managerial problems. In the beginning, as one railroad expert wrote, "management had been personal and autocratic; the superintendent, a man gifted with energy and clearness of perception, moulded the property to his own will. But as the properties grew, he found himself unable to give his personal attention to everything. Undaunted, he sought to do everything and do it well. He ended by doing nothing."

In 1854 Erie Railroad employee Daniel McCallum sought solutions to these problems and developed a more efficient system of management. He divided the railway into manageable geographic units with a communication system to route information effectively. Management was separated from daily operations, and responsibilities were divided on a functional basis. Later the Louisville and Nashville Railroad adopted a cost-accounting system. These efforts to deal with the special problems of the industry created new management styles that would aid other large-scale businesses.

The power and influence of the railroads touched many phases of American life. Some actions benefited the nation but were taken in a high-handed manner. For example, before the 1880s each location determined its time by the position of the sun. Even in cities fairly close together clocks were set differently; New York City and Boston were twelve minutes apart. To simplify schedules, in 1883 railroad men established four time zones—without consulting any branch of government.

Such arbitrary power alarmed the American public. Some of the freewheeling railroad barons aggravated fears. Vanderbilt once remarked, "What do I care about the law? Hain't I got the power?" Another time a member of the Pennsylvania legislature reportedly said, "Mr. Speaker, I move we adjourn unless the Pennsylvania Railroad has some more business to conduct." The railroad industry pioneered the accumulation and use of economic power. Others followed in their footsteps, often corrupting politics. Popular outcries eventually forced congressional action to curb their excesses. The first national regulatory agency, the Interstate Commerce Commission, oversaw the railroads. All the basic industries followed similar paths, but each added new features in the march toward economic consolidation.

Steel

On his way from being a thirteen-year-old immigrant worker in a textile mill to receiving a half billion dollars from J. P. Morgan, Andrew Carnegie made a stop in the railroad industry. From 1853 to 1865 he learned good management techniques as he rose through the ranks with the Pennsylvania Railroad. By the time he resigned in 1865, Carnegie was superintendent of its western division and had made investments that brought him an annual income of almost $50,000.

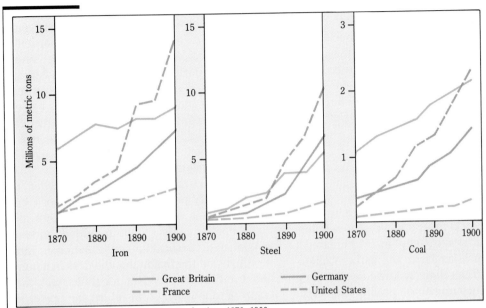

Figure 16.4   Iron, Coal, and Steel Production, 1870–1900
Carl N. Degler, *The Age of Economic Revolution.* Copyright © 1977 by Scott, Foresman and Co.

For the next seven years he dabbled in various industries until he settled on steel as the vehicle for his ambition and acumen. Carnegie often boasted that he knew almost nothing about making steel. He hired experts to do that. What he did know was how to run a company and make money. His shrewdness took all variables into account. For example, he built his steel mill in Homestead—just outside the Pittsburgh city limits—which unlike the city was serviced by two railroads. He could therefore wrangle over rates, an opportunity not shared by his competitors in the city.

The key to Carnegie's success was his ability to cut costs without lowering quality. He used such traditional measures as wage cuts and increased hours for workers, but he also constantly explored new methods to increase productivity. When told that a plant had broken all records the previous week, he replied, *"Congratulations! Why not do it every week?"* By not focusing on short-term profits, he was willing to invest in expensive new technology to lower long-term costs of production. Reportedly, he opened one board meeting with the question, "Well, what shall we throw away this year?"

Such action gave Carnegie a competitive edge, which he enhanced by vertical integration. Buying the sources of his raw materials—iron ore and coke—he both lowered their cost to him and controlled his supplies. Not content merely with this "backward integration," he also practiced "forward integration" by acquiring many of the transportation facilities needed to distribute his product. This vertical integration lowered final prices by cutting out profit-taking by suppliers and shippers.

Carnegie effectively used all the economies of scale available to large firms. Soon he was able to undersell and destroy most of the dozens of steel companies that had blossomed in response to the increased demand by railroads and industry. He also was a master at exploiting downturns in the business cycles. Most of his acquisitions were made during depressions, when prices were lower.

Competitors and labor movements suffered from Carnegie's actions, but the result was better steel at cheaper prices. The "survival of the fittest" did bring tangible benefits for society. As Carnegie once noted, "Two pounds of iron-stone mined upon Lake Superior and transported nine hundred miles to Pittsburgh; one pound and one half of coal, mined and manufactured into coke, and transported to Pittsburgh; a small amount of manganese ore mined in Virginia and brought to Pittsburgh . . . these four pounds of materials [are] manufactured into one pound of steel, for which the consumer pays one cent." Such cheap steel aided the expansion of the railroads and the rise of other industries.

Petroleum

Just as Carnegie eliminated most of his rivals in steel, John D. Rockefeller organized oil refining. The success of "Drake's folly" in 1859 created a "black gold" rush similar to the earlier California gold rush. The relatively low cost of drilling wells at first encouraged the proliferation of so many small companies that output and prices fluctuated dramatically. After entering the oil business in 1862, John D. Rockefeller founded the Standard Oil Company of Ohio in 1870. This giant corporation was capitalized at $41 million. Competition, however, still created chaos, and Rockefeller lamented that "the butcher, the baker, and the candlestick maker began to refine oil."

To Rockefeller the answer lay in consolidation. "The time was ripe for it. It had to come," he later wrote, "though all we saw at the moment was the need to save ourselves from wasteful conditions." In 1872 he began to use the South Improvement Company to combat waste. It was a combination of oil refiners and railroad directors aimed at dividing the oil carriage trade between the railroads. In return for a guaranteed share of the shipments, Rockefeller convinced the railroads to give rebates, which secretly returned a part of the published rail rates to the oil refiners. Eventually Rockefeller was

John D. Rockefeller

able to obtain rebates not only on the oil he shipped but also on the shipments of his competitors. Thus Rockefeller, like Carnegie, could undersell his competitors, whom he often bought out during times of economic depression. Like Carnegie also, he cut costs by vertical integration—buying such operations as barrel-making companies and pipelines. He meticulously lowered production costs while maintaining quality. "Nothing in haste, nothing ill done," was his motto.

Such techniques allowed Rockefeller to control ninety percent of the oil business, but legal problems arose from Standard Oil's far-flung holdings. His solution added another weapon in the arsenal for consolidation. In 1882 he convinced the major stockholders in a number of refineries to surrender their stock to a board of nine trustees. In return they received trust certificates that entitled them to a share of the joint profits of all the refineries. The benefits of this device were readily apparent. Pools had no legal standing and could be manipulated by some members to the detriment of other members. In a trust, however, competitive actions were of no benefit. Everyone shared all losses and gains.

Soon trusts began popping up like crabgrass throughout the economy. By 1888 a corporate lawyer wrote:

> It is currently reported and believed that the "Trust" monopolies have drawn within their grasp not only kerosene oil and cotton seed oil, but sugar, oatmeal, starch, white corn meal, straw paper, . . . whiskey, rubber, steel, . . . wrought iron, pipes, iron nuts, stoves, lead, copper, envelopes, paper bags, paving pitch, cordage, coke, reaping and binding and mowing machines, plows, glass, and water works. And the list is growing day by day. Millions of dollars, in cash and property, are being drawn into the vortex.

Andrew Carnegie was not the only American to hate the trusts and pools. Their proliferation sparked a public uproar which eventually led to the passage of the Sherman Antitrust Act of 1890. Industrialists abandoned trusts, but consolidation continued. One metamorphosis was the interlocking directorate, where competing companies shared nearly identical boards of directors. Another version was the holding company, where one firm held enough shares of a company's stock to obtain controlling interest. None of the dodges fooled the public. Like the railroads, the conglomerates, regardless of what they were called, eventually provoked further legislative attempts to curb their awesome power.

Meat Packing

Drastic transformations occurred in consumer industries as well as basic industry, as can be seen in the meat-packing business. There the interplay of new technology and new organization also ushered in new marketing techniques. Once again, the railroads played a key role by opening up the grazing ranges of the Great Plains. Because of its rail network, Chicago quickly became the major funnel through which cattle were distributed from West to East. From its Union Stock Yards, cows were shipped to abattoirs or slaughterhouses on the outskirts of eastern cities. The meat from the slaughtered animals was then distributed through local butchers to city residents.

There were several problems with such a distribution system, chief of which was the deterioration of the stock during long train journeys. Until the development of the refrigerated car, however, the only alternative was pickling or curing meat—processes that had already made Chicago the pork-packing center, but which were not as well suited to beef. Cattle dealer Gustavus Swift realized the possibilities opened up by refrigerated cars. Not only could fresh meat be shipped more safely, but by centralizing slaughtering, waste products could be utilized. Profits were increased by making horns into buttons and hooves into glue. Eventually Swift formed glue, fertilizer, soap, and glycerine factories. People said that Swift used every part of a pig except the squeal.

Local butchers and wholesalers usually lacked refrigerated storage facilities, so Swift established his own warehouses, bypassing wholesale distributors and their cut of the profits. Swift had to overcome consumer resistance to the idea of buying meat weeks after the animal was slaughtered in a distant city. Local

Because the emergence of gigantic trusts concentrated economic power into relatively few hands, many people saw the trusts as the real "bosses of the Senate."

butchers often fed consumer distrust; New York shops frequently displayed signs reading "No Chicago beef sold here." Swift responded with a major advertising campaign stressing the superiority of western beef. His mass marketing tactics proved successful. By the late 1890s six packers supplied almost ninety percent of all meat shipped in interstate commerce, and abattoirs virtually disappeared.

Swift also pioneered in mass production, employing assembly lines. The slaughtering and packing process was subdivided into numerous distinct jobs. Workers repeated one particular action as carcasses moved along on overhead conveyor belts. There was little wasted motion, and, as one of Swift's superintendents noted, "If you need to turn out a little more, you speed up the conveyor a little and the men speed up to keep pace."

Motion picture star Charlie Chaplin later parodied such tactics in the movie "Modern Times." In it, a too-rapid conveyor created comic chaos. The waste of time, however, was no laughing matter to industrial managers. Engineer Frederick J. Taylor laid the foundations of "scientific management" with his time-and-motion studies. Stopwatch in hand, Taylor observed the workers and then divided the manufacturing process into units that allowed for little wasted motion. He believed his ideas would benefit labor as well as management. Instead, his aim "to induce men to act as nearly like machines as possible" promoted monotony and displaced workers—especially higher paid skilled ones.

Most business leaders did not really advocate free enterprise fueled by competition. To them competition meant chaos, and they sought to eliminate it. J. P. Morgan, one historian wrote, "felt that the American economy should ideally be like a company organizational chart, with each part in its proper place, and the lines of authority clearly designated. He did not really believe in the free enterprise system, and like most ardent socialists, he hated the waste, duplication, and clutter of unrestrained competition." Morgan and other bankers often stepped in during economic panics to reorganize bankrupt companies. They chewed up failing companies and railroads and spat them out as single supercorporations. The result was a more orderly economy, but at the price of centralizing vast economic power into the hands of a few unelected individuals. As one wit quipped when U. S. Steel was formed, "God created the world in 4004 B.C. and J. P. Morgan reorganized it in 1901."

ECONOMIC MODERNIZATION IN THE SOUTH AND WEST

Although most industrialization occurred in the Northeast, all regions experienced profound changes as a national, interdependent economy emerged. In that process a world based on personal relationships was displaced by a more impersonal world based on contractual relationships. Just as the local cobbler was replaced by large factories mass producing shoes, the largely self-sufficient farmer who sold a little surplus locally to buy the cobbler's shoes gave way to cash-crop farmers who bought factory-made shoes by mail-order catalog—never seeing the people who made or sold them. At the same time, his crops went to feed urban masses hundreds of miles away—none of whom he knew personally.

Some of the forces feeding the growth of industry also fueled agricultural expansion. Rural population kept growing, although not as rapidly as urban population. Both the number of farms and farmers more than doubled at the same time that farmers became a minority of the population. Most of these new farmers were in the West, which was being tamed and exploited in the late nineteenth century. Demand by the urban masses for food sparked a farming revolution based upon mechanization and scientific agriculture. One region, however, did not share equally in the benefits of economic modernization. For a variety of reasons the South failed to keep pace with the rest of the nation. Despite numerous efforts to forge a "New South," the region slipped further and further behind.

Western Expansion

The transcontinental railroads were not originally meant to "open up" the West. They were laid across what was called the "Great American Desert" in order to link the east and west coasts. The perceived worthlessness of the Plains was reflected in the willingness to give much of it away—to the Indians and later to the railroads. The mining frontier first altered perceptions of the region's value. Confrontations between miners and Indians foreshadowed the expulsion of the Indians from land which had been "given" them "forever" before whites realized its real worth.

Miners starred in the first act of the drama of western expansion and were followed by other casts of actors. The railroads played a significant role in creating new ways to exploit the land. In addition to mineral wealth, the region had two other plentiful resources: grass and cows. Railroads provided the means to get the cattle to eastern cities, where urban residents wanted more meat to eat. The result was the birth of western ranching.

At first, ranching, like placer mining, did not require much capital. Both the cows and the grass were free. By 1860 some five million head of wild Texas longhorns had descended from cattle imported by Spanish colonists. They displaced the buffaloes that were being hunted

Technology had a huge impact on farming. Machinery increased both production and the growing burden of debt, which began to crush many farmers when agricultural prices fell.

to virtual extinction. In fact, cattle were so plentiful that they were considered almost worthless in the West. However, steers sold for $30 to $50 a head in Chicago. All that was needed was a way to get them there.

James G. McCoy realized the potential for profit and established the first "cowtown" at Abilene, Kansas, where he built stock pens and loading chutes. Cowboys drove cattle there for shipment by rail to Chicago. Other cowtowns arose as some six million head of cattle endured the "long drive" to those sites between 1866 and 1888.

As longhorns could not be easily captured or herded on foot, the methods of the Mexican gauchos were copied and the American cowboy was born. Herding cattle while mounted on horses was hard, dirty work frequently undertaken by poor whites and blacks. One partici-

pant wrote, "It was tiresome grimy business for the attendant punchers, who travelled over in a cloud of dust, and heard little but the constant chorus from the crackling of hoofs and ankle joints, from the bellows, lows, and bleats of the trudging animals." Romantic stories both whitened as well as glorified the cowboy. Actually, the heyday of the cowboy was rather brief, for ranching, like mining, was soon transformed into an organized business.

Profits from a successful drive were very good—about forty percent. This naturally attracted eastern investors, and soon the long drives declined as better methods were found. The lean rangy longhorns were better suited to enduring the long drive than to producing choice, juicy steaks. They became even less desirable after being herded long distances. As the rail network expanded into Texas, ranchers

In the hey-day of the open range, thousands of wild cattle were rounded up to be driven to cow towns for shipment to the East.

switched from rounding up stray cattle to raising and breeding the longhorns with superior imported stock to improve the quality of the beef.

The cattle breeders needed large tracts of grassland for grazing and usually just appropriated land from the public domain. Most centered their operations around stream banks and claimed all the adjoining grasslands. During this open range era, high profits attracted even more investors. Eventually the ranchers joined other segments of the economy that were outproducing demand. As the Plains became overgrazed, beef prices dropped from $30 to $10 a head in 1885 and 1886. Poorer producers were driven out by these low prices, challenges to their land claims by sheepherders and farmers, and bad weather. A winter of terrible blizzards following the scorching summer in 1885 led to the death of ninety percent of western cattle.

After sometimes bloody battles for supremacy between these economic competitors, the "Wild West" was largely tamed by the 1890s. Ranchers who remained established legal title to their grazing lands, fenced them in with barbed wire, and practiced scientific breeding

and feeding of their stock. The forces of economic consolidation had reached ranching—making it a business requiring large amounts of capital.

Land legislation of the era aided the monopolization of ranching by a relatively few "cattle barons." Large tracts of public lands were given away or sold cheaply through such acts as the Homestead Act of 1862, the Timber Culture Act of 1873, and the Desert Land Act of 1877. Enacted to promote socially desirable goals, all had large loopholes that were exploited by cattlemen and land speculators. To promote settlement, the Homestead Act gave 160 free acres to those who would cultivate it for five years. The Desert Land Act granted 640 acres at $1.25 an acre to anyone who would irrigate the land. The Timber Culture Act, based on the theory that the trees increased rainfall, awarded 160 acres to anyone who would plant trees on a quarter of the land. Cattlemen and speculators fraudulently claimed to have met the terms of the grants or hired dummy entrymen to stake claims for them. A bucket of water was sometimes the only basis for claims of irrigation. Lumber barons in California, Nevada, Oregon, and Washington simi-

Because of the scarcity of trees in the Plains, settlers built homes from "bricks" of sod. With walls two to three feet thick, the houses were gloomy but provided cozy and solid protection from the elements.

larly utilized the Timber and Stone Act of 1878. Thus much of the newly discovered wealth of the West ended up in hands of a few winners in the great land lottery.

While the mining, cattle, and lumber frontiers offered some quick, easy riches before being transformed into capital-intensive businesses, the farming frontier required more patience to make any profits. By the time farmers arrived in the new West, much of the best land had already been appropriated. Most of the 274 million acres distributed under the terms of the Homestead Act were eventually purchased by bona fide settlers from speculators and cattlemen. Other farmers bought land from the railroads, which promoted settlement to increase traffic in isolated areas. To lure settlers the roads often provided easy credit terms and extolled western opportunities in flyers and speeches.

Many farming pioneers soon learned that railroad propaganda sometimes overstated the promise of the West. When they arrived, they discovered a shortage of wood and water but an overabundance of severe weather, insects, and social isolation. The houses they built of "bricks" cut from thick prairie sod were func-

tional but bleak. At first, many farmers managed only to eke out a bare subsistence. Eventually, however, western farmers were caught up in the forces of change that transformed agriculture as dramatically as other sectors of the economy.

The Changing Nature of Farming

When Congress passed the Homestead Act in 1862, most of the arable land east of the Mississippi was already taken. The established farmers of the Old Northeast adapted fairly well to the changing economy and were generally prosperous. Most did not try to compete with the new wheat and corn areas of the West. Instead they turned their efforts to supplying the rapidly growing urban areas with fresh vegetables, dairy products, poultry, and pigs. They also profited from rising land values by selling extra acres to residential and industrial developers at high prices. Although they may not have liked all the changes, most received a reasonable share of the fruits of economic expansion. The same could not be said for many farmers in the West and South.

$5,000 REWARD

JESSE JAMES
For Train Robbery

THE "WILD WEST"

At 6 P.M. April 5, 1892, a mysterious train, its shades tightly drawn, pulled out of Cheyenne, Wyoming bound for Casper, 200 miles to the northwest. Aboard the train were 46 heavily armed vigilantes. The train had been chartered by Wyoming's cattle kings to put an end to cattle rustling in remote Johnson County. Among the passengers were 22 hired gunmen and two newspaper reporters. At Casper, the vigilantes debarked from their train and mounted on horseback. Their mission: to kill Johnson County settlers suspected of cattle rustling.

For more than two decades, the cattlemen had accused the homesteaders of land grabbing and cattle theft. Juries refused to convict the small stockmen, and the cattle barons responded by taking the law into their own hands. In one

incident, on the night of July 20, 1889, ten cattlemen captured two homesteaders and hanged them from a stunted pine tree. Altogether six or seven suspected rustlers were shot or hanged. Despite lynchings and shootings, rustling continued, and in the summer of 1891, the cattle barons decided to launch an armed invasion of Johnson County and kill the most notorious rustlers. Members of the Wyoming Stock Growers' Association were asked to provide names of suspected rustlers. They compiled a list of 70 purported cattle thieves.

On Saturday, April 9, 1892, the vigilantes shot and killed two suspected rustlers at K C Ranch near the southern edge of Johnson County. Word of the killings quickly spread, and a band of two

hundred homesteaders formed a posse to avenge the murders. At the T A Ranch 14 miles south of Buffalo, the posse surrounded the vigilantes.

Before the vigilantes could be captured, however, Wyoming's acting governor and the state's senators sent frantic telegrams to President Benjamin Harrison declaring that a state of insurrection existed in Johnson County and that the United States cavalry be sent in to quell the disturbances. Early on Wednesday, April 13, the cavalry rode to the rescue and escorted the invaders out of Johnson County. Several federal marshals and state officials were among the vigilantes who were charged with first degree murder, but the charges eventually were dropped. The Johnson County war was over.

Today, it is commonly assumed that the roots of violence in American society lie in our frontier heritage. According to popular mythology—disseminated by dime novels, pulp newspapers, and television and movie westerns—the frontier was a lawless land populated by violent men: outlaws, stage coach robbers, gunslingers, highwaymen, vigilantes, claim jumpers, cattle rustlers, horse thieves, Indian fighters, border ruffians, and mule skinners.

How lawless was the Wild West? Certain forms of violence *were* indeed common: warfare between Indians and whites, attacks on Chinese and Mexican minorities, vigilantism, rowdyism, drunkenness, opium addiction, gambling, vigilante executions, stage coach robberies, and gunfights. Racially-motivated acts of brutality represented the ugliest side of frontier violence. In 1871, in one of the most gruesome incidents, ranchers in California's Sacramento Valley tracked 30 Digger Indians into a cave and shot them, saving the children for last because they "could not bear to kill them with [a] 56-calibre Spencer rifle. 'It tore them up so bad.'" Instead, they were shot with a 38-calibre Smith and Wesson revolver.

Chinese immigrants faced particular hostility. In Los Angeles, on October 24, 1871, a white mob stormed the city's Chinatown district and murdered between 20 and 25 Chinese men and women. In Rock Springs, Wyoming Territory, on September 2, 1885, a heavily armed white mob attacked the town's Chinatown, set fire to the Chinese coal miners' shacks, and fired bullets at fleeing workers, killing 50, ten percent of the town's Chinese population. A few days later, in Seattle, Washington Territory, a mob killed Chinese hop pickers while they were asleep in their tents. In November, a Tacoma mob routed Chinese immigrants out of their dwellings and loaded them into wagons and dumped them outside of town.

Blacks and Hispanics also encountered frontier violence. In 40 Texas counties, at least 373 black freedmen were lynched or murdered between June 1865 and June 1868. In California, some 15,000 Mexican, Chilean, and Peruvian gold hunters were driven out of the gold fields by threats of lynching, branding, whippings, and ear croppings. Said one white miner: "Give 'em a fair jury trial and rope 'em with all the majesty of the law."

Vigilante lynchings represented another widespread form of frontier violence. The lack of courts of law and police forces in the West gave rise to committees of vigilance—extralegal committees organized to suppress and punish crime summarily—in frontier regions. These committees banded together to punish murderers, counterfeiters, corrupt government officials, and horse and cattle thieves. In a single year in California, 1855, 47 people were executed by mobs, 9 by legal tribunals, and 10 by sheriffs or police officers. Between 1865 and 1890, 27 vigilante movements arose in Texas pursuing outlaws like John Wesley Hardin. A final wave of vigilantism originated in rural southern Indiana in 1887. Known as the White Cap movement, local rural committees flogged drunks, prostitutes, and men who failed to support their families.

The most notorious perpetrators of frontier violence were the outlaws and gunmen, like Belle Starr, Billy the Kid, Black Bart, Frank and Jesse James, John Wesley Hardin, the Younger Brothers, Butch Cassidy and the Sundance Kid, and the Dalton Gang, who held up stage coaches and trains, robbed banks, and stole horses and cattle. Hardin and the Jameses—who ironically were the sons of ministers—as well as the Younger brothers learned outlaw strategy as Confederate guerillas during the Civil War. Hardin, who was probably the most prolific murderer, shot and killed over twenty men between 1868, when he was 15, and 1878, when he was finally captured and incarcerated in a Texas prison. Frank and Jesse James, America's most renowned bank and train robbers, staged at least 26 daring robberies between 1866 and 1881 in Missouri, taking in half a million dollars. Black Bart (born Charles E. Boles)

robbed 27 stage coaches in 28 attempts in California between 1875 and 1882, using an empty shotgun as his only weapon.

Most popular accounts of western banditry, however, appear to be grossly exaggerated and romanticized. Bat Masterson, who, according to legend, killed 30 men in gunfights, actually killed three. Billy the Kid, who supposedly killed one man for each of his 21 years of life, also apparently killed three.

Kansas's cattle towns, legend holds, witnessed a killing every night. But in fact in Abilene, Caldwell, Dodge City, Ellsworth, and Wichita, a grand total of 45 homicides took place during a 15 year span, 1.5 homicides per cattle trading season, never exceeding 5 in one year. In Deadwood, South Dakota, where Wild Bill Hickok was shot in the back while playing poker in 1876, only four homicides—and no lynchings—took place in the town's most violent year. And in Tombstone, Arizona, the site of the shootout at the OK Corral, where Marshal Virgil Earp and his brothers Wyatt and Morgan, backed by gambler Doc Holliday, hurled the Clanton Brothers "into eternity in the duration of a moment," only five men were killed in the city's deadliest year.

Despite the omnipresence of rifles, knives, and revolvers and the prevalence of saloons, gambling houses, and bordellos, rape, robbery and burglarly were relatively rare. "We could go to sleep in our cabins," wrote one miner, "with our bag of gold dust under our pillows minus locks, bolts or bars, and feel a sense of absolute security."

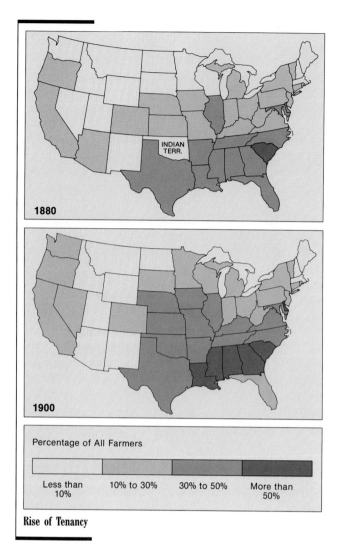

Percentage of All Farmers

Less than 10% | 10% to 30% | 30% to 50% | More than 50%

Rise of Tenancy

success resulted mainly from abnormally wet summers in the 1870s and 1880s, as they learned when conditions returned to normal. During the good times, however, optimism flourished. As one Kansas official noted: "Most of us crossed the Mississippi with no money but with a vast wealth of hope and courage. Haste to get rich has made us borrowers, and the borrowing has made booms, and the booms have made men wild, and Kansas became a vast asylum covering 80,000 square miles." Then came the droughts. By 1900 two-thirds of the homesteaders had failed, and farmers returned east with signs saying, "In God We Trusted; In Kansas We Busted."

In the South, the Civil War brought several changes that crippled agriculture. Wartime devastation destroyed half the region's farm equipment and killed one-third of its draft animals. The death of slavery also ended the plantation system, and replacements had to be found. The number of farms doubled from 1860 to 1880, but the number of landowners remained the same. The size of the average farm dropped from 347 acres to 156 acres, as sharecropping and tenancy rose. The farms were not only smaller but also frequently worked by people who did not own them. In other words, at the very time the rest of the economy was consolidating, southern agriculture was marching off in the opposite, less efficient direction. Another problem was a shortage of cash, which forced southern farmers to borrow against future crops. Crop liens and high credit prices kept a lot of black and white farmers trapped in a cycle of debt and poverty.

Many Plains and southern farmers became losers in the economic modernization of agriculture. Nevertheless, both the winners and the losers were playing essentially the same game. That game was the commercialization of farming. Most of the rules were the same as those for manufacturers: specialization, new technology, mechanization, expanded markets, heavier capital investment, and reliance on interstate transportation. Most of these changes were wholeheartedly embraced by farmers of that generation—until they fell behind their industrial cousins in the expanding economy.

Most farmers agreed with a farm journal's assertion, "Agriculture, like all other business, is

The challenges of farming were much greater in the West, and when they were finally met, overproduction depressed prices. Cultivation of the West required new agricultural techniques and adaptations to the environment. The scarcity of trees not only dictated the building of sodhouses but also made the cost of fencing prohibitive. Until the development of barbed wire in 1872, crops were not easily protected from the millions of roaming cattle.

A more serious problem was the lack of water. Farmers came to believe they had found solutions by using new varieties of seed, pumping water from far below the ground surface with windmills, and using cultivation techniques known as "dry farming." In reality their

better for its subdivision, each one growing that which is best suited for his soil, climate, and market." Specialization became apparent in the decline of subsistence farming and the growing importance of cash crops. Although general farming continued, most farmers planted more of their acreage in the single crop best suited for their land and market. Outside of the South, cash crops were usually supplemented by small gardens and stock raising. In Dixie cotton reigned supreme, and tenant farmers were often forced by landowners and merchants to plant all available acres with cotton. Most, however, specialized by choice.

Technology and mechanization also revolutionized agriculture. Inventions came to the farms as rapidly as to the factories and increased productivity just as dramatically. After the mechanization of wheat farming, the hours required to farm an acre dropped from sixty-one to three, and the per acre cost of production fell from $3.65 to $.66. Machines entered every phase of agriculture, and by 1890 some 900 companies were manufacturing such items as hay loaders, cord binders, seeders, rotary plows, mowers, and combines. Farmers began to learn "scientific agriculture" at land-grant colleges which Congress established under the Morrill Land Grant Act of 1862. Agricultural researchers explored ways to increase production and found new uses for overabundant crops at agricultural experiment stations funded by the Hatch Act of 1887. Obviously, farmers were not opposed to all government aid to the economy.

As in manufacturing, mechanization brought economies of scale to agriculture, but they were not as easily exploitable. Although some bonanza farmers in the Dakotas cultivated 100,000 acres and more, the average farm remained 150 acres large. The farms of the West were usually much larger than average because dry farming techniques produced low yields per acre. To succeed, a western farmer needed more acres, and to work those acres he needed more machines; both cost money. Thus, like businessmen, they needed access to capital. Unable to sell shares in their enterprise, most obtained personal loans with their land, machinery, and crops as collateral. Unfortunately, as production increased, prices fell, and

to counteract lower profits farmers further expanded production in a self-defeating downward spiral. Mortgage indebtedness grew two and one-half times faster than agricultural wealth.

One solution to overproduction was to expand markets, which required cheap and reliable transportation facilities. Railroads, therefore, had as much impact in agriculture as in industry. Instead of selling surplus food to the local cobbler, American farmers fed distant urban masses at home and abroad; twenty percent of agricultural production was exported. This also meant that farmers' profits hinged on many factors beyond their control—such as the size of harvests in Argentina. Marketing became a key to success; one farm editor declared, "The work of farming is only half done when the crop is out of the ground."

Most farmers realized and, at first, even celebrated their status as businessmen. Agricultural expansion was as dramatic as that of industry, yet farmers began to lose ground. In 1860 farmers owned fifty percent of the nation's wealth and received thirty percent of the national income. By 1910 those figures had dropped to twenty percent and eighteen percent. At the same time farmers were becoming a minority of the population. As they discovered that they could not adapt as well as industrialists to the new economic order, they began to assert the superiority of rural culture. They stressed farmers' ties to the soil and heralded individualism and self-sufficiency as truly American characteristics. Their ties to the soil, however, were really not very binding; in 1910 more than half of all farmers had lived less than five years on the land they were farming. Most farms were indeed individually owned and operated, but if farmers retained the outward forms of economic individualism, their functions were far removed from that of the independent, self-sufficient yeoman farmer.

The New South

Like the farmers, most Southerners wholeheartedly endorsed the new economic order at first. Some even saw the South's salvation in the destruction of slavery. In 1870, South Carolinian Edwin DeLeon proclaimed "a New South, whose wants and wishes, ends and aims, plans and purposes, are as different from those of 1860, as though a century instead of a decade only, divided the two."

Dramatic changes were indeed taking place in the South. Railroad development increased at a rate greater than the nation at large. The textile industry rapidly blossomed; the number of spindles in the region increased 900 percent from 1880 to 1900. Birmingham grew into a major producer of raw steel, and by 1890 southern steel and iron made up almost 20 percent of the national total. At the same time southern agriculture was recovering. Cotton production exceeded prewar records by the 1870s.

In the 1880s, James B. Duke introduced a major new industry to the region and followed a path similar to other captains of industry. Duke was a North Carolina tobacco grower when he encountered a machine that rolled cigarettes in 1881. He bought the patent and proceeded to change American tastes to suit his purposes. Prior to then most tobacco users either chewed the weed or smoked pipes or cigars. Duke enclosed "trading cards" featuring pictures and stories of popular heroes in packs of cigarettes to lure youngsters into smoking. At the same time Duke was buying out competitors and in 1890 created a trust through which he controlled 150 companies in an almost perfect monopoly until 1911 federal antitrust actions disbanded the trust.

Though entirely homegrown, Duke's enterprise had no distinctly southern characteristics. DeLeon had predicted another kind of development, writing, "The Northerner will carry South his thrift, his caution, his restless activity, his love of new thing; the Southerner will temper these with his reckless liberality, his careless confidence, his fiery energy, and his old-time conservatism; and both will be benefited by the admixture."

His vision was a much romanticized version of what actually happened. The North's major contribution to southern industrialism was capital. The growing timber business was almost exclusively northern-owned and operated, and railroad expansion as well as coal and iron production depended heavily on northern investment. Southern contributions included lower wage scales, longer hours, and paternalistic mill towns that controlled the lives of laborers drawn mainly from the poor white population. Blacks were totally excluded or relegated to menial positions in most southern industries. Not only did southern workers receive as little as half of what Northerners were paid, but some were not paid at all. Under the region's "convict-lease" system, the states rented out convicted criminals (often black) to private interests, providing a cheap labor source that often displaced paid labor.

The need for northern capital led to propaganda campaigns by such southern spokesmen as Henry W. Grady, the editor of the *Atlanta Constitution*. He wrote and traveled extensively to proclaim the unlimited opportunities of the "New South." Grady envisioned three major changes from the Old South: diversified farming, industrialization, and racial accommodation and cooperation. To win support for these changes, New South spokesmen linked the new order to the virtues of romanticized versions of the Old South and the "Lost Cause" of the Confederacy. Confederate heroes were named to boards of directors and appeals to southern nationalism were made. As one historian wrote, the "romance of the past was used to underwrite the materialism of the present."

Southern industrial expositions were also used to lure outside investment. At the Cotton States Exposition of 1895 in Atlanta, a black spokesman for the New South emerged. Booker T. Washington, principal of Tuskegee Normal and Industrial Institute in Macon County, Alabama, was asked to give an address by the exposition's white organizers. His speech, which came to be called the "Atlanta Compromise," rivaled those of Grady in its optimistic appraisal of southern potential. It also outlined a basis of racial cooperation. If whites would allow blacks educational and economic opportunity, Washington promised that blacks "will buy your surplus land, make blossom the waste places in your fields, and run your factories." He urged blacks to make themselves economically indispensable to whites and forego agitation for political and social rights. Their economic importance would bring them white acceptance—and the rights they desired.

Booker T. Washington (left) founded Tuskegee Institute in Alabama where blacks could receive instruction in agriculture and the trades to prepare them for advancement in the "New South." Above, black women learn upholstery and mattress making.

Washington practiced what he preached. Tuskegee was a model New South institution, focusing on industrial education and promoting diversified farming. It boasted the only all-black agricultural experiment station. As its director, George Washington Carver advocated the utilization of undeveloped southern resources and sought to expand markets for such crops as peanuts and sweet potatoes.

Despite all the New South optimism, the region's economic position in the nation continued to slip. Cotton remained king, and the inefficiencies of sharecropping continued. Racial discrimination blighted southern efforts at economic modernization. The progress that was made did not alter the South's position at the bottom of the economic ladder. Although the South's share of national manufacturing doubled between 1880 and 1920, it rose only to ten percent of the total—roughly the same percent it had at the start of the Civil War. Per capita income increased twenty-one percent, but fell from sixty percent of that of the North in 1860 to forty percent in 1900. As happened in the

West, the South's reliance on northern capital kept the region in a colonial economic relationship with the majority of profits going elsewhere. The disparity between the winners and losers was even greater than elsewhere—aided by political favoritism. By the end of the century farmers would lead a major revolt against the entrenched economic powers and seek political solutions to their problems.

CONCLUSION

In one generation the United States became the economic colossus of the world. After a heated period of intense competition, the merger movement forged supercorporations that controlled the majority of their industries. There were many positive benefits of this economic expansion and consolidation. In some cases people were able to buy superior goods at cheaper prices. As Edwin Atkinson noted in 1886, "Did Vanderbilt keep any of you down

CHRONOLOGY OF KEY EVENTS

1859 First oil well at Titusville, Pennsylvania

1867 First shipment of cattle from Abilene, Kansas, to Chicago

1869 Transcontinental railroad completed

1872 Social Darwinist William Graham Sumner began career at Yale; Andrew Carnegie entered steel business

1873 Panic started six-year depression

1874 Barbed wire patented

1876 Alexander Graham Bell invented telephone; Philadelphia Centennial Exhibition

1879 Thomas Edison invented incandescent light bulb

1881 Tuskegee Institute founded by Booker T. Washington

1882 John D. Rockefeller established Standard Oil Trust

1883 *Santa Clara County* v. *The Southern Pacific Railroad*

1886 Severe drought ended cattle boom

1888 George Eastman invented hand-held camera

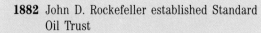

1889 Andrew Carnegie published article entitled "The Gospel of Wealth"

1893 Panic started five-year depression; Chicago Columbian Exposition

1895 Booker T. Washington's "Atlanta Compromise"

1901 J. P. Morgan founded United States Steel

by saving you two dollars and seventy-five cents on a barrel of flour, while he was making fourteen cents?"

Social mobility did increase. Although some skilled artisans slipped downward on the social ladder, upward mobility rates usually doubled the downward rates. Of course not all shared equally. Few made the transition from rags to riches that Carnegie accomplished. Most industrial leaders instead came from rather privileged backgrounds. The majority were relatively well-educated Protestants of native birth.

Average annual incomes also rose steadily for almost all classes of workers. On the other hand those wage increases rarely equaled the rising cost of living. Nevertheless, most families' standard of living improved, because more members of the family worked for wages. Items

that had been considered luxuries soon became viewed as necessities.

At the same time, individuals paid huge social costs for these advancements. Some people paid a disproportionate share of these costs. Patterns of working and living dramatically changed. Many workers found themselves in a new status that imperiled their independence. Personal relationships were being replaced by impersonal, contractual arrangements. Shady corporate practices corrupted public morality. As Henry Demarest Lloyd noted in 1881, Standard Oil "has done everything with the Pennsylvania legislature except refine it." In short, all aspects of life underwent profound transformation, and the story of the late nineteenth century is the story of adaptation and adjustment to the new social and economic order.

REVIEW SUMMARY

During the second half of the nineteenth century, America underwent a dramatic economic transformation, emerging as the world's leading industrial power. Major factors in the nation's rapid rise were:

- a wealth of natural resources
- a productive population
- the inventive genius necessary to harness these assets

Popular opinion and government policy favored the expanding industries in their quest for wealth. In this unabashedly pro-business environment, the railroads and other major industries followed similar paths.

- overexpansion
- competitive conflict
- modernization
- consolidation into a small number of major firms or trust

The economic changes of the period affected everyone, but the South and West reaped fewer benefits than the East, and many farmers began to see themselves as losers in the new order.

SUGGESTIONS FOR FURTHER READING

AMERICA: LAND OF PLENTY

Samuel P. Hayes, *The Response to Industrialism, 1885–1914* (1967); Nathan Rosenberg, *Technology and American Economic Growth* (1972); Elting E. Morison, *From Know-How to Nowhere: The Development of American Technology* (1974) and *Men, Machines, and Modern Times* (1966); Robert Bruce, *Bell: Alexander Graham Bell and the Quest of Solitude* (1973); Leo Marx, *The Machine in the Garden* (1964); George H. Daniels, *Science and Society in America* (1971); Siegfried Giedion, *Mechanization Takes Command* (1948); Robert Higgs, *The Transformation of the American Economy* (1971); D. F. Noble, *America by Design* (1977).

A FAVORABLE CLIMATE

Sidney Fine, *Laissez-faire and the General Welfare State* (1956); Richard Hofstadter, *Social Darwinism in American Thought*, rev. ed. (1955); Robert McCloskey, *American Conservatism in the Age of Enterprise* (1951); James Weinstein, *The Corporate Ideal in the Liberal State* (1960); Louis Galambos and Barbara Barrow Spence, *The Public Image of Big Business in America* (1975); T. Jackson Lears, *No Place of Grace: Antimodernism and the Transformation of American Culture* (1981); W. Elliot Brownlee, *Dynamics of Ascent*, rev. ed. (1979); Milton Friedman

and Anna J. Schwartz, *Monetary History of the United States, 1867–1960* (1963); Thomas C. Cochran, *Business in American Life* (1972).

ECONOMIC GROWTH AND DEVELOPMENT

John F. Stover, *American Railroads* (1970); Thomas Cochran, *Railroad Leaders, 1845–1890* (1953); George R. Taylor and Irene D. Neu, *The American Railway Network, 1861–1890* (1956); Joseph F. Wall, *Andrew Carnegie* (1970); Harold C. Livesay, *Andrew Carnegie and the Rise of Big Business* (1975); Peter Temin, *Iron and Steel in Nineteenth Century America* (1964); David F. Hawkes, *John D.: Founding Father of the Rockefellers* (1980); Allan Nevins, *Study in Power: John D. Rockefeller* (1953); Andrew Sinclair, *Corsair: The Life of J. Pierpont Morgan* (1981); George Wheeler, *Pierpont Morgan and Friends* (1973); Matthew Josephson, *The Robber Barons* (1934); Jonathan Hughes, *The Vital Few* (1966); Francis L. Eames, *The New York Stock Exchange* (1968).

ECONOMIC MODERNIZATION IN THE SOUTH AND WEST

Frederick Jackson Turner, *The Frontier in American History* (1920); Ray A. Billington, *Westward Expansion* (1967); William S. Greever, *Bonanza West: Western Mining Rushes* (1963); Robert V. Hine, *The American West* (1973); Julie Roy Jeffrey, *Frontier Women* (1979); Thomas D. Clark, *Frontier America* (1969); Henry Nash Smith, *Virgin Land: The West as Symbol and Myth* (1950); Terry G. Jordan, *Trails to Texas: Southern Roots of Western Cattle Ranching* (1981); David Dary, *Cowboy Culture* (1981); J. M. Shaggs, *The Cattle Trading Industry* (1973); Robert R. Dykstra, *The Cattle Towns* (1968); Roger D. McGrath, *Gunfighters, Highwaymen, and Vigilantes: Violence on the Frontier* (1984); Fred A. Shannon, *The Farmer's Last Frontier* (1963); Gilbert C. Fite, *The Farmer's Frontier, 1865–1900* (1966); Lewis Atherton, *The Cattle Kings* (1961); Philip Durham and E. L. Jones, *The Negro Cowboys* (1965); R. M. Robbins, *Our Landed Heritage* (1942); P. W. Gates, *History of Public Land Law Development* (1968); Everett Dick, *The Sod-House Frontier, 1854–1890* (1937); Allan G. Bogue, *From Prairie to Corn Belt* (1963); C. Vann Woodward, *Origins of New South, 1877–1913* (1951) and *The Strange Career of Jim Crow*, rev. ed. (1974); Orville Vernon Burton and Robert C. McMath, Jr., eds., *Towards a New South?: Post-Civil War Southern Communities* (1982); John S. Ezell, *The South since 1865* (1975); Dewey Grantham, Jr., *The Democratic South* (1963); Steven Hahn, *The Roots of Southern Populism: Yeoman Farmers and the Transformation of the Georgia Upcountry, 1850–1890* (1983); Melton A. McLaurin, *Paternalism and Protest: Southern Cotton Mill Workers and Organized Labor* (1971); Paul Gaston, *The New South Creed* (1970); Thomas D. Clark and Albert D. Kirwan, *The South Since Appomattox* (1967); J. Morgan Kousser, *The Shaping of Southern Politics* (1974).

Making a New America

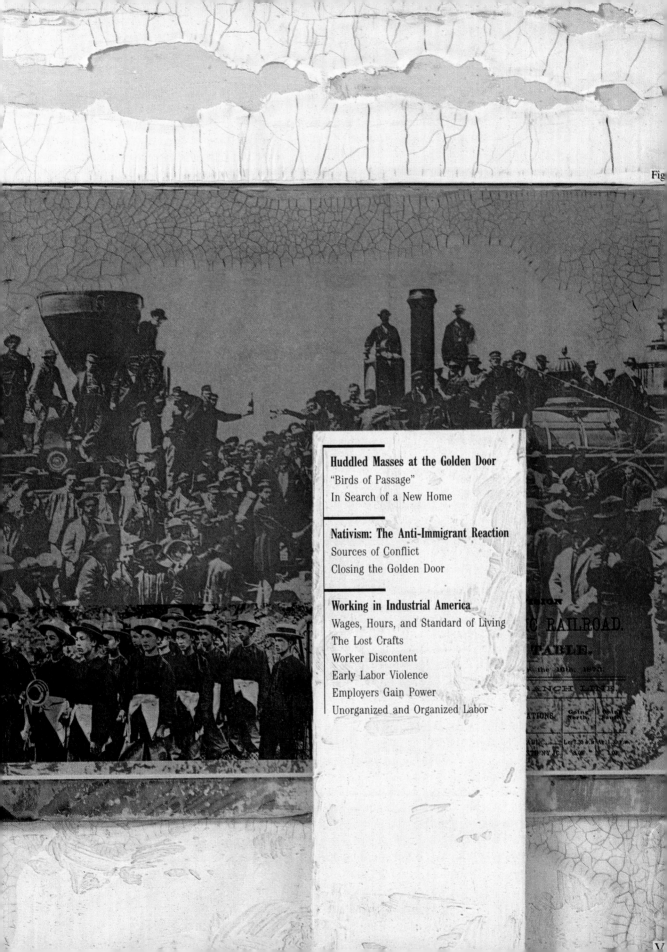

The opium dens of late nineteenth-century San Francisco were as quiet as death. Opium smokers expected the drug to induce a tranquil passive state. Under the influence of the thick white smoke, users did not talk or sing or quarrel or fight. They did not desire the companionship of the opposite sex or the still beauty of art. They only sought to sink into their own inner isolated world. Jean Cocteau, a French writer who was once addicted to the drug, remarked "Opium is the only vegetable substance that communicates the vegetable state to us."

Some Chinese who came to the United States during the second half of the nineteenth century found solace in the stillness of the opium dens. In 1876, George W. Duffield, a policeman in San Francisco's Chinatown, told a California Senate Committee investigating the social, moral, and political effects of Chinese immigration, "Ninety-nine Chinamen out of one hundred smoke opium." In his diatribe Duffield claimed that the new Asian immigrants actively supported gambling dens and houses of prostitution. White native-born witnesses insisted that Chinese immigration had contributed significantly to crime and moral decay in San Francisco.

Perhaps Charles Wolcott Brooks, who spent several years in China, best articulated the views of the city authorities. He was asked: "Do you think they have any particular love for our [American] institutions?" He replied: "I don't think they have any at all. They come purely as a matter of gain—as a matter of dollars and cents. If it is profitable, they will come. If it is not profitable, they will not come. The very fact of their retaining their own dress and customs, and keeping themselves so entirely separate, as a people, shows that they have not. . . . The Chinese come abroad not to spend, but to accumulate. They maintain their own customs and language. . . . The Chinese . . . hate us most cordially. . . ."

The Chinese may not have developed any emotional attachment to America or its institutions. After all, most never planned to stay in the United States. They loved the villages of their homeland that they left behind, and they valued their own ageless Chinese customs. In America they sought the opportunity to work—not voting rights, education, or assimilation, and no work was beneath them. They resignedly accepted the most menial jobs in the mines, on the railroad construction gangs, and in the booming western cities.

Most never planned to stay in the United States. Home was always thousands of miles away. Since they only came to America to accumulate money, the Chinese immigrants lived as inexpensively as possible. They slept in huge halls, where as many as one thousand men could sleep on matted floors. Often three men would share one mat, sleeping in eight-hour shifts. By this method, a Chinese man could reduce the cost of his room to ten cents a month. When not sleeping, he worked, and he sent most of his earnings back to his family in China, to whom he intended to return someday.

The majority left their wives in China. In America there were twenty Chinese men for every Chinese woman. Occasionally the men would return to China long enough to impregnate their wives, but then it was back to America again for more "coolie" labor and Yankee dollars. If a Chinese man survived this difficult existence until he was fifty or sixty years old, he would return to China for good, respected by his family and village. If, as often happened, he died young in America, his bones would be sent back to China, and they too would be respected by his family and village.

Immigration, then, could in no way be interpreted as a rejection of China. In reality, it was a defense of the Chinese way of life, for the money sent home helped preserve the traditional order. America was not a sacred idea, but a means to an end, and, of course, sometimes a very lonely country. It was no wonder that opium, prostitution, and suicide were shadowy attractions of San Francisco's Chinatown.

Americans failed to understand the mind of the Chinese immigrant. To them, the Chinese were just non-Western, non-Christian, and non-White aliens. Although railroad builders and mine owners regarded the Chinese as good, inexpensive laborers, native-born American workers believed they brought down wages for all workers. Every major American labor organizer of the period, from T. V. Powderly and Samuel Gompers to Eugene Debs and Henry George, called for federal action to restrict Chinese immigration. Some leaders charged that the "coolies" so depressed wages that women in white working families had to resort to prostitution to avoid starvation.

The most vocally anti-Chinese Americans were the Irish-Americans, new immigrants themselves. The Chinese, they asserted, were corrupt, despotic, cunning, deceitful, cruel, and hopelessly depraved. In addition, they were dirty and a threat to public health. They falsely blamed outbreaks of syphilis, cholera, leprosy, and other nameless contagions on Chinese immigrants.

Labor leaders, Irish politicians, the Catholic church, Eastern editorialists, California workers—all agreed, the Chinese should—*must*—be excluded from the United States as undesirable, unassimilable aliens. In 1882, Congress responded with the Chinese Exclusion Act, which suspended Chinese immigration. It was the first time that America closed its doors to any immigrants for ethnocultural reasons.

Later, other immigrant groups shared experiences similar to the Chinese. Native-born Americans saw other ethnic groups as beyond reform, as not having the "right stuff" to become Americans. Again and again labor leaders, religious authorities, and old-line Americans joined forces in opposition to certain groups of immigrants. The entire process culminated in 1924 with the passage of the National Origins Act.

Yet immigrants contributed greatly to the growth of industrial America. They and their fellow workers—native-born white and black Americans—built the railroads that crisscrossed the country; mined the gold and silver that made other men rich; and labored in the oilfields, steel mills, coal pits, packing plants, and factories that made such names as Rockefeller, Carnegie, Swift, and Westinghouse famous. Without these men and their companions, there would have been no industrialization. In the process they made the United States into an ethnically rich nation.

Until the Chinese Exclusion Act thousands of Chinese traveled to the United States. Most were men; rarely did women and families come along too.

HUDDLED MASSES AT THE GOLDEN DOOR

On October 28, 1886, President Grover Cleveland traveled to New York Harbor to watch the unveiling of the Statue of Liberty. A gift from France, Frederic Auguste Bartholdi's grand statue was meant to symbolize solidarity between the two republics, but that was not how Americans and incoming immigrants interpreted the sculpture. For them it was a simple symbol of welcome, with the statue's torch lighting the path to a better future. At the base of the statue the words of Emma Lazarus emphasized the promise of America:

> Give me your tired, your poor,
> Your huddled masses yearning to breathe free,
> The wretched refuse of your teeming shore.
> Send these, the homeless, tempest-tossed to me,
> I lift my lamp beside the golden door!

For immigrants who arrived in America from Europe, the Statue of Liberty was both a sign of welcome and an indication of a new life.

In popular theory, the promise of America exerted a powerful pull on Europe and Asia. The United States stood for political freedom, social mobility, and economic opportunity. Since the first settlers landed in Jamestown, millions of immigrants had responded to the American magnet. At no time was immigration as great as in the late nineteenth and early twentieth centuries. Between 1860 and 1890 more than ten million immigrants arrived on America's shores. Between 1890 and 1920 over fifteen million more arrived.

America was not the only country to lure immigrants from Europe. Millions more immigrated to Australia, New Zealand, South Africa, Canada, Brazil, Argentina, and other underpopulated areas of the globe. In truth, seen in its worldwide context, the United States pull was less powerful than the European push. During the nineteenth century almost every European country experienced a dramatic population increase. Advancements in medicine and public health standards reduced infant mortality rates and increased life expectancies, but available land and food could not increase to meet the new population demands. Almost every European country, from Ireland in the northwest to Greece in the southeast, experienced the same phenomenon. First came a population boom; twenty years later, when the baby boomers reached maturity, immigration increased sharply.

Historians have divided immigration to the United States into two categories: old and new. The source of the old immigration was northern and western Europe—England, Ireland, France, Germany, and Scandinavia. Except for the Irish, they were mostly Protestants, always white, a majority were literate, and most had lived under constitutional forms of governments. Assimilation for them was a relatively easy process. The new immigration stemmed from eastern and southern Europe. Greeks, Poles, Russians, Italians, Slavs, Turks—they found assimilation more difficult. Politically, religiously, and culturally, they differed greatly from the earlier immigrants as well as native-born Americans.

The shift from "old" to "new" occurred during the 1880s. For example, in 1882, when 788,992 immigrants arrived in America, most were Germans, British, and Scandinavians; eighty-seven percent came from northern and western Europe. By 1907 this pattern had changed. That year when 1,285,349 immigrants landed in America, more than eighty percent were from southern and eastern Europe.

Certainly, a geographic shift in origin of immigration to the United States took place,

but more than geography differentiated the old and the new immigration. Their reasons for leaving Europe, visions of America, settlement patterns, and occupational choices varied dramatically.

By the late nineteenth century, the motives and the opportunity to emigrate to America were present in southern and eastern Europe. With the abolition of serfdom, peasants were free to emigrate; and with the rise in population, young men faced job, land, and food shortages. Finally, railroads and steamships made travel faster and less expensive. Indeed, during the 1880s British and German steamships hauled immigrants across the Atlantic for as little as $8, and by the turn of the century the trip only took five and a half days. In short, the conditions were right for the push to emigrate to America.

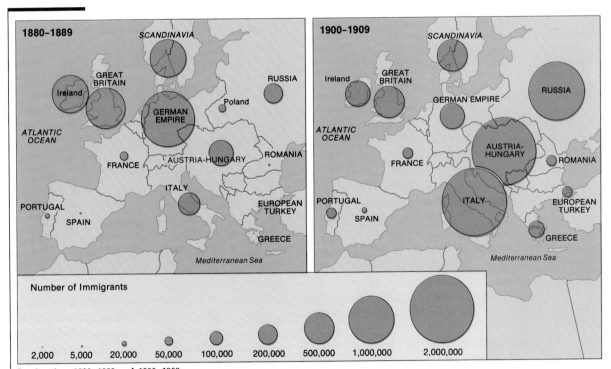

Immigration, 1880–1889 and 1900–1909
The source of old immigration was primarily northern and western Europe—England, Ireland, France, Germany, and Scandinavia. By the late 1880s a wave of new immigrants began to arrive from eastern and southern Europe.

The influx of "new" immigrants included Greeks, Poles, Russians, Slavs, Italians, and Turks. Many had trouble assimilating to life in America.

"Birds of Passage"

Essentially two types of immigrants came to America. "True" immigrants formed one group, migrant workers comprised the other. The people in the second group, often called birds of passage, were like the Chinese. They never intended to make the United States their home. Unable to earn a livelihood in their home countries, they came to America, worked and saved, and then returned home. Most were young men in their teens and twenties. They left behind their parents, young wives, and children, indications that their absence would not be too long. Before 1900, immigration officials estimated that seventy-eight percent of Italian immigrants and ninety-five percent of Greek immigrants were men. Many of them traveled to America in the early spring, worked until the late fall, and then returned to the warmer climates of their southern European homes for the winter. Some immigrants came to America fully intending to return home but for one reason or another—

love, hardship, early death—didn't. Overall, twenty to thirty percent of all immigrants did return.

The activity of the birds of passage can be clearly seen in Italian immigration patterns. Starting during the 1870s, Italian birth rates began to rise and mortality rates fell. Population pressure became severe, especially in *Il Mezzogiorno*, the southern and poorest provinces of Italy. Known as "the land that time forgot," the social customs and family patterns of *Il Mezzogiorno* seemed timeless. Life revolved around *la famiglia* ("the family"), and *l'ordine della famiglia* ("the rules of family behavior and responsibility") was a sacred code. Unfortunately for the people in *Il Mezzogiorno*, the central government, dominated by Northerners and concerned only with northern interests, did not forget the impoverished southern provinces. Heavily taxed and hurt by high protective tariffs on northern industrial goods, southern Italians sunk deeper into poverty. Cynically but realistically they noted the sad truth of the old expression *la legge va contra i cristiani* ("the law works against the people").

The law and population pressures already worked against the region; soon nature also joined the opposition forces. A series of natural disasters rocked southern Italy during the first decade of the twentieth century. Earthquakes caused untold devastation in the provinces of Basilicata and Calabria. Vesuvius erupted and buried a town near Naples. Then Etna erupted. The worst tragedy, however, was the 1908 earthquake and tidal wave that struck the Strait of Messina between Sicily and the Italian mainland. The disaster destroyed hundreds of villages and killed tens of thousands of people. In the city of Messina alone, more than 100,000 people perished.

The kinds of jobs that Italian men sought reflected their attitude toward America. They did not look for careers. Occupations that provided opportunity for upward economic mobility were alien to them. Unlike most of the earlier emigrants to America, they did not want to farm in America or even own land, both of which implied a permanence that did not figure in their plans. Instead, Italians headed for the cities, where labor was needed and wages were relatively good. Few jobs were beneath them. Native-born Americans commented that the Italian birds of passage readily accepted "work no white man could stand." Expecting their stay in America to be short, they lived as inexpensively as possible under conditions that native-born families considered intolerable.

Italians were particularly attracted to heavy construction jobs. One study of Italians in America noted in 1905, Italians gravitated toward "work that is simple and monotonous . . . that can be performed by men disposed in a gang, under the more or less military supervision of a foreman, so that the worker becomes himself like a part of a machine. . . ." Contracted out by a professional labor broker known as a *padrone,* Italians supplied the muscle that dug tunnels and canals, laid railroad tracks, and constructed bridges and roads. So important were they to the construction business that in 1905 the Industrial Commission concluded that "it would be a difficult thing . . . to build a railroad of any considerable length without Italian labor." As early as 1890, ninety percent of New York's public works employees and ninety-nine percent of Chicago's street workers were Italian.

While they received good wages, their homes in Italy were seldom forgotten. One nostalgic Italian admitted, "Doctor, we brought to America only our brains and our arms. Our hearts stayed there in the little house in the beautiful fields of our Italy." And for women, adjustment to America was even more difficult. They often wore black clothing, an old country practice which symbolized self-sacrifice, misery, and determination. Edward Corsi, the son of immigrants who became President Franklin Roosevelt's commissioner of immigration, recalled that his mother never adjusted to America: "She loved quiet, and hated the noise and confusion. . . . She spent her days, and the waking hours of the nights, sitting at one outside window staring up at the little patch of sky above the tenements. She was never happy here, though she tried. . . ."

Italians were not the only birds of passage. The same forces—population pressure, unemployment, hunger, and the breakdown of agrarian societies—sent Greeks, Slavs, Chinese, Japanese, Mexicans, French Canadians, and inhabitants of scores of other nations to the United States. Seeking neither permanent homes nor citizenship, they desired only an opportunity to work for a living, hoping to save enough money to return to a better life in their old home. Always the land they coveted was in Europe or Asia, not in the United States.

Slavs, and especially Poles, dramatized this pattern of temporary migration—the desire to use America as a means of improving their lot in their home country. Strong and robust, they preferred the work that paid the best—usually the most dangerous and physically exhausting. After disembarking at east coast ports, Slavs generally headed directly to the mill and mining towns of Pennsylvania and the Midwest. They found the wages they were after in the stockyards of Chicago, the coal mines of Scranton, and the steel mills of Pittsburgh and Buffalo. In 1910 a Pittsburgh steel worker earned between

Most of the miners from Pennsylvania to California were immigrants from Europe and Asia. Anxious to improve their standard of living in their homeland, these immigrants would accept dangerous, but high-paying jobs.

$2.28 and $2.41 for a twelve-hour day; a miner in the same area earned between $2.40 and $3.00 for eight hours of work. For an unskilled laborer, that was considered good pay.

Unlike the Italians who preferred to work in sociable gangs and above ground, Poles readily accepted the hard lonely labor of the mines and steel mills. The extra money was enough compensation for the danger of underground or indoor work. Employers quickly noted this Slavic inclination. In 1909 a Pittsburgh newspaper advertisement solicited "Tinners, Catchers, and Helpers. To work in open shops. Syrians, Poles, and Romanians Preferred." Such an advertisement attracted hundreds of hardy Slavs in search of good wages and the fast route home.

In Search of a New Home

In contrast to the birds of passage, several million other immigrants came to America with no intention of ever returning to the land of their birth. These were the permanent immigrants, for whom America offered political and religious freedom as well as economic opportunity. The promise of America was especially appealing to members of ethnic and religious minorities who were persecuted, abused, and despised in their homelands. Germans from Slavic countries, Greeks from Romania, Serbs from Hungary, Turks from Bulgaria, Poles from Russia—for these men and women home held few warm associations.

A fine case in point is Czarist Russia, a country notoriously and historically inhospitable to many minorities. In 1907, 250,000 "Russians" emigrated from Russia. But who were these "Russians"? Over 115,000 were Jews, and another 73,000 were Poles. Others were Finns, Germans, and Lithuanians. Only a small fraction of the Russian immigrants were of Russian ethnic stock. In short, for Russia true immigration was generally an alternative for minorities.

The Jews were the prototypical true immigrants. Like the Irish-Catholics a generation before, they fled near unbearable hardships. From the thirteenth century, millions of Jews had maintained a relatively stable communal life in Poland. Then during the eighteenth cen-

tury Russia, Prussia, and Austria conquered and divided Poland. Most of the Polish Jews fell under Russian rule, and the quality of their lives took an immediate, drastic, downward turn. Russian authorities drove Jews out of commerce and forced them into an area known as the Pale of Settlement. There they toiled to farm in the poor soil of the steppes or earn a living as artisans or craftsmen in impoverished villages. There, too, Russian officials burned their books, disrupted their religious practices, and occasionally even broke up their families. Particularly painful were the Russian conscription laws, which took thousands of boys between the ages of twelve and eighteen for periods of military service up to twenty-five years.

Starting in the early 1880s, conditions for Jews in Russia rapidly deteriorated from bad to worse to intolerable. Laws restricted Jewish businesses, prevented Jewish land ownership, and limited Jewish education. Pogroms, a form of legally sanctioned mob attacks against Jews, killed and injured thousands of persons. Sometimes at the whim of authorities, Russian Cossacks burned Jewish houses and destroyed Jewish possessions.

For Jews, then, immigration offered a chance for a far better life than existed for them in the Pale of Settlement. Dr. George M. Price, one of the several million Jews who left Russia for America during the late nineteenth century, expressed the feelings of these immigrants for their homeland. In his diary he wrote: "Sympathy for Russia? How ironical it sounds! Am I not despised? Am I not urged to leave? Do I not hear the word zhid (Jew) constantly? Can I even think that some consider me a human capable of thinking and feeling like others? Do I not rise daily with the fear lest the hungry mob attack me? . . . It is impossible . . . that a Jew should regret leaving Russia."

Because they came to the United States to stay, the form of Jewish immigration differed substantially from that of the birds of passage. For them immigration was not simply a young man's alternative. Jews, as all other true immigrants, tended to come to America in family units. Men and women, young and old—they were all represented. They brought their life savings and most valuable possessions with them, never expecting to see again what they left behind. As a result, the move to America was financially and physically taxing. And once in America, whole families had more expenses than the young male birds of passage.

Since America was now their home, Jewish men looked for jobs offering future opportunities rather than simply the opportunity to work for wages. They were not drawn to the steel mills and mines, or even to jobs in construction. They desired skilled, not unskilled, labor. Many Jews had skills, for the uncertain life of the Russian Pale had taught them not to depend on land or commerce. There, a Jew's greatest possession was the ability to do something that could not be taken away. This meant a skilled craft. In the Pale and in America Jews were tailors and seamstresses, cigar makers and toy makers, tanners and butchers, carpenters, joiners, roofers, and masons, coppersmiths and blacksmiths. They had the knowledge and ability to perform the thousands of skilled tasks needed in an urban environment. The available statistical evidence reinforces this point. Where seventy-five percent of Italians and Poles entering the United States between 1899 and 1910 were unskilled laborers or farmers, sixty-seven percent of all Jews were skilled workers.

Not all new immigrants arrived on the east coast. These Jewish immigrants disembarked at the port in Galveston, Texas.

NATIVISM: THE ANTI-IMMIGRANT REACTION

Sometimes an isolated event, by itself not historically important, can illuminate like a flash of lightning the social landscape and beliefs of a particular time. Certainly this is true with the *Hennessy* case. In 1890 a feud between gangs on the New Orleans docks turned violent. Joe and Pete Provenzano were arrested and tried for attempting to massacre the rival gang. The trial took a sensational turn when David Hennessy, the New Orleans superintendent of police, asserted in 1891 that he had evidence that a secret Sicilian organization known as the Mafia was involved in the affair. Shortly after Hennessy made his bold charges, five armed men gunned him down. Before he died, Hennessy was heard to say, "The dagos shot me."

The crime raised a hue and cry against Sicilians, and local police arrested scores, urged on by Mayor Joseph Shakespeare's instructions to "arrest every Italian you come across, if necessary." The mayor told the public, "We must teach these people a lesson that they will not forget for all time." Eleven Sicilians were brought to trial, but a jury failed to convict them. Undaunted, a local mob promptly took matters into their own hands and shot or clubbed to death nine and hanged two of the suspects. As far as most natives of New Orleans were concerned, justice had been done.

Many Americans seemed to agree. Editorialists praised the mob action and damned the vile "un-American" Italians. Soon the affair sent ripples across diplomatic waters. Italy protested the mob action, but Washington refused to take any action. Anti-Italian rhetoric became ugly and wild rumors ricocheted like bullets. Some said that the Italian fleet was headed toward America's east coast; others claimed that uniformed Italians were going through military drills in the streets of New York City. One thing was clear, noted an editorialist in the *Review of Reviews,* Congress had to pass immigration legislation to keep out "the refuse of the murderbreeds of Southern Europe."

The *Hennessy* case soon faded from the front pages of American newspapers. Italy did not attack the United States, and Congress did not immediately push through a restrictive immigration policy. But the emotions it generated and revealed were very real. Native-born Americans harbored deep suspicions of and resentments toward immigrants, especially those from southern and eastern Europe. If American industrialists saw in the immigrants a bottomless pool of dependable inexpensive labor, other Americans saw something far different and much less promising. Workers saw competition. Protestants saw Catholics and Jews. Educators saw illiterate hordes. Politicians saw peasants, unfamiliar with the workings of republicanism, democracy, and constitutionalism, and, what was even worse, perhaps contaminated by a belief in socialism, communism, or anarchism. Social Darwinists saw a mass of dark-skinned, thick-browed, bentbacked people who were far "below" northern and western Europeans on the evolutionary ladder. In short, native-born Americans, heirs of a different culture, religion, and complexion, saw something alien and inferior, perhaps even dangerous.

They reacted accordingly. They posted signs: "No Jews or Dogs Allowed." They called the Chinese "coolies," and the Mexicans "bean heads." Overall, they created an atmosphere of hostility that too often spilled over into open violence. During an 1895 labor conflict in the southern Colorado coal fields, a group of American miners killed six Italians. In 1891 in a New Jersey mill town, 500 tending boys in a glass works rioted when the management hired fourteen young Russian Jews. When Slavic coal miners went on strike in 1897 in eastern Pennsylvania, local citizens massacred twenty-one Polish and Hungarian workers. On the west coast, Chinese workers were subject to regular and vicious attacks. Especially during economic hard times, native-born Americans lashed out against the new immigrants.

Sources of Conflict

Nativism, as this anti-immigrant backlash was called, took many forms. Racial nativism, the subject for thousands of books and articles, is the best remembered. University professors such as Wisconsin's Edward Alsworth Ross and popular writers such as Madison Grant decried the new immigrants as biologically less advanced than the Americans who traced their ancestry back to northern and western Europe. "Observe immigrants," Ross wrote in *The Old World in the New,* "in their gatherings, washed, combed, and in their Sunday best. You are struck by the fact that from ten to twenty percent are hirsute, low-browed, big-faced persons of obviously low mentality. . . . These ox-like men are descendants of those who always stayed behind." Using such criteria as complexion, size of cranium, length of forehead, and slope of shoulders, the immigrants from southern and eastern Europe were judged inferior to most native-born Americans. That university professors and scientists accepted such theories of innate racial and ethnic inferiority gave credibility to these notions.

Religious differences reinforced ethnic variations. Overwhelmingly Catholic and Jewish, the new immigrants challenged the Protestant orthodoxy in America. Anti-Catholicism, noted a leading student of nativism, "blossomed spectacularly" during the late nineteenth century. Many Americans regarded the Pope as the antiChrist and Catholics as his evil minions. And it was widely believed that the authoritarian bent of the Catholic mind made it incompatible with democratic institutions. As the Reverend Josiah Strong observed in his best-selling book *Our Country: Its Possible Future and the Present Crisis* (1885), there was "an irreconcilable difference between papal principles and the fundamental principles of our free institutions."

Native-born Americans viewed Jews with even greater suspicion, attributing the characteristics of Shakespeare's Shylock to Jews as a whole. "Money is their God," wrote leading journalist and social critic Jacob Riis. Other writers commented that Jews were tactless, tasteless, and pushy. Eventually many social clubs, country clubs, hotels, and universities excluded Jews, arguing that money alone could not purchase respectability.

The *Leo Frank* case painfully demonstrated the ubiquitous anti-Semitism in American society. Frank, a Cornell University graduate and a son of a wealthy New York merchant, managed an Atlanta pencil factory. In 1914 one of the factory hands, Mary Phagan, was found murdered on the premises. Frank was tried and convicted on flimsy evidence, but the case soon became an international cause célèbre. After reviewing the case the governor of Georgia commuted Frank's death sentence to life imprisonment. The action outraged native Georgian whites. They boycotted Jewish merchants and clamored for Frank's blood. Finally, a group of citizens from Mary Phagan's home town took Leo Frank from a state prison, transported him 175 miles across the state, and coldly hanged him. As news of the hanging spread, people gathered to gaze at the sight and shout "Now we've got you! We've got you now!" In the 1980s, new evidence in the Phagan case proved Frank innocent, and Georgia's Board of Pardon's granted him a posthumous pardon. But dispassionate justice was scarce in the weeks after Frank's death.

Orators used the *Leo Frank* case as an object lesson. Tom Watson, the fiery Georgia politician, warned listeners, "From all over the world, the Children of Israel are flocking to this country, and plans are on foot to move them from Europe *en masse* . . . to empty upon our shores the very scum and dregs of the *Parasite Race*." Like Josiah Strong and Edward Alsworth Ross, Tom Watson believed that Congress should stop the flow of immigrants before America was flooded by the waves of eastern and southern Europeans.

Many congressmen agreed with Watson. They too harbored strong suspicions of the new immigrants. For them, political fears mixed naturally with racial and religious misgivings. They tended to equate immigration with radicalism and suspected that every boat that docked at Ellis Island contained a swarm of socialists, communists, and anarchists prepared to foment revolution. As unfounded as their fears were, they could always point to isolated cases of radicalism among immigrants. They drew attention, for example, to Leon Czolgosz, born only months after his eastern European immigrant parents arrived in America. Discontent and unable to adjust to American life, Czolgosz became a convert to revolutionary anarchism. On September 6, 1901, he attended the Pan-American Exposition in Buffalo and waited patiently in a receiving line to shake hands with President William McKinley. When he reached McKinley, Czolgosz smiled, lifted up a gun, and shot the president twice through his tuxedo vest. Questioned about his action, Czolgosz confessed, "I don't believe in the Republican form of government and I don't believe we should have any rulers. It is right to kill them." Such actions and statements seemed to confirm the worst fears of antiradical nativists.

The strongest resentments against the new immigrants, however, were purely economic. American workers, particularly the unskilled, believed that the immigrants depressed wages by their willingness to "work cheap." An iron worker complained, "Immigrants work for almost nothing and seem to be able to live on wind—something which I can not do." Even skilled workers maintained that the birds of passage immigrants were unwilling to support any union efforts to improve working conditions in America. Samuel Gompers, head of the American Federation of Labor, said that the immigration problem in America was "appalling." He believed that the immigrants from eastern and southern Europe and from Asia were ignorant, unskilled, and unassimilable. Calling for strong restrictive legislation, he said, "Some way must be found to safeguard America."

In short, by the 1890s, when a terrible depression had disrupted the normal economic and social course of America, the new immigrants became a convenient scapegoat for the nation's myriad ills. Americans were swept along by a wave of xenophobic fear. It was a time when people elevated racial prejudice and

American laborers blamed their low wages and poor working conditions on immigrant workers. Labor competition added to the nativist reaction.

rumors to universal truths. Native-born Americans blamed crime on Italians and prostitution on the Chinese; they claimed that the social ills of America's expanding cities—corruption, poor sanitation, violence, crime, disease, pollution—were the fault of the new immigrants. And they looked to the federal government for relief and protection.

Closing the Golden Door

The first immigrants to be attacked were those who were most different from native-born Americans and the most unskilled. Certainly this was the case with the Chinese. Between 1868 and 1882 more than 160,000 Chinese entered the United States. They laid down railroad tracks and mined for gold, silver, and coal. Unlike native-born Americans and most members of other immigrant groups, they did not consider cooking, washing, and ironing as "women's work," and in these areas they were particularly successful. Perhaps even too successful.

Lee Chew, who as a boy in China dreamed of obtaining wealth in "the country of the American wizards," immigrated as a young man to the United States. In America he found opportunity. He worked and saved and sacrificed. In America he also discovered that Chinese were subject to the worst forms of exploitation and abuses. Like blacks in the South and Indians in the West, white Americans cheated and sometimes violently attacked the Chinese. "Americans are not all bad," Lee noted, "nor are they wicked wizards. Still . . . their treatment of us is outrageous."

During the depression of the mid-1870s the Chinese came under increasingly bitter and violent attacks. At the forefront of the nativistic onslaught were the Irish, themselves recent immigrants, who competed with the Chinese for unskilled labor. Irish political leaders in America demanded an end to Chinese immigration into the United States. But by the provisions of the Burlingame Treaty (1868) with China, the Chinese were free to immigrate and to establish American citizenship.

Eventually Congress responded to the pressure for restriction. In 1880 China gave the United States the right "to regulate, limit or suspend," though not to prohibit, the immigration of workers. Quickly the golden door slammed shut. In 1882 the Chinese Exclusion Act suspended Chinese immigration for ten years and drastically restricted the rights of the Chinese already in the United States. In 1892 Congress extended the act for another ten years, and then in 1902 extended it indefinitely. The legislation established a precedent for the future exclusion of other immigrants. By the 1890s, most Americans agreed that the country should restrict "undesirable" immigrants. But how, for example, could Congress close America's door to southern and eastern Europeans while leaving it open for northern and western

Europeans? To achieve this end, politicians proposed a literacy test. As early as the late 1880s economist Edward W. Bemis proposed that the United States exclude all male adults who could not read and write their own language. He maintained that such a law would effectively stop the flow of eastern and southern Europeans into America. The idea soon had the backing of the influential Republican Senator Henry Cabot Lodge of Massachusetts and the equally important Immigration Restriction League.

In 1896, Lodge pushed through Congress a literacy test bill, which would have excluded any adult immigrant unable to read forty words in his language. Lodge's timing was poor. The bill reached the desk of Democratic President Grover Cleveland two days before his second term expired. Cleveland promptly vetoed the measure. The bill, Cleveland suggested, tested prior opportunities and America stood for open opportunities. In short, the bill fell pitifully below American ideals.

Cleveland's veto did not end the demand for restrictive legislation, nor did it even kill the idea of a literacy test. Presidents William Howard Taft and Woodrow Wilson vetoed similar pieces of legislation. In 1917, on the eve of America's entry into World War I, Wilson vetoed a literacy test bill on the grounds that it was "not a test of character, of quality, or of personal fitness." Nevertheless Congress passed the act over Wilson's veto.

World War I chilled an already cold climate for immigrants from southern and eastern Europe. Those who were born in the polyglot Austro-Hungarian Empire were now considered the enemy. Others were watched with deep suspicion. This was especially true after the 1917 Bolshevik Revolution in Russia. Once again American authorities regarded Jews from Russia as potential revolutionaries. Responding to this fear, in 1918 and 1920 Congress passed legislation to exclude or deport anarchists and other "dangerous radicals."

The fight over restriction ended with a clear win for nativism in the generation-long battle. In the early 1920s Congress discovered its own solution: the quota system. The Emergency Quota Act (1921) limited immigration according to a nation-based quota system. It

In 1882 Congress passed the Chinese Exclusion Act, which barred Chinese laborers from entering the United States for ten years.

provided that no more than three percent of any given nationality in America in 1910 could annually immigrate to the United States. In 1924 the National Origins Act lowered the quote to two percent of each nationality residing in America in 1890. By using 1890 as the base year, the act was clearly aimed at restricting eastern and southern Europeans, for there were far less of the new immigrants in America in 1890 than in 1910. Although in 1927 the base year was changed to 1920, the National Origins Act had achieved its desired result. The golden door was no longer fully open to eastern and southern Europeans, and it was completely closed to Asians. An important era in American history had ended.

WORKING IN INDUSTRIAL AMERICA

If during the 1920s restrictionists won an important battle, they lost their self-proclaimed war. They longed for a rural, white, Protestant, ethnically homogeneous America, but the war they waged took the form more of a rear guard action than an offensive. Between 1870 and 1920 America had changed dramatically. It became a richly complex, ethnically diverse, industrial country. In fact, even before 1900 its cities were the most cosmopolitan in the world. In 1880 more than eighty-seven percent of the inhabitants of Chicago were immigrants and their children. In other major American cities the statistics were similar: Milwaukee and Detroit, eighty-four percent; New York and Cleveland, eighty percent; St. Louis and San Francisco, seventy-eight percent. By contrast, ninety-four percent of the inhabitants of London in 1910 came from England and Wales.

These new immigrants provided the muscle for America's spectacular industrial growth. They laid railroad track, built bridges and roads, mined coal, silver, and gold, and made steel. Once again, statistics tell at least part of the story. In 1919 more than ninety percent of the anthracite coal miners were immigrants from eastern and southern Europe. Of the 14,359 workers in Carnegie's steel plants in the Pittsburgh area, 11,694 were eastern and southern Europeans. Indeed, without immigrant labor American industrialization would have moved forward at a far slower pace.

Wages, Hours, and Standard of Living

Was it worth it after all? Was the price paid by native-born and immigrant labor for industrialization worth the benefits they received? This is not a simple question to answer; in fact, each laborer might have answered it differently. But in their answers there would have been common themes. Unquestionably industrialization extracted a heavy toll from the laborers, who suffered psychologically and emotionally in industrial America. It changed not only how, when, and where they worked, but also how

they regarded work and how they perceived themselves. Equally unquestionably, however, industrialization transformed the United States into the most prosperous country in the world. To some degree, laborers shared in that prosperity and increase in material comfort.

Wages played an important role in a laborer's attitude toward work. In general, wages rose and prices fell during the late nineteenth and early twentieth centuries. Exactly how much is a question of heated historical debate. Clarence Long, an economic historian, in his study of wages and earnings in the late nineteenth century, estimated that when adjusted for changes in the price level, real daily wage rates rose from about $1 in 1860 to $1.50 in 1890, and real annual earnings increased from approximately $300 in 1860 to more than $425 in 1890. Other students of the subject believe Long's estimates are overly optimistic and that wages tended to stagnate, especially in the large textile industries. Even Long, however, admits that the pace of wages and earnings lagged well behind the spectacular growth in the American economy.

Even with the modest improvements in wages, laborers fought a continual battle with poverty. More often than not, the prosperity of a family depended on how many members of that family worked. Carroll D. Wright, chief of the Massachusetts Bureau of the Statistics of Labor, expressed the matter plainly in 1882: "A family of workers can always live well, but the man with a family of small children to support, unless his wife works also, has a small chance of living properly."

Take, for example, the case of two coal miners studied in 1883 by agents for the Illinois Bureau of Labor Statistics. Both were hardworking union men who earned wages of $1.50 per day. The first worked only thirty weeks in 1883, and his total income was $250. He lived with his wife and five children in a $6 per month, two-room tenement apartment. During the year he spent only $80 on food, mainly bread, salted meat, and coffee. His apartment was crowded but neat, and his children attended public school. In 1883, at least, he made barely enough to allow his family to maintain a minimal standard of living. His existence was

The family economy was an important part of survival in America. This family earned extra money by arranging artificial flowers at home.

precarious. Strikes, lay-offs, sickness, or injury could easily throw him and his family into abject poverty.

The second miner worked full time in 1883 and earned $420. He had a wife and four children, three of whom were also miners, and they brought home an additional $1000. They lived comfortably in their own six-room house perched on an acre of land. They ate well, spending $900 a year on food. Steak, butter, potatoes, bacon, and coffee comprised a typical breakfast. They bought books and enjoyed a full leisure life. The material quality of life, then, often depended on circumstances other than occupation or wages.

The most important factor in determining the well-being of a working-class family was how many members of the family worked. Fathers and sons, mothers and daughters, and often aunts, uncles, and grandparents—all contributed to the "family economy." To be sure, the nature of the "family economy" created

concern. Carroll D. Wright in the United States Census of 1880 warned, "the factory system necessitates the employment of women and children to an injurious extent, and consequently its tendency is to destroy family life and ties and domestic habits, and ultimately the home."

In truth, the opposite was probably true. Without the income earned by wives and children, families faced greater threats to their unity. Economically, families worked as a single entity; the desires of any particular individual often had to be sacrificed for the good of the family. This meant that women and children worked, families took in boarders, and all earnings were used for a common end. Far from destroying the family, the "family economy" often strengthened it.

During the first decade of the twentieth century, social workers conducted numerous studies to determine how much a family or a single individual needed to sustain a typical working-class existence for a year. Estimates for New York City ranged between $800 and $876 for a family of four, $505 for a single man, and $466 for a working woman. Many of New York's laborers fell painfully below the recommended minimum. Single women lived particularly difficult lives. A New York study concluded that women earned about half as much as men, and that the majority made less than $300 per year. One woman worker described her meager existence: "I didn't live, I simply existed. I couldn't live that [which] you could call living. . . . It took me months and months to save up money to buy a dress or a pair of shoes. . . . I had the hardest struggle I ever had in my life."

What was true for women was equally valid for blacks, Asians, and Mexicans in America. They were given the most exhausting and dangerous work, paid the least, and were fired first during economic hard times. For a black sharecropper farming a patch of worked-over soil in Mississippi, or a Chinese miner carrying nitroglycerin down a hole in a Colorado mountain, or a Mexican working on a Texas ranch, $300 per year would have seemed a kingly sum.

There were clear divisions even among workers. At the top ranks were the highly skilled laborers. Mostly English-speaking, generally Protestant, and almost exclusively white, they were paid well, had good job security, and considered themselves elite craftsmen. Below them were the semiskilled and unskilled workers. Most were immigrants from southern and eastern Europe, spoke halting if any English, and were Catholics or Jews. They lacked job security and had to struggle for a decent existence. At the bottom of the semiskilled and unskilled category were the nonwhite and women workers, for whom even a decent existence was normally out of reach.

Like wages, hours varied widely. The central question workers asked was, "How much of a person's life should be devoted to work?" Long hours were not a new phenomenon tied to industrial America. Farm workers and artisans often labored from sunup to sundown, but the tempo and quality of their labor was different. Farm work was governed by the season and the weather. During summer months and harvest, work was intense, but it slowed down during the shorter days of winter. There was always time for fishing, horse racing, visiting, and tavern-going. The rhythms of the preindustrial workshop similarly mixed work with fellowship. If the work days were long, they were also sociable. As they worked, laborers talked, joked, laughed, and even drank. In fact, laborers considered rum drinking an integral aspect of work. As Richard O'Flynn recalled, "The rum barrel was always near the work—ready for distribution, by this means they kept the men hard at work all day."

Nor was time measured out in teaspoons for the preindustrial laborer. Punctuality was not the golden virtue it became during industrialization. In the early nineteenth century, household clocks were rare and many of them possessed only a single hand. Large-scale production of household clocks did not begin in America until the 1830s, and it was not until the Civil War that cheap, mass-produced pocket watches became readily available. Certainly the idea of punching a time clock exactly on time was alien to the preindustrial worker, who might think in terms of hours but not in terms of minutes.

Preindustrial labor, then, had a more relaxed atmosphere. This is not meant to romanticize it. Farm work and shop labor could be hard and dangerous, but there were no sharp lines between labor and leisure. Gambling, storytelling, singing, debating, and drinking formed a crucial part of the work day. Thrift, regularity, sobriety, orderliness, punctuality—hallmarks of an industrial society—were virtues not rigorously observed.

The new concept of time changed not only how people worked but also how they regarded labor. The great architectural feature of nineteenth and early twentieth-century New England mill towns was the giant, looming bell towers of the factories. At George Pullman's model factory outside Chicago, the bell tower was a solid Victorian structure whose clock face reflected in a pool in front of it. Before clocks and watches, the bell towers served a utilitarian function. They told the laborers when to get out of bed, be at work, eat lunch, and go home. The importance of time was literally drilled home in a brochure prepared by the International Harvester Corporation to teach Polish laborers the English language. "Lesson One" read:

I hear the whistle. I must hurry.
I hear the five minute whistle.
It is time to go into the shop.
I take my check from the gate board and hang it
on the department board.
I change my clothes and get ready to work.
The starting whistle blows.
I eat my lunch.
It is forbidden to eat until then.
The whistle blows at five minutes of starting
time.
I get ready to go to work.
I work until the whistle blows to quit.
I leave my place nice and clean.
I put all my clothes in the locker.
I must go home.

The lesson perfectly describes the ideal industrial worker. He is at work on time, labors continuously until a whistle tells him to eat, keeps himself and his workplace clean, and goes straight home after work. In short, he is punctual, hard-working, clean, and sober.

Given this new standard of work and time demanded by factory owners, laborers were reluctant to work the preindustrial dawn to dusk day. In 1889 hundreds of trade unionists paraded through the streets of Worcester, Massachusetts, behind a banner which read: "Eight Hours for Work, Eight Hours for Rest, Eight Hours for What We Will." That was their goal, and a popular song of the day captured the ideal.

> We mean to make things over;
> We're tired of toil for naught;
> We may have enough to live on,
> But never an hour for thought.
>
> We want to feel the sunshine,
> We want to smell the flowers;
> We are sure that God has willed it,
> And we mean to have eight hours.

The reality, however, fell far short of the ideal. It is difficult to generalize about hours because they varied considerably from occupation to occupation. In 1890, for example, bakers averaged over 65 hours a week, steelworkers over 66, and canners nearly 77. Working in a steel mill blast furnace was a twelve-hour-a-day, seven-day-a-week job, including one

During the late nineteenth century, laborers fought unsuccessfully for an eight-hour workday.

twenty-four hour continuous shift and one day off every two weeks. Even as late as 1920 skilled workers still averaged 50.4 hours a week and the unskilled 53.7 hours. Before the 1930s, workers regarded the idea of an eight-hour day or even a ten-hour day as an unattainable dream.

For women, the new ideals of industrial America created even more work. The increased emphasis on cleanliness led to a greater demand for tidy homes. As a result, women devoted more time to cleaning, dusting, and scrubbing. In addition, the growing availability of washable cotton fabrics increased the amount of laundering housewives performed. Finally, more varied diets meant women spent more time plucking feathers from chickens, soaking and blanching hams, roasting coffee beans, grinding whole spices and sugar, and cooking meals. By 1900 the typical housewife worked six hours a day on just two tasks: meal preparation and cleaning.

HOUSEWORK IN NINETEENTH-CENTURY AMERICA

Housework in nineteenth-century America was harsh physical labor. Preparing even a simple meal consumed great time and energy. Prior to the twentieth century, cooking was performed on a coal or wood burning stove. Unlike an electric or a gas range, which can be turned on with the flick of a single switch, cast iron and steel stoves were exceptionally difficult to use.

Ashes from an old fire had to be removed. Then, paper and kindling had to be set inside the stove, dampers and flues had to be carefully adjusted, and a fire lit. Since there were no thermostats to regulate the stove's tempera-

ture, a woman had to keep an eye on the contraption all day long. Any time the fire slackened, she had to adjust a flue or add more fuel.

Throughout the day, the stove had to be continually fed with new supplies of coal or wood—an average of fifty pounds a day. At least twice a day, the ash box had to be emptied, a task which required a woman to gather ashes and cinders in a grate and then dump them into a pan below. Altogether, a housewife spent four hours every day sifting ashes, adjusting dampers, lighting fires, carrying coal or wood, and rubbing the stove with thick black wax to keep it from rusting.

It was not enough for a housewife to know how to use a cast iron stove. She also had to know how to prepare unprocessed foods for consumption. Prior to the 1890s, there were few factory prepared foods. Shoppers bought poultry that was still alive and then had to kill and pluck the birds. Fish had to have scales removed. Green coffee had to be roasted and ground. Loaves of sugar had to be pounded, flour sifted, nuts shelled, and raisins seeded.

Cleaning was an even more arduous task than cooking. The soot and smoke from coal and wood burning stoves blackened walls and dirtied drapes and carpets. Gas and kerosene lamps left smelly deposits of black soot on furniture and curtains. Each day, the lamps' glass chimneys had to be wiped and wicks trimmed or replaced. Floors had to be scrubbed, rugs beaten, and windows washed. While a small minority of well-to-do families could afford to hire a cook at $5 a week, a waitress at $3.50 a week, a laundress at $3.50 a week, and a cleaning woman and a choreman for $1.50 a day, in the overwhelming majority of homes, all household tasks had to be performed by a housewife and her daughters.

Housework in nineteenth-century America was a full-time job. Gro Svendsen, a Norwegian immigrant, was astonished by how hard the typical American housewife had to work. As she wrote her parents in 1862:

> We are told that the women of America have much leisure time but I haven't yet met any woman who thought so! Here the mistress of the

house must do all the work that the cook, the maid and the housekeeper would do in an upper class family at home. Moreover, she must do her work as well as these three together do it in Norway.

Before the end of the nineteenth century, when indoor plumbing became common, chores that involved the use of water were particularly demanding. Well-to-do urban families had piped water or a private cistern, but the overwhelming majority of American families got their water from a hydrant, a pump, a well, or a stream located some distance from their house. The mere job of bringing water into the house was exhausting. According to calculations made in 1886, a typical North Carolina housewife had to carry water from a pump or a well or a spring eight to ten times each day. Washing, boiling, and rinsing a single load of laundry used about 50 gallons of water. Over the course of a year she walked 148 miles toting water and carried over 36 tons of water.

Homes without running water also lacked the simplest way to dispose of garbage: sinks with drains. This meant that women had to remove dirty dishwater, kitchen slops, and, worst of all, the contents of chamberpots from their house by hand.

Laundry was the household chore that nineteenth century housewives detested most. Rachel Haskell, a Nevada housewife, called it "the Herculean task which women all dread" and "the great domestic dread of the household."

On Sunday evenings, a housewife soaked clothing in tubs of warm water. When she woke up

the next morning, she had to scrub the laundry on a rough washboard and rub it with soap made from lye, which severely irritated her hands. Next, she placed the laundry in big vats of boiling water and stirred the clothes about with a long pole to prevent the clothes from developing yellow spots. Then she lifted the clothes out of the vats with a washstick, rinsed the clothes twice, once in plain water and once with bluing, wrung the clothes out and hung them out to dry. At this point, clothes would be pressed with heavy flatirons and collars would be stiffened with starch.

The last years of the nineteenth century witnessed a revolution in the nature of housework. Beginning in the 1880s, with the invention of the carpet sweeper, a host of new "labor-saving" appliances were introduced. These included the electric iron (1903), the electric vacuum cleaner (1907), and the electric toaster (1912). At the same time, the first processed and canned foods appeared. In the 1870s, H. J. Heinz introduced canned pickles and sauerkraut; in the 1880s Franco-American Company introduced the first canned meals; and in the 1890s, Campbell's sold the first condensed soups. By the 1920s, the urban middle class enjoyed a myriad of new household conveniences, including hot and cold running water, gas stoves, automatic washing machines, refrigerators, and vacuum cleaners.

Yet despite the introduction of electricity, running water, and "labor-saving" household appliances, time spent on housework did not decline. Indeed, the typical full-time housewife today spends just as much time on

housework as her grandmother or great-grandmother. In 1924, a typical housewife spent about 52 hours a week in housework. Half a century later, the average full-time housewife devoted 55 hours to housework. A housewife today spends less time cooking and cleaning up after meals, but she spends just as much time as her ancestors on housecleaning and even more time on shopping, household management, laundry, and childcare.

How can this be? The answer lies in a dramatic rise in the standards of cleanliness and childcare expected of a housewife. As early as the 1930s, this change was apparent to a writer in the *Ladies Home Journal:*

> Because we housewives of today have the tools to reach it, we dig every day after the dust that grandmother left to spring cataclysm. If few of us have nine children for a weekly bath, we have two or three for a daily immersion. If our consciences don't prick us over vacant pie shelves or empty cookie jars, they do over meals in which a vitamin may be omitted or a calorie lacking.

The Lost Crafts

Although workers complained regularly about wages and hours, they were equally disturbed by several other results of industrialization. The late nineteenth-century industries differed from the preindustrial workshop in four important areas: size, discipline, mechanization, and displacement of skill. The new factories were huge; they employed hundreds, even thousands, of laborers. In 1850 the McCormick reaper plant in Chicago employed about 150 workers; in 1900 the work force had grown to more than 4000; and in 1916 the plant housed 15,000 workers. During that latter year, the Ford Motor Company works at Highland Park, Michigan, employed 33,000 workers. Increasingly, giant industries dominated the American economy.

These huge plants demanded an organized, disciplined work force. The informality of the preindustrial workshop, with only a handful of employees, was an inevitable casualty. During those earlier times, for example, a cigar maker might go to the shop early in the morning, sip his *café con leche* and roll fifty cigars including a few smokes for himself. At noon he retired to a saloon and played pinochle while eating a leisurely lunch and then returned to his bench for another four hours. There he talked and joked with his co-workers with the hum of the other voices and the click of the cutting blade as background. In the industrial factories workers were carefully regulated to ensure maximum productivity. Work became formalized and structured, and between the owner and the worker several levels of bureaucrats began to emerge.

Mechanization of work led to both the large factories and the incredible boom in productivity. It also caused an erosion of certain skilled trades. Imaginative inventors designed machines that performed tasks previously done by skilled craftsmen. A simple cigar mold, for example, allowed an unskilled worker to bunch cigar tobacco, a job once handled by a skilled tobacco roller. Where once a single tailor took a piece of cloth, cut it, fashioned it, sewed it, and made a pair of pants, by 1859 a Cincinnati clothing factory had divided the process into seventeen different semiskilled jobs. The replacement of skilled craftsmen by semiskilled laborers was a characteristic of the factory system. As one historian has observed, "the typical factory hand became a machine operator or fractionated workman, toiling at a single bit of the manufacturing process."

By the end of the century, it appeared to many observers that all work was being mechanized and moving toward the factory mode. Even farmers followed the mechanization march. By the early 1880s, one Dakota Territory wheat farm—or "food factory" as a critic called it—stretched over 30,000 acres, used two hundred reapers and thirty steampowered threshers, and employed one thousand field hands. Workers did not know their bosses, but this impersonality of labor was offset by a remarkable increase in output.

Worker Discontent

In the long run, industrialization brought much to many. Between 1860 and 1920 the volume of manufactured goods increased almost fourteen fold. Consumer goods which once only the rich could afford came into the purchasing range of the middle class. Newspapers and magazines advertised, and department stores displayed, a wide variety of factory products.

From a worker's perspective, however, industrialization was often an inhumane process. Factory labor tended to be monotonous, and machines made work more dangerous. Industrial accidents were alarmingly common, and careless or tired workers sacrificed their fingers, hands, arms, and sometimes even lives. To make matters even worse, owners often assumed an uncaring attitude toward their laborers. Concerned with production quotas and cost efficiency, owners seemed insensitive to workers' needs; and in fact, many *were* insensitive. As one factory manager proclaimed, "I regard my people as I regard my machinery. So long as they can do my work for what I choose to pay them, I keep them, getting out of them all I can. What they do or how they fare outside my walls I don't know, nor do I consider it my business to know. They must look out for themselves as I do myself."

Department stores changed shopping habits for Americans. They offered standardized products at prices affordable to the masses.

Where once workers determined their production and work pace, now factory managers with stopwatches made laborers account for their time by seconds. Workers particularly resented scientific time-motion experts, who strove to get the maximum production out of every laborer. One worker expressed the feelings of many others: "We don't want to work as fast as we are able to. We want to work as fast as we think it's comfortable for us to work. We haven't come into existence for the purpose of seeing how great a task we can perform through a lifetime."

Workers did not passively accept industrialization and the changes that enormous process caused. At almost every step they resisted change, and they had formidable weapons at their disposal. On one level, resistance entailed a simple, individual decision not to change completely. Factory managers demanded a steady, dependable work force, but they were plagued by chronic absenteeism. Immigrant workers refused to labor on religious holidays, and in some towns factories had to shut down on the day the circus arrived. Across America, heavy drinking on Sunday led to "blue Mondays," a term used to describe absenteeism.

Another form of individual protest was simply quitting. Most industrial workers changed jobs at least every three years, and in many industries the annual turnover rate was over 100 percent. Some quit because they were bored, "forced to work too hard," or because they were struck by spring wanderlust and simply wanted to move. Others quit because of severe discipline, unsafe working conditions, or low wages. Compulsive quitting was a clear indication that perhaps twenty percent of the work force never came to terms with industrialization.

Quick to quit workers were similarly quick to take collective action. The late nineteenth century witnessed the most sustained and violent industrial conflict in the nation's history.

Strikes were as common as political corruption during the period. Between 1881 and 1890, the Bureau of Labor Statistics estimated that 9668 strikes and lockouts had occurred. In 1886, 1432 strikes and 140 lockouts involved 610,024 workers. Although most of the conflicts were relatively peaceful, some were so violent that citizens across the nation feared that America was moving toward another revolution.

Early Labor Violence

An examination of several conflicts indicate clearly the relative power of industrialists and workers. An early violent conflict occurred in the anthracite coal region of eastern Pennsylvania. The late 1860s and early 1870s were troubled times for this socially and ethnically divided area. Mine owners competed ruthlessly against each other, and they all distrusted the miners and their union, the Workingmen's Benevolent Association (WBA). Added to economic and class tensions, the area was torn by ethnic conflicts. American born Scots-Irishmen owned most of the mines, and Welshmen and Englishmen served as mine superintendents. Increasingly, however, the miners were Irish-Catholic immigrants. Old World prejudices thus mingled with New World economics.

Matters became worse when the depression of the mid-1870s hit the area. Led by Franklin B. Cowen, president of the Reading Railroad, the mine owners came together and agreed to observe common policies regarding prices, wages, and union negotiations. Competition thus reduced, the owners cut wages and increased work loads. This sort of oppression was nothing new to the Irish, and they responded much as they had in the Old Country. More important than the WBA were the Ancient Order of Hibernians, a secret fraternal society of Irish immigrants, and its inner circle, the Molly Maguires. While the WBA battled the owners at the negotiation table, the Molly Maguires waged a violent guerrilla war. They disrupted the operation of several mines and attacked a handful of mining officials.

Because it was secretive, little is known about the Mollies. However, Cowen and the owners were able to infiltrate the group with a secret agent, James McParland. While McParland was gathering information, the WBA went on strike. Disorder and violence followed. Using the local press, Cowen convinced much of the community that a direct link existed between the WBA, the Mollies, and the bloodshed. His tactic worked and the strike was broken.

A short time later, Cowen used McParland's testimony to destroy both the Mollies and the WBA. Altogether, twenty Mollies were convicted and executed. Throughout their sensational trials, Cowen again linked Molly activities with the WBA. It was a scenario that industrialists would use again and again. The greatest weapon against strikers was the community's fear of violence. If an industrialist could convince the public that unions promoted violence, then they could characterize their own union busting tactics as a sincere defense of law and order. Cowen used the tactic successfully in 1875 and 1876.

The same depression that convulsed the Pennsylvania coal fields shook the rest of the country as well. To keep from going under, many businessmen cut rates and attempted to recoup their losses by reducing labor costs. This was true especially in the highly competitive railroad business. Repeatedly, workers suffered wage cuts, and as usually unskilled wages were slashed more than the skilled.

During the dog days of mid-July, 1877, the Baltimore and Ohio Railroad announced its third consecutive ten percent wage cut. Angry, frustrated, hot, hungry, and led by the new Trainmen's Union, railroad workers along the line went on strike. When trouble followed, Baltimore and Ohio workers seized an important junction at Martinsburg, West Virginia. There the workers battled first local, then state, and finally federal law authorities.

From Martinsburg the strike spread north and west. Railroad workers walked off their jobs and trains, vital to the American economy, sat unused and deserted. The strike paralyzed transportation in the Midwest and much of the industrial northeast. It seemed there was violence and destruction everywhere. In Baltimore the state militia shot into a mob and killed ten persons; in Pittsburgh rioters burned 2000 freight cars, looted stores, and torched railroad buildings; in Buffalo, Chicago, and Indianapolis workers and police engaged in bloody battles.

When local police and state militiamen failed to quell the problems, President Rutherford B. Hayes ordered federal troops to do the job. Eventually, superior force restored peace and the trains started rolling again. Like most spontaneous strikes, the Great Strike of 1877 failed. But the anger it revealed frightened America. Although some authorities labeled the disturbances as the work of communist agitators, more thoughtful observers realized it was caused by legitimate grievances. For owners and workers alike, the strike was a lesson. Owners learned that workers were not merely passive partners in the industrial process. Labor learned that, when pressed, the federal government was not neutral—it would side with capital.

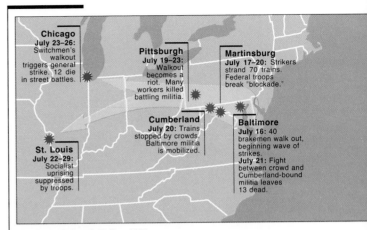

The Great Railroad Strike, 1877
The spontaneous uprising that followed the railroad strike of 1877 paralyzed two-thirds of the nation's trackage for two weeks and destroyed millions of dollars worth of railroad property.

Employers Gain Power

Between 1877 and 1886 industrialists grew in organizational and economic power. In the steel, oil, coal, railroad, and meat industries ruthless competition and consolidation produced industrial giants. Workers could not match the power of Rockefeller, Carnegie, and Swift. They controlled their industries; they were the victors in the competitive industrial wars. They were confident men who believed that they knew what was best for themselves and their workers, and their confidence bred arrogance. A sense of superiority and self-righteousness ran through their public statements. For example, one textile company manager confidently declared, "There is such a thing as too much education for working people . . . I have seen cases where young people were spoiled for labor by being educated to a little too much refinement."

The power of industrialists can be seen in the famous Haymarket Square Riot of 1886. In 1885 skilled molders won a strike at McCormick Harvester Machine Company in Chicago. Reacting angrily to the union's activities, McCormick introduced pneumatic molders which could be run by unskilled workers. Again in 1886, the skilled workers went on strike, but this time the result was different. The combined forces of

McCormick and local police ensured the safety of an army of strikebreakers and the plant's output continued until the strike was broken.

Tempers, however, remained high, and violence resulted. In May, after the strike ended, police and workers clashed once again, and a handful of laborers were killed and wounded. Disturbed by the violent force used by police in defense of industrialists' positions, August Spies, a Chicago anarchist and labor agitator, called for a protest meeting in Haymarket Square. The meeting was held on May 4 under rainy skies and before a small and generally unenthusiastic crowd. The speeches were dull and the listeners were peaceful. But as the meeting was breaking up, local police unexpectedly charged the crowd. Then somebody—to this day no one knows who—threw a bomb into the melee, killing police and protesters alike.

Industrialists, city officials, ministers, and the local press convinced a bewildered public that the bombing was a prelude to anarchistic revolution. Police arrested eight local radicals, including Spies, and charged them with conspiracy. There was no real evidence against them, but the mood of the authorities was so biased that no evidence was needed. The eight

In 1886 Illinois police attempted to break up a meeting of labor leaders and sympathizers. A riot ensued when someone threw a bomb into the fray, killing seven policemen and four workmen.

were tried, convicted, and sentenced to be hanged. One man committed suicide in his cell, three were eventually pardoned, but four were executed. For radicals, labor agitators, and unionists, the message was clear: police and public opinion were on the side of the industrialists.

The excessive violence of the Molly Maguires, the Great Strike of 1877, and the Haymarket Square Riot was not necessarily typical of disputes between labor and management. Although labor violence continued unabated in the 1890s with such dramatic episodes as the Homestead Strike and the Pullman Strike (see Chapter 18), often late nineteenth-century labor disputes were settled peacefully. In most cases, however, management won the conflicts. Only in small towns, where prolabor and anti-industrial sentiment knew no class lines, did labor battle management on anything approaching even terms.

Unorganized and Organized Labor

Historians have used the term "robber barons" to characterize late nineteenth-century industrialists. Whether "robber" is accurate or not is debatable, but "baron" is a fitting description. They controlled their industries as medieval barons ruled their fiefs. Their word was usually final, and such a modern concept as democracy found an unsympathetic environment inside factory walls. A Pennsylvania coal miner described accurately what workers experienced behind those walls: "They find monopolies as strong as government itself. They find capital as rigid as absolute monarchy. They find their so-called independence a myth, and that their subjection to power is as complete as when their forefathers were part and parcel of the baronial estate."

Unfortunately, during the last third of the nineteenth century labor was unable to form an organization powerful enough to deal with capital on equal terms. Before 1900, most unions were weak, and their goals were often out of touch with the changing American economy. In addition, the labor force itself was divided along ethnic, racial, gender, and craft lines. It was during this period, then, that labor attempted to overcome its own divisions and fumbled its way toward a clearer vision of what were its own best interests.

Before the 1870s most American unions were locally rooted, craft-based organizations. They were geared to the small Jacksonian workshop, not to the large modern factory. The first union to attempt to organize all workers was the short-lived National Labor Union (NLU). Founded in Baltimore in 1866, the NLU sought to give the worker a voice in national affairs. Its program was ambitious. Besides shorter hours and higher wages, it supported women's and blacks' rights, monetary reform, and worker-owned industries. As one of their leaders said, the "only way by which the toiling masses can protect themselves against the unjust claims and soul-crushing tyranny of capital" was for "themselves to become capitalists." It disdained the emerging industrial capitalism. Referring to capital, its leader, William Sylvis, wrote to Karl Marx: "We have made war upon it, and we mean to win it. If we can we will win through the ballot box; if not, we will resort to sterner means. A little bloodletting is sometimes necessary in desperate cases." Rich in ideas and solution, however, the NLU was poor in organization and finances. The NLU, whose reach exceeded its grasp, died during the depression of the mid-1870s.

The vision of the NLU was carried on by the Noble and Holy Order of the Knights of Labor. Begun in 1869 as a secret fraternal order as well as a union, the Knights remained small and unimportant until 1878 when it went public. Led by Terence V. Powderly, a machinist and former mayor of Scranton, Pennsylvania, in 1881 the Knights opened its membership not only to "any person working for wages but to anyone who had at any time worked for wages." The Knights excluded only bankers, lawyers, liquor dealers, speculators, and stock brokers, whom they viewed as money manipulators and exploiters.

Complete worker solidarity was the Knight's goal. "An injury to one is an injury to all," they proclaimed. They welcomed and spoke for all laborers—women and men, black and white, immigrant and native, unskilled and skilled. Like the NLU, the Knights rejected industrial capitalism and favored cooperatively owned industries. "The aim of the Knights of Labor," Powderly emphasized, "is to make each man his own employer." Although critics at the time labeled the Knights "wild-eyed, utopian visionaries," they are best understood in the context of exploited workers searching for a less exploitive alternative to industrial capitalism. If their statements were extreme, their suffering was real.

Powderly was an able leader who had a clear view of the future and was able to express the fears and ambitions of American labor. He called for reforms of the currency system, the

The Knights of Labor attempted to organize all workers—skilled and unskilled, white and black, and native-born and immigrant.

abolition of child labor, regulation of trusts and monopolies, an end to alien contract labor networks, and government ownership of public utilities. By nature a diplomatic, good-natured man, he favored peaceful arbitration of labor disputes and opposed strikes. He also opposed the formation of narrow trade unions, instead advocating that skilled workers should assist the unskilled. Harmony and fellowship ultimately dominated his vision of America's future. Consensus not conflict was his goal.

The Knights' rhetoric found sympathetic listeners among American workers. During the early 1880s membership rolls grew. Then came 1884, the beginning of what labor historians have called "the great upheaval." Strikes erupted in the coal fields of Pennsylvania and Ohio and the railroad yards of Missouri and Illinois. The labor conflicts continued into 1885 and 1886. Labor won some, but by no means all, of the strikes. Although its role was small, the Knights were associated with several of the important labor victories. By mid-1886 perhaps 750,000 workers had joined the Knights.

From that high point, however, the decline was rapid. Administrative and organizational problems surfaced, and Powderly's relatively conservative leadership was opposed by more radical members, who fully accepted strikes and conflict. In 1886, the Haymarket Square bombing branded all unions as un-American and violent in the public mind. By 1893, when Powderly was driven from office, the Knights' membership had declined alarmingly. Weakened and divided, it failed to survive the depression of the mid-1890s.

Unlike the Knights and the NLU, the American Federation of Labor (AFL) did not aspire to remake society. Its leaders accepted industrial capitalism and rejected partisan politics and the dreams of radical visionaries. Instead they concentrated on practical, reachable goals—higher wages, shorter work days, and improved working conditions. Most importantly, they only recruited skilled laborers, recognizing that easily replaceable unskilled workers were in a poor position to negotiate with employers.

Formed in 1886 by the coming together of skilled trade unions, the AFL was led ably by

Samuel Gompers, a Jewish immigrant from England who had been the president of a New York cigar makers' union. Like many cigar makers, Gompers was well, if informally, educated. Cigar-rolling was a quiet job, and the rollers often employed one of their number as a reader. As a boy Gompers not only learned a skill but he absorbed the leading political,

Samuel Gompers

economic, and literary ideas of his day. "In fact," Gompers later wrote, "these [readings and] discussions in the shops were more like public debating societies or . . . 'labor forums.'" The workers discussed the works of Marx and Engels, and Gompers even learned German so that he could fully understand German socialists—but he never joined the socialist movement. He maintained that the transition from capitalism to socialism would be glacially slow. Far better, he felt, to strive for the attainable than talk, dream, and wait for the utopian.

As the head of the AFL, a post he held for almost forty years, Gompers used his considerable "moral power" and organizational ability to fight for achieveable goals. American laborers were divided over religious, racial, ethnic, gender, and political issues, but they all desired higher wages, more leisure time, and greater liberty. Working out of his eight-by-ten office, and using tomato boxes for filing cases, Gompers battled for those unifying issues. He focused on the world around him, not the best of all possible worlds. For this reason, he opposed "theorizers" and "intellectuals" in the labor movement. Once effectively organized, he maintained, labor could deal with capital on equal terms.

Gompers's approach toward working with capital and organizing labor proved successful in the long run. Before 1900, however, the AFL was no more successful than the Knights or the NLU. In fact, workers benefited little from unions before the turn of the century. All together,

CHRONOLOGY
OF KEY EVENTS

1866 National Labor Union formed in Baltimore

1869 Knights of Labor formed secretly in Philadelphia

1870 Census reports there are 39.8 million people in the United States

1877 Great Railway Strike

1882 Chinese Exclusion Act

1882 First Labor Day celebrated in New York City

1885 Reverend Josiah Strong's *Our Country* published

1886 Statue of Liberty dedicated

1886 Haymarket Square Riot in Chicago

1886 American Federation of Labor formed in Columbus, Ohio, Samuel Gompers elected president

1891 Hennessey case in New Orleans ignited anti-Italian emotions

1892 Homestead, Pennsylvania, Strike

1894 Pullman Strike

1900 Census reports there are 75.9 million people in the United States

1901 Leon Czolgosz assassinates William McKinley

1914 Leo Frank case

1921 Emergency Quota Act

1924 National Origins Act

---

less than five percent of American workers joined trade unions, and the major areas of industrial growth were the least unionized. Nevertheless, the experimentation during the late nineteenth century taught workers valuable lessons. To combat the power of capital, labor needed equal power. During the twentieth century labor would move closer to that power.

CONCLUSION

In 1986 the Statue of Liberty was given a good cleaning. Its copper was shined as much as copper turned green can be shined, and its struc-ture was refortified. America celebrated, and television newscasters recited once again Emma Lazarus's poem "The New Colossus"— or as one commentator called it "her 'huddled masses' poem." Few asked the question, "What are we celebrating?"

What America celebrated was nothing less than the emergence of modern America. In 1876 when France shipped the Statue of Liberty to the United States, the country, despite a recent civil war, was remarkably uniform. Most Americans traced their ancestry to Great Britain, worshipped in a Protestant church, and lived on farms or in small villages. If they were divided, it was along political and economic lines, not along ethnic and religious ones. The United States was not a world leader. Its navy was small, its diplomats uninfluential, and its industry still largely underdeveloped.

By 1900 America had changed radically. Unprecedented immigration had transformed the country into the most diverse nation in the world. Italians, Slavs, Serbs, Greeks, Chinese—a host of immigrants crowded into American cities. Catholics and Jews worked alongside Protestants in the country's expanding industries. For some it was an exciting, hopeful time; for others a painful, disillusioning one. Old America gave way to a New America with startling speed. In fact, most Americans in 1900 had not yet adjusted to the massive changes. What role would the new immigrants play in American life? What rights did workers have in the large industries? These and other questions would be answered in the next century.

REVIEW SUMMARY

During the late nineteenth and early twentieth centuries, immigration to America soared. European and Asian immigrants came for a variety of reasons, settled primarily in cities, and provided the muscle for American industrialization.

  - many Italian, eastern European, and Chinese immigrants were "birds of passage," returning to their native land after working in America
  - other immigrants, like the Jews, made new homes in America

Some native-born Americans responded to the increasing rate of immigration by:

  - attacking the immigrants for their religious and political beliefs
  - complaining that the immigrants lowered wages and weakened the country's Anglo-Saxon traditions
  - eventually pressuring Congress into passing restrictionist legislation

Regardless of the conflict, however, the immigrants gradually entered the larger society, and America was enriched in the process.

SUGGESTIONS FOR FURTHER READING

OVERVIEWS AND SURVEYS

Leonard Dinnerstein and David Reimers, *Ethnic Americans* (1975); H. U. Faulkner, *Politics, Reform, and Expansion* (1959); John Garraty, *The New Commonwealth* (1968); Ray Ginger, *The Age of Excess* (1965); Oscar Handlin, *The Uprooted* (1951); Samuel Hays, *The Response to Industrialism, 1885–1914* (1957); Alan M. Kraut, *The Huddled Masses* (1982); H. W. Morgan, ed., *The Gilded Age;* Robert Wiebe, *The Search for Order, 1877–1914* (1967).

HUDDLED MASSES AT THE GOLDEN DOOR

Rodolfo Acuña, *Occupied America: A History of Chicanos,* 2nd ed. (1981); Josef J. Barton, *Peasants and Strangers* (1975); Rowland Berthoff, *British Immigrants in Industrial America, 1790–1950* (1953); John W. Briggs, *The Italian Passage* (1978); Jack Chen, *The Chinese of America* (1980); Alexander DeConde, *Half Bitter, Half Sweet: An Excursion into Italian-American History* (1971); Richard Gambino, *Blood of My Blood* (1975); Caroline Golab, *Immigrant Destinations* (1977); Irving Howe, *World of Our Fathers* (1976); Maldwyn Allen Jones, *American Immigration* (1960) and *Destination America* (1976); Thomas Kessner, *The Golden Door* (1977); Harry Kitano, *Japanese Americans* (1969); Joseph Lopreato, *Italian Americans* (1970); Carey McWilliams, *North from Mexico* (1948); Ande Manners, *Poor Cousins* (1972); Charles C. Moskos, Jr., *Greek Americans* (1980); Cecyle S. Neidle, *America's Immigrant Women* (1975); Humbert Nelli, *Italians in Chicago, 1880–1930* (1970) and *The Business of Crime* (1976); William Petersen, *Japanese Americans* (1971); Moses Rischin, *The Promised City: New York's Jews, 1870–1914* (1962); Andrew Rolle, *The Immigrant Upraised* (1968) and *The Italian Americans* (1980); Theodore Saloutos, *The Greeks in the United States* (1963); Philip Taylor, *The Distant Magnet* (1971); Stephan Thernstrom, *Poverty and Progress* (1964) and *The Other Bostonians* (1969); Maurice Violette, *The Franco-Americans* (1976); Joseph Wytrawal, *America's Polish Heritage* (1961) and *The Poles in America* (1969); Helena Znaniecka Lopata, *Polish Americans* (1976).

NATIVISM: THE ANTI-IMMIGRANT REACTION

Robert Carlson, *The Quest for Conformity* (1975); Leonard Dinnerstein, *The Leo Frank Case* (1968); Milton M. Gordon, *Assimilation in American Life* (1964); Mark Haller, *Eugenics* (1963); Leo Hershkowitz, *Tweed's New York* (1977); John Higham, *Strangers in the Land* (1955); Gerd Korman, *Industrialization, Immigrants and Americanizers* (1967); Richard M. Linkh, *American Catholicism and European Immigrants, 1900–1924* (1975); Paul Mc-

Bride, *Culture Clash* (1975); Seymour Mandelbaum, *Boss Tweed's New York* (1965); Stuart Creighton Miller, *The Unwelcome Immigrant* (1969); Thomas J. Pavlak, *Ethnic Identification and Political Behavior* (1976); Diane Ravitch, *The Great School Wars* (1974); Alexander Saxton, *The Indispensable Enemy* (1971).

WORKING IN INDUSTRIAL AMERICA

Paul Avrich, *The Haymarket Tragedy* (1984); David Brody, *Steelworkers in America* (1960); Wayne G. Broehl, Jr., *The Molly Maguires* (1964); Robert V. Bruce, *1877: Year of Violence* (1959); John R. Commons et al., *History of Labor in the United States,* 4 volumes (1918–1935); Victor Greene, *The Slavic Community on Strike* (1968); Gerald Grob, *Workers and Utopia* (1961); Herbert Gutman, *Work, Culture, and Society* (1975); Alice Kessler-Harris, *Out to Work: A History of Wage-Earning Women in the United States* (1982); David Katzman, *Seven Days a Week: Women and Domestic Service in Industrializing America* (1978); Stuart B. Kaufman, *Samuel Gompers and the Origins of the AFL* (1973); Harold Livesay, *Samuel Gompers and Organized Labor in America* (1978); David Montgomery, *Beyond Equality* (1967) and *Workers' Control in America* (1979); Daniel Rodgers, *The Work Ethic in Industrial America 1850–1920* (1978); Gerald Rosenblum, *Immigrant Workers* (1973); Roy A. Rosenzweig, *Eight Hours for What We Will* (1983); Nick Salvatore, *Eugene V. Debs, Citizen and Socialist* (1982); David Shannon, *The Socialist Party of America* (1967); Peter Shergold, *Working-Class Life* (1982); Leslie Woodcock Tentler, *Wage-earning Women* (1979); Norman Ware, *The Labor Movement in the United States, 1860–1895* (1929).

End of the Century Crisis,

1877–1896

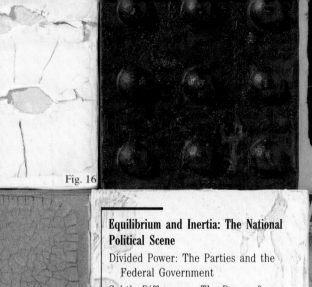

Fig. 16

On July 9, 1896, William Jennings Bryan rose to speak to the delegates at the Democratic National Convention in Chicago. "I thought I had never seen a handsomer man," a reporter wrote, "young, tall, powerfully built, clear-eyed, with a mane of black hair which he occasionally thrust back with his hand." A champion of expanding the currency by coining silver, Bryan attacked supporters of a gold standard as elitist oppressors of the debt-ridden masses. He enthralled the crowd from the beginning, but his closing words created pandemonium. "We will answer the demand for a gold standard," Bryan roared, "by saying to them: 'You shall not press down upon the brow of labor this crown of thorns, you shall not crucify mankind upon a cross of gold.'" As he spoke his fingers first traced the course of imaginary trickles of blood from his temples. He closed with his arms outstretched as if he were nailed to a cross.

When he dropped his arms, he had won the Democratic nomination and cinched the victory of the party's silverites over President Grover Cleveland's "Gold Democrats." The Cleveland supporters left Chicago unwilling to accept Bryan's "foul pit of repudiation, socialism, [and] anarchy," as one declared. Another said, "I am a Democrat still—very still." Since the Republicans had nominated William McKinley and adopted a gold standard and high tariff platform, the voters had a clearer choice than anytime since 1860. Silver became a symbol in 1896 for a number of popular grievances. It represented, among other things, rural values, the common people, and a growing discontent with northeastern political domination.

In his campaign Bryan capitalized on his oratorical genius and electrifying charisma. He began August 7 on a grueling round of appearances. By November he had traveled over 18,000 miles, visiting 27 states and giving 600 talks. His youth—he was thirty-six—sustained him as he made his own travel arrangements, bought his own tickets, carried his own bags, rode in public cars, and walked from train stations to hotels late at night. He was often called upon to give unscheduled speeches; when one Indiana crowd awakened him, he spoke in his nightgown.

Such actions seemed necessary because Bryan was only able to raise the meager sum of around $500,000, and nearly half of the Democratic newspapers opposed him. Taking his campaign directly to the people, Bryan appealed to sectional and class animosities. He did not mince words: "Probably the only passage in the Bible read by some financiers is that about the wise men of the East. They seem to think that wise men have been coming from that direction ever since."

With a Republican campaign fund of over $3.5 million, McKinley wisely refused to follow Bryan's course. "I might just as well put up a trapeze in my front lawn and compete with some professional athlete as to go out speaking against Bryan," he said. Between June and November, McKinley left his home in Canton, Ohio, for only three days. Railroads provided cheap excursion rates to Canton so that every day except Sunday, people—sometimes as many as 50,000—thronged to McKinley's lawn where he conducted his "front porch" campaign. The gatherings were hardly spontaneous. His skillful staff organized the groups by occupation or interest, screened each delegation's remarks, and planned each event in detail down to brass bands and banners.

Unlike Bryan's speeches, McKinley's were calm and dispassionate, stressing national unity rather than diversion. "We are all dependent on each other, no matter what our occupation may be," he declared. "All of us want good times, good wages, good markets; and then we want good money always." From his front porch he addressed some 750,000 people from thirty states, but he did not have to rely on merely this. The Republicans spent more for printing than Bryan raised for his entire campaign. By the campaign's end Republicans sent 200 million pamphlets to 15 million voters. Some 250 paid speakers toured 27 states, and a group of former Union army generals, calling themselves a "Patriotic Heroes Battalion," rallied veterans along the route of a flag-draped train.

On election day Bryan and his wife rose at 6:30 A.M. and voted at a local fire station in Omaha, Nebraska. He then gave seven speeches in his hometown before collapsing, exhausted, in bed that evening. McKinley walked to his

In the 1896 election, Republicans sought to convince voters that Bryan was a radical who threatened American values and institutions, while McKinley (shown in the campaign poster above) would guarantee stability, order, and integrity.

polling place and stood in line to vote. He then returned home to wait for the returns—his lawn and porch in worse shape than he was. All over the nation politicians and just plain people waited to find out which man and party would preside over the dawning of the twentieth century.

The election came in a decade of turbulence which saw violence toward the labor movement, rising racial tensions, militant farmers, and discontented unemployed workers—all of which became worse after a major depression began in 1893. The social fabric seemed to be unraveling rapidly, which is why the election of 1896 was considered so important.

Following Reconstruction, national politics were colorful but not very significant. Since no important policy differences separated the two major parties, the campaigns revolved around personalities, gimmicks, emotional slogans, and local issues. As elections were trivialized, they also became a major source of entertainment, and voters turned out in record numbers. This triumph of style over substance in politics, as well as culture, led the era to be labeled the

"Gilded Age." By 1890 both the Democratic and Republican parties had lost touch with the sentiments of large blocks of voters. The losers in the great national race toward economic modernization began to question the assumptions behind it. Their voices rose in the 1890s, but unable to unite around a viable agenda, they failed to win many battles in the closing years of the nineteenth century. The issues they raised, however, appeared regularly on the political agendas of the twentieth century.

EQUILIBRIUM AND INERTIA: THE NATIONAL POLITICAL SCENE

American politics have often seemed odd to Europeans. Never was this more true than in the closing decades of the nineteenth century. The apparent lack of ideological bases of American political parties bewildered them. In his 1898 book, *The American Commonwealth,* Lord James Bryce wrote that "neither party has any principles, any distinctive tenets. Both have traditions. Both claim to have tendencies. Both have certainly war cries, organizations, interests enlisted in their support. But those interests are in the main the interests of getting or keeping the patronage of government. . . . All has been lost, except office or the hope of it."

Bryce was an astute observer. The apparent paradoxes of Gilded Age politics become more understandable, however, in the light of the relative strengths of the major parties, the nature of current political ideology, and the organization and functions of the parties.

Divided Power: The Parties and the Federal Government

From the crucible of the Civil War and Reconstruction both the Democratic and Republican parties emerged with sizable and stable constituencies. For the twenty years between 1876 and 1896 they shared a rare equality of political power. Elections were so close, that until 1896 no president won office with a majority of the popular vote. Two (Hayes and Harrison) even entered the presidency without a plurality. The average popular vote margin was one and one-half percent. Republicans occupied the White House for twelve years, Democrats for eight. Only during three two-year periods did the same party control the presidency and both houses of Congress—Democrats once and Republicans twice. Most of the time Congress itself was split, with Democrats generally taking the House and the Republicans the Senate. Very few seats shifted parties in any given election.

The party division of Congress inevitably weakened the presidents of the era. None were elected to consecutive terms. Novelist Thomas Wolfe called them "the lost Americans" and noted that "their gravely vacant and bewhiskered faces mixed, melted, swam together" in the public mind. Lord Bryce claimed none of them "would have been remembered had he not been President." To be fair, all were competent men, some with distinguished war records, most with considerable public service. One reason they were so forgettable was the era's concept of the presidency. Most agreed with Cleveland's assertion that the office "was essentially executive in nature." "I did not come here to legislate," he said. Presidents were only supposed to execute efficiently and honestly the policies determined by Congress—occasionally vetoing ill-advised legislation. Even though these presidents were able to turn back many of the encroachments on presidential authority that began in Johnson's term, none considered it his duty to propose legislation.

Some found the office frustrating. After James Garfield moved from leadership roles in the House of Representatives to the presidency, he lamented, "I have heretofore been treating of the fundamental principles of government, and here I am considering all day whether A or B should be appointed to this or that office." Even representatives and senators were frequently frustrated, however, because congressional action was often stalemated. In the House, outdated, complex rules hampered action. Party discipline was practically impotent in both houses, and since neither controlled both houses for more than a two-year term, there was little possibility of formulating and enacting any coherent legislative program.

The paucity of legislative action can also be explained by the popular rejection of activist government at the start of the Gilded Age. Widely accepted doctrines of laissez-faire and Social Darwinism circumscribed the appropriate role of government. William Graham Sumner once proclaimed that government had "at bottom . . . two chief things . . . with which to deal. They are the property of men and the honor of women. These it has to defend against crime." Both parties basically accepted a limited vision of federal responsibility. When vetoing a small appropriation for drought relief in Texas, Democrat Cleveland asserted that "though the people support the Government, the Government should not support the people." Republican leader Roscoe Conkling claimed that the only duty of government was "to clear the way of impediments and dangers, and leave every class and every individual free and safe in the exertions and pursuits of life."

Such antigovernment sentiment tended to increase the power of the judicial branch. Many saw the courts as a bastion against governmental interference, and they certainly fulfilled that role. On the basis of the Fourteenth Amendment, judges were especially active in striking down state laws to regulate business. They also narrowly interpreted the constitution on federal authority—ruling that the power to tax did not extend to personal incomes and that the power to regulate interstate commerce applied only to trade, not manufacturing. Congress also defaulted to the judiciary by enacting vague laws which relied upon the courts for both definition and enforcement.

Subtle Differences: The Bases of Party Loyalty

One consequence of the equality of power shared by the Democrats and Republicans was the reluctance of either party to chance losing voters by articulating clear positions on most contemporary issues. Perhaps this reluctance was also based on the memories of the divisive 1860 election and its devastating impact on Democratic and national unity. In addition, during the early stages few Amerians criticized industrialization and economic modernization, and there was widespread consensus on quite a few issues.

Most members of both parties did not question the pace or cost of industrialization. They also saw little need for the federal government to play a major role in regulating the economy. When a Democratic president replaced a Republican one in 1893, Henry Frick wrote Andrew Carnegie, "I cannot see that our interests are going to be affected one way or another by the change in administration." Indeed businessmen had so little to fear from either party that they contributed generously to both.

Until 1896 the parties did share numerous similarities. Both were lead by wealthy men but still tried to appeal to wage earners and farmers as well as merchants and manufacturers. Most members of both believed in protective tariffs and "sound currency." Both rejected economic radicalism and positive programs to aid workers. Presidents of both parties sent federal troops to break up strikes.

Ironically, for all their similarities the parties evoked fierce loyalty from a heterogeneous mix of people. One reason party platforms were so innocuous as to be interchangeable is that both parties were composed of factions and coalitions of "strange bedfellows." Because of its past and abolitionist connection the Republican party retained the support of activist reformers, idealists, and blacks. Yet most Republicans came from established "old stock" families, and the more wealth a man had, the more likely he was to vote Republican. It was a curious combination of "insiders" and "outsiders."

The Democrats were even more mixed. The party's constituents often were united only by its members' opposition to the Republicans on various grounds. One Republican leader complained, "The Republican party does things, the Democratic party criticizes; the Republican party achieves, the Democratic party finds fault." Several generations later Will Rogers quipped, "I don't belong to an organized party; I'm a Democrat." His words were certainly true of the Gilded Age. The party contained such disparate elements as southern whites, Catholics, Jews, and immigrants.

For historical and cultural reasons party loyalty was frequently determined by the three factors of region, religion, and ethnic origin. The regional factor was most evident in the support by white Southerners of the Democratic party. To vote for the party of abolition and Reconstruction was considered treason and a threat to white supremacy. On the other hand the Republicans could count on heavy support from New England for the opposite reasons. To New Englanders, the Democrats were the party of traitorous rebellion against the Union. Because the Republicans could not expect to receive any southern white votes, this was one issue they did need to tiptoe around. They frequently "waved the bloody shirt," reminding Northerners that the Democrats had caused the Civil War. In 1876 one Republican declared, "Every man that tried to destroy this nation was a Democrat . . . . Soldiers, every scar you have on your heroic bodies was given you by a Democrat."

For various reasons immigrants had long gravitated toward the Democratic party. Many were members of the poorest classes which traditionally voted Democratic. In the 1850s anti-immigration Know-Nothing party members joined the Republican ranks, reinforcing immigrants' ties to the Democrats. Most of the "new immigrants" of the Gilded Age settled in cities controlled by Democratic political machines that won their loyalty by meeting the immigrants' needs. As immigration swelled, increasing Democratic strength, Republicans became more and more restrictionist. In fact, immigration policy was one of the very few substantive issues on which the parties took clearly different stands.

Religious affiliations also helped determine party loyalty—partly because of the positions on immigration. Many of the late nineteenth-century immigrants were Catholics and Jews who were suspicious of the Protestant-dominated Republican party. There were also fundamental differences in the religious orientation of most Republicans and Democrats. Republicans tended to belong to *pietistic* sects that based salvation on good works and moral behavior. Democrats, on the other hand, leaned toward *ritualistic* religions based on faith and observance of church rituals. Pietistic Republicans frequently sought to legislate morality, supporting prohibition of alcohol and enforcement of Sunday blue laws, which barred various activities on the sabbath—including baseball. Many Democrats did not believe that personal morality could or should be a matter of state concern. A Chicago Democrat explained, "A Republican is a man who wants you t' go t' church every Sunday. A Democrat says if a man wants t' have a glass of beer on Sunday he can have it."

The roots and constituencies of the parties created differences in their outlooks. The Republicans became the "party of morality," the Democrats the "party of personal liberty." Democrats not only rejected government interference in their personal life, they were also more suspicious of government activism of any sort. Some quoted the eighteenth-century Democrat Albert Gallatin's dictum: "We are never doing as well as when we are doing nothing."

In reality though the differences and divisions *within* parties was as great, and sometimes greater, than those between the two. The Democrats could count on the South for all its electoral votes, but southern Democrats frequently broke party ranks when voting on legislation. They sometimes voted with western Republicans on acts favorable to farmers. They were, however, fundamentally conservative men of Whiggish tendencies who usually voted with northern Republicans on fiscal and economic issues, as well as on immigration restriction. In a bizarre political arrangement, southern Democrats also voted with northern Republicans at times in order to receive a share of the spoils of office.

The Republicans were even more deeply divided into factions. One group, lead by Roscoe Conkling of New York, was labeled the "Stalwarts." Followers of James G. Blaine of Maine were called "Half-breeds." The only significant item of dispute between the two was who would receive the numerous jobs appointed by the president. The distribution of patronage was a prime function of both parties of the era. Thus the division was bitter. When Conkling was asked if he intended to campaign for Blaine in 1884, he snapped that he did not engage in criminal activities.

There was one faction of the Republican party that did have some ideological basis. It was composed of reformers whose primary concern was honest and effective government. They had bolted the party in 1872 because of the corruption of the Grant regime, and they bolted again in 1884. Party regulars ridiculed them, calling them "goo-goos" for their idealistic good government crusade. They were finally labeled "Mugwumps," and a joke asserted that they had their "mugs" on one side of the fence and their "wumps" on the other.

The divisions in the Republican party reflected the fact that the politicians of the day were less concerned with issues and ideology than with winning office and distributing patronage. Lord Bryce observed that American politicians could be distinguished from European ones by the fact "that their whole time is frequently given to political work, that many of them draw an income from politics . . . that . . . they are proficient in the acts of popular oratory, of electioneering, and of party management."

The Business of Politics: Party Organization

If most elected leaders of the Gilded Age did not seem to take substantive issues seriously, they were very earnest about their political careers. They worked hard at both "party management" and "electioneering." The result was the largest voter turnout in the nation's history. In the elections from 1860 to 1900 an average of seventy-eight percent of eligible voters cast ballots. Outside of the South, where blacks were increasingly prevented from voting and where the Democratic nomination determined the general election, the turnout sometimes reached ninety percent.

Party organization was geared to get out the vote. The parties were structured like pyramids with ward or precinct meetings at the base. At these all party members were allowed to attend. They generally elected representatives to county committees, which then sent members to the state committees that conducted the ongoing business of the party and nominated state candidates for office. At the top were the national committees. National conventions, where representation was based on the electoral votes of the states, met every four years to select national candidates, draft platforms, and vote on party rules. On election day thousands of local party workers mobilized and called on designated lists of voters to ensure that their party's supporters went to the polls. In 1884 Indiana Republicans appointed 10,000 such "district men."

There was one main difference in Republican and Democratic party organization. Republicans generally depended on strong state orga-

Urban political machines used money from graft to finance personalized services for their constituents in return for votes. Here New York's Tammany Hall machine hold a free barbecue for voters.

Many cartoonists attacked the corruption of machine politics. In this one, Richard Croker, head of the New York City machine, is pictured as a sun surrounded by corrupt satellites.

nization, and Democrats tended to rely on urban political machines to win and control votes. Since city governmental structures did not keep pace with the huge population increases, machines based on ward captains provided many of the services for which government would later be held responsible. The machine also aided immigrants and rural migrants to adjust to city life. One ward boss noted: "There's got to be in every ward somebody that any bloke can come to—no matter what he's done—and get help. Help, you understand, none of your law and justice, but help." The politicians were paid in votes from the people, bribes from legal and illegal businesses, and graft from contractors. The system worked so well that the Democrats usually carried the big cities.

For both parties recruiting and maintaining party voters was a game for professionals. In Pennsylvania, Republican workers compiled a list of 800,000 voters with notations as to their reliability as voters. Politics was also a rough and frequently corrupt game. Conkling warned, "Parties are not built by deportment, or by ladies' magazines, or gush." In 1888 when Benja-

min Harrison proclaimed, "Providence has given us the victory," Republican party boss Matt Quay snorted, "Providence hadn't a damn thing to do with it." Quay then added that Harrison "would never know how close a number of men were impelled to approach the gates of the penitentiary to make him president." Electoral corruption was not limited to one party. In the same year a Mississippi Democrat admitted: "it is no secret that there has not been a full vote and a fair count in Mississippi since 1875, that we have been preserving the ascendancy of white people by revolutionary methods. In other words, we have been stuffing ballot boxes, committing perjury, and here and there in the state carrying the elections by fraud and violence."

Gilded Age politics was not dull. One could almost claim that the business of politics was entertainment. One observer remarked, "What the theatre is to the French, or the bull fight . . . to the Spanish . . . [election campaigns] and the ballot box are to *our* people." The drama of emotional tent meetings rivaled circuses. The pageantry of parades also provided excitement. Almost everyone got caught up in the elections, frequently displaying such paraphernalia as buttons, handkerchiefs, hats, banners, and posters emblazoned with their party's symbol or slogan. In 1888 one tobacco company enclosed a picture of one of the twenty-five presidential hopefuls in its packages. Politics was undoubtedly the prime form of mass entertainment.

Many politicians surely must have enjoyed their status as "media stars" and folk heroes. For some, whose ethnic or class backgrounds closed conventional doors of opportunity, politics provided a vehicle of upward social mobility, similar to professional entertainment and athletics or trade union leadership. Yet politics as a vocation offered other rewards. Elected and appointed officials not only received salaries but also openly accepted gifts from lobbyists and free passes from railroads. They sometimes used their governmental status to promote their private interests. James G. Blaine of Maine expressed no qualms about accepting stock concessions from an Arkansas railroad that he had aided in getting a federal land grant. One quip claimed that the United States had the best Congress money could buy.

In such an environment the so-called spoils system was sure to flourish. Rewarding party workers with government jobs, regardless of qualifications, began in the antebellum period. It grew between 1865 and 1891 as federal positions tripled, from 53,000 to 166,000. Indeed, presidents spent much of their time making some 100,000 appointments—most of which were in the postal service. That number of jobs provided incentives to precinct and ward bosses to get out the vote, even though party victory in national elections rarely made much difference otherwise.

Style over Substance: Presidential Campaigns, 1880–1892

After the disputed election of 1876 almost created a constitutional crisis, the presidency was snatched from Democrat Samuel J. Tilden and given to Rutherford B. Hayes. A series of bargains were needed for the acceptance of the dubious findings of the electoral commission that named Hayes president. Thus from the start, his administration was tainted with snide references to him as "His Fraudulence" and "Old 8 to 7." He was actually honest, competent, and did much to establish the Republican party as the "party of morality" after the corruption of the Grant regime. His wife also helped to link Republicans with morality by her refusal to serve strong drinks—earning her the label of "Lemonade Lucy."

Hayes sought to set some standards for federal officeholders; his actions, however, mainly alienated fellow Republicans, and he refused to run for a second term in 1880. Stalwarts hoped to run Grant again, but the Republican convention became deadlocked. On the thirty-sixth ballot the party turned to a "dark-horse" candidate, James A. Garfield, a veteran Ohio congressman. To conciliate the Stalwarts, Chester A. Arthur, a Conkling henchman, became the vice-presidential nominee.

The Democrats nominated an even more obscure figure, General Winfield Scott Hancock, whose only claim to fame was being a hero of the Battle of Gettysburg. He was described as "a good man weighing 250 pounds." Garfield was also bland, but he had the advantage of a log cabin birth and a brief career on a canal towpath—which gave rise to a popular Republican campaign slogan, "from the towpath to the

Gimmicks in Gilded Age political campaigns, such as this Bryan donkey, stirred public interest, resulting in the highest voter turnouts in the nation's history.

White House." The 1880 election was one of the closest of the century in popular vote. Garfield received a mere 39,000 vote plurality out of almost 10 million ballots cast. The margin of victory may well have been the result of Hancock's candor in calling tariffs "a local issue." This alarmed many businessmen, some of whom made lavish contributions to Garfield's campaign. They later exacted payment for their aid by influencing the appointment of federal judges who were pro-business.

Like Hayes, Garfield soon became embroiled in patronage issues. Only four months after his inauguration he was shot twice by a deranged office seeker named Charles Guiteau, who explained, "I am a Stalwart. Arthur is now President of the United States." A native of Vermont, Arthur attended Union College, became an abolitionist lawyer, and then held a series of appointed offices. Considered by many to be a party and civil service hack, Arthur surprised them by becoming a champion of patronage and tariff reform. He also astounded them by vetoing two bills that were popular with Republicans. However, Congress passed both the $28 million river and harbor bill and the Chinese Exclusion Act over his veto.

In this cartoon, Grover Cleveland's illegitimate child is used to impugn "Grover the Good's" well-known political integrity.

When 1884 brought the next presidential election, Arthur's actions had won him more favor from the public than from his party. The Republicans bypassed him and chose James G. Blaine, who was far from bland. He was so handsome and charismatic that a colleague's wife once remarked, "Had he been a woman, people would have rushed off to send expensive flowers." Indeed, Blaine had almost all the qualities of a successful presidential candidate: a phenomenal memory for names and faces, eloquent oratory, and a quick wit. He was, however, a tainted political commodity. While in Congress he had become very rich without any visible means of outside income. Copies of letters circulated that seemed to indicate Blaine was up for sale to the railroads. He was more than the mugwumps could stomach.

Realizing the potential advantage of a mugwump defection, the Democrats selected Grover Cleveland, a reform governor of New York. He was neither physically attractive nor charismatic. He did have one appealing quality, however. He was honest. As one supporter explained, "We love him for the enemies he has made." Yet Cleveland and Blaine did not disagree on the major issues. Therefore, their campaign revolved around personalities and became one of the most scurrilous in the nation's history.

Blaine's tainted past was obvious fodder for the Democrats' campaign. At torchlit rallies Democrats chanted: "Blaine! Blaine! James G. Blaine! Continental liar from the state of Maine!" Unable to find a shred of evidence to challenge Cleveland's honesty, Republicans publicized a more personal scandal. As a bachelor, Cleveland had supported an illegitimate child since 1874, even though his paternity was questionable. Thus Republicans countered Democratic chants with "Ma! Ma! Where's my pa? Going to the White House? Ha! Ha! Ha!" In the end Cleveland's victory may have come as the result of an indiscretion by a Blaine supporter who labeled the Democrats as the party of "rum, Romanism, and rebellion." Even though Blaine's mother was Catholic, Democrats were able to rally Catholic voters to win key states.

A strange thing happened during Cleveland's presidency—a real, live issue emerged.

Like most Democrats, Cleveland had long been less enthusiastic about high tariffs than Republicans. While in office he found that existing tariff rates were producing treasury surpluses that tempted congressmen to propose programs and appropriations which he considered dangerous expansions of federal activities. A moralistic man, Cleveland was deeply opposed to governmental involvement in the economy and social issues. Thus he became an advocate of tariff reduction.

In 1888 the Democrats renominated Cleveland and wrote tariff reduction into their platform. The Republicans chose Benjamin Harrison and cheerfully picked up the gauntlet—denouncing Cleveland's "free trade" as unpatriotic. They also promised generous pensions to veterans. Voters at last were given some choice on a real issue. The result was a viciously corrupt and close election. Harrison's campaign chairman, Matt Quay, proceeded to "put the manufacturers of Pennsylvania under the fire and fry all the fat out of them." He asked them to make large contributions to the Republican party as insurance premiums against lowered tariff rates. When Cleveland lost, many blamed his defeat on taking too clear a stand on an issue. Actually, by 1890 many people had begun to demand legislative action on a number of the issues the major parties had so studiously avoided.

THE SEARCH FOR LEGISLATIVE ANSWERS TO EMERGING PROBLEMS

Politics provided great entertainment, but there were always people who wanted more. Often local political activity was considerably more vibrant than the political inertia at the national level. As discontent arose, many problems were first tackled on the city, county, and state levels before becoming a part of the national agenda. Such issues as the currency and tariffs could only be solved at the national level. Others such as demands for clean government were undertaken at all levels. On the whole, the states responded more vigorously than the national government to the problems created by

Support for high tariffs began to erode, especially among Democrats, with the growth in the 1880s of treasury surpluses—which many feared would lead the government to undertake questionable activities.

economic changes—only to have the Supreme Court sometimes tie their hands. Actions by the federal Congress were often timid and perhaps deliberately unenforceable.

The Crusade Against Corruption in Government

"The present era of indelible rottenness is not Democratic, it is not Republican, it is national. Politics are not going to cure more ulcers like these, nor the decaying body they fester upon." This indictment of American government was penned in 1873 in a novel by Mark Twain and Charles Dudley, which gave the era its label of the Gilded Age. Because of the pervasiveness of the corruption, some saw no way out. "All being corrupt together," E. L. Godkin, editor of *The Nation*, wrote, "what is the use of investigating each other?"

There was certainly corruption at all levels of government—from the graft-financed urban machines to the notorious spoils system at the national level. In both cases only a minority of voters was disturbed by the conditions at first. For many people machine politics served a number of useful purposes, such as providing needed goods and services and reconciling conflicting interests. Machines also provided training grounds for politicians, whose professionalism and party discipline were useful in state legislatures and Congress as they rose through the ranks.

Nevertheless, the machines were never fully accepted as legitimate—especially among the urban elite. Professionals, old-stock families, wealthy businessmen, and intellectuals preferred government, as Mugwump Charles Schurz said, "which the best people of this country will be proud of." Such a government would be run by experts with business-like efficiency. The mugwumps played an important role in defining the machines as "problems" instead of solutions and won some municipal victories. They led the successful campaign for Australian secret ballots to eliminate the means of parties' keeping tabs on voters. "Clean government" had its costs. Mugwump support for restrictions on alien voting rights and for literacy tests for suffrage led to the first reduction of the franchise in a half a century.

On the national level their prime concern was the graft and corruption emanating from the spoils system. Hayes's actions to improve the quality of political appointees lost him his party's support, and not until after the revulsion at Garfield's assassination did Congress finally take action. With the support and encouragement of President Arthur, Congress enacted the Pendleton Act in 1883. It outlawed political contributions by officeholders and established competitive examinations for federal positions to be given by the Civil Service Commission. The act was rather timid—only applying to about ten percent of government employees. It was also not passed from purely unselfish motives. Since it was to apply only to future appointees and protect incumbents, the Democrats called it "a bill to perpetuate in office the Republicans who now control the patronage of the Government." In the same manner, every president after its enactment increased the number of covered positions—usually to prevent his appointees from being removed. The political system was becoming modernized, but some questioned whether it was being improved.

Regulating the Railroads and Trusts

One corrupting influence on government was the role of the railroads, which bragged about buying congressmen as one would cattle. In addition, railroad actions frequently determined who would succeed and who would fail economically. All shippers did not pay the same fares. Rebates gave advantages to such men as John D. Rockefeller. Also, although average rates declined during the late 1870s and through the 1880s, that decline was not shared equally. Where lines competed and pools failed, rate wars slashed fares to incredibly low rates. On the other hand, where monopolies existed, shippers paid murderously high rates. Because of competitive conditions, one could frequently pay less for long hauls than for short hauls. The losers, including farmers, urban businessmen, and bankers, became increasingly angry and demanded relief.

Action to regulate the railroads began at the state level. Beginning with the establishment of a regulatory commission in Massachusetts in 1869, by 1880 fourteen states had railroad commissions. The most active advocate of regulation was the Patrons of Husbandry—a farmers' group organized into local chapters called "granges." The Grangers and their allies, especially in the Midwest, got stronger legislation enacted that set maximum rates and charges within their states.

The railroad men naturally attacked these so-called Granger laws through the courts. At first they lost. In the 1877 *Munn* v. *Illinois* decision, the Supreme Court ruled that when "private property is affected with a public interest it . . . must submit to be controlled by the public for the common good." Nevertheless, it was difficult for states to regulate railroads chartered by other states and doing business across state lines. Then in the 1886 *Wabash* case the Supreme Court took away their rights to even try—by ruling that only Congress had the right to regulate interstate commerce.

Pressure began to build for federal action, and Congress responded to the demands with the Interstate Commerce Act, which Grover Cleveland signed in February, 1887. It prohibited pools, rebates, and rate discriminations; provided that all charges by the railroads should be "reasonable and just"; and established the Interstate Commerce Commission. The commission was significant as the first federal regulatory agency, but its power was woefully limited. It could investigate charges against the railroads and issue "cease and desist" orders, which could only be enforced by the courts.

Conservative courts soon nullified ninety percent of the commission's orders, and between 1887 and 1905 the Supreme Court decided against the ICC in fifteen of sixteen cases. By 1892 railroad attorney Richard S. Olney wrote, "The Commission, as its functions have now been limited by the Courts, is, or can be made of great use to the railroads. It satisfies the popular clamor for a government supervision of railroads, at the same time that such supervision is almost entirely nominal. . . . It thus becomes a sort of protection against hasty and crude legislation hostile to railroad interests. . . . The part of wisdom is not to destroy the Commission but to utilize it." One railroad executive admitted, "There is not a road in the country that can be accused of living up to the rules of the Interstate Commerce Commission."

A similar symbolic victory was won over the trusts. Again action started on the state level; by the mid-1880s fifteen southern and western states had passed antitrust legislation. Of course, companies simply incorporated in more sympathetic states. The laws were both ineffective and likely to be overturned by federal courts, but they did reflect popular distaste for the monopolies. Congress responded to these rumblings by enacting the Sherman Antitrust Act in 1890. On the surface it seemed to doom the trusts, prohibiting any "contract, combination in the form of trust or otherwise, or conspiracy in restraint of trade or commerce." Once again appearances were deceiving, but not to all the congressmen who passed it. One senator explained that the congressmen had wanted to pass "some bill headed 'A bill to Punish Trusts' with which to go to the country" to aid their reelection.

Until 1901 the act was virtually unenforced; the Justice Department instituted only four-

Public anger over railroad power finally pushed Congress to pass the Interstate Commerce Act in 1887.

teen suits and failed to get convictions in most of them. The Supreme Court also emasculated the law in *United States* v. *E. C. Knight Co.* (1895), ruling that it applied to commerce but not manufacturing. Thus the subject of the suit, a sugar trust controlling ninety-eight percent of the industry, was not in violation. Indeed, the only effective use made of the act in its first decade was as a tool to break up labor strikes by court injunctions.

Tariff and Currency Debates

As the election of 1888 between Cleveland and Harrison shows, the tariff was one issue on which the parties did differ. That difference was more illusionary than real, however. Regardless of party, congressmen voted their constituents' interests, which made few of them consistent on the issue. "I am a protectionist for every interest which I am sent here by my constituents to protect," one Democratic senator explained. Supporters of protectionism were those who sold on the domestic markets; opponents depended on foreign markets. Both groups included some farmers and manufacturers from every region.

The tariff became an issue during Cleveland's first term—primarily because he feared the consequences of the treasury surpluses that tariffs produced. In 1887 at his urging, the Democratic House enacted moderate reductions, but the Republican Senate blocked the bill. Cleveland then proceeded to make the tariff a focus of his reelection bid in 1888. Republicans erroneously interpreted his narrow defeat as a mandate for protectionism. Congress then enacted the McKinley Tariff, which raised the average duties to the highest level yet. The Republicans misread public sentiment. The unpopular McKinley Tariff helped the Democrats win the presidency and both houses of Congress in the 1892 elections. The new Congress passed a ten percent reduction in the Wilson-Gorman Tariff. Reformers were disappointed with the moderation of the cuts but were appeased by a provision of the act placing a two percent tax on incomes. That provision, however, was declared unconstitutional in *Pollock* v. *The Farmer's Loan and Trust Co.* in 1895.

The currency issue, which was destined to become the most heated, was also the most complex. At its root was a long period of deflation following the Civil War. The level of prices dropped because the production of goods was growing faster than the supply of money. More goods than the money with which to buy them reduced prices. Farmers are not necessarily hurt by a general deflation if all prices fall equally and their debt level is low. Wheat, corn, and cotton prices, however, declined more than other prices. Farmers had also borrowed heavily to expand production, and they were caught in a debt squeeze with their mortgage payments remaining high while the prices they received fell. A farmer who borrowed $1000 to buy a farm in 1868 on a twenty-five-year mortgage found that he had to produce over twice as much cotton to make the mortgage payment in 1888. Although he received virtually nothing for doubling his efforts, his creditor received not only interest for the use of his money but

also additional bonanza—dollars worth twice as much as the ones he lent.

Debtors of all occupations began blaming their problems on deflation and saw inflation of the currency as the cure. For them inflation was a moral issue—a question of justice. One way this could happen was to increase the number of legal tender paper "greenbacks" issued during the war. Instead, Congress voted to gradually retire the greenbacks already in circulation. Even the organization of a Greenback party, which ran James B. Weaver for president in 1888, did not change congressional minds.

Before the issuance of greenbacks, the nation had been on a bimetallic standard since the 1790s. The dollar was based on both gold and silver, and for years dollars were coined at a 16 to 1 mint ratio. In other words a dollar contained sixteen times as much silver as gold. By the 1870s this ratio did not reflect the market prices of the metals. Silver prices were so high that producers sold it on the open market rather than take it to the mint to be coined. Unable to buy silver at that ratio, Congress passed the Coinage Act of 1873 that ended the minting of silver.

Soon after, the discovery of large deposits of silver drove prices down. Then it was in the interest of both silver producers and inflationists to return to the coining of silver at 16 to 1. Together they formed a large lobby that wrested minor concessions from Congress. The Bland-Allison Act of 1878 and the Sherman Silver Purchase Act of 1890 required the government to buy fixed amounts of silver, but neither inflated the currency significantly. Once again Congress responded to popular pressure with essentially cosmetic actions. On issues without powerful supporters, it could hardly be expected to act courageously.

Legislative Activity on Minority Rights and Social Issues

To Afro-Americans the Republicans remained the party of black rights, but following the election of 1876 the party did less and less to earn that label. By 1890, however, conditions finally moved some Republicans to action. Dismayed by increasing southern assaults on the black vote, Senator Henry Cabot Lodge and others drafted a federal elections Bill. It sought to protect voter registration and guarantee fair congressional elections by establishing mechanisms to investigate charges of voting fraud and to deal with disputed elections.

Southern white response was rapid and bitter. The *Florida Times-Union* charged: "The gleam of federal bayonets will again be seen in the South." The *Mobile Register* warned that the Bill "would deluge the South in blood." Northern Democrats lent their support to southern outrage. Cleveland exclaimed, "It is a dark blow at the freedom of the ballot." Although in 1890 Republicans controlled both houses of Congress, they finally bartered away the Lodge Election Bill to gain support for the McKinley Tariff. Protection of manufacturers was more important to them than the protection of blacks.

In that same year Republicans also let the Blair Education Bill die. Providing for federal aid to schools, mostly black, that did not get a fair share of local and state funds, the Blair Bill marked the last glimpse of the party's dying abolitionist roots as well as the dethronement of party idealism. The Fifty-first Congress was seeking to alleviate treasury surpluses to protect tariffs, but in the end the only group to receive substantial aid was Union Army veterans, who were voted pensions by the so-called billion dollar Congress in 1890.

Other measures of the era affected minorities—but usually in a negative way. Southern white Democrats enacted discriminatory legislation against blacks at the local and state level. A movement for immigration restriction, usually initiated by Republicans, led to the Chinese Exclusion Act of 1882 and other legislation banning certain categories of immigrants and giving the federal government control of overseas immigration. In 1887 the Dawes Act attacked the tribal roots of American Indian culture, and resulted unintentionally in making Native Americans dependent wards of the state.

The status of women also began to enter the political agenda in the form of the women's suffrage movement. After an 1869 split in the movement, the National Women Suffrage Association, led by Elizabeth Cady Stanton and Susan B. Anthony, fought for the vote on the national level through the courts and a proposed constitutional amendment. At the same time the American Woman Suffrage Association sought victories at the state level.

By 1890, when the groups merged to form the National American Woman Suffrage Association, the victories of both groups were limited. NWSA lost an 1874 Supreme Court decision resulting from a suit filed by Virginia Minor against a St. Louis registrar for denying her the right to vote. The Court ruled that citizenship did not automatically confer the vote and that suffrage could be denied specific groups, such as criminals, the insane, and women. In 1878 Anthony did succeed in getting a constitutional amendment introduced into the Senate which stated that "the right to vote shall not be denied or abridged by the United States or by any state on account of sex." It continued to be submitted for the next eighteen years but was usually killed in committee and only rarely reached the floor of the Senate.

There was more success on the state and local level. By 1890 nineteen states allowed women to vote on school issues, and three states extended women the franchise on tax and bond issues. Referenda were held in eleven states, but only the territory of Wyoming had granted women full political equality. Three states—Colorado, Utah, and Idaho—adopted women's suffrage during the 1890s, but then the movement seemed to lose steam. As male resistance mounted, no other state acted until 1910. Many men agreed with a Texas senator that "equal suffrage is a repudiation of manhood."

Although most social issues received short shrift at the federal level, at the local and state level some received passionate attention. The two main ones—education and prohibition— were essentially Republican issues. An Iowa Republican slogan called for "a school house on every hill, and no saloon in the valley." Many were alarmed by the increased use of alcohol— annual consumption of beer rose from 2.7 to 17.9 gallons per capita from 1850 to 1880. Republicans moved beyond the educative temperance movement to attempt to make drinking alcohol a crime. They also sought to increase compulsory school attendance, but their efforts were often linked to moves to undermine parochial schools and schools that taught immi-

In 1869 Wyoming became the first territory to allow women to vote in all territorial elections. It later refused to enter the Union without woman suffrage.

grants in their native tongues. In most areas these Republican actions backfired, losing more voters than they gained. For example, Republicans had once predicted "Iowa will go Democratic when Hell goes Methodist," but in 1890 the state fell to their opponents.

By 1890 very little effective legislation had been adopted to deal with the problems arising from a pluralistic society experiencing rapid social change. This resulted partly from a political equilibrium that bred inertia. At the same time concepts of the limited nature of governmental responsibility did not provide impetus for action. Nevertheless, public demands for change were growing. No group challenged the status quo more than the farmers.

THE FARMERS REVOLT

Cries for change naturally emanated from the losers in the new economic order. Among the greatest losers were American farmers. Their

failure to thrive in the expanding economy convinced many that the cards had been stacked against them. After seeking various solutions to their problems, farmers turned to politics—taking up Populist leader Mary E. Lease's cry "to raise less corn and more hell." Their success was limited, but they led the first American mass movement to reject Social Darwinism and laissez-faire. They also promoted the "radical" idea that "it is the duty of government to protect the weak, because the strong are able to protect themselves." Some even questioned basic tenets of industrial capitalism.

Grievances: Real and Imagined

In 1887 North Carolina editor Leonidas L. Polk summed up the views of many farmers: "There is something radically wrong in our industrial system. There is a screw loose. . . . The railroads have never been so prosperous, and yet agriculture languishes. The banks have never done a better . . . business, and yet agriculture languishes. Manufacturing enterprises never made more money, . . . and yet agriculture languishes. Towns and cities flourish and 'boom,' . . . and yet agriculture languishes."

The basic cause of the farmers' problems was the decline of agricultural prices—primarily because of overproduction. Farmers had a hard time believing, however, that they could produce too much. Kansas governor Lorenzo Dow Lewelling wondered how "there were hungry people . . . because there was too much bread" and "so many . . . poorly clad . . . because there was too much cloth."

Overproduction was an abstract, invisible enemy; many farmers sought more tangible, personal villains—the railroads, bankers, and monopolists. As "Sockless" Jerry Simpson claimed, "It is a struggle between the robbers and the robbed." Farmers believed they were being robbed by high freight and credit costs, an unfair burden of taxation, middlemen who exploited their marketing problems, and an inadequate currency.

Although there was no conspiracy by the "monopolists" to fleece the farmers, their grievances did contain a germ of truth. Freight rates were higher for farmers in the West because of the long distances to markets and the scattered

THE POLITICAL POOR RELATION - AN UNWELCOME GUEST

By the late 1880s many farmers were already suffering from severe economic dislocation. This 1889 cartoon shows a poor, hungry farmer gazing at a banquet of tariff-gorged industrialists while McKinley pours whiskey.

and seasonal nature of grain shipments. Although western farmers generally paid the same interest rates as easterners, they were more dependent on mortgages to finance their operations than the corporations. Southern farmers also paid dearly through higher credit prices for goods obtained by crop liens. The high level of debt carried by farmers increased their marketing problems. All the crops in a region were usually harvested at the same time, and farmers had to sell them immediately to pay off loans. Middlemen took advantage of the glutted markets to buy the crops at low prices for resale when the prices rose. Sometimes their profit margin was greater than that of the farmer who had labored long and hard to produce the goods. The unfairness of this galled farmers because they lived dreary lives, isolated from the excitement and modern conveniences of the city. The isolation was especially hard on the women, who were, as one writer noted, "not

much better than slaves. It is a weary, monotonous round of cooking and washing and mending and as a result the insane asylum is $\frac{1}{3}$d filled with wives of farmers."

Governmental policy also seemed to hurt more than help. Property taxes hit farmers harder because of the tangible nature of their property. The tariffs generally hurt most farmers by both raising the prices they paid for goods and making it harder for them to sell their crops on the international market. The deflationary policy of the federal government especially hurt the farmers because of their great indebtedness. Every economic downturn brought a wave of farm foreclosures and frustration. Thousands of dreams died slowly, as one Kansas farmer's letter reveals.

At the age of 52 years, after a long life of toil, economy and self-denial, I find myself and family virtually paupers. With hundreds of cattle, hundreds of hogs, scores of good horses, and a

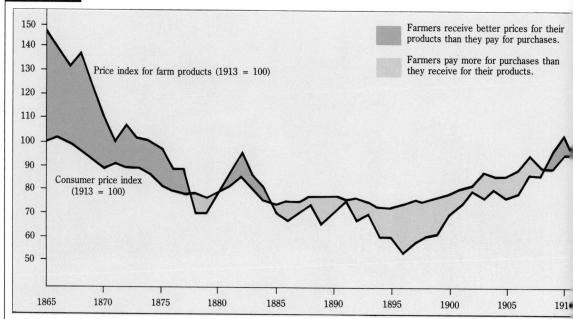

Figure 18.1
Price Indexes for Consumer and Farm Products, 1865-1913

farm that rewarded the toil of our hands with 16,000 bushels of golden corn, we are poorer by many dollars than we were years ago. What once seemed a neat little fortune and a house of refuge for our declining years . . . has been rendered valueless.

The Farmers Organize

In the age of economic consolidation farmers realized early the need to unite and cooperate. They were never able, however, to do so as effectively as the industrialists and railroads, due to their greater geographic separation as well as a frontier-bred individualism. The first national farm organization was the Patrons of Husbandry. It was founded in 1867 by Oliver Kelley, a United States Department of Agriculture employee. His action illustrated that the federal government was not totally insensitive to farm problems. Organized into local Granges that sponsored lectures, dances, and picnics, the group met a deep hunger for social interaction, and the membership grew to over one million by 1874.

The Grangers soon moved beyond their social functions to address the economic grievances of the farmers. Grangers' actions focused on railroad regulation and cooperatives, both of which met with some success. They were responsible for numerous state laws that established railroad commissions. Grangers viewed cooperatives as one solution to the high prices paid by farmers and the low prices paid to farmers. Buying cooperatives were formed to buy in bulk directly from manufacturers, eliminating retail markups. In some places granges established cooperative banks, grain elevators, cotton gins, insurance companies, processing plants, and even plants to manufacture farm implements. Sales cooperatives aimed at increasing crop prices by joint marketing.

Granger victories and successes were generally short-lived and limited. The Supreme Court nullified the Granger laws in the *Wabash* case of 1886. Most of the cooperatives were short on capital and skilled management and were hampered by the continued individualism of many farmers. They were no match against the unrelenting attacks by private business. In

Popular Protest Since the Civil War

Grand Demonstration of Workingmen, New York City (September 5, 1882).

Women have been at the
forefront of protest movements through the years.
Their causes have ranged
from worker solidarity rallies
at a May Day parade around
1900 (above, left) to marching for the ERA in recent
years (right). American Indians (above, right) have protested violations of treaty
rights and have organized
movements to reclaim their
land. Black Americans have
long been seeking redress of
grievances. During demon-
strations in Birmingham in
1963, blacks faced the fire
department's high pressure
hoses (opposite, top); Americans often gather in Washington, D. C. to commemorate
the 1963 march for civil
rights and Martin Luther
King's vision of the fulfillment of the American dream
(opposite, bottom).

In the 1960s automobile bumper stickers proclaimed "America—Love It or Leave It" and "My Country—Right or Wrong." The implication was that patriotic people do not criticize their nation or its government. Many believed that to do so was actually "un-American." If, however, protest is considered unamerican," then in the years since the Civil War many Americans have earned that label. In fact, so many people have used their constitutional right to petition their government in various ways that protest has been a vital ingredient in the national heritage. It has often served, to paraphrase Thomas Jefferson, to provide "fertilizer for the tree of liberty."

With tactics ranging from armed insurrection to peaceful marches, Americans of practically every class and occupation have sought to change conditions. One can more easily list groups that have *not* engaged in organized protest than to name those who did. In general the only groups exempt from most protest activities include those individuals who were either satisfied with the status quo or had the influence and means to make changes through the political process or by the use of wealth. The professional and industrial elite have usually had the power, prestige, and pocketbooks to reach their goals through such means as advertising and propaganda campaigns, lobbying legislatures, and financing the election of officeholders sympathetic to their cause.

At various times in the nation's history almost every other group has found voting an unavailable or inadequate method to meet their needs. Some, such as blacks and women, were denied the ballot box as a vehicle for change. Others, such as the farmers of the 1890s and 1920s, discovered their votes were insufficient to elect a government responsive to their problems. Organized protest thus provided a voice for the disfranchised and a tool for political minorities—groups that at one time or another actually constituted a majority of the American people. Indeed, protest has

Economic protest has taken many different forms during the years since the Civil War. In 1932 striking dairymen set up blockades against the delivery of milk (right). Farmers (below) were quick to lead marches or demonstrations to help make their views known. Picketing is a frequent form of protest, as these striking tobacco workers showed in Pittsburgh in 1913 (opposite, top). Violence erupted in 1914 when coal miners in Ludlow went on strike against the Colorado Fuel and Iron Company. Evicted from company-owned housing, the miners moved into tent colonies which were later destroyed by the state militia and company guards. Here (opposite, center), Red Cross members survey the damage. Sit-down strikes were also weapons in the arsenal of labor protest, such as this one at the Fisher body plant in Flint, Michigan, in 1937 (opposite, bottom).

served as a check on the tyranny of the majority and as a balance to the undue influence of elite minorities. In the twentieth century protest has become widely accepted—almost institutionalized—and may well provide an outlet for frustration that has helped to prevent the rampant terrorism plaguing some other nations.

American protestors are a diverse lot; their goals and methods have been as different as their backgrounds. Farmers have sought various kinds of governmental subsidies to offset their competitive disadvantages in the modern economy. Industrial workers have organized strikes and boycotts to protect themselves from exploitation and to receive a larger share of the fruits of their labor. Women struggled for the right to vote; they have also demanded a greater role in the economy and society. Some women sought protective legislation, which others denounced as legal straightjackets preventing equal rights. While most groups have battled to be included more fully in the "American dream," Native Americans have often protested their forced "Americanization" and cried for more independence. The most persistent and patient protestors have been black Americans. As one of the largest groups to accept American institutions and values, but to be denied their fruits for centuries, they have a long and rich tradition of protest, which has served as an inspiration to other groups. Black Power was followed with Brown Power, Grey Power, and Gay Power.

Organized protest, like reform, never entirely disappears but seems to peak in cycles. It appears to flourish when two ingredients are present: grievances and hope. Satisfaction and total despair both provide barren ground for action. Indeed, the existence of protest implies some faith in the system. Black Americans provide a striking example of the interplay of hope and grievances. Their protest efforts have never ceased but reached

crescendos at the turn of the century and in the 1960s. In the first instance, hopes had been raised by the successes of Reconstruction but grievances grew as white Southerners sought to limit and reverse black advancement. Protest quieted down only after southern whites had diminished hope by creating a legalized system of repression based on disfranchisement, segregation and lynching. The upheaval of the 1960s followed such victories as the desegregation of the armed forces and favorable Supreme Court rulings, especially the Brown decision of 1954. By 1960, however, blacks realized that the walls of segregation were not going to tumble very quickly without further efforts on their part.

To an amazing degree organized American protest since the Civil war has been essentially peaceful. Most violence has been the result of efforts by authorities to stop movements—such as the violence against labor strikers in the 1890s and against Birmingham blacks in 1963. When violence did occur in protest activities, it was usually directed against property rather than people. Labor sometimes engaged in sabotage of management property, and blacks in urban ghettos burned down white-owned buildings in the 1960s. There have been, of course, some exceptions. Splinter groups of both the anarchists and the Weathermen set off bombs that killed individuals. As before the Civil War, much of the violent mob action has been directed at minorities. Both the activities of the Klan during Reconstruction and white mobs in numerous race riots at the turn of the century and later led to deaths of hundreds of blacks.

Most leaders of organized protest by minority groups have been reluctant to use violence. They seem to believe that effective propaganda should inspire rather than outrage the public. The genius of such organizers and spokesmen as Martin Luther King, Jr., is that they utilized widely cher-

Issues of intense personal concern or matters of principle often bring people together to achieve a common goal. Protestors blocked the road at Diablo Canyon as a response to the proliferation of nuclear power (above). Parents in Boston, Massachusetts, rallied against court-ordered busing in their school district (left). At Stanford University a number of students formed a group protesting dilution of the core reading list to include more non-Western material for Western Culture courses (opposite, top). People striving for equal housing and employment opportunities are shown at an Operation PUSH meeting (opposite, center). In March 1988 students at Gallaudet University, a federally run school for the hearing impaired, protested when a hearing president was chosen to head the school (opposite, bottom).

ished ideals to challenge the status quo. King did not ask Americans to repudiate their values—only to live up to them. Even those who wanted to make fundamental changes, such as socialist leader Eugene V. Debs, often phrased their demands to appeal to one set of popular beliefs to invalidate another.

Practically every available tactic has been employed by protestors. Marches have always been popular for diverse groups: the Ku Klux Klan, women suffragettes, army veterans demanding early bonuses, unemployed workers seeking government aid, and blacks urging civil rights legislation. Although the March on Washington of 1963 has become the best known, it was only one of many times the nation's capital has been beset by large groups.

Some marches have ended in occupations, as did the Bonus Army of 1932. Other grounds and buildings have been taken over without the preliminary act of marching. Students of the 1960s occupied college administration buildings. Farmers in the 1930s forcefully closed down courthouses to prevent foreclosure proceedings. Native Americans in the American Indian Movement laid siege to the town of Wounded Knee, South Dakota, in 1973. Workers staged 477 sit-down strikes in 1937, refusing both to work or to leave the factory.

Sparked by four black college students who sat down at the Woolworth's lunch counter in Greensboro, North Carolina, the sit-in movement of the 1960s was another form of occupation. It also illustrates another facet of protest—civil disobedience. Through the years, hundreds had been arrested for trespassing or parading without a permit. Black Americans perfected civil disobedience as a tactic of change in America. By openly and deliberately breaking segregation laws, and by being willing to go to jail for violating "unjust laws," blacks made segregation both more visible and expensive. The peace movement of

the Vietnam years followed their lead, burning their draft cards as a symbol of their unwillingness to obey conscription laws during an "unjust war."

Women broke no laws when they mocked "Miss America" contests, but their action displays the importance of symbolism in protest. The raised, clenched fist of the Black Power movement said much without words. The impact of such symbolism was evident in the response to the raised fists of black

athletes at the 1968 Olympics. Songs, as well as symbols, have been an integral part of protest. From "Buddy, Can You Spare a Dime?" of the Great Depression to "We Shall Overcome" in the 1960s, songs have eloquently expressed both the frustrations and the aspirations of suffering peoples.

Protestors have often met with either repression or ridicule. Many times their actions have had few immediate, positive results. Given the strength of the spirit of con-

servatism in American culture, however, what is remarkable are the successes. Segregation is now illegal; compulsory military service is no longer required; practically every adult can vote; women explore space and run for vice-president on a major party ticket; government at all levels has become more responsive to the rights and needs of minorities. Without the influence of protest, America would indeed be a different kind of place "to love or leave."

Anti-Vietnam War protest did eventually make a difference.

the late 1870s the Grangers declined and soon reverted to farm social clubs.

Economic grievances remained, and the farmers' organizational response shifted to the Alliance movement. Milton George, the editor of the Chicago-based *Western Rural,* organized a northwestern Alliance in 1880. Never very effective, by the late 1880s it was mainly a paper organization. In the South, however, the Alliance movement was more radical and more successful. Starting in 1877 as a frontier farmers' club in Lampasas County, Texas, it grew into the Grand State Alliance in 1879. Beginning in 1886, under the new leadership of Dr. Charles W. Macune, the southern Alliance spread rapidly by organizing new locals and absorbing existing farm groups in other regions as well as the South. At the same time a separate Colored Alliance was established. By 1890 the southern Alliance was a national organization with about 1.5 million members—and an additional 1 million members in its colored affiliate.

Like the Grangers, Alliancemen sought to establish cooperatives, mostly without long-term success. They also conducted wide-ranging social and educational programs and boasted about 1000 affiliated newspapers. Self-help, however, proved inadequate; in 1890 they turned to political action. Southern Alliancemen tried to capture their state Democratic parties rather than supplant them. In the Northwest and Great Plains farmers were not burdened with such intense party loyalty or the complication of the racial issue. Thus they established independent third parties. Regardless of the form of the organization, Alliancemen sought to enact a number of political solutions to their problems.

The Agrarian Agenda

The demands of the farmers mixed rhetoric, radicalism, and realism. Their words were filled with anger that had flared white-hot after years of smouldering resentment. No one voiced that anger better than Kansas homesteader Mary E. Lease.

> Wall Street owns the country. It is no longer a government of the people, by the people and for the people, but a government of Wall Street, by Wall Street and for Wall Street. The great common people of this country are slaves, and monopoly is the master. The West and South are bound and prostrate before the manufacturing East . . . . Our laws are the output of a system which clothes rascals in robes and honesty in rags. The parties lie to us and the political speakers misled us. We were told two years ago to go to work and raise a big crop, that was all we needed. We went to work and plowed and planted; the rains fell, the sun shone, nature smiled, and we raised the big crop that they told us to; and what came of it? Eight-cent corn, ten-cent oats, two-cent beef and no price at all for butter and eggs—that's what came of it.

Their words rang with a rejection of aspects of capitalism that in retrospect seems radical. They spoke in a language that divided the nation into "haves" and "have-nots." "There are but two sides," one manifesto proclaimed. "On the one side are the allied hosts of monopolies, the money power, great trusts and railroad corporations. . . . On the other are the farmers, laborers, merchants and all the people who produce wealth. . . . Between those two there is no middle ground." To farmers, government either stood by idly or actively aided the monopolists as the "fruits of the toil of millions are stolen to build up colossal fortunes for a few." The result was that from "the same prolific womb of governmental injustice we breed the two great classes—tramps and millionaires." They also saw a division between the toiling masses who produced wealth and the parasitic capitalists who exploited it. In response they proclaimed that "wealth belongs to him who creates it."

Their rhetoric earned scorn from critics who labeled the leaders "hayseed socialists." There were some unsavory aspects to the movement. A few agrarians espoused simplistic and often anti-Semitic conspiracy theories. Other flamboyant demagogues such as "Pitchfork Ben" Tillman of South Carolina exploited rural anger for their personal political ambitions. Thus, with a mixture of contempt and fear, critics called the rural reformers "crackpot radicals."

By Gilded Age standards farmer demands were indeed radical even though most have been adopted in the twentieth century. Their most socialistic ideas called for government ownership and operation of the railroads and the telegraph and telephone. These demands, however, did not reflect a desire for state ownership of all productive property. As landowners, farmers rejected socialism, but some did believe that these transportation and communication facilities were "natural monopolies" that could only be run efficiently under centralized management and were too important to the public good to be in the hands of a private monopoly.

The remainder of the agrarian political agenda reflected a rather realistic and moderate response to the farmers' problems. To ease their credit crisis they advocated an inflated, more flexible currency and the subtreasury plan. Considered by the Alliancemen to be the keystone of their program, subtreasuries (federal warehouses) were to be constructed as places where farmers could store their crops and receive treasury notes amounting to eighty percent of the crops' market value. Relieved from the pressure to sell immediately, farmers could wait for prices to rise to sell their crops and then pay back their subtreasury advances plus small interest and storage fees. Farmers saw the plan as a solution to the twin evils of the crop lien and depressed prices at harvest time.

Farmers believed that many of their ailments could be relieved by a more responsive, activist government. They therefore proposed political changes to "restore the government of the Republic to the hands of 'the plain people,' with which class it originated." Among the proposed changes were initiative and referendum, direct primaries, the use of a secret ballot, and the direct election of United States senators by the people rather than the state legislatures. Such political reforms were meant to expand government actions "to the end that oppression, injustice, and poverty shall eventually cease in the land." To finance government programs farmers called for a graduated income tax based upon the ability to pay.

Although the farmers failed to address the fundamental problem of overproduction, adoption of the agrarian demands could have relieved somewhat the agricultural distress fueling their anger. Thus the farmers became increasingly involved in political organization.

Emergence of the Populist Party

In 1890 Alliancemen entered politics in the West and the South with remarkable success. Under independent party banners, western Alliancemen elected a governor in Kansas, gained control of four state legislatures, and sent United States senators from Kansas and Nebraska. Working through the existing Democratic state parties, southern Alliancemen elected four governors, seven legislatures, forty-four congressmen, and several senators.

Western Alliancemen interpreted this success as a mandate to establish a national third party. At a May 1891 meeting in Cincinnati they failed to convince the southern Alliancemen to join them. By 1892, however, the Southerners became disillusioned with Alliance-backed Democrats who failed to support the subtreasury; they soon overcame their apprehension of third parties. The Alliances joined hands in St. Louis to create the People's or Populist party. In July 1892 the Populist party's national convention in Omaha drafted a platform and gave its presidential nomination to James B. Weaver of Iowa, a former Union general and greenback supporter. To symbolize the unity of the party they nominated former Confederate officer James G. Field for vice-president.

The majority of the Populists were small-scale farmers in the South and West whose farms were minimally mechanized. Most relied on a single cash crop, had unsatisfactory access to credit, and lived in social isolation some distance from towns and railroads. In other words their existence was marginal in all respects. The majority owned some land, but sizable numbers of sharecroppers and tenant farmers joined the party. Prosperous, large-scale, diversified farmers found little appeal in the party's platforms or activities.

The Populists realized the need to broaden the base of its constituency. Therefore, the Omaha platform included planks to appeal to urban workers. They advocated an eight-hour day, immigration restriction, and the abolition of the Pinkerton system that supplied strike breakers to management. One plank promised "fair and liberal" pensions to veterans. In the South some Populists, such as Tom Watson of Georgia, sought to woo black voters. "You are kept apart," he told audiences of black and white farmers, "that you may be separately fleeced of your earnings. You are made to hate each other because upon that hatred is rested the keystone of the arch of financial despotism which enslaves you both."

The Populists conducted colorful campaigns, which one Nebraska Democrat called a blend of "the French Revolution and a western religious revival." Their anger fostered a revolutionary spirit that appealed to large numbers of farmers. In 1892 Weaver became the first third-party candidate to win over one million votes. He also carried Kansas, Colorado, Idaho, and Nevada for a total of twenty-two electoral votes. Populist strength in such mining states as Colorado reflected the appeal to silver miners of the party's demand for inflation by means of the free and unlimited coinage of silver at 16 to 1. On the other hand, the Populists failed to carry a single southern state, largely because of voting fraud and the Democrats' cries of white

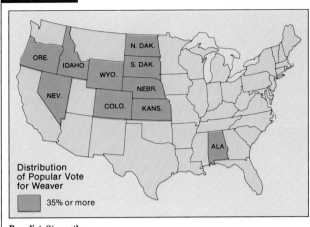

Distribution of Popular Vote for Weaver

35% or more

Populist Strength

supremacy as well as their ability to control a large number of black votes through economic intimidation. Nevertheless, it was a remarkable showing for a new party, revealing the extent of popular discontent. The next year brought the panic of 1893, which produced more discontent and gave the Populists great hopes for the election of 1896.

Disillusionment and anger pushed Alliance members into politics—a move that culminated in the Populist party in 1892.

DEPRESSION AND TURBULENCE IN THE 1890s

Social harmony became somewhat strained in the late 1880s with such violent episodes as the Haymarket Square Riot of 1886. Economic "losers," mainly workers and farmers, were already becoming restless. The depression following the panic of 1893 intensified their suffering. Naturally turbulence increased, setting the stage for the election of 1896, where an attempt was to be made to unite the losers in a quest for political power.

The Roots and Results of the Depression

While the Populists made their bid for office in the election of 1892, the two major parties featured a rerun of the election of 1888. Once again Cleveland and Harrison faced each other over the issue of the tariff. This time, however, the outcome was different, and Cleveland entered the White House—just in time for the panic of 1893.

The depression started in Europe and spread to the United States as overseas buyers reduced their purchases of American goods. Many foreign investors also became alarmed over the possible impact of the Sherman Silver Purchase Act. Their unloading of some $300 million of investments caused American gold to leave the country to pay for these securities. Thus supplies of currency dropped—leading rapidly to falling prices. There had also been serious overexpansion of the economy, especially in railroad construction. Confidence faltered, the stock market crashed, and banks failed.

The panic ushered in a depression in which unemployment reached twenty percent of the workforce. Farm prices dropped to new lows, and farm foreclosures reached new highs. Sharp wage cuts and massive layoffs took place in virtually every industry. Henry Adams lamented, "Men died like flies under the strain, and Boston grew suddenly old, haggard, and thin." Still opposed to direct federal aid, President Cleveland's only response to the suffering was repeal of the Sherman Silver Purchase Act;

an attempt at tariff reduction; and the sale of lucrative federal bonds to a banking syndicate, headed by J. P. Morgan, aimed at protecting the nation's gold reserves. To many, his actions seemed both misguided and inadequate.

Expressions of Worker Discontent

Violence had begun to escalate in labor-management relations in the late 1880s and continued into the 1890s. In 1892, for example, Andrew Carnegie and the Amalgamated Association of Iron and Steel Workers clashed at Carnegie's Homestead plant outside of Pittsburgh. In an effort to crush the union, Carnegie slashed wages, and, expecting a confrontation, he fortified his steel mills, hired strikebreakers, and employed the Pinkerton Agency to protect them. This done, Carnegie departed for Scotland on a fishing trip and left Henry Clay Frick to do battle with organized labor.

On July 5, strikers and Pinkerton Agents fought their first battle. The smoke from cannons, rifles, dynamite, and burning oil filled the hot summer air. Ten men were killed and another seventy were wounded, but the workers won this first engagement. Frick appealed to the governor of Pennsylvania for help; the governor dispatched 8000 militiamen to Homestead "to protect law and order"—a phrase normally used as a synonym for defense of industrialists' property.

The fighting continued until late July when an anarchist from Chicago named Alexander Berkman decided to take matters into his own hands. He went to Frick's office, shot the manager twice, and stabbed him seven times before being subdued. Frick lived and police arrested Berkman. Although Berkman had no connections with the steel union, the local and national press linked unionism with radicalism. Shortly afterward, strikebreakers went to work and the union was defeated and destroyed by the powerful forces of capital, government, and press.

During the depression, employers frequently cut wages to preserve profits. In 1894 the workers in the Pullman plant at Chicago found their wages reduced several times while their rent for company-owned housing remained the same. When management refused to negotiate with the union, members of the

American Railway Union (ARU) refused to handle any cars made in the Pullman plant. The boycott totally disrupted railroad traffic in the Midwest. Railroad executives appealed to Governor John Altgeld for help, but the liberal politician refused to interfere. The executives then turned to Attorney General Richard Olney, a former railroad corporation lawyer. Olney and President Cleveland responded quickly. They used the excuse of protecting the mails to come to the aid of the railroad managers. Over Altgeld's protest, the government sent 2000 troops to the Chicago area, and a federal court issued a blanket injunction which virtually ordered union leaders to discontinue the strike. When ARU president Eugene V. Debs defied the injunction, he was imprisoned. Only after federal troops arrived did violence occur. Within two days, bitter fighting had broken out, railcars were burned, and over $340,000 worth of damage had been done to railroad property. Force—absolute, final, and federal—crushed the Pullman strike.

Such unified repressive force drove some workers to the left. Prior to 1894, the Socialist Labor Party had been miniscule in membership. Badly divided, it was led by the abrasive Daniel DeLeon. After the Pullman strike Eugene V. Debs emerged from prison a socialist—and at the same time made socialism more respectable. Born in Indiana in 1855, the balding Debs had the common touch and delivered with a Hoosier twang a version of socialism based upon distinctly American values. The movement thus acquired a fiery and effective orator. "Many of you think you are competing," Debs would declare. "Against whom? Against Rockefeller? About as I would if I had a wheelbarrow and competed with the Sante Fe [railroad]." Around the nucleus of his personality the larger and stronger Socialist Party of America began to form and directly challenge unrestrained capitalism.

The mass suffering during the depression also provoked some to ask the federal government to provide work for the unemployed. One such person was Jacob S. Coxey, a short, quiet Ohio businessman who advocated putting men to work on the roads. They were to be paid by the printing of $500 million in legal tender paper money, which would also help to inflate

Worker discontent boiled over in the 1890s but was met with stubborness and violence by business management. Here strikebreakers gather to defeat the Homestead strike.

the currency. He organized the Army of the Commonwealth of Christ to march to Washington and demand action. When about 500 of them straggled into the capital on May 1, 1894, their leader was arrested for walking on the grass. Federal authorities beat and arrested his troops. Although "Coxey's Army" fell far short of his dream of a demonstration of 400,000 jobless workers, their actions did get the attention of the public. Forty-three newspaper reporters accompanied them, reporting almost every detail of the march. One journalist quipped, "Never in the annals of insurrection has so small a company of soldiers been accompanied by such a phalanx of recording angels."

Deteriorating Race Relations

The turbulent 1890s was also one of the worst decades of racial violence in the nation's history. That violence stemmed from class as well as race conflict. Following Reconstruction, southern Bourbon Democrats in some states had forged a rather strange alliance with black

"RISE BROTHERS! ":
THE BLACK RESPONSE TO JIM CROW

Afro-Americans had long struggled against white prejudice and repression. During Reconstruction constant vigilence was needed to protect and expand newly won rights. Some efforts were in vain, but black successes had helped to curb the growth of segregation. For example, blacks in Savannah, Georgia, succeeded in desegregating their city's streetcar system in 1872 by boarding the so-called white cars, threatening legal action, and boycotting the Jim Crow cars. Beginning in the 1890s, however, a rising tide of virulent white racism eventually confounded black attempts to resist being made into second-class citizens. With a new determination white Southerners stripped blacks of the right to vote, passed segregation laws, and lynched blacks who refused to cooperate.

Once whites had won the battle and the smoke had cleared from the battlefields, a mythology of black submission and acceptance arose. Booker T. Washington became a symbol of black cooperation and accommodation. Selected passages of his 1895 Atlanta address were heralded as the "will of blacks." Other voices were ignored. Few quoted the words of John Hope in the year following the "Atlanta Compromise." Then a professor at a black college in Nashville, Hope exhorted his fellow blacks:

Rise, Brothers! Come let us possess this land. Never say 'Let well enough alone.' Cease to console yourself with adages that numb the moral sense. Be discontented. Be dissatisfied. . . . Be restless as the tempestuous billows on the boundless sea. Let your dissatisfaction break mountain-high against the walls of prejudice and swamp it to the very foundation. Then we shall not have to plead for justice nor on bended knee crave mercy; for we shall be men. Then and not until then will liberty in its highest sense be the boast of our Republic!

Instead of passive acceptance, the response of many blacks to the new wave of discrimination was to employ every available tactic to protest the loss of their rights. Before disfranchisement was completed, black officeholders made impassioned speeches and lobbied their white colleagues in opposition to discriminatory legislation. Activists organized local "Negro Rights," "Emancipation," and "Colored Uplift" groups that wrote strongly worded resolutions and organized petition drives. Individuals and groups launched legal challenges in the courts. Some tested the new laws by breaking them. Protest meetings were held. Boycotts of newly segregated facilities occurred in such diverse southern cities as New Orleans, Savannah, Jacksonville, and Richmond. The black press often fearlessly attacked white actions; a Bay Minette, Alabama, paper counseled, "The best remedy for lynching is a good Winchester rifle." Finally, a few engaged in the ultimate protest—armed resistance.

Two examples illustrate the nature and results of black protest at the turn of the century. The first, a Savannah streetcar boycott in 1906, enjoys many similarities to the Montgomery bus boycott of 1955—the main exception being the outcome. The second, the story of Robert Charles, indicates that this early civil rights movement had its share of martyrs, as did the movement a half century later.

At the beginning of the twentieth century whites and blacks of Savannah were proud that their city had been immune to the lynching virus. By 1906 it was also one of the few southern cities without a single Jim Crow law on its books. Race relations were better than average but not ideal. Although fifty-four percent of the city's 72,000 residents were black, the white minority exercised a firm, if benevolent, control over the black majority. There were only three black public officials, and they held positions allotted to blacks by law. Nevertheless, the black community had spawned a leadership class that commanded some respect from the white establishment and enjoyed some political clout. Thus they had been able to turn back all previous attempts to enact segregation.

The year 1906, however, brought increased racial tension throughout the South with several outbreaks of violence in such places as Brownsville, Texas, and Atlanta, Georgia. In Georgia white prejudice was aroused by the bitter gubernatorial campaign of Hoke Smith. Savannah whites began to urge their leaders to get into the "new order of things" and exclude blacks from both politics and social contact with whites. On September 12, 1906, the city adopted a law that required separate seating in streetcars and empowered the police to arrest anyone sitting in the wrong place.

The black elite of the leading black ministers, physicians, and businessmen had already formed a committee to lobby against the ordinance. Once the law was passed, they immediately organized a boycott. In the churches, ministers urged compliance, and the black Savannah *Tribune* declared: "Let us walk! walk! and save some nickels . . . Do not trample on your pride by being 'jim crowed.' Walk! " Black hackmen reduced their fares for boycotters from 25 cents to 10 cents. One group attempted to form the United Transportation Company to compete with white lines. Those rich enough to own wagons drove themselves and friends to town.

Many who could get no other transportation heeded the words of the leaders and walked. It was reported that the mayor's secretary had given his maid carfare to bring two large suitcases from his home to city hall. When she arrived late and soaked with perspiration, he discovered that she had followed the advice of her minister and refused to ride the streetcar. The local white paper noted that trolley after trolley went by with the back seats vacant. The boycott was almost total.

City authorities responded much like those of Montgomery did in 1955. They cracked down on unlicensed hacks and harassed licensed ones. Blacks remained firm for some time—even after it became apparent that the boycott was not going to change white minds. As late as May 1908, two years after the start of the boycott, the streetcar line admitted that no more than eighty percent of blacks had returned to the cars. Without action by the federal government, even economic loss could not persuade whites to abandon segregation.

While Savannah blacks suffered inconvenience to protest the enfringement of their rights, Robert Charles paid a much higher price. In his twenties in 1900, he was a quiet, intense young man who worked at odd jobs and supported black emigration to Africa as a response to white prejudice in the South. He read a lot and collected weapons, but broke no laws. One night in July he sat on a front porch in New Orleans talking quietly with a friend. Close to midnight three police officers arrived with drawn pistols and flailing billy clubs to announce his arrest.

Charles responded to the unjust arrest by drawing his gun and shooting one of the officers. Wounded himself, he then fled—not to safety but to rearm. Grabbing a rifle, Charles moved from one hiding place to another. Along his trail he left five dead police officers and a dozen wounded ones. A mob of over one thousand joined police in the manhunt, frequently firing indiscriminately into the black community. Finally surrounded, Charles was burned out of his hiding place and immediately riddled with bullets. As was customary, the mob then badly mutilated the body. They killed the man but not the spirit. Newspaper woman Ida Wells-Barnett investigated the incident and ended her report with the words: "The white people of this county may charge that he was a desperado, but to the people of his own race Robert Charles will always be regarded as the 'hero of New Orleans.'" Later his willingness to fight police brutality with retaliatory violence would be renewed by the Black Panthers in the 1960s.

Even heroic actions failed to protect black rights from the onslaught of discrimination at the dawn of the new century. Nevertheless these men and women added to the heritage of black protest that would reap rewards a half century later—when sympathetic media coverage changed public opinion and the federal government finally decided that it was in the national interest to protect the rights of all citizens.

Republicans. In return for the protection of the Bourbons and a share of the lesser offices, blacks helped those conservative, elitist whites to beat back challenges from lower-class whites. Tom Watson was right when he told black and white farmers that the Bourbons were using race as a wedge to keep them apart.

The Bourbon-black alliance could work only for as long as it was in the interests of upper-class whites to support black rights and votes. There were few external pressures to do so as the Republican party and all three branches of government deserted blacks. Although the Populists failed to unite blacks and whites on the basis of class interests, the attempt led to considerable bloodshed. Whites shed white blood, but more frequently they spilled black blood. Lynching became a tool for controlling both black votes and actions. Under the pretext of "maintaining law and order" vigilante mobs hanged, mutilated, and burned blacks in increasing numbers. During the decade of the 1890s an average of two to three blacks were lynched each week.

Jacob S. Coxey led his army of unemployed workers into Washington, D.C., where Coxey was arrested and his army dispersed by club-wielding police.

It is probably not coincidental that attempts to limit black voting began in earnest precisely at the time that farmer unrest arose. Mississippi led the way in finding ways to skirt the Fifteenth Amendment. Without mentioning "race, color, or previous condition of servitude," the 1890 Mississippi constitution established poll taxes, literacy tests, and residency requirements that depleted the ranks of black voters. A key element of the literacy tests was a requirement that voters be able to explain what they read to the satisfaction of the voter registrars; blacks found registrars extremely hard to satisfy. The Supreme Court displayed its disregard for black rights by upholding the so-called Mississippi Plan in *Williams* v. *Mississippi.* Other states soon adopted similar measures. Later, to woo lower-class white voters, grandfather clauses were added—exempting from these requirements anyone who would have been eligible to vote in 1860. That provision applied to all adult white males and to no blacks.

Once whites stripped away black political power other black rights toppled. With no need to cater to black voters, whites soon began to pass discriminatory legislation. Most wanted segregation as a means of racial control, but the Fourteenth Amendment raised constitutional questions. The Supreme Court removed that barrier. After several rulings that limited constitutional protection of black rights, in the 1896 *Plessy* v. *Ferguson* decision the Court finally ruled that public accommodations for blacks could be "separate but equal." With segregation legalized, southern whites rather frantically passed "Jim Crow" laws to legally require the separation of the races for the next two decades. When the frenzy stopped, some states had even passed laws prohibiting interracial checker playing and requiring textbooks used in black schools to be stored in separate rooms from those used in white schools.

Segregation and the exclusion of blacks from public facilities had long existed in a haphazard way—based upon custom. Converting this informal and inconsistent arrangement into a legalized system of repression spawned violence, and no one stepped in to protect blacks. The popularity of Booker T. Washington's 1895 "Atlanta Compromise" with its plea for racial cooperation is easily understandable under the

CHRONOLOGY OF KEY EVENTS

1869 Patrons of Husbandry founded; first Granger law

1873 Coinage Act

1877 *Munn* v. *Illinois*

1881 Garfield assassinated; Arthur becomes president

1882 Chinese Exclusion Act

1883 Pendleton Act

1884 Mugwump movement; Cleveland elected

1886 *Wabash* Case

1887 Interstate Commerce Act; Dawes Act; Farm prices plummet

1888 Greenback Party nominated Weaver; Harrison elected

1890 Farmers' Alliance entered politics; Sherman Antitrust Act; National American Woman Suffrage Association formed; Mississippi constitution disfranchised blacks; McKinley Tariff; Sherman Silver Purchase Act

1892 Populist Party formed; Cleveland elected Homestead strike

1893 Panic followed by depression

1894 Pullman strike; Coxey's "army"

1895 *United States* v. *E.C. Knight Co.; Pollock* v. *The Farmer's Loan and Trust Company*

1896 *Plessy* v. *Ferguson*; McKinley defeats Bryan

1897 Dingley Tariff

1900 Gold Standard Act

---

conditions it was delivered. Both whites and blacks were eager to find a way out of the bloodshed.

Fissures seemed to be opening up along quite a number of the seams in American society. It was enough to provoke one of the major parties to respond somewhat to popular demands in 1896; and that created a dilemma for the Populists.

The Tide Is Turned: The Election of 1896

After the Republicans nominated William McKinley and the Democrats chose William Jennings Bryan, the Populists were left with an impossible choice. When Bryan and the Democrats endorsed silver, the Populists had their thunder stolen. They had hoped to ride silver to power because of the growing popularity of the issue. William H. Harvey's pro-silver book, *Coin's Financial School*, had become a best-

seller in 1894. Rather than picking up silverite bolters from the major parties, as the Populists expected, however, they were faced with a real problem. To nominate someone else would split the silver votes and ensure a victory for McKinley. Yet to nominate Bryan meant a loss of their identity and momentum.

Many Populists argued fervently against "fusion" with the Democrats, who focused almost exclusively on silver at the expense of the rest of the Populist demands. Watson and others viewed the obsession with silver as "a trap, a pitfall, a snare, a menace, a fraud, a crime against common sense and common honesty." In the end they bit the bullet and nominated Bryan for president but chose Tom Watson for vice-president rather than the Democratic choice, Arthur Sewall.

"God's in his Heaven, all's right with the world!" Republican campaign manager Mark Hanna wired McKinley when he learned of the Republican victory. McKinley carried the popular vote, 7.1 million to 6.5 million and the electoral votes, 271 to 176. The defeat of Bryan and the silver forces brought an end to political equilibrium. Millions of Democrats left their party, and the Republican party became the majority party. Republicans won the presidency in seven of the nine contests between 1896 and 1928, and controlled both houses of Congress seventeen of the next twenty sessions. One basic reason for the Republican victory of 1896 was the bad luck of the Democrats to be in power when the depression came. Republicans gleefully noted in 1894, "We were told in the old times that the rich were getting richer and the poor were getting poorer. To cure that imaginary ailment our political opponents have brought on a time when everybody is getting poorer."

The Populists of course suffered the most from the election results: their party disappeared. Their attempt to unite farmers and labor, blacks and whites, failed. Like the Socialists and other radicals, the Populists were never able to recruit organized labor to forge a broad-based working-class movement. American Federation of Labor president Samuel Gompers and other labor leaders argued that farmers were capitalists, not wage earners, and that their goals were not compatible with labor's interests. For example, the inflation that farmers wanted would raise food prices to the detriment of workers already living close to the margin. In the South race proved to be more important than class, and disillusioned white Populists such as Tom Watson turned to bitter Negrophobia following their defeat. They joined gladly with the Bourbons to curtail black suffrage. Ironically, the Bourbons stirred up racism to defeat the Populists and then proved to be unable to put the genie back into the bottle. In many states they were replaced by less elitist, bigoted demagogues.

Americans had come to a turning point in 1896 and chose the conservative path. The Republican administration quickly raised duties with the Dingley Tariff of 1897. Three years later the Currency Act officially put the nation on the gold standard by requiring all money to be redeemable in gold. Ironically, new discoveries of gold and more efficient extracting methods brought the inflation that farmers had

sought from silver. Prosperity began to return, and the Republicans could point with pride to their slogan, "The Full Dinner Pail." That prosperity also emasculated the agrarian movement as rising prices eased farmers' economic distress. And such inventions and services as the telephone and rural free delivery of the mail decreased the isolation and boredom of their lives—especially after mail-order catalogs began to arrive from Montgomery Ward's and Sears, Roebuck.

CONCLUSION

After Reconstruction, national politics entertained the masses rather than solved the emerging problems of industrialization. The two major parties differed little in their laissez-faire support of business and seemed more concerned with the spoils of office than with the suffering of farmers, workers, and minorities. Political inertia bred crises as problems remained unresolved. Finally, a democratic challenge to unrestrained capitalism arose from the losers in the race toward economic modernization. Led by disgruntled farmers, the Populists sought to unite large segments of the American population on the basis of class interest. As a result, the election of 1896 provided a real choice for American voters.

The conservative victory brought about the death of Populism, but many of the problems the farmers addressed in the 1890s continued into the twentieth century. Time vindicated their demands. A large number of their rejected solutions were adopted in the first two decades of the new century; most of their remaining agenda was enacted in modified forms during the New Deal of the 1930s. Attention was first diverted, however, by prosperity and an aggressive foreign policy.

REVIEW SUMMARY

Between the elections of 1876 and 1896 the major political parties failed to confront the problems of an industrializing society. Political inertia resulted from several causes:

> a rare equality of power between the major parties

weak presidencies

bipartisan acceptance of laissez-faire philosophy

Although Congress did enact some reformist legislation, the laws did little to reduce social inequalities. Farmers, who experienced severe hardship in an economy oriented to the needs of industrialists, manifested their anger by:

organizing Granges and Alliances

forming the Populist party

Depression swelled the ranks of the discontented in the 1890s. Misery led to violence until one party, the Democrats, finally gave some attention to the pressing social issues of the day. However, the Republican victory in 1896 ensured that major change would not occur at that time.

SUGGESTIONS FOR FURTHER READING

EQUILIBRIUM AND INERTIA: THE NATIONAL POLITICAL SCENE

Vincent P. DeSantis, *The Shaping of Modern America, 1877–1916* (1975); John A. Garraty, *The New Commonwealth, 1877–1890* (1968); Morton Keller, *Affairs of State: Public Life in Nineteenth Century America* (1977); Harold U. Faulkner, *Politics, Reform, and Expansion, 1890–1900* (1959); Ray Ginger, *The Age of Excess* (1975); John M. Dobson, *Politics in the Gilded Age* (1972); H. Wayne Morgan, *From Hayes to McKinley* (1966); Leonard D. White, *The Republican Era, 1869–1901* (1958); David J. Rothman, *Politics and Power: The United States Senate, 1869–1901* (1966); Robert D. Marcus, *GOP: Political Structure in the Gilded Age, 1880–1896* (1971); Richard Jensen, *The Winning of the Midwest* (1971); Horace S. Merrill, *Bourbon Democracy in the Midwest, 1865–1896* (1967); Paul Kleppner, *The Cross of Culture: A Social Analysis of Midwestern Politics, 1850–1900* (1970); J. Rogers Hollingsworth, *The Whirligig of Politics: The Democracy of Cleveland and Bryan* (1963); John Allswang, *Bosses, Machines, and Urban Voters* (1977); R. Hal Williams, *Years of Decision: American Politics in the 1890s* (1978).

THE SEARCH FOR LEGISLATIVE ANSWERS TO EMERGING PROBLEMS

John G. Sproat, *The Best Men: Liberal Reformers in the Gilded Age* (1968); Gerald W. McFarland, *Mugwumps, Morals, and Politics 1884–1920* (1975); Ari A. Hoogenboom, *Outlawing the Spoils: The Civil Service Movement* (1961); Walter T. K. Nugent, *Money and American Society* (1968); Tom E. Terrill, *The Tariff, Politics, and American Foreign Policy, 1874–1901* (1973); Allen Weinstein, *Prel-* *ude to Populism: Origins of the Silver Issue, 1867–1878* (1970); A. M. Paul, *Conservative Crisis and the Role of Law: Attitudes of Bar and Bench, 1887–1895* (1969); Aileen Kraditor, *The Ideas of the Woman's Suffrage Movement, 1890–1920* (1965); Eleanor Flexner, *Century of Struggle: The Women's Rights Movement in the United States* (1959); Stanley P. Hirshson, *Farewell to the Bloody Shirt: Northern Republicans and the Southern Negro* (1962); Vincent P. DeSantis, *Republicans Face the Southern Question, 1877–1897* (1959); Justus D. Doenecke, *The Presidencies of James A. Garfield and Chester A. Arthur* (1981); Lewis L. Gould, *The Presidency of William McKinley* (1980); Mary R. Dearing, *Veterans in Politics* (1952).

THE FARMERS REVOLT

Lawrence Goodwyn, *Democratic Promise: The Populist Movement in America* (1976); John D. Hicks, *The Populist Revolt* (1931); Richard Hofstadter, *The Age of Reform* (1954); Norman Pollack, *The Populist Response to Industrial America* (1966); Robert McMath, Jr., *Populist Vanguard: A History of the Southern Farmers Alliance* (1975); Bruce Palmer, *Man Over Money: The Southern Populist Critique of American Capitalism* (1980); Sheldon Hackney, *Populism to Progressivism in Alabama* (1969); J. Morgan Kousser, *The Shaping of Southern Politics* (1974); Walter T. K. Nugent, *The Tolerant Populists* (1963); Peter H. Argersinger, *Populism and Politics: William Peffer and the People's Party* (1974); Allan G. Bogue, *Money at Interest: The Farm Mortgage on the Middle Border* (1955); Paolo Coletta, *William Jennings Bryan: Political Evangelist* (1964); C. Vann Woodward, *Tom Watson: Agrarian Rebel* (1938); Charles Morrow Wilson, *The Commoner: William Jennings Bryan* (1970); Martin Ridge, *Ignatius Donnelly* (1962); Norman Pollack, ed., *The Populist Mind* (1967); Paul W. Glad, *McKinley, Bryan, and the People* (1964) and *The Trumpet Soundeth: William Jennings Bryan and His Democracy* (1964); Steven Hahn, *The Roots of Southern Populism* (1983).

DEPRESSION AND TURBULENCE IN THE 1890s

Charles Hoffman, *The Depression of the Nineties: An Economic History* (1970); Samuel T. McSeveney, *The Politics of Depression* (1972); Donald L. McMurry, *Coxey's Army* (1929); Ray Ginger, *Bending Cross: A Biography of Eugene V. Debs* (1969); Nick Salvatore, *Eugene V. Debs: Citizen and Socialist* (1982); John P. Diggins, *The American Left in the Twentieth Century* (1973); J. Morgan Kousser, *The Shaping of Southern Politics: Suffrage Restriction and Establishment of the One-Party South, 1880–1910* (1974); C. Vann Woodward, *The Strange Career of Jim Crow*, rev. ed. (1974); Howard N. Rabinowitz, *Race Relations in the Urban South, 1865–1900* (1978); Robert F. Durden, *The Climax of Populism: The Election of 1896* (1965); Stanley L. Jones, *The Election of 1896* (1964).

Imperial America, 1870–1900

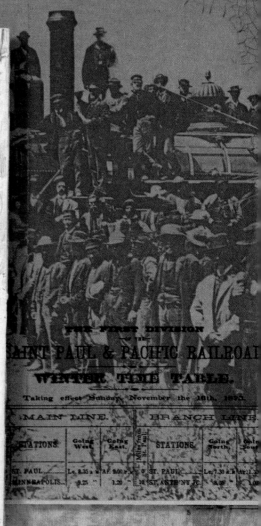

THE FIRST DIVISION
OF THE
SAINT PAUL & PACIFIC RAILROAD
WINTER TIME TABLE.
Taking effect Sunday, November the 16th, 1873.

MAIN LINE.				BRANCH LINE.		
STATIONS	Going West	Going East	Miles from St. Paul	STATIONS	Going North	Going South
ST. PAUL	Le. 8.35	Ar. 5.00	0	ST. PAUL	Le. 7.30	Ar.
MINNEAPOLIS	9.25	1.25	10	ST. ANTHONY		

Dreams of expansion came easily to Americans during the nineteenth century. For most of the century they expanded westward, moving into Texas and Kansas, pushing across the Great Plains, and occupying California and the Pacific Northwest. But they did not restrict their dreams to the millions of acres between Mexico and Canada. They cast covetous eyes toward Central America and the islands of the Caribbean and the Pacific. Plans to annex Nicaragua, Cuba, Santo Domingo, the Virgin Islands, Hawaii, and Samoa fired politicians' imaginations. Before the Civil War, the debate over slavery blocked expansionist efforts. Once the Union was preserved, however, expansionists returned to their plans with revived energy and enthusiasm.

President Ulysses Grant had a pet expansionist project of his own. He eyed the Dominican Republic, the eastern two-thirds of the Caribbean island of Santo Domingo. Annexation, he maintained, would benefit America in a number of ways. The island was rich in mineral resources, possessed an important natural harbor, and its inhabitants were eager to buy American products. Most importantly for Grant, who was ever mindful of America's race problem, the Dominicans were black. The island could serve as a frontier for black Americans, a retreat from Klan harassment.

With so much to gain, Grant put his full political weight behind annexation. His conduct was less than presidential. First, he sent his personal secretary and close friend Orville Babcock to Santo Domingo on a "fact finding" mission. Unimpressed by the islanders, Babcock reported: "The people are indolent and ignorant. The best class of people are the American Negroes who have come here from time to time." But he was convinced that the Dominican Republic was a commercial and strategic prize worthy of annexation. What was more, Bonaventura Baez, the unscrupulous president of the republic, was anxious to sell his country. With the money he would make from the transaction, Baez hoped to move and establish residence in Paris or Madrid, because, as Babcock noted, the Dominican Republic was "a dull country."

Unrest at home added fuel to Baez's willingness to sell. His government was threatened both by neighboring Haiti and a strong force of Dominican rebels. So difficult was Baez's position, Babcock had to order a United States Navy ship to protect the Baez government during the annexation negotiations, which were completed in the late fall of 1869. The promise of American dollars had convinced Baez that his country should belong to the United States.

Grant was pleased. The treaty of annexation, however, would have to be ratified by the Senate, a body more difficult to satisfy than Baez's government. An informal man, Grant decided to forgo presidential protocol and personally visit Charles Sumner, the chairman of the Senate Foreign Relations Committee. On the evening of January 2, 1870, Grant made an unannounced call at Sumner's Washington home on Lafayette Park. Later Sumner recalled that Grant was drunk. Drunk or sober, Grant was certainly in earnest. He energetically discussed the need to annex the Dominican Republic. Sumner listened then replied: "Mr. President, I am an Administration man, and whatever you do will always find in me the most careful and candid consideration." Grant departed for his short walk back to the White House believing he had won Sumner's full support. In fact, he had only won the powerful Massachusetts senator's "candid consideration."

After consideration and considerable investigation, Sumner decided that the entire annexation scheme was distasteful. He was disturbed by Babcock's and Baez's unethical financial dealings and was enraged that the United States Navy had been used to keep the Dominican president in power. Sumner was not a man to mince words. Labeled "probably the most intolerant man that American history has ever known," he accused Grant of being "a colossus of ignorance." Finally by a vote of 5 to 2, the Foreign Relations Committee voiced its disapproval of the treaty of annexation.

Grant was furious. His son later recalled, "I never saw Father so grimly angry." Known for his bulldog tenacity during the Civil War, Grant was not about to quit. He hinted that if the United States did not take the Dominican Republic, one of the European powers would, and he reported the results of a rigged plebiscite in which the Dominicans supposedly supported annexation by the suspicious vote of 15,169 to 11, but Grant's efforts failed. On June 30, 1870, the Senate rejected the treaty. Defining America's duty toward the island, Sumner said, "Our duty is as plain as the Ten Commandments. Kindness, beneficence, assistance, aid, help, protection, all that is implied in good neighborhood, these we must give freely, bountifully, but their independence is as sacred to them as is ours to us."

The failed attempt to annex the Dominican Republic is important for the themes it underscored. It demonstrated both the desire for expansion by the president and his advisors and the power of Congress in foreign affairs. During the remainder of the century the scenario would be repeated again and again, often with different results. Gradually during this period, presidents wrested more control over foreign affairs from Congress. And Congress, for its part, accepted a more expansionist foreign policy. As presidents and Congress found common ground, America expanded outward into the Caribbean and the Pacific. The expansion took different forms. Sometimes the United States annexed countries outright. Other times America remained content to exercise less forceful control over nominally independent countries. The results were the same. The United States ultimately acquired an overseas empire and expanded its influence over the Western Hemisphere.

Area of Grant's Expansionist Scheme

During the turn of the century, the United States increasingly tried to influence world affairs. Here, Uncle Sam assumes a forceful attitude.

CONGRESSIONAL CONTROL AND THE REDUCTION OF AMERICAN POWER

Foreign Service

In 1869 when Grant took office, congressmen and other Americans held the State Department and the diplomatic service in low esteem. No majestic building housed the State Department. Instead the department was headquartered in a former orphan asylum. Nor was the post of secretary of state as great a prize as it had been. Once regarded as a stepping stone to the presidency, politicians increasingly viewed the post as a reward for outstanding party men or the refuge for defeated presidential aspirants. Even the diplomats themselves did not escape criticism. One newspaper editor said the diplomatic service was too often used as "gilt edged pigeon holes for filing away Americans, more or less illustrious, who are no longer particularly wanted at home."

The irreverent treatment of the State Department reflected a congressional and national mood. Concerns over the currency, civil service reform, Reconstruction, taxation, the tariff, Indian fighting, and railroad building dwarfed interest in foreign affairs. As late as 1889, Henry

Cabot Lodge, whose interests in foreign affairs were great, could write: "Our relations with foreign nations today fill but a slight place in American politics, and excite . . . a languid interest. We have separated ourselves so completely from the affairs of other people." During the 1870s and 1880s, when a powerful Congress largely dictated foreign policy, the spirit of Washington's Farewell Address and the Monroe Doctrine guided the country. Washington had counciled America to steer clear of foreign entanglements and Monroe had made isolationism a national obsession. Separated from a powerful Europe by the cold North Atlantic, Congress saw no reason to spend time or money on the State Department or foreign affairs.

Using its control over the budget as a sword, Congress trimmed the State Department to the bone. In 1869, Congress allowed the State Department a paltry thirty-one clerks; by 1881 presidential efforts had succeeded in raising that number to a still inadequate fifty. Politicians who considered the foreign service "a nursery of snobs" viewed diplomats as an expensive, nearly useless luxury. A few reformers even advocated the abolition of the foreign service. They argued that two oceans protected America and that they could hire international lawyers to handle any really serious international crises.

Reduction of the Military

The sword that trimmed the State Department was also used on America's army and navy. When the Civil War ended and peace returned to the country, Congress quickly reduced America's military might. The result made the United States a weaker country. In 1865 America had the largest and perhaps the most powerful navy in the world. To be sure, it was a ragtag navy, comprised of just about any vessel that would float. Ranging from the powerful ironclad *Monitor* to modest yachts, the United States Navy numbered 971 vessels. Within nine months of Appomattox, the auctioneer and the axe reduced that number to 29.

As Congress watched unconcerned, the navy declined intellectually as well as physically. To begin with, there were far too many officers. Although America's navy was less than

one tenth as large as Great Britain's, it contained almost twice as many officers. With promotions based strictly upon length of service, any officer who lived long enough could become an admiral. The system almost guaranteed poor leadership. While the world's best navies converted to steel and steam, American naval leaders remained tied to wood and sails. As one American officer from the period recalled, "To burn coal was so grievous an offense in the eyes of the authorities that for years the coal-burning captain was obliged to enter in the logbook in *red ink* his reasons for getting up steam and starting the engines." Quickly the American navy became a joke. In 1881 authorities claimed, with some justification, that a single modern ship of the Chilean navy could destroy the entire United States fleet.

The men appointed as the secretaries of the navy did nothing to help matters. They were mostly political appointees who knew little and cared less about ships. One historian noted that Richard W. Thompson of Indiana, whom Rutherford B. Hayes appointed Secretary of the Navy, was "so densely ignorant of naval affairs that he expressed surprise upon learning that ships were hollow."

The power and effectiveness of the army was similarly reduced. On May 23, 1865, with the Civil War just ended, Union bluecoats marched down Pennsylvania Avenue in a victory parade. There were over 100,000 soldiers. It took an hour for General Meade's cavalry to pass the reviewing stand. "Marching twelve abreast, the general's infantry consumed another five hours." The next day thousands of General Sherman's men repeated the performance, marching briskly "like the lords of the world!"

The sight would not be repeated for over fifty years. Demobilization occurred quickly and haphazardly. In May 1865 the army contained 1,034,064 volunteers; by November 1866 only 11,043 remained in uniform. Eventually Congress slashed the number of even the regular troops. By the end of Reconstruction, Congress had reduced the army to a distant echo of its former self. In 1876 the maximum strength stood at 27,442 troops.

Certainly in 1876 the United States did not need an active foreign service and a powerful army and navy to secure its borders. No countries threatened America. Geography defended the United States, and the European balance of power discouraged foolish European designs on any part of the Western Hemisphere. At the same time, the relative weakness of America's foreign service, army, and navy discouraged the United States from attempting to extend its influence beyond its own borders. All in all, most congressmen were entirely happy with the situation.

Seward's Dreams

Not everyone in government agreed with congressional leadership in foreign affairs. Regularly during the 1860s and 1870s, presidents or their secretaries of state called for a more forceful, expansionist foreign policy. William Henry Seward of New York, who served as secretary of state for Lincoln and Johnson, was such a man. A cold and vain man with a weak chin and a prominent nose, Seward dreamed of an American empire which would dominate the Pacific and Caribbean basins. During his term as secretary of state, he advocated a vigorous expansionism. He negotiated with Denmark to purchase the Danish West Indies (Virgin Islands), with Russia to buy Alaska, and with Santo Domingo for the Dominican harbor of Samana Bay. In addition, his plan for an American empire encompassed Haiti, Cuba, Iceland, Greenland, Honduras's Tigre Island, and Hawaii.

Congress balked. It did not share Seward's vision. During Seward's term, America did acquire the Midway Islands in the middle of the Pacific Ocean, but few Americans even noticed the addition. The purchase of Alaska in 1867 drew more comments, most of which were negative. Congressmen grumbled over the treaty. Some senators claimed that $7.2 million was too much money for a frozen wasteland that only Eskimos and seals could love. Others cracked jokes about "Johnson's Polar Bear Garden" and "Frigidia." But in the end the Senate, influenced by a few well-placed bribes, reluctantly ratified the treaty.

Articulate and aggressive anti-imperialists blocked the remainder of Seward's dreams. During the late 1860s and the 1870s congressional power was at a high tide. Seward and President Andrew Johnson were no match for

When the United States purchased Alaska in 1867, Americans considered the deal a wasteful folly.

Sumner and Thaddeus Stevens and their colleagues in Congress. Congressmen consistently found other issues more pressing than foreign affairs. They freely gave money to railroad construction companies and Union veterans; such gifts contributed significantly to their reelection. But they drew America's purse strings tight when confronted with most expansionist schemes.

THE SPIRIT OF AMERICAN GREATNESS

Although Congress was reluctant to endorse expansionist schemes, during the last third of the nineteenth century many other citizens had become convinced that the United States had to adopt a more aggressive and forceful foreign policy. Their reasons varied. Some believed expansion would be good for American business. Others felt America had a duty to spread its way of life to less fortunate countries. Still others maintained that economic and strategic security required that the country acquire overseas bases. Behind all the arguments, however, rested a common assumption: the United States was a great and important country, and it should start acting the part.

American Exceptionalism

For many Americans it started with God's plan. The idea of American exceptionalism—that the nation houses God's chosen people—has deep roots in the country's history. Puritan concepts of "a city upon the hill" mixed easily with talk of the greatness of republicanism and democracy and the Manifest Destiny of America. The teachings of Social Darwinists added "scientific proof" to the concept of American exceptionalism. With such Darwinian phrases as "natural selection" and "survival of the fittest," American intellectuals praised the course of American history. Even Charles Darwin himself was not immune to the lure of American exceptionalism. In *The Descent of Man* (1871), he wrote: "There is apparently much truth in the belief that the wonderful progress of the United States, as well as the character of the people, are the results of natural selection: The more energetic, restless, and courageous men from all parts of Europe have emigrated during the last ten or twelve generations to that great country . . . "

Such ideas found warm reception in America. Darwin's theories were more readily accepted in the United States than they were in England. However, there was a dark side to American exceptionalism, and this, too many Americans were quick to endorse: If white Anglo-Saxon Americans were biologically superior, then other races and other nations had to be inferior. During the late nineteenth century, such Social Darwinists as Gobineau in France and John Fiske in the United States helped to make racism intellectually acceptable. Catering to Anglo-Saxon audiences, Social Darwinists advanced one pseudo-scientific theory after another to "prove" the superiority of Anglo-Saxons.

From the idea of superiority to the acceptance of domination was a short step. If Americans were God's and Darwin's chosen people, why shouldn't they dominate and uplift less fortunate countries and peoples? This was the question that advocates of a more aggressive American foreign policy asked their audiences. Senator Albert J. Beveridge of Indiana spoke for many Americans when he told Congress,

> God has not been preparing the English-speaking and Teutonic peoples for a thousand years for nothing but vain and idle self-admiration. No! He has not made us the master organizers of the world to establish a system where chaos reigns. He has given us the spirit of progress to overwhelm the forces of reaction throughout the earth. He has made us adept in government that we may administer government among savage and senile peoples.

Sense of Duty

Religious leaders also noted the duty that American exceptionalism implied. Talk of the "White Man's Burden" was rife during the period. Protestant missionaries carried their faith and beliefs to the far corners of the world. The benefits of their message extended well beyond preaching salvation and saving souls. They also extolled the virtues of American civilization, which included everything from democracy and rule by law to sanitation, material progress, sewing machines, and cotton underwear. Defining good and bad, progress and savagery by American standards, they attempted to alter

Many foreign missions sought to unite the people of the world by extolling the virtues of American civilization.

native customs and beliefs to conform to a single American model.

Popular writer and religious leader Reverend Josiah Strong voiced what other missionaries and true believers acted upon. In 1885 Strong published *Our Country: Its Possible Future and Present Crisis,* a book which quickly sold 170,000 copies and was translated into dozens of languages. "The Anglo-Saxon," Strong wrote, "is the representative of two great ideas . . . civil liberty [and] a pure *spiritual* Christianity." These two ideas, he added, are destined to elevate all mankind, and "the Anglo-Saxon . . . is divinely commissioned to be . . . his brother's keeper." He firmly believed that it was America's destiny and duty to expand and spread its influence. Quoting the Bible while speaking to Anglo-Saxon Americans, he intoned, "Prepare ye the way of the Lord!"

Search for Markets

Strong's message was not lost on the business leaders of America. They fully agreed that missionaries should preach the benefits of American material progress as well as the glories of the Protestant faith. Looking south toward Latin America and west toward Asia, American businessmen and farmers saw vast virgin markets for their industrial and agricultural surpluses. Sensing that American markets offered few new opportunities, they entertained fabulous visions of hungry Latin Americans and shoeless Chinese. They fully agreed with the able American diplomat John A. Kasson who warned the readers of the *North American Review* in 1881: "We are rapidly utilizing the whole of our continental territory. We must turn our eyes abroad, or they will soon look inward upon discontent."

During the late nineteenth century, Kasson's words seemed particularly apt. Although the United States became the leading industrial and agricultural country in the world, domestic consumption did not keep pace with the galloping production. In addition, throughout the period the government pursued tight money policies, and the real income of laborers made only modest gains. The result was a boom and bust economy which witnessed spectacular growth as well as severe depressions. In fact, in the twenty-five years after 1873, the country suffered through depressions during 1873–1878, 1882–1885, and 1893–1897.

In part, the United States was a victim of its own spectacular success. Increased production without increased consumption led only to glutted markets and falling prices. For example, in 1870 Americans produced 4,300,000 bales of cotton; by 1891 that figure had grown to 9,000,000. In 1871 a pound of cotton sold for 18 cents; by 1891 the price had dropped to 7 cents. The story was the same for wheat, meat, tobacco, and corn. Increasingly, farmers—and industrialists—looked toward foreign markets. Too often, export trade spelled the difference between prosperity and bankruptcy. The future of America, many economic leaders believed, would be determined by the ability of the government to find and secure new markets.

During the depression years, the lure of foreign trade proved particularly strong. Depressions meant farm foreclosures and industrial unemployment, problems which led to social unrest. The Grange and Populist movements, the two largest agrarian revolts, originated in cotton and wheat areas during depression years. And such labor confrontations as the violent railroad strikes of 1877, Chicago's Haymarket Riot of 1886, and the Pullman Strike of 1894 occurred during lean economic times. For many Americans the issue was simple: The United States must acquire foreign markets or face economic hardship and revolution at home. As one industrial spokesman put it: The time has come for the United States to pursue "an intelligent and spirited foreign policy," one in which the government would "see to it" that the country has adequate foreign markets. If force proved necessary, then so be it.

The State Department was in full agreement. William Henry Seward and Hamilton Fish, Johnson's and Grant's secretaries of state, believed firmly that America needed new markets. Seward called the potentially bottomless markets of Asia "the prize," and he wanted the United States to acquire islands in the Pacific as stepping stones toward that prize. He similarly believed that the United States should extend its economic control to include Canada and Latin America. Hamilton Fish agreed with the hoarse-voiced, cigar-chewing Seward. Although like Seward he had to contend with a cautious, isolationist Congress, Fish made several important strides toward the Asia markets. During his term as secretary of state, the United States signed treaties with Hawaii and Samoa, two Pacific island groups which would later become part of the American empire.

During the late 1870s and 1880s, economic hard times quickened the search for new markets. William Evarts, Rutherford B. Hayes's secretary of state, valued a good story. He once told a British Minister that George Washington had been able to throw a dollar across the Rappahannock River because a dollar went farther in those days. Evarts also valued dollars, and he felt Americans needed far more of them. As secretary of state, he worked toward an American commercial empire. "The vast resources of our country need an outlet," he told the nation. He hoped that unexploited Asian and Latin American markets would guarantee continual economic growth and social tranquility for all Americans.

James G. Blaine and Frederick T. Frelinghuysen, who served as secretaries of state for Garfield and Arthur, concentrated their efforts on Latin American markets. Blaine later recounted that during his short stay in the State Department in 1881 he followed two principles: "first, to bring about peace . . . ; second, to cultivate such friendly commercial relations with all American countries as would lead to a large increase in the export trade of the United States." When Blaine was forced out of office after Garfield's assassination, Frelinghuysen continued his policies. He successfully negotiated bilateral reciprocity treaties with many Latin American countries. These treaties lowered tariffs and thus stimulated trade between the United States and Latin America.

By the mid-1880s, efforts in favor of expansion combined with economic and social problems at home convinced Congress to reevaluate its isolationist policies. The West was settled, the Indians defeated, the Union reconstructed, and the railroads built. It was now time to look at our oceans not as defense barriers but as paths toward new markets and increased prosperity. A final problem, however, remained. America's navy and merchant marine seemed woefully unfit for the challenge.

The New Navy

By 1880 the United States Navy was a sad joke. Ill-informed officers commanded obsolete wooden ships. Both men and vessels should have been retired years before. The English writer and wit Oscar Wilde was close to the truth when he had one of his fictional characters reply to an American woman who complained that her country had no ruins and no curiosities: "No ruins! No curiosities! You have your Navy and your manners!"

If America hoped to compete for world markets, it had to upgrade its navy. During the 1880s and early 1890s advocates of a New Navy moved Congress to action. The transformation from a "heterogeneous collection of naval trash" to a great navy occurred in two stages. The facelift began in 1883, during the administration of Chester A. Arthur. Prodded by the president, Congress passed an act providing for three small cruisers and a dispatch boat. These ships were the beginning of the famous White Squadron. More vessels soon followed. Under the direction of President Grover Cleveland and his able secretary of the navy, William Whitney, the White Squadron grew in size and naval bureaucracy and fleet personnel improved.

By 1890 great gains had been made, but serious problems remained. The White Squadron was not a world class navy. The ships built were lightly armored, fast cruisers, ideal for hit-and-run missions but inadequate for any major naval engagement. While England and Germany were building large, heavily armored battleships capable of bombarding and damaging coastal cities, the United States continued to think of naval warfare in terms of commerce raiding.

Benjamin F. Tracy, Benjamin Harrison's secretary of war, was determined to change American naval thinking. Although careful to note that he wanted a fleet not for "conquest, but defense," Tracy had a very modern view of what defense entailed. To adequately defend

During the late nineteenth century, the United States dramatically upgraded its navy. Steel ships replaced ones previously made of wood.

America's interests, Tracy called for ships which could "raise blockades" and attack an enemy's coast, "for a war, though defensive in principle, may be conducted most effectively by being offensive in its operations." In fact, Tracy maintained the proper defense might even include shooting first: "The nation that is ready to strike the first blow will gain an advantage which its antagonist can never offset." Such a first strike definition of defense meant one thing: The United States needed to build modern, armored battleships. Tracy wanted two battleship fleets, one for the Atlantic and another for the Pacific.

Personal tragedy momentarily sidetracked Tracy. In February 1890 his wife and youngest daughter burned to death in a fire which destroyed Tracy's Washington home. But Tracy's program was kept alive in Congress by such "Big Navy" advocates as Senator Eugene Hale of Maine and Representative Henry Cabot Lodge of Massachusetts. They found Congress in the mood to act. As one senator said, "You can not negotiate without a gun." In 1890, Congress appropriated money for the construction of three first-class battleships and a heavy cruiser. It was the beginning of a new, very much offensive navy for the United States. Reviewing his accomplishments in 1881, Tracy boasted: "The sea will be the future seat of empire. And we shall rule it as certainly as the sun doth rise."

Talk of empire, navy, trade, and national greatness came together in 1890 in the publication of a monumentally important book, *The Influence of Sea Power upon History*, by Captain Alfred Thayer Mahan. Mahan, who was attached to the Naval War College, was more comfortable around books than on ships. Although he had served throughout the world, he had the look, temperament, and inclinations of a college don. His masterpiece set forward the simple thesis that naval power was the key to national greatness. Taking Greece, Rome, and England as examples, he attempted to demonstrate that countries rise to world power through expanding their foreign commerce and protecting that commerce with a strong navy.

Without a powerful navy, Mahan emphasized, a nation can never enjoy full prosperity and security. Without a strong navy, in short, no nation could ever hope to be a world power.

Shaping Public Opinion

Mahan's writings and Tracy's proposal were applauded by American politicians and businessmen who felt it was time for the United States to assume the rights and responsibilities of world power status. These were important men—men of wealth, prosperity, education, and influence. Some like Whitelaw Reid, editor of the New York *Tribune*, helped shape public opinion through their editorials. Others like Henry Cabot Lodge, Theodore Roosevelt, Albert J. Beveridge, and John Hay were powerful politicians and administrators. They were vocal nationalists who believed that the United States was destined to be the greatest of world powers. Increasingly after 1890, these and other men of like mind dominated and shaped America's foreign policy, and "public opinion" followed their lead. "After all," noted Secretary of State Walter Q. Gresham in 1893, "public opinion is made and controlled by the thoughtful men of the country."

These expansionists often shared common experiences and beliefs. Most were prosperous Republicans from old-line American families, and most had traveled abroad widely. Anglo-Saxon by heritage, they tended to be ardent Anglophiles, full of praise for Great Britain's imperial efforts. They believed that the United States should join "Mother England" in administering to the "uncivilized" corners of the globe. As Beveridge noted, without the work of Anglo-Saxons "the world would relapse into barbarism and night . . . . We are trustees of the world's progress, guardians of its righteous place."

Lodge and other expansionists called for a bold foreign policy, what they termed the "large policy." They advocated the construction of a canal through Central America to allow American ships to move between the Atlantic and Pacific oceans more rapidly. To protect the canal, the United States would have to exert control over Cuba and the other strategically located Caribbean islands. Next America would have to acquire coaling stations and naval bases across the Pacific. Secure bases in Hawaii, Guam, Wake Island, and the Philippines would allow the Unites States to exploit the seemingly limitless China market. Finally, a powerful navy would have to protect the entire American empire.

In the end, then, all of their plans returned to the theme of a strong navy. Like his friend Mahan, priggish Lodge was a student of history. "It is the sea power which is essential to the greatness of every splendid people," he said. It had enabled Rome to crush the Carthaginians, England to defeat Napoleon, and the North to win the Civil War. Without the power of a strong navy, Lodge believed that America could never experience real peace and security: "All the peace the world has ever had has been obtained by fighting, and all the peace that any nation . . . can ever have, is by readiness to fight if attacked." For Lodge as for Tracy, thoughts of peace and war often ran together and appeared in the same sentences.

THE EMERGENCE OF AGGRESSION IN AMERICAN FOREIGN POLICY

Proponents of the New Navy and the "large policy" talked loudly about peace. But their talk of peace, like their foreign policy and naval ambitions, was couched in aggressive language. "To be prepared for war is the most effectual means to promote peace," said Theodore Roosevelt. The more they talked about peace, the closer war seemed. It is not surprising that the United States launched a more belligerent foreign policy at the same time it was building and launching more powerful ships. The two developments originated from the same source: a ready acceptance of force as the final arbiter of international disputes. Before the turn of the century, the acceptance of force would lead to the Spanish-American War of 1895, and between 1885 and 1897, during the presidencies of Benjamin Harrison and Grover Cleveland, the same attitudes almost caused several other wars. The Spanish-American War was not an aberrant event. Rather it was the result of a more aggressive American foreign policy, one aimed at acquiring both world respect and an empire.

Confronting the Germans in Samoa

Changing American attitudes toward foreign policy were first seen in Samoa, a group of fourteen volcanic islands lying 4000 miles from San Francisco along the trade route to Australia. Throughout the nineteenth century, American whalers stopped in Samoa, and its two splendid natural harbors, Apia and Pago Pago, had often provided refuge for ships caught in Pacific storms. If the natives were quarrelsome among themselves, they were exceptionally friendly with Americans.

American interest in Samoa was decidedly more mercenary. In 1872 an American negotiated a treaty with a tribal chief to grant the United States rights to a naval station at Pago Pago. Although an anti-expansionist Senate took no action on the treaty, expansionists kept trying. In 1878 the Senate did ratify a similar treaty, which formally committed the United States to Samoa. Unfortunately for the United States, Germany and England were also determined to influence events on the islands.

America's chief rival for Samoa was Germany. Like the United States, Germany was just beginning to think in terms of empire. German chancellor Otto von Bismarck decided that Samoa should belong to Germany, and as a result of the intricacies of European politics, England sided with the "iron chancellor." President Cleveland and his secretary of state, Thomas F. Bayard, firmly disagreed. Germany and the United States were set on a collision course.

When a conference between the three countries held in Washington in 1887 failed to solve the problem, war seemed closer still. Neither Germany nor the United States had much money invested in the islands, but both felt their national pride was at stake. "We must show sharp teeth," remarked Bismarck. Cleveland decided to show part of America's new White Squadron. He dispatched three warships to Samoa. Nature, however, had the most powerful weapon. On the morning of March 16,

MORE BLUSTER THAN BLOOD.

America's attempt to gain the Samoan Islands as a coaling station along the route to Australia led to a diplomatic crisis with Germany.

1889, a typhoon swept across Samoa, destroying the American and German warships anchored in Apia harbor.

The violent winds seemed to calm the ruffled emotions of the United States and Germany. "Men and nations," wrote the New York *World,* "must bow before the decrees of nature." The same year as the typhoon, Germany, the United States, and England met for another conference, this one in Berlin. Without consulting the Samoans, they decided to partition the islands. Everyone seemed satisfied—except the Samoans who were deprived of their independence and saddled with an unpopular king. The plan lasted until 1899, when Germany and the United States ended the facade of Samoan independence and officially made colonies of the islands. The United States was granted Tutuila, with the harbor of Pago Pago, and several smaller islands. Many expansionists believed that America's aggressive stand against Germany had paid handsome dividends.

Teaching Chile a Lesson

American expansionists had something to gain from their confrontation with Germany over Samoa. Pago Pago was, after all, "the most perfectly landlocked harbor that exists in the Pacific Ocean." It was an ideal coaling station for ships running between San Francisco and Australia. American troubles with Chile, however, are more difficult to understand. Trade and strategic policy played small roles. More than anything else, touchy pride and jingoism pushed the United States toward war with Chile.

Had people not died, the background to the confrontation would have been amusing. In 1891 a revolutionary faction, which the United States had opposed, gained control of the Chilean government and initiated a foreign policy which was unfriendly toward America. Shortly thereafter, on October 16, 1889, an American cruiser, the *Baltimore* anchored off the coast of Chile, sent about one hundred members of its crew ashore on leave at Valparaiso. Many of the sailors did what sailors normally do on leave. They retired to a local saloon—in this particular case, to the True Blue Saloon—and drank. An officer who arrived on the scene later said that the men had gone ashore "for the purpose of getting drunk" and that by evening they were "probably drunk, properly drunk." As the men left the saloon, a riot broke out. An angry, anti-American mob attacked the sailors, killing two and injuring sixteen. To make matters worse, the Chilean police, who had done nothing to halt the fighting, carried the surviving Americans off to jail.

It was an unfortunate affair, and the United States loudly protested, demanding a formal apology and "prompt and full reparation." The Chilean government refused. President Harrison, a former general who had worn Union blue during the Civil War and who prided himself on his patriotism and was easily swayed by jingoism, threatened to break off diplomatic relations—a serious step toward war—unless the United States received an immediate apology. When his secretary of state, James G. Blaine, tried to counsel moderation, Harrison angrily replied, "Mr. Secretary, that insult was to the uniform of United States sailors."

Public opinion sided with Harrison. *The New York Sun* commented that "we must teach men who will henceforth be called snarling whelps of the Pacific that we cannot be snapped at with impunity." And angry young Theodore Roosevelt insisted, "For two nickels he would declare war himself . . . and wage it sole." Finally the Chilean government backed down. It apologized for the attack on the sailors and paid an indemnity of $75,000.

The threat of force had again carried the day. Advocates of the New Navy and aggressively nationalistic Americans cheered Harrison's actions. The foreign policy of the United States was becoming increasingly belligerent and strident. Few Americans heeded Edwin L. Godkin, editor of the influential *Nation* who wrote, "The number of men and officials in this country who are now ready to fight somebody is appalling. Navy officers dream of war and talk and lecture about it incessantly. The Senate debates are filled with predictions of impending war and with talk of preparing for it at once . . . . Most truculent and bloodthirsty of all, jingo editors keep up a din day after day about the way we could cripple one country's fleet and destroy another's commerce, and fill heads of boys and silly men with the idea that war is the normal state of a civilized country."

The Hawaiian Pear

Throughout the late nineteenth century, Hawaii figured prominently in American foreign policy planning. Earlier in the century, the islands had been a favorite place for American missionaries. Many went to Hawaii to spread Christianity and ended up settling and raising their families in the tropical paradise. More important still was the location of the islands. Not only were they ideally situated along the trade routes to Asia, but they offered a perfect site for protecting the Pacific sea lanes to the American west coast and the potential locations of an isthmus canal. In Hawaii, missionary, economic, and strategic concerns met in complete harmony.

By the mid-1880s, Congress was willing to accept expansionists' dreams for Hawaii. In 1884 a treaty between Hawaii and the United States set aside Pearl Harbor for the exclusive use of the American navy. After some debate

Congress ratified the treaty in 1887, and Hawaii officially became part of American strategic planning. By that time the islands were already economically tied to the United States. An 1875 treaty had admitted Hawaiian sugar into the United States duty-free, giving the islanders a two cents per pound advantage over other foreign producers. The legislation encouraged American speculators to invest in Hawaiian sugar and to import Chinese and Japanese laborers to the islands to work on the large plantations. The investments returned incredibly high dividends, and for a time business boomed.

Problems arose suddenly in 1890. The McKinley Tariff Act of that year removed all tariffs on foreign sugar and protected domestic sugar producers by awarding American sugar a bounty of two cents per pound. Hawaiian sugar prices plummeted. The American minister in Honolulu estimated that the McKinley Tariff cost Hawaiian producers $12 million. Added to this, in 1891 the government of the islands changed. Queen Liliuokalani ascended to the throne. A poet and a composer, she expressed interest in humanitarian work and initiated a strong anti-American policy. She wanted to purge American influences in Hawaii and disenfranchise all white men except those married to native women.

The white population in Hawaii reacted quickly. On January 17, 1893, three days after the queen dismissed the legislature and proclaimed a new constitution, white islanders overthrew her government. Supported by the American minister in Honolulu, John L. Stevens, and aided by American sailors and marines, the revolution was fast, almost bloodless, and successful. Stevens then proclaimed Hawaii an American protectorate and wired his superiors in Washington that "the Hawaiian pear is now fully ripe, and this is the golden hour for the United States to pluck it."

The revolutionaries in Hawaii favored prompt American annexation of the islands. In Washington, the Harrison administration, which was due to leave office on March 4, agreed. It negotiated a treaty of annexation with "indecent haste" and sent it to the Senate for ratification. Public sentiment cheered Harrison's actions, and the cry, " . . . Liliuokalani give us your little brown hannie!" swept the country.

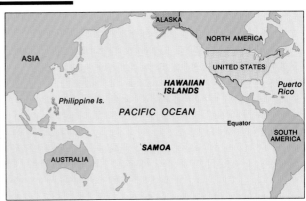

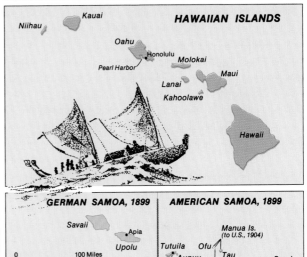

Hawaii and Samoa

Before the Senate could ratify the treaty, Cleveland took office. An anti-imperialist, Cleveland had grave misgivings about the revolution, America's reaction, and the treaty. Five days after his inauguration, he recalled the treaty from the Senate and sent a special agent, James H. Blount of Georgia, to Hawaii to investigate the entire affair. After a careful investigation, Blount reported to Cleveland that the majority of native Hawaiians opposed annexation and that on moral and legal grounds the treaty was unjustified. Cleveland accepted Blount's report and killed the treaty.

This did not end the controversy. A white American minority continued to govern Hawaii. To correct the situation, Cleveland sent another

Queen Liliuokalani of Hawaii was a strongly national-istic ruler who was deposed by a group of American businessmen.

representative, Albert S. Willis, to Hawaii to convince the new government to step down and allow Queen Liliuokalani to return to the throne. Willis failed in his mission. "Queen Lil" refused to promise full amnesty for the revolutionaries if she were returned to power. "My decision would be," she said, "as the law directs, that such persons should be beheaded." In addition, President Sanford B. Dole, head of a large Hawaiian pineapple corporation, refused to leave office. In the end, Cleveland washed his hands of the entire matter, and the revolutionaries proclaimed an independent Hawaiian republic on July 4, 1894. Four years and three days later, during the early weeks of the Spanish-American War, the United States finally annexed Hawaii.

Facing Down the British

Potentially the most serious conflict America faced during the 1890s originated in a dispute over a strip of land in a South American jungle.

Venezuela and British Guiana shared a common border; the dispute was over exactly where that border was located. Both sides claimed land which the other side said was theirs. For almost fifty years this dispute remained peacefully unsettled, but the discovery of gold in the region in the 1880s increased the importance of the issue. It was a rich deposit—the largest nugget ever discovered, 509 ounces, was found there—and both Britain and Venezuela wanted it for their own. In response to Venezuelan requests to help, several times the United States offered to arbitrate the matter, and each time Britain refused the offer.

By June 1895 Cleveland and his new secretary of state, Richard Olney, had decided that Britain's actions were in violation of the spirit, if not the letter, of the Monroe Doctrine. Both men were short tempered. Ever since a cancer operation had left him with an artificial jaw of vulcanized rubber, Cleveland had been irritable. And Olney, who had persuaded Cleveland to use federal troops to put down the Pullman Strike in Chicago the year before, was a man of strong ideas who did not shrink from the use of force. In a strongly worded message to Great Britain, Olney warned, "Today the United States is practically sovereign on this continent, and its fiat is law upon the subjects to which it confines its interposition." Olney demanded that Britain submit the dispute to arbitration, hinting that the United States might intervene militarily if its wishes were not honored.

Lord Salisbury, Britain's prime minister, foreign secretary, and consummate aristocrat, waited four months to reply to Olney's note, and then answered, in effect, that the dispute did not involve either the United States or the Monroe Doctrine and would America kindly mind its own business. Olney was furious. Americans throughout the country felt insulted. Cleveland, who was duck hunting in North Carolina when Salisbury's response reached Washington, returned to the capital, read the message, and became "mad clean through." In a special message to Congress, he asked for funds to establish a commission to determine the actual Venezuelan boundary, and he insisted that he would use force if necessary to maintain that boundary against any aggressors. Both houses of Congress unanimously approved Cleveland's

A LITTLE MONROE DOCTORING MIGHT BE GOOD FOR HIM.

Preoccupied with larger diplomatic problems in England and South Africa, Britain agreed to arbitration to settle the Venezuela border dispute.

request. The excitement of war was in the air. Although he was in London during much of the controversy, Senator Henry Cabot Lodge captured the mood of America when he wrote a friend, "War is a bad thing no doubt, but there are worse things both for nations and for men."

The violence of America's reaction surprised Salisbury and British officials. England certainly did not want war, particularly at that time when it was becoming involved in a conflict in South Africa. Salisbury reversed his position and allowed a commission to arbitrate the dispute. In the end, the arbitral tribunal gave Britain most of the land it claimed.

America, however, felt it was the real winner. Cleveland had faced the British lion and won. The Monroe Doctrine and American prestige soared to new heights. More important for the future, Cleveland's actions, coupled with his handling of the Hawaiian revolution, significantly increased the power of the president over foreign affairs. Relations between the United States and Britain would quickly im-

prove, and relations between America and Venezuela would rapidly deteriorate, but future presidents would not soon relinquish their control over foreign policy.

THE WAR FOR EMPIRE

Spirit of the 1890s

During the Venezuela Crisis many Americans seemed to openly invite and look forward to the prospect of war. Theodore Roosevelt, who was determined to be the first in war even if he were the last in peace, wrote: "Let the fight come if it must; I don't care whether our sea coast cities are bombarded or not; we would take Canada." For Roosevelt, war would be an ennobling experience. It would test and validate American greatness. "All the great masterful races," Roosevelt wrote, "have been fighting races; and the minute that a race loses the hard fighting virtues, then . . . it has lost its proud right to stand as the equal of the best."

Throughout the 1890s other Americans echoed Roosevelt's war cries. Viewed as a whole, it was a decade of strident nationalism and aggressive posturing. It was also a troubled and violent decade. Racked by the depression of 1893, frustrated by the problem created by monopolies, and plagued by internal strife, Americans turned on each other, often with violent results. Strikes in Pullman, Illinois, and Homestead, Pennsylvania, saw laborers battle federal and state authorities. Populist protest dramatized the widening gulf between city and country, rich and poor. Anarchists and socialists talked about the need for violent solutions to complex problems.

Popular culture in America reflected this aggressive mood. As Roosevelt denounced "the soft spirit in the cloistered life" and "the base spirit of gain," Americans looked to arenas of conflict for their heroes. They glorified boxers like the great John L. Sullivan, who held the heavyweight championship of the world between 1882 and 1892. They cheered as violence increased on the Ivy League football fields. They admired body builders like Bernarr Macfadden and Eugene Sandow, who was heralded as the most perfectly developed man in the world. In the first issue of *Physical Culture*,

THEODORE ROOSEVELT AND THE ROUGH RIDERS

Aboard the *Yucatan,* anchored off the coast of Cuba, Theodore Roosevelt received the news on the evening of June 21, 1898. He and his men, a volunteer cavalry regiment dubbed the Rough Riders, had received their orders to disembark from the safety of the ship and join the fighting ashore. It was a welcomed invitation, celebrated with cheers, war-dances, songs, boasts, and toasts. "To the Officers—may they get killed, wounded or promoted," urged one toast which captured the mood aboard the ship.

Roosevelt and many men of his generation looked forward to war, greedily anticipating the chance to prove their mettle in battle. They had been raised on stories of the Civil War, stories that over the years had taken on the golden gloss of time. Tales of Shiloh, Chancellorsville, Antietam, and Gettysburg; of Robert E. Lee, Ulysses S. Grant, and Stonewall Jackson; of battles won and causes lost had fired their imaginations. The Spanish-American War was their chance to experience firsthand what they had long only heard about from their fathers' and uncles' lips.

Few men wanted the war more than Roosevelt. Son of a wealthy New York family, he was competitive by nature and enjoyed all physical sports. He also loved history, writing books about American wars and heroic deeds. And for Roosevelt there was perhaps even a deeper motivation. During the Civil War his father, the man he admired above everyone else, had hired a substitute soldier to serve for him. Thousands of other wealthy men had done the same, but for Theodore such a course was unmanly. During war, he believed, able bodied men should be in a uniform, not dressed in mufti. He would not repeat his father's mistake. When the Spanish-American War was declared, TR quickly resigned his post as assistant secretary of the navy and joined the fray. In his own mind, he could do nothing else. In *The Rough Riders,* his memoirs of the war, he quoted a poem by Bret Harte, whose last verse was:

> "But when won the coming battle,
> What of profit springs therefrom?
> What if conquest, subjugation,
> Even greater ills become?"
> But the drum
> Answered, "Come!"

And come Roosevelt did.

The men who followed him were kindred spirits. They were rough riders, the men who with Roosevelt formed the First United States Volunteer Cavalry regiment. Some were Ivy Leaguers from Harvard, Yale, and Princeton who belonged to the most exclusive clubs in Boston and New York City. Many had been college athletes, stars in football, tennis, and track and field, men for whom war was a grand playing field. Others were Westerners—cowboys, hunters, frontier sheriffs, Indian fighters, Texas Rangers, prospectors—"a splendid set of men," wrote Roosevelt, "tall and sinewy, with resolute, weather-beaten faces, and eyes that looked a man straight in the face without flinching." Such men were accustomed to riding horses, shooting rifles, and living off the land.

Bucky O'Neill was something of a Rough Rider ideal. Indian fighter and sheriff of Prescott, Arizona, Bucky could shoot with the hunters, exchange stories with the prospectors, and philosophize with the college graduates. Roosevelt once overheard Bucky and Dr. Robb Church, the former Princeton football player who served as the surgeon for the Rough Riders, "discussing Aryan word roots together, and then sliding off into a review of the novels of Balzac, and a discussion as to how far Balzac could be said to be the founder of the modern realistic school of fiction." Once when Bucky and Roosevelt were leaning on the ship's railing searching the Caribbean sky for the Southern Cross, the old Indian fighter asked, "Who would not risk his life for a star?" TR agreed that great risk was part of greatness.

Brimming with enthusiasm, perhaps a bit innocent in their naivete, the Rough Riders viewed Cuba as a land of stars, a place to win great honors or die in the pursuit. Like many of his men, TR believed "that the nearing future held . . . many chances of death, of honor and renown." And he was ready. Dressed in a Brooks Brothers uniform made especially for him and with several extra pairs of spectacles sewn in the lining of his Rough Rider hat, Roosevelt prepared to meet his destiny.

In a land of beauty, death often came swiftly. As the Rough Riders and other soldiers moved inland toward Santiago, snipers fired upon them. The high-speed Mauser bullets seemed to come out of nowhere, making a *z-z-z-z-z-eu* as they moved through the air or a loud *chug* as they hit flesh.

Since the Spanish snipers used smokeless gunpowder, no puffs of smoke betrayed their positions.

During their first day in Cuba, the Rough Riders experienced the "blood, sweat, and tears" of warfare. Dr. Church looked "like a kid who had gotten his hands and arms into a bucket of thick red paint." Some men died, and others lay where they had been shot dying. The reality of war strikes different men differently. It horrifies some, terrifies others, and enrages still others. Sheer exhilaration was the best way to describe Roosevelt's response to the death and danger. Even sniper fire could not keep TR from jumping up and down with excitement.

On July 1, 1898, the Rough Riders faced their sternest task. Moving from the coast toward Santiago along the Camino Real, the main arm of the United States forces encountered an entrenched enemy. Spread out along the San Juan Heights, Spanish forces commanded a splendid position. As American troops emerged from a stretch of jungle, they found themselves in a dangerous position. Once again the sky seemed to be raining Mauser bullets and shrapnel. Clearly the Heights had to be taken. Each hour of delay meant more American casualties.

The Rough Riders were deployed to the right to prepare to assault Kettle Hill. Once in position, they faced an agonizing wait for orders to charge. Most soldiers hunched behind cover. Bucky O'Neill, however, casually strolled up and down in front of his troops, chain-smoked cigarettes, and shouted encouragement. A sergeant implored him to take cover. "Sargeant," Bucky remarked, "the Spanish bullet isn't made that

will kill me." Hardly had he finished the statement when a Mauser bullet ripped into his mouth and burst out of the back of his head. Even before he fell, Roosevelt wrote, Bucky's "wild and gallant soul had gone out into the darkness."

Finally the orders came. On foot the Rough Riders moved up Kettle Hill toward the Spanish guns. It was a slow, painful, heroic charge. Bullets, sounding "like the ripping of a silk dress," cut down a number of Roosevelt's men. But unable to stop the push of the American forces, the Spanish gave way, leaving their fortified positions and running for safety.

From the heights of Kettle Hill, Roosevelt watched another United States attack on nearby San Juan Hill. Once again feeling the wolf rising in his heart, he led his men toward the new objective. Again the fighting was difficult. But again the Spanish gave way. By the end of the day, American forces had taken the San Juan Heights. Before them was Santiago and victory. "The great day of my life," as TR called it, was over.

"Another such victory like that of July 1," wrote Richard Harding Davis, "and our troops must retreat." Indeed, casualties ran high, and the Rough Riders suffered the heaviest losses. But the fighting helped to break the Spanish resistance. It was the last really difficult day of fighting in the war. Perhaps more importantly, the day made Roosevelt a national hero. Aided by his ability at self-promotion, TR used the event as a political stepping stone. "I would rather have led the charge," he later wrote, "than served three terms in the U.S. Senate."

Macfadden declared, "Weakness Is a Crime." In saloons across the country, Sullivan defiantly boasted, "I can lick any sonofabitch in the house." And in the parlors of the wealthy, Roosevelt stressed, "Cowardice in a race, as in an individual, is the unpardonable sin." Between Sullivan and Roosevelt, and the Americans that admired both men, was a bond forged by the love of violence and power.

This attitude led to the glorification of war and jingoistic nationalism. During the mid-1890s a remarkable interest in Napoleon gripped the nation; between 1894 and 1896 twenty-eight books were written about the Corsican general. In public schools throughout the country, administrators instituted daily flag salutes and made the recitation of the new pledge of allegiance mandatory. Even the popular music of the day had a particularly martial quality. Such marches as John Philip Sousa's "Stars and Stripes Forever" (1897) and "A Hot Time in the Old Town" (1896) captured the aggressive, patriotic, and boisterous mood of the country.

As the disputes with Germany, Chile, and Great Britain demonstrated, neither the American people nor its leaders feared war. The horrors of the Civil War were dying with the generation which had known them. A younger generation of men, filled with romantic and idealized conceptions of battle and heroism, now openly sought a war of their own. In Washington some politicians even began to view war as a way to unite the country, to quell the protests of angry farmers and laborers.

The Cuban Revolution

Often times the mood of a nation governs the reaction to and interpretation of events. Such was the case with America's attitude toward the Cuban Revolution. In 1895, while Sousa was writing energetic marches and Americans were cheering new boxing heroes, an independence revolt broke out in Cuba. It was not the first time the Cubans took up arms in pursuit of independence. During the Ten Years' War (1868–1878) Cuban patriots had unsuccessfully fought for their independence against their Spanish rulers. The war was bloody and violent,

and Cubans actively sought American support; but the United States, guided by a policy of isolationism, steered clear.

By 1895, however, cautious isolationism was out of beat with Sousa's and Roosevelt's aggressive tempo. From the start, Americans expressed far more than casual interest in the rebellion. To be sure, American business was concerned. Americans had invested over $50 million in Cuba, and the annual trade between the two countries totaled almost $100 million. Once the revolution started, insurgents burned crops in the fields, and the trade between Cuba and the United States slowed to a trickle. Overall, however, economics played a relatively unimportant role in forming America's attitude toward the revolution.

Humanitarianism was a far more important factor. Americans cheered the underdog. In Cuba's valiant fight, they saw a reenactment of their own war for independence. And the resourceful Cubans made sure that Americans stayed well supplied with stories of Spanish atrocities and Cuban heroism. The Cuban junta—or central revolutionary committee—established a base in New York City and Tampa, Florida, and daily provided American newspapers with stories aimed at sympathetic American hearts.

Not all the stories were false. The Cuban—and Spanish—suffering was real enough. Unable to defeat the Spanish army in the field, Cuban revolutionaries resorted to guerilla tactics. They burned sugar cane fields and blew up mills. They destroyed railroad tracks and bridges. They vowed to win their independence or destroy Cuba in the process. One of their leaders, General Maximo Gomez, aptly stated the guerillas' and Cuba's position: "The chains of Cuba have been forged by her own richness, and it is precisely this which I propose to do away with soon." Supported by the populace, the guerillas succeeded in turning Cuba into an economic and military nightmare for Spanish officials.

In 1896 Spain sent Governor-General Valeriano Weyler y Nicolau to Cuba to crush the rebellion. A man of ruthless clarity, he understood the nature of guerilla warfare. Guerillas could not be defeated by conventional engagements. Their generals did not imitate the tactics of Napoleon; they were not concerned with flanking maneuvers and cavalry charges. Their weapons were patience and endurance and popular support. Weyler knew this, and he decided to fight the guerillas on their own terms.

His first plan was to rob the guerillas of their base of support, the rural villages and the sympathetic peasants. He divided the island into districts and herded Cubans into guarded camps. It was a policy that the United States would later use to fight guerillas in the Philippines and Vietnam, but Weyler was brutal in his execution of it. He forced over a half million Cubans from their homes and crowded them into shabbily constructed and unsanitary camps. The food was bad, the water worse. Disease spread with frightful speed and horrifying results. Perhaps 200,000 Cubans died in the camps as Weyler earned the sobriquet "the Butcher." After inspecting the camps, Senator Renfield Proctor of Vermont reported on the plight of the Cuban people to Congress: "Torn from their homes, with foul earth, foul air, foul water, and foul food or none, what wonder that one-half have died and that one-quarter of the living are so diseased that they cannot be saved? . . . Little children are still walking about with arms and chest terribly emaciated, eyes swollen, and abdomens bloated to three times the natural size."

The Yellow Press

In the United States reports of the suffering Cuban masses filled the front pages of newspapers. In New York City, William Randolph Hearst's New York *Journal* and Joseph Pulitzer's New York *World* used the junta's lurid stories as ammunition in a newspaper war. Newspaper reporters freely engaged in "yellow journalism," exaggerating conditions which were in truth depressingly sad and inhumane. Most stories had a sensational twist. One particularly incendiary drawing by Frederic Remington, the famous western artist sent to Cuba by Hearst, pictured three leering Spanish officials searching a nude Cuban woman. Hearst ran the picture five columns wide on the second page of the *Journal,* and the edition sold close to

This *New York Journal* sketch by Frederick Remington of Spanish officials searching a woman on an American steamer shocked the country.

one million copies, the largest newspaper run in history until then. Neither the picture nor the story, however, mentioned that Spanish women—not men—conducted the search. Such coverage biased American opinion against Spain. It also sold newspapers. When Hearst bought the *Journal* in 1895 it had daily circulation of 77,000 copies; by the summer of 1898 sales had increased to over 1.5 million daily.

"Yellow journalism" persuaded many Americans to call for United States intervention in the Cuban Revolution. Grover Cleveland, however, was not easily moved by newspaper reports. His administration wanted to protect American interests in Cuba but was dead set against any sort of military intervention in the conflict. Without recognizing the revolutionaries, he worked to convince Spain to grant "home rule." Spain was unconvinced. But Cleveland was unprepared to move beyond vague warnings. When he left office in early 1897, the revolution in Cuba raged as violently as ever.

McKinley Moves Toward War

Cleveland passed the Cuban problems to his successor William McKinley. Like Cleveland, McKinley deplored war. He had fought bravely in the Civil War, and he knew the horrors of war firsthand. For McKinley, arbitration was the civilized way to settle disputes. War was a poor and wasteful alternative. Before he would even consider military intervention, McKinley was determined to exhaust every peaceful alternative.

McKinley displayed strength and patience. As many influential Americans called for United States intervention, McKinley worked diplomatically to end the fighting. For a time it appeared that his efforts would succeed. In October 1897 a new government in Spain moved toward granting more autonomy to Cuba. It removed Weyler and promised to end his hated reconcentration program. Spain, said McKinley, was following "honorable paths." Patience and cool heads, he hoped, would carry the day.

Spain moved with glacial slowness. Some of its reforms were half-hearted, others were merely designed to calm American emotions. In Cuba the bloodshed continued. As Spanish officials and Cuban revolutionaries ignored or denounced Spain's "honorable paths," pressure on McKinley to take stronger action mounted. By January of 1898 the president looked as defeated as his diplomatic efforts. He had to take drugs to sleep, his skin was pasty, and his dark eyes seemed to be sinking farther back into his head. During February two events would end any hope of a diplomatic solution and lead to the Spanish-American War.

William Randolph Hearst had often told his reporters: "Don't wait for things to turn up. Turn them up!" He did just that in early February 1898. With the help of the Cuban junta, Hearst acquired a private letter from Enrique Dupuy de Lome, the Spanish minister in the United States, to a Spanish friend of his in Cuba. The letter contained de Lome's unguarded and undiplomatic opinion of McKinley. Reprinted on the front page of the *Journal* on February 9, 1898, Hearst labeled the letter: "Worst insult to the United States in Its History." De Lome called McKinley "weak and a bidder for the admiration of the crowd." He accused the American president of being a hypocrite and a "would-be politician." Even worse, De Lome suggested that Spain's new peace policy was mere sham and propaganda.

The letter hit the American public like a bombshell. Although de Lome resigned, America was in no mood to forget and forgive. Former Secretary of State Richard Olney wrote his old boss Grover Cleveland, "I confess [that] some expressions of his letter stagger me and, if they . . . mean that Spain has been tricking us as regards autonomy and other matters incidental to it, I should have wanted the privilege of sending him his passports before he had any chance to be recalled or resign." Olney expressed the mood of the nation. As one of the leaders of the Cuban junta noted, "The de Lome letter is a great thing for us."

Less than one week later a second event rocked America. On the still evening of February 15, an explosion ripped apart the *Maine,* a United States battleship anchored in Havana Harbor. The ship quickly sank, killing 350 officers and men. An investigation in 1898 ruled that an external explosion had sunk the *Maine.* In a 1976 study, Admiral Hyman G. Rickover blamed the sinking on an internal explosion. In truth, no one knows the who, how, and why answers. Americans at the time, however, were not in an impartial or philosophical mood. They blamed Spain. One diplomatic historian commented, "'Remember the *Maine*!' became a national watch word . . . In a Broadway bar a man raised his glass and said solemnly, 'Gentlemen, remember the *Maine*!' Through the streets of American cities went the cry, 'Remember the *Maine*! To Hell with Spain!'"

War was in the air, and it is doubtful if McKinley or any other president could have long preserved peace. Congress was ready for war. On March 6, McKinley told a leading congressman, "I must have money to get ready for war." Congress responded on March 8 by passing the "Fifty Million Bill" (the amount of McKinley's request) without a single dissenting vote. Although McKinley continued to work for a diplomatic solution to the crisis, his efforts lacked his earlier energy and optimism. By early April, diplomacy had reached its end.

The sinking of the *Maine* was one of the major events leading to the Spanish-American War. It is still uncertain who or what sank the *Maine*.

On April 11, an exhausted McKinley sent a virtual war message to Congress. He asked for authority to use force to end the Cuban war. His message mixed talk of commerce with lofty humanitarianism. America must take up the "cause of humanity," he wrote, and stop the "very serious injury to the commerce, trade, and business of our people, and the wanton destruction of property."

On April 19 Congress officially acted. It proclaimed Cuba's independence, demanded Spain's evacuation, and authorized McKinley to use force to achieve those results. In the Teller Amendment, Congress added that the United States had no intention of annexing Cuba for herself. For some Americans it was a great and noble decision. Senator Albert Beveridge, one of the great speakers of his day, intoned: "At last, God's hour has struck. The American people go forth in a warfare holier than liberty— holy as humanity." For the men and boys who would have to fight the battles, the war would soon seem considerably less noble.

The Spanish-American War

There is no simple explanation for the Spanish-American War. Economics and imperial ambitions certainly played a part, but no more so than did humanitarianism and selfless concern for the suffering of others. McKinley tried to find a peaceful solution, but he failed. Some historians and many of his contemporaries have viewed McKinley as a weak, hollow president, a messenger boy for America's financial community. A Washington joke in the late 1890s ran, "Why is McKinley's mind like a bed?" Answer: "Because it has to be made up for him every time he wants to use it." Such was not the case. McKinley did have a vision—a peaceful vision—of America's role in world affairs. But the unpredictability of events and the mood of the nation were more powerful than the president.

In theory America had prepared for war with Spain. In 1897 the Navy Department had drawn up contingency plans for a war against Spain for the liberation of Cuba. It had envisioned a war centered mainly in the Caribbean, but the navy had plans to attack the Philippine Islands, which belonged to Spain, and even the coast of Spain, if necessary. In the Caribbean, the navy planned to blockade Cuba and assist an army invasion of the island. On paper, neatly written and soundly reasoned, America was well prepared for a war that seemed more of a military exercise than a deadly struggle.

In reality, the military was not physically ready for war. The process of mobilizing troops was chaotic and the training given volunteers was inadequate. In addition, the army faced severe supply shortages. Volunteers suffered the most. They were herded into camps, often without such basic equipment as tents and mess kits. Long before they ever faced enemy guns or even saw Cuba, they battled wet uniforms, bad food, and deadly sanitary conditions. Far more volunteers died in stateside camps than were killed by Spanish bullets.

For black troops, regular and volunteers, racism exasperated already difficult conditions. They too were plagued by spoiled beef, thick wool uniforms, and unsanitary conditions. Also, since most of the large camps were located in the South—in places such as Tampa, New Orleans, Mobile, and Chickamauga Park, Tennessee—they also had to battle Jim Crow laws and other forms of racial hostility. They saw signs that proclaimed "Dogs and niggers not allowed" and were pelted by rocks. Once in the camps, they were given the lowest military assignments. George W. Prioleau, a black chaplin, noted: "Talk about fighting and freeing poor Cuba and of Spain's brutality; of Cuba's murdered thousands, and starving reconcentradoes. Is America any better than Spain?"

While the agony of mobilization was taking place, the navy moved into action. During the tense weeks before the United States went to

All black troops fighting in Cuba were commanded by white officers, much to the dissatisfaction of the black soldiers.

war against Spain, Theodore Roosevelt, then acting secretary of the navy, wired his friend Commodore George Dewey, leader of America's Asiatic Squadron: "KEEP FULL OF COAL. IN THE EVENT OF DECLARATION OF WAR [WITH] SPAIN, YOUR DUTY WILL BE TO SEE THAT THE SPANISH SQUADRON DOES NOT LEAVE THE ASIATIC COAST, AND THEN OFFENSIVE OPERATIONS IN PHILIPPINE ISLANDS." Dewey had been anxiously waiting for just that order. He was a warrior, and he looked forward to war. One historian remarked that "Dewey looked like a resplendent killer falcon, ready to bite through wire, if necessary, to get at a prey."

Biting through wire was not necessary. He only had to sail to Manila Bay. At the break of light on the morning of May 1, 1898, he struck. In a few hours of fighting, he destroyed Spain's Asiatic fleet. It was a stunning victory. Only one American died, and he of heat prostration manning a ship's overworked boiler. "You have made a name for the nation, and the Navy, and yourself," Roosevelt wrote Dewey. Americans rejoiced in the quick victory. Newspapers were filled with stories of American heroics and poems praised Dewey. One not very accomplished poet captured the public mood:

> Oh, dewey was the morning
> Upon the first of May,
> And Dewey was the Admiral,
> Down in Manila Bay.
> And dewey were the Spaniard's eyes,
> Them orbs of black and blue;
> And dew we feel discouraged?
> I do not think we dew.

Not every victory came so easily. Closer to home in the Caribbean theater, the war was much more prosaic. The main Spanish forces in Cuba were in control of the strategically important Santiago Bay. To defeat the Spanish it would take the combined efforts of the army and the navy. With this in mind, McKinley ordered Major General William R. Shafter, commander of the all-regular 5th Corps, from Tampa to Santiago. The trip to Cuba set the tone for the entire expedition. Delays, confused orders, and other problems slowed the process. Some 17,000 American troops were forced to spend nineteen days on crowded transports, sweating in their woolen uniforms, eating unappetizing travel rations, and thinking about what lay ahead. Finally, toward the end of June, and with the help of Cuban rebels, American troops landed at Daiquiri and Siboney.

From there they moved toward Santiago. The distance was not great. Santiago Bay was only about fifteen miles from the coastal town of Siboney. But the road to Santiago was little more than a rutted, dirt trail. When it rained wagons became mired in the mud, streams swelled and made fording treacherous, and the troops suffered in the jungle humidity. Slowly the army moved forward, more concerned with broken wagons and tropical diseases than Spanish soldiers.

On July 1, American soldiers learned first hand the horrors of battle. Between the American position and Santiago were Spanish troops in the tiny hamlet of El Caney and along the San Juan Heights, a ridge to the east of Santiago. From the first, American plans broke down in the face of stiff Spanish opposition. There were no romantic charges, no idealized warfare. The American troops that struggled up Kettle and San Juan hills moved very slowly and suffered alarming casualties. Although outnumbered more than ten to one, Spanish soldiers made United States troops pay for every foot they advanced. After America finally secured the enemy positions, correspondent Richard H. Davis wrote, "Another such victory as that of July 1 and our troops must retreat."

General Shafter was frankly worried and even considered retreat. Grossly overweight and gout-ridden, Shafter had neither the disposition nor the ability to lead an energetic campaign. Fortunately for him, Spain's forces in

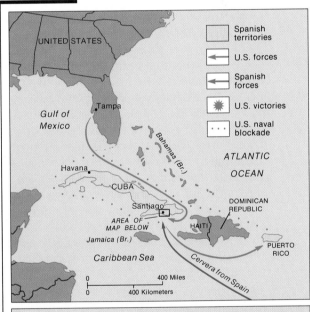

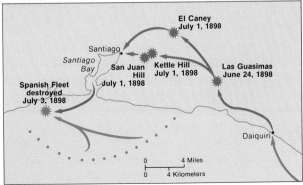

Spanish-American War, Cuban Theater

Cuba were even less ready to fight. In Santiago, Spanish soldiers faced shortages of food, water, and ammunition. On July 3, the Spanish squadron tried to break an American blockade and force its way out of Santiago Bay. The act was a suicidal move. American guns destroyed the Spanish fleet and killed some 500 Spanish sailors. Only one American died in the decisive engagement. When his men broke out in a yell of joy, Captain Philip of the *Texas* said, "Don't cheer, men, the poor devils are dying."

Little fighting remained. On July 17 the leading Spanish general in Cuba surrendered to Shafter. Timid in war, Shafter was petty in victory. He refused to permit any naval officers to sign the capitulation document, nor would he allow any Cubans to participate in the surrender negotiations and ceremonies. It was a sad moment. The Cubans who had fought so long and bravely for their independence were denied the glory of their success.

Before the full Spanish surrender, the United States extended its influence in the Caribbean. In late July, General Nelson G. Miles invaded Puerto Rico, Spain's other Caribbean colony. Without any serious resistance, United States forces took the island. Finally, on August 12, Spain surrendered, granting Cuban independence and ceding Puerto Rico and Guam to the United States. Both countries agreed to settle the fate of the Philippines at a postwar peace conference to be held in Paris.

For America, it had been a short, successful war. Spanish bullets killed only 379 Americans, the smallest number in any of America's wars. Disease and other problems cost over 5000 more lives. If the army's mobilization had been chaotic, its troops had performed heroically under fire. And the navy, which took most of the credit for winning the war, demonstrated the wisdom of its planners. All in all, many Americans agreed with United States Ambassador to England John Hay that it had been a "splendid little war."

There was nothing little about the consequences of the war. With the Spanish-American War the United States became an imperial power. The war increased America's appetite for overseas territories. The McKinley administration used the war to annex Hawaii and part of Samoa. In addition, at the Paris Peace Conference the United States wrested the Philippines, Puerto Rico, and Guam from Spain. Although the United States paid Spain $20 million for the Philippines, there was no question that Spain was forced to negotiate under duress.

Freeing Cuba

Many Americans favored the annexation of Cuba. In the land grab that ended the war, the idealism of the Teller Amendment and the war's beginning was all but forgotten. When the war ended, United States troops stayed in Cuba, and the country was ruled by an American-run military government. Particularly under General Leonard Wood, the military government helped Cuba recover from its terrible conflict with Spain. Wood restored the Cuban economy and promoted reforms in the legal system, education, sanitation, and health care. Neither Wood nor McKinley, however, was willing to grant Cuba its immediate independence. In his annual message of December 1898, McKinley noted that American troops would stay in Cuba until "complete tranquility" and a "stable government" existed on the island.

In 1903 the United States finally recognized Cuban independence; and it was a limited independence at that. According to the Platt Amendment to the Army Appropriation Bill of 1901, Cuba could exercise self-government, but it could sign no treaties that might limit its independence. Should, in the judgment of the United States, Cuban independence ever be threatened, the Platt Amendment authorized the United States to intervene in Cuba's internal and external affairs. In short, for Cuba, independence had the look and feel of an American protectorate.

The Imperial Debate

Compared to the Philippines, Cuba was a minor problem. McKinley's decision to annex the Philippines pleased some Americans and angered many more. Businessmen who dreamed of the rich China markets applauded McKinley's decision. Naval strategists similarly believed it was a wise move. They argued that if the United

States failed to take the Philippines, then one of the other major powers probably would. Germany, Japan, and England had already expressed interest in the strategically located islands. Finally, Protestant missionaries favored annexation to facilitate their efforts to Christianize the Filipinos. That the Filipinos already favored Roman Catholicism did not seem to dampen the fervor of the Protestant missionaries.

Opposed to the annexation of the Philippines was a heterogeneous group of Americans who called themselves anti-imperialists. The group included such notable Americans as agrarian leader William Jennings Bryan, steel magnate Andrew Carnegie, labor organizer Samuel Gompers, writers Mark Twain and William Dean Howells, reformers Lincoln Steffens and Jane Addams, university presidents Charles W. Eliot of Harvard and David Starr Jordan of Stanford, and politicians George Frisbie Hoar of Massachusetts and "Pitchfork Ben" Tillman of South Carolina.

Their reasons for being anti-imperialists were as varied as their occupations and backgrounds. Some were high-minded idealists who believed that the Filipinos had the right to govern themselves. Others had more selfish reasons for opposing annexation. Samuel Gompers, for example, feared that annexation would lead to an influx of Filipino workers into the United States and hurt the American labor movement. Still others opposed annexation for base racial grounds. Vividly remembering the difficulties of Reconstruction, many Southerners and Northerners believed that annexation would only lead to renewed racial problems. The annexation of "dependencies inhabited by ignorant and inferior races," noted the *Nation* editor E. L. Godkin, could only lead to trouble.

During early 1899 the imperial debate raged. Journalists editorialized, speakers pontificated, and humorists detailed the absurdities of both sides. Mark Twain asked, "Shall we . . . go on conferring our Christianity upon the peoples that sit in darkness, or shall we give those poor things a rest? Shall we bang right ahead in our old-time, loud, pious way . . . or shall we sober up and sit down and think it over first." Twain's thoughtful questions about all the up-

roar changed very few opinions. Even Andrew Carnegie's offer to write a personal check for $20 million to buy the independence of the Philippines failed to end the debate. Ultimately, imperialists and anti-imperialists had different visions for America, and no bridge could span the gulf between.

The issue was settled on February 6, 1899, when the Senate voted on the Treaty of Paris. Strained tempers were evident in the tense atmosphere. Imperialist Senator Henry Cabot Lodge called the treaty fight the "closest, most bitter, and most exciting I have ever known, or ever expect to see in the Senate." For a time it appeared that the imperialists would not be able to muster the two-thirds majority needed to ratify the treaty. Anti-imperialist and titular leader of the Democratic party William Jennings Bryan ironically saved the imperialist cause. Not wanting to prolong the war by rejecting the treaty, he urged Democratic anti-imperialists to vote for ratification. In the close vote of 57 to 27 the Senate ratified the treaty. Undoubtedly Bryan hoped to use the issue of Philippine independence to capture the presidency in 1900, but such was not the case. With ratification of the treaty, the issue lost its sense of urgency and Americans grew tired of the debate.

The War to Crush Filipino Independence

Filipino independence, however, was not an abstract debate in the Philippines. Imperialist arguments about duty, destiny, defense, and dollars were lost on independence-minded Filipinos, led by Emilio Aguinaldo, who had fought bravely against the Spanish both before and after Dewey arrived in Manila. They had battled for their own independence, not to replace Spain with the United States as their colonial master. When it was clear that the United States did not have Filipino interests at heart, Aguinaldo and his followers resumed their fight for independence. Like the Cubans, freedom was a cause which they held dear. Like the Spanish, the United States was not willing to grant that freedom.

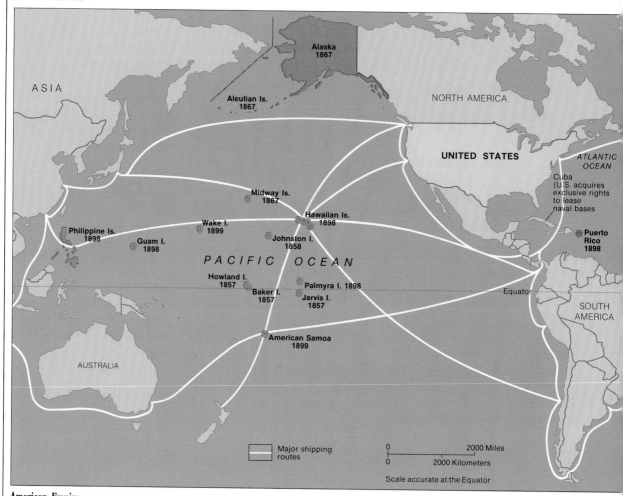

American Empire

With the Treaty of Paris, the United States gained an expanded colonial empire that included Puerto Rico, Alaska, Hawaii, part of Samoa, Guam, the Philippines, and a chain of Pacific islands.

Between 1899 and 1902 American troops and Filipino revolutionaries fought an ugly and destructive colonial war. Mark Twain's *The War Prayer* captured the mood of the fighting: "O Lord our God, help us to tear their soldiers to bloody shreds with our shells . . . , blast their hopes, blight their lives, protract their bitter pilgrimage." American soldiers faced a difficult task. Some did not know what they were fighting for, whose interests they were defending, or what rights they were protecting. Others regarded the Filipinos as subhuman. They referred to them as "niggers" and "gugus," and

they regarded the notion of Philippine independence as a joke.

Black American troops fighting to destroy Filipino freedom faced an even greater and more painful dilemma. Many black soldiers readily identified with Filipino aspirations. Some white officers even suspected, as journalist Stephen Bonsel noted in 1907, that "the negro soldiers were in closer sympathy with the aims of the native populations than they were with those of their white leaders and the policy of the United States." Although the majority of black troops professionally followed the orders of their white officers, an unusually large number deserted. Once again, Bonsel suggested the reason. The white soldier "deserted because he was lazy and idle and found service irksome"; blacks deserted "for the purpose of joining the insurgents," with whose struggle they identified.

For black and white soldiers alike, however, the actual fighting was bloody and frustrating. Aguinaldo's men were efficient guerrilla warriors. They fought only when victory was certain, usually ambushing small patrols. They burned bridges, destroyed railroads, sniped, and sabotaged. They filled pits with sharpened stakes and tortured prisoners. Some American captives had their ears cut off, and many Filipinos who supported the United States were hacked to death with bolos or buried alive. Aguinaldo's hope was that eventually the game would not be worth the prize, and that the American president would call his troops home.

McKinley was not about to do any such thing, and American troops proved just as vicious as the Filipino insurgents. Atrocities committed by American soldiers became alarmingly common. Americans used the "water cure" to obtain information. This entailed forcing a prisoner to drink gallons of water and then stepping on or punching his bloated stomach to empty it quickly. In one especially violent campaign General Jacob H. Smith ordered his subordinates to take no prisoners: "I wish you to kill and burn . . . the more you kill and burn the better it will please me. I want all persons killed who are capable of bearing arms in actual hostilities against the United States." In the last category he included any male ten or older.

In another campaign, American leaders used the same tactics which had made the Spanish General Weyler infamous in Cuba. They tried to destroy the guerrilla base by herding more than 300,000 civilians into concentration zones. Death and disease, starvation and suffering increased in the concentration centers. "Suburbs of hell" was what one American commander called them. For many observers, the difference between Spanish actions in Cuba and American actions in the Philippines was a matter of degree and not kind. Philosopher William James wrote, "We are destroying

Emilio Aguinaldo, shown here as a prisoner on a United States gunboat, helped in the fight against the Spanish and also struggled to liberate his country from the United States.

the lives of these islanders by the thousands, their villages and their cities . . . 'No life shall you have, we say, except as a gift from our philanthropy after your unconditional surrender to our will . . .' Could there be a more damning indictment of that whole bloated ideal termed 'modern civilization' than this amounts to?" Along the same line, industrialist and anti-imperialist Andrew Carnegie told a United States peace commissioner in the Philippines, "You seem to have about finished your work of civilizing the Filipinos. About 8000 of them have been completely civilized and sent to Heaven."

Aguinaldo hoped that Bryan would defeat McKinley for the presidency in 1900 and thereby install an anti-imperialist in the White House. The November election dashed Aguinaldo's hopes. Five months later American troops captured the Filipino leader. This coupled with American reform efforts designed to improve transportation, education, and public health in

Philippine insurgents were often rounded up by American soldiers and locked in prison camps. Many saw little difference between their Spanish and American masters.

the Philippines doomed the Philippine independence movement. On July 4, 1902, the war was officially ended. The American victory was complete. However, approximately 4200 Americans and over 20,000 Filipino soldiers had died. Perhaps another 200,000 Filipino civilians died of famine, disease, and war-related incidents. The United States paid Spain $20 million for the Philippines, but it cost another $400 million to crush the Philippine independence movement.

Keeping the Doors Open

The struggle against the Filipinos led to congressional investigations and shocked many Americans. Political and business leaders, however, continued to believe that the Philippines were worth the fight, because the islands were of strategic importance both as a military base and a stepping stone toward the Asian markets. Yet policy makers understood the popular mood; they knew that the American public would be hostile to any United States military venture into China *just* to support trade.

To prevent other countries from carving up China, in 1899 Secretary of State John Hay issued an "open door" note. The note was an attempt to prevent further European partitioning of the Manchu empire and to protect the principle of open trade in China. Under the terms of the Open Door Policy, all countries active in China would respect each other's trading rights by imposing no discriminating duties and closing no ports within their spheres of influence. Although most European countries expressed little interest in Hay's Open Door Policy—which, after all, benefited the United States the most—in 1900 Hay announced that the European powers had accepted his proposal.

The Chinese themselves had other plans. In the late spring of 1900 a group of Chinese nationalists, known as Boxers, besieged the Legation Quarter in Peking, calling for the expulsion or death of all westerners in China. The Boxers, whose Chinese name better translates as

In 1900 the United States sent troops to help put down the Boxer Rebellion in China. Here American soldiers march across the sacred ground of the Forbidden City in Peking.

"Righteous and Harmonious Fists," were a quasi-religious organization that believed deeply in magic and maintained that all its members were impervious to western bullets. As a joint European and American rescue force proved, bullets could and would kill Boxers. By late summer, 1900, westernizers had crushed the Boxer Rebellion.

Additional troops in China threatened Hay's Open Door Policy. On July 3, 1900, during the tensest moment of the Boxer Rebellion, he issued a second open door note, calling on all western powers to preserve "Chinese territorial and administrative entity" and uphold "the principle of equal and impartial trade with all parts of the Chinese Empire." Once again, few European countries paid attention to Hay's Open Door Policy. Mutual distrust and the fear of provoking a general European war—more than any American plan—prevented the major European powers from dismembering China. Out of Hay's Open Door Policy notes came the idea that the United States was China's protec-

tor. It was another example of the increasingly active role the United States had taken in world affairs.

CONCLUSION

Thirty-two years separated the inauguration of Ulysses S. Grant and the assassination of William McKinley, but during that generation, America and the presidency changed radically. Part of the change can be attributed to growth—industry boomed, the population swelled, agricultural production increased. The growth was also psychological. Perhaps a more appropriate term would be maturation. During those years many Americans achieved a new sense of confidence, and their vision broadened. After 250 years of looking westward across America's seemingly limitless acres of land, they began to look toward the oceans and consider the possibilities of a new form of expansion. They also began to follow the imperial examples of En-

CHRONOLOGY OF KEY EVENTS

1868 Burlingame Treaty with China encourages Chinese immigration to the United States	**1891** Chilean crisis moves U.S. close to war, but Chile finally apologizes
1873 American ship *Virginius* seized in Cuba by Spanish officials, fifty-three crew members executed	**1893** After the Hawaiian Revolution President Cleveland refuses to annex the islands; in 1894 U.S. recognizes the Hawaiian Republic
1875 U.S. and Hawaii sign commercial treaty—in 1887 the U.S. will acquire the right to build a naval base at Pearl Harbor	**1895** U.S. and Great Britain clash over the Venezuelan boundary issue
1878 U.S.–Samoa treaty grants the U.S. the right to use Pago Pago Harbor as a coaling station	**1898** Battleship *Maine* sunk in Havana Harbor helping to lead to Spanish-American War
1882 U.S. recognizes and signs trade agreement with Korea	**1899** Secretary of State John Hay issues his first Open Door Note
1885 Reverend Josiah Strong publishes *Our Country*	**1900** Hawaii made a U.S. territory; Boxer Rebellion
1890 Captain Alfred Thayer Mahan publishes *The Influence of Sea Power upon History*	**1902** Philippine-American War ends with a U.S. victory

gland, France, Italy, and Germany. Talk of world power, world outlook, world responsibilities colored their rhetoric.

This outward thrust was accompanied and enhanced by the growth of presidential power. Grant worked hard for the annexation of the Dominican Republic, but Congress blocked his efforts. By the turn of the century, however, Congress clearly expected the president to lead the nation in the area of foreign affairs. Harrison, Cleveland, and McKinley, as well as their advisors, firmly guided America's foreign affairs. Although the presidents pursued different policies, they agreed that America should have a greater influence in world affairs. None questioned the fundamental fact that the United States was and should be a world power.

Many questions, nevertheless, remained unanswered. What were the rights of a world power? What were its responsibilities? What were its duties? Neither Harrison, Cleveland, nor McKinley gained much experience in running a colonial administration. The limits and possibilities of American power had yet to be defined and explored. The next three presidents—Roosevelt, Taft, and Wilson—would help to define how America would use its new power.

REVIEW SUMMARY

Between 1870 and 1900 the United States shed its isolationist past and embarked on a new course which emphasized an aggressive, internationalist foreign policy. As the president assumed more control over foreign affairs, the United States increased its presence in the Caribbean and the Pacific. Influencing America's outward push were

the drive for markets
a sense of mission
the development of a "new navy"
ever sharper clashes of interest with Germany, Chile, Great Britain, Hawaii, and Spain as the United States became more involved in world affairs

America's aggressive mood increased during the 1890s, and the period culminated in the war with Spain. By 1900 the United States had acquired an empire and become a world power.

SUGGESTIONS FOR FURTHER READING

OVERVIEWS AND SURVEYS

Robert L. Beisner, *From the Old Diplomacy to the New, 1865–1900* (1976) and *Twelve Against Empire* (1968); Alexander DeConde, *A History of American Foreign Policy* (1963); Foster R. Dulles, *Prelude to World Power: American Diplomatic History, 1860–1900* (1965); Robert H. Ferrell, *American Diplomacy* (1969); Walter LaFeber, *The New Empire: An Interpretation of American Expansion* (1963); Richard Hofstadter, *The Paranoid Style in American Politics and Other Essays* (1965); R. W. Leopold, *The Growth of American Foreign Policy* (1967); Thomas G. Paterson, *American Foreign Policy* (1977); Milton Plesur, *America's Outward Thrust* (1971); Robert H. Wiebe, *The Search for Order, 1877–1920* (1967); William A. Williams, *The Tragedy of American Diplomacy* (1972) and *The Roots of the Modern American Empire* (1969).

CONGRESSIONAL CONTROL AND THE REDUCTION OF AMERICAN POWER

C. S. Campbell, Jr., *Special Business Interests and the Open Door Policy* (1951); David Donald, *Charles Sumner and the Rights of Man* (1970); Allan Nevins, *Grover Cleveland* (1932) and *Hamilton Fish* (1936); Ernest N. Paolino, *The Foundations of the American Empire: William Henry Seward and U.S. Foreign Policy* (1973); David Pletcher, *The Awkward Years* (1963); Tom E. Terrill, *The Tariff, Politics, and American Foreign Policy, 1874–1901* (1973)

THE SPIRIT OF AMERICAN GREATNESS

Henry Blumenthal, *France and the United States* (1970); Alexander E. Campbell, *Great Britain and the United States, 1895–1903* (1960); Warren I. Cohen, *America's Response to China* (1971); James A. Field, Jr., *America and the Mediterranean World, 1776–1882* (1969); John Garraty, *Henry Cabot Lodge* (1953); Bradford Perkins, *The Great Rapprochement: England and the United States, 1895–1914* (1968); Thomas J. McCormick, *China Market* (1967); Paul A. Varg, *The Making of a Myth: The United States and China, 1897–1912* (1968); Marilyn B. Young, *Rhetoric of Empire: American China Policy, 1895–1901* (1968)

THE EMERGENCE OF AGGRESSION IN AMERICAN FOREIGN POLICY

William R. Braisted, *The United States Navy in the Pacific, 1897–1909* (1958); R. P. Gilson, *Samoa 1830 to 1900* (1970); John A. S. Grenville, *Lord Salisbury and Foreign Policy* (1964); Kenneth J. Hagan, *American Gunboat Diplomacy and the Old Navy, 1877–1889* (1973); Walter R. Herrick, *The American Naval Revolution* (1966); William A. Russ, Jr., *The Hawaiian Revolution* (1959); Ronald Spector, *Admiral of the New Empire: The Life and Career of George Dewey* (1974); Margaret Sprout, *The Rise of American Naval Power* (1939); Merze Tate, *The United States and the Hawaiian Kingdom* (1965)

THE WAR FOR EMPIRE

Frank Freidel, *The Splendid Little War* (1958); John M. Gates, *Schoolbooks and Krags* (1973); Willard B. Gatewood, Jr., *"Smoked Yankees" and the Struggle for Empire* (1971) and *Black Americans and the White Man's Burden, 1898–1903* (1975); L. L. Gould, *The Presidency of William McKinley* (1980); David Healy, *U.S. Expansionism* (1970); Gerald F. Linderman, *The Mirror of War: American Society and the Spanish-American War* (1974); Ernest R. May, *Imperial Democracy* (1961) and *American Imperialism* (1968); Stuart C. Miller, *"Benevolent Assimilation": The American Conquest of the Philippines, 1899–1903* (1982); H. Wayne Morgan, *From Hayes to McKinley* (1969), *The Gilded Age* (1970), *William McKinley and His America* (1963), and *America's Road to Empire* (1965); Julius W. Pratt, *Expansionists of 1898* (1936); Goran Rystad, *Ambiguous Imperialism* (1975); Daniel B. Schirmer, *Republic or Empire* (1972); E. Berkeley Tompkins, *Anti-Imperialism in the United States* (1970); David F. Trask, *The War With Spain* (1981); Richard E. Welch, Jr., *Response to Imperialism* (1979); Leon Wolff, *Little Brown Brother* (1961).

Fig. 16

CHAPTER 20

The Rise of an Urban Society and City People

Andrew Borden had, as the old Scotch saying goes, short arms and long pockets. He was cheap, not because he had to be frugal but because he hated to spend money. He had dedicated his entire life to making and saving money, and tales of his unethical and parsimonious business behavior were legendary in his home town of Fall River, Massachusetts. Local gossips maintained that as an undertaker he cut off the feet of corpses so that he could fit them into undersized coffins that he had purchased at a very good price. Andrew, however, was not interested in rumors or the opinions of other people; he was concerned with his own rising fortunes. By 1892 he had amassed over half a million dollars, and he controlled the Fall River Union Savings Bank as well as serving as the director of the Globe Yard Mill Company, the First National Bank, the Troy Cotton and Manufacturing Company, and the Merchants Manufacturing Company.

Andrew was rich, but he didn't live like a wealthy man. Instead of living alongside the other prosperous Fall River citizens in the elite neighborhood known as The Hill, Andrew resided in an area near the business district called the flats. He liked to save time as well as money, and from the flats he could conveniently walk to work. For his daughters Lizzie and Emma, whose eyes and dreams focused on The Hill, life in the flats was an intolerable embarrassment. Their house was a grim, boxlike structure that lacked comfort and privacy. Since Andrew believed that running water on each floor was a wasteful luxury, the only washing facilities were a cold-water faucet in the kitchen and a laundry room water tap in the cellar. Also in the cellar was the only toilet in the house. To make matters worse, the house was not connected to the Fall River gas main. Andrew preferred to use kerosene to light his house. Although it did not provide as good light or burn as cleanly as gas, it was less expensive. To save even more money, he and his family frequently sat in the dark.

The Borden home was far from happy. Lizzie and Emma, ages thirty-two and forty-two in 1892, strongly disliked their stepmother Abby and resented Andrew's penny-pinching ways.

Lizzie especially felt alienated from the world around her. Although Fall River was the largest cotton-manufacturing town in America, it offered few opportunities for the unmarried daughter of a prosperous man. Society expected a woman of Lizzie's social position to marry, and while she waited for a proper suitor, her only respectable social outlets were church and community service. So Lizzie taught a Sunday School class and was active in the Woman's Christian Temperance Union, the Ladies' Fruit and Flower Mission, and other organizations. She kept herself busy, but she wasn't happy.

In August, 1892, strange things started to happen in the Borden home. They began after Lizzie and Emma learned that Andrew had secretly changed his will. Abby became violently ill. In time so did the Borden maid Bridget Sullivan and Andrew himself. Abby told a neighborhood doctor that she had been poisoned, but Andrew refused to listen to her wild ideas. Shortly thereafter, Lizzie went shopping for prussic acid, a deadly poison she said she needed to clean her sealskin cape. When a Fall River druggist refused her request, she left the store in an agitated state. Later in the day, she told a friend that she feared an unknown enemy of her father's was after him. "I'm afraid somebody will do something," she said.

On August 4, 1892, Bridget awoke early and ill, but she still managed to prepare a large breakfast of johnnycakes, fresh-baked bread, ginger and oatmeal cookies with raisins, and some three-day-old mutton and hot mutton soup. After eating a hearty meal, Andrew left for work. Bridget also left to do some work outside. This left Abby and Lizzie in the house alone. Then somebody did something very specific and very grisly. As Abby was bent over making the bed in the guest room, someone moved into the room unobserved and killed her with an ax.

Andrew came home for lunch earlier than usual. He asked Lizzie where Abby was, and she said she didn't know. Unconcerned, Andrew, who was not feeling well, lay down on the parlor sofa for a nap. He never awoke. Like Abby, he was slaughtered by someone with an ax. Lizzie "discovered" his body, still lying on the sofa. She called Bridget, who had taken the back

izzie Borden was found
ot guilty.

stairs to her attic room: "Come down quick; father's dead; somebody came in and killed him."

Experts have examined and reexamined the crime, and most have reached the same conclusion: Lizzie killed her father and stepmother. In fact, Lizzie was tried for the gruesome murders. However, despite a preponderence of evidence, an all male jury found her not guilty. Their verdict was unanimous and was arrived at without debate or disagreement. A woman of Lizzie's social position, they affirmed, simply could not have committed such a terrible crime.

Even before the trial started, newspaper and magazine writers had judged Lizzie innocent for much the same reasons. As one expert on the case noted, "Americans were certain that well-brought-up daughters could not commit murder with a hatchet on sunny summer mornings." Criminal women, they believed, originated among the lower classes and even looked evil. A criminologist writing in the *North American Review* commented, "[The female criminal] has coarse black hair and a good deal of it. . . . She has often a long face, a receding forehead, overjutting brows, prominent cheek bones, an exaggerated frontal angle as seen in monkeys and savage races, and nearly always square jaws." They did not look like round-faced Lizzie, and they did not belong to the Ladies' Fruit and Flower Mission.

Jurors and editorialists alike judged Lizzie according to their preconceived notions of Victorian womanhood. They believed that such a woman was gentle, docile, and physically frail, short on analytical ability but long on nurturing instincts. "Women," wrote an editorialist for *Scribner's*, "are merely large babies. They are shortsighted, frivolous and occupy an intermediate stage between children and men . . . ." Too uncoordinated and weak to accurately swing an ax and too gentle and unintelligent to coldly plan a double murder, women of Lizzie's background simply had to be innocent because of their basic innocence.

Even as Lizzie was being tried and found innocent, Victorian notions were being challenged. In the larger cities of America, a new culture was taking form, one based on freedoms, not restraints. In this new climate, anything was possible, or so at least some people claimed. Immigrants could become millionaires and women could vote and hold office. Rigid Victorian concepts crumbled under the weight of new ideas; but the new freedoms came with a high price. In both the cities and the culture that flourished within them, a new order had to be constructed out of the chaos of freedom.

NEW CITIES AND NEW PROBLEMS

Transforming the Walking City

Andrew Borden was a throwback to older urban residential patterns. He would have felt comfortable with the physical layout of the mid nineteenth-century walking city. In an age before reliable mass transportation, when only the rich could afford a carriage, the majority of city dwellers had to walk to and from work. This simple fact dictated the type of cities that emerged in America. They were compact and crowded, normally limited to about two miles from center city or the distance a person could walk in half an hour. Even America's largest cities—New York, Philadelphia, and Boston—conformed to these standards.

Inside these cities, houses, businesses, and factories were strewn about willy-nilly. Tightly packed near the waterfront were shops, banks, warehouses, and business offices, and not far away were the residences of the people who owned those enterprises or worked in them. There was little residential segregation. If the rich occupied the finest houses in the center city, the poor lived in the alleys and dirty streets close by. In city life, people dealt with people in this congested, highly personalized world. Rich and poor, native-born and immigrant, black and white—they all walked along the same streets and worked in the same area.

Booming industrialism during the last third of the century shattered this arrangement. As industrialists built their new plants in or near existing cities, urban growth accelerated at an alarming rate. Like twin children, factories and cities grew and matured together, each helping the other to reach its physical potentials. In 1860, before America's industrial surge, twenty percent of the population lived in cities. By 1900, forty percent of the country's population were urban dwellers. And in 1920 the figure exceeded fifty percent. At the same time, the numbers of large cities (those with a population of over 100,000) increased at an even faster rate. In 1860, America had only nine large cities. The numbers rose to thirty-eight in 1900 and sixty-eight in 1920.

Immigrant as well as native sources fueled the urban explosion. Although most of the late nineteenth-century immigrants came from rural communities, they settled in America's industrial heartland (see Chapter 17). As late as 1920, eighty-seven percent of Irish immigrants, eighty-nine percent of the Russians, eighty-four percent of Italians and Poles, eighty percent of Hungarians, and seventy-five percent of Austrians, British, and Canadians lived in cities. Added to these were the native-born migrants who moved from rural poverty to the cities. For every industrial worker who moved to the countryside, twenty farmers moved to urban America. Just as in Europe and Asia, rural opportunities in the United States were dwindling at the same time rural population was growing. Thus ten farm sons moved to the cities for each son who became a farm owner.

Black migration from the rural South to the urban North further expanded the labor pool in the industrial cities. Slow at first, it increased each decade, as blacks left the land of their bondage determined to forge a better life for themselves and their families in the northern cities. Between 1897 and 1920 almost one million blacks left the South, and of those, eighty-five percent settled in the urban North.

City Technology

Even the largest of the walking cities was unprepared to meet the demands the newcomers placed on it. Cities were already crowded, and construction technology was not yet sufficiently advanced to accommodate the recent arrivals. But in time engineers and scientists discovered ways to allow cities to expand. During the half century after 1870, horizontal and vertical growth changed the skyline and living conditions of urban America.

Better transportation facilities solved the basic limitation of the walking city. As early as the 1830s the horse-drawn omnibus permitted a handful of wealthier urbanites to escape life in the crowded center city. Usually pulled by one or two horses, an omnibus carried twelve to twenty passengers along a fixed route for between six and twelve cents. Faster than walking, it was also more expensive, certainly beyond the means of an unskilled laborer who earned less than one dollar a day. Similarly the commuter railroads, which also dated back to the 1830s and 1840s and cost between twelve

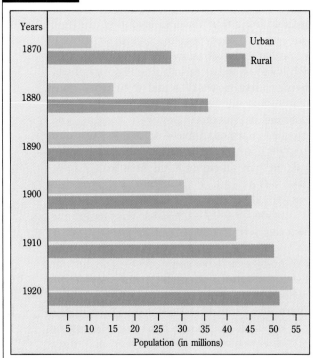

Figure 20.1
Urban and Rural Population, 1870–1920

During the early decades of the twentieth century hundreds of thousands of blacks fled the rural south for the cities of the industrial north.

and twenty-five cents to ride, served only the wealthier classes. Constructed and owned by entrepreneurs, omnibuses and commuter railways existed only for the comfort of people who could pay.

The horse railway expanded the city for the middle-class urbanites, white-collar workers, and skilled tradesmen. For five cents, these horse-drawn omnibuses carried passengers over steel rails at a speed of six to eight miles per hour. By the 1880s, over 300 American cities had constructed horsecar lines, and they significantly expanded the size of cities. Now a person could live five miles from his or her place of work and still travel there in half an hour. The age of walking was almost over.

The horsecar was not always as safe or as comfortable as its developers planned. Travelers complained about pickpockets, tobacco juice, and overcrowding. Describing the activity

of pickpockets, one passenger suggested, "Before boarding a car, prudent persons leave their purses and watches in the safe deposit company and carry bowie knives and derringers." To make the pickpocket's task easier, entrepreneurial conductors overloaded their cars, occasionally packing eighty persons into a car designed for twenty-five. Novelist William Dean Howells observed, "Men and women are indecently crushed without regard for the personal dignity we prize."

Drivers and horses suffered even worse fates. Underfed, overworked horses struggled day after day until they dropped from exhaustion, at which point they were unhitched and left to die. The drivers fared little better. In New York City during the early 1880s they worked sixteen-hour days for $12 a week. Exposed to the weather in the front or rear of the cars, they suffered terribly in the winter as cold winds

Traffic jams are nothing new in America. This grid-lock at Dearborn and Randolph Streets in Chicago occured before the widespread use of automobiles.

whipped their faces and froze their fingers around the reins. One streetcar conductor, hardened by years of work, remarked, "I feel that I could almost digest cobble stones." When the conductors demanded a twelve-hour day, a young New York assemblyman and future president, Theodore Roosevelt, labeled them "communistic" and suggested that no men who asked to be so coddled were worthy of their sex.

For hillier cities like San Francisco and Pittsburgh, the cable car, introduced during the 1870s, proved a blessing for man and horse alike. Pulled by a moving underground cable, engineers believed it would be the public transportation of the future—but its problems were considerable. Expensive to install and quick to break down, the cable car soon became a victim of the electric trolley, which was cheaper to run and more dependable.

In 1880, Frank Sprague, a young engineer, converted the horse car network of Richmond,

Virginia, to electricity. Drawing electrical current from overhead wires, trolleys could operate in stop and go traffic and travel at average speeds of ten to twelve miles per hour. American cities quickly climbed aboard the electric bandwagon. By 1902, ninety-seven percent of urban transit mileage had been electrified. Trolleys connected not only city with suburb but also city with city. By 1920 a person could travel from Boston to New York entirely by trolley.

Called "one of the most rapidly accepted innovations in the history of technology," trolleys were not without their problems. The overhead wires gave cities a weblike appearance, and in the winter the electric wires snapped from the cold and created serious dangers. In addition, they sometimes frightened horses and thus worsened traffic problems. Altogether, by the 1890s, the mixture of horse cars, cable cars, and trolleys jostling each other and pedestrians on city streets created immense traffic jams.

English science fiction writer H. G. Wells found Chicago streets in 1906 "simply chaotic—one hoarse cry for discipline."

Clogged streets inspired engineers to search for other transportation solutions. Looking above and below ground, they designed elevated railway lines and subways. Electricity powered both, and each helped to ease mass transportation for the masses. The Chicago "el" (elevated railway) and the New York City subway satisfied the minds of urban traffic engineers and even occasionally stirred the souls of artists. W. Louis Sonntag, Jr., painted a beautiful watercolor of New York City's Bowery in 1895, capturing the wonder of the age of electricity. Illuminated by electric lights, an el and a trolley pass in the night.

While mass transportation allowed cities to spread miles beyond their cores, steel and glass permitted cities to reach for the sky. At mid-century, few buildings were higher than five stories. Church spires still dominated the urban skyline. Buildings, like cities themselves, were personal; they didn't dwarf the individual. That, however, soon changed. As a real estate columnist wrote in the *Chicago Tribune* in 1888: "In real estate calculations, Chicago has thus far had but three directions, north, south, and west, but there are indications now that a fourth is to be added and that it is to cut a larger figure in the coming decade than all the others. The new direction is zenithward. Since water hems in the business center on three sides and a nexus of railroads on the south, Chicago must grow upward."

Using traditional brick and masonry construction, architects could not design buildings much higher than ten stories. In 1885 New York architect William LeBaron Jenney solved the problem by using cast iron and steel, the product that was transforming America into an industrial giant. Using light masonry over an iron and steel skeleton, Jenney built the Home Insurance Building in Chicago, which although only ten stories was the first true skyscraper in history. Steel, light masonry, and eventually glass revolutionized building construction.

Louis Henri Sullivan, who had once worked for Jenney, demonstrated the architectural possibilities of the skyscraper. Working in Chicago, a town that had been almost totally destroyed by the great 1871 fire, Sullivan became the leading exponent of skyscraper technology, turning his back on classical models and preaching the doctrine that "form follows function." Quick-tempered and difficult to work with, Sullivan nonetheless designed many of the most beautiful and practical skyscrapers in America, including the Wainwright Building in St. Louis and the Transportation Building in Chicago.

Skyscrapers changed the profile of American cities as surely as industrialism altered the American landscape. Returning to America from Europe in 1906, novelist Henry James observed "the multitudinous skyscrapers standing up to the view . . . like extravagant pins in a cushion already overplanted, and stuck in as in the dark, anywhere and anyhow." What disturbed James's sensibilities excited most Amer-

This watercolor of New York City's Bowery at night by W. Louis Sonntag, Jr., shows how steam, steel, and electricity played a major part in transforming cities.

icans. The skyscraper, many reasoned, was America out to prove that its reach did not exceed its grasp. In fact, businessmen and industrialists even used skyscrapers to glorify their own accomplishments. Bigger was best, and the race to the sky was on. In 1913, President Woodrow Wilson pressed the button which lit up the Woolworth Building. At 792 feet, it was the largest building in America, a monument to five- and ten-cents king Frank Woolworth. This architectural history book and hauntingly beautiful structure truly was "the Cathedral of Commerce."

The Segregated City

With the outward and upward growth of cities came an end to the more personal walking city. Mass transportation freed the upper and middle classes from having to live in the city core. Voicing their opinion with their feet, they scampered for the "streetcar suburbs," where popular theory held that the water was purer, the trees fuller, and the air fresher. They commuted to work and no longer mixed daily with their economic inferiors.

The working class moved into areas and even houses deserted by wealthier families. In New York City the large stately brownstone homes which had served the upper classes were subdivided into small apartments to satisfy the new demand for inexpensive housing. Of course, architects had not built the houses to be used as multi-unit apartments, and numerous problems resulted.

Ethnic groups and races, like economic classes, tended to stake out neighborhoods in the new, larger cities. For the first time, black ghettos emerged in the major northern cities, and in Chicago, New York, Boston, and Philadelphia, English became a foreign language in ethnic neighborhoods. These neighborhoods reproduced in their finer details Old World conditions. Familiar faces, food, churches, and speech comforted lonely immigrants. Even Old World prejudices survived in the ethnic neighborhoods. Greeks from Athens continued to regard Spartans as stupid and pugnacious, and northern Italians maintained their belief that southern Italians were lazy and untrustworthy.

Since members of the ethnic working class were too poor for even moderately priced mass transit, they tended to settle close to their places of work. In New York City, Jews and Italians lived within walking distance from the Lower East Side garment factories. In Chicago, the Poles and Lithuanians who worked in the meat packing industry awoke in the morning and went to sleep at night close to the sound of dying animals and the stench of stockyard filth.

Just as new residential trends separated rich and poor, the central business district underwent important changes. Prices for central city real estate shot up astronomically, sometimes as much as one thousand percent a decade in the late nineteenth century. Only businesses and industries could afford the new prices, and the central cities were turned over to high income businesses, banks, warehouses, railroad terminals, and the recently developed department stores. It became an area where money was made, not where people lived.

The Problems of Growth

By the 1890s, British observers despaired over what had become of the once small American cities. The uncontrolled growth, they suggested, had created ugliness on an almost unprecedented scale. English traveler Charles Philips Trevelyan graphically described the horrors of industrial Pittsburgh:

> A cloud of smoke hangs over it by day. The glow of scores of furnaces light the river banks by night. It stands at the junction of two great rivers, the Monongahela which flows down in a turbid yellowy stream, and the Allegheny which is blackish . . . All nations are jumbled up here, the poor living in tenement dens or wooden shanties thrown up or dumped down with little reference to roads or situation, whenever a new house is wanted. It is a most chaotic city, and as yet there is no public spirit or public consciousness to make conditions healthy or decent.

Rudyard Kipling sounded a similar note after visiting Chicago. Although he had seen the suffering and overcrowded conditions of Bombay

Of Pittsburgh in the 1890s, one critic observed, "The realm of Vulcan couldn't be more filthy with burning fires spurting flames on every side."

and Cairo, Kipling was appalled by the Windy City: "This place is the first American city I have encountered . . . Having seen it, I urgently desire never to see it again."

Trevelyan's and Kipling's judgments were not the rantings of anti-American foreigners. Numerous American observers echoed their opinions. American cities were unprepared for the incredible growth they experienced during the late nineteenth century. Housing, clean water, competent police, and adequate public services were all in short supply. To make matters worse, the people who moved to the cities usually came from rural areas and were uninitiated in the ways of city life. Finally, health standards were low everywhere and scientists had barely begun to study the problems and diseases created by crowded urban conditions.

Housing presented the most pressing problem. The immigrants disembarking at the ports

of entry and the farmers arriving at the train depots had to have some place to live. The situation created opportunities as well as problems. The building industry was one of the great urban boom industries, and its leaders largely determined the shape and profile of the modern city. Like the other "captains of industry," they worked in an essentially unregulated economic world, bent upon maximizing their profits and equipped with a lofty disregard of public opinion.

In urban housing money talked. The rich could afford good housing. In New York City, the wealthy built opulent mansions up Fifth Avenue along Central Park. High ceilings, European furnishings, and spacious rooms were commonplace, and even the new apartments of the upper classes were designed and constructed by gifted architects and craftsmen. Along Central Park West at Seventy-second Street, the Dakota Apartments still stand as a standard for "the good life." Like the Woolworth Building, it is one of the beautiful architectural triumphs of the period.

Tenements, poorly built and shabbily equipped, greeted urban newcomers without money. They were designed to cram the largest number of people into the smallest amount of space. Like skyscrapers, they made use of vertical space by piling family upon family into small, poorly-lighted, badly-ventilated apartments. By 1900 portions of the Jewish Tenth Ward in New York's Lower East Side had reached population density levels of 350,000 persons to one square mile and as many as one person per square foot in the most crowded areas. This was perhaps the highest density in world history.

Dumbbell tenements, with their narrow air wells at each side, were the most notorious examples of exploitive urban housing. Architectural critic Lewis Mumford claimed they "raised bad housing into an art." Although they conformed to the Tenement Reform Law of 1879, which required all rooms to have access to light and air, they made maximum use of standard 25 by 100 feet urban lots. The problems inherent in the dumbbell tenement were obvious from the first, but the design was not outlawed in New York until 1901.

Tenement life on the lower East side of New York was overcrowded, filthy, and dangerous. For the wealthy, city life could be quite luxurious, as the rooms of Alexander T. Stewart's Fifth Avenue mansion show.

Street conditions, unlike housing, were more democratic in that they plagued rich and poor alike. People dumped their trash and horses unloaded their own particular pollution onto the dirty city thoroughfares. Spring rains turned them into fetid quagmires, and winter freezes left them with hard deep ruts. In addition, well into the 1870s, pigs roamed the streets of most cities, rooting for food in the garbage and further polluting the environment. Indeed, when trolleys began to replace horses as the primary form of urban transportation, editorialists predicted that the age of air pollution would soon come to an end. Yet as late as 1900, there were still 150,000 horses in New York City, each producing between twenty and thirty pounds of manure a day.

Waste not dumped onto the streets often found its way into the rivers which flowed through the major cities or the harbors which bordered them. By the turn of the century, thirteen million gallons of sewage were emptied each day into the Delaware River, the major source for Philadelphia's drinking water. At Baltimore, according to H. L. Mencken, the bay smelled like a "billion polecats." This paled in comparison to Pittsburgh's rivers. The Golden Triangle, where the Allegheny and Monongahela rivers meet to form the Ohio River, could have just as aptly been dubbed the black triangle because of the industrial waste poured into it.

The establishment of dump sites did little to solve the terrible garbage problem. The Reverend Hugh Miller Thompson described the conditions in a New Orleans dump to a meeting of the American Public Health Association in 1879: "Thither were brought the dead dogs and cats, the kitchen garbage and the like, and duly dumped. This festering, rotten mess was picked over by rag-pickers and wallowed over by pigs, pigs and humans contesting for a living in it, and as the heaps increased, the odors increased also, and the mass lay corrupting under a tropical sun, dispersing the pestilential fumes where the winds carried them."

Between 1880 and 1914, the years of the greatest amount of immigration, the garbage problem worsened. According to a 1905 study, Americans produced more trash than any other peoples. An American city dweller, for example, produced an average 860 pounds of mixed rubbish each year, compared to 450 pounds per capita in English cities and 319 pounds in German cities. Viewed in a more graphic way, one 1912 report noted that if the refuse of New York City was gathered in one place, "the resulting mass would equal in volume a cube about one eighth of a mile on an edge. This surprising volume is over three times that of the great pyramid of Gizeh, and would accommodate one hundred and forty Washington monuments with ease."

Overcrowded housing, polluted streets and rivers, uncollected garbage—these problems and others contributed to the notoriously unhealthy urban environment. Unfortunately advances in medicine and public health lagged behind technological and industrial progress. Diseases ranging from yellow fever and smallpox to diphtheria and typhoid claimed victims by the thousands. In 1878 a yellow fever epidemic moved along the Mississippi River; 5150 people died in Memphis and another 3977 died in New Orleans. Known as the American Plague, the disease struck without warning and often led to a rapid but painful death. Walter Reed's discovery in 1900 that the disease was carried by the *Aedes aegypti* mosquito led to a cure for the dreaded scourge.

The smallpox virus proved a more persistent problem. Although not as deadly as yellow fever, it struck more people and left millions of faces scarred by pockmarks. Like diphtheria and scarlet fever, smallpox flourished in the overcrowded and garbage-strewn cities. During the late nineteenth century, health wardens unsuccessfully tried to limit the diseases. Often party hacks, they owed their jobs to their political loyalty rather than their knowledge of public health. Asked to define "hygiene," one worthy health official replied, "It is a mist rising from wet ground."

Death, suffering, and massive inconvenience prodded city officials to move toward a more systematic approach to their problems. It was a slow transition, involving the replacement of political appointees with trained experts. Yet during the late nineteenth century remarkable progress was made, particularly after the discovery of the germ theory in the 1880s which linked contagious disease to environmental conditions.

Health officials and urban engineers vigorously attacked the sewage and water problems. Discussing the importance of a good sewer system, one Baltimore engineer noted in 1907 that Paris is "the center of all that is best in art, literature, science, and architecture, and is both clean and beautiful. In the evolution of this ideal attainment, its sewers took at least a leading part . . . ." Without good sewers and clean drinking water, urban civilization was almost a contradiction of terms. To improve conditions, cities replaced cesspools and backyard privies with modern sewer systems, and most large cities turned to filtration and chlorination to assure pure water supplies.

From Private City to Public City

In housing, pure water, and clean streets, the battle lines in most cities were drawn between individual profits and public need. Individual entrepreneurs shaped the modern American city. They laid the horsecar and trolley lines, constructed the skyscrapers, apartments, and tenements, and provided water for the growing urban populations. Like their industrial counterparts, they worked, planned, and invested, fully expecting to earn huge profits. Their pocketbooks came before their civic responsibilities. The result was that they provided good housing and services for only those city dwellers who could pay.

Historians have termed this type of city the "private city." Allowing the profit motive to determine urban growth created numerous problems. It led to such waste and inefficiency as competing trolley lines, where promoters could

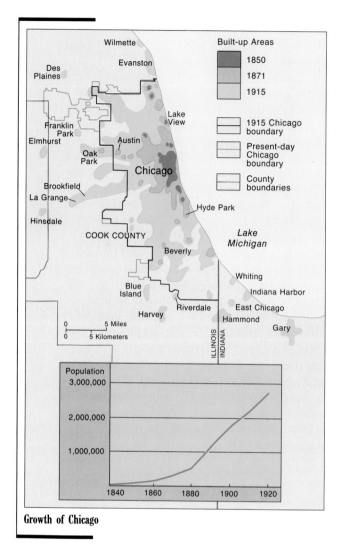

Growth of Chicago

turn a profit, and such inconveniences as poorly cleaned streets, where there was little money to be made. But most important, it stood contrary to planned urban growth. Urban entrepreneurs were generally unconcerned about the city as a whole. They regarded parks as uneconomic use of real estate and battled against the idea of zoning. In the end, they contributed to the ugliness and problems of Pittsburgh, New York, Chicago, and other American cities.

By the turn of the century, urban engineers and other experts began calling for planned urban growth and more concern for city services. Advocates of the "public city," they wanted efficient, clean, healthy cities where rich and poor could enjoy a decent standard of

life. They formed a professional class. Most were college educated, and they brought knowledge, administrative expertise, and taste for bureaucracy to government service. After 1900 they would increasingly dominate the quest for better services and public responsibility, but in many cities their voices were heard too late. The scars of the "private city" remained on the urban landscape.

CITY CULTURE

Nightlife

It was almost like magic. At 3:00 P.M. on September 4, 1882, Thomas Edison's chief electrician threw the switch on the inventor's Pearl Street station. Four hundred electric lights went on. Wall Street buildings were for the first time illuminated by the clearest of all artificial lighting. "It was not until 7 o'clock, when it began to be dark that the electric light made itself known and showed how bright and steady it was," commented a *New York Times* reporter. In the *Times* offices, where fifty-two Edison lights illuminated the night, "it seemed almost like writing by daylight." Just as trolleys spelled the end for the horsecar, electric lights eventually replaced gas lights, candles, and oil lamps.

Electricity soon bathed America's leading cities in white light, making night day and giving it a timeless quality. In the rural regions life revolved around the sun. Farmers awoke with the sun, labored during the hours of daylight, and went to sleep soon after the sun disappeared over the horizon. Although one's labor changed depending on the season, the order of one's day was changeless. In cities and industries night became more than just a time to rest. Labor and leisure claimed their share of the night.

This new nightlife fired the imaginations of urbanites. If nighttime labor proved a plague for the working class, nighttime leisure animated the lives of the wealthy. For Broadway's "fast set," the real fun began after the theaters closed. They moved down the Great White Way, stopping at one of the exclusive restaurants for a late-night dinner. Surrounded by electric lights and mirrors, they dined on meals available only in urban centers. They ate shrimp

Late in the century, when electricity and steel came into wide use, the face of American cities was greatly altered. Here Herald Square is illuminated at night.

mornay, beef marguery, canape of crab meat, bisque de creme, and other such exotic dishes. At restaurants like Delmonico's, eating became a refined pleasure and not just a physical necessity.

City eating habits, as much as electric lights, demonstrated the yawning gap between the values of an older rural America and those of the emerging urban society. In 1840 critics of presidential candidate Martin Van Buren attacked him for his eating habits. William Henry Harrison, his opponent who subsisted on "raw beef without salt," ridiculed Van Buren's taste for strawberries, raspberries, celery, cauliflower, and French cooking, claiming that democratic virtue thrived only on crude, tasteless food. The American diet, however, expanded along with the nation's cities. Lorenzo Delmonico, the Swiss immigrant who founded New York's most famous restaurant, popularized ices and green vegetables and cooked food which rivaled the best in Paris.

It is difficult to imagine the impression electric lights and fruit salads made on the people who lived in or visited American cities. They underscored a style of life clearly different from what existed in rural America. City life presented a strange new world which inspired American writers, painters, and musicians with feelings of excitement and revulsion. This ambivalent reaction formed the basis of a new urban culture. A culture, which like a mixed salad, combined the energies and experiences of all city people—black and white, male and female, immigrant and native-born.

From the Genteel Tradition to Realism and Naturalism

Frank Norris was born in Chicago, grew up in San Francisco, and lived for a time in Paris. He restlessly moved about the world looking for action. As a reporter he traveled to Cuba to cover the Spanish-American War and to South

Africa to chronicle the Boer War. In his journalism and in his novels, he told the truth, and he fed his readers bloody slices of the real world. He battled "false views of life, false characters, false sentiments, false morality, false history, false philosophy, false emotions, false heroism." Shortly before he died at thirty-two of appendicitis in 1902, he boasted, "I never truckled. I never took off the hat to fashion and held it out for pennies. I told them the truth. They liked it or they didn't like it. What had that to do with me? I told them the truth."

The truth. How literature had changed during the previous generation! At the end of the Civil War, the American literary tradition had little to do with harsh truth. Controlled by a literary aristocracy in Boston, literature conformed to the "genteel tradition." Great writers endeavored to reinforce morality, not portray reality. Real life was too sordid, corrupt, and mean; it was far too coarse, violent, and vulgar. Literature, these arbitors decided, should transcend the real and anchor to the ideal. James Russell Lowell, one of the leaders of the genteel tradition, spoke for his fellow writers when he commented that no man should describe any activity that would make his wife or daughter blush. Sex, violence, and passion were taboo.

Out of rural America came the first challenge to the genteel tradition. Such local colorists as Bret Harte, who set his stories in the rough mining camps of the West, emphasized regional differences and used regional dialects to capture the flavor of rural America. In their own way, the local colorists were as confined by their approaches to writing as the defenders of the genteel tradition. Although their characters used real American speech, they were hardly realistically presented. Humor and innocence were the hallmarks of local colorists.

Only Mark Twain, whose real name was Samuel Langhorne Clemens, transcended the genre. Like a local colorist, he used regional dialects, humor, and sentimentality in all his novels, but he also explored the darker impulses of human nature. *Huckleberry Finn* (1885), his classic work, exposes the greed, violence, corruption, alcoholism, and racism in American society. As Huck and runaway slave Jim travel down the Mississippi River toward freedom,

Mark Twain, one of the greatest nineteenth century novelists, often drew attention to the problems of his time.

they encounter a society based upon a perversion of Christian ethics and the Golden Rule. Nowhere is Twain more insightful than when he deals with American racism. In one scene, Huck invents a story about a riverboat explosion. A woman asks if anyone was injured. "No'm," Huck responds. "Killed a nigger." Relieved, she replies, "Well, it's lucky; because sometimes people do get hurt."

The greatest success and failure of Mark Twain is that he never outgrew his obsession with life on the Mississippi River. Except perhaps in his *Connecticut Yankee,* the impact of industrialism and city life on the American character did not much interest Twain. It did, however, fascinate most of the other great writers of his generation. Equipped with camera eyes and critical minds, they wanted to show American life in all its harsh and sordid reality. Realism, the name of their movement, soon replaced the genteel sentimentality of the previous generation. Defined as "the truthful treatment of material" by its leader William Dean Howells, Realism centered on average individuals dealing with concrete ethical choices in realistic circumstances. Even style became secondary. "Who cares for a fine style," Norris wrote in 1899. "Tell your yarn and let your style go to the devil. We don't want literature, we want life."

As Realism matured in the largely unregulated and highly competitive cities it turned into Naturalism. A more pessimistic movement, Naturalism portrayed the individual as a helpless victim, battered defenseless by natural forces beyond his control. Influenced by the writings of Charles Darwin, Karl Marx, and eventually Sigmund Freud, naturalists described a world in which biological, social, and psychological forces determined a person's fate. They were particularly interested in how the uncaring forces of industrialization and urbanization determined the course of individual lives. Even when they wrote about the problems of rural America, the power of factory and city worked in the shadows.

Describing the Urban Jungle

The premier naturalistic writer was Theodore Dreiser. Unlike most earlier American novelists, he was not the product of Protestant, Anglo-Saxon, middle-class respectability. His German-Catholic immigrant father's life was the flip side of the American success story. After a promising beginning, he and his family slid deeper and deeper into poverty. As a boy and a young man, Theodore knew what it was like to subsist on potatoes and fried mush, and all his life he dreaded winter, which reminded him of the most painful days of poverty. Sympathetic to those who had similarly suffered, he wrote, "Any form of distress—a wretched, down-at-heels neighborhood, a poor farm, an asylum, a jail, or an individual or group of individuals anywhere that seemed to be lacking in the means of subsistence or to be devoid of the normal comforts of life—was sufficient to set up in me thoughts and emotions which had a close kinship to actual and severe physical pain."

Dreiser left home at sixteen and went to Chicago, where he became first a journalist and then a novelist. Unlike better educated writers, Dreiser had no genteel tradition to shed or rebel against. With his plodding style and atrocious English, Dreiser lacked every writing tool except genius. His first novel, *Sister Carrie* (1900), unflinchingly describes the effect of modern urban society on the lives of one woman and one man. Carrie travels to Chicago in search of happiness, which she equates with material possessions, but discovers only poverty, exploitation, and hardship. Like the course of Dreiser's own family, the likeable, friendly Carrie sinks ever deeper into physical and moral despair.

Theodore Dreiser

Although Frank Norris praised the novel, it shocked most readers accustomed to the genteel tradition. Doubleday Page and Company published *Sister Carrie* but did not advertise it. As a result it sold only 456 copies, and Dreiser's royalties amounted only to a depressing $68.40. With time, however, Americans recognized Dreiser's genius and read his novels as realistic treatments of modern industrial society.

Like Dreiser, Stephen Crane was also interested in the effect poverty and urban life had on the individual character. His first novel, *Maggie: A Girl of the Streets* (1893), traces the life of a girl raised in a New York City slum. In rapid order, she loses her innocence, her virginity, and her life. It was not a story of a character being rewarded or punished. Maggie was an honest, cheerful person, but that was not the issue. She was a victim of her environment, and issues of personal good or evil were at best irrelevant. Poverty determined Maggie's and later Carrie's fate.

Taken together, naturalistic writers challenged the traditional idea that individuals had the power to control their own destiny. Rugged individualism, that cherished frontier ideal, seemed poor protection against the forces of urban poverty and industrial exploitation. Carrie was no match for the sweatshop owner, and Maggie's innocence was merely a target in her environment. Although neither *Maggie* nor *Sister Carrie* was a blueprint for reform, both suggested a pressing need for change. The same private city that offered opportunity for the wealthy held little promise for the poor.

Painting Urban Reality

During the 1830s and 1840s nationalistic Americans began to develop a truly national culture. Unlike Europe, America did not have proud literary, artistic, or musical traditions. America had produced no Parthenon, no Rembrandt, no

Everett Shinn's *The Laundress* presents American urban life in an impressionistic style.

Beethoven. What America did have was land, thousands of miles of wild land. It was an asset which became the basis of American culture. Writers wrote about it, and artists painted it. James Fenimore Cooper created Natty Bumppo, the virtuous frontier hero. Artist Thomas Cole endowed the American wilderness with a religious quality. Indeed, after visiting Europe, Cole reported that plowed fields and mountain castles had ruined the Old World landscape. "American scenery," he wrote, "has features, and glorious ones, unknown to Europe. The most distinctive, and perhaps the most impressive, characteristic of American scenery is its wildness."

American artists shared with American writers and social critics a general aesthetic and philosophical dislike of the city. As Americans moved West, artists continued to focus on the landscape. Albert Bierstadt exaggerated the drama of the Rocky Mountains, but his pictures thrilled eastern and western Americans alike. Even the great, late nineteenth-century realists—Winslow Homer, Thomas Eakins, and John LaFarge—continued the traditional anti-urban bias. To be sure, Eakins's work demonstrated a profound respect for the machine, but his admiration did not extend to the city.

By the end of the century, however, the varied urban landscape began to intrigue artists. Steel bridges, colorful immigrant costumes, smoke-filled, congested streets, clashing boxers, washed clothes hanging between tenements, pigeons soaring over flat apartment roofs—each demonstrated the everyday beauty of the city. The energy, conflict, and power of the city seemed to explode with artistic possibilities. When a critic noted that in George Bellows's *Stag at Starkey's* the fighters' faces are hidden, Bellows replied, "Who cares what a prize fighter looks like. It's his muscles that count."

Appropriately enough, the center of this new movement was New York City. The leader of the school—often described as "ash can" because of its urban orientation—was Robert Henri, an artistic and political radical. Skyscrapers thrilled him, and he saw beauty in the most squalid slum. He was joined by such other artists who shared his love of city life and political radicalism as John Sloan, George Luks, Maurice Prendergast, Everett Shinn, W. J. Glackens, and Ernest Lawson. Their paintings were generally in the impressionistic style, but they were more concerned with content than technique. As George Luks sneered at a critic, "Technique, did you say? My slats! Say, listen, you—it's in you or it isn't. Who taught Shakespeare technique? Guts! Guts! Life! Life! That's my technique."

Like Theodore Dreiser, who admired the Ash Can School, Henri and his followers used their talent to show problems in the growing cities. Bellows's *Cliff Dwellers* portrayed teeming life but also overcrowded tenement conditions. His *Steaming Streets* underscored the problems of urban traffic. And George Luks's *Hester Street* illuminated the excitement but also the packed conditions of the Jewish section of Lower New York.

Maturing along with the ash can painters was a second school of artists who also gained inspiration from the urban landscape. Labeled modernists, they championed the pure freedom of nonrepresentational abstract painting. Their intellectual leader was Alfred Stieglitz, whose studio at 291 Fifth Avenue in New York was used to exhibit the modernist paintings of Georgia O'Keeffe, Marsden Hartley, John Marin, Max Weber, and Arthur Dove. Like the ash-canners, they too were drawn to the conflict and power of the city. Describing the city as the theme for abstract art, John Marin observed, "I see great forces at work, great movements, the large buildings and the small buildings, the warring of the great and the small . . . While these powers are at work . . . I can hear the sound of their strife, and there is great music being played."

In 1913 the ash-canners and the modernists participated in the most important art exhibition in American history. Held at the Sixty-Ninth Regiment Armory in New York, the show also included works by Cezanne, Van Gogh, Picasso, Marcel Duchamp, Georges Braque, and Juan Gris, the leaders of the European post-impressionists. The Armory Show drew some criticism; Duchamp's cubist *Nude Descending a Staircase* was called "an explosion in a shingle factory." Other critics and collectors maintained that the exhibition marked a new age for

John Marin's *Brooklyn Bridge* presents the dynamics of urban life in the clashing tension of this abstract painting.

American art. "The members of this association have shown you that American artists—young American artists, that is—do not dread . . . the ideas or the culture of Europe," noted leading collector John Quinn. "This exhibition will be epoch-making." Its more important result was to fuse European and American art movements. It further signaled the ascendancy of the modernists who dominated the next generation of American art.

The Sounds of the City

Modern American music began in the nation's large cities, and from the very first was the language of the oppressed. Before the late nineteenth century, critics regarded American music as decidedly inferior to European music. America had produced no great classical composers in the European tradition, and what music it did create was largely the sounds of work and worship. Uninfluenced by European traditions, American blacks adapted the rhythms and melodies of Africa to meet American conditions. Out of this marriage came the work songs of Mississippi slaves, the street cries of Charleston fish and fruit vendors, and the religious spirituals. Unlike the European music which was based on a twelve-note scale, African music centered on rhythmical complexity and used notes that did not conform to the standard scale. Repetition, call-and-response, and strong beat became the hallmarks of black American music. Stephen Foster and minstrel shows helped to popularize the music with white audiences.

The two traditions, African and European, existed independently in the United States until the 1890s, when they were suddenly thrown together in New Orleans. As in most southern cities, Jim Crow laws passed during the 1890s legally and forcefully separated the races in New Orleans. For the history of Ameri-

can music this process had unexpected results. It forced together blacks from very different backgrounds. Before the 1890s wealthy half-white, half-black Creoles had lived in the affluent downtown section of New Orleans and followed European musical traditions. Segregation, however, forced them uptown, where poorer blacks who followed African musical traditions lived. Although Creoles and poor blacks did not mix socially, they did forge new musical styles.

The result was jazz, a musical form based upon improvisation within a structured band format which used both African and European traditions. Such early New Orleans jazz bands as Buddy Bolden's Classic Jazz Band and Joe "King" Oliver's Creole Jazz Band pioneered the style. Playing in an era before recorded music, Bolden was considered to be particularly talented. He had lived in the uptown region even before segregation, where Baptist churches stood next to voodoo parlors and music provided the background for prayer, work, and play. Bolden's style was characterized by a

Jazz combined European and Afro-American music styles into a new musical form. Here King Oliver's Creole Jazz Band poses for a rare picture.

powerful, moody grace that mesmerized audiences. But Bolden's music came from the soul of a troubled man. Plagued by syphilis and alcoholism, in 1907 he went bezerk during a street parade and spent the rest of his life in a mental hospital.

Storyville, the New Orleans red-light district, provided employment for the jazz musicians. Freed from manual labor during the day, they honed their musical skills and explored the possibilities of their instruments. Charlie "Sweet Lovin'" Galloway, Ferdinand "Jelly Roll" Morton, Robert "Baby" Dodds, Bunk Johnson, Sidney Bechet, Alphonse Picou, and, especially, Louis Armstrong entertained Storyville customers. Called the "Gibraltar of commercialized vice . . . twenty-four blocks given over to human degradation and lust," Storyville was also the mecca of jazz musicians.

The black musicians who worked in Storyville made far more than even skilled laborers. On an average night, fifty musicians played in Storyville; during carnival season as many as seventy-five worked. The very best "professors," who played in the most exclusive houses, made between ninety and one thousand dollars a week. Band members' earnings ranged from thirty to one hundred dollars a week. Alphonse Picou recalled the days before Storyville was officially closed with fond nostalgia: "Those were happy days, man, happy days. Buy a keg of beer for one dollar and a bag of food for another. . . . Talking 'bout wild and wooly! There were two thousand registered girls and must have been ten thousand unregistered. And all crazy about clarinet blowers."

Jazz flourished in Storyville, but so too did ragtime and the blues. Ragtime, a syncopated piano style, needed only one performer and was therefore popular as cafe and bordello entertainment. Tony Jackson, Scott Joplin, and Jelly Roll Morton played ragtime piano with style and grace. Joplin, a Texas-born black who had formal musical training, wrote several scores of popular rags, and Morton developed a piano swing beat. Blues musicians, mostly blacks raised outside of European traditions, performed in cheap saloons and expressed the pain of life in an hostile world.

During World War I government officials closed Storyville as a health hazard. As the houses of prostitution closed their doors, the talented black musicians headed north—to St. Louis, Chicago, Memphis, Kansas City, and New York. They continued to play jazz and the form continued to evolve. White musicians, trained in the European tradition, soon put their imprint on the American musical form. Bix Beiderbecke from Davenport, Iowa, for example, formed a Chicago-based jazz band. He used more instruments, replaced the African banjo with the guitar, and moved away from improvisation.

Although larger jazz bands dominated music during the next generation, they were an outgrowth of the New Orleans sound. It was also the result of the mixture of European and African traditions. It could only have happened in the fertile atmosphere of the cities, where old and new, black and white, immigrant and native-born combined to create new literary, artistic, and musical forms.

ENTERTAINING THE MULTITUDES

City sports, like city music, were loud and raucous. It moved to the beat of the trolley cars and steel wheels on steel tracks, not horses' hoofs on dusty farm roads. Before the urbanization of the late nineteenth century, the sports and games that Americans played tended to be informal and participant oriented. Rules varied from region to region, and few people even considered the standardization of rules desirable. By 1900 this cozy informality had changed dramatically. Entertainment became a major industry, and specialized performers competed for the right to entertain the multitudes.

Of Fields and Cities

"Baseball," wrote Mark Twain, "is the very symbol, the outward and visible expression of the drive and push and struggle of the raging, tearing, booming nineteenth century." It captured the bustle and hustle of city life. More than any other sport of the period, baseball was an urban game. All of the early professional teams were located in cities and most of the paid players were products of the cities.

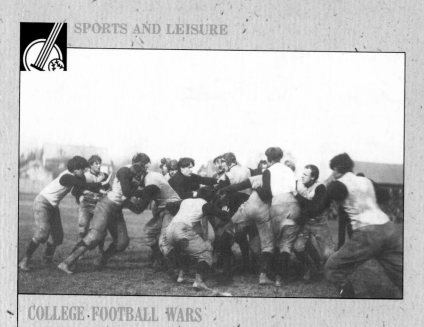

COLLEGE·FOOTBALL·WARS

Although the year was 1905, the story is hauntingly familiar. It deals with colleges, football, and corruption. Henry Beach Needham in an article in *McClure's* charged that college football had become a professional endeavor, that players were paid performers who cared little for their studies. Take, for example, James J. Hogan, Yale's captain and star player who knew how to make the most out of an "amateur" sport. At the age of twenty-seven, he agreed to play football for Yale. In return, Yale paid his tuition, gave him a $100 a year scholarship, housed him in rooms at its most luxurious dormitory, and fed him at the University Club. In addition, Hogan and two other players received all the profits from the sale of game programs, and Hogan was appointed the American Tobacco Company's

agent in New Haven and received a commission on every package of cigarettes sold in the area. Finally, after each season—but during the school term—Hogan was given a ten-day vacation trip to Cuba.

Hogan's case was by no means unique. In an age of unregulated football competition, it was each school for itself, each player for himself. Money talked and school spirit was for the students in the stands. Players were more mercenaries than students; their loyalty was constantly on the auction block. Andrew Smith demonstrated this principle in 1902. On October 4, Smith played an exceptional game for Pennsylvania State University against a powerhouse Penn team. By that next Monday he had transferred schools and was practicing with Penn, a college which had also "drafted" players from Middlebury, Colorado College, La-

fayette, and Peddie. Of course, at least Lafayette College had little cause for complaint. Fielding H. Yost, who coached the University of Michigan for three decades, recalled his undergraduate days at West Virginia. During one season, an undefeated Lafayette had "hired" Yost to play against the also unbeaten Penn. After the game, Yost "transferred" back to West Virginia.

Critics charged that football was undermining the very ethics which college professors were laboring to instill into students. As early as 1893, E. L. Godkin, editor of the influential *Nation*, noted that the leading colleges were losing their educational orientation and becoming "huge training grounds for young gladiators, around whom as many spectators roar as roared in the Flavian amphitheatre." More than a decade later, Charles W. Eliot, president of Harvard, complained bitterly that each fall undergraduates at his university seemed totally obsessed by football, talking about or thinking about little else. Godkin and Eliot found a kindred spirit in John S. Mosby, who had led the Confederate Mosby's Raiders during the Civil War. Although he had been suspended from Virginia in 1853 for shooting a fellow student, Mosby continued to think of the school as his alma mater. In 1909 the old raider wrote, "I do not think football should be tolerated where the youth of the country are supposed to be taught literature, science and humanity. The game seems to overshadow everything else at the University."

Mosby's letter was prompted by another football problem—violence. By the turn of the century, the number of athletes killed or injured in football games had reached an alarming level. In 1909 Virginia halfback Archer Christian died shortly after being injured in a game against Georgetown. As Mosby asked, "I believe that cockfighting is unlawful in Virginia: Why should better care be taken of a game chicken than a school boy?" Other critics pondered the same question, for during the 1909 season thirty boys were killed and 216 seriously injured in football games.

The most publicized death of that season was Army's captain Eugene Byrne. He was fatally injured in a game against Harvard. The event was so shocking that the game was immediately halted, and the Army-Navy game of that year was canceled. Buried with full military honors, thousands mourned Byrne's senseless death and questioned the place of college football in American society.

Football brutality was a serious problem. The nature of the game emphasized violence. Unlike today when the team with the ball has four plays to make a ten-yard first down, during the late-nineteenth and early-twentieth centuries the offensive team had three plays to make a five yard first down. In addition, passing was severely restricted both by the rules and by tradition. As a result, coaches emphasized "mass plays" which directed the maximum amount of force against one isolated player or point on the field. The flying wedge was the most notorious mass play. The play entailed players grouping themselves in a V formation and starting to run before the ball was put into play. Then at the last moment the ball

was snapped and passed to a player within the wall of the wedge. The wedge of runners then crashed into their stationary opponents. Given that equipment was crude—players often played without helmets and no helmet had a facemask—this brute use of massed force injured hundreds of players each year.

If the flying wedge and other mass plays were not bad enough, referees rarely enforced rules against slugging, kicking, and piling-on. Victory was the supreme object; and any method seemed justified in the pursuit of that goal. One Princeton player confessed to a reporter that he and his teammates were coached to eliminate dangerous opponents during the early minutes of a game. A writer for the *Nation* believed this ruthless drive for victory illustrated a fundamental American characteristic: "The spirit of the American youth, as of the American man, is to win, 'to get there,' by fair means or foul; and the lack of moral scruple which prevades the struggles of the business world meets with temptations equally irresistible in the miniature contests of the football field."

By the end of the terribly brutal 1905 season many educators, journalists, and politicians had decided that college football served no educational good and did considerable harm. Professor Shailer Mathews of Chicago's Divinity School labeled football "a social obsession—a boy-killing, education-prostituting, gladiatorial sport." Even though President Theodore Roosevelt stepped in and tried to clean up the game and officials altered the rules of the sport, a number of universities

chose to drop football from their athletic programs. Columbia, Union, Northwestern, Stanford, and California led the abolitionist movement.

Between 1905 and 1910 critics continued to level charges of brutality, commercialism, and corruption against football. The 1905 rules had not lessened the violence, and death continued to shock concerned Americans. In 1910 the rules of football were once again altered. In the most important change, the forward pass as we know it today was legalized. Although football conservatives continued for several years to ignore the new offensive weapon, in 1913 the pass came into its own. That year a highly regarded Army team filled an open date in its schedule with a small Indiana school called Notre Dame. During the game Notre Dame quarterback Charley Dorais threw perfectly timed passes to his favorite end Knute Rockne. The result was a 35–13 upset by the Irish of Notre Dame. By the end of the season other teams had adopted the new tactic and passes filled the autumn air. The age of the mass play was over.

Passing made football even more exciting, and after 1913 criticism of the sport generated little support. Of course, brutality, commercialism, and corruption continued, but such scandals led more to attacks on individual schools than against football as a college sport. Indeed, by 1917 football reigned unrivaled as college's supreme sport and public spectacle.

Baseball was the leading sport of the late nineteenth century. It brought a sense of America's rural past into the country's urban present.

The mythology of the sport, however, harkened back to America's past. The myth lingers still that Abner Doubleday "invented" baseball in 1839 when he laid out the first baseball diamond in the pastoral village of Cooperstown, New York. The United States Post Office gave semi-official recognition to the myth in 1939 when it issued a commemorative stamp honoring the centennial anniversary of the event. In fact, if anyone can be said to have invented a sport that actually evolved, it was Alexander J. Cartwright, Jr., a New York City stationery and book store owner who in 1845 set down the first written rules for the game.

The symbols of the game also recalled America's rural past. Unlike most modern sports, no clock governed the pace of a baseball game. In crowded, dirty cities, baseball was played on open, grassy fields with such bucolic names as Sportsman Park, Ebbets Field, and the Polo Grounds. (Yankee Stadium, opened in 1923, was the first baseball enclosure to veer

from the rural tradition.) The sport even had fences and bullpens and was played during the planting and harvesting seasons of spring, summer, and fall.

If the symbols and mythology of baseball were rural, the game itself was very urban. Team managers, like their industrialist counterparts, preached the values of hard work, punctuality, thrift, sobriety, and self-control to their players. Baseball, they emphasized, was like modern life, ruthlessly competitive and demanding sacrifice for the "good of the team." As Mr. Clayton, a character in an 1891 baseball novel, explained, "We can't work and we can't play, we can't learn and we can't make money, without getting some of other people's help." Like modern corporate society, then, modern sports reinforced the ideal of teamwork.

During the last third of the nineteenth century, as men like Rockefeller and Carnegie struggled to bring order to their industrial empires, modern baseball took form. Rules were standardized. In the early years of baseball a base runner could be thrown out by hitting him with the ball as he ran between the bases. Organizers outlawed such violent relics of the past. Owners attempted to make the sport suitable for the urban middle class. They banned the spit ball, arranged games to fit the urban professionals' schedules, fined players for using profanity, and encouraged women to attend the games.

Most important, they formed competitive professional leagues centered in the industrial cities of America. In 1869 Harry Wright took his all-professional Cincinnati Red Stockings on a barnstorming tour. Traveling on the recently completed Transcontinental Railroad, they played teams from New York City to San Francisco and compiled a record of fifty-seven wins, no losses, and one tie. Over 23,000 fans watched their six-game series in New York, and almost 15,000 spectators attended a single game they played in Philadelphia. In Washington, D.C., President Ulysses S. Grant commended them on their accomplishments. During the year the team traveled 11,877 miles by rail, stage, and boat and entertained more than 200,000 spectators.

The Cincinnati club taught the rest of America, as one journalist commented, that "steady, temperate habits and constant training are all conditions precedent to all first class professional organizations." It also demonstrated to entrepreneurs that there was money to be made in professional sports. In 1876 William A. Hulbert and several associates formed the National League, which was organized around owners and clubs, not players. In business terms, the league was a loosely organized cartel designed to eliminate competition among franchises for players. Eventually, league officials devised the "reserve clause," which effectively bound a player to the team that held the rights to him. This further undermined the ability of a player to negotiate for a higher salary. Although the National League was known as a "rich man's" league because it charged a fifty-cents admission price, it was certainly not a rich player's league.

In 1890 the players revolted and formed the Players' League. Headed by lawyer and star player John Montgomery Ward, the Players' League was an experiment in workers' control of an industry. In words similar to those used by workers in other industries the players' "manifesto" of 1889 claimed, "There was a time when the [National] League stood for integrity and fair dealing. Today it stands for dollars and cents . . . Players have been bought, sold, and exchanged, as though they were sheep, instead of American citizens . . . by a combination among themselves, stronger than the strongest trusts, they [the owners] were able to enforce the most arbitrary measures, and the player had either to submit or get out of the profession in which he had spent years in attaining a proficiency." Lofty in ideals, the Players' League was badly managed and lasted only one year.

With the failure of the Players' League, the National League increased its control over professional baseball. It either crushed rival leagues or absorbed them. In 1903, for example, after a short business war the National League entered into a partnership with the American League. The only losers were the players, whose salaries decreased with the absence of competition. Nevertheless, the popularity of the sport soared. By 1909, when William Howard Taft established the precedent for the president opening each season by throwing out the first ball, baseball had become the national pastime.

"I Can Lick Any Sonofabitch in the House"

Only boxing rivaled baseball in popularity during the late nineteenth century. Like baseball, boxing began the period as a largely unstructured sport, but by 1900 entrepreneurs had reorganized the activity into a profitable business. Although boxing remained illegal in most parts of America, it produced some of the first national sports heroes.

Bare-knuckle boxing, the forerunner of modern boxing, was a brutal, bloody sport. It involved two men, who fought bare-fisted until one could not continue. A round lasted until one of the men knocked or threw down his opponent. At that point both men rested for thirty seconds and then started to fight again. Fights

John L. Sullivan won the heavyweight title in 1882 after a grueling seventy-five round victory over Jake Kilrain.

came the greatest known American athlete during the nineteenth century. "Excepting General Grant," one newspaperman wrote, "no American has received such ovations as Sullivan." Born in Boston of Irish immigrant parents, Sullivan was a loud boastful man who loved to drink and fight. He often walked into a saloon and claimed he could outfight and outdrink "any sonofabitch in the house." After he won the bare-knuckle world heavyweight title in 1882, tales of his punching power and his unrestrained attacks on Victorian morality spread across the country. Politicians, actors, writers, and merchants avidly followed his exploits, but Sullivan never lost touch with his immigrant, working-class origin. In Irish Boston, Sullivan's elevated standing went unquestioned. Comparing the Boston of old and new, one poet wrote:

> Just fancy what mingled emotions
> Would fill the Puritan heart
> To learn what renown was won for his town
> By means of the manly art!
> Imagine a Winthrop or Adams
> In front of the bulletin board,
> Each flinging his hat at the statement that
> The first blood was by Sullivan scored.

During the 1880s, Sullivan watched his sport move toward greater respectability. Boxing, like baseball, underwent a series of reforms. The traditional challenge system for arranging fights was replaced by modern promotional techniques pioneered by New Orleans athletic clubs. Fighters deserted bare fisted combat and started wearing gloves. Most important of all, professional boxers adopted the Marquis of Queensberry Rules, which standardized a round at three minutes, allowed a one minute rest period between rounds, and outlawed all wrestling throws and holds. The new rules also replaced the fight to the finish with a fight to a decision over a specified number of rounds. Although the new rules did not lessen the violence of the sport, they did provide for more orderly bouts.

The Queensberry Rules resembled the recently adopted factory innovations. Just as workers lost control of the pace of work, fighters no longer could determine the pace of action. Under the old rules prize fighters could

could and often did last over one hundred rounds and as long as seven or eight hours. After such a fight it took months for the men to recover.

Boxers, unlike baseball players, often emerged from poor immigrant families. Irish-Americans dominated the sport during the late nineteenth century, and they used boxing—as well as gambling, drinking, and prostitution—as "one of the queer ladders of social mobility in American life." Such men as John Morrissey, James C. Heenan, and John L. Sullivan became national legends during the period. Morrissey, for instance, was born in Ireland, lived in poverty in Troy, New York, gained fame as a prize fighter, and eventually became a leading New York gambler and politician. By the time he died he had served two terms in Congress and made a fortune.

The Great John L. (John L. Sullivan), however, eclipsed Morrissey in popularity. He be-

tacitly agree to slow down the action in order to catch their breath or simply exchange boasts and oaths. Now a bell and a referee told them when to fight and when to rest. The factory system had effectively invaded boxing.

John L. Sullivan won the last bare-knuckle championship contest. In 1887 he defeated Jake Kilrain in a fight held near Richberg, Mississippi. It was an illegal fight, but it attracted spectators from all social classes. Bat Masterson, the gun-fighter and gambler, served as timekeeper, and he was joined at ringside by wealthy sons of southern aristocrats, gamblers, and sporting men of every variety. The fight lasted for seventy-five rounds, and both boxers drank whiskey between rounds. After winning the epic fight, Sullivan gained even greater fame.

Sullivan lost the title in 1892 to James J. Corbett in a legal gloved contest fought in New Orleans. Nicknamed "Gentleman Jim," Corbett's scientific boxing style and smooth manners outside the ring demonstrated that boxing had gained increased respectability. In fact, by the 1890s boxing was no longer a working-class sport. Like baseball, it had become an organized, structured, and profitable business. All that was left of the older sport was the legend of the Great John L.—the boisterous, crude, lovable, man-child. As he told future novelist Theodore Dreiser shortly after the Corbett fight: "I'm ex-champion of the world, defeated by that little dude from California, but I'm still John L. Sullivan—ain't that right. Haw! Haw! They can't take that away from me, can they? Haw! Haw! Have some more champagne boy."

The Excluded Americans

Although promoters talked about the democratic nature of sports, this was far from the case. To be sure, a number of Irish and German men—often immigrants or sons of immigrants—prospered in professional sports. Far more Americans were excluded from the world of sports.

In large cities the lines between social classes tended to blur, much to the discomfort of the wealthy who struggled to separate themselves from the hoi polloi. The rich moved to the suburbs and employed other methods of residential segregation to isolate themselves. An uncommon amount of intermarrying was another tactic. They also used sports and athletic clubs to set themselves apart. "Gentlemen and ladies," as they styled themselves—they only wanted to compete against opponents of similar dress, speech, education, and wealth.

One way to exclude the masses was to engage in sports which only the very rich could play. Yachting and polo demanded nearly unlimited free time, expensive equipment, and a retinue of hired helpers. The New York Yacht Club was founded in 1884 and was soon joined by a "succession of gentlemen ranking high in the social and financial circles" of the city. By the 1890s every major eastern seaboard city had its exclusive yacht club, and each summer the richest yacht owners sailed their splendid vessels to Newport, Rhode Island, the most exclusive of the summer colonies.

Athletic clubs devoted to track and field, golf, and tennis were similarly exclusive. The members of Shinnecock Hills, one of the oldest golf clubs in America, prided themselves on the beauty of their course as well as their own social standing. Such exclusive clubs catered to more than the members' athletic concerns. Each club had an elaborate social calendar filled with dress balls and formal dinners. When they did schedule sporting events, participation and the privilege of watching were normally on an invitation only basis.

To prevent the various social classes from mixing too freely in athletics, wealthy patrons advocated the code of amateurism, which separated the greedy professionals—who often came from the poorer classes—from the more prosperous athletes who participated in a sport simply for the love of the game. The revival of the Olympic Games in 1896 strengthened the amateur code. Thus when it was discovered that Jim Thorpe, an Oklahoma Indian from a reservation school who won the decathlon and the pentathlon in the 1912 Stockholm Games, had played baseball for a minor league professional team during the summer of 1909, the International Olympic Committee stripped him of his medals.

Although amateurism was a subtle attack on the working class, sports leaders moved more forcefully against blacks. During the 1870s and 1880s, blacks and whites competed in sports against each other on a fairly regular basis. A number of blacks even rose to become world champions. Marshall W. "Major" Taylor was hailed as the "Fastest Bicycle Rider in the World"; Isaac Murphy rode horses to three Kentucky Derby victories; and George Dixon and other blacks won boxing titles. During the 1890s, however, blacks and whites were segregated in most sports.

Jim Crow laws came to boxing during this period. John L. Sullivan steadfastly refused to fight black boxers. In 1892 he issued his famous challenge to fight all contenders: "In this challenge I include all fighters—first come, first served—who are white. I will not fight a Negro. I never have and I never shall." True to his word, the Boston Strong Boy never did. The same year, lightweight champion George Dixon administered a frightful beating to white challenger Jack Skelly in New Orleans. After the fight, the editor of the *New Orleans Times-Democrat* wrote that it was "a mistake to match a negro and a white man, a mistake to bring the two races together on any terms of equality, even in the prize ring." After 1892 the number of "mixed bouts" declined rapidly.

Organized baseball also excluded blacks during the 1890s. During the 1880s several owners integrated their professional baseball teams, but the trend toward segregation that led to the landmark court case, *Plessy* v. *Ferguson* (1896), overtook baseball. In 1889 baseball's *Sporting News* announced that "race prejudice exists in professional baseball ranks to a marked degree, and the unfortunate son of Africa who makes his living as a member of a team of white professionals has a rocky road to travel." The observation was accurate. By 1892 major-league baseball was all white, and it would remain so until Jackie Robinson broke the "color barrier" in 1945.

Cultural expectations and stereotypes also limited the development of women athletes. Scientists spoke and wrote confidently about women's "arrested evolution." Compared to men, they were considered weak and uncoordi-nated, athletically retarded because of their narrow sloping shoulders, broad hips, underdeveloped muscles, and short arms and legs. Although they might ride a bicycle or gently swing a croquet mallet, men ridiculed women who were interested in serious competitive athletics.

Even during the 1890s, when the tall, commanding Gibson Girl became the physical ideal and women became more interested in sports and exercise, women's athletics developed along different lines than men's. Male and female physical educators considered women to be uncompetitive and decided that women's sports should serve a utilitarian function. Sports, they emphasized, should promote a woman's physical and mental qualities and thus make her more attractive to men. They also believed that sports and exercise would sublimate female sexual drives. As renowned physical educator Dudley A. Sargent noted: "No one seems to realize that there is a time in the life of a girl when it is better for her and for the community to be something of a boy rather than too much of a girl."

But tomboyish behavior had to stop short of abrasive competition. Lucille Eaton Hill, director of physical training at Wellesley College, urged women to "avoid the evils which are so apparent . . . in the conduct of athletics for men." She and her fellow female physical educators encouraged widespread participation rather than narrow specialization. In short, women left spectator and professional sports to the men. Indeed, not until 1924 were women allowed to compete in Olympic track and field events, and even then on a limited basis.

From Central Park to Coney Island

Like sports, parks changed to satisfy new urban demands. Mid-nineteenth-century park designers felt uneasy about the urban environment. In parks they saw an antidote for the tensions and anxieties caused by living in cities. Frederick Law Olmstead, the most famous park architect, believed cities destroyed community ties and fostered ruthless competition. He designed Central Park to serve as a rural retreat in the

Coney Island provided a temporary escape from the pressures of urban life. Its sense of informality and sheer excitement attracted people of every class.

midst of New York. Surrounded by rolling hills and quiet lakes, city dwellers would be moved toward greater sociability. "No one who has closely observed the conduct of the people who visit [Central] Park," Olmstead declared, "can doubt that it exercises a distinctly harmonizing and refining influence upon the most unfortunate and most lawless classes of the city—an influence favorable to courtesy, self-control, and temperance."

The quiet world offered by Central Park, however, was too tame for many urbanites. They wanted more excitement. This was clearly seen at the World's Columbian Exposition of 1893 in Chicago. The most popular area of the World's Fair was the Midway, the center of commercial amusements. Visitors eagerly rode the Ferris wheel, visited the "40 Ladies from 40 Nations" exhibition, and watched "Little Egypt" perform her exotic dances. Parks that amuse, not soothe, attracted the most people.

Entrepreneurs were quick to satisfy the public's desire for entertainment. During the 1890s a series of popular amusement parks opened in Coney Island. Unlike Central Park, which was constructed as a rural retreat, the Coney Island parks glorified the sense of adventure and excitement of the cities. They offered exotic, dreamland landscapes; wonderful, novel machines; and a free, loose social environment. At Coney Island men could remove their coats and ties, and both sexes could enjoy a rare personal freedom. As one immigrant claimed, for the young "privacy could be had only in public."

Coney Island also encouraged new values. If, as Olmstead believed, Central Park reinforced self-control, sobriety, and delayed gratification, Coney Island stressed the emerging consumer-oriented values of extravagance, gaiety, abandon, revelry, and instant gratification. It attracted working-class Americans who longed for at least a taste of the "good life." If a person could never hope to own a mansion in Newport, he could for a few dimes experience the exotic pleasures of Luna Park or Dreamland Park.

Even the rides in the amusement parks were designed to create illusions and break down reality. Mirrors distorted people's images and rides threw them off balance. At Luna Park, the "Witching Waves" simulated the bobbing of a ship at high sea, and the "Tickler" featured spinning circular cars which threw riders together. "Such rides," wrote a student of Coney Island, "served in effect as powerful hallucinogens, altering visitors' perceptions and transforming their consciousness, dispelling everyday concerns in the intense sensations of the present moment. They allowed customers the exhilaration of whirlwind activity without physical exertion, of thrilling drama without imaginative effort."

The Magic of the Flickering Image

Coney Island showed workers that machines could liberate as well as enslave. It offered an escape from an oppressive urban landscape to an exotic one. The motion picture industry, however, offered a less expensive, more convenient escape. During the early twentieth century it developed into a major popular culture form, one that reflected the hopes and ambitions, fear and anxieties of an urban people.

In 1887 when Thomas Edison moved his research laboratory from Menlo Park to Orange, New Jersey, he gave W. K. L. Dickson, one of his leading inventors, the task of developing a motion picture apparatus. Edison envisioned a machine "that should do for the eye what the phonograph did for the ear." Working closely with Edison, Dickson developed the Edison kinetophonograph, a machine capable of showing film in synchronization with a phonograph record. The idea of talking pictures, however, was not as popular as the moving pictures themselves. After further refinements by Edison and other inventors, silent moving pictures became a commercial reality.

The first movies, as the new form was soon called, presented brief vaudeville turns or

Early Nickelodeans were cramped and uncomfortable, but they provided endless leisure enjoyments for immigrant and native-born Americans.

glimpses of everyday life. Such titles as *Fred Ott's Sneeze, Chinese Laundry, The Gaiety Girls Dancing, Dentist Scene,* and *Highland Dance* tell the full content of each three or four minute film. Still the movies attracted considerable interest, and film makers began to experiment with such new techniques as editing and intercutting separate "shots" to form a dramatic narrative. In 1903 the release of Edwin S. Porter's *The Great Train Robbery,* the first western and the first film to exploit the violence of armed robbery, fully demonstrated the commercial possibilities of the invention. Although *The Great Train Robbery* ran only twelve minutes, it mesmerized audiences.

During the first decade of the twentieth century, movies developed a strong following in ethnic, working-class neighborhoods. Local entrepreneurs converted stores and saloons into nickelodeons and introduced immigrants to a silent world of promise. Movies provided inexpensive and short escapes from the grimmer realities of urban life. Describing the experience of visiting a nickelodeon, Abraham Cahan, editor of the *Jewish Daily Forward*, wrote in 1906: " . . . people must be entertained and five cents is little to pay. A movie lasts half an hour. If it isn't too busy you can see it several times. They open in the afternoon and customers, mostly men and women, eat fruit and have a good time." In addition, since the movies were silent, they required no knowledge of English to enjoy.

Ministers, the political right, and other guardians of traditional Victorian morality criticized the new form of entertainment. Movies, said Nebraska's superintendent of schools Joseph R. Fulk, "engendered idleness and cultivated careless spending" at the "expense of earnest and persistent work." Worse yet, they stirred "primitive passions," encouraged "daydreaming," and fostered "too much familiarity between boys and girls." Soon local boards of censorship formed to protect innocent boys and girls, and perhaps not so innocent men and women, from being corrupted by movies.

In the cities, censorship movements ultimately failed. Furthermore, attempts by white, native-born American businessmen to control the new industry similarly failed. Ironically, while films were attracting middle-class audiences, control of the industry shifted to immigrant entrepreneurs, most of whom were born in Eastern Europe. They proved better able than native-born businessmen to develop the possibilities of the medium. They emerged from a culture that valued laughter, cooperation, and entertainment. These attitudes allowed them to make movies that appealed to Americans.

Committed to giving the people what they wanted, they were less committed to the traditional Victorian code of morality. As Samuel Goldwyn, one of the Big Eight, observed, "If the audience don't like a picture, they have a good reason. The public is never wrong. I don't go for all this thing that when I have a failure, it is because the audience doesn't have the taste or education, or isn't sensitive enough. The public pays the money. It wants to be entertained.

That's all I know." To better entertain the public, the Big Eight started producing feature length films and moved the industry from the East Coast to sunny Hollywood, where they could shoot outdoors and, incidentally, escape union difficulties. While such "stars" as Charlie Chaplin, Douglas Fairbanks, and Mary Pickford captured the hearts of America, the Big Eight forged a multi-million dollar industry.

The Agony of Painless Escape

Coney Island and movie theaters provided one form of escape, and the criticism of both was fairly uniform. James Gibbons Huneker, a leading cultural critic of the period, feared the surrender of reason and repression that Coney Island encouraged. "Unreality," he commented, "is as greedily craved by the mob as alcohol by the dipsomaniac; indeed, the jumbled nightmares of a morphine eater are actually realized at Luna Park." And Maxim Gorky, the Russian writer and revolutionary who visited America in 1906, suggested that mass amusement acted as an opiate of the people. At the same time as popular culture was exploring the theme of mechanized instant gratification, however, Americans were seeking escape in other, more ominous forms.

Like the whirring machines at Coney Island and the flickering images on the silent, silver screen, the mindless escape of narcotics attracted millions of Americans. During the late nineteenth and early twentieth centuries, as the nation underwent the trauma of industrialization and urbanization, Americans took drugs in unprecedented amounts. Apologists blamed this development on the Civil War. They claimed that soldiers became addicted to morphine after using the drug as a pain killer. Yet France, Germany, Great Britain, Russia, and Italy also fought wars in the second half of the nineteenth century, and their drug addiction rates were far below those of the United States.

Part of the problem was that before 1915 there were few restrictions on the importation and use of opium, its derivatives, and cocaine.

1869 First all-professional baseball team, the Cincinnnati Red Stockings, founded for a railroad barnstorming tour of America

1869 Rutgers defeats Princeton 6 to 4 in first intercollegiate football game

1870 Atlantic City Boardwalk completed

1871 Great Chicago Fire destroys much of the city's downtown, killing about 300 people

1872 Montgomery Ward & Company, the first mailorder house, opens in Chicago

1873 *The Gilded Age* by Mark Twain and Charles Dudley Warner published

1873 Andrew Hallidie invents cable car for use in San Francisco

1873 Yellow fever, cholera, and smallpox epidemics erupt in southern cities

1876 The National League, the first professional baseball league, founded

1878 Thomas Edison patents phonograph and records "Mary Had a Little Lamb"

1879 Frank W. Woolworth opens first successful 5-and-10-cent store in Lancaster, Pennsylvania

1882 John L. Sullivan wins heavyweight championship of the world

1883 Brooklyn Bridge completed at a cost of $15 million

1884 Mark Twain publishes *The Adventures of Huckleberry Finn*

1886 United States Lawn Tennis Association established

1887 First successful electric trolley line built by Frank J. Sprague in Richmond, Virginia

1888 Edward Bellamy publishes *Looking Backward, 2000–1887*

1889 Walter Camp selects first all-American football teams

1890 Jacob A. Riis publishes *How the Other Half Lives* exposing slum life

1891 James A. Naismith invents the sport of basketball

1891 Thomas Edison patents a kinetoscopic camera for taking moving pictures

1891 First Boston Marathon run from Hopkinton, Massachusetts, to Boston

1893 World's Columbian Exposition in Chicago opens

1893 Stephen Crane writes *Maggie: A Girl of the Streets*

1894 United States Golf Association established

1895 First professional football game played in Latrobe, Pennsylvania

1896 Olympic Games revived in Athens, Greece

1900 Theodore Dreiser writes *Sister Carrie*

1913 Armory Show held in New York City

Physicians prescribed opiates for a wide range of ailments, and patent medicine manufacturers used morphine, laudanum, cocaine, or heroin in their concoctions. William Hammond, former surgeon general of the army, swore by cocaine and drank a wine glass of it with each meal. The Hay Fever Association officially recommended cocaine as an effective remedy. Coca-Cola used cocaine as one of its secret ingredients, and the Parke Davis Company produced coca-leaf cigarettes, cheroots, and a Coca Cordial. Vin Mariani, a wine product containing cocaine, was endorsed by Pope Leo XIII, was advertised as "a perfectly safe and reliable diffusable stimulant and tonic; a powerful aid to digestion and assimilation; admirably adapted for children, invalids, and convalescents."

Cocaine in particular was regarded as a wonder drug. One manufacturer claimed that it could "supply the place of food, make the coward brave, the silent eloquent, free the victims of the alcohol and opium habits from their bondage, and, as an anesthetic, render the sufferer insensitive to pain . . . " But by the late 1890s its harmful effects had become obvious. Journalists and government officials linked it to urban crime and racial unrest in the South. Eventually, angry citizens and the federal and state governments launched the first great American crusade against cocaine. It culminated with the Harrison Anti-Narcotic Act (1914), which controlled the distribution of opiates and cocaine; but drug addiction remained a problem in cities well into the 1920s.

Robert Louis Stevenson's *Dr. Jekyll and Mr. Hyde,* which he wrote under the influence of cocaine, described the dangers of challenging society's standards and altering one's personality, but in America's cities a new culture had taken shape. It opposed Victorian restraints, glorified the freedoms of urban life, and at the same time worried about the implications of a liberated life-style. Social, as well as economic, freedom came with a price. By the 1890s many Americans believed some new form of regulations was needed to check the social and economic freedom unleashed in urban America.

CONCLUSION

A. T. Stewart, Rowland H. Macy, Marshall Field, John Wanamaker—their very names conjure visions of miles and miles of consumer goods. They brought order to shopping and emphasized standardization of products. In their department stores in New York, Chicago, and Philadelphia, customers could purchase readymade clothes, jewelry, toys, sheet music, cutlery, and a wide range of other products. Serving urban markets and satisfying urban desires, they provided a safe haven for urban shoppers. Inside one of the great department stores, consumers isolated themselves from the garbage in the streets, the filth in the air, and the sounds of traffic and commerce which dominated the outside world.

Both the orderly world of the department store and the chaotic one of the streets were the products of urban entrepreneurs who fashioned the modern cities. In pursuit of profits they were capable of producing dazzling monuments to commerce and terrible tributes to greed. The same spirit that built the Woolworth Building and the Dakota Apartments also constructed dumbbell tenements. By 1900, their days of absolute dominance were numbered. Although they would remain a vital part of American capitalism, in the future they would be rivaled by governmental planners—people who wanted to extend the smooth, efficient order of the department store to the outside streets.

The emergence of the great cities changed American life. To be sure, they exerted an economic domination, but their influence was still greater. Eventually, they came to dominate the American imagination. In the cities, the clash of ideas and beliefs, of peoples and traditions created an exciting, new heterogeneous culture. The result was evident at places such as Coney Island and the Armory Show, it was visible in many of the movies, and it was audible at a New Orleans jazz cafe. As the nineteenth century drew to a close, a new culture was clearly emerging. It would add a new element to the new century.

REVIEW SUMMARY

The decades before and after 1900 saw America move away from its rural heritage and become a predominantly urban society. The process was often confusing and painful, but the cultural and physical results excited many Americans. The development of the rapidly growing cities was determined by

> the rise of new mass transit and construction technologies and architectural ideas, which permitted cities to expand outward and upward
>
> the needs of individual entrepreneurs, whose urban initiatives often worked to the disadvantage and discomfort of the poorer residents

Both high and popular culture reflected the centrality of the city in American life.

> writers, painters, and musicians began to explore urban themes and receive inspiration from urban life
>
> new spectator sports and amusement parks catered to the urban multitudes

Along with industrialization, urbanization changed the focus of American life.

SUGGESTIONS FOR FURTHER READING

OVERVIEWS AND SURVEYS

Daniel J. Boorstin, *The Americans: The Democratic Experience* (1973); Sean Cashman, *America in the Gilded Age* (1984); Howard P. Chudacoff, *The Evolution of American Urban Society* (1981); Charles N. Glaab and A. Theodore Brown, *A History of Urban America* (1983); David R. Goldfield and Blaine A. Brownell, *Urban America* (1979); Raymond A. Mohl, *The New City* (1985); Lewis Mumford, *The City in History* (1967); Benjamin Rader, *American Sports* (1983); Robert H. Walker, Jr., *Life in the Age of Enterprise, 1865–1900* (1970); Sam Bass Warner, Jr., *The Urban Wilderness* (1972); Robert H. Wiebe, *The Search for Order, 1877–1920* (1967).

NEW CITIES NEW PROBLEMS

Andrew Alpern, *Apartments for the Affluent* (1975); Nelson M. Blake, *Water for the Cities* (1956); Charles W. Cheape, *Moving the Masses* (1980); Howard Chudacoff, *Mobile Americans* (1972); Dean R. Esslinger, *Immigrants and the City* (1975); David M. Fine, *The City, The Immigrant and American Fiction, 1880–1920* (1977); Kenneth Fox, *Better City Government* (1977); Frederic Cople Jaher, *The Urban Establishment* (1982); Maury Klein and Harvey A. Kantor, *Prisoners of Progress: American Industrial Cities, 1850–1920* (1976); Roger Lane, *Policing the City* (1967) and *Violent Death in the City* (1979); Blake McKelvey, *The Urbanization of America, 1860–1915* (1963); Clay McShane, *Technology and Reform* (1974); Harold M. Mayer and Richard C. Wade, *Chicago* (1969); Martin V. Melosi, *Garbage in the Cities* (1982) and (ed.) *Pollution and Reform in the American Cities, 1870–1930* (1980); Gilbert Osofsky, *Harlem: The Making of a Ghetto, 1890–1920* (1967); Bradley R. Rice, *Progressive Cities* (1977); Laura Wood Roper, *FLO: A Biography of Frederick Law Olmsted* (1973); Martin J. Schiesl, *The Politics of Efficiency* (1977); Allan H. Spear, *Black Chicago* (1967); Elizabeth Stevenson, *Park Maker: A Life of Frederick Law Olmsted* (1977); Jon C. Teaford, *The Municipal Revolution in America* (1975), *City and Suburb* (1979), and *The Unheralded Triumph: City Government in America, 1870–1900* (1984); Joel A. Tarr, *Transportation Innovation and Changing Spatial Patterns in Pittsburgh, 1850–1934* (1978); David Ward, *City and Immigrants* (1971); Sam Bass Warner, Jr., *Streetcar Suburbs* (1962).

CITY CULTURE

Gunther Barth, *City People* (1980); Lois W. Banner, *Women in Modern America* (1974) and *American Beauty* (1983); Paul Boyer, *Urban Masses and Moral Order in America, 1820–1920* (1978); Carl W. Condit, *The Chicago School of Architecture* (1964) and *The Rise of the Skyscraper* (1952); Carl N. Degler, *At Odds: Women and the Family in America* (1980); Blanche H. Gelfant, *The American City Novel* (1954); Justin Kaplan, *Mr. Clemens and Mark Twain* (1966); Alfred Kazin, *On Native Ground* (1942); O. W. Larkin, *Art and Life in America* (1949); Neil Leonard, *Jazz and the White Americans* (1962); David J. Pivar, *Purity Crusade: Sexual Morality and Social Control, 1868–1900* (1980); William O'Neill, *Divorce in the Progressive Era* (1973); W. J. Rorabaugh, *The Alcoholic Republic* (1979); Sheila M. Rothman, *Woman's Proper Place* (1978); William J. Schafer and Johannes Riedel, *The Art of Ragtime* (1977); Vincent Scully, *American Architecture and Urbanism* (1969); Larzer Ziff, *The American 1890s* (1966).

ENTERTAINING THE MULTITUDES

Melvin L. Adelman, *A Sporting Time* (1986); Reid Badger, *The Great American Fair* (1979); David F. Burg, *Chicago's White City of 1893* (1976); Dominick Cavallo, *Muscles and Morals: Organized Playgrounds and Urban Reform, 1880–*

1920 (1981); John E. DiMeglio, *Vaudeville U.S.A.* (1970); Perry Duis, *The Saloon* (1983); Lewis A. Erenberg, *Steppin' Out: New York Nightlife and the Transformation of American Culture, 1890–1930* (1981); Charles E. Funnell, *By the Beautiful Sea* (1983); Elliott Gorn, *The Manly Art* (1986); Stephen Hardy, *How Boston Played: Sport, Recreation, and Community, 1865–1915* (1982); Neil Harris, *Humbug: The Art of P. T. Barnum* (1973); Michael T. Isenberg, *John L. Sullivan and His America* (1988); John F. Kasson, *Amusing the Millions, Coney Island at the Turn of the Century* (1978); Jackson Lears, *No Place of Grace: Antimodernism and the Transformation of American Culture, 1880–1920* (1981); Lary May, *Screening Out the Past: The Birth of Mass Culture and the Motion Picture Industry, 1896–1929* (1980); Donald J. Mrozek, *Sport and American Mentality, 1880–1910* (1983); Russel B. Nye, *The Unembarrassed Muse* (1970); Steven A. Riess, *Touching Base: Professional Baseball and American Culture in the Progressive Era* (1980); Randy Roberts, *Papa Jack: Jack Johnson and the Era of White Hopes* (1983); Robert Sklar, *Movie-Made America* (1975); Dale A. Somers, *The Rise of Sports in New Orleans, 1850–1900* (1972).

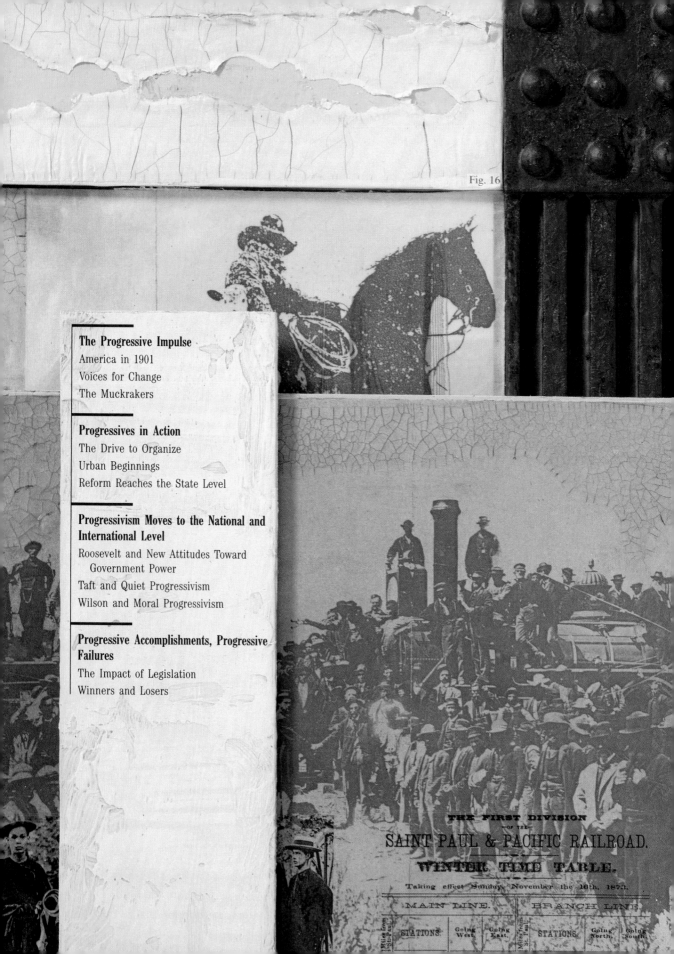

Fig. 16

THE FIRST DIVISION
OF THE
SAINT PAUL & PACIFIC RAILROAD.
WINTER TIME TABLE.
Taking effect Sunday, November the 30th, 1873.

MAIN LINE. BRANCH LINE.

Miles from St. Paul	STATIONS.	Going West.	Going East.	Miles from St. Paul	STATIONS.	Going North.	Going South.

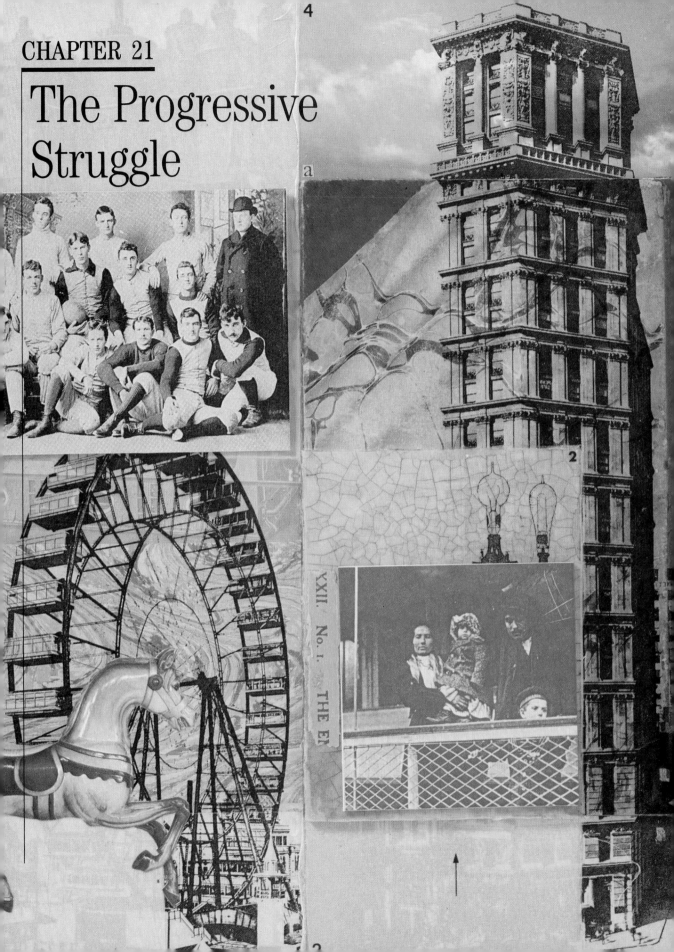

CHAPTER 21
The Progressive Struggle

imes had changed by 1902 when George F. Baer declared "anthracite mining is business and not a religious, sentimental or academic proposition." Those tough-minded words might have won public approval at an earlier time, but many believed that Baer, spokesman for mine owners in Pennsylvania, was merely pig-headed. His words were in response to a request by John Mitchell of the United Mine Workers for arbitration of a labor dispute. There was an unusual amount of support for the coal miners' position. Exposes had increased popular awareness of miserable working conditions, and the union's demands seemed reasonable: a nine-hour day, recognition of the union, a ten to twenty percent increase in wages, and a fair weighing of the coal mined. Mitchell repeatedly reiterated the miners' willingness to accept arbitration, both before and after fifty thousand miners walked out of the pits in May 1902.

Skillfully led, the coal miners stood firm month after month. By September coal was running short and prices were rising. With winter approaching, empty coal bins began multiplying, even in schools and hospitals. Baer remained stubborn. "The rights and interests of the laboring man," he declared, "will be protected and cared for—not by the labor, but by the Christian men to whom God in his infinite wisdom has given the control of property interests in this country." This proclamation of the Gospel of Wealth fell on deaf ears. Newspaper after newspaper expressed disgust with the mine owners, and some tentatively suggested government ownership of the mines.

On October 3, President Theodore Roosevelt, in a wheelchair as a result of an accident, presided over a conference in the White House. Attending were Mitchell, Baer, Attorney General Philander C. Knox, and other labor leaders and mine operators. Baer was not in a mood to be cooperative. "We object to being called here to meet a criminal," he told a reporter, "even by the President of the United States." Refusing to speak directly to Mitchell, Baer urged Roosevelt to prosecute UMW leaders under the Sherman Act and to use federal troops to break the strike—as Cleveland had done in the 1894 Pullman strike. While Mitchell "behaved like a gentleman" according to Roosevelt, Baer was obstinate, concluding one diatribe against unions by calling "free government . . . a contemptible failure if it can only protect the lives and property and secure comfort of the people by compromise with violators of law and instigators of violence and crime."

Roosevelt became so irritated with Baer that he declared, "If it wasn't for the high office I hold I would have taken him by the seat of the breeches and the nape of the neck and chucked him out of that window." When the owners returned to Pennsylvania, they took actions which indicated they might use force to break the strike. Roosevelt's response was to begin preparations to send ten thousand federal troops to take over and operate the mines. This action jolted opponents of state socialism who induced banker J. P. Morgan to get involved. Serving as a broker, Morgan was able to patch together a compromise under which the miners returned to work and Roosevelt appointed a commission to arbitrate.

The commission and its findings illustrate a number of aspects of the turn-of-the-century reforms labeled "Progressivism." Originally, the commission was to consist of an army engineer, a mining engineer, a businessman "familiar with the coal industry," a federal judge, and an "eminent sociologist"—reflecting a progressive tendency to call upon "experts" to conduct public affairs. Its composition was also decidedly pro-business, and even the addition of two other members and the appointment of a labor leader as the "eminent sociologist" did not redress this imbalance. As a result its findings were essentially conservative: a ten percent wage increase and reduction of working hours to eight a day for a handful of miners and to nine for most. The union did not receive recognition, and the traditional manner of weighing coal was continued. The commission also suggested a ten percent increase in the price of coal. Business influence on other progressive responses to social problems generally produced similar moderate solutions that frequently brought industrialists as many benefits as losses.

Nevertheless, Roosevelt's actions did add some new rules to the game. For the first time a president did not give knee-jerk support to business. Government became not merely a champion of the status quo but also an arbiter

President Roosevelt, surrounded here by coal miners after the 1902 strike, set a new precedent by threatening the use of force against management rather than labor.

of change. The retreat from laissez-faire was propelled by demands of the middle class and workers. By 1902 many middle-class citizens had rejected the heavy-handed tactics of management, which often ended in chaos and conflict. They sought a more orderly, stable, and just society through government intervention. Workers also began to flex their political muscles, electing sympathetic mayors in a number of cities. Like the coal miners, Americans of all classes were learning the limits of individualism and joining together in organizations to accomplish their goals. National leaders such as Roosevelt began to recognize the need for change in order to preserve stable government and the capitalistic system. Roosevelt justified his actions in 1902 to save "big propertied men . . . from the dreadful punishment which their folly would have brought upon them." He stood, he declared, "between them and socialistic action." For a variety of motives, a plethora of legislation was enacted—sometimes with unintended results.

THE PROGRESSIVE IMPULSE

Americans exalted progress as a basic characteristic of their nation's distinctiveness. Technology was reshaping the human environment in dramatic ways. The pace of change was dizzying. Then in the late 1890s people seemed to stop, catch their breath, and look around at their brave, new world. Much filled them with pride, but some of what they saw seemed outmoded or disruptive. Problems, however, appeared eminently solvable. Modern minds were explaining and harnessing natural forces. Could they not also understand and control human behavior? Could they not eliminate conflict and bring harmony to competing interests through some simple adjustments in the system? Americans increasingly answered "Yes" and called themselves "Progressives." Many agreed with Thomas Edison's observation, "We've stumbled along for awhile, trying to run a new civilization in old ways, but we've got to start to make this world over."

America in 1901

The twentieth century opened with a rerun of the 1896 election between William Jennings Bryan and William McKinley. Although the outcome was the same, much was different. "I have never known a Presidential campaign so quiet," Senator Henry Cabot Lodge noted. By 1900 the crises of the 1890s had largely passed. Prosperity had returned and was shared by many. The nation also reveled in its new-found international power following the Spanish-American War. The social fabric seemed to be on the mend, but memories of the depression still haunted Americans, and society's blemishes appeared more and more intolerable to many.

As the nation reached adulthood a number of ugly moles and warts had indeed erupted. Maldistribution of wealth and income persisted. One percent of American families possessed nearly seven-eighths of its wealth. Four-fifths of

Breaker boys employed by the mines worked in dirty, dismal, and dangerous surroundings that robbed them of their childhood.

Americans lived on a subsistence level while a handful lived in incredible opulence. In 1900, Andrew Carnegie earned about $23 million; the average working man earned $500. The wealth of a few was increased by the exploitation of women and children. One out of five women worked for food rather than fulfillment, earning wages as low as $6 a week. The sacrifice of the country's young to the god of economic growth was alarming. One reporter undertook to do a child's job in the mines for one day and wrote, "I tried to pick out the pieces of slate from the hurrying stream of coal, often missing them; my hands were bruised and cut within a few minutes; I was covered from head to foot with coal dust, and for many hours afterwards I was expectorating some of the small particles of anthracite I had swallowed."

Working conditions were equally horrifying in other industries, and for many Americans housing conditions were as bad or worse. One investigator described a Chicago neighborhood, remarking on the "filthy and rotten tenements, the dingy courts and tumble down sheds, the foul stables and dilapidated outhouses, the broken sewer pipes, the piles of garbage fairly alive with diseased odors." At the same time the Vanderbilts summered in a "cottage" of seventy rooms, and wealthy men partied in shirts with diamond buttons worth thousands of dollars.

The middle class enjoyed neither extreme. Its members did have their economic grievances, however. Prosperity increased the cost of living by thirty-five percent in less than a decade, while many middle-class incomes remained fairly stable. Such people were not poor, but they believed they were not getting a fair share of the prosperity. Many came to blame the monopolies and watched with alarm as trusts proved to be immune to the Sherman Act and proliferated rapidly. Between 1898 and 1904 nearly three-fourths of trusts and seven-eighths of their capital came into being. Decreasing competition seemed to threaten America's status as the land of opportunity.

People came to believe that they had to find political solutions to the nation's problems. To achieve that goal they had to wrestle government from the hands of a few and return it to the "people." The great democratic experiment seemed to have run afoul. Wealthy industrialists bought state and federal legislators; urban political machines paid for votes with money from bribes; southern elections had become both bloody and corrupt.

Most problems were not new in 1901; neither were the proposed solutions. What came to be called Progressivism was rooted in the Gilded Age. Whereas reform had been a sideshow earlier, it now became a national preoccupation. Progressivism was more broadly based and enjoyed larger appeal than any previous reform movement. The entire nation had experienced war or depression, never reform. One reason it did so was the diversity and pervasiveness of the voices calling for change.

Public distaste for trusts flourished during the Progressive era—fueled by journalistic attacks on them and cartoons such as these.

Voices for Change

Social Darwinism, laissez-faire economics, and the Gospel of Wealth never enjoyed total acceptance. Throughout the Gilded Age challenges and alternative visions had chipped away at their bases of support. By 1900, Americans had done nothing less than to reinterpret their understanding of their world. Under the old, classical interpretation the universe was governed by absolute and unchangeable law. There was divine logic to all and truth was universal—the same at all times and in all places. Mankind's chore was to discover these truths, not to devise new ones. Under this vision public policy should be aligned with natural laws; to attempt to change the course of those laws through man-made law was to court disaster. Such logic justified the concentration of wealth as well as the lack of governmental regulation of business and assistance to the poor and weak.

The earlier challengers offered rather radical or simplistic alternatives. In 1879 Henry George wrote *Progress and Poverty.* As the title implies, he early recognized the unequal distribution of the fruits of economic growth. His solution was a "single tax" on what he called the "unearned increment" of land values. He wanted to tax those who benefited from land speculation and rising property values without producing anything. In essence he attacked the premise of capitalism that one could

use money to make more money without providing other goods or services. In *Looking Backward* (1888) Edward Bellamy provided a glimpse of a utopian society based upon a state-controlled economy propelled by cooperation rather than competition. The writings of such people profoundly influenced the Populists, the Socialists, and many who called themselves progressive.

Although critics dismissed the likes of George as crackpots, some respectable voices arose from the arts and literature, academia, the legal world, organized religion, and journalism. Realist writers described the world as it was, not as it should be. Instead of romantic heroes battling for abstract ideals, their characters were ordinary people dealing with concrete problems. The naturalists portrayed the powerlessness of the individual against the uncaring forces of urbanization and industrialization. Artists of the "ash can" school painted urban scenes teeming with problems as well as life. Thus art and literature became mirrors of social concerns (see Chapter 20).

A revolution was also taking place in the academic world. Two of the most important changes were the democratization of higher education and the revolt against formalism. From 1870 to 1910 the number of colleges and universities nearly doubled, and their enrollment grew from 52,000 in 1870 to 600,000 in 1920. Higher education became less elitist, white, religious, and male as women came to account for 47.3 percent of students in 1920 and black enrollment grew to over 20,000. Their professors became increasingly middle class as well. Such students and teachers had less interest in supporting the status quo.

Also undermining the status quo was the revolt against formalism. Previous academics had sought to explain the world by formulating abstract, universal theories. The new scholars, especially in the emerging social sciences, turned this approach on its head. They began instead by collecting concrete data. In field after field that data did not support the so-called natural laws propounded by their predecessors. Knowledge, philosopher and educator John Dewey proclaimed, was "no longer an immobile solid; it has been liquefied."

Theories had proscribed limits to human action; facts became weapons for change. Classical economists asserted that self-interested economic decisions by individuals in a freely competitive economy provided natural regulation of markets through the laws of supply and demand. The new economists, calling themselves "institutional economists," conducted field research to learn how the economy actually worked. Their findings challenged the laissez-faire doctrines of the classicists on two levels: that free competition existed and that human decisions were based on purely economic motivations. To continue policies based on competition was absurd in an economy dominated by monopolies. In *Theory of the Leisure Class* (1899) and *The Instinct of Workmanship* (1914) economist Thorstein Veblen demonstrated the power of noneconomic motives. For example, vanity prompted the rich to indulge in "conspicuous consumption" well beyond their economic needs. For many economists "natural laws" were, in the words of Richard T. Ely, "used as a tool in the hands of the greedy."

A group of sociologists called themselves "Reform Darwinists" and rejected Spenser's Social Darwinism as another tool of exploitation. They accepted evolutionary principles and the influence of environment but denied that people were merely pawns manipulated by natural forces. Human intelligence was an active

These women in a physics class illustrate the growing presence of women in college during the Progressive era.

factor that could control and change the environment, especially when people worked together. A leading Reform Darwinist, Frank Lester Ward, thus proclaimed, "The individual has reigned long enough. The day has come for society to take its affairs into its own hands and shape its own destinies."

Ward's call for "rational planning" and "social engineering" in his *Dynamic Sociology* (1883) was echoed by Frederick W. Taylor, an efficiency advisor to management. His time and motion studies lowered production costs, and he asserted, "The fundamental principles of scientific management are applicable to all kinds of human activities." The goal of most such social scientists was a more orderly society, as was expressed by Walter Lippmann, who called upon society "to introduce plan where there has been clash, and purpose into the jungles of disordered growth."

Legal scholars joined the assault on formalism in both books and court decisions. During the Gilded Age, courts had read laissez-faire principles into the Constitution. Decisions striking down regulatory and reform legislation invoked abstract principles such as the sanctity of property rights and contracts. In theory all such rights were equal before the law; reality was a different matter. For example, in *Lochner* v. *New York* (1905) the Supreme Court struck down a New York law limiting bakers' working hours. The law, the court ruled, violated the bakers' rights to bargain freely and to make contracts. Most workers, however, had no real power to bargain and maintaining that myth merely increased management's already overwhelming advantage.

A new breed of jurist, many of whom were disciples of Dean Roscoe Pound of the Harvard Law School, challenged laissez-faire justice. Pound advocated "sociological jurisprudence," calling for "the adjustment of principles and doctrines to the human conditions they are to govern rather than assumed first principles." Supreme Court Justice Oliver Wendell Holmes, Jr., agreed. He rejected the idea that laws had ever been the logical result of pure, universal principles. "The life of the law has not been logic;" he wrote, "it has been experience." Laws had been and should be based on "the felt necessities of the time." Lawyer Louis D. Brandeis successfully argued their ideas in 1908. The Supreme Court upheld a ten-hour law for women working in Oregon laundries in *Muller* v. *Oregon*, primarily because of social research documenting the damage done to women's health by long hours.

As Americans began to reject absolute truths and universal principles, the question remained of how to determine right from wrong and good from bad. The answer came from philosopher William James with his doctrine of pragmatism. Ideas, he argued, were to be judged by the results. An idea that produced a socially desirable end was right and good. Philosophical thought was useless unless it was directed at solving problems. Pragmatism was a distinctly American philosophy and found many adherents. One of them, John Dewey, applied its principles to education. Earlier schools that stressed rote memorization of a static body of facts, he believed, were unable to meet the needs of individuals in a dynamic, changing environment. Instead, education should be based on experience and directed toward personal growth. In schools modeled after Dewey's Laboratory School at the University of Chicago, students engaged in activities which taught problem solving by doing rather than reading.

The literary and intellectual currents of the era helped to set the stage for reform by combining optimism, idealism, and a tough-minded practicality. Yet the educated elite were probably reflecting rather than shaping public opinion. Priests and preachers influenced far more people than professors. The impact of organized religion on Progressivism was profound. It was no coincidence that Teddy Roosevelt's supporters marched around the hall singing "Onward Christian Soldiers" at their 1912 convention.

The confrontation between the church and the city produced the Social Gospel movement. The impact of environment was brought home to urban clergymen who saw bodies ravaged before souls could be saved. As a young Baptist minister in the dismal New York neighborhood "Hell's Kitchen," Walter Raushenbusch described the poor coming to his church for aid.

"They wore down our threshold, and they wore away our hearts . . . one could hear human virtue cracking and crunching all around."

For Raushenbusch and many others like him there was no conflict between science and religion. "Translate the evolutionary theses into religious faith," he declared, "and you have the doctrine of the Kingdom of God." Following the lead of William Graham Taylor at the Chicago Theological Seminary, theology schools added courses in Christian sociology to teach "the application of our common Christianity to . . . social conditions." The Social Gospelers used the tools of scientific inquiry to root out and solve human problems in order to usher in the "Kingdom of God on Earth." Many settlement house workers, such as Jane Addams, sought to put their faith into action for "the joy of finding the Christ that lieth in man, but which no man can unfold save in fellowship." The Social Gospelers advocated a kind of sacred humanism.

Jane Addams

Progressivism was dominated by, but not limited to, Protestantism. The 1893 encyclical, *Rerum Novarum*, by Pope Leo XIII inspired such Catholic priests as Father John A. Ryan to declare "a small number of very rich men have been able to lay upon the masses of people a yoke little better than slavery itself" and "no practical solution of this question will ever be found without the assistance of the church." Such Catholics as Alfred E. Smith and Robert F. Wagner became prominent progressive politicians. Others such as Jewish lawyer Louis Brandeis illustrated that the reform sentiment was not exclusively Christian either.

The Muckrakers

A final spark to ignite public interest in reform was popular journalism. The expansion of education and cities provided a mass audience for low-priced magazines. Such journals as *Collier's* and *McClure's* sold for ten cents and could only succeed if large numbers of people bought them. Their editors quickly rediscovered people's fascination with evil and launched series of exposés. Investigative reporters peeked beneath all sorts of rocks and brought to light corruption in almost every

McClure's Magazine

facet of society. Their vivid, indignant accounts sold magazines but appalled some of the elite such as Teddy Roosevelt, who compared the writers to the character in John Bunyan's *The Pilgrim's Progress* who was too engrossed in raking muck to look up and accept a celestial crown. Thus these chroniclers came to be called muckrakers.

Most of the exposés came out serially in magazines, others were books, but all titillated the public. John Spargo wrote on child labor, "Statistics cannot express the withering of child lips in the poisoned air of factories; the tired strained look of child eyes that never dance to the glad music of souls tuned to Nature's symphonies." The United States Senate, according to David Graham Phillips, "betrayed the public to that cruel and vicious spirit of Mammon [money] which has come to dominate the nation." Further, he argued, "The United States Senate is a larger factor than your labor and intelligence, you average American, in determining your income. And the Senate is a traitor to you!" State legislatures were little better, as was shown by William Allen White's investigation in Missouri. "The legislature met biennially, and enacted such laws as the corporations paid for and such as were necessary to fool the people." In *Following the Color Line*, Ray Stannard Baker exhorted, "Whether we like it or not the whole nation . . . is tied by unbreakable bonds to its Negroes, its Chinamen, its slum-dwellers, its thieves, its murderers, its prostitutes. We cannot elevate ourselves by driving them back either with hatred, violence or neglect; but only by bringing them forward: by service." Ida Tarbell called Standard Oil "one of the most gigantic and dangerous conspiracies ever attempted." In similar, stirring words Lincoln Steffens denounced urban politics in *The Shame of the Cities*, and Upton Sinclair described the horrifying conditions in the meat-packing industry in *The Jungle*.

One might believe these men and women were cynical mudslingers, but that was not how they saw themselves. "We muckraked," said Baker, "not because we hated our world, but because we loved it. We were not hopeless, we were not cynical, we were not bitter." The public sometimes missed the intended message. Sinclair's goal in *The Jungle* was a socialist critique of the exploitation of labor in the meat-packing industry, but as he ruefully noted, "I aimed at the nation's heart and hit it in the stomach." After a few years, muckraking tended to degenerate into sloppy research and wild, unsubstantiated charges. Yet the publishers of the over 2000 muckraking books and articles who aimed at the nation's pocketbooks, hit a number of Americans in the heart.

Ida Tarbell became one of the most influential muckrakers after the 1904 publication of her *History of the Standard Oil Company.*

PROGRESSIVES IN ACTION

Voices of change echoed a genuine transformation of popular sentiment. Americans of all classes began calling themselves "progressives" and sought to reform whichever social evil captured their attention. Most believed problems could be legislated away; their typical response to injustice or sin was "There ought to be a law." At the same time they rejected the individualism of Social Darwinism and believed progress would come through cooperation rather than competition. Thus they organized themselves by droves into groups which shared their own particular vision of human progress.

The diversity of the organizations founded reflect the breadth of reform activity. Indeed, so varied were the aims of people calling themselves progressive that to call Progressivism a movement is a mistake. There was little unity except in the idea that people could improve society. Most progressives, however, were middle-class moderates who abhorred radical solutions. Motivated by a fear and hatred of class conflict, such progressives sought to save the capitalists from their own excesses and thereby salvage the system. Their goal was an orderly and harmonious society.

The Drive to Organize

Organizing was a major activity at the turn of the century. Such professional groups as the American Medical Association and the American Historical Association began to emerge in modern form. These groups reflected the rise of a new professionalism which helped to create a body of "experts" to be tapped by progressives wanting to impose order and efficiency on social institutions. The organizations themselves also acted to bring change. The AMA was reorganized in 1901, and by 1910 its membership had increased from 8400 to over 70,000. Its major goal was to improve the standards of the profession. Government aid was obtained with the passage of laws requiring licenses to practice medicine. In 1910 a study financed by the

Carnegie Foundation recommended minimum standards for medical education. The widespread acceptance of its report closed the doors of dozens of marginal medical schools—several of which trained minority doctors. The end result of the new professionalism in most fields was to limit the number of practitioners, which did help weed out incompetents, but also increased the incomes of the remainder and often reduced minority participation. In other words, order, stability, and improved standards were achieved at the cost of decreased opportunity.

Given the religious bent of progressive thought, a number of church-related organizations also arose. One of the most important was the Federal Council of Churches of Christ in America. Founded in 1908, it was an interdenominational group which advocated safer working conditions, the abolition of child labor, shorter work weeks and higher wages, workmen's compensation, old-age pensions, and "the most equitable division of the products of industry that can ultimately be devised."

To a large extent middle-class women led in the organization of reform. Technology and domestic help lessened the burdens of running a home for these women, but a stigma remained on paid employment. Women's clubs provided an outlet for the energies and abilities of many competent and educated women. Local organizations flourished and formed the General Federation of Women's Clubs in 1890. In the next two decades reform groups mainly founded and led by women sprang up.

The majority of activist, middle-class women became involved in movements closely linked to their assigned social roles as guardians of morality and nurturers of the family. Many worked through religious groups such as the Young Women's Christian Association. Numerous others joined in a resurgence of prohibitionism. Americans had always drunk a lot of alcohol, and consumption peaked between 1911 and 1915. By the 1890s earlier movements had faded, leaving only three states with prohibition laws. After a quarter of a century of inactivity, the Women's Christian Temperance Union revived and by 1898 had 10,000 local branches. It was joined by the Anti-Saloon League (organized in 1893) and such church organizations as the Temperance Society of the Methodist Episcopal church.

Some of the prohibitionists were Protestant fundamentalists who considered the consumption of alcohol a sin; others were concerned with its social impact. Urban reformers constantly saw the consequences of alcohol abuse in domestic violence, accidents, and pauperism. Alcohol was the root of so many social problems that to ignore it was like "bailing water out of a tub with the tap turned on; letting the . . . liquor traffic run full blast while we limply stood around and picked up the wreckage." The AMA reported the physical devastation of alcoholism. Many in the Anti-Saloon League were also dismayed by the part played by drinking establishments in machine politics.

The idea of legislating morality for the good of society spilled over into the sexual sphere. A major area of concern was prostitution, and its opponents had a variety of motivations. Some stressed its role in the spread of venereal disease. Others deplored the exploitation of women and the double standard that allowed only men sexual freedom. For some it was morally wrong; to others it was just one more social evil—a product of environment rather than original sin. Many linked it with immigration as they did alcohol abuse. The crusade against the age-old problem had deep roots, but at the turn of the century it followed a typically progressive path. Muckraking journalists enraged the public with lurid accounts of "white slavery" rings that kidnapped young women and forced them into prostitution. The first step was to pressure local governments to establish commissions to study the problem. Most reports stressed the economic roots. One prostitute asked an investigator, "Do you suppose I am going back to earn five or six dollars a week in a factory, when I can earn that amount any night and often much more?"

Some people believed prostitution was merely a symptom of a larger disease, and they became "purity crusaders." Dr. Will K. Kellogg wrote "The exorbitant demands of the sexual appetites encountered among civilized people are not the result of a normal instinct, but are due to the incitements of an abnormally stimulating diet, including alcohol, the seduction of prurient literature and so-called art, and the temptations of impure associations." After a national Purity Congress in 1895, the purity crusaders lobbied not only for the prohibition of alcohol and prostitution but also for such things as censorship and the regulation of narcotics.

There were two aims of progressive social reform: control and justice. Women were deeply involved in social justice movements as well as control movements like prohibition. Middle-class women had long dominated humanitarian work, but during the 1890s their work took on a new aggressiveness. Women came to believe that aid to the poor was an inadequate response; they wanted to attack the causes of poverty. They sought to improve wages and working conditions, especially for women, and to protect children from exploitation. To this end, they started several organizations. The National Consumers League, led by former Illinois factory inspector Florence Kelly, lobbied for protective legislation for women and children as well as better working and living conditions for all. Kelly became a leading advocate of child labor laws and was joined in this cause by Alabama clergyman Edgar Gardner Murphy, who proposed the formation of the National Child Labor Committee in 1904. Like most progressives, child labor reformers gathered data and made photographs to document horrors for legislators at the local, state, and finally federal level.

A similar path was followed by many organizations that studied various urban problems and proposed solutions. The National Municipal League (1895) was a forum for improving city government. The National Housing Association (1910) sought to obtain building codes with minimum health and safety standards and proposed federally subsidized housing. The American Association for Labor Legislation and the American Association for Old-Age Security lobbied for protective legislation for labor and pension plans.

Some reformers were not content to be merely advocates for the poor and the weak; they wanted to get directly involved with such people to educate them and organize them to

Alarmed by the unhealthy child-care practices of many immigrants, visiting nurses went to immigrant homes to teach such things as the proper bathing of babies.

help themselves. Here again middle-class women played a key role. Foremost among such activities was the settlement house movement. Following the lead of Jane Addams, many young college-educated women moved into slum neighborhoods to live and work with those they sought to help. "From the first," Addams wrote, "it seemed understood that we were ready to perform the humblest neighborhood services. We were asked to wash the newborn babies, and to prepare the dead for burial, to nurse the sick, and to 'mind the children.' "

More than unselfishness motivated such women. One worker confessed that settlement houses gratified her "thirst to know how the other half lives." Some educated women wanted more freedom than marriage and part-time volunteer work seemed to offer. One appeal of settlement work was that it was not controlled by men. The result was a growing social feminism that cut across class lines. An example was the founding of the National Women's Trade Union League in 1905. Through it wealthy supporters organized women workers, joined their strikes, and trained leaders.

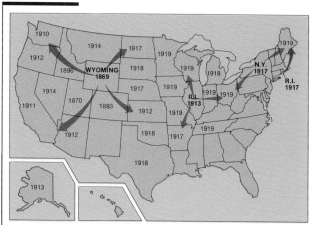

Woman Suffrage

Between 1869 and 1919, states gradually allowed women the right to vote in presidential elections as a result of the Nineteenth Amendment.

At first such activity seemed to draw attention away from the suffrage movement. Women's roles in progressive reforms, however, convinced many people that women not only deserved the right to vote but also that their political participation would be socially beneficial. Jane Addams asserted, "If women have in any sense been responsible for the gentler side of life which softens and blurs some of its harsher conditions may they not have a duty to perform in our American cities?" Arguments based on women's "special role," however, cut both ways. In articles with such titles as "Famed Biologist's Warning on the Peril in Votes to Women," writers charged that voting was so "unnatural" for women that pregnant women would miscarry and nursing mothers' milk would cease to flow. As during the fight for ratification of the Equal Rights Amendment in the 1970s, not all opponents were male. Mrs. A. J. George of the National Association Opposed to Woman Suffrage declared, "The Woman-suffrage movement is an imitation-of-man movement, and as such, merits the condemnation of every normal man and woman."

In the face of such opposition suffragists began to escalate their demands for the vote. Many became convinced that only national action could be effective. Thus the National American Woman Suffrage Association, led by Carrie Chapman Catt after 1915, began a broad-based campaign for a federal amendment. More militant women followed the young Quaker, Alice Paul, who founded the National Women's party in 1914. She accepted the tactics of British suffragists who had picketed, gone on hunger strikes, and actively confronted both politicians and police.

Another branch of the social justice movement sought to improve relations between blacks and whites. White southerners had continued to seek forms of racial control to replace slavery. Their solution became a three-legged stool: legal segregation, disfranchisement, and violence. From the beginning, blacks resisted white efforts. In city after city Afro-Americans utilized almost every tool and tactic that would prove successful in the 1960s. They marched, they lobbied legislative bodies, they petitioned, they challenged discriminatory legislation in courts, and they boycotted segregated streetcars. Under the leadership of Booker T. Washington, they also tried conciliation. Nothing stemmed the rising tide of racism.

As conditions grew worse, Washington seemed to grow even more accommodating, at least in public. Behind the scenes he supported protest activities—using code names and secret funds. Educated blacks, however, became increasingly disenchanted with his public performance. They also resented his suppression of dissent by his fellow blacks. His influence with white politicians and philanthropists as well as his control of much of the black press gave him incredible power, which he used ruthlessly on occasion. The so-called anti-Bookerite radicals found their spokesperson in W. E. B. Du Bois. Unlike Washington, who had been born into slavery and educated at an industrial school, Du Bois was born to free parents in Massachusetts and became the first black to receive a doctorate from Harvard.

Gifted with staggering intellectual brilliance, Du Bois expressed the frustrations and dreams of his fellow blacks in *The Souls of Black Folks* (1903). Of being black in America, he wrote, "one ever feels his twoness—an American, a Negro, two souls, two thoughts, two

Women employed a variety of tactics in their fight for the vote. Here Dr. Anne Shaw and Carrie Chapman Catt led 20,000 marchers down 5th Avenue in New York City.

unreconciled strivings, two warring ideals in one dark body." In that book he also penned a polite but devastating critical analysis of Washington's leadership. Among other things, he objected to Washington's failure to recognize the importance of the vote, his emphasis on industrial education at the expense of higher education, his reluctance to criticize as well as praise white actions, and his willingness to give up previously won rights.

Relations between the two men deteriorated steadily after 1903, even though only immediate methods and not ultimate goals separated them. Both wanted the full acceptance of blacks as first-class citizens. To Washington the best route was self-help and educating the masses. To these ends, he made Tuskegee Institute into an impressive institution staffed entirely by blacks. Du Bois, on the other hand, was more integrationist and believed the key to black advancement was in cultivating what he called the "Talented Tenth." To him more of the

limited education funds should go to train the most able ten percent of blacks for leadership—through liberal arts and professional schooling.

By 1905 their differences became so great that Du Bois joined William Monroe Trotter in forming the Niagara Movement. It was an organization devoted to two main objectives: opposition to Washington's leadership and demands for "full manhood rights." Only about fifty educated blacks—mainly Northerners—joined, and the movement struggled to exist in the face of unrelenting sabotage by Washington. It played an important role, however, in convincing northern white progressives that an alternative to Washington was desirable. Then whites in Springfield, Illinois, went on a rampage against blacks. Concerned whites joined with Du Bois to found the National Association for the Advancement of Colored People in 1909. At first the group was led and dominated by whites; Du Bois was the only black to hold a responsible position, as editor of its journal *The*

W. E. B. Du Bois, shown here in the editorial offices of the *Crisis* at the New York headquarters of the NAACP, was at first the only black to hold a significant office in the organization.

Crisis. The organization eventually became more black over time, but the focus of its activities remained essentially the same: education and propaganda, court challenges to discrimination, and lobbying for such legislation as a federal antilynching law.

Immigration policy became another source of organization. The American Protective Association (1887) sought to control and limit the access of the "teeming masses yearning to be free." Members lobbied for literacy tests and quotas. One described a boatload of immigrants, saying "in every face there was something wrong—lips thick, mouth coarse, upper lip too long, cheek bones too high, chin poorly formed, the bridge of the nose hollowed, the base of the nose tilted, or else the whole face prognathous." While many Americans recoiled from the nation's pluralistic nature, others welcomed it. One wrote, "our dream of the United States ought not to be a dream of monotony" but instead an "orchestration of mankind." Thus some progressives formed the North American League for Immigrants to "protect the newcomers from unscrupulous bankers, steamship captains and fellow countrymen."

Even if most were middle class, progressives obviously came from all classes, and within classes there was a diversity of responses to the modernizing society and economy. Many businessmen organized to fight regulatory and labor legislation in such groups as the National Association of Manufacturers and the American Anti-Boycott Association. Others, however, joined moderate reformist groups such as the Reform Municipal Voters League and the Chamber of Commerce. Even more liberal was the National Civic Federation founded in 1901. With wealthy Republican politician Mark Hanna as president and labor leader Samuel Gompers as vice-president, the group accepted unionization and sought to bring together employers, employees, and the general public to discuss industrial problems.

The drive to organize pervaded all society, creating such diverse groups as the Boy Scouts of America (1910), the Rotary Club (1915), the National Collegiate Athletic Association (1906), the National Birth Control League (1915), and even the Aero Club of America (1905) to popularize "ballooning as a sport, especially among the more wealthy class." Americans came to believe in cooperative efforts to reach goals. In unprecedented numbers they also began to look to government for answers—starting at the city level and moving up to Washington.

Urban Beginnings

Progressivism was largely a response to modernization so it first confronted the most visible problems—most of which were found in the cities. Incredibly rapid rises in urban populations outpaced the ability of "small-town" governments to meet the challenges. Political machines provided needed services but came under attack in the 1890s as inefficient and corrupt. Progressivism began to emerge in cities even while most attention was being focused on the rural-based Populists. Middle- and upper-class reformers demanded governments operated "on a strict business basis" and run "not by partisans, either Republican nor Democratic, but by men who are skilled in business management and social service."

Urban reformers' victories included the secret ballot and voter registration in some cities. Then in 1900 a model for efficient, nonpartisan city government emerged from the chaos created by a devastating hurricane that killed over 6000 people in Galveston, Texas. Local government broke down and the state legislature appointed a five-man commission to run the city. The idea spread to over 400 cities by World War I. A refinement was added in 1913 when in the wake of a disastrous flood, Dayton, Ohio, hired a city manager to do the day-to-day work of running the city.

The cost of efficiency was decreased democracy. Indeed, some urban reformers were openly antidemocratic. One wrote in 1901, "Ignorance should be excluded from control. City business should be carried on by trained experts selected on some other principle than popular suffrage." The ward system under which aldermen were elected by district was seen as a problem because, as a Chicago businessman noted in 1911, "Men of successful experience and ability large enough to do justice to public affairs will seldom live and bring up families in the poorer wards." Such reformers sought naively to take "politics" out of government, but by "politics" they often meant the voice of people not like them. Nevertheless, these goals contradicted broader support for democracy, and by 1914 most city commissioners were required to run for election—often, however, in at-large elections rather than by districts.

Middle-class progressives sometimes found their will thwarted by lower-class voters. Breaking up urban machines often destroyed the informal welfare networks that met the needs of the poor. When that happened, the poor rejected the new efficiency. In 1901, the Tammany Hall machine recaptured New York with the campaign slogan "To hell with reform." Poor immigrants did not accept that their ignorance and "foreign ways" were at the root of urban problems. "It is not so much the under crust," one declared, "as the upper crust that endangers the interests of the people."

In a number of cities mayors were elected who sympathized with working-class desires. Tom L. Johnson, elected mayor of Cleveland in 1901, rejected Americanization efforts to impose middle-class morality on the poor. "I am not trying to enforce Christianity," he proclaimed, "only make it possible." To this end he expanded social services and brought about the public ownership of the waterworks, gas and electric utilities, and public transportation—reducing their costs to the poor. After his election 1899, Mayor Samuel "Golden Rule" Jones sought to establish the "Cooperative Commonwealth, the Kingdom of Heaven on Earth," in Toledo, Ohio. Until his death in 1904, he worked to provide free kindergartens, free playgrounds, free golf courses, and free concerts. He also reformed the police department, substituting light canes for the heavy clubs carried by patrolmen and prohibiting the jailing of people without charges. He made some powerful enemies and once declared, "Everyone is against me but the people." Most urban liberals depended on working-class voters.

The move toward public ownership of utilities was avidly supported by the Socialists, who showed growing strength on the local level. In 1910 a Socialist was elected mayor of Milwaukee, and in the next year 70 others were elected in towns and cities across the nation. By 1912 about 1000 held offices in 33 states and 160 cities. Their rising power, however, helped trigger a backlash by middle-class voters who favored regulatory commissions to public ownership.

THE WHITE PLAGUE

During the Progressive Era, the rise of scientific ways of thinking cleared the way for reformers and health officers to launch a campaign against the disease most identified with industrialization—tuberculosis (TB). During the nineteenth century, TB was aptly called "the Captain of All the Men of Death." It killed more people and caused more sickness than any other disease in the western world. Its very name conjures up images of fetid sweatshops and sulphurous mills where men, women, and children had their health broken by long working hours and physical exhaustion; of urban slums and overcrowded tenements rotten with disease; and, finally, of emaciated, ghost-like wretches, feverish with infection, gasping for breath, coughing up mouthfuls of blood, and staring hollow-eyed into space waiting for death.

In a sense, TB mirrors the complexity of the Industrial Revolution, for just as the transformation of the economy was multifaceted, TB is not one but many diseases. TB is merely the generic name for a host of infections caused by *tubercle bacilli*, isolated in 1882 by Robert Koch, the famous German scientist. The most common (and most feared) is pulmonary tuberculosis, a chronic, debilitating disease of the lungs; it can kill its victims in a few months but usually requires several years to complete the task. Other common forms of the disease include meningeal TB, which produces an inflammation of the membranes surrounding the brain; TB of the spine, which causes a hunchback deformity of the spine; lupus, TB of the skin; and miliary TB, a generalized infection that occurs when the *tubercle bacilli* are distributed by the bloodstream throughout the body, producing small nodules on most organs.

Because the term "tuberculosis" did not appear in print until around 1840, most Americans knew the disease as consumption, which seemed the perfect metaphor for describing how the victims of the disease gradually wasted away from debilitating fever, weight loss, night sweats, chronic cough, and copious sputum, decorated toward the end with the bright red blood spots that denoted advanced pulmonary tuberculosis.

In less polite society, "consumptives" were called "lungers," a term of derision. Throughout the nineteenth century, many people associated TB with poverty and attached a social stigma to the disease. Others believed that TB was caused by some hereditary defect. For them, the perplexing problem was why the disease hit some families harder than others. In Ralph Waldo Emerson's family, for example, he and three of his brothers suffered from the disease, while his fellow transcendentalist, Henry David Thoreau, lost a father, a sister, and a grandfather to TB before dying from the disease himself.

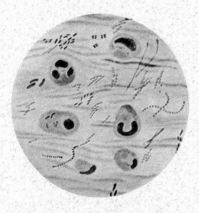

Paradoxically, despite its dreadful symptoms and terrifying ability to wipe out entire families, TB was romanticized on both sides of the Atlantic. For many writers, it became a metaphor for comparing decay in nature to disease in man. Thus, Henry Thoreau, upon seeing the first splashes of red in the green maple leaves of autumn, could write in 1852 in his *Journal Intime:* "Decay and disease are often beautiful, like . . . the hectic glow of consumption."

In fact, the Age of Romanticism's much heralded "doom and gloom" may have derived at least in part from the sadness and melancholy caused by the deaths of loved ones from TB—especially the death of young adults for whom the disease had a special affinity. John Keats, the quintessential romantic poet, succumbed to TB at 26; Emily Brontë, author of the powerful *Wuthering Heights,* was cut down tragically at 30. The novels of the day, Charles Dickens's *David Copperfield,* for one, are positively littered with the corpses of people killed in the bloom of youth by the "White Plague."

The disease also broke its share of hearts in the theater and at the opera. Alexander Dumas lamented the death from TB of a beautiful heroine in *La Dame aux Camelias,* which in its English translation became the play, *Camille, or the Fate of a Coquette,* later adapted by Verdi for the opera as *La Traviata.* An identical fate befell the heroine in the play, *La Boheme,* which inspired Puccini's opera of the same name.

Under the spell of this heart-wrenching romanticism, writers, poets, and artists created a new and profoundly twisted ideal of feminine beauty: the dying angel, smitten by consumption, whose physical appeal was somehow enhanced by her malady. One gravely ill woman confided to her diary, "I cough continually! But for a wonder, far from making me look ugly, this gives me an air of languor that is very becoming." As depicted by writers, the dying female consumptive was, to her fingertips, an exquisitely fragile creature, the very embodiment of both the romantic and the Victorian ideal of frail feminine beauty. Her languid pallor was rendered even more pale by the generous application of whitening powders; and her slender body, with its swan-like neck and elongated limbs, was adorned in thin, sheer white clothing of cotton or linen, giving her appearance an ethereal quality, as a spirit not quite of this earth.

Numerous artists struggled to capture this image on canvas, including Gabriel Rossetti of the Pre-Raphaelite school, who idealized tall, slender women "with cadaverous bodies and sensual mouths." Reducing this image to a word portrait, Henry James described Janet Burden, one of the leading Pre-Raphaelite models, as "strange, pale, livid, gaunt, silent, and yet in a manner graceful and picturesque." To another observer the same woman looked "as if she had walked out of an Egyptian tomb at Luxor."

As the nineteenth century grew to a close, however, the romantic view of life gradually lost its hold on the public's imagination. Instead of celebrating TB, writers, joined by health reformers, saw TB through the lens of realism. They linked the disease to poverty, unsafe working conditions, overcrowded housing, poor diet, and the failure of government to safeguard the public's health. Rather than glorifying consumptives, this change in attitude depicted them as the victims of a cruel, punishing illness. TB was no longer something to spark the artistic imagination; it was now a microbial insult to mankind and an indictment against the society that tolerated it.

Urban Progressivism was obviously not a coherent, unified movement. Different groups at different times succeeded in different cities. Social services were cut to lower business taxes in some cities and expanded in others. In most cities the evils of overcrowded, unhealthy tenements were attacked with such things as building codes, with varying degrees of success. By the turn of the century, however, more and more people began to look to the states to solve problems.

Reform Reaches the State Level

Regardless of their objectives, many urban reformers eventually dabbled in state politics. The city had little power and the federal government seemed too remote. Thus the states became major battlegrounds for reform. The form and leadership of state Progressivism was as diverse and complex as urban Progressivism. In the South most progressives worked through the Democratic party; in the Midwest and on the Pacific Coast progressives captured the Republican party. In the industrial Northeast progressives emerged in both major parties, but the Democrats were the more successful. In some cases progressive governors, such as Al Smith of New York, were the products of urban machines that embraced reform to hold onto their electorates. Others, such as Robert LaFollette of Wisconsin, were Republican regulars who bypassed party leaders to ride reform to power. In the South reform governors were elected by startlingly diverse constituencies. In Mississippi small town lawyer and editor James K. Vardaman was elected by the "redneck" vote of poor farmers. In Georgia the urban middle class were the main supporters of Hoke Smith, publisher of the *Atlanta Journal.*

State progressives pursued four major goals: establishing "direct democracy"; protecting the public by regulating the economy; increasing state services; and social control. Reformers passed many laws but the impact of legislation was not always what they expected. One progressive creed was dramatically stated by William Allen White: "The voice of the people is indeed the will of God." By World War I most states had adopted political procedures designed to give the people a more direct say in running the government. Initiative allowed voters to propose legislative changes, usually by petition; referendum gave the public a mechanism to vote directly on controversial legislation; recall provided a way to remove elected officials. Many states also established direct primaries. Other states adopted measures to cleanse electoral procedures: secret ballots, voter registration, and corrupt practices legislation. The drive for direct democracy culminated in the Seventeenth Amendment (1913) which substituted popular election of senators for election by state legislatures.

Victories of women suffragists at the state level also expanded democracy. After the 1890s their efforts seemed to stall, and no new state gave women the vote until Washington did so in 1910. California acted the next year, and four other western states followed suit by 1916. That year Jeannette Rankin was elected to Congress from Montana. These victories encouraged the efforts to obtain a constitutional amendment.

Born on a Montana ranch in 1880 and graduated from the University of Montana in 1902, Jeannette Rankin was elected to Congress in 1916.

Progressive actions to protect the public and regulate the economy took many forms. In the West, especially, the emphasis was on regulating railroads and utilities, reflecting the Populist heritage. Legislatures created commissions to regulate the rates charged by both. At the same time, taxes on corporations were increased. For example, after LaFollette's election in Wisconsin in 1900, state revenues from taxes on railroads grew from $1.9 million to $3.4 million.

In the industrialized states, workmen's compensation became a major goal. Horror stories about industrial accidents had long abounded, and muckrakers further inflamed the public. Then in 1911 a major tragedy chilled the hearts of Americans. A fire broke out at the Triangle Shirtwaist Company in New York just thirty minutes before closing time. The doors were locked to prevent the women who worked there from leaving early, and many fire escape ladders were either broken or missing. By the time the flames were doused, 147 workers, mainly women and girls, had lost their lives—47 had jumped to their deaths, littering the street with bodies. The Triangle fire was the worst example of escalating industrial accident rates. The only recourse for most maimed workers or their widowed spouses was to sue the company, which for many was not a realistic option. Some did get high settlements, however, which represented an unpredictable cost to businessmen. Thus the idea of mandatory insurance grew in popularity with support of many factory owners. Between 1910 and 1916, 32 states enacted workmen's compensation laws.

The work of the National Child Labor Committee and other organizations moved states to legislate protection for women and children. Progressives gathered evidence of the harm done to both by long working hours and unsafe, unhealthy conditions. State action was necessary, they argued, for two reasons: women and children could not protect themselves and the nation's future depended on the health of both. By 1916, thirty-two states had laws regulating the hours worked by women and children, eleven had specified minimum wages for women, and every state regulated child labor in some manner. Other protective legislation included building and sanitary codes.

Lining the street, the bodies of some of the 147 people killed in the Triangle fire served as a horrific reminder of the cost of inadequate safety measures.

A number of states also expanded social services and funding for education. Because of lobbying by settlement house workers, some twenty states by 1914 had provided mother's pensions to widows or abandoned wives with dependent children. The sums paid were meagre—ranging from $2 to $15 a month for the first child and lesser amounts for the rest. A major area of educational reform was the expansion of compulsory education to the high school level. Support often came from businessmen, who saw public education as a means of preparing individuals for an industrial society. One result of their aims was that very few public schools were modeled on John Dewey's progressive educational doctrines. Instead of promoting personal development, education in the industrialists' minds should inculcate discipline and punctuality. Hence school bells trained one for factory whistles and giving letter grades taught the value of individual initiative. Governments also made school organization more business-like with increased power given to school superintendents and principals, who were expected to be trained in management techniques.

The flip side of state social justice legislation was increased efforts at social control. Prohibitionists won many victories in the states, especially in the South. That region provided fertile soil because of the strength of Protestant fundamentalism and the so-called race problem. One southern prohibitionist argued that blacks were "a child race in the South, and if drunkenness causes three-fourths of the crime ascribed to it, whiskey must be taken out of the Negro's hands," and that it was the duty "of the stronger race to forego its own personal liberty for the protection of the weaker race." Between 1907 and 1909 Georgia, Mississippi, North Carolina, Tennessee, and Alabama adopted state prohibition, and by 1916 fourteen other states had joined them.

The move toward social control infected all regions. Between 1907 and 1917, sixteen states passed laws authorizing sterilization of various categories of allegedly unfit individuals. Social control measures were usually directed at minorities, so the South naturally offered the extreme examples, but California progressives excluded Asians almost as ruthlessly. Southern whites trumpeted segregation as a reform—with the approval of many northern progressives. Even race relations muckraker Ray Stannard Baker wrote, "As for the Jim Crow laws in the South, many of them, at least, are at present necessary to avoid clashes between the ignorant of both races." Segregation was enacted under progressive governors—a paradox only if the general progressive tendency toward social control is ignored.

In most ways southern Progressivism was for whites only. Increased school funding was common, but the bulk went to educating white children. The discrepancies between the amounts spent accelerated, making even more of a lie of the *Plessy* v. *Ferguson* (1896) formula of "separate but equal" facilities. In 1919 southern states spent an average of $12.16 per white student and $3.29 per black student. Racism remained a potent force. As governor of Mississippi from 1903 to 1907 James K. Vardaman pursued progressive reforms in such areas as convict-lease, school funding, and railroad regulation. At the same time he defended lynching, saying "We would be justified in slaughtering every Ethiop on earth to preserve unsullied the honor of one Caucasian home."

The legacy of Progressivism in the states was mixed, as were the motives of reformers.

Regardless of their goals, most came to look to the federal government for help. One reformer expressed their frustration. "When I was in the city council . . . fighting for a shorter work day, [my opponents] told me to go to the legislature; now [my fellow legislators] tell me to go to Congress for a national law. When I get there and demand it, they will tell me to go to hell."

PROGRESSIVISM MOVES TO THE NATIONAL AND INTERNATIONAL LEVEL

When McKinley was reelected in 1900, few expected a national reform leader; but for a quirk of fate they would have been right. As the 1900 Republican convention rolled around, party leaders realized they had a problem. Theodore Roosevelt had become a national hero in the wake of the Spanish-American War, but he angered party regulars by supporting regulatory legislation as governor of New York. When they decided to "bury" Roosevelt in the vice-presidency, Mark Hanna warned, "Don't you realize that there's only one life between that madman and the White House?" On September 6, 1901, anarchist Leon Czolgosz shot McKinley. Eight days later that one life was gone, and Roosevelt was president. It was not immediately apparent, however, that he would usher in reform. Many remembered that during the Pullman strike Roosevelt had suggested shooting the strikers. Most therefore did not expect the action he took in the 1902 coal strike. That year, however, became the first in a decade and a half of snowballing reform that would bring a massive amount of legislation and four constitutional amendments by 1920.

Roosevelt and New Attitudes Toward Government Power

Roosevelt became the most forceful president since Lincoln, but few men have looked or sounded less presidential. He was short, nearsighted, beaver-toothed, and talked in a high-pitched voice. A frail, asthmatic child, he seemed intent on proving his manliness. Thus his life became a robust adventure of sports, hunting, and camping. Once while president he

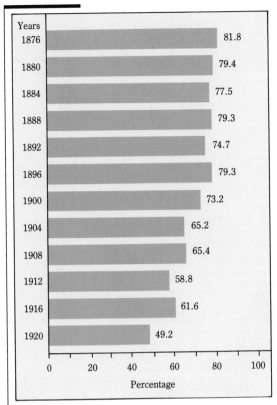

Figure 21.1
Voter Participation in Presidential Elections, 1876-1920

self as a conservative but declared, "The only true conservative is the man who resolutely sets his face toward the future." To preserve what was vital, one had to reform.

Roosevelt shared two progressive sentiments. One was that government should be efficiently run by able, competent people. The other was that industrialization had created the need for expanded governmental action. "A simple and poor society," he observed, "can exist as a democracy on the basis of sheer individualism. But a rich and complex society cannot so exist." The results of the two sentiments were that Roosevelt reorganized and revitalized the executive branch, modernized the army command structure and the consular service, and pursued the federal regulation of the economy that has characterized twentieth-century America.

Although he was later remembered more for "trust-busting" and his "Square Deal," Roosevelt considered conservation his greatest domestic accomplishment. It was the topic of his first presidential address. "We are prone to think of the resources of this country as inexhaustible; this is not so," he later warned Con-

took a foreign diplomat skinny-dipping in the Potomac. His exuberance, vitality, and wit captivated most Americans. They called him "Teddy" and named a stuffed bear after him. To understand him, an observer declared, one had to remember "the president is really only six years old." He was not a simple man, however. His hobbies included writing history books, and he displayed a keen intellect that he had honed at Harvard.

Born into an aristocratic Dutch family in New York, Roosevelt rejected a leisurely life for the rough and tumble world of politics, which his friends declared was an occupation for saloonkeepers and such. "I answered," he wrote in his autobiography, "that if this were so it merely meant that the people I knew did not belong to the governing class, and that I intended to be one of the governing class." His privileged background made him an unlikely candidate for reformer, yet he ended up making reform both fun and respectable. He saw him-

Theodore Roosevelt had a strong ally for his conservation efforts in John Muir, a western naturalist who helped establish Yosemite National Park.

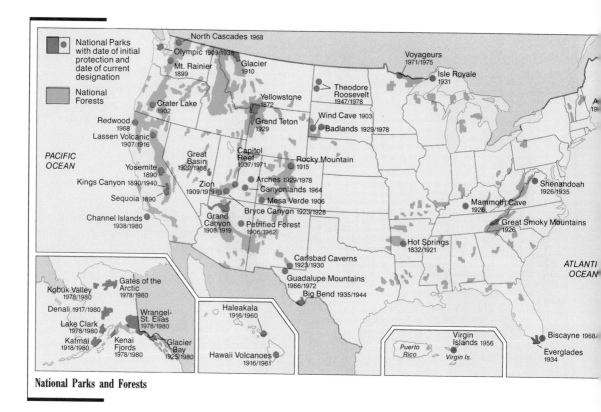

National Parks and Forests

gress. In 1902 he backed the Newlands Reclamation Act, which set aside the proceeds from public land sales for irrigation and reclamation projects. He also used presidential power to add almost 150 million acres to national forests and to preserve valuable coal and water sites for national development. With his ally, chief forester Gifford Pinchot, he sponsored a National Conservation Congress in 1908.

Some businessmen disliked Roosevelt's conservation policies, and he aggravated others by two actions in 1902. The first was his handling of the coal strike, which served notice that the government could no longer be counted upon to come automatically to the aid of management in labor disputes. The second was a suit against Northern Securities Company under the Sherman Antitrust Act. His "trust-busting" was an answer to progressive prayers. Antimonopoly was a strong component of Progressivism. Most agreed with Louis Brandeis that "If the Lord had intended things to be big, he would have made men bigger—in brains and character." Antitrust action had not been un-

dertaken on a large scale in the cities and states only because federal action seemed required.

Northern Securities was a wise choice for action. It was a highly unpopular combination of northwestern railroad systems engineered by such heavyweights as James J. Hill and J. P. Morgan. The suit infuriated Hill, who complained, "It seems hard that we should be compelled to fight for our lives against the political adventurers who have never done anything but pose and draw a salary." In 1904 the Supreme Court ordered the company's dissolution. That same year in a case against the major meat packers, the Court also reversed the E. C. Knight ruling that exempted manufacturing from federal antitrust law.

The rulings pleased Roosevelt, who rejected the Court's earlier narrow, strict interpretations of the Constitution. He believed instead that the Constitution "must be interpreted not as a straight-jacket . . . but as an instrument designed for the life and healthy growth of the Nation." In his desire to expand federal power, he was once credited with asking "What's the Constitution between friends?" Yet Roosevelt was not a true convert to trust-busting.

"This is an age of combination," he wrote, "and any effort to prevent all combination will be not only useless, but in the end vicious." At the same time he believed "of all the forms of tyranny the least attractive and the most vulgar is the tyranny of mere wealth." Thus he attacked trusts that abused their power and left alone trusts that acted responsibly. He preferred to negotiate differences, and to do so he established in 1904 a Bureau of Corporations within the Department of Commerce and Labor, which had been created the year before.

Campaigning on the slogan of a "Square Deal," Roosevelt easily defeated the Democratic candidate Alton B. Parker in the 1904 presidential election. Now elected in his own right he launched into expanding the regulatory power of the federal government. His top priority was to control more effectively the railroads by expanding the power of the Interstate Commerce Commission—over the objection of conservative Republican senators. In 1903, the Elkins Act had already been passed to eliminate rebates, but Roosevelt wanted to go further and

Without federal regulation, meat packers exploited workers and allowed rats and other contaminants to be processed with meat to make sausage.

give the ICC the power to set rates. Through shrewd political maneuvering he got this with the Hepburn Act of 1906, although he had to give up his demand for limited court review of rate decisions.

The publication of Upton Sinclair's *The Jungle* in that same year caused an uproar by consumers for regulation of the food and drug industries. In the Agriculture Department a chemist, Harvey W. Wiley, had long been analyzing food products for chemical adulteration and had tested additives on volunteers known as the "Poison Squad." The data were supplemented by an investigation of the meat-packing industry ordered by Roosevelt, which proved Sinclair's charges of filth and contamination. Congress then passed the Pure Food and Drug Act and the Meat Inspection Act on the same day in 1906.

Roosevelt's vigor extended not only to domestic politics but also to international relations. Progress and order could benefit the world as well as the nation. In addition, imperialism was not dead; the Spanish-American War

Cartoons such as this earned Roosevelt the title of "trust-buster," but he was actually only opposed to trusts that abused their power.

had left a legacy of increased power and influence. Order having been restored in Cuba and the Philippines by 1903, Roosevelt launched the United States into the role of policeman. His doctrine was to "speak softly and carry a big stick," but he really only lived up to the second half of the slogan.

Possession of the Philippines brought with it concern over turbulent Asian politics. Most alarming was the emergence of Japan after its unexpected victories in the Russo-Japanese War (1904–1905). Often playing the role of arbiter at home, Roosevelt shifted his arena and mediated the crisis at the Portsmouth, New Hampshire, conference in August 1905—an action that won him a Nobel Peace Prize. Japan remained a formidable rival, however, and agreements were reached to respect each other's Asian interests. In the Pacific, Roosevelt's "big stick" was displayed by conspicuous stops there during a 1907 tour of America's "Great White Fleet."

Within the Western Hemisphere Roosevelt was even less reluctant to threaten or use force. In 1906 he responded to Cuban demonstrations against the Platt Amendment and insurrection by sending in marines, who stayed until 1909. "I am doing my best," he declared, "to persuade the Cubans that if only they will be good they will be happy. I am seeking the very minimum of interference necessary to make them good." The marines could be very persuasive.

Progress and strategic considerations also demanded that a canal in Central America link the Atlantic and Pacific oceans. Roosevelt was determined to make it happen. There were two possible routes: one through Nicaragua and one across the Panamanian isthmus, which belonged to Colombia. A start had been made in Panama by a French company, which ran out of funds and was reorganized as the New Panama Canal Company. The new company's major asset was its concession from Colombia that extended to 1904.

Opened to traffic on August 15, 1914, the Panama Canal's construction was a monumental engineering accomplishment. It was 40.3 miles long and cost more than $365 million to build.

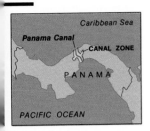

Panama Canal

Three commissions appointed to determine the route recommended Nicaragua, primarily because the New Panama Canal Company demanded $190 million for its rights, property, and previous work. Its stockholders, mainly Americans, were frantic to convince Congress to choose the Panamanian route. They dropped their demand to $40 million, contributed profusely to campaign funds, and hired a full-time lobbyist—Philippe Bunau-Varilla, the French chief engineer of the original company. In June 1902, Congress authorized efforts to secure the rights to a Panamanian canal.

The Hay-Herran Treaty provided the United States with rights to a six-mile-wide zone in return for a $10 million payment to Colombia and an annual rental fee of $250,000 to begin nine years after the ratification of the treaty. As in America, ratification required the consent of the Colombian senate, which in August 1903 rejected the treaty unanimously—probably to delay it until 1904 when the New Panama Canal Company's concession expired and Colombia might receive some of the $40 million earmarked for the company.

Roosevelt was furious. "The blackmailers of Bogota," he roared, should not be allowed "permanently to bar one of the future highways of civilization." He drafted a message to Congress proposing to take the canal zone by force but never delivered it. Another solution was found. Bunau-Varilla engineered a revolution by Panamanians—providing them with a national constitution, flag, and anthem as well as assurances that the United States would not let their revolt fail. He was right. Most Colombian troops were prevented from even getting to the so-called revolution by the U.S.S. *Nashville*. Three days after its start, Roosevelt recognized the independence of the Republic of Panama. The American secretary of state and the French citizen Bunau-Varilla, who had demanded to be made ambassador to the United States, then quickly drafted the Hay-Bunau-Varilla Treaty with essentially the same terms as the Hay-

Herran Treaty—only now the payment went to the rebels, not Colombia.

People all over the world were enraged by American actions. At first Roosevelt denied any part in the revolution, but he eventually admitted, "I took the Canal Zone and let Congress debate; and while the debate goes on the Canal does also." In 1914 the canal was completed—a monument to both progress and Yankee imperialism.

It was a big investment, one that needed protection. Foreign military vessels could not be allowed to threaten it. At the same time, however, Latin American countries sometimes fell behind in debt payments to such European powers as Britain and Germany. As a result those two nations blockaded Venezuela in 1902–1903. In 1904, Roosevelt announced that the United States would thenceforth assume responsibility to see that the nations of the Caribbean behaved themselves and paid their debts. Thus European intervention would not be necessary. Known as the Roosevelt Corollary to the Monroe Doctrine, this policy justified United States intervention in such places as the Dominican Republic, Nicaragua, and Haiti. Roosevelt's "big stick" diplomacy established America as the "police of the Western Hemisphere"— a role that would last long into the twentieth century.

By 1908 Roosevelt had left his indelible mark on the nation and decided not to run for reelection. He cast his support to William Howard Taft, who easily defeated William Jennings Bryan, the Democratic nominee and loser for the third time. Roosevelt then retired and went to hunt lions in Africa—a move that led J. P. Morgan to toast "Health to the Lions."

Taft and Quiet Progressivism

William Howard Taft brought to the presidency a distinguished record of public service. An Ohio lawyer, he had served as a federal judge, the first civil governor of the Philippines, and secretary of war. He, however, did not look presidential; he weighed over 350 pounds, leading to rumors that a special bathtub was to be installed in the White House. Unlike his predecessor he was far from charismatic and indeed

At his inauguration in 1909, William Howard Taft did not realize the challenges he faced from a divided Republican party in Congress.

quite shy; legalistic and precise, he was neither a firey writer nor speaker. In short, he was incapable of rallying the public for any cause, and reformers were especially skeptical. As a judge he had been called the "injunction standard bearer" by labor leaders. When soldiers shot into the crowd at the Haymarket riot, he confided, "they have only killed six as yet. This is hardly enough to make an impression."

Indeed Taft was essentially more conservative than Roosevelt, especially in his view of governmental power. "The lesson must be learned," he argued, "that there is only a limited zone within which legislation and governments can accomplish good." Further, he declared, "We can, by passing laws which cannot be enforced, destroy that respect for laws . . . which has been the strength of people of English descent everywhere." On the other hand, his respect for the law extended to the Sherman Act. "We are going to enforce that law or die in the attempt," he promised, and far more cases were prosecuted in his administration than during the so-called trust-buster Roosevelt's tenure.

In his own quiet way Taft was as sympathetic to reform as Roosevelt. He supported the eight-hour day and favored legislation to improve mine safety. He also urged passage of the Mann-Elkins Act of 1910, which increased the rate-setting power of the ICC and extended its jurisdiction to telephone and telegraph companies. The Sixteenth and Seventeenth amendments were initiated under his presidency. Purity crusaders also won a victory in 1910 with the passage of the Mann Act, which made it illegal to transport women across state lines for "immoral purposes."

Nevertheless, Taft was not forceful enough to preside effectively over the growing divisions within the Republican party. The conservatives, led by the powerful Senator Nelson W. Aldrich, were determined to draw the line against further reform. At the same time, progressive Republicans such as Robert LaFollette and George Norris were growing rebellious. Conflict came on several fronts. The first was the tariff. In his campaign Taft had promised a lower tariff, but in the end accepted the much compromised Payne-Aldrich Tariff. While placing many nonessential items on the duty-free list, it actually raised some key duties. It disappointed reformers immensely. Listing such duty-free items as silkworm eggs, canary bird seed, hog bristle, leeches, and skeletons, the political humorist Finley Peter Dunne had his fictional bartender, Mr. Dooley, proclaim, "The new tariff puts these familyer commodyties within the reach iv all." Taft had suffered a defeat but foolishly did not admit it, calling the tariff the "best" ever passed. In reality he backed down on his pledges because he believed the president should not interfere unduly with the legislative branch. He also simply had an accommodating personality. One Republican griped, "The trouble with Taft is that if he were Pope he would think it necessary to appoint a few Protestant Cardinals."

Caught in the middle of several conflicts, Taft eventually alienated the progressive wing of his party and Teddy Roosevelt. He first supported and then abandoned party insurgents who challenged the power of conservative Speaker of the House "Uncle Joe" Cannon.

Later, when Gifford Pinchot protested a sale of public lands by Secretary of the Interior Richard A. Ballinger, Taft fired him. That action infuriated conservationists and Roosevelt, who was also irritated by Taft's antitrust prosecutions. Roosevelt believed that a case had been pursued against U.S. Steel to embarrass him. The investigation exposed a deal he made with J. P. Morgan in 1907 in return for the banker's aid in stemming a financial panic.

One area in which Taft continued Roosevelt's policy was in Latin America, at least in objectives if not in methods. Called dollar diplomacy, Taft's approach in the Caribbean was to use dollars instead of bullets to ensure stability and order. He wanted American capital to replace European capital in Latin America in order to increase United States influence there. When British bondholders wanted to collect their debts from Honduras in 1909, Taft asked American financiers to assume the debt. In 1910 he convinced New York bankers to take over the assets of the National Bank of Haiti. When needed, however, Taft also wielded a big stick. He refused to recognize a revolution in Nicaragua until the leaders agreed to accept American credits to pay off British debts and sent marines to punctuate his point.

By 1912 progressive Republicans were ready to bolt the party if Taft were renominated, and Roosevelt declared his intention to run. The fight for the nomination became bitter. Taft called Roosevelt's supporters "political emotionalists or neurotics." Roosevelt labeled Taft's people as "men of cold heart and narrow mind, who believe we can find safety in dull timidity and dull inaction." As president Taft was able to control the convention. The defeated Roosevelt walked out with his supporters and formed a third party, known as the Progressive or Bull Moose Party.

Many leading reformers attended the Progressive convention, which often resembled a religious revival with hymn-singing and marches. Its platform endorsed such wide-ranging reforms as abolition of child labor; federal old-age, accident, and unemployment insurance programs; an eight-hour day; and woman suffrage. At Roosevelt's request, how-

"Ye're me Circulation. Ye're Small, Hinpissy, but ye're Silict."

The Irish barkeeper "Mr. Dooley" was the creation of Finley Peter Dunne, a political humorist who used Dooley to satirize politicians and public opinion.

ever, a plank supporting black equality was deleted. Calling the major parties "husks with no real soul," he accepted its nomination.

With the Republicans divided, Democratic chances of recapturing the White House increased. A former Republican senator lamented that the only unanswered question was "Which corpse gets the most flowers?" The scent of victory led to a hard fight for the Democratic nomination, which New Jersey's progressive governor, Woodrow Wilson, won on the forty-sixth ballot. The Socialist party nominated Eugene V. Debs, making it a four-way race.

As soon became apparent, the real battle was between Wilson and Roosevelt. It was marked by an unusually high level of debate over the proper role of government in a modern, industrialized society. Wilson declared, "What this country needs above everything else is a body of laws which will look after the men who are on the make rather than the men who are already made." Labeling his program "New Freedom," his aim was the restoration of competition and his tool was to be trust-busting.

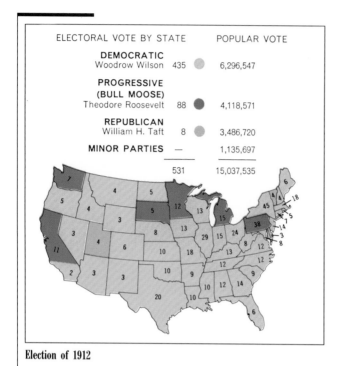

ELECTORAL VOTE BY STATE   POPULAR VOTE

DEMOCRATIC
Woodrow Wilson   435   6,296,547

**PROGRESSIVE
(BULL MOOSE)**
Theodore Roosevelt   88   4,118,571

REPUBLICAN
William H. Taft   8   3,486,720

MINOR PARTIES   —   1,135,697

531   15,037,535

Election of 1912

Wilson and Moral Progressivism

As the third Progressive-era president, Woodrow Wilson differed from his predecessors in both appearance and leadership style. He looked very much like the moralistic professor he was. The son and grandson of Presbyterian ministers, Wilson was raised in the South and practiced law in Atlanta before receiving his doctorate from Johns Hopkins University in Baltimore. His book, *Congressional Government,* was published in 1895, and he became president of Princeton University in 1902 before being elected governor of New Jersey. His religion was an important factor in his personality. "My life would not be worth living," he declared, "if it were not for the driving power of religion."

Wilson was not the kind of man whom people named stuffed animals after or gave nicknames. His self-righteousness was not endearing. One politician noted that when Wilson "said something to me . . . I didn't know whether God or him was talking." Although much less charismatic, Wilson did resemble Roosevelt in being a better speaker than Taft and in his view of the role of the president. Roosevelt had called the presidency a "bully pulpit," and Wilson agreed that the president should be the "political leader of the nation" because "his is the only national voice in politics." Unlike Taft, he argued that the president must be "as much concerned with the guidance of legislation as with the just and orderly execution of the laws."

Wilson's activism coincided with the growing demands for further reform. Investigations and amendments launched earlier came to fruition during his presidency. The result was an outpouring of legislation. In 1913, his first year in office, the Sixteenth Amendment was ratified, allowing the imposition of a federal income tax. This was accomplished as a provision of the Underwood Tariff passed in a special session of Congress that year. Wilson called the session to redeem a campaign pledge to lower duties as part of the New Freedom goal of restoring competition. During the tariff hearings lobbyists were so plentiful Wilson complained, "a brick wouldn't be thrown without hitting one of

Roosevelt, on the other hand, believed that big business was not necessarily bad, but proclaimed, "Somehow or other we shall have to work out methods of controlling the big corporations *without* paralyzing the energies of the business community." His answer was "New Nationalism"—the expansion of federal regulatory activities to control rather than dismantle the trusts. Big government would offset the power of big business. Their rhetoric differed sharply, but in their presidencies each practiced a little of both "New Freedom" and "New Nationalism."

The split in the Republican party enabled the Democrats to capture not only the White House but also the Senate. Democrats also consolidated their control of the House so Wilson entered the presidency with his party in power. Nevertheless, Wilson did not receive a majority of the popular vote. He got 6.3 million votes; Roosevelt, 4.1 million; Taft, 3.5 million; and Debs nearly 1 million. In the electoral college, however, Wilson won an impressive 435 votes to Roosevelt's 88 and a mere 8 for Taft.

them." This time, however, they did not all prevail. Congress significantly lowered duties for the first time since the Civil War. To recoup lost revenues, a graduated tax of from one to six percent was placed on personal incomes of $4000 and over.

Congress passed banking reform the same year. Following the panic of 1907 congressional investigations were launched. Everyone, including bankers, had come to believe the nation's banking system needed to be stabilized by governmental action. The question was how it was to be done. Wall Street wanted a centralized system owned and controlled by bankers. Others wanted a more decentralized system owned or controlled by the government. The Federal Reserve Act of 1913 was a compromise. It established the Federal Reserve System of twelve regional banks owned by bankers but under the control of a presidentially appointed Federal Reserve Board.

Prohibitionists won their first national victory with the Webb-Kenyon Act of 1913. It allowed dry states to interfere with the transportation of alcohol across their state lines. The next year those concerned with the large amounts of narcotics in patent medicines rejoiced over the passage of the Harrison Narcotic Act. It required a doctor's prescription for the sale of a list of controlled substances. Congress also compelled manufacturers of these drugs to register with the government and maintain sales records.

In 1914 Congress also took actions to deal with monopolies and to regulate business. In September it established the Federal Trade Commission to replace the Bureau of Corporations. The five-person body was charged with investigating alleged violations of antitrust law and could issue "cease and desist" orders against corporations found guilty of unfair trade practices. The next month the Clayton Act sought to close some of the loopholes of the Sherman Act and prohibited a number of business practices such as price discrimination. One provision declared that labor unions were not to be considered illegal combinations in restraint of trade—a move to undermine the use of court injunctions against strikers.

A pious professor, Woodrow Wilson brought both competence and a grim moral determination to the presidency.

At that point Wilson believed he had accomplished his agenda. He was not a supporter of further labor legislation or farm-credit plans. A firm opponent of paternalism, he said, "The old adage that God takes care of those who take care of themselves is not gone out of date. No federal legislation can change that thing. The minute you are taken care of by the government you are wards, not independent men." As the election of 1916 approached, however, progressives reminded Wilson of the importance of the farm and labor vote. Legislation to win those votes soon followed. Farmers were given the Federal Farm Loan Act, which provided them low-interest credit, and legislation giving federal supplemental funding for agricultural specialists in each county. Labor got the Keating-Owen Child Labor Act, which barred from interstate commerce goods made by children under sixteen; the Adamson Act, which established an eight-hour day for railroad workers; and the Workman's Compensation Act,

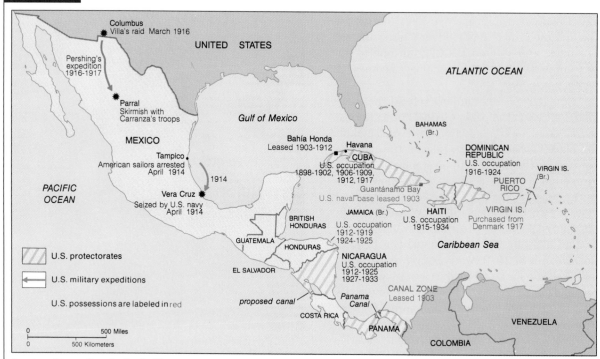

American Interventions in the Caribbean

Early in the twentieth century, the United States policed the Western Hemisphere and often took action when it judged Latin American countries were not running their affairs properly.

which provided protection to federal employees. Progressives were also pleased by Wilson's appointment of Louis Brandeis to the Supreme Court. All helped to ensure victory over the Republican nominee Charles Evans Hughes.

Wilson's moralism did not stop at national boundaries. Indeed his sermonistic foreign policy has sometimes been called "missionary diplomacy." His gospel was American-style democracy. "When properly directed," he declared, "there is no people not fitted for self-government." That direction was to come from the United States. He spoke of "releasing the intelligence of America for the service of mankind" and proclaimed "every nation needs to be drawn into the tutelage of America."

The rhetoric was different from his predecessors, but the results were the same. Renouncing both big stick and dollar diplomacy, Wilson continued to maintain stability and order to the south by similar measures. He sent marines to the Dominican Republic and Haiti,

and kept them in Nicaragua. His interventionism ran into more trouble in Mexico, where the overthrow of long-time dictator Porfirio Diaz in 1911 began a cycle of revolution. Just before Wilson entered office Victoriano Huerta came to power through assassination—an action that repulsed the moralistic Wilson. To the surprise of many, Wilson refused to extend diplomatic recognition to Huerta's government. Such recognition was generally routine whenever a government could demonstrate control; it did not imply approval.

Wilson simply refused to accept what he called a "government of butchers." He wrote one diplomat, "The United States intends not merely to force Huerta from power but to exert every influence it can to secure Mexico a better government under which all contracts and business concessions will be safer than they have ever been." Americans considered protection of contracts and concessions very important—they controlled seventy-five percent of Mexico's mines, sixty percent of its oil, and seventy percent of its rubber. Wilson's tactics escalated from diplomatic pressure to landing troops at Veracruz—a move that infuriated Mexicans more than Huerta's despotism. Even after Huerta was overthrown, civil war continued between the government forces of Venustiano Carranza and rebels led by Pancho Villa.

In an attempt to draw America into the fracas, Villa launched a raid into New Mexico in March 1916. The tactic worked, and Wilson sent an expedition to capture Villa. Led by General John Pershing, American troops failed to find him. Soon they were 300 miles deep into Mexican territory—an action that led to the brink of war with Carranza's government in January 1917. By then, however, America was being drawn into World War I, and Wilson decided to withdraw the troops. In the end he got basically the kind of government he wanted for Mexico, but Mexicans continued to believe that their government was their business and deeply resented the American intervention.

American involvement in World War I diverted attention from more than Mexico. Domestic reform took a backseat to "making the world safe for democracy." Yet war always brings changes on the homefront. Thus the nation shifted gears, but Progressivism did not entirely die. Indeed prohibitionists, woman suffragists, and immigration restrictionists won their greatest victories in the wake of war.

PROGRESSIVE ACCOMPLISHMENTS, PROGRESSIVE FAILURES

The twentieth century began with great optimism about the power of human beings to shape their destinies. Progress, people believed, could be legislated. Efficient, noncorrupt government could provide order and stability, promote social justice, and improve personal morals. Groups organized to promote their goals, and more and more of them began to win their objectives. In the 1920s, however, some realized that legislation had not always had its desired effect, that not everyone had benefited equally and that change had been far from radical.

In April 1914 Woodrow Wilson sent American troops to Vera Cruz on a flimsy pretext—but really to destabilize Huerta's government.

The Impact of Legislation

Measured by direct results most Progressive reforms proved disappointing. In some cases unintended consequences actually worked against the intended goals of laws. This often occurs when ideals confront reality. Solving one problem frequently creates another. Nevertheless, progressives established important precedents that opened doors to later, more effective reform.

Attempts to promote direct democracy were among the least effective. Direct election of senators did not seem to alter the kinds of people elected. Initiative, referendum, and recall were rarely used, and not by the so-called people. The expense and organization needed for petition drives were beyond the reach of any but well-financed pressure groups. An unintended result of democratization was to increase the power of urban machines. Bosses may have had to work a little harder, but most

Table 21.1

Progressive Legislation and Amendments

Act	Date	Significance
Newlands Reclamation Act	1902	Set aside proceeds from public land sales for irrigation and conservation projects
Elkins Act	1903	Outlawed railroad rebates
Hepburn Act	1906	Gave ICC power to set rates
Pure Food and Drug Act	1906	Set purity standards for foods and drugs
Meat Inspection Act	1906	Provided for government inspection of meat packing operations
Payne-Aldrich Tariff	1907	Failed attempt at tariff reform
Mann-Elkins Act	1910	Increased power of ICC and put telegraph and telephone companies under its jurisdiction
Mann Act	1910	Made transporting women across state lines "for immoral purposes" illegal
Sixteenth Amendment	1913	Made personal income taxes constitutional
Underwood Tariff	1913	Significantly reduced tariffs for the first time since the Civil War and imposed an income tax
Seventeenth Amendment	1913	Provided for election of U.S. senators by the people rather than state legislatures
Federal Reserve Act	1913	Established twelve federal reserve banks and the Federal Reserve
Webb-Kenyon Act	1913	Allowed states to prevent transportation of alcohol across their borders
Harrison Narcotic Act	1914	Made the sale of some drugs illegal without a doctor's prescription
Federal Trade Commission Act	1914	Established FTC to administer antitrust legislation
Clayton Act	1914	Attempted to close some loopholes in Sherman Antitrust Act
Federal Farm Loan Act	1916	Provided low-interest loans to farmers
Keating-Owen Child Labor Act	1916	Barred goods made by children under the age of sixteen from interstate commerce
Adamson Act	1916	Established eight-hour day for railroad workers
Workman's Compensation Act	1916	Provided job-related injury and death insurance for government employees

were still able to dominate primaries as well as elections. The move toward popular voting increased the political power of populous cities—and the machines that controlled them. The greatest failing of the movement was a dramatic drop in voter participation. Nevertheless, in some states, such as Wisconsin, government did become more responsive to public needs, and urban machines often adopted reform measures to maintain power.

Other kinds of urban reforms had varying results. In some, government did indeed become more efficiently and economically run. The competency and honesty of officials generally increased. An occasional consequence, however, were cuts in social services in less affluent neighborhoods. This was more likely to happen where the commissioner-manager system was adopted—usually in mid-size cities without a tradition of machine politics. In other cities municipally-owned utilities lowered rates, which provided real relief for the poor.

Attempts to regulate the railroads on either the state or national level rarely produced dramatic benefits for the general public. The chief advocates and beneficiaries of railroad regulation were frequently large shipping interests who did not share lower costs with consumers. With the Hepburn Act, Roosevelt did accomplish his primary goal of giving the ICC the power to set rates. The provision allowing court review of its decisions, however, made the act more significant as a precedent for expanded governmental power than as an immediate solution to problems. The courts ruled in favor of the railroads in most rate disputes.

Antimonopoly actions also did not always produce the intended results. For example, the break-ups of Standard Oil and the American Tobacco Company did not increase competition or lower prices. Perhaps the only legislation to fulfill the promise of New Freedom was the Underwood Tariff, and it was reversed by the tariff legislation of the 1920s. The Clayton Act was widely, and correctly, considered too vague for effective enforcement. The general counsel of the American Anti-Boycott Association analyzed the provision to exempt labor organizations from antitrust legislation and declared that the law "makes few changes in existing law

as relating to labor unions, injunctions and contempts of court, and those are of slight practical importance." Later court decisions proved his assessment accurate.

The Federal Trade Commission did not become an aggressive watchdog either. One of Wilson's cabinet members reported that the president viewed it as "a counsellor and friend to the business world" rather than as "a policeman to wield a club over the head of the business community." His appointments were fairly conservative, and the appointments of the 1920s were even more so. In the end the FTC proved beneficial to big business by protecting firms from unexpected suits and by outlawing many "unfair trade practices," many of which had promoted competition at the expense of stability. On the other hand, the FTC was also an important precedent.

Proclaimed victories for labor frequently turned out to be more symbolic than real. In the arbitration of the 1902 coal strike, for example, what the United Mine Workers did *not* receive is very significant: the union did not win recognition. As the 1920s would show, organized labor did not emerge from the Progressive era any stronger. Yet the symbolism can be important. The precedent that the government would not automatically support the demands of management was later built upon during the New Deal.

Some labor legislation brought benefits but also produced unintended results. Child Labor Laws in combination with compulsory education legislation decreased the number of children from ages ten to fifteen who were working for wages from one in five in 1900 to one in twenty by 1930. During those same years the number of students enrolled in secondary education increased by 800 percent. Both were desirable results, but in the short run at least, the poor received a mixed blessing. The income of a family's children was often crucial to its welfare, and no alternatives were provided. As one historian noted, "Child labor laws treated the symptoms and made the disease—poverty—worse." Much the same can be said about limits imposed on women's working hours. Laws establishing minimum wages for women helped to offset earning losses somewhat, but such laws, like the Child Labor Act, were declared unconstitutional in the 1920s.

Workman's compensation laws were an improvement over existing procedures but were not an unqualified victory of labor over management. Indeed, businessmen eventually welcomed relief from the growing number of suits instituted by hungry lawyers on a contingent fee basis. By agreeing to take a percentage of any damage awards and to charge no fee for lost cases, attorneys made it possible for poor workers to take legal action. The award schedule in most compensation plans provided payments far below what some lawyers had been winning in court. Workers, however, were guaranteed at least some compensation. For the industrialists, a predictable premium replaced the uncertainty of court actions, decreasing the risks and increasing stability in the cost of doing business.

The establishment of the Federal Reserve System also enhanced order and stability. Everyone benefited from the maintenance of cash reserves for emergencies, a more flexible currency, and national check clearing facilities. The banking system became more resistant to panics but, as 1929 would prove, not immune to them. Wall Street was not a big loser. Three of the five seats on the Federal Reserve Board went to large bankers, and the New York Federal Reserve bank quickly came to dominate the system. The new system, in other words, was a significant improvement but far from a radical change.

From consumers' points of view, the Pure Food and Drug Act and the Meat Inspection Act were great victories. After the rise of mass production and mass marketing, only federal action could provide adequate protection from adulteration of the nation's foodstuffs. Unintended beneficiaries, however, were the large drug and meat-packing companies which could more easily afford the increased expenses of meeting required production standards. Thus the effect was anticompetitive. Lobbying by the big meat packers also affected the final form of the legislation. Their victories included government payment of inspection costs and the deletion of the requirement to date canned meat. Like much Progressive legislation, the final act

did provide protection for consumers, but in a way agreeable to big business. Swift, one of the largest meat packers, even endorsed its passage in an advertisement declaring, "It is a wise law."

Other Progressive legislation left mixed legacies. Roosevelt's conservation measures prevented wanton squandering of resources but also aided the larger lumber companies. Morality legislation made undesirable activities illegal, but at the same time more profitable for organized crime. It also fostered widespread disrespect for the law. With a maximum rate of six percent, the income tax did little to redistribute the huge fortunes of such men as J. P. Morgan, but did establish an important tool for later use. A significant precedent was set by the Adamson Act, through which the federal government first dabbled in wage and hour legislation. Many other Progressive reforms were illusory or short termed. In the 1920s lax enforcement and hostile court decisions reversed many of them. Nevertheless, laissez-faire had suffered an irreversible blow. That was a major accomplishment and perhaps as much as many progressives wanted.

Winners and Losers

Before the era was ended, people from almost every class and occupation had sought to take advantage of the climate of change to promote their interests. Obviously not all were equally successful. Few were unqualified winners or losers, but some gained far more than others, and some lost more than they gained. Clearly, large corporations were among the biggest winners. One historian labeled the movement "the triumph of conservatism." Given the basic conservatism of all three presidents and most congressmen, as well as the resources and influence of big business, this may have been inevitable. It was not, however, the original intention of all legislation. To label most progressives as conservative is a gross mistake.

Other winners included members of the growing body of middle-class technocrats. At all levels of government the search for orderly, efficient management by experts created new job opportunities for engineers, health professionals, trained managers, and other experts. Re-

CHRONOLOGY
OF KEY EVENTS

1899 Veblen published *Theory of the Leisure Class*; Samuel "Golden Rule" Jones elected mayor of Toledo

1900 City commission established in Galveston, Texas

1901 McKinley assassinated; Roosevelt becomes president

1902 Newlands Reclamation Act; *Northern Securities* case; Coal strike

1903 Hay-Bunau-Varilla Treaty; W. E. B. Du Bois published *Souls of Black Folks*

1904 National Child Labor Committee formed; Roosevelt Corollary to the Monroe Doctrine

1905 *Lochner* v. *New York*

1906 Upton Sinclair published *The Jungle*; Hepburn Act; Pure Food and Drug Act; Meat Inspection Act

1908 Taft elected; *Muller* v. *Oregon*

1909 National Association for the Advancement of Colored People (NAACP) formed

1910 Mann-Elkins Act

1911 Triangle fire

1912 Wilson elected

1913 Sixteenth and Seventeenth amendments ratified; Underwood Tariff; Federal Reserve Act

1914 Panama Canal completed; Federal Trade Commission established; Clayton Act

1916 Jeannette Rankin elected to Congress; Child Labor Act; Adamson Act; Mexican intervention

forms that diminished the influence of political parties also increased the power of special interest groups working for particular social and economic goals. Consumers of all classes shared benefits from government regulation.

In general most of the winners were white, urban, Protestant, and middle class. This was true even though working-class ethnics won victories in some cities and states. They and small businessmen were among those who both lost and gained. Afro-Americans came closest to being unqualified losers. For blacks, the only lasting advances came from establishing organizations. The NAACP survived to become an important force later in the century, and self-help organizations provided aid to many blacks. Other victories were mainly token; the defeats were concrete.

In the South, and often in the North as well, blacks were clearly losers on the local level. At the same time black relations with the federal government also deteriorated. Of the three presidents, Roosevelt was the most sympathetic to blacks. In 1901, he invited Booker T. Washington to dine at the White House, consulted with him on some southern appointments, and named a few blacks to federal positions. His actions hardly reflected an acceptance of black equality, however. He believed, "as a race and in the mass they are altogether inferior to whites." One of his speeches to Congress seemed to condone lynching. Most disturbing to blacks was his handling of an incident in Brownsville, Texas, in 1906. There, a shoot-out occurred between white townspeople and black soldiers. No one could determine exactly what happened, but that did not deter Roosevelt from ordering dishonorable discharges for 167 black soldiers without court martial.

When Taft became president, he approved of southern disfranchisement and appointed white-supremacist Republicans to federal jobs. These actions by the two Republicans convinced some blacks, including W. E. B. Du Bois, to support Wilson in 1912. They made a mistake. The influence of Wilson's southern upbringing and advisors became apparent when he allowed his cabinet to segregate federal employees and to demote black officeholders—especially those "who boss white girls." Jim Crow moved to Washington, and Wilson's defense of those actions indicated the blindness and paternalism of many white progressives on race:

> It is true that the segregation of the colored employees in the several departments was begun upon the initiative and at the suggestion of the heads of departments, but as much in the interest of the negroes as for any other reason, with the approval of some of the most influential negroes I know, and with the idea that the friction, or rather the discontent and uneasiness, which had prevailed in many departments would thereby be moved. It is as far as possible from being a movement *against* the negroes. I believe it to be in their interest.

It seems that white progressives often seemed to feel they knew the best interests of those not like them—at home and abroad.

CONCLUSION

At the start of the new century, Americans confronted the urban squalor, poverty, powerful monopolies, corrupt and inefficient government, disorder, and despair that had accompanied the forces of modernization. They were determined to do something to achieve more social justice and stability. Numerous solutions were proposed and victories won. In the end, however, Americans rejected radicalism and ignored major problems.

Once again the nation resolutely refused to come to terms with its ethnic and cultural diversity. Rather than protect minorities, most actions infringed on their personal liberties and sought to control rather than accommodate their differences. Women won some victories, but the majority of Americans did not accept the radical feminists' vision of true equality. Socialists' dreams of a peaceful, democratic redistribution of the country's wealth fell on deaf ears. In the end, there was no significant change in the distribution of either wealth or power. The United States had weeded and tidied up its social garden, not replanted it. Although that garden produced bitter fruit for some people, many Americans benefited. Also, the vigor and diversity of progressive actions brought to light many problems and provided later generations with a body of experience in dealing with them.

REVIEW SUMMARY

By the close of the nineteenth century many Americans were seeking solutions to the problems created by a rapidly expanding economy and population. Voices for change arose from numerous sources—intellectual as well as popular. Calling themselves "progressive," people undertook:

> to organize themselves into groups
> to press government at all levels for action
> to seek more order, stability, and justice in society

Beginning in the cities and then moving to the state and national levels many laws were passed to:

> curb the power of trusts and railroads
> give "the people" more voice in government
> enforce morality
> bring order and fairness to taxation and banking

In the end most legislation proved ineffective and sometimes had unintended consequences. However, laissez-faire government had been attacked and important precedents set for the future.

SUGGESTIONS FOR FURTHER READING

THE PROGRESSIVE IMPULSE

Harold U. Faulkner, *The Quest for Social Justice, 1898–1914* (1931); David W. Noble, *The Progressive Mind*, rev. ed. (1981); James Weinstein, *The Corporate Ideal in the Liberal State, 1900–1918* (1968); Richard Abrams, *The*

Burdens of Progress (1978); Frank Tariello, *The Reconstruction of American Political Ideology* (1982); John L. Thomas, *Alternative America: Henry George, Edward Bellamy, Henry Demarest Lloyd, and the Adversary Tradition* (1983); Robert Wiebe, *The Search for Order* (1968); John W. Chambers, *The Tyranny of Change: America in the Progressive Era* (1978); Richard Hofstadter, *Age of Reform* (1955); William R. Hutchinson, *The Modernist Impulse in American Protestantism* (1976); Lawrence Veysey, *The Emergence of the American University* (1970); David W. Marcell, *Progress and Pragmatism* (1974); Thomas Haskell, *The Emergence of Professional Social Science* (1977); Louis Filler, *The Muckrakers*, rev. ed. (1980); Arthur Ekirch, *Progressivism in America* (1974); Jerold S. Auerbach, *Unequal Justice: Lawyers and Social Change in Modern America* (1976); Robert M. Cruden, *Ministers of Reform: The Progressive Achievement in American Civilization, 1889–1920* (1982); Samuel Haber, *Efficiency and Uplift: Scientific Management in the Progressive Era* (1964); Samuel Konefsky, *The Legacy of Holmes and Brandeis* (1956); Morton White, *Social Thought in America: The Revolt Against Formalism* (1975); David Riesman, *Thorstein Veblen* (1963); Harold S. Wilson, *McClure's Magazine and the Muckrakers* (1970).

PROGRESSIVES IN ACTION

Norman H. Clark, *Deliver Us from Evil: An Interpretation of Prohibition* (1976); James H. Timberlake, *Prohibition and the Progressive Crusade* (1963); Walter I. Trattner, *Crusade for the Children* (1970); Ruth Rosen, *The Lost Sisterhood: Prostitution in America, 1900–1919* (1982); Allen F. Davis, *Spearheads for Reform: The Social Settlements and the Progressive Movement, 1890–1914* (1967) and *American Heroine: Jane Addams* (1973); Roy Lubove, *The Progressives and the Slums, 1890–1917* (1962); Nancy S. Dye, *As Equals and Sisters, Feminism, the Labor Movement, and the Women's Trade Union League of New York* (1980); August Meier, *Negro Thought in America, 1880–1915* (1963); Louis R. Harlan, *Booker T. Washington: The Making of a Black Leader, 1856–1901* (1972) and *The Wizard of Tuskegee, 1901–1915* (1983); Charles F. Kellogg, *NAACP* (1970); Elliott M. Rudwick, *W. E. B. DuBois* (1969); Ellen Condliffe Lagemann, *A Generation of Women: Education in the Lives of Progressive Reformers* (1979); David P. Thelen, *Robert LaFollette and the Insurgent Spirit* (1976) and *The New Citizenship: Origins of Progressivism in Wisconsin* (1972); Irwin Yellowitz, *Labor and the Progressive Movement in New York City* (1965); John D. Buenker, *Urban Liberalism and Progressive Reform* (1973); Bradley R. Rice, *Progressive Cities: The Commission Government Movement* (1972); Melvin G. Holli, *Reform in Detroit: Hazen Pingree and Urban Politics*

(1969); George E. Mowry, *California Progressives* (1951); Sheldon Hackney, *Populism to Progressivism in Alabama* (1969); Dewey Grantham, *Southern Progressivism: The Reconciliation of Progress and Tradition* (1983); Richard L. McCormick, *From Realignment to Reform: Political Change in New York State, 1893–1910* (1981); Bruce M. Stave, *Urban Bosses, Machines, and Progressive Reformers* (1984); and Rene J. Dubos, *The White Plague: Tuberculosis, Man, and Society* (1952).

PROGRESSIVISM MOVES TO THE NATIONAL AND INTERNATIONAL LEVEL

Lewis L. Gould, *Reform and Regulation: American Politics from Roosevelt to Wilson* (1986); John M. Blum, *The Republican Roosevelt*, rev. ed. (1954); William Harbaugh, *The Life and Times of Theodore Roosevelt* (1961); George E. Mowry, *The Era of Roosevelt* (1958); G. Wallace Chessman, *Theodore Roosevelt and the Politics of Power* (1969); James Penick, Jr., *Progressive Politics and Conservation: The Ballinger-Pinchot Affair* (1968); Paolo E. Coletta, *The Presidency of William Howard Taft* (1973); James Holt, *Congressional Insurgents and the Party System* (1969); John M. Blum, *Woodrow Wilson and the Politics of Morality* (1956); Arthur S. Link, *Wilson*, 5 vols. (1947–1965) and *Woodrow Wilson and the Progressive Era* (1954); John Milton Cooper, Jr., *The Warrior and the Priest: Woodrow Wilson and Theodore Roosevelt* (1983); John D. Buenker, *The Income Tax and the Progressive Era* (1985); James Oliver Robertson, *No Third Choice: Progressives in Republican Politics, 1916–1921* (1983); Lester Langley, *The United States and the Caribbean* (1980); Whitney Perkins, *Constraints of Empire: The United States and Caribbean Intervention* (1981); Walter LaFeber, *The Panama Canal* (1979); Howard K. Beale, *Theodore Roosevelt and the Rise of America to World Power* (1956); Dana G. Munro, *Intervention and Dollar Diplomacy in the Caribbean, 1900–1921* (1964); P. Edward Haley, *Revolution and Intervention: The Diplomacy of Taft and Wilson with Mexico, 1910–1917* (1917); John Womack, *Zapata and the Mexican Revolution* (1968); Robert E. Quirk, *An Affair of Honor: Woodrow Wilson and the Occupation of Vera Cruz* (1962).

PROGRESSIVE ACCOMPLISHMENTS, PROGRESSIVE FAILURES

Gabriel Kolko, *The Triumph of Conservatism* (1963); Robert Wiebe, *Businessmen and Reform* (1962); Paul D. Casdorph, *Republicans, Negroes, and Progressives in the South, 1912–1916* (1981); John Dittmer, *Black Georgia in the Progressive Era, 1900–1920* (1977); Jack Temple Kirby, *Darkness at the Dawning: Race and Reform in the Progressive South* (1972).

126

a

900 L
400
W

EUROPE VIA LIVERPOOL
LUSITANIA

Fig. 55

Production Possibility
Curve 2

1914
1918

1914   1918

Guns

CHAPTER 22

The United States and World War I

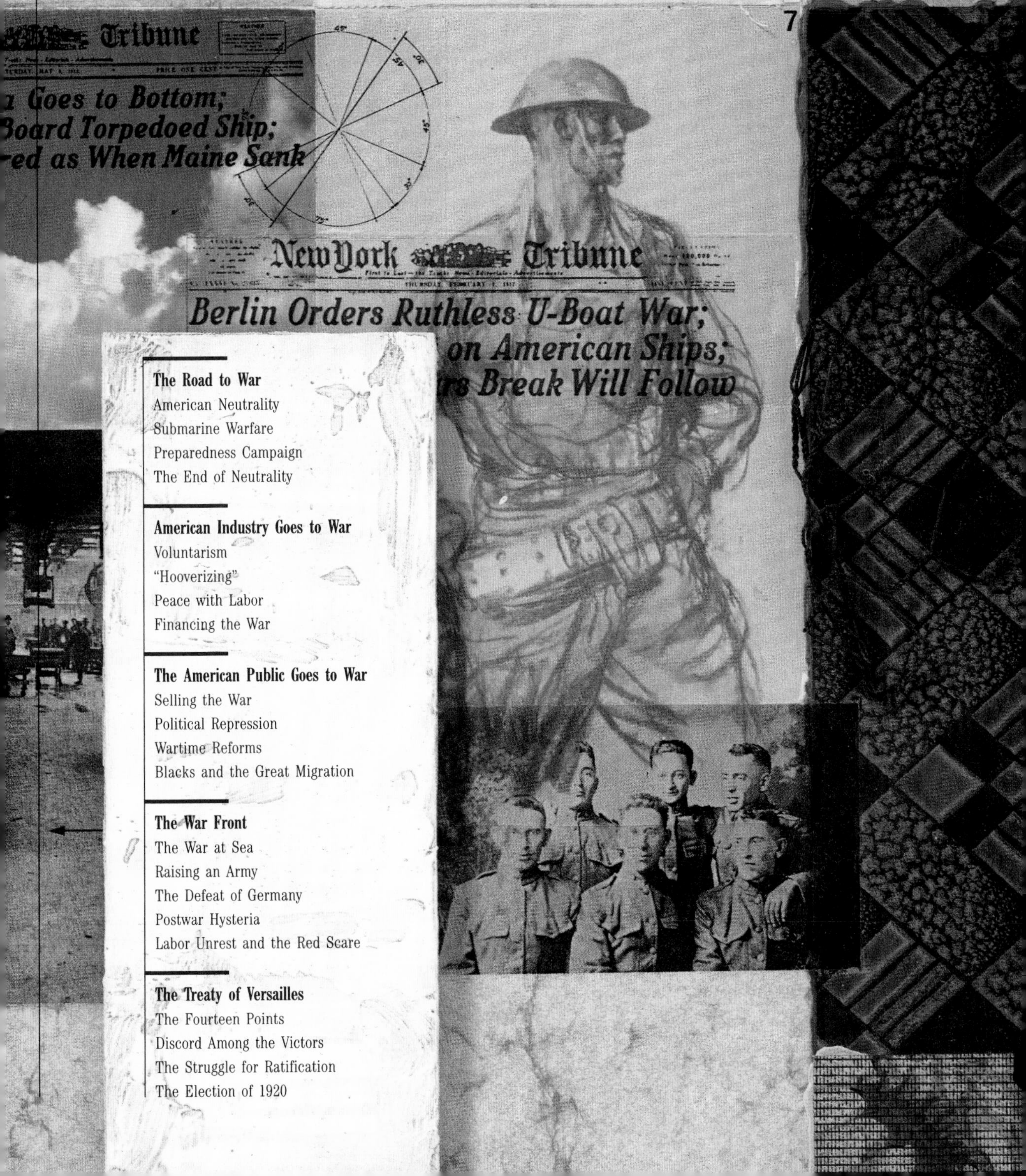

a Goes to Bottom;
Board Torpedoed Ship;
ed as When Maine Sank

New York ⚓ Tribune

Berlin Orders Ruthless U-Boat War;
on American Ships;
rs Break Will Follow

To disillusioned writers of the 1920s Randolph Bourne was "the intellectual hero of World War I." His appearance was anything but heroic. Theodore Dreiser called Bourne "as frightening a dwarf as I had ever seen." An unusually messy forceps delivery crushed one side of Bourne's skull at birth, leaving him with a misshapen ear, a partially paralyzed face, and a mouth permanently askew in a horrible grimace. Then, when he was four, an attack of spinal tuberculosis twisted his frame and left him a hunchback dwarf.

Bourne's brain, however, was razor sharp. He started reading at the age of two, and by the time he entered school, he had devoured entire books, including the Bible. A brilliant student, Bourne attended Columbia University where he studied under Franz Boaz, the father of cultural anthropology; John Dewey, the famed educator and apostle of pragmatism; and Charles A. Beard, the historian who stressed the economic motives of the founding fathers.

Bourne left college on the eve of World War I determined to become a writer. It was a period of intense intellectual ferment, and its undisputed center was New York's Greenwich Village, where self-styled literary radicals had declared war on the smugness and the optimism of American culture. Bourne joined them and contributed to such new magazines, as *The New Republic, The Seven Arts,* and *The New Masses.* Bourne made his reputation as a critic of World War I.

He loathed President Woodrow Wilson, whom he labeled "an indubitably intellectualized president," and he directed his choicest barbs at fellow intellectuals who supported the Wilson administration's conduct of neutrality and later the war. In effect, he charged them with not debating the pros and cons of Wilson's policies and not subjecting the president's high-sounding rhetoric to the fierce scrutiny required to sharpen public debate. They were "opening the sluices and flooding the public with the sewage of the war spirit." When they accused Randolph Bourne of not understanding the realities of war, he wrote: "In a time of faith, skepticism is the most intolerable of all insults."

Bourne refused to endow the war with lofty purposes. He was not a knee-jerk pacifist; he knew that some wars were unavoidable, perhaps even necessary. Rather, Bourne was an independent thinker who regarded Woodrow Wilson's policies as vague and misguided. World War I was not a struggle to make the world safe for democracy, he insisted; it was nothing more than "frenzied mutual suicide." To those who argued that this war would be different, that the war could be converted into an instrument of progress and democracy, Bourne replied that World War I would unleash "all the evils that are organically bound up with it." America's allies would reject Wilson's call for a "peace without victory," Bourne cautioned, because "War determines its own end—victory." Instead of supporting a just peace, they would try to win the war and "then grab what they can."

At home there would be "clumsily levied taxes and the robberies of imperfectly controlled private enterprises," suppression of civil liberties and the growth of big government. "War is the health of the State," he declared. "It automatically sets in motion throughout society those irresistible forces for uniformity, for passionate cooperation with the Government in coercing into obedience the minority groups and individuals which lack the larger herd sense."

Unlike many of his contemporaries, Bourne feared the power of the state. During wartime that power grew exponentially, making it "the inexorable arbiter and determinant of men's businesses and attitudes and opinions." The individual would lose every conflict with the state. Bourne denied that America could rely on "individual offerings of good will and enterprise" to conduct the war. "It will be coercion from above that will do the trick rather than patriotism from below," he warned.

Most alarming of all, the war would kill reform by diverting public attention from the unfinished work of progressivism. It would "leave the country spiritually impoverished because of the draining away of sentiment into the channels of war." Finally, Bourne scoffed at the idea that his opposition to the war was unpatriotic. Patriotism to him was "merely the emotion that fills the herd when it imagines itself engaged in massed defense or massed attack."

A few days after the Armistice was signed in 1918, Bourne died, a victim of the influenza epidemic that killed 500,000 Americans that winter. Although he had no visible impact on Wilson's administration or its conduct of the war, the questions Bourne raised about the relationship between war and society were prophetic. World War I was a terrible human tragedy.

THE ROAD TO WAR

On June 28, 1914, in Sarajevo, the provincial capital of Bosnia, in the Balkans, terrorists assassinated Archduke Franz Ferdinand, the heir to the Austro-Hungarian throne. A complicated system of alliances pitting the Triple Entente of France, Russia, and Great Britain against the Central Alliance of Germany and Austria-Hungary triggered a chain reaction that started World War I. Austria blamed Serbian nationalists for the killing and declared war on Serbia. When Russia and France mobilized to support their ally, Germany immediately declared war on them. After Germany invaded Belgium, England entered the war on the side of France and Russia. In the Far East, Japan, England's ally since 1902, also went to war against Germany.

Both sides anticipated a swift victory. After Germany's offensive through France and Belgium was halted at the River Marne in September 1914, however, the Great War bogged down in the trenches. Congealed lines of men, stretching from the English Channel to the Swiss border, formed an unmovable battle front across northern France. There they remained throughout 1915—four million men burrowed into the ground, ravaged by tuberculosis, plagued with lice and rats, staring at each other across barren expanses called "no man's land" and fighting pitched battles over narrow strips of blood-soaked earth.

Airplanes, tanks, hand grenades, and poison gases distinguished the war from earlier conflicts, but the machine gun was the most potent killer. One machine gunner had the fire-

Within weeks of the assassination of Archduke Franz Ferdinand, Germany, Turkey, and Austria-Hungary were at war with England, France, and Russia.

power of hundreds of soldiers; the German high command called it "the essence of concentrated infantry." The grim cycle repeated itself countless times: officers cried "Attack!"; men rose in waves; and the opposing forces opened fire with machine guns, spewing out death at the rate of eight bullets per second. In minutes, thousands of men lay wounded or dead, savage evidence of how efficiently military technology and insane tactics could combine to slaughter a generation of young men. When the war ended, Germany had lost 1,800,000 men; Russia, 1,700,000; France, 1,385,000; Austria-Hungary, 1,200,000; and Great Britain, 947,000.

American Neutrality

Most people were surprised when the war erupted. Not since the defeat of Napoleon had there been a large-scale war in Europe. Many observ-

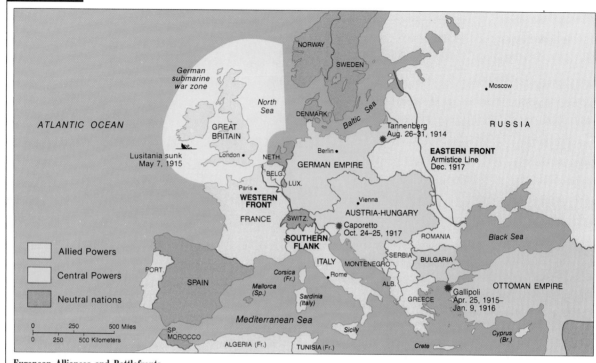

European Alliances and Battlefronts

ers regarded armed conflict as an anachronism, a dead relic rendered unthinkable by human progress. They believed the major powers were too advanced morally and materially to fight. Peace societies abounded on both sides of the Atlantic, nurturing visions of a world without war, and the Hague Conferences of 1899 and 1907 seemed to bear out their optimism by codifying international law and establishing procedures for the peaceful resolution of conflict.

World War I shattered those naive assumptions, but President Wilson's declaration of neutrality reassured most Americans, who did not believe their interests and security hinged on the war's outcome. Steeped in a long tradition of noninvolvement and comforted by the protection of the Atlantic, they hoped to escape

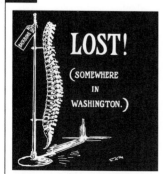

Many Americans were divided over the prospect of war.

Europe's insanity. A New York *Sun* editorial declared that "it would be folly for the country to sacrifice itself to the frenzy of dynastic politics and the clash of ancient hatreds which is urging the Old World to destruction."

Yet Americans were deeply divided over the war from the outset. Ties of language and culture prompted many to side with the Allies, and, as the war progressed, the British adeptly exploited these bonds. After the German invasion of neutral Belgium, for example, British propagandists had a field day depicting the Germans as sadistic brutes who committed atrocities against civilians. The Central Powers had their sympathizers, too. Approximately one-third of the nation, 32 million people, were either foreign born or the children of immigrants, and more than 10 million derived from the nations of the Central Powers. Millions of Irish-Americans sided with the Central Powers because of their hatred for England.

Standing between these factions was President Wilson. He knew practically nothing about foreign policy when he took office. His own experience as a scholar and as a progressive governor had been limited to domestic politics, and he tried to apply the same principles of liberal reform to foreign affairs. At the least, Wilson's approach to foreign affairs was both legalistic and moralistic. He expected nation states to behave like gentlemen; and, above all, that meant living up to the letter of international law and respecting the rights of every nation.

Wilson's declaration of neutrality insisted that the public be "neutral in fact as well as in name." Privately, his sympathies lay with the Allies, especially Great Britain, whose culture and government he had long admired. His closest advisors, Robert Lansing, who later served as his secretary of state; Walter Hines Page, ambassador to the Court of St. James; and Colonel Edward House, his alter ego, were all pro-British. Yet the president knew that the war's causes were complicated and obscure; simple prudence dictated that the United States must avoid taking sides.

Domestic politics reinforced Wilson's resolve to stay out of the war. In 1914 the United States stood at the end of two decades of bitter social and political debate. Labor unrest, the rise of huge corporations, the antitrust movement, and the arrival of 12 million new immigrants since the turn of the century had produced deep fissures in American society. "Every reform we have won will be lost if we go into this war," declared Wilson in 1914.

Control of the seas posed the greatest threat to American neutrality. The British navy controlled the sea lanes and attempted to blockade Europe. They mined the North Sea and started seizing American vessels bound for neutral countries, often without offering compensation. In 1916 Britain "blacklisted" some eighty-seven American companies accused of trading with Germany and censored the mail coming from Europe to the United States. Coupled with England's ruthless suppression of the Irish Rebellion in 1916, these actions infuriated Wilson, who privately denounced the English as "poor Boobs."

The protests left the British cold. They interpreted Wilson's ardent defense of neutral rights as petty, legalistic quibbling. England was fighting for its life. What were a few confiscated cargoes in comparison? Still, the British realized they could not push Wilson too far; they needed American trade to survive; so they tried to enforce the blockade as tightly as possible without rupturing relations with the United States.

Economic self-interest limited Wilson's options. He could have ended the controversy over neutral rights immediately by clamping an embargo on trade with the belligerents, but he refused because the trade was stimulating the American economy. The United States had been in a recession when Wilson entered office in 1913, and the war had increased the volume of trade with the Allies from $824 million in 1914 to $3.2 billion in 1916. Commerce with the Central Powers declined from $169 million to $1.15 million.

The huge volume of trade quickly exhausted the Allies' cash reserves, forcing them to ask the United States for credit. Secretary of State William Jennings Bryan, a near pacifist, opposed their requests, declaring: "Money is the worst of contrabands—it commands all other things." After hesitating for several months, President Wilson agreed in October 1915 to permit loans to belligerents, a decision that favored Great Britain and France far more than Germany. By 1917 American loans to the Allies had soared to $2.25 billion; loans to Germany stood at a paltry $27 million. The United States became a creditor nation for the first time, creating a strong economic interest in an Allied victory.

Submarine Warfare

Germany had no choice but to intimidate American shippers. On February 4, 1915, Germany proclaimed a "war zone" around the British Isles. All enemy merchant ships there would be torpedoed without warning; and neutral ships would be in danger, too. The Germans were bluffing—they had only four U-boats in the area. The submarine was preeminently a weapon of terror and intimidation, and the Germans intended to use it as an instrument of psychological warfare until they could build enough ships to make good their threats.

At the time, the submarine was a new technology which blatantly contradicted international law. Vessels on the high seas intending to make war against another vessel were required

The German U-boat, a terrifying new weapon of the war, attacked silently and without warning.

German diplomat in Washington warned that "there will be hell to pay."

On May 1, 1915, the German Embassy took out full-page ads in New York newspapers warning Americans not to travel on Allied ships. Undeterred, 197 Americans sailed for the British Isles on board the *Lusitania,* the queen of the Cunard fleet. On May 17, 1915, a German U-boat torpedoed the *Lusitania* off the coast of Ireland, and she sank in eighteen minutes, killing 1198 persons, 128 of them Americans. Here was a harsh test of America's neutrality. The public was shocked and outraged. It did not seem to matter that the *Lusitania* was transporting munitions in her hull and carrying secret orders to ram submarines on sight. The New York *Nation* called the sinking "wholesale murder on the high seas," and a small minority of Americans, led by Theodore Roosevelt, demanded war.

Wilson reacted with toughness and patience. He pressed the Germans to apologize for the sinking, compensate the victims, and pledge to stop attacking merchant ships. The Germans met Wilson halfway. In February 1916 they expressed regret over the *Lusitania* and agreed to pay an indemnity. However, the Imperial Government refused to stop sinking merchant ships without warning, explaining that its survival depended on full use of the submarine. Wilson was happy to have the matter ended, but the issue of submarine warfare had not been resolved. "I can't keep the country out of war," Wilson admitted privately. "Any little German lieutenant can put us into war at any time by some calculated outrage."

The president was right to be concerned. On March 24, 1916, a submarine attacked the *Sussex,* an unarmed French passenger ship. The *Sussex* reached port, but eight people were killed and seven Americans seriously wounded. Wilson announced that the United States would sever diplomatic relations unless Germany promised to stop sinking all merchant and passenger ships without warning. Anxious to keep the United States neutral, the Germans agreed. The so-called *Sussex* pledge reduced tensions between the United States and Germany for the remainder of 1916, but again the fragile peace depended on German restraint.

by law to warn their intended victim, allow time for passengers to get into lifeboats and clear the area, and then rescue survivors after the sinking. Merchant vessels with contraband had to be "visited and searched" before any attack. These regulations were impossible for the U-boat. It was a guerrilla of the seas whose effectiveness rested on the element of surprise. Because surfacing to warn the enemy meant certain destruction, the Germans ignored international law.

Woodrow Wilson did not. To his legalistic mind, the German U-boats were guilty of criminal acts. In unusually blunt language, he warned Berlin that it would be held "strictly accountable" for American lives. While international law did not guarantee the safety of neutrals who traveled on belligerent ships, Wilson acted as though it did. With the United States demanding that Germany treat a single American passenger as a shield to an entire merchant ship, a

Preparedness Campaign

Wilson's critics argued that the best way to ensure peace was to prepare for war. The pugnacious Teddy Roosevelt accused the president of conducting "milk and water" diplomacy, while another critic sneered that the Germans were "standing by their torpedoes, the British by their guns, and Wilson by strict accountability." As Tin Pan Alley produced songs with titles such as "I Did Not Raise My Boy to Be a Coward," the National Security League, headed by General Leonard Wood, organized volunteer military training programs across the country.

Wilson also had critics on the left who feared the drift toward war. Socialists like Eugene V. Debs and Morris Hillquit interpreted the war as a struggle for assets among capitalist nations. Radicals like anarchist Emma Goldman and "Big Bill" Haywood, head of the Industrial Workers of the World, opposed the war on similar grounds and advocated violent resistance to preparedness. Liberal reformers like Randolph Bourne and Oswald Garrison Villard were convinced that war would destroy the spirit of progressivism. Professional peace crusaders like social worker Jane Addams and Hamilton Holt, head of the League to Enforce Peace, opposed war in general on moral grounds. In the Midwest, the Nonpartisan League, a radical farmers' political party, adopted a pro-German stand.

The forces for preparedness had the upper hand. In June 1916 Congress passed the National Defense Act (Hay Act), increasing the army from 90,000 to 220,000 men. A few months later Congress passed the Naval Construction Act, appropriating more than $500 million for new ships. Though of small importance militarily, both acts drew fire from the antipreparedness forces in Congress who feared that armaments would lead to war. The preparedness campaign forced Wilson to run to catch up with public opinion. Though he had opposed preparedness early in his administration, Wilson shifted ground and lobbied for both bills.

Despite his support for military preparedness, Wilson ran as the peace candidate in the election of 1916. The Republicans chose Charles Evans Hughes over the fiery Theodore Roosevelt. A member of the progressive wing of the GOP, Hughes was a former governor of New York who had earned a solid reputation as a liberal. His nomination reflected the GOP's determination to regain progressive support and avoid the split that had put Wilson in the White House four years earlier. Though his campaign speeches criticized the president soundly, Hughes had a hard time explaining how his policies differed. Wilson, by contrast, ran squarely on his record. The Democratic platform stressed the president's legislative victories for progressive reform, his patient handling of the Mexican crisis, and, above all, his declaration of neutrality. "He kept us out of war" became the Democrats' rallying cry.

The race was extremely close. On election eve the New York *Times* and the New York *World* both conceded victory to Hughes, who went to bed believing he had won. He ran well in traditional Republican strongholds such as the Midwest (he won Illinois, Indiana, and Michigan) and the large eastern states. However, Wilson won in the electoral college by a vote of 277 to 254. With a popular vote margin of 9.1 million to Hughes's 8.5 million, Wilson carried

As the peace candidate in the 1916 election, Wilson advocated military preparedness but continued to say, "I am not expecting this country to get into the war."

the Solid South, Ohio, Maryland, and New Hampshire. But he owed his victory to voters west of the Mississippi River where he took every state except Oregon, Iowa, South Dakota, and Minnesota. The Democratic party's strength in 1916 rested on an ethnic-worker-farmer coalition. Wilson carried the Solid South, the labor vote in the Northeast and Midwest, the old-line progressives, and substantial numbers of western farmers.

Interpreting his reelection as a vote for peace, Wilson attempted to mediate. On December 18, 1916, he asked the belligerents to list their war aims and state their terms for peace. The following month he declared that both sides should embrace his demands for a "peace without victory." Randolph Bourne was right. Above all else, the belligerents were interested in complete victory. Neither side welcomed his overture. The Germans announced they would not permit neutrals at the conference table. The British, too, publicly rejected Wilson's offer. Privately, a high-ranking British official confided to Walter Hines Page, the American ambassador: "Everybody is mad as hell," and called Wilson an "ass."

The End of Neutrality

Any hope of a negotiated settlement ended when Germany announced that after February 1, 1917, all vessels caught in the war zone, neutral or belligerent, armed or unarmed, would be sunk without warning. Driven to desperation by the British blockade and unable to break the impasse on land, Germany had decided to risk everything on the U-boats' starving Britain into submission. The German high command expected the United States to declare war in retaliation, but they were confident their submarines could deliver a knockout blow before America could mobilize.

Here, then, was the ultimate test of "strict accountability." Members of his cabinet pressed Wilson to declare war, but he broke diplomatic relations instead. Critics accused him of shaking first his fist and then his finger, but Wilson regarded war as a ghastly alternative. He could not bring himself to act. For weeks he was indecisive and confused, unable to accept the fact

that "strict accountability" demanded war once the Germans started sinking American ships.

The Zimmermann telegram finally snapped Wilson out of his daze. On January 16 British code breakers intercepted a secret message from Arthur Zimmermann, the German foreign minister, to the German ambassador to Mexico, proposing an alliance between Germany and Mexico in the event that Germany went to war with the United States. Germany promised to help Mexico recover the territory it had lost in the 1840s, roughly the present-day states of Texas, New Mexico, and Arizona. The British revealed the scheme to Wilson on February 24, hoping to draw the United States into the war.

The president was now convinced that German militarism threatened American security. For years Americans had been concerned about Germany's economic penetration of world markets, as well as her strong military tradition. The Zimmermann telegram convinced millions of people that German intentions and American national security were at odds. For Wilson in particular, German U-boats violated international law and threatened the long-held American commitment to freedom of the seas. Finally, and perhaps most important to the president, Germany was prepared to conquer England and destroy Anglo political institutions.

Late in February Wilson asked Congress for permission to arm American merchant ships. The House approved, but eleven pacifists in the Senate filibustered against the bill. Dismissing his Senate opponents as "a little band of willful men, representing no opinion but their own," Wilson issued an executive order on March 12, arming merchant ships and instructing them to shoot submarines on sight.

The United States and Germany were virtually at war. At this critical juncture the Russian Revolution erupted. The czar fell, and in his place stood the provisional government of a Russian Republic, complete with a representative parliament. With the only autocratic regime among the Allies swept away, the war seemed to pit democracy against despotism.

Pale and solemn, Wilson delivered his war message to Congress on April 2. The United States "had no quarrel with the German people," he insisted, but their "military masters" had to be defeated in order to make the world "safe for democracy." Congress interrupted his address several times with thunderous applause. The next day the Senate approved the war resolution, 82 to 6; the House followed on April 6, 373 to 50. The president signed the declaration on April 7, 1917, and America was at war.

Why did Wilson fail to keep America at peace? True, cultural ties with Great Britain predisposed the United States to favor the Allies, and enormous volumes of trade strengthened these sympathies. Culture and trade were not the decisive issues, however. Wilson's strong defense of freedom of the seas meant that the United States was bound to clash with Germany once its U-boats started sinking American ships. The other critical factor was Wilson's desire to dictate the peace. By entering the war, the United States would be guaranteed a place at the peace table. "I hate this war," an anguished Wilson confided to one of his aides, "and the only thing I care about on earth is the peace I am going to make at the end of it."

Most Americans supported the declaration of war. John Dewey, the famed educator, spoke for Progressives when he announced that the war was an ugly reality which had to be converted into an instrument for benefiting mankind. Randolph Bourne disagreed. "If the war is too strong for you to prevent," he asked, "how is it going to be weak enough for you to control and mould to your liberal purposes?"

AMERICAN INDUSTRY GOES TO WAR

Administration officials believed that America's major contribution to the war would be economic, not military. Production had to be raised to supply the Allies and outfit an army. Yet no one, in or out of government, had a thorough understanding of the economy. President Wilson responded "with a smile of incredibility" when a leading economist at Columbia University estimated the war might cost as much as $10 billion in its first year. Wilson badly underestimated both the size and the cost of the task at hand.

Voluntarism

The country was nearly as unprepared for war in 1917 as it had been in 1914. Decisions had to be made about mobilization, but there was no consensus on the proper role of government in society. One group of Progressives had long demanded more government regulation, but another group simply wanted to break up the large industrial monopolies and then let the free market govern the economy. Conservatives opposed any growth of government power at the expense of business. Caught between these differing views, Wilson hesitated to mobilize by decree. Instead, he tried to create a system of economic incentives that would permit him to manage the war through a spirit of voluntarism.

It took almost a year to organize an effective war administration. Wilson established a war cabinet with six key boards, conferring broad power on the central government. The War Industries Board (WIB), under the leadership of Bernard M. Baruch, a Wall Street financier, assumed the task of managing the economy. Baruch's team of 100 businessmen (many of them volunteer "Dollar-A-Year" men) fixed prices, set priorities, and reduced waste. To increase production, they appealed to the profit motive. Baruch reasoned that "you could be forgiven if you paid too much to get the stuff, but you could never be forgiven if you did not get it, and lost the war." The WIB set prices artificially high, permitting profits to triple during the war. One steel executive confessed: "We are all making more money out of this war than the average human being ought to."

The Fuel Administration, the War Trade Board, the Shipping Board, and the U.S. Railroad Administration used similar policies. Under the slogan "Mine More Coal," the Fuel Administration increased production by two-fifths and conserved supplies through voluntary "lightless nights" and "gasless Sundays." The Railroad Administration ended the chaos that had snarled the rail system during the early months of the war, spending more than $500 million on equipment and repairs. By offering large profits to railroads and high wages to workers, it established a rail system under national control.

THE FIRST DAY OF THE SOMME

During the American Civil War, Richard J. Gatling hoped to become wealthy by selling the Union army his hand-cranked machine gun. His weapon could unleash up to 200 rounds a minute, as compared to the 2 to 3 rounds a minute from a rifled musket being loaded and fired by a well-trained soldier. Gatling considered his weapon "providential," the ultimate device, he wrote to Abraham Lincoln, for "crushing the rebellion." After the war Gatling even spoke of social benefits. His machine gun would ease the pain and suffering of war. Only one soldier would be needed "to do as much battle duty as a hundred" because of his gun's "rapidity of fire." His weapon would "supersede the necessity of large armies, and consequently exposure to battle and disease would be greatly diminished."

Hiram Maxim, another inventor, offered a major improvement in 1884 when he demonstrated a mechanism that would permit a machine gun to fire automatically,

simply by depressing the trigger. Because of such technological breakthroughs, water-cooled machine guns capable of shooting 600 rounds a minute were commonplace in the arsenal of weapons used by armies engaged in World War I. These Maxim guns, as they were called, could spray an area with bullets and easily outduel companies of soldiers trained well enough to fire their breechloading rifles 15 times a minute. The machine gun proved to be an effective killing weapon.

More sophisticated weapons did not, as Richard Gatling had assured his customers, result in any reduction in the size of wartime armies. During Europe's Age of Industrialization, the major powers built up ever larger military forces, as if only huge masses of troops could defeat the enhanced firepower of new weapons such as the machine gun.

When the armies of Europe first collided in August 1914 after

Germany's penetration through Belgium, a stark reality became clear. Firepower, both in the form of small arms and large artillery, was so overwhelming that neither side could defeat the other without virtual annihilation. What emerged were opposing lines of trenches along the Western Front, running without interruption south from the North Sea all the way through France to the border of Switzerland. For the next three years, combat became a horrible contest in which one or the other side tried to break through these trench lines.

The Battle of the Somme was in many ways typical. Up until June 1916 this sector in northeastern France was inactive. German divisions had been present since September 1914 and had constructed three defensive lines of trenches running back from "no-man's land," an area some 500 to 1000 yards wide on the other side of which were trenches manned by the Allies—the British to the north and the French to the south of the Somme River. Because of a fearsome struggle occurring far to the south at Verdun, the Allied high command, after preliminary planning, decided in May 1916 to mount a massive offensive in the Somme sector.

If German lines could be permanently ruptured, then it would be possible to roll up enemy divisions on their flanks. Divisions of the German army would face surrender or retreat, thus breaking the military deadlock in favor of the Allies. But to breach the German trenches in coordinated fashion along fifty miles involved detailed planning, considering the thousands of troops and massive firepower that the Allies faced.

Further, surprise attacks were impossible. German artillery and machine gun operators had the capacity to obliterate waves of soldiers trying to cross no-man's land, even before they reached the barbed wire placed in front of the German trenches. The only alternative was to prepare the way with an extended artillery bombardment.

The Battle of the Somme erupted with a seven-day cannonade. Before it was over British artillery dumped 2,960,000 rounds fired by a crew of 50,000 gunners on the German trenches. By the evening of the second day, wrote an observer, "some sectors of the German front line were already unrecognizable and had become crater fields." The next day the British started releasing clouds of chlorine gas, hoping that it would seep down into dugouts twenty or more feet below ground where German soldiers were living, surviving, and listening carefully for the climactic fury of the bombardment, the sure sign that the infantry assault was to begin.

At 6:30 A.M., on July 1, one hour before infantry troops were to advance, the cannonade reached "an intensity as yet unparalleled . . . along the whole front." German soldiers noticed the difference and knew the moment of reckoning was near. The whole course of the battle would depend upon their ability to get back above ground, set up their machine guns, and begin firing before enemy infantry overran them. It was a moment for which they had repeatedly trained.

As zero hour approached, thousands of British and French soldiers made final preparations in their trenches. Their assignment was to secure control of the second German line by the end of the day. Soon they would be climbing up scaling ladders and jumping over the top, then listening for the sounds of whistles from their platoon leaders to guide them across no-man's land. Most found themselves "sweating at zero hour," supposedly from "nervous excitement." Many had attended church services the previous day. Explained one British soldier, "I placed my body in God's keeping, and I am going into battle with His name on my lips." Everyone received a warm breakfast and a healthy ration of rum to settle their nerves.

Promptly, at 7:30 A.M., the race began. Over the top went hundreds of thousands of British and French troops. Up out of their dugouts came German soldiers. In most areas the Germans were ready with time to spare. Their machine gun and artillery fire cut one-third of the British battalions to shreds before they reached what remained of the first German trenches.

British soldiers who survived witnessed unbelievable sights. One watched as "two men suddenly rose into the air vertically, 15 feet perhaps," as a German shell hit the ground ahead of him. "They rose and fell with the easy, graceful poise of acrobats," he noted, as they died. Another saw men "falling forward," stating that it was "some time before I realized they were hit." In one company only three soldiers made it to the barbed wire. Their leader, a lieutenant, looked around in amazement and said: "God, God, where's the rest of the boys?"

Hardly over the top, a British sergeant heard the "patter, patter" of German machine guns. "By the time I'd gone another ten yards," he explained, "there seemed to be only a few men left around me; by the time I had gone twenty yards, I seemed to be on my own. Then I was hit myself." This sergeant was among the fortunate. In some sectors, British soldiers who evaded machine gun fire and reached the other side "were burned to death by [German] flame throwers."

From the British perspective, the battle went poorly on July 1, 1916. At the end of the day, they had not captured the German second line, but they had suffered 60,000 casualties, including 21,000 dead, most in the first hour of the attack. The Germans, who got the bulk of their machine guns up and operating, experienced only 6000 casualties by comparison. But the battle had just begun, and it would rage in fits and starts until November 18, when the Allies decided that a break in the Somme sector was not attainable. By that time the British had suffered 420,000 casualties, the French an estimated 200,000. No one knows exactly how many soldiers the Germans lost, but a fair guess would be in the 500,000 to 600,000 range. Yet virtually no ground had been lost or gained.

It is not surprising, then, that the Allies rejoiced when the Americans finally entered the war. They needed more than loans and war goods to win. Field Marshal Joseph Joffre, the former French commander in chief, said it all when he arrived in the United States after Congress declared war in April 1917. Stated Joffre with his usual bluntness: "We want men, men, men."

"Hooverizing"

Agricultural production came under the jurisdiction of the Food Administration. Herbert Hoover, its director, was a mining engineer and self-made millionaire who had served with distinction as head of relief operations in Belgium. Appealing to the spirit of patriotism, he preached "the gospel of the clean plate." Americans "Hooverized" with wheatless Mondays and Wednesdays, meatless Tuesdays, and porkless Thursdays and Saturdays.

No foe of profits, Hoover set farm prices at high levels to encourage production. He stabilized the grain market by guaranteeing farmers a minimum price and he purchased raw sugar and then sold it to refineries at a fixed rate. The policies worked. Overall, real farm incomes rose thirty percent during the war, and despite bad wheat crops in 1916 and 1917, food production increased by one quarter, domestic food consumption fell, and America's food shipments to the Allies tripled.

Peace with Labor

The administration also made concessions to labor. At his own request, Wilson addressed the American Federation of Labor (AFL) conven-

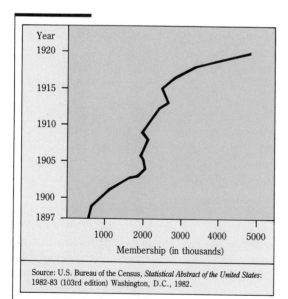

Year

Source: U.S. Bureau of the Census, *Statistical Abstract of the United States: 1982-83 (103rd edition)* Washington, D.C., 1982.

Figure 22.1
Labor Union Membership, 1897–1920

tion in November 1917, the first time a president had so honored the trade union movement. Flanked by a guard of soldiers to dramatize the solemnity of the occasion, he delivered an eloquent plea for industrial peace. Important policy shifts followed. Gradually, Wilson recognized labor's right to organize and engage in collective bargaining, and he sanctioned other key demands, including the eight-hour workday. To settle labor disputes, Wilson created the National War Labor Board (WLB), with ex-president William Howard Taft and Frank B. Walsh, a liberal lawyer, as its chairmen. Though it lacked legal authority, the WLB had the president's backing and a commitment from industry and labor to accept its decisions. During the war the WLB heard 1241 cases affecting 711,500 workers.

While the administration embraced the AFL, it opposed militant unions like the Industrial Workers of the World (IWW). From the textile mills of New England to the logging camps of the Pacific Northwest, the "Wobblies" demanded higher wages and better working conditions, and they went out on strike to win them. Because the Wobblies frequently employed the rhetoric of class warfare to dramatize their demands, their strikes frightened many Americans who believed social revolution was underway. Warning that strikes would cripple the war effort, shrewd businessmen played upon these fears to demand suppression of the so-called radical unions. The Wobblies were "traitors," they sneered, and the IWW stood for "I Won't Work."

Samuel Gompers, president of the AFL, was determined to separate his union from the militant workers. He seized Wilson's olive branch and pledged not to strike for the duration of the war. The AFL supported the war effort like superpatriots and joined the administration's attack on socialist critics of the war both at home and in Europe. Indeed, the AFL even accepted money from the government. Gompers's policies paid handsome dividends. The AFL won a voice in homefront policy, and union men were placed in wartime agencies where they pushed for the eight-hour day and staved off pressure from employers bent on preserving the open shop. Real income of manufacturing workers and coal miners rose by

IWW strikes, like the Oliver Steel Strike in Pittsburgh, did little to help the war effort at home. In response, the AFL pledged not to strike for the war's duration.

one-fifth between 1914 and 1918. By 1919 almost half of the American labor force had achieved a forty-eight-hour week (compared to one-eighth in 1915). Finally, the AFL expanded its membership from 2.7 million in 1916 to 4 million in 1919.

Financing the War

While business and labor both profited from the war, neither group could agree on how it should be financed. By 1920 the war had cost $33.5 billion—thirty-three times the federal government's revenues in 1916. Conservatives favored a regressive tax policy—consumption taxes, borrowing, and, if necessary, a slight increase in income taxes. Reformers and radicals called for a progressive tax policy—inheritance and excess profits taxes coupled with higher income taxes. Wilson walked the middle ground, but the heaviest burdens fell on the wealthy through taxes on large incomes, corporate profits, and estates. By 1919 the tax burden in the highest income brackets had risen to seventy-seven percent.

Much of the war's price tag fell on a small minority of wealthy people who had not been taxed heavily before 1916; and, in so doing, the war brought a permanent reversal in the sources of tax revenues. Before the war nearly three-quarters of federal revenues had come from excise and customs taxes; the remainder came from a modest income tax and from other duties on wealth such as estate taxes. After the war, the ratios were reversed. America's tax structure shifted from taxing consumption to taxing wealth, proof that progressives were winning the struggle to make upper-income groups pay a large share of the cost of government. On the tax issue Randolph Bourne was wrong.

Taxes, however, financed only one-third of the war. Inflation and the spirit of voluntarism surrounding the heavily publicized sales of bonds temporarily concealed the war's real price. The policy of opting for incentives rather than statutory controls increased voluntarism, but it also obscured the real dislocations of the war on the economy. The national debt rose from $1 billion in 1915 to $20 billion in 1920.

THE AMERICAN PUBLIC GOES TO WAR

Though willing to use the state to coerce individual citizens, Wilson opposed any action that might alter the nation's economic system. A fiscal conservative who wanted to keep the role of the state to a minimum, he struggled to preserve the tradition of little government interference in the economy. Like most of his contemporaries, Wilson preferred to see real authority and control exercised by the private sector. Ironically, World War I took a giant step toward augmenting the power of the central government.

Selling the War

Wilson's decision to substitute voluntarism for state controls had profound social consequences. By refusing to impose statutory controls on industry, he placed the burden of supporting the war on the profit motive and the public's sense of patriotism. To be sure, this policy avoided the clash between the administration and industry that would have resulted from strict government control over the economy, but it did so at a huge cost to civil liberties.

Government coercion was directed at public opinion, not at industry. Because he doubted the loyalty of many ethnic Americans, Wilson established the Committee on Public Information (CPI) to mobilize public support for the war. Its chairman was George W. Creel, an able and energetic journalist, who created America's first propaganda agency. Creel immediately drafted a voluntary censorship agreement with newspapers that permitted them to cover the war but kept sensitive military information out of print. The CPI hired hundreds of musicians, writers, and artists to stage a patriotic campaign, and it sponsored 75,000 speakers who delivered four-minute war pep talks in vaude-

Hollywood and Tin Pan Alley did their part to encourage patriotism by putting out scores of war films and a large number of music pieces like the one shown here.

ville and movie theaters across the country. Americans could not take in a movie without being told to love the state and hate the enemy.

Indeed, the CPI found a powerful ally in Hollywood. Quick to perceive that patriotism spelled profits, studio moguls cranked out scores of war films with titles such as *The Prussian Cur, The Claws of the Hun,* and *To Hell with the Kaiser.* Crude propaganda pieces all, these films bombarded workers and immigrants with the message that the Allies were good and the Central Powers evil. Moreover, movie stars such as Douglas Fairbanks, Mary Pickford, and Charlie Chaplin toured the country selling war bonds, while Tin Pan Alley did its best to foster patriotism, too, by pumping out a series of catchy tunes with titles like "Keep the Home Fires Burning" and "Over There." All in all, World War I offered impressive evidence of film's potential for shaping public opinion.

Popular culture reflected the CPI's influence. Truth became the first casualty; language lost meaning, and stereotypes abounded. Suddenly, dissent meant treason, Germans were Huns, and German-Americans were all spies for the fatherland. It did not matter that the vast majority of German-Americans supported the United States; the CPI consistently attacked their loyalty. At its best the CPI may have sold war bonds, discouraged war stoppages, and convinced the public to support the war; at its worst it fostered an American witch hunt.

As passions rose, Americans lashed out at all things German. In the name of patriotism, musicians no longer played Bach and Beethoven, and schools stopped teaching the German language. Americans renamed sauerkraut "liberty cabbage"; dachshunds, "liberty hounds"; and German measles, "liberty measles." Cincinnati, with its large German-American population, even removed pretzels from the free lunch counters in saloons. Vigilante attacks on anyone suspected of being unpatriotic were common. German-speaking families were afraid to talk on the street, and not without reason; many became the victims of mob violence. Workers who refused to buy war bonds often suffered harsh retribution, and attacks on labor protestors were nothing short of brutal. The legal system backed the suppression. Juries routinely released defendants accused of violence against individuals or groups critical of the war.

Political Repression

The government fueled the hysteria. In June 1917 Congress passed the Espionage Act, giving postal officials authority to ban newspapers and magazines from the mails and threaten individuals convicted of obstructing the draft with $10,000 fines and twenty years in jail. The following year, Congress grew even more repressive. The Sedition Act of 1918 made it a federal offense to use "disloyal, profane, scurrilous, or abusive language" about the Constitution, the government, the American uniform, or the flag. The government prosecuted over 2100 people under these acts. Randolph Bourne's belief that civil rights would fall victim to the power of the state rang true.

Cartoons like this helped increase the already strong anti-German sentiment of many, and German-Americans were often badgered, beaten, and killed.

Political dissenters bore the brunt of the repression. Eugene V. Debs, who urged socialists to resist militarism, was imprisoned for nearly three years. The Industrial Workers of the World were singled out for especially harsh treatment. In September 1917 the Justice Department staged massive raids on IWW officers, arresting 169 of its veteran leaders. The administration's purpose was, as one attorney put it, "very largely to put the IWW out of business." The courts then handed down stiff prison sentences. The government had won.

The Supreme Court later approved the attacks on civil liberties. Its leading libertarian, Oliver Wendell Holmes, upheld the Espionage Act in *Schenck* v. *United States* (1919) by comparing the denial of free speech during the war to the prohibition against "a man falsely shouting fire in a theater and causing panic." In a second case, *Abrams* v. *United States* (1919), Holmes reversed himself and argued against the Sedition Act, returning to his support for "free trade in ideas." He was outvoted seven to two.

World War I did not cause repression; it merely intensified old fears. Many Americans clung to the image of the United States as a strong, isolated country, inhabited by old stock, white, middle-class Protestants. Their vision no longer reflected reality, but the war offered them a chance to lash out at those who had changed America. Immigrants, radical labor organizers, socialists, anarchists, communists, critics of any kind, became victims of intolerance.

Wartime Reforms

The war hysteria bred a curious alliance between superpatriots and old style reformers. The Prohibitionists had little difficulty turning World War I to their advantage. They had been winning victories at the state level since the middle of the nineteenth century, but their first federal victory came in 1917 when Congress prohibited the use of grain for the production of alcoholic beverages, arguing that foodstuffs were needed to feed American soldiers and the Allies. To supply an additional push, the Prohibitionists joined the anti-German craze, portraying America's enemies as beer-guzzling Huns and warning that German-Americans controlled the nation's breweries. The "drys" finally won when Congress passed the Eighteenth Amendment in 1917. The final state ratified the amendment two months after the Armistice, and the Volstead Act, which banned the manufacture and sale of alcoholic beverages, took effect one year later.

Like prohibition, women's suffrage benefited from the emergency atmosphere of World War I. Although radical suffragists, led by Alice Paul of the National Women's Party, refused to support the war as long as women could not vote, most women's organizations backed the war effort. Wilson appointed suffragists Carrie Chapman Catt and Anna Howard Shaw as directors of the Women's Committee of the Council of National Defense. As thousands of women went to work in the defense industries, the Department of Labor formed a special unit to collect data on female workers. After the war the Women's Bureau campaigned for federal legislation protecting women workers. Because military officials refused to give women regular appointments in the medical corps, thousands of women joined the Red Cross and the American Women's Hospital Service and served overseas as nurses, physicians, clerks, and ambulance drivers. In 1918 the army established the

Members of the National Women's Party, led by Alice Paul (on the balcony), celebrate their right to vote at their headquarters in Washington, D.C. in 1920.

During the war, many women took jobs previously held by men. Here a group of women repair an automobile in a factory.

Army Corps of Nurses to provide similar services to wounded United States soldiers.

The leaders of the women's movement demanded the vote as a reward for their patriotic support of the war. Although Woodrow Wilson had long opposed women's suffrage, political reality was forcing his hand. Most western states had already extended the right to vote to women. Illinois followed suit in 1914 and Rhode Island and New York in 1917. With so many women now eligible to vote, President Wilson did not want the question to become an issue in the upcoming elections. Alice Paul, head of the National Women's Party, had organized around-the-clock picketing in front of the White House. In 1918 Wilson publicly came around to the idea, telling the Senate that the vote for women "is vital to the winning of the war." In 1919, shortly after the Armistice, Congress passed the Nineteenth Amendment, granting women the right to vote. Ratification followed in the summer of 1920.

Apart from the vote, however, World War I brought no permanent changes for women. At the outset women hoped that the war would open important new jobs for them. Instead, the rise in employment opportunities was meager and brief. Of the million women who found jobs in war-related industries, most were already in the workforce. Labor unions opposed hiring women and tolerated their presence solely as a wartime necessity. Industrial jobs, the unions insisted, were for men and should be returned to them as soon as the war ended. As the Central Federated Union of New York put it: "the same patriotism which induced women to enter industry during the war should induce them to vacate their positions after the war." Fewer than half of the women who took jobs in heavy industry during the war still held them in 1919, and the number of women in the workforce was smaller in 1920 than it had been in 1910.

Blacks and the Great Migration

Blacks hoped to use the war to improve their status. Most black newspapers backed the war. Even the militant black intellectual W. E. B. Du Bois urged blacks to "close ranks" with whites, declaring, "If this is our country, then this is our war." Du Bois hoped that blacks, by demon-

The 369th infantry regiment returned from war in February 1919. They were awarded the *Croix de Guerre* (war cross) for bravery in the Meuse-Argonne.

strating patriotism and bravery, could win public respect and earn better treatment after the war.

At first military leaders even denied blacks the privilege of dying for their country. The marines accepted no blacks; the navy used them only as mess boys; and the army planned to make them servants. When the National Association for the Advancement of Colored People (NAACP) and other black organizations protested, however, the army agreed to compromise. Following the Civil War example, the army created black regiments commanded by white officers. Those black regiments that were committed to battle fought well, but most black soldiers in Europe were used to move supplies. While two-thirds of the American Expeditionary Force saw combat, only one-fifth of the black troops did so.

Back home the record was equally mixed. In decades following the Civil War a steady trickle of blacks had left the South to search for jobs in northern cities. During World War I that

trickle became a flood. Plagued by the boll wee-
vil, low cotton prices, and unrelenting white
repression, sharecroppers were ripe for a
change. When labor agents appeared in 1916
promising jobs in the North, blacks responded
eagerly. By November 1918 the "Great Migration" had brought half a million southern blacks
to the "Land of Hope."

Many found jobs in northern factories and
packing houses. The Chicago packing houses
had been ninety-seven percent white in 1901,
but by 1918 they employed 10,000 blacks—
over twenty percent of the workforce. Virtually
all white in 1900, the northern steel industry
was ten percent black by 1920. But regardless
of the industry, discrimination forced blacks to
the bottom of the ladder, where they took over
the menial, back-breaking jobs that had been
vacated by Slavic and Italian workers, the most
recent wave of immigrants.

The Great Migration angered southern
whites. The price of cotton tripled during the
war; southern planters, fearing the loss of their
labor force, resorted to intimidation and mob
violence to stop the exodus. A mob in Mississippi, for example, derailed a train to prevent
blacks from leaving. Like their ancestors who
had taken the underground railroad to freedom,
many blacks who moved to the North during
World War I had to travel under cover of darkness.

Northern whites opposed the Great Migration, too. Manufacturers welcomed cheap black
labor (especially as strikebreakers), but most
northerners felt threatened by the newcomers.
Middle-class whites feared changes in the racial
composition of their society, while immigrants
resented the competition for jobs and encroachment on their neighborhoods. Increasingly, Northerners turned to segregation, discrimination, and violence, and blacks, hoping
for a better life in the North, fought back. Race
riots erupted in twenty-six cities in 1917, including northern communities such as Philadelphia and southern towns like Houston. The
most serious race riot occurred in East St.
Louis, where at least thirty-nine blacks were
killed.

Clearly, World War I meant different things
to different groups: for the administration, a

test of the limits of voluntarism; for businessmen and technocrats, a chance to pull the le-
vers of government; for nativists and superpatriots, an excuse to lash out at "undesirable"
elements; for radicals and dissenters, repression and hardship; for manufacturers and farmers, high profits; for reformers, victories on
women's suffrage and prohibition; for trade unions, the right to organize for better pay; and for
blacks, a chance to escape from southern poverty.

THE WAR FRONT

The United States entered World War I without
a large army or the ships to transport one to
Europe. Six weeks before Congress declared
war, the army had not even drafted plans to
organize a large military force. Most Americans
thought that the Allies were winning and hoped
that the United States' contribution could be
limited to material, financial credits, and moral
support. In truth, the Allies were ready to collapse. The French army was in the throes of
mutiny. Soldiers were tired of suicidal assaults
ordered by inept generals, and the U-boat offensive had reduced Britain to a six-week supply of food. (Allied losses for 1917 stood at 6.5
million tons of shipping.)

The War at Sea

The situation was desperate and Wilson ordered the United States Navy to help the British. American ships relieved the British of patrolling the Western Hemisphere, while another
portion of the fleet steamed to the north Atlantic to combat the submarine menace. Six destroyers reached Ireland on May 4; thirty-five
ships had arrived by July; and 343 ships patrolled the seas surrounding England by the
war's end.

American and British commanders disagreed sharply on how best to defend merchant
ships. The British believed in "the needle in the
haystack" theory—dispersing individual vessels widely at sea and then shooting them
through carefully patrolled channels for the last
leg of the journey. The policy had not worked.
In April alone shipping losses totaled 881,027

Life in the trenches, as depicted by the British soldiers in 1916, was often cramped, uncomfortable, and miserable. Many men tried to make the best of it by surrounding themselves with personal effects.

tons. The Americans proposed a convoy system—using warships to escort merchant ships to Great Britain. The British reluctantly agreed, and by December the convoy system had cut losses in half.

Raising an Army

Wilson's response to the Allies' cries for land forces was more cautious. His choice to lead the American Expeditionary Force (AEF) was Major John J. "Black Jack" Pershing. Despite urgent requests from Allied commanders, Pershing refused to send raw recruits to the front. He also rejected demands that American units be integrated as replacements into British and French regiments. Instead, Pershing insisted on keeping American troops as independent units under his command. To bolster Allied morale while the army trained, the War Department hurriedly dispatched the First Division

to France, where it marched through Paris on July 4, 1917, to the cheers of thousands.

A bitter debate erupted over how to raise the American army. Confronted with heavy pressure from Theodore Roosevelt and others who favored a volunteer army, Wilson insisted on conscription. Opponents argued that the draft was unnecessary and undemocratic. Responding to the selective service bill, Congressman Champ Clark of Missouri minced no words: "... there is precious little difference between a conscript and a convict." Despite widespread fears that the draft threatened democracy, Congress passed the Selective Service Act on May 18, 1917. Unlike the Civil War, there were no draft riots. More than 23 million men registered during World War I, and 2,810,296 were inducted into the armed services.

To assign these men to the right military tasks, the army launched an ambitious program of psychological testing. The man who devel-

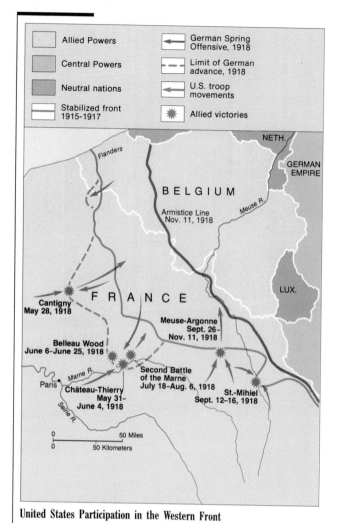

Legend:

- Allied Powers
- Central Powers
- Neutral nations
- Stabilized front 1915–1917
- German Spring Offensive, 1918
- Limit of German advance, 1918
- U.S. troop movements
- Allied victories

NETH.

GERMAN EMPIRE

Flanders

B E L G I U M

Armistice Line Nov. 11, 1918

Meuse R.

LUX.

Cantigny May 28, 1918

F R A N C E

Meuse-Argonne Sept. 26– Nov. 11, 1918

Belleau Wood June 6–June 25, 1918

Marne R.

Paris

Second Battle of the Marne July 18–Aug. 6, 1918

Château-Thierry May 31– June 4, 1918

Seine R.

St.-Mihiel Sept. 12–16, 1918

0   50 Miles
0   50 Kilometers

United States Participation in the Western Front

oped and presided over this program was Robert M. Yerkes, a Harvard-trained psychologist and former president of the American Psychological Association. Yerkes was a brilliant organizer and a forceful promoter of his profession. Since most scientists regarded psychology as a "soft" discipline (in many universities it was housed in the philosophy department), Yerkes saw the war as an opportunity to establish the academic legitimacy of psychology by providing a vital service to the nation. "If the Army machine is to work smoothly and efficiently," he declared, "it is as important to fit the job to the man as to fit the ammunition to the gun."

Yerkes and his associates all believed that intelligence was hereditary and quickly developed a large-scale mental testing program. Two separate tests were devised. Army Alpha was for those who could read English; Army Beta was for men who failed the Alpha test or were illiterate in English. The Alpha test included questions that became the stock and trade of mental testing—untangling sentences, supplying the next number of a sequence, making analogies, and so forth. The Beta test used pictures to examine the same skills. Both tests could be completed in less than an hour, and both could be administered to large groups of men. During the war, 1.75 million recruits took the tests.

Though Yerkes insisted that the tests measured native intelligence, they did not. They were biased in favor of academic skills. Men who knew their way around a school room scored higher than those who did not. "It was touching," one examiner observed, "to see the intense effort . . . put into answering questions, often by men who had never held a pencil in their hands." Still, the army needed some means of sorting out its huge number of draftees, and mental testing appeared to be fair and democratic. Actually, it reinforced the class structure of American society. Native-born whites achieved the highest scores, while blacks and recent immigrants consistently scored lower.

Apart from selecting officers, the army made little use of the test data. Ordinary soldiers were not assigned tasks on the basis of test scores. After the war, however, Yerkes boldly proclaimed that mental testing had "helped to win the war." All it really accomplished was to sell the public on the idea of mental testing and lay the groundwork for a thriving peacetime industry. After the war, numerous businesses adopted mental tests to screen personnel, and many colleges started requiring them for admission. Few legacies of the war had a more lasting or widespread impact on American society.

The Defeat of Germany

As the American army trained, the situation in Europe deteriorated. The mutiny within the French army was spreading (ten divisions were now in revolt); the Eastern Front had dissolved when the Bolsheviks, who had seized power in November, took Russia out of the war by signing a separate peace treaty with Germany; and the German and Austrian forces had all but routed the Italian armies. In fact, by late 1917 the war had come down to a race between American mobilization and Germany's war machine.

On March 21, 1918, General Erich Von Ludendorff launched a massive offensive on the Western Front in the Valley of the Somme. Committing more than 600 artillery pieces to the attack, the Germans struck the British and then the French. Badly bloodied, the Allied forces lost ground. With German troops barely fifty miles from Paris, Marshal Ferdinand Foch, the leader of the French army, assumed command of the Allied forces.

On July 15, 1918, the German army mustered its forces for one last drive on Paris. After three days of heated battle, Foch's Allied troops, aided by 85,000 American soldiers, turned them back. Foch launched a furious counteroffensive that lasted until August 6. Allied troops, strengthened by American divisions, hit the Germans hard in a series of bloody assaults, pushing them back to the Belgian border by the end of October.

The "Yanks" started arriving in large numbers in July and August and by mid-August, they occupied the southern tip of the Western Front. The American First Army, under the command of General Pershing, began its first independent action on September 12, capturing 16,000 Germans in three days. By the end of September, Pershing commanded an army of 1,200,000 and the American forces manned about one-fourth (approximately eighty-five miles) of the Western Front.

Overall, American forces made the crucial difference in the war. The German forces were numerically superior when American troops first arrived, but by the end of the war the Allies could field 600,000 more men than the Germans.

Buoyed by the fresh manpower, the Allies pressed their advantage. They launched a major offensive in the summer of 1918, and

American troops began arriving in Europe throughout 1918. Here the 69th Infantry from New York say their farewells.

On November 11, 1918 American troops celebrated the news of the armistice on the Western Front while the Western world rejoiced at home.

within a few months the Central Powers were on the verge of collapse. The Austro-Hungarian Empire asked for peace; Turkey and Bulgaria stopped fighting; and Germany requested an armistice, hoping Wilson would give them enough time to withdraw to a more defensible position. Instead, he insisted that the German forces leave France and Belgium and surrender all arms. In a direct slap at the Kaiser, Wilson announced that he would negotiate only with a democratic regime in Germany. Though the military leaders and the Kaiser wavered, the German people had suffered enough. A brief revolution forced the Kaiser to abdicate, and a civilian regime seized control of the government.

Germany's new rulers immediately accepted the armistice and agreed to negotiate a treaty. At 11:00 A.M., November 11, 1918, the guns stopped. At the moment of peace, German and Allied soldiers entered the no man's land to gossip and trade souvenirs. Throughout the Western world, crowds filled the streets to celebrate peace.

Postwar Hysteria

Peace did not restore stability to the United States. Jubilation over the Armistice quickly dissolved into fear, unleashing the forces of conformity, vigilantism, and repression. The attack centered on blacks, organized labor, and political dissidents—the very groups that old-stock citizens blamed for the changes in American society which they found most threatening. The Wilson administration either led the attacks or did nothing to stop them. Big government had found new enemies at home to replace those abroad. Echoing Bourne's earlier warnings, Frederick Howe, the commissioner of immigration under President Wilson, would later write: "I became distrustful of the state. It seemed to want to hurt people; it showed no concern for innocence; it aggrandized itself and protected its powers by unscrupulous means."

Hopes for improved race relations after the war were dead. Tensions rose in the North because of competition between whites and blacks for jobs and housing. In the South, whites feared the returning 400,000 black veterans who had been trained in the use of firearms. Many of the black veterans had served in France where they were treated with respect. Southern whites feared that they would demand the same treatment at home. Determined to keep blacks repressed, southern whites instituted a reign of terror. In 1919 ten black veterans were lynched (several still in uniform); fourteen were burned at the stake. All told seventy lynchings occurred in the first year of peace.

The heat of summer brought tensions to a boil, and race riots broke out in twenty-five cities. The worst violence erupted on a Chicago beach where seventeen-year-old Eugene Williams strayed into waters claimed by whites. A rock-throwing mob kept him from reaching shore, and Williams drowned. Fighting broke out when police refused to arrest his killers. Thirteen days of street violence followed, leaving 38 dead, 578 injured, and 1000 families homeless.

Black and white liberals were dismayed by the growing violence. In Atlanta, they established the Commission on Interracial Cooperation to promote better race relations. The NAACP, which had emerged from the war as the leading representative of black Americans, advised blacks to defend themselves until a solution could be found that combined peace with justice. W. E. B. Du Bois urged black veterans to put their military training to use, exhorting them to "return fighting." The sad truth, however, was that the black masses could not defend themselves from white attacks, any more than civil rights organizations could destroy segregation, end discrimination, or abolish lynch law. Not until the federal government committed itself to the defense of civil rights would black Americans be safe in their homes or have any chance at equality.

Labor Unrest and the Red Scare

Labor was another troublespot. Most American workers had demonstrated their patriotism by not striking during the war, but the Armistice ended their trust in management. High inflation, job competition from returning veterans, and government policies all contributed to labor's discontent. Of the three, inflation was the most serious. Food prices more than doubled between 1915 and 1920; clothing costs more than tripled. President Wilson had made peace with trade unions only as a wartime necessity. After the fighting stopped, he removed wartime controls on industry. Correctly interpreting this as a green light from the White House, business leaders closed ranks to roll back the wartime concessions they had made to workers.

The first strike came just four days after the Armistice. In New York the Amalgamated Clothing Workers walked out for a fifteen percent wage hike and a forty-four-hour week. To the surprise of most observers, the workers won. A tidal wave of strikes then swept the country. Textile workers, actors, and telephone operators went out; a general strike paralyzed Seattle; the bituminous miners struck; 365,000 steelworkers staged the biggest strike the nation had ever seen; and in Boston the police

even walked out. By the end of 1919 more then four million workers (a staggering twenty percent of the workforce) had staged over 3600 strikes nationwide.

The strikes left the labor movement in shambles. Well-established unions like the skilled workers of the American Federation of Labor came through the turmoil in good shape. Unions of unskilled workers in the mass production industries, like the United Mine Workers or the steel workers, were easily defeated. The message was clear: without government backing, organized labor was no match for the united strength of the anti-union employers. The upshot was that the labor movement lost 1.5 million members.

The strikes frightened middle- and upper-class Americans, who feared the country was on the verge of revolution. The government made it worse by claiming that the strikes were instigated by Communists. The Bolshevik revolution had taken Russia out of the war by 1918, angering large numbers of Americans. Then in March 1919, the Bolsheviks organized the Third International and called for socialists and workers in Europe and the United States to seize control of their government and join the worldwide revolution. When Communist revolts in Eastern Europe followed, Americans braced themselves for trouble at home.

A bomb scare brought public fear to a head. Just before May Day, 1919, authorities discovered twenty bombs in the mail of prominent capitalists, including John D. Rockefeller and J. P. Morgan, as well as government officials like Postmaster General Burleson and Justice Oliver Wendell Holmes. A month later, bombs exploded in eight American cities. Anarchists were probably responsible, but the public blamed the communists. Ironically, most American radicals denounced the violence.

Fear sparked by the labor unrest, communism, and the bombings plunged the United States into the "Red Scare" of 1919 and early 1920. Every threat to national security, real or imagined, fed public fear. The nation had lost confidence in its ability to survive without use of police state tactics. Civil liberties became the first victim of the hysteria, for the Bill of Rights was all but suspended. Again, Randolph Bourne's warnings haunted the country.

Vigilantism flourished. Juries across the country acquitted individuals accused of violent acts against communists. In the Washington lumber town of Centralia, American Legionaires stormed the IWW office on Armistice Day. Four attackers died in the fight, and townspeople lynched an IWW member in reprisal. Four other Wobblies were sentenced to long terms for murder. The Centralia raid triggered assaults on IWW officers across the state, culminating in the arrests of over 1000 Wobblies. Federal authorities then moved to break the IWW's back by arresting 165 Wobblie leaders—many of whom received prison sentences of up to twenty-five years.

Congress was no more tolerant. In May 1919 the House of Representatives refused to seat Victor Berger, a Milwaukee socialist, after he was convicted of sedition. The House again denied him his seat following a special election in December 1919. Not until his reelection in 1922, after the government dropped it charges, did Congress seat him.

Attorney General A. Mitchell Palmer led the attack on radicalism. Ambitious to become president in 1920, Palmer hoped to ride a wave of public hysteria against radicalism into the White House. To root out sedition, he created a General Intelligence Division (the precursor of the FBI) in the Justice Department under the direction of J. Edgar Hoover. Hoover collected the names of thousands of known or suspected communists and made plans for a coordinated government attack on their headquarters.

In November 1919 Palmer struck with lightning speed at radicals in twelve cities. The raids netted 250 arrests, a small taste of what was to come. A second series of raids in thirty-three cities followed in January. This time Palmer's men arrested more than 4000 alleged Communists, many of whom were jailed without bond, beaten, and denied food and water for days. Local authorities freed most of them in a few weeks, except for 600 aliens, who were deported.

Palmer insisted that he was ridding the country of the "moral perverts and hysterical neurasthenic women who abound in commu-

nism." To cooler heads, however, his tactics gave off the unmistakable odor of a police state. Charles Evans Hughes denounced the raids as "violations of personal rights which savor of the worst practices of tyranny." Suddenly on the defensive, Palmer tried to rally public support by predicting a huge outburst of terrorist attacks on May Day, 1920. Federal troops went on alert and police braced themselves in cities across the country, but May Day came and went without incident. Suddenly Palmer looked more like dead wood than presidential timber. His bid for the White House fizzled, and the Red Scare had largely spent its fury.

THE TREATY OF VERSAILLES

The Fourteen Points

Long before the military outcome of the war had become clear, the Allies started planning for peace. As early as 1915 Britain and France had signed secret treaties imposing a harsh peace on Germany. Their plans were totally at odds with Wilson's call for "peace without victory." Wilson felt a punitive treaty would sow the seeds of future wars. Repeatedly during the war, Wilson had elaborated his ideas on the interdependence of democracy, free trade, and liberty, and on January 8, 1918, he unveiled the Fourteen Points, his personal formula for peace.

Five of the points were general. Wilson called for "open covenants openly arrived at," freedom of the seas, free trade, arms reduction, and self determination. Other points demanded partial or full independence for minorities and a recognition of the rise of nationalist sentiments. The fourteenth point, which Wilson considered the heart of his plan, called for an international organization to promote world peace by guaranteeing the territorial integrity of all nations. The fairness of the terms, Wilson hoped, would command the support of the Allies and strengthen the hand of peace advocates within Germany.

Wilson's foreign policy was his version of liberal capitalism, the New Freedom projected

Table 22.1

Woodrow Wilson's Fourteen Points, 1918: Success and Failure in Implementation

1. Open covenants of peace openly arrived at	Not fulfilled
2. Absolute freedom of navigation upon the seas in peace and war	Not fulfilled
3. Removal of all economic barriers to the equality of trade among nations	Not fulfilled
4. Reduction of armaments to the level needed only for domestic safety	Not fulfilled
5. Impartial adjustment of colonial claims	Not fulfilled
6. Evacuation of all Russian territory; Russia to be welcomed into the society of free nations	Not fulfilled
7. Evacuation and restoration of Belgium	**Fulfilled**
8. Evacuation and restoration of all French lands; return of Alsace-Lorraine to France	**Fulfilled**
9. Readjustment of Italy's frontiers along lines of Italian nationality	Compromised
10. Self-determination for the former subjects of the Austro-Hungarian Empire	Compromised
11. Evacuation of Rumania, Serbia, and Montenegro; free access to the sea for Serbia	Compromised
12. Self-determination for the former subjects of the Ottoman Empire; secure sovereignty for Turkish portion	Compromised
13. Establishment of an independent Poland, with free and secure access to the sea	**Fulfilled**
14. Establishment of a League of Nations affording mutual guarantees of independence and territorial integrity	Not fulfilled

Source: Data from G. M. Gathorne-Hardy, *The Fourteen Points and the Treaty of Versailles* (Oxford Pamphlets on World Affairs, no. 6, 1939), pp. 8-34; Thomas G. Paterson et al., *American Foreign Policy, A History Since 1900*, 2nd ed., Vol. 2, pp. 282-93.

on a world stage. His call for freedom of the seas and free trade would protect free market capitalism from monopolistic restrictions, and open huge markets to booming American industries. Self-determination would offer independence to Europe's minorities as well as please millions of recent immigrants back in the United States, most of whom were drifting into the Democratic party. The League of Nations would give the world the ability to police aggression and relieve the United States of that responsibility. As far as Wilson was concerned, the Fourteen Points were perfect: they offered peace, freedom, and profits.

When the tide of war turned in favor of the Allies in 1918, peace forces within Germany agreed to surrender on the basis of the Fourteen Points. They overthrew the Kaiser's regime, paving the way for Wilson to make good on his promise of a peace without victory. The president's personal prestige was at its peak when the Armistice was declared. During the war, Democrats and Republicans had closed ranks behind his leadership under the slogan,

"politics is adjourned." Europeans saw Wilson as the moral leader of the Western democracies, and his authority rested not only on words but on might. Economically, the United States was now the most powerful nation on earth. It had been spared the devastation of war; its economy was booming; and its armed forces, in sharp contrast to exhausted armies of Europe, had barely geared up for battle.

Wilson was his own worst enemy in marshaling support for his peace plans. His first mistake was the "October Appeal," in which he asked voters to support Democratic candidates at the polls in 1918 if they wished him to continue as their "unembarrassed spokesman." The request offended Republicans who had supported the administration during the war. When the voters gave Republicans a narrow majority (primarily reflecting local issues), Wilson looked as if he had lost a national referendum on his leadership.

The American Peace Commission's composition further alienated Congress. Wilson broke precedent by personally heading the commission, a role no previous president had assumed. Then he named only one Republican to the five-man commission; the other three men were loyal Democrats and personal associates. The failure to include a prominent Republican senator was a serious tactical error, for the treaty had to be approved by two-thirds of the Senate.

Discord Among the Victors

The American delegation arrived in Europe early in January 1919, where along with the other delegates they confronted three basic issues: territory, reparations, and future security. On each of these issues, Wilson and the Allies disagreed. Early in the war the Allies decided to divide Germany's territorial possessions among themselves, but the Fourteen Points called for self-determination. Devastated by the war, the Allies (especially France) wanted to saddle Germany with huge reparations to pay for the war. The Fourteen Points rejected punishment, arguing it would only lead to future wars. On

the issue of security, France wanted Germany dismembered, while the other Allies favored treaties and alliances.

Only five nations had an important voice in the proceedings. Prime Minister David Lloyd George of Great Britain proved to be Wilson's staunchest ally. Yet he also defended Britain's colonial ambitions and insisted upon reparations. Premier Georges Clemenceau, the "Tiger" of France, was determined to break up the German empire and bleed the German people dry in order to rebuild France. He wryly remarked, "God gave us the Ten Commandments and we broke them. Wilson gave us his Fourteen Points—we shall see."

Premier Vittorio Orlando of Italy, the most urbane of the delegates, was bent upon pressing Italy's territorial ambitions in the Tyrol and on the Adriatic. When Wilson refused to sanction Italy's sovereignty over the largely Yugoslav population near Fiume, Orlando stormed out of the peace conference in disgust. The final important negotiator was Count Nobuaki

At the January peace conference in Paris, Wilson met with Prime Minister David Lloyd George, Premier Vittorio Orlando, and Premier Georges Clemenceau.

Makino, the ambitious spokesman for Japan, who wanted control of German interests in the Far East. He complicated Wilson's task by insisting upon a statement of racial equality in the League of Nations charter.

V. I. Lenin

The Russians were conspicuously absent at Versailles. Allied leaders, furious at the Bolsheviks for negotiating a separate peace with Germany at Brest-Litovsk in March 1918, were adamant that V. I. Lenin's "Red" government would have no voice at the peace conference. Indeed, the Allies had earlier decided to intervene militarily in the Russian Revolution, and even as their spokesmen met in Versailles, Allied armies were fighting in Russia on the side of the "White" or anticommunist movements.

Personally, Wilson despised the Bolsheviks (too undemocratic), and, in keeping with his response to Huerta's regime in Mexico, he refused to extend diplomatic recognition to Lenin's government. To help rescue a Czech army trapped by the Germans in northern Russia, Wilson sent 5000 soldiers to the Soviet Union in 1918, where they joined up with British troops. To help evacuate the Czech army out through Vladivostok, Wilson sent a 9000 man army to Siberia in 1919. Wilson hoped that the presence of American troops in Russia would save the Czech army, limit any Japanese hopes for expansion in Siberia, and perhaps even help the anticommunist forces. The last American troops did not withdraw until 1922.

For their part, the Bolsheviks failed to draw any distinction

American Military Forces in Russia, 1918

between the American and the other western invaders and resented them all with a passion. Yet the presence of American troops on Russian soil was not the only explanation for the intense hatred that developed between Lenin and Wilson. As a result of the Bolshevik Revolution, Lenin emerged as Wilson's chief rival for world leadership. In sharp contrast to the liberal democracy and the limited social change of Wilson, Lenin championed communism, social revolution, and radical change. Wilson was determined to see that his vision of the world's future, not Lenin's, carried the day at Versailles.

To achieve any treaty at all, Wilson had to compromise. Though he fought gallantly, he was repeatedly thwarted by the combined strength of the others. In the end he tried to scale down their demands and pinned his hopes on the League of Nations. Under the territorial compromise, the Allies got control of Germany's colonies as "mandates" under the supervision on the League of Nations. Japan was allowed to keep Germany's Pacific islands under mandate and to assume the German economic interest in China's Shantung peninsula. In Eastern Europe, the delegates created the nation states of Poland, Yugoslavia, Czechoslovakia, Estonia, Latvia, Lithuania, and Finland. Europe's political map for the first time roughly resembled its linguistic and cultural map.

Security proved more difficult to negotiate. Over the misgivings of most delegates, Wilson succeeded in making the League of Nations an integral part of the final treaty. France remained dubious and demanded a buffer zone, not a convention. To meet Clemenceau's terms, France got control of Alsace-Lorraine for ten years, and the coal-rich Saar Basin was demilitarized permanently and placed under the League of Nations for fifteen years. After Wilson and Lloyd George both signed security treaties guaranteeing these arrangements, France, in return, grudgingly agreed to join the League of Nations.

Despite promises of a just peace, the treaty imposed a harsh settlement on Germany, burdening the country with a $34 billion reparations bill, far more than Germany could pay. In addition, Germany lost territories that contained German people: Alsace-Lorraine to

Europe after World War I

members "to respect and uphold the territorial integrity and independence of all members of the League."

The Struggle for Ratification

Wilson knew that the treaty faced stiff opposition back home. In February thirty-nine Senate Republicans had signed a petition warning that they would not approve the League in its present form. To court domestic support, Wilson persuaded the other delegates in Europe to acknowledge the Monroe Doctrine, omit domestic issues from the League's purview, and permit member states to withdraw after two years' notice. Though he worked to include provisions the Senate wanted, Wilson was not willing to separate the League and the treaty. In March he warned: "When the treaty comes back, the gentlemen on this side will find the covenant not only in it, but so many threads of the treaty tied to the covenant that you cannot dissect the covenant from the treaty without destroying the whole vital structure."

Senate opposition was divided into three groups. The first, the fourteen "irreconcilables," were staunch isolationists who wanted the United States to remain unaligned and uninvolved. Led by William Borah of Idaho, they objected to Article 10 which called for the mutual protection of the territorial integrity of all member states. Henry Cabot Lodge of Massachusetts spoke for the second group of critics known as the "strong reservationists." Basically in favor of the treaty, they wanted to modify the League to accommodate isolationist sentiments. The third group of opponents, the "limited reservationists," were the most numerous. They were concerned about Article 10 but could have been satisfied by minor alterations. With their backing and the support of Senate Democrats, Wilson could have easily secured the passage of the treaty.

Polls showed that most Americans favored the League in some form. All Wilson had to do was compromise with the Senate and the treaty would pass. Instead, he returned to Washington in July itching for a fight, and he grew more stubborn and frustrated as the summer wore

France, the Saar Basin to a League protectorate, a corridor containing the port of Danzig to Poland, and Upper Silesia to Czechoslovakia. The war guilt clause in the reparations bill blamed Germany for the war. Germany's war machine was completely dismantled and any plans for future rearmament were strictly forbidden. Germany felt betrayed. Clearly, this was not a peace based upon the Fourteen Points. Rather, it brought to life Bourne's predictions of victors who "grab what they can."

The compromises permitted all the delegates to sign the peace treaty. Wilson accepted the territorial and punitive provisions in order to ensure the adoption of the League of Nations, which he hoped would secure world peace and eventually redress the treaty's inequities. The League consisted of an Assembly that included all member states, and an executive council composed of the United States, Great Britain, France, Italy, Japan, and four other states to be elected by the Assembly. Article 10 was the League's core, for it pledged all

on. Dismissing his opponents as "blind and little provincial people," Wilson declared that the "Senate must take its medicine." His use of a medical metaphor was telling, for Wilson's health had deteriorated under the strain of the war. In fact, in Paris he had suffered a severe attack of indigestion that was probably a mild stroke.

Against his doctor's warnings, Wilson decided to take his case to the people. In September 1919 he began a nationwide tour, covering 8000 miles in thirty-three days and delivering thirty-two major addresses. He started in the Midwest where opposition to the treaty was strongest, gradually moving west where he met cheering crowds. Totally exhausted, Wilson collapsed on September 25 in Pueblo, Colorado. He returned to Washington where four days later he suffered a severe stroke paralyzing the left side of his body. In all probability, Wilson sustained enough neurological damage to warp his personality and impair his judgment. Unable to work, he did not meet his cabinet for more than six months. Since the law made no provision for removing an incapacitated president, Wilson's wife and a few close aides ran the government, operating under a cloak of silence about the president's condition.

As the Senate vote on the treaty approached, Wilson remained adamant, telling his wife: "Better a thousand times to go down fighting than to dip your colours to dishonorable compromise." He ordered all Democrats to vote against the treaty if it contained any changes. The treaty came to a vote one year, one week, and one day after the Armistice. The Democrats defeated the revised version of the treaty, 55–39; a few minutes later Republicans defeated the treaty without changes, 39–53. The "irreconcilables" were elated.

Wilson was clearly to blame for the Senate's failure to reach a compromise. When supporters of the treaty tried again in March, nearly half of the Democrats disobeyed the president and voted for a revised version of the treaty. But twenty-three followed Wilson's orders, and the treaty fell seven votes short of adoption. The Republicans were elated, proclaiming (in a parody of Wilson's 1916 slogan), "He kept us out of peace."

The refusal of the Senate to ratify the Treaty of Versailles and join the League of Nations is satirized in this cartoon.

An admirer of the British parliamentarian system, Wilson then hatched a bizarre scheme which showed just how much he had lost contact with reality. He wanted fifty-seven recalcitrant senators to resign and stand immediately for reelection. If they were replaced by pro-League people, Wilson would have his ratification; if a majority of them were reelected, Wilson would resign the presidency. At the urging of his advisors, Wilson dropped the proposal.

The Election of 1920

Unable to accept defeat, Wilson then decided to make the election of 1920 a "solemn referendum" on the League: the election of a Democrat would signify approval of the treaty; a Republican victory would mean the treaty's death. It was a dubious test at best of the public's support of the treaty. National elections rarely rest on a single issue. Instead, they turn on a myriad of issues, most of which are quite local in character.

When the Democratic convention met in San Francisco, the delegates ignored Wilson's pathetic anglings for a third term and nominated Governor James M. Cox of Ohio. To round out the ticket, they selected the assistant secretary of the navy, Franklin D. Roosevelt, for vice-president, largely to capitalize on the magic Roosevelt name. The Republican candidate was Senator Warren G. Harding of Ohio. A stalwart party regular on domestic issues, Harding had voted for the Treaty of Versailles with the Lodge reservation.

While Cox barnstormed the country, Harding campaigned from his front porch in Ohio. His campaign managers were afraid to turn him loose on the election circuit for fear of what he might say. As one wag put it, "Thank God only one of them can be elected." Cox campaigned unequivocally for the League of Nations and the Treaty of Versailles. Harding, by contrast, waffled shamelessly, announcing that he opposed the League, but favored an "association of nations." Thus, the election of 1920 was not a "solemn referendum" on the League, for the issue was hopelessly confused. Indeed, the League had become a dead issue. Most voters simply wanted to repudiate Wilson and wartime excesses. And they did just that, giving Harding the largest electoral victory (61 percent of the popular vote) since Washington's election. Harding received 16,152,200 votes to Cox's 9,147,353. Eugene V. Debs, the Socialist candidate, won 919,799 votes (at the time he was serving a prison term in the Atlanta federal penitentiary for opposing American involvement in the war). In the Electoral College, Harding's victory was more impressive: 404 to 127.

The Republicans won because the fragile coalition that Wilson had built in 1916 fell apart. Many Democrats, disillusioned by the costs of the war, either stayed at home or switched parties. Angered by the Treaty of Versailles, ethnic Americans (Germans, Italians, and the Irish in particular) abandoned the Democrats in droves. Their defection cost the Democrats the nation's urban centers. Western states and the Midwest went Republican as well, for despite their wartime prosperity, many farmers were convinced that Wilson's agricultural policies had favored cotton growers in the South over the grain producers of the Midwest. The Solid South alone remained a bastion of Democratic strength, but it did not have nearly enough votes to elect a president.

Harding interpreted his victory as a mandate to reject the League. America never joined the League of Nations, opening the way for those who later blamed the United States for the rise of fascism in Italy and Nazism in Germany. Some even went so far as to claim that America's failure to join the League caused World War II. If the United States had only joined, they insisted, the League would have been able to deter German and Japanese aggression by presenting a united front. But what good was a united front if none of its members was prepared to fight? The critics failed to recognize that the French and the English were not willing to use force to impose collective security—neither was the United States, in or out of the League. Congress had the upper hand in making foreign policy until the very eve of World War II, and it was determined to prevent the United States from being drawn into another European war. The war's main legacy, then, was not peace without victory, but bitterness and suspicion.

CONCLUSION

World War I made Randolph Bourne a prophet. His overpowering conviction that war obliterates idealism and brings out the darker side of the human spirit was borne out by the changes in American life between 1914 and 1919. Before the war, the United States had primarily been an isolated, Western Hemisphere country, preoccupied with life on this side of the Atlantic. The Industrial Revolution had begun its transformation of the economic landscape, but most Americans still earned a living farming their own land. Although the progressive movement had campaigned to use government to eliminate gross economic abuses, the power of the state remained quite miniscule compared to the private sector. And although the United States had been concerned about its cultural pluralism, there was still more consensus than paranoia, more accord than conflict.

CHRONOLOGY OF KEY EVENTS

1914 Archduke Ferdinand assassinated; World War I begins

1915 Sinking of the *Lusitania;* Resignation of Bryan; Wilson permits loans to belligerents

1916 *Sussex* pledge; National Defense Act; Wilson reelected

1917 Zimmermann telegram; U.S. declares war; Selective Service Act; Espionage Act; AEF First Division marches through Paris; Justice Department raids the IWW; Wilson addresses the AFL

1918 Wilson unveils the Fourteen Points; Final German offensive fails; Armistice signed; Influenza epidemic; Death of Randolph Bourne

1919 Versailles negotiations; Nineteenth Amendment grants women the right to vote; Volstead Act; Race riots in American cities; Red Scare and Palmer raids begin; Wilson collapses while touring the U.S. to promote the League of Nations

1920 Versailles Treaty defeated in Senate; National debt reaches $20 billion; Harding elected president

World War I changed everything, accelerating social and economic changes and unleashing extraordinary fears. When the war ended, the United States had become the premier economic power on earth, with global interests requiring protection. Those responsibilities were terrifying to a country lulled into a sense of security by three centuries of geographic isolation. To prosecute the war, the federal government had assumed unprecedented powers, but when the war's instabilities triggered fears of labor unions, anarchists, communists, and immigrants, the state turned its powers on the minorities, assaulting civil liberties in the name of conformity. Rather than make global political commitments commensurate with its new economic interests, the United States refused to ratify the Treaty of Versailles or join the League of Nations.

In 1920 the country was exhausted and confused. When Republican presidential candidate Warren G. Harding promised a return to "normalcy" in 1920, it struck a responsive chord. Millions of Americans thought it meant resurrecting rural villages and a small farm economy, restoring an Anglo-Protestant culture, and forgetting about the rest of the world. The 1920s would prove them wrong.

REVIEW SUMMARY

During World War I the United States adopted new policies in order to mobilize its strength.

> the government secured voluntary cooperation of industry and agriculture through economic incentives
>
> it won the support of labor by recognizing labor's demands and granting some key demands
>
> it employed a progressive tax structure and a savings bond program to finance the war
>
> it organized a propaganda campaign to promote anti-German sentiments
>
> through conscription it raised an army that was to be independent of the command of its European allies

The war and its immediate aftermath had far-reaching consequences for American society.

> blacks abandoned the South for work in northern cities
>
> despite their military service, blacks experienced only token reform in civil rights
>
> after the war the government cracked down on labor
>
> women enjoyed new opportunities in the workplace and the Nineteenth Amendment established female suffrage
>
> a red scare swept the nation
>
> the war brought new prosperity, deadening the spirit of reform and minimizing interest in internationalist projects

SUGGESTIONS FOR FURTHER READING

OVERVIEWS AND SURVEYS

Randolph S. Bourne, *War and the Intellectuals: Collected Essays, 1915–1919* (1964); Foster R. Dulles, *America's Rise to World Power, 1898–1954* (1955); Robert H. Ferrell, *Woodrow Wilson and World War I, 1917–1921* (1985); Lloyd C. Gardner, *Safe for Democracy: The Anglo-American Response to Revolution, 1913–1923* (1984); Otis L. Graham, Jr., *The Great Campaigns: Reform and War in America, 1900–1928* (1971); Ellis W. Hawley, *The Great War and the Search for a Modern Order: A History of the American People and Their Institutions, 1917–1933* (1979); Manfred Jones, *The United States and Germany: A Diplomatic History* (1984); William E. Leuchtenburg, *The Perils of Prosperity, 1914–1932* (1958); Arthur S. Link,

Wilson (5 vols.; 1947–1965); Emily S. Rosenburg, *Spreading the American Dream: American Economic and Cultural Expansion, 1890–1945* (1982); Bernadotte Schmitt and Harold C. Vedeler, *The World in the Crucible: 1914–1919* (1984); Daniel M. Smith, *The Great Departure: The United States in World War I, 1914–1920* (1965); James R. Vitelli, *Randolph Bourne* (1981); and Edwin A. Weinstein, *Woodrow Wilson: A Medical and Psychological Biography* (1981).

THE ROAD TO WAR

Robert W. Cherny, *A Righteous Cause: The Life of William Jennings Bryan* (1985); Kendrick A. Clement, *William Jennings Bryan, Missionary Isolationist* (1982); John W. Coogan, *The End of Neutrality: The United States, Britain, and Maritime Rights, 1899–1915* (1981); John M. Cooper, Jr., *The Vanity of Power: American Isolation and the First World War, 1914–1917* (1969); John M. Cooper, Jr., *The Warrior and the Priest: Woodrow Wilson and Theodore Roosevelt* (1983); Patrick Devlin, *Too Proud to Fight: Woodrow Wilson's Neutrality* (1974); Ross Gregory, *The Origins of American Intervention in the First World War* (1971); George F. Kennan, *The Decision to Intervene* (1958); George F. Kennan, *Russia Leaves the War* (1956); N. Gordon Levin, Jr., *Woodrow Wilson and World Politics: America's Response to War and Revolution* (1968); Arthur S. Link, *Woodrow Wilson: Revolution, War and Peace* (1979); Ernest R. May, *The World War and American Isolation, 1914–1917* (1959); and Barbara Tuchman, *The Guns of August* (1962).

AMERICAN INDUSTRY GOES TO WAR
THE AMERICAN PUBLIC GOES TO WAR

Rodolfo Acuna, *Occupied America* (1980); Allan M. Brandt, *No Magic Bullet: A Social History of Venereal Disease in the United States Since 1880* (1985); Zechariah Chafee, *Free Speech in the United States* (1941); Valerie Jean Conner, *The National War Labor Board: Stability, Social Justice, and the Voluntary State in World War I* (1983); Wayne Cornelius, *Building the Cactus Curtain: Mexican Migration and U.S. Responses from Wilson to Carter* (1980); Robert E. Cuff, *The War Industries Board: Business-Government Relations During World War I* (1973); Charles Gilbert, *American Financing of World War I* (1970); Maurine Wiener Greenwald, *Women, War, and Work: The Impact of World War I on Women Workers in the United States* (1980); David M. Kennedy, *Over Here: The First World War and American Society* (1980); K. Austin Kerr, *Organized for Prohibition: A New History of the Anti-Saloon League* (1985); Daniel J. Kevles, *In the Name of Eugenics: Genetics and the Uses of Human Heredity* (1985); Frederick C. Luebke, *Bonds of Loyalty: German-Americans and World War I* (1974); John F. McClymer, *War and Welfare: Social Engineering in America, 1890–*

1925 (1980); Paul L. Murphy, *World War I and the Origin of Civil Liberties in the United States* (1979); H.C. Peterson and Gilbert C. Fite, *Opponents of War, 1917–1918* (1957); William Preston, Jr., *Aliens and Dissenters: Federal Suppression of Radicals, 1903–1933* (1953); Stephen Skowronek, *Building a New American State: The Expansion of National Administrative Capacities, 1877–1920* (1982); Stephen Vaughn, *Holding Fast the Inner Lines: Democracy, Nationalism, and the CPI* (1980); and Neil A. Wynn, *From Progressivism to Prosperity: World War I and American Society* (1986).

THE WAR FRONT

Arthur E. Barbeau and Florette Henri, *The Unknown Soldiers: Black American Troops in World War I* (1974); Edward W. Coffman, *The War to End Wars: The American Military Experience in World War I* (1968); Harvey DeWeerd, *President Wilson Fights His War: World War I and the American Intervention* (1968); and Russell F. Weigley, *The American Way of War: A History of United States Military Strategy and Policy* (1973).

SOCIAL UNREST AFTER THE WAR

Wesley M. Bagby, *The Road to Normalcy: The Presidential Campaign and Election of 1920* (1962); David Brody, *Labor in Crisis: The Steel Strike of 1919* (1962); Stanley Coben, *A. Mitchell Palmer: Politician* (1963); Paul Fussell, *The Great War and Modern Memory* (1975); Robert K. Murray, *The Red Scare: A Study in National Hysteria, 1919–1920* (1955); Burl Noggle, *Into the Twenties: The United States from Armistice to Normalcy* (1974); Francis Russell, *A City in Terror: 1919, the Boston Police Strike* (1975); Arthur M. Schlesinger, Jr., *The Crisis of the Old Order, 1919–1933* (1957); and William Tuttle, Jr., *Race Riot: Chicago and the Red Summer of 1919* (1970).

THE TREATY OF VERSAILLES

Thomas A. Bailey, *Woodrow Wilson and the Great Betrayal* (1945); Thomas A. Bailey, *Woodrow Wilson and the Lost Peace* (1944); Warren F. Kuehl, *Seeking World Order* (1969); N. Gordon Levin, Jr., *Woodrow Wilson and World Politics: America's Response to War and Revolution* (1968); Charles L. May, Jr., *The End of Order, Versailles, 1919* (1980); Arno J. Mayer, *Politics and Diplomacy in Peacemaking: Containment and Counterrevolution at Versailles, 1918–1919* (1967); Arno J. Mayer, *Wilson vs. Lenin: Political Origins of the New Diplomacy, 1917–1918* (1969); Ralph A. Stone, *The Irreconcilables: The Fight Against the League of Nations* (1970); and William C. Widenor, *Henry Cabot Lodge and the Search for an American Foreign Policy* (1980).

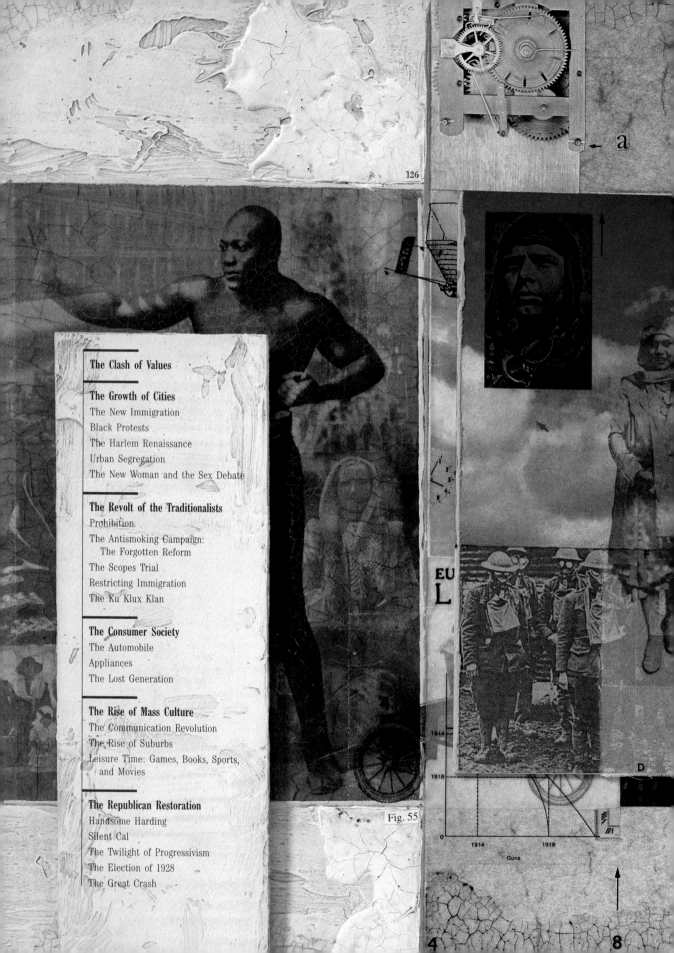

126

a

EU
L

1914

1918

Fig. 55

D

1914   1918

Guns

4   8

CHAPTER 23

Modern Times, The 1920s

HD: Plane director of all common normals

Common normal
Common generator

*T*n 1898 the Physicians Club of Chicago held a symposium on "sexual hygiene" to provide its members with some practical tips on marriage counseling. Confronted by an increasing number of married women who were inquiring about birth control, Chicago physicians offered this advice: "Get a divorce and vacate the position for some other woman, who is able and willing to fulfill all a wife's duties as well as to enjoy her privileges." Most Americans agreed. They did not believe that sex should be separated from procreation. To the male custodians of morality, birth control challenged patriarchy. Some warned it would lead to sexual promiscuity and an epidemic of venereal diseases, while others charged that it would raise the divorce rate and thereby weaken the family. Many women condemned birth control just as soundly. Taught from childhood to embrace the cult of domesticity, they accepted childbearing as their "biological duty" and rejected birth control as immoral and radical.

By 1950, however, most Americans regarded birth control as a public virtue rather than a private vice. The person most responsible for this amazing transformation was Margaret Sanger (1879–1966), a petite redhead with soft brown eyes, an iron will, and the soul of a firebrand. From 1914 to 1937 Sanger campaigned to make birth control morally acceptable. She built a network of clinics where women could get accurate information about contraception and obtain inexpensive, reliable birth control devices. After World War II, she helped organize the international planned parenthood movement and played a key role in the development of "the pill." Margaret Sanger probably had a greater influence on the world than any other American woman.

Sanger's mother, Margaret Higgins, bore eleven children, all ten pounders or more. Michael Higgins, her father, was a free-thinking Irishman who worked as a stonecutter, but preferred to hang around pubs proclaiming his faith in socialism and doubts about God. Her mother died of pulmonary tuberculosis at the age of forty-three; her father lived to be eighty-four. Sanger believed for the rest of her life that her mother's suffering could have been prevented by effective family planning.

An unhappy marriage also pushed Sanger toward reform. While still in nursing school, she married William Sanger, an architect and would-be artist, and they set up housekeeping in Greenwich Village, a bohemian colony in New York City. After bearing three children in rapid succession, Sanger overcame her own struggle with tuberculosis, finished school, and began a nursing career. Through her husband, she met the leaders of radical politics in New York, including the anarchist, Emma Goldman, and the Wobbly, William D. "Big Bill" Haywood. Feeling trapped by married life and determined to achieve her own identity, Margaret plunged into New York's labor movement. As her marriage to William slowly dissolved, she devoted herself to the families of the working poor.

Sanger was convinced that large families placed a terrible economic burden on the poor, and she sympathized with the countless women, rich and poor, who desperately wanted to control their fertility. After watching several working-class women bleed to death from back alley abortions, Sanger came to regard birth control as the most important issue of her day, not because she opposed abortion but because birth control would make them, as well as unwanted babies, unnecessary. When male labor leaders failed to include contraception on their reform agenda, Sanger left the labor movement and resolved to make birth control her life's work.

On the eve of World War I, Sanger launched a one-woman crusade for contraception. She lectured to anyone who would listen and offered birth control devices to anyone in need. In 1921 she organized the American Birth Control League, which opened scores of clinics in major American cities. Next Sanger recruited physicians and social workers to agitate for repeal of the Comstock Act of 1873, a federal law making it illegal to send birth control information or devices through the mail. In addition, she attracted several wealthy feminists to the birth control movement, and their support financed research on the relative safety and effectiveness of different kinds of contraceptives.

Sanger was a key figure in the transition to modern times. Her career illustrates how the reform spirit of the Progressive Era not only

After spending a year absorbing medical opinions and learning about contraceptives, Margaret Sanger began publishing the journal *Woman Rebel*.

survived the conservative climate of the 1920s but touched the lives of future generations. While most reforms were essentially political, birth control was a social movement that involved feminists, philanthropists, social workers, physicians, and scientists. No legacy of progressivism was more far-reaching. The birth control movement reformed sexual mores, redefined the proper role of women in society, and redistributed power within the family.

THE CLASH OF VALUES

The 1920s was a confusing decade. In the wake of the Great War's carnage and failed promises, people were at odds. Wets battled drys, atheists ridiculed fundamentalists, White, Anglo-Saxon Protestants (WASPs) denounced the "new immigrants," whites lashed out against blacks, and practically everyone sensed a decline in morality. Rural folks debated the dubious morals of city dwellers, while farmers glowered at industrialists. Midwesterners and southerners expressed their skepticism about the Golden East, with its sprawling cities teeming with immigrants. World War I had left people disillusioned and skeptical about human nature, but at the same time they were intoxicated with

economic prosperity and the potential of the future.

The 1920s "New Era" was a transitional decade when Americans debated which of their traditional values to preserve and which to modify or abandon. The choices were disconcerting, and relatively few people recognized these conflicts for what they were—unavoidable growing pains of a nation struggling to come to grips with cultural pluralism and modernization.

THE GROWTH OF CITIES

The most dramatic and visible change in the American landscape was the rise of the cities. According to the census of 1920, more Americans lived in cities than in the country for the first time in the nation's history. Most urbanites lived in small towns and cities, but a surprising number resided in metropolitan areas—large cities with 50,000 or more people. During the 1920s nearly 15 million Americans moved to the cities. The South remained largely rural, but its rate of urbanization increased more than other areas, rising from twenty-five percent in 1920 to thirty-two percent in 1930, a clear indication of what the future held in store for the "Sun Belt."

Most new arrivals to the cities came from the country. Farms lost 10,184,000 residents between 1920 and 1940. Even those who remained on the land did not necessarily escape the city's influence. Electrical power scattered industries over broad areas, and as the automobile increased labor's mobility, many rural folk commuted to jobs in nearby mill towns and cities.

Urban growth drove up land values and reshaped the skyline of America's cities, especially in central business districts. In New York and Chicago, the amount of office space more than doubled during the 1920s. Skyrocketing land prices forced architects to build "up" instead of "out," launching the first great era of skyscrapers. New York's ornate Woolworth Building, rising 55 stories and 760 feet above ground level, was completed in 1914, offering the prototype for the new "Woolworth Gothic" skyscrapers that quickly dominated Manhat-

The Woolworth Building in New York City, shown here under construction in 1912, set the trend for skyscrapers in numerous cities throughout the 1920s.

tan's skyline. Soon Chicago had its 34-story, Gothic-topped Tribune Tower on Michigan Avenue, and other skyscrapers quickly appeared in Pittsburgh, Cleveland, Kansas City, and San Francisco. America's cities were starting to look alike.

The New Immigration

The new cities were inhabited by new immigrants. Immigration patterns to the United States began to change in the 1880s, with fewer and fewer people arriving from northern and western Europe and more and more coming from southern and eastern Europe. Instead of being Protestants, they were Roman Catholic, Eastern Orthodox, and Jewish. Old stock had grown accustomed to immigrants from Germany, Scandinavia, and the British Isles, but they were confused by the arrival of Poles, Lithuanians, Czechs, Slovaks, Magyars, Ukrainians,

Russians, Serbians, Croatians, Italians, Greeks, and Armenians.

The new immigrants poured into the industrial cities of the Northeast and Midwest, filling them with new sights, sounds, and smells, all of which were alien to native Americans. The outbreak of war in Europe temporarily stopped the flow of immigrants in 1914, but in 1919 the trickle became a flood again. Between 1919 and 1926, more than 3.2 million immigrants poured into the United States. Protestants resented the influx of Catholics and Jews; labor unions feared the competition for jobs; and eugenicists prophesied the corruption of American stock.

Black Protests

Black protests did little to allay those fears. A number of black organizations adopted a much more active profile in protesting discrimination. Closely identified with Booker T. Washington's conciliatory approach to race relations, the National Urban League, organized in 1911 by social workers, white philanthropists, and conservative blacks, concentrated on getting jobs for urban blacks. During the 1920s the league stressed the new opportunities that increased prosperity would bring to urban blacks, but a report from the Atlanta League on training blacks to be better janitors revealed the true employment picture. Blacks made scant progress on the job front during the 1920s.

The National Association for the Advancement of Colored People (NAACP), formed in 1909, left economic issues to the Urban League and concentrated on civil rights and legal action. The NAACP won important decisions from the Supreme Court against the grandfather clause (1915) and restrictive covenants (1917). Except for W. E. B. Du Bois, who became the director of publicity, the NAACP's top officers during its early years were white liberals. After World War I, however, the leadership gradually shifted to blacks.

Under the capable direction of James Weldon Johnson, its first black secretary, the NAACP fought against school segregation in northern cities during the 1920s, and lobbied hard, though unsuccessfully, for a federal antilynching bill. Though progress in these areas would not come until after World War II, the NAACP established itself between the wars as the nation's leading civil rights organization.

Black radicals dismissed the Urban League and the NAACP as too conservative. A. Philip Randolph, the brilliant editor of the militant Socialist monthly, the *Messenger,* saw prejudice as the inevitable consequence of a capitalist system that drove a wedge between black and white workers. To end discrimination and achieve racial equality, he called for a "New Negro" who would meet violence with violence. Randolph also urged blacks to seek admission into the trade unions. His great accomplishment during the 1920s was the organization of the Brotherhood of Sleeping Car Porters. After years of bitter opposition, the Pullman Company recognized the Brotherhood in 1937 as the porters' bargaining agent. Though Randolph spoke for the black masses, his appeal was limited to the college educated, black elite. Most blacks neither read nor understood his intellectual theories.

Marcus Garvey appealed to a different group of blacks. A flamboyant and charismatic figure from Jamaica, Garvey preached racial pride and black separatism instead of integration. He declared that God and Jesus were both black and exhorted his followers to glorify their African heritage and to revel in the beauty of their black skin.

In 1914 Garvey organized the Universal Negro Improvement Association (UNIA) to promote black migration to Africa. Under the slogan, "Africa for the Africans, at home and abroad," the UNIA opened branches in many American cities and in several foreign countries after World War I. Its Black Star Steamship Line sold stock to thousands of members with the promise of helping blacks migrate to Africa. Garvey also advocated complete economic self-sufficiency for blacks remaining in the United States. He told his followers to buy only from black-owned businesses, and the UNIA opened a chain of laundries, groceries, restaurants, a hotel, a doll factory (whose products all had black bodies), and a printing plant.

The UNIA collapsed in the mid-1920s after the Black Star Line went bankrupt. Garvey was charged with mail fraud, jailed, and finally deported, but this "Black Moses" left a rich legacy. At a time when magazines and newspapers were filled with advertisements for hair straighteners and skin lightening cosmetics, Garvey's message of racial pride struck a responsive chord in many black Americans.

Marcus Garvey

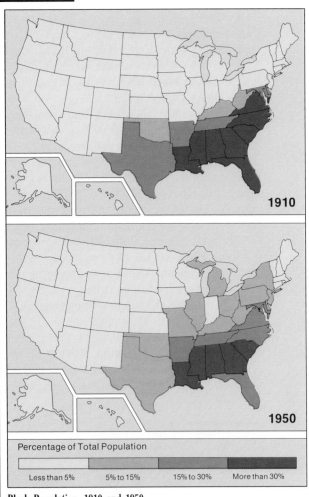

Percentage of Total Population

Less than 5%   5% to 15%   15% to 30%   More than 30%

Black Population, 1910 and 1950

The Harlem Renaissance

The movement for black pride found its cultural expression in the Harlem Renaissance. Located in New York's upper Manhattan, Harlem attracted black intellectuals who had migrated there from small towns or rural areas where they had felt stifled and oppressed. Langston Hughes, poet laureate of the Harlem Renaissance, captured the exhilaration of arriving in Harlem: "I can never put on paper the thrill of the underground ride to Harlem. I went up the steps and out into the bright September sunlight. Harlem! I stood there, dropped my bags, took a deep breath, and felt happy again."

By the 1920s the Harlem Renaissance was in bloom. Langston Hughes probed the past in his elegant poem, "The Negro Speaks of Rivers," while Countee Cullen struck an ironic note in "Yet Do I Marvel," where he pondered God's ways and declared: "Yet do I marvel at this curious thing: To make a poet black and bid him sing." In *Cane*, a compilation of short stories, poems, and vignettes, Jean Toomer, perhaps the most gifted prose writer of the renaissance,

The Harlem Renaissance, led by W. E. B. Du Bois and James Johnson, a professor of literature, soon attracted a large number of black intellectuals.

explored the lives of blacks who toiled in Georgia's sawmills in the 1880s.

For all its artistic promise, the Harlem Renaissance had little influence over the black masses, most of whom never knew it existed. "The ordinary Negroes hadn't heard of the Negro Renaissance," Hughes later lamented. "And if they had, it hadn't raised their wages any." In fact, the Harlem Renaissance often reflected the stereotypes of its white patrons, who were fascinated by the cult of the primitive during the 1920s. They underwrote the Harlem Renaissance by providing scholarships, prizes, and grants to aspiring young black artists who all too often were expected to reinforce white stereotypes of black culture. The leaders of the Harlem Renaissance shied away from such controversial social issues as "passing" and all but ignored jazz, one of the most important black contributions to American culture.

Urban Segregation

In 1910 three-fourths of the nation's blacks lived on farms, and nine-tenths of them lived in the South. That profile started changing dramatically during World War I. Hoping to escape the tenant farming, sharecropping, and peonage of the South, they left for jobs in the North. During the 1920s 1.5 million blacks moved to the cities, some to such southern cities as Houston, Memphis, Atlanta, and Birmingham, but most went to major northern metropolises such as New York, Philadelphia, Cleveland, and Chicago. By 1930, one of five American blacks lived in the North.

The large influx of blacks intensified housing shortages, making competition for limited housing still another source of friction between blacks and whites. In city after city, whites closed ranks against blacks, blocking access to their neighborhoods. White realtors refused to show blacks houses in white areas. And many cities adopted residential segregation ordinances. After the Supreme Court declared these ordinances unconstitutional in 1917, however, whites formed so-called neighborhood improvement associations. Trading upon their members' fears of reduced property values, they adopted the restrictive covenant, an agreement binding property owners of a given area not to sell to blacks. Whites who dared sell to blacks were vulnerable to law suits by "damaged" neighbors. Not until 1948 did the Supreme Court strike down judicial support for deed restrictions, making them impossible to enforce.

Zoning laws offered a more subtle means of segregating blacks. They were originally designed to keep businessmen and industries out of residential neighborhoods. The Supreme Court upheld zoning laws in 1926, and by 1930, 981 American cities had adopted them. After the Court's ruling, new zoning laws addressed not only land usage but the height and shape of buildings, specifying rigid construction requirements that virtually precluded low income groups from building or buying homes in well-to-do neighborhoods. By the 1930s zoning restrictions had become the tool of choice for segregating certain groups on the basis of wealth.

Racial animosity, neighborhood covenants, and zoning restrictions confined blacks to certain areas within the cities. Between World War I and World War II, scores of American cities developed black cores. By 1930 New York and Chicago, the cities with the largest black populations, had wards that were ninety-five percent black. Cities within cities, these "black metropolises" were ghettos not unlike the ethnic ghettos of the late nineteenth and early twentieth centuries.

The New Woman and the Sex Debate

"If all girls at the Yale prom were laid end to end, I wouldn't be surprised," remarked Dorothy Parker, the official wit of New York's smart set. Parker's quip captured the public's perception that sexual mores were changing dramatically during the 1920s. As early as 1913 an editor for *Current Opinion* complained that America had struck "Sex O'Clock," and a few years later a writer for *The Atlantic* warned of the "obsession of sex which has set us all a-babbling about matters once excluded from the amenities of conversation." Practically every newspaper had articles on prostitution,

venereal disease, sex education, birth control, and the rising divorce rate—not to mention somber warnings against "racial suicide" by eugenicists who feared that "inferior stocks of people" might take over the country by outbreeding their social betters.

City life contributed to the new attitudes. With its crowded anonymity, urban culture allowed for a release of sexual energy because community restraints on individual behavior were much weaker than in rural villages and small towns. The cities also promoted secular, consumer values and more easily tolerated diversity—ethnic, religious, and sexual.

If cities created a new environment for sexual values, the new psychology of Sigmund Freud provided the ideas. A Vienna physician, Freud revolutionized academic and popular thinking about human behavior by arguing that unconscious sexual anxieties explain more about the way people act than all of their rational protestations. Freud also claimed that those sexual fears develop in infancy and stay with people throughout their lives. During the 1920s, Freud was the center of attention among physicians, academics, advice columnists, women's magazines, and preachers, all of whom debated the virtue or vice of his notions.

"the new woman"

The image of the "flapper" said it all— the liberated woman who bobbed her hair, painted her lips, raised her hemline, and danced the Charleston. The public's anxiety about "fast" women reached all the way down to adolescent girls. One fretful mother told sociologists Robert and Helen Lynd, "My son has been asked to a dance by three different girls and there is no living with him," while another complained, "It's the girls' clothing. We can't keep our boys decent when girls dress that way."

More alarming than women's dress was their behavior. When Lewis Terman of Stanford

THE SEXUAL REVOLUTION OF THE EARLY 1900s

During the late 1800s, public sexual attitudes in the United States were rooted in a moral code that is known as "civilized sexual morality." This sexual code condemned public discussion of sexual matters, held that sexual relations outside of marriage were the worst of sins, and declared that the only legitimate purpose of sexual relations was reproduction. Foreign travelers were invariably struck by Americans' sexual prudery. In the United States, they reported, a chicken breast was called a bosom and a piano leg was called a limb and was covered with lace trousers.

This strict sexual code drew support from a large medical literature claiming that loss of semen through masturbation or excessive sexual intercourse would produce "urinary difficulties, disorders of the genital organs, spinal diseases, weakness of the brain, loss of

memory, epilepsy, insanity, apoplexy, abortions, premature births, and extreme feebleness, morbid predispositions, and an early death of offspring." Respected physicians warned that women were too frail physically and too sensitive spiritually to engage in frequent intercourse and that "the majority of women (happily for them) are not very much troubled with sexual feelings of any kind." Above all, physicians warned that individuals who engaged in sexual relations outside of marriage ran a high risk of contracting incurable venereal diseases.

The Victorian sexual code was, of course, a public ideal, not an accurate description of reality. Prostitution flourished in turn-of-the-century America. Every large city had at least one red-light district. Early twentieth-century vice commissions estimated that there were "not less" than a quarter of a million prostitutes in the country.

In Chicago, an estimated quarter of the city's males visited prostitutes annually, and paid them $15 million a year. Pornography was also widespread.

Nor were nineteenth century women necessarily the prudish, sexually ignorant figures popularized in Victorian mythology. A sex survey of forty-five well-educated women, mainly born before 1870, reported that most enjoyed intercourse and experienced orgasm.

Nevertheless, the values of "civilized sexual morality" dominated polite society and received strong public backing. A "purity crusade" had arisen in the 1860s and 1870s in response to proposals to legalize and regulate prostitution. In almost every major city in the country, former abolitionists like William Lloyd Garrison, feminists like Susan B. Anthony, temperance advocates, and ministers joined forces to defeat legalized prostitution. Prostitution, they argued, exploited poor women to satisfy male lust and endangered respectable women, who were often infected with syphilis and gonorrhea by their husbands.

In later years, the purity forces broadened their aims. In addition to fighting prostitution, they also sought to protect the family by outlawing abortion, restricting the sale of alcohol, stamping out pornography, censoring nudity in the arts, enforcing the Sabbath through enactment of "blue laws," suppressing the use of narcotics, and stopping the flow of birth control information through the mails.

The self-appointed leader of the purity forces was a staunch antivice crusader named Anthony Comstock. As a youth, Comstock had been so upset by an impulse toward masturbation that he feared he might be driven to commit suicide. He became active in the Young Men's Christian Association in New York and was shocked by the prevalence of prostitutes and the sight of vendors selling obscene books.

In 1873, Comstock persuaded Congress to pass a federal law banning from the mails "every obscene, lewd, lascivious or filthy book, pamphlet, paper, letter, writing, print or other publication of an indecent character." Comstock was then appointed special agent of the Post Office and charged with responsibility for arresting those who used the mail in violation of the law. "Morals, not art or literature," Comstock declared, and he proceeded to destroy 500,000 reproductions of art and arrest 3000 persons for obscenity. He took credit for hounding sixteen persons to their deaths.

By 1910, Comstock and the purity forces had achieved many of their legislative goals. They had successfully pushed for state laws to restrict divorce; raised the age of consent for sexual intercourse (from seven in some states, to eighteen); imposed tests for venereal disease prior to marriage; and criminalized abortion. The purity crusaders also won passage of a federal statute that defined the mailing of birth control information a felony.

The years just before World War I witnessed a series of sharp challenges to the nineteenth-century code of sexual purity. Radical new ideas about marriage were publicized and debated. Swedish feminist Ellen Key preached a scheme of "unwed motherhood"; Edith Ellis, wife of British sex researcher Havelock Ellis, advocated trial marriage and

"semi-detached marriage" where each spouse occupied a separate domicile; still others advocated "serial marriage" and easier divorce. Greenwich Village bohemians and political radicals advocated free love. Psychologists, including Havelock Ellis, G. Stanley Hall, and Sigmund Freud, attacked the notion that women lacked sexual impulses.

Sexual conduct was also changing rapidly. The first scientific sex surveys indicated that women who came to maturity after the turn of the century were much more likely than their mothers to engage in sex before marriage and outside it. Women who were born around 1900 were two to three times as likely to have premarital intercourse compared to women born before 1900. They were also more likely to experience orgasm. Among men, premarital sexual experience did not increase, but it was less limited to prostitutes.

Public alarm over the changes occurring in American sexual experience culminated in the 1910s in an explosion of concern over "white slavery"—prostitution—and the "black plague"—venereal disease. A torrent of lurid books appeared—with such titles as The Traffic in Souls, The House of Bondage, and The Shame of a Great Nation—which explained how innocent young girls were seduced by panderers and, through the use of a chloroformed cloth, a hypodermic needle, or a drugged drink, forced into prostitution. Congress attacked the problem of "white slavery" in 1910 by adopting the Mann Act, which made it a crime to transport women across state lines for immoral purposes. During the first World War, Congress went further and provided states with federal funds to set up

facilities in which to detain and rehabilitate women apprehended as prostitutes.

During the 1920s, the drift toward sexual liberalization continued. Journalists wrote in bewilderment about a new social phenomenon, the flapper, the independent, assertive, pleasure-hungry young woman, "making love lightly, boldly, and promiscuously." Systematic sex surveys showed that the incidence of premarital intercourse was continuing to rise and that an increasing number of young women had slept with men other than their future husband. Meanwhile, contraceptive practices were also changing dramatically. Instead of relying heavily upon douching or coitus interruptus as a form of birth control, younger women were using the more effective and less disruptive diaphragms.

Growing sexual permissiveness evoked a sharp reaction. Religious journals denounced popular dance styles as "impure, polluting, corrupting, debasing, destroying spirituality, [and] increasing carnality." A bill was introduced in the Utah state legislature to fine and imprison women who wore skirts on the streets "higher than three inches above the ankle." In the Ohio legislature it was proposed that cleavage be limited to two inches and that the sale of any "garment which unduly displays or accentuates the lines of the female figure" be prohibited. Four states and many cities established censorship boards to review films and many other cities broke up red-light districts and required licenses for dance halls. But despite these efforts, a sexual revolution had begun that has continued until this day.

University questioned 777 middle-class women in 1938, he discovered that seventy-four percent of those born between 1890 and 1900 remained chaste until marriage, while the figure dropped to thirty-two percent among those born after 1910. The more exhaustive research of Alfred C. Kinsey revealed a similar pattern. Between 1938 and 1952 Kinsey and his co-workers at Indiana University interviewed 5940 white females from all social classes. Women born after 1900 were twice as likely to have had premarital sex as their mothers, with the most pronounced changes occurring in the generation reaching maturity at the end of World War I and in the early 1920s.

Sexual permissiveness had eroded Victorian values, but the "new woman" was less of a challenge to traditional morality than her critics feared. She was not promiscuous; she merely practiced a "permissiveness with affection." Her sexual experience before marriage was limited (usually no more than two or three partners, one of whom she married), and she was just as committed to marriage as her mother's generation. In practice, this meant a narrowing of the double standard of morality. Instead of turning to prostitutes, men made love with their sweethearts.

But that was where the changes stopped. The "new woman" still accepted the traditional roles of wife and mother. In fact, the most striking theme of women's history in the 1920s is its continuity with the past. Whether one looked at politics, the workplace, or the home, the status of women remained fundamentally unchanged. Nowhere was the absence of change more evident than in politics. Most feminists had viewed politics as the key to ending discrimination against women, arguing that the vote would bring other reforms in its train. After the Nineteenth Amendment passed, there was a great deal of talk about female voters uniting to clean up politics, reform society, and end discrimination in the marketplace so that women could compete on an equal footing with men.

None of these hopes was realized during the 1920s. Women failed to organize into a bloc vote, and apart from a few state and local elections where the female vote did prove decisive, there was no evidence that women voted differently than men. Even more galling to feminists, there was considerable evidence that substantial numbers of women failed to vote at all. Throughout the 1920s significantly fewer women voted than men.

Nor did women reform the marketplace. According to the census of 1920, there were over 8 million women (the figure rose to more than 10 million by 1930) employed in 437 different types of jobs. But 57 percent of the female work force was composed of black and foreign-born women, and domestic service was the largest occupation, followed by secretaries, typists, and clerks—all low paying jobs. Though female workers made significant progress in organizing the garment industry, their efforts to form labor unions in other industries failed. The American Federation of Labor (AFL) was openly hostile to women because it did not want females competing with men for jobs.

Female professionals, too, made little progress. They consistently received less money

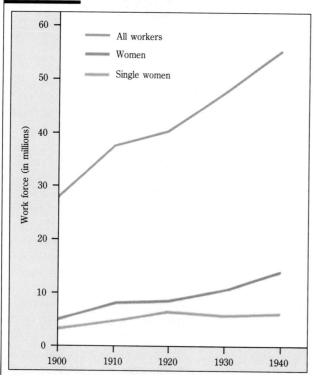

Figure 23.1
Women in the Work Force, 1900-1940

than their male counterparts, and while the proportion of female workers in the professions rose from roughly twelve percent to fourteen percent between 1920 and 1930, more than seventy-five percent of them were concentrated in "female" occupations—teaching and nursing. The percentage of female lawyers and architects remained constant between 1910 and 1930 (about three percent), while the total number of female doctors declined from 9015 to 6825. There were only 60 female certified accountants and 151 female dentists in the entire country in the late 1920s.

Most Americans saw working women as an anomaly. Young women could work during the interlude between leaving home and marriage, but they were expected to make homemaking their career after marriage. While economic necessity forced poor women to continue working after marriage, most middle-class women of the 1920s abandoned any hope of combining careers with marriage. If anything, the 1920s was a flight from feminism and a resurgence of domesticity. As one article put it, "the office woman, no matter how successful, is a transplanted posey." The proper role for women, a college president advised, was "to strengthen and beautify and sanctify the home."

America had not resolved the basic conflict between equal rights for women and the sexual division of labor which confined women to the domestic sphere. Feminists had secured the vote, but it soon became clear that a great deal more was needed to overcome inequality.

THE REVOLT OF THE TRADITIONALISTS

The rise of the cities, the appearance of ghettoes, the mass influx of Catholic and Jewish immigrants, the black migration north, the appearance of civil rights and black pride groups, and the changes in sexual mores all posed a threat to traditional white Protestants living in rural areas. They vented their fears and frustrations in the 1920s by leading zealous campaigns against alcohol, smoking, evolution, immigrants, and radicals.

Prohibition

Like the sex debate, the controversy over prohibition exposed deep fissures in American society. Though many urbanites supported prohibition, big cities with large ethnic populations generally opposed it, while small towns and rural areas (especially in the Midwest and Bible-belt South) supported it. The key was the class, ethnic, and religious makeup of the community, not merely whether the community was rural or urban.

At first the apparent success of prohibition muted its critics. Distilleries and breweries shut down, saloons locked their doors, arrests for drunkenness declined, and alcohol-related deaths all but stopped. Compliance, however, had less to do with piety and public support than the law of supply and demand; illegal liquor was in short supply and its price was higher than the average worker could afford.

Private enterprise filled the void. Smugglers served the needs of wealthy imbibers who could afford the best liquor and wine, but the less affluent had to rely on small-time operators producing for local consumption. Due to high shipping and storage costs, it was more expensive to produce beer or wine, so the price of liquor, relative to other alcoholic beverages, declined. Drinking habits shifted accordingly: The consumption of hard liquor rose, while beer and wine decreased.

Much of the hard liquor sold was either of poor quality or downright poisonous. According to one widely circulated story, a potential buyer who sent a liquor sample to a laboratory for analysis was shocked when the chemist replied: "Your horse has diabetes." For others the problem of "killer batches" was anything but funny. Hundreds, perhaps thousands, died from drinking concoctions with names like "Jackass Brandy" and "Soda Pop Moon."

Neither federal nor state authorities had enough funds to enforce prohibition. The Federal Prohibition Bureau began the 1920s with 1520 agents and by 1930 the number had grown to only 2836. Lax enforcement, coupled with huge profits, enticed large-scale operators to enter the business. Organized crime, of course, had long been a fixture of urban life,

Under Prohibition, otherwise law-abiding citizens visited speakeasies, smuggled alcohol, and often carried hip flasks filled with bootleg liquor.

with gambling and prostitution as its base, but small-time, local operators managed these vices. Liquor demanded production plants, distribution networks, and sales forces, attracting large-scale operators with the capital and business skills to tackle big-time bootlegging.

Bootlegging proved to be a gold mine for organized crime. By the late 1920s syndicates sold 150 million quarts of liquor each year, generating revenue in excess of $2 billion annually (more than two percent of the gross national product). Chicago's Al Capone had a gross income of $60 million in 1927 and employed an army of workers. A ruthless figure accused of ordering numerous gangland killings, he preferred to think of himself as a businessman. "All I do is supply a public demand," he insisted. "I do it in the best and least harmful way I can."

Opponents of prohibition were right in insisting that it could not be enforced. Where prohibition was popular it was well-enforced; where it was not, particularly in large cities, prohibition became a joke and people openly flaunted it. On more than one occasion journalists saw President Warren Harding's bootlegger drive to the backdoor of the White House and unload cases of liquor in broad daylight.

In 1923 New York became the first state to repeal its enforcement law, and six states followed suit by 1930. Others remained firm supporters of prohibition, prompting Walter Lippmann to conclude: "The high level of lawlessness is maintained by the fact that Americans desire to do so many things which they also desire to prohibit." Not until the 1930s, when the Great Depression gave the country something really serious to worry about, did prohibition lose steam. After a presidential commission reported that prohibition was indeed unenforceable, Congress finally repealed it on December 5, 1933. Liquor control became a state and local matter.

The Antismoking Campaign: The Forgotten Reform

"Prohibition is won," exclaimed the evangelist Billy Sunday in 1920, "Now for tobacco!" Sunday's challenge was the battle cry for religious groups, educators, moral crusaders, and health advocates seeking to follow up the victory over demon rum with a crusade against "our Lady Nicotine."

Opposition to tobacco was hardly new. King James I denounced smoking in 1603 as "A custom loathsome to the eye, hateful to the nose, harmful to the brain, [and] dangerous to the lungs." During the nineteenth century, the antitobacco campaign was an appendage of the prohibition movement, and critics of the "vile weed" denounced pipes, cigars, plugs, and snuff with equal venom. After the introduction of machine-made cigarettes in the 1880s, however, opponents concentrated their fire on the "little white slavers," declaring that cigarettes were much more damaging to health than previous forms of tobacco because smokers inhaled fumes that were literally poison.

As early as the Civil War, some cities had banned smoking in restaurants, theaters, public buildings, trolleys, and railway cars. Antismokers organized the National Anti-Cigarette League in 1903. Scores of prominent leaders joined the crusade, including David Starr Jordan, the president of Stanford University, who told audiences, "Boys who smoke cigarettes are like wormy apples"; and the lecturer Elbert Hubbard who declared, "Cigarette smokers are men whose future lies behind them." Between 1896 and 1923 fourteen states, mainly in the Midwest, outlawed the sale of cigarettes, and there were calls for a constitutional amendment prohibiting them nationwide.

Smokers had little to fear. By the end of the 1920s every state had repealed its laws against cigarette sales. The crusade against tobacco was the last hurrah of the prohibition movement, and it failed because prohibition was a legal fiasco and because the public considered smoking the lesser vice. Nor did the style of the antismokers help their cause. Many Americans dismissed them as moral zealots and opponents of individual liberty who were too quick to expand the power of the state over private behavior.

Unlike drinkers, who were often defensive, smokers strongly defended their right to smoke. The tobacco industry supported them and opposed every effort to restrict the sale of cigarettes, spending millions of dollars on advertisements reassuring smokers that they were sophisticated, sexy, and even healthy. They drove home the message that smoking was a matter of individual choice free from state control. Not until the 1950s when scientists linked smoking to lung cancer did the antismoking movement reappear.

The Scopes Trial

The opponents of alcohol and tobacco also attacked the teaching of evolution in public schools. They got their day in court in the celebrated "Monkey Trial." When the Tennessee legislature passed a law against the teaching of evolution in public schools, John T. Scopes, a biology teacher in the small town of Dayton, deliberately violated the statute to provoke a test case. He was brought to trial in the summer of 1925. William Jennings Bryan, rural America's defender of the faith, volunteered as a witness for the prosecution, and Clarence Darrow, the famous trial lawyer and self-proclaimed agnostic, headed a legal team retained by the American Civil Liberties Union to defend Scopes.

To accommodate the throngs of reporters and sightseers, the judge held court in a vacant lot where the cries of hot dog vendors added to the carnival atmosphere. The outcome was

GATHERING DATA FOR THE TENNESSEE TRIAL

Religious fundamentalists led the crusade against Darwin's theory of evolution. The Scopes trial enthralled people on both sides of the debate.

never in doubt. Scopes admitted he had broken the law. He was convicted and fined $100, though Tennessee's Supreme Court rescinded the fine on a technicality. What gave the trial its drama was the clash between Bryan and Darrow, and the opposite images of America they represented.

Bryan took the stand for the prosecution as an expert witness on science and religion, and his simple, direct answers to Darrow's sarcastic questions revealed an unshakable faith in the literal truth of the Bible. Though Darrow sought to belittle his testimony as "fool ideas that no intelligent Christian on earth believes," Bryan insisted that "it is better to trust in the Rock of Ages than to know the ages of rocks." Journalists had a field day ridiculing Bryan, who died a few weeks after the trial ended, but the many fundamentalists for whom he spoke thought that he had carried the day. The Scopes trial exposed how little tolerance secular and fundamentalist groups had for each other.

Restricting Immigration

Concern about the teaching of evolution was matched only by a surge in nativism in the 1920s. A broad coalition of people believed that foreigners posed a grave threat to the United States. Organized labor, bent upon protecting high wages, resented competition from cheap labor; staunch nativists and superpatriots alike warned that foreign influences would pollute the American character; social workers argued that their caseload of disadvantaged people was already at the breaking point; and assorted businessmen regarded immigrants as dangerous agents of radicalism.

Together, these groups argued that the United States could no longer serve as the world's safety valve. After a stopgap immigration law in 1921 failed to stop the flow, Congress passed the National Origins Act of 1924. It established an immigration quota of two percent of each national group counted in the 1890 census. Since southern and eastern Europeans had not arrived in large numbers until the turn of the century, the law gave western and northern Europeans a big edge over the "new immi-

grants." Great Britain and Ireland, for example, could send 65,731 a year, but Italy only 5802.

Asians suffered the harshest treatment. Bowing to pressure from the West Coast, Congress excluded them entirely, even though diplomatic agreements with China and Japan had virtually stopped immigration from the Far East. (Ironically, the quota system would have allowed fewer than 150 Japanese to enter the United States annually.) The Japanese people deeply resented the insult. Japan boycotted American goods, a patriotic Japanese committed harikari in front of the American Embassy in Tokyo, and the Japanese ambassador in Washington resigned in protest.

Hostility to immigrants was also at work in the Sacco and Vanzetti case. On April 15, 1920, two unidentified gunmen robbed a shoe factory in South Braintree, Massachusetts, murdering a paymaster and a guard. The crime occurred at the peak of the Red Scare in the United States, when the Justice Department was investigating two Italian immigrants, Nicola Sacco and Bartolomeo Vanzetti, both avowed anarchists. Jus-

The *Sacco and Vanzetti* case, shown here in a painting by Ben Shahn, brought about violent protest in America as well as abroad.
Ben Shahn, *Bartolomeo Vanzetti and Nicola Sacco.* (1931-32) Tempera on paper over composition board, 10½ x 14½". Collection the Museum of Modern Art, New York. Gift of Mrs. John D. Rockefeller, Jr.

tice Department officials advised local police authorities of their presence in Massachusetts, and on May 5 they were arrested and charged with robbery and murder. Although the prosecution failed to prove that the two men had committed the crime, their political views were paraded before the jury, and on July 14, 1921, they were convicted and sentenced to death.

Their conviction brought a storm of protest from the Italian-American community, liberals, and civil rights advocates. Sacco-Vanzetti defense funds were established in the United States and Europe, and such distinguished people as Albert Einstein, Felix Frankfurter, H. G. Wells, and George Bernard Shaw protested the sentence. They demanded a review of the case, claiming that Sacco and Vanzetti had been convicted not because of the evidence but because of their political views. For six years they were able to secure stays of execution. Early in July 1927 Governor Alvan T. Fuller of Massachusetts appointed a blue-ribbon commission, headed by Harvard president Abbott Lawrence Lowell, to investigate the case. At the end of the month the commission upheld the conviction. Sacco and Vanzetti, asserting their innocence to the very end, went to the electric chair on August 23, 1927, sending out as their last message the words "This is our career, and our triumph." Following their deaths, protesters attacked American embassies across Europe, setting off a debate on their innocence that has reverberated down to this day.

The Ku Klux Klan

Fear of political radicals and ethnic minorities found its most strident voice during the 1920s in the Ku Klux Klan, a secret organization that stood for "100 percent pure Americanism" and limited its membership to white, native-born Protestants. Organized on Thanksgiving night, 1915, in a ceremony beneath a burning cross on a mountaintop in Georgia, the revived Klan was, in the words of its founder and imperial wizard, Colonel William Joseph Simmons, a "living memorial" to the Klan of Reconstruction days. An insurance salesman, part-time Methodist minister, and perennial booster of fraternal societies, Simmons had no political agenda. Under his inept leadership, the Klan remained a small southern organization teetering on the edge of bankruptcy. During its first five years, the Klan had only 5000 members.

That changed in 1920 when Simmons hired two advertising specialists, Edward Young Clark and Elizabeth Tyler, to market the Klan. They did nothing to change the product. The Klan remained, as before, a loosely knit web of vigilante groups, with no national program. Its policy was set at the local level, varying from community to community to accommodate local prejudices, be they directed at blacks, Catholics, Jews, Mexicans, Orientals, foreigners or "Reds." Clark and Tyler hired an army of organizers to canvas the country selling memberships in the Klan. (Membership cost ten dollars; the sheet was four dollars extra.) Working on commission and molding their pitch to match their clientele, they were astoundingly successful. By 1921 the Klan had become a national organization with over 90,000 paying members; by 1925 it claimed a membership of 5 million! An amazed southern newspaper editor called the "idea of selling people their own prejudices almost equal to the old bunco game of selling a hick the Capitol."

The Klan, however, was not just a band of rural rednecks. True, the Klan was strongest (and most violent) in the South, but it also had a large following in the Southeast, the Far West, and the Midwest. Moreover, the Klan showed considerable strength in several large urban areas, including Chicago, Indianapolis, and Detroit. Its natural habitat was not the countryside but middling towns and small cities. Most members were not "poor white trash" but members of the lower middle class from old stock, respectable families.

In its heyday (1921–1926), the Klan was a political force to be reckoned with. At the state level, it controlled or influenced the election of governors and legislators in Alabama, Georgia, Arkansas, Texas, Oklahoma, California, Oregon, Indiana, and Ohio. In fact, the Klan's strength extended into Pennsylvania, New York, and parts of New England. Yet, its vision was essen-

The Klan was not just limited to the southern countryside. Here they parade through the main streets of a town as a crowd watches.

tially negative. Except for an Oregon statute requiring Catholic children to attend public schools (later declared unconstitutional), the Klan did not inspire a single law.

Night ridings, cross burnings, tar and featherings, public beatings, and lynchings were the Klan's stock in trade, but the objects of its wrath were not limited to ethnic and religious offenders. In addition to nativism, its attacks reflected the public's anxieties about the decline in private behavior. The Klan lashed out against wife beaters, drunkards, bootleggers, gamblers—anyone who violated time-honored standards of morality.

In the end, poor leadership and the absence of a political program destroyed the Klan. KKK elected officials offered no constructive legislation. Even more damaging, several of its leaders were involved in sex scandals, while others were indicted for corruption. By 1930 voters had turned Klansmen out of office, Klan membership had fallen to 50,000, and the forces of nativism were in full retreat. The country had abandoned a grass roots movement which stood for Americanism but smacked of fascism. Most Americans were too preoccupied with the

economy to invest a lot of energy in the Klan. The cross burnings and racism retreated into obscurity, only to wait for another opportunity to go public again.

THE CONSUMER SOCIETY

Despite all the sources of tension in the United States during the 1920s, a new force for social cohesion was at work. America was rapidly evolving a consumer culture that blunted regional differences and imposed similar tastes and lifestyles. Propelled by revolutions in transportation, advertising, communications, and entertainment, a new consumer society emerged during the 1920s as the dominant cultural motif of modern America.

The Automobile

"Why on earth do you need to study what's changing this country," a Midwesterner asked the Lynds in 1924. "I can tell you what's happening in just four letters: A-U-T-O!" The man was right. In 1900 only 8000 motor vehicles were registered in the United States and the automobile was little more than a rich man's toy; by 1920 their number had risen to more than 9 million. By 1925 Ford had lowered the price of his sturdy Model A's to less than $300, about three-months pay for the average urban worker. That year registrations reached 19,940,724, and by 1930 Americans owned 26,531,999 cars (more than one automobile for every five people).

No previous form of transportation (except walking) had been so widely available. In Muncie, Indiana, a town of 11,000, only 125 families owned a horse and carriage in 1890. Most people walked. By the time of the Lynds' study in 1924, however, two out of three families in Muncie owned an automobile. The great American love affair with the automobile was underway: One working class housewife told the Lynds, "I'll go without food before I'll see us give up the car."

Enthusiasts claimed the automobile promoted family togetherness through evening rides, picnics, and weekend excursions. Critics decried family squabbles between parents and teenagers over use of the automobile, the ap-parent decline in church attendance resulting from all-day Sunday outings, and budget pressures working families faced to support their automobile habit. Others felt distressed about the blurring of class lines—blue-collar families riding around just like rich folks. Worst of all, charged critics, the automobile gave young people too much freedom and privacy. Nearly ninety percent of the automobiles sold in the United States by 1927 were enclosed. These "portable bedrooms" removed courtship from the family parlor and gave couples a private room they could take anywhere.

Critics also blamed the automobile for undermining public devotion to thrift. In the past, people had been taught to live within their means. That meant paying cash for consumer goods or doing without. The automobile changed this. An ad in a midwestern newspaper showed a kindly banker advising a young couple to buy an automobile on time, predicting that the purchase would raise their horizons, which, in turn, would boost their earning power. Long before New Dealers started quoting John Maynard Keynes, Madison Avenue was telling Americans to spend themselves rich.

With the huge increase in automobile sales and the rise of the consumer society, filling stations,
like this one in New York City, often sold groceries and sandwiches, too.

Appliances

Madison Avenue struck another bonanza in appliances. The key to the market was electricity. Prior to World War I only one-fifth of America's households had electricity, but by 1929 the proportion had risen to two-thirds, and by 1940, to over four-fifths. Electric refrigerators, washing machines, vacuum cleaners, and toasters quickly took hold. By 1929 one of four homes had electric vacuum cleaners; one in five had toasters.

Appliances eased the sheer physical drudgery of housework, but they did not shorten the average housewife's work week. The modern housewife was expected to do more because the standards she was asked to meet kept rising. In the 1920s and 1930s she fell under the guidance of advice columnists, the ads of soap manufacturers who brought her favorite "soap" operas into her home, and the precepts of appliance manufacturers. All equated cleanliness with motherly love and tried to make women who did not keep spotless homes feel like failures. Sheets had to be changed weekly; the house had to be vacuumed daily.

Social pressure expanded household chores to keep pace with the new technology. The irony did not stop there. Touted as labor saving devices, household appliances actually stopped the trend toward the centralization of certain jobs, like laundry and baking. Far from liberating women, appliances actually imposed new pressures and expectations on them.

The Lost Generation

For a few Americans, the consumer culture was thoroughly disgusting. Disillusioned by the collapse of Wilsonian idealism, the hypocrisy of prohibition, and the upsurge of nativism, a new generation of American writers felt alienated. America had become a nation of conspicuous consumption awash in materialism and devoid of spiritual vitality. The "Lost Generation" despised the narrow-mindedness of small town life, with its complacency, its conformity, and, above all, its devotion to the all-mighty dollar.

No writer captured these themes better than Sinclair Lewis, the first American to win the Nobel Prize for literature. In *Main Street*

Ernest Hemingway

F. Scott Fitzgerald

(1920), he mingled satire with caricature when he declared: "Main Street is the climax of civilization. That this Ford might stand in front of the Bon Ton Store, Hannibal invaded Rome and Erasmus wrote in Oxford cloisters." In *Babbitt* (1922), a scathing portrait of the small town businessmen, Lewis coined a term for the spiritual conformity that became synonymous with following the crowd.

H. L. Mencken's view of American life was even more cynical. As editor of *Mercury* magazine, he produced hundreds of essays mocking practically every aspect of American life. To him the South was "the Sahara of the Bozart," a "gargantuan paradise of the fourth rate," and the middle class was the "booboisie." Mencken directed some of his choicest barbs at reformers, the same crowd whose efforts had led to the bloodshed of World War I and the gangsters of Prohibition. "If I am convinced of anything," he snarled, "it is that Doing Good is in bad taste."

The two other premier literary figures in the 1920s were F. Scott Fitzgerald and Ernest Hemingway. In such novels as *The Great Gatsby* (1925) and *Tender Is the Night* (1929), Fitzgerald exposed the decadence and materialism of American culture. His best known character Jay Gatsby was destroyed by his own integrity in a morally bankrupt society. Hemingway placed great value on toughness and "manly virtues," and *The Sun Also Rises* (1926) and *A Farewell to Arms* (1929) emphasized meaningless death and the importance of stoically facing the absurdities of the universe.

THE RISE OF MASS CULTURE

New technology assisted the birth of consumer society, and a new cultural currency, based on leisure and entertainment, first appeared in the 1920s.

The Communication Revolution

In 1897 the United States had less than one telephone for every hundred residents, but by 1914 the number had risen to one in ten, and by 1930 it stood at one in six. Americans averaged over 64 million calls per day in 1929, and a person in New York could talk with someone in London for about $10 a minute that same year. The telephone marked the beginning of the transition from the written to the electronically transmitted word, brought the home in closer contact with the outside world, and reduced household visiting among neighbors.

The impact of the radio was even greater— it drew the nation together by bringing news, entertainment, and advertisements to millions of listeners. With the organization of the National Broadcasting Corporation (NBC) in 1926 and the Columbia Broadcasting System (CBS) the following year, radio developed into a national industry, offering the same programs from coast to coast. In 1929 over 10 million households owned radios, well over one-third of the families in the country, and Americans spent a staggering $85 million on radio equipment in that year alone.

The radio offered something for everyone. Not only did it report news events minutes after they happened, but it brought politics to life as Americans got to hear the voices of their political leaders or listen to Will Rogers poke gentle fun at them. Serial adventures such as "The Green Hornet" and "The Lone Ranger" appealed to the entire family, while sports broadcasts were pitched at male audiences. The "soaps" dominated weekday programming, as millions of housewives listened to "Portia Faces Life" and "Life Can Be Beautiful."

The radio helped create mass culture by blunting regional differences. Listeners heard the same news reporters, serial shows, and sporting events delivered in the same dialect.

They heard the same advertisements telling them what to buy; and no other media had the power to create folk heroes so quickly. When Charles Lindbergh, the "Lone Eagle," became the first person to fly nonstop across the Atlantic from New York to Paris in 1927, the radio brought his incredible feat into American homes and made him a celebrity overnight.

The radio also reinforced national prejudices. "Amos and Andy," which first aired in 1929, was one of the most popular shows of the Depression. Its portrait of black life spread vicious racial stereotypes into homes whose occupants knew little about black people. Other minorities fared no better. The Italian gangster, the blood-thirsty Indian, the Mexican with the sing-song voice, the tight-fisted Jew, and the Irish thug became stock characters in radio programming.

The Rise of Suburbs

Americans were not just buying the same products and listening to the same programs. They were also living together in new housing arrangements. Paralleling the black ghettoes was the growth of white suburbs. Havens for the wealthy and upper middle class, and usually characterized by the presence of a variety of white ethnic groups, suburbs grew at a much faster rate than center cities. Indeed, the 1920s saw an explosion in both the number and the size of so-called satellite cities and bedroom communities. Between 1920 and 1930 the population of Beverly Hills, a Los Angeles suburb, increased 2485 percent; Shaker Heights, a Cleveland suburb, 1000 percent; and Elmwood Park, a Chicago suburb, 717 percent.

Transportation developments gave birth to the suburbs in the 1920s. Until then, urban growth was constrained by the need of workers to live near their jobs. After the Civil War, trolleys and streetcars greatly expanded labor's mobility, permitting workers to move beyond the walking radius surrounding factories. Metropolitan growth followed the trolley tracks as suburbs sprang up along the commuter lines.

The automobile accelerated the trend. No longer dependent on public transportation, workers enjoyed much wider latitude in deciding where to live. Though suburbs had once been the exclusive domain of the well-to-do, the automobile enabled working-class families to move there too. Those who hoped to escape the city's congestion by moving to the suburbs were quickly disappointed. The sharp rise in road construction following the Federal Highway Act of 1916 produced complicated lateral traffic flows within cities. Traffic congestion became worse. City planners counterattacked with traffic circles, synchronized stop lights, divided dual highways, and grade separation of highways from city streets, but nothing could free motorists from the rush hour and holiday traffic jam. Whether one looked at the size and shape of cities or the flow of people within them, the automobile's tire tracks could be seen in virtually every urban area of America.

Leisure Time: Games, Books, Sports, and Movies

Thanks to the unprecedented prosperity of the 1920s, Americans had more money for leisure activities than ever before. Spending for entertainment more than doubled during the 1920s, reaching $4.3 billion in 1929. The average worker devoted seven hours a week to play. Much of the time and money went for parlor games—mahjong sets, crossword puzzles, and the like. Contract bridge was the most durable of the new pastimes, followed closely by photography. Americans hit golf balls, played tennis, and bowled. Dance crazes swept the country. The fox trot gave way to the Charleston, which in turn was replaced by the jitterbug.

While Lewis, Mencken, Fitzgerald, and Hemingway found much to criticize, millions of Americans preferred a new popular literature, even though it reflected the confusion of the decade. In 1914, Edgar Rice Burroughs wrote *Tarzan of the Apes*, and it was a runaway bestseller. During the next twenty years, he wrote forty other novels, most of them about Tarzan. For an American concerned about urbanization and industrialization, the adventures of a lone white man in "dark Africa" revived the spirit of the frontier and individualism.

The novels of Zane Grey were no less popular. His book *Riders of the Purple Sage* appealed to an America looking back nostalgically at its frontier heritage, a time when life seemed simple. Between 1918 and 1934, Grey wrote twenty-four books and became the most well-known writer of popular fiction in the country. He used a tried but true formula: lots of romance, lots of action, and a moralistic struggle between good and evil, all put in a western setting. Grey's villains were universally greedy, dishonest, and immoral, and his heroes were just the opposite—they always triumphed.

The 1920s was a decade of contrasts, and popular fiction was no exception. People wanted virtuous heroes and old-time values in their fiction, but a lot of them also wanted to be titillated. One of the major publishing trends of the 1920s was the boom in "confession magazines." The rise of the city, the liberated woman, and the impact of the movie industry had all relaxed Victorian standards, and into the vacuum came the confession magazine— borderline pornography with stories of romantic success and failure, divorce, fantasy, and adultery. Writers survived the cuts of the censors by couching their stories in moral lessons advising readers to avoid similar mistakes in their own lives. The most successful of the confession magazines was Bernard McFadden's *True Story*, whose subscription list soared from 10,000 in 1919 to more than two million in 1926.

Another rage of the 1920s was spectator sports. Because the country yearned for individual heroes to stand out larger than life in an increasingly impersonal, organized society, prize fighting enjoyed a huge following, especially in the heavyweight division where hard punchers like Jack Dempsey became national idols. Team sports flourished in colleges and high schools, but even then Americans focused on individual superstars, people whose talents or personalities earned them a cult following. Notre Dame emerged as a college football powerhouse in the 1920s, but it was head coach Knute Rockne and his "pep talks" on dedication and persistence which became part of the fabric of American popular culture. Harold "Red" Grange, the "Galloping Ghost" halfback for the University of Illinois, single-handedly put professional football on the cultural map when he signed a contract with the Chicago Bears in 1926 and barnstormed around the country.

Spectator sports became popular in the 1920s and those who emerged as heroes of the day included men like "Red" Grange of the University of Ilinois and "Babe" Ruth of the New York Yankees.

Baseball was even more popular. Fans spent countless hours of calculating, memorizing, and quizzing one another on baseball statistics. The sport's undisputed superstar was George Herman "Babe" Ruth, the "Sultan of Swat." The public loved Ruth for his unparalleled skills as well as his personal weaknesses. Ruth held the major league record for most scoreless innings pitched in a World Series (when he was a member of the Boston Red Sox), and then led the New York Yankees to victory in four World Series and set four home run records, hitting sixty in his best year. While hitting or pitching as nobody had before, Ruth was also known for his gargantuan appetite and capacity to drink himself into a stupor. His beer belly was as patented as his swing.

Ruth transformed baseball in the 1920s because the public needed the change. Until the 1920s, baseball was the game of Ty Cobb— defense, base hits, and stolen bases. Ruth changed it all in 1919 when he hit twenty-nine home runs, the most ever in a single season, and an astonishing fifty-four in 1920. Between 1915 and 1930, the total number of home runs in major league baseball increased from 384 a

year to 1565. Stolen bases were cut in half. Baseball became the game of the big hitter, the superstar, and no hitter was bigger, literally and figuratively, than Babe Ruth. He made baseball the "national pastime."

Americans spent ten times more on movies than on spectator sports. Movie attendance leveled off at 90 million per week in 1929, in a population of 120 million. Movies were big business, and the industry could afford to produce huge spectacles. Cecil B. DeMille's *Ten Commandments,* with its "cast of thousands" and dazzling special effects, demonstrated the new medium's ability to hold audiences spellbound. Comedies were popular, whether highly sophisticated pieces such as *Sinners in Silk,* featuring young men and women sharing in new sexual freedom, or slapstick masterpieces starring Charlie Chaplin, Buster Keaton, or Harold Lloyd. Ironically, the slapstick comedies provided the most significant social commentary of the 1920s, spoofing the pretensions of the wealthy and presenting sympathetic portraits of the poor.

Like the radio and sports, movies helped create a new popular culture, with common

Harold Lloyd, who had a disfigured hand, usually performed his own stunts high above city streets in his movies.

speech, dress, behavior, and heroes; and like the radio, Hollywood did its share to denigrate minority groups. Mexicans appeared as sleepy-eyed peasants, while the only parts for blacks went to actors like Stepin Fetchit, who got rich playing superstitious, blithering idiots. The wooden box and the silver screen both molded and mirrored mass culture.

THE REPUBLICAN RESTORATION

While social, economic, and cultural life during the 1920s was characterized by enormous change, politics at the national level was an attempt to turn back the clock a generation. During the 1920s. Republican leaders promised to restore prosperity, and most Americans went along with the conservative rhetoric, hoping to find in politics the stability they were missing in society and culture.

Talk about trust busting and the need to regulate big business gave way in "New Era" politics to hope for a partnership between government and industry, one that would promote the interests of American corporations at home and abroad. Politicians of the 1920s saw themselves as managers who understood economic growth. In place of government regulation, they put their confidence in cooperation through the exchange of information among voluntary associations in every segment of the economy.

The GOP controlled American politics in the 1920s, and its victories rested squarely on the votes of traditional Republicans. Though strongest in the rural states of the Midwest, the GOP was a potent political force in the Far West and in much of New England. Socially, it remained the party of old stock, Protestant, middle, upper-middle, and upper-class Americans; occupationally, it drew its strength from bankers, professionals, business managers, and large farmers.

Handsome Harding

The presidents of the New Era were, by and large, mediocre politicians. Senator Warren G. Harding of Ohio, who led off the decade, suited the times perfectly. Handsome enough to be a movie star, he not only looked great but told the voters what they wanted to hear. Harding promised Americans a return to "normalcy," which meant "not heroism but healing, not agitation but adjustment, not surgery but serenity." Democrat William McAdoo likened Harding's speeches to "an army of pompous phrases moving over the landscape in search of an idea." Harding's critics missed the point: Americans listened to his words and found reassurance. He appeared to be a moderate, responsible leader who would avoid extremes and guide the country into a decade of prosperity. Harding trounced the Democratic candidate, Governor James M. Cox of Ohio, 16,143,407 to 9,130,328, carrying every state outside the Democratic South.

Harding remained in office what he had been before, a fun-loving man who liked to hit golf balls, play poker, drink whiskey, and shoot the breeze with old pals. He left government to his cabinet members and the Court, staffed by political conservatives all. They approached government as managers, equating the public's interests with those of big business. Secretary of State Charles Evans Hughes championed American business interests abroad with unbridled enthusiasm; Andrew Mellon, secretary of the treasury, denounced government regulation and slashed taxes on the rich; Henry Wallace, the secretary of agriculture, organized conferences between farmers and bureaucrats under the Bureau of Agricultural Economics; and William Howard Taft presided over a Supreme Court that limited labor's right to picket, threw out minimum wages for women, and overturned a national child labor law.

The most important figure of the "New Era" was Herbert Hoover, secretary of commerce under both Harding and his successor, Calvin Coolidge. A world famous engineer and self-made millionaire, Hoover abhorred destructive competition and waste in the economy, which he proposed to eliminate through "associationism." Toward that goal, he promoted voluntary trade associations to foster cooperation in nearly every major industry and agricultural commodity through educational conferences, research commissions, trade practice controls, and ethical standards. (By 1929 more than two thousand trade associations were busily at work trying to implement Hoover's vision of a stable and prosperous economy.) Hoover's other major initiative was to convert the Commerce Department into a planning agency for businessmen. Working in cooperation with private groups such as the National Bureau of Economic Research, the Commerce Department conducted studies and compiled statistics to aid corporate planning.

Not all of Harding's appointments matched Hoover's talent and vision. Harding's father once chided him: "It's a good thing you weren't born a girl. Because you'd be in a family way all the time. You can't say no." The president found it especially hard to say "no" to old friends and cronies, members of the so-called Ohio Gang, when they asked for government jobs. In the end, this motley assortment of political hacks and hangers-on plunged his administration into disgrace.

Within two years after Harding assumed office, major scandals (involving bribes and kickbacks) erupted in the Justice Department and in the Veterans Bureau. Shortly after these

Harding's administration was fraught with scandals involving bribes and kickbacks among many of the men in his cabinet.

disclosures, Harding died of a cerebral embolism on August 2, 1923. More misdeeds soon came to light, including the infamous Teapot Dome oil scandal. Albert B. Fall, a wealthy senator from New Mexico whom Harding had appointed as secretary of the interior, was convicted of accepting $360,000 in bribes in exchange for leasing drilling rights on federal naval oil reserves. He became the first cabinet member in American history convicted for crimes in office. There was more. Attorney General Harry Daugherty was accused of accepting payoffs for selling German chemical patents controlled by the Alien Property Office. Daugherty was forced to resign.

In retrospect, two things stand out about the scandals. First, none involved partisan attacks on private individuals or on political opponents. Harding simply appointed men who were personally corrupt. Second, the public seemed indifferent to the scandals. Harding's successor, Calvin Coolidge, managed to convert the scandals into a political asset by convincing the public that he had moved swiftly to punish the wrongdoers.

The election of 1924 symbolized, in a variety of ways, the tensions and concerns of the 1920s. Despite the Harding scandals, President Calvin Coolidge was riding the crest of the prosperity wave. Meeting in New York to nominate their own candidate, the Democrats were badly split between William Gibbs McAdoo, the son-in-law of Woodrow Wilson and former secretary of the treasury, and Alfred Smith. McAdoo represented the southern, rural wing of the party, which opposed immigration and evolution and supported prohibition, Protestantism, and the Ku Klux Klan. Al Smith, governor of New York, was the flag bearer for the northern urban wing, which opposed immigration restriction, prohibition, and the Ku Klux Klan. After 102 ballots in the sweltering Madison Square Garden, the Democrats turned to a compromise candidate, Wall Street attorney John W. Davis. By that time, they had all but committed suicide, at least as far as 1924 was concerned.

A coalition of labor leaders, social workers, and former Progressives bolted both major parties and formed the Progressive Party, nominating Wisconsin Senator Robert La Follette for president. Their platform called for government ownership of natural resources, abolition of child labor, elimination of monopolies, and increased taxes on the rich. In the end, no issue was as potent as the GOP prosperity crusade. Coolidge won the election with 15,725,016 votes to Davis's 8,385,586 and La Follette's 4,822,856.

Silent Cal

Coolidge was a stern-faced, tight-lipped New Englander, whom Alice Roosevelt Longworth said looked like he had been "weaned on a pickle." Born in Plymouth Notch, Vermont, where five generations of Coolidges had worked the same family farm, he epitomized the rural values threatened by immigration, urbanization, and industrialization. After graduating from Amherst College, Coolidge opened a law office in Northampton, Massachusetts, where he embarked on a political career that led to the governorship of the Bay State. When

Calvin Coolidge, often referred to as the "do-nothing president" holds a press conference at his home in Vermont.
From Stefan Lorant's *The Glorious Burden*

he ruthlessly crushed the Boston police strike in 1919 by calling out the National Guard, Coolidge gained a reputation as a staunch conservative and won the number two slot on the Republican ticket in 1920.

Coolidge was a do-nothing president. In the words of Irving Stone, "He aspired to become the least President the country had ever had; he attained his desire." Coolidge went to bed early, slept ten hours a night, napped every afternoon, and seldom worked more than four hours a day. In part his sloth stemmed from a metabolic need for rest, but it also derived from a deep philosophical belief in the wisdom of inactivity. "Four-fifths of all our troubles in this life would disappear," sighed Coolidge, "if we would only sit down and keep still."

Harding and Coolidge idealized rich businessmen. Coolidge, in particular, was consumed by a reverence for the corporate elite. "The man who builds a factory builds a temple," said Coolidge. "The man who works there, worships there." It follows, then, that government should do everything in its power to promote business interests. While Coolidge set the tone for his administration, he left it to his cabinet members, the courts, and Congress to devise strategies for consummating the marriage between business and government.

Business leaders had contributed $8 million to the GOP's campaign chest in 1920; in return they expected the federal government to roll back the gains organized labor had made during World War I. The courts led the attack. In 1921 Harding named William Howard Taft as chief justice of the Supreme Court. Taft's judicial philosophy embraced the sanctity of private property as the highest ideal of the republic. Under Taft, the Court took a narrow view of federal power, assigning the responsibility for protecting individual citizens to the states. During the 1920s the Court outlawed picketing, upheld the yellow-dog contract, overturned national child labor laws, and abolished minimum wage laws for women.

The Twilight of Progressivism

The government's tilt toward business signaled a retreat from progressivism. The Democrats were in disarray, and Teddy Roosevelt's wing of the GOP was all but dead. Still, the reform impulse did not disappear entirely during the 1920s. A small band of beleaguered reformers, led by Robert La Follette of Wisconsin and George Norris of Nebraska, kept progressivism alive in Congress. They worked for child labor laws, regulation of wages and working hours for women, and farm relief. In 1922, Congress passed the Capper-Volstead Act, which freed farm cooperatives from the threat of antitrust prosecution, clearing the way for production restrictions and price-fixing. The farm bloc failed to enact the McNary-Haugen Bill, which would have raised farm prices by having the government purchase farm surplus and then sell them in foreign markets. Congress passed the measure twice, but Coolidge vetoed it both times. In addition, progressives defeated an attempt by private investors (led by Henry Ford) to build a hydroelectric dam across the Tennessee River at Muscle Shoals, Alabama, thus preserving the task of developing electricity in the region for public utilities.

Social welfare advocates had some temporary success at the national level. In 1912 President William Howard Taft created the Children's Bureau in the Department of Labor because of the country's high rate of infant mortality. In 1918 the bureau discovered that 16,000 women had died in childbirth and 250,000 children had failed to survive their first year. The Children's Bureau began campaigning for a federal program to improve prenatal and neonatal care. The social work establishment, along with Margaret Sanger and birth control advocates, supported the idea, and although the American Medical Association opposed it, President Warren G. Harding backed it. In 1921 Congress passed the Sheppard-Towner Act, which appropriated $1.5 million in 1922 for state hygiene instruction programs. The program lasted for seven years until President Calvin Coolidge refused to fund it any longer.

Progressives had better luck at the state and local level. Social workers and women's groups spearheaded the campaigns, sponsoring a broad range of welfare legislation. By 1930 forty-four states provided assistance to women with dependent children, and thirty-four states adopted workmen's compensation laws. Under the leadership of Governor Alfred Smith, New

York granted women a forty-one-hour work week and instituted the nation's first public housing program.

Opponents denounced welfare legislation as state intervention which increased production costs for states that passed reforms and left them unable to compete with those that did not. Asked to choose between social welfare programs and jobs, Congress and the states in most instances chose jobs. The public did not care that reform had been largely abandoned. As one coed told a pollster: "We're not out to benefit society . . . or to make industry safe. We're not going to suffer over how the other half lives."

The Election of 1928

Coolidge announced his retirement from politics in 1928 with the terse statement, "I do not choose to run." With his exit the Republicans embraced Herbert Hoover, while the Democrats turned to Alfred E. Smith. Since the platforms of both parties were nearly identical, the election turned on personalities and images of America. Few elections have pitted opponents who better defined the two faces of America—one rural, the other urban.

A native of Iowa, Hoover depicted himself as a simple farmboy who, through hard work and pluck, had grown up to be wealthy and famous. During the campaign he told folksy tales of an idyllic boyhood spent in rural America, replete with nostalgic glimpses of swimming holes, hunting and fishing trips, and moonlight romps in fresh snow. His childhood, however, was more complicated than that. Orphaned as a boy, Hoover was shuttled back and forth between a variety of relatives until he went to Stanford University. He graduated with a degree in mining in 1893, and after laboring in the mines during the depression that year, he got an engineering job with an international firm. Brilliant and talented, he was a millionaire twelve years later. The very portrait of the self-made man, Hoover represented a safe, familiar world.

Though he celebrated rural values, Hoover was also a spokesman for the future. A leading advocate of scientific progressivism, Hoover accepted the reality of industrialization, technology, governmental activism, and global markets. He stood in sharp contrast to the passive roles played by Harding and Coolidge in the 1920s. Hoover believed the president should lead—that the federal government had the responsibility to coordinate the competing interests of a modern economy, and that technology, logic, and expertise, in both the public and private sectors, could make economic prosperity a permanent feature of American life.

Smith offered a vivid contrast. The son of immigrants, he was an Irish Catholic from Hell's Kitchen in New York City who had started public life with nothing and climbed the political ladder as a faithful son of Tammany Hall. Smith sported his eastern accent and mannerisms with the same pride that he tipped his brown derby hat. A foe of prohibition, he spoke for urban, ethnic Americans. Smith too represented the future, not so much in terms of science, technology, and organization, but in terms of cultural pluralism and urbanization. The future of America was in the cities, and the cities were full of new ethnic groups struggling for acceptance and the good life. Still caught between its past and the future, the Democratic party was badly divided between its rural and urban wings. Smith made no bones about his loyalties.

Not that it made much difference who the Democrats ran. Thanks to the economy, the Republicans were unbeatable in 1928; but Smith was hurt by his failure to bridge the North-South, urban-rural split in the party, by anti-Catholic sentiment, and by his own attacks on prohibition. The anti-Catholic campaign fractured the solid South, as six states in Dixie defected to Hoover. Aided by prosperity, religious bigotry, and the dry vote, Hoover coasted to an easy victory, swamping Smith by 21,392,190 votes to 15,016,443.

Yet, even in defeat, Smith's campaign revealed the most significant political change of the 1920s—the growing power of urban and ethnic voters in the Democratic party. Smith carried the twelve largest cities in the United States by a margin of 38,000 votes. Equally important, many new voters showed up at the polls for the first time, as total voter turnout

The Changing American Landscape
PART TWO

CENTRAL PARK.

Central Park, previously rocky and dotted with a few farms and unsightly squatter's shanties, was described as "an area of beauty, charming as the Garden of the Lord" by 1863.

After being away from America for twenty years, locked in a self-imposed exile in Europe, writer Henry James returned in 1904 to his native land. Much of the land and the people were unchanged; New England cultural predelictions and rocky soil seemed hard and changeless. But in the cities of America there was the look and feel of novelty; there America had changed. In New York City, James found "the power of the most extravagant of cities, rejoicing . . . in its might, its fortune, its unsurpassable conditions. . . . " Viewed from the Hudson River "the multitudinous sky-scrapers standing up . . . like extravagant pins in a cushion already overplanted" seemed "rather surprised, as yet, at itself." For James and other travelers American cities shocked, thrilled, and frightened sometimes all at once. The cities were huge, overcrowded, ugly, and dirty; they were also huge, spacious, glorious, and beautiful. In New York City only a score or so blocks separated the squalid slums of the Lower East Side from the bucolic tranquility of Central Park.

Unlike Europe, where urban planning had its roots in centuries-old traditions, the profit motive largely governed the development of American cities. Where wealth resided, luxury and stateliness were the order of the day. For the "Four Hundred" of New York Society—the individuals whom social arbiters named as the best of New York's best—city life sparkled. Along Upper Fifth Avenue between 42nd Street and 92nd Street were the city "homes" of the leaders of New York's (and often the nation's) society, business, commerce, and industry. Dubbed the Gold Coast, "French" chateaux, "castles on the Rhine," and Cornelius Vanderbilt's block-long gothic palace shouldered each other for their place in the sun.

Public pleasure grounds dotted the areas. Central Park was a milestone in the history of American parks and landscaping. Its undulating lawns connected to tree-lined boulevards and residential avenues were answers to the spreading ugliness and congestion of urban life.

In the same cities as the wealthy, but in a very different world, were the domiciles of the poor and working class. Overcrowded and in various stages of decay, the tenement houses of New York, Philadelphia, Boston,

By 1911 downtown New York (bottom) was a modern city, incorporating all the scientific and engineering advances of the day—skyscrapers, bridges, elevators, electric lights, subways, and automobiles. With electricity came night life: Broadway stage productions, moving pictures, and entertainment at fancy roof-top gardens such as that of the Hotel Astor on Times Square (below). As the city grew uptown, multiple dwellings replaced shanties; The Dakota, a luxurious apartment building, shared its view of Central Park with the poor and their barnyard animals (left).

Improved means of transportation brought real estate development outside the city. The apartment house began to appear on the outskirts of the city, but with the amenities of the country—the architect called them "garden apartments." Railroads, then automobiles, and highways encouraged subdivision of the land. Shown below is Wilshire Boulevard, looking toward downtown Los Angeles in 1922.

and Chicago seemed to bear witness to the notion that people can live anywhere. If the tenements seemed part of James's romantic pincushion from afar, they permitted no romantic illusions up close. To be in the land of tenements, wrote novelist William Dean Howells, "is to inhale the stenches of the neglected street, and to catch the yet fouler and dreadfuller poverty-smell which breathes from the open doorways. . . . It is to see the work-worn look of mothers, the squalor of the babies, the haggish ugliness of the old women, and the slovenly frowziness of the young girls." Howells might have added, it was also to see vacant lots and sides of wagons used as toilets and mattresses crowded on rooftops.

Close to the tenements were the industries which over time made living in cities uncomfortable and unhealthy for rich and poor alike. Pittsburgh presented an ideal case in point. By the second decade of the twentieth century, its three rivers were choked to death by generation accumulation of slag, chemicals, and human filth. Added to this was the smoke, smog, and grime which turned day into night. As one commentator observed, "Pittsburgers became used to this drab existence, to a life without beauty, without joy, full of obstacles, hazards, and unpleasantness." Visitors to Pittsburgh marveled at the city's phantasmic qualities, especially its shroud of darkness

The building boom of suburban communities led to growing decay and environmental problems. Contrasting with the new, neat suburbs, such as Mineola, Long Island, (below) were the dilapidated, decaying city dwellings shown in this view (right) of Cincinnati in the 1930s. By the mid-1940s, air pollution had become so bad in Pittsburgh that 9:20 A.M. looked more like 9:20 P.M. (bottom).

which often descended around noon and like a wet blanket muffled footsteps and voices. The total effect of Pittsburgh, noted one journalist, was that of "an esthetic abortion, a municipal hovel, a mining town on a vast scale." Or, as O. Henry observed, it was the "low-downest" hole in the surface of the earth.

To escape the problems of the cities, individuals with enough money moved to the outskirts and commuted to the cities to work. In the East, where the move was well under way by the turn of the century, trolleys and trains carried people from outlying areas to the city and back. Often sedate villages were transformed into "bedroom" suburban communities. For example, Old Greenwich, Connecticut, was a shipping, shipbuilding, and potato farming village in 1800. In the 1830s it became a picturesque summer resort area. The railroad boom in the second half of the nineteenth century turned Old Greenwich into a suburb of New York City. Chestnut Hill outside Philadelphia and Lake Forest outside Chicago similarly developed from villages into suburbs. The advent of the automobile brought more construction to the urban fringe, including the apartment house, which migrated from the central city to the outskirts with new architectural groupings: building facades set back from the street; grass and shrubs on a parkway; interior courts and gardens.

The post-war economic boom began to reflect the extent of the automobile's influence on American life. Roadside gas stations and cabins began appearing along the highways (above). In suburban, rural, and city areas, drive-in restaurants became popular attractions (left). Rebuilding America took on large proportions in the 1960s and still continues today. Cities like Philadelphia (bottom, right) began to revitalize historic areas with modern offices and apartment buildings to complement renovated historic structures. Planned communities, such as Reston, Virginia, combine urban life in a country setting (below), while shopping malls (right) continue to evolve and replace the small town business communities in varying forms.

In the West, the growth and configuration of cities was dependent on the automobile and the highways on which it traveled. Midwesterners who moved to the West Coast in the 1920s and 1930s wanted houses, not apartments, and western land developers had the space to satisfy their desires. The automobile allowed western cities to expand *away* from the nucleus, and even without a nucleus. It permitted the city to sprawl outward like a giant amoeba. Assessing the work of real estate developers, one historian noted, "No plan, no systematic order dominated their vision, nothing but immediate and short-term profit. And many of the resultant communities in their garish and impermanent and unlovely aspect reflected this headlong rush to build." This pattern seen first in Los Angeles in the 1920s was subsequently repeated in San Francisco, Seattle, Portland, Denver, Albequerque, El Paso, Phoenix, Tucson, Dallas, and Houston. Carey McWilliams has suggested that the people who built these cities were eternal villagers who sought to recreate the midwestern village in western cities, to have at once both city and country life. The automobile allowed them to explore that dream.

Fast-food restaurants, drive-in theaters, and shopping malls changed the look of suburban America in the 1960s and 1970s; urban renewal altered cities and planned communities brought some order to suburban growth. The development of riverfront and harbor areas in such cities as Pittsburgh, Cincinnati, and Baltimore have brought shoppers back into the cities. And new pollution standards have encouraged people to restore the stately city houses and apartments. Increasingly in the 1980s, Americans are fleeing the suburbs for the cities.

This process of gentrification is an attempt to recapture a lost America—an urban America of solid brownstones with parlors and high ceilings. The same aesthetic standards are beginning to be applied to the country's highways. Limits on billboard ads have once again permitted travelers an unobstructed view of nature. Can America reclaim its lost landscape? A note of hopeful change comes from a recent study listing Pittsburgh, once one of the country's ugliest cities, as the "best" city in which to live in America.

The phrase from the song, "America the Beautiful," "from sea to shining sea" once conjured visions of breathtaking natural beauty. The juxtaposition of the man-made landscape and nature's would suggest that man may need to ponder his relationship to the environment.

rose from forty-nine percent to fifty-seven percent. Most of them came from industrial, urban communities in the North. This meant that hyphenated Americans were rapidly acquiring the habit of voting. They were voting Democratic, shrinking the influence of the rural element in the party, as well in the nation.

erbert Hoover

Herbert Hoover's election was the climax of New Era politics. He was the apostle of total cooperation between government and business. "Given a chance to go forward with the policies of the last eight years," he declared shortly after entering the White House, "we shall soon with the help of God be in sight of the day when poverty will be banished from this nation." Optimistic businessmen, bankers, and stockbrokers echoed Hoover's promises, predicting a future of prosperity and progress. The stock market crash was just around the corner.

The Great Crash

Economic historians have been hard pressed to explain why the Jazz Age ended in financial disaster. Employment was high, prices were stable, and production soared. Manufacturing output nearly doubled between 1921 and 1929, and the real wages of industrial workers rose by about seventeen percent. Not everyone prospered, to be sure. Strapped with long-term debts, high taxes, and a sharp drop in crop prices, farmers lost ground throughout the decade, never matching their income of 1920. Most blacks and Hispanics lived in poverty, large numbers of poor whites haunted southern Appalachia, and virtually every large American city had its ghetto. Still, more people were comfortable, well-to-do, or rich during the 1920s than ever before in American history.

The most remarkable feature of the decade was greed, or in the words of economist John Kenneth Galbraith, the public's "inordinate de-sire to get rich quickly with a minimum of physical effort." The Florida land boom of 1925–1926 was the most spectacular monument to investment irresponsibility. Land prices in Florida rose exponentially until two devastating hurricanes in 1926 showed in the words of Frederick Lewis Allen "what a Soothing Tropic Wind could do when it got a running start from the West Indies." In the wake of the damage the land boom collapsed and prices fell back to earth, bringing financial disaster to those who had assumed that providence had selected Florida's marshlands as the perfect instrument for making them wealthy.

The passion for speculation surfaced even more dramatically in the Great Bull Market. Beginning in the last six months of 1924 the price of securities began to rise, and while there were periodic dips over the next few years, the stock market continued to climb upward until 1928 when the rate of increase switched from measured steps to vaulting leaps. During the summer of 1928 alone, the value of stocks went up more than a hundred points. With the price of individual stocks rising as much as twenty points in a single day and five million shares changing hands, it was not uncommon for the ticker tapes to run two hours behind.

Credit financed the Great Bull Market. Margin buying allowed the purchaser of securities to pay only a fraction of their face value. The actual securities would then be left with the broker as collateral for the loan that paid for them, but the purchaser retained full title to them at their face value, including the right to sell them at a profit as the market rose. Speculators could get all the benefits of ownership without paying the full purchase price. In 1926 trading in the stock market stood at $451 million; by 1929 it had leaped to $1.1 billion. Brokers' loans stood at $3.5 billion in 1926; by 1929 they had jumped to $8.5 billion, eloquent testimony that borrowing for investment had transmuted itself into an orgy of speculation. Contrary to later mythology, most speculators were wealthy people or members of the upper middle class. The average American did not own stocks, let alone play the market.

Federal Reserve Board monetary policy did not help matters. Board members found them-

This newspaper headline from October 25, 1929 claims what everyone feared. The downward spiral continued through 1932 when prices were 80 percent below their 1929 highs.

selves in a real dilemma. If they raised interest rates to stifle the speculative boom, they risked slowing down the economy and creating unemployment. If they lowered interest rates in order to stimulate the economy, they would only make securities speculation worse. Confused and uncertain, the Federal Reserve Board pursued contradictory policies. Between 1927 and 1929 the board raised and lowered interest rates several times in a futile attempt to stop the Wall Street orgy without slowing the economy. Private greed and government impotence were combining to create a catastrophe.

A few days before he left office in 1929, Coolidge reassured the public that stocks were "cheap at current prices." Others were not so sure. Financial analysts for the *New York Times* warned investors that the huge gap between stock prices and the rate of economic growth was bound to end in disaster. The bubble burst in the September and October of 1929 when the market finally crashed. By November the value of the average stock had dropped fifty percent, reducing the wealth of their owners by an estimated $30 billion. With the exception of a brief flirtation with stability in 1931, the mar-

ket continued its downward spiral for the next several years. Overall, the index of common stocks dropped from 26 points in 1929 to 6.9 points in 1932.

But the Great Crash did not cause the Great Depression. Whole segments of the American economy, including agriculture, banking, manufacturing, and foreign trade, were already depressed when the stock market crashed. Farming had been depressed ever since the end of World War I. Burdened by the heavy debts they had assumed to finance wartime production increases, farmers were trapped in 1919 when European agriculture revived. Global farm production was up and commodity prices were down. Farm income declined, and to recover their losses and make their debt payments, individual farmers increased production. The collective result of millions of farmers increasing production was larger surpluses and lower prices. It was a vicious cycle which persisted throughout the decade. The decline in farm income reverberated throughout the rest of the economy; they stopped buying farm implements, tractors, automobiles, furniture, and consumer goods from the mail order houses.

Millions of farmers were forced to default on their debts, placing tremendous pressure on the banking system. Between 1920 and 1929 more than 5000 of the country's 30,000 banks failed. Afraid to put their money in banks, large numbers of people began hoarding cash, which by 1930 totaled more than $1 billion out of circulation. When the stock market crashed in 1929 and continued down until 1933, the banking system saw more of its assets destroyed. Between 1929 and 1933, when the entire banking system collapsed, another 5000 banks went under. Bankers were frightened and cautious, unwilling to make loans even to worthy borrowers.

Thousands of small businesses were unable to secure working capital loans and failed. Thousands of others failed because they had lost their working capital in the stock market. Instead of reinvesting some of their profits during the 1920s back into the business and expanding their capacity, they gambled it in the securities markets. When the crash came in

1929, they lost money which should have gone into new factories, technologies, and distribution systems. Unable to raise their own cash or borrow it, these small businesses closed their doors and laid off their workers.

Labor's position was similarly weak. Because wage increases during the 1920s did not keep pace with the rise in corporate profits, purchasing power could not absorb the supply of consumer goods. The economic irony of the 1920s revolved around the business community's promotion of the consumer culture through advertising while at the same time refusing to give workers the wage increases they needed to buy the products. Like farmers, workers did not have enough purchasing power to sustain the economy.

The invention of installment buying was another culprit. Between 1919 and 1927 the total volume of installment debt increased from $100 million to $7 billion. Consumers went on a spending binge, encouraged by "buy now and pay later" advertising. Demand for automobiles

and furniture was especially great, and those industries expanded rapidly in the early 1920s. Later in the decade, consumer demand for cars and furniture reached a saturation point. By 1927 both industries found themselves with excess capacity and began laying off workers.

Finally, Republican tariff policies depressed foreign trade. Anxious to protect American industries from foreign competition after World War I, Congress passed the Emergency Tariff Act of 1921, the Fordney-McCumber Tariff of 1922, and the Hawley-Smoot Tariff of 1930, all of which successively raised tariff rates to unprecedented levels. Combined with serious weaknesses in the European economies, the American tariffs stifled international trade and contributed to the economic malaise.

The declines in purchasing power created a vicious cycle. Drops in consumer spending led inevitably to reductions in production and worker layoffs. Those workers then spent less and the cycle repeated itself. Business bankruptcies increased and even healthy concerns

Soup kitchens and bread lines throughout many cities did their best to serve the lines of hungry families, while thousands of people went from town to town in search of jobs.

1920	Election of Harding; Urban population exceeds rural population for the first time
1921	Capper-Volstead Act protects farm coops from antitrust persecution; Taft becomes Chief Justice
1923	Harding dies; New York becomes the first state to repeal enforcement of prohibition
1924	National Origins Act; Coolidge elected; Senate probes Teapot Dome scandal
1925	Ku Klux Klan membership reaches 5 million; Scopes Monkey Trial; *The Great Gatsby* published; Almost 20 million automobiles registered in the U.S.
1926	Supreme Court upholds zoning laws; National Broadcasting Corporation (NBC) organized; Stock market trading reaches $451 million

1927 Lindbergh flies solo across the Atlantic; Sacco and Vanzetti executed

1928 Hoover elected

1929 Two-thirds of all U.S. homes have electricity; Stock market crash

postponed investment. The depression did not seize the country in an instant; it infected the land gradually, like a slow-growing cancer. From Maine to California, in numbers that seemed incredible, businesses failed, banks folded, and corporations slashed production, cut wages, and laid off employees. The national income dropped from $88 billion in 1929 to $40 billion in 1933, by which time 13 million Americans (twenty-five percent of the workforce) were unemployed.

Measured in human terms, the Great Depression was the greatest economic catastrophe in American history. It struck urban and rural areas, blue- and white-collar families alike. In the nation's cities, unemployed men took to the streets to sell apples or shine shoes. By the end of 1930, New York City had thirty-three soup kitchens, serving lines of hungry families that stretched for blocks. Thousands of men, many of whom deserted their wives and children, hopped freight trains and wandered from town to town looking for jobs or handouts.

Unlike most of Western Europe, the United States had no federal system of unemployment insurance. The burden fell on state and municipal governments working in cooperation with private charities such as the Red Cross and the Community Chest. Created to handle temporary problems, these groups lacked the resources to alleviate the massive suffering created by the Great Depression. In the rural South, relief funds were virtually nonexistent. A social worker in Alabama considered herself fortunate when the county appropriated $300 to serve 5000 unemployed, starving people.

Conditions in the urban North were little better. Most city charters did not permit public funds to be used for work relief. Philadelphia provided relief to only one needy family in five, and those families lucky enough to receive assistance got less than $20 a month. New York supplied less than $10 a month per family. Most small and medium sized cities offered no assistance. By the fall of 1931 relief programs were bankrupt in most cities. Adding insult to injury, several states disqualified relief clients from voting; while other cities forced them to surrender their automobile license plates. The nation was trapped in the middle of an economic disaster.

CONCLUSION

Janus, the two-faced god of antiquity, offers an intriguing symbol for America in the 1920s. The nation's image was divided, with one profile looking optimistically to the future, while the other stared longingly at the past. Caught between the disillusionment of World War I and the economic malaise of the Great Depression, the decade witnessed a gigantic struggle between an old and a new America, a time when the past was visibly, almost tangibly, giving way to the future. Instead of a land of farms and villages, the United States had become a country of factories and cities. The Protestant values of America suddenly had new rivals, not just the Catholicism and the Judaism of the new immigrants, but the secularism of modern culture. Although most Americans wanted to retreat into an isolationist shell and disregard the outside world, the country had acquired global territorial and economic interests which required protection.

Tradition gave way to innovation as a modern society emerged. Country against city, native against immigrant, worker against farmer, Protestant against Catholic, fundamentalist against liberal, conservative against progressive, wet against dry, Victorian against libertarian—all the issues of the 1920s reflected different images of the same struggle, a colossal identity crisis in which the United States came to terms with modern society. But what World War I started, the Great Depression interrupted. The intense cultural debates of the 1920s gave way to the equally intense economic debates of the 1930s. Cultural politics took a back seat to the politics of survival.

REVIEW SUMMARY

In the postwar decade the nation struggled between traditional and modern values.

- a spirit of nativism led to immigration laws, urban segregation, persecution of minorities, and the resurgence of the Ku Klux Klan
- women experienced new sexual and professional freedom
- moral reforms ended in failure
- new outlooks such as existentialism and Freudian psychology competed with a religious fundamentalism
- Americans moved further in the direction of a mass-consumption society
- progressive reform retreated to the local and state levels as laissez-faire ideology came to dominate national politics
- seeming prosperity concealed deep flaws in the national economy

SUGGESTIONS FOR FURTHER READING

OVERVIEWS AND SURVEYS

Frederick Lewis Allen, *Only Yesterday: An Informal History of the Nineteen-Twenties* (1930); Paul A. Carter, *Another Part of the Twenties* (1977); Paul A. Carter, *The Twenties in America* (1968); Ellis Hawley, *The Great War and the Search for Modern Order* (1979); John D. Hicks, *Republican Ascendency, 1921–1933* (1960); William E. Leuchtenburg, *The Perils of Prosperity, 1914–1932* (1958); and Geoffrey Perrett, *America in the Twenties: A History* (1982).

POLITICS

LeRoy Ashby, *The Spearless Leader: Senator Borah and the Progressive Movement in the 1920s* (1972); Gary Dean Best, *The Politics of American Individualism: Herbert Hoover in Transition, 1918–1921* (1976); David Burner, *Herbert Hoover: A Public Life* (1979); David Burner, *The Politics of Provincialism: The Democratic Party in Transition, 1918–1932* (1968); Clarke Chambers, *Seedtime of Reform, 1918–1933* (1956); Paula Elder, *Governor Alfred E. Smith: The Politician as Reformer (1983);* William Harbaugh, *Lawyer's Lawyer: The Life of John W. Davis* (1973); John D. Hicks, *Republican Ascendency, 1921–1932* (1960); Matthew Josephson and Hannah Josephson, *Al Smith: Hero of the Cities* (1970); Allen Lichtman, *Prejudice and the Old Politics: The Presidential Election of 1928* (1979); Richard Lowitt, *George W. Norris* (1971); Donald R. McCoy, *Calvin*

Coolidge: The Quiet President (1967); Robert K. Murray, *The Harding Era: Warren G. Harding and His Administration* (1969) and *The Politics of Normalcy* (1973); George Nash, *The Life of Herbert Hoover—the Engineer* (vol. 1; 1983); Burl Noggle, *Teapot Dome: Oil and Politics in the 1920s* (1962); Francis Russell, *The Shadow of Blooming Grove: Warren G. Harding in His Times* (1968); Andrew Sinclair, *The Available Man: The Life Behind the Masks of Warren Gamaliel Harding* (1965); David P. Thelen, *Robert M. La Follette and the Insurgent Spirit* (1976); William Allen White, *A Puritan in Babylon: The Story of Calvin Coolidge* (1940); and Joan Hoff Wilson, *Herbert Hoover: Forgotten Progressive* (1975).

BUSINESS AND ECONOMICS

Irving Bernstein, *The Lean Years: A History of the American Worker, 1920–1933* (1960); David Brody, *Workers in Industrial America: Essays on the Twentieth Century Struggle* (1980); Alfred Chandler, *Strategy and Structure: Chapters in the History of American Industry* (1962); James J. Flink, *The Car Culture* (1975); Kenneth T. Jackson, *Crabgrass Frontier: The Suburbanization of the United States* (1985); Sanford M. Jacoby, *Employing Bureaucracy: Managers, Unions, and the Transformation of Work in American Industry, 1900–1945* (1985); Robert H. Zieger, *Republicans and Labor, 1919–1929* (1969); Donald Pope, *The Making of Modern Advertising* (1983); Jim Potter, *The American Economy Between the Wars* (1974); James Protho, *The Dollar Decade: Business Ideas in the 1920s* (1954); John B. Rae, *The Road and the Car in American Life* (1971); and George Soule, *Prosperity Decade: From War to Depression, 1917–1929* (1947).

NATIVISM AND MORAL REACTIONISM

David Chalmers, *Hooded Americans: The First Century of the Ku Klux Klan, 1865–1965* (1965); Robert A. Divine, *American Immigration Policy, 1924–1952* (1954); Norman Furniss, *The Fundamentalist Controversy, 1918–1931* (1954); Ray Ginger, *Six Days or Forever? Tennessee v. John Thomas Scopes* (1974); Vivian Gornick, *The Romance of American Communism* (1977); John Higham, *Strangers in the Land: Patterns of American Nativism, 1860–1925* (1955); Kenneth T. Jackson, *The Ku Klux Klan in the City, 1915–1930* (1969); Lawrence Levine, *Defender of the Faith: William Jennings Bryan, the Last Decade, 1915–1925* (1965); Robert K. Murray, *Red Scare: A Study in National Hysteria, 1919–1920* (1955); William Preston, Jr., *Aliens and Dissenters: Federal Suppression of Radicals, 1903–1933* (1961); Andrew Sinclair, *Prohibition* (1962); and William Young and David E. Kaiser, *Postmortem: New Evidence in the Case of Sacco and Vanzetti* (1985).

RACIAL MINORITIES

Rodolfo Acuña, *Occupied America: A History of Chicanos* (1981); Albert Camarillo, *Chicanos in a Changing Society: From Mexican Pueblos to American Barrios in Santa Barbara and Southern California, 1848–1930* (1979); Nathan Huggins, *Harlem Renaissance* (1971); Ira Katznelson, *Black Men, White Cities* (1973); Kenneth Kusmer, *A Ghetto Takes Shape: Black Cleveland, 1870–1930* (1976); David Levering Lewis, *When Harlem Was in Vogue* (1981); Manning Marable, *W.E.B. Du Bois: Black Radical Democrat* (1986); Matt S. Meier and Feliciano Rivera, *The Chicanos* (1972); Gilbert Osofsky, *Harlem: The Making of a Ghetto: Negro New York, 1890–1930* (1965); Kenneth Philp, *John J. Collier and the Crusade for Indian Reform, 1920–1954* (1977); Ricardo Romo, *East Los Angeles: History of a Barrio* (1983); Theodore Vincent, *Black Power and the Garvey Movement* (1971); and Nancy Weiss, *The National Urban League, 1910–1940* (1974).

WOMEN AND THE FAMILY

W. Andrew Achenbaum, *Shades of Gray: Old Age, American Values, and Federal Policy Since 1920* (1983); William H. Chafe, *The American Woman: Her Changing Social, Economic, and Political Role* (1983); Mark Thomas Connelly, *The Response to Prostitution in the Progressive Era* (1980); John D'Emilio and Estelle Friedman, *Intimate Matters* (1988); David H. Fischer, *Growing Old In America* (1978); Penina Migdal Glazer and Miriam Slater, *Unequal Colleagues: The Entrance of Women into the Professions, 1890–1940* (1987); Linda Gordon, *Woman's Body, Woman's Right: A Social History of Birth Control in America* (1976); David Kennedy, *Birth Control in America: The Career of Margaret Sanger* (1970); J. Stanley Lemons, *The Woman Citizen: Social Feminism in the 1920s* (1973); Elaine Tyler May, *Great Expectations: Marriage and Divorce in Post-Victorian America* (1980); James Reed, *From Private Vice to Public Virtue: The Birth Control Movement and American Society Since 1830* (1978); Ruth Rosen, *The Lost Sisterhood: Prostitution in America* (1982); Anne Firor Scott, *The Southern Lady: From Pedestal to Politics, 1830–1930* (1972); Leslie W. Tentler, *Wage-Earning Women: Industrial Work and Family Life in the United States, 1900–1930* (1979); and Winifred D. Wandersee, *Women's Work and Family Values, 1920–1940* (1980).

FARMERS AND THE SOUTH

J. D. Black, *Agricultural Reform in the United States* (1930); Gilbert Fite, *George N. Peek and the Fight for Farm Parity* (1954); John D. Hicks and Theodore Saloutos, *Twentieth Century Populist: Agricultural Discontent in the Midwest, 1900–1939* (1964); Don S. Kirshner, *City and Country: Rural Responses to Urbanization in the 1920s* (1970); and George B. Tindall, *The Emergence of the New South, 1913–1945* (1967).

THE RISE OF MASS CULTURE

Erik Barbouw, *A Tower of Babel: A History of Broadcasting in the United States to 1933* (1966); Loren Baritz, ed., *The Culture of the Twenties* (1971); Robert Crunden, *From Self to Society: Transition in American Thought, 1919–1941* (1972); Paula Fass, *The Damned and the Beautiful: American Youth in the 1920s* (1977); Frederick Hoffman, *The Twenties: American Writing in the Postwar Decade* (1962); Fred J. McDonald, *Don't Touch That Dial* (1979); Roderick Nash, *The Nervous Generation: American Thought, 1917–1930* (1970); Randy Roberts, *Jack Dempsey, the Manassa Mauler* (1979); Philip T. Rosen, *The Modern Stentors: Radio Broadcasters and the Federal Government, 1920–1934* (1980); and Robert Sklar, *Movie-made America: A Cultural History of American Movies* (1976).

THE COMING OF THE DEPRESSION

William J. Barber, *From New Era to New Deal: Herbert Hoover, the Economists, and American Economic Policy, 1921–1933* (1985); David Burner, *Herbert Hoover: A Public Life* (1979); Martin L. Fausold, *The Presidency of Herbert Hoover* (1985); John Kenneth Galbraith, *The Great Crash, 1929* (1955); Ellis W. Hawley, *The Great War and the Search for a Modern Order* (1979); C. P. Kinderberger, *The World in Depression, 1929–1939* (1973); William E. Leuchtenburg, *The Perils of Prosperity, 1914–1932* (1958); Albert U. Romasco, *The Poverty of Abundance: Hoover, the Nation, and the Depression* (1965); Jordan A. Schwartz, *Interregnum of Despair: Hoover's Congress and the Depression* (1970); Richard N. Smith, *An Uncommon Man: The Triumph of Herbert Hoover* (1984); Robert Jobel, *The Great Bull Market* (1968); Peter Temin, *Did Monetary Forces Cause the Great Depression?* (1976).

CHAPTER 24

The Age of Roosevelt

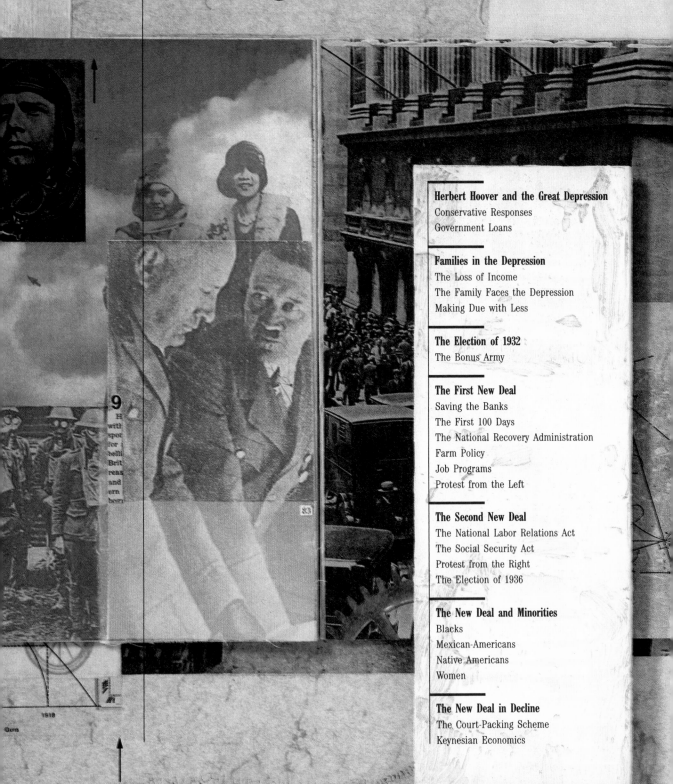

Locust. 52

2

Fig. 115(a)

Fig. 113(b)

To fans of authentic folk music, Woodrow Wilson "Woody" Guthrie was a "Shakespeare in overalls," the finest American frontier ballad writer of the twentieth century. Guthrie himself, however, downplayed his importance, insisting "All you can write is what you see." He must have seen plenty, for according to Alan Lomax, the distinguished musicologist, Guthrie knew America's plain folk better than anyone. His singing voice—droning, nasal, and high-pitched—was definitely an acquired taste, but the words of Guthrie's songs were pure poetry. In lyrics at once simple and penetrating, he sang of vagabonds who wandered the land in search of work, of union men who saw their comrades on the picket lines fall beneath the blows of company goons, and of farmers who watched with horror as their land dried up, blew away, and turned the skies of the Southwest into a Dust Bowl. In short, he put to music the hardships and struggles of working-class Americans caught up in the Great Depression.

Guthrie drew his material from his life. Born in 1912, Woody (his mother named him after Woodrow Wilson who won the Democratic nomination a week before his birth) grew up in Oklahoma and the Texas panhandle in a family star-crossed by disasters. When he was still a boy his older sister died from setting herself on fire after an argument with their mother; his father, once a prosperous land speculator, sank into alcoholism as land prices plummeted following the collapse of the oil boom; and his mother slowly slipped into madness and had to be committed to the state mental hospital where she died of Huntington's chorea, the illness that later claimed Woody.

In the face of these tragedies the Guthrie household simply dissolved, and Woody was left pretty much on his own. By nature shy and a bit of a loner, he passed the time by learning to play the guitar and harmonica. Guthrie soon discovered that he had a natural talent for music and for making people laugh, and he started playing on streetcorners for the small change people tossed into his cigar box. Eventually, he dropped out of school and became a drifter, driven by an internal restlessness that would keep him on the road for the rest of his life.

Guthrie spent the Great Depression riding the rails, playing his music on a revolving stage of one-night stands, and visiting "his" people, the "Okies" and "Arkies," along the boxcars, hobo jungles, and squalid migrant camps from Oklahoma to California. As he crisscrossed the country, he saw families sleeping on the ground and children with distended bellies who cried from hunger while guards hired to protect the orchards prevented them from eating fruit that lay rotting on the ground. Over time a quiet anger began to eat at him and he blamed the nation's "polli-Tish-uns" for not doing more to relieve the people's suffering. In private he even spoke of strapping on six-guns, robbing banks, and giving the money to starving people, like the Robin Hood figure, "Pretty Boy Floyd," in one of his ballads.

By 1940, Guthrie had made his debut in New York City, where he recorded several albums and became something of a cult figure. By this time his repertoire of Dust Bowl ballads had grown to include a variety of protest songs, including an endless assortment of union songs. His home-grown radicalism made him an instant hit with Socialist and Communist intellectuals and entertainment figures who saw his music as a powerful weapon in the class struggle. To them, Guthrie was an authentic folk hero, the very embodiment of the proletarian artist.

Woody Guthrie often inscribed the phrase, "This machine surrounds hate and destroys it" on his guitars.

A father and his sons try to make their way through the blinding dust during a dust storm in Cimarron County, Oklahoma, in April 1936.

In truth, Guthrie's political views were more radical than those of most Americans. Nevertheless, he aptly fulfilled his role as the "voice of the people" by putting to music the most important themes to emerge in American life during the 1930s—the common man's defiant pride and will to survive in the face of adversity, and the extraordinary love that Americans felt for their country. In the opening verse of "Dust Can't Kill Me," for example, Guthrie has an anguished mother proclaim:

> That old dust storm killed my baby,
> But it won't kill me, lord.
> No, it won't kill me.

In "God Blessed America" (which later generations of Americans would come to recognize by the first line of the first verse, "This land is your land, this land is my land"), Guthrie sang of "endless skyways," "golden valleys," "diamond deserts," and "wheat fields waving," evoking the country's grandeur with a poet's sense of beauty. What gave the song its power, however, was his insistence that America belonged to the people: every verse closed with the refrain, "God blessed America for me."

Thus, even in the depths of the Great Depression, Guthrie found much of enduring value in America. Somehow the nation was surviving without blowing itself apart, and he gave much of the credit to the people. In ballad upon ballad, he celebrated the fortitude, dignity, and strength of Americans. Woody Guthrie was right to praise the people in his songs. They were the glue that held things together while President Roosevelt experimented with policies and programs that would promote relief, recovery, and reform. The New Deal was important, but it rested squarely on the support of the people.

HERBERT HOOVER AND THE GREAT DEPRESSION

Like previous leaders, Hoover regarded recessions as inevitable. The prevailing economic theory held that intervention was both unnecessary and unwise. Periodic dips, it was argued, formed a natural part of the business cycle. Financial panics in 1837, 1857, 1873, 1893, and 1907 had failed to elicit much action from the administrations. Left to itself, the economy would recover. Hoover disagreed. Although he thought the Great Crash was a temporary slump in a fundamentally healthy economy, Hoover believed that the president should try to facilitate economic recovery.

Conservative Responses

First, Hoover resorted to old-fashioned "jawboning." Shortly after the stock market crash, he held a series of meetings with business and labor leaders, stressing the need to sustain prices, wages, and employment. In response, industrial leaders promised to maintain prices and wages, and labor spokesmen pledged not to strike or demand higher wages. While Hoover

remained hopeful that voluntary measures would suffice, it became apparent by the end of 1930 that businessmen could not maintain employment.

Next, the president tried cheerleading. The contrast between Hoover's speeches and conditions in the country was jarring. In the spring of 1930, just before unemployment figures rose sharply, he assured Americans: "The worst effects of the crash upon unemployment will have passed during the next sixty days." Hoover kept insisting that the economy was fundamentally sound, that the hard times would be short-lived, and that recovery was just around the corner. Critics regarded his rosy pronouncements as proof that he was insensitive to the unemployed and the dispossessed, and gradually the public came to share that view. People called the shantytown slums that grew up on the edges of cities "Hoovervilles." Newspapers became "Hoover blankets" and empty pockets turned inside out, "Hoover flags."

Hoover was neither cruel nor insensitive. A humane man, he was privately tormented by the suffering of the poor. Yet he could not bring himself to sanction large-scale federal public works programs because he honestly believed that recovery depended upon the private sec-

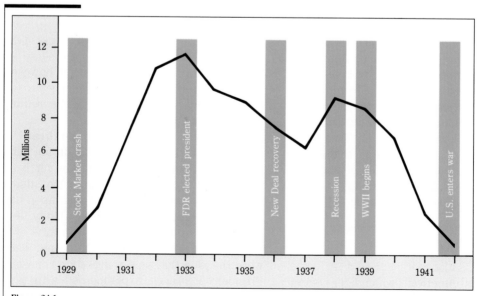

Figure 24.1
Unemployment, 1929-1942

tor, because he wanted to maintain a balanced budget, and because he feared the "dole" (as he termed federal relief programs) would undermine the people's moral character by making them dependent. He did not realize that the sheer size and complexity of the nation's economic problems rendered meaningless old shibboleths like "self-reliance" and "rugged individualism."

Government Loans

When jawboning and cheerleading failed to revive the economy, Hoover reluctantly adopted other measures. In 1932 Congress created the Reconstruction Finance Corporation (RFC) to loan $2 billion to banks, savings and loan associations, railroads, and life insurance companies. Assuming that the depression was caused by lack of credit, they believed that loan money would "trickle down" through the money markets to businesses which would then increase production and hire workers. The same principle applied to the Federal Home Loan Bank System (FHLBS), which Congress created in July 1932 to lend up to $500 million to savings and loan associations to revive the construction industry.

By early 1933 Hoover's antidepression agencies had loaned out all of their money, but by then the economy was collapsing. Thousands of banks throughout the country had gone bankrupt and the unemployment rate had reached twenty-five percent. The money from the RFC and FHLBS had not trickled down because the real problem in the economy was not the supply of credit but the lack of demand for goods. It was a vicious cycle. Unemployed workers could not buy goods, so businessmen cut back production and laid off more workers. Businessmen did not approach bankers for working capital loans, because they were not interested in increasing production. Therefore, the government loan money, which Hoover had hoped would revive the economy, simply rotated back and forth between financial institutions and the RFC and FHLBS. In the meantime, life got worse for millions of people.

Down to the bitter end, Hoover refused to admit that people were starving in America,

High unemployment rates meant decreased demand for goods and services, which in turn lead to more unemployment—by this time thousands of banks were bankrupt.

even while critics were placing the responsibility squarely at the White House door. Here was proof that Hoover was a great engineer, sneered one critic, for "in a little more than two years he has drained, ditched, and damned the United States."

FAMILIES IN THE DEPRESSION

The Great Depression did not affect everyone the same way. As many as forty percent of Americans, however, lived through these years without experiencing real hardships. A few were so wealthy that they were unaware of the suffering of others. For most Americans, however, the depression touched their lives daily. "Mass unemployment," as one journalist observed, "is both a statistic and an empty feeling in the stomach." The unemployment figures reveal how many Americans felt these pains: when Franklin D. Roosevelt took office in 1933, one quarter of the nation's families had no breadwinner. That figure fluctuated during the 1930s, but it did not drop below 14.3 percent until 1941.

The Loss of Income

For all but the most fortunate, the Great Depression meant a decline in family income. In 1929 the average American family earned $2300; by 1933 they earned $1500, a thirty-five percent drop. Most of the decline came from unemployment, but it also reflected reduced wages for those who kept their jobs. By 1933 nine out of ten companies had cut wages (some by as much as fifty percent), and more than half of all employers had converted their workforce from full- to part-time jobs, averaging roughly sixty percent of the normal work week.

These figures were so devastating because most Americans relied on salaries or wages. As late as 1870, half the work force was self-employed (on farms, for the most part), but by 1923 three out of four Americans worked for salaries or wages, leaving them especially vulnerable to economic changes. In fact, the depression forced Americans to develop a new category of poor people: in addition to the traditional poor, who included single parents, the elderly, tenant farmers, and the disabled, officials now spoke of the "new" poor—middle- and working-class people who lost their jobs and slid into poverty as a result of the depression.

The Family Faces the Depression

The depression had a powerful impact on families. It forced many couples to delay marriage; it produced a sharp drop in the divorce rate (many couples could not afford to maintain separate households or pay legal fees to obtain divorces); and it caused the birthrate to fall below the replacement level for the first time in American history.

Traditional roles within the family changed. Many fathers found their status lowered by the

Table 24.1

Depression Shopping List: 1932 to 1934

Automobiles		Household Items		Toys	
Pontiac Coupe	$ 585.00	Silverplate flatware, 26 pieces	$ 4.98	Doll carriage	$ 4.98
Chrysler Sedan	995.00	Double-bed sheets	.67	Sled	1.45
Dodge	595.00	Bath towel	.24	Tricycle	3.98
Studebaker	840.00	Wool blanket	1.00	Bicycle	10.95
Packard	2150.00	Wool rug (9' × 12')	5.85	Fielder's glove & ball	1.25
Chevrolet 1/2-ton pick-up truck	650.00	**Appliances**		**Food**	
Clothing		Electric iron	$ 2.00	Sirloin steak/lb.	$ .29
Women's		Electric coffee percolator	1.39	Rib roast/lb.	.22
Mink coat	$ 585.00	Electric mixer	9.95	Bacon/lb.	.22
Leopard coat	92.00	Vacuum cleaner	18.75	Ham/lb.	.31
Cloth coat	6.98	Electric washing machine	47.95	Chicken/lb.	.22
Wool dress	1.95	Gas stove	23.95	Pork chops/lb.	.20
Wool suit	3.98	Electric sewing machine	24.95	Salmon (16 oz. can)	.19
Wool sweater	1.69	**Furniture**		Milk (quart)	.10
Silk stockings	.69	Dining room set, 8-piece	$ 46.50	Butter (per lb.)	.28
Leather shoes	1.79	Lounge chair	19.95	Eggs (dozen)	.29
Men's		Double bed & mattress	14.95	Bread (20 oz. loaf)	.05
Overcoat	$ 11.00	Mahogony coffee table	10.75	Coffee (per lb.)	.26
Wool suit	10.50	Chippendale sofa	135.00	Sugar (per lb.)	.05
Trousers	2.00	Louis XV walnut dining table	124.00	Rice (per lb.)	.06
Shirt	.47	Wing chair	39.00	Potatoes (per lb.)	.02
Pullover sweater	1.95	Grand piano	395.00	Tomatoes (16 oz. can)	.09
Silk necktie	.55			Oranges (per dozen)	.27
Stetson hat	5.00			Corn Flakes (8 oz. box)	.08
Shoes	3.85			**Air Travel**	
				New York to Chicago, round trip	$ 86.31
				Chicago to Los Angeles, round trip	207.00

Great Depression. For them unemployment meant a loss of power as primary decision makers. In fact, large numbers of men who were unable to fulfill their roles as breadwinners lost their self-respect, became immobilized, and stopped looking for work, while others took their frustrations out in drink and became self-destructive or abusive to their families. Still others walked out the door, never to return. A survey in 1940 revealed that more than 1.5 million married women had been deserted by their husbands.

In contrast to men, many women found their status enhanced by the depression. Despite the historic opposition to outside employment for married women, they entered the work force in large numbers. Black women, in particular, found it easier than their husbands to find jobs. Most went to work as domestic servants, clerks, secretaries, sales persons, textile workers and the like. And just as unemployment eroded men's status, employment brought women more power. It changed the way they saw themselves and the way others saw them, and it redistributed authority within the family. The fact that women brought home paychecks strengthened their voice in family decisions.

Older people were especially hard hit by the depression. The number of senior citizens had increased sharply since the Civil War. In 1860, for example, only one American in forty was sixty-five or older; by 1940, that figure had risen to one in fifteen. For most senior citizens, a longer life span meant financial dependency. According to a government survey in 1937, less than thirty-five percent of elderly Americans were financially secure; nearly half had to rely on relatives for support.

Making Do with Less

The Great Depression also drew many families closer together. The stresses, conflicts, and role changes which proved to be so threatening to some families were balanced for others by the sense of unity that derived from sharing struggles and coping with adversity. As one observer said: "Many a family has lost its automobile and found its soul." Families had to devise strate-

gies for getting through hard times, for their survival depended on it. Their stories, as Woody Guthrie knew instinctively, shed as much light on the Great Depression as anything that happened in Washington.

Consider the case of the Jewell Jones family of Bauxite, Arkansas, a small mining town near the center of the state. Though they never went hungry, they depended upon contributions from each family member. The father brought home $3 for one day's work in the mines, while the mother earned $2 a week scrubbing floors in the company hospital. The couple's two sons added a few extra dollars by working as caddies at a nearby golf course, and their three daughters helped tend the family garden, can produce, and slaughter chickens and a calf each year.

There were few luxuries. The father made toys for the children, and the mother sewed most of their clothes, which were carefully mended and handed down from child to child. Shoes were an exception. The Jones children each got a pair of "store-bought" shoes when school began in the fall (plenty large so they would fit all year). When the soles wore out, they had to continue to wear the tops even though their bare feet touched the ground. Looking back on those hard times fifty years later, one of the daughters recalled:

> One year there came a terrible snowstorm and Momma wouldn't let me go to school because my shoes were worn out and my feet would freeze. I cried and cried because I had a perfect attendance that year. So I was just bawling when Winfred [the older brother] took Mamma into the kitchen, talked to her, and then came out smiling. "Don't cry, Sissy," he said. "You can go to school." He carried me the whole way [about three miles round trip] on his back. You see, he was a football star in high school, and the company had bought him football shoes. So he could walk on the snow.

Like many other American families, the Joneses made it through the depression by pulling together.

In a sense, the Joneses were lucky because they were able to hold their own. Others, like Benjamin Isaac's family of Chicago, Illinois, lost ground. Prior to the depression, Ben had

Thousands of people suddenly found themselves homeless during the Depression and many gathered in hobo colonies like this New York City "Hooverville."

earned a comfortable living selling clothing door-to-door on credit, collecting by the week. Most of his customers, he recalled, were middle-class folks who bought freely and paid their bills promptly. After the depression struck, however, Ben watched his weekly collections drop from $400 to $15. Suddenly, he could not pay the rent and had to move his wife and three children out of their spacious apartment into a $15 a month flat. "I'm telling you," he lamented, "today a dog wouldn't live in that place. Such a dirty, filthy, dark place."

Shortly after they moved in, their landlord abandoned the building and the city turned off the water. For the next two months, his wife had to carry water from another building to cook, wash, bathe, and flush the toilet. Their diet suffered, too. Though they were able to buy a good cut of meat on occasional Sundays, their meat ration for the rest of the week was half a pound of baloney.

Ben's most painful memory of the depression was going on relief. Over time they lost all their family resources, including car which had to be sold to buy food. Unemployed and destitute, Ben finally asked for help:

> I didn't want to go on relief. Believe me, when I was forced to go to the office . . . the tears were running out of my eyes. I couldn't bear myself to take money from anybody for nothing. If it wasn't for those kids—I tell you the truth—many a time it came to my mind to go commit suicide [rather] than go ask for relief. But somebody had to take care of those kids.

Ben was not able to find a steady job for the remainder of the depression. After their public assistance ran out, he turned to selling razor blades and shoe laces door-to-door. Some days his total earnings did not exceed fifty cents. Yet somehow the Isaac family held together and survived.

Like the Joneses and the Isaacs, other families pooled their incomes, moved in with other family members in order to cut expenses, bought day-old bread, ate in souplines, and did without things they could not afford. Many families drew comfort from their religions, sustained by the hope that things would turn out well in the end, while others placed their faith in themselves, in their own dogged will to survive—which so impressed observers like Woody Guthrie. But increasingly, many looked to the federal government for some help.

THE ELECTION OF 1932

Franklin D. Roosevelt won the Democratic nomination in June 1932. At first glance he did not look like someone who could relate to suffering people; he had spent his entire life in the lap of luxury. A fifth cousin of Teddy Roosevelt, he was born in 1882 to a wealthy family in Dutchess County, New York. His mother's favorite child, Roosevelt enjoyed a privileged youth. He attended Groton, an exclusive private school, Harvard (where his professors did not regard him as a serious student), and Columbia Law School. Blessed with a famous family political name, Roosevelt entered public service in 1910 as a state senator in New York. President Wilson appointed him as assistant secretary of the navy in 1913, and his status as the rising star of the Democratic party was confirmed when James Cox chose him as his running mate in the presidential election of 1920.

Handsome and outgoing, Roosevelt had a bright political future. Then disaster struck. In 1921, he developed polio. The disease left him paralyzed from the waist down and confined to a wheelchair for the rest of his life. Instead of retiring, however, Roosevelt threw himself into a rehabilitation program and labored diligently to return to public life. "If you had spent two years in bed trying to wiggle your toe," he later observed, "after that anything would seem easy."

Buoyed by an exuberant optimism and devoted political allies, Roosevelt won the governorship of New York in 1928, one of the few Democrats to survive the Republican landslide. He surrounded himself with able advisors, many of whom were college professors or social workers who had spent their lives fighting urban poverty. Together they converted New York into a laboratory for testing political reforms, including conservation, old age pensions, public works projects, and unemployment insurance.

In his acceptance speech before the Democratic convention in Chicago in 1932, Roosevelt promised "a New Deal for the American people." The band then struck up "Happy Days Are Here Again" and the delegates cheered. Actually, the speech contained little in the way of concrete proposals. Few intellectuals had a high opinion of him. Walter Lippmann, described Roosevelt as "a pleasant man who, without any important qualifications for the office, would very much like to be President."

The people saw Roosevelt differently. During the campaign, he calmed their fears and gave them hope. Even a member of Hoover's administration had to admit: "The people seem to be lifting eager faces to Franklin Roosevelt, having the impression that he is talking intimately to them." Charismatic and utterly charming, Roosevelt radiated confidence. He

Roosevelt was charming and charismatic and many people felt he was genuinely interested in their concerns. Here Roosevelt meets with a miner during his 1932 campaign.

even managed to turn his lack of a blueprint into an asset. Instead of offering plans, he advocated the experimental method. "It is common sense to take a method and try it," he declared, "if it fails, admit it frankly and try another."

The Republicans stuck with Hoover. Dejected and embittered, he projected despair and failure. (One observer quipped that "if you put a rose in Hoover's hand, it would wilt.") Advocating the same measures that had failed to bring relief since 1929, Hoover challenged Roosevelt to debate the problems that confronted the country. Instead of accepting the challenge, Roosevelt remained silent and watched Hoover end what little chance he had for reelection by his callous treatment of the "Bonus army."

The Bonus Army

The "Bonus army" was a bedraggled collection of unemployed veterans and their families who marched on Washington in the spring of 1932. Calling themselves the Bonus Expeditionary Force (BEF), a parody of the American Expeditionary Force (AEF), they came to lobby Con-

Bonus army recruits poured in from every part of the country during the spring and summer of 1932. Here a contingent marches through New York City.

gress for immediate payment of their war service bonuses, which were not due until 1945. More than 15,000 strong, they erected a shanty-town and camped out in vacant lots and empty government buildings. Though the House gave them what they wanted, the Senate killed the bill after President Hoover lobbied against it, prompting one veteran to shout in disgust, "We were heroes in 1917, but we're bums today."

Most then left Washington, D.C., but a few thousand stayed on because they had no other place to go. At Hoover's request, Congress appropriated $100,000 to help pay their expenses home. Late in July, however, the District of Columbia police tried to evict some bonus marchers from government buildings, and a riot broke out in which two policemen and two marchers died. Secretary of War Patrick Hurley urged Hoover to declare martial law, but the president refused. He did not want to attack the veterans. Instead, he told Hurley to have General Douglas MacArthur use federal troops to remove them from the government buildings to their camps nearby. MacArthur exceeded these orders badly. Using tanks, tear gas, rifle fire, sabers, and torches, he attacked the veterans and drove them from the city. (Newsmen captured the melee in vivid photographs which papers carried the next day.)

Hoover was appalled at what happened. Privately, he blamed both Hurley and MacArthur; publicly, he accepted the blame and even argued that the bonus marchers had posed a real threat of insurrection. The public was outraged by the excessive use of force, and Hoover encountered bitter resentment everywhere he tried to campaign that summer. In Detroit the crowds of unemployed auto workers chanted, "Down with Hoover, Slayer of Veterans." Upon hearing the news of the Bonus army incident, Franklin D. Roosevelt remarked: "Well, this will elect me."

Roosevelt buried Hoover in November. He won 22,809,638 votes to Hoover's 15,758,901, and 472 to 59 electoral votes. In addition, the new Congress was overwhelmingly Democrat— 311 to 119 seats in the House and 60 to 35 in the Senate. The hefty Democratic majority in the House included 131 freshmen from Republican districts. Roosevelt attracted new groups of voters—young people, women, and ethnics.

A Protestant, Roosevelt also recaptured the South for the Democratic party, and he carried every state but seven in the Northeast. (Pennsylvania was the only large state he lost.) Many Republicans apparently stayed at home. Despite their overwhelming disdain for Hoover, however, voters stayed within the two-party system, soundly rejecting candidates on the left. The Socialist nominee received only 880,000 votes; the Communist party's candidate, only 100,000.

THE FIRST NEW DEAL

The New Deal was a jumble of hastily improvised legislation and executive orders, which, as one historian put it, somehow added up to "more than the sum of its parts." Most of the legislation was economic and came in three spurts: the first in 1933, the second in 1935, and the last in 1938. From beginning to end, it was an intensely personal enterprise unified only by Roosevelt's personality. The ideas behind particular measures came from his advisors, for Roosevelt never pretended to be an original thinker. Instead of a well-defined political philosophy, he had a vague commitment to moderate reform, leavened with keen political instincts and a desire to help people.

Roosevelt's greatest asset was his ability to persuade, and no president has ever encountered a Congress so eager to follow. As one representative put it: "I had as soon start a mutiny in the face of a foreign foe as . . . [go] against the program of the President." Even Senator Arthur H. Vandenberg, a leading Republican conservative, announced that the situation called for a "dictator." No one was exactly sure what Roosevelt should do, but the country preferred anything to inactivity. On inauguration day Will Rogers exclaimed: "If he burned down the Capitol we would cheer and say, 'Well, at least he got a fire started anyhow.'"

In his inaugural address on March 4, 1933, Roosevelt told the public, "the only thing we have to fear is fear itself." Promising decisive action, he called Congress into a special session and demanded "broad executive power to wage a war against the emergency, as great as the power that would be given me if we were in fact

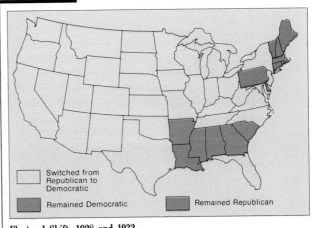

Electoral Shift, 1928 and 1932

invaded by a foreign foe." It was a ringing speech summoning the nation to battle, and across America public anticipation surged as people waited to see what the new president would do.

Saving the Banks

Roosevelt's first target was the banking crisis. In the months before he took office, America's banking system had all but disintegrated. Hundreds of banks had collapsed, wiping out the life savings of nearly 10 million people. Thirty-eight states had closed their banks, and banks in the remainder were operating on reduced schedules. On March 5 Roosevelt declared a "National Bank Holiday," stopping all banking transactions. A few days later he sent to Congress, the Emergency Banking Relief Bill, a conservative set of reforms that had been drafted with the assistance of Hoover's advisors. Immediately approved by Congress, the new law permitted solvent banks to reopen under government supervision. More important, it gave the Reconstruction Finance Corporation power to buy the stock of troubled banks and keep them open until they could be reorganized. Finally, it gave the president broad powers over the Federal Reserve System.

To generate support for his programs, Roosevelt appealed directly to the people. Using radio the way later presidents would exploit

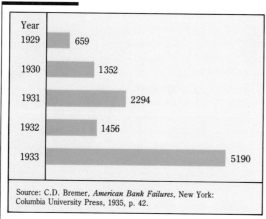

Year	
1929	659
1930	1352
1931	2294
1932	1456
1933	5190

Source: C.D. Bremer, *American Bank Failures*, New York:
Columbia University Press, 1935, p. 42.

Figure 24.2
Bank Failures, 1929-1933

television, he conducted the first of many "fireside chats" on March 12 over a national network heard by 60 million Americans. With serene assurance, he explained what he had done in plain, simple terms and told the public to have "confidence and courage." When the banks reopened the following day, the public demonstrated its faith by making more deposits than withdrawals. One of Roosevelt's key advisors did not exaggerate when he later boasted, "Capitalism was saved in eight days."

Three months later the administration followed up with the Banking Act of 1933. In addition to mandating a separation of investment banking from commercial banking to protect depositors from unsound new investment projects, the law established the Federal Deposit Insurance Corporation (FDIC). One of the real weaknesses of the banking system in the 1920s and 1930s was the frequency with which panic-stricken depositors made "runs" on their own banks, forcing liquidation of assets and often default. The FDIC, by guaranteeing payment of all deposits up to $2500 (in 1934 it was raised to $5000), was designed to restore some stability to the financial markets.

The First 100 Days

Banking reform was just the beginning. During the first "100 Days" of Roosevelt's term, Congress jammed through fifteen major bills, more

legislation than any preceding session had passed in history. (see Table 24.2, p. 789). Most of the early bills of the "100 Days" were conservative and deflationary. During his first days in office, Roosevelt opposed deficit spending to finance government programs. Cutting federal spending, imposing a consumer tax on beer, and helping large bankers at the expense of small bankers—these were measures that Hoover could have supported. In fact, like his predecessor, Roosevelt hoped to maintain a balanced budget. That hope proved to be impossible to achieve; the demands imposed by the depression were simply too great.

The later bills of the "100 Days" represented a change in direction. Distancing himself from Hoover's tight money policies, Roosevelt provided relief to debtors and exporters by devaluating the dollar, abandoning the gold standard, and ordering the Federal Reserve System to ease credit. This major shift reflected the declining clout within his administration of conservatives like Lewis Douglas, the budget director, and the growing influence of a group of advisors who came to be known as the "brain trust."

The brain trust, whose members included Rexford G. Tugwell (generally regarded as the architect of the first New Deal), Raymond Moley, and Adolph A. Berle, Jr., was composed of bright young economists and college professors who supplied Roosevelt with economic ideas and oratorical ammunition. They insisted that "bigness" was the natural product of a mature industrial economy. Instead of busting trusts, government should accept consolidations, impose national economic planning on private corporations, and enforce regulations that would promote open and fair competition. Under their tutelage, Roosevelt launched two major reforms that became the backbone of the first New Deal: one was aimed at industry, the other at agriculture.

The National Recovery Administration

The National Recovery Administration (NRA), established by the National Industrial Recovery Act (NIRA), was in Roosevelt's words "the most

Table 24.2

Legislation Enacted During the Hundred Days, March 9-June 16, 1933	
March 9	Emergency Banking Relief Act
March 22	Beer-Wine Revenue Act
March 31	Unemployment Relief Act
May 12	Agricultural Adjustment Act
May 12	Federal Emergency Relief Act
May 18	Tennessee Valley Authority Act
May 27	Securities Act of 1933
June 5	Gold Repeal Joint Resolution
June 13	Home Owners' Refinancing Act
June 16	Farm Credit Act
June 16	Banking Act of 1933
June 16	Emergency Railroad Transportation Act
June 16	National Industrial Recovery Act

important and far-reaching legislation ever passed by the American Congress." It distilled three decades of federal efforts to define a working relationship between government and industry. Philosophically, the NRA had much in common with Teddy Roosevelt's "New Nationalism"; it rejected Woodrow Wilson's "New Freedom," which erred in the judgment of New Dealers by attempting to regulate industry too closely; it drew its labor policies from Bernard Baruch's experiences with the War Labor Board of World War I; and it embraced Herbert Hoover's trade association movement (although Hoover opposed it because it replaced voluntary cooperation with government coercion).

The NRA's ultimate goal was economic planning to remove the major causes of economic instability—ruinous competition, overproduction, labor-management confrontations, and price fluctuations. Under the NRA, boards of industrial leaders, labor representatives, and government officials would draft codes of competition that would limit production, assign quotas among individual producers, and impose strict price guidelines. In practice, the guidelines were legalized price fixing and offered businessmen the chance to rationalize markets. To attract labor's support, Section 7A of the NIRA guaranteed maximum hours, minimum wages, and the right of collective bargaining. In short, the NRA proposed to restore economic health by letting industry regulate itself and offering government sanction to labor unions.

General Hugh Johnson, Roosevelt's choice to head the NRA, worked hard to win support for the new agency, and under his tireless prodding, it got off to a promising start. By midsummer, 1933, over 500 industries had signed codes covering 22 million workers; and by the end of the summer the nation's ten largest industries had been won over, as well as hundreds of smaller businesses ranging from dog food producers to burlesque houses. All across the land businesses displayed the "Blue Eagle," the insignia of the NRA, in their windows, and General Johnson was confident that the public would boycott businesses that did not.

The success was short-lived. Johnson proved to be overzealous and alienated many businessmen by attacking NRA critics as "chiselers." Instead of creating a smooth-running corporate state, Johnson presided over a chorus of endless squabbling. Since representatives of big business dominated the boards, they drafted codes that favored their interests over those of small competitors. Aware that the NRA lacked the staff to monitor compliance with the codes, many small businessmen simply ignored them. Even though they controlled it from the outset, many leaders of "big business" also opposed the NRA. At the bottom, the NRA was government telling businessmen what to do and they resented it.

Labor did not benefit from it much either. On the positive side, the codes abolished child labor and established the precedent of federal regulation of minimum wages and maximum hours. In addition, the NIRA gave a boost to the labor movement by drawing large numbers of unskilled workers into unions. For example, John L. Lewis of the United Mine Workers (UMW), which merged with the garment trade unions in 1938 to form the Congress of Industrial Organizations (CIO),

John L. Lewis

pointed to Section 7A as proof that the New Deal supported the labor movement. During the NRA's first year, Lewis expanded the UMW's membership from 150,000 to 500,000. On the negative side, however, the NRA codes set wages in most industries well below what labor demanded, and large occupational groups, such as farm workers, were not covered by the codes. The "National Run Around" pleased no one.

The NIRA, the bill that created the NRA, also sought to promote industrial recovery through "pump-priming," a favorite scheme of the "brain trusters." The object was to stimulate the economy through large public works construction projects. Title II of the NIRA appropriated $3.3 billion for public projects, but the administration was too cautious. Harold Ickes, secretary of the interior and director of the Public Works Administration (PWA), was a cautious administrator who insisted upon meticulous planning. He was determined to eliminate waste and political influence in the public projects. Although the PWA eventually spent $3 billion, Ickes's prudence prevented funds from being distributed fast enough to have any measurable impact on the economy.

Roosevelt backed Ickes, hoping that unspent PWA funds could be returned to the federal budget. (As a result, public construction lagged. As late as 1936 it reached only sixty percent of its predepression level.) Other New Deal agencies followed the same pattern. While the New Deal was remarkably scandal free, it often worked at cross purposes with itself, permitting concern for potential corruption to hamper prompt and decisive action.

Farm Policy

Roosevelt had more success with agriculture. He sympathized with farmers, who had watched their income fall sixty percent between 1929 and 1933, leaving them with crops they could not sell and mortgages they could not meet. To make matters worse, their current woes followed a decade of hard times in the 1920s. Small wonder that farmers looked back wistfully to the prosperity they had enjoyed on the eve of World War I and tried to regain it

through their repeated calls for "parity," in which farm prices enjoyed the same proportional relationship to industrial prices as they had in 1914.

The New Deal attacked the nation's farm problems on several fronts. The Rural Electrification Administration brought electricity to much of the hinterland. Between 1935 and 1942 the proportion of farms with electricity rose from eleven to thirty-five percent. The Soil Conservation Service helped farmers battle erosion; the Farm Credit Administration offered some relief from farm foreclosures; and the Commodity Credit Corporation permitted farmers to use stored products as collateral for loans. Roosevelt's most ambitious farm program, however, was the Agriculture Adjustment Act (AAA).

Like the NRA, the AAA sought a partnership between the government and major producers. Roosevelt's basic approach was to raise prices by reducing the supply of farm goods. Secretary of Agriculture Henry Wallace borrowed the idea from farmers in the Midwest who were already experimenting with "farm holidays" in an effort to raise prices by holding goods off the market. Under the AAA, the large producers, acting through farm cooperatives, would agree upon a "domestic allotment" plan setting total output and assigning acreage quotas to each producer. Participation would be voluntary. Farmers who thought they could make it without government subsidies were free to go their own way, but those who cut production to comply with the quotas would be paid for land left fallow. These payments, in turn, would be financed by a tax on middlemen and processors, which meant that the AAA would be largely self-supporting.

Unfortunately for its backers, the AAA was a public relations disaster. Because the 1933 crops had already been planted by the time Congress established the AAA, the administration ordered farmers to plow their crops under. Farmers collected over $100 million for mowing down 10 million acres of cotton. To forestall a glut in the hog market, the government purchased and slaughtered 6 million shoats and 200,000 pregnant sows, burying over 9 million pounds of pork. True, the government salvaged one million pounds for the needy, but the public neither understood nor forgave the waste. Future reductions were achieved by planning rather than destruction, but the AAA's image never recovered. To the jobless, it was cruel to pay farmers to destroy food and cut production while hunger stalked the streets.

Overall, the AAA's record was mixed. Farm income doubled between 1933 and 1936, but the main beneficiaries were large farmers. The AAA did little to help sharecroppers and tenant farmers, the groups hardest hit by the agricultural crisis. In fact, the unintended effect of federal farm policies was to increase the flight of small farmers from the land. More than 700,000 southern farmers were sharecroppers and tenant farmers who rented land in return for money or a share of the harvest. When landlords signed the acreage reduction contracts, more than 50,000 families were quickly thrown off the land. Between 1932 and 1935, three million Americans abandoned farming and moved to the city.

Nor was the AAA successful in solving overproduction. Thanks to technological breakthroughs—principally the widespread use of chemical fertilizers and the increased mechanization of farm tasks—the reductions produced by allotment plans were more than offset by dramatic increases in crop yields per acre. The pattern of subsidy and surplus so familiar to post–World War II America was already in place by the late 1930s.

Job Programs

Even the most optimistic New Dealers knew that programs like the NRA and the AAA would not end the depression overnight. To offer short-term assistance to the unemployed, Roosevelt reluctantly embraced welfare programs. Congress authorized the Civilian Conservation Corps in March 1933 to assist two of the president's favorite causes—improving national parks and employing young people. By midsummer, the government had employed 300,000 young men between the ages of eighteen and twenty-five who were hard at work planting saplings, building fire towers, stocking depleted streams, and restoring historic battle-

For $30 a month, workers in the CCC planted trees and dug drainage ditches. Federal work relief programs like these helped many retain their self respect.

fields. All told, 2650 CCC camps were built, and by 1942, 2.5 million men had served in Roosevelt's "Tree Army."

The CCC was the most popular New Deal program. It offered young men fresh air, exercise, healthy food, and educational programs. In addition to room and board, they received a modest wage, most of which was sent home to their families or set aside in a savings account to help finance college. Though clearly a public relations triumph, the CCC's economic impact was small. It excluded women, imposed rigid quotas on blacks, and offered employment to only a small number of the young people who needed work.

The Civil Works Administration (CWA), established in November 1933, ran the most ambitious relief programs. At its helm stood Harry Hopkins, the unorthodox social worker who had headed Roosevelt's relief program in New York State. Hopkins did not fit the traditional "Jane Addams" image of the social worker. He was divorced, played the horses, and cursed fluently, but even his critics admitted that Hopkins could get things done. When he arrived for work and found his office not ready, he set up a desk in the hallway and spent $5 million dollars in two hours channeling relief funds through state and local agencies. Within a month, the CWA put 2.6 million men to work, and within two months 4 million men were building 250,000 miles of road, 40,000 schools, 150,000 privies, and 3700 playgrounds.

In March 1934, however, Roosevelt scrapped the CWA because (like Hoover) he was afraid of creating a permanent dependent class. In a rare display of social ignorance, Roosevelt blithely observed: "No one is going to starve during warm weather." Actually, official statistics later revealed that 110 Americans starved to death in 1934.

Roosevelt had underestimated the seriousness of the crisis. As government funding slowed down and economic indicators leveled off in 1934, the situation worsened and a series of violent strikes erupted. Communists fomented unrest among farm workers coast to coast; a general strike closed down San Francisco for four days; and a British correspondent reported that Toledo was "in the grip of civil war." On Labor Day, 1934, garment workers launched the single largest strike in the nation's history. All across the land, Roosevelt was attacked for not doing enough to combat the depression, criticisms which did not go unheeded in the White House.

Neither did the results of the 1934 congressional elections. The Democrats won thirteen new House seats and nine new Senate seats, a clear mandate for bolder action. After the elections, the Republicans controlled less than one-third of the seats in Congress and a paltry seven governorships. Many of the newly elected Democrats were self-proclaimed activists, prompting an elated Harry Hopkins to exclaim: "Boys— this is our hour. We've got to get everything we want—a works program, social security, wages and hours, everything—now or never."

Following the congressional elections, Roosevelt abandoned his hopes for a balanced budget. Government planning and the proposed alliance with business were dead, leaving only one other road to recovery—government spending. Privately, he called the dole "a narcotic, a subtle destroyer of the human spirit."

Yet there seemed no other choice. Influenced by the CCC model, he decided to put more men to work on government jobs rather than give them a free ride.

In January 1935 Congress created the Works Progress Administration (WPA), Roosevelt's program to employ 3.5 million workers at a "security wage"—twice the level of welfare payments but well below union scales. To head the new agency, Roosevelt again turned to Harry Hopkins. Since the WPA's purpose was to put men to work quickly, Hopkins opted for labor-intensive tasks, creating jobs that were often makeshift and inefficient. While critics charged that "WPA" stood for "We Piddle Along," in truth the agency built many worthwhile projects. In its first five years alone, the WPA constructed or improved 2500 hospitals, 5900 schools, 1000 airport fields, and nearly 13,000 playgrounds. By 1941 it had provided jobs to forty percent of the nation's unemployed, pumping $11 billion into the economy.

Among the most popular of the various WPA programs were those designed to celebrate America—the land and its people, past and present. With the economy in shambles, America seemed all the more precious, and people wanted to preserve it. While folksingers like Woody Guthrie honored America in ballads, others wanted to catalog it, photograph it, paint it, record it, and write about it.

The federal government nurtured and directed the resurgence of patriotism. In photojournalism, for example, the Farm Security Agency (FSA) hired scores of talented photographers, including Dorothea Lange, Walker Evans, and Ben Shahn, to create a pictorial record of America. They produced a raft of "I've seen America" books, and among the 27,000 photographs they shot, only a handful showed people who appeared broken in health or in spirit. The faces in most of the photographs were the images of survivors, people in whom dignity had triumphed over despair.

In fact, the celebration of "the people" became the New Deal's dominant cultural motif. The WPA organized a number of programs to interview ordinary people in order to save their stories for posterity, programs which had the added benefit of putting writers, artists, actors, and other creative people to work. In addition to sponsoring an impressive set of guides to the states, the Federal Writers Project dispatched a battery of folklorists into the backcountry in search of tall tales and other "American Stuff." Oral historians collected slave narratives, and musicologists compiled an amazing collection of folk music. (Woody Guthrie was the subject of an extensive interview and three-album recording session.) Other WPA programs included the Theatre Project, which produced the "living newspaper," a running commentary on everyday affairs, and the Art Project, which decorated the nation's libraries and post offices with murals of muscular workmen, bountiful wheatfields, and massive machinery. These programs made many lasting contributions to the country's intellectual life. In addition, they established the precedent of federal support to the arts and the humanities, laying the groundwork for future federal programs designed to encourage the life of the mind in America.

Protest from the Left

The WPA marked the height of Roosevelt's control over Congress during the first New Deal. Following its passage, Congress dallied for several months over the remainder of his program. Opposition came from both the right and the left. Conservatives attacked the NRA and New Deal labor policy, while liberals accused Roosevelt of not doing enough to help the poor. Not one but three figures stepped forward to challenge Roosevelt: Huey Long, a Louisiana senator; Francis Townsend, a retired California physician; and Father Charles Coughlin, a Catholic priest from Detroit.

Of the three, Huey Long attracted the widest following. For those who insisted America needed a dictator, Louisiana's self-styled "Kingfish" was the pick of the field. Long took his nickname from one of the characters on the hit radio show, "Amos and Andy." A fiery campaigner, he was a spellbinding orator in the tradition of southern populism, and he was intensely ambitious. As governor and then senator, he ruled Louisiana with an iron hand. He also attacked the big oil companies, increased state spending on public works, and

WPA artists included Jackson Pollock, William de Kooning, and Ben Shahn. Here Louis Ross and his assistants paint a mural for the WPA Building at the 1939 World's Fair.

improved the public school system. The people of Louisiana loved him. Though he had backed Roosevelt in 1932, Long quickly broke ranks over the conservative nature of the New Deal.

Early in 1934 Long announced his "Share Our Wealth" program. Promising to make "Every Man a King," he threatened to soak the rich by imposing a stiff tax on inheritances over $5 million and levying a 100 percent tax on annual incomes over $1 million. The confiscated funds, in turn, would be distributed to the people, guaranteeing every American family an annual income of no less than $2000—more than enough to buy "a radio, a car, and a home." By February 1935 Long's followers had organized over 27,000 "Share Our Wealth" clubs. Roosevelt had to take him seriously, for a Democratic poll revealed that the "Kingfish" might attract three to four million voters to an independent presidential ticket.

Like Long, Father Charles Coughlin was an early supporter who later turned on the New Deal. Known as the "radio priest," he spoke to the nation from his Catholic parish in Royal Oak, Michigan, a Detroit suburb. By 1934 Coughlin's weekly mail was larger than the president's and his radio audience was estimated at 30 million. In a rich, warm voice, he blamed the depression on bankers and Jews and challenged Roosevelt to solve the crisis by nationalizing the banks and by promoting monetary inflation. When Roosevelt refused to heed his advice, Coughlin stopped referring to the New Deal as "Christ's Deal" and denounced it as the "Pagan Deal." In 1934 he broke with Roosevelt and formed the National Union for Social Justice.

Roosevelt's least strident opponent was Dr. Francis Townsend, a decent man whose opposition to the New Deal flowed less from personal ambition than from honest disagreements. A public health officer in Long Beach, California, he found himself unemployed at the age of sixty-seven with only $100 in savings. Townsend saw many people in similar straits in California—elderly migrants from the Midwest with no jobs and no resources. What finally drove him to act, however, was the sight of three old women rummaging through garbage cans for scraps. Their plight, coupled with his own financial difficulties, convinced him that old age relief was the key to ending the depression.

In January 1934 Townsend announced his plan for "Old Age Revolving Pensions, Limited," demanding that every citizen over sixty be given a $200 monthly pension. In return, the recipients had to retire and spend their entire pension every month within the United States. As Townsend described it, younger adults would inherit the jobs that would open, and the economy would be stimulated by the increased purchasing power of the elderly. Critics lambasted Townsend, arguing that it was ludicrous to spend $24 billion out of a national income of only $40 billion to benefit a mere nine percent of the population; but many Americans found the plan refreshingly simple, and no doubt agreed with Townsend when he replied, "I'm not in the least interested in the cost of the plan." By 1936 Townsend claimed to have 3.5 million followers.

Roosevelt could not afford to ignore so many voters. Acting alone, Long, Coughlin, and Townsend might not have enough support to defeat Roosevelt, but their challenge was real. In a close election, they commanded more than enough votes to tip the scales in favor of a Republican candidate. To remain in office, Roosevelt had to review his program in the light of their criticisms.

THE SECOND NEW DEAL

Alarmed by his critics, Roosevelt slowly abandoned his dream of a coalition uniting all Americans behind the New Deal. Previously, he had seen himself as an honest broker attempting to reconcile the conflicting demands of widely diverse interest groups. Now Roosevelt began inching toward the left. The Supreme Court gave him a shove in the same direction. On May 26, 1935, the Court struck down the NRA in *Schechter* v. *United States*—the "sick chicken" case. In *Schechter* the Court ruled unanimously that the federal government did not have the power to regulate the sale of poultry in Brooklyn. Far from being interstate commerce, the sale was a local transaction and therefore outside Congress's regulatory power. The Court reprimanded both Roosevelt and Congress for expanding federal authority where it did not belong. Roosevelt was furious. He accused the court of returning the nation "to the horse-and-buggy definition of interstate commerce."

In June Roosevelt refused to dismiss Congress for summer vacation, insisting that they swelter in the Washington heat until they had passed his new legislative agenda. The result was the "Second Hundred Days."

The National Labor Relations Act

The National Labor Relations Act (Wagner Act) came first. Senator Robert F. Wagner of New York, the bill's sponsor, seized the opportunity to replace Section 7A of the NIRA with what he called "labor's Magna Carta." Down to this point Roosevelt had resisted any drastic shift in government labor policy, but once the Wagner

Act's passage seemed assured, he swallowed his personal misgivings about strengthening labor at the expense of management and gave it his belated blessing. It passed overwhelmingly. The NLRA was government's most important concession to labor to date. It guaranteed labor's right to organize by creating the National Labor Relations Board (NLRB), which had the power to conduct labor elections, determine bargaining units, and restrain business from "unfair labor practices."

The Wagner Act inspired an unprecedented burst of labor organizing. Philip Murray of the United Mine Workers (UMW) organized the Steel Workers' Organizing Committee. Sidney Hillman established the Textile Workers' Organizing Committee. Late in 1936 Walter Reuther and the United Automobile Workers (UAW) launched the famous "sit-down" strikes in which workers occupied factories but refused to work. The automobile companies reacted to the strikes with violence, but the union prevailed. In February 1937 General Motors gave in and recognized the union. UAW membership increased from 30,000 members to more than 400,000 in less than a year. When the Steel Workers' Organizing Committee signed up 350,000 workers by 1937, the United States Steel Corporation capitulated to the union's demands. The umbrella organization for the UMW, UAW, Steel Workers' Organizing Committee, Textile Workers' Organizing Committee, and the Amalgamated Clothing Workers (and other unions) was the Congress of Industrial Organizations (CIO), first formed in 1936 and led by John L. Lewis. The Wagner Act had put the full force of the federal government behind the right of labor to bargain collectively.

The Social Security Act

The Social Security bill came next. A goal of reformers since the progressive era, it was aimed at alleviating the plight of the visible poor—dependent children, the elderly, and the handicapped. Senator Robert Wagner of New York and Congressman David Lewis of Pennsylvania, both of whom had firsthand knowledge of poverty, sponsored the bill, and Roosevelt signed it on August 15, 1935.

Roosevelt signed the Social Security Bill into law on August 15, 1935, even though many believed that it could not fulfill its promises.

A major political victory for Roosevelt, the Social Security Act was a triumph of social legislation. It stole Francis Townsend's thunder by offering workers sixty-five or older monthly stipends based on previous earnings (the first payments were not due to begin until 1940), and it gave the indigent elderly small relief payments, financed by the federal government and the states. In addition, the bill provided assistance to blind Americans and those with other handicaps, and to dependent children who did not have a wage-earning parent. It also established the nation's first federally sponsored system of unemployment insurance. Both the retirement system and the unemployment insurance were financed by mandatory payroll deductions levied equally on employees and employers.

Critics who demanded "cradle to grave" protection as the birthright of all Americans faulted Social Security on several counts. The payments it authorized, they noted, were pitifully small (initially, they ranged from $10 to $85 a month); its retirement system excluded

Table 24.3	
Later New Deal Legislation	
1934	Farm Mortgage Refinancing Act
	Gold Reserve Act
	Civil-Works Emergency Relief Act
	Home Owners' Loan Act
	Farm Mortgage Foreclosure Act
	Bank Deposit Insurance Act
	Silver Purchase Act
	Securities Exchange Act
	Labor Dispute Joint Resolution
	Railway Pension Act
	Communication Act
1935	Emergency Relief Appropriation Act
	Wagner-Connery Labor Relations Act
	Social Security Act
	Public Utility Holding Company Act
	Work Relief Act
1937	National Housing Act
	Bankhead-Jones Farm Tenancy Act
1938	Fair Labor Standards Act

such occupational groups as migrant workers, civil servants, domestic servants, merchant seamen, day laborers, and employees of charitable, religious, and educational institutions; its budget came from a regressive tax scheme that placed a disproportionate tax burden on the poor; and, most troubling of all, it failed to provide health insurance. Conservatives, however, insisted that the Social Security Act went too far down the road to socialism, complaining it was a clear example of government's assuming duties that belonged to individuals or their families.

Social Security committed the government to a social welfare role by providing the first federally sponsored "floor" for elderly, disabled, dependent, and unemployed Americans. By so doing, it greatly expanded the public's sense of entitlement—the support they expected the government to give all its citizens. Defending the compromises he was forced to make as "politics all the way through," Roosevelt boasted that "no damn politician can ever scrap my social security program."

The remaining "must legislation" of the Second Hundred Days included utilities regulation, banking reform, and a new tax proposal. These issues had more symbolic than real importance. On the whole the second New Deal merely sought to make capitalism more humane. In the words of William Allen White, a distinguished American journalist, such measures were "long past due," as a "belated attempt to bring the American people up to the modern standards of English-speaking countries." Roosevelt never contemplated, much less achieved, a social revolution. He made no attacks on private property; the well-to-do retained their privileges; wealth was not redistributed.

Neither was there any compelling evidence that a majority of Americans wanted him to do more. Despite the severe economic hardships of the depression, most Americans still supported capitalism. In fact, the Parker Brothers brought out a new board game in 1935 called Monopoly. It was a real estate game that invited players to acquire private property, convert their property into monopolies, and then drive their competitors to the wall through exorbitant rents. Monopoly was not only an instant hit but went on to become the most popular board game in American history.

Protest from the Right

Many businessmen and wealthy Americans felt that capitalism was threatened and pointed to the Second Hundred Days as proof. William Randolph Hearst ordered his newspapers to substitute "Raw Deal" for "New Deal." Firmly committed to a balanced budget, conservatives viewed heavy government spending as sacrilege, and they were appalled by the growth of the bureaucracy in Washington, D.C. In 1932 the number of civilian federal employees in the nation's capital stood at 73,445, but by 1936 the number had soared to 122,937. (By 1940 it had climbed to 139,770—nearly double what it had been in 1932.) Conservatives feared that the government's growth would increase its power at the expense of states' rights and individual liberties, and they were terrified that Roosevelt would raise rich people's taxes to finance his relief programs for the poor.

"*Mother, Wilfred wrote a bad word!*"

This 1938 *Esquire* cartoon captures the mood of disapproval among many at the time.

Many wealthy Americans regarded Roosevelt as a traitor to his class; they saw the election of 1936 as their chance to save America. Mark Sullivan, a conservative journalist, warned readers that 1936 might be "the last presidential election America may ever have," and confessed his despair over the public's failure "to see that the New Deal is to America what the early phase of Nazism was to Germany."

The Election of 1936

To carry its banner in 1936, the GOP picked Alfred M. Landon of Kansas, the only Republican governor to survive the 1934 elections. Landon was far more liberal than many of his backers. He opposed the KKK, backed business regulation, and supported many New Deal programs. A poor public speaker, his campaign was not helped by the fact that he offered few alternatives to Roosevelt's programs. As their campaign song, the Republicans chose Stephen Foster's "Oh! Susanna." Clearly, the appeal of the soft-spoken, sincere "Kansas Coolidge" was nostalgia.

The GOP's only hope was for a third party to stop Roosevelt. That hope proved groundless. Huey Long's organization fell apart after he was assassinated in 1935, and Roosevelt's swift reconciliation with Louisiana politicians became known as the "Second Louisiana Purchase." Francis Townsend's campaign, already weakened by passage of the Social Security Act in 1935, collapsed in the spring of 1936 under charges of corruption; and by 1936 Father Coughlin had been reduced to an abusive name-caller who had been publicly rebuked by the Catholic church. By the time the remnants of their followers met to form the Union party, they were no longer a threat. They nominated William Lemke, the radical farm advocate, as their presidential nominee.

By contrast, the Democrats were riding high. Always a brilliant campaigner, Roosevelt enjoyed the race. Embracing the rhetoric of the left, he lashed out at "economic royalists" who opposed the New Deal, and he promised even greater reforms. The economy was on his side. In 1936 industrial output was almost twice as high as in 1933, the national income half again as much. When Landon heard the third quarter economic report he privately conceded defeat.

On election night Roosevelt's inner circle gathered at Hyde Park to hear the news: approximately sixty-one percent of the eligible voters had cast ballots—27,752,869 for the president, 16,674,665 for Landon, and 882,479 for Lemke. Roosevelt carried every state but Maine and Vermont. James A. Farley, the president's political manager, joked, "As Maine goes, so goes Vermont," while another New Deal insider boasted: "If Roosevelt had given one more speech he would have carried Canada." In Congress the victory was equally lopsided: 331 to 89 in the House and 76 to 16 in the Senate. So many Democrats were elected to Congress that twelve freshman senators had to sit on the Republican side.

Thus, the new Democratic coalition was firmly in place by 1936. It was based on poor people, labor, urban ethnics, the traditional Democratic South, blacks, and intellectuals. It would shape the contours of American politics for decades to come.

THE NEW DEAL AND MINORITIES

The depression hit minority groups especially hard. The "last hired, first fired" syndrome affected them from the very beginning of the downturn. Discrimination was rampant. Detroit denied blacks relief on a routine basis, and Houston refused to accept relief applications from blacks and Mexican-Americans. In Atlanta "black shirts" marched downtown in 1930 carrying banners proclaiming: "Niggers back to the cotton fields—city jobs are for white folks." Such incidents tended to be the rule, not the exception.

Blacks

Of the groups that formed the Democratic coalition, the New Deal benefited blacks the least. From a purely political standpoint, Roosevelt at first had little reason to reward blacks. In the election of 1932 he received only twenty-one percent of the black vote; the overwhelming majority of black voters showed their traditional loyalty to the party of Lincoln. During Roosevelt's first administration, however, one of the most dramatic voter shifts in American history occurred, and in 1936, seventy-five percent of black voters supported the Democrats.

Blacks turned to Roosevelt in large measure because the New Deal's spending programs offered them some relief from the depression, and in part because the GOP had done little to reward their earlier support. Overall, however, Roosevelt's record on civil rights must have made many blacks wonder why they bothered to change. Equal rights for blacks was not a priority of either major party, and the vast majority of white Americans did not think that race relations needed to be reformed. In that sense Roosevelt reflected his times. Instead of using the New Deal programs to promote racial

equality, the administration consistently bowed to discrimination.

Part of the problem was simply politics. In order to pass the major New Deal relief legislation, Roosevelt needed to maintain the fragile coalition between the northern and southern wings of the Democratic party. He worried that vigorous promotion of civil rights for blacks would alienate southern whites and fracture the coalition. Time and time again, Roosevelt backed away from equal rights in order to maintain the loyalty of southern whites.

The NRA's programs, for example, offered whites the first crack at jobs and authorized separate and lower pay scales for blacks. To disillusioned blacks, the NRA stood for "Negros Ruined Again." The FHA refused to guarantee mortgages for blacks who tried to buy in white neighborhoods; and CCC camps were strictly segregated, as was much of the TVA. Furthermore, the Social Security Act excluded precisely those job categories that blacks traditionally filled. One NAACP writer became so disgruntled with Roosevelt's record that he charged: "The New Deal [is] the same raw deal."

Since forty percent of all black workers were sharecroppers and tenant farmers, the AAA acreage reduction programs were disastrous. White landlords could make more money by leaving land untilled and blacks out of work, than by putting land into production. As a result, more than 100,000 blacks were forced off the land in 1933 and 1934. When sharecroppers and tenants were allowed to stay, they often received little or no AAA payments because the money was funneled to them through white landlords. In 1934 white liberals and black leaders organized the Southern Tenant Farmers' Union to protest the plight of sharecroppers, including blacks, but when demanded direct AAA payments to tenants, the white commercial farmers were up in arms and the administration backed down.

Black leaders were especially angered by Roosevelt's failure to act on two of their key demands: an antilynching bill and a bill abolishing the poll tax. Roosevelt cited political necessity to excuse his administration's timid record on civil rights. When questioned by Walter White, head of the NAACP, about the antilynching bill, he replied: "I just can't take that risk." Conservative southern Democrats had seniority in Congress and controlled all the committee chairmanships, he explained, and if he tried to fight them on the race question, they would block his bills.

The New Deal did record some pluses on civil rights. Roosevelt named Mary Bethune, the black educator, to the advisory committee of the National Youth Administration (NYA), and thanks to her efforts, blacks received a fair share of NYA funds. The WPA was colorblind, and blacks in northern cities benefited from its work relief programs. Harold Ickes, a strong supporter of civil rights, poured federal funds into black schools and hospitals in the South. Black leaders would have preferred integrated facilities but agreed that separate facilities were better than no facilities. Moreover, Ickes's department became the home of the much publicized "Black Cabinet," including Clark Foreman as his personal assistant and Robert C. Weaver and William H. Hastie, two bright young lawyers. Together they formed a pressure group that pushed the administration to end segregation.

Still, most blacks appointed to New Deal posts were tokens—advisors on Negro affairs

A member of the advisory committee for the National Youth Administration, Mary McLeod Bethune meets here with Eleanor Roosevelt.

in one department or another. At best they achieved a new visibility in government. Instead of being brought in from the outside for consultations and then sent home, they now had permanent positions within the administration.

Mexican-Americans

Fewer in number and scattered throughout the Southwest, Mexican-Americans had less political clout than blacks. Like blacks, however, they too faced problems during the Great Depression. AAA acreage reduction programs affected migrant workers in somewhat the same way it affected sharecroppers and tenant farmers. Many were laid off, either because of the slow economy, the AAA, or job competition in the fields from unemployed whites. Still the New Deal did help in some ways. The Farm Security Administration set up camps for migrant farm workers in California, and the FERA, CCC, and WPA hired unemployed Mexican-Americans on relief jobs.

Many people of Mexican descent did not qualify for relief assistance, however. Mexican aliens, of course, could not get assistance, but Mexican-American migrant workers also had trouble because they did not live long enough in the same place to meet residency requirements. Also, legal statutes excluded agricultural workers from the benefits of workmen's compensation, Social Security, and the National Labor Relations Act. All told, the New Deal did very little for migrant farm workers, and since so many Mexican-Americans labored in the fields, they were not helped much by federal government programs.

Mexican-Americans also faced a unique problem during the 1930s. As unemployment became more and more severe, labor unions began to protest the presence of Mexican workers in the United States. Unions demanded deportation, and federal, state, and local authorities gave in to the pressure. Los Angeles began deporting Mexicans and Mexican-Americans alike to prevent them from applying for relief. "The Mexicans are trash," declared one California official. "They have no standard of living. We herd them like pigs." Eventually, more than 400,000 people of Mexican descent were de-

"THE TUSKEGEE SYPHILIS STUDY"

The South in the 1930s was the section of the United States that most resembled the underdeveloped nations of the world. Its people (white and black) remained mostly rural; they were less well educated than other Americans; and they made decidedly less money.

As a group, black Americans in the South were among the poorest of the poor: virtual paupers, chronically unemployed, without benefit of sanitation, adequate diet, or the rudiments of hygiene. They suffered from a host of diseases, including tuberculosis, syphilis, hookworm, pellagra, rickets, and rotting teeth; and their death rate far exceeded that of whites.

Despite their need, few blacks received proper medical care. In fact, many black Americans lived outside the world of modern medicine, going from cradle to grave without ever seeing a doctor. There was a severe shortage of

black physicians, and many white physicians refused to treat black patients. In addition, there were only a handful of black hospitals in the South, and most white hospitals either denied blacks admission or assigned them to segregated wings that were often overcrowded.

But poverty was as much to blame as racism for the medical neglect of black Americans. Medical care in the United States was offered on a fee-for-services basis, and the simple truth was that many blacks were too poor to be able to afford medical care.

To combat these and other problems, the federal government in 1912 united all its health-related activities under the Public Health Service (PHS). Over the next few decades, the PHS distinguished itself by launching attacks on hookworm, pellagra, and a host of other illnesses. In no field was it more active than in its efforts to fight venereal diseases.

Health reformers knew that syphilis was a killer, and that it was also capable of inflicting blindness, deafness, and insanity on its victims. Furthermore, they saw the disease as a serious threat to the family because they associated it with prostitution and with loose morals in general, which added a moral dimension to their medical concerns.

Taking advantage of the emergency atmosphere of World War I, progressive reformers pushed through Congress in 1918 a bill to create a special Division of Venereal Diseases within the PHS. The PHS officers who launched this new offensive against syphilis began with high motives, and their initial successes were impressive. By 1919, they had established over 200 health clinics, which treated over 64,000 patients who could not otherwise have afforded health care.

In the late 1920s, the PHS joined forces with the Rosenwald Fund (a private philanthropic foundation based in Chicago) to develop a syphilis control program for blacks in the South. Most doctors assumed that blacks suffered a much higher infection rate than whites because blacks abandoned themselves to sexual promiscuity. And once infected, the argument went, blacks remained infected because they were too poor and too ignorant to seek medical care.

To test these theories, PHS officers selected communities in six different southern states, examined the local black populations to ascertain the incidence of syphilis, and offered free treatment to those who were infected. This pilot program had hardly gotten underway, however, when the stock market collapse forced the Rosenwald Fund to terminate its support, and the PHS was left without sufficient funds to follow-up its syphilis control work among blacks in the South.

Macon County, Alabama, was the site of one of those original pilot programs. Its county seat, Tuskegee, was the home of the famed Tuskegee Institute. It was in and around Tuskegee that the PHS had discovered an infection rate of thirty-five percent among those tested, the highest incidence in the six communities studied. In fact, despite the presence of the Tuskegee Institute, which boasted a well-equipped hospital that might have provided low cost health care to blacks in the region, Macon County was home to the worst poverty and the most sickly residents the PHS uncovered anywhere in the South.

It was precisely this ready-made laboratory of human suffering that prompted the PHS to return to Macon County in 1932. Since they could not afford to treat syphilis, the PHS officers decided to document its damage on its victims by launching a scientific study of the effects of untreated syphilis on black males. Many white Southerners (including physicians) believed that although practically all blacks had syphilis, it did not harm them as severely as it did whites. PHS officials knew that syphilis was a serious threat to the health of black Americans, and they intended to use the results of the study to pressure southern state legislatures into appropriating funds for syphilis control work among rural blacks.

Armed with these good motives, the PHS launched the Tuskegee Study in 1932. It involved approximately 400 black males, who tested positive for the disease, and

200 non-syphilitic black males to serve as controls. In order to secure cooperation, the PHS told the local residents that they had returned to Macon County to treat people who were ill. The PHS did not inform them that they had syphilis. Instead, the men were told that they had "bad blood," a catch-all phrase which rural blacks used to describe a host of ailments.

While the PHS had not intended to treat the men, state health officials demanded, as the price of their cooperation, that the men be given at least enough medication to render them noninfectious. Consequently, all of the men received a little treatment. No one worried much about the glaring contradiction of offering treatment in a study of untreated syphilis because the men had not received enough treatment to cure them. Thus, the experiment was scientifically flawed from the outset.

Although the original plan called for a one year experiment, the Tuskegee Study continued until 1972—partly because many of the health officers became fascinated by the scientific potential of a long-range study of syphilis. No doubt others rationalized the study by telling themselves that the men were too poor to afford proper treatment, or that too much time had passed for treatment to be of any benefit. The health officials, in some cases, may have seen the men as clinical material rather than human beings.

At any rate, the Tuskegee Study killed approximately 100 black men who died as a direct result of syphilis, scores went blind or insane, and still others endured lives of chronic ill health from syphilis-

related complications. Throughout their suffering, the PHS made no effort to treat the men, and on several occasions took steps to prevent them from getting treatment on their own. As a result, the men did not receive penicillin when that "wonder drug" became widely available after World War II.

During those same four decades, however, civil protests raised America's concern for the rights of black people, and the ethical standards of the medical profession changed dramatically. PHS officials published no fewer than thirteen scientific papers on the experiment (several of which appeared in the nation's leading medical journals), and it was the subject of numerous sessions at medical conventions.

The Tuskegee Study ended in 1972 because a "whistle-blower" in the PHS named Peter Buxtun leaked the story to the press. At first health officials tried to defend their actions, but public outrage quickly silenced them, and they agreed to end the experiment. As part of an out-of-court settlement, the survivors were finally treated for syphilis. In addition, the men, and the families of the deceased, received small cash payments.

The forty year death-watch had finally ended, but its legacy can still be felt today. In the wake of its hearings, Congress enacted new legislation to protect the subjects of human experiments. The Tuskegee Study left behind a host of unanswered questions about the social and racial attitudes of the medical establishment in the United States. It served as a cruel reminder of how class distinctions and racism could negate ethical and scientific standards.

ported during the 1930s. Since many were United States citizens—the American-born husbands, wives, or children of Mexican aliens—the deportations constituted a gross violation of civil liberties.

Native Americans

A brighter spot in the New Deal's treatment of ethnic minorities was the so-called Indian New Deal. In 1933 President Roosevelt appointed John Collier as commissioner of Indian affairs. Collier had Congress create the Indian Emergency Conservation Program, a CCC-type project for the reservations, and by the time World War II broke out, more than 85,000 Indians had worked on the project, building 1742 dams and reservoirs, 12,230 miles of fence, 91 lookout towers, and 9737 miles of fire trails. They conducted pest control projects on 1,315,870 acres of land and removed poisonous weeds from 263,129 acres of reservation farm and grazing land. Collier also saw to it that the PWA, WPA, CCC, and NYA actively hired Native Americans.

Collier had long been an opponent of the fifty-year-old government allotment program, in which tribal lands had been broken up and distributed to individual Native Americans and whites. In 1934 Congress reversed that program by passing the Indian Reorganization Act, which terminated the allotment program, provided funds for tribes to purchase new land, offered government recognition of tribal constitutions, and ended prohibitions on the use of Native American languages, tribal ceremonies, and traditional dress on the reservations. That same year, the Johnson-O'Malley Act provided for federal grants to local school districts, hospitals, and social welfare agencies to assist Native Americans.

Women

Women fared somewhat better than other minorities under the New Deal. In the case of black women, race proved to be a more important factor than gender. Prior to the depression, women had dominated the field of social work, as well as the voluntary associations that cared for the poor and unemployed. Since many of the same skills were needed to combat the depression, women joined the throngs of professionals who rushed to Washington to work in the New Deal.

Once there, women formed a tightly knit network of professionals who worked hard to promote each other's careers. Frances Perkins, the secretary of labor, was the first woman in American history to hold a cabinet appointment. As the director of the Women's Division of the Democratic Committee, Molly Dewson helped place women throughout the administration. By 1939 women held one-third of the positions in the independent agencies and almost one-fifth of the positions in the executive departments.

Eleanor Roosevelt deserves much of the credit for the progress made by minorities. The first president's wife to stake out an independent public position, she provided the social conscience of the New Deal. Few people knew how difficult public appearances were for her, for she had to overcome an almost pathological shyness to voice her sympathies and convictions, but overcome it she did. In 1933 alone she traveled 40,000 miles, visiting families, investigating work conditions, and checking welfare programs. In fact, she seemed to appear everywhere: a *New Yorker* cartoon of the 1930s showed a startled coal miner at the bottom of a pit exclaiming: "For gosh sakes, here comes Mrs. Roosevelt!"

She worked tirelessly to influence her husband and the heads of government agencies to secure employment for well-qualified women and blacks. More courageous than her husband and less restricted politically, she was willing to take a public stand on civil rights. When the Daughters of the American Revolution refused in 1939 to grant the black contralto Marian Anderson permission to sing in Constitution Hall, Mrs. Roosevelt arranged for a concert on the steps of the Lincoln Memorial on Easter Sunday.

Philosophically, Roosevelt appeared to move closer to his wife's vision of society after the election of 1936. In his second inaugural address, he promised to press for new social legislation. "I see one-third of a nation ill-housed, ill-clad, ill-nourished," the president told the country. Yet Roosevelt's second term was destined to bog down into a political stalemate on social issues. He wasted his energies on an ill-conceived battle with the Supreme Court and an abortive effort to purge the Democratic party. Then he turned his attention to the international scene.

THE NEW DEAL IN DECLINE

The Court-Packing Scheme

The New Deal and the Supreme Court had been on a collision course for several years when Roosevelt decided to move against it. In 1935 the Court had ruled the NRA unconstitutional; in 1936 it had struck down the AAA in *Butler v. United States*. Roosevelt was convinced that the Supreme Court was out of step with the other two branches of government: the executive and the legislative branches were tugging in opposite directions. To remedy this problem, Roosevelt decided to force his opponents on the Supreme Court to resign so he could replace them with justices more sympathetic to his policies. On February 5, 1937, Roosevelt announced a plan to add a new member to the Supreme Court for every judge who had reached the age of seventy without retiring (six justices were over seventy). To offer a carrot with the stick, Roosevelt also announced plans for a generous pension program for retiring federal judges.

The court-packing scheme was a political disaster. Conservatives and liberals alike were appalled by Roosevelt's attack on the separation of powers, and critics accused him of trying to assume dictatorial powers. Fortunately, the Court itself ended the crisis—"the switch in time that saved nine," as one wit quipped. In five-to-four votes, the Court upheld a Washington state minimum wage law (much like the one it had overthrown in New York), and, even more surprising, the Court ruled that the Wagner Act was constitutional. Two more close decisions, one upholding compulsory unemployment insurance and the other old age pensions,

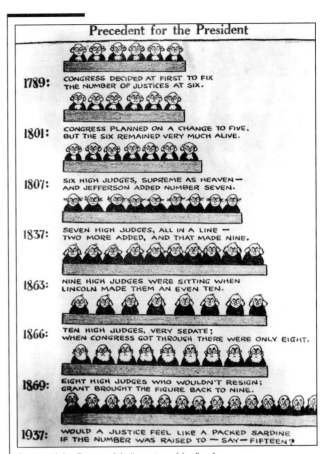

Outraged by Roosevelt's "court-packing" scheme, many conservatives and liberals argued that it could set a dangerous precedent for the future.
Precedent for the President—a 1937 copyright cartoon by Herblock

offered further proof that the Court had softened its opposition to the New Deal.

Roosevelt remained too obsessed with the battle to realize that he had won the war. He pushed the court-packing bill until the end of July, squandering his strength on a struggle that had long since become a political embarrassment. In the end, the only part of the president's plan to gain congressional approval was the pension program. Once it passed, Justice Willis Van Devanter, the most obstinate advocate of states' rights on the Court, resigned. In fact, by 1941 Roosevelt was able to name five justices to the Supreme Court, including Hugo Black and William O. Douglas. The new "Roosevelt Court" significantly expanded the government's role in the economy and civil liberties.

Keynesian Economics

Roosevelt made another blunder in 1937. A debate was raging in the administration over economic policy. One group, led by Secretary of the Treasury Henry Morganthau, wanted severe spending cuts to balance the federal budget and restore business confidence. A second group, led by WPA head Harry Hopkins and Marriner Eccles, governor of the Federal Reserve Board, were enchanted by the ideas of English economist John Maynard Keynes. Keynes argued that the federal government should spend its way out of the depression by creating purchasing power through tax cuts and new spending programs. Reassured by good economic news in 1936, the president sided with the budget balancers and late in 1937 implemented severe cutbacks in government spending programs.

The consequences were immediate. By early 1938 economic conditions dipped nearly as low as they had been in 1932, and just as he had reaped the credit for the recovery of 1936, Roosevelt got blamed for the depression of 1937–38. Republicans, weary of hearing about "Hoover's depression," relished the chance to decry "Roosevelt's depression." Finally, on April 14, 1938, Roosevelt switched his loyalties to Keynes's advocates and asked Congress to resume spending. Congress responded with huge appropriations for the PWA and welfare funds for the states. As it had before, public spending helped blunt the worst effects of the troubled economy, but it took the massive spending of World War II to end the depression and restore the nation to a firm economic footing.

Roosevelt's third blunder was his abortive attempt to purge the Democratic party of conservative senators who had opposed various portions of the New Deal. In the off-year election of 1938, Roosevelt campaigned against five southern senators, all of whom won reelection. Some of them, like "Cotton Ed" Smith of South Carolina, probably would not have been reelected had the president kept silent. The attempted purge intensified the conservative-liberal split within the Democratic party and demonstrated that it was possible to defy the

president and still be reelected. It also weakened the Democratic coalition at a time when conservative support was needed for military preparedness to meet the growing threat from Europe.

By the end of 1938 the reform spirit was gone. Even Harry Hopkins admitted that Americans had become "bored with the poor, the unemployed, and the insecure." In Congress a conservative alliance of southern Democrats and northern Republicans blocked all efforts to expand the New Deal. Yet if Roosevelt could not pass any new measures, it was equally true that his opponents could not dismantle his programs. The New Deal ended in a political stalemate.

CONCLUSION

Economically, the New Deal was largely a failure. Its programs were inefficient and unwieldy, offering too little too late; and it did nothing to alter the distribution of wealth and little to end the depression. By 1939 national productivity had barely reached 1929 levels, and 10 million men and women were still unemployed. Roosevelt simply could not bring himself to support the level of federal spending needed to trigger a recovery. Government spending remained below $10 billion a year, with deficits on the scale of $4 billion a year. Indeed, despite the handwringing and wailing of conservatives, huge deficits did not become a feature of the federal budget until World War II, when federal spending leaped to $95 billion a year, with deficits of over half that amount. World War II, not the New Deal, snapped America out of the depression, for then and only then did the economy recover and unemployment disappear.

Yet whatever its economic shortcomings, the New Deal made an enormous difference in peoples' lives. The Social Security program, while it ignored many, made the government responsible for old age pensions and for offering welfare to those unable to care for themselves. The NIRA and the Wagner Act encouraged the growth of unions; minimum wage laws put a floor under wages for many workers; and child labor was finally abolished in industry

hronology
OF KEY EVENTS

1932 The Bonus Army is driven from Washington; Roosevelt elected

1933 National Bank Holiday; Emergency Banking Relief Act; National Industrial Recovery Act; Agriculture Adjustment Act; Tennessee Valley Authority; Repeal of Twenty-first Amendment

1934 Securities and Exchange Commission created; Indian Reorganization Act; Establishment of the Southern Tenant Farmers' Union; Challenge from Huey Long, Father Coughlin, and Francis Townsend

1935 Works Progress Administration (WPA) is established; The National Recovery Administration is declared unconstitutional in the "sick chicken" case; The Second Hundred Days; The Wagner Act; The Social Security Act; Huey Long assassinated; The Congress of Industrial Organizations (CIO) is created

1936 Agriculture Adjustment Act is declared unconstitutional; Roosevelt reelected; Beginning of United Auto Workers' sit-down strike

1937 General Motors recognizes the United Auto Workers; The court-packing scheme; Roosevelt adopts Keynesian spending policies

1938 Congress sets 40 cents an hour minimum wage

(though it remained in agriculture). While the New Deal stopped far short of providing equal treatment under the law for black Americans, it did offer them a measure of relief from the depression and a new visibility in government. Women fared somewhat better than blacks, thanks to the new employment opportunities that became available in New Deal agencies.

Much of the government's new role radiated from the White House. The situation when Roosevelt took office was so dire that it required decisive action, and he responded in kind. Through his high visibility and expert handling of the media, he created the image of a compassionate leader and a bold innovator; and no other president to date could match his skill at persuading Congress to follow his programs.

More and more, the public came to expect the other branches of government to support his initiatives. Presidential power was further augmented by Roosevelt's administrative style—creating special agencies to handle specific problems and placing people in charge who could get the job done.

Above all the New Deal convinced the public that the federal government was responsible for restoring and safeguarding the nation's economic health. Prior to the New Deal there was a good chance that if someone were asked how the government affected them, they would think in terms of the state government, or even their local government. Federal policies simply did not impinge that much on the public. The New Deal changed all that. FDR's alphabet soup of programs and agencies made the federal government such a daily presence in people's lives that they now expected Washington to involve itself in everything from farm subsidies to regulating the sale of stocks and securities.

Anyone comparing the political economy of 1940 with its 1920 counterpart notices two dramatic changes. First, by 1940 the federal government had claimed responsibility for stable prices and full employment by coordinating the economy, and second, Keynesian fiscal policies had largely replaced older ideas about balanced budgets and laissez-faire in stimulating purchasing power, production, and employment. The New Deal had transformed the landscape of public policy in the United States.

REVIEW SUMMARY

The Great Depression created serious dislocations in American society:

> the decline of the industrial sector led to massive unemployment
>
> the collapse of farm prices devastated rural communities
>
> loss of income caused many men to desert their families and take to the road
>
> women assumed increasing family responsibilities, both as wage-earners and decision-makers

Franklin D. Roosevelt's New Deal (1932–1940) introduced new powers and responsibilities to the federal government:

> the government made itself supervisor of the banking system
>
> it took on the role of economic planner for both the industrial and farming sectors
>
> it tempered unemployment through civilian job programs
>
> it provided minor reforms for blacks, women, and Mexican-Americans, and enacted a truly revolutionary program favoring tribal organization for Native Americans
>
> under pressure from leftist critics, it established the rights of labor and created the social security system

In general, the federal government assumed responsibility as the protector of the nation's social and economic welfare. But by 1940 the New Deal had spent most of its momentum, and the nation began to turn its attention to the conflicts in Europe and Asia.

SUGGESTIONS FOR FURTHER READING

HERBERT HOOVER AND THE GREAT DEPRESSION

William J. Barber, *From New Era to New Deal: Herbert Hoover, the Economists, and American Economic Policy, 1921–1933* (1985); David Burner, *Herbert Hoover: A Public Life* (1979); Roger Daniels, *The Bonus March: An Episode of the Great Depression* (1971); Martin L. Fausold, *The Presidency of Herbert Hoover* (1985); Ellis W. Hawley, *The Great War and the Search for a Modern Order* (1979); Robert L. Heilbroner and Aaron Singer, *The Economic Transformation of America*, 2nd ed. (1984); William E. Leuchtenburg, *The Perils of Prosperity, 1914–1932* (1958); Donald J. Lisio, *The President and Protest: Hoover, Conspiracy, and the Bonus Riot* (1974); Albert U. Romasco, *The Poverty of Abundance: Hoover, the Nation, and the Depression* (1965); Jordan A. Schwartz, *Interregnum of Despair: Hoover's Congress and the Depression* (1970); and Richard N. Smith, *An Uncommon Man: The Triumph of Herbert Hoover* (1984).

FRANKLIN ROOSEVELT AND THE NEW DEAL

John Barnard, *Walter Reuther and the Rise of the Auto Worker* (1983); James M. Burns, *Roosevelt: The Lion and the Fox* (1956); Paul K. Conkin, *The New Deal*, 2nd ed. (1975); Frank Friedel, *Launching the New Deal* (1973); Otis L. Graham, Jr., *The New Deal: The Critical Issues* (1973); Joseph Lash, *Eleanor & Franklin* (1971); William E. Leuchtenburg, *Franklin D. Roosevelt and the New Deal* (1963); Robert S. McElvaine, *The Great Depression: America, 1929–1941* (1984); David Milton, *The Politics of U.S. Labor: From the Great Depression to the New Deal* (1980); Albert U. Romasco, *The Politics of Recovery: Roosevelt's New Deal* (1983); and Arthur Schlesinger, Jr., *The Age of Roosevelt*, 3 vols. (1957–1960).

NEW DEAL POLICIES AND STRATEGIES

Bernard Bellush, *The Failure of the NRA* (1977); Marion Clawson, *New Deal Planning: The National Resources Planning Board* (1981); Phillip J. Funigiello, *Toward a National Power Policy: The New Deal Electric Utility Industry, 1933–1941* (1973); Ellis Hawley, *The New Deal and the Problem of Monopoly: A Study in Economic Ambivalence* (1966); Robert F. Himmelberg, *The Origins of the National Recovery Act* (1976); Roy Lubove, *The Struggle for Social Security, 1900–1935* (1968); Thomas McCraw, *TVA and the Power Fight, 1933–1939* (1971);

Michael Parrish, *Security Regulation and the New Deal* (1970); James T. Patterson, *America's Struggle Against Poverty* (1981); James T. Patterson, *The New Deal and the State: Federalism in Transition* (1969); and John Salmond, *The Civilian Conservation Corps, 1933–1942: A New Deal Case Study* (1967).

LABOR

John Barnard, *Walter Reuther and the Rise of the Auto Worker* (1983); Cletus E. Daniel, *Bitter Harvest: A History of California Farmworkers, 1870–1941* (1981); Melvin Dubofsky and Warren Van Tine, *John L. Lewis: A Biography* (1977); Sidney Fine, *Sit-Down: The General Motors Strike of 1936–1937* (1969); James A. Hodges, *New Deal Labor Policy and the Southern Cotton Textile Industry, 1934–1941* (1986); David Milton, *The Politics of U.S. Labor: From the Great Depression to the New Deal* (1980); and Ronald W. Schatz, *The Electrical Workers: A History of Labor at General Electric and Westinghouse, 1923–1960* (1983).

PROTEST AND CULTURAL HISTORY

Andrew Bergmen, *We're in the Money: Depression America and Its Films* (1971); Alan Brinkley, *Voices of Protest: Huey Long, Father Coughlin, and the Great Depression* (1982); Harvey Klehr, *The Heydey of American Communism: The Depression Decade* (1984); Joe Klein, *Woody Guthrie: A Life* (1980); Abraham Holzman, *The Townsend Movement, A Political Study* (1963); Jerre Mangione, *The Dream and the Deal: The Federal Writers' Project, 1935–1943* (1972); James T. Patterson, *Congressional Conservatism and the New Deal* (1967); Richard H. Pells, *Radical Visions and American Dreams: Cultural and Social Thought in the Depression Years* (1973); Richard Polenberg, *Reorganizing Roosevelt's Government . . . 1936–1939* (1966); Leo Ribuffo, *The Old Christian Right: The Protestant Far Right from the Great Depression to the Cold War* (1983); Studs Terkel, *Hard Times: An Oral History of the Great Depression* (1970); Frank A. Warren, *An Alternative Vision: The Socialist Party in the 1930s* (1976); and T. Harry Williams, *Huey Long* (1969).

WOMEN AND THE FAMILY

William H. Chafe, *The American Woman: Her Changing Social, Economic, and Political Role, 1920–1970* (1972); Glen H. Elder, Jr., *Children of the Great Depression: Social Change in Life Experience* (1974); Alice Kessler-Harris, *Out to Work: A History of Wage-Earning Women in the United States* (1982); Steven Mintz and Susan Kellogg, *Domestic Revolutions: A Social History of American Family Life,* 1988; Lois Sharf, *To Work and to Wed: Female Employment, Feminism, and the Great Depression* (1980); Winifred D. Wandersee, *Women's Work and Family Values, 1920–1940* (1981); and Susan Ware, *Beyond Suffrage: Women in the New Deal* (1981).

MINORITY GROUPS

Dan T. Carter, *Scottsboro: A Tragedy of the Modern South* (1969); William H. Harris, *Keeping the Faith: A. Philip Randolph, Milton P. Webster, and the Brotherhood of Sleeping Car Porters, 1925–37* (1977); Abraham Hoffman, *Unwanted Mexican Americans in the Depression, Repatriation Pressure, 1929–1939* (1974); James H. Jones, *Bad Blood: The Tuskegee Syphilis Experiment—A Tragedy of Race and Medicine* (1981); Lawrence C. Kelly, *The Assault on Assimilation: John Collier and the Origins of Indian Policy Reform* (1983); Kenneth Philp, *John Collier's Crusade for Indian Reform, 1920–1954* (1977); Mark Reisler, *By the Sweat of Their Brows: Mexican Immigrant Labor in the United States, 1900–1940* (1976); Nancy J. Weiss, *Farewell to the Party of Lincoln: Black Politics in the Age of FDR* (1983); Raymond Wolters, *Negroes and the Great Depression: The Problem of Economic Recovery* (1970); and Raymond L. Zangrando, *The NAACP Crusade Against Lynching, 1909–1950* (1980).

AGRICULTURE AND THE SOUTH

David E. Conrad, *The Forgotten Farmers: The Story of the Sharecroppers in the New Deal* (1965); Frank Friedel, *F.D.R. and the South* (1965); Donald H. Grubbs, *Cry from the Cotton: The Southern Tenant Farmers Union and the New Deal* (1971); R. Douglas Hurt, *The Dust Bowl: An Agricultural and Social History* (1982); Jack Temple Kirby, *Rural Worlds Lost: The American South, 1920–1960* (1987); Richard Kirkendall, *Social Scientists and Farm Politics in the Age of Roosevelt* (1966); Paul Wertz, *New Deal Policy and Southern Rural Poverty* (1978); Theodore M. Saloutos, *The American Farmer and the New Deal* (1982); Walter J. Stein, *California and the Dust Bowl Migration* (1973); George B. Tindall, *The Emergence of the New South, 1913–1945* (1967); and David Worster, *Dust Bowl: The Southern Plains in the 1930s* (1979).

CHAPTER 25

The End of Isolation: America Faces the World, 1920-1945

When he saw the production of American industry during World War II, Winston Churchill declared, "Nothing succeeds like excess!" The British prime minister was right; while Allied armies won the decisive battles of World War II, the Allied victory rested squarely on America's economic productivity. The gross national product went from $91 billion in 1939 to $166 billion in 1945, and industrial production rose by ninety-six percent, an astonishing growth rate. By 1943 United States production outstripped all its enemies combined; by 1944 it was twice as great.

No one symbolized the economic miracle better than Henry J. Kaiser. A man of stout frame, formidable jowls, and a pronounced paunch, Kaiser had an unparalleled gift for making money. Before the war his Six Companies consortium built Boulder Dam and sank the piers for the Golden Gate Bridge. Such spectacular feats of engineering more than supported the boasts of his son, Edgar, who proudly declared: "We are building an empire." When World War II erupted, Kaiser used his experience with government contracts and government officials to quickly emerge as one of the leading industrial architects of the Allied victory.

Kaiser built ships—tankers, small aircraft carriers, troop ships, and Liberty ships, the basic cargo carrier of the war. Speed was his watchword, and he would not tolerate delays in production schedules. In 1941 it took 355 days to build a Liberty ship. With prefabricated parts and assembly-line methods, Kaiser trimmed it down to fifty-six days in 1943. By 1945 his ten shipyards had more than $3 billion in government contracts and turned out a ship a day. With enemy submarines sinking everything in sight, what counted was speed and large-scale production, not efficiency, cost, or quality.

Kaiser's shipyards were a microcosm of American society. Teeming with people who had left small towns and farms to seek jobs in defense industries, they employed 125,000 men and women who faced problems ranging from overcrowded housing to nonexistent child care. Kaiser devised ingenious ways to attract workers. He paid good wages, built a modern hospi-

tal or clinic near every shipyard, enrolled workers and their families in an excellent health plan, and experimented with round-the-clock nurseries and child-care centers.

After the war Kaiser boasted that he was the very epitome of rugged individualism and dynamic capitalism, but his success was really a form of "welfare capitalism." Government loans financed his shipyards, and cost-plus government contracts guaranteed his profits. He was one of the founders of what would later be called the military-industrial complex. Still, his concern for the health of his workers and their families was a blend of capitalism and compassion, a model of corporate management that survived long after the last of his shipyards was placed in mothballs.

DIPLOMACY BETWEEN THE WARS

World War I's horrible casualties, disappointments over the Treaty of Versailles, the United

One of the biggest producers of war goods was Henry Kaiser. Almost one quarter of America's entire wartime output of merchant shipping came from his shipyards.

States failure to join the League of Nations, and the Red Scare all left the public hostile to foreign crusades. Americans wanted to pretend that events in Europe did not affect them. "The people have had all the war, all the taxation, and all the military service they want." declared President Calvin Coolidge in 1925. During the 1920s and much of the 1930s, the United States concentrated on improving its status in the Western Hemisphere and making sure that Americans would never again fight someone else's war.

The Isolationist Mirage

Throughout the 1920s, the Republican administrations debated and ultimately refused to join the League of Nations or the World Court. Such commitments threatened to entangle the United States too deeply in global politics. In December 1921 Secretary of State Charles Evans Hughes convened a disarmament conference in Washington, D.C. The Five Power Naval Pact of 1922 established a ten-year moratorium on the construction of battleships and set current tonnage for battleships at a ratio of 5:5:3 for the United States, Great Britain, and Japan; 1.75 for France and Italy. To win support for what the Japanese delegates called a ratio of "Rolls-Royce, Rolls-Royce, Ford," the United States and Great Britain agreed not to improve their fortifications in the Far East, especially in the Philippines. In 1922 the United States also signed the Nine Power Pact, an agreement to preserve the "Open Door" in China, and the Four Power Treaty committing the United States, Great Britain, France, and Japan to consult before war threatened to erupt in Asia.

The other major attempt to prevent future armed conflict was the naive crusade to outlaw war in the 1920s. The French foreign minister, Aristide Briand, and Secretary of State Frank B. Kellogg, negotiated an agreement, ultimately signed by sixty-two nations, renouncing war as an instrument for resolving international disputes. Defensive wars, however, were allowed. The Kellogg-Briand Pact of 1928 earned Kellogg the Nobel Peace Prize, but few people had illusions about it. Nations always claim to fight defensive wars.

When Secretary of State Kellogg signed the Kellogg Peace Treaty in Paris, many people knew that it would not actually prevent wars.

The Good Neighbor Policy

In addition to their attempts to prevent conflicts in Europe and the Far East, the Republicans tried to improve relations with Latin America. During the 1920s, this effort, subsequently dubbed the "Good Neighbor Policy," had its ups and downs, but it was at least a beginning. The United States pulled the marines out of the Dominican Republic in 1924 and from Nicaragua in 1925, only to send them back to Nicaragua a few months later when a revolution broke out.

The real test came in Mexico. After the election of Alvaro Obregón as president of Mexico in 1920, the Mexican government expropriated American-owned oil properties. The oil companies demanded government intervention, but in 1927 President Coolidge appointed Dwight Morrow, a partner in the firm of J. P. Morgan and Company, as ambassador. Mexicans expected the worst; one newspaper declared, "after Morrrow come the marines." They were wrong. Morrow liked Mexico. One of his first actions was to change the sign on the embassy to read "United States Embassy" rather than "American Embassy." It was a small gesture, but it was not lost on the Mexicans, who had long resented the United States arrogance in appropriating a continental adjective. Morrow's diplomacy paid handsome dividends, and in 1927 Mexico once again recognized American-owned oil properties.

President Hoover continued the policy of careful diplomacy. He planned to withdraw marines from Nicaragua and Haiti and resisted pressure from Congress to establish a customs receivership in El Salvador when the government there defaulted on its bonds. In 1930 Hoover approved a document written by Undersecretary of State J. Reuben Clark. The Clark Memorandum repudiated the Roosevelt Corollary to the Monroe Doctrine, which for twenty-five years had justified United States intervention in Latin America.

In his first inaugural address, President Franklin D. Roosevelt dedicated the United States "to the policy of the good neighbor," giving the new relationship with Latin America a name. Secretary of State Cordell Hull stunned Latin America in December 1933 at the Seventh Pan-American Conference, declaring that "no state has the right to intervene in the international or external affairs of another." The marines left Nicaragua in 1933 and Haiti in 1934. In the Hull-Alfara Treaty of 1934, the United States surrendered the "right to intervene" and Panama finally gained its political independence. When Mexico expropriated foreign oil properties in 1938, Roosevelt refused to intervene. The Good Neighbor Policy did not solve all the problems with Latin America. Fears of American military might and economic influence still remained, but the Good Neighbor Policy promoted better relations just when hemispheric solidarity was needed to meet the threat of global war.

THE COMING OF WORLD WAR II

Conflict in the Pacific

Japan was the aggressor in the Far East. Chronically short of raw materials and desperate to establish a political and cultural hegemony in Asia, the Japanese looked enviously at Manchuria, China, Indochina, and the East Indies, where they could find iron ore, coal, rice, rubber, and petroleum. In 1931 Japan invaded Manchuria and reduced the province to a puppet state renamed Manchuko. The invasion violated the Nine Power Treaty and the Kellogg-Briand Pact, but President Hoover refused to apply economic sanctions, fearing they might hurt American exports and lead to war—and military intervention was out of the question. Instead, he applied the Stimson Doctrine (named after Secretary of State Henry L. Stimson), which refused to extend diplomatic recognition to the Manchuko government. Japan was not impressed.

Japan withdrew from the League of Nations in 1933. The next year Japan terminated the Five Power Treaty of 1922 which had limited its naval power in the Pacific. When Japan walked out of the London Naval Conference in 1935, naval disarmament was dead. Japan was now free to build an Asian empire.

In 1937 Japan invaded China, a clear violation of the Nine Power Treaty, the Kellogg-Briand Pact, and the Four Party Treaty. In December 1937 Japanese aircraft bombed the *Panay*, a United States gunboat. Desperate to keep out of an Asian war, the United States offered a feeble protest and quickly accepted Japan's apology.

The Rome–Berlin Axis

The situation was even worse in Europe where Adolf Hitler had risen to power on the backs of a devastated German economy and humiliated national psyche. The Treaty of Versailles had saddled Germany with a reparations bill of more than $33 billion in 1921. Germany was completely unable to make the interest payments, let alone the principal and the economy

Benito Mussolini and Adolph Hitler share their diplomatic triumph over France and England in Munich in 1938.

went into a tailspin marked by severe unemployment and hyperinflation. Charles Dawes, a prominent American banker, worked out the Dawes Plan in 1924 reducing the reparations bill and providing Germany with an American loan. In 1929 the so-called Young Plan, developed by American banker Owen D. Young, reduced reparations to $2 billion, but even that was too much when the Great Depression hit in 1929. Poverty-stricken and blamed for World War I, Germans wanted desperately to reclaim their national pride. Adolph Hitler promised to restore all that and more.

During the 1930s Germany repudiated the Treaty of Versailles and reasserted its military might in Europe. Hitler came to power in 1933 and immediately took Germany out of the League of Nations. In 1935 he rearmed Germany and started a peacetime draft. Benito Mussolini, whose fascist party had won control of Italy in 1922, attacked helpless Ethiopia in 1935. Germany and Japan signed the Anti-Comintern Pact (forerunner of a full-scale military alliance) in 1936, and Germany and Italy formed the Rome-Berlin Axis. That same year German troops reoccupied the Rhineland (the area between the Rhine River and France). Intent on reuniting all the German-speaking peo-

ple of Europe in the "Third Reich," Hitler annexed Austria in 1938, and later in the year seized the German-speaking Sudetenland in western Czechoslovakia.

The attacks went virtually unchallenged. The League of Nations failed to act and its member states offered only feeble protests. The cautious response reflected the mood of a war-weary world. Everyone hoped the Germans, Italians, and Japanese would be satisfied with their acquisitions and stop expanding. It was a hopelessly naive dream.

In the United States isolationist sentiment was strong and the government was preoccupied with the Great Depression. Hoping to expand foreign trade, President Franklin D. Roosevelt extended diplomatic recognition to the Soviet Union in 1933, provoking the wrath of isolationists and anticommunists alike. Rather than participate in the London Economic Conference of 1933, which tried to stabilize international currencies, Roosevelt surprisingly announced the United States intention to stay off

Axis Takeovers in Europe, 1936-1939

the gold standard. The British were outraged at his economic nationalism. Meanwhile, in the Senate, Gerald P. Nye, a Republican from North Dakota, opened an investigation in 1934 which eventually charged international bankers and weapons manufacturers with manipulating American entrance into World War I in order to increase profits. He never substantiated his charges, but for three years the headlines fanned the flames of isolationism.

Although Roosevelt believed that the United States had important international commitments, he was limited by isolationists in Congress. Between 1935 and 1937, Congress passed three separate neutrality laws that clamped an embargo on arms sales to belligerents, forbade American ships to enter war zones and prohibited them from being armed, barred Americans from traveling on belligerent ships, and restricted trade with belligerents on nonembargoed exports to a "cash and carry" basis. In October 1937 President Roosevelt delivered a speech in Chicago in which he referred to the need to "quarantine the aggressors," but he retreated into silence as soon as it became clear that the public did not support vigorous action.

Adolf Hitler took advantage of Europe's and America's indecisiveness. On August 24, 1939, Germany and the Soviet Union signed the Nazi-Comintern Pact, a nonaggression treaty. His eastern flank protected, Hitler invaded Poland on September 1, 1939. Two days later, France and Great Britain honored their treaty obligations to defend Poland and declared war on Germany. World War II had formally begun.

Poland was no match for Germany. Though its people fought bravely, Poland fell in a few weeks, and then the land fighting in Europe stopped for several months. The Sitzkrieg (Phony War or Bore War) ended in April 1940, when German tanks swept through Denmark and Norway. Hitler's next victim was the Netherlands, which fell in five days.

Most observers expected Germany to stop there, for the next target was France, with an army of three million men poised behind the Maginot Line, a military engineering feat of miles of concrete underground installations. Undeterred, Germany attacked France in May.

Hitler's armies devastated Poland with their tremendous force and firepower. Here soldiers drive through a town battered by repeated bombings.

Hitler outflanked the supposedly invincible Maginot Line by slicing his tank divisions through the Ardennes forest. France surrendered in June, and only a heroic boatlift at Dunkirk saved 300,000 British and French troops from being captured. Pro-German elements organized a new government, Vichy France, but Charles de Gaulle fled to London, declared himself the leader of Free France, and established a government in exile.

England then braced itself for invasion. To soften them up, Hitler ordered his Luftwaffe (air force) to bomb Britain mercilessly. Throughout the fall of 1940, CBS's Edward R. Murrow, speaking from the rooftops of London, kept Americans glued to their radios with stirring reports of the dog fights. British fighter pilots ultimately won the Battle of Britain, establishing control of the air space over the British Isles. As 1940 ended, Great Britain, though knocked to its knees and badly bloodied, had survived. Americans watched the bloodshed with the gravest concern. During the first year of the war bookstores sold out their entire stock of Rand McNally's European maps as people tried to keep abreast of the German Blitzkrieg (lightening war).

President Roosevelt responded to the war by proclaiming neutrality. Unlike Wilson, however, he said nothing about being "neutral in thought as well as in action." Roosevelt felt a German victory would threaten America's future security, and when France fell, he resolved to save England at all costs—including war.

Isolationism and the Election of 1940

Soon after the German invasion of Poland in 1939, Roosevelt pushed a fourth Neutrality Act through Congress. It modified the 1937 law by permitting belligerents to purchase war materials if they paid cash and carried the goods away in their own ships, a pro-British stipulation since England controlled the Atlantic. Using private companies as go-betweens and acting on his own authority, Roosevelt then rushed thousands of planes and guns to Britain. In September 1940 he persuaded Congress to pass the first peacetime draft in American history and signed an executive agreement with Great Britain transferring fifty destroyers in exchange for ninety-nine year leases on eight British bases in the Western Hemisphere. Most Americans supported the destroyers-for-bases deal. When the first ships slipped out of Boston harbor, motorists on the Charleston Bridge blew their horns, while pedestrians along the shore cheered.

Isolationists opposed the tilt toward Britain. Strongest in the Midwest, they represented the entire spectrum of political thought, including Republicans such as Senators Arthur Vandenberg of Michigan and Robert Taft of Ohio; Democrats such as Joseph Kennedy, ambassador to Great Britain, and Progressives such as Wisconsin's Senator Robert La Follette. They offered several antiwar arguments—some compelling, others specious. Betraying a deep strain of anti-Semitism, aviator Charles Lindbergh, accused Jews of trying to push the United States into war with Germany. Vandenberg warned against the growth of executive power, anticipating later concerns about the "imperial presidency." Their most powerful argument was that Europe's war did not threaten "fortress America." German planes and tanks could never attack the United States. While most isolationists despised the Nazis, they insisted that America should sit this war out because its security was not endangered.

World War II was a major issue in the election of 1940. After easily being renominated, Roosevelt dumped Vice-President John Garner, who had opposed a third term for the president. As his new running mate, Roosevelt picked Secretary of Agriculture Henry A. Wallace. The Republicans passed over their front runners (isolationists all) to nominate a dark horse candidate, Wendell L. Willkie of Indiana. Head of a large public utilities holding company, Willkie was a liberal Republican who had been a Democrat most of his life.

The election was one of the dirtiest in American history. Willkie faced such a barrage of missiles when he spoke in the big Democratic cities that the *New York Times* issued daily reports of the objects thrown and the hits registered. (The projectiles ranged from rotten eggs to a five-pound steel wastebasket that split open the head of a teenage girl.) When cries of state socialism failed to stir the public, Willkie said that Roosevelt would plunge the nation into war if reelected. Roosevelt assured American parents on the eve of the election: "I have said this before, but I shall say it again and again: Your boys are not going to be sent into any foreign wars."

It was the closest presidential election since 1916. Roosevelt defeated Willkie 27 million votes to 22 million votes, and 449 electoral votes to 82. Democrats gained seven votes in the House, but Republicans picked up five in the Senate. As New York City Mayor Fiorello La Guardia put it, Americans preferred "Roosevelt with his known faults to Willkie with his unknown virtues."

After the election, Churchill informed Roosevelt that England could no longer buy war supplies. Consequently, the president replaced "cash and carry" with "lend-lease." In a press conference, he said lend-lease was like offering a garden hose to a neighbor whose house was on fire, arguing that after the fire had been extinguished, the neighbor would return the hose. Isolationists saw things differently. "Lending war equipment is a good deal like lending chewing gum," said Senator Taft of Ohio. "You don't want it back."

Roosevelt submitted the lend-lease bill to Congress in January 1941, setting off months of debate. The nastiest comment came from Senator Burton Wheeler, who called lend-lease a "Triple A foreign policy that would plow under every fourth American boy." Americans argued about lend-lease in barber shops, board meetings, and grocery stores across the country. Early in March, Congress passed the bill and Roosevelt signed it on March 11, 1941. With "this legislation," he declared, "our country has determined to do its full part in creating an adequate arsenal of democracy."

To cement the Anglo-American bond, Roosevelt met with Churchill in August 1941 on board the U.S.S. *Augusta* off the coast of Newfoundland. The agreement they reached, known as the Atlantic Charter, pledged a mutual effort on behalf of democracy, freedom of the seas, arms reductions, and a just peace. The United States and Great Britain were now virtually allies.

If supporting the British seemed necessary, however, many Americans balked at helping the Russians. After Hitler's June 1941 invasion of the Soviet Union, Russia became an ally, prompting Roosevelt to extend lend-lease to them. Soviet critics were outraged, but Churchill supported the decision wholeheartedly, declaring, "If Hitler invaded Hell, I would make at least a favorable reference to the Devil in the House of Commons." In November 1941, the United States allocated one billion dollars in lend-lease to the Soviets. By 1945 America's al-

Kneeling in prayer near the Capitol in Washington, D.C., members of the "Mother's Crusade" against the lend-lease bill plead for Congress not to pass the measure.

lies had received $50 billion, four times the amount loaned to the allies in World War I.

In April 1941 the United States went beyond financial assistance by constructing bases in Greenland. During the summer American destroyers began escorting convoys as far as Iceland; and to protect convoys the rest of the way, the American navy tracked German submarines and signaled their locations to British destroyers. In September a German submarine attacked the *Greer*, an American destroyer which had been tracking it. Roosevelt told the public the *Greer* had been on an innocent mail run to Ireland. He then ordered the navy to "shoot on sight" any German ships in the waters surrounding Ireland. Roosevelt stopped short, however, of asking Congress for a formal declaration of war.

Pearl Harbor

Thanks to the public's preoccupation with Europe, Roosevelt had a relatively free hand in the Far East. Here the problem centered on Japan's determination to build the Greater East Asia Co-Prosperity Sphere, a Japanese empire including large parts of China, Southeast Asia, and the western Pacific. Japan wanted to expand, but that goal clashed with the two main pillars of America's Far Eastern policy: preservation of the "Open Door" for trade, and the protection of China's territorial integrity.

After Japan invaded China in 1937, relations deteriorated rapidly. The United States did little more than ask Japan to withdraw, but Tokyo refused, insisting that the United States stop all aid to Chiang Kai-shek, the leader of the Chinese government. In July 1939 Secretary of State Cordell Hull, aware that American exports were fueling the Japanese war machine, threatened to impose economic sanctions. Roosevelt rejected an embargo on all war materials out of fear that Japan would attack the Dutch East Indies to secure the oil it needed. His fears were not misplaced. Germany's defeat of France in 1940 gave Japan an unprecedented opportunity. In September 1940 the pro-German Vichy government of France "invited" Japan to occupy northern Indochina, an obvious step toward the Dutch East Indies. Roose-

velt was convinced Japan wanted to bring all of Asia under its control, threatening America's quest for free markets. Late in September he placed an embargo on scrap iron and steel, hoping that economic sanctions would strengthen moderates in Japan who wished to avoid conflict with the United States.

Instead, radical militants in Japan seized power. Japan then promptly negotiated the Tripartite Pact with Germany and Italy, becoming one of the Axis Powers. To protect its northern flank, Japan signed a five-year nonaggression pact in April 1941 with Stalin. Following these diplomatic maneuvers, Japan occupied bases in southern Indochina. Roosevelt saw the noose tightening around the Dutch East Indies, the Philippines, and British Malaya, and in July 1941 he retaliated by freezing Japanese assets in the United States and by cutting off steel, oil, and aviation fuel exports to Japan.

Roosevelt's economic sanctions hurt Japan. Striving to secure the materials its military needed, Japan negotiated with the United States throughout 1941. The United States insisted that Japan immediately withdraw from Indochina and China, a move which would have all but ruined Japan's dream of the economic and strategic security of the Greater East Asia Co-Prosperity Sphere. The Japanese offered some minor concessions. They promised not to attack further to the south, not to attack the Soviet Union in the north, and not to declare war against the United States if Germany and America went to war. But they also insisted that the United States abandon Chiang Kai-shek. Roosevelt refused. In October 1941 the Japanese government fell and General Hideki Tojo, the leader of the militants, seized power. War was imminent.

In November 1941 Tokyo offered to compromise on several points if Washington would soften its demands. Secretary of State Cordell Hull refused. Having already decided on war if the United States rejected its terms, Tokyo gave the final approval on December 1 for an air strike on Pearl Harbor. Months earlier American cryptographers had broken the Japanese diplomatic code, though not the military code. In December the volume of diplomatic cables increased, raising American suspicions, and on

In a little more than an hour, the surprise attack at Pearl Harbor had killed more than twenty-four hundred American sailors and sunk eight battleships, including the USS *Arizona* pictured here.

December 6 they intercepted a hostile sounding message from Tokyo to the Japanese ambassador in the United States.

Most military experts expected the Japanese to strike the British and Dutch West Indies. They were wrong. At 8:00 A.M. on Sunday morning, December 7, 1941, Japanese planes hit Pearl Harbor, executing the most daring surprise attack in military history. In less than two hours the base was reduced to flames, two battleships were sunk and six others heavily battered, the remainder of the fleet was damaged or destroyed, and more than 2400 Americans were dead. Japanese losses, in contrast, were minimal.

It was a costly victory. Japan's hopes of destroying American aircraft carriers were foiled when routine maneuvers took the flattops out to sea before the attack. More important, the attack united the American public as nothing else could have. Opposition to Roosevelt simply evaporated. Speaking for his fellow isolationists, Senator Wheeler shouted: "The only thing to do now is to lick the hell out of them." On December 8 Congress declared war on Japan with but one dissenting vote. Germany declared war on the United States on December 11.

AMERICA AT WAR

Practically everyone agreed on what had to be done: stimulate the economy, raise an army, and win the war. Yet the complexity of the economic problems were mind-boggling. New plants had to be built and existing ones expanded; raw materials had to be procured and distributed where they were needed; labor had to be kept on the job; production had to be raised; and all of this had to be done without inflation.

Economic Mobilization

President Roosevelt made the switch from reformer to war leader with ease, telling reporters that "Dr. New Deal" had to be replaced by "Dr. Win-the-War." Like President Wilson before him, Roosevelt hoped to accomplish the job with a minimum of government controls. He, too, would fail. World War II created a huge, and for the most part permanent, federal bureaucracy.

In January 1942 Roosevelt created the War Production Board (WPB) to "exercise general responsibility" over the economy. To lead the agency, he selected Donald Nelson, the highly respected head of Sears, Roebuck and Company. Roosevelt refused, however, to make Nelson the "czar" of American industry, reserving that power for himself. Leading industrialists responded coolly to the call for economic conversion. Profits were already booming because of the war in Europe, and they did not wish to jeopardize their position in the domestic market by converting their factories to military production. Others worried about getting stuck with inflated capacity after the war ended. As one business executive cautioned, "Guns are not windshield wipers."

The automotive industry was the test case for conversion, for Detroit's assemly lines were needed for tanks and planes. Detroit also consumed eighty percent of the nation's rubber, eighteen percent of its steel, and fourteen percent of its copper. When Roosevelt issued a call for 50,000 airplanes a year, however, Detroit first ran for cover. Automotive sales had shot up by forty percent in 1941, and industry executives were not eager to risk their profits. To gain their support, Washington offered even greater profits. The military suspended competitive bidding, used cost-plus contracts, guaranteed low-cost loans for retooling, and paid huge subsidies for plant construction and equipment. Detroit made the switch. Aircraft production leaped from 6000 planes in 1940 to 47,000 in 1942; by 1943 it had jumped to 86,000; and by the end of the war it exceeded 100,000, more than doubling Roosevelt's goal. Secretary of War Henry Stimson defended Detroit's huge

Tanks roll on the assembly line at the Chrysler-operated tank arsenal near Detroit.

defense profits, explaining that "in a capitalist country, you have to let business make money out of the process or business won't work."

Consumer industries profited as well. Robert W. Woodruff of Coca-Cola made the five cent drink the most widely distributed consumer product in the world. He convinced the army that soldiers needed Coke to refresh their fighting spirit. Backed by government subsidies, the company built an international network of plants, and then purchased them at a fraction of their cost after the war, ensuring its postwar supremacy in the soft drink industry.

Most military contracts went to big business because large-scale production simplified buying. At Roosevelt's insistence the Justice Department stopped prosecuting antitrust violators shortly after Pearl Harbor, despite clear evidence that international cartels—especially those involved in the development of synthetic rubber—had impeded the war effort. Not until 1944 did Roosevelt permit the Justice Department to resume antitrust prosecutions, and his reason for doing so was not to protect small businessmen or consumers, but to block business arrangements that might endanger national defense in the future.

Government policies accelerated business consolidations. Overall, industrial profits doubled, but small industries shared little in the gains. In 1940 the top 100 companies had produced thirty percent of America's industrial output; by 1943, they produced seventy percent and the other 175,000 companies the rest. Congressional hearings, chaired by Senator Harry S Truman from Missouri, disclosed that the conglomerates were squeezing out small businesses. Congress tried to help small businesses by establishing the Smaller War Plants Corporation in 1943, but these industries simply lacked the capital to convert to war production and the political connections to borrow enough money to retool.

Government financed research became a new industry. When the war began, Germany enjoyed scientific and technological superiority, especially in tanks and artillery. To counter their advantage, Roosevelt created the Office of Scientific Research and Development (OSRD) in June 1942. Its most ambitious project was the development to the atomic bomb. Alerted by Albert Einstein of the need to beat the Germans, Roosevelt put over $2 billion and 500,000 workers into the Manhattan Project, the atomic bomb's code name.

Federal funds also supported the development of radar, flame throwers, antiaircraft artillery, rockets, and penicillin. New blood plasma techniques permitted 13 million pints of blood to be collected. Moreover, antimalarial drugs and insecticides, including DDT, dramatically reduced the incidence of mosquito-carried diseases among troops in the Mediterranean and Pacific. As a result, the death rate of wounded soldiers who reached medical installations was half that of World War I. Even more amazing, the noncombat-related death rate among troops was virtually the same as the domestic death rate.

American agriculture performed equally impressively. To encourage production, Roosevelt allowed farmers to make large profits by setting crop prices at 110 percent of parity, defined as the ratio between agricultural prices and manufactured goods prices during the agricultural boom years of 1910 to 1914. Good weather, mechanization, and a dramatic increase in the use of fertilizers did the rest. Cash income for farmers jumped from $2.3 billion in 1940 to $9.5 billion in 1945. Most profits went to large-scale operators with the capital to buy expensive machinery and fertilizers. Many small farmers, saddled with huge debts from the depression, left their farms for jobs in defense plants or the armed services. Altogether, over 5 million farm residents (seventeen percent of the total) left rural areas during the war.

Overall, the war brought unprecedented prosperity. Per capita income rose from $373 in 1940 to $1074 in 1945, and total personal income went from $81 billion to $182 billion during the same years. American workers never had it so good. The total income of families increased even more dramatically when large numbers of women joined the workforce, creating millions of double-income families.

In fact, the war brought Americans more money than they could spend. The production of consumer goods could not keep pace with the new buying power. During 1942 the difference between disposable income and available goods approached $17 billion. There were shortages of everything—hair curlers, toasters, dishes, diapers, and spoons. As early as 1943 many manufacturers were reduced to accepting postwar orders. General Electric's ad the month of the Normandy invasion announced, "Now we'll be glad to put your name down for earliest available data on postwar air conditioning and refrigeration equipment."

Steeped in the values of a consumer society, Americans emerged from the Depression with a backlog of desires only to face empty shelves. Most people accepted the deprivations stoically, but others hoarded what they could— shoes, canned goods, used tires, and other scarce products. If stores did not have what they wanted, some customers simply grabbed anything. On December 7, 1944, the third anniversary of Pearl Harbor, Macy's set a new sales record when many of its stores sold down to the bare shelves.

Controlling Inflation

The shortages led to inflation. Prices rose eighteen percent between 1941 and the end of 1942, with an increase of eleven percent in food prices alone in 1942. Fearful that inflation would destroy the economy, Congress created the Office of Price Administration (OPA) in January 1942, to control prices. The OPA quickly defined the ceiling for individual merchants as the highest price they had charged for a particular item in March 1942.

Since the success of price controls depended on the rationing of scarce goods, the OPA also introduced ten major rationing programs in 1942. For staple products in short supply, the OPA issued ration cards and coupons to more than 120 million people. To get sugar, meat, butter, bacon, cheese, alcohol, canned goods, and shoes, shoppers had to hand coupons to retailers, who found the whole system hopelessly cumbersome. Gasoline, too, was rationed; drivers without special credentials were allotted only three gallons a week. For a society intoxicated with the automobile—weekend rides and cruising Main Street—three gallons was a hardship. Relying on voluntarism and patriotism, the OPA also extolled the virtues of self-sacrifice, telling people to "Use it up, wear it out, make it do, or do without." There was often a good bit of Yankee ingenuity to the rationing. When the OPA announced that the cloth for women's bathing suits had to be cut by ten percent, manufacturers responded with the two-piece bathing suit. A bare midriff had suddenly become patriotic.

Rationing was only one of the anti-inflation programs. Washington also tried to reduce demand by reducing purchasing power. War bond sales were targeted at working-class families. Secretary of the Treasury Henry Morgenthau rejected a poster that showed a woman in a mink coat buying war bonds. He told the artist to draw a woman in overalls. The campaign was successful. In addition to helping finance the war, war bonds by 1944 absorbed more than seven percent of the real personal income of Americans.

Tax reform also limited inflation. Fewer than four million Americans had filed tax re-

At a consumer conservation booth in West Dundee Township, Illinois, women are given "food for thought" in an attempt to help the war effort.

turns in 1939, and most blue-collar workers that year had paid no income taxes at all. To cool off consumer purchasing power, Congress passed the Revenue Act of 1942, which raised corporate taxes, increased the excess profits tax from sixty to ninety percent, and levied a flat five percent withholding tax on anyone who earned more than $642 a year. By mid-1943 most American workers had taxes deducted weekly from wages, and the number of tax returns at the end of the year leaped to 30 million. The federal government reduced the public's buying power, forced citizens to pay more than forty percent of the war's total cost as the war progressed, and laid the foundation for the modern tax structure.

The administration also resorted to wage controls. The War Labor Board (WLB), established in 1942, had the power to set wages, hours, and working conditions, but it had to work on a case-by-case basis and was quickly swamped by wage disputes. A test case was needed to establish national guidelines, and steel workers offered such a case. In the summer of 1942, workers in several steel mills demanded a dollar-a-day raise. In response, the

WLB adopted what came to be called the "Little Steel" formula. Using January 1, 1941, as the starting point, it permitted a fifteen percent hike in wages to compensate for the cost of living increases to May 1942, but prohibited additional pay increases for the duration of the war. This meant that the steel workers received only a five and one-half percent raise (about 44 cents a day) because they had already secured additional increases earlier in the year. The Little Steel formula was not inflationary because workers in other industries had already secured the maximum increase.

In practice, however, the Little Steel formula did not freeze wages. It applied only to hourly wages, not weekly totals. Thus, while wage rates increased a modest twenty-four percent during the war, the weekly paychecks of workers, thanks to overtime, rose seventy percent.

Price controls were the final weapon against inflation, but they were not used until labor demanded government action. In October 1942 Roosevelt appointed James F. Byrnes, his chief utility advisor, head of the Office of Economic Stabilization, later renamed the Office of War Mobilization. Byrnes instituted broad price freezes in the spring, and by the summer prices had stopped climbing. To placate consumers still further, Byrnes rolled back prices ten percent on selected agricultural products, including meat and butter.

These programs brought inflation under control. After 1942 the annual inflation rate was only one and one-half percent. Still the administration's methods pleased no one. Everyone groused about taxes; manufacturers and farmers resented price controls, which they saw as an attack on their profits; and labor bitterly decried wage freezes, which they regarded as an attack on their incomes.

World War II was a boon to workers. It created 17 million new jobs at the exact moment when 15 million men and women entered the armed services. Unemployment virtually disappeared. In 1939 over 8 million people (seventeen percent of the workforce) were out of work, but between 1939 and 1941 most traditional breadwinners got their jobs back. After Pearl Harbor, labor was at an absolute premium, drawing into the workforce previously unemployed and underemployed groups such as women, teenagers, blacks, the elderly, and the handicapped.

The war also gave labor unions a boost. Under the benevolent hand of government protection, unions rebounded from their sharp decline of the 1920s and 1930s. Union membership jumped from 10.5 million to 14.75 million during the war. The WLB enforced "maintenance of membership" agreements in all shops with defense contracts. Newly hired workers were given fifteen days to resign from the union. If they did not, the company had to collect their union dues. This represented a compromise between management's insistence upon an open shop (workers could join or drop the union at will) and labor's demand for a closed shop (all employees had to belong to the union).

Still, labor unrest rose throughout the war. After Pearl Harbor union officials pledged not to strike for the duration, but inflation and wage restrictions soon eroded their good will. Work stoppages rose from 2960 in 1942 to 4956 in 1944, though most were brief and did not harm the war effort. In 1943, however, coal miners went on strike and railroad workers threatened to follow. According to John L. Lewis, the fiery president of the United Mine Workers, the reason for the strike was simple: the average mine worker earned only $1700 in 1942 (well below the national average) and deserved a raise.

Lewis won a hefty pay increase for his men. By 1944 their wages averaged $2535 a year, the first time in history coal miners earned more than most manufacturing workers. The victory, however, weakened public support for labor. Most Americans condemned strikes as unpatriotic, and Roosevelt considered drafting or jailing the strikers. Lewis had supported Wendell Willkie in 1940, so there was no love lost between the president and the union leader. Privately, Roosevelt offered to resign as president if Lewis promised to commit suicide, but publicly Roosevelt was a model of restraint with labor leaders. After all, labor was a vital element of his political coalition.

Congress was far less sympathetic. Over Roosevelt's veto, it passed the Smith-Connally

Act, which banned strikes in war industries, authorized the president to seize plants useful to the war effort, and limited political activity by unions. "In doing so," declared *Time* magazine, "it dealt Franklin Roosevelt the most stinging rebuke of his entire career, his worst domestic defeat of World War II." The Smith-Connally Act proved unworkable. It rested on the mistaken belief that strikes were caused by a handful of unruly labor barons, when in reality they resulted from the pressure of rank-and-file workers.

The Smith-Connally Act reflected a conservative turn, both in Congress and in the country at large. Democratic voters failed to turn out in large numbers in the congressional elections of 1942, as full employment seemed to take the steam out of blue-collar voting. In addition, soldiers away from home were not permitted to vote. Though the Democrats continued to maintain a thin majority throughout the war, a coalition of Republicans and conservative Democrats after 1942 could defeat any measure. Secretary of the Treasury Morgenthau did not exaggerate when he complained: "I can get all my New Dealers in the bathtub now."

Beginning in 1943 Roosevelt's opponents led a successful attack against the New Deal, refusing to fund the Civilian Conservation Corps, the Works Progress Administration, the National Youth Administration, and the National Resources and Planning Board. Conservatives argued that these agencies had dangerously expanded federal power and were no longer needed. With reform in retreat, the Republicans were optimistic about the election of 1944. On the first ballot at their convention, they chose Thomas E. Dewey, the dapper young governor of New York. (Harold Ickes quipped that forty-two-year-old Dewey had thrown his diaper into the ring.) Dewey accepted the New Deal as part of American life, but argued against expanding it. Like Roosevelt, he supported an international organization after the war, but remained hazy on specifics. In fact, Dewey supported all of Roosevelt's foreign policy initiatives.

Despite his declining health, Roosevelt easily won renomination for a fourth term. In March 1944 doctors discovered that he was suffering from high blood pressure, creating a special concern about his choice of a running mate. He dumped Vice-President Henry Wallace, the ardent internationalist whom critics had denounced for advocating "the Century of the Common Man" after the war. In his place, Roosevelt selected Harry S Truman, a little known senator from Missouri who had chaired the Senate hearings on wartime industrial profits.

The campaign revitalized Roosevelt. After delivering a flurry of vague speeches about ending poverty at home, he unveiled plans for a "GI Bill of Rights" promising liberal unemployment benefits, educational support, medical care, and housing loans for veterans. Congress approved it overwhelmingly in 1944. Republicans rallied their forces to defeat a federal voting bill that allowed soldiers to cast absentee ballots. A Bill Mauldin cartoon aptly captured the disappointment of GIs, as Willie consoled his buddy by saying, "That's okay, Joe, at least we can take bets."

The smart money was on FDR. Roosevelt easily won reelection. Unwilling to switch leaders while at war, the public stuck with Roosevelt to see the crisis through. The president received 25,611,936 votes to Dewey's 22,013,372, and he won in the Electoral College by 432 to 99.

Molding Public Opinion

Roosevelt was determined to avoid the mistakes of World War II. He did not want propaganda to fuel hate and arouse false hopes. Shortly before Pearl Harbor, Roosevelt established the Office of Facts and Figures under Archibald MacLeish, the Librarian of Congress. A gentle poet, MacLeish became ensnared in bureaucratic struggles with government agencies, the armed services, and the Office of Strategic Services for control of war policy. By 1944 the government had all but abandoned its efforts to shape public opinion about the war.

Private enterprise filled the void. Movies, comic strips, newspapers, books, and advertisements reduced the war to a struggle between good and evil—Americans versus the Japanese and the Germans. The Japanese bore the brunt of the propaganda, especially during the first two years of fighting. Caricatured with thick glasses and huge buck teeth, public portraits of the Japanese grew more ugly and vicious. Deeply engrained racism fed the stereotypes, reviving old fears of the "yellow peril."

Attitudes toward the Germans were more complex. Without racism to heighten the passions, blame fell upon Adolf Hitler. Americans were slow to believe charges of Nazi atrocities, but the disbelief gradually faded before eye witness reports from GIs and news correspondents at the front. American views shifted accordingly. Gradually, they came to blame not just the Nazis, but all Germans for the war.

Movies were the most important instrument of propaganda, but Hollywood made little effort to confront the war's complexities. Instead, the industry churned out a series of simple morality plays. War films showed exhausted, shell-shocked troops who battled the enemy to the end. Films like *Back to Bataan, Thirty Seconds Over Tokyo,* and *Guadalcanal Diary* showed a few Americans outfighting the hordes of Japanese. Hollywood also produced sympathetic portraits of America's allies, including the sentimental *Mrs. Miniver,* which portrayed the British as kind and determined, and won seven Academy Awards in 1942. Hollywood produced 982 movies during the war, enough for three new movies each week at the neighborhood theater.

Popular culture both fed and reflected the desire to win the war and get the boys back. Soldiers abroad knew only that they wanted to return to Mom, and, as one GI told cartoonist Bill Mauldin, to a "piece of blueberry pie." Mauldin's characters Willie and Joe fought because they had to—not to build a new world but to return to the goodness of America—baths, steaks, and their wives.

SOCIAL CHANGE DURING THE WAR

World War II brought about important changes in American life—some subtle, others profound. Above all it set people in motion, pulling them off their farms, out of small towns, and packing them into large urban areas. Urbanization had virtually stopped during the Depres-

"Joe, yestiddy ya saved my life an' I swore I'd pay ya back. Here's my last pair of dry socks."

Bill Mauldin's cartoon characters, Willie and Joe, were popular not only at home, but also among soldiers abroad.

sion, but the war saw the number of Americans who lived in cities leap from forty-six to fifty-three percent.

War industries sparked the urban growth. Detroit's population, for example, exploded as the automotive industry switched to war vehicles. Washington, D.C., became another boom town, as tens of thousands of new workers staffed the swelling ranks of the bureaucracy. The most dramatic growth occurred in California. Of the 15 million civilians who moved across state lines during the war, over 2 million went to California to work in defense industries.

Women

Women were especially affected by the war. The most visible change was the sudden appearance of large numbers of women in uniform. The military organized them into auxiliary units with special uniforms, their own officers, and, amazingly, equal pay. By 1945 over 140,000 had joined the Women's Army Corps (WACs); 60,000 the Army Nurses Corps; 100,000 the navy (WAVEs); 14,000 the Navy Nurses Corps; 23,000 the marines; and 13,000 the Coast Guard. Most either filled traditional women's roles, such as nursing, or replaced men in noncombat situations.

Women also substituted for men on the home front. During the war 6.3 million women entered the labor force, and for the first time in history married working women outnumbered single working women. While these figures were dramatic, the fact remains that women working outside the home still constituted a minority of married women. Though women comprised thirty-seven percent of the civilian workforce in 1945, only twenty-two and one-half percent of married women worked outside the home. Still, the war challenged the public's image of proper female behavior, as "Rosie the Riveter" became the popular symbol of women who abandoned traditional jobs as domestic servants and store clerks to work in construction and heavy industry.

Most observers expected women to retreat to the kitchen when the men returned home. Yet a Women's Bureau survey in 1943 showed that seventy percent of working women hoped to keep their jobs after the war. Many women liked the economic freedom that came with wages (sales of women's clothing doubled during the war), while others insisted that they had to work to improve their family's standard of living, anticipating arguments for the two-income family after the war.

Women had to pay a high price for their economic independence. Outside employment did not free them from domestic duties. The same women who put in full days in offices and factories went home to cook, clean, shop, and take care of the children. They had not one job, but two, and the only way they could fill both was to become "superwomen" who sacrificed recreation and sleep.

Even a "superwoman" could not occupy two places at once, which raised the question that haunted many Americans, "Who's minding the children?" A few industries, such as Kaiser Steel, offered day-care facilities, but most

During the war, a growing number of women not only joined the armed services, but also helped out in the labor force at home by filling jobs normally held by men.

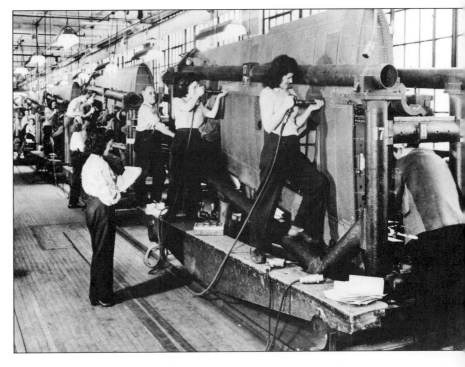

women made their own arrangements. Whether relatives or babysitters filled the void, child-care problems often arose, with a corresponding rise in the incidence of "latchkey" children.

Social critics had a field day with women. Social workers blamed working mothers for the rise in juvenile delinquency during the war. Every week brought new complaints about lack of modesty, self-indulgence, drinking, dress standards, and sexual promiscuity—and just as many spirited defenses praising women on all scores. A woman could flip through practically any magazine and find herself lauded, criticized, and analyzed. "Choose any set of criteria you like," wrote the famous anthropologist Margaret Mead in 1946, "and the answer is the same: women and men are confused, uncertain and discontented with the present definition of women's place in America." Still, most women elected to stick with the familiar. A 1943 poll revealed that seventy-three percent of young women planned to become housewives and mothers, eighteen percent hoped to combine family and career, and only nine percent intended to pursue careers as singles.

Marriage and birth rates reflected the preference for traditional roles. From 1941 to 1945, the marriage rate oscillated between 93 and 105 marriages per 1000 women between the ages of seventeen and twenty-nine, well above the 89.1 for those women during the "normal" years of 1925 to 1929. The birth rate increased, too, rebounding sharply from the all-time low of 18 to 19 per thousand people during the depression. In 1943 it jumped to 22.7, and by 1946 it reached 25, where it remained with modest fluctuations for the rest of the decade. Overall, the "baby boom" did not signal a return to large families; rather, it showed that women were marrying at younger ages and starting their families earlier in life.

Hasty marriages between young partners often proved brittle. Wartime separations forced newlyweds to develop new roles and become self-reliant, and many couples later found it difficult to reestablish their relationship. Rather than remain in unhappy marriages, they often opted for divorce. In 1946 the American courts granted a record 600,000 divorces. By 1950 the divorce rate stood at one-quarter of the marriages, well above the prewar levels.

Americans had not turned sour on marriage. The divorce rate had been climbing steadily (except during the depression when many people could not afford to get married or divorced) since 1900. Furthermore, most Americans who divorced during the 1940s promptly remarried. They had rejected their mates, not marriage.

Minorities

World War II also accelerated long-developing social changes for blacks. Blacks moved to cities and went to work in factories. Indeed, more than one million blacks migrated to the North during the war (twice the number who did so in World War I), and more than two million found work in defense industries. Yet blacks continued to be the last hired and the first fired, and other forms of discrimination remained blatant, especially in housing and employment.

Black leaders vigorously fought discrimination. Months before America entered the war, they pressed Washington to abolish discrimination in defense industries. In the spring of 1941, A. Philip Randolph, president of the Brotherhood of Sleeping Car Porters, called for 150,000 blacks to march on Washington. Embarrassed and concerned, Roosevelt issued an executive order prohibiting discrimination in defense industries and creating the Fair Employment Practices Commission (FEPC). But the FEPC's small staff lacked the power and resources to back up its decisions. During the war most complaints were not even processed, and contractors ignored thirty-five of the forty-five compliance orders issued by the FEPC.

Blacks fared no better in the public sector. Most blacks in the federal bureaucracy worked as janitors, and the armed services treated blacks as second-class citizens. The marines excluded blacks; tried to use them as servants; and the army created separate black regiments commanded by white officers. The Red Cross even segregated blood plasma.

Not surprisingly, racial tensions deepened during the war. Black GIs increased from 100,000 in 1941 to 700,000 in 1944. Many joined the armed services hoping to find social mobility. Instead, they found segregation and discrimination. They resented white officials who denounced Nazi racism but remained silent about discrimination against blacks. Northern blacks stationed in the South found race relations shocking. Charleston's buses carried these signs: "Avoid Friction. Be Patriotic. White passengers will be seated from front to rear, colored passengers from rear to front."

Conditions in the civilian sector were equally tense. As urban areas swelled with defense workers, housing and transportation shortages created hot spots of racial hatred. In 1943 a riot broke out in Detroit in a federally sponsored housing project. Polish-Americans wanted blacks barred from the new apartments, named, ironically, in honor of the black abolitionist and poet Sojourner Truth. White soldiers from a nearby base joined the fighting, and other federal troops had to be brought in to dispel the mobs. The violence left thirty-five blacks and nine whites dead.

Similar conflicts erupted across the nation, exposing in each instance a basic contradiction: white Americans espoused equality but practiced discrimination. One black told Swedish social scientist Gunnar Myrdal, "just carve on my tombstone, here lies a black man killed fighting a yellow man for the protection of a white man." A 1942 survey of America's blacks showed that many sympathized with the Japanese struggle to expel white colonialists from the Far East. Significantly, the same survey showed that a majority of white industrialists in the South preferred a Germany victory to racial equality for blacks.

The rising social tensions prompted many blacks to join civil rights organizations. The National Association for the Advancement of Colored People (NAACP) intensified its legal campaign against discrimination, and its membership grew from 50,000 to 500,000 as large numbers of blacks and middle-class whites demanded equality for blacks.

Some blacks, however, accused the NAACP of being too slow and conciliatory. The Congress of Racial Equality (CORE), organized in 1942, used sit-ins instead of legal action. These tactics had some success in the North, but the South's response was brutal. In Tennessee, for example, Bayard Rustin, who later became a prominent civil rights leader in the 1950s, was savagely beaten for refusing to move to the back of the bus. Although their short-term gains were modest, blacks forged a new set of demands and tactics that helped shape the civil rights movement after the war.

Federal officials did little to advance civil rights. Personally, Roosevelt was sympathetic to blacks, but he feared losing the support of the Solid South if he moved too rapidly on the race issue. Thus, while he admitted black leaders to the White House to hear their grievances, all they left with were promises. Eleanor Roosevelt remained the conscience of the administration, expressing openly her sympathy for civil rights, but the president was not willing to take the political risks needed to end discrimination and promote racial equality.

World War II affected Mexican-Americans no less than blacks. Almost 400,000 Mexican-Americans served in the armed forces. As soldiers, they expanded their contacts with Anglo society, visiting new parts of the country and meeting for the first time large groups of people who held fewer prejudices against them. For others, jobs in industry provided an escape hatch from the desperate poverty of migratory farm labor. In New Mexico, for example, about one-fifth of the rural Mexican-American population left for war-related jobs.

The need for farm workers grew dramatically after Pearl Harbor. To meet that demand, the United States established the *bracero* (work hands) program in 1942, and by 1945 several hundred thousand Mexican workers had immigrated to the Southwest. Commercial farmers welcomed them, but the labor unions resented them. That resentment generated animosity and discrimination for Mexicans and Mexican-Americans alike.

In Los Angeles, the tensions between Anglos and Mexicans erupted in violence. Mexican youth gangs took to wearing flamboyant "zoot suits," tattooing their left hands, and celebrating their ethnicity. In June 1943 hundreds of Anglo sailors on liberty from the harbors at San Pedro and Long Beach went downtown on liberty in Los Angeles. They resented what they considered the arrogance of the "zooters," and riots broke out for several nights. Police ignored the Anglo attackers and the local press treated the incident as if Mexican-American gangs had precipitated it. The riots continued for several days until military police ordered the sailors back to their ships.

Despite the violence and discrimination, the poor of all races benefited from World War II. Thanks to full employment and progressive taxation, income was redistributed in favor of those on the bottom. The top five percent's share of disposable income actually fell from twenty-three percent in 1939 to seventeen percent in 1945. Before the war there had been twelve families with an income under $2000 for every family with an income over $5000; after the war the ratio was almost even. Poor people derived their gains largely from the state of the economy (the need for soldiers and workers), not from government policy or the efforts of organized labor.

Fear of Enemy Aliens

On December 8, 1941, Roosevelt issued an executive order concerning enemy aliens. In addition to suspending naturalization proceedings for Italians, Germans, and Japanese immigrants, it required them to register, restricted their mobility, and prohibited them from owning items like cameras and shortwave radios that might be used for sabotage. In practice, however, the government was anything but even-handed, for racial attitudes influenced how public policy was applied; Germans and Italians were treated fairly, but Japanese suffered gross injustices.

According to the 1940 census, there were 600,000 Italian aliens in the United States. In general, the government treated them well, administering the enemy alien laws compassionately. On Columbus Day, 1942 (just before the congressional elections), Roosevelt lifted their enemy alien designation and established simplified naturalization procedures. The German aliens received similar treatment. Though less numerous (264,000) and not as politically important to the Democrats, they were treated with respect.

Jewish refugees complicated the German question. Reflecting a powerful strain of anti-Semitism, Congress in 1939 refused to raise immigration quotas to admit 20,000 Jewish children fleeing Nazi oppression into the United

States. As the wife of the United States Commissioner of Immigration remarked at a cocktail party, "20,000 children would all too soon grow up to be 20,000 ugly adults."

Instead of relaxing immigration quotas, American officials tried in vain to persuade Latin American countries and Great Britain to admit Jewish refugees. Other officials, such as Assistant Secretary of State Breckinridge Long, the man in charge of administering immigration policy, argued that the best way to rescue the Jews was to win the war. Bitterly anti-Semitic in his private views, Long insisted that any relaxation of the quota system would permit Nazi spies to slip into the country with the legitimate refugees. While the futile debates dragged on, Hitler's death camps killed helpless victims at the rate of 2000 an hour. As late as 1944, American officials consistently downplayed reports of genocide in the press, but they knew the truth. Air reconnaissance missions had taken scores of photographs of the death camp at Auschwitz, and military intelligence officers knew the location of several other concentration camps.

Nazi Concentration Camps

Finally, in January 1944, Secretary of the Treasury Henry Morgenthau, the only Jew in the Cabinet, presented to Roosevelt the "Report to the Secretary on the Acquiescence of this Government in the Murder of the Jews." In response, Roosevelt created the War Refugee Board, which, in turn, set up refugee camps in Italy, North Africa, and the United States. The American effort offered too little, too late. During the eighteen months of the War Refugee Board's existence, Hitler killed far more Jews than it saved.

Like Jews, Japanese-Americans suffered from intense discrimination. Barred from immigrating to the United States by the Immigration Act of 1924, they totaled 260,000 people, 150,000 of them in Hawaii and 110,000 on the West Coast, where most worked as small farmers or businessmen serving the Japanese community. After Pearl Harbor, rumors spread that a Japanese invasion was imminent, with Japanese-Americans poised to strike as a fifth column for the invasion.

On February 19, 1942, Roosevelt authorized the Department of War to designate military areas and to exclude any or all persons from them. Authorities immediately moved against Japanese aliens. Because the Japanese were a major population group in Hawaii and the backbone of the local economy, they were excluded from relocation. On the West Coast, however, military authorities ordered the Japanese to leave, drawing no distinction between aliens and citizens. Forced to sell their property for pennies on the dollar, most suffered severe financial losses, and relocation proved next to impossible, for no other states would take them. The governor of Idaho opposed any migration to his state, declaring: "The Japs live like rats, breed like rats and act like rats. We don't want them."

When voluntary measures failed, Roosevelt created the War Relocation Authority. It resettled 100,000 Japanese-Americans across ten camps in seven western states. Called relocation camps, they were concentration camps resembling minimum security prisons. In them, American citizens who had committed no crimes were imprisoned behind barbed wire, put in ramshackle wooden barracks where they lived one family to a room, and furnished with nothing but cots and bare light bulbs. Food, medical care, and schools were all inadequate.

Japanese-Americans of all ages, tagged like pieces of luggage, awaited their relocation to one of ten detention camps in seven western states. This family was from Hayward, California.

Nearly 18,000 Japanese-American men left those camps to fight for the United States Army. Most served with the 100th Infantry Battalion and the 442nd Regimental Combat Team. In Italy, the 442nd sustained nearly 10,000 casualties, with 3600 Purple Hearts, 810 Bronze Stars, 550 Oak Leaf Clusters, 342 Silver Stars, 123 divisional citations, 47 Distinguished Service Crosses, 17

Military Area (exclusion zone)
■ Internment camps

Japanese-American Internment Camps

Legions of Merit, 7 Presidential Unit Citations, and 1 Congressional Medal of Honor. In short, they fought heroically and became the most decorated military unit in World War II. In one of the most painful scenes in American history, Japanese-American parents, still in the concentration camps, were awarded posthumous Purple Hearts for their dead sons.

Some Japanese-Americans protested their treatment, claiming gross civil rights violations. Citing national security considerations, the Supreme Court backed the government six to three in *Korematsu* v. *U.S.* (1944). But in a dissenting opinion, Frank Murphy charged that federal policy had fallen "into the ugly abyss of racism." On December 18, 1944, in the *Endo* case, the Supreme Court decided that a civilian agency, the War Relocation Authority, had no constitutional authority to incarcerate law-abiding citizens. Two weeks later the federal government began closing down the camps, ending one of the most blatant violations of civil liberties in American history.

THE WAR IN EUROPE

The Grand Alliance

America's entrance into World War II forged the Grand Alliance of the United States, Great Britain, Free France, and the Soviet Union. It was from the beginning an uneasy alliance, born of necessity and filled with tension.

Britain's objectives were Europe-centered, approaching international affairs in spheres-of-influence, balance-of-power terms. The British wanted the war to weaken all the other continental powers, giving Britain the dominant role in redrawing the postwar map of Europe, especially in Poland and the Balkans, where they hoped to erect a barrier against Soviet expansion. Above all, Churchill insisted that Britain must emerge from the war with its empire intact.

France's goals reflected the vision of one man—General Charles de Gaulle, who was determined to restore France to greatness. By nature aloof, enigmatic, suspicious, and stubborn, he was equally charismatic and forceful. Like Churchill, he fought to retain his country's empire, and as the war progressed American officials came to regard de Gaulle as a political extremist. In policy disputes, he often sided with the British to oppose American and Soviet demands.

Joseph Stalin was the undisputed leader of the Soviet Union. A former seminary student and the son of a cobbler, Stalin had not only survived the turbulent years following the Bolshevik revolution, but had crushed all rivals to become Lenin's successor. Iron-willed and deeply paranoid, Stalin was a formidable negotiator—ruthless and brutal, devious and shrewd. He was determined to destroy Germany so that German troops would never again threaten the Soviet Union. Stalin also insisted that postwar Russia include parts of Poland and Finland and all of the Baltic states. Eastern Europe would then form a buffer against future aggression from the West, and provide colonies to be exploited in rebuilding the Soviet economy.

Roosevelt's war objectives were a curious blend of vague principles and political realities. He endorsed a new League of Nations, supported open markets, opposed colonialism, and pushed for democratic elections to counter spheres of influence. Among these goals, he was most concerned with securing free markets and opposing colonialism, aims which reflected his remarkable ability to join political principle with economic advantage. Yet Roosevelt was nothing if not pragmatic. He often compromised his principles in order to preserve Allied cooperation. Roosevelt's style of leadership influenced his diplomacy. Of all the Allied leaders he had the most exaggerated sense of his abilities as a diplomat. Disliking the rough and tumble of hard bargaining, he relied too heavily on personal charm and tried to avoid clashes by postponing arguments with the other leaders.

From the outset, then, the Grand Alliance was riddled with dissent. Each of the allies had separate agendas, many of which were mutually exclusive. Given their conflicting interests, the Allies were bound to have difficulty coordinating military strategy and agreeing upon postwar goals.

Early Axis Victories

After Pearl Harbor, the United States confronted the problem of waging global war. Before the conflict ended, the United States had troops and supplies scattered around the world. The war would cost America one million casualties, and over 300,000 deaths. The financial price was equally high: $350 billion in all—about $250 million a day at the peak of the fighting.

The first six months after Pearl Harbor were disastrous. Japanese forces captured Guam, Wake Island, the Philippines, Hong Kong, and Malaya and slashed deep into Burma, cutting the Burmese Road, which was China's lifeline to the West. General Douglas MacArthur, though vowing to return, was driven from the Philippines in March 1942. In a matter of months the Japanese had conquered a vast expanse extending from the Gilbert Islands through the Solomons and from New Guinea to Burma, leaving India and Australia vulnerable to attack.

In Europe, the Allied cause was hardly more encouraging. German submarines sank over 500 American merchant ships in the first

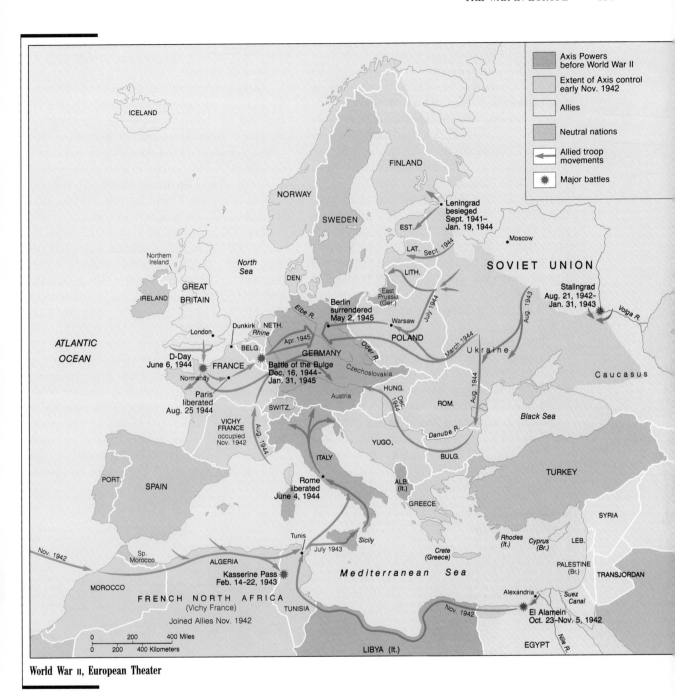

World War II, European Theater

ten months of 1942. With their lend-lease supplies threatened, the British stood in danger of collapsing before America could mobilize. On the Russian front, the Germans made short work of Stalin's divisions as they pressed toward Stalingrad, and the news from North Africa was equally bleak. On May 26, 1942, Field Marshal Erwin Rommel, known as the "Desert Fox" began his sweep toward the Suez Canal. A brilliant strategist, he slashed almost to Alexandria before being halted by the British. In short, Axis victories in the Pacific, Russia, and Africa made it clear that the war would be long and costly.

Stemming the German Tide

Despite the public rage over Pearl Harbor, Roosevelt agreed with Churchill and Stalin that defeating Germany was the top priority. The decision rested on two considerations: it would be difficult to dislodge Hitler from Europe if Britain fell; and Stalin needed to be placated. Throughout the war, Stalin remained suspicious, fearing that his allies planned to let the Germans and the Russians kill one another. As the Germans drove deep into Russian territory in 1942, he demanded that a second front be opened immediately to force Germany to divide her armies, thus taking some of the pressure off Russia. As one observer remarked, Soviet Foreign Minister V. M. Molotov knew only four words of English: "yes," "no," and "second front."

By the autumn of 1942 the Allies stopped Germany in the west, and the tide of battle began to turn on the Eastern Front as well. In September Germany lost twelve divisions at Stalingrad. In November the Red Army counterattacked, launching the drive to push the Germans back across the Ukraine. Despite Russia's victories and Stalin's pleas for a second front, the Allies, at Churchill's insistence, attacked the Germans in North Africa instead of France. Stalin saw this as a betrayal and his suspicions deepened.

Allied victories in Africa seemed to confirm Churchill's wisdom. British Field Marshal Sir Bernard Montgomery drove the Germans back to Tunis in October, and in November 1942 General Dwight David Eisenhower led a force of 400,000 Allied soldiers in a full-scale invasion of North Africa (Operation Torch). The German and Italian forces fought bravely. By the end of the campaign the Axis armies had lost 349,000 soldiers killed or captured, while the Allies had suffered only 70,000 casualties. Complete victory came on May 12, 1943, when the remnants of the Axis armies surrendered. Germany and Italy had suffered a major defeat and the Mediterranean was now open to Allied shipping.

Cheered by the North African victory, Allied leaders had to decide where to attack next. In January 1943 Churchill and Roosevelt met in Casablanca, French Morocco, without Stalin, who was invited but refused to attend, pleading that he could not leave Russia at this critical juncture of the war. Fearing that a premature invasion of France might bog down into trench-style warfare, Churchill argued for an invasion

The tide turned for the Allied forces when remnants of the Axis armies surrendered at El Alemein and the Mediterranean opened for Allied shipping.

of Sicily and then Italy. The United States initially opposed the plan (Operation Husky), arguing that it would delay the invasion of France without accomplishing any decisive results; but Churchill's views prevailed. As one of the United States' chief military advisors remarked at the time: "We came, we listened, and we were conquered."

Since they had again delayed the invasion of France, Churchill and Roosevel tried to reassure Stalin. They renewed their pledge to open a second front in Europe and vowed that they would make peace with the Axis powers only on the basis of unconditional surrender. While the "unconditional surrender" agreement was made public on the last day of the conference, Stalin was kept in the dark for several months about the other agreements reached at Casablanca, including the decision to postpone the second front.

Sicily fell in August 1943 after a campaign of slightly more than a month. Shortly before its surrender, Mussolini was deposed and placed under arrest. (German paratroopers later rescued him and installed him as head of the Italian government in German-occupied Italy.) The king of Italy appointed as the leader of the new government Marshal Pietro Badoglio, an old fascist who had led the Italian invasion of Ethiopia. Under Badoglio, Italy promptly surrendered on September 8, 1943, and then immediately switched sides and declared war on Germany.

The fighting in Italy was fierce. The terrain was mountainous, and the Germans offered savage resistance. Though the Italian campaign ultimately secured the Mediterranean, tied up German troops, and secured air bases for flights over central Europe, Stalin deeply resented the commitment of Allied troops there instead of France. Furthermore, he held Badoglio in contempt and strongly objected to his sudden rehabilitation as an Ally. Was this the way the Allies intended to treat former fascists, permitting them to become leaders in Allied dominated governments? Since Soviet troops had played no role in the Italian campaign, Roosevelt and Churchill would not permit the Russians to participate in organizing an occupation government in Italy.

Meanwhile, Russia was winning the war on the Eastern Front. By October 1943 Soviet troops had recorded stunning victories in the battles of Leningrad and Stalingrad. American aid did not arrive in time to contribute to these victories, but American weapons, vehicles, clothing, and food were crucial to subsequent Soviet offensives. Keeping Russia supplied was no longer a problem because the Allies had won the Battle of the Atlantic. Radar, air patrols, and destroyer escorts neutralized the German submarines, lowering shipping losses from 514,744 tons in March 1943 to 199,409 tons in May.

The Teheran Conference

Buoyed by military success, Stalin was conciliatory when he met Roosevelt and Churchill in November 1943 in Teheran, the capital of Iran. It was their first face-to-face meeting. The agenda focused on the long-awaited second front and the shape of the postwar world. In response to Stalin's demands, they set May 1944 as a target date for "Operation Overlord"—the invasion of France. To increase the chances of success, Stalin promised to coordinate Russia's spring offensive with the invasion.

The Teheran Conference dissolved into bitter controversy over postwar issues. Stalin demanded Soviet control over Eastern Europe, and he insisted that Germany be divided into several weak states. Churchill demanded democratic governments in Eastern Europe, especially in Poland, for which England had gone to war. He wanted no part in emasculating Germany, arguing that a strong Germany was vital to the balance of power in postwar Europe. While Churchill fought Stalin over Eastern Europe, he bristled at any criticism of Britain's intent to reoccupy her colonies.

Roosevelt tried to be the conciliator at Teheran. He agreed to the partition of Germany, and while he supported Churchill's plans for Eastern Europe, Roosevelt was enough of a realist to know that Russia had the inside track there. Convinced that he could handle "Uncle Joe," he decided to leave the postwar settlement to an international organization dominated by the victors. The Teheran Conference yielded little but an airing of the leaders' demands; nothing was settled but the opening of the second front.

In preparation for the invasion, the Allies adopted saturation bombing, dropping 2,697,473 tons of bombs on German territory, killing 305,000 civilians, and damaging over 5.5 million homes. The raids were extremely costly. In a single week in February 1944 the Americans lost 226 bombers and 2600 crewmen. All told, Allied airmen suffered 158,000 fatalities. The bombing was supposed to wipe out the German war machine and break the people's will to resist. In fact, the bombs often missed military targets and killed innocent civilians. Missions like the firebombing of nonindustrial Dresden, which killed 100,000 people, did much to convince the Germans that Hitler's ravings about the evil Allies were true. The bombings only stiffened the German will to fight.

Liberating Europe

As the bombers pounded Germany the Allies concluded their preparations for the long-awaited invasion. Over 3 million soldiers massed in England under the command of General Dwight D. Eisenhower, a gifted strategist who was also adept at soothing the sensitive egos of other Allied commanders. D-day came on June 6, 1944. After two weeks of desperate fighting on the beaches of Normandy, the Allies began to push inland. Quickly achieving air mastery, they broke out of the bottleneck on the Normandy peninsula at the end of June. A month later Allied troops were sweeping across Europe in a race for Berlin. Paris was liberated in August, and by mid-September the Americans had crossed the German border.

On December 16, 1944, the Germans launched a desperate counteroffensive. Allied forces were concentrated north and south of the Ardennes Forest in eastern France, leaving the forest itself lightly defended. In what became known as the Battle of the Bulge, German armored divisions drove sixty miles through the gap to the Franco-Belgian border. The American 1101st Airborne Division held them off at Bastogne until General George Patton's Third Army moved in for the kill. When the battle was over, the Americans had suffered 77,000 casualties while inflicting 120,000 on the Germans.

LANDINGS ON D-DAY: The Longest Day

For the Allies in World War II, the D-day landing of June 6, 1944, was the long-planned, long-anticipated blow against Nazi Germany. Originally scheduled for 1942, it had been pushed back first to 1943 and finally to 1944. Although both the Soviet Union and impatient Americans had clamored for an earlier invasion, Prime Minister Winston Churchill of Great Britain, who remembered the difficulties of Dunkirk, counseled caution.

The cross-channel invasion was a risky proposition and an immense undertaking. During early 1944 the Allies moved thousands of aircraft, tanks, trucks, jeeps, and men into southeastern England, moving soldiers to joke that if the invasion was long postponed, England would tilt and sink into the Channel. Then there were the imponderables which defied careful planning: weather, visibility, the state of the Channel.

As much as possible General Dwight D. Eisenhower, who was the overall commander of the invasion, tried to deceive the Germans into believing that the invasion would take place at the Pas de Calais, around Boulogne, Calais, and Dunkirk. It appears that Hitler did believe that the Allies would strike at the Pas de Calais. Instead, Ike centered his attack further to the west, along the French coast between Cherbourg and Le Havre. Altogether, the Allies assaulted five beaches and dropped paratroopers and airborne infantry into three sites.

Further east, British paratroopers were given the task of securing the left flank by gaining control of the Orne River. American paratroopers were given the job of securing the right flank along the Merderet River. In between these two points, the Allies landed on five beaches: Sword (British), Juno (Canadian), Gold (British), Omaha (American), and Utah (American). All totalled, 2,876,000 soldiers, sailors, and airmen; 11,000 aircraft; and over 2000 vessels played a role in the invasion.

At several beaches, especially Utah, the Allies met little opposition. At others, notably Omaha, the story was different and losses were heavy. More than 2000 Americans were killed or wounded securing Omaha beach on June 6. But by the end of that "longest day" the Allies had accomplished their goal. They were back in France and ready to move east toward Germany.

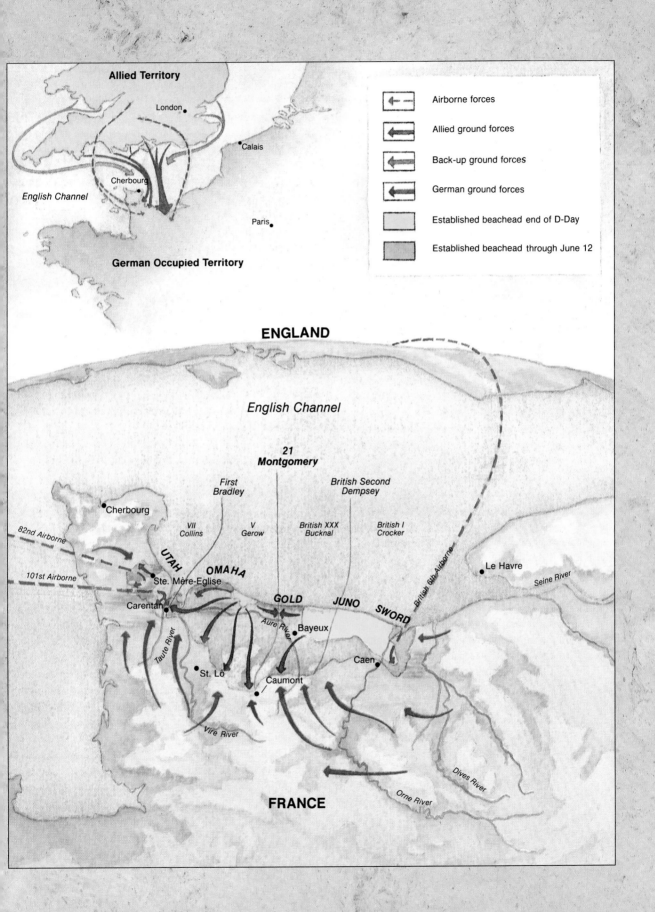

Allied Territory

London

Calais

Cherbourg

English Channel

Paris

German Occupied Territory

Airborne forces

Allied ground forces

Back-up ground forces

German ground forces

Established beachead end of D-Day

Established beachead through June 12

ENGLAND

English Channel

21
Montgomery

First
Bradley

British Second
Dempsey

Cherbourg

82nd Airborne

VII
Collins

V
Gerow

British XXX
Bucknal

British I
Crocker

101st Airborne

UTAH

OMAHA

Ste. Mère-Eglise

GOLD

JUNO

SWORD

British 6th Airborne

Le Havre

Seine River

Carentan

Aure River

Bayeux

Caen

Taute River

St. Lô

Caumont

Vire River

Dives River

Orne River

FRANCE

A Coast Guard combat photographer shot this panorama of the French invasion beach as supplies and reinforcements were funneled ashore for the conquest of the Cherbourg Peninsula.

More important, the German capacity to launch another offensive had been destroyed.

True to his word, Stalin simultaneously launched the spring offensive. His troops engaged the Germans in furious combat all across Eastern Europe, tying up men and materials that otherwise might have been hurled against the Allies. Indeed, Russian troops battled three German divisions for every single German division that opposed the invasion. By January 1945 the Russians had captured Warsaw, and by February they were forty-five miles from Berlin.

The Yalta Conference

With victory in Europe at hand, Roosevelt, Churchill, and Stalin met in February 1945 at Yalta, a resort on the Russian Black Sea, to settle the shape of the postwar world. They quickly concurred on the partition of Germany, including a zone for French occupation, but they agreed on little else. No action was taken on Stalin's demand for the permanent dismemberment of Germany, and no decision was reached on reparations. Stalin wanted Germany to pay $20 billion in reparations, half of which was to go to Russia. Churchill opposed him, rejecting any plan that would leave Germany financially prostrate after the war.

Eastern Europe was the most divisive issue at Yalta. As early as December 1941, Stalin had told the British that Russia would join an anti-German alliance only if they would sanction Soviet control over the Baltic states (Estonia, Lithuania, and Latvia), as well as portions of Finland, Poland, and Romania. Stalin expected British support. In October 1944 he and Churchill had met secretly in Moscow to strike a deal on Eastern Europe. Unbeknownst to Roosevelt, they agreed to divide Eastern Europe into British and Soviet spheres for the duration of the war. Russia was to have the dominant voice over Romania, Great Britain over Greece, and Yugoslavia was to be controlled jointly.

Stalin initially kept his part of the bargain. In December 1944, amidst street fighting in Athens to drive out Axis troops, British and Greek troops suddenly turned on the Greek communists who had been their allies. Stalin did not lift a finger to prevent their slaughter. No doubt he expected the British to repay his restraint over Greece by supporting his designs on Eastern Europe.

At Yalta, Stalin announced his intentions for eastern Poland. To compensate Poland and to weaken Germany, he demanded that Poland receive a large chunk of Germany. Reminding Churchill and Roosevelt that they had excluded him from any role in forming the Italian government, Stalin made it clear that the shoe was now on the other foot. He would tolerate no interference in Eastern Europe.

Confronted by Roosevelt's and Churchill's bitter opposition, Stalin agreed to a face-saving compromise: Russia would permit free elections in Poland and include democratic forces in a new government there. Stalin tacked so many amendments on the Polish compromise that one of Roosevelt's chief military aides complained the Russians "could stretch it all the way from Yalta to Washington without technically breaking it." In place of an enforcement mechanism, the agreement stipulated that the three powers would consult and reach a unani-

Stalin, Roosevelt, and Churchill met at Yalta in February 1945 to discuss the state of the postwar world.

mous decision on any action. In other words, Stalin won a veto over the Western powers in Eastern Europe.

Yalta's record on the remaining issues was less ambiguous. Stalin promised to enter the war against Japan within three months of Germany's surrender, and he renewed his pledge to join the United Nations. Roosevelt considered both concessions important victories because he wanted Russia's help in defeating Japan and because he remained hopeful that the United Nations could resolve disputes between the United States and the Soviet Union peacefully after the war ended.

Roosevelt has been denounced for his role at Yalta, but there was little more he could have done. The Russians refused to lose at the conference table what they had won on the battlefield. In the words of one psychologist, the Soviets reduced all reality to the "searing experience of World War II." The war had destroyed 1700 towns and 70,000 villages; it had left 25 million Russians homeless. Another 7.5 million Soviet military personnel and 10 million civilians died; more than 600,000 had starved to death during the seige of Leningrad alone. More Russians had died at Stalingrad than the United States had lost in all theaters of the war combined. Stalin was determined to protect Russia from future attack. Force alone could have compelled him to vacate Eastern Europe, and most Americans did not want to fight Russia. Looking back at Yalta, Churchill remarked, "Our hopeful assumptions were soon to be falsified. Still, they were the only ones possible at the time."

Allied victories came rapidly after the Battle of the Bulge. On March 4, American troops reached the Rhine River, and in April they met the Russian army sixty miles south of Berlin. After Roosevelt's death on April 12, however, Stalin immediately tested the new president, Harry S Truman. Stalin ordered the execution of democratic leaders in Eastern Europe and replaced them with Communist governments. Truman was outraged by Stalin's disregard for the Yalta agreements, but like Roosevelt he was not willing to fight the Soviets to save Eastern Europe.

Despite his anger, Truman ignored Churchill's pleas to occupy Prague and Berlin before the Red Army. Instead, he accepted the advice of General Eisenhower to finish off Germany. On April 22 Russian troops reached Berlin and occupied the city after house-to-house fighting. On April 30 Hitler committed suicide, and Germany surrendered one week later. The Allies celebrated V-E (Victory in Europe) Day on May 8, 1945.

THE WAR IN THE PACIFIC

Though Europe received top priority, American forces stopped Japanese advances in the Pacific by late summer of 1942. Two decisive naval battles, Coral Sea and Midway, turned the tide. In May, a Japanese troop convoy sailed into the Coral Sea between New Guinea and Australia to capture Port Moresby. The United States Navy intercepted and destroyed the convoy, preventing the attack and forcing Japan to reconsider her plans for invading Australia.

Island-Hopping

Two months later, at Midway Island in the Central Pacific, the Japanese launched an aircraft carrier offensive to cut American communications and isolate Hawaii to the east. American naval intelligence, however, had finally broken the Japanese military code and Admiral Chester Nimitz's ships were ready. Beginning June 3, a furious battle ensued, and by June 6, the Japanese had lost three destroyers, a heavy cruiser, and four carriers. The Americans lost one carrier (the *Yorktown*) and a destroyer. The Battle of Midway broke the back of Japanese naval power.

On August 7, 1942, the American land offensive began when the 1st Marine Division attacked Guadalcanal in the Solomon Islands. They captured the air strip on Guadalcanal, and following months of bloody fighting, the Japanese left the island in February, giving the Allies a secure supply line to Australia. The victory at Guadalcanal protected the American eastern flank so that General Douglas MacArthur, commander of Southeast Pacific forces, could begin his march through New Guinea on his way back to the Philippines.

Japanese advances in China proved more difficult to halt. Allied troops had to cut a new road through the mountainous terrain of Burma to supply Chiang Kai-shek's army, but the real problem was that China was racked by civil war, and Chiang fought harder against the Communist forces headed by Mao Tse-tung than he did against the Japanese. The head of Allied forces in China, General Joseph Stillwell ("Vinegar Joe"), nicknamed Chiang "Peanut," but Roosevelt maintained the illusion that Chiang Kai-shek was a strong leader, destined to lead a powerful country.

Despite setbacks in China, the Allies won major victories in the South Pacific, where they moved on Japan from two directions. In the southeast, General MacArthur seized Lae on the northern coast of New Guinea in September 1943, and from there, instead of making frontal assaults on Japanese strongpoints, he leapfrogged up the coast, taking isolated positions and forcing the Japanese to leave their fortifica-

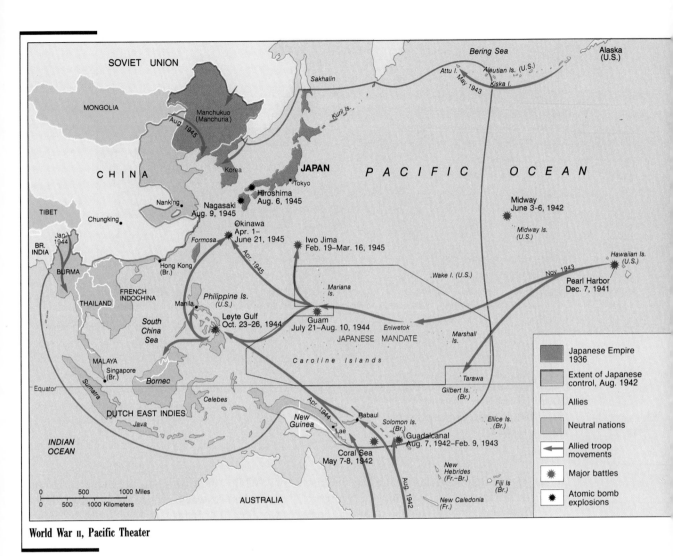

World War II, Pacific Theater

tions to attack. The Japanese expected MacArthur to attack their impregnable, 100,000 man fortress at Rabaul on New Britain. Instead, he isolated and bypassed it. By July 1944 MacArthur's forces controlled all of New Guinea.

Meanwhile, Admiral Chester Nimitz's naval and marine forces in the Central Pacific, were "island-hopping" all the way to Japan, conquering important positions, building an airstrip, and from there attacking the next island. The first island group to receive an amphibious assault was the Gilberts. Late in November, the marines attacked Tarawa, a tiny island three miles long and 600 yards wide. It was a bloody

battle. The Japanese troops fought to the death, and the marines took 3301 casualties in three days of fighting.

With the Gilberts secured, Nimitz assaulted the Marshall Islands in February 1944. The Japanese offered only light resistance there because they wanted to make a stand at the Marianas Islands. The Marianas were important to the United States. Guam, the southernmost of the Marianas, had been seized by Japan just after Pearl Harbor, and retaking it would have enormous symbolic significance. More important, the Marianas were close enough to Japan for B-29 bombing raids. Japan realized their sig-

General MacArthur, commander of Southeast Pacific forces, splashed ashore on October 21, 1944 in the Philippines with the 96th Division.

nificance and defended the islands to the last man. The battle took place in July and August 1944. When it was over, the Japanese had lost 50,000 troops and 450 of their best fighter pilots; the government of Hideki Tojo had fallen. B-29s began regular bombing raids over Japan in November 1944.

On October 21, 1944, General MacArthur invaded the Philippines, splashing ashore with the 96th Division for the benefit of photographers. That same month the navy won a stunning victory at the Battle of Leyte Gulf, where the Japanese lost four carriers, three battleships, eight destroyers, and nine cruisers, virtually their entire remaining battle fleet. American submarines now controlled Pacific shipping lanes, cutting the Japanese islands off from military and food supplies. In January, United States forces invaded Luzon, the main island of the Philippines. Victory came five months later. MacArthur's troops had killed 240,000 Japanese soldiers.

While MacArthur was attacking the Philippines, Nimitz was bearing down on Iwo Jima. If Iwo Jima fell, fighter planes would be able to link up with B-29s heading out of the Marianas and protect them in their raids on Japan. The 3rd, 4th, and 5th Marine Divisions attacked Iwo Jima in February 1945, and early in March the island was in American hands. The cost of the attack was high. Four thousand marines lost their lives.

The fighters then joined the B-29s over Japan, allowing the bombers to reduce armaments and increase bombloads. By the end of the war American pilots had dropped 160,000 tons of bombs on Japan. Japan's population density, combustible building materials, and limited industrial capacity made strategic bombing more effective than in Europe. Bombs killed over 330,000 civilians (86,000 in the firebombing of Tokyo alone) and destroyed over forty percent of the buildings in sixty-five cities. Japanese war production fell dramatically—oil by eighty-three percent and aircraft engines by seventy-five percent.

In June 1945 American troops attacked Okinawa, 350 miles south of Japan. Japanese resistance became more and more fierce. Kamikaze attacks (suicide flights by Japanese pilots) rose dramatically. Of the 4000 planes lost by the Japanese at Okinawa, 2800 were kamikaze missions. Japan's soldiers were just as tenacious. Many fought to the death rather than surrender. When Okinawa fell in June, more than 130,000 Japanese soldiers had died there.

With the outcome of the war no longer in doubt, many moderate Japanese wanted to avoid an invasion. With the peace party growing in strength, Hideki Tojo resigned in July 1944, but strong factions within the military vowed to fight to the death. In an effort to save Japan, the Emperor switched his support to the peace party in February 1945. He then sent out peace feelers to Stalin, who in turn conveyed them to Truman in July 1945.

Truman and the Dawn of the Atomic Age

Few presidents have been asked to conduct diplomacy with less preparation than Harry S Truman. He had risen to power as a loyal machine politician in Kansas City. As vice-president and former senator from Missouri he knew next to nothing about foreign affairs. Roosevelt had kept Truman largely in the dark, neither seeking his counsel nor confiding in him. When Roosevelt's death elevated him to the White House, Truman told reporters: "I felt like the moon, the stars, and all planets had fallen on me." Yet Truman was determined to be a strong president, to make decisions resolutely—qualities which had both advantages and disadvantages.

Potsdam, a suburb of Berlin, was Truman's first international conference and the last wartime meeting of the Allied leaders. When the conference convened in July 1945, Truman had been in office long enough to believe that Roosevelt had been too soft with Stalin. Truman was convinced that Stalin was a liar who only understood force. Yet Truman was not willing to

risk a showdown over Eastern Europe, primarily because his military advisers insisted that the United States still needed Russia's help against Japan.

If Truman stopped short of provoking a showdown over Eastern Europe, he still pushed the Russians hard at Potsdam. During the negotiations, Truman learned that American scientists had successfully tested the first atomic bomb. Hoping to impress Stalin, Truman told him in a conversation one evening that the United States had just developed a new weapon of awesome power. Stalin blithely replied that he trusted the United States would make good use of it against Japan. Thus, Truman's first effort at "nuclear diplomacy" was largely a failure. Far from being intimidated, Stalin had stood his ground.

Deadlocked on Eastern Europe, Truman and Stalin turned their attention to Japan. The sole accomplishment of the conference was the Potsdam Declaration of July 26, demanding immediate "unconditional surrender" and warning that the only alternative was "prompt and utter destruction."

This was too vague to give the Japanese ample warning of what lay in store. Some scientists who had helped develop the bomb, joined by several key political figures, advised Truman not to use it. They foresaw the bomb's implications for a postwar arms race with the Soviet Union. Others, arguing from a moral position, insisted that the United States should warn the Japanese about the bomb's terrifying power, giving them an opportunity to surrender. As a compromise, a few suggested dropping the bomb on an uninhabited Pacific island, with neutral observers at a safe distance to report its destructive force.

Truman rejected these alternatives. The atomic bomb was the most jealously guarded secret of World War II, and Truman had no intention of sharing the secret with anyone. He rejected the idea of a test demonstration because his scientists could not guarantee the bomb would explode. In the end, Truman decided to drop the bomb.

Military considerations played a large role in his decision. According to the best intelligence reports, an invasion of the Japanese Is-

HIROSHIMA AND NAGASAKI

On July 16, 1945, the Atomic Age became reality. The place was Alamagordo Air Force Base near Los Alamos, New Mexico. The occasion was the first successful explosion of an atomic bomb. Observers witnessed "a blinding flash that lighted the entire northwestern sky." Next came "a huge billow of smoke," followed by "an enormous ball of what appeared to be fire and closely resembled a rising sun." Dr. J. Robert Oppenheimer, the chief scientist at Los Alamos whose team had designed the weapon, was so overwhelmed by the scale of the blast that he thought of a Hindu quotation: "Now I am become death, destroyer of worlds."

Back in 1939, two brilliant scientists, Albert Einstein and Enrico Fermi, both of whom had fled fascism and anti-Semitism in Europe, warned President Roosevelt that German nuclear physicists under

Adolf Hitler's control might well be trying to develop such a bomb. Roosevelt realized the implications, and he set in motion what became the "Manhattan Project," a top secret effort involving civilian scientists and army engineers to apply the theory of nuclear fission to a bomb. Hitler's scientists never succeeded, but now in July 1945, with the war over in Europe, the United States had a weapon with the potential to threaten civilization itself. The question was whether the bomb would be used against Japan, the last of the Axis powers still at war.

The Japanese were a formidable foe. Since 1942, United States troops had been rolling back their empire, all the way to the shores of Japan and the Chinese mainland by the summer of 1945. The toll of casualties was horrendous. Japanese soldiers fought with a

sense of personal honor that struck Americans as fanatical. They would not surrender when beaten but would fight to their death. To do otherwise would be to disgrace themselves, their families, and their emperor, whom they considered a god.

At first, in defending Pacific islands like Guadalcanal (August 1942–February 1943), Japanese soldiers mounted suicidal *banzai* charges. They ran forward in waves at United States troops, inflicting massive damage before being shot down. Later, on islands like Iwo Jima (February–March 1945), they used elaborate networks of deep bunkers and tunnels to wreak havoc, so much so that United States casualties started to reach the fifty percent range. By 1945, the Japanese were unleashing *kamikaze* raids in which pilots sacrificed themselves for the glory of the empire by dive bombing their planes into United States naval vessels. In the bloody battle of Okinawa (April–June 1945), *kamikazes* flew some 2800 planes into ships, inflicting 10,000 casualties and sinking 28 vessels, besides damaging 325 other ships.

American soldiers, as well as the public at large, neither understood nor respected Japanese martial values. Explained a marine corps general, to shoot "a Jap . . . was like killing a rattlesnake." Almost universally Americans used terms of racial derision to describe an enemy who had not only mounted the "sneak attack" on Pearl Harbor but who now refused to surrender when beaten.

Such attitudes affected the development of a comprehensive United States war plan, known as DOWNFALL, constructed on the assumption that only a full-scale invasion of Japan would bring total victory in the Pacific. The first phase of the plan, called Operation OLYMPIC, involved an assault on Kyushu, the southernmost island of Japan, to begin in November 1945. The joint chiefs of staff presented OLYMPIC to President Truman in June and stated that American casualties could reach 268,000 (out of 767,000 participants). The Japanese still had 2.3 million soldiers ready to fight and another 4 million citizens trained in the use of arms. If they battled to the death, as they had so far, American casualties would exceed 1 million by the time American troops conquered the main island of Honshu in 1946 or 1947.

Because of the bloody price everyone expected to pay, high ranking officials in the United States were anxious to involve Russia—to attack through Manchuria—in the final crushing of Japan. At Yalta in February 1945, President Roosevelt secured pledges of Soviet assistance. But then at Potsdam in July, President Truman seemed much less interested. Having just learned of the test results at Los Alamos, Truman told Joseph Stalin of "a new weapon of unusual destructive force." Stalin, however, would not be cast aside. He still wanted the territory (the lower half of Sakhalin Island, the Kurile islands, and certain considerations in Manchuria) promised at Yalta. The Soviet leader thus "hoped" that the United States "would make good use" of the weapon "against the Japanese," but, as he made clear, the Russians would not be denied their part in the invasion or the promised territory.

Meanwhile, a committee of scientists and military officers were at work in selecting possible targets. Some advocated a demonstration at a pre-announced neutral site as a way of forcing the Japanese into surrender, but others feared what might happen should the bomb prove to be a dud. All leverage would then be lost. Finally, with great reluctance, these advisors agreed that there was "no acceptable alternative to direct military use" of the bomb.

In public, Truman never admitted to any qualms about the decision to use the new weapon, but in private he wondered how "we as the leader of the world for the common welfare" could employ "this terrible bomb." Yet he accepted the responsibility for many reasons. He wanted to save hundreds of thousands of American lives by avoiding a full invasion of Japan against soldiers who fought like "savages, ruthless, merciless, and fanatic." Likely, too, Truman and his advisors feared the expansionism of the Communist regime of Joseph Stalin. Using the bomb might prove a great point of leverage in dealing with the Soviets in the days ahead.

While Truman and others considered the alternatives, a select unit of the Army Air Force, flying B-29s, made a series of practice bomb runs over Japan. Since these planes did not attack, as they had so often before in firebombing cities like Tokyo, no one paid much attention. Then on August 6, 1945, at a few minutes past 8:00 A.M., three B-29s at 31,600 feet of altitude appeared over Hiroshima. Colonel Paul Tibbets, piloting the lead bomber, *Enola Gay*, turned the controls over to Major Thomas Ferebee, the bombardier officer, who completed the run. It took forty-five seconds, as *Enola Gay* banked away as fast as it could,

for the atomic bomb to reach the ground. As the fireball erupted toward the sky, 100,000 Japanese citizens, including thousands of soldiers assigned to the Second General Army with its headquarters just 2000 yards from ground zero, died instantly. Three days later, with no Japanese indication of a willingness to surrender, a second bomb flattened Nagasaki and killed 35,000 people.

Dropping two atomic bombs gave peace advocates in Japan the muscle they needed to overcome the militarists. When on August 10 Emperor Hirohito agreed to seek peace terms, the war faction reluctantly acceded, but not before an attempt on the sacred emperor's life. Final resistance collapsed, however, after General Anami Korechika, the war minister, upheld his honor by committing suicide on August 14. He could not face hearing Hirohito's proclamation of surrender.

When American troops training for Operation OLYMPIC learned about the surrender, they rejoiced. "We would not be obliged to run up the beaches near Tokyo assault-firing while being mortared and shelled," wrote one of them. "We are going to live. We are going to grow up to adulthood after all." Yet they did not realize how different the world would be with nuclear weapons in the hands of the two superpowers to emerge from World War II. For a moment, however, General Douglas MacArthur seemed to understand. After the Japanese surrender ceremony on September 2, 1945, he stated: "We have had our last chance. If we do not devise some greater and more equitable system, Armageddon will be at our door."

lands might cost one million casualties, with the Japanese suffering several times that figure. Ironically, the bomb had the potential to save countless lives on both sides by ending the war immediately. Truman's decision to drop the bomb was also influenced by the growing friction between the Americans and the Soviets. He hoped to impress the Russians with America's might so that they would be easier to deal with after the war.

Following Japan's rejection of the Potsdam Declaration, Truman gave the final order. On August 6 a single B-29 flew over Hiroshima and dropped an atomic bomb that decimated 4.4 square miles and killed 70,000 people. On August 8 the Soviets entered the war against Japan, making good on Stalin's promise at Yalta. When the first bomb failed to produce a surrender, Truman ordered a second strike. On August 9 Nagasaki was obliterated, killing another 80,000 Japanese. The following day Japan sued for peace. Like V-E day, V-J Day (Victory over Japan) triggered a spontaneous national celebration in the United States. Tens of millions of Americans hit the streets in a mass expression of joy and relief. On September 2, 1945, General MacArthur accepted the unconditional surrender of Japan aboard the battleship *Missouri* in Tokyo Bay. Truman refused to permit the Russians to attend the ceremony or to play any role in creating an occupation government for Japan.

World War II was over. The fascist governments had been destroyed; their military machines had been crushed; their economies had been shattered; their major cities lay in ruins; and their people faced starvation. The Allies were hardly less devastated, except for the United States, which emerged from the war stronger than ever. Much of the world had to be reordered and rebuilt, but the conflicts between the Americans and the Russians that emerged during the war raised grave doubts over the prospects for future cooperation.

This photo of the remains of the Nagasaki Medical College shows the almost total destruction of the atomic blast. The buildings that remain standing were made of reinforced concrete.

CHRONOLOGY OF KEY EVENTS

1921 Washington Conference produces the Nine Power Treaty and the Four Power Treaty

1922 Mussolini assumes power in Italy

1931 Japan invades Manchuria

1933 Hitler assumes power in Germany

1936 Anti-Comintern Pact; Rome-Berlin Axis formed

1937 Roosevelt signs the Neutrality Act; Japan attacks the U.S.S. *Panay* in China

1938 Germany annexes Austria; Hitler appeased at the Munich Conference; Germany seizes the Sudetenland

1939 Nazi-Comintern Pact; Invasion of Poland; Beginning of World War II

1940 Germany occupies France; Roosevelt reelected

1941 Lend-Lease policy allows the U.S. to support Great Britain; Germany invades Russia; Japanese attack Pearl Harbor; U.S. enters the war

1942 Congress of Racial Equality (CORE) organized; U.S. defeats Japan at Guadalcanal; Beginning of Nisei internment in U.S.

1943 United Mine Workers strike; Allied victory in North Africa; Invasion of Italy

1944 D-day, the Allied invasion of Normandy; MacArthur returns to the Philippines

1945 Yalta Conference; Roosevelt dies; V-E day; First atomic bomb dropped on Hiroshima; V-J day

CONCLUSION

When World War II erupted in Europe, President Roosevelt knew that most Americans supported the Allies. So did he, but his freedom to act was severely limited by isolationists in Congress. For more than two years, Roosevelt struggled to preserve the fiction of neutrality while providing programs to assist the Allies. After the attack on Pearl Harbor, isolationist opposition crumbled and the public united behind the war. The United States joined Great Britain, Free France, the Soviet Union, and China to defeat the Axis Powers—Germany, Japan, and Italy. Yet apart from the need to crush the enemy, the Allies agreed upon little. Throughout the war, they clashed over military strategy and postwar objectives, disagreements that anticipated the conflicts of the postwar era.

The impact of World War II on the American economy was enormous, and it even ended the Great Depression. Fueled by government contracts, the economy expanded dramatically, soaring to full employment and astounding the world with its productivity. The war accelerated corporate mergers, as well as the trend toward large-scale units in agriculture. Labor unions also grew during World War II. The government adopted pro-union policies, continuing the New Deal's sympathetic treatment of organized labor. Keynesian economic principles, which held that manipulation of federal government spending and taxation policies could control unemployment and prices, had first emerged during the New Deal. It was during

World War II that these principles were firmly implanted as public policy.

The Democrats reaped a political windfall from the war. Roosevelt rode the wartime emergency to unprecedented third and fourth terms, preserving the New Deal coalition among voters so effectively that people wondered if the Republicans would ever elect another president. Despite political victories, however, the Democrats could not recapture congressional support for liberal reforms. The reform spirit was largely gone—a victim, it seemed, of the country's unmistakable swing to the right in politics.

The war's social consequences were varied. For most people, it had a disruptive influence—separating families, overcrowding housing, and creating a shortage of consumer goods. The war also set people in motion, accelerating the movement from the countryside to the cities; and it redefined roles and opened new opportunities for women and minority groups. Yet sexual and racial barriers remained, highlighting the reforms left unfinished at home even as American troops fought totalitarian states abroad.

The most important legacy of the war was the growth in the power of the federal government. Presidential power expanded enormously, presaging the postwar rise of what critics termed the "imperial presidency." Much of the president's energies went into formulating and directing a revolution in American foreign policy. Gone forever was the notion of fortress America, isolated and removed from world affairs. In its place stood a strong internationalist state, determined to exercise power on a global scale.

REVIEW SUMMARY

The United States entered World War II only after a series of policies designed to preserve the illusion of world peace and (later) neutrality

- it organized a series of treaties outlawing war in the 1920s
- it mended relations with Latin America
- it adopted a "cash and carry" arms policy which was eventually replaced with the policy of "lend-lease"

After the attack on Pearl Harbor, America mobilized for war on the industrial, civilian, and military fronts by

- using research grants and cost-plus contracts to push industry to new levels
- managing labor through the War Labor Board
- employing war rationing and price controls
- providing new opportunities for blacks and women in the military and war-related industry
- interning Japanese-Americans in relocation camps
- establishing a military alliance with Russia and Britain

The end of World War II marked America's emergence as the world's foremost economic power and the sole possessor of the atomic bomb.

SUGGESTIONS FOR FURTHER READING

OVERVIEWS AND SURVEYS

Selig Adler, *The Uncertain Giant: American Foreign Policy Between the Wars* (1969); Albert R. Buchanan, *The United States and World War II* (2 vols.; 1964); Martha Hoyle, *A World in Flames: A History of World War II* (1970); Robert Leckie, *The Wars of America* (2 vols.; 1981); Studs Terkel, ed., *"The Good War": An Oral History of World War Two* (1984); Russell F. Weigley, *The American Way of War: A History of United States Military Strategy and Policy* (1973); and Gordon Wright, *The Ordeal of Total War, 1939–1945* (1968).

DIPLOMACY BETWEEN THE WARS

Charles Chatfield, *For Peace and Justice: Pacifism in America, 1914–1941* (1971); Charles DeBenedetti, *The Peace Reform in American History* (1980); Charles DeBenedetti, *Origins of the Modern American Peace Movement, 1915–1929* (1978); Robert H. Ferrell, *Peace in Their Time* (1952); Erwin F. Gellman, *Good Neighbor Diplomacy: United States Policies in Latin America, 1933–1945* (1979); Manfred Jonas, *Isolationism in America, 1935–1941* (1966); Joan Huff Wilson, *American Business and Foreign Policy, 1920–1933* (1971); John E. Wiltz, *In Search of Peace: The Senate Munitions Inquiry, 1934–36* (1963); and Bryce Wood, *The Making of the Good Neighbor Policy* (1961).

THE COMING OF WORLD WAR II

Thomas A. Bailey and Paul B. Ryan, *Hitler vs. Roosevelt: The Undeclared Naval War* (1979); Robert J. Butow, *Tojo and the Coming of the War* (1961); Warren I. Cohen,

America's Response to China: An Interpretive History of Sino-American Relations (1971); Wayne S. Cole, *America First: The Battle Against Intervention, 1940–1941* (1953); Wayne S. Cole, *Roosevelt and the Isolationists, 1932–1945* (1983); James V. Compton, *The Swastika and the Eagle: Hitler, the United States, and the Origins of World War II* (1967); Robert Dallek, *Franklin D. Roosevelt and American Foreign Policy, 1932–1945* (1979); Robert A. Divine, *Illusion of Neutrality* (1982); Robert A. Divine, *Second Chance: The Triumph of Internationalism During World War II* (1967); Herbert Feis, *The Road to Pearl Harbor: The Coming of the War Between the United States and Japan* (1950); Akira Iriye, *After Imperialism: The Search for a New Order in the Far East, 1921–1931* (1965); Warren F. Kimbell, *The Most Unsordid Act: Lend-Lease, 1939–1941* (1982); William L. Langer and S. Everett Gleason, *The Challenge to Isolation: The World Crisis of 1937–1940 and American Foreign Policy* (1952); Joseph P. Lash, *Roosevelt and Churchill, 1939–1941: The Partnership that Saved the West* (1976); Martin V. Melosi, *The Shadow of Pearl Harbor: Political Controversy Over the Surprise Attack, 1941–1946* (1977); Keith L. Nelson, *Victors Divided: America and the Allies in Germany, 1918–1923* (1975); Gordon W. Prange, *At Dawn We Slept: The Untold Story of Pearl Harbor* (1981); David Reynolds, *The Creation of the Anglo-American Alliance, 1937–1941: A Study in Competitive Cooperation* (1982); Bruce Russett, *No Clear and Present Danger: A Skeptical View of the United States Entry into World War II* (1972); Michael Schaller, *The U.S. Crusade in China, 1936–1945* (1979); John E. Wiltz, *From Isolation to War, 1931–1941* (1968); and Roberta Wohlstetter, *Pearl Harbor: Warning and Decision* (1962).

AMERICA AT WAR

John Morton Blum, *V Was for Victory: Politics and American Culture During World War II* (1976); Eliot Janeway, *Struggle for Survival* (1951); Paul A.C. Koistinen, *The Hammer and the Sword: Labor, the Military, and Industrial Mobilization, 1920–1945* (1979); Nelson Lichtenstein, *Labor's War at Home: The CIO in World War II* (1983); Richard Lingeman, *Don't You Know There's a War On? The American Home Front, 1941–1945* (1970); Donald Nelson, *Arsenal of Democracy: The Story of American War Production* (1946); Richard Polenberg, *The War and Society: The United States, 1941–1945* (1972); Harold G. Vatter, *The U.S. Economy in World War II* (1985); and Gerald T. White, *Billions for Defense: Government Finance by the Defense Plant Corporations During World War II* (1980).

SOCIAL CHANGES DURING THE WAR

Karen Anderson, *Wartime Women: Sex Roles, Family Relations, and the Status of Women During World War II* (1981); Chester W. Gregory, *Women in Defense Work During World War II: An Analysis of the Labor Problem and Women's Rights* (1974); Susan M. Hartmann, *The Home Front and Beyond: American Women in the 1940s* (1982); Leila J. Rupp, *Mobilizing Women for the War: German and American Propaganda, 1939–1945* (1978); A. Russell Buchanan, *Black Americans in World War II* (1977); Dominic J. Capeci, Jr., *The Harlem Riot of 1943* (1977); Dominic J. Capeci, Jr., *Race Relations in Wartime Detroit: The Sojourner Truth Housing Controversy of 1942* (1984); Richard M. Dalfiume, *Desegregation of the U.S. Armed Forces: Fighting on the Front, 1939–1953* (1969); Mauricio Mazon, *The Zoot-Suit Riots: The Psychology of Symbolic Annihilation* (1984); August Meier and Elliot Rudwick, *CORE . . . 1942–1968* (1973); Gunnar Myrdal, *An American Dilemma* (1944); Neil Wynn, *The Afro-American and the Second World War* (1976); Robert Shogun and Thomas Craig, *The Detroit Race Riot* (1964); Roger Daniels, *Concentration Camps USA: Japanese Americans and World War II* (1971); Richard Drinnon, *Keeper of Concentration Camps: Dillon S. Myer and American Racism* (1987); Audrie Girdner and Anne Loftig, *The Great Betrayal: The Evacuation of the Japanese-Americans During World War II* (1969); and Peter H. Irons, *Justice at War: The Story of the Japanese American Internment Cases* (1983).

THE WAR IN EUROPE

Robert Beitzell, *The Uneasy Alliance: America, Britian and Russia, 1941–1943* (1972); James McGregor Burns, *Roosevelt: Soldier of Freedom* (1970); Diane Shaver Clemens, *Yalta* (1970); Kent Roberts Greenfield, *American Strategy in World War II: A Reconsideration* (1967); Eric Larrabee, *Commander in Chief: Franklin Delano Roosevelt, His Lieutenants, and Their War* (1987); Ronald Schaffer, *Wings of Judgment: American Bombing in World War II* (1985); Bradley F. Smith, *The Shadow Warriors: O.S.S. and the Origins of the C.I.A.* (1983); Gaddis Smith, *American Diplomacy During the Second World War, 1941–1945* (1965); John Snell, *Illusion and Necessity: The Diplomacy of World War II* (1963); and Mark A. Stoler, *The Politics of the Second Front: American Military Planning and Diplomacy in Colation Warfare, 1941–1943* (1973).

THE WAR IN THE PACIFIC

Gar Alperovitz, *Atomic Diplomacy: Hiroshima and Potsdam* (1965); Robert Butow, *Japan's Decision to Surrender* (1954); Herbert Feis, *The Atomic Bomb and the End of World War II* (1966); Greg Herkin, *The Winning Weapon: The Atomic Bomb in the Cold War, 1945–1950* (1980); Robert Jungk, *Brighter Than a Thousand Suns: A Personal History of the Atomic Scientists* (1958); Dan Kurzman, *Day of the Bomb: Countdown to Hiroshima* (1986); Martin J. Sherwin, *A World Destroyed: The Atomic Bomb and the Grand Alliance* (1975); Ronald H. Spector, *Eagle Against the Sun: The American War With Japan* (1984).

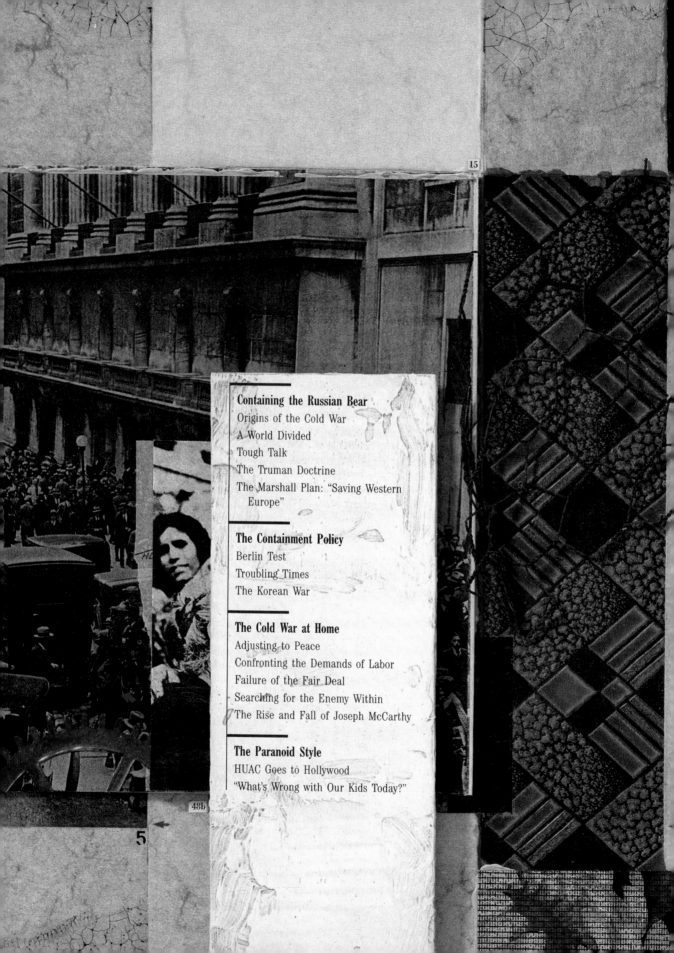

CHAPTER 26

Waging Peace and War

U.S. SHIP SUNK BY

NO LIVES LOST ABOARD
TORPEDOED TRANSPORT

Fig. 113(bb)

It was Sunday, August 27, 1948. Whittaker Chambers appeared calm as he answered questions on *Meet the Press*, a weekly radio news show. The appearance, like most of Chambers's life, was a deception. He knew he was on enemy ground, and that questions were the ammunition of the war. "I sought not to let myself be crowded," he later recalled, "not to lose my temper during the baiting." Chambers sat very still, waiting for the inevitable question. He didn't have to wait long. Edward T. Folliard, a reporter for the Washington *Post*, asked, "Are you willing to say now that Alger Hiss is or ever was a Communist?" Chambers paused a second before answering, for the answer could open him up to a slander or libel suit. Then came his terse, important reply: "Alger Hiss was a Communist and may be now." Like his questioners, Chambers also knew how to use words as weapons.

The road to *Meet the Press* had begun for Chambers a generation and a lifetime before 1948. It was paved with unhappiness. His father, Jay, was almost a stranger in his own house. For a time Jay left his wife Laha; after three years he returned. He demonstrated no love or affection for his wife or children. Whittaker remembers that Jay—who never allowed his children to call him "Papa"—dined alone and seldom spoke, except perhaps to say "don't." Home experiences left Chambers rebellious and feeling unwanted. He was forced to withdraw from Columbia for writing a mildly sacrilegious play, and he flirted with radical political philosophies, moved through a succession of love affairs, and kicked about Europe. In 1926 his brother Richard committed suicide. It was the most painful event in Chambers's life. For several months he was inconsolable. Almost as a form of therapy, he committed himself fully to another family—the communist party. During his time of troubles, it gave his life a direction and a purpose.

During the late 1920s and early 1930s, as the United States sank deeper and deeper into the Great Depression, other Americans joined Chambers in the Communist party. Feeling betrayed by the capitalistic order, they looked toward the Soviet Union for economic and political inspiration. Under Joseph Stalin, Russia appeared less affected by the depression than the capitalistic West. Still more Americans joined the Communist party because only Russia seemed to be standing up against the fascist threat posed by Hitler, Mussolini, and Franco. For Chambers and his comrades, then, the Red Star represented the future and the best hope of the world.

Chambers met Alger Hiss in 1934, when they both belonged to the same communist "cell" in Washington, D.C. In appearance and personality they were almost perfect opposites. Chambers was overweight and sloppy; his clothes always seemed rumpled, and his face had a sleepy, slightly disinterested cast. Hiss was cut from different cloth. Handsome, thin, aristocratic looking, Hiss's career was marked by ambition and achievement. He was an honors student at Johns Hopkins and Harvard Law School; he was a favorite of future Supreme Court justice Felix Frankfurter; he clerked for the legendary Oliver Wendell Holmes. Popular with influential superiors and his co-workers, Hiss obviously had been singled out as one of the best and brightest, as one who would succeed. And he did. He acted as a counsel for the Agricultural Adjustment Administration, worked for the Senate committee investigating the munitions industry, went to the Yalta Conference with President Roosevelt, helped to organize the United Nations, and served as the president of the Carnegie Endowment for International Peace.

During his impressive career, Hiss worked with Whittaker Chambers for the Communist party. While Hiss served as a legal assistant for the Senate committee investigation of the munitions industry, he became close friends with Chambers. Hiss allowed Chambers to use his Washington, D.C., apartment for two months, gave him an automobile, and even permitted him to stay in his home on several occasions. Although Hiss would later deny that he knew Chambers—and then admit that he knew him slightly under a different name—the evidence is clear on one point: the bureaucrat and spy had formed a close friendship. It was during that period of friendship in the mid-1930s, Chambers later testified, that Hiss began to give him secret government documents.

The conviction of Alger Hiss (left)—accused of being a spy in the 1930s by Whittaker Chambers (right)—caused many Americans to believe the nation was threatened by internal subversion.

Like many of his American comrades, Chambers abandoned the ideology of Communism and lost faith in the Soviet Union during the late 1930s. There were sound reasons for his break with the CP. For the true believers of the early 1930s, the Soviet Union was the light that failed. By 1938 news of Stalin's purges, which would eventually lead to the death of millions of Russians, had reached the West. Such gross disregard for humanity shook many American communists. In addition, in 1939 Stalin signed a nonaggression pact with Hitler's Germany. Once seen as the bulwark against Nazi expansion, Russia now joined Germany in dividing Poland. Although during World War II the United States and the Soviet Union were forced together as allies, communist ideology ceased to attract many American followers.

Chambers not only quit the Communist party, he turned against it with vengeful wrath. As an editor for *Time* magazine, he openly criticized communist tactics and warned about the evils of the Soviet Union. Time only increased his rage. Finally in 1948 he went before the House Un-American Activities Committee (HUAC) and told his life story, carefully naming all his former CP friends and associates. Of all the people he named, the one who attracted the

most attention was the brilliant young New-Dealer Alger Hiss.

Of course Hiss denied Chambers's allegations. He too appeared before HUAC. Well-dressed and relaxed despite a too tight collar, he testified, "I am not and never have been a member of the Communist Party . . . I have never followed the Communist Party line, directly or indirectly. To the best of my knowledge, none of my friends is a Communist." As he answered questions, he smiled and confidently stood on his record of public service. Unlike his nervous, rumpled accuser, Hiss was the picture of placid truthfulness. His testimony satisfied most of the committee members, even the Republicans.

He satisfied most, but not all. After hearing both Chambers and Hiss, Richard Nixon, a junior congressman from California, still wasn't sure Hiss was as innocent as he seemed. As one psycho-historian bluntly put it, Hiss "was everything Nixon was not." Nixon's struggling background contrasted sharply with Hiss's career, and Nixon believed Hiss treated him "like dirt." At Nixon's insistence, Hiss and Chambers were brought together face to face before HUAC. At that meeting, Chambers demonstrated his encyclopedic knowledge about Hiss, his family, and his life. He discussed the furniture in Hiss's house and Hiss's hobbies. He showed beyond any doubt that he had been close to Hiss. For once Hiss's confident equanimity vanished. He challenged Chambers to make his accusations in public, where he would not be protected against a libel suit.

Chambers accepted the challenge, and on *Meet the Press* he repeated his charges. Hiss hesitated for a month and then sued Chambers for defamation. During the involved trials which followed, Chambers proved his case. He even produced a series of classified, microfilmed documents which he had stored in a hollowed-out pumpkin on his Maryland farm. Experts testified that the classified documents had been written in Hiss's hand or typed on Hiss's Woodstock typewriter. Hiss was indicted for perjury by a federal grand jury. Although the first trial ended in a hung jury, the second trial was far less satisfactory for Hiss. In January 1950 he was found guilty and sentenced to five years in prison.

The Hiss-Chambers affair was one of the major episodes of the late 1940s. It was a time of momentous changes. America reversed its isolationist tradition in world affairs and accepted the responsibilities and problems of world leadership. Across the globe it clashed with Russia over a series of symbolic and real issues. Labeled the Cold War, these ideological and economic battles affected American domestic and foreign policy. During the late 1940s and early 1950s Americans attacked the communist threat inside as well as outside the United States. In an atmosphere charged with fear, anxiety, paranoia, and hatred, the United States waged peace and war with equal emotional intensity.

CONTAINING THE RUSSIAN BEAR

During World War II, when the United States and the Soviet Union were allies, Joseph Stalin was known as Uncle Joe. The media portrayed him as a stern but fair leader and pictured communism as strikingly like capitalism. Even Hol-

lywood cooperated in this image-making process. Warner Brothers's *Mission to Moscow* (1943), Sam Goldwyn's *North Star* (1943), MGM's *Song of Russia* (1943), and Frank Capra's *Battle of Russia* all emphasized pro-Soviet themes. *Mission to Moscow* was particularly kind to Stalin, who appeared on screen as a gentle, pipe-smoking, sad-eyed friend of America.

In reality Stalin was a determined, ruthless leader who had over the years systematically eliminated his actual and suspected political rivals. Between 1933 and 1938 he removed over 850,000 members of the Communist party, and perhaps one million more died in labor camps. He was apparently suspicious of almost everyone inside and outside of Russia. If his attitude was extreme, it was not totally irrational. Twice in his lifetime Russia had been invaded from the West. Twice Germans had pushed into his country, killing millions upon millions of Russians. Russia suffered an estimated 12,150,000 casualties in World War I and 27,500,000 in World War II. For Stalin, the West stood unalterably opposed to communism. He would take what he could from the West, but he would never trust westerners.

Stalin, however, was not the only suspicious world leader. The newest western leader, President Harry Truman, was wary of Stalin, but did not exactly regard him as the enemy, at least not in 1945. After all, Russia and America had been allies during World War II. When Truman took office on April 12, 1945, he assumed he could deal with Stalin. Advisors told him that Stalin was a tough, no-nonsense leader. These were characteristics that the tough, no-nonsense Truman could appreciate. His first meeting with Stalin at Potsdam confirmed his initial assessment of the Russian leader. "I like Stalin," Truman wrote his wife Bess. "He is straightforward. Knows what he wants and will compromise when he can't get it."

Potsdam was the light before the long dark tunnel. Truman was overly optimistic about his ability to work with Stalin. Totally different backgrounds and philosophies separated the two leaders from the start, and the directions in which they led their countries drove them further apart. The United States and the Soviet

The onset of the Cold War was due in part to the growing divergence between the United States and the Soviet Union after World War II. At Potsdam, Britain's Prime Minister Clement Attlee, President Truman, and Stalin tried unsuccessfully to decide the future of Poland and Germany.

Union emerged from World War II as the two most powerful countries in the world. Both countries were inexperienced as world leaders, but both knew exactly what they wanted, and what they wanted guaranteed future conflicts. The Cold War was the result.

Origins of the Cold War

For western leaders and their diplomats, World War II had a successful but not a neat ending. Too many questions were left unanswered, too many issues unresolved. At Yalta and then at Potsdam the leaders of Russia, England, and the United States discussed the future of Poland and Germany, but they arrived at no firm conclusions. Afraid of further straining the already uneasy wartime alliance, they decided to leave such thorny issues to the future. The future arrived in August 1945 after America dropped two atomic bombs on Japan. The fates of Eastern Europe and Germany were as yet undetermined as was the relationship between the United States and the Soviet Union.

When Germany invaded Poland in early September 1939, England and France came to the aid of Poland. Russia did not. Instead, Russia invaded Poland from the east and gobbled up a large section of the country. In 1941, however, Germany invaded Russia and forced Stalin to join the Grand Alliance against Hitler. For the remainder of World War II, Russia battled heroically against Germany on the Eastern Front. The West contributed massive amounts of weapons and supplies in this theater of war; but it was the Red Army working alone that drove the Germans out of Eastern Europe. When the war ended, Russia controlled all of Eastern Europe from Stettin on the Baltic Sea to Trieste on the Adriatic Sea.

Had Russia liberated Eastern Europe, or simply replaced Germany as the master of the region? That was the crucial question of 1945. The debate centered on the fate of Poland. Truman insisted that the Soviets allow free and democratic elections in Poland. Certainly, Truman conceded, Russia had the right to expect any Polish government to be friendly toward the Soviet Union, but he expected Stalin to give Poland its complete freedom. In America Poland's fate was no abstract diplomatic issue. Millions of Americans of Eastern European origins pressed Truman to take a tough stand. Truman complied. He told Soviet Foreign Minister V. M. Molotov that America would not tolerate Poland being made into a Russian puppet state. His speech was salted with profanity—"words of one syllable," Truman described them—and Molotov remarked, "I have never been talked to like that in my life."

Truman's mule-skinner language, however, did not impress Stalin. The Soviet leader had survived a harsh youth, a brutal prison term, a lonely exile, a revolution, and two world wars. He was not now about to give away Poland or any other territory the Red Army occupied simply because of Truman's colorful phrases. Twice during the twentieth century Germany had invaded Russia through Poland. Stalin was determined it would never happen again. As he had bluntly stated at Yalta, "For the Russian people, the question of Poland is not only a question of honor but also a question of security . . . of life and death for the Soviet Union."

Confronted by an inflexible opponent, Truman played his trump card. He threatened to cut off economic aid to the Soviet Union. Devastated by World War II, Russia needed the aid, but Stalin believed Poland was even more important. Rather than abandon Poland, Russia accepted the loss of American money. In the end, Truman was powerless. Americans would certainly not accept a war with Russia to reliberate Poland, and the Soviet Union was not about to leave Poland voluntarily. Although there was no war, there was one important casualty: relations between America and Russia were strained to the breaking point.

A World Divided

The controversy over Poland indicated the direction of postwar Soviet-American relations. The two countries were divided by substantial issues, the most important of which was the degree of control over other nations. At the end of the war both nations occupied large areas of land. America's control was based on the strength of its economy as much as its military position. Even as the country demobilized, American leaders were confident that they could use foreign aid to exert influence on the future development of the world. Russia's control in all of Eastern Europe—Hungary, Romania, Bulgaria, and Czechoslovakia, as well as Poland—depended on the physical presence of the Red Army. Stalin freely granted America and England their spheres of influence, but he wanted the West to recognize his own.

Truman refused. A believer in national self-determination and the virtues of democracy, he opposed Stalin's use of military force as a diplomatic weapon. As he told Averell Harriman, America's ambassador to the Soviet Union, the United States might not expect to obtain one hundred percent of what it wanted, but "we should be able to get eighty-five percent." The irony of the United States position was clearly seen by political commentator Walter Lippmann: "While the British and the Americans held firmly . . . the whole position in Africa and the Mediterranean . . . and the whole of Western Germany . . . they undertook by negotiation and diplomatic pressure to reduce Russia's position in Eastern Europe . . . ."

Approaching issues from different perspectives, Russia and America arrived at different conclusions. After World War II ended, they agreed on very little. The fate of Germany illustrates the basic conflict between the two powers. Russia wanted to punish Germany by stripping the country of its industry and imposing harsh reparation payments. Only a prostrate Germany, unarmed and unthreatening, would satisfy Stalin. As Truman lost confidence in the Soviet Union, he came to believe in the need for a strong Germany to act as a block against Russian expansion. The result of these conflicting approaches was a divided Germany. Occupied by the Red Army, East Germany became a Soviet satellite. West Germany fell under the American, British, and French sphere of influence and soon became part of the postwar democratic alliance.

Control over atomic weapons also divided the two powers. America developed and used the first atomic bomb but realized that future world safety depended upon some plan to control the awesome potential of the weapon. Truman seemed favorable to international control

"Don't mind me—just go right on talking."   FEB. '47

Warning of worldwide destruction, this cartoon implies that the U.S. could not maintain its atomic weapon monopoly.
from *The Herblock Book* (Beacon Press, 1952)

of the world's fissionable materials publicly. Privately he used the threat of the bomb in his negotiations with the Soviet Union. America, Secretary of War Henry L. Stimson commented, wore the "weapon rather ostentatiously on our hip." Stalin reacted with suspicion and bitterness to this contradictory policy, distrusting any atomic control plan that originated in the United States. At a high-level meeting in the Kremlin he announced his own plan: "A single demand of you, comrades: Provide us with atomic weapons in the shortest possible time. You know that Hiroshima has shaken the whole world. The equilibrium has been destroyed. Provide the bomb. It will remove a great danger from us." The result was an atomic arms race, not international cooperation.

By early 1946 United States-Soviet relations were irreparably strained. In February 1946, Stalin warned all Soviet citizens that there would never be a lasting peace with the capitalistic West. Economic sacrifices and perhaps more warfare lay ahead. Justice William

Douglas labeled the speech "the declaration of World War III." The next month Winston Churchill traveled to Fulton, Missouri, to give a lecture of his own. With Truman by his side, he announced that "from Stettin in the Baltic to Trieste in the Adriatic, an iron curtain has descended across the continent." Only a combined Anglo-American effort could lift the curtain. Fortunately, Churchill emphasized, "God has willed" the atomic bomb to America. Dramatic words and ominous warnings, threats and counterthreats—the Cold War clearly had been declared.

Tough Talk

Although real issues divided America and Russia, the emotionally charged rhetoric and the emergence of Cold War myths hardened the battle lines. Truman lacked the skill and the language of a diplomat, and like leaders before and after him he was trying to avoid the mistakes of the immediate past. Truman's advisors encouraged the president to take a hard line toward Russia. Remembering how the British and the French had given in to Hitler at the Munich Conference of 1938, American foreign policy makers were determined not to allow history to repeat itself. Equating Stalin's goals with Hitler's, however, was a grave mistake. Stalin was concerned more with security than expansion; he wanted to protect his country from a future attack, not initiate World War III. As George Kennan, America's leading expert on the Soviet Union, later observed, "The image of a Stalinist Russia poised and yearning to attack the West, and deterred only by our possession of atomic weapons, was largely a creation of the Western imagination."

The Munich example and the get-tough talk turned American public opinion against Russia. Leading American diplomat Dean Ache-

George Kennan

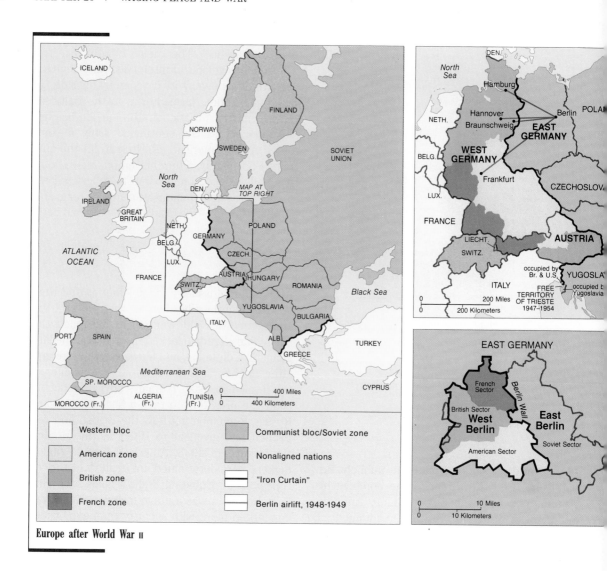

Europe after World War II

son warned, "I think it is a mistake to believe that you can, at any time, sit down with the Russians and solve problems." Comments of this sort were aired over and over in public as the media formed a new, more menacing image of Stalin. The pipe in hand and sad, soft eyes of Uncle Joe quickly faded in late 1945 and early 1946. News stories emphasized confrontation, conflict, and controversy. Talk turned no longer toward how to avoid an explosive conflict but rather how to win it. In the mind of the public, Russia soon became the once and future enemy of America.

The Truman Doctrine

America's rise as a world power was paralleled by Britain's decline. England, like much of the rest of Europe, suffered terribly during World War II. Its economy was shattered, and burned-out buildings and miles of fresh graveyards gave silent testimony to the country's physical and human losses. By early 1947 Britain could no longer stand as the leader of the Western democracies. On Friday, February 21, 1947, England passed the torch to America. The British ambassador in Washington requested an emergency meeting with Secretary of State George C. Marshall. He had "a piece of blue paper" to deliver. The quaint phrase meant in diplomatic parlance a formal and important message. Simply put, the ambassador announced that Britain could no longer economically support Greece and Turkey in their fight against communist rebels. If the two countries were to be kept as Western allies, the United States had to aid their cause. Emphasizing this point, the message concluded, "Unless urgent and immediate support is given to Greece, it seems probable that the Greek Government will be overthrown and a totalitarian regime of the extreme left will come into power."

Truman was prepared to assume the burden, but there were doubts whether the country was. Republicans had regained control of Congress in the November 1946 elections, and they were not anxious to shoulder expensive new foreign programs. In addition, rapid demobilization after World War II had drastically reduced the size and effectiveness of the American military forces. Still, something had to be done. Truman's advisors and congressional leaders, recommended that he speak directly to the American people. But as Republican Senator Arthur Vandenberg warned, to win public support the president would have to "scare the hell out of the American people."

On March 12, 1947, Truman appeared before a joint session of Congress and described the Greek situation as a battle between the forces of light and the legions of darkness. "At the present moment in world history nearly every nation must choose between alternative ways of life," he said. "One way of life is based upon the will of the majority, and is distinguished by free institutions, representative government, free elections, guarantees of individual liberty, freedom of speech and religion, and freedom from political oppression. The second way of life is based upon the will of a minority forcibly imposed upon the majority. It relies upon terror and oppression . . . ." Congress sounded its approval as Truman came to his climactic sentence: "I believe that it must be the policy of the United States to support free peoples who are resisting attempted subjugation by armed minorities or outside pressures." La-

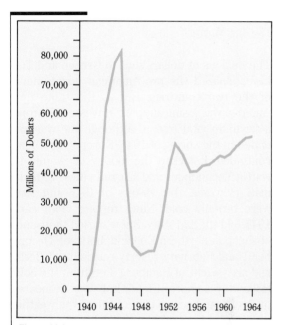

Figure 26.1
National Defense Budgets, 1940–1964

beled the Truman Doctrine, the statement set the course United States foreign policy would follow during the next generation.

Specifically, Truman called for economic aid to "save" Greece and Turkey. Congress responded by appropriating $400 million. By later standards it was a paltry sum, but it was a significant beginning. In the future, America would send billions of dollars in economic and military aid to countries fighting communism, even though the leaders of some of those nations were themselves dictators. In Truman's morality play, however, "anti-communists" and "free peoples" became synonymous.

Although Truman succeeded in getting aid for Greece and Turkey and in arousing the American public, a few foreign policy experts believed that his scare tactics did more harm than good. George Kennan deplored the sweeping language of the Truman Doctrine which placed United States aid to Greece "in the framework of a universal policy rather than in that of a specific decision addressed to a specific set of circumstances."

The Marshall Plan: "Saving Western Europe"

The millions of dollars sent to Greece and Turkey stabilized the pro-American governments of the two countries. But at the same time America was losing support in Western Europe, a far more vital region. Although the war had ended in the spring of 1945, Europe's problems continued. It lacked the money to rebuild its wartorn economies and scarred cities. To make matters worse, the winters of 1946 and 1947 were brutally cold. News reports from early 1947 told the sad story. Snow buried thousands of sheep in northern England; between December 1 and February 8, forty residents of Berlin and sixty-eight of Hamburg died from the cold; Holland was short of food; Italy was inundated by floods; and across the continent the weather report was always the same: "cold or very cold." The winter hardships fueled the Communist party, which made marked gains. Anne O'Hare McCormick told Americans in the *New York*

Under the Marshall Plan, one of many shipments to arrive overseas was this load of 209 American-made tractors delivered to France.

Times, "The extent to which democratic government survives on [the] continent depends on how far this country is willing to help it survive."

Truman concurred, and so did his advisors. They were distressed by the growth of anti-Americanism in Europe, an area that figured prominently in their postwar economic plans. The image of America had changed from loyal ally to selfish exploiter. Describing the typical occupation soldier in Germany, an army chaplain wrote, "There he stands in his bulging clothes, fat, overfed, lonely, a bit wistful, seeing little, understanding less—the Conqueror, with a chocolate bar in one pocket and a package of cigarettes in the other . . . . The chocolate bar and the cigarettes are about all that he, the Conqueror, has to give the conquered."

At the Harvard University commencement on June 5, Secretary of State Marshall announced a plan to give Europe more. After describing the severe problems facing Europe, Marshall suggested that America could not afford to send a Band-Aid to cover the deep European wounds. Europe needed massive economic blood transfusions. He told his audience that the cost might well range upward to $17 billion. Without America's help, however, "economic, social, and political deterioration of a very grave character" would result. And from a more selfish point of view, America needed a strong democratic Europe to provide rich markets for American goods and to act as a check against Russian westward expansion.

Congress trimmed the Marshall Plan down to $12.5 billion, but few Europeans quibbled about the difference. The program put food in the mouths of hungry children, coal in empty furnaces, and money in near-empty banks. Americans were proud of the Marshall Plan, and Europeans were moved by it. Winston Churchill judged it "the most unsordid act in history." And Hugh Gaitskell, British chancellor of the exchequer, noted: "We are not an emotional people . . . and not very articulate, but these characteristics should not . . . hide the real and profound sense of gratitude toward the American people." All told, the Marshall Plan greatly restored America's prestige abroad.

THE CONTAINMENT POLICY

Money, even billions of dollars, could not substitute for a concrete foreign policy to guide United States actions: an explicit policy that mixed the international idealism of the Truman Doctrine and the economic realism of the Marshall Plan with the will to meet the real or perceived Russian threat. The policy was not long in coming. In July 1947, the journal *Foreign Affairs* contained an article entitled "The Sources of Soviet Conduct" by "Mr. X." The article provided a blueprint for the policy of containment, which would influence American foreign policy for at least the next generation.

"Mr. X" was George Kennan, the government's foremost authority on Russian history (see p. 855). Educated at Princeton University, Kennan had spent his adult life in the United States foreign service where he carefully studied the Soviet scene. During World War II he was stationed in Moscow, and was able to observe Soviet political behavior. Although he believed Russians were a "great and appealing people," he distrusted the Soviet government. In February 1946, he expressed his views of the Soviet Union in an 8000 word telegram to his superiors in Washington, and in the 1947 *Foreign Affairs* article, Kennan made his views public. He regarded communism as a pseudoreligion, a movement that simply could not be totally eliminated. It could, however, be *contained* to its present borders by a politically, economically, and militarily active United States. What was needed was "the adroit and vigilant application of counterforce at a series of constantly shifting geographical and political points, corresponding to the shifts and maneuvers of Soviet policy."

Although Kennan later remarked that he was talking about the political containment of a political threat, in 1947 his article was read as primarily a military blueprint. As such, it satisfied hard-liners but was challenged by many other politicians and respected political commentators. Walter Lippmann challenged Kennan's policy in *The Cold War: A Study in U. S. Foreign Policy* (1947). Containment, Lippmann commented, allowed Russia largely to decide when and where its battles against America would take place. If followed it might well lead America into a land war in Asia where the idea of victory would be a cruel delusion. Lippmann found it "hard to understand how Mr. X could have recommended such a strategic monstrosity."

Containment involved confronting the spread of communism across the globe and as Americans soon learned, it came with a heavy price. It meant supporting our allies around the world with billions of dollars in military and economic aid, and it meant thousands of Americans dying in foreign lands. Since containment was a defensive policy, it involved permanent Cold War without any hope of ultimate victory. Unlike World War I and World War II, the Cold War emphasized the doctrine of limited wars fought for limited goals. An in this arrangement, Kennan noted, "Man would have to recognize . . . that the device of military coercion would have . . . only relative—never an absolute—value in the pursuit of political objectives." It was a policy bound to breed frustration and anxiety—certain to influence domestic as well as foreign policy.

Berlin Test

During the late 1940s containment seemed to fit American needs. An early test of it came in Berlin, a divided city located in the heart of East Germany, deep within the Russian zone. Nikita Khrushchev called democratic West Berlin a "bone in the throat" of Russia. In June 1948, Stalin decided to remove the bone by stopping all road and rail traffic between West Germany and Berlin. It was a crisis tailor-made for the containment policy. Stalin had picked the time and place. Now Truman had to decide upon a response.

He chose the sky. Stalin could close highways and railways, but he could not legally close the skyways. For almost one year America and Britain kept West Berlin alive and democratic by a massive airlift. Food, coal, clothing, and all other essentials were flown daily into Berlin. It was an heroic feat, a triumph of technology. Western pilots logged 277,264 flights

The Soviet blockade in Berlin was broken by the airlift during 1948–49. Over 7000 tons of food and fuel were provided for West Berliners during the crisis.

into West Berlin; they hauled in 2,343,315 tons of food, fuel, medicine, and clothing. Finally on May 12, 1949, Stalin lifted his blockade of West Berlin. Containment had passed an important test.

Troubling Times

Truman scored a series of triumphs during 1947 and 1948. The Truman Doctrine, the Marshall Plan, and the Berlin Airlift strengthened his popularity at home and United States prestige abroad. In the election of 1948 Truman won a remarkable upset victory over Thomas E. Dewey. Then in 1949 eleven of the Western democracies joined the United States in signing the North Atlantic Treaty Organization (NATO), a mutual defense pact. NATO signified America's position as the leader of the Western Alliance, and it conformed to the containment policy. But difficult times for Truman, containment, and America lay ahead. In late August 1949, American scientists detected traces of radioactive material in the Soviet atmosphere. The cause was as clear as a mushroom-shaped cloud. Russia had the bomb—a full decade before American intelligence expected it.

On September 22 Truman told the public: "We have evidence that an atomic explosion occurred in the USSR." Although the press tried to downplay the story, a wave of anxiety swept the country. Physicist Harold C. Urey told reporters, "There is only one thing worse than one nation having the atomic bomb— that's two nations having it." There was another thing even worse: the fact that one of the nations which had the bomb also had the Red Army.

Between 1945 and 1949 the threat of the bomb had given teeth to American policy. It was America's check to the Red Army, and United States policy makers seldom allowed Soviet leaders to forget it. In 1945 then Secretary of State James F. Byrnes told his Soviet counterpart V. M. Molotov, "If you don't cut out all this stalling and let us get down to work, I am going to pull an atomic bomb out of my hip pocket and let you have it." Now Molotov had one in his hip pocket. Truman responded by asking his scientists to accelerate the development of a hydrogen bomb; and Congress responded by voting appropriations for Truman's latest defense requests. Of such events and decisions arms races have their humble origins.

On the heels of the Russian bomb came more unwelcome news—the establishment of the communist government in China after a bitter civil war. The war between Mao Tse-tung's and Chou En-lai's Communists and Chiang Kai-shek's Nationalists had been raging since the 1930s. The United States had strongly backed Chiang during the civil war, providing him with more than $3 billion in aid between 1945 and 1949. But the aid was unable to prop up a government that was structurally unsound, inefficient, and corrupt. In the first week of May 1949, Chiang fled across the Formosa Strait to Taiwan, and on September 21, Mao proclaimed Red China's sovereignty. With Chiang in Taiwan and Mao on the mainland, China became a tale of two countries.

The Truman administration tried to put the best face possible on the turn of events. Secretary of State Dean Acheson issued a thousand-page White Paper explaining how Mao had won the civil war. It detailed the rampant corruption in the Nationalist government and Chiang's many mistakes. Assessing the role of the United States in the outcome of the conflict Acheson

The celebration of the first anniversary of Mao Tse-tung's rule in 1950 brought many to the streets of Peking.

concluded, "Nothing that this country did or could have done within the reasonable limits of its capabilities could have changed that result . . . it was the product of internal Chinese forces, forces which this country tried to influence but could not."

For the American public, however, that explanation was not good enough. The China most Americans knew, as one historian put it, was associated with "Pearl Buck's peasants, rejoicing in the good earth . . . dependable, democratic, warm, and above all pro-American." It was an image that American missionaries confirmed during the 1920s and 1930s and one which journalists supported during World War II. Americans were told that there were two types of Asians—the good Chinese and the evil Japanese. In 1941 *Time* magazine even ran an article entitled "How to Tell Your Friends From the Japs." It confidently reported, "the Chinese expression is likely to be more placid, kindly, open; the Japanese more positive, dogmatic, arrogant."

Republicans and supporters of Chiang in America blamed Truman for "losing" China. Led by Henry Luce, the influential publisher of *Time* and *Life* who was the China-born son of

The Cold War took on a new dimension in 1949 when Americans learned that Russia had broken the U.S. nuclear monopoly.

American missionaries, an informal group known as the China Lobby blasted the Truman administration. They claimed "egg-sucking phony liberals" had "sold China into atheistic slavery." The China Lobby believed that America had far more influence than it actually had, that a country that contained six percent of the earth's population could control the other ninety-four percent. They were wrong, but millions of Americans took their loud cries seriously.

"China lost itself," Acheson countered. "We picked a bad horse," Truman admitted. But given the political pressure at home, Truman was not about to change mounts in the middle of the race. Reversing America's traditional policy of recognizing *de facto* governments whether approved or not, Truman refused to recognize the communist People's Republic of China. Instead he insisted that Chiang's Nationalist government on Taiwan was the legitimate government of China. It was an unrealistic policy, but one that future presidents found politically difficult to reverse. The United States and the People's Republic of China did not establish formal relations until 1979.

The Korean War

The rhetoric of the Truman administration tended to simplify complex issues, intensify the Cold War rivalry and to tie foreign policy to domestic politics. Failure abroad could have calamitous consequences for politicians at home. "If you can't stand the heat, get out of the kitchen," Truman often said. By 1950 the kitchen had become hotter. After "China fell," Truman was more than ever determined to contain communism.

The mood of the Truman administration is clearly evident in National Security Council Paper Number 68 (NSC 68), one of the most important documents of the Cold War. Completed in April of 1950, it expressed the views of foreign policy planner Paul Nitze and Dean Acheson that communism is a monolithic world movement directed from the Kremlin; it advocated "an immediate and large-scale build-up in our military and general strength of our allies with the intention of righting the power balance and in the hope that through means other than all-out war we could induce a change in the nature of the Soviet system." NSC 68 extended

American occupation troops stationed in Japan joined South Korean allies in a retreat to the southeast area of Korea where they managed to hold off the North Korean forces.

the Truman Doctrine and called for America to protect the world against the spread of communism. The cost would be great—NSC 68 estimated it at twenty percent of the gross national product—but planners warned that without the commitment America faced the prospect of a world moving toward communism.

Truman realized that NSC 68 "meant a great military effort in time of peace. It meant doubling or tripling the budget, increasing taxes heavily, and imposing various kinds of economic controls." And he doubted whether Congress would accept such a peacetime build-up. He never got a chance to find out, for in June 1950 America went to war in Korea.

Korea, like Germany, was a divided country. North of the 38th parallel, Communist Kim Il Sung governed North Korea. Supported by the Soviet Union, Kim forged a modern, disciplined army during the late 1940s. In South Korea, seventy-five-year-old President Syngman Rhee who received strong aid and support from the United States, opposed any reconciliation with the communist North Korea. But, as Secretary of State Acheson noted in an unfortunate speech before the National Press Club on January 12, 1950, South Korea lay outside America's primary "defense perimeter." As far as military security of South Korea was concerned, Acheson emphasized, should "an attack occur the initial resistance" must come from "the people attacked."

On June 25, 1950, the attack occurred. In an orderly, coordinated offensive, North Korea sent 90,000 men across the 38th parallel into South Korea. They faced a weak, disorderly South Korean army, aptly described as "little more than a constabulary." It was a mismatch of epic proportions, and South Korean troops quickly mounted an all-out retreat. As the monsoon rains drenched the rice paddies and mountains, Korea moved swiftly toward unification under Kim's communist government.

Why did North Korea attack? At the time, the Truman administration believed that the Soviets directed the assault. It regarded Kim as little more than a puppet whose strings were manipulated in Moscow. There is little evidence, however, to support this contention. More likely internal Korean politics dictated the

In October 1950, when hopes were high for total victory in Korea, Truman met with General MacArthur at Wake Island.

course of events. Kim's position in North Korea was by no means secure. He faced organized opposition from a Democratic Front for the Unification of the Fatherland. The invasion of South Korea, therefore, may have been launched to undercut that movement. Certainly Kim informed Stalin of the impending invasion, but the idea and the timing were probably his own.

Truman had just finished a Saturday dinner in Independence, Missouri, when Acheson telephoned him with news of the invasion. His reaction was as rapid and as certain as North Korea's attack. Since both Koreas were technically wards of the United Nations, the Truman administration took the matter to the Security Council. With the Soviet Union absent (it was boycotting the United Nations over the refusal of the organization to seat the People's Republic of China), the Security Council by a 9 to 0

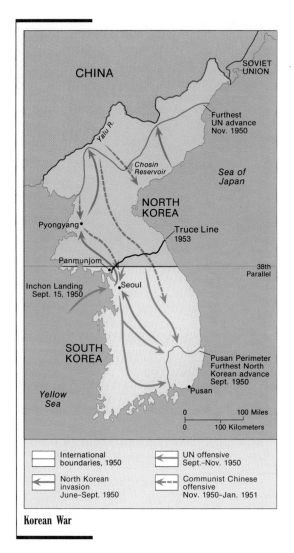

Korean War

Truman that ground forces would not be needed. Truman's advisors seemed convinced that the Asians would turn and run at the first show of Western force. Although the bombs destroyed miles of roads and bridges, they did not slow the North Korean advance.

On June 30, Truman took the fateful step of ordering American occupation troops stationed in Japan to proceed to Korea. They soon joined their South Korean allies in a headlong retreat. For six weeks the allies fell steadily back until they stabilized a perimeter in southeast Korea around the port city of Pusan. With their offensive halted, North Korean troops mounted a siege. To the surprise of the world, the Pusan perimeter held firm.

For American soldiers it had been a painful and disappointing two months. They were fighting in an unfamiliar country for an unsatisfactory objective. Truman's announced goal was simply to restore the 38th parallel as the border between the two Koreas. Victory then was defined as a stalemate. Corporal Stephen Zeg of Chicago expressed the feeling of other soldiers when he commented, "I'll fight for my country, but I'll be damned if I see why I'm fighting to save this hellhole."

But fighting they were, and General Douglas MacArthur was determined to reverse the military situation of the war. A bold, even arrogant man, firmly fixed in his opinions and certain of his ability to command in battle, MacArthur decided to split his forces and launch a surprise attack against the North Koreans' rear. On the morning of September 15, 1950, American marines began an amphibious attack on Inchon, a port city, wrote one historian, "about as large as Jersey City, as ugly as Liverpool, and as dreary as Belfast." MacArthur's military advisors warned him against the move, noting that Inchon possessed every natural and geographic handicap. MacArthur, however, was confident of victory. It was a bold, risky maneuver—a bold, risky, successful maneuver.

Faced with an enemy to their front and their rear, North Korean troops retreated across the border. By the beginning of October those North Korean soldiers who were not captured or killed were above the 38th parallel. Truman had achieved his stated objective. But

vote condemned the North Korean assault and demanded an immediate ceasefire. Encouraged by the United Nations's prompt action, Truman pledged American support to South Korea and strengthened the military position of the United States in Asia.

Truman termed the conflict a "UN police action" and, in fact, a number of United Nations members sent troops, but for all practical purposes it was a war that initially matched the United States and South Korea against North Korea. Air force advisors told Truman that they could stop the North Korean advance by bombing the communist supply line. They convinced

the warrior in MacArthur wanted more—he wanted victory on the battlefield. And he said so, loudly and publicly. In private the Truman administration was moving toward MacArthur's position. Containment was giving way to a policy of liberation. After receiving MacArthur's reassurances at a private meeting on Wake Island, Truman decided to allow United States forces to move across the 38th parallel and "liberate" North Korea. Like MacArthur's Inchon landing, it was a bold plan, predicated on the widely held American belief that Red China would not intervene in the conflict.

This time boldness failed. North Korea was a difficult country to invade. The American army had no reliable maps and mountainous terrain rendered traditional military tactics impossible. In addition, as MacArthur's forces moved recklessly north toward Manchuria, Chinese officials sent informal warnings to the United States that unless the advance stopped, their country would enter the fray. MacArthur ignored Chinese warnings and his own intelligence reports and kept moving.

Communist China struck in late November. Over 300,000 troops poured across the border and attacked unprepared American forces. An advance force of marines near the Chosin Reservoir was cut off from the main army. They made the best of a bad situation. "The enemy is in front of us, behind us, to the left of us, and to the right of us," Colonel Lewis B. "Chesty" Puller told his regiment. "They won't escape *this* time." Puller's bravado, however, could not hide the terrible truth. The entry of Communist China had brought a whole new war.

Winning the war was now out of the question. Only MacArthur continued to talk about an absolute victory. If a nation was going to fight a war, he sermonized, it should fight to win. In Washington, however, the Truman administration was shifting back to the pre-Inchon policy of containment. When MacArthur publicly criticized the administration's newest approach, an angry Truman recalled him and replaced him with General Matthew B. Ridgway. In America Truman's sacking of Mac raised a firestorm of protest. An April 1951 Gallup poll reported that sixty-six percent of Americans disapproved of Truman's firing of

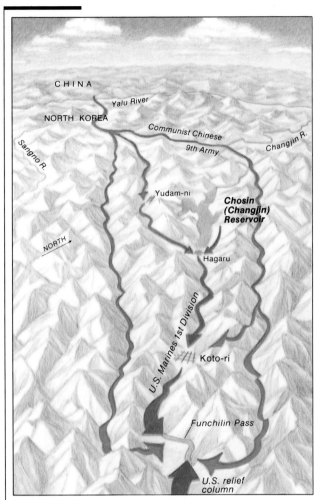

Marine Breakout from Chosin Reservoir
The Communist Chinese Forces (100,000) had set a trap for the Marines (20,000) at Chosin Reservoir. The Marines doggedly fought their way out of the mountains in weather that ranged from −30°F at night to about 0° during the day.

the general, and then in October, fifty-six percent indicated that they believed Korea was a "useless war."

The Korean War dragged on until July 10, 1951, when formal peace negotiations began, but it proved to be a long, difficult process. While diplomats talked, American soldiers fought and died. All together, 34,000 Americans were killed and 103,000 wounded during the

Korean War. When Truman left office in early 1953 the carnage still continued. Finally on July 23, 1953, the war ended as it began, with North Koreans above the 38th parallel and South Koreans below it. It was a victory for Truman's containment policy, but for millions of Americans it somehow tasted like defeat.

THE COLD WAR AT HOME

Commie for a day. It was a theme idea. It answered the question, "What would it be like to live under a Soviet-type, communist dictatorship?" On May Day 1950, at Mosinee, Wisconsin, American Legionnaires disguised themselves as Russian soldiers and staged a mock communist takeover of their town. They arrested and summarily locked up the mayor and clergymen, nationalized all businesses, confiscated all firearms, and rid the library of rows of objectional books. They even forced Mosinee residents to alter their eating habits. The local restaurants served only potato soup, dark bread, and black coffee, and only Young Communist Leaguers were permitted to eat candy. Eventually Mosinee patriots "liberated" their town, and at dusk they held a mass democratic rally amidst much patriotic music and the burning of communist literature.

For most of Mosinee's citizens it was an edifying experiment. "We really learned about what 100 percent communism would be like," one resident observed. They concluded that life under communism was hardly worth living. Many found intolerable the lack of such basic freedoms as privacy, speech, press, religion, and decent food. One participant noted, confessed, "I know some people who even drove to [neighboring] Wausau to get something to eat. In Russia I guess you wouldn't be able to get anything else anywhere."

There is an element of humor to Mosinee's Red May Day. But behind the events was a national mood that was far from funny. As Truman waged the Cold War abroad, Cold War issues gradually came to dominate the American domestic scene. During the ensuing Red Scare,

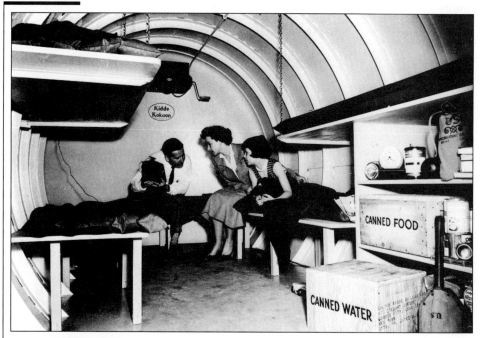

H-bomb shelters could take care of a family for three to five days and were big selling items in the 1950s. This deluxe model came equipped with five bunks and air mattresses.

the fear of communism disrupted American life, and the freedoms that Americans took for granted came under attack. At home as well as abroad, Americans battled real and imagined communist enemies.

Adjusting to Peace

Truman and his advisors approached the end of World War II with their eyes on the past. They were uneasy about the future. Memories of the Great Depression and the painful social and economic adjustment after World War I clouded their thinking. They knew that massive wartime spending, not the New Deal, had ended the decade of depression, and they worried that peace might bring more economic suffering. Peace with prosperity was their goal.

The solution to the problems of converting back to a peacetime economy, Truman believed, lay in the continuation, at least for a time, of wartime government economic controls. During the war the Office of Price Administration (OPA) had controlled prices and held inflation in check. After Japan surrendered, Truman asked Congress to continue price controls and outlined a program for economic reconversion. To ensure future prosperity, Truman advocated such economic measures as a sixty-five-cents-an-hour minimum wage, nationalization of the housing industry, and stronger fair employment practices legislation.

Congress responded half-heartedly. It did pass the Employment Act of 1946. Although it was less than Truman had requested, it did provide the institutional framework for more government control over the economy. The act created the Council of Economic Advisors to help "promote free competitive enterprise, to avoid economic fluctuations . . . and to maintain employment, production, and purchasing power." During the decades after 1946, the council exerted a powerful influence over economic policy.

On the other hand, Republicans and Southern Democrats balked against a return to more "New Dealism." One influential congressman even accused Truman of "out-dealing the New Deal." Instead, Congress destroyed the OPA by relaxing its controls, a policy that created immediate inflation. Congress's refusal to pass Truman's economic package did not tumble America into another depression. In truth, the American economy was basically sound. Wartime employment and wartime saving had created a people whose money was burning holes in their pockets. They wanted peacetime goods—automobiles, houses, Scotch whiskey, nylon stockings, and red meat. Given the demand and the short supply, inflation was inevitable. In addition, the short supply of consumer goods increased black market activities. Americans offered bribes for preferential treatment from car salesmen, butchers, and landlords. But as industries converted to peacetime production, consumer supplies rose to meet the new demands.

Confronting the Demands of Labor

The death of the OPA led to demands for higher wages as well as higher prices. During the war labor unions had taken "no strike" pledges, and through their efforts America became the "arsenal of democracy." Workers labored long and hard, agreeing to speed-ups and higher production quotas. Less than .0006 of one percent of total production time was lost to strikes.

The end of the war signaled the start of the strike season as workers demanded rewards for their wartime efforts and their loss of overtime pay. During 1946 over five million laborers struck, and 107,476,000 man-days were lost to strikes. If labor's cause was just, its timing was disastrous. After clashing repeatedly with an obstreperous Congress, Truman was in no mood to coddle labor. When two national railway brotherhoods threatened to disrupt the transportation system, Truman proposed to draft the workers. On national radio he announced, "The crisis at Pearl Harbor was the result of action by a foreign enemy. The crisis tonight is caused by a group of men within our country who place their private interests above the welfare of the nation." Confronted by hostile public opinion and an unsympathetic president, the brotherhoods went back to work.

Labor was angry. United Mine Workers leader John L. Lewis told reporters, "You can't mine coal with bayonets." As winter approached, Lewis took his men out on strike. The prospect of a cold winter created anxiety, and Truman reacted angrily. He threatened to take over the mines and lashed out publicly at the defiant Lewis. Finally Truman appealed directly to the miners, asking them to go back to work for the good and warmth of the nation. It worked. Lewis called off the strike. Truman's prestige and confidence soared.

Truman's gains were labor's losses. The congressional elections of 1946, which brought the conservative Republican-controlled Eightieth Congress, added to labor's problems. Led by Robert Taft, Congress pushed through the Taft-Hartley Labor Act of 1947, which was passed over Truman's veto. It outlawed the closed shop, gave presidents power to delay strikes by declaring a "cooling-off" period, and curtailed the political and economic power of organized labor. The act signified the conservative mood of the country.

It was a bad period for all workers, but for female workers it was especially hard. During the war they had filled a wide range of industrial jobs, but returning soldiers quickly displaced them. Some accepted the change and returned to their prewar occupations. Others resented the loss of their relatively high-paying jobs. What was worse, when new jobs opened employers hired and trained younger males rather than rehire the experienced females. Thus while male workers complained about the antilabor mood of the country, unemployed women laborers lamented the antifemale prejudices among employers.

Failure of the Fair Deal

Political experts expected America to vote Republican in the 1948 presidential elections. Truman's policies had angered liberals, labor, Southerners, and most of Congress. Moreover, Democrats had occupied the White House since 1933. Republicans reasoned that it was time for a change. They nominated Thomas E. Dewey of New York, the GOP candidate in 1944. The Democrats stayed with Truman, even though large numbers of Southerners and liberals deserted the party to follow third party movements.

An underdog from the start, Truman rolled up his sleeves and took his cause to the people. His train was the seventeen-car "Presidential Special." The rear car was the *Ferdinand Magellan*, the bullet-proof, steel-and-concrete reinforced presidential car that had been made for Roosevelt during the war. It weighed 285,000 pounds—enough to crush every other car in the train had the engineer stopped suddenly. It moved across the country, and at each stop Truman blasted the "do-nothing" Eightieth Congress. "If you send another Republican Congressman to Washington, you're a bigger bunch of suckers than I think you are," he lectured. "Give 'em hell, Harry!" was the popular refrain. By contrast, Dewey sat tight, seemingly more concerned with his fastidious appearance than his bland speeches. His cold personality failed to move American voters. "I don't know which is the chillier experience—to have Tom ignore you or shake your hand," noted a Truman supporter. "You have to get to know Dewey to dislike him," added another.

By election day Truman had closed the gap. The old Roosevelt coalition—midwestern farmers, urban ethnics, organized labor, blacks, and Southerners—remained sufficiently strong to send Truman back to the White House. The election was a testimony to the legacy of FDR as well as Truman's scrappiness, and to the often overlooked fact that Democrats outnumbered Republicans in the nation.

"Keep America Human With Truman," read one of his campaign posters. In 1949 he announced a plan to do just that. Known as the Fair Deal, the legislative package included an expansion of Social Security, federal aid to education, a higher minimum wage, federal funding for public housing projects, a national plan for medical insurance, civil rights legislation for minorities, and other measures to foster social and economic justice. As Truman explained, "I expect to give every segment of our population a fair deal."

Congress took Truman's package, stripped off the wrapping, threw away some of the contents, and sent it back to the president for his signature. Congress did extend Social Security, raise the minimum wage to seventy-five cents an hour, and further develop several New Deal programs. But the more original proposals of the Fair Deal—civil rights legislation, a national health insurance program, an imaginative farm program, and federal aid to education—were rejected by a Congress, that opposed anything defined as "creeping socialism."

Truman, as well as Congress, contributed to the ultimate failure of the Fair Deal to achieve its objectives. To be sure, Republicans and Southerners joined forces in opposition to civil rights and government spending programs. But on domestic issues Truman demonstrated an almost total inability to work with Congress. In addition, by 1949 foreign policy dominated the president's attention and claimed an increasing share of the federal budget.

Searching for the Enemy Within

While Congress removed the heart from Truman's Fair Deal, Cold War winds were chilling the country's political landscape. The tough diplomatic rhetoric of Truman, Acheson, and other policymakers encouraged Americans to view the rivalry between the Soviet Union and the United States in simplistic terms. America became the "defender of free people," Russia the "atheistic enslaver of millions." Every time a world event did not go America's way, it was seen as a Soviet victory. In this world of black-and-white thinking, the suspicion that "enemies within" America were secretly aiding the Russian cause took shape. Soon talk of American "atomic spies" giving information to the Russians and State Department officials sabotaging United States foreign policy became common.

Were spies working against American interest to further the Soviet cause? Unquestionably, yes. In 1945 Igor Gouzenko, a Soviet embassy official in Ottawa, defected to the West, carrying with him documents which detailed a communist spy ring working in Canada and the United States. The evidence led to the arrests of two British physicists, Dr. Alan Munn May and Dr. Klaus Fuchs, who had worked on the Manhattan Project. Fuchs implicated a group of American radicals—Harry Gold, David Greenglass, Morton Sobell, and Julius and Ethel Rosenberg. Clearly these individuals had passed atomic secrets to the Soviets during the war. Whether or not this information helped Russia to develop an atomic bomb is largely conjecture.

The damage done by British spies Kim Philby, Guy Burgess, and Donald Maclean is more certain. All these men held high British diplomatic and intelligence posts and were privy to sensitive American CIA and British Secret Intelligence Service (SIS) information. In 1951 Burgess and Maclean defected to Russia. In 1963 Philby joined them. There is considerable circumstantial evidence that the information they passed to Russia severely compromised American Cold War intelligence, and perhaps may have been influential in the Chinese intervention into the Korean War.

There were certainly spies; but the issue soon outgrew the question of mere espionage, and became an instrument of partisan politics. Republicans accused Democrats of being "soft" on communism—in fact, of harboring spies in the State Department and other government agencies. Richard M. Nixon, who was elected to Congress in 1946, announced that Democrats were responsible for "the unimpeded growth of the communist conspiracy in the United States." As proof Republicans pointed to the "fall" of China, the atomic bomb in Russia, and Alger Hiss in the State Department.

Truman reacted to the criticism by establishing a federal employee loyalty program that authorized the FBI to investigate all government employees. Although the search disclosed no espionage or treason, thousands of employees were forced to resign or were fired because their personal lives or past associations did not meet government inspection. Homosexuality, alcoholism, unpaid debts, contribution to left-wing causes, support of civil rights—all became grounds for dismissal.

Truman also used the anticommunism issue to drum up support for his foreign policy. At the end of World War II public opinion polls revealed that few Americans regarded communism as a serious problem. Republican charges

Widespread protesting, both for and against Julius and Ethel Rosenberg, was common after their conviction—and subsequent execution—for treason in 1951.

and Truman's loyalty program, however, encouraged citizens to profess one hundred percent Americanism. In 1947 the president sent a special "Freedom Train" across the country to exhibit important national documents, including the Truman Doctrine. By 1950 communism had become a more visible issue at home as well as abroad.

Ethel and Julius Rosenberg paid the supreme price. They were Communists, and at least one—Ethel—may have been a spy, but the death penalty was not mandatory for their crime. Judge Irving R. Kaufman, nevertheless, made an example of them. Their "diabolical conspiracy to destroy a God-fearing nation," Kaufman charged, had given Russia the bomb "years before our best scientists predicted." He ordered the couple's execution for treason. On June 19, 1953, the Rosenbergs, parents of two young sons, died in the electric chair.

The Rise and Fall of Joseph McCarthy

More than any other person, Wisconsin Senator Joseph McCarthy capitalized on the anticommunism issue. Although he did not join the crusade until 1950, the entire movement bears the name "McCarthyism." His career, which caused so much suffering for so many, illuminated the price the country had to pay for temporarily placing anticommunism above the Constitution.

Elected to the Senate in 1946, McCarthy spent four years in relative obscurity, all the while demonstrating his incompetency and angering his colleagues. Then on February 9, 1950, he gave a Lincoln's Birthday address in Wheeling, West Virginia. Warning his audience about the threat of communism to America, he boldly announced, "While I cannot take the time to name all of the men in the State Department who have been named as members of the Communist Party and members of a spy ring, I have in my hand a list of 205 . . . a list of names that were known to the Secretary of State and who nevertheless are still working and shaping the policy of the State Department." McCarthy had no real list; he had no names. Simply put, he was lying. But within days he became a national sensation.

McCarthy dealt in simple solutions for complex problems. He told Americans that the United States could control the outcome of world affairs if it would get the Communists out of the State Department. It was those "State Department perverts," those "striped-pants diplomats" who "gave away" Poland, "lost" China, and allowed Russia to develop the bomb. It was the "bright young men who are born with silver spoons in their mouths" who were "selling the Nation out." His arguments found receptive ears among Catholics who had relatives in Eastern Europe, political outsiders in this country who resented the power of the "Ivy League Eastern Establishment," supporters of Chiang, and pragmatic Republicans who wanted to return to the White House in 1952. And with the outbreak of the Korean War in the early summer of 1950, Joseph McCarthy's support grew.

McCarthy's origins were humble; he worked his way through high school and a Catholic college and intentionally cultivated the image of a bull in a china closet. With his beetle brow, he looked the part of a movie villain. He was in all ways the opposite of Secretary of State Dean Acheson, whose Ivy League degrees, waxed mustache, and aristocratic accent were a flapping red flag to McCarthy. Throughout the early 1950s McCarthy bitterly attacked "Red Dean" and the State Department. But in the end, McCarthy ferreted out no Communists, espionage agents, or traitors.

McCarthy's basic tactic was never defend. Caught in a lie, he told another; when one case dissolved, he created another. He attacked Truman and Eisenhower, Acheson and Marshall, the State Department and the United States Army. No authority or institution frightened him. In 1954 his campaign against the army became so bitter that the Senate arranged special hearings. Televised between April 22 and June 17, the Army-McCarthy hearings attracted a high audience rating. It was the first time that most Americans saw McCarthy in action—the bullying of witnesses, the cruel innuendo, the tasteless humor. At one point he attempted to ruin a young lawyer's career in order to discredit the lawyer's associate, Joseph Welch, the army's chief counsel. Welch tried to stop McCarthy but couldn't. Appalled, the chief counsel interrupted, "Until this moment, Senator, I think I never really gauged your cruelty or your recklessness . . . . If it were in my power to forgive you for your reckless cruelty, I would do so. I like to think I am a gentle man, but your forgiveness will have to come from someone other than me . . . . Have you no sense of decency, sir, at long last?"

He didn't, and a large television audience saw that he didn't. McCarthy's downfall was as rapid as his rise. When the polls showed that his popularity had swung sharply downward, his colleagues mounted an offensive. On December 2, 1954, the Senate voted to "condemn" McCarthy for his un-Senatorial behavior. Newspapers

Senator Joseph McCarthy's downfall came about as a result of his unsubstantiated charges of communist infiltration throughout the country.

THE KEFAUVER COMMITTEE

In May 1950, at the very moment that Senator Joseph McCarthy was beginning his crusade against the domestic political threat posed by communism, the United States Senate created a special committee to investigate another "enemy within": organized crime. The nation appeared to be in the midst of an unprecedented wave of lawlessness. A memorandum to the president reported that a serious crime was committed in the United States every 18.7 seconds. Aggravated assault was up 68.7 percent over prewar averages; rape was up 49.9 percent. Burglary, murder, robbery, prostitution, gambling, and racketeering all were on the increase. Criminologists attributed the postwar crime wave to such factors as wartime disruption of families, shortages of

goods during and after the war, and a continuing public demand for illicit gambling. But journalists, citizen crime commissions, and the Federal Bureau of Narcotics identified another villain, organized crime.

Estes Kefauver, an ambitious forty-seven-year-old first term Tennessee Democratic senator, originally proposed a congressional investigation of organized crime in January 1949. The Truman administration, already rocked by charges of fiscal mismanagement, financial irregularities, and favors to businessmen, feared that any inquiry might link urban Democratic political machines to criminal activities. For a time, the administration succeeded in blocking a potentially embarrassing investigation. But on April 6, 1950, the bodies of two gangsters were

found in a Kansas City, Missouri, Democratic political club under a photograph of President Truman. The Democratic-controlled Senate quickly authorized the investigation of organized crime.

For the next fifteen months, the committee held hearings in fourteen major cities and took testimony from more than 800 witnesses. The committee immediately attracted national attention by linking individuals close to Florida's Democratic governor, Fuller Warren, to a book-making syndicate controlled by Al Capone's mob in Chicago. Subsequent hearings in Kansas City and Chicago revealed widespread examples of political corruption and influence peddling.

Television made the Kefauver committee's hearings among the most influential in American history. While the Kefauver committee did not hold the first televised congressional hearings (it was actually the fifth congressional committee to allow TV cameras into a hearing room), it was the first to attract a massive number of viewers. As many as twenty to thirty million Americans watched spellbound as crime bosses, bookies, pimps, and hitmen appeared on their television screen. They listened intently as the committee's chairman informed them that "there is a secret international government-within-a-government" in the United States, controlling gambling, vice, and narcotics traffic and infiltrating legitimate businesses, protected by corrupt police officers, prosecutors, judges, and politicians.

The high point of the investigation occurred in New York City, where the committee held televised hearings beginning on March 12, 1951, and lasting eight days. Over fifty witnesses testified before the committee, but public interest centered on the alleged boss of the New York underworld Frank Costello, alias Francisco Castaglia, alias Frank Severio. Costello was purportedly head of the organized crime family previously headed by Vito Genovese and Charles Luciano.

In his initial appearance before the committee, Costello's lawyer objected to having his client's face televised. Technicians proceeded to focus the cameras on Costello's hands. The result was television at its most powerful. As committee counsel Rudolph Halley fired questions, Costello was seen nervously ripping sheets of paper to shreds, drumming his fingers on the table top, and clenching his fist.

During the New York hearings, the television viewing daytime audience grew from a miniscule 1.5 percent of homes to a phenomenal 26.2 percent. In the New York metropolitan area an average of 86.2 percent of all individuals watching television watched the hearings, twice the number that had watched the World Series the previous October. The New York City electric company had to add a generator to supply power for all the television sets in use. Commented *Life* magazine: "The week of March 12, 1951, will occupy a special place in history. . . . [People] had suddenly gone indoors into living rooms, taverns, and clubrooms, auditoriums and back-offices. There, in eerie half-light, looking at millions of small frosty screens, people sat as if charmed. . . . Never before had the atten-tion of the nation been riveted so completely on a single matter."

The Kefauver committee failed to produce effective crime-fighting legislation, but it did heighten public awareness of the problem of political corruption and organized crime and generated pressure to enforce existing law. In the aftermath of the committee's investigation, more than 70 local crime commissions were established. The Special Rackets Squad of the FBI launched 46,000 investigations, and by 1957, federal prosecutors had won 874 convictions and recovered $336 million. The committee's hearings were largely responsible for the defeat of proposals to legalize gambling in Arizona, California, Massachusetts, and Montana.

The investigation was important in one other respect. The Kefauver committee played a vital role in popularizing the myth that organized crime in the United States was an alien import, brought to the United States by Italian, and especially by Sicilian, immigrants in the form of the Mafia, a highly centralized, secret organization, which used violence and deceit to prey on the weaknesses and vices of the public. In its report, the committee asserted that much of the responsibility for gambling, loan sharking, prostitution, and narcotics trafficking lay in two major syndicates with close business relations with the Mafia.

In fact, the committee's conclusion—that organized crime was rooted in a highly centralized ethnic conspiracy—was in error. Most organized crime in the United States is organized on a municipal and regional, rather than a national, basis. And many groups have used crime as a route out of poverty, a "queer ladder of social mobility."

Prohibition and the Great Depression offered opportunities for criminals mirroring the whole ethnic mosaic of America. Bootlegging and speakeasies offered huge financial returns and gangsters quickly moved into large-scale gambling, narcotics, prostitution, protection, extortion, bribery, contract killing, and business and labor racketeering. By the end of the 1920s, one of the largest criminal organizations, Al Capone's in Chicago, took in more than $100 million annually and had half the city's police on its payroll. Organized crime is an American phenomenon whose power and prosperity lies in the fact that it caters to vices that the public refuses to give up.

stopped printing his outlandish charges. He sank back into relative obscurity, and died on May 2, 1957.

The end of the Korean War and McCarthy's downfall signaled the end of the Red Scare. The Cold War remained, but most Americans soon realized that there was no domestic communist threat. They learned that an occasional spy was part of the price that free societies pay for their personal freedom, and that "McCarthyism" can be the result of a curtailment of that freedom.

THE PARANOID STYLE

A certain "paranoid style" permeated the early Cold War years. Defining the term historian Richard Hofstadter wrote,

> "It is, above all, a way of seeing the world and of expressing oneself. . . . The distinguishing thing about the paranoid style is . . . that its exponents see . . . a 'vast' or 'gigantic' conspiracy as *the motive force* in historical events. . . . The paranoid spokesman sees the fate of this conspiracy in apocalyptic terms—he traffics in the birth and death of whole worlds, whole political orders, whole systems of human values. . . . Since what is at stake is always a conflict between absolute good and absolute evil, the quality needed is not a willingness to compromise but the will to fight things out to the finish.

The nature of the fight against Communism contributed to the paranoid style. Politicians warned Americans that Communism silently and secretly destroyed a country from within. Although directed from Moscow, its aim was subversion through the slow destruction of a country's moral fiber. No one knew which institution it would next attack, or when. It might be the State Department or the YMCA; it might be the presidency, the army, the movie industry, or the Cub Scouts. Politicians counseled vigilance. They told Americans to watch for the unexpected, to suspect everyone and everything. As a result, between 1945 and 1955 a broad spectrum of institutions, organizations, and individuals came under suspicion.

HUAC Goes to Hollywood

The House of Representatives established the Un-American Activities Committee (HUAC) in the late 1930s to combat subversive right-wing and left-wing movements. Its history was less than distinguished. From the first it tended to see subversive Communists everywhere at work in American scoiety. HUAC even announced that the Boy Scouts were Communist infiltrated. During the late 1940s HUAC picked up the tempo of its investigations, which it conducted in well publicized sessions. Twice during this period HUAC traveled to Hollywood to investigate Communist infiltration in the film industry.

HUAC first went to Hollywood in 1947. Although it didn't find the party line preached in the movies, it did call a group of radical screen writers and producers into its sessions to testify. Asked if they were Communists, the "Hollywood Ten" refused to answer questions about their political beliefs. As Ring Lardner, Jr., one of the Ten, said, "I could answer . . . but if I did, I would hate myself in the morning." They believed that the First Amendment protected them. In the politically charged late 1940s, however, their rights were not protected. Those who refused to testify were sent to prison and blacklisted.

HUAC went back to Hollywood in 1951. This time it called hundreds of witnesses from both the political right and the political left. Conservatives told HUAC that Hollywood was littered with "Commies." Walt Disney even recounted attempts to have Mickey Mouse follow the party line. Of the radicals, some talked but most didn't. To cooperate with HUAC entailed "naming names"—that is, informing on one's friends and political acquaintances. Again, those who refused to name names found themselves unemployed and unemployable.

The HUAC hearings and blacklisting convinced Hollywood producers to make strongly anticommunist films. Between 1947 and 1954 they released more than fifty such films. Most were second-rate movies, starring third-rate actors. The films assured Americans that Communists were thoroughly bad people—they didn't have children, they exhaled cigarette

The House Committee on Un-American Activities conducted an investigation of communist activities in Hollywood that included testimony by such notable actors as Ronald Reagan.

I Was a Teenage Werewolf (1957) seemed closer to uncontrollable beasts than civilized adults. As Tony tells a psychiatrist, "I say things, I do things—I don't know why."

FBI reports and congressional investigations reinforced the theme of adolescent moral decline. J. Edgar Hoover, head of the FBI, linked the rise in juvenile delinquency to the decline in the influence of family, home, church, and local community institutions. Youths had moved away from benign authority toward temptations of popular culture, which, Hoover said, "flout indecency and applaud lawlessness."

Frederic Wertham, a psychiatrist who studied the problem extensively, agreed, emphasizing particularly the pernicious influence of comic books. He believed that crime and horror comic books fostered racism, fascism, and sexism in their readers. In his book *Seduction of the Innocent* (1954), Wertham even linked homosexuality to the reading of comics. Describing how the comic *Batman* could lead to homosexuality, Wertham quoted one of his male patients: "I remember the first time I came across the page mentioning the 'secret bat cave.' The thought of Batman and Robin living

smoke too slowly, they murdered their "friends," and they went berserk when arrested.

If the films were bad civics lessons, they did have an impact. They seemed to confirm HUAC's position that communists were everywhere, that subversives lurked in every shadow. They reaffirmed the paranoid style and helped to justify McCarthy's harangues and Truman's Cold War rhetoric.

"What's Wrong with Our Kids Today?"

At the same time it turned out films about serious but bumbling Communists, Hollywood produced movies that contributed to the fear that something was terribly wrong with the youth of America. Films such as *The Wild One* (1954), *Blackboard Jungle* (1955), *Rebel Without a Cause* (1955), and *Blue Denim* (1959) portrayed adolescents as budding criminals, emerging homosexuals, potential fascists, and pathological misfits—everything but perfectly normal kids. On close inspection, cultural critics concluded that something was indeed wrong with American youth, who like Tony in

Movies like *Rebel Without a Cause* starring James Dean depicted the futility and hopelessness of American youth in the 1950s.

together and possibly having sex relations came to my mind . . . I felt I'd like to be loved by someone like Batman or Superman." Far from being an unheard voice, Wertham's attack generated congressional investigations of and local attacks against the comic book industry.

For a number of critics, sports were an antidote to the ills of wayward youths. "Organized sport is one of our best weapons against juvenile delinquency," remarked J. Edgar Hoover. Youths who competed for championship trophies felt no inclination to compete for "wrist watches, bracelets and automobiles that belong to other people." Nor would they turn to Communism. As Senator Herman Walker of Idaho bluntly put it, "I never saw a ballplayer who was a Communist."

Given these widespread beliefs, the sports scandals of the early 1950s shocked the nation and raised fresh questions about the morality of American adolescents. In February 1951, New York authorities disclosed that players for the City College of New York (CCNY) basketball team had accepted money to fix games. By the time the investigations ended, Long Island University, New York University, Manhattan College, St. John's, Toledo, Bradley, and Kentucky were implicated in the scandal, which involved forging transcripts and paying players as well as fixing games.

In August 1951, the scandal moved to football. This one involved academic cheating, not pointshaving, and was confined to one school—the United States Military Academy at West Point. Altogether, Academy officials dismissed ninety cadets, half of them football players, for violations of the school's honor code. "These acts," said Senator Harry F. Byrd of Virginia, "have struck a blow at the morals of the youth of the country which will last for a long time."

The West Point scandal especially struck at the nation's heart, for half a world away in Korea American soldiers were battling to contain Communism. What of their moral fiber? They too had read comics, watched films written by left-wing screen writers, and been exposed to the "subversive" influences. Did they have the "right stuff"? These questions swirled around the Korean prisoner of war (POW) controversy. Early reports suggested the American POW's in Korea were different from, and infe-

rior to, those of World War II. Journalists portrayed them as undisciplined, morally weak, susceptible to "brain-washing," uncommitted to traditional American ideals, and prone to collaborate with their guards. POW's experiences seemed to confirm that something indeed was wrong with the kids of America.

What was wrong? Who was corrupting the youth of America? The Republican *Chicago Tribune* blamed the affair on the New Deal. The Communist *Daily Worker* said it was the fault of Wall Street, bankers, and greedy politicians. The paranoid style, after all, had no party affiliation. Other Americans, without being too specific, simply felt that there was some ominous force working within America against America.

Adherents to the paranoid style dealt more with vague perceptions than concrete facts. They reacted more to what seemed to be true than to what actually was true. In fact, sociologists and historians have demonstrated that Korean POWs behaved in much the same way as POWs from earlier wars. And during the late 1940s and 1950s juvenile delinquency was not on an upswing. Alien subversive forces were not undermining American morality. In retrospect, we know this. But the rhetoric of the Cold War and McCarthyism created a political atmosphere which proved fertile for the paranoid style.

CONCLUSION

By 1953 and 1954 there were indications of a thaw in the Cold War. First came the death of Joseph Stalin, which was officially announced on March 5, 1953. Shortly thereafter Georgi Malenkov told the Supreme Soviet, the highest legislative body of the Soviet Union: "At the present time there is no disputed or unresolved question that cannot be settled peacefully by mutual agreement. . . . This applies to our relations with all states, including the United States of America." That summer the Korean War ended in a stalemate that allowed both the United States and the Communist forces to save face. In America, 1954 saw the fall of McCarthy. Certainly these events did not end the paranoid style in either America or Russia, but they did ease the tension.

CHRONOLOGY OF KEY EVENTS

1945 United Nation opens in San Francisco; U.S. troops enter Korea south of the 38th parallel replacing the Japanese; Potsdam conference held to consider the post-war world

1946 Winston Churchill's iron curtain speech in Fulton, Missouri, expresses Cold War tensions; National Steel Strike

1947 Truman announces the Truman Doctrine and calls for aid to Greece and Turkey; Marshall Plan extends economic aid to Western Europe; Taft-Hartley Act passed over Truman's veto

1948 The United States recognizes the state of Israel; Whittaker Chambers accuses Alger Hiss of being a member of the Communist party; Berlin Airlift sustains West Berlin for almost a year

1949 North Atlantic Treaty Organization (NATO) established; George Orwell publishes *1984*, predicting the spread of totalitarian governments; American Cancer Society warns that cigarette smoking may cause cancer; Bikinis introduced as bathing suits; The communists under Mao Tse-tung drive Nationalists off the Chinese mainland

1950 Senator Joseph McCarthy charges that there are communists in the State Department; North Korea invades South Korea—Truman sends U.S. forces to support South Korea; Truman authorizes the Atomic Energy Commission to produce the hydrogen bomb

1951 Truman relieves General Douglas MacArthur of his command in Korea; Julius and Ethel Rosenberg sentenced to death for conspiring to give the Soviet Union classified U.S. military documents; Jerome D. Salinger's *Catcher in the Rye* is published

1952 Hydrogen bomb successfully tested; Hollywood introduces three-dimensional (3-D) movies

1953 Soviet Premier Joseph Stalin dies, leading to a power struggle in Russia

1954 Senate holds Army-McCarthy hearings

In addition, by 1954 both the United States and the Soviet Union had become more comfortable in their positions as world powers. Leaders in both countries had begun to realize that neither side could readily win the Cold War. Between 1945 and 1954 each had carved out spheres of influence. Russia and its sometime-ally China dominated most of Eastern Europe and the Asian mainland. America and its allies controlled Western Europe, North and South America, most of the Pacific, and to a lesser extent Africa, the Middle East, and Southeast Asia. Throughout much of the Third World, however, emerging nationalistic movements challenged both United States and Soviet influences.

In the United States, the containment policy was seldom even debated. The Truman Doctrine and muscular internationalism governed foreign policy decisions, but economic and political questions lingered. How much would containment cost? Where would the money come from? Which Americans would pay the most? Would it mean the end of liberal reform? During the next decade American leaders would wrestle with these and other questions.

REVIEW SUMMARY

The World War II alliance between the Soviet Union and the United States broke apart in the late 1940s. The result was the Cold War, an ideological conflict that led to a series of crises throughout the world. Domestically, the Cold War led to widespread infringement of civil liberties in the name of anticommunism. Early postwar conflict involved

> the fate of Poland and Eastern Europe
> control of atomic weapons
> American postwar loans

The position of the United States in regard to these questions was defined by the Truman Doctrine, the Marshall Plan, the formation of NATO, and the policy of containment. Later events both abroad and at home would serve to intensify the Cold War

> the "fall" of China
> Soviet acquisition of the atomic bomb
> the Korean War
> the sudden rise of McCarthyism

The Cold War became the dominant foreign policy issue in postwar America.

SUGGESTIONS FOR FURTHER READING

OVERVIEWS AND SURVEYS

Stephen Ambrose, *Rise to Globalism: American Foreign Policy, 1938-1980* (1980); William H. Chafe, *The Unfinished Journey* (1986) and *The American Woman* (1972); Alexander DeConde, *A History of American Foreign Policy* (1963); Robert H. Ferrell, *American Diplomacy* (1969); Alonzo Hamby, *The Imperial Years* (1976); Godfrey Hodgson, *America in Our Time* (1975); Walter LaFeber, *America, Russia, and the Cold War* (1976); R. W. Leopold, *The Growth of American Foreign Policy* (1967); William

Leuchtenburg, *A Troubled Feast* (1983); Thomas G. Paterson, *American Foreign Policy* (1977); Richard Polenberg, *One Nation Divisible* (1980); Emily and Norman Rosenberg, *In Our Time* (1982); Frederick F. Siegel, *Troubled Journey* (1984); William A. Williams, *The Tragedy of American Diplomacy* (1972) and *The Roots of the Modern American Empire* (1969); Lawrence Wittner, *Cold War America* (1979); Howard Zinn, *Postwar America, 1945-1971* (1973).

CONTAINING THE RUSSIAN BEAR

Dean Acheson, *Present at the Creation: My Years in the State Department* (1969); Gar Alperovitz, *Atomic Diplomacy* (1965); James Aronson, *The Press and the Cold War* (1970); Stanley D. Bachrack, *The Committee of One Million: "China Lobby" Politics, 1953-1971* (1976); Richard J. Barnet, *The Giants: Russia and America* (1977); Charles E. Bohlen, *Witness to History, 1929-1969* (1973); Ronald J. Caridi, *The Korean War and American Politics* (1969); Bernard C. Cohen, *The Public's Impact on Foreign Policy* (1973); Bruce Cumings, *The Origins of the Korean War* (1981); Lynn Etheridge Davis, *The Cold War Begins: Soviet-American Conflict Over Eastern Europe* (1974); Robert J. Donovan, *Conflict and Crisis* (1977) and *Tumultuous Years* (1982); A. W. DePorte, *Europe Between the Superpowers: The Enduring Balance* (1979); Herbert Feis, *From Trust to Terror: The Onset of the Cold War* (1971); Robert H. Ferrell, *George C. Marshall* (1966); D. F. Fleming, *The Cold War and Its Origins* (two volumes, 1961); John L. Gaddis, *The United States and the Origins of the Cold War, 1941-1947* (1972) and *Strategies of Containment: A Crucial Appraisal of Post-War American National Security Policy* (1982); Lloyd C. Gardner, *Architects of Illusion: Men and Ideas in American Foreign Policy, 1941-1949* (1970); Marshall I. Goldman, *Detente and Dollars: Doing Business with the Soviets* (1975); Akira Iriye, *The Cold War in Asia* (1974); Burton Kaufman, *Trade and Aid* (1982); Joyce and Gabriel Kolko, *The Limits of Power: The World and U. S. Foreign Policy, 1945-1954* (1972); Bennett Kovrig, *The Myth of Liberation; East-Central Europe in U. S. Diplomacy and Politics Since 1941* (1973); Bruce Kuklick, *American Policy and the Division of Germany* (1972); Ralph B. Levering, *The Public and American Foreign Policy, 1918-1978* (1978); Vojtech Mastny, *Russia's Road to the Cold War, 1941-1945* (1979); Ernest R. May, *The Truman Administration and China, 1945-1949* (1975); David S. McLellan, *Dean Acheson* (1976); Thomas Paterson, *On Every Front: The Making of the Cold War* (1979); David Rees, *Korea: The Limited War* (1964); Martin Sherwin, *A World Destroyed: The Atomic Bomb and the Grand Alliance* (1975); Gaddis Smith, *Dean Acheson* (1972); John W. Spanier, *The Truman-MacArthur Controversy and the Korean War* (1965); Harry S. Truman, *Memoirs*, 2 vols. (1955, 1956); Adam B. Ulam, *Expansion and*

Coexistence: The History of Soviet Foreign Policy, 1917-1973 (1974); William Welch, *American Images of Soviet Foreign Policy* (1970); Allen S. Whiting, *China Crosses the Yalu: The Decision to Enter the Korean War* (1960); Lawrence Wittner, *American Intervention in Greece, 1943-1949* (1982); Daniel Yergin, *Shattered Peace* (1977).

THE COLD WAR AT HOME

David Brody, *Workers in Industrial Society* (1981); Edwin R. Bayley, *Joe McCarthy and the Press* (1981); David Caute, *The Great Fear: The Anti-Communist Purge Under Truman and Eisenhower* (1978); Alistair Cooke, *A Generation on Trial* (1950); Robert Ferrell, *Harry Truman and the Modern American Presidency* (1982); Richard Freeland, *The Truman Doctrine and the Origins of McCarthyism* (1972); Richard M. Fried, *Men Against McCarthy* (1976); Charles L. Fontenay, *Estes Kefauver* (1980); Walter Goodman, *The Committee* (1968); Joseph Bruce Gorman, *Kefauver* (1971); Robert Griffith, *The Politics of Fear* (1970); Alonzo Hamby, *Beyond the New Deal: Harry S. Truman and American Liberalism* (1973); Susan M. Hartmann, *Truman and the 80th Congress* (1971); Richard S. Kirkendall, *Harry S. Truman, Korea, and the Imperial Presidency* (1975); Stanley I. Kutler, *The American Inquisition: Justice and Injustice in the Cold War* (1982); R. Alton Lee, *Truman and Taft-Hartley* (1966); Samuel Lubell, *Future of American Politics* (1952); Maeva Marcus, *Truman and the Steel Seizure Case* (1977); Allen J. Matusow, *Farm Policies and Politics in the Truman Administration* (1967); William Howard Moore, *The Kefauver Committee and the Politics of Crime* (1974); David Oshinsky, *A Conspiracy So Immense: The World of Joe McCarthy* (1983); James T. Patterson, *Mr. Republican: A Biography of Robert A. Taft* (1972); Thomas C. Reeves, *The Life and Times of Joe McCarthy* (1982); Richard H. Rovere, *Senator Joe McCarthy* (1959); Michael Rogin, *McCarthy and the Intellectuals* (1967); Edward L. and Frederick H. Schapsmeier, *Prophet in Politics: Henry A. Wallace and the War Years, 1940-1965* (1971); Athan Theoharis, *Seeds of Repression: Harry S. Truman and the Origins of McCarthyism* (1972); Allen Weinstein, *Perjury: The Hiss-Chambers Case* (1978); Theodore Wilson, "The Kefauver Committee" in *Congress Investigates,* eds. Arthur M. Schlesinger, Jr., and Roger Bruns (1975).

THE PARANOID STYLE

Eric Goldman, *The Crucial Decade and After* (1961); Richard Hofstadter, *The Paranoid Style in American Politics and Other Essays* (1965); Victor Navasky, *Naming Names* (1980); Nora Sayre, *Running Time: Films of the Cold War* (1982).

Fig. 287

73

103

COMPANY

CHAPTER 27

Ike's America

Figure 1-3. Equator, Latitude, and Parallels of Latitude

Mose Wright stood and surveyed the courtroom. Most of the faces he saw were white. The two accused men were white. The twelve jurors were white. The armed guards were white. Slowly Wright, a sixty-four-year-old black sharecropper, extended his right arm. "Thar he," Wright answered, pointing at J. W. Milam. He then pointed at Roy Bryant, the second defendant. In essence, Wright was accusing the two whites of murdering Emmett Till, his fourteen-year-old grandson—accusing them in a segregated courtroom in Sumner, Mississippi. Wright later recalled that he could "feel the blood boil in hundreds of white people as they sat glaring in the courtroom. It was the first time in my life I had the courage to accuse a white man of a crime, let alone something as terrible as killing a boy. I wasn't exactly brave and I wasn't scared. I just wanted to see justice done."

It was 1955, but the march of racial justice in the South had been painfully slow. In 1954 the Supreme Court of the United States in the landmark *Brown* v. *Board of Education of Topeka* decision had ruled that segregated schooling was "inherently unequal." News of the *Brown* decision drew angry comments and reactions from all corners of the Jim Crow South. Mississippi Senator James Eastland told his constituents that the decision destroyed the Constitution of the United States and counseled, "You are not obliged to obey the decisions of any court which are plainly fraudulent . . . ." Throughout Dixie, Klansmen burned crosses while other white leaders hastily organized Citizens' Councils. Self-proclaimed protectors of white America vowed "to make it difficult, if not impossible, for any Negro who advocates desegregation to find and hold a job, get credit, or renew a mortgage."

Into this racially charged atmosphere came Emmett Till in August 1955. Taking a summer vacation from his home on the South Side of Chicago, he rode a train to visit relatives living near Money, Mississippi. Emmett had known segregation in Chicago, but nothing like what he discovered in Money, where shortly before his arrival a black girl had been "flogged" for "crowding white people" in a store.

Emmett's mother told him what to expect and how to act: "If you have to get on your knees and bow when a white person goes past, do it willingly." But Emmett had a mind and a mouth of his own. In Chicago, he told his cousins, he was friends with plenty of white people. He even had a picture of a white girl, *his* white girl, he said. "Hey," challenged a listener, "there's a [white] girl in that store there. I bet you won't go in there and talk to her."

Emmett accepted the challenge. He entered Bryant's Grocery and Meat Market, browsed about, and bought some candy. As he left, he said, "Bye, Baby" to Carolyn Bryant. Outside an old black man told Emmett to scat before the woman got a pistol and blew "his brains out." The advice sounded sage enough, so Emmett beat a hasty retreat.

A few days later Roy Bryant returned to Money after trucking shrimp from Louisiana to Texas. What his wife told him is unknown, but it was enough to make him angry. After midnight that Saturday night, he and his brother-in-law, J. W. Milam, drove to Mose Wright's unpainted cabin. They demanded the "boy who done the talkin'." Mose tried to explain that Emmett was from "up nawth" and unfamiliar with Southern ways. The logic of the argument was lost on the two white men, one of whom told Mose that if he caused trouble he would never see his next birthday.

Various stories have been told about what happened during the next few hours. One thing is for certain: Emmett Till did not live to see daybreak. According to Milam and Bryant's account, they had only meant to scare the northern youth. But Emmett did not beg for mercy. Therefore they *had* to kill him. "What else could we do? " Milam asked. "He was hopeless. I'm no bully; I never hurt a nigger in my life. I like niggers in their place. I know how to work 'em. But I just decided it was time a few people got put on notice."

Three days later Emmett's body was found in the Tallahatchie River. A gouged out eye, crushed forehead, and bullet in his skull gave evidence to the beating he took. Around his neck, attached by barbed wire, was a seventy-five pound cotton gin fan. At the request of his mother, the local sheriff sent the decomposing body to Chicago for burial.

Mamie Bradley, Emmett's mother, grieved openly and loudly. Contrary to the wishes of

Mississippi authorities, she held an open casket funeral. Thousands of black Chicagoans attended the viewing, and the black press closely followed the episode. *Jet* magazine even published a picture of the mutilated corpse. In the black community the Till murder case became a cause célèbre. In a land that valued justice, would any be found in Mississippi?

In Money white Southerners rallied to Bryant and Milam's side. Supporters raised a $10,000 defense fund, and southern editorials labeled the entire affair a "Communist plot" to destroy southern society. By the time the trial started, American interest seemed focused on Mississippi. Few people, however, expected that Bryant and Milam would be judged guilty, because few expected any blacks would testify against white men in Mississippi.

Mose Wright proved the folly of common wisdom. He dramatically testified against the white men. So did several other relatives of Emmett Till. But in his closing statement, John C. Whitten, one of the five white attorneys, told the all-white, all-male jury: "Your fathers will turn over in their graves if [Milam and Bryant are found guilty] and I'm sure that every last Anglo-Saxon one of you has the courage to free these men in the face of that [outside] pressure."

The jury returned a "not guilty" verdict. On that day in 1955 there was no justice in Sumner, Mississippi. Michigan Congressman Charles Diggs, who sat with other blacks in the rear section of the segregated courtroom, recalled, "I certainly was angered by the decision, [but] I was not surprised by it. And I was strengthened in my belief that something had to be done about the dispensation of justice in that state." Roy Wilkens of the NAACP remarked that "there is in the entire state no restraining influence of decency, not in the state capital, among the daily newspapers, the clergy, not among any segment of the so-called lettered citizens."

But if there was no justice that day, there were clear signs of change. A black man had demanded justice in white-controlled Mississippi. Soon—very soon—other voices would join Mose Wright's. Their peaceful but insistent cries would be heard over the surface quiet of Dwight Eisenhower's America. They would force America to come to terms with its own

Mose Wright and his three boys attended the trial of Bryant and Milam in Sumner, Mississippi. They had seats in the "colored" section of the courtroom.

ideology. After an heroic struggle against fascism and during a cold conflict against communism, Americans no longer could ignore racial injustice and inequality at home.

It was time for a change. During the late 1940s and the 1950s the process began. Slow, painful, poignant, occasionally uplifting—the march toward justice moved forward. It was part of other significant social and economic changes taking place in America. Against the backdrop of Eisenhower's calm assurances, a new country was taking shape.

QUIET CHANGES

Most white Americans during the late 1940s and the early 1950s were unconcerned about the struggles of their black compatriots. Perhaps some admired Jackie Robinson's efforts on the baseball field, but few made the connection between integration in sports and civil rights throughout society. Other concerns seemed more urgent. In November 1952 the Korean

Eisenhower won the nomination at the Republican convention in 1952 and easily won the election over the Democratic candidate, Adlai Stevenson.

War was dragging into its third year, and the chances for a satisfactory peace were fading. Joseph McCarthy was still warning Americans about the communist infiltration of the United States government. Political corruption had stained the Truman administration. At the polls Americans were ready to vote for change.

I Like Ike

Republicans certainly felt it was time for change. The Democrats had occupied the White House for the previous twenty years. In 1952 they ran Governor Adlai Stevenson of Illinois for the presidency. A political moderate and a vocal anticommunist, the witty, sophisticated Stevenson was burdened by Truman's unpopularity. His Republican opponent was Dwight David Eisenhower, a moderate, anticommunist war hero. The Republican campaign strategy was summarized in a formula—K_1C_2. Eisenhower promised that if elected he would first end the war in Korea then battle communism and corruption at home. The nation re-

sponded. Eisenhower was swept into office. He even carried several southern states and cut into the urban-ethnic coalition of the Democrats.

The country responded to Eisenhower. "I Like Ike" campaign buttons and posters captured the public sentiment. And there was much to like. Few people had advanced so far while making so few enemies. Ike's was the classic Horatio Alger success story. Although born in Texas, he was raised in Abilene, Kansas, the northern terminus of the Chisholm Trail. An accomplished athlete and a good student, Ike earned an appointment to West Point, where he graduated in 1915 among "the class on which the stars fell." (Fifty-nine of the 164 graduates of the class would rise to the rank of brigadier general or higher.)

As an army officer, Eisenhower demonstrated rare organizational abilities and a capacity for complex detail work. If by 1939 he had only risen to the rank of lieutenant colonel, he had impressed his superiors. With the outbreak of World War II, he was promoted with startling rapidity. In fact, in 1942 General George Marshall passed over 366 more senior officers to promote Eisenhower to major general and appoint him commander of the European theater of operations. It was Ike who planned and oversaw America's invasions of North Africa, Sicily, and Italy and who led the combined British-American D-Day invasion. By the end of the war, Ike was a four-star general and an international hero.

Ike's ability to win the loyalty of others and work with people of diverse and difficult temperaments would serve him well as a politician. But during the early postwar years, he expressed no interest in holding political office. "I cannot conceive of any set of circumstances that could drag out of me permission to consider me for any political post from dog catcher to Grand High Supreme King of the Universe," he told a reporter in 1946. And indeed there is no evidence that Ike had ever voted or had any party affiliation before running for the presidency on the Republican ticket in 1952.

Eisenhower did have strong beliefs concerning America's domestic and foreign policy. His fiscal conservativism led him to the Republican party, and his internationalism convinced him to run for the presidency. He did not want to see an isolationist Republican elected in 1952, and the early front-runner was isolationist Robert Alphonso Taft, the powerful Ohio senator. Once Ike had defeated Taft for the nomination, his victory over Stevenson was almost anticlimactic.

Almost overnight the image of Eisenhower was transformed from one of a master military organizer to one of mumbling, bumbling, smiling incomprehensibility. Reporters commented upon his friendly smile, engaging blue eyes, and his mangled syntax. As a young officer he wrote striking speeches for Douglas MacArthur, and as a World War II general he impressed reporters with the precision of his thought. Commenting on Ike's speaking style, FDR's press secretary said, "He knows his facts, he speaks freely and frankly, and he has a sense of humor, he has poise, and he has command."

Had Eisenhower somehow sunk into senility upon taking office? Certainly not. He sensed that the country needed a rest from twenty years of active presidents. Rather than an earth shaker, the country needed a "dirt smoother." The result was the "hidden hand leadership" of Ike. In public he seemed everyone's favorite grandfather and golfing buddy, friendly, outgoing, quick to please, but only slightly interested in being president. Although he had read widely in both military history and the classics, he insisted publicly that he only read westerns, and those not too closely.

"Dynamic Conservatism"

Eisenhower brought the military chain of command system to the White House. He was in charge, and he kept the major decisions of his administration in his own hands. But he left the detail work and the political battling to his subordinates. The most important person after Eisenhower in this command structure was Sherman Adams, the former governor of New Hampshire who served as Ike's chief of staff. Adams determined who got to see the president and what issues were placed before him. Although forced to resign in 1958 for influence peddling, Adams pioneered modern White House administration.

Ike saw himself as a foreword-looking Republican. He called himself a conservative, "but an extremely liberal conservative," one who was concerned with fiscal prudence but not at the expense of human beings. Ike termed his approach "Modern Republicanism" and "dynamic conservativism," by which he meant, "conservative when it comes to money matters and liberal when it comes to human beings." In practice this approach led the Eisenhower administration to cut spending but not to attempt any rollback of New Deal social legislation.

George Humphrey, a conservative Ohio industrialist, served as Eisenhower's treasury secretary. More conservative than Eisenhower, Humphrey believed that the federal government should shift more fiscal responsibilities to the state and private sectors. He did succeed in getting Congress to abolish the Reconstruction Finance Corporation (see Chapter 23) and turn over off-shore oil rights to the seaboard states. The *New York Times* called this latter piece of legislation, the Submerged Land Act, "one of the greatest and surely the most unjustified give-away programs in all the history of the United States." On the whole, however, Eisenhower's domestic programs were hardly reactionary.

During Ike's two terms the country made steady and at times spectacular economic progress. In 1955 the minimum wage was raised from seventy-five cents to one dollar per hour, and during the 1950s the average family income rose fifteen percent and real wages were up twenty percent. "American labor has never had it so good," AFL-CIO chief George Meany told his associates in 1955. Although the population increased by 28 million people, the country was on the whole better housed and fed than ever before. The output of goods and services rose fifteen percent. Especially for white Americans, "modern Republicanism" seemed a viable alternative to New Dealism.

A Country of Wheels

If Eisenhower labored to curtail the role of the federal government in some areas, he expanded it in other places. As an expert on military logistics, Ike frequently expressed concern about the sad state of the American highway system. During World War II he had been impressed by Hitler's system of *Autobahnen* which allowed the German dictator to deploy troops to different parts of Germany with incredible speed. From his first days in office, Eisenhower worked for legislation to improve America's highway network.

The highway lobby agreed. A loose collection of pressure groups formed the lobby, including representatives from the automobile, trucking, bus, oil, rubber, asphalt, and construction industries. Following the philosophy that what was good for General Motors was good for the country, the highway lobby pushed for a new federally subsidized interstate highway system. Not only would such a project provide millions of new jobs, it would contribute to a safer America by making it easier to evacuate major cities in the event of a nuclear attack.

As a result of presidential and lobby pressure, in 1956 Congress passed the National Sys-

tem of Interstate and Defense Highways Act, the most significant piece of legislation enacted under Eisenhower. As planned, the system would cover 41,000 (later expanded to 42,500) miles, cost $26 billion, and take thirteen years to con-

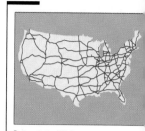

Interstate Highways

struct. Although it took longer to complete and cost far more than Congress projected, it did provide the United States with the world's most extensive superhighway system.

More than any other piece of legislation, it also changed America. After Congress passed the 1956 bill, cultural critic Lewis Mumford wrote, "When the American people, through their Congress, voted . . . for a $26 billion highway program, the most charitable thing to assume is that they hadn't the faintest notion of what they were doing." Mumford realized that this commitment to internal combustion engines would alter the culture and landscape of America; and it has. It accelerated the decline of the inner city and the flight to the suburbs. The downtown portion of cities, once thriving with commerce and excitement, rapidly turned into ghost towns. As downtown businesses, hotels, and theaters closed, suburban shopping malls with multi-screen cinemas and roadside motels began to dot the American highway landscape. Drive-in theaters, gasoline service stations, house trailers, mobile homes, and multi-car garages signified the birth of a new extended society, one without center or focus.

Home architecture exemplified America's mobile-minded culture. The garage, once separated from and located behind the house, achieved a new position. By the 1960s the average home devoted more space to the family automobiles than to individual family members. With access to the house itself—usually through the kitchen—the garage had become an integrated part of the house and the car an important member of the family.

America's commitment to highways and cars created numerous problems. Mass transportation suffered most conspicuously. Street cars and commuter railroads languished, as did the country's major interstate railroads. Since highway construction was financed by a nondivertible gasoline tax, government often ignored mass transit. In the years since the end of World War II, seventy-five percent of government expenditures for transportation have gone for highways as opposed to one percent for urban mass transit. As a result, those without the use of automobiles—the old, the very young, the poor, the handicapped—became victims of America's automobile obsession.

Ike, Dulles, and the World

For Eisenhower, "modern Republicanism" was more than simply a domestic economic credo. It also implied an internationalist foreign policy. As with domestic policy, in foreign policy Ike preferred to operate behind the scenes. But he did make all major foreign policy decisions.

The point man for Ike's foreign policy was Secretary of State John Foster Dulles. When Eisenhower asked Dulles to head the State Department, he remarked, "You've been training yourself to be Secretary of State ever since you were nine years old." And so he had. An interest in foreign affairs was part of the Dulles heritage. John Foster's maternal grandfather had served as Benjamin Harrison's secretary of state, and one of his uncles, Robert Lansing, had held the same job under Woodrow Wilson. In 1919 as a young man, Dulles had been part of the American delegation to the Versailles Peace Conference, and in later years, as a member of the prestigious Wall Street law firm of Sullivan and Cromwell, he represented clients with international interests. After World War II, he helped to organize and then served as a delegate to the United Nations. In addition, throughout his life Dulles was a careful student of foreign affairs and international politics. Eisenhower noted, there was "only one man I know who has seen *more* of the world and talked with more people and *knows* more than [Dulles] does—and that's me."

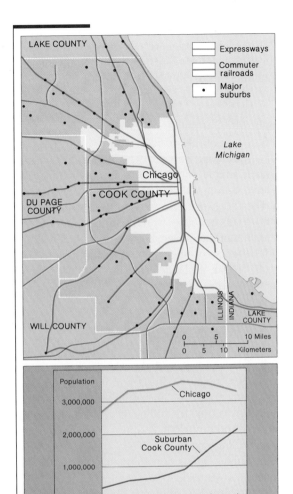

Suburban Growth

Dulles's experience and knowledge was somewhat offset by his rigidity and excessive moralism. If Americans felt comfortable calling President Eisenhower "Ike," not even close friends called Dulles "Jack." Plain and as unpolished as granite, Dulles took himself, his Presbyterian religion, and the world seriously. One Washington correspondent described him as "a card-carrying Christian," and he frequently delivered lectures on the evils of "atheistic, materialistic Communism." He tended to see opposition to communism in religious terms. A friend recalled a conversation in which China's Chiang Kai-shek and South Korea's Syngman Rhee were criticized. Offended, Dulles announced: "No matter what you say about them, those two gentlemen are modern-day equivalents of the founders of the church. They are Christian gentlemen who have suffered for their faith."

Although Eisenhower and Dulles had strikingly different public styles, they shared a common vision of the world. Both were internationalists and cold warriors who believed that the Soviet Union was the enemy and that the United States was and should be the protector of the free world. Peace was their objective— but never a peace won by appeasement. To keep honorable peace, both were willing to consider the use of nuclear weapons and go to the brink of war. As Dulles said in 1956, "You have to take some chances for peace, just as you must take chances in war."

Occasionally Dulles's impassioned anticommunist rhetoric obscured the actual policies pursued by the Eisenhower administration. In public Dulles rejected the Containment Doctrine as a "negative, futile and immoral policy" and advocated the "liberation" of Eastern Europe. It was time to "roll back" the Iron Curtain, he said, and if nuclear weapons were needed to achieve America's objectives—well, then, so be it. In public Dulles constantly flexed his—and America's—muscles.

In reality, Eisenhower's objectives were far more limited and his approach toward foreign policy much more cautious. Eisenhower supported containment, but not as practiced by Truman. In Eisenhower's eyes, Truman's approach was unorganized and far too expensive. If America continued Truman's shotgun policies, the costs would soon become higher than Americans would be willing to pay. A change, Ike maintained, was needed.

Eisenhower termed his adjustments of the Containment Doctrine the "New Look." Ike's program began with the idea of saving money. To do this he decided to emphasize nuclear weapons over conventional weapons, assuming that the next major war would be a nuclear conflict. This "more bang for the buck" program drew angry criticism. Congressional hawks claimed that Eisenhower was "putting too many eggs in the nuclear basket," and liberals suggested that the program would inevitably lead to nuclear destruction.

Through strong foreign alliances, Eisenhower built bases for nuclear weapons and encouraged resistance to communist expansion.

Whatever the criticisms, the New Look did save money. While air and missile forces were expanded, the army's budget was trimmed of all of its fat and much of its bone. In fact, if Eisenhower had had his way, the army would have been completely reorganized. The results of Eisenhower's approach were dramatic. In 1953 defense cost $50.4 billion. By 1956 Eisenhower had reduced the defense budget to $35.8 billion. In addition, during the same period troop levels were reduced by almost one third (see Figure 26.1, p. 857).

Future presidents did not so much reverse Eisenhower's approach as enlarge it. They continued the nuclear buildup started by Eisenhower, and at the same time insisted upon increased spending on conventional weapons. The result was an ever escalating defense budget.

The New Look took an unconventional approach to conventional warfare. Ike had learned from Truman's mistakes in Korea. America could not send weapons and men to all corners of the world to contain communism. It was a costly, deadly policy. Instead, the New Look emphasized the threat of massive retaliation to keep order, and reinforced America's position with a series of foreign alliances which encouraged indigenous troops and peoples to resist communist expansion. Finally, Eisenhower used the CIA as a covert foreign policy arm. Through timely assassinations and political coups engineered by the CIA, Eisenhower was able to prevent—or at least forestall—the emergence of anti-America regimes. While historians argue about the morality of the CIA's covert operations, they were very much a part of the New Look.

A New Face in Moscow

The world changed dramatically a few months after Eisenhower took office. On March 5, 1953, Joseph Stalin, the Soviet dictator whom Ike knew personally, died. Always fearful of rivals, Stalin did not groom a successor. The result was a power struggle within the Kremlin, from which Nikita Khrushchev emerged as the winner.

Khrushchev looked like a cross between a Russian peasant and Ike himself. Short, rotund, and bald, he had a warm smile and alert eyes. Unlike Stalin, Khrushchev enjoyed meeting people, making speeches, and traveling abroad. If occasionally he lost his temper and uttered belligerent remarks—he once even took off his shoe and pounded it on a table at the United Nations—Khrushchev did try to lessen the tensions between the Soviet Union and the United States.

Ike shared Khrushchev's dream for peaceful coexistence between the two world leaders. In fact, Eisenhower used Stalin's death as an opportunity to extend an olive branch. Russia peacefully responded. During 1955 the nations resolved several thorny issues. Russia repatriated German prisoners of war who had been held in the Soviet Union since World War II, established relations with Greece and Israel, and gave up its claims to Turkish territory. Its most significant action was to withdraw from its occupation zone of Austria. It was the only time that the Soviet Union has given back territory

to a noncommunist state that it had seized during the war.

The cold winter of the Cold War seemed to be over. Khrushchev condemned Stalin's excesses, and Eisenhower talked guardedly about a new era of cooperation. In July 1955, the two leaders met in Geneva, Switzerland, for a summit conference. Actually, the meeting achieved few tangible results, but the two leaders seemed to be working toward the same peaceful ends. Against Dulles's advice, Eisenhower even smiled when posing for pictures with the Russians. "A new spirit of conciliation and cooperation" had been achieved, Ike announced. Unfortunately, "the Spirit of Geneva" would not survive the confrontations ahead.

1956: The Dangerous Year

Neither Eisenhower nor Khrushchev was completely candid. While working for "peaceful coexistence," both still had to satisfy critics at home. In Washington, Dulles continued to call

Nikita Khrushchev, Soviet Premier, pounds the table with his fist at the September 23, 1960, General Assembly session.

for the "liberation" of Eastern Europe and to hint that the United States would rally behind any Soviet dominated country that struck a blow for freedom. In reality, Eisenhower was not about to risk war with Russia to come to the defense of Poland, Hungary, or Czechoslovakia.

At the same time, Khrushchev's speeches often promised more than he would or could deliver. On February 24, 1956, for example, Khrushchev delivered a remarkable speech before the Twentieth Party Congress. For four hours, he condemned Stalin's domestic crimes and foreign policy mistakes, endorsed "peaceful coexistence" with the West, and indicated that he was willing to allow greater freedom behind the "iron curtain." Although the speech was supposed to be secret, the CIA obtained copies and distributed them throughout Eastern Europe.

Poland took Khrushchev at his word and moved in a more liberal, anti-Stalinist direction. Wladyslaw Gomulka, who represented the nationalistic wing of the Polish Communist party, gained power in Poland and moved his country away from complete Soviet domination. Claiming that "there is more than one road to socialism," Gomulka announced that Poles would defend with their lives their new freedoms. Since Poland did not attempt to withdraw from the Soviet bloc, Khrushchev allowed Poland to move along its more liberal course.

What Poland had won, Hungary wanted— and perhaps a bit more. On October 23, 1956, students and workers took to the streets in Budapest loudly demanding changes. As in Poland, they forced a political change. Independent Communist Imre Nagy replaced a Stalinist leader. The Soviets peacefully recognized the

Before the crushing Soviet onslaught on November 4, Hungarian freedom fighters rushed toward Budapest in an attempt to fight off Soviet forces.

new government. Pressing his luck, Nagy then announced that he planned to pull Hungary out of the Warsaw Pact—the Soviet-dominated defense community—and allow opposition political parties.

Khrushchev sent Soviet tanks and soldiers into Budapest to crush what he now termed a "counterrevolution." Students with bricks and hastily made Molotov cocktails were no match for the Red Army. The Soviets killed Nagy along with hundreds of demonstrators and brutally restored their control over Hungary. All the while, the Eisenhower administration just watched, demonstrating that the notion of "liberation" was mere rhetoric, not policy. Hungary, said Ike, was "as inaccessible to us as Tibet."

Actually, at the time of the Russian move into Budapest, Eisenhower was more concerned with the troubled Western alliance. The source of the problem was Egypt, whose nationalistic leader, President Gamel Abdel Nasser, was struggling to remain neutral in the Cold War. The United States had attempted to win Nasser's favor by promising to finance the construction of the Aswan High Dam on the Nile. But when Nasser recognized the People's Republic of China and pursued amicable relations with the Soviet Union, the Eisenhower administration withdrew the proposed loan. Neither Dulles nor Eisenhower was happy with Nasser's fence-sitting diplomacy.

Nasser struck back. On July 26, he nationalized the Suez Canal, which Ike believed was essential to the security of Western Europe. If Eisenhower was upset, British and French leaders were outraged, loudly claiming that the seizure threatened their Middle Eastern oil supplies. Eisenhower counseled caution, but Britain, France, and Israel resorted to "drastic actions." On October 29, Israel invaded Egypt and Britain and France used the hostilities as a pretext to seize the Suez Canal.

Eisenhower was furious. He interrupted his reelection campaign to return to Washington. One observer reported, "The White House crackled with barracks-room language." Ike told Dulles to inform the Israelis that "goddamn it, we're going to apply sanctions, we're going to the United Nations, we're going to do everything that there is so we can stop this thing."

And in a severe "tongue-lashing" he reduced British Prime Minister Anthony Eden to tears.

Eisenhower stood on the high ground, where he was uncomfortably aligned with the Soviet Union. Without law there can be no peace, he claimed, adding, "and there can be no law—if we were to invoke one code of international conduct for those who oppose us—and another for our friends." Cut off from American support and faced with angry Soviet threats, Britain, France, and Israel halted their operations on November 6, the same day Eisenhower was overwhelmingly reelected for a second term.

Taken together, the Hungarian and the Suez crises strained America's relations with Russia and its Western allies. "The spirit of Geneva" was being replaced by a more hostile mood. Nowhere was this better seen than in the 1956 Olympic Games, held in Melbourne, Australia, only two weeks after the November incidents. Egypt, Lebanon, and Iraq refused to take part in any Games which included Britain, France, and Israel. And in the water polo competition, a match between the Soviet Union and Hungary quickly deteriorated into a form of aquatic warfare.

The Troubled Second Term

In foreign affairs, Eisenhower's second term was less successful than his first. Age and health may have contributed to this turn of events. During his first four years in office, Ike suffered a heart attack and a bout with ileitis, which entailed a serious operation. During his second term, he was more apt to take vacations and play golf and bridge with his close friends. John Foster Dulles's health was also declining. During the Suez Crisis doctors discovered that he had cancer. Acute physical pain punctuated his last years as secretary of state and less than four years later he was dead.

Sputnik and Sputtering Rockets

More than ill health plagued Ike's foreign policy. Russian technological advances created a mood of edginess in American foreign policy and military circles. In 1957 the Soviet Union successfully placed a tiny transmitter encased in a 185-pound steel ball into an orbit around earth. They called the artificial satellite Sputnik—Russian for "fellow traveler"—but the humor of the name was lost on most Americans, who were too concerned about Soviet rocket advances to laugh.

Less than one month later, Russia launched its second Sputnik, this one built on a larger and grander scale. It weighed 1120 pounds, contained instruments for scientific research, and carried a small dog named Laika who was wired with devices to gauge the effects of extragravitational flight on animal functions. If the first Sputnik demonstrated that the Soviets had gained the high ground, the second indicated that they intended to go higher and to place men in space.

Before the end of 1957, the United States tried to respond with a satellite launch of its own. Code-named Vanguard, the satellite was placed on the top of a three-stage navy rocket which was ignited on December 6. Describing

DOG DAZE

Americans panicked when the Soviets launched the artificial satellite Sputnik in October 1957. The nation had lost its previously unquestioned superiority.

the "blast off," a historian wrote, "It wobbled a few feet off the pad and exploded. The grapefruit-sized American rival to Sputnik fell to the ground and beeped its last amid geysers of smoke." It was the first of a series of highly publicized American rocket launches which ended with the sputtering sound of failure.

Sputnik forced Americans to question themselves and their own values. Had the country become soft and overly consumer oriented? While Russian students were studying calculus, physics, and chemistry, had American students spent too much time in shop, home economics, and driver education classes? More importantly, did Sputnik give the Soviet Union a military superiority over the United States? If a Russian rocket could put a thousand-pound ball in orbit could the same rocket armed with nuclear warhead hit a target in the United States? Such questions disturbed ordinary Americans and United States policy makers alike.

In truth, Americans overrated the importance of Sputnik. It was not all that it seemed. As Wernher von Braun, one of America's leading German rocket scientists, would later demonstrate, launching a satellite was no great accomplishment. It simply took rockets with great thrust. Delivering a warhead to a specific target was quite another matter. That entailed sophisticated guidance systems, which Russia had certainly not developed.

Sputnik then did not demonstrate Soviet technological superiority. It did, however, indicate the willingness of Soviet leaders to place military advancement ahead of the physical well-being of their citizens. As a French journalist noted, the price of Sputnik was "millions of pots and shoes lacking." Then, as well as today, Russia lagged behind the West in diet, health care, education, housing, clothing, and transportation.

American policy makers reacted to the illusion of Soviet success. Congress appropriated more money for "defense-related" research and funneled more dollars into higher education in the United States. In fact, Sputnik was a tremendous boon for education. The Eisenhower administration jumped into the "space race" determined to be the swiftest. A leading historian of space measured the success of Eisen-

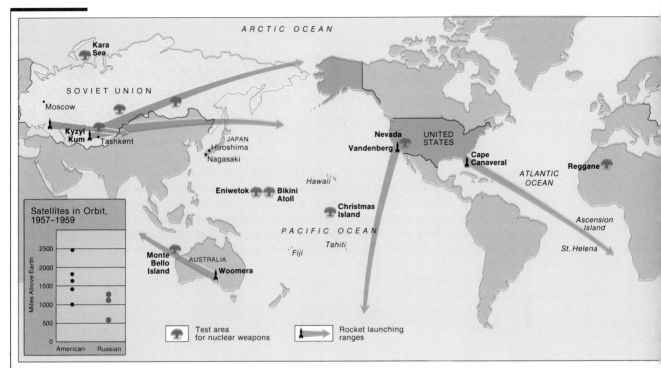

Rockets and Satellites, 1957–1959

The reaction of the United States to Sputnik led to a proliferation of rockets and satellites in both the USSR and the U.S. in the late 1950s.

hower's effort by noting, "more new starts and technical leaps occurred in the years before 1960 than in any comparable span. Every space booster and every strategic missile in the American arsenal, prior to . . . the 1970s, date from these years."

Third World Challenges

If Sputnik was largely an illusionary challenge, nationalist movements in the Third World created more serious problems. Eisenhower's response to such movements varied from case to case. On the one hand, he opposed Britain and France's efforts to use naked physical aggression to whip Egypt into line. On the other hand, Ike employed covert CIA operations to achieve his foreign policy goals. In 1953 the CIA planned and executed a coup d'état which replaced a popularly elected government in Iran with a pro-American regime headed by Shah Mohammad Reza Pahlevi. One year later the CIA masterminded the overthrow of a leftist government in Guatemala and replaced it with an unpopular but strongly pro-American government.

To keep order in what he believed were areas vital to American interests, Eisenhower would even resort to armed intervention. In 1958, Lebanese Moslems backed by Egypt and Syria, threatened a revolt against the Bierut government dominated by the Christian minority. President Camille Chamoun appealed to Eisenhower for support. Concerned with Middle Eastern oil, Ike ordered marines from America's Sixth Fleet into Lebanon. Once order was restored and Lebanese politicians had agreed on a successor to Chamoun, Ike withdrew American troops from Lebanon. But like the CIA activities in Guatemala and Iran, short-term benefits came with long-term costs. Increasingly, the United States became identified with unpopular, undemocratic, and intolerant right-wing regimes. Such actions tarnished America's image in the Third World.

The problems of Eisenhower's approach toward the Third World were clearly seen in his handling of the Cuban Revolution. In 1959, revolutionary Fidel Castro overthrew Fulgencio Batista, a right-wing dictator who had encouraged American investments in Cuba at the expense of the Cuban people. Before the revolution, in fact, American companies owned ninety percent of Cuban mining operations, eighty percent of its utilities, and forty percent of its sugar operations. Castro quickly set about to change the situation. He confiscated land and properties in Cuba owned by Americans, executed former Batista officials, and moved leftward.

Instead of waiting for Cuba's anti-American feelings to subside, Eisenhower decided to move against Castro. He gave the CIA permission to plan an attack on Cuba by a group of anti-Castro exiles, a plan which would culminate with the disastrous Bay of Pigs invasion (see Chapter 28). As one of his last acts as president, in 1961 Eisenhower severed diplomatic relations with Cuba. Such actions only increased Castro's anti-American resolve and further drove him into the arms of the Soviet Union.

Ultimately, the Truman and Eisenhower brands of containment were unsuccessful in dealing with nationalistic independence movements. Such movements have dominated the post–World War II world. Between 1944 and 1974, for example, seventy-eight countries won their independence. These included more than one billion people, or close to one-third of the world's population. By using a political yardstick to evaluate these movements, American presidents since Truman have made critical mistakes that have lowered the image of the United States in the Third World.

Not with a Bang, But a Whimper

Going into his last year in office, Eisenhower hoped to improve upon the foreign policy record of his second term. Since his last meeting with Khrushchev in Geneva, the Cold War had

intensified. In particular, the Soviets were once again threatening to cut off Western access to West Berlin, an action which Eisenhower feared might lead to a nuclear war. To solve the problem—or at least to neutralize it—Khrushchev visited the United States and had private talks with Eisenhower at Camp David, where the two agreed to a formal summit set for May 1960 in Paris.

The summit never took place. Just before the meeting the Soviets shot down an American U-2 spy plane over their territory. So sophisticated was the plane's surveillance equipment, it could read a newspaper headline from ten miles above the earth's surface. During the previous few years, U-2 missions had kept Eisenhower abreast of Soviet military developments and convinced him that Sputnik posed no military threat to the United States. Nevertheless, the existence of such planes was a military secret, and U-2 pilots had strict orders to self-destruct their planes rather than be forced down in enemy territory.

Assuming that the pilot had followed orders, Eisenhower responded to the Soviet charges of spying by publicly announcing that Russians had shot down a weather plane which had blown off course. Unfortunately for Ike, the pilot, Francis Gary Powers, had not followed orders, and the Soviets had him and the wreckage of his plane. Trying to save the summit, Khrushchev offered Eisenhower a way to save face. The Soviet leader indicated that he was sure that Eisenhower had not known about the flights. Eisenhower, however, accepted full personal responsibility and refused to apologize for actions which he deemed were in defense of America. Rather than appear soft himself, Khrushchev refused to engage in the Paris summit.

Eisenhower's presidency ended on this note of failure. A chance to improve Russian-American relations had been lost. But the end of his presidency should not obscure his positive accomplishments. He had ended one war, kept America out of several others, limited military spending, and presided over seven and a half years of relative peace. Like George Washington, when Eisenhower left office he issued warnings to America about possible future

When U-2 pilot Gary Powers was shot down over Russia, plans for a Soviet-American summit meeting in Paris came to a grinding halt.

problems. In particular, he noted, the "military-industrial complex"—an alliance between government and business—could threaten the democratic process in the country. As Eisenhower remarked early in his presidency, "Every gun that is made, every warship launched, every rocket fired signifies, in the final sense, a theft from those who hunger and are not fed, those who are cold and are not clothed."

WE SHALL OVERCOME

When Dwight Eisenhower took office in early 1953 almost everywhere in the United States racism—often institutionalized, sometimes less formal—was the order of the day. Below the Mason-Dixon line it reached its most virulent form in the Jim Crow laws that governed the everyday existence of southern blacks. Whites framed the Jim Crow laws to separate the races and to demonstrate white superiority and black inferiority to all. Jim Crow dictated that whites and blacks eat in separate restaurants, drink from separate water fountains, sleep in separate hotels, and learn in separate schools. In some states, the separate schoolbooks of black and white children were stored in separate closets so as to avoid contamination by touch.

Jim Crow subjected blacks to daily bouts of degradation and soul-destroying humiliation. Blacks had to give way on sidewalks to whites, tip their hats and speak respectfully. Blacks addressed whites of all ages as Mr., Mrs., or Miss; whites addressed blacks of all ages by their first names. Although the underpinning of the Jim Crow laws was the "separate but equal" doctrine enunciated in *Plessy* v. *Ferguson* (1896), both blacks and whites realized that subjugation, not equality, was the object of the laws. And Jim Crow leaped over national boundaries. When a waitress at a Howard Johnson's in Dover, Delaware, refused to serve a glass of orange juice to the finance minister of Ghana because of his color, America's image abroad was tarnished.

Segregation affected whites as well as blacks. Melton A. McLaurin, a historian who grew up in Wade, North Carolina, recalled that

Jim Crow laws were not only limited to restaurants or hotels in cities. This roadside sign makes it clear that segregation existed outside metropolitan areas, too.

race relations in the South in the mid-1950s were much as they had been in the 1890s. Jim Crow etiquette touched all relations between both races. "Blacks who had to enter our house," McLaurin noted, "for whatever reason, came in the back door. Unless employed as domestic servants, blacks conducted business with my father or mother on the back porch or, on rare occasions, in the kitchen. Blacks never entered our dining or living areas . . . except as domestics. . . . When a black person approached a doorway at the same time as a white adult, the black stepped back and sometimes even held the door open for the white to enter. The message I received from hundreds of such signals was always the same. I was white; I was different; I was superior. It was not a message with which an adolescent boy was apt to quarrel."

North of Dixie the situation was not much better. To be sure, rigid Jim Crow laws did not exist, but informally blacks were excluded from the better schools, neighborhoods, and jobs. Whites argued that the development of ghettos was a natural process, not some sort of racist agreement between white realtors. Such, however, was not the case. William Levitt, the most famous post–World War II suburban housing developer, attempted to keep blacks out of his developments. A passage in the New York Levittown covenant read: "No dwelling shall be used . . . by members of other than the Caucasian race, but the employment and maintenance of other than Caucasian domestic servants shall be permitted." Even after the courts struck down such restrictions, Levitt instructed his realtors not to sell to blacks.

When Ike left office in 1961, segregation remained largely unchanged. In that year, John Howard Griffin's best-selling book *Black Like Me* gave white America a stark look at the daily life of millions of black Americans. After darkening his skin chemically, Griffin traveled about the South to experience what it was like to live as a black in Jim Crow America. He described the humiliating search for places to sleep, eat, and even relieve himself in a land where facilities were not only separate and unequal but for blacks often nonexistent. Griffin's tale shocked and shamed many whites who never realized—or even considered—the plight of black Americans.

During Eisenhower's years in office, however, blacks did make significant strides in their quest for civil rights. In particular, during the decade after 1954 blacks won a series of legal victories which in theory if not always in practice buried Jim Crow. They were years of joy and years of sadness, when the best as well as the worst aspects of the American character were clearly visible.

Taking Jim Crow to Court

World War II underscored the yawning gap between the promise and reality of life in America. Fighting against Nazi racist theories helped to draw attention to real racial problems at home. At the start of the war defense industry managers refused to hire blacks and the races were segregated in the armed services. The war and a threat by black leader A. Philip Randolph to organize a protest march on Washington led to some changes. Executive Order 8802 prohibited discrimination in the war industries. But the outbreak of the Detroit race riot during the hot summer of 1943 demonstrated that blacks were dissatisfied with racial conditions at home. "Our war is not against Hitler and Europe," claimed one black columnist, "but against the Hitlers in America." And blacks drafted to fight against Japan foresaw the irony of many of their fates: "Here lies a black man killed fighting a yellow man for the glory of a white man."

After the war conditions improved at a snail's pace. With an eye upon black Democratic northern voters, Truman established the President's Committee on Civil Rights which issued several reports that most white politicians ignored. While Truman called for "fair employment throughout the federal establishment" and ordered the racial desegregation of the armed services, southern politicians proclaimed the need to return to the embrace of Jim Crow. "No Negro will vote in Georgia for the next four years," Eugene Talmadge promised after he was elected governor of Georgia. And in Congress, Southerners like Senator Theodore G. Bilbo railed against Truman's moderate racial reforms. Opposing Truman's plan for universal military training, Bilbo exhorted, "If you draft Negro boys into the army, give them three good meals a day and let them shoot craps and drink liquor around the barracks for a year, they won't be worth a tinkers dam thereafter."

By the late 1940s blacks realized that they would have to lead the fight against racial injustice. In the early years of the battle, the NAACP spearheaded the struggle. But the organization faced a number of problems, both within and outside the black community. For example, many blacks believed the NAACP was racist and elitist. The organization was staffed by educated middle-class blacks who seemed out of touch with the majority of their race. Worse yet, many blacks like radical Marcus Garvey continued to charge that the NAACP was staffed by light-skinned blacks because it accepted the theory that mulattos were more aggressive, enterprising, and ambitious than their pure-blooded counterparts.

Outside of the black community, the NAACP encountered a hostile white society. In Congress, Southern Democrats—there were no Southern Republicans—opposed any assault on segregation—the prevailing form of institutionalized racism.

Given this racial climate, the NAACP moved cautiously. Instead of attacking segregation head on, the organization chose to chip away at the legal edges of Jim Crow. The separate but equal doctrine was particularly vulnerable. In *Missouri ex rel Gaines* (1939), *Sweatt* v. *Painter* (1950), and *McLaurin* v. *Board of Regents* (1950), the NAACP lawyer demonstrated the impossibility, even the absurdity, of applying the separate but equal yardstick to graduate education and law schools. In all three cases, the Supreme Court agreed. If, the court implied, separate but equal educational systems were to be continued, then states had to pay more than lip service to equality.

In grade school and high school education, just as in graduate education, the South translated separate but equal to read "separate and highly unequal." In South Carolina's Clarendon County, for example, seventy-five percent of the students were black, but the white minority received sixty percent of the educational funds. On the average, the county spent $179 per year on each white student and $43 per year on each black student. Where were the separate but equal standards, asked NAACP lawyers.

Intellectual and financial considerations were not the only factors that precluded equality. Psychologists argued that segregation instilled feelings of inferiority among black children. Black psychologist Kenneth Clark conducted a simple test with black children attending segregated schools. He showed the children two dolls, one black and the other white. In one case, of the sixteen children tested, ten said they liked the white doll better, eleven added that the black doll looked "bad," and nine remarked that the white doll looked "nice." Recalling the tests, Clark noted, "The most disturbing question—and the one that really made me, even as a scientist, upset—was the final question: 'Now show me the doll that's

INTEGRATION IN SPORTS

On April 18, 1946, the sports world focused on a baseball field in Jersey City, an industrial wasteland on the banks of the Passaic River. It was the opening day for the Jersey City Giants of the International League. Their opponents were the Montreal Royals, the Brooklyn Dodgers' leading farm team. Playing second base for the Royals was Jackie Roosevelt Robinson, a pigeon-toed, highly competitive, marvelously talented black athlete. The stadium was filled with curious and excited spectators, and in the press box sportswriters from New York, Philadelphia, Baltimore, and cities further

west fidgeted with their typewriters. It was not just another season opening game. Professional baseball, America's national game, was about to be integrated.

Since the late-nineteenth century professional baseball and most other professional team sports had prohibited competition between whites and blacks. White athletes played for the highest salaries, in the best stadiums, before the most spectators. During the same years black teams barnstormed the country playing where they could and accepting what was offered. For blacks, the pay was low, the stadiums rickety, and the playing conditions varied between bad and dangerous. The *Plessy* v.

Ferguson ideal of "separate but equal" was a cruel joke.

During the period of forced segregation whites stereotyped black athletes. Since colonial times, whites had maintained that blacks were instinctive rather than thoughtful, physical rather than intellectual, complacent rather than ambitious. As athletes, whites believed blacks were physically gifted but lazy, undisciplined, and wholly lacking in competitive drive. Disregarding the success of black athletes in individual sports, whites clung to the racist theory that nature had fashioned blacks to laugh and sing and dance and play, but not to sacrifice, train, work, compete, and win.

The most successful black athletes and teams catered to these stereotypes. The Harlem Globetrotters, for example, played the role of Sambo in sweats. Started in 1927 by white Chicago entrepreneur Abe Saperstein, the all-black Harlem Globetrotters basketball team presented black athletes as wide-eyed, toothy, camera-mugging clowns. White audiences loved their antics—Marques Haynes dribbling circles around his hopeless white opponents while the rest of the Trotters stretched out on the floor feigning sleep; Meadowlark Lemon hiding the basketball under his jersey and sneaking down the court to make a basket; Goose Tatum slam-dunking while reading a comic book; all of them cavorting around with deflated, lopsided, or balloon balls, throwing confetti-filled water buckets on an indulgent crowd, and deviously getting away with every conceivable infraction of the rules.

Saperstein insisted that "his boys" conform off as well as on the court. As a Trotter veteran told new teammate Connie Hawkins, "Abe don't care what you do with colored, but don't let him catch you with no white broads . . . And don't let him see you with a Cadillac. He don't stand for that either." Nor did Saperstein allow his players to contradict whites. He wanted only "happy darkies," not "uppity niggers," on his team.

The Indianapolis Clowns were the Harlem Globetrotters of baseball. They played in grass skirts and body paint and engaged in comedy as much as baseball. Pregame routines included acrobatics and dancing, exaggerated black English, minstrel slapstick, and grinning, always lots of grinning. How could any reasonable person expect major league performances out of people playing baseball in grass skirts and war paint?

Jackie Robinson came to bat in the first inning. His very presence had ended segregation in "organized baseball." Now he wanted to strike a blow against the racist stereotyping. Nervous, he later recalled that his palms seemed "too moist to grip the bat." He didn't even swing at the first six pitches. On the seventh pitch he hit a bouncing ball to the shortstop who easily threw him out. It was a start of sorts.

In the third inning Robinson took his second at-bat. With runners on first and second, he lashed out at the first pitch and hit it over the left field fence 330 feet away. In the press box Wendell Smith and Joe Bostic, two black reporters for the *Amsterdam News*, "laughed and smiled . . . Our hearts beat just a little faster and the thrill ran through us like champagne bubbles." According to

another account, among the white sportswriters "there were some very long faces."

Robinson wasn't through for the day. In the fifth inning he had a bunt single, stole second, advanced to third on a ground ball, and, faking an attempt to steal home, forced a balk and scored. It was a virtuoso performance. During the remainder of the game he had two more hits, another stolen base, and forced a second balk. In the field he was tough, intense, and smart, a reverse image of the stereotypical black athlete. It was a fine day for Robinson and his supporters. "Baseball took up the cudgel of democracy," Bostic wrote, "and an unassuming, but superlative Negro boy ascended the heights of excellence to prove the rightness of the experiment. And prove it in the only correct crucible for such an experiment—the crucible of white hot competition."

The success of Jackie Robinson in baseball led to the integration of the other major professional sports. In 1946 the Cleveland Rams moved their football franchise to Los Angeles and to boost ticket sales signed blacks Kenny Washington and Woody Strode, both of whom had played football with Robinson at UCLA. Professional football thus became integrated. In 1950 the Boston Celtics of the National Basketball Association signed Chuck Cooper of Duquesne to a professional contract, and the New York Knicks signed Nat "Sweetwater" Clifton away from the Harlem Globetrotters, despite Abe Saperstein's bitter protests. The same year the United States Lawn Tennis Association allowed blacks to compete at Forest Hills. In a relatively short time

integration came to American professional sports.

The process was not without individual pain. Robinson especially became the object of hate mail, death threats, and racial slurs. Opposition runners spiked him and pitchers threw at him. Off the field he faced a life of segregated restaurants, clubs, theaters, and neighborhoods. Patient, witty, and quick to forgive, he endured extraordinary humiliation. He became an American hero, but he paid dearly. Throughout the 1946 and 1947 seasons Robinson was plagued by headaches, bouts of depression, nausea, and nightmares. Talking about the pressures on her husband, Rachel Robinson recalled, "There were the stresses of just knowing that you were pulling a big weight of a whole lot of people on your back . . . I think Jackie felt . . . that there would be serious consequences if he didn't succeed and that one of them would be that nobody would try again for a long time." Of course, the other black players also confronted trials on and off the field, but as Robinson's teammate Roy Campanella said, "nothing compared to what Jackie was going through."

Integration in sports preceded integration in society at large. But whether in sports or the civil rights movement, racial gains were paid for by individuals willing to risk serious hardships. Change seldom came easily and the struggle never ended quickly. In baseball, for example, as late as 1988 many white bureaucrats still resisted the idea of black managers, resorting to the same racial stereotyping that had plagued blacks for over three hundred and fifty years in America.

While some children attended segregated schools, others such as these black children in West Memphis, Arkansas, were crammed into the sanctuary of a church to hold classes.

most like you.' Many of the children became emotionally upset when they had to identify with the doll they had rejected. These children saw themselves as inferior, and they accepted the inferiority as part of reality." When asked that question, one child even smiled and pointed to the black doll: "That's a nigger. I'm a nigger."

It was inhumane to continue such psychological damage, the NAACP concluded. In 1952 the NAACP consolidated a series of cases under the name of the first case—*Brown* v. *Board of Education of Topeka*—which challenged the very existence of the separate but equal doctrine. The Supreme Court listened to the arguments and began their extended deliberation. Then in September 1953, Chief Justice Fred M. Vinson, who seemed to be leaning against ending segregation, died of a heart attack.

President Eisenhower named Earl Warren to take Vinson's place. It was a political, not an ideological, appointment. Formerly governor of California, Warren had helped Ike win the Republican nomination in 1952. Appointment as Chief Justice of the United States was a fine reward. On the surface, minorities had little reason to suspect that Warren would be on their side. During World War II he had been active in the relocation of 100,000 Japanese-Americans into internment camps; but in the years after that action, Warren realized that it had been a mistake. The *Brown* case offered him a second chance.

After working to achieve unanimity in the court, Warren read the Court's decision on May 17, 1954. "Does segregation of children in public schools solely on the basis of race, even though the physical facilities and other tangible factors may be equal, deprive children of the minority group of equal educational opportunities?" Warren asked. "We believe it does," he answered. "To separate them from others of similar age and qualifications solely because of their race generates a feeling of inferiority as to their status in the community that may affect their hearts and minds in a way very unlikely ever to be undone." In public education, he concluded, the "separate but equal" doctrine has no place. "Separate educational facilities are inherently unequal."

The *Chicago Defender* labeled the *Brown* decision "a second emancipation proclamation," and the *Washington Post* called it "a new birth of freedom." But such Court decisions have to be enforced. As Charles Houston, a leading NAACP lawyer, remarked, "Nobody needs to explain to a Negro the difference between the law in the books and the law in action."

A Failure of Leadership

A year after the *Brown* decision, the Supreme Court ruled that schools should desegregate "with all deliberate speed." It was a vague phrase, a cautious phrase, a legally meaningless phrase. Perhaps it was the price Warren had to pay for the previous year's unanimous verdict. In any case, the second decision placed the burden of desegregation into the hands of local, state, and national leaders. If the process was to be accomplished with the minimum amount of conflict, those leaders would have to be firm in their resolve to see justice done. Such, however, would not be the case.

On the national level, Eisenhower moved uncomfortably and cautiously on the issue of civil rights and desegregation. Born in Texas and reared in the white Midwest, Ike spent most of his life in a segregated army. He did not see racism as a great moral issue, and he was unresponsive to the black demand for equality. In truth, Eisenhower believed that the *Brown* decision had been a mistake, for which he blamed Earl Warren. He later asserted that the appointment of Warren had been the "biggest damn fool mistake" he had ever made. When questioned about the decision in 1954, he claimed, "I don't believe you can change the hearts of men with laws or decisions."

The brand of Ike's leadership and his ambitions for the Republican party further weakened his response. His behind-the-scenes approach—the "hidden hand" style—led him to avoid speaking out clearly and forcefully on the subject. Moral outrage was not his style. In addition, he was popular in the South and harbored hopes of bringing that section of the country into the Republican party. Therefore, instead of deploring the killing of Emmett Till and other atrocities by southern whites against blacks, Eisenhower kept quiet.

In the South, Eisenhower's silence was often as deadly as bullets. If Eisenhower had acted decisively in support of the *Brown* v. *Board of Education* decision—if he had placed the full weight of his office behind desegregation—there is some evidence that the South would have complied peacefully with the verdict. By not acting forcefully, however, Eisenhower strengthened the position of Southerners who equated desegregation with death. "Ending segregation," Governor James F. Byrnes of South Carolina said, "would mark the beginning of the end of civilization in the South as we have known it." Governor Herman Talmadge agreed, adding that integration would also inevitably lead to intermarriage and the "mongrelization of the races."

The Little Rock crisis demonstrated the failure of national and state leadership. In 1957 in Little Rock, Arkansas, school officials were ordered to desegregate. As they prepared to do so, Governor Orville Faubus, locked in a reelection fight, intervened. He announced that any integration attempt would disrupt public order and sent in the National Guard to prevent black children from entering Central High. While Eisenhower quietly tried to maneuver behind the scenes, a crisis brewed. On the morning of September 23, 1957, when black children attempted to attend school, they were inhospitably greeted by an angry mob chanting, "two, four, six, eight, we ain't going to integrate."

Television turned the ugly episode into a national drama. Millions of Americans for the first time witnessed violent racism as angry whites moved around the defenseless black children like hungry sharks. Disturbed by the episode, poet Robert Lowell wrote, "When I crouch to my television set, the drained faces of Negro school-children rise like balloons." For the first but not last time, television aided the cause of civil rights by conveying the human suffering caused by racism.

To restore order, Eisenhower federalized the Arkansas National Guard and sent one thousand paratroopers from the 101st Airborne Division to Little Rock. It was the first time since Reconstruction that a president ordered troops to the South. Although their presence desegregated Central High in 1957, the following year Faubus closed Little Rock's public schools, declaring "I stand now and always in opposition to integration by force or at bayonet point." Taken together, Faubus's shortsighted political moves and Eisenhower's refusal to take action until public order had been disrupted created a crisis that more thoughtful leadership could have avoided.

The Word from Montgomery

The failure of white leaders convinced blacks that court orders would not magically produce equal rights. The fight would be difficult, the march long. On a cold afternoon in Montgomery, Alabama, Rosa Parks, a well-respected black seamstress, who was active in the NAACP took a significant stride toward equality. She boarded a bus and sat in the first row of the "colored" section. The white section of the bus quickly filled, and according to Jim Crow rules, blacks were expected to give up their seats rather than force whites—male or female—to stand. The time came for Mrs. Parks to give up her seat. She stayed seated. When told by the bus driver to get up or he would call the police, she said, "You may do that." Later she recalled that the act of defiance was "just something I had to do." The bus stopped, the driver summoned the police, and Rosa Parks was arrested.

Black Montgomery rallied to Mrs. Parks's side. Like her, they were tired of riding in the back of the bus, tired of giving up their seats to whites, tired of having their lives restricted by Jim Crow. Local black leaders decided to organize a boycott of Montgomery's white-owned and white-operated bus system. They hoped that economic pressure would force changes

Paratroopers escorted black students to and from school in Little Rock, Arkansas, after violence erupted when the schools were told to desegregate.

which court decisions could not. For the next 381 days, more than ninety percent of Montgomery's black citizens participated in an heroic and successful demonstration against racial segregation. The common black attitude toward the protest was voiced by an elderly black woman when a black leader offered her a ride. "No," she replied, "my feets is tired, but my soul is rested."

To lead the boycott, Montgomery blacks turned to the new minister of the Dexter Avenue Baptist Church, a young man named Martin Luther King, Jr. Reared in Atlanta, the son of a respected and financially secure minister, King had been educated at Morehouse College, Crozier Seminary, and Boston University, from which he earned a doctorate in theology. King was an intellectual, excited by ideas and deeply influenced by the philosophical writings of Henry David Thoreau and Mahatma Gandhi as well as the teachings of Christ. They believed in the power of nonviolent, direct action.

King's words as well as his ideas stirred people's souls. At the start of the Montgomery boycott he told his followers:

> There comes a time when people get tired. We are here this evening to say to those who have mistreated us so long that we are tired—tired of being segregated and humiliated, tired of being kicked about by the brutal feet of oppression . . . We've come here tonight to be saved from the patience that makes us patient with anything less than freedom and justice . . . If you protest courageously and yet with dignity and Christian love, in the history books that are written in future generations, historians will have to pause and say "there lived a great people—a black people—who injected a new meaning and dignity into the veins of civilization."

In King, civil rights had found a genuine spokesman, one who preached a doctrine of change guided by Christian love not racial hatred. "In our protest," he observed, "there will be no cross burnings. No white person will be taken from his home by a hooded Negro mob and brutally murdered. There will be no threats and no intimidation."

The success of the Montgomery boycott inspired nonviolent black protests elsewhere in the South. Increasingly, young blacks took the

Rosa Parks's arrest for refusing to move to the back of the bus led to citywide bus boycotts throughout 1956. Martin Luther King, Jr., was one of the first to ride the buses when the Supreme Court ordered integration.

lead. Violence and biased law enforcement did not stop the protesters. Indeed, during the next two months, demonstrations erupted in fifty-four cities in nine states. The protesters were arrested, jailed, beaten, and even knocked off their feet by high-pressure fire hoses, but still they protested.

The protests were widely reported in the country's newspapers and televised nightly on the news shows. They confronted Americans everywhere with the stark reality of segregation. Ignorance of the situation became an impossibility; and as the violence continued, pressure mounted on white national politicians to take decisive action. By the early 1960s the word from Montgomery had reinforced the *Brown* decision. It was time for freedom to become a reality. (See Chapter 29 for fuller treatment of civil rights.)

THE SOUNDS OF CHANGE

Beginning in the late 1960s, American advertisers started to market a new commodity—the fifties. They marketed it as a Golden Decade, a carefree time before the assassination of John F. Kennedy, the Vietnam War, and Watergate. According to the popular myth, kids in the 1950s thought "dope" referred to a dull-witted person, parents married for life, and major family problems revolved around whether or not sis had a date for the prom. This image of the decade has taken different forms. *Happy Days* presented it on television; *American Grafitti* and *Diner* (set in the early '60s) detailed it on the silver screen. It was an age of innocence, tranquility, and static charm. In truth, however, that carefully packaged Golden Decade never existed. Instead, the decade was alive with dynamic, creative tensions.

Father Knows Best

The stock television situation comedy of the 1950s centered on a white family with a happily married husband and wife and two—or sometimes three—well-adjusted children. Most often, the family lived in a white, two-story suburban home, from which the father ventured daily to his white-collar job. The wife did not work outside the house—there was no need since the husband made a comfortable living. In any case, the shows emphasized, wives were also mothers, and mothers were supposed to stay home and tend the children. *Father*

Television programs of the 1950s often centered around a happy, well-adjusted family with two or three children living in suburbia.

Knows Best was the classic example of this genre. It ran from 1954 to 1962 and signaled an optimistic outlook through its title song, "Just Around the Corner There's a Rainbow in the Sky."

The picture these sitcoms presented of America was not entirely inaccurate. Starting after World War II, Americans moved steadily toward the suburbs, which during the 1950s grew six times faster than cities. Several factors contributed to this migration. The high price of urban real estate had driven industries out of the cities, and as always in American history, the population followed the jobs. By 1970 suburban areas had more manufacturing jobs than the central cities. In addition, developers built abundant, inexpensive homes, which newly married couples, aided by VA and FHA loans, purchased. Of the thirteen million homes constructed during the 1950s, eleven million were built in the suburbs.

Nor was the television image of predominantly white suburban families misleading. A far greater percentage of whites than blacks moved to the suburbs. In 1950 blacks comprised 12.5 percent of America's urban population and 4.9 percent of the country's suburban population. By 1970 the urban figure had climbed to 20.5 percent and the suburban number declined modestly to 4.8 percent. Housing and job restrictions worked to keep blacks in the central cities while allowing whites to fill the suburban areas.

Even the image of the suburban housewife preoccupied with her husband and her family was socially sanctioned. American women in the 1950s had babies as never before. The population of the United States increased by under 10 million in the 1930s, 19 million in the 1940s, and a staggering 30 million in the 1950s. During the 1950s the nation's growth rate approached that of India. The best-sellers list even indicated America's concern with children. Between 1946 and 1976 the pocket edition of Dr. Benjamin Spock's *Baby and Child Care* sold over 23 million copies, ranking it behind only the Bible and the combined works of Mickey Spillane and Dr. Seuss.

During the age of remarkable fertility, popular writers glorified the role of the mother. The best-seller *Modern Woman: The Lost Sex* went as far as to say that an independent woman was "a contradiction in terms." The ideal woman, writers observed, was content being a wife and a mother or, in a word, a homemaker. "Women must boldly announce," wrote novelist Sloan Wilson, "that no job is more exacting, more necessary, or more rewarding than that of housewife and mother." In the 1950s women married younger and had children sooner than they had in the previous two decades.

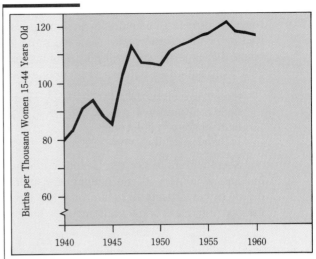

Figure 27.1
American Birth Rate, 1940-1960

The Other Side of the Coin

Father Knows Best and other shows portray an ideal world where serious problems seldom intrude and where life lacks complexity. In fact, the move to suburbia and the changes in family life forced Americans to reevaluate many of their beliefs.

Cultural critics, for example, claimed that life in suburbia fostered mindless conformity. Lewis Mumford described suburbs as "a multitude of uniform, unidentifiable houses, lined up

Table 27.1

Population of Metropolitan Areas by Region, Size, and Race, 1950-1970				
Year		Inner City	Suburbs	Black Population as percent of Inner City	Black Population as percent of Suburbs
1950	White	43,001,634	33,248,836		
	Black	6,194,948	1,736,521	12.5	4.9
	Other	216,210	102,531		
1970	White	49,430,443	71,148,286		
	Black	13,140,331	3,630,279	20.5	4.8
	Other	1,226,169	843,303		
Historical Statistics of the United States, Bicentennial Edition, vol. 1, p. 40.					

inflexibly, at uniform distances, on uniform roads, in a treeless communal wasteland, inhabited by people of the same class, the same income, the same age group." And a popular song called the suburban homes:

> Little boxes on the hillside,
> Little boxes made of ticky tacky
> Little boxes on the hillside,
> Little boxes all the same.

Some writers feared the United States had become a country of unthinking consumers driven by advertisers to desire only the latest gadget. Americans bought automobiles, houses, and electrical appliances as never before. Thirty percent more Americans owned homes in 1970 than in 1940. Between 1945 and 1960 the number of cars in the country increased by 133 percent and the use of electricity tripled. Indeed, the buying of homes, cars, televisions, and electrical appliances fueled the tremendous economic growth between 1945 and 1970. Clearly buying was good for the American economy, but was it beneficial to the individuals who spent more and more of their time in their cars and watching their televisions? Cultural observers despaired.

Many women also expressed frustration about their roles as wives and mothers. One poll of the 1934 graduates of the best women's colleges reported that one out of every three women felt unfulfilled. Although many women worked, cultural stereotyping prevented most of them from rising to the higher paying, more prestigious positions. In addition, noted Betty Friedan, those women who did place a career above marriage or family were regarded as abnormal.

The problems of suburban life were explored in numerous films, novels, articles, and advice books. The film *Invasion of the Body Snatchers* (1956) is an outstanding example of the fear that suburbia had created a nation of conformists. In the movie, the inhabitants of the town Santa Mira are turned into emotionless shells by giant pods from outer space. Like abusers of Miltown or Thorazine—the most popular adult drugs of the 1950s—the pod-people utterly lack individuality. As one explains, podism means being "reborn into an untroubled world, where everyone's the same." In that world, "there is no need for love or emotion." For such cultural critics as David Riesman, author of *The Lonely Crowd* (1955), America's acceptance of conformity threatened to make podism a form of reality.

The critics, however, overreacted to the "suburban threat." If the houses looked the same, the people were individuals—even if they often banded together to try to form suburban communities. In the suburbs, white working-class families could afford for the first time to purchase homes and live middle-class lives. This was a real accomplishment. The

Suburban housing developments like this one illustrated the conformity that cultural critics feared was becoming more common in the country.

problems that critics observed in the suburbs—the tendency toward conformity, cultural homogeneity, materialism, and anxiety over sex roles—were urban problems as well.

The Meaning of Elvis

The harshest critics of "suburban values" were American youths. Their criticism took different forms. Some of it was thoughtful and formalized, the result of the best efforts of young intellectuals. At other times it took a more visceral form, a protest that came from the gut rather than the mind. Of the second type of protest, none was more widely embraced by youths—or roundly attacked by adults—than rock and roll.

Rock and roll was the bastard mulatto child of a heterogeneous American culture. It combined black rhythm and blues with white country music. It was made possible by the post–World War II demographic changes. The movement of southern blacks and whites to the cities of the upper South and North threw together different musical traditions and forged an entirely new sound. Its lyrics and heavy beat challenged the accepted standards of "good taste" in music. Giving voice to this challenge, black rock-and-roll artist Chuck Berry sang:

> Well, I'm gonna write a little letter, gonna mail it to my local D.J.
> Yes, it's a jumpin' little record I want my jockey to play
> Roll over Beethoven, I gotta hear it again today
> You know my temp'rature's risin' and the jukebox blowin' a fuse
> My heart's beatin' rhythm and my soul keeps singin' the blues
> Roll over Beethoven and tell Tchaikovsky the news.

Confronting conventional morality, rock and roll was openly vulgar. The very term—"rock 'n' roll"—had long been used in blues songs to describe lovemaking, and early black rock-and-roll singers glorified physical relationships. Little Richard sang:

> Well, Long Tall Sally she's built for speed, she got
> Everythin' that Uncle John needs.

Elvis Presley, one of the great pioneers of rock and roll music, was the target of much controversy throughout his entire life.

And in another song, he boasted:

> I'm gonna RIP IT UP!
> I'm gonna rock it up!
> I'm gonna shake it up. I'm gonna ball it up!
> I'm gonna RIP IT UP and ball tonight.

From its emergence in the early 1950s, rock and roll generated angry criticism. In the South, white church groups attacked it as part of an NAACP plot to corrupt the morals of southern youths and foster integration. In Hartford, Connecticut, Dr. Francis J. Braceland described rock and roll as "a communicable disease, with music appealing to adolescent insecurity and driving teenagers to do outlandish things . . . It's cannibalistic and tribalistic." Particularly between 1954 and 1958, there were numerous crusades to ban rock and roll from the airways.

Most of the critics of rock and roll focused on Elvis Presley, who more than any other artist most fully fused country music with rhythm and blues. In his first record, he gave the rhythm and blues song "That's All Right Mama" a country feel and the country classic "Blue

1947 Jackie Robinson integrates professional baseball

1954 Gamal Abdel Nasser comes to power in Egypt; Ernest Hemingway wins Nobel Prize for literature

1955 American Federation of Labor and Congress of Industrial Organizations merge to form the AFL-CIO; Start of the Montgomery bus boycott; rock and roll attacked as "immoral"

1956 Congress passes the Federal Aid Highway Act; Soviets suppress the anticommunist revolution in Hungary; Suez Crisis erupts during Eisenhower's bid for reelection; Elvis Presley emerges on the national music scene

1957 President Eisenhower sends federal troops to desegregate Central High School in Little Rock, Arkansas; Jack Kerouac publishes *On The Road*; Congress passes Civil Rights Act prohibiting discrimination in public places based on race, color, religion, or national origins

1958 U.S. Marines sent to Lebanon to restore order

1959 Alaska and Hawaii become 49th and 50th states; Vice-president Richard Nixon engages in "kitchen debate" with Soviet Premier Khrushchev; Fidel Castro comes to power in Cuba; Berry Gordy, Jr., starts Motown Records

1960 U-2 pilot Francis Gary Powers shot down over Soviet territory

---

Moon Over Kentucky" a rhythm and blues swing. It was a unique exhibition of genius. In addition, Presley exuded sexuality. When he appeared on the Ed Sullivan Show, network executives instructed cameramen to avoid shots of Elvis's suggestive physical movements. Finally, Presley upset segregationists by performing "race music." Head of Sun Records Sam Phillips had once claimed, "If I could find a white man who had the Negro sound and the Negro feel, I could make a million dollars." Presley was that white man.

In the end, however, the protests implicit in Elvis Presley and rock and roll were largely co-opted by middle-class American culture. Record producers, most of whom were white, smoothed the jagged edges of rock and roll. Sexually explicit black recordings were rewritten and rerecorded—a process known as "covering"—by white performers and then sold to white youths. Black singer Joe Turner, for example, recorded "Shake, Rattle and Roll" for a black audience. Its lyrics ran:

> Get out of that bed,
> And wash your face and hands.
> Get into the kitchen,
> Make some noise with the pots and pans.
> Well you wear low dresses,
> The sun comes shinin' through.
> I can't believe my eyes,
> That all of this belong to you.

The white group Bill Haley and the Comets "covered" the song for a white audience. The new version stated:

> Get out in that kitchen,
> And rattle those pots and pans.
> Roll my breakfast
> 'Cause I'm a hungry man.
> You wear those dresses,
> Your hair done up so nice.
> You look so warm,
> But your heart is cold as ice.

In the second recording all references to beds and bodies have been eliminated; by 1959 rock and roll had become an accepted part of mainstream American culture.

A Different Beat

Rock-and-roll artists never rejected the idea of success in America. If they challenged conventional sexual mores and tried to create a unique sound, they accepted the rewards of success in a capitalistic society. Elvis Presley translated success into a steady stream of Cadillacs and conventional, unchallenging films. Not all youth protests, however, were so easily absorbed into middle-class culture. The Beat movement, for example, questioned the values at the heart of that culture.

The Beat Generation extolled the very thing that conventional Americans abhorred, they rejected what the others prized. Beats scorned materialism and traditional family life, religion, sexuality, and politics. They renounced the American Dream. Instead, they valued spontaneity and intuition, searching for truth through Eastern mysticism and drugs. Although whites formed the rank and file of the Beat Generation, they glorified the supposedly "natural" life of black Americans, a life representing (at least for whites) pure instinctual drives. They adopted black music and the jive words of the black lexicon. *Cat, solid, chick, Big Apple, square,* were all absorbed into the Beat vocabulary.

Educated at Columbia and Berkeley, Allen Ginsberg was one of the leading writers of the Beat Generation.

Allen Ginsberg was the leading poet of the Beat Generation. A graduate of Columbia University, where he was influenced by the lifestyle of New York City lowlifes and artists, Ginsberg moved to San Francisco in the mid-1950s. There, surrounded by kindred souls, Ginsberg came to accept his homosexuality and preached a life based on experimentation. He also developed an authentic poetic voice. In 1955 he wrote "Howl," the prototypical Beat poem. Written under the influence of drugs, "Howl" is a literary kaleidoscope, a breathless succession of stark images and passionate beliefs. In a unique but soon to be widely imitated style, Ginsberg declared,

> I saw the best minds of my generation destroyed
>   by madness, starving hysterically naked,
> dragging themselves through the negro streets
>   at dawn
> looking for an angry fix . . .

Ginsberg even questioned accepted Cold War beliefs. He wrote:

> America you don't really want to go to war.
> America it's them bad Russians.
> Them Russians them Russians and them China-
>   men. And them Russians.
> Them Russians want to eat us alive.
> America this is quite serious.
> America this is the impression I get from looking
>   in the television set.
> America is this correct?

Ginsberg and Jack Kerouac, the leading Beat novelist, outraged adults but discovered followers on college campuses and in cities across America. They tapped an underground dissatisfaction with the prevailing blandness of conventional culture. In this their appeal was similar to that of rock and roll. Both were scattering seeds which would bear fruit during the next decade.

CONCLUSION

Ike's America was both more and less than what it seemed. In foreign and domestic affairs, Eisenhower appeared to allow his subordinates to run the country, when in reality he made the important decisions. Whether it was national highways or the Middle East, Eisenhower's vision of order helped shape American policy. He was more influential than most Americans during the 1950s realized.

If Eisenhower was more active than he appeared, then the country was more dynamic than it seemed on the surface. Although critics railed against the conformity of suburban America, everywhere there were signs of change. During the 1950s blacks quickened the pace of their struggle for equality and youths experimented with alternatives to traditional behavior. And increasingly these two rebellions merged to form a distinct subculture. During the 1960s, the war in Vietnam would give a political edge to that subculture.

REVIEW SUMMARY

Between 1952 and 1960, during the two terms of Dwight Eisenhower, America experienced quiet but profound changes. Although Eisenhower continued the policy of containment and kept America at peace, at home the stage was being set for the great social and political confrontations of the 1960s.

> the Eisenhower administration expanded America's highway system, leading to great social and cultural changes
>
> the Civil Rights movement made tremendous legal gains and found a leader in Martin Luther King, Jr.
>
> "beats" and rock-and-rollers challenged American cultural norms

In short, beneath the quiet surface of Ike's America, great movements were taking shape.

SUGGESTIONS FOR FURTHER READING

OVERVIEWS AND SURVEYS

Stephen Ambrose, *Rise to Globalism: American Foreign Policy, 1938–1980* (1980); William H. Chafe, *The Unfinished Journey* (1986) and *The American Woman* (1972); Alexander DeConde, *A History of American Foreign Policy* (1963); Robert H. Ferrell, *American Diplomacy* (1969); Alonzo Hamby, *The Imperial Years* (1976); Godfrey Hodgson, *America in Our Time* (1975); Walter LaFeber, *America, Russia, and the Cold War* (1976); R. W. Leopold, *The Growth of American Foreign Policy* (1967); William Leuchtenburg, *A Troubled Feast* (1983); Thomas G. Paterson, *American Foreign Policy* (1977); Richard Polenberg, *One Nation Divisible* (1980); Emily and Norman Rosenberg, *In Our Time* (1982); Frederick R. Siegel, *Troubled Journey* (1984); William A. Williams, *The Tragedy of American Diplomacy* (1972) and *The Roots of the Modern American Empire* (1969); Lawrence Wittner, *Cold War America* (1979); Howard Zinn, *Postwar America, 1945–1971* (1973).

QUIET CHANGES

Charles Alexander, *Holding the Line* (1975); Stephen Ambrose, *Eisenhower, Vol. 1 and 2.* (1983, 1984); Robert A. Caro, *The Power Broker: Robert Moses and the Fall of New York* (1974); Chester L. Cooper, *The Lion's Last Roar: Suez, 1956* (1979); Robert A. Divine, *Eisenhower and the Cold War* (1981); Robert J. Donovan, *Eisenhower* (1956); Fred I. Greenstein, *The Hidden-Hand Presidency: Eisenhower as Leader* (1982); Townsend Hoopes, *The Devil and John Foster Dulles* (1973); Peter Lyon, *Eisenhower: Portrait of the Hero* (1974); John B. Rae, *The Road and the Car in American Life* (1971); Mark Rose, *Interstate* (1979); Walt W. Rostow, *The Stages of Economic Growth* (1959); James Sundquist, *Politics and Policy: The Eisenhower, Kennedy, and Johnson Years* (1968).

WE SHALL OVERCOME

Jervis Anderson, *A. Philip Randolph* (1973); Numan V. Bartley, *The Rise of Massive Resistance: Race and Politics in the South During the 1950s* (1959); Jack Bass, *Unlikely Heroes* (1981); Sally Belfrage, *Freedom Summer* (1965); William Berman, *The Politics of Civil Rights in the Truman Administration* (1970); Albert Blaustein and Clarence Clyde Ferguson, Jr., *Desegregation and the Law* (1962); Robert Conot, *Rivers of Blood, Years of Darkness* (1967); William Chafe, *Civilities and Civil Rights: Greensboro, North Carolina, and the Black Struggle for Freedom* (1980); Richard Dalfiume, *Desegregation of the U.S. Armed Forces* (1969); David Garrow, *Protest at Selma* (1976); Peter Goldman, *The Death and Life of Malcolm X* (1974); Alex Haley, *Autobiography of Malcolm X* (1966); Richard Kluger, *Simple Justice* (1976); Steven Lawson, *Black Ballots* (1977); David L. Lewis, *King* (1970); Manning Marable, *Race, Reform, and Rebellion: The Second Reconstruction in Black America, 1945–1982* (1984); Donald R. McCoy and Richard Ruetten, *Quest and Response: Minority Rights and the Truman Administration* (1973); Melton A. McLaurin, *Separate Pasts: Growing Up White in the Segregated South* (1987); August Meier and Elliot Rudwick, *CORE: A Study in the Civil Rights Movement, 1942–1968* (1973); Anne Moody, *Coming of Age in Mississippi* (1970); Benjamin Muse, *The American Negro Revolution* (1970); Gunnar Myrdal, *An American Dilemma* (1944); Stephen B. Oates, *Let the Trumpet Sound: The Life of Martin Luther King, Jr.* (1982); William L. O'Neill, *American High: The Years of Confidence, 1945–1960* (1986); James Peck, *Freedom Ride* (1962); Howell Raines, *My Soul Is Rested* (1977); Morton Sasna, *In Search of the Silent South*

(1977); Harvard Sitkoff, *The Struggle for Black Equality* (1983); Howard Zinn, *The Southern Mystique* (1962).

THE SOUNDS OF CHANGE

Kent Anderson, *Television Fraud* (1978); Erik Barnouw, *Tube of Plenty* (1982); Carl Belz, *The Story of Rock* (1969); William Chafe, *Women and Equality* (1977); Bruce Cook, *The Beat Generation* (1971); Marcus Cunliffe, *The Literature of the United States* (1967); Scott Donaldson, *The Suburban Myth* (1969); Betty Friedan, *The Feminine Mystique* (1963); John Kenneth Galbraith, *The Affluent Society* (1958); Herbert Gans, *The Levittowners* (1957); Michael Harrington, *The Other America* (1962); Molly Haskins, *From Reverence to Rape* (1978); Will Herberg, *Protestant,* *Catholic, Jew* (1955); Jerry Hopkins, *The Rock Story* (1970); Pauline N. Kael, *I Lost It at the Movies* (1965); Marcus Klein, *The American Novel Since World War II* (1970); David Marc, *Demographic Vistas: Television in American Culture* (1984); Greil Marcus, *The Mystery Train* (1982); Douglas Miller and Marion Nowak, *The Fifties: The Way We Really Were* (1977); James Patterson, *America's Struggle Against Poverty, 1900–1980* (1983); Ned Polsky, *Hustlers, Beats, and Others* (1985); David Potter, *People of Plenty* (1954); David Riesman, *The Lonely Crowd* (1958); Stephen M. Rose, *The Betrayal of the Poor: Transformation of Community Action* (1972); I. F. Stone, *The Haunted 50's* (1963); Michael Wood, *America in the Movies* (1975).

Fig. 287

CHAPTER 28
Vietnam and the Crisis of Authority

Ho Chi Minh was born roughly eighteen thousand miles from America but he might as well have come from a different planet. Ho was a tiny man, a frail, thin splinter of a man. He was gentle, and in public always deferential. Even after he had come to sole power in North Vietnam, he steadfastly avoided all the trappings of authority. Instead of uniforms or the white sharkskin suit of the mandarin, Ho favored the simple shorts and sandals worn by the Vietnamese peasants. He was sure of who he was—certain of his place in Vietnamese history—and he had no desire to impress others with his position. To his followers, he was "Uncle Ho," the kind, bachelor relative who treated all Vietnamese citizens like the children he never had.

Ho was born in 1890 in a village in a central province of Vietnam and originally named Nguyen Sinh Cung. In 1911 Ho left Vietnam and began a generation-long world odyssey. Signing aboard a French freighter, he moved from one port to the next. For a time he stayed in the United States, visiting Boston, New York City, and San Francisco. He was amazed not only by America's skyscrapers but also by the fact that immigrants in the United States enjoyed the same legal rights as American citizens. He was also struck by the impatience of the American people, their expectations of immediate results. (Later, during the Vietnam War, Ho would say to his military leaders, "Don't worry, Americans are an impatient people. When things begin to go wrong, they'll leave.")

After three years of almost constant travel, Ho settled in London, where he served the rich at the elegant Carlton Hotel. He lived in squalid quarters and learned that poverty existed even in the wealthiest, most powerful countries. Then it was on to Paris, where he came in contact with the French left. There he studied, and his nationalist ambitions became tinged with revolutionary teachings. He was still in Paris when the Great War ended and the world leaders came to Versailles for the Peace Conference. Inspired by Woodrow Wilson's call for national self-determination, Ho wrote that "all subject peoples are filled with hope by the prospect that an era of right and justice is opening to them . . . in the struggle of civilization against barbarism." Ho wanted to meet Wilson; he wanted to plea for independence for his country. Wilson ignored his request; Vietnam remained France's colony. Ho moved on— farther east and further left.

Disillusioned with France and socialism, Ho traveled to Moscow, where Lenin had declared war against imperialism. In the Soviet Union Ho embraced communism. In the ideology he saw a road to his ultimate goal, the liberation of Vietnam. By the early 1920s he was actively organizing Vietnamese exiles into a revolutionary force. He continued to travel—to Western Europe, back to Russia, to China, back to Russia, to Thailand, back to the West. He lived a life of secrecy, moving from place to place, changing his name, renouncing anything even remotely resembling a personal life. No wife, no children, few friends—only a cause. As he advised one Vietnamese returning to the homeland, "The colonialists will be on your trail. Keep away from our friends' homes and don't hesitate to pose as a degenerate if it will help put the police off the scent . . . "

In 1941 Ho returned to Vietnam. The time was right, he believed, to free Vietnam once and for all from colonial domination. The Japanese had forced out the French; now Ho and his followers would force out the Japanese. Once again Ho allied himself with the United States. Working alongside American OSS agents, Ho proved his mettle. He impressed the OSS agents with his bravery, intelligence, and unflagging

Ho Chi Minh

devotion to his course. On September 2, 1945, borrowing passages from the American Declaration of Independence, Ho declared Vietnamese independence.

The French had different plans for Vietnam, but Ho's struggle continued. In candid moments he admitted that he didn't expect to live to see Vietnam fully independent. Yet he knew that the struggle of others would eventually secure independence. Ho had patience. It was a quality that the West—first France and then the United States—found difficult to understand.

That was only one of the qualities of Ho and of the Vietnamese that the West didn't understand. A deep intellectual chasm divided Vietnam and the West. The West viewed history as a straight line in which progress was the governing principle. Emphasizing technological advancements and material improvements, Westerners glorified change and prized individualism.

The Vietnamese were products of different beliefs. Notions of competition, invention, and technological change were anathema to tradition-bound Vietnamese. For a thousand years they had survived using the same rice cultivating methods. Often, however, the margin between survival and death was a razor's edge. Unlike the United States, Vietnam did not have fertile frontier areas to settle. To make do with the land they had, the Vietnamese organized life around villages and practiced cooperative existence. Rich people were considered selfish because their wealth *had* to be gained at the expense of others. As one authority explained, "the idea remains with the Vietnamese that great wealth is antisocial, not a sign of success but a sign of selfishness."

Like wealth, individualism threatened the corporate nature of village life, based on duties, not individual rights, and on social harmony more than individual justice. Even their language excluded the idea of individualism. Vietnamese has no personal pronoun equivalent to the Western *I, je, ich.* A person speaks of oneself in relationship to the person being addressed—for example, as "your teacher," "your brother," "your wife."

Nor did Vietnamese believe in intellectual freedom, which fostered debate and discord, rather than community stability. Americans considered Soviet communism evil because it discouraged the exchange of free ideas; Ho Chi Minh was drawn to the doctrine because it provided a set of answers not subject to questioning. Ho Chi Minh was the product of that closed

world. America was the prophet of an open world. During the period between 1954 and 1973, United States officials became convinced that they had to "save" Vietnam from Ho Chi Minh and his communist brand of nationalism. Given Vietnamese leadership, traditions, and desire for independence, the American intervention in Vietnam was almost certain to fail.

THE ILLUSION OF GREATNESS

Television's President

John Fitzgerald Kennedy was made for television. His tall, thin body gave him the strong vertical line that cameras love, and his weather-beaten good looks appealed to women without intimidating men. He had a full head of hair, and even in the winter he maintained a tan. Complementing his appearance was his attitude. He was always "cool" in public. This too was tailor-made for the "cool medium" television. Wit, irony, and understatement, all delivered with a studied nonchalance, translate well on television. Table thumping, impassioned speech, and even earnest sincerity just do not work on television.

In the 1960 presidential race Kennedy challenged his Republican opponent Richard M. Nixon to a series of television debates. At the time, Kennedy faced an uphill battle. Young, handsome, and wealthy, Kennedy was considered by many to be singularly unprepared to make an effective president. His undistinguished political record stood in stark contrast to Nixon's work in Congress and eight years as Eisenhower's vice-president. In addition, Kennedy was Catholic and Americans had never elected a Catholic president. Behind in the polls, Kennedy needed a dramatic boost. Thus the challenge. Against the advice of his campaign manager, Nixon accepted.

The first debate was held in Chicago on September 26, 1960, only a little more than a month before the election. Nixon arrived looking ill and weak. During the previous six weeks he had banged his kneecap, which became infected, spent several weeks at the Walter Reed Hospital, and then caught a bad chest cold that

During the Kennedy-Nixon debates, John Kennedy demonstrated that for television politics, style was more important than substance.

Nixon fought back. He perspired, scored debating points, produced memorized facts, and struggled to win; but his efforts were "hot"— bad television. Instead of hearing a knowledgeable candidate, viewers saw a nervous, uncertain man, one whose clothes didn't fit and whose face looked pasty and white. In contrast, what Kennedy said sounded statesmanlike, and he *looked* very good. Kennedy was the clear winner. Only later did Nixon realize that the telecast had been a production, not a debate.

The polls registered the results. For the first time during the campaign, Kennedy inched ahead of Nixon in a Gallup poll. Republicans realized the impact of the debate. Senator Barry Goldwater called it "a disaster." Most of the people who were undecided before watching the debate voted for Kennedy. That proved to be the margin of victory. Only one-tenth of one percent separated the two candidates. Perhaps the most important result of the election, however, was not Kennedy's victory but the demonstration of the power of television. It came into its own in 1960.

The "Macho" Presidency

In his inaugural address Kennedy issued threats and challenges as well as making promises. Proud to be the first American president born in the twentieth century, proud to be the torch bearer for "a new generation," Kennedy wanted the world to know where he stood: "Let every nation know, whether it wishes us well or ill, that we shall pay any price, bear any burden, meet any hardship, support any friend, oppose any foe to assure the survival and the success of liberty." And who would pay, bear, meet, support, and oppose? On this point too Kennedy was clear: "And so, my fellow Americans: ask not what your country can do for you—ask what you can do for your country."

After the blandness and mangled syntax of Eisenhower's addresses, here was a speaker of rare ability, here were speeches beautifully phrased. Kennedy probably asked for more sacrifice and promised more rewards than any president since Woodrow Wilson. Only years after his death did people begin to ask if he was serious or if he was more concerned with how

left him hoarse and weak. All and all, by the day of the debate he looked like a nervous corpse— pale, twenty pounds underweight, and haggard. Makeup experts offered to hide his heavy beard and soften his jowls, but Nixon accepted only a thin coat of Max Factor's "Lazy Shave," a pancake cosmetic.

Kennedy looked better, very much better. He didn't need makeup to appear healthy, nor did he need special lighting to hide a weak profile. He did, however, change suits. He believed that a dark blue rather than a gray suit would look better under the bright lights. Kennedy was right, of course, as anyone who watches a nightly news program must realize.

The debate started. Kennedy spoke first. Although he was nervous, he intentionally slowed down his delivery. His face was controlled and cool. He smiled with his eyes and perhaps the corners of his mouth and his laugh was a mere suggestion of a laugh. His body language was perfect. As for what he said, Kennedy disregarded the prearranged ground rules and shifted what was supposed to be a debate on domestic issues to one on foreign policy

he said something than what he said. Indeed, he was attracted to verbal sleight-of-hand tricks: "If a free society cannot help the many who are poor, it cannot save the few who are rich. . . . Let us never negotiate out of fear, let us never fear to negotiate." Like the television debates, such statements emphasized style over substance.

Who was the speaker? Competition and an aggressively masculine view of the world ran through the life of John F. Kennedy. He was the son of a multimillionaire who demanded excellence of all his sons and who believed that as Boston Irish Catholics they had to try harder and be tougher than their Protestant neighbors. This was particularly difficult for John Kennedy, who suffered throughout his life from a series of illnesses and physical problems, including Addison's disease and chronic back trouble. His brother Bobby recalled, "At least one-half of the days that he spent on this earth were days of intense physical pain."

But he never used—and his father never accepted—pain as an excuse for inactivity. At Harvard University he played football, boxed, swam, and ran, and during vacations at the family home in Hyannis Port he roughhoused with his brothers and sisters. Throughout his life, Kennedy maintained this physical view of life. To impress the Kennedys, one associate remembered, you had to "show raw guts, fall on your face now and then. Smash into the house once in a while going after a pass. Laugh off twisted ankles or a big hole torn in your best suit."

Kennedy's macho ethos extended to his attitude toward women. Like his father, he regarded sexual conquests as a sign of manhood and considered females first and foremost as sexual objects. When he wanted companionship and conversation he turned to his male friends.

Kennedy brought this masculine attitude to his presidency. He surrounded himself with advisors who shared his energetic approach to work and play. He seemed charged with a sense of urgency and was fond of the Churchill quote, "Come then—let us to the task, to the battle and toil—each to our part, each to our station. Let us go forward together in all parts of the [land]. There is not a week, nor a day, nor an hour to be lost." In his own speeches Kennedy stressed the theme that America was entering a period of crisis: "In the long history of the world, only a few generations have been granted the role of defending freedom in its maximum danger. I do not shrink from this responsibility—I welcome it." Without crisis, Kennedy believed, no person could achieve greatness, and he desired greatness. As he wrote in his Pulitzer Prize-winning *Profiles in Courage,* "Great crises produce great men, and great deeds of courage."

Something Short of Camelot

From the very first, journalists associated the Kennedy administration with Camelot. According to the popular legend, King Arthur and his Knights of the Round Table established in the realm of Camelot a period of unparalleled peace and prosperity. Although Kennedy himself encouraged the Camelot comparisons, the record of his administration fell short of the ideal.

John F. Kennedy, the first president born in the twentieth century, brought youth, charm, and glamour to the White House.

Several factors worked to limit the success of Kennedy's domestic programs. To begin with, Kennedy lacked political support in Congress. While his party held a solid majority in the House, 101 of 261 Democratic representatives came from southern and border states, and they normally voted with conservative Republicans. Added to this problem was Kennedy's distaste for legislative infighting. He limited his domestic agenda to such traditional Democratic proposals as a higher minimum wage, increased social security benefits, and modest housing and educational programs. In his inaugural address he did not even mention poverty or race. In the final analysis, Kennedy was so concerned with the "crises abroad" that he did not want to risk any of his political capital on unpopular domestic reforms.

There were small successes. Congress raised the minimum wage, expanded Social Security, and appropriated a few billion dollars for public housing and aid to economically depressed areas. But such legislation hardly amounted to the "new frontier" Kennedy promised. These gains were offset by the setbacks, which Kennedy accepted perhaps too stoically. Congress defeated the president's plan for federal aid to education, a health insurance plan for the aged, and programs to help migrant workers, unemployed youths, and urban commuters.

Black Americans were especially disappointed with Kennedy's performance. They had, after all, supplied Kennedy's margin of victory in the 1960 election. But once elected JFK was slow in using his office to further the cause of civil rights.

For blacks, the early 1960s were difficult, violent years that tested their resolve. White segregationists confronted blacks' nonviolent

Police often used snarling dogs, fire hoses, clubs, and electric cattle prods against civil rights demonstrators.

desegregation efforts with unprovoked ferocity. In city after city violence erupted. NAACP organizer Medgar Evers was shot down outside his home in Jackson, Mississippi. Four black girls were killed when a Birmingham church was bombed. Police authorities sprayed black protesters with high-pressure fire hoses and unleashed attack dogs upon them. (See Chapter 29 for a fuller treatment of the fight for civil rights.)

Through his first two years in office, Kennedy remained largely silent. To win southern congressional support he even backed the nomination of a Mississippi jurist who had once referred to blacks as "chimpanzees" for a seat on the federal bench. Although Attorney General Robert Kennedy aided protesters when federal laws were violated, JFK and the FBI staked out a conservative position. As one historian noted, "Civil rights workers were assaulted and shot at—systematically, often openly, frequently by law enforcement officials themselves. And through it all, in virtually every case, federal authorities did nothing."

In 1963 Kennedy changed his position. In part this about-face was the impact of Bobby's prodding. In part it was the result of television, which daily showed shocking examples of brutality in the South and accelerated the demand for change. In late May 1963, Kennedy eloquently announced his new position. It should be possible, he said, "for American students of any color to attend any public institution without having to be backed up by troops . . . but this is not the case. . . . We preach freedom around the world . . . but are we to say to the world . . . that we have no second-class citizens except Negroes, that we have no class or caste system, no ghettos, no master race except with respect to Negroes?"

Perhaps Kennedy was convinced that the time had come for "the nation to fulfill its promise." Perhaps, as his supporters claim, in 1963 Kennedy was beginning to fulfill his own promise. His death in late 1963 left questions unanswered, potential unrealized. Judged by his accomplishments, however, Kennedy's Camelot, like King Arthur's, existed largely in the realm of myth.

Cuba Libre Revisited

Foreign affairs consumed Kennedy's interest. Unlike domestic politics, international conflicts were more clear-cut, and the divisions between "us" and "them" more certain. Foreign affairs also allowed Kennedy to express his masculine view of the world. They permitted JFK to employ the Kennedy approach to difficult decisions, which he once described as calculate the odds, make your choice, and "grab [your] balls and go."

In his approach to the world, Kennedy generally continued the essential Cold War policies of Truman and Eisenhower. He accepted the strategy of containment and the notion that the Soviet Union would take advantage of any sign of weakness by the United States. He was also suspicious of conventional diplomatic channels, preferring to listen to his young advisors rather than seasoned State Department officials.

Kennedy's handling of the Cuban Revolution revealed his bellicose tendencies. Like Eisenhower, Kennedy was dismayed by the success of Fidel Castro. Just as Americans during the 1890s had cried *Cuba Libre,*" on taking office Kennedy began to search for a way to "free" Cuba, this time from Castro's communism rather than Spain's colonialism. His desire to strike a blow against communism led him to embrace a CIA plan to overthrow Castro. If the CIA had successfully planned coups in Guatemala, Iran, and Laos, Kennedy reasoned, then perhaps it could do the job in Cuba.

The CIA plan entailed training and transporting a force of Cuban exiles to Cuba, where they would launch a counterrevolution against Castro. It was a plan that even the joint chiefs of staff believed would probably fail. Even worse, the plan was one of the worst kept secrets in the Western Hemisphere. One historian noted, "Washington knew because the CIA had to drum up broad support in the government for it. Miami knew because the CIA had done everything but take out classified ads to get volunteers. Guatemala knew because the exile brigade was training there, as a local newspaper pointed out. And Castro knew because everyone else did—except the American people."

Kennedy's plan for the Bay of Pigs backfired.

The invasion on April 17, 1961, at the Bay of Pigs was an unmitigated disaster. The Cuban people did not rise up to join the invaders, who were trapped on the beaches. Nor would Kennedy authorize United States air support for the exile forces. As a result, all but three hundred of the fifteen hundred invaders were killed or captured. If anything, the Bay of Pigs fiasco strengthened Castro's position in Cuba.

The Bay of Pigs invasion, however, did not end Kennedy's problems with Cuba. In the fall of 1962 a far more serious crisis arose when the Soviet Union began to install intermediate-range ballistic missiles (IRBMs) in Cuba. Instead of trying to work quietly through proper diplomatic avenues—a process that would have taken time and might have hurt the Democrats in the upcoming election—Kennedy announced the alarming news to an anxious television audience. After showing the public the American cities that the missiles could destroy, Kennedy said that he would not permit the Soviet ships transporting the weapons to enter Cuban waters. "The people were assured," a scholar commented, "that he would run any risk, including thermonuclear war, on their behalf." Such assurances created a genuine mood of crisis in the country.

Behind the scenes, Kennedy and Soviet Premier Nikita Khrushchev searched for a way to defuse the crisis. During the entire affair Bobby Kennedy counseled level-headed restraint and Khrushchev eschewed any shoe-pounding antics. In the end, the world leaders achieved a solution. Khrushchev agreed to remove the missiles under United Nations inspection in return for an American pledge not to invade Cuba. The Kennedy administration interpreted the result as a victory. "We're eyeball to eyeball and I think the other fellow just blinked," Secretary of State Dean Rusk ob-

served during the episode. And, indeed, the Soviet Union could hardly disagree. The Missile Crisis provided the ammunition to force Khrushchev out of power.

The two "superpowers" had stood at the brink, gazed into the abyss, and stepped back. And for what? "When all is said and done," observed one historian, "it seems that President Kennedy had risked ultimate disaster in service to a crisis that was more illusory than real, at least in military terms."

Again, the unsatisfactory "perhaps" reappeared. Perhaps Kennedy learned more from the Cuban Missile Crisis than he had from the Bay of Pigs invasion. Friends of Kennedy claimed that he reached maturity during the crisis and that it motivated him to move toward détente with the Soviet Union. In several 1963 speeches he called for "not merely peace in our time but peace for all time" and a "world safe for diversity." And he did support a treaty banning all atmospheric testing of nuclear weapons. Perhaps Kennedy had come to a new maturity.

The tragedy is that nobody can ever know. On November 22, 1963, Lee Harvey Oswald assassinated Kennedy in Dallas, Texas. The event moved the nation. Walter Cronkite cried on television, and millions of Americans cried in their homes. Once again, television gave the event a mythical quality—showing his grieving wife, his barely understanding children, his solemn funeral. Americans mourned together, eyes fixed on their television sets; and immediately commentators began to evaluate Kennedy's presidency in terms of not what was but what might have been.

VIETNAM: AMERICA'S LONGEST WAR

How did it start? And when? Even while the war in Vietnam tore at the heart of America in the 1960s most Americans, including some foreign policy experts, were not exactly sure of the answers to such basic questions. Johnson said he was continuing Kennedy's policy, who had continued Eisenhower's, who had continued Truman's, who had acted as he believed Roose-

Shocked and saddened, Americans everywhere shared the loss felt by President Kennedy's widow and two young children.

velt would have acted. The answers stretch back into time.

A Small Corner of a Bigger Picture

Struggle, like a mighty river, runs through the history of Vietnam. Ironically, part of Vietnam's troubles was the result of the richness of its own land. Its agricultural products (especially rice) and mineral deposits lured invaders from the East and West. China, the giant to its north, came first. For two thousand years Vietnam battled China for its own independence. The French came next. During the seventeenth, eighteenth, and nineteenth centuries, French traders and missionaries penetrated Vietnam, establishing their control over the country in the name of *la mission civilisatrice*. This "civilizing mission," however, robbed the Vietnamese of the wealth of their land and their independence. France's rules of governing

Vietnam—described as "a lot of subjugation, very little autonomy, a dash of assimilation"—created discontent among the Vietnamese, some of whom welcomed the Japanese who took over the country during World War II.

In 1945 the Vietnamese declared their independence, but the same year the French returned, bent upon the resubjugation of the country. The struggle continued, with the Communist Vietminh under Ho Chi Minh controlling the north of the country and the French the south. Between 1945 and 1954 both sides suffered terrible losses in the bitter guerrilla warfare.

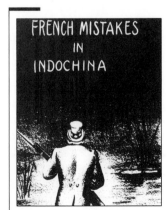

Many felt America was ignoring France's mistakes.

The United States faced a difficult decision. During World War II, Franklin Roosevelt had favored Vietnamese independence and aided Ho's fight against the Japanese. He recognized that the age of colonialism was doomed, and he wanted the United States identified with anticolonialism. At the same time, however, Roosevelt believed that a strong postwar Western Europe was essential to American security, and he did not want to alienate Britain or France by pressing too hard for an end to empires.

On Roosevelt's death, Harry Truman inherited FDR's problems. Even more than his former boss, he advocated a strong Western Europe, even if it had to base that strength upon the continuation of empires. It was a Cold War decision. The United States, Truman maintained, "had no interest" in "championing schemes of international trusteeship" that would weaken the "European states whose help we need to balance Soviet power in Europe."

In the game of Cold War politics, Vietnam became a pawn. Truman wanted French support against Russia. France wanted Vietnam. Truman willingly agreed to aid France's ambitions in exchange for France's support. The success of Mao Tse-tung's communist revolution in China strengthened America's support of the French in Vietnam. Obsessed with the idea of an international communist conspiracy, Truman and his advisors contended that Stalin, Mao, and Ho were united by the single ambition of world domination. They overlooked the historical rivalries that pulled Russia, China, and Vietnam apart. As Ho Chi Minh once told his people, "It is better to sniff French dung for a while than eat China's all our life."

By the late 1940s, the United States had assumed a large part of the cost of France's effort to regain its control over Vietnam. The price escalated during the early 1950s. By 1952 the United States was shouldering roughly one-third of the cost of the war, and between 1950 and 1954 America contributed $2.6 billion to France's war effort. But it was not enough. France was unable to defeat Ho's Vietminh.

In 1954 the war reached a crisis stage. In an effort to lure the Vietminh into a major engagement, the leading French commander moved 12,000 soldiers to Dien Bien Phu, a remote out-post in a river valley in northwest Vietnam. The Vietminh surrounded the fort and moved artillery pieces to the hills above the French airstrip. From there they mounted a siege of Dien Bien Phu. As the months passed, French manpower and prestige suffered punishing blows. Inside Dien Bien Phu, latrines overflowed, food supplies ran out, water spoiled, and unburied bodies fouled the air. Finally, on May 7, 1954, the last French commander surrendered.

During the siege the French continually asked President Eisenhower for military aid, but he refused to act without the support of Congress and Britain. Neither favored American military intervention. Senator Lyndon Johnson of Texas expressed the majority view in Congress when he opposed "sending American G.I.s into the mud and muck of Indochina on a blood-letting spree to perpetuate colonialism and white man's exploitation in Asia." As a result, France gave up its attempt to recolonize Vietnam. At the peace talks in Geneva, the countries involved agreed to hold elections in the summer of 1956 to reunify Vietnam.

Although Eisenhower would not militarily aid France, he quickly supported the independent government established in South Vietnam under the leadership of Ngo Dinh Diem. In America, where he spent several years in a Catholic seminary, Diem was known as an anticommunist and a nationalist. In Vietnam, where he had not been for twenty years, he was hardly known at all. As a popular leader, he had no appeal. Imperious, often paranoid, overly reliant on his own family, Diem, a Catholic in an overwhelmingly Buddhist nation, successfully alienated almost everyone who came into contact with him. Even United States intelligence sources rated his chances of establishing order in South Vietnam as "poor."

Diem, nevertheless, was America's man. Why? Because he was an anticommunist and a nationalist, and, as John Foster Dulles said, "because we know of no one better." Lyndon Johnson put it more bluntly in 1961: "Diem's the only boy we got out there." And even Eisenhower supported Diem militarily and politically. Vietnam became a test case, an opportunity for the United States to battle communism in Asia with dollars instead of Americans. When the time came to hold the unification election, Diem, with American backing, refused. Instead, to show his popularity he held "free" elections in South Vietnam, where he received an improbable 98.2 percent of the popular vote, including 605,000 votes from Saigon's 405,000 registered voters.

Diem's absolutist policies created problems. By the end of 1957, Vietminh guerrillas in South Vietnam were in open revolt. Two years later, North and South Vietnam resumed hostilities. The United States increased its aid, most of which went to improving the South Vietnamese military or into the pockets of corrupt officials. The United States spent little money on improving the quality of life of the peasants. Nor did the United States object strongly to Diem's dictatorial methods. Diem once said that the sovereign was "the mediator between the people and heaven," and he demanded absolute obedience.

By the end of Eisenhower's second term America had become fully committed to Diem and South Vietnam. To be sure, problems in Vietnam were not America's major concern. In fact, most Americans were unaware of their country's involvement there. More than anything, Vietnam was a small corner of a bigger picture. United States policy there was determined by larger Cold War concerns. America's presence in Vietnam, however, would soon be expanded.

Kennedy's Testing Ground

On taking office, John Kennedy reaffirmed his country's commitment to Diem and South Vietnam. He announced his intention to be even more aggressive than Truman or Eisenhower. In Vietnam Kennedy saw an opportunity to "prove" his nation's resolve and strength. In the end, South Vietnam as a country, was less important to Kennedy than the challenge it presented.

Kennedy believed that the United States needed a fresh military approach. Eisenhower's "massive retaliation" was too limited. It was of no use in a guerrilla war like Vietnam. Kennedy labeled his approach "flexible response," and it entailed the development of conventional and

counterinsurgency (antiguerrilla) forces as well as a nuclear response. Vietnam rapidly became the laboratory for counterinsurgency activities, a place for such Special Forces units as the Green Berets to develop their own tactics. To achieve this end, Kennedy expanded the Special Forces from 2500 to 10,000 men.

To "win" in Vietnam, Kennedy realized that he would have to strengthen America's presence there. In November of 1961 he decided to deploy American troops to South Vietnam. By the end of 1961, 3205 American "advisors" were in Vietnam. Kennedy increased this force to 9000 in 1962 and 16,000 in 1963. Although several of his advisors questioned this military escalation, arguing that once the United States committed troops it would be more difficult to pull out of the conflict, Kennedy remained firm in his desire to "save" South Vietnam.

As the American involvement deepened, Diem's control over South Vietnam declined. He alienated peasants by refusing to enact meaningful land reforms and Buddhists by passing laws to restrict their activities. Responding to Diem's pro-Catholic policies, Buddhists began organized protests. They conducted hunger strikes and nonviolent protests. Several Buddhist monks engaged in self-immolation. In full view of American reporters and cameras, one burned himself to death on a busy, downtown Saigon intersection. Although the gruesome sight shocked Americans, Diem's sister-in-law, Madame Nhu, laughed at the "barbecues," offering gasoline and matches for more fiery deaths.

More fiery deaths followed. Protests mounted. Outside of Saigon, Diem exerted little influence; the Kennedy administration soon reached the conclusion that without Diem South Vietnam had serious problems, with Diem the country was doomed. In sum, Diem had to go. Behind the scenes, Kennedy encouraged Vietnamese generals to overthrow Diem. On November 1, 1963, Vietnamese army officers arrested and murdered him and his brother. Although Kennedy did not approve of the assassination, the United States quickly aided the new government.

Three weeks later Kennedy was assassinated in Dallas. Several friends of Kennedy have suggested that he had begun to reevaluate his Vietnam policy and that after the 1964 election he would have started the process of American disengagement. In a moment of insight, Kennedy himself had observed, "The troops will march in; the bands will play; the crowds will cheer; and in four days everyone will have forgotten. Then we will be told we have to send more troops. It's like taking a drink. The effect wears off, and you have to take another." But whatever Kennedy's plans or insights, he had increased United States involvement in Vietnam.

Unfortunately for Kennedy's successor, the prospects for South Vietnam's survival were less than they had been in 1961. By 1963 South Vietnam had lost the fertile Mekong Delta to the Vietcong, as the communist guerillas in the South were known, and with it most of the country's rural population. From the peasants' perspective, the Saigon government stood for heavy taxes, no services, and military destruction; and increasingly they identified the United States with Saigon. Such was the situation Lyndon Johnson inherited.

Texas Tough in the Tonkin Gulf

Lyndon Baines Johnson was a complex man— shrewd, arrogant, intelligent, sensitive, vulgar, vain, and occasionally cruel. He loved power, and he knew where it was, how to get it, and how to use it. "I'm a powerful sonofabitch," he told two Texas congressmen in 1958 when he was the most powerful legislator on Capitol Hill. Everything about Johnson seemed to emphasize or enhance his power. He was physically large, and seemed even bigger than he was, and he used his size to persuade people. The "Johnson Method" involved "pressing the flesh"—a back-slapping, hugging sort of camaraderie. He also used symbols of power adroitly, especially the telephone which had replaced the sword and pen as the symbol of power. "No gunman," remarked one historian, "ever held a Colt .44 so easily" as Johnson handled a telephone.

A legislative genius, Johnson had little experience in foreign affairs. Reared in the poverty of the Texas hill country, educated at a small teachers' college, and concerned politi-

cally with domestic issues, before becoming president LBJ had expressed little interest in foreign affairs. "Foreigners are not like the folks I am used to," he often said, and whether it was a joke or not he meant it. He was particularly uncomfortable around foreign dignitaries and ambassadors, often receiving them in groups and scarcely paying attention to them. "Why do I have to see them?" he once asked. "They're [Secretary of State] Dean Rusk's clients, not mine."

Yet to say Johnson had little experience in foreign affairs is not to suggest that he did not have strong opinions on the subject. Like most politicians of the period, Johnson was an unquestioning Cold Warrior. In addition, along with accepting the domino theory and a monolithic view of communism, Johnson cherished a traditionally southern notion of honor and masculinity. It was his duty, he maintained, to honor commitments made by earlier presidents. "We are [in Vietnam] because . . . we remain fixed on the pursuit of freedom, a deep and moral obligation *that will not let us go.*" Leaving Vietnam, Johnson believed, would be a dishonorable act, dangerous for the nation's future. As he often said, "If you let a bully come into your front yard one day, the next day he will be up on your porch and the day after that he will rape your wife in your own bed."

Furthermore, Johnson believed that any retreat from Vietnam would destroy him politically. Soon after becoming president, he told America's ambassador to Vietnam, "I am not going to be the President who saw Southeast Asia go the way China went." No, he would not "lose" Vietnam and allow Republican critics to attack him as they had Truman. "I knew," LBJ later noted, "that Harry Truman and Dean Acheson had lost their effectiveness from the day the communists took over China." Johnson was determined to win the war, to "nail the coonskin to the wall."

Before winning in Vietnam, however, he had to win in the United States. The presidential election in 1964 was his top priority. He was pitted against Barry Goldwater, the powerful Arizona senator from the Republican Right. "Extremism in the defense of liberty is no vice," Goldwater said, and if elected he promised to defend South Vietnam at any cost. Democrats transformed his campaign slogan "In Your Heart, You Know He's Right," to "In Your Heart, You Know He Might," by which they meant that Goldwater might start a nuclear war. Goldwater did little to discourage such thinking. In his campaign he labored to make "nukes" socially acceptable, even coining the uncomfortably comforting phrase "conventional nuclear weapon."

Johnson's campaign strategy was to appear as the thoughtful, strong moderate. He would not lose Vietnam, he told voters, but neither would he use nuclear weapons or "send American boys nine or ten thousand miles from home to do what Asian boys ought to be doing themselves." Johnson promised that if elected he would create a "Great Society" at home and honor American commitments abroad. As usual, he knew what the voters wanted to hear, and they rewarded him with a landslide victory in the November election.

Behind the scenes, however, the Johnson administration was maneuvering to obtain a free hand for conducting a more aggressive war in Vietnam. He did not want a formal declaration of war, which might frighten voters. Rather he desired a quietly passed resolution giving him the authority to deploy American forces. Such a resolution would allow him to act without the consent of Congress. Johnson and his advisors were planning to escalate American involvement in the Vietnam War, but they hoped it would go unnoticed.

Johnson used two reported North Vietnamese attacks on the American destroyer *Maddox* as a pretext for going before Congress to ask for the resolution. Actually, he was less than truthful about the circumstances of the attack. The first attack occurred in the Tonkin Gulf in early August 1964 when the *Maddox* was thought to be aiding a South Vietnamese commando raid into North Vietnam, a violation of that country's sovereignty. When North Vietnamese torpedo boats attacked, the *Maddox* returned fire, sinking one of the communist ships and crippling two others. The *Maddox* lost only ammunition. The second of the Tonkin Gulf attacks probably never occurred. Assaulted by high waves, thunderstorms, and freak atmospheric conditions, the *Maddox's* sonar equipment apparently malfunctioned, registering twenty-two invisible

enemy torpedoes. No enemy ships were visually sighted, and none of the electronically sighted torpedoes hit the *Maddox* or its accompanying ship the *C. Turner Joy*. Soon after the incident the commander of the *Maddox* reached the conclusion that no attack had ever taken place.

Johnson realized the dubious nature of the second attack. He told an aide, "Hell, those dumb stupid soldiers were just shooting at flying fish." Nevertheless, he pressed Congress for a resolution. American ships, he emphasized, had been repeatedly attacked, and he wanted authorization to "take all necessary measures" to repel attacks, prevent aggression, and protect American security. It was a broad resolution; Johnson said that it was "like Grandma's nightshirt—it covered everything." Almost without debate, the Senate passed the resolution on August 7 with only two dissenting votes and the House of Representatives endorsed it unanimously. You "will live to regret it," Wayne Morse, who voted against it in the Senate, told the resolution's supporters. In the years that followed, as Johnson used his new powers to escalate the war, Morse's vote and prediction were vindicated, for the Tonkin Gulf Resolution allowed Johnson to act in an imperial fashion.

Neck Deep in Big Muddy

Lyndon Johnson liked to personalize things. Once a military aide tried to direct Johnson to the correct helicopter, saying "Mr. President, that's not your helicopter." "Son, they're all my helicopters," Johnson replied. So it was with the Vietnam War. He did not start the war, but once reelected he quickly made it "his war." Over the war he exercised complete control. One authority on the war described Johnson's role:

> He made appointments, approved promotions, reviewed troop requests, determined deployments, selected bombing targets, and restricted aircraft sorties. Night after night, wearing a dressing gown and carrying a flashlight, he would descend into the White House basement "situation room" to monitor the conduct of the conflict . . . often, too, he would doze by his bedside telephone, waiting to hear the outcome of a mission to rescue one of "my pilots" shot down over Haiphong or Vinh or Thai Nguyen. It was his war.

Lyndon Johnson—and much of his generation—believed that war came from weakness, and he vowed that he would not lose the war in Vietnam.

When he became president it was still a relatively obscure conflict for most Americans. Public opinion polls showed that seventy percent of the American public paid little attention to United States activities in Vietnam. At the end of 1963 only 16,300 United States military personnel were in Vietnam; the number rose to 23,300 by the end of 1964. Most of the soldiers there, however, were volunteers. Only a few people strongly opposed America's involvement. All this would change dramatically during the next four years.

With the election behind him, in early 1965 Johnson started to reevaluate the position of the United States. In Saigon crisis followed crisis as one unpopular government gave way to the next. Something had to be done, and Johnson's advisors suggested two courses. The military and most of LBJ's foreign policy experts called for a more aggressive military presence in Vietnam, including bombing raids into North Vietnam and more ground troops. Other advisors, notably Under Secretary of State George Ball, believed the United States was making the same mistakes as France had made. Escalating the war could create serious problems. "Once on the tiger's back," Ball noted, "we cannot be sure of picking the place to dismount."

Johnson chose the first course, claiming it would be dishonorable not to come to South Vietnam's aid. In February 1965, Vietcong troops attacked the American base in Pleiku, killing several soldiers. Johnson used the assault as a pretext to commence air raids into the North. Codenamed "Rolling Thunder," the operation was designed to use American technological superiority to defeat North Vietnam. At first, Johnson limited United States air strikes to enemy radar and bridges below the 20th parallel. But as the war dragged on, he ordered "his pilots" to hit metropolitan areas. Between 1965 and 1973, American pilots flew more than 526,000 sorties and dropped 6,162,000 tons of bombs on enemy targets. (As a point of contrast, the total tonnage of explosives dropped in World War II was 2,150,000 tons.) As a result, much of the landscape of North Vietnam took on a lunar look.

However, the bombs did not lead to victory. Ironically, the bombing missions actually strengthened the communist government in North Vietnam. As a United States intelligence report noted, the bombing of North Vietnam "had no significantly harmful effects on popular morale. In fact, the regime has apparently been able to increase its control of the populace and perhaps even to break through the political apathy and indifference which have characterized the outlook of the average North Vietnamese in recent years."

The massive use of air power also undermined United States counterinsurgency efforts. Colonel John Paul Vann, an American expert on counterinsurgency warfare noted, "The best weapon 'for this type of war' . . . would be a knife. . . . The worst is an airplane. The next worst is artillery. Barring a knife, the best is a rifle—you know who you're killing." By using bombing raids against the enemy in both the North and South, United States forces inevitably killed large numbers of civilians, the very

While bombing raids in North Vietnam did little to weaken the morale of the communist government there, the number of American troops sent to Vietnam almost tripled over a three-year period.

people they were there to help. For peasants everywhere in Vietnam, United States jets, helicopters, and artillery "meant more bombing, more death, and more suffering."

A larger air war also led to more ground troops. As Johnson informed Ambassador Maxwell Taylor, "I have never felt that this war will be won from the air, and it seems to me what is much more needed and will be more effective is a larger and stronger use of rangers and special forces and marines." Between 1965 and 1968 the escalation of American forces was dramatic. When George Ball warned in 1965 that 500,000 American troops in Vietnam might not be able to win the war, other members of the Johnson administration laughed. By 1968 no one was laughing. Ball's prediction was painfully accurate. Escalation of American troops and deaths went hand and hand. The year end totals for the United States between 1965 and 1968 were:

1965: 184,300 troops; 636 killed.
1966: 385,300 troops; 6644 killed.
1967: 485,600 troops; 16,021 killed.
1968: 536,000 troops; 30,610 killed.

But still there was no victory.

To Tet and Beyond

Throughout the escalation Johnson was less than candid with the American people. He argued that there had been no real change in American policy and that victory was in sight. Any reporter who said otherwise, he roundly criticized. Increasingly he demanded unquestioning loyalty from his close advisors. Such demands led to an administration "party line." As the war ground on, the "party line" bore less and less similarity to reality.

In late 1967, General William Westmoreland returned to America briefly to assure the public that he could now see the "light at the end of the tunnel." In his annual report Westmoreland commented, "The year ended with the enemy increasingly resorting to desperation tactics; . . . and he has experienced only failure in these attempts." At the time, the American press focused most of its attention on the battle of Khe Sanh, and Westmoreland assured everyone that victory there was certain.

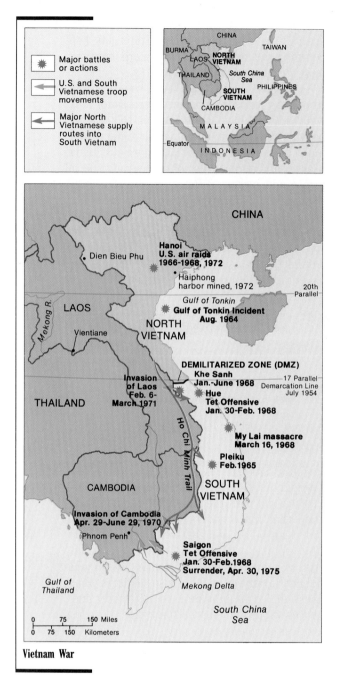

Vietnam War

tainly the Tet Offensive bode well for North Vietnam. A Vietcong suicide squad broke into the United States embassy in Saigon, and Vietnamese communists mounted offensives against every major target in South Vietnam, including five cities, sixty-four district capitals, thirty-six provincial capitals, and fifty hamlets.

For what it was worth, the United States repelled the Tet Offensive. For a month the fighting was ferocious and bloody, as the rivals fought in highly populated cities and almost evacuated hamlets. In order to retake Hue, the ancient cultural center close to the border between North and South Vietnam, allied troops had to destroy the city. One observer recorded that the city was left a "shattered, stinking hulk, its streets choked with rubble and rotting bodies." In another village, where victory came at a high price, the liberating American general reported, "We had to destroy the town to save it." Both sides suffered terribly. But after the allies cleared the cities of enemy troops, General Westmoreland judged the episode a great allied victory.

If technically the Tet Offensive was a military defeat for North Vietnam, it was also a profound psychological victory. Johnson, his advisors, and his generals had been proclaiming that the enemy was on the run, almost defeated, tired of war, ready to quit. Tet demonstrated that the contrary was true. Upset and confused, Walter Cronkite, the national voice of reason, expressed the attitude on his nightly newscast: "What the hell is going on? I thought we were winning the war?" The Tet Offensive, more than any other single event, turned the media against the war and exposed the widening "credibility gap" between official pronouncements and public beliefs. NBC anchorman Frank McGee reported that the time had come "when we must decide whether it is futile to destroy Vietnam in the effort to save it."

After Tet, Americans stopped thinking about victory and turned toward thoughts of how best to get out of Vietnam. "Lyndon's planes" and "Lyndon's boys" had been unable to achieve Lyndon's objectives. For Johnson this fact was politically disastrous. In the polls his popularity plummeted, and in the New Hampshire primary peace candidate Eugene McCarthy received surprisingly solid support.

Then with a suddenness which caught all America by surprise, North Vietnam struck into the very heart of South Vietnam. On the morning of January 30, 1968, North Vietnam launched the Tet Offensive. "Tet," the Vietnamese holiday which celebrates the lunar new year, traditionally is supposed to determine family fortunes for the rest of the year. Cer-

Too intelligent a politician not to realize what was happening, on the night of March 31, LBJ went on television and made two important announcements. First, he said that the United States would limit its bombing of North Vietnam and would enter into peace talks any time and at any place. And second, Johnson surprised the nation by saying, "I shall not seek, and I will not accept the nomination of my party for another term as your President." A major turning point had been reached. The gradual escalation of the war was over. The period of deescalation had started. Even in official government circles, peace had replaced victory as America's objective in Vietnam.

The Politics of a Divided Nation

If Johnson's fall seemed remarkably swift, and if it seemed as if he were surrendering power without a fight, it was because he knew that his policies had badly divided the nation. LBJ honestly believed he had pursued the only honorable course in Vietnam, that he had had America's best interests at heart. His problem, however, was *not* that his intentions were dishonorable but that his *modus operandi*—the style of his leadership—involved great duplicity. Instead of fully committing the United States by calling up the reserves and National Guardsmen and by pushing for higher taxes to pay for the war, Johnson gambled that a slow, steady escalation would be enough to force North Vietnam to accept a negotiated peace. All during the build-up, LBJ assured the American people that he was not drastically changing policy and, besides, victory was in sight. But he could not mislead all the people all the time, and after the Tet Offensive he knew that he could not mislead most of the people any more.

Dissatisfaction with Johnson's policy surfaced first among the young, the very people who were being asked to fight and die for the cause. Most of the young men who were drafted did serve, and most served bravely. In the early years of "Lyndon's war," many soldiers sincerely believed that they were fighting—and dying—to preserve freedom and nourish democracy in Southeast Asia. One career soldier, who did his first tour in Vietnam in 1966, recalled the idealism of his experience. He talked

enthusiastically about American contributions to the improvements in South Vietnamese village life. But by his last tour, in 1970, his idealism had died. As he told a friend, "I'm still ready to serve—any time. But as a killing machine, not a humanitarian."

As the war lengthened, an ever growing number of soldiers shared in this disillusionment. The disillusionment took different forms. Some soldiers turned to drugs to relieve the constant stress and fear that the war engendered. Journalist Michael Herr has written eloquently about the horrors of the war: "sachel charges and grenades blew up jeeps and movie houses, the VC (Vietcong) got work inside all the camps as shoe shine boys and laundresses, . . . they'd starch your fatigues . . . then go home and mortar your area. Saigon and Cholan and Danang held such hostile vibes that you felt that you were being dry sniped every time someone looked at you . . . ." Drugs and sex helped some soldiers—many just boys away from home for the first time—to cope with the nature of a guerrilla war. One GI recalled that R & R was really I & I—"intoxication and intercourse." In such an atmosphere boys became men, fast. "How do you feel," Herr asked, "when a nineteen-year-old kid tells you from the bottom of his heart that he has gotten too old for this kind of shit?"

Other soldiers reacted by viewing all Vietnamese as the enemy. In part the nature of the war against the Vietcong caused this attitude. In a village of "civilians" any man, woman, or child *might* be the enemy. "Vietnam was a dark room full of deadly objects," wrote Herr, "and the VC were everywhere all at once like spider cancer . . . ." Tension and anxiety were as ever present as olive drab.

Empty government phrases, however, also contributed to the problem. How could soldiers win the "hearts and minds" of villagers one day and rain napalm on them the next? Reacting to the surface idealism of United States policy, one experienced soldier commented, "All that is just a *load* man. We're here to kill gooks, period." The My Lai massacre, which saw American soldiers kill more than one hundred (the official figure was 122 but it was probably many more) South Vietnamese civilians, was the sad extension of this attitude.

THE AMERICAN MOSAIC

CESAR CHAVEZ AND *LA CAUSA*

In early April 1962, a thirty-five-year-old community organizer named Cesar Estrada Chavez set out single-handedly to organize impoverished migrant farm laborers in the California grape fields. He, his wife, and their eight children packed their belongings into a dilapidated nine-year-old station wagon, and moved to Delano, California, the center of the nation's table grape industry. Over the next two years, Chavez spent his entire life savings of $1200 creating a small social service organization for Delano's field laborers. Its services included immigration counseling, citizenship classes, funeral benefits, credit to buy cars and homes, assistance with voter regis-

tration, and a cooperative to buy tires and gasoline. As the emblem of his new organization, the National Farm Workers Association, Chavez chose a black Aztec eagle inside a white circle on a red background.

Chavez's sympathy for the plight of migrant farm workers came naturally. He was born in Yuma, Arizona, in 1927, one of five children of Mexican immigrants. When he was ten years old, his parents lost their small farm and the family was forced to become migrant fruit pickers in Arizona and California. There were times when the family had to sleep in their car or camp under bridges. When young Cesar was able to attend school (he attended more

than thirty mostly segregated schools), he was often shunted into special classrooms set aside for Mexican-American children.

In 1944, when he was seventeen, Chavez joined the navy, and served for two years on a destroyer escort in the Pacific. After his war service he married, spent two years as a sharecropper raising strawberries, followed by work in apricot orchards and in a lumber camp. Then in 1952 his life took a fateful turn. He joined a social service organization, known as the Community Service Organization, during a voter registration drive. The Community Service Organization aimed to educate and organize the poor so that they could solve their own social and economic problems. After founding CSO chapters in Madera, Bakersfield, and Hanford, California, Chavez was named the organization's general director in 1958. Four years later, he broke with the organization when it rejected his proposal to establish a farm workers union.

Most labor leaders considered Chavez's goal of creating the first successful union of farm workers in United States history an impossible dream. Not only did farm laborers suffer from high rates of illiteracy and poverty (average family earnings were just $2000 in 1965), they also experienced persistently high rates of unemployment (traditionally around nineteen percent) and were divided into a variety of ethnic groups (Mexican, Arab, Filipino, and Puerto Rican). Making unionization even more difficult were the facts that farm laborers rarely remained in one locality for very long and were easily replaced by inexpensive Mexican day laborers, known as *braceros,* who were trucked into California and the Southwest at harvest time.

Moreover, farm workers were specifically excluded from the protection of the National Labor Relations Act of 1935 (the Wagner Act). Unlike other American workers, farm workers were not guaranteed the right to organize, had no guarantee of a minimum wage, and had no federally guaranteed standards of work in the fields. State laws requiring toilets, rest periods, and drinking water in the fields were largely ignored.

In September 1965 Chavez was drawn into his first important labor controversies. The Filipino grape pickers went on strike. "All right, Chavez," asked one of the Filipino grape pickers' leaders, "are you going to stand beside us, or are you going to scab against us?" Despite his fear that the National Farm Workers Association was not sufficiently well organized to support a strike (it had less than $100 in its strike fund), he assured the Filipino workers that members of his association would not go into the field as strikebreakers. *Huelga!*—the Spanish word for strike—became the grape pickers' battle cry.

Within weeks, the labor strike began to attract national attention. Unions, church groups, and civil rights organizations offered financial support for *La Causa,* as the farmworkers' movement became known. In March 1966 Chavez led a 250-mile Easter march from Delano to Sacramento to dramatize the plight of migrant farm laborers. That same year, Chavez's National Farm Workers Association merged with an AFL-CIO affiliate to form the United Farm Workers Organizing Committee.

A staunch apostle of nonviolence, Chavez was deeply troubled by the violent incidents that marred the strike. Some growers raced tractors along the roadside, covering the strikers with dirt and dust. Others drove spraying machines along the edges of their fields, spraying insecticide and fertilizer on the picketers. Local police officers arrested a minister for reading Jack London's definition of a scab ("a two-legged animal with a corkscrew soul, a water-logged brain, and a combination backbone made of jelly and glue"). Some strikers, in turn, intimidated strikebreakers by pelting them with marbles fired from slingshots and by setting fire to packing crates.

In an effort to quell the escalating violence and to atone for the militancy of some of his union's members, Chavez began to fast on February 14, 1968. For five days he kept the fast a secret. Then, in an hour-long speech to striking workers, he explained that continued violence would destroy everything the union stood for. He said that the "truest act of courage, the strongest act of manliness, is to sacrifice ourselves for others in a totally nonviolent struggle for justice." For twenty-one days he fasted; he lost thirty-five pounds and his doctor began to fear for his health. He finally agreed to take a small amount of boullion and grapefruit juice and medication. On March 11, he ended his fast by taking communion and breaking bread with Senator Robert F. Kennedy.

The strike dragged on for three years. To heighten public awareness of the farm workers' cause, Chavez in 1968 initiated a boycott of table grapes. It was the boycott that pressured many of the grow-

ers into settling the strike. An estimated 17 million American consumers went without grapes in support of the farm workers bargaining position. By mid-1970, two-thirds of California grapes were grown under contract with Chavez's union.

In the years following its 1970 victory, Chavez's union has been beset by problems from within and without. Union membership dwindled from a high of more than 60,000 in 1972 to a low of 5000 in 1974 (it has since climbed back to around 30,000), and many of Chavez's top lieutenants resigned or were fired. Meanwhile, public concerns for the plight of migrant farmworkers declined.

Whatever his union's current problems, however, Chavez's achievements remain nothing short of remarkable. As a result of his efforts, the most back-breaking tool used by farm workers, the short hoe, was eliminated and the use of many dangerous pesticides in the grape fields was prohibited. His efforts also brought about a seventy percent increase in real wages from 1964 to 1980, and establishment of health care benefits, disability insurance, pension plans, and standardized grievance procedures for farm workers. He helped secure passage of the nation's first agricultural labor relations act in California in 1975, which prohibited growers from firing striking workers or engaging in bad-faith bargaining. Thanks to his efforts, migrant farm laborers won a right held by all other American workers: the right to bargain collectively.

By the late 1960s civil rights activism and antiwar protests had emerged on college campuses throughout the country.

At home, university students, most of whom had draft exemptions, also reacted to the war and Johnson's policies. They were the earliest and most vocal critics of the Vietnam War. If they lacked a coherent ideology, they were strong in numbers and energy. Between 1946 and 1970 enrollments in institutions of higher education had climbed from 2 million to 8 million. Although not all the students protested against the war, the most politically active ones did. As politicians they formed a curious breed—segregated from society as a whole, freed from adult responsibilities, bound to no real constituency, and encouraged by their teachers to think critically. Most student protesters were from upper middle-class families and could afford the intellectual luxury of being political idealists. (Youth culture as a whole will be discussed in greater detail in Chapter 29.)

Led by such leftist groups as Students for a Democratic Society (SDS), university students called for a more just society in which political life was governed by morality not greed. During the early 1960s they focused on the civil rights movement, participating in freedom rides and voter registration drives. By the mid-1960s, however, they were increasingly shifting their attention to America's "unjust and immoral" war in Southeast Asia; and with the shift their numbers swelled. In 1962 only ten universities had an SDS chapter, and each chapter had only a handful of members. By 1968 the organization boasted more than 100,000 members. By then, too, older voices had joined the student chorus of condemnation.

It was the older voices, energized by the idealism of youth, that led to Johnson's decision not to seek reelection in 1968. For many, it seemed as if the future of American politics belonged to the proponents of peace and morality. Students flocked to presidential candidate Gene McCarthy's peace cause. They cut their long hair, shaved their beards ("be clean for Gene"), put on coats and ties, and worked for McCarthy's campaign. After Johnson pulled his hat out of the ring, Robert Kennedy announced his candidacy. Although McCarthy supporters saw Kennedy as a political opportunist, he spoke eloquently for the cause of humanity and peace. When students at a Catholic university called for more bombings, RFK asked, "Do you understand what that means? It means you are voting to send people, Americans and Veitnamese to die

Eugene McCarthy

Although he was slow to declare his candidacy, Bobby Kennedy soon became the darling of the antiwar movement.

. . . . Don't you understand that what we are doing to the Vietnamese is not very different than what Hitler did to the Jews." Bobby, who enjoyed midnight bull sessions on the meaning of existence and looked at ease with his tie loosened and his shirt sleeves rolled above his elbows, spoke a language that radical students understood. He exhibited the passion and commitment that McCarthy lacked. By the conclusion of the campaign, Kennedy had become the foremost peace candidate, and representative of the young.

At his victory celebration after the California primary, Kennedy said, "We are a great country, an unselfish country, and a compassionate country. I intend to make that my basis for running." Moments later a fanatic Palestinian shot him in the head. With Bobby died the dreams of many Americans for a moral society.

Columnist Murry Kempton spoke for many people: "I have liked many public men immensely, but I guess [RFK] is the only one I have ever loved."

The Democratic party went to the Chicago Convention without a candidate. There they battled among themselves—young and old; radical, liberal, and conservative. In the streets, outside the convention hall, police beat protesters in full view of television cameras. An official commission later termed it a "police riot." Inside the convention hall the fighting was largely verbal, but it was just as intense and bitter. Abraham Ribicoff, a senator from Connecticut, accused Chicago's mayor Richard Daley of allowing the police to use "Gestapo tactics" in the street; Daley accused Ribicoff of having unnatural relations with his mother. In the end, the Democratic party chose Hubert Humphrey,

At the Democratic convention in Chicago, police attacked thousands of unarmed, middle-class, antiwar college students in what was later termed a "police riot."

Johnson's liberal vice-president, as their presidential candidate. Instead of change, the Democratic party chose a representative of the "old politics."

In a more tranquil convention in Miami, the Republican party endorsed Richard M. Nixon, who promised when elected to honorably end the Vietnam War, move against forced busing of black children to white schools, and restore "law and order." More calm and relaxed than ever before, the "new Nixon claimed to speak for the great majority of Americans who obeyed the nation's laws, paid their taxes, regularly attended church, and loved their country. Although Humphrey finished the campaign strong, Nixon's appeal to traditional values had an undeniable attraction. And on election day, Nixon scored a close victory.

THE TORTUOUS PATH TOWARD PEACE

During the presidential campaign of 1968, Richard Nixon expected the American voter to accept certain things on faith. First, he asked them to believe that he had a plan to honorably end the war in Vietnam. Second, he hoped that they would "buy" his new public image—the "new Nixon," experienced, statesmanlike, mature, secure, and ever so well adjusted. Most Americans probably did not believe either in the "new Nixon" or his pledge to "bring us together." On election day only twenty-seven percent of eligible voters cast their ballot for him, but in 1968 that proved enough votes to win the election.

Outsiders on the Inside

If Nixon had developed "new" characteristics, those qualities had not forced out the "old." Richard Nixon still considered himself something of an outsider, a battler against an entrenched political establishment. Reared on the West Coast in humble circumstances, he had to overcome considerable obstacles in his rise to power. In the process certain character traits emerged. He was a hard worker—careful, studious, with a tendency toward perfectionism. No detail was too small for his consideration. In addition, he did not shy away from an unpopular task. During his years as Eisenhower's vice-president, Nixon had proved particularly adept as a political hatchet man. He was also a loner—shy, introverted, humorless, uncomfortable in social situations. He was essentially a man of action, one who for most of his career carried a list of things to do in the inside pocket of his suit coat.

As a restless outsider, Nixon harbored a heightened suspicion of political insiders. Throughout his career he had been an outspoken critic of State Department officials and other establishment bureaucrats. On taking office he therefore surrounded himself with close advisors who held non-Cabinet titles. Cabinet appointees, and particularly his secretary of state, William Rogers, had almost no voice in key decisions. Personal aides H. R. Haldeman and John Ehrlichman—called the "Germans" by the White House press corps—advised Nixon on domestic political issues. Vice-President Spiro Agnew assumed the role of the administration's hatchet man so well that he became known as "Nixon's Nixon." He attacked the Establishment with the ferocity of a professional wrestler verbally abusing an archrival. The "sniveling, hand-wringing power structure," he said, "deserves the violent rebellion it encourages." As for foreign affairs, Nixon relied on his national security advisor, Henry Alfred Kissinger.

Most commentators regarded Kissinger as a strange ally for Nixon. Kissinger, after all, taught at Harvard, was a close associate of Nelson Rockefeller—Nixon's longtime Republican opponent—and had even offered to work for Nixon's Democratic opponent Hubert Humphrey. "Look," Kissinger said in 1968, "I've hated Nixon for years." Yet even while Kissinger was courting Humphrey, he was secretly working for Nixon's election. No matter who won in 1968, Kissinger would be on the victorious side. It was a piece of Machiavellian maneuvering that Nixon might have appreciated.

Beneath Kissinger's sophisticated exterior, he shared with Nixon fundamental characteristics and beliefs. Like Nixon, Kissinger's path to power was not a traditional one. A German Jew, he had lived for five years (between the ages of ten and fifteen) in Nazi Germany; he had been verbally and physically abused by his Aryan classmates. With the rest of his family, he fled to the United States during the late 1930s. After serving as an army translator-interrogator during World War II, he enrolled as a scholarship student at Harvard, from where he graduated *summa cum laude* in 1950 and was awarded his Ph.D. in 1954. His dissertation, later published as *A World Restored*, examined the ideas and policies of the conservative world leaders and diplomats who reconstructed Europe after the social and political upheavals caused by the Napoleonic Wars. During the late 1950s and 1960s, Kissinger wrote, taught, and emerged as a leading expert on foreign affairs.

Vain, irreverent, articulate, and intellectual, Kissinger shared Nixon's desire to alter the very nature of the country's foreign relations and to make history. Neither particularly enjoyed being part of a committee process, and the diplomacy of secrecy and intrigue attracted both. For all their surface differences, the shy politician and the flamboyant scholar were kindred spirits who combined to form an impressive team. As one historian observed, "each filled a vital gap in the other's abilities. Kissinger had no gift for American politics; he needed to serve a President who could manipulate the electorate into supporting his policies. Nixon benefited from Kissinger's good press contacts since his own were disastrous."

Vietnamization: The Idea and the Process

During his campaign Nixon had promised "peace with honor" and suggested that he had a secret plan to achieve those ends. Controversy surrounded just what that plan entailed. Several historians have suggested that Nixon's plan was an updated version of Eisenhower's plan to end the Korean War. In 1953 when Ike took office, he publicly called for peace while secretly sending a message to Chinese and North Korean leaders that if they stalled at the peace talks, he was prepared to use nuclear weapons to end the war. Nixon told his White House aide H. R. Haldeman that his plan was similar to Eisenhower's. He wanted North Vietnam to believe that he was a "madman." "I want the North Vietnamese to believe I've reached the point where I might do anything to stop the war,"

Nixon told Haldeman. "We'll just slip the word to them that 'for God's sakes, you know Nixon is obsessed about communists. We can't restrain him when he's angry—and he has his hand on the nuclear button'—and Ho Chi Minh himself will be in Paris in two days begging for peace." The "madman theory" helps to explain Nixon's dramatic shifts during his first four years in office as he moved between the poles of peacefully concluding the war and violently expanding the conflict.

One thing was certain, however, Nixon knew that he could not continue Johnson's policy. "I'm not going to end up like LBJ," he remarked, "holed up in the White House afraid to show my face on the street." The country needed something new. Whatever else he did, Nixon realized that to ensure some semblance of domestic tranquility he would have to begin to remove American troops from Vietnam. In May 1969, he announced, "The time is approaching when the South Vietnamese forces will be able to take over some of the fighting fronts now being manned by Americans." That summer he drummed harder on the idea of the South Vietnamese fighting their own war. In what had become known as the "Nixon Doctrine," the president insisted that Asian soldiers must carry more of the combat burden. Certainly the United States would continue to materially aid any anticommunist struggle, but the aid would not include the wholesale use of American troops.

The Nixon Doctrine formed the foundation of Nixon's Vietnamization policy. Working from the questionable premise that the government of Nguyen Van Thieu was stable and prepared to assume greater responsibility for fighting the war, Nixon announced that he planned to gradually deescalate American military involvement. Increasingly United States aid would be limited to war material, military advice, and air support. He coupled Vietnamization with a more strenuous effort to move along the peace talks.

At the same time as he extended the olive branch, he expanded the nature of the conflict. Hoping to slow down the flow of North Vietnamese supplies and soldiers into South Vietnam, Nixon ordered American B-52 pilots to

LOGISTICS IN A GUERILLA WAR: The Longest War

The Vietnam War was a logistical nightmare for the United States. Fought 9000 miles from America's shores, the United States had to ship hundreds of tons of supplies daily from the United States to bases in the Pacific and finally to fortified positions along the coast of Vietnam. Once the supplies were in Vietnam, they had to be protected from Vietcong guerillas, who blended into the civilian population and often obtained jobs on U.S. bases. As a result, although American forces established defense perimeters around their bases, the areas were never totally secure. Bombs in U.S. movie theaters or even mess halls were haunting reminders of the unpredictability of guerilla warfare.

North Vietnam sent much of its supplies south along the Ho Chi Minh Trail. Following a traditional series of trails through mountains and jungles from North Vietnam into Laos and Cambodia and finally emptying into South Vietnam, the Ho Chi Minh Trail was widened into a road capable of handling heavy trucks and thousands of troops. Along the trail, support facilities, often built underground to escape American detection and air strikes, included operating rooms, fuel storage tanks, and supply coaches. Throughout the war, United States forces tried but failed to effectively disrupt the flow of supplies and soldiers south.

The Vietcong tunnel complex created even more problems for American troops. The tunnels allowed Vietcong troops to appear and disappear almost by magic. The most famous tunnel complex was under Cu Chi, approximately twenty-five miles northeast of Saigon. It contained conference rooms, sleeping chambers, storage halls, and kitchens. United States forces bombed, gassed, and defoliated the Cu Chi area, but failed to destroy the tunnels. The "tunnel rats"—South Vietnamese soldiers and short, wiry GI combat engineer SWAT teams—fought heroically in the tunnels, but they too were unable to destroy the complexes. In the end, the unconventional nature of the Vietnam War guaranteed frustration and made it America's longest war.

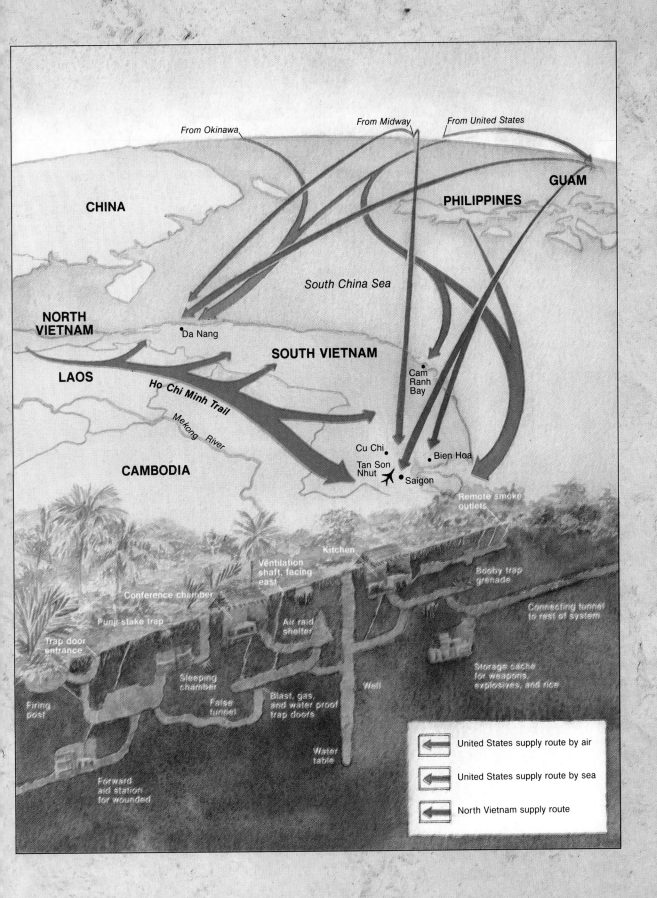

bomb the Ho Chi Minh Trail both in Vietnam and in Cambodia. He kept this violation of Cambodian neutrality secret from the American public. It was a bold move, but not very productive. The bombs only reduced the flow of men and supplies by approximately ten percent.

When both increased bombings of North Vietnam and Kissinger's peace talks with North Vietnamese officials failed to end the war, Nixon resorted to harsher military efforts. After watching *Patton,* his favorite movie, on board the presidential yacht *Sequoia,* he decided to "go for all the marbles" and send American ground forces to Cambodia to destroy communist supply bases. On the night of April 30, 1970, he went on television and told the American people of his plan. Ignoring previous American violations of Cambodia neutrality, he said that United States policy had been "to scrupulously respect the neutrality of the Cambodian people," while North Vietnam had used the border areas for "major base camps, training sites, logistics facilities, weapons and ammunition factories, airstrips and prisoner-of-war com-

pounds," as well as their chief military headquarters. As a result, Nixon announced a joint American and South Vietnamese "incursion" into Cambodia's border regions to be limited to sixty days. In an attempt to rally American support, Nixon emphasized that the country's honor and even manhood were at stake: "We will not be humiliated, we will not be defeated. If when the chips are down the U.S. acts like a pitiful helpless giant, the forces of totalitarianism will threaten free nations and free institutions throughout the world. It is *not our power but our will* that is being tested tonight."

Militarily the "incursion" fell far short of success. If American forces captured a few stockpiles of weapons, they did not uncover much else. But the "incursion" had dangerously enlarged the battlefield. More importantly, the invasion of Cambodia reignited the fires of the peace movement at home. Throughout the country, colleges and universities shut down in protest. Students raged at what they believe was an "immoral, imperialist policy." At Kent State University in Ohio a volley of gunshots

In the spring of 1970 National Guardsmen fired into a group of protesting students at Kent State University killing four.

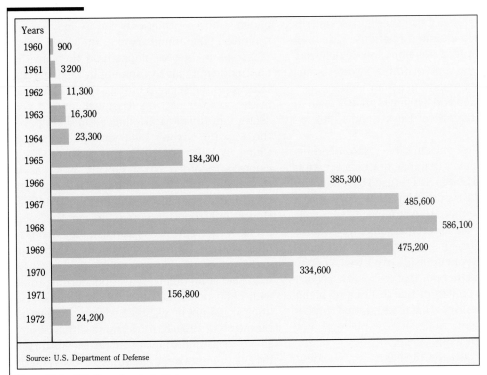

Years	
1960	900
1961	3 200
1962	11,300
1963	16,300
1964	23,300
1965	184,300
1966	385,300
1967	485,600
1968	586,100
1969	475,200
1970	334,600
1971	156,800
1972	24,200

Source: U.S. Department of Defense

Figure 28.1   U.S. Troop Levels in Vietnam
U.S. Department of Defense.

fired by Ohio National Guardsmen broke up a peaceful demonstration. The shots killed four students and wounded nine others. Less than two weeks later, policemen shot two more innocent students at Jackson State College in Mississippi. Instead of victory or even peace, Nixon's efforts had further divided America.

As an effective policy, Vietnamization was an utter failure. To be sure, the policy allowed Nixon to bring home American combat troops. When Nixon took office 540,000 American troops were in Vietnam; four years later only 70,000 remained. But American reductions were not accompanied by a marked improvement in the South Vietnamese Army (ARVN). This was clearly illustrated by the unsuccessful 1971 ARVN invasion into Laos. If anything, South Vietnam became more dependent on the United States during the years of Vietnamization. By 1972 South Vietnam's only product and export was war, and even this commodity was of inferior quality.

A "Decent Interval"

By 1972 Nixon simply wanted to end the war with as little embarrassment as possible. As a viable country, South Vietnam was hopeless. Without an active United States military presence, the country's demise was a forgone conclusion. Negotiations presented the only way out. Nixon and Kissinger hoped to arrange for a peace that would permit the United States and South Vietnam to save face and allow a "decent interval" of time to ensue between the American departure and the collapse of the government in Saigon. In the pursuit of the goal, Nixon changed the character of American foreign policy.

The Soviet Union and the People's Republic of China aided and advised North Vietnam. Yet the two large communist nations were hardly allies themselves. In fact, the Sino-Soviet split demonstrated to American leaders the fallacy of the old Cold War theme of a monolithic communist movement. Nixon and Kissinger were astute enough to use the Sino-Soviet rift to improve United States relations with both countries. Improved relations, they believed, would move the United States several steps closer to an "honorable" peace in Vietnam. Unfortunately, Nixon and Kissinger greatly overestimated the influence of Russia and China on North Vietnam.

From his first days in office, Nixon had his eyes on the People's Republic of China, a nation that the United States had refused to recognize. One Nixon aide reported in 1969, "You're not going to believe this, but Nixon wants to recognize China." It seemed remarkable, for Nixon's Cold War record—his opposition to any concession to the communists—was well known. But Nixon understood that his very record would protect him from public cries of being soft on communism; Nixon knew that unlike Truman, Kennedy, and Johnson, he did not have a Nixon to worry about.

Nixon approached China like a man holding a vase from the Ming dynasty, mixing caution with slow careful movements. In fact, both China and the United States walked on egg shells. Mao Tse-tung told reporter Edgar Snow that he "would be happy to talk with [Nixon]

In 1972 Richard Nixon visited China in an attempt to improve relations with that country. It was the first step toward achieving détente with the Soviet Union.

either as a tourist or as President." And Mao ended China's athletic isolation in 1971 by sending a table tennis team to the world championships in Nagoya, Japan, and then inviting an American team to compete in Peking. Capitalizing on the success of Ping-Pong diplomacy, in the summer of 1971 Kissinger made a very secret trip to China. Kissinger's mission paved the way for Nixon's own very public trip to China in February 1972. American television cameras recorded Nixon's every move as he toured the Great Wall, the Imperial Palace, and the other sites of historic China. For the White House, one reporter noted, "It was the social event of the year." Constantly smiling and bubbling with excitement, Nixon thoroughly enjoyed the event, going so far as quoting Chairman Mao at an official toast and learning to eat with chopsticks. Although full diplomatic relations would not be established until Jimmy Carter did so in 1979, Nixon's trip to China was the single most important event in the history of the relations between the United States and the People's Republic of China.

Concerned about the growing rapprochement between China and America, the Soviet Union sought to move closer to the United States. Once again, Nixon and Kissinger were pleased to oblige. In late May 1972, after many months of preparatory talks, Nixon traveled to Moscow to sign an arms control treaty with Leonid Brezhnev. The Strategic Arms Limitation Treaty of 1972 (SALT I) certainly did not preclude a future nuclear war between the superpowers. Although it froze Intercontinental Ballistic Missile (ICBMs) deployment, it did not alter the buildup of the more dangerous Multiple Independent Re-entry Vehicles (MIRVs), which, according to one historian "was about as meaningful as freezing the cavalry of the European nations in 1938 but not the tanks." As so often has been the case during the Cold War, SALT I provided more a warm breeze than the real heat wave necessary for a complete thaw.

In other areas the United States and the Soviet Union made more substantial progress. American businessmen forged inroads into the Russian market. Pepsi-Cola executives, metallurgy and ammonia dealers, computer and machine tools traders, and electric gear and mining equipment salesmen all benefited from the improved relations between America and Russia. Some farmers also reaped significant rewards, when disastrous harvests at home led the Soviet Union to purchase several billion dollars worth of American wheat, corn, and soybeans. And, of course, cultural and athletic exchanges and competition provided entertainment for millions of Americans and Russians alike.

Thus although Nixon had not been able to end the Vietnam War, his 1972 triumphs in Russia and China gave him more influence with North Vietnam's major allies. His visits to Peking and Moscow also dazzled American voters. In 1972 Nixon easily defeated Democratic candidate George McGovern, capturing sixty-one percent of the popular vote and 521 of the 538 votes of the electoral college. Nixon's success with blue-collar workers, conservative Catholics, and Southerners signified the end of the New Deal coalition.

Once reelected, Nixon again focused on Vietnam. A month before the election, Kissinger had announced, "Peace is at hand," but no sooner was Nixon safely reelected than the peace talks broke down once again. Nixon's response was more and heavier bombing of North Vietnam. Starting on December 18 and continuing for the next ten days, the Christmas bombings—code named Operation Linebacker II— killed over two thousand civilians, leveled a hospital, and destroyed large parts of Hanoi. Critics charged that Nixon was attempting to "wage war by tantrum" and that the bombings served no military purpose. Some even suggested that Nixon had become mentally unbalanced. Military authorities, however, maintained that the bombings quickened the pace of the peace process. When the bombings concluded the warring nations resumed peace talks.

In a week North Vietnam and the United States hammered out a peace, one that was strikingly similar to the October proposal. On January 23, 1973, America ended its active participation in the Vietnam War. Nixon quickly claimed that he had won an honorable peace, that his "secret plan" had worked, even if it had taken four years and claimed the lives of 21,000

American, 107,000 South Vietnamese, and more than 500,000 North Vietnamese soldiers. And, of course, the lives of many thousands of Vietnamese civilians. As one historian commented, "In all likelihood, the peace accords that were finally signed in January 1973 could have been negotiated four years earlier. In the name of credibility, honor, and patriotism, hundreds of thousands of lives had been lost."

America left the war in 1973, but the war did not end then. All the peace provided for was a "decent interval" between America's withdrawal and North Vietnam's complete victory. Almost as soon as the ink on the "peace treaty" was dry, North and South Vietnam were once again at war. Finally, in the spring of 1975 South Vietnamese forces collapsed. In March North Vietnam forces took Hue and Da Nang; by late April they were close to Saigon. On April 21 President Thieu publicly lambasted the United States, resigned, and beat a hasty retreat from his country. On April 30 South Vietnam formally announced its unconditional surrender. Vietnam was finally unified. Free elections in 1956 might have accomplished the same results.

The End of a Presidency

The year 1972 saw Nixon make a bid for greatness. He traveled to Peking and then to Moscow, giving Americans a glimpse of the possibility of a real and lasting peace. Quoting Chairman Mao he told Chinese officials, "So many deeds cry out to be done, and always urgently. . . . Seize the day, seize the hour." In the November elections the American public—or at least sixty-one percent of the public that voted—expressed their approval by casting their vote for Nixon. No one would have guessed that two and a half years later Nixon, a politician who loved being president, would resign in disgrace.

Watergate has become synonymous with political scandal. On June 17, 1972, all Watergate meant for Washingtonians was a plush office, shopping, and apartment complex that housed the Democratic party's national headquarters. That night Frank Wills, a night watchman, apprehended and arrested five men who had broken into the Democratic headquarters. As was later revealed, the break-in was part of series of unethical and illegal activities conducted by the Committee for the Re-election of the President (CREEP). Although Nixon probably had no foreknowledge of the crime, several of his closest aides did, and they soon told him. With an election less than half a year away, Nixon responded by obstructing and impeding the course of justice. During the next week, he urged the CIA to keep the FBI off the case on the grounds that it involved national security. And he counseled his aides to lie under oath, if necessary: "I don't give a [expletive deleted] what happens," he told his former attorney general, John Mitchell, who was then his campaign manager, "I want you all to stonewall it, let them plead the Fifth Amendment, cover-up, or anything else . . . ."

The break-in did not hurt Nixon's campaign. Between the activities of the burglars and the president were layers of officials and issues which had to be carefully peeled away. That would take time and energy. *Washington Post* reporters Bob Woodward and Carl Bernstein had both. They sensed that the break-in was only part of a larger scandal. Slowly they pieced together part of the story. Federal judge John Sirica helped the ends of justice by sentencing the uncooperative burglars to long jail terms. To lessen their time in prison, some of the burglars began to tell the truth, and the truth illuminated a path leading to the White House.

If Nixon had few real political friends, he had legions of enemies. Over the years he had offended or attacked many of the Democrats— and a number of the prominent Republicans— of his day. Indeed much of his political success had been based on dividing Americans—black and white, rich and poor, liberal and conservative—against themselves. His detractors latched onto the Watergate issue with the tenacity of a bulldog. House Majority Leader Tip O'Neill told a congressional ally in early 1973, "All my years tell me what's happening. They did so many bad things during that campaign that there is no way to keep it from coming out . . . . The time is going to come when impeachment is going to hit this Congress."

The Watergate scandal led to the downfall of Richard Nixon. Here the Ervin Committee questions Nixon aide H. R. Haldeman.

The Senate appointed a special committee, the Ervin Committee, to investigate the Watergate scandal, which attempted to assess White House involvement. Most of Nixon's top aides continued the cover-up. John Dean, counsel to the president, did not. Throughout the episode he had kept careful notes, and in a quiet, precise voice he told the Ervin Committee that the president was deeply involved in the cover-up. The matter was still not solved. All the committee had was Dean's word against the other White House aides.

On July 16, a relatively minor White House employee dropped the biggest bombshell. Alexander Butterfield testified that since early 1971 Nixon had used a voice-activated tape-recording system to record all Oval Office conversations. Whatever Nixon and his aides had said about Watergate in the Oval Office, therefore, was faithfully recorded on tape.

Nixon tried to keep the tapes from the Ervin Committee by invoking executive privilege and interpreting that doctrine to imply that a president had a right to keep confidential *any* White House communication, whether or not it involved sensitive diplomatic or national security matters. Special prosecutor Leon

Jaworski disagreed, arguing, "Who is to be the arbiter of what the Constitution says? Now, the President may be right in how he reads the Constitution. But he may also be wrong. And if he is wrong, who is there to tell him so? . . . This nation's Constitutional form of government is in serious jeopardy if the President, *any* President, is to say that the Constitution means what *he* says it does, and if there is no one, not even the Supreme Court, to tell him otherwise." The Supreme Court agreed with Jaworski, and after hearing arguments from both sides ordered Nixon to turn over the tapes.

Still Nixon hesitated; but Congress was in no mood for further delay. On July 27, 1974, the House Judiciary Committee, headed by Peter Rodino, recommended that the House impeach Nixon for obstruction of justice, abuse of power, and refusal to relinquish the tapes. The end was near and with little support in the Senate Nixon saw the futility of resistance. On August 5 he obeyed the Supreme Court ruling and released the tapes, which confirmed Dean's detailed testimony. He had been involved in a cover-up; he had obstructed justice. Four days later, on August 9, in a tearful farewell Nixon became the first American president to resign from office. The following day, Vice-President Gerald Ford, who had replaced Spiro Agnew after he had resigned over his involvement in an unrelated scandal, became the new president. "Our long national nightmare," he said, "is over."

CONCLUSION

Trying to describe Nixon and the Watergate scandal, Henry Kissinger noted that in the end, "The spider got entangled in his own web." Nixon, who aspired to greatness, ended his presidency in disgrace. To be sure, he could look back on his years in office and take pride in several of his accomplishments, especially the better relations he forged with China and Russia. However, his handling of the Vietnam War, domestic opposition, and the Watergate cover-up demonstrated the "old" Nixon continued to shadow the "new." Although he promised to bring Americans together, he ended by polarizing the nation.

On August 9, 1974, Richard Nixon resigned the presidency after being threatened with the release of his secret tapes and impeachment.

So, too, Johnson had divided the nation. His vision of a better, more just society—the Great Society (see Chapter 29)—was dashed on the rocks of Vietnam. There was in Johnson's position the essence of tragedy. As he later explained to biographer Doris Kearns, "I knew from the start that I was bound to be crucified either way I moved. If I left the woman I really loved—the Great Society—in order to get involved with the bitch of a war on the other side of the world, then I would lose everything at home . . . . but if I left that war and let the communists take over South Vietnam, then I would be seen as a coward and my nation would be seen as an appeaser and we would both find it impossible to accomplish anything for anybody anywhere on the entire globe." In Johnson's view he was like a Puritan wrestling with the question of his own salvation:

> Damned if you do,
> Damned if you don't.
> Damned if you will,
> Damned if you won't.

Of course, LBJ further injured his cause by refusing to tell the American people the whole truth.

CHRONOLOGY OF KEY EVENTS

1945 Ho Chi Minh proclaims the independence of Vietnam

1961 CIA-planned Bay of Pigs invasion fails to overthrow Castro; Alan Shephard becomes first American in space

1962 Supreme Court rules that public schools cannot require prayers; John Glenn becomes the first American to orbit the Earth; Wilt Chamberlain sets NBA scoring record with 100 points in one game

1965 President Johnson orders air attacks on North Vietnam; Malcolm X assassinated

1966 Truman Capote pioneers the nonfiction novel with *In Cold Blood*; Miniskirts come into fashion.

1967 Antiwar protestors march on Washington, D.C.; Israel defeats Egypt, Syria, and Jordan in the six-day war

1968 Tet Offensive; President Johnson ends bombing of North Vietnam and announces he will not seek reelection; Arthur Ashe becomes first black to win United States Men's Tennis Championship.

1970 Antiwar protestors are fired upon by National Guard troops at Kent State University; President Nixon sends U.S. troops into Cambodia.

1971 Cigarette advertisements banned from television

1972 Police arrest five men for breaking into the Democratic Party National Headquarters in the Watergate Complex; President Nixon visits Communist China

1973 Senate committee headed by Samuel J. Ervin probes links between the Watergate break-in and the White House

---

Vietnam, then, destroyed Johnson's presidency, and it helped to undermine Nixon's. It was a war that left scars—on the men who fought in it and on the people who opposed and supported it; on Americans and on Vietnamese; and on United States foreign policy and its position in the world. For almost thirty-five years the United States had been actively involved in Indochina, but its influence in the region effectively ended in 1975. The Vietnam War, like the Communist victory in China in 1949, undercut America's position in Asia.

The most constructive outcome of the war was the lessons it taught. Congress learned that it had to take a more active role in foreign affairs. The War Powers Act (1972), which requires the president to account for his actions within thirty days of committing troops in a foreign war, demonstrated that the Tonkin Gulf Resolution had taught Congress a painful lesson. Ho Chi Minh's nationalism taught policy makers that communism was not a monolithic movement, and that not all small nations are dominos. Perhaps politicians, policy makers, and citizens alike even learned that national policy should be based on the realities of individual situations and not Cold War stereotypes.

REVIEW SUMMARY

In Vietnam, the United States Cold War ideologies confronted a determined Third World nationalist movement. In supporting an unpopular, anticommunist government in South Vietnam, America by slow steps became deeply embroiled in a war which led to widespread destruction, political disillusionment, and social discontent.

America became involved in Vietnam when it supported France's effort to recolonize the region after World War II

John Kennedy made the country a test case for containment

Lyndon Johnson escalated America's involvement in Vietnam

The process of disengagement from the war was also gradual.

> after the 1968 Tet Offensive the United States began its long withdrawal from the conflict Richard Nixon completed the American pullout, and North Vietnam reunified the country in 1975

Vietnam demonstrated the limits of both American military power and the policy of containment.

SUGGESTIONS FOR FURTHER READING

OVERVIEWS AND SURVEYS

Stephen Ambrose, *Rise to Globalism: American Foreign Policy, 1938–1980* (1980); William H. Chafe, *The Unfinished Journey* (1986) and *The American Woman* (1972); Alexander DeConde, *A History of American Foreign Policy* (1963); Robert H. Ferrell, *American Diplomacy* (1969); Alonzo Hamby, *The Imperial Years* (1976); Godfrey Hodgson, *America in Our Time* (1975); Walter LaFeber, *America, Russia, and the Cold War* (1976); R. W. Leopold, *The Growth of American Foreign Policy* (1967); William Leuchtenburg, *A Troubled Feast* (1983); Thomas G. Paterson, *American Foreign Policy* (1977); Richard Polenberg, *One Nation Divisible* (1980); Emily and Norman Rosenberg, *In Our Time* (1982); Frederick F. Siegel, *A Troubled Journey* (1984); William A. Williams, *The Tragedy of American Diplomacy* (1972) and *The Roots of the Modern American Empire* (1969); Lawrence Wittner, *Cold War America* (1979); Howard Zinn, *Postwar America, 1945–1971* (1973).

THE ILLUSION OF GREATNESS

Carl M. Brauer, *John F. Kennedy and the Second Reconstruction* (1977); Herbert S. Dinerstein, *The Making of a Missile Crisis: October 1962* (1976); Theodore Draper, *Castro's Revolution* (1962); Louise FitzSimons, *The Kennedy Doctrine* (1970); Henry Fairlie, *The Kennedy Promise* (1976); Allen Matusow, *The Unraveling of America* (1984); Bruce Miroff, *Pragmatic Illusions: The Presidential Politics of JFK* (1976); Jack Newfield, *Robert F. Kennedy: A Memoir* (1976); Victor Navasky, *Kennedy Justice* (1971); Jack M. Schick, *The Berlin Crisis, 1958–1962* (1971); Arthur Schlesinger, Jr., *A Thousand Days* (1965); Theodore Sorenson, *Kennedy* (1965); Richard Walton, *Cold War and Counterrevolution* (1972); Garry Wills, *The Kennedy Imprisonment* (1983); Peter Wyden, *Bay of Pigs* (1980)

VIETNAM: AMERICA'S LONGEST WAR

Larry Berman, *Planning a Tragedy* (1982); Peter Braestrup, *Big Story* (1978); David Burner et al., *A Giant's Strength* (1971); Philip Caputo, *A Rumor of War* (1977); Robert Caro, *The Path to Power* (1982); Harry Caudill, *Night Comes to the Cumberlands* (1963); Warren Cohen, *Dean Rusk* (1980); Chester Cooper, *The Lost Crusade: America in Vietnam* (1970); Robert A. Divine, ed., *Exploring the Johnson Years* (1981); Ronnie Dugger, *The Politician* (1982); Bernard Fall, *Street Without Joy* (1964) and *The Two Vietnams* (1967); Frances FitzGerald, *Fire in the Lake* (1972); Philip Geyelin, *Lyndon B. Johnson and the World* (1966); Todd Gitlin, *The Whole World Is Watching* (1981); Eric Goldman, *The Tragedy of Lyndon Johnson* (1969); David Halberstam, *The Making of a Quagmire* (1965) and *The Best and the Brightest* (1972); Michael Herr, *Dispatches* (1977); George Herring, *America's Longest War* (1981); Seymour Hersh, *My Lai: A Report on the Massacre and Its Aftermath* (1971); Stanley Karnow, *Vietnam, A History* (1984); Doris Kearns, *Lyndon Johnson and the American Dream* (1977); Christopher Lasch, *The Agony of the American Left* (1969); Guenther Lewy, *America in Vietnam* (1978); Abraham Lowenthal, *The Dominican Intervention* (1972); Roger Morris, *Uncertain Greatness* (1978); Don Oberdorfer, *Tet!* (1971); William L. O'Neill, *Coming Apart* (1974); George Reedy, *The Twilight of the Presidency* (1971); Neil Sheehan, ed., *The Pentagon Papers* (1971); Kathleen J. Turner, *Lyndon Johnson's Dual War: Vietnam and the Press* (1981); Tom Wicker, *JFK and LBJ* (1969)

THE TORTUOUS PATH TOWARD PEACE

Carl Bernstein and Robert Woodward, *All the President's Men* (1974); Fawn Brodie, *Richard Nixon* (1981); John Dean, *Blind Ambition: The White House Years* (1976); Rowland Evans and Robert Novak, *Nixon and the White House: The Frustration of Power* (1973); Lloyd C. Gardner, ed., *The Great Nixon Turnaround* (1973); Stephen Graubard, *Kissinger: Portrait of a Mind* (1973); Robert Hartmann, *Palace Politics* (1980); Seymour Hersh, *The Price of Power* (1983); Leon Jaworski, *The Right and the Power: The Prosecution of Watergate* (1976); David Landau, *Kissinger: The Uses of Power* (1972); J. Anthony Lukas, *Nightmare: The Underside of the Nixon Years* (1976); Bruce Mazlish, *In Search of Nixon* (1972); Joe McGinnis, *The Selling of the President* (1969); Richard Nixon, *RN: The Memoirs of Richard Nixon* (1978); Kevin P. Phillips, *The Emerging Republican Majority* (1969); Thomas Powers, *The Man Who Kept the Secrets: Richard Helms and the CIA* (1979); William Safire, *Before the Fall* (1975); William Shawcross, *Sideshow* (1979); Jonathan Schell, *The Time of Illusion* (1975); Arthur M. Schlesinger, Jr., *The Imperial Presidency* (1973); Edward R. F. Sheehan, *The Arabs, Israelis, and Kissinger* (1976); John Sirica, *To Set the Record Straight* (1979); Marshall Frady, *Wallace* (1970); Theodore H. White, *Breach of Faith: The Fall of Richard Nixon* (1975).

CHAPTER 29
The Struggle for a Just Society

PEACE IN VIETNAM
VIETVETS FOR PEACE

93.

51

STUDENT POWER

2   4   3

Toward the end Phil Ochs started to lose it all—his voice, his looks, his sanity, his reason for living. During the 1960s Phil had been a widely respected writer and singer of protest songs, obscured only by the giant shadow cast by Bob Dylan. But whereas Dylan's career moved beyond the protest phase, Ochs's never did. After the election of Richard Nixon in 1968, Phil became something of a dinosaur, a relic of another age. By the early 1970s he knew he was out of joint with the new times. It was then that his life began to unwind, slowly at first and more rapidly toward the end.

In the fall of 1973 he traveled to Africa, which he believed had the most revolutionary potential. Fascinated by the Ugandan dictator Idi Amin, Phil told reporters that he planned to go to Uganda. In Tanzania, while walking alone on a beach at night, Phil was attacked by three men. They robbed him, beat him, and ruptured his vocal cords. The money and wounds were insignificant and superficial, but the damage to his voice was serious—he lost his upper range.

Back in the United States the downward plunge continued. He drank far too much and put on a layer of fat. Friends noted that he looked ill. Phil himself was convinced that he had stomach cancer and was going to die. His behavior was aberrant as well. He boasted that he was a CIA agent and convinced himself that the Mafia was after him. He began to carry weapons—hammers, lead pipes, knives, guns. He seldom slept and his body itched constantly. Nervously, he would scratch himself bloody, become enraged when he couldn't sleep, and throw furniture and punch walls.

He even took to calling himself John Train, claiming that Phil Ochs was dead. He confessed to a friend: "On the first day of summer, 1975, Phil Ochs was murdered in the Chelsea Hotel by John Train. . . . I killed Phil Ochs. The reason I killed him was, he was some kind of genius but he drank too much and was a boring old fart. For the good of societies, public and secret, he needed to be gotten rid of . . . he was no longer needed and useful."

John Train was occasionally arrested for minor offenses, and he was deserted by almost all of Phil Ochs's friends. Those friends who remained hoped that some miracle would bring back Phil Ochs. It never happened. On April 9, 1976, John Train/Phil Ochs committed suicide by hanging himself from a bathroom door.

In many ways, Phil Ochs's career—his voyage from social and political commitment to complete disillusionment—paralleled the fate of his generation. When he enrolled as a freshman at Ohio State University in the fall of 1958 he was a rebel looking for a cause. With his hair slicked back and collar turned up on his red leather jacket he presented a passable James Dean look-alike. Although his major was journalism, his primary concern centered on finding his own voice as a poet and singer. He found inspiration for both in left-wing politics. In his early songs he praised Fidel Castro, condemned capitalism, and complained about the impersonality of large universities. Like other students across the nation he was determined to have his say. In "I'm Going to Say It Now," Phil wrote:

Oh I am just a student, sir
And I only want to learn
But it's hard to see through the risin' smoke
Of the books that you like to burn.
So I'd like to make a promise
And I'd like to make a vow
Then when I've got something to say, sir
I'm gonna say it now.

He had something to say, but Ohio State wasn't the place to say it. In 1962 he headed for Greenwich Village, to the coffee houses, clubs, and bars along Bleecker and MacDougal streets, where folk singers were beginning to capture national attention. Civil rights was his first cause. He sang in concerts staged to encourage voter registration among blacks. He even journeyed to Mississippi, where he alternately searched for an "average Mississippian" to talk to and feared that he was going to be killed. Back in the Village he introduced a new song, "Here's to the State of Mississippi":

For underneath her borders the Devil draws no line
If you drag her muddy rivers nameless bodies you will find
And the fat trees of the forest have hid a thousand crimes

And the calendar is lying when it reads the present time,
Here's to the land you've torn out the heart of
Mississippi find yourself another country to be
part of.

When the war in Vietnam heated up Phil
discovered another cause. He sang on college
campuses, where he was hailed as a folk rock
star. Between songs he talked to the audience:
". . . here's a protest song . . . a song that's so
specific that you cannot mistake it for bullshit.
Speaking of bullshit . . . I'd like to dedicate this
song to McGeorge Bundy." Everyone laughed.
But the songs and the talk didn't end the war.

By the late 1960s
Phil began to lose his
audience, especially as
students deserted the
"causes" in order to
"tune in, turn on, and
drop out." Students
found new prophets.
Timothy Leary, a Har-
vard University psy-
chologist, preached the
virtues of LSD, a hallu-
cinogenic drug first fab-
ricated in 1938. Even
though the drug was
outlawed in 1966, LSD
continued to attract
people—mostly stu-
dents—who had given
up the struggle to cre-

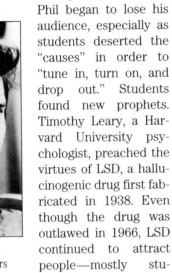

Phil Ochs was one of the
leading writers and singers
of protest music.

ate a better society for the quest of self-discov-
ery. Ken Kesey, author of the popular novel
One Flew Over the Cuckoo's Nest, replaced
Leary as the guru of LSD. He and his followers,
the Merry Pranksters, were products of postwar
affluence and were more concerned with passing the "acid test" than working to register
black voters or end the war in Vietnam.

For the Kesey crowd, Phil was merely
quaint. And Phil, who was frightened by any
drug harder than marijuana, realized that the
"chemical revolution" did not support any sort
of meaningful political revolution. He even believed that the government encouraged students to take drugs to dissipate their political

energies. Commenting on drugs and politics in
"Outside of a Small Circle of Friends" he wrote:

Smokin' marijuana is more fun than drinkin'
beer
But a friend of ours was captured
And they gave him thirty years
Maybe we should raise our voices, ask somebody
why
But demonstrations are a drag
And besides we're much too high

New trends in music also left Phil behind.
The folk clubs in the Village closed, and most of
the singers either died or moved to the West
Coast. The Beatles revived rock and roll and
folk singers were pushed into the background,
surfacing only for the occasional protest rally.
Even Dylan gave up his ragged clothes and
acoustic guitar for a black leather jacket and an
electric guitar. The best of the new music
aligned itself with the drug counterculture, not
the political left. In 1967 the Beatles released
Sargeant Pepper's Lonely Hearts Club Band,
which was widely regarded as a prophetic
statement. Timothy Leary called the Beatles
"evolutionary agents sent by God, endowed
with a mysterious power to create a new human
species." On one of the album's best cuts, John
Lennon sang, "I'd love to turn you on."

In the United States the counterculture
turned to the drug-laden San Francisco sound.
The Grateful Dead and the Jefferson Airplane
appealed to the "flower children" who moved to
San Francisco's Haight-Asbury district. The
Dead's Jerry Garcia recalled those days in the
mid-1960s when good drugs were more important than good music: "Thousands of people,
man, and helplessly stoned, all finding themselves in a roomful of other thousands of people, none of whom any of them were afraid of. It
was magic, far out, beautiful magic."

It might have been magic, but it didn't get
voters registered or end wars. This search for
wisdom without learning mocked the social and
political values Phil Ochs supported. Social responsibility, progress, commitment, and sacrifice played no part in the world of the hippies.
Phil did not belong in that world, and he knew
it. After the failure of the New Left (see
pp. 966-967) to influence the 1968 Demo-

cratic Convention in Chicago, Phil had a tombstone made for himself and pictured it on his *Rehearsals for Retirement* album:

> Phil Ochs (American)
> Born: El Paso, Texas 1940
> Died: Chicago, Illinois 1968

How right he was.

Phil Ochs died disillusioned. Some of the causes he supported—the end of racial inequality and an America without poverty—fell short of their goals. Some protest movements ran their course or fizzled out. Others, however, such as the minority liberation movements, simply kept evolving. If individuals dropped out, the movements survived and changed to meet new realities. And in the end, if great change was not achieved, real progress was made.

THE STRUGGLE FOR RACIAL JUSTICE

For black Americans in 1960 the statistics were grim. Their average life span was seven years less than white Americans. Their children had only half the chance of completing high school, only one-third the chance of completing college, and one-third the chance of entering a profession when they grew up. On average, black Americans earned half as much as white Americans and were twice as likely to be unemployed.

Table 29.2

High School Graduates (Percentage of Population Age 25-29)			
	1960	*1966*	*1970*
Blacks			
Male	36	49	54
Female	41	47	58
Whites			
Male	63	73	79
Female	65	79	76

Despite a string of court victories during the late 1950s, many black Americans were still second-class citizens. Six years after the landmark *Brown* v. *Board of Education* decision, just forty-nine southern school districts had desegregated and less than 1.17 percent of black schoolchildren in the eleven states of the old Confederacy attended public school with white classmates. Less than a quarter of the South's voting age black population could vote, and in certain southern counties blacks could not vote or serve on grand juries or trial juries, or frequent all-white beaches, restaurants, barber shops, hotels, and apartments.

In the North, too, black Americans suffered humiliation, insult, embarrassment, and discrimination. Many neighborhoods, businesses, and unions almost totally excluded blacks. In northern cities black unemployment soared as labor saving technology eliminated many semi-

Table 29.1

Income Distribution 1960, 1969 (Percentage)				
	Blacks and Other Nonwhites		*Whites*	
	1960	*1969*	*1960*	*1969*
Under $3000	38	20	14	8
$3000-4999	22	19	14	10
$5000-6999	16	17	19	12
$7000-9999	14	20	26	22
$10,000 and over	9	24	27	49

skilled and unskilled jobs that historically provided many blacks with work. Black families were experiencing severe strain; the proportion of black families headed by women had jumped from eight percent in 1950 to twenty-one percent in 1960. "If you're white, you're right," a black folk saying went; "if you're brown stick around; if you're black, stay back."

During the 1960s, however, a growing hunger for full equality arose among black Americans. Dr. Martin Luther King, Jr., gave voice to the new mood: "We're through with tokenism and gradualism and see-how-far-you've-comeism. We're through with we've-done-more-for-your-people-than-anyone-else-ism, We can't wait any longer. Now is the time."

Freedom Now

On Monday, February 1, 1960, four black freshmen at North Carolina Agricultural and Technical College—Ezell Blair, Jr., Franklin McClain, Joseph McNeill, and David Richmond—walked into the F. W. Woolworth store in Greensboro, North Carolina, and sat down at the lunch counter. They asked for a cup of coffee. A waitress told them that she would only serve them if they stood.

Instead of walking away, the four college freshmen stayed in their seats until the lunch counter closed. The next morning, the four college students reappeared at Woolworth's, accompanied by twenty-five fellow students. On Wednesday, student protesters filled sixty-three of the lunch counter's sixty-six seats. The sit-in movement had begun.

Although the student protesters ascribed to King's doctrine of nonviolence, their opponents did not. On one Saturday a group of white Nashville youths attacked the sit-in protesters. As one student described the confrontation, "Curiously, there were no police inside the store when the white teenagers and others stood in the aisles insulting us, blowing smoke in our faces, grinding out cigarette butts on our backs and finally pulling us off our stools and beating us. Those of us pulled off our seats tried to regain them as soon as possible, but none of us fought back in anger." When the police finally arrived, they arrested the black protesters, not the white tormenters.

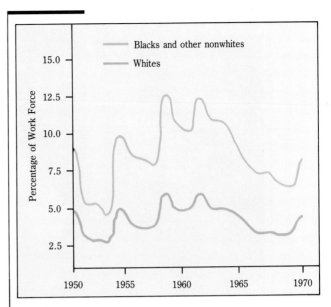

Figure 29.1
Unemployment 1950-1970

By the end of February, lunch counter sit-ins had spread through thirty cities in seven southern states. In Charlotte, North Carolina, a storekeeper unscrewed the seats from the lunch counters. Other stores roped off seats so that every customer had to stand. Alabama, Georgia, Mississippi, and Virginia, hastily passed antitrespassing laws to stem the outbreak of sit-ins. Despite these efforts, the nonviolent student protests spread across the South. Students attacked segregated libraries, lunch counters, and other public facilities.

In April, 142 student sit-in leaders from eleven states met in Raleigh, North Carolina, and voted to set up a new group to coordinate the sit-ins, the Student Non-Violent Coordinating Committee (SNCC). Martin Luther King told the students that their willingness to go to jail would "be the thing to awaken the dozing conscience of many of our white brothers." The president of Fisk University echoed King's judgment: "This is no student panty raid. It is a dedicated universal effort, and it has cemented the Negro community as it has never been cemented before."

By the end of 1960, 70,000 people had taken part in sit-ins in over one hundred cities

Lunch counter sit-ins in 1960 sparked an advance in the crusade against Southern segregation. Such passive resistance tactics proved very effective.

in twenty states. Police arrested and jailed more than 3600 protestors, and authorities expelled 187 students from college because of their activities. Nevertheless, the new tactic worked. On March 21, 1960, lunch counters in San Antonio, Texas, were integrated. By August 1, lunch counters in fifteen states had been integrated. By the end of the year, protestors had succeeded in integrating eating establishments in 108 cities.

The Greensboro sit-in initiated a new, activist phase in black Americans' struggle for equal rights. Fed up with the slow, legalistic approach that characterized the civil rights movement in the past, southern black college students began to attack segregation directly. Instead of relying upon court decisions or federal intervention to bring equal rights, students used nonviolent direct action to win civil rights for black Americans.

In the upper South, federal court orders and student sit-ins successfully desegregated lunch counters, theaters, hotels, public parks, churches, libraries, and beaches. In three states, however—Alabama, Mississippi, and South Carolina—segregation in restaurants, hotels, and bus, train, and airplane terminals remained intact. In those states, young civil rights activists launched new assaults against segregation.

To the Heart of Dixie

In early May 1961, thirteen men and women, black and white, set out from Washington, D. C., on two buses. They called themselves "freedom riders" and they wanted to demonstrate that despite a federal ban on segregated travel on interstate buses, segregation prevailed throughout much of the South. The freedom riders' trip was sponsored by the Congress of Racial Equality (CORE), a civil rights group dedicated to breaking down racial barriers through nonviolent protest. Dedicated disciples of the philosophy of Mahatma Gandhi, the freedom riders were willing to endure jail and suffer beatings to achieve integration. "We can take anything the white man can dish out," said one black freedom rider, "but we want our rights . . . and we want them now."

In Virginia and North Carolina, the freedom riders met little trouble. Black freedom riders were able to use white rest rooms and sit at white lunch counters. But in Winnboro, South Carolina, police arrested two black freedom riders and outside Anniston, Alabama, a white hurled a bomb through one of the bus's windows, setting the vehicle on fire. Waiting white toughs beat the freedom riders as they tried to escape the smoke and flames. Eight other whites boarded the second bus and assaulted the freedom riders before police restrained the attackers.

In Birmingham, Alabama, another mob attacked the second bus with blackjacks and lengths of pipe. In Montgomery, a club-swinging mob of 100 whites attacked the freedom riders; and a group of white youths poured an inflammable liquid on one black man and ignited his clothing. Local police arrived ten minutes later, state police an hour later. Explained Montgomery's police commissioner: "We have no intention of standing police guard for a bunch of troublemakers coming into our city."

In Washington, President Kennedy hastily deputized 400 federal marshals and Treasury agents and flew them to Alabama to protect the freedom riders' rights. The president publicly called for a "cooling-off period," but conflict continued. When freedom riders arrived in Jackson, Mississippi, twenty-seven were arrested for entering a "white-only" washroom and were sentenced to sixty days on the state prison farm.

The threat of racial violence in the South led the Kennedy administration to pressure the Interstate Commerce Commission to desegregate air, bus, and train terminals. In more than 300 southern terminals, signs saying "white" and "colored" were taken down from waiting room entrances and lavatory doors.

Civil rights activists' next major aim was to open state universities to black students. Although many southern states opened their universities to black students without incident, others were stiff-backed in their opposition to integration. A major breakthrough occurred in

James Meredith receiving his diploma at the University of Mississippi. His admission provoked a riot by 2500 white students.

September 1962, when a federal court ordered the state of Mississippi to admit James Meredith—a nine-year veteran of the Air Force—to the University of Mississippi in Oxford. Ross Barnett, the state's governor, promised on statewide television that he would "not surrender to the evil and illegal forces of tyranny" and would go to jail rather than permit Meredith to register for classes. Barnett flew into Oxford, named himself special registrar of the university, and ordered the arrest of federal officials who tried to enforce the court order.

James Meredith refused to back down. A "man with a mission and a nervous stomach," Meredith was determined to get a higher education. "I want to go to the university," he said. "This is the life I want. Just to live and breathe—that isn't life to me. There's got to be something more." Meredith arrived at the campus in the company of police officers, federal marshals, and lawyers. Angry white students waited, chanting, "Two, four, six, eight—we don't want to integrate."

Four times James Meredith tried unsuccessfully to register. He finally succeeded on the fifth try, escorted by several hundred federal marshals. The ensuing riot left two people dead and 375 injured, including 166 marshals. Ultimately, President Kennedy sent 16,000 troops to put down the violence.

"Bombingham"

By the end of 1961, protests against segregation, job discrimination, and police brutality had erupted from Albany and Atlanta, Georgia, to Jackson, Mississippi; Nashville, Tennessee; and Birmingham, Alabama. The symbol of unyielding resistance to integration was George C. Wallace, a former state judge and a onetime state Golden Gloves featherweight boxing champion, who won the Alabama governorship on an extreme segregationist platform. Promising that he would refuse to obey "any order to mix races in our schools," Wallace offered to "stand in the schoolhouse door" and if need be go to jail before permitting integration. At his inauguration in January 1963, Wallace declared: "I draw the line in the dust and toss the gauntlet before the feet of tyranny, and I say segregation now, segregation tomorrow, segregation forever."

It was in Birmingham, Alabama, that civil rights activists faced the most determined resistance. A sprawling steel town of 340,000 known as the "Pittsburgh of the South," Birmingham had a long history of racial acrimony. In open defiance of Supreme Court rulings, Birmingham had closed its thirty-eight public playgrounds, eight swimming pools, and four golf courses rather than integrate them. Calling Birmingham "the most thoroughly segregated city in the United States," the Reverend Dr. Martin Luther King, Jr., announced in early 1963 that he would lead demonstrations in the city until "Pharaoh lets God's people go." King and his followers demanded fair hiring practices, an end to segregation, and amnesty for previously arrested civil rights demonstrators.

Day after day, well dressed and neatly groomed men, women and children marched against segregation—only to be jailed for demonstrating without a permit. On April 12, King

himself was arrested—and while in jail wrote a scathing attack on those who asked black Americans to wait patiently for equal rights. A group of white clergymen had publicly criticized King for staging "unwise and untimely" demonstrations. King wrote out his reply on pieces of toilet paper and newspaper margins. "I am convinced," King wrote in his "Letter from a Birmingham Jail," "that if your white brothers dismiss us as 'rabble rousers' and 'outside agitators'—those of us who are working through the channels of nonviolent direct action—and refuse to support our nonviolent efforts, millions of Negroes, out of frustration and despair, will seek solace and security in black nationalist ideologies, a development that will lead inevitably to a frightening racial nightmare."

For two weeks, all was quiet, but in early May demonstrations resumed with renewed vigor. On May 2 and again on May 3, more than a thousand of Birmingham's black children marched for equal rights. In response, Birmingham's police chief, Theophilus Eugene "Bull" Connor, unleashed police dogs on the children and sprayed them with 700 pounds of water pressure—shocking the nation's conscience. Tension mounted as police arrested 2543 blacks and whites between May 2 and May 7, 1963. Under intense criticism, the Birmingham Chamber of Commerce reached an agreement on May 9 with black leaders to desegregate public facilities in ninety days, hire blacks as clerks and salespersons in sixty days, and release demonstrators without bail in return for an end to the protests.

King's goal was nonviolent social change, but the short-term result of protest was violence and confrontation. On May 11, white extremists firebombed an integrated motel. That same night, a bomb destroyed the home of Martin Luther King's brother. Shooting incidents and racial confrontations quickly spread across the South. Over the next ten weeks there were more than 750 riots in 186 cities and towns. In June, an assassin, armed with a Springfield rifle, ambushed thirty-seven-year-old Medgar Evers, the NAACP field representative in Mississippi, and shot him in the back. "I'm not afraid of dying," Evers had once said. "It might do some good."

In September, an explosion destroyed Birmingham's Sixteenth Street Baptist Church, killing four black girls and injuring fourteen others. Segregationists had planted ten to fifteen explosives under the steps of the fifty-year-old church building. That same day, a sixteen-year-old black Birmingham youth was shot from behind by a police shotgun, and a thirteen-year-old boy was shot while riding his bicycle. All told, ten people died during racial protests in 1963; thirty-five black homes and churches were fire bombed; and twenty thousand people were arrested during civil rights protests.

Kennedy Finally Acts

The eruption of violence in Birmingham and elsewhere finally forced the Kennedy administration to introduce legislation to guarantee black civil rights. Kennedy proposed a bill that required the desegregation of public facilities, outlawed discrimination in employment and voting, and allowed the attorney general to initiate school desegregation suits.

A hundred years after the Emancipation Proclamation, Kennedy declared, American blacks are still not "fully free. They are not yet freed from the bonds of injustice, they are not yet freed from social and economic oppression." As a result, "fires of frustration and discord are burning in every city, North and South." New laws against discrimination "are needed at every level."

During the 1960 campaign, Kennedy promised new civil rights legislation and declared that as president he would end housing discrimination with a "stroke of the pen." A few weeks before the election, Kennedy broadened his black support by helping to secure the release of Martin Luther King, Jr., from an Atlanta jail where he had been imprisoned for leading an antisegregation demonstration.

Kennedy's administration did file twenty-eight suits to protect black voting rights (compared to ten suits filed during the Eisenhower years), but it was not until November 1963, that Kennedy took steps to end housing discrimination with a "stroke of a pen"—after he had received hundreds of pens from frustrated civil rights leaders.

The March on Washington

The violence that erupted in Birmingham and elsewhere in 1961 and 1962 alarmed many veteran civil rights leaders. In December 1962, two veteran fighters for civil rights—A. Philip Randolph and Bayard Rustin—met at the office of the Brotherhood of Sleeping Car Porters in Harlem. Both men were pacifists, eager to rededicate the civil rights movement to the principle of nonviolence. Both men wanted to promote passage of Kennedy's civil rights bill, school desegregation, federal job training programs, and a ban on job discrimination. Thirty-two years before, Randolph had threatened to lead a march on Washington unless the federal government ended job discrimination against black workers in war industries. Now Rustin revived the idea of a massive march for civil rights and jobs.

On August 28, 1963, more than 200,000 people gathered around the Washington Monument and marched eight-tenths of a mile to the Lincoln Memorial. As they walked, the marchers carried placards reading: "Effective Civil Rights Laws—Now! Integrated Schools—Now! Decent Housing—Now!" and sang the civil rights anthem, "We Shall Overcome." At the Lincoln Memorial, folk singers Joan Baez, Bob Dylan, and Peter, Paul, and Mary sang spirituals and civil rights songs.

Ten speakers spoke to the crowd, but the event's highlight was an address by Martin Luther King. King concluded his eloquent speech with a moving description of his dream for America.

> "I have a dream," he declared, "that one day on the red hills of Georgia the sons of former slaves and the sons of former slaveowners will be able to sit down together at the table of brotherhood. . . . I have a dream that one day this nation will rise up and live out the true meaning of its creed: 'We hold these truths to be self-evident; that all men are created equal' . . . .

On August 28, 1963, over 200,000 blacks and whites gathered for a day-long rally at the Lincoln Memorial to demand an end to racial discrimination.

The Civil Rights Act of 1964

For seven months, debate raged in the halls of Congress. In a futile effort to delay the Civil Rights Bill's passage, opponents proposed more than 500 amendments and staged a protracted filibuster in the Senate. On July 2, 1964—a year and a day after President Kennedy had sent it to Congress—the Civil Rights Act was enacted into law. As finally passed, the act prohibited discrimination in voting, employment, and public facilities such as hotels and restaurants, and it established the Equal Employment Opportu-

nity Commission (EEOC) to prevent discrimination in employment on the basis of race, religion, or sex. Ironically, the provision barring sex discrimination had been added by opponents of the civil rights act in an attempt to kill the bill.

Although most white Southerners accepted the new federal law without resistance, many violent incidents occurred. Angry whites vented their rage in shootings and beatings; but despite such incidents, the Civil Rights Act was a success. In the first weeks under the 1964 civil rights law, segregated restaurants and hotels from Dallas to Charleston and from Memphis to Tallahassee opened their doors to black patrons. Over the next ten years, the Justice Department brought legal suits against more than 500 school districts charged with racial discrimination and more than 400 suits against hotels, restaurants, taverns, gas stations, and truck stops.

Voting Rights

The 1964 Civil Rights Act prohibited discrimination in employment and public accommodations. But many blacks were denied an equally fundamental constitutional right—the right to vote. The most effective barriers to black voting were state laws requiring prospective voters to read and interpret sections of the state constitution. In Alabama, voters had to provide written answers to a twenty-page test on the Constitution and state and local government. Questions included: Where do presidential electors cast ballots for president? Name the rights a person has after he has been indicted by a grand jury.

In an effort to bring the issue of voting rights to national attention, Martin Luther King, Jr., in early 1965 launched a voter registration drive in Selma, Alabama, a city of 29,500 people—14,400 whites and 15,100 blacks. Despite the fact that the federal government had filed a voting rights suit in 1961, Selma's voting rolls were ninety-nine percent white and one percent black.

For seven weeks, King led hundreds of Selma's black residents to the county court house to register to vote. In the first attempt to register black voters, more than 400 blacks marched to the county courthouse. They were stopped by County Sheriff James Clark, armed with a billy club and a cattle prod, who herded the marchers into a nearby alleyway. In succeeding weeks, Clark jailed nearly 2000 black demonstrators for contempt of court, juvenile delinquency, and parading without a permit. When King himself was arrested, he could accurately state that "there are more Negroes in jail with me than there are on the voting rolls." After a federal court ordered Clark not to interfere with orderly registration, the sheriff forced black applicants to stand in line for up to five hours before being permitted to take a "literacy" test. Not a single black voter was added to the registration rolls.

The demonstrations spread to nearby Marion, where fifty state troopers and white toughs attacked 400 black demonstrators. During the attack a young black man named Jimmie Lee Jackson was shot in the stomach; he died eight days later. King responded by calling for a march from Selma to the state capitol of Montgomery, fifty miles away.

On Sunday, March 7, 1965, black voting-rights demonstrators prepared to march. "I can't promise you that it won't get you beaten," King told them, ". . . but we must stand up for what is right!" Led by John Lewis, head of SNCC, and Hosea Williams, an official of King's Southern Christian Leadership Conference, the demonstrators, marched double file and headed toward the Edmund Pettus Bridge, across the Alabama River. As they crossed the bridge, 200 state police with tear gas, night sticks, and whips attacked them.

The five-day march from Selma to Montgomery finally resumed March 21, with protection from over 100 federal marshals, 1000 military police, and 1900 federalized Alabama National Guardsmen. The marchers chanted: "Segregation's got to fall . . . you never can jail us all." On March 25, a crowd of 25,000 gathered at the state capitol to celebrate the march's completion. Martin Luther King, Jr., addressed the crowd and called for an end to segregated schools, poverty, and voting discrimination. "I know you are asking today, 'How long will it take?' . . . How long? Not long, because no lie can live forever."

After nearly 2000 blacks were arrested for trying to register to vote in Selma, Alabama, demonstrators (including Martin Luther King) began a protest march from Selma to Montgomery.

Still, the violence continued. Within hours of the march's end, four Ku Klux Klan members shot and killed a thirty-nine-year-old white civil rights volunteer from Detroit named Viola Liuzzo. President Johnson expressed the nation's shock and anger. "Mrs. Liuzzo went to Alabama to serve the struggle for justice," the president said. "She was murdered by the enemies of justice who for decades have used the rope and the gun and the tar and the feather to terrorize their neighbors."

Two measures adopted in 1965 helped safeguard the voting rights of black Americans.

Table 29.3

Black Voter Registration Before and After the Voting Rights Act of 1965

State	1960	1966	Percent Increase
Alabama	66,000	250,000	278.8
Arkansas	73,000	115,000	57.5
Florida	183,000	303,000	65.6
Georgia	180,000	300,000	66.7
Louisiana	159,000	243,000	52.8
Mississippi	22,000	175,000	695.4
North Carolina	210,000	282,000	34.3
South Carolina	58,000	191,000	229.3
Tennessee	185,000	225,000	21.6
Texas	227,000	400,000	76.2
Virginia	100,000	205,000	105.0

U.S. Bureau of the Census, *Statistical Abstract of the United States: 1982-83* (103d edition) Washington, D.C., 1982.

On January 23, the states completed ratification of the Twenty-fourth Amendment to the Constitution barring a poll tax in federal elections. At the time, five southern states still had a poll tax. On August 6, President Johnson signed the Voting Rights Act which prohibited literacy tests and sent federal examiners to seven southern states to register black voters. Within a year, 450,000 southern blacks registered to vote.

Black Nationalism and Black Power

At the same time that such civil rights leaders as Martin Luther King fought for racial integration, other black leaders emphasized separatism and identification with Africa. Black nationalist sentiment was not something new. At the end of World War I, millions of black Americans were attracted by Marcus Garvey's call to drop the fight for equality in America and instead "plant the banner of freedom on the great continent of Africa."

One of the most important expressions of the separatist impulse during the 1960s was the rise of the Black Muslims, which attracted 100,000 members. Founded in 1931, in the depths of the Depression, the Nation of Islam appealed to the growing numbers of urban blacks living in poverty.

The Black Muslims elevated racial separatism into a religious doctrine and declared that whites were doomed to destruction. "The white devil's day is over," Black Muslim leader Elijah Muhammad cried. "Now he's worried, worried about the black man getting his revenge." Unless whites acceded to the Muslim demand for a separate territory for themselves, Muhammad said, "your entire race will be destroyed and removed from this earth by Almighty God. And those black men who are still trying to integrate will inevitably be destroyed along with the whites."

The Black Muslims did more than vent anger and frustration. The organization was also a vehicle of black uplift and self-help. The Black Muslims called upon black Americans to "wake up, clean up, and stand up" in order to achieve true freedom and independence. The Muslims encouraged the creation of black businesses and forbade alcohol and cigarettes.

The most controversial proponent of black nationalism was Malcolm X. The son of a Baptist minister who had been an organizer for Marcus Garvey's United Negro Improvement Association, he was born Malcolm Little in Omaha, Nebraska, and grew up in Lansing, Michigan. A reformed drug addict and criminal, Malcolm X learned about the Black Muslims in prison. After his release in 1952, he adopted the name Malcolm X to replace "the white slave-master name which had been imposed upon my paternal forebears by some blue-eyed devil." He quickly became one of the Black Muslim's most eloquent speakers, denouncing alcohol, tobacco, and extramarital sex.

Condemned by some whites as a demagogue for such statements as "If ballots won't work, bullets will," Malcolm X was a popular speaker on college campuses. He gained widespread public notoriety by attacking the Reverend Dr. Martin Luther King as a "chump" and a castrating Uncle Tom; advocating self-defense against white violence; and emphasizing black political power.

Malcolm X's main message was that discrimination led many black Americans to despise themselves. "The worst crime the white man has committed," he said, "has been to teach us to hate ourselves." Self-hatred caused black Americans to lose their identity, straighten their hair, and become involved in crime, drug addiction, and alcoholism.

In March 1964 (after he violated an order and publicly rejoiced at the assassination of President John F. Kennedy), Malcolm X withdrew from Elijah Muhammad's organization and set up his own Organization of Afro-Americans. Less than a year later, his life ended. On February 21, 1965, in front of 400 followers, he was shot and killed, apparently by followers of Black Muslim leader Elijah Muhammad, as he prepared to give a speech in New York City.

Inspired by Malcolm X's example, young black activists increasingly challenged the traditional leadership of the civil rights movement and its philosophy of nonviolence. Several factors contributed to a new spirit of nationalism and radicalism. Many young blacks lost faith in white liberals and interracial political activity when the 1964 Democratic party presidential convention refused to unseat an all-white delegation from Mississippi. A white backlash against civil rights also contributed to an upsurge of militancy. In 1964 Alabama Governor George Wallace, an avowed segregationist, entered three Northern Democratic presidential primaries and gained between one-third and one-half of the vote. Between mid-1964 and mid-1965, the Ku Klux Klan made its largest membership gains ever.

The single greatest contributor to the growth of militancy was the violence perpetrated by white racists. One of the most publicized incidents took place in June 1964, in Philadelphia, Mississippi, and led many young black civil rights workers to lose faith in nonviolence. On June 21, three civil rights workers—two whites, Andrew Goodman and Michael Schwerner, and one black, James Chaney—disappeared in the murky, snake-infested swamps of eastern Mississippi, where the charred shell of their station wagon was found. Earlier that day, the three had been stopped by police on the outskirts of Philadelphia, on a charge of driving 65 m.p.h. in a 30 m.p.h. zone. Six weeks later, the badly decomposed bodies

of the three young men were found buried in a dam six miles southwest of Philadelphia—all three had been beaten, then shot. In December, the sheriff and deputy sheriff of Neshoba County, Mississippi, along with nineteen others, were arrested on charges of violating the three men's civil rights, but six days later the charges were dropped. At the funeral of the three civil rights workers, black leader David Dennis angrily declared: "I'm sick and tired of going to the funerals of black men who have been murdered by white men. . . . I've got vengeance in my heart . . . ."

In 1966 two key civil rights organizations—the Student Nonviolent Coordinating Committee (SNCC) and the Congress of Racial Equality (CORE)—embraced black nationalism. In May, Stokely Carmichael, who had been born in Trinidad, was elected chairman of SNCC. He proceeded to transform SNCC from an interracial organization committed to nonviolence and integration into an all-black organization committed to "black power." "Integration is irrelevant," declared Carmichael. "Political and economic power is what the black people have to have." Although Carmichael initially denied that "black power" implied racial separatism, he eventually called on blacks to form their own separate political organizations. "To ask Negroes to get in the Democratic party," he declared, "is like asking Jews to join the Nazi party." One SNCC leader, James Foreman, demanded that white churches and synogogues pay black Americans $3 billion in "reparations."

In July 1966—one month after James Meredith, the black air force veteran who had integrated the University of Mississippi, was ambushed and shot while marching for voting rights in Mississippi—CORE also endorsed black power and repudiated nonviolence. In 1967 the organization deleted the word "multiracial" from its constitution, and the next year, CORE's national chairman, Roy Innis, announced that the group had become "once and for all . . . a Black Nationalist Organization" committed to "separation" of the races.

Of all the groups advocating racial separatism and black power, the one that received the widest publicity was the Black Panther party. Formed in October 1966, in Oakland, California,

A major achievement of the black power movement was the creation of black studies programs in universities across the country.

the Black Panther party was an armed revolutionary socialist organization advocating self-determination for black ghettos. "Black men," declared one party member, must unite to overthrow their white "oppressors," becoming "like panthers—smiling, cunning, scientific, striking by night and sparing no one!" The Black Panthers gained public notoriety by entering the gallery of the California State Assembly brandishing guns.

Separatism and black nationalism attracted no more than a small minority of black Americans. Public opinion polls indicated that only about fifteen percent of black Americans identified themselves as separatists and that the overwhelming majority of blacks considered Martin Luther King their favored spokesperson.

The older civil rights organizations such as the NAACP rejected separatism and black power. To veteran civil rights workers, black power meant abandoning nonviolence and integration and embracing, in King's words, "a nihilistic philosophy." Since blacks comprised just ten percent of the nation's population, said King, "we can't win violently. We have neither the instruments nor the techniques at our disposal, and it would be totally absurd for us to believe we could do it."

Yet despite their relatively small following, black power advocates exerted a powerful and positive influence upon the civil rights movement. In addition to giving birth to a host of community self-help organizations, supporters of black power spurred the creation of black studies programs in universities and encouraged black Americans to take pride in their racial background and recognize that "black is beautiful." A growing number of black Americans began to wear "Afro" hairstyles and take African or Arabic surnames. Singer James Brown captured the new spirit: "Say it loud— I'm black and I'm proud."

In an effort to maintain support among more militant blacks, veteran civil rights leaders began to address the problems of the poor blacks who lived in the nation's cities. The civil rights movement, Martin Luther King declared, had made only "surface changes" in the lives of black Americans. He said it did no good to be allowed to eat in a restaurant if you had no money to pay for a hamburger. King began to denounce the Vietnam War as "an enemy of the poor"; described the United States as "the greatest purveyor of violence in the world today"; and predicted that "the bombs that [Americans] are dropping in Vietnam will explode at home in inflation and unemployment." He urged a radical redistribution of wealth and political power in the United States in order to provide medical care, jobs, and education for all of the country's people. And he spoke of the need for a second "March on Washington" by "waves of the nation's poor and disinherited," who would "stay until America responds . . . [with] positive action." The time had come for radical measures "to provide jobs and income for the poor."

The Civil Rights Movement Moves North

On August 11, 1965, five days after President Lyndon Johnson signed the Voting Rights Act, the arrest of a twenty-one-year-old for drunk driving ignited a riot in Watts, a predominantly black section of Los Angeles. The violence lasted five days and resulted in 34 deaths, 3900 arrests, and the destruction of over 744 buildings. Rioters smashed windows, hurled bricks and bottles from rooftops, and threw molotov cocktails into buildings. Looters stripped store shelves of clothing, liquor, groceries, and furniture and burned credit records.

Over the next four summers, more than 150 major urban riots erupted in such cities as Buffalo, Chicago, Cincinnati, Des Moines, Detroit, Milwaukee, Newark, and Washington, D.C. The worst violence occurred during the summer of 1967, when riots occurred in 127 cities.

The assassination of Martin Luther King, Jr., in Memphis, Tennessee, on April 4, 1968, touched off the last major wave of rioting. Violence erupted in 168 cities, leaving 46 dead, 3500 injured, and $40 million worth of damage. In Washington, D.C., fires burned within three blocks of the White House.

In 1968 President Johnson appointed a commission to examine the causes of the race riots of the preceding three summers. Led by Illinois Governor Otto Kerner, the commission attributed racial violence to "white racism" and its heritage of discrimination and exclusion. Joblessness, poverty, a lack of political power, decaying and dilapidated housing, police brutality, and poor schools bred a sense of frustration and rage that had exploded into violence. The commission warned that unless major steps were taken, the United States would inevitably become "two societies, one black, one white—separate and unequal."

Until 1964 most white Northerners regarded race as a peculiarly southern problem that could be solved by extending voting rights to southern blacks and desegregating southern schools, buses, and lunchrooms. After 1964 the nation learned that discrimination and racial prejudice were nationwide problems—that black Americans were demanding not just de-segregation in the South but equality in all parts of the country. The nation also learned that resistance to black demands for equal rights was not confined to the Deep South, but existed in the North as well.

On February 3, 1964, 460,000 New York City students boycotted classes, staging a one-day protest against school segregation. A month later, black demonstrators staged a sit-in on New York City's Triborough Bridge, blocking traffic; demonstrators in Cleveland chained themselves together at construction sites to protest job discrimination. In 1965 Martin Luther King targeted housing discrimination in Chicago, which forced blacks to live in racial ghettos. Through marches and demonstrations, blacks forced Chicago Mayor Richard Daley and the Chicago Real Estate Board to negotiate. Anti-black riots exploded in Chicago's streets. King declared that he had "never seen anything so hostile and hateful [in the South] as I've seen here today."

In the North, however, blacks suffered not from *de jure* (legal) segregation, but primarily from *de facto* discrimination in housing, schooling, and employment—discrimination which lacked the overt sanction of law. "De facto segregation," wrote James Baldwin, "means that Negroes are segregated but nobody did it." The most obvious example of de facto segregation was the fact that the overwhelming majority of northern black schoolchildren attended predominantly black inner-city schools while most white children attended schools with an overwhelming majority of whites. In 1968—fourteen years after the *Brown* v. *Board of Education* decision—federal courts began to order busing as a way to deal with de facto segregation brought about by housing patterns. In April 1971, in the case of *Swann* v. *Charlotte-Mecklenburg Board of Education*, the Supreme Court upheld "bus transportation as a tool of school desegregation."

The Great Society and the Drive for Black Equality

No American president ever showed a stronger commitment to improving the position of black Americans than Lyndon Baines Johnson, the first Southerner to reside in the White House in half a century. As president he prodded Congress to pass a broad spectrum of civil rights laws, ranging from the Civil Rights Act of 1964 and the Voting Rights Act of 1965 to the 1968 Fair Housing Act barring discrimination in the sale or rental of housing. LBJ also took direct steps to require employers to take "affirmative action" to ensure that black Americans were not discriminated against in employment or promotions. Executive Order 11246, issued in 1965, required government contractors to ensure that job applicants and employees are not discriminated against. It required all contractors to prepare an "affirmative action plan" to achieve these goals.

Johnson broke many other color barriers. In 1966, he named the first black cabinet member, Secretary of Housing and Urban Development Robert Weaver. That same year, he appointed the first black woman, Constance Baker Motley, to the federal bench. In 1967 he appointed Thurgood Marshall as the first black American to serve on the Supreme Court. But Johnson's longest-lasting legacy was a battery of domestic antipoverty programs.

LBJ had a vision for America. During the 1964 campaign he often spoke about it. He envisioned an America "where no child will go unfed and no youngster will go unschooled;

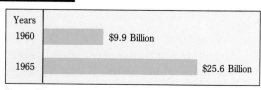

Figure 29.2
Federal Spending on Social Programs, Excluding Social Security

Years		
1960		$9.9 Billion
1965		$25.6 Billion

where every child has a good teacher and every teacher has good pay, and both have good classrooms; where every human being has dignity and every worker has a job; where education is blind to color and employment is unaware of race . . . ." Johnson called his vision the Great Society. In a 1964 speech at the University of Michigan, LBJ decisively declared that problems of housing, income, employment, and health were ultimately a federal responsibility. When Johnson left the presidency in 1969, his Great Society program had transformed the federal government. At the end of the Eisenhower presidency in 1961, there were only forty-five domestic social programs. By the end of the Johnson administration, the number had climbed to 435.

To combat poverty, the federal government raised the minimum wage and enacted programs to train poorer Americans for new and better jobs, including the 1964 Manpower Development and Training Act, and the Economic Opportunity Act, which established such programs as the Job Corps and the Neighborhood Youth Corps. To assure adequate housing, in 1966 Congress adopted the Model Cities Act to attack urban blight; set up a cabinet level Department of Housing and Urban Development; and began a program of rent supplements.

To promote education, Congress passed the Higher Education Act in 1965 providing student loans and scholarships; the Elementary and Secondary Schools Act of 1965 to pay for textbooks; and the Educational Opportunity Act of 1968 to help the poor finance college education. To address the nation's health needs, the Child Health Improvement and Protection Act of 1968 provided for prenatal and

Before becoming the first black Supreme Court Justice in 1967, Thurgood Marshall presented the legal arguments against school segregation that resulted in the *Brown* v. *Board of Education* decision.

postnatal care; the Medicaid Act of 1968 paid for the medical expenses of the poor; and Medicare, established in 1965, extended medical insurance to older Americans under the Social Security System.

When President Johnson announced his Great Society program in 1964, he promised substantial reductions in the number of Americans living in poverty. When he left office, he could legitimately argue that he had delivered on his promise. In 1960 forty million Americans, twenty percent of the population, were classified as poor. By 1969, their number had fallen to twenty-four million, twelve percent of the population. Johnson also pledged to qualify the poor for new and better jobs, to extend health insurance to the poor and elderly to cover hospital and doctor costs, and to provide better housing for low income families. Here, too, Johnson could say he had delivered. Infant mortality among the poor, which had barely declined between 1950 and 1965, fell by one-third in the decade after 1965 as a result of expanded federal medical and nutritional programs. Before 1965, twenty percent of the poor had never seen a doctor; by 1970 the figure had been cut to eight percent. The proportion of families living in houses lacking indoor plumbing also declined steeply, from twenty percent in 1960 to eleven percent a decade later.

Despite the widespread view that "in the war on poverty, poverty won," substantial progress had in fact been made. During the 1960s median black family income rose fifty-three percent; black employment in professional, technical, and clerical occupations doubled; and average black educational attainment increased by four years. The proportion of blacks below the poverty line fell from fifty-five percent in 1960 to twenty-seven percent in 1968. The black unemployment rate fell thirty-four percent. The country had taken major strides toward extending equality of opportunity to black Americans.

White Backlash

Ghetto rioting, the rise of black militancy, and resentment over Great Society social legislation combined to produce a backlash among many whites. In the wake of the riots, many whites fled the nation's cities. The Census Bureau estimated that 900,000 whites moved each year from central cities to the suburbs between 1965 and 1970.

Commitment to bringing black Americans into full equality weakened. In 1968 Alabama Governor George Wallace ran for president on the newly formed American Independent party ticket, declaring he would repeal "so-called civil rights laws." Wallace drew nearly 10 million votes in the election, 13.5 percent of the total votes cast, and won sufficient support in such northern states as Illinois and Ohio to swing these states to Republican candidate Richard Nixon.

During his 1968 campaign for the White House, Nixon promised to eliminate "wasteful" federal antipoverty programs, and to name "strict constructionists" to the Supreme Court. Once in office, the new president moved quickly to keep his commitments. In an effort to curb Great Society social programs, Nixon did away with the Model Cities program and the Office of Economic Opportunity. "The time may have come," declared a Nixon appointee, "when the issue of race could benefit from a period of benign neglect." The number of investigations

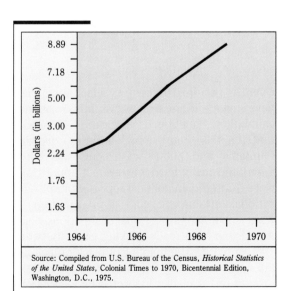

Source: Compiled from U.S. Bureau of the Census, *Historical Statistics of the United States*, Colonial Times to 1970, Bicentennial Edition, Washington, D.C., 1975.

Figure 29.3
Federal Aid to Education, 1964-1970

Vicious Circle

During the 1960s, American cities suffered from high levels of unemployment and crime, deteriorating systems of parks and sanitation, and chronic budgetary problems.
Copyright 1969 by Herblock in *The Washington Post*

pects being interrogated by police have a right to legal counsel.

As president, Nixon promised to alter the balance between the rights of criminal defendants and society's rights. He selected Warren Burger, a moderate conservative, to replace Earl Warren as Chief Justice of the United States and then successively nominated two conservative white Southerners for a second Court vacancy, only to have both nominees rejected (one for financial improprieties, the other for alleged insensitivities to civil rights). He eventually named four justices to the high court: Burger, Harry Blackmun, Lewis Powell, and William Rehnquist.

Under Chief Justice Burger and his successor William Rehnquist, the Supreme Court clarified the remedies that can be used to correct for past racial discrimination. In 1974 the Court limited the use of school busing for purposes of racial desegregation by ruling that busing could not take place across school district lines. In 1977 in the landmark *Bakke* case, the court held that educational institutions could take race into account when screening applicants—but could not use rigid racial quotas. In 1979 in the controversial *Weber* "reverse-discrimination" case, the court ruled that employers and unions could legally establish voluntary programs, including the use of quotas, to aid minorities and women in employment.

The Struggle Continues

Over the past quarter century, black Americans have made impressive social and economic gains. State-sanctioned segregation in restaurants, hotels, courtrooms, libraries, drinking fountains, and public washrooms was eliminated and many barriers to equal opportunity were shattered. In political representation, educational attainment, and representation in white collar and professional occupations, black Americans have made striking gains. Between 1960 and 1988 the number of black officeholders swelled from just 300 to nearly 6600 and the proportion of blacks in professional positions quadrupled. Black mayors now govern many of the nation's largest cities, including Chicago, Detroit, Los Angeles, Philadelphia, and Wash-

to determine whether communities were in compliance with school desegregation fell off sharply, from sixteen in 1969, the year Nixon took office, to zero in 1974. The administration urged Congress not to extend the Voting Rights Act of 1965 and to end a fair housing enforcement program.

President Nixon also made a series of Supreme Court appointments that brought to an end the activist era of the Warren Court. During the 1960s, the Supreme Court greatly increased the ability of criminal defendants to defend themselves. In *Mapp* v. *Ohio* (1961), the high court ruled that evidence secured by the police through unreasonable searches must be excluded from trial. In *Gideon* v. *Wainright* (1963), it declared that indigent defendants have a right to a court appointed attorney. In *Escobedo* v. *Illinois* (1964), it ruled that sus-

ington, D.C. Respect for black culture has also grown. The number of black performers on television and in film has increased, though most still appear in sitcoms or crime stories. Today, the most popular television performer (Bill Cosby), the most popular movie star (Eddie Murphy), and many of the most popular musicians and sports stars are black.

Nevertheless, full equality remains an unrealized dream; millions of black Americans still do not share fully in the promise of American life. According to census figures, blacks still suffer twice the unemployment rate of whites and earn only about half as much. The poverty rate among black families is three times that of whites, the same ratio as in the 1950s. Forty percent of black children are raised in fatherless homes and almost half of all black children are born into families earning less than the poverty level.

Separation of the races in housing and schooling remains widespread. Nationally, less than a quarter of all black Americans live in integrated neighborhoods and only about thirty-eight percent of black children attend racially integrated schools. And despite great gains in political influence, blacks still do not hold political offices in proportion to their share of the population. In 1987 there were only 400 black state legislators, compared to 7466 white state legislators, and altogether blacks still make up less than two percent of the nation's officeholders.

While the United States has eliminated many obstacles to black progress, much remains to be done if the country is to attain Martin Luther King's dream of a nation where

> all of God's children, black man and white man, Jew and Gentile, Protestant and Catholic, will be able to join hands and sing in the words of the old Negro spiritual, 'Free at Last, Free at Last, Thank God Almighty, I'm Free at last.'

THE YOUTH REVOLT

During the '60s, there was a sudden explosion in the number of teenagers and young adults. As a result of the depressed birthrates during the 1930s and the postwar baby boom, the

Tom Bradley, the son of a sharecropper, became the first black mayor of Los Angeles in 1973, winning more than fifty-six percent of the total vote.

number of young people aged fourteen to twenty-five jumped forty percent in a decade, until they constituted twenty percent of the nation's population. The nation's growing number of young people received far more schooling than their parents. Over seventy-five percent graduated from high school and nearly forty percent went on to higher education.

The skepticism of youth toward corporate and bureaucratic authority, their strong emotional identification with the underprivileged, and their intense desire for stimulation and instant gratification shaped the nation's politics, dress, music, and film. Unlike their parents, who had grown up amid the hardships of the Depression and the patriotic sacrifices of World War II, young people of the 1960s grew up during a period of rapid economic growth. Taking economic security for granted, they sought personal fulfillment and tended to dismiss the success-oriented lives of their parent's generation. "Never trust anyone over 30," was a popular saying.

At no earlier time in American history had the gulf between the generations seemed so wide. Blue jeans, long hair, psychedelic drugs, casual sex, hippie communes, campus demonstrations, and rock music all became symbols of the distance separating youth from the world of conventional adulthood.

The New Left

Late in the spring of 1962, five dozen college students gathered at a lakeside camp near Port Huron, Michigan, to discuss politics. For four days and nights the members of an obscure student group known as Students for a Democratic Society (SDS) talked passionately about such topics as civil rights, foreign policy, and the quality of American life. At five o'clock on the morning of June 16 the gathering ended. The participants had agreed upon a political platform that expressed their sentiments. This manifesto, one of the pivotal political documents in American history, became known as the Port Huron Statement.

The goal set forth in the Port Huron Statement was the creation of a radically democratic political movement in the United States that rejected levels of authority and bureaucracy. In its most important paragraphs, the document called for "participatory democracy"—direct individual involvement in the decisions that affected their lives. This notion would become the battle cry of the student movement of the 1960s—a movement that came to be known as the New Left.

The Port Huron Statement's chief author was Tom Hayden. Hayden was born on December 11, 1939, in Royal Oak, Michigan, a predominantly Catholic working class suburb of Detroit. From an early age, Hayden had questioned established authority. In high school, his idols were critics of conventional society, such as the hero of J. D. Salinger's *Catcher in the Rye* and *Mad Magazine's* Alfred E. Neuman. At the University of Michigan he edited the university's student newspaper. Hayden spent much of 1961 in the South, worked with SNCC, and was once badly beaten by local whites in McComb, Mississippi.

During the 1960s, Tom Hayden became one of the key figures in the New Left. In 1968 he flew to North Vietnam as a protest against the Vietnam War. The next year he gained further notoriety as one of the Chicago Seven defend-

ants who were acquitted on charges of conspiring to disrupt the 1968 Democratic Presidential Convention. Briefly, Hayden dropped out of politics, moved to Venice, California, and lived under a pseudonym. Later, he married actress Jane Fonda and became a member of the California legislature.

During the 1960s, thousands of young college students, like Tom Hayden and Phil Ochs, became politically active. The first issue to spark student radicalism was the impersonality of the modern university. Students questioned university requirements, restrictions on student political activities, and dormitory rules that limited the hours that male and female students could socialize with each other. Restrictions on students handing out political pamphlets on university property led to the first campus demonstrations that broke out at the University of California at Berkeley and soon spread to other campuses. Mario Savio, leader of the Berkeley Free Speech Movement, succinctly summarized the feelings of many student radicals:

> The university is well structured, well tooled, to turn out people with all the sharp edges worn off, the well-rounded person . . . . This means that the best among the people who enter must for four years wander aimlessly much of the time questioning why they are on campus at all, doubting whether there is any point in what they are doing, and looking forward toward a very bleak existence afterward in a game in which all of the rules have been made up, which one cannot really amend.

Involvement in the civil rights movement in the South initiated many students into radical politics. In the early 1960s, many white students from northern universities began to participate in voter registration drives, freedom schools, sit-ins, and freedom rides in order to help desegregate the South. For the first time, many witnessed poverty, discrimination, and violence first hand.

Student radicalism also drew inspiration from a literature of social criticism that flourished in the 1950s. Popular films, like "Rebel Without a Cause," portrayed sensitive, directionless, alienated youths unable to conform to the conventional adult values of suburban and

In the late summer of 1964 the first major student demonstrations took place at the University of California at Berkeley. Student protests against war, racism, and poverty continued throughout the country into the '70s.

corporate America. Sophisticated works of social criticism, by such maverick sociologists, psychologists, and economists as Herbert Marcuse, Paul Goodman, Michael Harrington, and C. Wright Mills, documented the growing concentration of power in the hands of social elites, the persistence of poverty in a land of plenty, and the stresses and injustices in America's social order.

Above all, student radicalism owed its support to student opposition to the Vietnam War. SDS held its first antiwar march in 1965 and attracted at least 15,000 protestors to Washington, and commanded wide press attention. Over the next three years, opposition to the war brought thousands of new members to SDS. The organization grew phenomenally, from fewer than a thousand members in 1962 to at least 50,000 in 1968. In addition to its antiwar activities, members of SDS also tried to organize a democratic "interracial movement of the poor" in the northern city neighborhoods.

Many members of SDS quickly grew frustrated by the slow pace of social change and began to look at violence as a tool to transform society. "I'm a nihilist! I'm proud of it, proud of it!" shouted a delegate at a 1967 SDS meeting in Princeton. "Tactics? It's too late. . . . Let's break what we can. Tear them apart." An underground newspaper, the *Berkeley Barb*, proclaimed that the "university cannot be reformed" and called for guerilla bands to sweep through "college campuses, busting up classrooms, and freeing our brothers from the prison of the university."

After 1968 SDS rapidly self-destructed. The Marxist-Leninist Progressive Labor party infiltrated the organization. SDS's final convention in 1969 degenerated into a shouting match, as factions tried to shout each other down with chants of "Ho, Ho, Ho Chi Minh!" and "Mao, Mao, Mao Tse-tung!" In 1969 the Weathermen, a surviving faction of SDS, attempted to launch a guerrilla war in the streets of Chicago—an incident known as the "Days of Rage"—to "tear pig city apart." Finally, in 1970 three members of the Weathermen blew themselves up in a Greenwich Village brownstone trying to make a bomb out of a stick of dynamite and an alarm clock.

The Making and Unmaking of a Counterculture

The New Left had a series of heroes—ranging from Marx, Lenin, Ho, and Mao to Fidel Castro, Che Guevera, and other revolutionaries. It also had its own uniforms, rituals, and music. Faded blue work shirts and jeans, wire-rimmed glasses, and work shoes were prescribed even if the dirtiest work the wearer performed was taking notes in a college class. The proponents of the New Left emphasized their sympathy with the working class—an emotion that was seldom reciprocated—and listened to labor songs that once fired the hearts of unionists, and to political protest folk music of Phil Ochs, Bob Dylan, and their crowd.

While the New Left labored to change the world and remake American society, other youths attempted to alter themselves and reorder consciousness. Variously labeled the counterculture, hippies, or flower children, they had their own heroes, music, dress, and approach to life.

In theory, supporters of the counterculture rejected individualism, competition, and capitalism. Adopting ideas from oriental religions rather unsystematically, they sought to become one with the universe. "The solution to the problem of identity is, get lost," wrote Norman O. Brown, whose books influenced the counterculture. All humanity, Brown believed, was part of a single entity, and a man or woman existed not as an individual but as part of the whole. As one interpreter of Brown explained, "Body existed, not as location or flesh, but as a field of energy; ego, character, personality were mere illusion. . . . Indeed, knowledge of the unity could be attained only by breaking the bonds of the ego, by having 'no self.' "

But how could one lose oneself? The process began with the act of rejection—of such liberal values as progress, order, reason, achievement, social responsibility; of competition, materialism, the work ethic, and other bourgeois "hang-ups." Rejection of monogamy

Many members of the counterculture chose to live in communes as a challenge to adult values, life-styles, and standards of living.

and releasing one's sexual energy also aided the process. If the counterculture did not invent sex, it claimed to have improved the patent. As in other aspects of the movement, the emphasis was on sharing. The traditional nuclear family gave way to the tribal or communal ideal, where members renounced individualism and private property and shared food, work, and sex. In such a community, love was a general abstract ideal rather than a focused emotion.

The quest for openness with the universe led many youths to experiment with hallucinogenic drugs. LSD had a particularly powerful lure. Under its influence, poets, musicians, politicians, and thousands of other Americans claimed to have tapped into an all-powerful spiritual force. After taking LSD, Henry Luce, founder and president of Time-Life, Inc., claimed that God told him all was right with America.

Perhaps some takers discovered profound truths, but by the late 1960s drugs had done more harm than good. The history of the Haight-Ashbury section of San Francisco illustrated the problems caused by drugs. In 1967 Haight was the center of the "counterculture," the home of the "flower children." During that "summer of love" the song "Are You Going to San Francisco" soared to the top of the pop chart, and in the "city of love" hippies ingested LSD, smoked pot, listened to "acid rock," and proclaimed the dawning of a new age. Even the Hell's Angels, an outlaw motorcycle group, temporarily joined the act, serving as the hippies' private police force. Notwithstanding *Time* magazine's description of Haight as "the vibrant epicenter of the hippie movement," the area was suffering from severe problems. High levels of racial violence, venereal disease, rape, drug overdoses, and poverty ensured more bad trips than good. "No doubt real love existed somewhere in the Haight," noted one historian. "But the case of the sixteen-year-old girl who was shot full of speed and raffled off in the streets was closer to the dominant reality."

Even music, which along with drugs and sex formed the counterculture trinity, failed to alter human behavior. In 1969 journalists hailed the Woodstock Music Festival as a symbol of love. But a few months later a group of Hell's Angels violently interrupted the Altamont Raceway music festival. As Mick Jagger sang "Sympathy for the Devil," an Angel stabbed a black man to death.

Like the New Left, the counterculture fell victim to its own excesses. Sex, drugs, and rock and roll did not solve the problems facing the United States; and by the end of the 1960s the counterculture had lost its force.

LIBERATION MOVEMENTS

The struggles of black Americans for racial justice inspired a host of other groups to seek full equality. Women, Mexican-Americans, Indians, and many other deprived groups protested against discrimination and organized to promote social change.

Women's Liberation Movement

Hosted by Jack Bailey, a gravel-voiced former carnival barker, it was one of the most popular daytime television shows of the 1950s. Five times a week, three women, each with a hardluck story, recited their tales of woe—diseases, retarded children, poverty—and the studio audience, with an applause meter, decided which woman was the most miserable. She became "Queen for a Day." Bailey put a crown on her head, wrapped her in a mink coat (which she got to keep for twenty-four hours), and told her about the new Cadillac she would get to drive (also for the next twenty-four hours). And then came gifts for the queen; a year's supply of Helena Rubinstein cosmetics; a Clairol permanent and once-over by a Hollywood make-up artist; and the electric appliances necessary for female happiness—a toaster oven, automatic washer, automatic dryer, and an iron. Altogether, everything a woman needed to be a prettier and better housewife.

One woman in the audience was Betty Friedan. A 1942 honors graduate of Smith College and former psychology Ph.D. candidate at the University of California at Berkeley, Friedan had quit graduate school, married, moved to the New York suburbs, and bore three children in rapid succession. American culture told her that husband, house, children, and electric appliances were true happiness. Betty Friedan was not happy; and she was not alone in her unhappiness.

In 1957 Friedan sent out a questionnaire to fellow members of her college graduating class. The replies amazed her. Again and again, she found women suffering from "a sense of dissatisfaction." Over the next five years, Friedan and other observers detected a widespread sense of discontent among American women. Doctors identified a new female malady, the housewife's syndrome, characterized by a mixture of frustration and exhaustion. CBS broadcast a television documentary entitled "The Trapped Housewife." *Newsweek* magazine noted that the nation's supposedly happy housewife was "dissatisfied with a lot that women of other lands can only dream of. Her discontent is deep, pervasive, and impervious to the superficial remedies which are offered at every hand." *The New York Times* editorialized, "Many young women . . . feel stifled in their homes." *Redbook* magazine ran an article entitled "Why Young Mothers Feel Trapped" and asked for examples of this problem. It received 24,000 replies.

Why, Friedan asked, were American women so discontented? In 1963 she published her answer in a book entitled *The Feminine Mystique.* This book, one of the most influential books ever written by an American, helped launch a new movement for women's liberation.

Sources of Discontent

During the 1950s, many American women reacted against the poverty of the Depression and the upheavals of World War II by placing renewed emphasis upon family life. Young women married earlier than their mothers had, and had more children and bore them faster. The average marriage age of American women dropped to twenty, a record low. The fertility rate rose fifty percent between 1940 and 1950—producing a population growth rate approaching that of India. Growing numbers of women decided to forsake higher education or a full-time career and achieve emotional fulfillment as wives and mothers. A 1952 advertisement for Gimbel's department store expressed the prevailing point of view. "What's college?" the ad asked. "That's where girls who are above cooking and sewing go to meet a man so they can spend their lives cooking and sewing." By "marrying at an earlier age, rearing larger families," and purchasing a house in the suburbs, young women believed, as *McCall's* magazine said, that they could find their "deepest satisfaction."

Politicians, educators, psychologists, and the mass media all echoed the view that women would find their highest fulfillment managing a house and caring for children. Many educators agreed with the president of Barnard College, who argued that women could not compete with men in the workplace because they "had less physical strength, a lower fatigue point, and a less stable nervous system." Women's magazines pictured housewives as happy with their tasks and depicted career women as neurotic, unhappy, and dissatisfied.

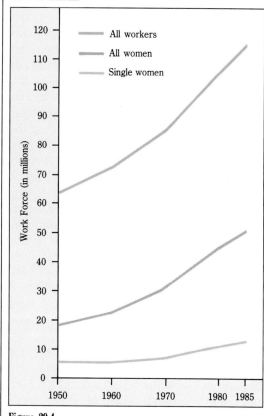

Figure 29.4
Women in the Work Force, 1950-1985

Already, however, a series of dramatic social changes were underway that would contribute to a rebirth of feminism. A dramatic upsurge took place during the 1950s in women's employment and education. More and more married women entered the labor force, and by 1960 the proportion of married women working outside the home was one in three. The number of women receiving college degrees also rose. The proportion of bachelor's and master's degrees received by women rose from just twenty-four percent in 1950 to over thirty-five percent a decade later. Meanwhile, beginning in 1957 the birthrate began to drop as women elected to have fewer children. A growing discrepancy had begun to appear between the popular image of women as fulltime housewives and mothers and the actual realities of many women's lives.

Feminism Reborn

Women in 1960 played a limited role in American government. Although women comprised about half of the nation's voters, there were no female Supreme Court justices, federal appeals court justices, governors, cabinet officers, or ambassadors. Only two of 100 United States senators and fifteen of 435 representatives were women. Of 307 federal district judges, two were women. Of 7700 members of state legislatures, 234 were women. Nor were these figures atypical. Only two American women had ever been elected governor, only two had ever served in the president's cabinet, and only six had ever served as ambassador.

Economically, women workers were concentrated in low-paying service and factory jobs. The overwhelming majority worked as secretaries, waitresses, beauticians, teachers, nurses, and librarians. Only 3.5 percent of the nation's lawyers were women, 10 percent of the nation's scientists, and less than 2 percent of the nation's leading business executives.

Lower pay for women doing the same work as men was commonplace. One out of every three companies had separate pay scales for male and female workers. A female bank teller typically made $15 a week less than a man with the same amount of experience and a female laundry worker made 49 cents an hour less than her male counterpart. Altogether, the earnings of women working fulltime averaged only about sixty percent of those of men.

In many parts of the country, the law discriminated against women. In three states—Alabama, Mississippi, and South Carolina—women could not sit upon juries. Many states restricted married women's right to make contracts, sell property, engage in business, control their own earnings, and make a will. Six states gave fathers preference in the custody of young children after a divorce.

In December 1961 President John F. Kennedy placed the issue of women's rights on the national political agenda. Eager to fulfill a debt to women voters—he had not named a single woman to a policy-making position—Kennedy established the first President's Commission on the Status of Women. Chaired by Eleanor Roo-

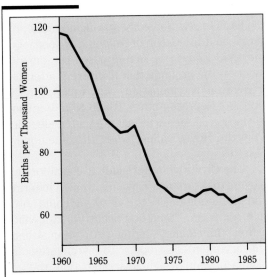

Figure 29.5
American Birth Rate, 1960-1985

sevelt, the commission was to recommend ways to combat "the prejudices and outmoded customs [that] act as barriers to the full realization of women's rights."

In 1963, the year that Betty Friedan published *The Feminine Mystique*, the commission issued its report. The report's recommendations included a call for an end to all legal restrictions on married women's right to own property, to enter into business, and to make contracts; equal opportunity in employment; and greater availability of child-care services.

The most important reform to grow out of the committee's investigations was the 1963 Equal Pay Act, which required equal pay for men and women who performed the same jobs under equal conditions. The Equal Pay Act was the first federal law to prohibit discrimination on the basis of sex.

The next year, Congress forged a new weapon in the fight against sex discrimination. Title VII of the 1964 Civil Rights Act prohibited discrimination in hiring or promotion based on race, color, religion, national origin, or sex by private employers and unions. As originally proposed, the bill only outlawed racial discrimination; but in a futile effort to block the measure, Representative Howard Smith of Virginia amended the bill to prohibit discrimination on the basis of sex. Some liberals including Representative Edith Green of Oregon, a cosponsor of the 1963 Equal Pay Act, opposed the amendment on the grounds that it diverted attention from racial discrimination—but it passed in the House of Representatives 168 to 133. "We made it! God Bless America!" shouted a female voice from the House gallery when the amendment passed.

The Civil Rights Act made it illegal for employers to discriminate against women in hiring and promotion unless the employer could show that sex was a "bona fide occupational qualification" (for example, hiring a man as an attendant for a men's restroom). To investigate complaints of employment discrimination, the act set up the Equal Employment Opportunity Commission (EEOC).

At first, the EEOC focused its enforcement efforts upon racial discrimination and largely ignored sex discrimination. The commission's director considered the provision prohibiting sex discrimination "a fluke . . . conceived out of wedlock" and the EEOC rejected a proposal that separate want ads for men and women be outlawed.

To pressure the EEOC to enforce the law prohibiting sex discrimination, Betty Friedan and 300 other women formed the National Organization for Women (NOW) in 1966, with Friedan as president. The organization pledged "to take action to bring women into full participation in the mainstream of American society now, exercising all the privileges and responsibilities thereof in truly equal partnership with men." NOW filed suit against the EEOC "to force it to comply with its own government rules." It also sued the country's 1300 largest corporations for sex discrimination, lobbied President Johnson to issue an executive order that would include women within federal affirmative action requirements, and challenged airline policies that required stewardesses to retire after they married or reached the age of thirty-two.

At its second national conference in November 1967, NOW drew up an eight-point bill of rights for women. It called for adoption of an Equal Rights Amendment (ERA) to the Constitution, prohibiting sex discrimination; equal educational, job training, and housing opportunities for women; and repeal of laws limiting access to contraceptive devices and abortion.

Two proposals produced fierce dissension within the new organization. One source of disagreement was the Equal Rights Amendment. The amendment consisted of two dozen words: "Equality of rights under the law shall not be denied or abridged by the United States or by any state on account of sex." It had originally been proposed in 1923 to mark the seventy-fifth anniversary of the Seneca Falls Women's Rights Convention and was submitted to Congress at almost every session. For over forty years, professional women, who favored the amendment, battled with organized labor and the Women's Bureau of the Labor Department, which opposed the amendment on the ground that it endangered "protective" legislation that set minimum wages and maximum hours for less-skilled women workers. At NOW's convention, women from the United Automobile Workers (UAW) opposed inclusion of the ERA in the Bill of Rights. When they lost, the UAW stopped providing NOW with office space and clerical services.

The other issue that generated controversy was the call for reform of abortion laws. In 1967 only one state—Colorado—had reformed nineteenth-century legal statutes which made abortion a criminal offense. Dissenters believed that NOW should avoid controversial issues which would divert attention away from economic discrimination.

Despite internal disagreements, NOW's membership grew rapidly, reaching 175,000 by 1988. The group broadened its attention to include such issues as the plight of poor and nonwhite women, domestic violence, rape, sexual harassment, the role of women in sport, and the rights of lesbians. At the same time, the organization claimed a number of achievements. Two victories were particularly important. In 1967, NOW persuaded President Lyndon Johnson to issue Executive Order 11375, which prohibited government contractors from discriminating on the basis of sex and required them to take "affirmative action" to ensure that women are properly represented in their workforce. The next year, the EEOC ruled that separate want ads for men and women were a violation of Title VII of the 1964 Civil Rights Act.

Radical Feminism

Alongside the National Organization for Women, other more radical feminist groups emerged during the 1960s among college students involved in the civil rights movement and the New Left. Women within these organizations for social change often found themselves treated as "second-class citizens," responsible for kitchen work, typing, and serving "as a sexual supply for their male comrades after hours." "We were the movement secretaries and the shit-workers," one woman recalled; "we were the earth mothers and the sex-objects for the movement men."

Women in the New Left also expressed unhappiness. "You are allowed to participate and to speak," noted one woman, "only the men stop listening when you do . . . How many times have you seen men get up and actually walk out of a room while a woman speaks, or begin to whisper to each other as she starts?" When women tried to raise the "woman question" at SDS's 1965 convention, men responded with "catcalls, storms of ridicule and verbal abuse, 'She just needs a good screw,' or . . . 'She's a castrating female.' "

In cities across the country, independent women's groups sprouted up in 1967. In the fall, at the first national gathering of women's groups at the National Conference for a New Politics, women demanded fifty-one percent of all committee seats in the name of minority rights. When men refused to meet their demand, the women walked out—signaling the beginning of a critical split between the New Left and the women's movement. The next year, radical women's groups appeared on the front pages of the nation's newspapers when they staged a protest of the Miss America pageant and provided a "freedom trash can," in which women could throw "old bras, girdles, high heeled shoes, women's magazines, curlers,

and other instruments of torture to women." They concluded their rally by crowning a sheep Miss America.

Women's liberation groups established the first feminist book stores, battered women's shelters, rape crisis centers, and abortion counseling centers. In 1971 Gloria Steinem and others published *Ms.*, the first national feminist magazine. The first 300,000 copies were sold out in eight days.

Radical new ideas began to fill the air. One women's liberation leader, Ti-Grace Atkinson, denounced marriage as "slavery," "legalized rape," and "unpaid labor." Meanwhile, a host of new words and phrases entered the language, such as *consciousness raising, Ms., bra burning, sexism,* and *male chauvinist pig.*

On August 26, 1970, the fiftieth anniversary of the ratification of the Nineteenth Amendment, the women's liberation movement dramatically demonstrated its growing strength by mounting a massive Strike for Equality. Members of virtually all feminist groups joined together in a display of unity and strength.

The Development of Feminist Ideology

Feminists subscribe to no single doctrine or set of goals. All are united, however, by a belief that women have historically occupied a subordinate position in politics, education, and the economic system. Modern feminist thought traces its roots to a book published by a famous French philosopher Simone de Beauvoir in 1949. Entitled *The Second Sex*, the book told of the assumptions, customs, educational practices, jokes, laws, and modes of speech that led young women to believe that they were inferior beings.

A decade and a half later, Betty Friedan made another important contribution to the development of feminist ideology. In *The Feminine Mystique*, she analyzed and criticized the role of educators, psychologists, sociologists, and the mass media in conditioning women to believe that they could only find fulfillment as housewives and mothers. By requiring women

THE MODERN FAMILY

Does a father have the right to give his children his last name even if his wife objects? Can an expectant mother obtain an abortion without her husband's permission? Should a teenager, unhappy with her parents' restrictions on her smoking, dating, and choice of friends, be allowed to have herself placed in a foster home? Should a childless couple be permitted to hire a "surrogate mother" who will be artificially inseminated and carry a child to delivery? These are among the questions that the nation's courts have had to wrestle with as the nature of American family life has, in the course of a generation, been revolutionized.

During the 1950s, the Cleavers on the television show "Leave It to Beaver" epitomized the American family. In 1960, over seventy percent of all American households were like the Cleavers: made up of a breadwinner father, a homemaker mother, and their kids. Today, "traditional" families with a working husband, a non-employed wife, and one or more children

make up less than fifteen percent of the nation's households. And as America's families have changed, the image of the family portrayed on television has changed accordingly. Today's television families run the gamut from two-career families like the Huxtables on "The Cosby Show" to two single mothers and their children on "Kate and Allie," and an unmarried couple who cohabitate in the same house on "Who's the Boss."

Profound changes have reshaped American family life in recent years. In a decade, divorce rates doubled. The number of divorces today is twice as high as in 1966 and three times higher than in 1950. The rapid upsurge in the divorce rates contributed to a dramatic increase in the number of single-parent households—or what used to be known as broken homes. The number of households consisting of a single woman and her children has tripled since 1960. A sharp increase in female-headed homes has been accompanied by a startling increase in the number of couples cohabitating

outside of marriage. The number of unmarried couples living together has quadrupled since 1970.

What accounts for these upheavals in family life? One of the most far-reaching forces for change has been a sexual revolution far more radical than the early-twentieth century "revolution in morals and manners." Contemporary Americans are much more likely than their predecessors to postpone marriage, to live alone, and to engage in sexual intercourse outside of marriage. Today, over eighty percent of all women say that they were not virgins when they married, compared to less than twenty percent a generation ago. Extramarital sex has also increased sharply. Back in the 1940s, just eight percent of married women under the age of twenty-five had committed adultery. Today the estimated figure is twenty-four percent. Meanwhile, the proportion of children born to unmarried mothers has climbed from just five percent in 1960 to over twenty percent today.

The roots of these developments were planted during the early 1960s, when a new openness about sexuality swept the nation's literature, movies, theater, advertising, and fashion. In 1960, the birth control pill was introduced, offering a highly effective method of contraception. Two years later, Grossinger's resort in New York State's Catskills Mountains introduced the first singles-only weekend, thereby acknowledging couples outside marriage. In 1964 the first "singles bar" opened in New York City; the musical "Hair" introduced nudity to the Broadway stage; California designer Rudi Gernreich created the first topless bathing suit; and bars began to feature topless waitresses and dancers. Sexually oriented magazines began to display full frontal nudity and filmmakers began to show simulated sexual acts on the screen. A new era of public sexuality was ushered in and as a result it became far easier and more acceptable to have an active social life and sex life outside of marriage.

At the same time, the nation's courts and state legislatures liberalized laws governing sex and contraception. In 1957, the Supreme Court narrowed the legal definition of obscenity, ruling that the portrayal of sex in art, literature, and film was entitled to constitutional protections of free speech, unless the work was utterly without redeeming social value. In 1962, Illinois became the first state to decriminalize all forms of private sexual conduct between consenting adults. In succeeding years, the Supreme Court struck down a series of state statutes that prohibited the prescription or distribution of contraceptives, and in 1973, in the case of *Roe* v. *Wade,* the high court decriminalized abortion. These legal decisions, to a large extent, took government out of the business of regulating private sexual behavior and defining the sexual norms according to which citizens were supposed to live.

Another factor reshaping family life has been a massive influx of mothers into the workforce. As late as 1940, less than twelve percent of white married women were in the workforce; today the figure is nearly sixty percent and over half of all mothers of preschoolers work outside the home. The major forces that have propelled women into the workforce include a rising cost of living, which spurred many families to seek a second source of income; increased control over fertility through contraception and abortion, which allows women to work without interruption; and rising educational levels, which lead many women to seek employment for intellectual stimulation and fulfillment.

As wives have assumed a larger role in their family's financial support, they have felt justified in demanding that husbands perform more childcare and housework. At the same time, fewer children have a full-time mother and as a result an increasing number of young children are cared for during the day by adults other than their own parent. Today, over two-thirds of all three-to-five-year-olds take part in a day-care, nursery school, or pre-kindergarten program, compared to one-fifth in 1970.

Feminism has been another major force that has transformed American family life. The women's liberation movement attacked the societal expectation that women defer to the needs of spouses and children as part of their roles as wives and mothers. Militant feminist activists like Ti-Grace Atkinson denounced marriage as "slavery" and "legalized rape." The larger mainstream of the women's movement articulated a powerful critique of the idea that childcare and housework were the apex of a woman's accomplishments or her sole means of fulfillment.

The feminist movement awakened American women to what many viewed as one of the worst forms of social and political oppression: sexism. The introduction of this awareness would go far beyond the feminists themselves. Although only a small minority of American women openly declared themselves to be feminists, the arguments of the women's movement drastically altered women's attitudes toward family roles, childcare, and housework. As a result of feminism, a substantial majority of women now believe that both husband and wife should have jobs, do housework, and take care of children.

The changes that have taken place in family life have been disruptive and troubling and have transformed the family into a major political battleground. Both liberals and conservatives have offered their own proposals about how the American family can best be strengthened. Conservative activists, fearful that climbing rates of divorce, single parenthood, and working mothers represent a breakdown of family values, launched a politically influential "pro-family movement" during the 1970s. They sought to restrict access to abortion, block ratification of the proposed Equal Rights Amendment to the Constitution, restrict eroticism on television, and limit teenagers' access to contraceptive information. Liberals have approached family issues from a different tack. Unlike conservatives, they are more willing to use government social policies to strengthen family life. Some of the proposals they have made to strengthen families include expanded nutritional and health programs for pregnant women, federal subsidies for day-care services for low-income families, uniform national standards for childcare centers, and a requirement that employers give parents unpaid leave to take care of a newborn or seriously ill child. Without a doubt, the family will remain one of the most heated political issues in the years to come.

to subordinate their own individual aspirations to the welfare of their husbands and children, said Friedan, the "feminine mystique" prevented women from achieving self-fulfillment and happiness.

In the years following the publication of *The Feminine Mystique*, feminists developed a large body of literature analyzing the economic, psychological, and social roots of female subordination. It was not until 1970, however, that the more radical feminist writings reached the broader reading public with the publication of Shulamith Firestone's *The Dialectic of Sex*, Germaine Greer's *The Female Eunuch*, and Kate Millet's *Sexual Politics*. These books argued that gender distinctions structure virtually every aspect of individual lives, not only in such areas as law and employment, but also in personal relationships, language, literature, religion, and individuals' internalized self-perceptions. They attributed female oppression to the ideology of male supremacy. "Women have very little idea how much men hate them," declared Greer. As examples of misogyny these authors cited pornography, grotesque portrayals of women in literature, sexual harassment, wife abuse, and rape.

Since 1970 feminist theory has exploded into many different directions. Today, there are more than thirty national feminist news and opinion magazines along with an additional twenty academic journals dealing with women's issues. Women's historians, feminist literary and film critics, and physical and social scientists have begun to ask exciting new questions about women's historical experience, sex and status differences between women and men, sex role socialization, economic and legal discrimination, and the depiction of women in literature.

The Supreme Court and Sex Discrimination

Despite its conservative image, the Supreme Court under Chief Justices Warren Burger and William Rehnquist has been active in the area of sex discrimination and women's rights. In contrast to the Warren Court, which ruled on only one major sex discrimination case—upholding a law that excluded women from serving on juries—the Burger and Rehnquist Courts considered numerous cases involving women's rights.

The Burger Court issued its first important discrimination decision in 1971. In its landmark decision, *Griggs* v. *Duke Power Company*, the Court established the principle that regardless of an employer's intentions, any employment practice is illegal if it has a "disparate" impact on women or minorities and "if it cannot be shown to be related to job performance." In subsequent cases, the Court legitimized the use of statistics in measuring employment discrimination and also approved the use of back pay to compensate the victims of discrimination.

The Court has not yet set an absolute rule that laws and employment practices must treat men and women the same. The Court's test for sex discrimination, adopted in 1976, is that to be constitutional, a policy that discriminates on the basis of sex must be "substantially related to an important government objective."

The Court's most controversial decision involving women's rights was delivered in 1973 in the case of *Roe* v. *Wade*. An unmarried, pregnant Texas waitress, assigned the pseudonym Jane Roe to protect her privacy, brought suit against Dallas district attorney Henry Wade to prevent him from enforcing a nineteenth-century Texas statute prohibiting abortion. The Court ruled on the woman's behalf and struck down the Texas law and all similar laws in other states. In its ruling, the Court declared that the decision to have an abortion is a private matter of concern only to a woman and her physician, and that only in the last three months of pregnancy could the government limit the right to abortion.

Many Americans—including many Catholic lay and clerical organizations—bitterly opposed the Supreme Court's *Roe* v. *Wade* decision and banded together to form the "right to life" movement, which ran Ellen MacCormack as a presidential candidate in the 1976 presidential primaries. The major legislative success of the "right to life" movement was adoption by Congress of the so-called Hyde Amendment,

Right-to-life groups, backed by fundamentalists, conservatives, and the Catholic church scored a victory
with the Hyde amendment. However, pro-choice
groups helped organize privately funded agencies and
clinics to allow women a choice.

which permitted states to refuse to fund abortions for indigent women.

The Equal Rights Amendment

In March 1972 the Congress passed an Equal
Rights Amendment (ERA) to the United States
Constitution, prohibiting sex discrimination,
with only eight dissenting votes in the Senate
and twenty-four in the House. Before the year
was over, twenty-two state legislatures ratified
the ERA. Ratification by thirty-eight states was
required before the amendment would be
added to the Constitution. Over the next five
years, only thirteen more states ratified the
amendment—and five states rescinded their
ratification. In 1978, Congress gave proponents
of the amendment thirty-nine more months to
complete ratification, but no other state gave its
approval.

The ERA had been defeated, but why? Initially, opposition came from organized labor,
which feared that the amendment would eliminate state "protective legislation," that established minimum wages and maximum hours for
women workers. Increasingly, however, resistance to the amendment came from women of
lower economic and educational status, whose
self-esteem and self-image were bound with
being wives and mothers and who wanted to
ensure that women who devoted their lives to
their families were not accorded lower status
than women who worked outside the home.

The leader of the anti-ERA movement was
Phyllis Schlafly, a Radcliffe-educated mother of
six from Alton, Illinois. A larger-than-life figure,
Schlafly earned a law degree at the age of fifty-
four, wrote nine books (including the 1964
best-seller *A Choice Not an Echo*), and created
her own lobbying group, the Eagle Forum.
Schlafly argued that the ERA was unnecessary
because women were already protected by the
Equal Pay Act of 1963 and the Civil Rights Act
of 1964, which barred sex discrimination, and
claimed that the amendment would outlaw separate public restrooms for men and women and
deny wives the right to financial support.

Impact of the Women's Liberation Movement

Since 1960 women have made enormous social gains. Gains in employment have been particularly impressive. During the 1970s, the number of working women climbed forty-two percent and much of the increase was in what traditionally was considered "men's" work and professional work. The percentage of lawyers who were women increased by 9 percentage points; the percentage of professors by 6 points; of doctors by 3.6 points. By 1986, women made up fifteen percent of the nation's lawyers, forty percent of all computer programmers, and twenty-nine percent of the country's managers and administrators.

Table 29.4

Occupation by Sex, 1972 and 1980 (Percentage)		
Occupation	*1972/Female*	*1980/Female*
Professional/Technical	39.3	44.3
Accountants	21.7	36.2
Computer specialists	16.8	25.7
Engineers	0.8	4.0
Lawyers and Judges	3.8	12.8
Life/Physical Scientists	10.0	20.3
Physicians/Dentists	9.3	12.9
Professors	28.0	33.9
Engineering/Science technicians	9.1	17.8
Writers/Artists/Entertainers	31.7	39.3
Sales	41.6	45.3
Real Estate Agents/Brokers	36.7	50.7
Clerks, retail	68.9	71.1
Clerical	75.6	80.1
Bookkeepers	97.9	90.5
Clerical supervisors	57.8	70.5
Office machine operators	71.4	72.6
Secretaries	99.1	99.1
Crafts Workers	3.6	6.0
Blue-collar supervisors	6.9	10.8
Machinists and Jobsetters	0.6	4.0
Tool and Die makers	0.5	2.8
Mechanics (except automobile)	1.0	2.6

U.S. Bureau of the Census, *Statistical Abstract of the United States: 1982-83* (103d edition) Washington, D.C., 1982.

Great strides have been made in undergraduate and graduate education. Discrimination against women students and faculty members was outlawed by Title IX of the Education Amendments Act of 1972. Today, for the first time in American history, women constitute a majority of the nation's college students and nearly as many women as men receive master's degrees. In addition, the number of women students receiving degrees from professional schools—including dentistry, law, and medicine—has shot upward.

Women have also made impressive political gains. In 1988 more than two dozen women served in Congress, more than eighty served as mayors of large cities, and more than a thousand serve in state legislatures. In 1984, for the first time, a major political party nominated a woman, Geraldine Ferraro, for the vice-presidency. Ten percent of the top appointed offices during the Reagan administration went to women and Sandra Day O'Connor was named the first woman to sit on the Supreme Court. Three women held cabinet posts and the president appointed a woman ambassador to the United Nations. By 1988 more than 15,000 women held elective office.

Despite all that has been achieved, however, problems remain. Most women today continue to work in a relatively small number of traditional "women's" jobs and a full-time female worker earns only 68 cents for every $1 paid to men. Even more troubling is the fact that large numbers of women live in poverty. The "feminization of poverty" was one of the most discouraging trends of the 1970s and 1980s. Today, nearly half of all marriages end in divorce and many others end in legal separation and desertion—and the economic plight of these women is often desperate. Although female-headed families constitute only fifteen percent of the United States population, they account for more than half of the poor population. Major gains have been achieved, but advances remain to be made.

Mexican-American Liberation

On election day, 1963, hundreds of Mexican-Americans in Crystal City, Texas, the "spinach

Table 29.5

Ratio of Divorces to Marriages, 1890-1980	
1890	1-17
1900	1-12
1910	1-11
1920	1-7
1930	1-5
1940	1-6
1950	1-4.3
1960	1-3.8
1970	1-3.5
1980	1-2

capital of the world," gathered near a statue of Popeye the Sailor to do something that many had never done before: vote. Although Mexican-Americans outnumbered Anglos two to one, Anglos controlled all five seats on the Crystal City council. For three years, organizers struggled to register Mexican-American voters. When the election was over, Mexican-Americans had won control of the city council. "We have done the impossible," declared Albert Fuentes, who led the voter registration campaign. "If we can do it in Crystal City, we can do it all over Texas. We can awaken the sleeping giant."

As the 1960s began, Mexican-Americans shared problems of poverty and discrimination with other minority groups. The median income of a Mexican-American family was just sixty-two percent of the median income of the general population, and four-fifths of employed Mexican-Americans were concentrated in semi-skilled and unskilled jobs, a third in agriculture.

Educational attainment lagged behind other groups (Mexican-Americans averaged less than nine years of schooling as recently as 1970), and Mexican-American pupils were concentrated in schools, with few Hispanic or Spanish-speaking teachers. Gerrymandered election districts and restrictive voting legislation resulted in the political underrepresentation of Mexican-Americans.

During the 1960s, a new militancy arose among Chicanos (Mexican-Americans). In 1962 Cesar Chavez began to organize California farm workers, and three years later, in Delano, California, he led his first strike. At the same time that Chavez led the struggle for higher wages, enforcement of state labor laws, and recognition of the farm worker union, Reies Lopez Tijerina fought to win compensation for the descendants of families whose lands had been seized illegally. In 1963 Tijerina founded the Alianza Federal de Mercedes (the Federal Alliance of Land Grants) in New Mexico to restore the legal rights of heirs to Spanish and Mexican land grants that had been guaranteed under the treaty ending the Mexican War.

In Denver, Rodolfo "Corky" Gonzales formed the Crusade for Justice in 1965 to protest school discrimination; provide legal, medical, and financial services and jobs for Chicanos; and foster the Mexican-American cultural heritage. La Raza Unida political parties arose in a number of small towns with large Chicano populations. On college campuses across the Southwest, Chicanos formed political organizations.

Through the efforts of men such as Cesar Chavez, Mexican-American farm workers organized successful strikes and were able to increase their hourly wages.

In 1968 Congress responded to the demand among Mexican-Americans for equal educational opportunity by enacting legislation encouraging school districts to adopt bilingual education programs to instruct non-English speakers in both English and their native language. In a more recent action, Congress moved in 1986 to legalize the status of many immigrants, including many Mexicans, who entered the United States illegally. The Immigration Reform and Control Act of 1986 provides permanent legal residency to undocumented workers who had lived in the United States since before 1982 and prohibits employment of illegal aliens.

Since 1960 Mexican-Americans have made impressive political gains. During the 1960s four Mexican-Americans—Senator Joseph Montoya of New Mexico and Representatives Eligio de la Garza and Henry B. Gonzales of Texas and Edward R. Roybal of California—were elected to Congress. In 1974 two Chicanos were elected governors—Jerry Apodaca in New Mexico and Raul Castro in Arizona—becoming the first Mexican-American governors since early in this century. In 1981 Henry Cisneros of San Antonia became the first Mexican-American mayor of a large city.

Today, the 10.5 million Mexican-Americans, the nation's second largest minority group, con-

tinue to struggle to expand their political influence, improve their economic position, and preserve their distinctive culture.

The Native American Power Movement

In November 1969, 200 Native Americans seized the abandoned federal penitentiary on Alcatraz Island in San Francisco Bay. For nineteen months Indian activists occupied the island in order to draw attention to conditions on the nation's Indian reservations. Alcatraz, the Native Americans said, symbolized conditions on reservations: "It has no running water; it has inadequate sanitation facilities; there is no industry, and so unemployment is very great; there are no health care facilities; the soil is rocky and unproductive." The activists, who called themselves Indians of All Tribes, offered to buy Alcatraz from the federal government for "$24 in glass beads and red cloth."

On Thanksgiving Day, 1970, 350 years after the Pilgrims' arrival, Wampanoag Indians, who had taken part at the first Thanksgiving, held a National Day of Mourning at Plymouth, Massachusetts. A tribal representative declared, "We forfeited our country. Our lands have fallen into the hands of the aggressor. We have allowed the white man to keep us on our knees." Meanwhile, another group of Native Americans established a settlement at Mount Rushmore, to demonstrate Indian claims to the Black Hills.

During the late 1960s and early 1970s, a new spirit of political militancy arose among the first Americans, just as it had among black Americans and women. No other group, however, faced problems as severe as Native Americans. In 1970 the Indian unemployment rate was ten times the national average, and forty percent of the Native American population lived below the poverty line. In that year, Native American life expectancy was just forty-four years, a third less than that of the average American.

Conditions on many of the nation's reservations were not unlike those found in underdeveloped areas of Latin America, Africa, and Asia. The death rate among Native Americans exceeded that of the United States population

Henry Cisneros, elected mayor of San Antonio in 1981, was interviewed by Walter Mondale in 1984 as a potential Democratic vice-presidential nominee.

as a whole by one-third. Half a million Indian families lived in unsanitary dilapidated dwellings, many in shanties, huts, or even abandoned automobiles.

On the Navajo reservation in Arizona, which is roughly the size of West Virginia, most families lived in the midst of severe poverty. The birth rate was very high; two-and-one-half times the overall United States rate and the same as India's. Living standards were low; the average family's purchasing power was about the same as a family in Malaysia. The typical house had just one or two rooms, sixty percent of the reservation's dwellings had no electricity, and eighty percent had no running water or sewers. Educational levels were low. The typical resident had completed just five years of school, and fewer than one adult in six had graduated high school.

During World War II, Native Americans began to protest against such conditions. In 1944 Native Americans formed the National Congress of American Indians (NCAI), the first major intertribal association. Among the group's primary concerns were protection of Indian land rights and improved educational opportunities for Native Americans. When Congress voted in 1953 to allow states to assert legal jurisdiction over Indian reservations without tribal consent and the federal government sought to transfer federal Indian responsibilities for a dozen tribes to the states (a policy known as "termination") and relocate Indians into urban areas, the NCAI led opposition to these measures. "Self-determination rather than termination!" was the NCAI slogan. Earl Old Person, a Blackfoot leader, commented, "It is important to note that in our Indian language the only translation for termination is to 'wipe out' or 'kill off' . . . how can we plan our future when the Indian Bureau threatens to wipe us out as a race? It's like trying to cook a meal in your tipi when someone is standing outside trying to burn the tipi down."

By the late 1950s a new spirit of Indian militance had arisen. In 1959 the Tuscarora tribe, which lived in upstate New York, successfully resisted efforts by the state power authority to convert reservation land into a reservoir. In 1961 the National Indian Youth Council, began to use the phrase "Red Power." It spon-

In Wounded Knee, South Dakota, members of the American Indian Movement occupied the town for over two months.

sored demonstrations, marches, and "fish-ins" to protest state efforts to abolish Indian fishing rights guaranteed by federal treaties. Native Americans in the San Francisco Bay area in 1964 established the Indian Historical Society to present history from the Indian point of view, while the Native American Rights Fund brought legal suits against states that had taken Indian land and abolished Indian hunting, fishing, and water rights in violation of federal treaties. Many tribes also took legal action to prevent strip mining or spraying of pesticides on Indian lands.

The best known of all Indian power groups was AIM, the American Indian Movement, formed by a group of Chippewas in Minneapolis in 1966 to protest alleged police brutality. In the fall of 1972, AIM led urban Indians, traditionalists, and young Indians along the "Trail of Broken Treaties" to Washington, D.C., seized the offices of the Bureau of Indian Affairs, and occupied them for a week in order to dramatize Indian grievances. In the spring of 1973, 200 heavily armed Indians took over the town of Wounded Knee, South Dakota, site of an 1890 massacre of 300 Sioux by the United States army cavalry, and occupied the town for seventy-one days.

1960 Black students stage the first sit-in; a Congressional subcommittee reports that 207 disk jockies in 42 cities received over $260,000 in "payola" to play records on the air; Food and Drug Administration approves the first public sale of the birth control pill

1961 Thirteen "freedom riders" set out from Washington, D.C.; Supreme Court rules in *Mapp* v. *Ohio* that evidence seized in unreasonable searches must be excluded from trial; President John F. Kennedy convenes the first presidential panel to examine the status of women

1962 James Meredith becomes the first black student at the University of Mississippi; Students for a Democratic Society agree upon the Port Huron Statement

1963 George Wallace elected governor of Alabama; Medgar Evers, NAACP field representative in Mississippi, is shot and murdered; President John F. Kennedy proposes a civil rights bill; march for civil rights in Washington, D.C.; Betty Friedan publishes *The Feminine Mystique*; Equal Pay Act requires equal pay for men and women who perform the same work under equal conditions; Supreme Court rules in *Gideon* v. *Wainright*

1964 Twenty-fourth Amendment is ratified; 464,000 students boycott New York City schools; Supreme Court rules congressional districts must be apportioned according to the principle of "one-man, one-vote"; Congress enacts the 1964 Civil Rights Act; University of California at Berkeley students strike to protest restrictions on campus political activities; Supreme Court rules in *Escobedo* v. *Illinois*

1965 Malcolm X assassinated; voter registration drive in Selma, Alabama; Voting Rights Act of 1965; riot breaks out in the Watts section of Los Angeles; SDS holds its first anitwar march; Executive Order 11246 requires government contractors to adopt affirmative action plans

1966 President Johnson nominates Dr. Robert Weaver to become the first black cabinet official; National Organization for Women founded

1967 A group led by Reis Tijerina seizes a county courthouse in New Mexico as part of a movement to reassert land claims granted by Spain and Mexico; the "Summer of Love" in San Francisco's Haight-Ashbury district; National Conference on the New Politics in Chicago; Thurgood Marshall sworn in as the first black Supreme Court justice

1968 George Wallace runs for the presidency on the American Independent party ticket; Martin Luther King, Jr., assassinated in Memphis, Tennessee

1969 500,000 young people attend a four-day rock concert near Woodstock, New York; Native Americans seize the abandoned federal penitentiary at Alcatraz

1970 Ohio National Guardsmen open fire on a group of Kent State University students; Mississippi police kill two black students at Jackson State University

1972 Congress approves an Equal Rights Amendment to the Constitution with only 32 dissenting votes; Title IX of the Educational Amendments Act

1973 American Indian Movement occupies Wounded Knee, South Dakota

1979 *Weber* "reverse discrimination" case

1984 Geraldine Ferraro becomes the first woman nominated by a major party for the vice-presidency

1986 Immigration Reform and Control Act

Indians are no longer a vanishing group of Americans. The 1980 census recorded an Indian population of 1.38 million in the United States, seventy-two percent over the figure reported in 1970 and four times the number recorded in 1950. About half of these people live on reservations, which cover 52.4 million acres in twenty-seven states, while most others live in urban areas. The largest Native American populations are located in Alaska, Arizona, California, New Mexico, and Oklahoma. As the Indian population has grown in size, individual Indians have claimed many accomplishments, including receipt of the Pulitzer Prize for fiction by N. Scott Momaday, a Kiowa.

Although Native Americans continue to face severe problems of employment, income, and education, they have demonstrated conclusively that they will not abandon their Indian identity and culture or be treated as dependent wards of the federal government.

CONCLUSION

During the 1960s, many groups, including black Americans, women, Mexican-Americans, and Native Americans, struggled for equal rights. Early in the decade, black college students, impatient with the slow pace of legal change, staged sit-ins, freedom rides, and protest marches to challenge legal segregation in the South. Passionately committed to a philosophy of nonviolent direct action, these students suffered beatings and went to jail to achieve integration. Their efforts led the federal government to pass the Civil Rights Act of 1964, prohibiting discrimination in public facilities and employment, and the Twenty-fourth Amendment to the Constitution and the Voting Rights Act in 1965, guaranteeing black voting rights.

Despite significant legal gains, many black Americans felt a growing sense of frustration and anger. The violence perpetrated by white racists and a growing white backlash against civil rights led black nationalists to downplay the goal of integration and instead emphasize black political power, community control of schools, creation of black businesses, and black pride. Frustration also grew in urban ghettos,

where the black poor faced problems of poverty, unemployment, and de facto segregation that were not addressed by civil rights legislation. In the summer of 1965, black frustration erupted into violence in Watts, a predominantly black district of Los Angeles, and over the next three years, over 150 major riots occurred.

In a far-reaching effort to reduce poverty, alleviate hunger and malnutrition, extend medical care, provide adequate housing, and enhance the employability of the poor, black and white, President Johnson launched his Great Society program in 1964. Although critics charged that federal public assistance, food subsidies, health programs, and child-care programs contributed to welfare dependence, family breakup, and an increase in out-of-wedlock births, the programs did succeed in cutting the proportion of families living in poverty in half.

The example of the civil rights movement inspired other groups to press for equal opportunity. The women's movement fought for passage of antidiscrimination laws, equal educational and employment opportunities, and a transformation of traditional views about women's place in society. Mexican-Americans battled for bilingual education programs in schools, unionization of farm workers, improved job opportunities, and increased political power. Native Americans pressed for control over Indian lands and resources, the preservation of Indian cultures, and tribal self-government.

REVIEW SUMMARY

During the 1960s, many groups of Americans struggled for equal rights

  black Americans used sit-ins, freedom rides, and protest marches to fight segregation

  northern blacks protested poverty, unemployment, and de-facto segregation

  college students staged demonstrations against the Vietnam War

  feminists demanded equal employment opportunities and an end to sexual discrimination

  Mexican-Americans protested discrimination in voting, education, and employment

  Native Americans demanded that the government recognize their land rights and the right of tribes to govern themselves

The federal government responded to calls for equal rights and opportunities by

- barring discrimination through the 1963 Equal Pay Act; the 1964 Civil Rights Act; the 1965 Voting Rights Act; and the Twenty-fourth Amendment
- enacting President Johnson's Great Society programs
- establishing affirmative action programs for women and minorities

SUGGESTIONS FOR FURTHER READING

OVERVIEWS AND SURVEYS

Ronald Berman, *America in the Sixties* (1968); Godfrey Hodgson, *America in Our Time* (1976); Allen J. Matusow, *The Unraveling of America* (1984); William L. O'Neill, *Coming Apart* (1971); Milton Viorst, *Fire in the Streets* (1979).

THE STRUGGLE FOR RACIAL JUSTICE

Floyd Barbour, *A New Black Consciousness* (1968); Rhoda Blumberg, *Civil Rights* (1984); Carl Brauer, *John F. Kennedy and the Second Reconstruction* (1977); Charles S. Bullock, III and Charles M. Lamb, eds., *Implementation of Civil Rights Policy* (1984); Paul Burstein, *Discrimination, Jobs, and Politics* (1985); Stokely Carmichael and Charles V. Hamilton, *Black Power* (1967); Clayborne Carson, *In Struggle: SNCC and the Black Awakening* (1981); Clayborn Carson, David J. Garrow, Vincent Harding, and Darlene Clark Hine, eds., *A Reader and Guide: Eyes on the Prize* (1987); William Chafe, *Civilities and Civil Rights* (1980); Eldridge Cleaver, *Soul on Ice* (1968); Joel Dreyfuss and Charles Lawrence, III, *The Bakke Case* (1979); Archie Epps, *Malcolm X and the American Negro Revolution* (1969); Joe R. Feagin and Harlan Hahn, *Ghetto Revolts* (1973); Robert Fogelson, *Violence as Protest* (1971); Philip S. Foner, ed., *The Black Panthers Speak* (1970); James Forman, *The Making of Black Revolutionaries* (1972); David J. Garrow, *Protest at Selma* (1978), *The FBI and Martin Luther King* (1981); and *Bearing the Cross: Martin Luther King, Jr., and the Southern Christian Leadership Conference* (1986); Paul Good, *The Trouble I've Seen* (1974); Robert H. Haverman, ed., *A Decade of Federal Antipoverty Programs* (1977); Len Holt, *The Summer that Didn't End* (1966); LeRoi Jones and Larry Neal, eds., *Black Fire* (1968); Richard Kluger, *Simple Justice: The History of Brown v. Board of Education and Black America's Struggle for Equality* (1976); Daniel Knapp and Kenneth Polk, *Scouting the War on Poverty* (1971); Steven F. Lawson, *In Pursuit of Power: Southern Blacks and Elec-*toral *Politics* (1985); Sar Levitan, *The Great Society's Poor Law* (1969); Sar Levitan and Robert Taggart, *The Promise of Greatness* (1976); David Lewis, *King* (1970); James W. Loewen and Charles Sallis, *Mississippi: Conflict and Change* (1982); August Meier and Elliot Rudwick, *CORE* (1980); Anne Moody, *Coming of Age in Mississippi* (1968); Alden Morris, *The Origins of the Civil Rights Movement* (1984); Charles Murray, *Losing Ground* (1984); Victor S. Navasky, *Kennedy Justice* (1971); Robert J. Norrell, *Reaping the Whirlwind: The Civil Rights Movement in Tuskegee* (1985); Stephen B. Oates, *Let the Trumpet Sound: The Life of Martin Luther King, Jr.* (1982); Malcolm X and Alex Haley, *The Autobiography of Malcolm X* (1966); James T. Patterson, *America's Struggle Against Poverty* (1981); Howell Raines, *My Soul Is Rested: Movement Days in the Deep South Remembered* (1977); John E. Schwarz, *America's Hidden Success* (1983); Cleveland Sellers, *The River of No Return* (1973); Harvard Sitkoff, *The Struggle for Black Equality* (1981); James Sundquist, *Politics and Policy* (1968); Pat Watter, *Down to Now* (1971); J. Harvie Wilkinson, III, *From Brown to Bakke* (1979); Juan Williams, *Eyes on the Prize: America's Civil Rights Years* (1987); William Julius Wilson, *The Truly Disadvantaged* (1988); Eugene Wolfenstein, *The Victims of Democracy: Malcolm X and the Black Revolution* (1981); Howard Zinn, *SNCC* (1965).

THE YOUTH REVOLT

E. J. Bacciocco, Jr., *The New Left in America* (1974); David Caute, *The Year of the Barricades: A Journey Through 1968* (1988); Peter Clecak, *America's Quest for the Ideal Self: Dissent and Fulfillment in the 60s and 70s* (1984) and *Radical Paradoxes* (1973); Morris Dickstein, *Gates of Eden: American Culture in the Sixties* (1977); John Diggins, *The American Left in the Twentieth Century* (1973); David Farber, *Chicago '68* (1988); Richard Flacks, *Youth and Social Change* (1971); Todd Gitlin, *The Whole World is Watching* (1981); Tom Hayden, *Reunion* (1988); Maurice Isserman, *". . . If I Had a Hammer"* (1987); Alexander Klein, ed., *Natural Enemies: Youth and the Clash of Generations* (1970); Lawrence Lader, *Power on the Left* (1979); James Miller, *"Democracy is in the Streets"* (1987); Charles Reich, *The Greening of America* (1970); Theodore Roszak, *The Making of a Counterculture* (1969); Kirkpatrick Sale, *SDS* (1973); Irwin Unger, *The Movement* (1974).

LIBERATION MOVEMENTS

Rudolpho Acuna, *Occupied America* (1981); William H. Chafe, *The American Woman* (1974) and *Women and Equality* (1977); Robert L. Daniel, *American Women in the Twentieth Century* (1987); Mark Day, *Forty Acres* (1971); Barbara Sinclair Deckard, *The Women's Movement* (1983); Vine Deloria, Jr., *Behind the Trail of Broken Treaties* (1974) and *Custer Died for Your Sins* (1969);

John Gregory Dunne, *Delano* (1967); Jo Freeman, *The Politics of Women's Liberation* (1975); Betty Friedan, *The Feminine Mystique* (1963); William Hodge, *The First Americans: Then and Now* (1981); Judith Hole and Ellen Levine, eds., *Rebirth of Feminism* (1972); Peter Iverson, *The Navajo Nation* (1981); Ethel Klein, *Gender Politics* (1984); Jacques E. Levy, *Cesar Chavez* (1975); Kristin Luker, *Abortion and the Politics of Motherhood* (1984); Peter Matthiessen, *In the Spirit of Crazy Horse* (1983) and *Sal si Puedes* (1972); Matt Meier and Feliciano Rivera, *The Chicanos* (1972); D'Arcy McNickle, *Native American Tribalism* (1973); Jean Maddern Pitrone, *Chavez, Man of the Migrants* (1971); Julian Samora, *Los Mojados* (1971); Stan Steiner, *The New Indians* (1968); Ronald B. Taylor, *Chavez and the Farm Workers* (1975); Wilcomb Washburn, *Red Man's Land/White Man's Land* (1971); Gayle Yates, *What Women Want* (1975); Winthrop Yinger, *Cesar Chavez* (1975).

A

COMPANY

CHAPTER 30
The Limits of American Power

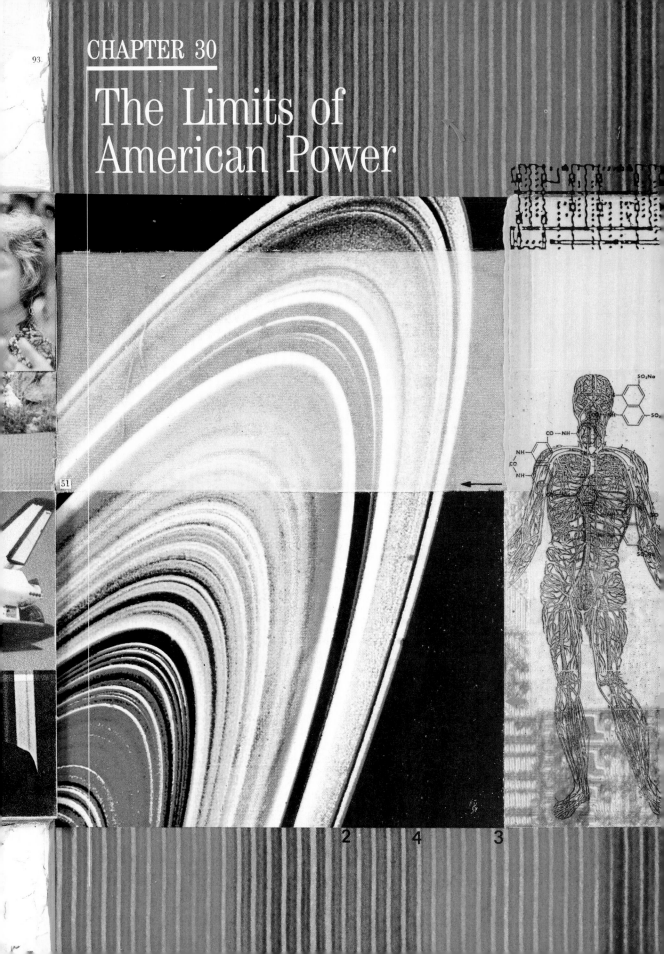

51

2   4   3

The face on the dust jacket is confident, almost arrogantly so. Proudly Italian in features, its expression is openly American. Lee Iacocca looks out at the reader with shrewd eyes and a smug, closed-mouth smile, as if to say, "I've about got this world figured out." His body language reaffirms the look. A thick, powerful slab of a man, he leans back in his leather executive chair, his hands locked behind his head, his arms spread outward like two V-shaped wings. Gold cufflinks and a gold Rolex add to the sum total: a successful, fully confident American businessman.

The irony of the picture is, of course, that Lee Iacocca is the most visible symbol of the American automobile industry, which in turn is the most prominent example of the failure of American industry to compete in a changing world economy. Once the car makers in Detroit produced automobiles that mirrored America's strength and power. They were big, heavy, comfortable, powerful cars, loaded with such expensive options as power windows, power brakes, and power steering. "Big cars mean big profits," went the Detroit saying. And the profits were big. Detroit manufacturers regularly sold eight million cars a year, ten or eleven million in a boomer year. The leading executives made millions, and they believed the future held unlimited promise.

For them, bigger was better. When an engineer at Chrysler designed a smaller, low-slung car, K. T. Keller, the company's top executive, remarked in disgust, "Chrysler builds cars to sit in, not to piss over." So what if they weren't energy efficient. So what if they only traveled ten to thirteen miles on a gallon of gas. Until 1973 gas was cheap. In 1950 one gallon of gas at the pump cost 27 cents; more than twenty years later in 1973 the price was 37 cents. Thus while the price of almost every other basic consumer commodity had doubled, the price of gas had remained about the same.

Detroit—the land of big cars and big money, of General Motors, Chrysler, and Ford—was Iacocca's world. "Cars were in my blood," he claimed. From 1946 to 1978 he worked for Ford, climbing the corporate ladder from salesman to zone manager, to district manager, to divisional head, to president of Ford. "At that time . . . it wasn't prestige or power I wanted. It was money," Iacocca later said. And he made money—millions for himself and billions for Ford.

In 1978 Henry Ford II, the grandson of the founder of the company, fired Iacocca. The reason is largely unknown. An imperious leader, Henry Ford II often acted without explaining the true motives behind his actions. Certainly for a man of Iacocca's ego, it was a painful experience. "Your timing stinks," he told Ford. "We've just made a billion eight for the second year in a row. That's three and a half billion in the past two years. But mark my words, Henry. You may never see a billion eight again. And do you know why? Because you don't know how the _ _ _ _ we made it in the first place!"

In Iacocca's angry words there was more truth than perhaps he even realized. By the late 1970s the American automotive industry had crashed into new economic realities. To begin with, the price of oil had become unstable. Although Middle Eastern oil had been inexpensive during the period between 1945 and the early 1970s, economic realities dictated that it *must* eventually rise dramatically. Each year more and more nations entered the industrial ranks; each year the consumption of oil increased; each year the limited supplies of oil decreased. Eventually, experts predicted, the price of oil would shoot up toward its true market value.

Lee Iacocca

Arab nationalism also entered into the equation. Oil, the lifeblood of modern industry, could be used as a political weapon. In 1973, after the failures of Egypt in the Yom Kippur war with Israel, Arabs struck at the United States with an oil embargo. The price of oil quickly rose from three dollars a barrel to twelve dollars. The auto industry was caught unprepared. Then in early 1979 the Shah of Iran, a strong United States ally, fled his country. In his place came the Ayatollah Khomeini, a bitter opponent of the United States. Once again the flow of oil west stopped, and once again prices rose.

The oil crises forced Americans to reevaluate the "bigger is better" axiom. While American auto makers had built heavy, luxury cars, European and Japanese manufacturers had developed smaller, fuel-efficient models. German front-wheel-drive cars, for example, eliminated the drive shaft, thus reducing the weight of the automobile and providing more interior room. Lighter cars meant smaller engines and less gas. In addition, front wheel drive responded better to the driver's touch. As the price of a gallon of gas charged toward the dollar mark, American drivers purchased increasing numbers of smaller, well-engineered foreign cars and allowed the Detroit dinosaurs to rust in the lots.

Foreign exporting policies similarly hurt American manufacturers. In Japan, the Ministry of International Trade and Industry (MITI) decided which Japanese industries would receive government subsidies, trade protections, and research and development aids. After World War II, MITI targeted autos, steel, chemicals, shipbuilding, and machinery manufacturing for special treatment. The results of this economic planning were spectacular. In the mid-1950s, Detroit producers considered Japanese cars an industry joke. Scratch the body of a Japanese car, went the Detroit quip, and you can still see the Budweiser labels. By 1982 little laughing was heard in Detroit. That year the fuel-efficient Japanese cars captured thirty percent of the United States market.

Men like Iacocca complained bitterly, and looked to their own government for help. After being fired from Ford, Iacocca accepted the top position at Chrysler. With the help of a 1.2 billion dollar loan from Washington, he put the ailing company on its feet again. But he continued to warn all Americans that the United States industrial base was in trouble. The days of limitless expansion were over. If the United States was going to rebuild its lost strength, it had to protect itself from unfair Japanese and European trade practices. "Japan is really doing nothing wrong," Iacocca wrote, "...they're simply dealing in their own self-interest. It's up to us to start dealing in *ours.*"

Iacocca's appeal has won him a number of supporters, many of whom have encouraged him to run for president. He remains confident about himself, but he is less certain about America. He has seen his country reach its height of economic and military influence, and then confront serious challenges. He believes America can regroup to meet the challenges, but he insists that it will entail economic changes. Many of the challenges are now clear, the final results are not.

THE LIMITS OF POWER

James Earl Carter, Jr., who favored the simpler and less austere name Jimmy, became president of the United States on January 20, 1977. In his inaugural ceremony he tried to establish a tone for his presidency. The country, he believed, was weary of the excesses brought about by Johnson and Nixon's imperial use of power. Their actions had led to the debacle in Vietnam and the abuses of Watergate. Carter wanted to assure Americans that he was one of them—elected by them and working for them. In an action to symbolically reinforce this point, Carter and his family walked the 1.2 miles between the Capitol and the White House rather than ride in a bullet-proof limousine. The crowd that lined the streets on that bitterly cold day shouted their approval. Some wept, and Carter himself shed tears.

Carter continued this humble approach to his office in his inaugural address. "We must once again have faith in our country—and in one another," he said. He asked for a commitment to a new, more humane political agenda—human rights, environmental quality, nuclear arms control, and the national and international search for peace and justice. Finally, he told his compatriots that they would have to get used to the idea that there were limits to American economic and political power: "We have learned that 'more' is not necessarily 'better,' that even our great nation has its recognized limits, and that we can neither answer all questions nor solve all problems . . . we must simply do our best."

Carter was not sure most Americans agreed with his words. In fact, he later wrote, "it was not possible even for me to imagine the limits we would have to face. In some ways, dealing with limits would become the subliminal theme of the next four years . . . ." Carter's assessment of his White House years was painfully accurate. Just as ordinary Americans faced economic limits during the 1970s and 1980s, Carter and his successor Ronald Reagan confronted serious limits in their conduct of foreign policy.

Peanuts and World Politics

Jimmy Carter had a warm, friendly smile and a seemingly easy-going disposition. In the 1976 presidential race he used both to his full advantage. Although his Republican opponent was Gerald Ford, Carter ran as much against Richard Nixon and Lyndon Johnson as against Ford. He ran as a man of the people, a political outsider, upset by the betrayal of America by Washington politicians. He promised to end government corruption, return to simpler traditions, and restore the government to the people. On election day, the voters responded more to Carter's faith in them than his policies, and by a narrow margin they sent Carter to the White House.

Carter was more than he seemed. Although he liked to picture himself as a simple "peanut farmer" from Plains, Georgia, and talk about his populist roots and "born again" Christian faith, Carter was a well-educated, complex man. He graduated in the top tenth of his United States Naval Academy class and participated in the navy's nuclear submarine program. After leaving the navy, he excelled as a businessman, politician, and administrator. In 1973 he was asked to join the prestigious Trilateral Commission, a group of executives drawn from the elites of the United States, Canada, Europe, and Japan whose purpose was to promote "orderly" economic development throughout the world.

Carter also brought serious liabilities to the White House. In the area of foreign affairs, he was the least-experienced president since World War II. Although he had foreign policy goals—the pursuit of human rights, detente with the Soviet Union, and the elimination of nuclear weapons—he had no concrete plan for achieving his goals. To more realistic and experienced foreign policy experts, Carter's promise to do his best seemed inadequate for the problems he was certain to face.

In domestic affairs Carter looked to his close friends—the "Georgia Mafia"—for advice. But in foreign affairs he sought experienced help. He selected Cyrus R. Vance as secretary of state and Zbigniew Brzezinski as national security advisor, both of whom had been members of the Trilateral Commission. Vance was a Washington insider, the prototypical establishment figure. A graduate of Yale Law School, and a gentlemanly tennis player, Vance practiced law in New York City. He had served as a foreign policy trouble-shooter in both the Kennedy and Johnson administrations. He had an ingrained sense of decency, infinite patience, and always sought the peaceful way out of a conflict.

Zbigniew Brzezinski—Zbig to his friends—was a product of different forces. The son of a pre–World War II Polish diplomat, he came to the United States with his family after the Soviet Union took over his homeland. Educated at Harvard—where he was the classmate of Henry Kissinger, another European emigre—Zbig's thesis was entitled "The Permanent Purge: Politics in Soviet Totalitarianism." In it and his later writings he emphasized the need for a firm policy toward Soviet expansionism. He believed that America was becoming soft and reluctant to use its substantial power. Brzezinski regretted this trend. As one historian observed, "In facing a choice between inflicting pain and trying reassurance as an approach to changing Soviet behavior, Brzezinski came down on the side of inflicting pain."

Opening Gambits

During the early years of the Carter administration the potential ideological conflict between Vance and Brzezinski did not surface. Unlike Henry Kissinger, Brzezinski was not interested in thrusting himself into the public spotlight; he enjoyed working behind the scenes, allowing Vance to receive the headlines. In addition, Brzezinski, Vance, and Carter agreed that there would be no bureaucratic fighting between the State Department and the NSC such as had plagued the Nixon administration. The three worked fairly well together during the first two years of Carter's presidency and achieved several foreign policy successes.

Carter owed part of his success to earlier administrations. In 1978, for example, Carter pushed through Congress the Panama Canal Treaty, which returned the Canal Zone to Panama. Some senators and many Americans opposed the treaty, agreeing with one senator that "We stole it [the Canal] fair and square." But Carter's firm stand on the issue improved the image of the United States in Latin America. Nevertheless, negotiations on the Panama Canal Treaty had started during the Johnson administration and had been supported by Nixon and Ford during the 1970s. Similarly, the full recognition of the People's Republic of China in 1979 simply consummated the process begun by Nixon in 1972.

Carter achieved other successes by being the right person in the right office at the right time. This was particularly true in the role the president played in the peace negotiations between Egypt and Israel. Since the founding of Israel in 1948, Egypt's foreign policy had been built around destroying the Jewish state. The two countries seemed to divide their time between fighting wars and planning to fight wars. The fighting resulted in an enlarged Israel and a weakened Egypt. Then in 1977, Anwar el-Sadat, the practical and far-sighted leader of Egypt, decided to seek peace with Israel. To demonstrate that his intentions were sincere, he even traveled to Israel and spoke with the Israeli Parliament. It was an act of rare political courage, for Sadat risked alienating Egypt from the rest of the Arab world without a firm commitment for a peace treaty with Israel.

Although both countries wanted peace, major obstacles had to be overcome. Sadat wanted Israel to retreat from the West Bank of the Jordan River and from the Golan Heights (which it had taken from Jordan in the 1967

Jimmy Carter's greatest triumph as president came with the signing of the Camp David Accords between Egypt and Israel.

war), recognize the Palestine Liberation Organization (PLO), provide a homeland for the Palestinians, relinquish its unilateral hold on the city of Jerusalem, and return the Sinai to Egypt. Such conditions were unacceptable to Israeli Prime Minister Menachem Begin. A member of a group that engaged in terrorist acts in the years prior to Israel's independence, Begin refused to consider recognition of the PLO or the return of the West Bank. By the end of 1977 Sadat's peace mission had run aground.

Enter Carter. He invited both men to Camp David, the presidential retreat in the Catoctin Mountains, for face-to-face talks. It was almost like a working holiday. They negotiated, played tennis, negotiated, watched movies, and negotiated. The world leaders and their teams of experts worked through the chilly autumn nights and the beautiful days. In the end they hammered out a peace.

To be sure, the peace was not perfect. They did not settle such important territorial issues as the West Bank, the Golan Heights, Jerusalem, and recognition of the PLO. But Begin did agree to return the Sinai to Egypt, and Egypt agreed to recognize Israel. For Carter it was a proud moment. No American president, Begin claimed, "has ever so involved himself in our problems." Unfortunately, the Camp David accords were denounced by the rest of the Arab Middle East, and in 1981 Sadat paid for his vision with his life when anti-Israeli Egyptian soldiers assassinated him.

No Islands of Stability

Carter's early years were not without their problems. During his campaign he had promised to speak out for human rights and move toward detente with the Soviet Union. In both areas he tried, but without much success. He did not want to jeopardize relations with America's right-wing allies—such as Iran, the Philippines, Indonesia, Chile, and South Korea—by pressing too hard on the human rights issue. And to criticize violations of human rights by United States enemies, such as the Soviet Union and Cuba, did little constructive good. In fact, such criticism detracted from the president's peaceful overtures toward Russia.

Taken as a whole, Carter's first two years represented the calm before the storm. His last two years presented a series of problems and heartaches, most of which centered around America's relations with Iran. Since the end of World War II, Iran had been a valuable friend of the United States in the troubled Middle East. In 1953 the CIA had worked to ensure the power of the young Shah, Mohammed Reza Pahlavi. And between 1953 and 1978 the Shah had oftentimes repaid the debt. He allowed the United States to establish electronic listening posts in northern Iran along the border of the Soviet Union, and during the 1973–1974 Arab oil embargo the Shah continued to sell oil to the United States. In addition, the Shah bought arms from the United States with, as one historian noted, "the abandon of an alcoholic using a credit card in a liquor store." These purchases helped the American balance-of-payment problem. All considered, few world leaders were more loyal to the United States.

Like previous American presidents, Carter was willing to overlook the Shah's violations of human rights. To demonstrate America's support of the Shah, Carter and his wife Rosalynn visited Iran for New Year's Eve. After being entertained at a lavish banquet, Carter made a toast, which crammed a series of mistaken assumptions into very few words. He spoke of Iran as "an island of stability in one of the most troubled areas of the world" and of the Shah as a great leader who had won "the respect and the admiration and love" of his people.

The Shah was popular among wealthy Iranians and Americans. In the slums of the southern section of Teheran and in the poverty-stricken villages of Iran, however, there was little respect, admiration, or love for the Shah. Led by a fundamentalist Islamic clergy and emboldened by want, the masses of Iranians turned against the Shah and his Westernization policy. And as Carter spoke, revolutionary sentiment stirred.

In early fall the revolutionary surge in Iran gained force. The Shah, who had once seemed so powerful and secure, was paralyzed by indecision, alternating between ruthless suppression and moving to liberalize his regime. In Washington, Carter was almost as indecisive as the Shah, alternating between Brzezinski's advice to firmly stand behind the Shah and State Department suggestions to cut losses and prepare to deal with a new government in Iran. Carter tried a little of both and not enough of either. One diplomatic historian commented, "President Carter inherited an impossible situation—and he and his advisors made the worst of it."

On January 16, 1979, the Shah left Iran for an extended "vacation" in Egypt. He never returned to his native land. In his wake, however, exiled religious leader Ayatollah Ruhollah Khomeini did return to Iran, preaching the doctrine that the United States was the "great Satan" behind the Shah. Relations between America and Iran were terrible, but Iranian officials claimed they could become infinitely worse if the Shah were admitted into the United States. Yet that was exactly what Henry Kissinger, David Rockefeller, Brzezinski, and others were advising Carter to do. When Carter learned that

After 444 days the Iranian hostage crisis ended, but not before it had virtually paralyzed Carter's administration and his chances for reelection.

the Shah needed to come to the United States for treatment of lymphoma, he extended a humanitarian invitation.

"You're opening a Pandora's box," the Iranian prime minister remarked when he heard the news. On November 4, 1979, Iranian "students" invaded the American embassy in Teheran and captured seventy-six Americans, thirteen of whom were freed several weeks later. The rest were held hostage for 444 days and were the objects of intense political interest and media coverage. Between 1972 and 1977 the three major networks had devoted only an average of five minutes per year to coverage of Iran; during the hostage crisis Iran coverage appeared every night.

Carter was helpless. Because Iran was not a stable country in any recognizable sense, it was impossible to pressure. Diplomatic historian Gaddis Smith wrote, "The powerless, with little to lose, have a special power." Carter devoted far too much attention to the almost insoluble problem. The hostages stayed in the public spotlight because Carter kept them there.

Divisions in the Carter administration became clear. Vance favored patient negotiations; Brzezinski advocated the use of force. American policy and international respect, Brzezinski argued, was more important than the lives of a handful of hostages. At first, Carter disagreed, saying, "The problem with all of the military options is that we could use them and feel good for a few hours—until we found out they had killed our people. And once we started killing people in Iran, where will it end?" But eventually Carter sided with Brzezinski and authorized a rescue attempt. (Vance later resigned in protest.) The rescue mission failed and Carter's position became even worse.

Perhaps the most important hostage was Carter himself. He was powerless to prevent the 1979 Soviet invasion of Afghanistan. His subsequent cancelation of America's participation in the 1980 Moscow Olympic Games and embargo of further shipments of grain and high-technology to the Soviet Union did nothing to help the Afghan people. And his failure to free the hostages hurt him in the 1980 presidential election. Negotiations finally brought the hostages' release, but not until Ronald Reagan had been president for half an hour.

The Iranian crisis demonstrated the limits of American power. In traditional foreign affairs the United States still exerted considerable influence, but it was almost powerless to deal with terrorism or terrorist governments. During his 1980 campaign Ronald Reagan promised to restore American power—to put America tall in the saddle once more—but he would soon discover what Carter already knew: rhetoric was no substitute for a new foreign policy based on changing world relationships.

The Actor As President

The only person who benefited from the hostage crisis was Reagan. But the reasons for his success in the 1980 election ran deeper than one foreign policy embarrassment. Carter's economic policy was as errant as his foreign policy. Changes in voting patterns also played into Reagan's hands. The poor stayed away from the polls and conservatives were energized by the "New Right," which revolutionized campaign tactics by its scientific use of direct mailings.

In the end, however, Reagan's greatest strength was his direct simplicity. He provided simple answers to complex problems. As an actor he was known more as a good script reader than a thinking, feeling, creative artist. His strengths were his warmth and voice. He acted in sixty-six movies and was remembered best for his performances in *The Knute Rockne*

While many critics questioned some of his policies, Ronald Reagan attracted the loyalty and affection of millions of Americans.

Story, Kings Row, and *The Winning Team.* Politically he moved from the near left to the far right, from being a New Deal Democrat to enlisting as a Goldwater Republican. Although he left the movies for politics and industry, he continued to be a good script reader. Between 1954 and 1962 he was a spokesman for General Electric. Elected governor of California in 1966, he proved an equally able spokesman for West Coast conservatives. In the election of 1980 he remained the good script reader. He promised to restore America's economic, social, and foreign policy greatness. At the very time that the country was facing new limits, he promised an America without limitations. Reagan's America was firmly rooted in the country's past, not its troubled present and uncertain future.

Reagan's foreign policy was equally steeped in America's past. He revived the image of the Soviet Union as the "evil empire." The Soviets, he asserted, "reserve unto themselves the right to commit any crime, to lie, to cheat."

They were behind all the unrest in the world. He chose a secretary of state who shared his beliefs, if not his ability to communicate. General Alexander Haig, an army officer who had served in a number of sensitive political posts, claimed that the Soviet Union was guilty of "training, funding, and equipping international terrorism." Haig and Reagan believed in peace, but not on Russia's terms. Peace and arms talks would have to wait, to use Haig's mangled syntax, upon Moscow's "reining in of what has been a hemorrhaging of risk-taking." And, Haig warned the Kremlin, "a change of the status quo would be met with the full range of power assets." Translated, the Reagan-Haig policy entailed a return to the coldest years of the Cold War. Even to earlier Cold Warrior and anti-Soviet George Kennan, Reagan's rhetoric was "childish, inexcusably childish, unworthy of people charged with responsibilities for conducting the affairs of a great power in an endangered world."

Old Rhetoric and New Realities

The rhetoric might have been the same, but the world was not. Back in the 1950s there had been a clarity about power, an ability to predict reactions, to identify friends and enemies. Secretary of State John Foster Dulles could "rattle the sabres" and expect the world to take him seriously, to cower and adjust accordingly. In economics, the United States reigned supreme, unrivaled in its ability to get its way. Money talked and the dollar ruled. Militarily, it was a bipolar world with two power centers, one in Washington and the other in the Kremlin. Both sides knew exactly with what and with whom they were dealing. And in terms of politics, NATO was aligned against the Warsaw Pact, and the emerging Third World was still under the control or at least the influence of the European imperial powers.

Life had changed by the 1980s. Global economic power had spread out in thirty years. Japan emerged as a genuine threat to American economic hegemony, and the oil crisis of the 1970s created a new power center in the Middle East, albeit one characterized by extraordi-

nary political and social instability. World political power had disintegrated since the 1950s. NATO was weakened by the withdrawal of France and the constant bickering between Greece and Turkey. The United States also found Israel an unpredictable ally, too independent and precipitous. It was the same in the communist world. The Warsaw Pact experienced strong stirrings of independence in Hungary; Polish workers in Solidarity challenged the party's dominance; and the People's Republic of China was no longer in the Soviet orbit.

The Third World seemed completely out of control. By the late 1980s, European imperialism was dead and the former colonies were dealing with their newfound independence. In Central America, peasant uprisings against conservative, military elites gained ground, especially when they received Cuban and Soviet military and economic assistance. The Islamic Revolution brought the Ayatollah Khomeini to power in Iran and threatened the rest of the

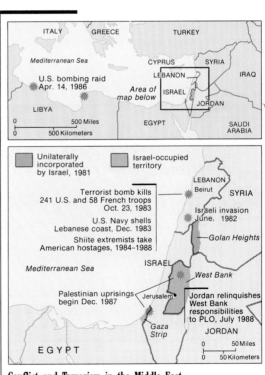

Conflict and Terrorism in the Middle East

Middle East with religious violence. Lebanon was destroyed as an independent nation. Vietnamese forces warred alternately with the Chinese, Cambodians, and Laotians; black Africa fought against the anticommunist government in South Africa; Iran and Iraq engaged in a decade-long death struggle; and South Koreans opposition political parties wrested power from their American-backed government. Into this political, economic, and social cauldron, President Reagan brought the anachronistic rhetoric of the Cold War.

During his first term, Reagan abandoned the policy of detente pursued by presidents Kennedy, Johnson, Nixon, Ford, and Carter, turning instead to a strategy of confrontation and military deterrence. Between 1981 and 1984 he doubled the defense budget from $130 billion to $260 billion. Most of the money went to nuclear weapons systems. Reagan called for deployment of the MX missile, construction of the B-1 bomber, and implementation of the Strategic Defense Initiative (Star Wars), a space missile defense system. In 1983 Reagan ordered warheads placed in 500 cruise missiles stationed in Western Europe, which made them operational. For a time he continued the grain

Increased spending on the Star Wars program (SDS), Reagan argued, would free the United States from reliance on the strategy of deterrence.

embargo on the Soviet Union, which Jimmy Carter imposed in response to the invasion of Afghanistan in 1979, and tried to establish an embargo on shipment of technically sophisticated equipment from NATO countries to Russia. Reagan also imposed economic sanctions on Poland when the government crushed the Solidarity workers' union in October 1981.

Reagan's attempt to resurrect American power in the face of "Soviet expansionism" similarly shaped his response to Middle East events. Ever since World War II, American interests in the Middle East had revolved around the survival of Israel and access to Persian Gulf oil supplies. The Arab oil embargo of 1973 forced the United States to seek closer ties with Saudi Arabia, Egypt, Kuwait, and the Arab Emirates, and in the process, relations with Israel deteriorated. The Soviet invasion of Afghanistan seemed to threaten Persian Gulf oil supplies, as did the Iran-Iraq war, especially when both countries began attacking oil tankers and threatening refineries.

In Lebanon, Muslims fought Christians, Jews battled Arabs, Syrian troops squared off against the Israeli army, and several factions of the PLO fought among themselves and against Israel. Consistent with his view of the Soviet Union as "the evil empire," Reagan saw Russia behind all the trouble. The Soviet Union maintained a strong military relationship with Syria, and Syria was a major military and economic support to the PLO factions, which in turn were using Lebanon as the battleground in their struggle against Israel. In 1982, after the Israelis first invaded and then withdrew from Lebanon, a contingent of French, Italian, and American troops were sent to Beirut in an attempt to maintain a tenuous peace.

Political instability reigned in Lebanon. No faction was clearly in charge. Early in 1983 a terrorist car bomb attack on the American embassy in Beirut killed sixteen American employees, and throughout the year PLO snipers fired on United States Marine positions. In September 1983 Reagan stationed a naval task force off the Lebanese coast, and when PLO sniper attacks continued, he ordered heavy artillery shelling of outposts in the hills surrounding Beirut. On October 23, 1983, a Muslim terrorist on

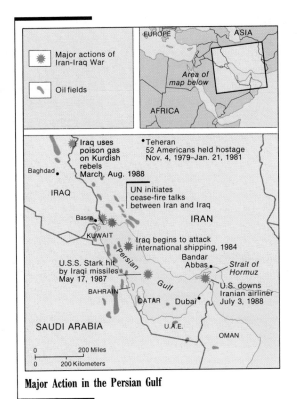

Major Action in the Persian Gulf

troubles for the United States, and Reagan was not about to let it happen again.

In October 1983 Prime Minister Maurice Bishop of Grenada, a small island nation in the Caribbean, was assassinated and a more radical Marxist government took power. Soviet money and Cuban troops came to Grenada, and when they began constructing an airfield capable of handling large aircraft, the Reagan administration decided to overthrow the communists and restore a pro-American regime. On October 25, just two days after the bombing of the marine headquarters in Beirut, 2000 American troops invaded Grenada, killed or captured 750 Cuban troops, and established a new government. Although most Latin American nations condemned the invasion as "Yankee imperialism," the Grenadans themselves approved of America's humbling of the "Marxist thugs." And the American public applauded it, perhaps even needed it psychologically at a time when the Middle East was generating so much frustration.

The problems in Central America were much stickier. In 1979 the conservative, corrupt government of Anastasio Somoza in Nicaragua

a suicide mission drove an explosive-laden truck into the marine headquarters, killing 241 American soldiers. The complexity of Lebanese politics confused and frustrated most Americans, and they reacted angrily to the deaths of the marines. But who was responsible? Who could be punished? Congress threatened to invoke the War Powers Act of 1973 and force Reagan to withdraw the troops from Lebanon; and in February 1984 he acquiesced, "redeploying" them to naval vessels in the Mediterranean. The marines were out of Lebanon.

Reagan saw events in the Caribbean and Central America in the same Cold War terms. For more than 150 years the Monroe Doctrine had governed American foreign policy, warning European powers to avoid intervention in the Western Hemisphere. Reagan was determined not to allow a communist government to take power in the Caribbean, Mexico, or Central America. Fidel Castro's successful revolution in Cuba in 1959, and his subsequent alignment with the Soviet Union, had created no end of

Reagan's policies in the Middle East were questioned after a terrorist bomb blast killed 241 marines in Beirut.

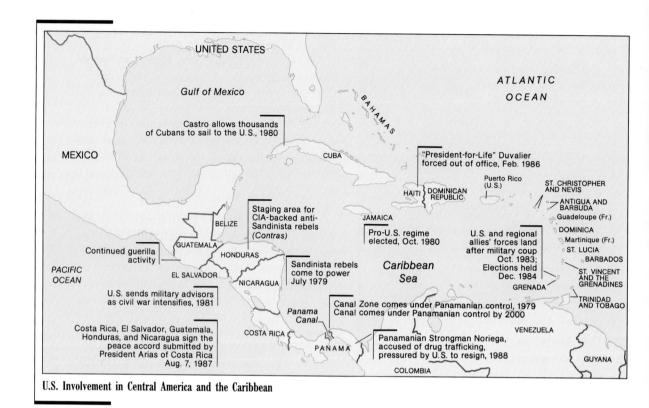

UNITED STATES

Gulf of Mexico

Castro allows thousands
of Cubans to sail to the U.S., 1980

MEXICO

*ATLANTIC
OCEAN*

BAHAMAS

CUBA

"President-for-Life" Duvalier
forced out of office, Feb. 1986

Puerto Rico
(U.S.)

HAITI   DOMINICAN
REPUBLIC

ST. CHRISTOPHER
AND NEVIS

ANTIGUA AND
BARBUDA

Guadeloupe (Fr.)

Staging area for
CIA-backed anti-
Sandinista rebels
(Contras)

BELIZE

GUATEMALA

JAMAICA

Pro-U.S. regime
elected, Oct. 1980

*Caribbean
Sea*

U.S. and regional
allies' forces land
after military coup
Oct. 1983;
Elections held
Dec. 1984

DOMINICA

Martinique (Fr.)

ST. LUCIA

BARBADOS

ST. VINCENT
AND THE
GRENADINES

Continued guerilla
activity

HONDURAS

*PACIFIC
OCEAN*

EL SALVADOR

NICARAGUA

Sandinista rebels
come to power
July 1979

GRENADA

TRINIDAD
AND TOBAGO

U.S. sends military advisors
as civil war intensifies, 1981

Costa Rica, El Salvador, Guatemala,
Honduras, and Nicaragua sign the
peace accord submitted by
President Arias of Costa Rica
Aug. 7, 1987

COSTA RICA

*Panama
Canal*

PANAMA

Canal Zone comes under Panamanian control, 1979
Canal comes under Panamanian control by 2000

Panamanian Strongman Noriega,
accused of drug trafficking,
pressured by U.S. to resign, 1988

VENEZUELA

GUYANA

COLOMBIA

U.S. Involvement in Central America and the Caribbean

was overthrown by leftist rebels (Sandanistas). For Reagan, the Sandanista victory in Nicaragua looked "like another Cuba." Worried that they might provide a military base for the Soviet Union as well as export revolution to El Salvador, Guatemala, and Honduras, the Reagan administration authorized covert CIA operations against Nicaragua, which resulted in the destruction of petroleum facilities and the mining of their harbors; and funneled money to the *contras,* pro-American guerilla fighting against the Sandanista regime. In neighboring El Salvador Reagan provided large-scale military assistance and advisors to help the government fight a growing left-wing insurgency.

Nicaraguan *contra* forces

Campaigning for reelection in 1984, Rea-

gan argued that four years of "toughness" with communists and Middle East fanatics had restored American credibility in the world. That credibility soon unraveled in a tangled web of deception involving both Central America and the Middle East. In 1984 Congress began refusing Reagan's requests for money to finance the *contra* guerillas. On the other side of the world, Moslem extremists in Lebanon began kidnapping American journalists, teachers, and diplomats, holding them hostage. Despite the greatest intelligence network in the world, the United States was unable to locate the hostages.

Terrorism was becoming more common. In December of 1985, Moslem extremists detonated bombs near the Israeli terminals at the Rome and Vienna airports, killing dozens of innocent people. CIA intelligence sources indicated that Muammar el-Qaddafi, the Libyan dictator, had financed the bombings. Early in 1986 Reagan severed all American economic ties with Libya; ordered all American workers to leave the country; froze all Libyan assets in the United States; and staged United States naval exercises off the Libyan coast in the Gulf of Sidra. When terrorists then exploded a bomb on April 6, 1986, in a West German discotheque frequented by American servicemen, Reagan blamed the event on Libya and retaliated with an air strike against military installations in Tripoli and Qaddafi's personal compound, killing dozens of civilians.

The attack seemed to subdue Qaddafi for a while, but it did not solve the problem of the hostages in Lebanon. Although Reagan had promised again and again to never negotiate with terrorists for the return of the hostages, he desperately wanted to secure their release. Early in the summer of 1986, it appeared that Iran was behind the kidnappings, or at least had strong connections with the terrorists. Iran was in the midst of its devastating war with Iraq and badly in need of sophisticated weapons. Against the advice of Secretary of State George Schultz (who had replaced Alexander Haig in 1983) and Secretary of Defense Caspar Weinberger, Reagan agreed to sell weapons to Iran in return for a release of the hostages. The arms sales were conducted in the strictest secrecy; any publicity that the United States was arming the Ayatollah Khomeini had the potential for political catastrophe.

The arms sales to Iran generated a $10 million profit, and National Security Advisor John M. Poindexter and his aide Lieutenant Colonel Oliver North diverted the money to finance the *contra* guerillas in Nicaragua. All this was done surreptitiously through the CIA intelligence network, and apparently with the support of CIA director William Casey. When news of the arms sales and diversion of funds reached the press in November 1986, the Reagan administration faced a political firestorm. Although Reagan denied knowing anything about the *contra* funds, polls indicated that most Americans did not believe him. For a president whose major asset had been credibility, the Iran-*contra* scandal was a disaster. Ronald Reagan, "the great communicator," was unable to convince most Americans of his innocence. Poindexter and North resigned their positions and

Controversy and unrest arose in the Reagan administration when no one would accept responsibility for the Iran-*contra* affair.

the ensuing scandal seriously weakened the influence of the president.

A major side effect of the Iran-*contra* affair, however, was a reevaluation of the administration position on arms control and nuclear weapons reductions. On October 11–12, 1986, a month before the news broke about Iran-*contra*, President Reagan met in Reykjavik, Iceland, with Soviet premier Mikhail Gorbachev to discuss limitations on nuclear weapons. By 1987 the total number of warheads for each nation approached 50,000. But when Gorbachev asked Reagan to postpone development of the "Star Wars," an antimissile defensive system based on using lasers and particle beams to destroy incoming missiles in outer space. The president refused, abruptly terminating the summit meeting but labeling it "a success" for home consumption.

Just one month later, desperate to regain control of his presidency, Reagan changed his mind and in the spring of 1987 offered Gorbachev the possibility of delaying implementation of Star Wars. The Soviet premier quickly resumed negotiations and prepared for another summit with Reagan, where both men hoped for a nuclear arms treaty. Both leaders needed the treaty. Reagan wanted to repair the damage

AIDS: A MODERN PLAGUE

The Names Project AIDS Quilt

Americans have long debated what to do about sexually transmitted diseases (STD). Health officials have insisted that STD is a medical problem that should be handled like any other communicable disease: through research, treatment, public education, and the vigorous application of modern techniques of epidemiology. Others have argued that STD is primarily a moral problem.

World War I brought the issue to a head. Army planners debated whether to concentrate on trying to prevent STD through educational propaganda against extramarital sex (accompanied by a crackdown on red-light districts), or whether to sanction the use of condoms and focus on medical treatment to cure infection. In the end, they elected to combine both approaches. Moreover, when the identical problem reappeared in World War II, the government promptly adopted the same solution: scary propaganda against extramarital sex, followed by condoms and treatment for soldiers who surrendered to temptation. Even the debate over treatment sounded like an echo. The discovery of penicillin precipitated another round of arguments over whether this new "wonder drug" should be given to soldiers who contracted STD, and the dispute was settled exactly as it had been in World War I: wayward souls received treatment.

Following World War II, public funding for STD work rose and the number of cases fell. The victory over STD, however, proved to be short-lived, for the infection rates tripled between 1950 and 1975. What happened? In part, health officials were victims of their own success. Given the power of new antibiotics, doctors stopped worrying as much about the social behavior that led to transmission, and they became less vigilant in their efforts to track down the partners of infected patients. Yet the doctors were not solely to blame. The public's apathy was reflected in reduced health budgets for STD work.

The lull ended in the 1980s with the appearance of acquired immune deficiency syndrome (AIDS), the most terrifying disease of modern times. As early as 1980, physicians began reporting a strange medical phenomenon among gay men, Haitians, hemophiliacs, and intravenous drug users. Patients from these groups were falling prey to fatigue, a puzzling combination of infections, a rare skin cancer known as Kaposi's sarcoma, and eventual death. No one recovered from the disease.

After prolonged and ill-funded research, AIDS was finally linked to a virus which probably originated in Zaire, spreading to the United States via Haiti. Additional research soon revealed that AIDS was not limited to any single group; rather, it threatened everyone. But why did it take so long to mobilize research efforts and public awareness? The explanation lies in long-standing attitudes about STD.

First and foremost, AIDS was widely regarded as a "gay" disease, and homosexuals were a favorite target of the "new right" and the "moral majority," whose political clout had helped put Ronald Reagan in the White House. Patrick Buchanan, White House Director of Communications, proclaimed that homosexuals had "declared war on nature, and now nature is extracting an awful retribution." By the time Reagan's administration took notice of AIDS in 1987, more than 21,000 Americans had died from the disease. Part of the reason lay in President Reagan's cutbacks in domestic programs: AIDS became another casualty of Reaganomics, another victim of the administration's hostility to social services. In the end, however, a series of shocking events forced the government to act: These included the discovery of AIDS contaminated hospital blood supplies; the appearance of AIDS in heterosexuals; and the surprisingly bold anti-AIDS campaign of Surgeon General C. Everett Koop.

Koop recommended AIDS education for school children "at the earliest date possible," and he further advocated the promotion and use of condoms. Conservatives were outraged and charged the government with attempting to promote immorality. But Koop and other public health officials held firm. The government sponsored television and radio commercials warning the public against "unsafe sex" and mailed an explicit brochure on AIDS to every household in America.

As the public's concern rose, various groups demanded that AIDS sufferers be quarantined. Though health authorities repeatedly stressed that casual contacts could not spread the disease, many people feared the worst. The objections of civil libertarians, who opposed quarantine, left them cold, as did the arguments of

those who rejected quarantine on practical grounds. (Where were tens of thousands of AIDS sufferers to be kept? Who was to pay for their care during this forced isolation?) While these arguments kept any serious movement for quarantine from developing, the public remained edgy. Some parents withdrew their children from schools where AIDS patients were enrolled, and AIDS sufferers found that many of their co-workers wanted them removed from their jobs.

Yet some of the reactions to AIDS within the gay community were no less extreme. Granted, most gay leaders struggled from the outset to publicize AIDS and to promote safe sex and monogamous relationships. But other gays reacted with denial. Some initially believed (or chose to believe) that AIDS was a heterosexual propaganda tactic designed to crush the nascent gay movement. To many, gay liberation meant not merely toleration of homosexuality but a celebration of sexuality, a reordering of values with greater emphasis on the long-suppressed pleasure principle. Multiple and unprotected contacts were the final necessary step to political freedom. Others proclaimed that AIDS could never hit them. And still others became resigned and carried on as usual. In the gay community they became known as Doris Days, after the actress famous for singing *"Que será, será."*

The end of the AIDS story cannot be written, for no one can predict the impact this deadly disease will have on American society. To date (1988), more than 60,000 Americans have been diag-

nosed with the disease, more than 34,000 have died from it, and another 1.5 million are believed to be infected. With a cure nowhere in sight, medical authorities expect to be confronted by literally hundreds of thousands of AIDS patients by the turn of the century. Their care will be both protracted and expensive. Who will pay for it?

Despite these grim realities, sex researchers report few changes in the public's private behavior, especially in those groups that are at high risk for contracting the disease. Though hard data are lacking, the experts agree that "unsafe sex" remains a common practice among many hetero-sexual adolescents and young adults, and the same holds true for some gays. Thus, even in the midst of this terrifying plague, modern-day health authorities, like their progressive ancestors, have found it difficult to modify behavior in order to prevent venereal infections. And like the progressives, many Americans today will no doubt continue to place their hopes on education and on the search for new medical advances with which to eradicate AIDS, debating all the while whether those who contract the disease should be helped or condemned.

President Reagan and Soviet leader Mikhail Grobachev attempted to reach some agreements about the nuclear arms race when they met in Reykjavik, Iceland.

to his reputation and leave office with a memorable success. Gorbachev wanted to divert "arms money" to the sagging Soviet economy. It was a far cry from the Cold War rhetoric Reagan had used in 1980.

THE ECONOMY OF LIMITED EXPECTATIONS

It was January 17, 1949. Standing idly on the dock, waiting for the work to begin, several longshoremen snickered in disbelief. The car looked ridiculously un-American. Tiny and ugly, it resembled half a walnut shell with wheels, or better yet, an insect, a "bug," a "beetle." Ben Pon, the official Volkswagen agent to the United States, was aboard the Dutch freighter *Westerdam* in New York harbor, holding a press conference to introduce the VW to American consumers. He called the car the "Victory Wagon," but skeptical reporters dubbed it "Hitler's car." It was. A generation of American moviegoers remembered seeing it in 1930s newsreels touting Germany's economic recovery. But how could it ever appeal to Americans? The VW was slow, dull, small, and fuel efficient, just when

Americans were lusting after fins, scoop grills, and chrome—lots of chrome. In 1949 Americans purchased 6,250,000 automobiles. Two were VWs. The longshoremen were right, but not for long. They were laughing at the future.

Calm Before the Storm

That future seemed bright in 1949. World War II inflation had subsided, and the country did not slide back into the Great Depression when the war ended in 1945. The European and Asian economies were still in shambles, while American factories produced ever-increasing volumes of goods. A global economy, driven by multinational corporations, was emerging, and because those companies were American-based in 1949, the United States found it easy to penetrate foreign markets.

Foreign aid made that even easier. The Marshall Plan was designed to prevent the spread of communism by reconstructing Europe's economy, but European consumers promptly spent the $10 billion on American goods—everything from machine tools and heavy equipment to Levis and Coca-Cola. Americans had no competition in 1949.

Except for the Korean War inflation in 1951, the 1950s was an economic oasis. Between 1950 and 1960, consumer prices rose an average of 2.3 percent annually, and with 1951 factored out, only 1.7 percent. Unemployment averaged 4.5 percent a year, a figure close to the magical 4 percent economists considered "full employment." Finally, real economic growth averaged 3.2 percent a year during the 1950s, enough to more than absorb population growth and price increases. Stable prices, full employment, and steady growth were the economic hallmarks of the 1950s.

But there were dark clouds on the horizon. By the late 1950s, the world economy had recovered from the war. Concerned by Cold War issues, the United States encouraged the economic development of Western Europe and Japan. By picking up their defense burden, the United States freed money which these nations used to rebuild their industrial plants and for research and development. Japan constructed an industrial base from scratch—new factories, new technologies, new ideas, new confidence. So did Germany. Compared to the aging factories in the "Rustbelt" of the United States, Japanese and European factories were state of the art—efficient, productive, and modern.

Another major disadvantage for the United States were wage levels. Labor costs in Japan and Western Europe were much lower. By the mid-1950s, workers in the United States earned four times as much as their counterparts in Japan and twice as much as European workers. With lower production costs and lower wage levels, Japanese and European companies were ready to open up the American market.

High wages and outdated factories led to declining productivity, the most serious problem in the post–World War II American economy. Productivity—the total volume of goods and services produced per hour of work—declined badly in the 1960s and 1970s. From a 3.1 percent annual increase between 1955 and 1962, productivity grew only 2.3 percent per year for the next decade, and grew only 1.1 percent per year between 1973 and 1977. In 1978 and 1979 it actually dropped 2 percent a year. In contrast, West German productivity increased 4 percent annually during the 1970s and Japan's an extraordinary 7 percent. With productivity declining, American goods became more and more expensive and less and less competitive in world markets.

The energy industry was also in trouble. Ever since the late nineteenth century, the United States had been energy self-sufficient, blessed with enormous reserves of coal, oil, natural gas, and hydroelectric power. But in the 1950s, the combination of cheap fuel and a consumer culture led to an orgy of consumption. With only six percent of the world's population, the United States accounted for one-third of global fuel consumption. Between 1950 and 1965, American energy consumption increased from 33 to 53 quadrillion BTUs, but production did not keep pace. Incentives for large-scale domestic production declined when the international oil companies found they could import high quality crude oil, at 6 cents a gallon, from the Middle East. Foreign oil was so cheap that coal-burning utilities made the expensive shift to oil and natural gas. Imports went to 8.5 million barrels a day in 1977, accounting for 48 percent of consumption. The nation had become dangerously vulnerable to foreign producers.

At the same time the economy was also undergoing major structural changes. After World War II, the United States entered the "post-industrial age." During the Industrial Revolution, the American economy had revolved around the extractive industries (coal, iron ore, timber, and oil) and heavy industries (railroads, steel, textiles, and automobiles). Beginning in the 1950s, the significance of mining and manufacturing declined, giving way to an economy based on services, high technology, and information.

The year 1955 was particularly symbolic. Labor leaders George Meany and Walter Reuther raised their hands in unity as the American Federation of Labor and the Congress of Industrial Organizations fused into the AFL-CIO, the largest labor union in the country. But that same year, white-collar workers outnumbered blue-collar workers for the first time. Union membership accounted for thirty-five percent of the nonagricultural workforce, but

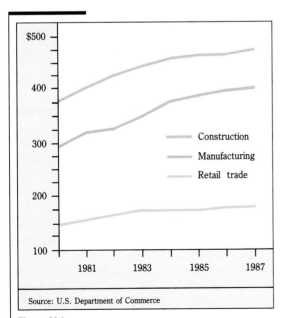

Source: U.S. Department of Commerce

Figure 30.1
Weekly Earnings

that number dropped to only twenty-five percent in the early 1970s. Those regions of the country dependent on heavy industry were in for a hard time.

Big cities lost their economic vitality after World War II. With manufacturing declining, factory closings in urban centers became increasingly common in the 1950s and 1960s. City life acquired a rigid class profile. In high rise buildings, white commuters from suburbs occupied the middle-class technical and professional positions, while resident blacks and Hispanics were left with low-paying, dead-end jobs. Unemployment rates among blacks and Hispanics were consistently two to three times as high as whites, generating an urban "underclass" dependent on welfare payments for survival. By the 1960s, most American cities had large, blighted ghettos inhabited by frustrated, unhappy people.

Weaknesses in the economy became visible late in the 1950s and early in the 1960s. Those two VWs sold in 1949 became 50,457 in 1956. Foreign car sales went from 50,000 in 1955, less than one percent of the market to 600,000 in 1959 (ten percent of the market). Japanese autos imported to the United States went from 26,000 in 1970 to 1,600,000 in 1979, making up

During the 1970s and 1980s, Japanese imports captured an ever-increasing share of the American automobile market.

25 percent of the American market; hundreds of thousands of Detroit auto workers received pink slips that year. The onslaught continued in the 1980s, with East European and Korean cars entering the United States. "Yugo" and "Hyundai" joined VW, Toyota, Datsun, and Honda in carving up the American market.

The steel industry compounded these economic troubles. Outmoded plants could not compete with Japanese and German products. In 1950 steel imports were virtually unknown; U.S. Steel, Bethlehem, and Republic Steel dominated the global market. By 1977 Japan was exporting $2.3 billion of steel to the United States. In 1980 imports accounted for nearly twenty-five percent of the American steel market.

The Storm

The impact of urban decay, the rise of a service economy, the decline of manufacturing, and the flood of imports were apparent early in the 1960s. After hovering at full employment levels in the 1950s, unemployment jumped to 6.6 percent in 1961 before dropping back only slightly in 1962 and 1963. It was disquieting to President John F. Kennedy and the Democrats, who had promised economic stability, but they were more alarmed in 1962 when the country's steel companies announced a major price increase. Roger Blough, head of United States Steel, personally visited the White House on April 10 to tell Kennedy of his decision. The president had been working for months with the steelworkers union to get them to agree to a modest wage increase in the interest of stable prices. They had agreed early in April. When Blough told Kennedy of the price increase, the president seethed with anger, saying, "My father once told me that all steel men were sons-of-bitches, and I did not realize until now how right he was." Over the next three days Kennedy "played hardball," ordering the Justice Department to begin an antitrust investigation and the FBI to look into the personal finances of steel company executives. On April 13, the steel companies rescinded the price increase.

On the advice of Walter Heller, head of the Council of Economic Advisors, Kennedy then adopted an approach to the recession based on the theories of British economist, Lord Keynes—increased government spending combined with a tax cut to boost consumer demand. The federal budget went from $92 billion in 1960 to $119 billion in 1964. The Kennedy tax reform package, which provided $11 billion to consumers spread out over a three-year period, passed Congress in 1964—after his assassination. Higher spending and tax cuts stimulated the economy, and unemployment dropped below five percent in 1964.

Billions of those dollars were spent in Vietnam. President Lyndon B. Johnson escalated the war in 1965, expecting it to be a brief affair, a relatively quick "mop-up" action to destroy the Vietcong and stabilize the government of South Vietnam. Instead, the war turned into an economic and foreign policy nightmare. Millions of young men answered draft calls, enlisted, or avoided the war by enrolling in college. By 1968 the war was costing $3 billion a month and the federal budget rocketed to $179 billion. Not surprisingly, with so many men in uniform or in college, unemployment fell to 3.5 percent. On the economic front, there seemed little to complain about.

America discovered pollution in 1969. That year, in Cleveland, Ohio, the Cuyahoga River caught fire. Each year steel plants, paper mills, mines, and city sewage systems along the river dumped a million tons of chemicals, metals, and organic pollutants into its waters. The river carried the mess through Ohio into Lake Erie. Methane gas bubbled off the surface of the river, and the top six inches were more oil, grease, and debris than water. When a steel mill dumped hot slag into the Cuyahoga in 1969, the river ignited over a stretch of several hundred yards and burned for several hours.

The burning of the Cuyahoga was a spectacular symbol of dangerous pollution. Automobile emissions polluted the atmosphere, endangering lives in cities like Los Angeles and Houston. Waterways were clogged with sludge; ecologists declared Lake Erie "dead" in 1969. Consumers produced a mountain of garbage every day, taxing landfill capacities. Chemical companies buried hazardous wastes in shallow pits.

Environmental pollution, including the collection and disposal of toxic waste, has been an important issue throughout the country since the late 1960s.

On April 1, 1969, environmentalists staged "Earth Day" demonstrations across the country, demanding stiff federal regulations limiting factory discharges into the air and water. Cleaning up the environment made long-range economic sense, but it was expensive in the short-run. Corporate and labor leaders opposed stiffer environmental regulations because the installation of pollution-reducing technology would drive up the cost of American products and make them even less competitive in world markets. Environmentalists responded that in the long run, failure to protect the fragile ecosystem would guarantee an economic and health catastrophe. Ironically, both groups were correct. The federal government established the Environmental Protection Agency to set pollution standards in the late 1960s, and the prices of American goods went up.

Stagflation

By the 1970s, the economy was suffering from *stagflation*—unemployment, inflation, and stagnant growth, all at the same time. Vietnam disguised the weaknesses in a mask of prosperity for a few years, but as early as 1968, economists and politicians expressed concern about the consumer price index. After more than fifteen years of stability, prices were on the rise again.

Inflationary pressures had been present before Vietnam. Aging factories, declining productivity, increasing wage levels, and expensive environmental regulations all pushed prices higher. Moreover, President Lyndon Johnson found it impossible to finance the Great Society and pay for the war without running up a huge budget deficit for fiscal 1968—$25 billion in a federal budget of $178 billion. The economy was operating at near full capacity; federal spending increased consumer purchasing power. Too much money was chasing too few goods. Consumer demand was outstripping the supply of goods and prices inched up more than four percent in 1968 and nearly six percent in 1970.

Johnson realized that he should either raise taxes or cut the Great Society, but he knew that economic issues created political problems.

Although the economic dilemma had to be addressed. Johnson was loathe to let the "bitch of a war" hurt his "lady." That left only a tax increase, but the war was already so unpopular that a tax increase to support Vietnam was politically out of the question. In a 1965 comment to his advisors, Johnson remarked: "I don't know much about economics, but I do know the Congress. And I can get the Great Society through right now—this is a golden time. We've got a good Congress and I'm the right President and I can do it. But if I talk about the cost of the war, the Great Society won't go through and the tax bill won't go through." The president settled for a modest income tax surcharge, hoping the war would be over soon enough to extricate himself—and the country—from the crisis. It was not to be. Inflation hit 6.5 percent in 1970 and fell back only slightly to 5.3 percent in 1971.

On top of the structural inflation and the price increases fueled by the war, the Arab oil boycott of 1973–74 and the Organization of Petroleum Exporting Countries (OPEC) price increases drove the consumer price index even higher. On October 6, 1973, the Middle East erupted in war for the fourth time in a generation when Egyptian and Syrian troops invaded Israeli-held territory in the Sinai Peninsula and Golan Heights. In what has since been known as the Yom Kippur War, American-supplied Israeli forces won a decisive victory over the Arabs.

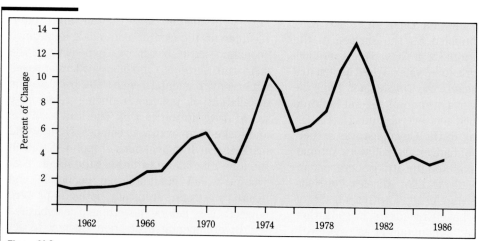

Figure 30.2
Consumer Price Index, 1960-1986

The Israeli victory soon turned into an American economic nightmare. In 1973 the United States imported millions of barrels of oil each day. The Saudi Arabian announcement on October 20, 1973, stopping all oil shipments to America created a real crisis, especially when other Persian Gulf exporters joined the boycott. It lasted until March 1974. Early that year, OPEC announced an increase in oil prices from $3 to $5 a barrel, and within three months the price was $12 a barrel. Fuel prices skyrocketed and farmers, manufacturers, and distributors passed on their higher costs by raising prices. The inflation rate jumped to seven percent in 1974.

That was only the beginning. When Islamic fundamentalists revolted against the Shah of Iran in 1979, the political instability disrupted Iranian oil production, removing 4 million barrels a day from world supplies and driving oil prices up to $34 a barrel. In 1980 the inflation rate hit thirteen percent; it raged at an eighteen percent annual level for the second quarter of 1980. To put inflation into more concrete terms, in 1960 a family with a combined yearly income of $9000 was considered upper class; by the mid-1980s the same amount was below the poverty line.

But this was stagflation, so even while prices were increasing rapidly, economic growth was slowing and unemployment was rising. Between 1969 and 1973, the Vietnam War wound down and millions of soldiers returned to the civilian workforce. Increased competition from foreign goods continued to cut into American employment, and OPEC price increases drained hundreds of billions of dollars of consumer purchasing power off to the Middle East. Unemployment went from 3.5 percent in 1969 to 5.9 percent in 1971 and 7.1 percent in 1974.

Stagflation was confusing. It contradicted the last forty years of Keynesian economic experience. Unemployment and inflation usually did not coexist. When unemployment was high, prices had been stable or even declining. Policymakers could increase government spending, reduce taxes, and expand the money supply, all of which augmented consumer purchasing power and created jobs, without having to

"It Gets Into Everything"

In the late 1970s oil became the central concern of domestic and foreign policy in the United States. Copyright 1979 by Herblock in the Washington Post.

worry about creating an inflation problem. When inflation had been the problem, jobs were plentiful. Policymakers could raise taxes, trim government spending, and contract the money supply, reducing consumer demand and the upward pressure on prices without producing a recession.

The problem with stagflation was the pain of its options. To attack inflation by reducing consumer purchasing power only made unemployment worse. The other choice was no better. Stimulating purchasing power and creating jobs also drove prices higher. Not surprisingly, economic policy during the 1970s was a nightmare of confusion and contradiction.

Richard Nixon was the first president to confront the problem, but instead of resorting to the typical Republican rhetoric of balanced budgets and spending cuts, he appeared on national television on June 11, 1971, and announced "I am a Keynesian." Most people in his own party were stunned, and Democrats were dumbfounded. Nixon was stealing their thunder. To solve the unemployment problem, he proposed fiscal 1971 and 1972 federal budgets that included $23 billion deficits each year, as well as expansionary monetary policies. But to prevent inflation from getting worse, Nixon imposed a ninety-day wage-price-rent freeze. Three months later, he launched phase two of his anti-inflation program, a mandatory set wage and price guideline, monitored by the federal government, which lasted until January 1973. They were followed by a third period of voluntary controls. Inflation stayed at about four percent during the freeze, but once the controls were lifted the consumer price index started up again. He imposed a sixty-day wage-price freeze in June 1973. The Arab oil boycott in October finished off the anti-inflation campaign. The last of the controls expired in April 1974, just four months before Nixon's resignation.

When Gerald Ford came into the White House in August 1974, he inherited an inflation

Even imposing wage-price freezes did not seem to help President Nixon curb the ever-increasing rate of inflation that plagued his administration.

rate in excess of ten percent and an unemployment rate of seven percent. At first, the Ford administration attacked the economic crisis in traditional Republican fashion, tightening up the money supply, raising interest rates, and limiting government spending. Ford wielded the veto pen with more frequency than any other president. In just over two years, he vetoed fifty-three congressional spending bills which he considered too expensive and inflationary. He also unveiled in 1975 his "WIN" (Whip Inflation Now) program, complete with "WIN" lapel buttons for members of the press corps. The press conference was a public relations disaster; nobody was convinced that Ford's WIN lapel buttons would do any good. Several days later, Chevy Chase performed a savage parody of the press conference on the popular television show *Saturday Night Live,* complete with his own rendition of Ford tripping over a WIN button. In the end, WIN proved to be no more than a series of ineffectual wage and price guidelines monitored by the federal government.

By 1975 the first round of OPEC price increases had already reverberated throughout the economy and inflation began to drop down to 6.6 percent, but unemployment soared to 9 percent. Now seeing unemployment as a more serious problem than inflation, the Ford administration reversed itself, stimulating the economy with lower interest rates, higher government spending, and a $22 billion tax reduction. Ford proposed a fiscal 1976 budget of $366 billion with a deficit of $66 billion, the largest since World War II. Such capricious economic policies did little to improve public confidence in the administration, and Ford paid for his vacillation when he lost the 1976 presidential election to Jimmy Carter and the Democrats.

Like others before him, Carter thought he had answers to the country's economic plight. He promised a balanced budget by 1980, a thorough administrative reorganization of the federal government, welfare reform, a huge windfall profits tax on oil companies to finance development of alternative energy sources, and energy conservation methods. Carter was politically naive, somehow assuming that Congress would be as amenable to his ideas as the Georgia legislature had been. Carter had won the election of 1976 campaigning against "politicians," and he brought a self-righteousness to Washington that did little to endear him to Congress. Hamilton Jordan, Carter's chief of staff, never even bothered to introduce himself to Congressman Tip O'Neill, speaker of the House of Representatives.

Carter proved inept in dealing with Congress, and it was not until the spring of 1980 that the energy package he proposed in 1977 saw the light of day. It provided new fuel efficiency standards for automobiles, huge government grants to develop alternative energy sources, and a windfall profits tax on oil companies to pay for it all. The real beneficiaries of the oil crisis had been the international oil companies. Rumors floated around the country that the oil companies were deliberately creating shortages by holding petroleum off the market in storage facilities. Jimmy Carter's proposal that their profits be taxed was a popular one. But it was too little, too late. Carter's dream of administrative reorganization died a quick death on Capitol Hill. So did the promise of a balanced budget. During the Carter administration, the federal government produced budget deficits totaling more than $150 billion and the Federal Reserve Board expanded the money supply. Under such stimulation unemployment declined to less than six percent.

But Carter stood helpless before inflation. OPEC pushed up oil prices in 1976, and by the end of 1979 they were $24 a barrel, 800 percent above 1973. Staggering inflation was not far behind, reaching 12.7 percent at the end of 1979. By that time the Iranian Revolution had cut world oil production, and petroleum prices began their climb to $34 a barrel in 1980. Inflation went to 13 percent annually.

Donning a sweater and appearing against the backdrop of a wood-burning fireplace, President Carter delivered several frank speeches to the American people, telling them that the days of cheap energy were over, as were the days of unlimited economic expansion. People would have to adjust to a simpler lifestyle if the demon of inflation was ever to be brought under control. It was exactly what Americans did not want to hear. They were upset about ($1.20 for a gallon of gas,) high electricity and heating bills, fuel shortages, and long lines outside service stations. As far as they were concerned, Carter was as inept in economic affairs as he was in dealing with the Iran hostage crisis. What they wanted was good news and hope, and in 1980 Ronald Reagan gave it to them.

Reaganomics

In the election of 1980, Republican candidate Ronald Reagan repeated one question a thousand times to the American people: "Are you better off today than you were four years ago?" With inflation at eighteen percent, the answer was obvious: "No." Reagan then proposed to make Americans better off with what he called "supply-side economics": the end of exorbitant union contracts, which would make American goods competitive once again; drastic cuts in federal spending and balanced budgets to restore business confidence; tax reductions to stimulate investment and purchasing power; and decontrol of those economic areas strangled by federal regulation so competition could be restored. Only then could stable prices and full employment be restored.

Reagan's attack on "inflationary" wage increases was more symbolic than real, but the symbol was a powerful one. In August of 1981, the 15,000-member Professional Air Traffic Controllers Organization, after specific warnings from Reagan, went on strike for higher pay and a shorter work week. Reagan gave them forty-eight hours to return to work, after which he promptly fired all those still at home. Union leaders condemned the firings, but America was no longer a union country; the economy was changing and most people backed Reagan. His popularity ratings soared.

The promise to cut federal spending and balance the federal budget ran head-on into powerful constituencies in Congress. Although Reagan managed to push through cuts in some federal social and educational programs, most of them, like Social Security and military retirement, were protected by automatic pay in-

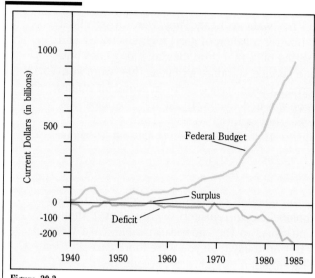

Figure 30.3
U.S. Budget Deficits, 1940-1985

creases tied to the consumer price index. Congressmen were simply unwilling to vote to cut those benefits. In those areas where he did have some authority, like defense spending, Reagan engineered massive increases. Between 1981 and 1987, the defense budget jumped from $165 billion a year to more than $330 billion, and for fiscal 1988, Reagan submitted the first *trillion-dollar* budget to Congress, complete with a staggering $225 billion deficit, which ended any dreams of a balanced budget.

Reagan was more successful with his tax policies. In 1981 he pushed through Congress a bill providing for a tax cut of five percent in 1981 followed by cuts of ten percent in 1982 and 1983. Critics charged that Reagan's tax policies benefited only middle and higher income groups, but Reagan's supporters argued back that the tax cuts would provide fresh investments to the economy and a boost in employment. In 1986 the administration then pushed through another tax bill, this one a "revenue neutral" measure which substantially reduced tax rates on individuals, increased rates on corporations, and closed a variety of nonproductive tax loopholes. The administration argued

that the bill would direct capital into productive areas of the economy.

Finally, Reagan set out to "liberate free enterprise from fifty years of liberal Democratic restraints." In 1982 Congress deregulated the banking industry and lifted ceilings on interest rates. Federal price controls on air fares were lifted as well. Congress deregulated the natural gas industry in 1983 by gradually removing federal price controls. The Department of Transportation postponed the application of expensive, federally mandated passive restraint systems and fuel efficiency standards for automobiles; the Environmental Protection Agency relaxed its interpretation of the Clean Air Act; and the Department of the Interior opened up large areas of the federal domain, including offshore oil fields, to private development.

The results of deregulation were mixed. Bank interest rates became more competitive, but smaller banks found it difficult to hold their own against larger institutions. Natural gas prices increased once decontrol set in, but so did production, easing some of the country's dependence on foreign fuel. Air fares on high-traffic routes between major cities dropped dramatically in the 1980s when price controls were lifted, but fares for short, low-traffic flights skyrocketed. Most critics agreed, however, that deregulation had restored some competition to the marketplace.

When Reagan entered the White House in January 1981, the inflation rate was running at 13 percent a year and unemployment stood at 7.4 percent. Unemployment shot up to 8.5 percent in 1982 and 10 percent in 1983, but then began a slow retreat which brought it back to 6.2 percent by 1987. The inflation rate fell from 13 percent in 1981 to less than 4 percent in 1987.

Reagan and the Republicans took credit for the achievement. The irony was how little connection there was between administration rhetoric and economic recovery. Reagan claimed that cuts in federal spending and balanced budgets would restore business confidence, reduce inflation, and stimulate production and employment. Unemployment and inflation had dropped, not as a result of a balanced budget

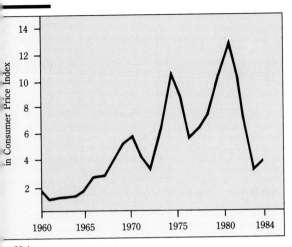

re 30.4
tion, 1960-1984

restrained the money supply until interest rates exceeded twenty percent. Impervious to political influence and the tendency of politicians to expand the money supply before elections in order to create jobs, Volker squeezed inflationary pressures out of the economy. Federal Reserve policies, combined with falling oil prices, pushed the inflation rate to below four percent in 1986, the lowest rate since early in the 1970s.

The country was not concerned about why the economy was improving. Reagan claimed credit for it and most Americans were willing to give it to him. In the presidential election of 1984, Reagan ran against Democratic candidates Walter Mondale and Geraldine Ferraro, and he asked one question again: "Are you better off now than you were four years ago? " The answer was a resounding "yes" and Reagan swamped his opponents, at least for the fifty-three percent of the electorate who turned out to vote. Along with Vice-President George Bush, Reagan received a fifty-nine percent plurality and outdistanced Mondale 525 to 13 in the Electoral College.

President Reagan returned to the White House riding a wave of unprecedented popularity. Inflation had dropped during his first administration largely because of declining oil prices, but in 1987, with world consumption rising and political instability reasserting itself in the Middle East, especially in Iran, oil prices began to rise again, reaching $22 a barrel at the end of the summer and heating up the consumer price index. Success on the employment front had been achieved only with extraordinary budget deficits. David Stockman, budget chief in the first Reagan administration, accused the president in 1987 of committing "fiscal carnage." Between 1981 and 1987, Stockman argued, the federal debt increased $1.5 trillion, three times the debt accumulated by all thirty-nine of Reagan's presidential predecessors. Most economists feared for the future, convinced that a continuation of such enormous budget deficits would mortgage the economy for a generation and perhaps trigger a "hyperinflation." Stable prices, full employment, and steady growth still appeared out of reach. America couldn't have it all.

but because of the greatest deficits in American history. Enormous federal spending, combined with tax cuts, had increased consumer purchasing power, stimulated production, and created jobs, just as Keynesian economics predicted.

And inflation, for a change, had not become more severe. Oil prices peaked in 1981 at $34 a barrel. The worldwide recession reduced global demand just when Iranian production was returning. New oil discoveries in Mexico, completion of the Alaskan pipeline with oil from the Prudhoe Bay field, and a wave of new drilling because of high prices increased world oil supplies. In the United States, more fuel-efficient automobiles, improved insulation in buildings and homes, and conservation reduced demand for oil. Suddenly, the world was awash in a sea of oil, and in the process, petroleum prices declined in 1982 and 1983, the price dropping to $25 a barrel. Inflation declined with oil prices. Late in 1985, oil prices nosedived, falling at their lowest point in 1986 to less than $9 a barrel.

With oil prices falling, the Federal Reserve Board exercised new authority over the money supply. Paul Volker became head of the Federal Reserve Board in 1979, and he ruled it with an iron hand. Determined to wipe out inflation, he

CHRONOLOGY OF KEY EVENTS

1973 Arab oil embargo	**1979** Shah of Iran forced to leave his country. Ayatallah Khomeini assumes control of the Iranian revolution; Soviet Union invades Afghanistan; Sandinista guerillas come to power in Nicaragua; Three Mile Island nuclear plant near Harrisburg, Pennsylvania, damaged in accident
1975 Cambodian Communists seize U.S. merchant ship *Mayaguez*. U.S. marines recapture ship and crew; North Vietanamese and Vietcong overrun South Vietnam; Communist Pathet Lao takes control of Laos; National Cancer Institute links cancer to air pollution	
	1980 U.S. boycotts Moscow Summer Olympics
1976 Chinese Communist Party Chairman Mao Tse-tung dies; *Rocky* wins Oscar for Best Picture; Alex Hailey publishes *Roots*	**1981** American hostages held in Iran released; President Reagan calls for an increased budget and construction of new weapons
1977 President Carter pardons most Vietnam War draft evaders; President Carter signs new Panama Canal Treaties; Gary Gilmore becomes first person to suffer death penalty in U.S. since 1967	**1983** Muslim terrorists on a suicide mission kill 241 American soldiers in Beirut; U.S. invades Grenada and overthrows a pro-Cuban Marxist government
	1986 U.S. launches air strikes against Libya in retaliation for terrorist attacks
1978 United States and Communist China establish full diplomatic relations; Camp David peace talks improve relations between Israel and Egypt; Films *The Deer Hunter* and *Coming Home* explore the trauma of the Vietnam War; Senate ratifies Panama Canal Treaties	**1987** Iran-Contra hearings
	1988 George Bush and Michael Dukakis nominated for president

TOWARD THE 1990s

During its last year in office, the Reagan administration suffered several serious setbacks but also won some important victories. In America, Reagan's own cabinet came under attack from critics who were concerned about the low level of ethics in politics. The charges were hardly new. Before 1988 CIA director William Casey, Secretary of Labor Raymond Donovan, Secretary of the Interior James Watt, and head of the Environmental Protection Agency (EPA) Ann Burford had been roundly criticized for their actions. Reporters even coined a special term— the "sleaze factor"—to describe ethical problems of Reagan's administration. Finally Reagan's long-time advisor, Attorney General Edwin Meese, was forced out of office in 1988. Interestingly enough, however, the various

scandals that rocked his administration did not significantly hurt Reagan's popularity. To the end of his second term, Reagan remained a popular president.

If charges of ethical and financial irregularities crippled the Reagan Administration at home, they did not greatly affect the president's foreign policy. Reagan abandoned his "evil empire" theme during his last year in office and moved to improve relations with the Soviet Union. The "spirit of Reykjavik" was revived in the spring of 1988 when Reagan traveled to Moscow for a summit meeting with Soviet Premier Mikhail Gorbachev. There the two leaders hammered out an important treaty that called for the gradual destruction of Russia's and America's intermediate range nuclear missiles. By the late summer of 1988 the citizens of the two countries were treated to the sight of the safe destruction of U.S. Pershing II missiles and Soviet SS20 missiles.

Motivated by Gorbachev's westernizing policies, the Soviet Union has moved cautiously toward greater openness, or *glasnost* as the change has been labeled. Turning away from the secretive policies of former Soviet leaders, Gorbachev has allowed protests in Latvia, Estonia, and Lithuania—the Baltic states under Soviet control—and openly criticized the barbarous excess of the Stalin regime. In addition, Gorbachev's policy of *perestroika* (administrative and economic restructuring) has produced greater openness and freedom in the Soviet Union. Coupled with the Soviet withdrawal from Afghanistan and the movement by Iran and Iraq toward ending their decade-long war, the prospect of better relations between the Soviet Union and the United States has improved.

Nonetheless, real challenges and dangers remain. The death of Pakistan's dictator and United States ally Mohammad Zia ul-Haq in a mysterious airplane explosion could lead to new hazards in that part of the world. And the Middle East remains a dangerously unstable area. But those problems will have to be dealt with by Reagan's successor.

For the most part, however, Democratic candidate Michael Dukakis and Republican candidate George Bush ignored important foreign policy issues during their presidential campaigns. They also glossed over America's serious economic troubles. Instead both ran bitter negative campaigns. Dukakis accused Bush's vice-presidential candidate, Dan Quayle, of using influence to stay out of the Vietnam War and to gain admission to the Indiana University law school. Bush in turn emphasized Dukakis's lack of experience and lack of interest in a strong national defense. On election day, however, the real choice was between change or a continuation of Reagan's policies, and the American electorate chose a continuation by George Bush.

CONCLUSION

In January 1988 *Newsweek* boldly announced "The Eighties Are Over." The article character-ized the 1980s as a time of greed, self-indulgence, and ostentatious displays of wealth: a time when financier Ivan Boesky claimed, "Greed is not a bad thing. You shouldn't feel guilty"; when Nancy Reagan spent $25,000 on her inaugural wardrobe and $209,508 on new White House china; when the circulation of *Money* magazine climbed from 800,000 to 1.85 million; when the prime-time soap opera about the super-rich, *Dallas*, reached number one in the ratings; and when Madonna had a pop music hit entitled "Material Girl." On television advertisers told consumers, "Yes, you can have it all, you deserve it all, all for you, yes . . . " President Reagan's message was similar. America could have it all—low taxes, public services, strong defense, eternal greatness. But expectations outran realities. As one journalist observed, "The peculiar amalgam that we now think of as the '80s lasted six years, 11 months and 15 days, finally collapsing with the Dow on October 19, 1987."

If 1984 was "The Year of the Yuppie," 1988 was "The Year of the Couch Potato." All signposts indicated that Americans were ready to move out of the fast lane and relax more. Diner food replaced West Coast *nouvelle cuisine,* which featured tiny portions of exquisitely arranged food. Walking edged out running for millions of Americans; the marathon craze actually peaked in 1982-1983. The cult of thinness began to lose its appeal. Professional trendsetter Faith Popcorn predicted Americans getting "a little fatter. One of the big trends is toward gaining weight. It shows health and it shows security." Finally, cocaine consumption and carefree spending started to decline, and interest in family life began its resurgence. Popular movies reflected these new attitudes. *Less Than Zero* and *Bright Lights, Big City* both tried to deglamourize cocaine. And *Fatal Attraction* portrayed the career-minded woman as a family-destroying psychopath. Filmmaker John Hughes remarked that audiences "want to see a woman dead who dares to attack the institution of family."

The more balanced outlook—the recognition of limitations—has even spilled over into national politics. During his last year in office, President Reagan reversed his earlier "evil empire" rhetoric and demonstrated a willingness to negotiate seriously with the Soviet Union. And the increase of voter interest in the 1988 elections indicated that Americans are concerned about the nation's and world's growing problems, which include a three-trillion-dollar deficit and political instability in the Middle East and Central America. Thoughtful Americans have grown skeptical of Rambo policies and the culture of greed. They realize that they have more meaningful traditions to guide them.

REVIEW SUMMARY

During the 1970s and 1980s the United States experienced troubling times. In foreign affairs, Third World countries added new complexities to the Cold War. At home economic problems created doubts about long-term prosperity. As a result, Americans seemed to face a future of diminished expectations. Jimmy Carter had his share of problems as president:

- although he contributed to the peace process in the Middle East, he was crippled by the Iran hostage crisis
- high inflation and unemployment plagued him at home
- higher fuel costs and industrial decline raised questions about the health of the American economy during his presidency

Ronald Reagan, too, has had mixed results during his administration:

- he controlled inflation and unemployment but greatly enlarged the national debt
- he was able to improve relations with the Soviet Union, but Third World troubles continued

Trade and deficit problems remain for a new generation of politicians to confront.

SUGGESTIONS FOR FURTHER READING

OVERVIEWS AND SURVEYS

Stephen Ambrose, *Rise to Globalism: American Foreign Policy, 1938-1980* (1980); William H. Chafe, *The Unfinished Journey* (1986) and *The American Woman* (1972); Alexander DeConde, *A History of American Foreign Policy* (1963); Robert H. Ferrell, *American Diplomacy* (1969); Alonzo Hamby, *The Imperial Years* (1976); Godfrey Hodgson, *America in Our Time* (1975); Walter LaFeber, *America, Russia, and the Cold War* (1976); R. W. Leopold, *The Growth of American Foreign Policy* (1967); William

Leuchtenburg, *A Troubled Feast* (1983); Thomas G. Paterson, *American Foreign Policy* (1977); Richard Polenberg, *One Nation Divisible* (1980); Emily and Norman Rosenberg, *In Our Time* (1982); Frederick F. Siegel, *A Troubled Journey* (1984); William A. Williams, *The Tragedy of American Diplomacy* (1972) and *The Roots of the Modern American Empire* (1969); Lawrence Wittner, *Cold War America* (1979); Howard Zinn, *Postwar America, 1945-1971* (1973).

THE LIMITS OF POWER

Alan M. Brandt, *No Magic Bullet: A Social History of Venereal Disease in the United States Since 1880* (1985); Zbigniew Brzezinski, *Power and Principle* (1983); Jimmy Carter, *Keeping Faith* (1982); Robert Dallek, *Ronald Reagan: The Politics of Symbolism* (1984); Wilbur Crane Eveland, *Ropes of Sand: America's Failure in the Middle East* (1980); Gerald R. Ford, *A Time to Heal* (1979); Haynes Johnson, *In the Absence of Power* (1980); Clark Mollenhoff, *The Man Who Pardoned Nixon* (1976); Richard M. Nixon, *United States Foreign Policy for the 1970s: Building for Peace* (1971); William B. Quandt, *Decade of Decisions* (1977); Richard Reeves, *A Ford, Not a Lincoln* (1975); Barry Rubin, *Paved with Good Intentions* (1980); Robert Scheer, *With Enough Shovels: Reagan, Bush and Nuclear War* (1983); Randy Shilts, *And the Band Played On: Politics, People, and the AIDS Epidemic* (1987); John Stockwell, *In Search of Enemies* (1976); Jerald TerHorst, *Gerald Ford and the Future of the Presidency* (1974); Cyrus Vance, *Hard Choices* (1983); Joseph G. Whelan, *Soviet Diplomacy and Negotiating Behavior: Emerging New Context for U.S. Diplomacy* (1979).

THE ECONOMY OF LIMITED EXPECTATIONS

Richard Barnet, *The Lean Years* (1980); Walter Dean Burnham, *The Current Crisis in American Politics* (1982); Alan Crawford, *Thunder on the Right: The New Right and the Politics of Resentment* (1980); Paul and Anne Ehrlich, *The End of Affluence* (1974); Nathan Glazer, *Affirmative Discrimination* (1975); David Halberstam, *The Powers That Be* (1979); Robert L. Heilbroner, *An Inquiry into the Human Prospect* (1975); Martin Melosi, *Coping With Abundance: Energy and Environment in Industrial America, 1820-1980* (1983); Kirkpatrick Sale, *Power Shift: The Rise of the Southern Rim and Its Challenge to the Eastern Establishment.* (1975); Allan P. Sindler, *Bakke, DeFunis and Minority Admissions: The Quest for Equal Opportunity* (1978); Robert Stobaugh and Daniel Yergin, eds., *Energy Future* (1980); Theodore White, *America in Search of Itself* (1982); J. Harvie Wilkinson, *From Brown to Bakke: The Supreme Court and School Integration, 1954-1978* (1979); William J. Wilson, *The Declining Significance of Race* (1978); Daniel Yergin and Martin Hillenbrand, eds., *Global Insecurity* (1982).

Appendix

The Declaration of Independence

In Congress, July 4, 1776

The Unanimous Declaration of the thirteen United States of America,

When, in the course of human events, it becomes necessary for one people to dissolve the political bonds which have connected them with another, and to assume, among the powers of the earth, the separate and equal station to which the laws of nature and of nature's God entitle them, a decent respect to the opinions of mankind requires that they should declare the causes which impel them to the separation.

We hold these truths to be self-evident: That all men are created equal; that they are endowed by their Creator with certain unalienable rights; that among these are life, liberty, and the pursuit of happiness; that, to secure these rights, governments are instituted among men, deriving their just powers from the consent of the governed; that whenever any form of government becomes destructive of these ends, it is the right of the people to alter or to abolish it, and to institute new government, laying its foundation on such principles, and organizing its powers in such form, as to them shall seem most likely to effect their safety and happiness. Prudence, indeed, will dictate that governments long established should not be changed for light and transient causes; and accordingly all experience hath shown that mankind are more disposed to suffer, while evils are sufferable, than to right themselves by abolishing the forms to which they are accustomed. But when a long train of abuses and usurpations, pursuing invariably the same object, evinces a design to reduce them under absolute despotism, it is their right, it is their duty, to throw off such government, and to provide new guards for their future security. Such has been the patient sufferance of these colonies; and such is now the necessity which constrains them to alter their former systems to government. The history of the present King of Great Britain is a history of repeated injuries and usurpations, all having in direct object the establishment of an absolute tyranny over these states. To prove this, let facts be submitted to a candid world.

He has refused his assent to laws, the most wholesome and necessary for the public good.

He has forbidden his governors to pass laws of immediate and pressing importance, unless suspended in their operation till his assent should be obtained; and when so suspended, he has utterly neglected to attend to them.

He has refused to pass other laws for the accommodation of large districts of people, unless those people would relinquish the right of representation in the legislature, a right inestimable to them, and formidable to tyrants only.

He has called together legislature bodies at places unusual, uncomfortable, and distant from the depository of their public records, for the sole purpose of fatiguing them into compliance with his measures.

He has dissolved representative houses repeatedly, for opposing, with many firmness, his invasions on the rights of the people.

He has refused for a long time, after such disolutions, to cause others to be elected; whereby the legislative powers, incapable of annihilation, have returned to the people at large for their exercise; the state remaining, in the mean time, exposed to all the dangers of invasions from without and convulsions within.

He has endeavored to prevent the population of these states; for that purpose obstructing the laws for naturalization of foreigners; refusing to pass others to encourage their migration hither, and raising the conditions of new appropriations of lands.

He has obstructed the administration of justice, by refusing his assent to laws for establishing judiciary powers.

He has made judges dependent on his will alone, for the tenure of their offices, and the amount and payment of their salaries.

He has erected a multitude of new offices, and sent hither swarms of officers to harass our people and eat out their substance.

He has kept among us, in times of peace, standing armies, without the consent of our legislatures.

He has affected to render the military independent of, and superior to, the civil power.

He has combined with others to subject us to a jurisdiction foreign to our constitution, and unacknowledged by our laws, giving his assent to their acts of pretended legislation:

For quartering large bodies of armed troops among us;

For protecting them, by a mock trial, from punishment for any murder which they should commit on the inhabitants of these states;

For cutting off our trade with all parts of the world;

For imposing taxes on us without our consent;

For depriving us, in many cases, of the benefits of trial by jury;

For transporting us beyond seas, to be tried for pretended offenses;

For abolishing the free system of English laws in a neighboring province, establishing therein an arbitrary government, and enlarging its boundaries, so as to render it at once an example and fit instrument for introducing the same absolute rule into these colonies;

For taking away our charters, abolishing our most valuable laws, and altering fundamentally the forms of our governments;

For suspending our own legislatures, and declaring themselves invested with power to legislate for us in all cases whatsoever.

He has abdicated government here, by declaring us out of his protection and waging war against us.

He has plundered our seas, ravaged our coasts, burned our towns, and destroyed the lives of our people.

He is at this time transporting large armies of foreign mercenaries to complete the works of death, desolation, and tyranny already begun with circumstances of cruelty and perfidy scarcely paralleled in the most barbarous ages, and totally unworthy the head of a civilized nation.

He has constrained our fellow-citizens, taken captive on the high seas, to bear arms against their country, to become the executioners of their friends and brethren, or to fall themselves by their hands.

He has excited domestic insurrection among us, and has endeavored to bring on the inhabitants of our frontiers the merciless Indian savages, whose known rule of warfare is an undistinguished destruction of all ages, sexes, and conditions.

In every stage of these oppressions we have petitioned for redress in the most humble terms; our repeated petitions have been answered only by repeated injury. A prince, whose character is thus marked by every act which may define a tyrant, is unfit to be the ruler of a free people.

Nor have we been wanting in our attentions to our British brethren. We have warned them, from time to time, of attempts by their legislature to extend an unwarrantable jurisdiction over us. We have reminded them of the circumstances of our emigration and settlement here. We have appealed to their native justice and magnanimity; and we have conjured them, by the ties of our common kindred, to disavow these usurpations, which would inevitably interrupt our connections and correspondence. They, too, have been deaf to the voice of justice and of consanguinity. We must, therefore, acquiesce in the necessity which denounces our separation, and hold them, as we hold the rest of mankind, enemies in war, in peace friends.

We, therefore, the representatives of the United States of America, in General Congress assembled, appealing to the Supreme Judge of the world for the rectitude of our intentions, do, in the name and by the authority of the good people of these colonies, solemnly publish and declare, that these United Colonies are, and of right ought to be, FREE AND INDEPENDENT STATES; that they are absolved from all allegiance to the British crown, and that all political connection between them and the state of Great Britain is, and ought to be, totally dissolved; and that, as free and independent states, they have full power to levy war, conclude peace, contract alliances, establish commerce, and do all other acts and things which independent states may of right do. And for the support of this declaration, with a firm reliance on the protection of Divine Providence, we mutually pledge to each other our lives, our fortunes, and our sacred honor.

JOHN HANCOCK

BUTTON GWINNETT	THOS. NELSON, JR.	RICHD. STOCKTON
LYMAN HALL	FRANCIS LIGHTFOOT LEE	JNO. WITHERSPOON
GEO. WALTON	CARTER BRAXTON	FRAS. HOPKINSON
WM. HOOPER	ROBT. MORRIS	JOHN HART
JOSEPH HEWES	BENJAMIN RUSH	ABRA. CLARK
JOHN PENN	BENJA. FRANKLIN	JOSIAH BARTLETT
EDWARD RUTLEDGE	JOHN MORTON	WM. WHIPPLE
THOS. HEYWARD, JUNR.	GEO. CLYMER	SAML. ADAMS
THOMAS LYNCH, JUNR.	JAS. SMITH	JOHN ADAMS
ARTHUR MIDDLETON	GEO. TAYLOR	ROBT. TREAT PAINE
SAMUEL CHASE	JAMES WILSON	ELBRIDGE GERRY
WM. PACA	GEO. ROSS	STEP. HOPKINS
THOS. STONE	CAESAR RODNEY	WILLIAM ELLERY
CHARLES CARROLL OF CARROLLTON	GEO. READ	ROGER SHERMAN
GEORGE WYTHE	THO. M'KEAN	SAM'EL. HUNTINGTON
RICHARD HENRY LEE	WM. FLOYD	WM. WILLIAMS
TH. JEFFERSON	PHIL. LIVINGSTON	OLIVER WOLCOTT
BENJ. HARRISON	FRANS. LEWIS	MATTHEW THORNTON
	LEWIS MORRIS	

The Constitution of the United States of America

PREAMBLE

We the people of the United States, in order to form a more perfect union, establish justice, insure domestic tranquillity, provide for the common defense, promote the general welfare, and secure the blessings of liberty to ourselves and our posterity, do ordain and establish this Constitution for the United States of America.

ARTICLE I

Section 1 All legislative powers herein granted shall be vested in a Congress of the United States, which shall consist of a Senate and a House of Representatives.

Section 2 The House of Representatives shall be composed of members chosen every second year by the people of the several States, and the electors in each State shall have the qualifications requisite for electors of the most numerous branch of the State Legislature.

No person shall be a Representative who shall not have attained to the age of twenty-five years, and been seven years a citizen of the United States, and who shall not, when elected, be an inhabitant of that State in which he shall be chosen.

Representatives and direct taxes shall be apportioned among the several States which may be included within this Union, according to their respective numbers, *which shall be determined by adding to the whole number of free persons, including those bound to service for a term of years and excluding Indians not taxed, three-fifths of all other persons.* The actual enumeration shall be made within three years after the first meeting of the Congress of the United States, and within every subsequent term of ten years, in such manner as they shall by law direct. The number of Representatives shall not exceed one for every thirty thousand, but each State shall have at least one Representative, *and until such enumeration shall be made, the State of New Hampshire shall be entitled to choose three, Massachusetts eight, Rhode Island and Providence Plantations one, Connecticut five, New York six, New Jersey four, Pennsylvania eight, Delaware one, Maryland six, Virginia ten, North Carolina five, South Carolina five, and Georgia three.*

Passages no longer in effect are printed in italic type.

When vacancies happen in the representation from any State, the Executive authority thereof shall issue writs of election to fill such vacancies.

The House of Representatives shall choose their Speaker and other officers; and shall have the sole power of impeachment.

Section 3 The Senate of the United States shall be composed of two Senators from each State, *chosen by the legislature thereof,* for six years; and each Senator shall have one vote.

Immediately after they shall be assembled in consequence of the first election, they shall be divided as equally as may be into three classes. The seats of the Senators of the first class shall be vacated at the expiration of the second year, of the second class at the expiration of the fourth year, and of the third class at the expiration of the sixth year, so that one-third may be chosen every second year, so that one-third may be chosen every second year; *and if vacancies happen by resignation or otherwise, during the recess of the legislature of any State, the Executive thereof may make temporary appointments until the next meeting of the legislature, which shall then fill such vacancies.*

No person shall be a Senator who shall not have attained to the age of thirty years, and been nine years a citizen of the United States, and who shall not, when elected, be an inhabitant of that State for which he shall be chosen.

The Vice-President of the United States shall be President of the Senate, but shall have no vote, unless they be equally divided.

The Senate shall choose their other officers, and also a President *pro tempore,* in the absence of the Vice-President, or when he shall exercise the office of President of the United States.

The Senate shall have the sole power to try all impeachments. When sitting for that purpose, they shall be on oath or affirmation. When the President of the United States is tried, the Chief Justice shall preside: and no person shall be convicted without the concurrence of two-thirds of the members present.

Judgment in cases of impeachment shall not extend further than to removal from the office, and disqualification to hold and enjoy any office of honor, trust or profit under the United States: but the party convicted shall nevertheless be liable and subject to indictment, trial, judgment and punishment, according to law.

Section 4 The times, places and manner of holding elections for Senators and Representatives shall be prescribed in each State by the legislature thereof; but the Congress may at any time by law make or alter such regulations, except as to the places of choosing Senators.

The Congress shall assemble at least once in every year, and such meeting *shall be on the first Monday in December, unless they shall by law appoint a different day.*

Section 5 Each house shall be the judge of the elections, returns and qualifications of its own members, and a majority of each small constitute a quorum to do business; but a smaller number may adjourn from day to day, and may be authorized to compel the attendance of absent members, in such manner, and under such penalties, as each house may provide.

Each house may determine the rules of its proceedings, punish its members for disorderly behavior, and with the concurrence of two-thirds, expel a member.

Each house shall keep a journal of its proceedings, and from time to time publish the same, excepting such parts as may in their judgment require secrecy; and the yeas and nays of the members of either house on any question shall, at the desire of one-fifth of those present, be entered on the journal.

Neither house, during the session of Congress, shall, without the consent of the other, adjourn for more than three days, nor to any other place than that in which the two houses shall be sitting.

Section 6 The Senators and Representatives shall receive a compensation for their services, to be ascertained by law and paid out of the treasury of the United States. They shall in all cases except treason, felony and breach of the peace, be privileged from arrest during their attendance at the session of their respective houses, and in going to and returning from the same; and for any speech or debate in either house, they shall not be questioned in any other place.

No Senator or Representative shall, during the time for which he was elected, be appointed to any civil office under the authority of the United States, which shall have been created, or the emoluments whereof shall have been increased, during such time; and no person holding any office under the United States shall be a member of either house during his continuance in office.

Section 7 All bills for raising revenue shall originate in the House of Representatives; but the Senate may propose or concur with amendments as on other bills.

Every bill which shall have passed the House of Representatives and the Senate, shall, before it become a law, be presented to the President of the United States; if he approve he shall sign it, but if not he shall return it with objections to that house in which it originated, who shall enter the objections at large on their journal, and proceed to reconsider it. If after such reconsideration two-thirds of that house shall agree to pass the bill, it shall be sent, together with the objections, to the other house, by which it shall likewise be reconsidered, and, if approved by two-thirds of that house, it shall become a law. But in all such cases the votes of both houses shall be determined by yeas and nays, and the names of the persons voting for and against the bill shall be entered on the journal of each house respectively. If any bill shall not be returned by the President within ten days (Sundays excepted) after it shall have been presented to him, the same shall be a law, in like manner as if he had signed it, unless the Congress by their adjournment prevent its return, in which case it shall not be a law.

Every order, resolution, or vote to which the concurrence of the Senate and House of Representatives may be necessary (except on a question of adjournment) shall be presented to the President of the United States; and before the same shall take effect, shall be approved by him, or being disapproved by him, shall be repassed by two-thirds of the Senate and House of Representatives, according to the rules and limitations prescribed in the case of a bill.

Section 8 The Congress shall have power

To lay and collect taxes, duties, imposts, and excises, to pay the debts and provide for the common defense and general welfare of the United States; but all duties, imposts and excises shall be uniform throughout the United States;

To borrow money on the credit of the United States;

To regulate commerce with foreign nations, and among the several States, and with the Indian tribes;

To establish an uniform rule of naturalization, and uniform laws on the subject of bankruptcies throughout the United States;

To coin money, regulate the value thereof, and of foreign coin, and fix the standard of weights and measures;

To provide for the punishment of counterfeiting the securities and current coin of the United States;

To establish post offices and post roads;

To promote the progress of science and useful arts by securing for limited times to authors and inventors the exclusive right to their respective writings and discoveries;

To constitute tribunals inferior to the Supreme Court;

To define and punish piracies and felonies committed on the high seas and offenses against the law of nations;

To declare war, grant letters of marque and reprisal, and make rules concerning captures on land and water;

To raise and support armies, but no appropriation of money to that use shall be for a longer term than two years;

To provide and maintain a navy;

To make rule for the government and regulation of the land and naval forces;

To provide for calling forth the militia to execute the laws of the Union, suppress insurrections, and repel invasions;

To provide for organizing, arming, and disciplining the militia, and for governing such part of them as may be employed in the service of the United States, reserving to the States respectively the appointment of the officers, and the authority of training the militia according to the discipline prescribed by Congress;

To exercise exclusive legislation in all cases whatsoever, over such district (not exceeding ten miles square) as may, by cession of particular States, and the acceptance of Congress, become the seat of government of the United States, and to exercise like authority over all places purchased by the consent of the legislature of the State, in which the same shall be, for erection of forts, magazines, arsenals, dock-yards, and other needful buildings;—and

To make all laws which shall be necessary and proper for carrying into execution the foregoing powers, and all other powers vested by this Constitution in the government of the United States, or in any department or officer thereof.

Section 9 *The migration or importation of such persons as any of the States now existing shall think proper to admit shall not be prohibited by the Congress prior to the year 1808; but a tax or duty may be imposed on such importation, not exceeding $10 for each person.*

The privilege of the writ of habeas corpus shall not be suspended, unless when in cases of rebellion or invasion the public safety may require it.

No bill of attainder or ex post facto law shall be passed.

No capitation, or other direct, tax shall be laid, unless in proportion to the census or enumeration herein before directed to be taken.

No tax or duty shall be laid on articles exported from any State.

No preference shall be given by any regulation of commerce or revenue to the ports of one State over those of another; nor shall vessels bound to, or from, one State, be obliged to enter, clear, or pay duties in another.

No money shall be drawn from the treasury, but in consequence of appropriations made by law; and a regular statement and account of the receipts and expenditures of all public money shall be published from time to time.

No title of nobility shall be granted by the United States: and no person holding any office of profit or trust under them, shall, without the consent of the Congress, accept of any present, emolument, office, or title, or any kind whatever, from any king, prince, or foreign state.

Section 10 No State shall enter into any treaty, alliance, or confederation; grant letters of marque and reprisal; coin money; emit bills of credit; make anything but gold and silver coin a tender in payment of debts; pass any bill of attainder, ex post facto law, or law impairing the obligation of contracts, or grant any title of nobility.

No State shall, without the consent of Congress, lay any imposts or duties on imports or exports, except what may be absolutely necessary for executing its inspection laws: and the net produce of all duties and imposts, laid by any State on imports or exports, shall be for the use of the treasury of the United States; and all such laws shall be subject to the revision and control of the Congress.

No State shall, without the consent of Congress, lay any duty of tonnage, keep troops or ships of war in time of peace, enter into any agreement or compact with another State, or with a foreign power, or engage in war, unless actually invaded, or in such imminent danger as will not admit of delay.

ARTICLE II

Section 1 The executive power shall be vested in a President of the United States of America. He shall hold his office during the term of four years, and, together with the Vice-President, chosen for the same term, be elected as follows:

Each State shall appoint, in such manner as the legislature thereof may direct, a number of electors, equal to the whole number of Senators and Representatives to which the State may be entitled in the Congress; but no Senator or Representative, or person holding an office of trust or profit under the United States, shall be appointed an elector.

The electors shall meet in their respective States, and vote by ballot for two persons, of whom one at least shall not be an inhabitant of the same State with themselves. And they shall make a list of all the persons voted for, and of the number of votes for each; which list they shall sign and certify, and transmit sealed to the seat of government of the United States, directed to the President of the Senate. The President of the Senate shall, in the presence of the Senate and House of Representatives, open all the certificates, and the votes shall then be counted. The person having the greatest number of votes shall be the President, if such number be a majority of the whole number of electors appointed; and if there be more than one who have such majority, and have an equal number of votes, then the House of Representatives shall immediately choose by ballot one of them for President; and if no person have a majority, then from the five highest on the list said house shall in like manner choose the President. But in choosing the President the votes shall be taken by States, the representation from each State having one vote; a quorum for this purpose shall consist of a member or members from two-thirds of the States, and a majority of all the States shall be necessary to a choice. In every case, after the choice of the President, the person having the greatest number of votes of the electors shall be the Vice-President. But if there should remain two or more who have equal votes, the Senate shall choose from them by ballot the Vice-President.

The Congress may determine the time of choosing the electors and the day on which they shall give their votes; which day shall be the same throughout the United States.

No person except a natural-born citizen, *or a citizen of the United States at the time of the adoption of this Constitution,* shall be eligible to the office of President; neither shall any person be eligible to that office who shall not have attained to the age of thirty-five years, and been fourteen years a resident within the United States.

In case of the removal of the President from office or of his death, resignation, or inability to discharge the powers and duties of the said office, the same shall devolve on the Vice-President, and the Congress may by law provide for the case of removal, death, resignation, or inability, both of the President and Vice-President, declaring what officer shall then act as President, and such officer shall act accordingly, until the disability be removed, or a President shall be elected.

The President shall, at stated times, receive for his services a compensation, which shall neither be increased nor diminished during the period for which he shall have been elected, and he shall not receive within that period any other emolument from the United States, or any of them.

Before he enter on the execution of his office, he shall take the following oath or affirmation:—"I do solemnly swear (or affirm) that I will faithfully execute the office of the President of the United States, and will to the best of my ability preserve, protect and defend the Constitution of the United States."

Section 2   The President shall be commander in chief of the army and navy of the United States, and of the militia of the several States, when called into the actual service of the United States; he may require the opinion, in writing, of the principal officer in each of the executive departments, upon any subject relating to the duties of their respective offices, and he shall have power to grant reprieves and pardons for offenses against the United States, except in cases of impeachment.

He shall have power, by and with the advice and consent of the Senate, to make treaties, provided two-thirds of the Senators present concur; and he shall nominate, and by and with advice and consent of the Senate, shall appoint ambassadors, other public ministers and consuls, judges of the Supreme Court, and all other officers of the United States, whose appointments are not herein otherwise provided for, and which shall be established by law: but Congress may by law vest the appointment of such inferior officers, as they think proper, in the President alone, in the courts of law, or in the heads of departments.

The President shall have power to fill up all vacancies that may happen during the recess of the Senate, by granting commissions which shall expire at the end of their next session.

Section 3   He shall from time to time give to the Congress information of the state of the Union, and recommend to their consideration such measures as he shall judge necessary and expedient; he may, on extraordinary occasions, convene both houses, or either of them, and in case of disagreement between them, with respect to the time of adjournment, he may adjourn them to such time as he shall think proper; he shall receive ambassadors and other public ministers; he shall take care that the laws be faithfully executed, and shall commission all the officers of the United States.

Section 4   The President, Vice-President and all civil officers of the United States shall be removed from office on impeachment for, and on conviction of, treason, bribery, or other high crimes and misdemeanors.

ARTICLE III

Section 1   The judicial power of the United States shall be vested in one Supreme Court, and in such inferior courts as the Congress may from time to time ordain and establish. The judges, both of the Supreme and inferior courts, shall hold their offices during good behavior, and shall, at stated times, receive for their services a compensation which shall not be diminished during their continuance in office.

Section 2   The judicial power shall extend to all cases, in law and equity, arising under this Constitution, the laws of the United States, and treaties made, or which shall be made, under their authority;—to all cases affecting ambassadors, other public ministers and consuls;—to all cases of admiralty and maritime jurisdiction;—to controversies to which the United States shall be a party;—to controversies between two or more States;—*between a State and citizens of another State;*—between citizens of different States;—between citizens of the same State claiming lands under grants of different States, and between a State, or the citizens thereof, and foreign states, citizens or subjects.

In all cases affecting ambassadors, other public ministers and consuls, and those in which a State shall be party, the Supreme Court shall have original jurisdiction. In all the other cases before mentioned, the Supreme Court shall have appellate jurisdiction, both as to law and fact, with such exceptions, and under such regulations, as the Congress shall make.

The trial of all crimes, except in cases of impeachment, shall be by jury; and such trial shall be held in the State where said crimes shall have been committed; but when not committed within any State, the trial shall be at place or places as the Congress may by law have directed.

Section 3 Treason against the United States shall consist only in levying war against them, or in adhering to their enemies, giving them aid and comfort. No person shall be convinced of treason unless on the testimony of two witnesses to the same overt act, or an confession in open court.

The Congress shall have power to declare the punishment of treason, but no attainder of treason shall work corruption of blood, or forfeiture except during the life of the person attainted.

ARTICLE IV

Section 1 Full faith and credit shall be given in each State to the public acts, records, and judicial proceedings of every other State. And the Congress may by general laws prescribe the manner in which such acts, records, and proceedings shall be proved, and the effect thereof.

Section 2 The citizens of each State shall be entitled to all privileges and immunities of citizens in the several States.

A person charged in any State with treason, felony, or other crime, who shall flee from justice, and be found in another State, shall on demand of the executive authority of the State from which he fled, be delivered up, to be removed to the State having jurisdiction of the crime.

No person held to service or labor in one State, under the laws thereof, escaping into another, shall, in consequence of any law or regulation therein, be discharged from such service or labor, but shall be delivered up on claim of the party to whom such service or labor may be due.

Section 3 New States may be admitted by the Congress into this Union; but no new State shall be formed or erected within the jurisdiction of any other State; nor any State be formed by the junction of two or more States, or parts of States, without the consent of the legislatures of the States concerned as well as of the Congress.

The Congress shall have power to dispose of and make all needful rules and regulations respecting the territory or other property belonging to the United States; and nothing in this Consitution shall be so construed as to prejudice any claims of the United States, or of any particular State.

Section 4 The United States shall guarantee to every State in this Union a republican form of government, and shall protect each of them against invasion; and on application of the legislature, or of the executive (when the legislature cannot be convened), against domestic violence.

ARTICLE V

The Congress, whenever two-thirds of both houses shall deem it necessary, shall propose amendments to this Constitution, or, on the application of the legislatures of two-thirds of the several States, shall call a convention for proposing amendments, which, in either case, shall be valid to all intents and purposes, as part of this Constitution, when ratified by the legislatures of three-fourths of the several States, or by conventions in three-fourths thereof, as the one or the other mode of ratification may be proposed by the Congress; provided *that no amendments which may be made prior to the year one thousand eight hundred and eight shall in any manner affect the first and fourth clauses in the ninth section of the first article;* and that no State, without its consent, shall be deprived of its equal suffrage in the Senate.

ARTICLE VI

All debts contracted and engagements entered into, before the adoption of this Constitution, shall be as valid against the United States under this Constitution, as under the Confederation.

This Constitution, and the laws of the United States which shall be made in pursuance thereof; and all treaties made, or which shall be made, under the authority of United States, shall be the supreme law of the land; and the judges in every State shall be bound thereby, anything in the Constitution or laws of any State to the contrary notwithstanding.

The Senators and Representatives before mentioned, and the members of the several State legislatures, and all executive and judicial officers, both of the United States and of the several States, shall be bound by oath or affirmation to support this Constitution; but no religious test shall ever be required as a qualification to any office or public trust under the United States.

ARTICLE VII

The ratification of the conventions of nine States shall be sufficient for the establishment of this Constitution between the States so ratifying the same.

Done in Convention by the unanimous consent of the States present, the seventeenth day of September in the year of our Lord one thousand seven hundred and eighty-seven and of the Independence of the United States of America the twelfth. In witness whereof we have hereunto subscribed our names.

GEORGE WASHINGTON,
President and Deputy from Virginia

New Hampshire
JOHN LANGDON
NICHOLAS GILMAN

Massachusetts
NATHANIEL GORHAM
RUFUS KING

Connecticut
WILLIAM S. JOHNSON
ROGER SHERMAN

New York
ALEXANDER HAMILTON

New Jersey
WILLIAM LIVINGSTON
DAVID BREARLEY
WILLIAM PATERSON
JONATHAN DAYTON

Pennsylvania
BENJAMIN FRANKLIN
THOMAS MIFFLIN
ROBERT MORRIS
GEORGE CLYMER
THOMAS FITZSIMONS
JARED INGERSOLL
JAMES WILSON
GOUVERNEUR MORRIS

Delaware
GEORGE READ
GUNNING BEDFORD, JR.
JOHN DICKINSON
RICHARD BASSETT
JACOB BROOM

Maryland
JAMES McHENRY
DANIEL OF ST. THOMAS JENIFER
DANIEL CARROLL

Virginia
JOHN BLAIR
JAMES MADISON, JR.

North Carolina
WILLIAM BLOUNT
RICHARD DOBBS SPRAIGHT
HU WILLIAMSON

South Carolina
J. RUTLEDGE
CHARLES C. PINCKNEY
PIERCE BUTLER

Georgia
WILLIAM FEW
ABRAHAM BALDWIN

Amendments to the Constitution

*The first ten Amendments (the Bill of Rights) were adopted in 1791.

AMENDMENT I

Congress shall make no law respecting an establishment of religion, or prohibiting the free exercise thereof; or abridging the freedom of speech, or of the press; or the right of the people peaceably to assemble, and to petition the government for a redress of grievances.

AMENDMENT II

A well-regulated militia being necessary to the security of a free State, the right of the people to keep and bear arms shall not be infringed.

AMENDMENT III

No soldier shall, in time of peace, be quartered in any house without the consent of the owner, nor in time of war, but in a manner to be prescribed by law.

AMENDMENT IV

The right of the people to be secure in their persons, houses, papers, and effects, against unreasonable searches and seizures, shall not be violated, and no warrants shall issue but upon probable cause, supported by oath or affirmation, and particularly describing the place to be searched, and the persons or things to be seized.

AMENDMENT V

No person shall be held to answer for a capital, or otherwise infamous crime, unless on a presentment or indictment of a grand jury, except in cases arising in the land or naval forces, or in the militia, when in actual service in time of war or public danger; nor shall any person be subject for the same offense to be twice put in jeopardy of life or limb; nor shall be compelled in any criminal case to be a witness against himself, nor be deprived of life, liberty, or property, without due process of law; nor shall private property be taken for public use without just compensation.

AMENDMENT VI

In all criminal prosecutions, the accused shall enjoy the right to a speedy and public trial, by an impartial jury of the State and district shall have been previously ascertained by law, and to be informed of the nature and cause of the accusation; to be confronted with the witnesses against him; to have compulsory process for obtaining witnesses in his favor, and to have the assistance of counsel for his defense.

AMENDMENT VII

In suits at common law, where the value in controversy shall exceed twenty dollars, the right of trial by jury shall be preserved, and no fact tried by a jury shall be otherwise reexamined in any court of the United States, than according to the rules of the common law.

AMENDMENT VIII

Excessive bail shall not be required, nor excessive fines imposed, nor cruel and unusual punishments inflicted.

AMENDMENT IX

The enumeration in the Constitution, of certain rights, shall not be construed to deny or disparage others retained by the people.

AMENDMENT X

The powers not delegated to the United States by the Constitution, nor prohibited by it to the States, are reserved to the States respectively, or to the people.

AMENDMENT XI [Adopted 1798]

The judicial power of the United States shall not be construed to extend to any suit in law or equity, commenced or prosecuted against one of the United States by citizens of another State, or by citizens or subjects of any foreign state.

AMENDMENT XII [Adopted 1804]

The electors shall meet in their respective States, and vote by ballot for President and Vice-President, one of whom, at least, shall not be an inhabitant of the same State with themselves; they shall name in their ballots the person voted for as President, and in distinct ballots the person voted for as Vice-President, and they shall make distinct lists of all persons voted for as President, and of all persons voted for as Vice-President, and of the number of votes for each, which lists they shall sign and certify, and transmit sealed to the seat of government of the United States, directed to the President of the Senate;—the President of the Senate shall, in the presence of the Senate and House of Representatives, open all the certificates and the votes shall then be counted;—the person having the greatest number of votes for President shall be the President, if such number be a majority of the whole number of electors appointed; and if no person have such majority, then from the persons having the highest numbers not exceeding three on the list of those voted for as

President, the House of Representatives shall choose immediately, by ballot, the President. But in choosing the President, the votes shall be taken by States, the representation from each State having one vote; a quorum for this purpose shall consist of a member or members from two-thirds of the States, and a majority of all the States shall be necessary to a choice. And if the House of Representatives shall not choose a President whenever the right of choice shall devolve upon them, before *the fourth day of March* next following, then the Vice-President shall act as President, as in the case of the death or other constitutional disability of the President.

The person having the greatest number of votes as Vice-President shall be the Vice-President, if such number be a majority of the whole number of electors appointed; and if no person have a majority, then from the two highest numbers on the list the Senate shall choose the Vice-President; a quorum for the purpose shall consist of two-thirds of the whole number of Senators, and a majority of the whole number shall be necessary to a choice. But no person constitutionally ineligible to the office of President shall be eligible to that of Vice-President of the United States.

AMENDMENT XIII [Adopted 1865]

Section 1 Neither slavery nor involuntary servitude, except as a punishment for crime whereof the party shall have been duly convicted, shall exist within the United States, or any place subject to their jurisdiction.

Section 2 Congress shall have power to enforce this article by appropriate legislation.

AMENDMENT XIV [Adopted 1868]

Section 1   All persons born or naturalized in the United States, and subject to the jurisdiction thereof, are citizens of the United States and of the State wherein they reside. No State shall make or enforce any law which shall abridge the privileges or immunities of citizens of the United States; nor shall any State deprive any person of life, liberty, or property, without due process of law; nor deny to any person within its jurisdiction the equal protection of the laws.

Section 2   Representatives shall be apportioned among the several States according to their respective numbers, counting the whole number of persons in each State, excluding Indians not taxed. But when the right to vote at any election for the choice of Electors for President and Vice-President of the United States, Representatives in Congress, the executive and judicial officers of a State, or the members of the legislature thereof, is denied to any of the male inhabitants of such State, being twenty-one years of age and citizens of the United States, or in any

way abridged, except for participation in rebellion, or other crime, the basis of representation therein shall be reduced in the proportion which the number of such male citizens shall bear to the whole number of male citizens twenty-one years of age in such State.

Section 3 No person shall be a Senator or Representative in Congress, or Elector of President and Vice-President, or hold any office, civil or military, under the United States, or under any State, who, having previously taken an oath, as a member of Congress, or as an officer of the United States, or as a member of any State legislature, or as an executive or judicial officer of any State, to support the Constitution of the United States, shall have engaged in insurrection or rebellion against the same, or given aid or comfort to the enemies thereof. Congress may, by a vote of two-thirds of each house, remove such disability.

Section 4 The validity of the public debt of the United States, authorized by law, including debts incurred for payment of pensions and bounties for services in suppressing insurrection or rebellion, shall not be questioned. But neither the United States nor any State shall assume or pay any debt or obligation incurred in aid of insurrection or rebellion against the United States, or any claim for the loss of emancipation of any slave; but all such debts, obligations, and claims shall be held illegal and void.

Section 5 The Congress shall have power to enforce, by appropriate legislation, the provisions of this article.

AMENDMENT XV [Adopted 1870]

Section 1 The right of citizens of the United States to vote shall not be denied or abridged by the United States or by any State on account of race, color, or previous condition of servitude.

Section 2 The Congress shall have power to enforce this article by appropriate legislation.

AMENDMENT XVI [Adopted 1913]

The Congress shall have power to lay and collect taxes on incomes, from whatever source derived, without apportionment among the several States, and without regard to any census or enumeration.

AMENDMENT XVII [Adopted 1913]

Section 1 The Senate of the United States shall be composed of two Senators from each State, elected by the people thereof, for six years; and each Senator shall have one vote. The electors in each State shall have the qualifications requisite for electors of [voters for] the most numerous branch of the State legislatures.

Section 2   When vacancies happen in the representation of any State in the Senate, the executive authority of such State shall issue writs of election to fill such vacancies: Provided, that the Legislature of any State may empower the executive thereof to make temporary appointments until the people fill the vacancies by election as the Legislature may direct.

Section 3   This amendment shall not be so construed as to affect the election or term of any Senator chosen before it becomes valid as part of the Constitution.

AMENDMENT XVIII [Adopted 1919; Repealed 1933]

Section 1   After one year from the ratification of this article the manufacture, sale, or transportation of intoxicating liquors within, the importation thereof into, or the exportation thereof from the United States and all territory subject to the jurisdiction thereof, for beverage purposes, is hereby prohibited.

Section 2   The Congress and the several States shall have concurrent power to enforce this article by appropriate legislation.

Section 3   This article shall be inoperative unless it shall have been ratified as an amendment to the Constitution by the legislatures of the several States, as provided by the Constitution, within seven years from the date of the submission thereof to the States by the Congress.

AMENDMENT XIX [Adopted 1920]

Section 1   The right of citizens of the United States to vote shall not be denied or abridged by the United States or by any State on account of sex.

Section 2   The Congress shall have power to enforce this article by appropriate legislation.

AMENDMENT XX [Adopted 1933]

Section 1   The terms of the President and Vice-President shall end at noon on the 20th day of January, and the terms of Senators and Representatives at noon on the 3d day of January, of the years in which such terms would have ended if this article had not been ratified; and the terms of their successors shall then begin.

Section 2   The Congress shall assemble at least once in every year, and such meeting shall begin at noon on the 3d day of January, unless they shall by law appoint a different day.

Section 3   If, at the time fixed for the beginning of the term of the President, the President-elect shall have died, the Vice-President-elect shall become President. If a President shall not have been chosen before the time fixed for the beginning of his term, or if the President-elect shall have failed to qualify, then the Vice-President-elect shall act as President until a President shall have qualified; and the Congress may by law provide for the case wherein neither a President-elect nor a Vice-President-elect shall have qualified, declaring who shall then act as President, or the manner in which one who is to act shall be selected, and such persons shall act accordingly until a President or Vice-President shall have qualified.

Section 4   The Congress may by law provide for the case of the death of any of the persons from whom the House of Representatives may choose a President whenever the right of choice shall have devolved upon them, and for the case of the death of any of the persons from whom the Senate may choose a Vice-President whenever the right of choice shall have devolved upon them.

Section 5   Sections 1 and 2 shall take effect on the 15th day of October following the ratification of this article.

Section 6   This article shall be inoperative unless it shall have been ratified as an amendment to the Constitution by the Legislatures of three-fourths of the several States within seven years from the date of its submission.

AMENDMENT XXI [Adopted 1933]

Section 1   The eighteenth article of amendment to the Constitution of the United States is hereby repealed.

Section 2   The transportation or importation into any State, Territory, or Possession of the United States for delivery or use therein of intoxicating liquors, in violation of the laws thereof, is hereby prohibited.

Section 3   This article shall be inoperative unless it shall have been ratified as an amendment to the Constitution by conventions in the several States, as provided in the Constitution, within seven years from the date of submission thereof to the States by the Congress.

AMENDMENT XXII [Adopted 1951]

Section 1   No person shall be elected to the office of President more than twice, and no person who has held the office of President, or acted as President, for more than two years of term to which some other person was elected President shall be elected to the office of President more than once. But this article shall not apply to any person holding the office of President when this article was proposed by the Congress, and shall not prevent any person who may be holding the office of

President, or acting as President, during the term within which this article becomes operative from holding office of President or acting as President during the remainder of such term.

Section 2   This article shall be inoperative unless it shall have been ratified as an amendment to the Consitution by the legislatures of three-fourths of the several States within seven years from the date of its submission to the States by the Congress.

AMENDMENT XXIII [Adopted 1961]

Section 1 The District constituting the seat of Government of the United States shall appoint in such manner as the Congress may direct:

A number of electors of President and Vice-President equal to the whole number of Senators and Representatives in Congress to which the District would be entitled if it were a State, but in no event more than the least populous State; they shall be in addition to those appointed by the States, but they shall be considered for the purposes of the election of President and Vice-President, to be electors appointed by a State; and they shall meet in the District and perform such duties as provided by the twelfth article of amendment.

Section 2   The Congress shall have the power to enforce this article by appropriate legislation.

AMENDMENT XXIV [Adopted 1964]

Section 1   The right of citizens of the United States to vote in any primary or other election for President or Vice-President, for electors for President or Vice-President, or for Senator or Representative in Congress, shall not be denied or abridged by the United States or any State by reason of failure to pay any poll tax or other tax.

Section 2   The Congress shall have the power to enforce this article by appropriate legislation.

AMENDMENT XXV [Adopted 1967]

Section 1   In case of the removal of the President from office or of his death or resignation, the Vice President shall become President.

Section 2   Whenever there is a vacancy in the office of the Vice President, the President shall nominate a Vice President who shall take office upon confirmation by a majority vote of both Houses of Congress.

Section 3 Whenever the President transmits to the President pro tempore of the Senate and the Speaker of the House of Representatives has written declaration that he is unable to discharge the powers and duties of his office, and until he transmits to them a written declaration to the contrary, such powers and duties shall be discharged by the Vice President as Acting President.

Section 4   Whenever the Vice President and a majority of either the principal officers of the executive departments or of such other body as Congress may by law provide, transmit to the President pro tempore of the Senate and the Speaker of the House of Representatives their written declaration that the President is unable to discharge the powers and duties of his office, the Vice President shall immediately assume the powers and duties of the office as Acting President.

Thereafter, when the President transmits to the President pro tempore of the Senate and the Speaker of the House of Representatives his written declaration that no inability exists, he shall resume the powers and duties of his office unless the Vice President and a majority of either the principal officers of the executive department[s] or of such other body as Congress may be law provide, transmit within four days to the President pro tempore of the Senate and the Speaker of the House of Representatives their written declaration that the President is unable to discharge the powers and duties of his office. Thereupon Congress shall decide the issue, assembling within forty-eight hours for that purpose if not in session. If the Congress, within twenty-one days after receipt of the latter written declaration, or if Congress is not in session, within twenty-one days after Congress is required to assemble, determines by two-thirds vote of both Houses that the President is unable to discharge the powers and duties of his office, the Vice President shall continue to discharge the same as Acting President; otherwise, the President shall resume the powers and duties of his office.

AMENDMENT XXVI [Adopted 1971]

Section 1   The right of citizens of the United States, who are eighteen years of age or older, to vote shall not be denied or abridged by the United States or by any State on account of age.

Section 2   The Congress shall have power to enforce this article by appropriate legislation.

Presidential Elections

Year	Candidates	Parties	Popular Vote		Electoral Vote	Voter Participation
1789	**GEORGE WASHINGTON**		*		69	
	John Adams				34	
	Others				35	
1792	**GEORGE WASHINGTON**		*		132	
	John Adams				77	
	George Clinton				50	
	Others				5	
1796	**JOHN ADAMS**	Federalist	*		71	
	Thomas Jefferson	Democratic-Republican			68	
	Thomas Pinckney	Federalist			59	
	Aaron Burr	Dem.-Rep.			30	
	Others				48	
1800	**THOMAS JEFFERSON**	Dem.-Rep.	*		73	
	Aaron Burr	Dem.-Rep.			73	
	John Adams	Federalist			65	
	C. C. Pinckney	Federalist			64	
	John Jay	Federalist			1	
1804	**THOMAS JEFFERSON**	Dem.-Rep.	*		162	
	C.C. Pinckney	Federalist			14	
1808	**JAMES MADISON**	Dem.-Rep.	*		122	
	C. C. Pinckney	Federalist			47	
	George Clinton	Dem.-Rep.			6	
1812	**JAMES MADISON**	Dem.-Rep.	*		128	
	De Witt Clinton	Federalist			89	
1816	**JAMES MONROE**	Dem.-Rep.	*		183	
	Rufus King	Federalist			34	
1820	**JAMES MONROE**	Dem.-Rep.	*		231	
	John Quincy Adams	Dem.-Rep.			1	
1824	**JOHN Q. ADAMS**	Dem.-Rep.	108,740	(30.5%)	84	26.9%
	Andrew Jackson	Dem.-Rep.	153,544	(43.1%)	99	
	William H. Crawford	Dem.-Rep.	46,618	(13.1%)	41	
	Henry Clay	Dem.-Rep.	47,136	(13.2%)	37	
1828	**ANDREW JACKSON**	Democratic	647,286	(56.0%)	178	57.6%
	John Quincy Adams	National Republican	508,064	(44.0%)	83	
1832	**ANDREW JACKSON**	Democratic	687,502	(55.0%)	219	55.4%
	Henry Clay	National Republican	530,189	(42.4%)	49	
	John Floyd	Independent			11	
	William Wirt	Anti-Mason	33,108	(2.6%)	7	

*Electors selected by state legislatures.

Year	Candidates	Parties	Popular Vote		Electoral Vote	Voter Participation
1836	**MARTIN VAN BUREN**	Democratic	765,483	(50.9%)	170	57.8%
	W. H. Harrison	Whig			73	
	Hugh L. White	Whig	739,795	(49.1%)	26	
	Daniel Webster	Whig			14	
	W. P. Magnum	Independent			11	
1840	**WILLIAM H. HARRISON**	Whig	1,274,624	(53.1%)	234	80.2%
	Martin Van Buren	Democratic	1,127,781	(46.9%)	60	
	J. G. Birney	Liberty	7069		—	
1844	**JAMES K. POLK**	Democratic	1,338,464	(49.6%)	170	78.9%
	Henry Clay	Whig	1,300,097	(48.1%)	105	
	J. G. Birney	Liberty	62,300	(2.3%)	—	
1848	**ZACHARY TAYLOR**	Whig	1,360,967	(47.4%)	163	72.7%
	Lewis Cass	Democratic	1,222,342	(42.5%)	127	
	Martin Van Buren	Free-Soil	291,263	(10.1%)	—	
1852	**FRANKLIN PIERCE**	Democratic	1,601,117	(50.9%)	254	69.6%
	Winfield Scott	Whig	1,385,453	(44.1%)	42	
	John P. Hale	Free-Soil	155,825	(5.0%)	—	
1856	**JAMES BUCHANAN**	Democratic	1,832,955	(45.3%)	174	78.9%
	John C. Frémont	Republican	1,339,932	(33.1%)	114	
	Millard Fillmore	American	871,731	(21.6%)	8	
1860	**ABRAHAM LINCOLN**	Republican	1,865,593	(39.8%)	180	81.2%
	Stephen A. Douglas	Democratic	1,382,713	(29.5%)	12	
	John C. Breckinridge	Democratic	848,356	(18.1%)	72	
	John Bell	Union	592,906	(12.6%)	39	
1864	**ABRAHAM LINCOLN**	Republican	2,213,655	(55.0%)	212	73.8%
	George B. McClellan	Democratic	1,805,237	(45.0%)	21	
1868	**ULYSSES S. GRANT**	Republican	3,012,833	(52.7%)	214	78.1%
	Horatio Seymour	Democratic	2,703,249	(47.3%)	80	
1872	**ULYSSES S. GRANT**	Republican	3,597,132	(55.6%)	286	71.3%
	Horace Greeley	Democratic; Liberal Republican	2,834,125	(43.9%)	66	
1876	**RUTHERFORD B. HAYES**	Republican	4,036,298	(48.0%)	185	81.8%
	Samuel J. Tilden	Democratic	4,300,590	(51.0%)	184	
1880	**JAMES A. GARFIELD**	Republican	4,454,416	(48.5%)	214	79.4%
	Winfield S. Hancock	Democratic	4,444,952	(48.1%)	155	
1884	**GROVER CLEVELAND**	Democratic	4,874,986	(48.5%)	219	77.5%
	James G. Blaine	Republican	4,851,981	(48.2%)	182	
1888	**BENJAMIN HARRISON**	Republican	5,439,853	(47.9%)	233	79.3%
	Grover Cleveland	Democratic	5,540,309	(48.6%)	168	

Year	Candidates	Parties	Popular Vote		Electoral Vote	Voter Participation
1892	**GROVER CLEVELAND**	Democratic	5,556,918	(46.1%)	277	74.7%
	Benjamin Harrison	Republican	5,176,108	(43.0%)	145	
	James B. Weaver	People's	1,041,028	(8.5%)	22	
1896	**WILLIAM McKINLEY**	Republican	7,104,779	(51.1%)	271	79.3%
	William J. Bryan	Democratic People's	6,502,925	(47.7%)	176	
1900	**WILLIAM McKINLEY**	Republican	7,207,923	(51.7%)	292	73.2%
	William J. Bryan	Dem.-Populist	6,358,133	(45.5%)	155	
1904	**THEODORE ROOSEVELT**	Republican	7,623,486	(57.9%)	336	65.2%
	Alton B. Parker	Democratic	5,077,911	(37.6%)	140	
	Eugene V. Debs	Socialist	402,283	(3.0%)	—	
1908	**WILLIAM H. TAFT**	Republican	7,678,908	(51.6%)	321	65.4%
	William J. Bryan	Democratic	6,409,104	(43.1%)	162	
	Eugene V. Debs	Socialist	420,793	(2.8%)	—	
1912	**WOODROW WILSON**	Democratic	6,293,454	(41.9%)	435	58.8%
	Theodore Roosevelt	Progressive	4,119,538	(27.4%)	88	
	William H. Taft	Republican	3,484,980	(23.2%)	8	
	Eugene V. Debs	Socialist	900,672	(6.0%)	—	
1916	**WOODROW WILSON**	Democratic	9,129,606	(49.4%)	277	61.6%
	Charles E. Hughes	Republican	8,538,221	(46.2%)	254	
	A. L. Benson	Socialist	585,113	(3.2%)	—	
1920	**WARREN G. HARDING**	Republican	16,152,200	(60.4%)	404	49.2%
	James M. Cox	Democratic	9,147,353	(34.2%)	127	
	Eugene V. Debs	Socialist	919,799	(3.4%)	—	
1924	**CALVIN COOLIDGE**	Republican	15,725,016	(54.0%)	382	48.9%
	John W. Davis	Democratic	8,386,503	(28.8%)	136	
	Robert M. LaFollette	Progressive	4,822,856	(16.6%)	13	
1928	**HERBERT HOOVER**	Republican	21,391,381	(58.2%)	444	56.9%
	Alfred E. Smith	Democratic	15,016,443	(40.9%)	87	
	Norman Thomas	Socialist	267,835	(0.7%)	—	
1932	**FRANKLIN D. ROOSEVELT**	Democratic	22,821,857	(57.4%)	472	56.9%
	Herbert Hoover	Republican	15,761,841	(39.7%)	59	
	Norman Thomas	Socialist	881,951	(2.2%)	—	
1936	**FRANKLIN D. ROOSEVELT**	Democratic	27,751,597	(60.8%)	523	61.0%
	Alfred M. Landon	Republican	16,679,583	(36.5%)	8	
	William Lemke	Union	882,479	(1.9%)	—	
1940	**FRANKLIN D. ROOSEVELT**	Democratic	27,244,160	(54.8%)	449	62.5%
	Wendell L. Willkie	Republican	22,305,198	(44.8%)	82	
1944	**FRANKLIN D. ROOSEVELT**	Democratic	25,602,504	(53.5%)	432	55.9%
	Thomas E. Dewey	Republican	22,006,285	(46.0%)	99	
1948	**HARRY S TRUMAN**	Democratic	24,105,695	(49.5%)	304	53.0%
	Thomas E. Dewey	Republican	21,969,170	(45.1%)	189	
	J. Strom Thurmond	State-Rights Democratic	1,169,021	(2.4%)	38	
	Henry A. Wallace	Progressive	1,156,103	(2.4%)	—	
1952	**DWIGHT D. EISENHOWER**	Republican	33,936,252	(55.1%)	442	63.3%
	Adlai E. Stevenson	Democratic	27,314,992	(44.4%)	89	

Year	Candidates	Parties	Popular Vote		Electoral Vote	Voter Participation
1956	**DWIGHT D. EISENHOWER**	Republican	35,575,420	(57.6%)	457	60.6%
	Adlai E. Stevenson	Democratic	26,033,066	(42.1%)	73	
	Other	—	—		1	
1960	**JOHN F. KENNEDY**	Democratic	34,227,096	(49.9%)	303	62.8%
	Richard M. Nixon	Republican	34,108,546	(49.6%)	219	
	Other	—	—		15	
1964	**LYNDON B. JOHNSON**	Democratic	43,126,506	(61.1%)	486	61.7%
	Barry M. Goldwater	Republican	27,176,799	(38.5%)	52	
1968	**RICHARD M. NIXON**	Republican	31,770,237	(43.4%)	301	60.6%
	Hubert H. Humphrey	Democratic	31,270,533	(42.7%)	191	
	George Wallace	American Indep.	9,906,141	(13.5%)	46	
1972	**RICHARD M. NIXON**	Republican	47,169,911	(60.7%)	520	55.2%
	George S. McGovern	Democratic	29,170,383	(37.5%)	17	
	Other	—	—		1	
1976	**JIMMY CARTER**	Democratic	40,828,587	(50.0%)	297	53.5%
	Gerald R. Ford	Republican	39,147,613	(47.9%)	241	
	Other	—	1,575,459	(2.1%)	—	
1980	**RONALD REAGAN**	Republican	43,901,812	(50.7%)	489	52.6%
	Jimmy Carter	Democratic	35,483,820	(41.0%)	49	
	John B. Anderson	Independent	5,719,722	(6.6%)	—	
	Ed Clark	Libertarian	921,188	(1.1%)	—	
1984	**RONALD REAGAN**	Republican	54,455,075	(59.0%)	525	53.3%
	Walter Mondale	Democratic	37,577,185	(41.0%)	13	
1988	**GEORGE H. BUSH**	Republican	48,883,809	(53.9%)	426	50.0%
	Michael S. Dukakis	Democratic	41,808,253	(46.1%)	111	

Vice-Presidents and Cabinet Members by Administration

The Washington Administration (1789-1797)

Vice-President	John Adams	1789-1797
Secretary of State	Thomas Jefferson	1789-1793
	Edmund Randolph	1794-1795
	Timothy Pickering	1795-1797
Secretary of Treasury	Alexander Hamilton	1789-1795
	Oliver Wolcott	1795-1797
Secretary of War	Henry Knox	1789-1794
	Timothy Pickering	1795-1796
	James McHenry	1796-1797
Attorney General	Edmund Randolph	1789-1793
	William Bradford	1794-1795
	Charles Lee	1795-1797
Postmaster General	Samuel Osgood	1789-1791
	Timothy Pickering	1791-1794
	Joseph Habersham	1795-1797

The John Adams Administration (1797-1801)

Vice-President	Thomas Jefferson	1797-1801
Secretary of State	Timothy Pickering	1797-1800
	John Marshall	1800-1801
Secretary of Treasury	Oliver Wolcott	1797-1800
	Samuel Dexter	1800-1801
Secretary of War	James McHenry	1797-1800
	Samuel Dexter	1800-1801
Attorney General	Charles Lee	1797-1801
Postmaster General	Joseph Habersham	1797-1801
Secretary of Navy	Benjamin Stoddert	1798-1801

The Jefferson Administration (1801-1809)

Vice-President	Aaron Burr	1801-1805
	George Clinton	1805-1809
Secretary of State	James Madison	1801-1809
Secretary of Treasury	Samuel Dexter	1801
	Albert Gallatin	1801-1809
Secretary of War	Henry Dearborn	1801-1809
Attorney General	Levi Lincoln	1801-1805
	Robert Smith	1805
	John Breckinridge	1805-1806
	Caesar Rodney	1807-1809
Postmaster General	Joseph Habersham	1801
	Gideon Granger	1801-1809
Secretary of Navy	Robert Smith	1801-1809

The Madison Administration (1809-1817)

Vice-President	George Clinton	1809-1813
	Elbridge Gerry	1813-1817
Secretary of State	Robert Smith	1809-1811
	James Monroe	1811-1817
Secretary of Treasury	Albert Gallatin	1809-1813
	George Campbell	1814
	Alexander Dallas	1814-1816
	William Crawford	1816-1817
Secretary of War	William Eustis	1809-1812
	John Armstrong	1813-1814
	James Monroe	1814-1815
	William Crawford	1815-1817
Attorney General	Caesar Rodney	1809-1811
	William Pinkney	1811-1814
	Richard Rush	1814-1817
Postmaster General	Gideon Granger	1809-1814
	Return Meigs	1814-1817
Secretary of Navy	Paul Hamilton	1809-1813
	William Jones	1813-1814
	Benjamin Crowninshield	1814-1817

The Monroe Administration (1817-1825)

Vice-President	Daniel Tompkins	1817-1825
Secretary of State	John Quincy Adams	1817-1825
Secretary of Treasury	William Crawford	1817-1825
Secretary of War	George Graham	1817
	John C. Calhoun	1817-1825
Attorney General	Richard Rush	1817
	William Wirt	1817-1825
Postmaster General	Return Meigs	1817-1823
	John McLean	1823-1825
Secretary of Navy	Benjamin Crowninshield	1817-1818
	Smith Thompson	1818-1823
	Samuel Southard	1823-1825

The John Quincy Adams Administration (1825-1829)

Vice-President	John C. Calhoun	1825-1829
Secretary of State	Henry Clay	1825-1829
Secretary of Treasury	Richard Rush	1825-1829
Secretary of War	James Barbour	1825-1828
	Peter Porter	1828-1829
Attorney General	William Wirt	1825-1829
Postmaster General	John McLean	1825-1829
Secretary of Navy	Samuel Southard	1825-1829

The Jackson Administration (1829–1837)

Vice-President	John C. Calhoun	1829–1833
	Martin Van Buren	1833–1837
Secretary of State	Martin Van Buren	1829–1831
	Edward Livingston	1831–1833
	Louis McLane	1833–1834
	John Forsyth	1834–1837
Secretary of Treasury	Samuel Ingham	1829–1831
	Louis McLane	1831–1833
	William Duane	1833
	Roger B. Taney	1833–1834
	Levi Woodbury	1834–1837
Secretary of War	John H. Eaton	1829–1831
	Lewis Cass	1831–1837
	Benjamin Butler	1837
Attorney General	John M. Berrien	1829–1831
	Roger B. Taney	1831–1833
	Benjamin Butler	1833–1837
Postmaster General	William Barry	1829–1835
	Amos Kendall	1835–1837
Secretary of Navy	John Branch	1829–1831
	Levi Woodbury	1831–1834
	Mahlon Dickerson	1834–1837

The Van Buren Administration (1837–1841)

Vice-President	Richard M. Johnson	1837–1841
Secretary of State	John Forsyth	1837–1841
Secretary of Treasury	Levi Woodbury	1837–1841
Secretary of War	Joel Poinsett	1837–1841
Attorney General	Benjamin Butler	1837–1838
	Felix Grundy	1838–1840
	Henry D. Gilpin	1840–1841
Postmaster General	Amos Kendall	1837–1840
	John M. Niles	1840–1841
Secretary of Navy	Mahlon Dickerson	1837–1838
	James Paulding	1838–1841

The William Harrison Administration (1841)

Vice-President	John Tyler	1841
Secretary of State	Daniel Webster	1841
Secretary of Treasury	Thomas Ewing	1841
Secretary of War	John Bell	1841
Attorney General	John J. Crittenden	1841
Postmaster General	Francis Granger	1841
Secretary of Navy	George Badger	1841

The Tyler Administration (1841–1845)

Vice-President	None	
Secretary of State	Daniel Webster	1841–1843
	Hugh S. Legaré	1843
	Abel P. Upshur	1843–1844
	John C. Calhoun	1844–1845

Secretary of Treasury	Thomas Ewing	1841
	Walter Forward	1841–1843
	John C. Spencer	1843–1844
	George Bibb	1844–1845
Secretary of War	John Bell	1841
	John C. Spencer	1841–1843
	James M. Porter	1843–1844
	William Wilkins	1844–1845
Attorney General	John J. Crittenden	1841
	Hugh S. Legaré	1841–1843
	John Nelson	1843–1845
Postmaster General	Francis Granger	1841
	Charles Wickliffe	1841
Secretary of Navy	George Badger	1841
	Abel P. Upshur	1841
	David Henshaw	1843–1844
	Thomas Gilmer	1844
	John Y. Mason	1844–1845

The Polk Administration (1845–1849)

Vice-President	George M. Dallas	1845–1849
Secretary of State	James Buchanan	1845–1849
Secretary of Treasury	Robert J. Walker	1845–1849
Secretary of War	William L. Marcy	1845–1849
Attorney General	John Y. Mason	1845–1846
	Nathan Clifford	1846–1848
	Isaac Toucey	1848–1849
Postmaster General	Cave Johnson	1845–1849
Secretary of Navy	George Bancroft	1845–1846
	John Y. Mason	1846–1849

The Taylor Administration (1849–1850)

Vice-President	Millard Fillmore	1849–1850
Secretary of State	John M. Clayton	1849–1850
Secretary of Treasury	William Meredith	1849–1850
Secretary of War	George Crawford	1849–1850
Attorney General	Reverdy Johnson	1849–1850
Postmaster General	Jacob Collamer	1849–1850
Secretary of Navy	William Preston	1849–1850
Secretary of Interior	Thomas Ewing	1849–1850

The Fillmore Administration (1850–1853)

Vice-President	None	
Secretary of State	Daniel Webster	1850–1852
	Edward Everett	1852–1853
Secretary of Treasury	Thomas Corwin	1850–1853
Secretary of War	Charles Conrad	1850–1853
Attorney General	John J. Crittenden	1850–1853
Postmaster General	Nathan Hall	1850–1852
	Sam D. Hubbard	1852–1853
Secretary of Navy	William A. Graham	1850–1852
	John P. Kennedy	1852–1853
Secretary of Interior	Thomas McKennan	1850
	Alexander Stuart	1850–1853

The Pierce Administration (1853–1857)

Vice-President	William R. King	1853–1857
Secretary of State	William L. Marcy	1853–1857
Secretary of Treasury	James Guthrie	1853–1857
Secretary of War	Jefferson Davis	1853–1857
Attorney General	Caleb Cushing	1853–1857
Postmaster General	James Campbell	1853–1857
Secretary of Navy	James C. Dobbin	1853–1857
Secretary of Interior	Robert McClelland	1853–1857

The Buchanan Administration (1857–1861)

Vice-President	John C. Breckinridge	1857–1861
Secretary of State	Lewis Cass	1857–1860
	Jeremiah S. Black	1860–1861
Secretary of Treasury	Howell Cobb	1857–1860
	Philip Thomas	1860–1861
	John A. Dix	1861
Secretary of War	John B. Floyd	1857–1861
	Joseph Holt	1861
Attorney General	Jeremiah S. Black	1857–1860
	Edwin M. Stanton	1860–1861
Postmaster General	Aaron V. Brown	1857–1859
	Joseph Holt	1859–1861
	Horatio King	1861
Secretary of Navy	Isaac Toucey	1857–1861
Secretary of Interior	Jacob Thompson	1857–1861

The Lincoln Administration (1861–1865)

Vice-President	Hannibal Hamlin	1861–1865
	Andrew Johnson	1865
Secretary of State	William H. Seward	1861–1865
Secretary of Treasury	Samuel P. Chase	1861–1864
	William P. Fessenden	1864–1865
	Hugh McCulloch	1865
Secretary of War	Simon Cameron	1861–1862
	Edwin M. Stanton	1862–1865
Attorney General	Edward Bates	1861–1864
	James Speed	1864–1865
Postmaster General	Horatio King	1861
	Montgomery Blair	1861–1864
	William Dennison	1864–1865
Secretary of Navy	Gideon Welles	1861–1865
Secretary of Interior	Caleb B. Smith	1861–1863
	John P. Usher	1863–1865

The Andrew Johnson Administration (1865–1869)

Vice-President	None	
Secretary of State	William H. Seward	1865–1869
Secretary of Treasury	Hugh McCulloch	1865–1869
Secretary of War	Edwin M. Stanton	1865–1867
	Ulysses S. Grant	1867–1868
	Lorenzo Thomas	1868
	John M. Schofield	1868–1869

Attorney General	James Speed	1865–1866
	Henry Stanbery	1866–1868
	William M. Evarts	1868–1869
Postmaster General	William Dennison	1865–1866
	Alexander Randall	1866–1869
Secretary of Navy	Gideon Welles	1865–1869
Secretary of Interior	John P. Usher	1865
	James Harlan	1865–1866
	Orville H. Browning	1866–1869

The Grant Administration (1868–1877)

Vice-President	Schuyler Colfax	1869–1873
	Henry Wilson	1873–1877
Secretary of State	Elihu B. Washburne	1869
	Hamilton Fish	1869–1877
Secretary of Treasury	George S. Boutwell	1869–1873
	William Richardson	1873–1874
	Benjamin Bristow	1874–1876
	Lot M. Morrill	1876–1877
Secretary of War	John A. Rawlins	1869
	William T. Sherman	1869
	William W. Belknap	1869–1876
	Alphonso Taft	1876
	James D. Cameron	1876–1877
Attorney General	Ebenezer Hoar	1869–1870
	Amos T. Ackerman	1870–1871
	G. H. Williams	1871–1875
	Edwards Pierrepont	1875–1876
	Alphonso Taft	1876–1877
Postmaster General	John A. J. Creswell	1869–1874
	James W. Marshall	1874
	Marshall Jewell	1874–1876
	James N. Tyner	1876–1877
Secretary of Navy	Adolph E. Borie	1869
	George M. Robeson	1869–1877
Secretary of Interior	Jacob D. Cox	1869–1870
	Columbus Delano	1870–1875
	Zachariah Chandler	1875–1877

The Hayes Administration (1877–1881)

Vice-President	William A. Wheeler	1877–1881
Secretary of State	William M. Evarts	1877–1881
Secretary of Treasury	John Sherman	1877–1881
Secretary of War	George W. McCrary	1877–1879
	Alex Ramsey	1879–1881
Attorney General	Charles Devens	1877–1881
Postmaster General	David M. Key	1877–1880
	Horace Maynard	1880–1881
Secretary of Navy	Richard W. Thompson	1877–1880
	Nathan Goff, Jr.	1881
Secretary of Interior	Carl Schurz	1877–1881

The Garfield Administration (1881)

Vice-President	Chester A. Arthur	1881
Secretary of State	James G. Blaine	1881

Secretary of Treasury	William Windom	1881
Secretary of War	Robert T. Lincoln	1881
Attorney General	Wayne MacVeagh	1881
Postmaster General	Thomas L. James	1881
Secretary of Navy	William H. Hunt	1881
Secretary of Interior	Samuel J. Kirkwood	1881

The Arthur Administration (1881–1885)

Vice-President	None	
Secretary of State	F. T. Frelinghuysen	1881–1885
Secretary of Treasury	Charles J. Folger	1881–1884
	Walter Q. Gresham	1884
	Hugh McCulloch	1884–1885
Secretary of War	Robert T. Lincoln	1881–1885
Attorney General	Benjamin H. Brewster	1881–1885
Postmaster General	Timothy O. Howe	1881–1883
	Walter Q. Gresham	1883–1884
	Frank Hatton	1884–1885
Secretary of Navy	William H. Hunt	1881–1882
	William E. Chandler	1882–1885
Secretary of Interior	Samuel J. Kirkwood	1881–1882
	Henry M. Teller	1882–1885

The Cleveland Administration (1885–1889)

Vice-President	Thomas A. Hendricks	1885–1889
Secretary of State	Thomas F. Bayard	1885–1889
Secretary of Treasury	Daniel Manning	1885–1887
	Charles S. Fairchild	1887–1889
Secretary of War	William C. Endicott	1885–1889
Attorney General	Augustus H. Garland	1885–1889
Postmaster General	William F. Vilas	1885–1888
	Don M. Dickinson	1888–1889
Secretary of Navy	William C. Whitney	1885–1889
Secretary of Interior	Lucius Q. C. Lamar	1885–1888
	William F. Vilas	1888–1889
Secretary of Agriculture	Norman J. Colman	1889

The Benjamin Harrison Administration (1889–1893)

Vice-President	Levi P. Morton	1889–1893
Secretary of State	James G. Blaine	1889–1892
	John W. Foster	1892–1893
Secretary of Treasury	William Windom	1889–1891
	Charles Foster	1891–1893
Secretary of War	Redfield Proctor	1889–1891
	Stephen B. Elkins	1891–1893
Attorney General	William H. H. Miller	1889–1891
Postmaster General	John Wanamaker	1889–1893
Secretary of Navy	Benjamin F. Tracy	1889–1893
Secretary of Interior	John W. Noble	1889–1893
Secretary of Agriculture	Jeremiah M. Rusk	1889–1893

The Cleveland Administration (1893–1897)

Vice-President	Adlai E. Stevenson	1893–1897
Secretary of State	Walter Q. Gresham	1893–1895
	Richard Olney	1895–1897

Secretary of Treasury	John G. Carlisle	1893–1897
Secretary of War	Daniel S. Lamont	1893–1897
Attorney General	Richard Olney	1893–1895
	James Harmon	1895–1897
Postmaster General	Wilson S. Bissell	1893–1895
	William L. Wilson	1895–1897
Secretary of Navy	Hilary A. Herbert	1893–1897
Secretary of Interior	Hoke Smith	1893–1896
	David R. Francis	1896–1897
Secretary of Agriculture	Julius S. Morton	1893–1897

The McKinley Administration (1897–1901)

Vice-President	Garret A. Hobart	1897–1901
	Theodore Roosevelt	1901
Secretary of State	John Sherman	1897–1898
	William R. Day	1898
	John Hay	1898–1901
Secretary of Treasury	Lyman J. Gage	1897–1901
Secretary of War	Russell A. Alger	1897–1899
	Elihu Root	1899–1901
Attorney General	Joseph McKenna	1897–1898
	John W. Griggs	1898–1901
	Philander C. Knox	1901
Postmaster General	James A. Gary	1897–1898
	Charles E. Smith	1898–1901
Secretary of Navy	John D. Long	1897–1901
Secretary of Interior	Cornelius N. Bliss	1897–1899
	Ethan A. Hitchcock	1899–1901
Secretary of Agriculture	James Wilson	1897–1901

The Theodore Roosevelt Administration (1901–1909)

Vice-President	Charles Fairbanks	1905–1909
Secretary of State	John Hay	1901–1905
	Elihu Root	1905–1909
	Robert Bacon	1909
Secretary of Treasury	Lyman J. Gage	1901–1902
	Leslie M. Shaw	1902–1907
	George B. Cortelyou	1907–1909
Secretary of War	Elihu Root	1901–1904
	William H. Taft	1904–1908
	Luke E. Wright	1908–1909
Attorney General	Philander C. Knox	1901–1904
	William H. Moody	1904–1906
	Charles J. Bonaparte	1906–1909
Postmaster General	Charles E. Smith	1901–1902
	Henry C. Payne	1902–1904
	Robert J. Wynne	1904–1905
	George B. Cortelyou	1905–1907
	George von L. Meyer	1907–1909
Secretary of Navy	John D. Long	1901–1902
	William H. Moody	1902–1904
	Paul Morton	1904–1905
	Charles J. Bonaparte	1905–1906
	Victor H. Metcalf	1906–1908
	Truman H. Newberry	1908–1909

Secretary of Interior	Ethan A. Hitchcock	1901–1907
	James R. Garfield	1907–1909
Secretary of Agriculture	James Wilson	1901–1909
Secretary of Labor and Commerce	George B. Cortelyou	1903–1904
	Victor H. Metcalf	1904–1906
	Oscar S. Straus	1906–1909
	Charles Nagel	1909

The Taft Administration (1909–1913)

Vice-President	James S. Sherman	1909–1913
Secretary of State	Philander C. Knox	1909–1913
Secretary of Treasury	Franklin MacVeagh	1909–1913
Secretary of War	Jacob M. Dickinson	1909–1911
	Henry L. Stimson	1911–1913
Attorney General	George W. Wickersham	1909–1913
Postmaster General	Frank H. Hitchcock	1909–1913
Secretary of Navy	George von L. Meyer	1909–1913
Secretary of Interior	Richard A. Ballinger	1909–1911
	Walter L. Fisher	1911–1913
Secretary of Agriculture	James Wilson	1909–1913
Secretary of Labor and Commerce	Charles Nagel	1909–1913

The Wilson Administration (1913–1921)

Vice-President	Thomas R. Marshall	1913–1921
Secretary of State	William J. Bryan	1913–1915
	Robert Lansing	1915–1920
	Bainbridge Colby	1920–1921
Secretary of Treasury	William G. McAdoo	1913–1918
	Carter Glass	1918–1920
	David F. Houston	1920–1921
Secretary of War	Lindley M. Garrison	1913–1916
	Newton D. Baker	1916–1921
Attorney General	James C. McReyolds	1913–1914
	Thomas W. Gregory	1914–1919
	A. Mitchell Palmer	1919–1921
Postmaster General	Albert S. Burleson	1913–1921
Secretary of Navy	Josephus Daniels	1913–1921
Secretary of Interior	Franklin K. Lane	1913–1920
	John B. Payne	1920–1921
Secretary of Agriculture	David F. Houston	1913–1920
	Edwin T. Meredith	1920–1921
Secretary of Commerce	William C. Redfield	1913–1919
	Joshua W. Alexander	1919–1921
Secretary of Labor	William B. Wilson	1913–1921

The Harding Administration (1921–1923)

Vice-President	Calvin Coolidge	1921–1923
Secretary of State	Charles E. Hughes	1921–1923
Secretary of Treasury	Andrew Mellon	1921–1923
Secretary of War	John W. Weeks	1921–1923
Attorney General	Harry M. Daugherty	1921–1923
Postmaster General	Will H. Hays	1921–1922
	Hubert Work	1922–1923
	Harry S. New	1923

Secretary of Navy	Edwin Denby	1921–1923
Secretary of Interior	Albert B. Fall	1921–1923
	Hubert Work	1923
Secretary of Agriculture	Henry C. Wallace	1921–1923
Secretary of Commerce	Herbert C. Hoover	1921–1923
Secretary of Labor	James J. Davis	1921–1923

The Coolidge Administration (1923–1929)

Vice-President	Charles G. Dawes	1925–1929
Secretary of State	Charles E. Hughes	1923–1925
	Frank B. Kellogg	1925–1929
Secretary of Treasury	Andrew Mellon	1923–1929
Secretary of War	John W. Weeks	1923–1925
	Dwight F. Davis	1925–1929
Attorney General	Henry M. Daugherty	1923–1924
	Harlan F. Stone	1924–1925
	John G. Sargent	1925–1929
Postmaster General	Harry S. New	1923–1929
Secretary of Navy	Edwin Derby	1923–1924
	Curtis D. Wilbur	1924–1929
Secretary of Interior	Hubert Work	1923–1928
	Roy O. West	1928–1929
Secretary of Agriculture	Henry C. Wallace	1923–1924
	Howard M. Gore	1924–1925
	William M. Jardine	1925–1929
Secretary of Commerce	Herbert C. Hoover	1923–1928
	William F. Whiting	1928–1929
Secretary of Labor	James J. Davis	1923–1929

The Hoover Administration (1929–1933)

Vice-President	Charles Curtis	1929–1933
Secretary of State	Henry L. Stimson	1929–1933
Secretary of Treasury	Andrew Mellon	1929–1932
	Ogden L. Mills	1932–1933
Secretary of War	James W. Good	1929
	Patrick J. Hurley	1929–1933
Attorney General	William D. Mitchell	1929–1933
Postmaster General	Walter F. Brown	1929–1933
Secretary of Navy	Charles F. Adams	1929–1933
Secretary of Interior	Ray L. Wilbur	1929–1933
Secretary of Agriculture	Arthur M. Hyde	1929–1933
Secretary of Commerce	Robert P. Lamont	1929–1932
	Roy D. Chapin	1932–1933
Secretary of Labor	James J. Davis	1929–1930
	William N. Doak	1930–1933

The Franklin D. Roosevelt Administration (1933–1945)

Vice-President	John Nance Garner	1933–1941
	Henry A. Wallace	1941–1945
	Harry S Truman	1945
Secretary of State	Cordell Hull	1933–1944
	Edward R. Stettinius, Jr.	1944–1945
Secretary of Treasury	William H. Woodin	1933–1934
	Henry Morgenthau, Jr.	1934–1945

Secretary of War	George H. Dern	1933–1936
	Henry A. Woodring	1936–1940
	Henry L. Stimson	1940–1945
Attorney General	Homer S. Cummings	1933–1939
	Frank Murphy	1939–1940
	Robert H. Jackson	1940–1941
	Francis Biddle	1941–1945
Postmaster General	James A. Farley	1933–1940
	Frank C. Walker	1940–1945
Secretary of Navy	Claude A. Swanson	1933–1940
	Charles Edison	1940
	Frank Knox	1940–1944
	James V. Forrestal	1944–1945
Secretary of Interior	Harold L. Ickes	1933–1945
Secretary of Agriculture	Henry A. Wallace	1933–1940
	Claude R. Wickard	1940–1945
Secretary of Commerce	Daniel C. Roper	1933–1939
	Harry L. Hopkins	1939–1940
	Jesse Jones	1940–1945
	Henry A. Wallace	1945
Secretary of Labor	Frances Perkins	1933–1945

The Truman Administration (1945–1953)

Vice-President	Alben W. Barkley	1949–1953
Secretary of State	Edward R. Stettinius, Jr.	1945
	James F. Byrnes	1945–1947
	George C. Marshall	1947–1949
	Dean G. Acheson	1949–1953
Secretary of Treasury	Fred M. Vinson	1945–1946
	John W. Snyder	1946–1953
Secretary of War	Robert P. Patterson	1945–1947
	Kenneth C. Royall	1947
Attorney General	Tom C. Clark	1945–1949
	J. Howard McGrath	1949–1952
	James P. McGranery	1952–1953
Postmaster General	Frank C. Walker	1945
	Robert E. Hannegan	1945–1947
	Jesse M. Donaldson	1947–1953
Secretary of Navy	James V. Forrestal	1945–1947
Secretary of Interior	Harold L. Ickes	1945–1946
	Julius A. Krug	1946–1949
	Oscar L. Chapman	1949–1953
Secretary of Agriculture	Clinton P. Anderson	1945–1948
	Charles F. Brannan	1948–1953
Secretary of Commerce	Henry A. Wallace	1945–1946
	W. Averell Harriman	1946–1948
	Charles W. Sawyer	1948–1953
Secretary of Labor	Lewis B. Schwellenbach	1945–1948
	Maurice J. Tobin	1948–1953
Secretary of Defense	James V. Forrestal	1947–1949
	Louis A. Johnson	1949–1950
	George C. Marshall	1950–1951
	Robert A. Lovett	1951–1953

The Eisenhower Administration (1953–1961)

Vice-President	Richard M. Nixon	1953–1961
Secretary of State	John Foster Dulles	1953–1959
	Christian A. Herter	1959–1961
Secretary of Treasury	George M. Humphrey	1953–1957
	Robert B. Anderson	1957–1961
Attorney General	Herbert Brownell, Jr.	1953–1958
	William P. Rogers	1958–1961
Postmaster General	Arthur E. Summerfield	1953–1961
Secretary of Interior	Douglas McKay	1953–1956
	Fred A. Seaton	1956–1961
Secretary of Agriculture	Ezra T. Benson	1953–1961
Secretary of Commerce	Sinclair Weeks	1953–1958
	Lewis L. Strauss	1958–1959
	Frederick H. Mueller	1959–1961
Secretary of Labor	Martin P. Durkin	1953
	James P. Mitchell	1953–1961
Secretary of Defense	Charles E. Wilson	1953–1957
	Neil H. McElroy	1957–1959
	Thomas S. Gates, Jr.	1959–1961
Secretary of Health, Education, and Welfare	Oveta Culp Hobby	1953–1955
	Marion B. Folsom	1955–1958
	Arthur S. Flemming	1958–1961

The Kennedy Administration (1961–1963)

Vice-President	Lyndon B. Johnson	1961–1963
Secretary of State	Dean Rusk	1961–1963
Secretary of Treasury	C. Douglas Dillon	1961–1963
Attorney General	Robert F. Kennedy	1961–1963
Postmaster General	J. Edward Day	1961–1963
	John A. Gronouski	1963
Secretary of Interior	Stewart L. Udall	1961–1963
Secretary of Agriculture	Orville L. Freeman	1961–1963
Secretary of Commerce	Luther H. Hodges	1961–1963
Secretary of Labor	Arthur J. Goldberg	1961–1962
	W. Willard Wirtz	1962–1963
Secretary of Defense	Robert S. McNamara	1961–1963
Secretary of Health, Education, and Welfare	Abraham A. Ribicoff	1961–1962
	Anthony J. Celebrezze	1962–1963

The Lyndon Johnson Administration (1963–1969)

Vice-President	Hubert H. Humphrey	1965–1969
Secretary of State	Dean Rusk	1963–1969
Secretary of Treasury	C. Douglas Dillon	1963–1965
	Henry H. Fowler	1965–1969
Attorney General	Robert F. Kennedy	1963–1964
	Nicholas Katzenbach	1965–1966
	Ramsey Clark	1967–1969
Postmaster General	John A. Gronouski	1963–1965
	Lawrence F. O'Brien	1965–1968
	Marvin Watson	1968–1969

Secretary of Interior	Stewart L. Udall	1963–1969
Secretary of Agriculture	Orville L. Freeman	1963–1969
Secretary of Commerce	Luther H. Hodges	1963–1964
	John T. Connor	1964–1967
	Alexander B. Trowbridge	1967–1968
	Cyrus R. Smith	1968–1969
Secretary of Labor	W. Willard Wirtz	1963–1969
Secretary of Defense	Robert F. McNamara	1963–1968
	Clark Clifford	1968–1969
Secretary of Health, Education, and Welfare	Anthony J. Celebrezze	1963–1965
	John W. Gardner	1965–1968
	Wilbur J. Cohen	1968–1969
Secretary of Housing and Urban Development	Robert C. Weaver	1966–1969
	Robert C. Wood	1969
Secretary of Transportation	Alan S. Boyd	1967–1969

The Nixon Administration (1969–1974)

Vice-President	Spiro T. Agnew	1969–1973
	Gerald R. Ford	1973–1974
Secretary of State	William P. Rogers	1969–1973
	Henry A. Kissinger	1973–1974
Secretary of Treasury	David M. Kennedy	1969–1970
	John B. Connally	1971–1972
	George P. Shultz	1972–1974
	William E. Simon	1974
Attorney General	John N. Mitchell	1969–1972
	Richard G. Kleindienst	1972–1973
	Elliot L. Richardson	1973
	William B. Saxbe	1973–1974
Postmaster General	Winton M. Blount	1969–1971
Secretary of Interior	Walter J. Hickel	1969–1970
	Rogers Morton	1971–1974
Secretary of Agriculture	Clifford M. Hardin	1969–1971
	Earl L. Butz	1971–1974
Secretary of Commerce	Maurice H. Stans	1969–1972
	Peter G. Peterson	1972–1973
	Frederick B. Dent	1973–1974
Secretary of Labor	George P. Shultz	1969–1970
	James D. Hodgson	1970–1973
	Peter J. Brennan	1973–1974
Secretary of Defense	Melvin R. Laird	1969–1973
	Elliot L. Richardson	1973
	James R. Schlesinger	1973–1974
Secretary of Health, Education, and Welfare	Robert H. Finch	1969–1970
	Elliot L. Richardson	1970–1973
	Caspar W. Weinberger	1973–1974
Secretary of Housing and Urban Development	George Romney	1969–1973
	James T. Lynn	1973–1974
Secretary of Transportation	John A. Volpe	1969–1973
	Claude S. Brinegar	1973–1974

The Ford Administration (1974–1977)

Vice-President	Nelson A. Rockefeller	1974–1977
Secretary of State	Henry A. Kissinger	1974–1977
Secretary of Treasury	William E. Simon	1974–1977
Attorney General	William Saxbe	1974–1975
	Edward Levi	1975–1977
Secretary of Interior	Rogers Morton	1974–1975
	Stanley K. Hathaway	1975
	Thomas Kleppe	1975–1977
Secretary of Agriculture	Earl L. Butz	1974–1976
	John A. Knebel	1976–1977
Secretary of Commerce	Frederick B. Dent	1974–1975
	Rogers Morton	1975–1976
	Elliot L. Richardson	1976–1977
Secretary of Labor	Peter J. Brennan	1974–1975
	John T. Dunlop	1975–1976
	W. J. Usery	1976–1977
Secretary of Defense	James R. Schlesinger	1974–1975
	Donald Rumsfeld	1975–1977
Secretary of Health, Education, and Welfare	Caspar Weinberger	1974–1975
	Forrest D. Mathews	1975–1977
Secretary of Housing and Urban Development	James T. Lynn	1974–1975
	Carla A. Hills	1975–1977
Secretary of Transportation	Claude Brinegar	1974–1975
	William T. Coleman	1975–1977

The Carter Administration (1977–1981)

Vice-President	Walter F. Mondale	1977–1981
Secretary of State	Cyrus R. Vance	1977–1980
	Edmund Muskie	1980–1981
Secretary of Treasury	W. Michael Blumenthal	1977–1979
	G. William Miller	1979–1981
Attorney General	Griffin Bell	1977–1979
	Benjamin R. Civiletti	1979–1981
Secretary of Interior	Cecil D. Andrus	1977–1981
Secretary of Agriculture	Robert Bergland	1977–1981
Secretary of Commerce	Juanita M. Kreps	1977–1979
	Philip M. Klutznick	1979–1981
Secretary of Labor	F. Ray Marshall	1977–1981
Secretary of Defense	Harold Brown	1977–1981
Secretary of Health, Education, and Welfare	Joseph A. Califano	1977–1979
	Patricia R. Harris	1979
Secretary of Health and Human Services	Patricia R. Harris	1979–1981
Secretary of Education	Shirley M. Hufstedler	1979–1981
Secretary of Housing and Urban Development	Patricia R. Harris	1977–1979
	Moon Landrieu	1979–1981

Secretary of Transportation	Brock Adams	1977–1979
	Neil E. Goldschmidt	1979–1981
Secretary of Energy	James R. Schlesinger	1977–1979
	Charles W. Duncan	1979–1981

The Reagan Administration (1981–1989)

Vice-President	George Bush	1981–1989
Secretary of State	Alexander M. Haig	1981–1982
	George P. Shultz	1982–1989
Secretary of Treasury	Donald Regan	1981–1985
	James A. Baker, III	1985–1988
	Nicholas Brady	1988–1989
Attorney General	William F. Smith	1981–1985
	Edwin A. Meese, III	1985–1988
	Richard Thornburgh	1988–1989
Secretary of Interior	James Watt	1981–1983
	William P. Clark, Jr.	1983–1985
	Donald P. Hodel	1985–1989
Secretary of Agriculture	John Block	1981–1986
	Richard E. Lyng	1986–1989
Secretary of Commerce	Malcolm Baldridge	1981–1987
	C. William Verity, Jr.	1987–1989
Secretary of Labor	Raymond Donovan	1981–1985
	William E. Brock	1985–1988
	Ann Dore McLaughlin	1988–1989
Secretary of Defense	Caspar Weinberger	1981–1988
	Frank Carlucci	1988–1989
Secretary of Health and Human Services	Richard Schweiker	1981–1983
	Margaret Heckler	1983–1985
	Otis R. Bowen	1985–1989
Secretary of Education	Terrel H. Bell	1981–1985
	William J. Bennett	1985–1988
	Lauro F. Cavazos	1988–1989
Secretary of Housing and Urban Development	Samuel Pierce	1981–1989
Secretary of Transportation	Drew Lewis	1981–1983
	Elizabeth Dole	1983–1987
	James L. Burnley, IV	1987–1989
Secretary of Energy	James Edwards	1981–1982
	Donald P. Hodel	1982–1985
	John S. Herrington	1985–1989

The Bush Administration (1989–   )

Vice-President	J. Danforth Quayle	1989–
Secretary of State	James A. Baker, III	1989–
Secretary of Treasury	Nicholas F. Brady	1988–
Attorney General	Richard Thornburgh	1988–
Secretary of Interior	Manuel Lujan, Jr.	1989–
Secretary of Agriculture	Clayton K. Yeutter	1989–
Secretary of Commerce	Robert A. Mosbacher	1989–
Secretary of Labor	Elizabeth H. Dole	1989–
Secretary of Defense	Richard Cheney	1989–
Secretary of Health and Human Services	Louis W. Sullivan	1989–
Secretary of Education	Lauro F. Cavazos	1988–
Secretary of Housing and Urban Development	Jack F. Kemp	1989–
Secretary of Transportation	Samuel K. Skinner	1989–
Secretary of Energy	James D. Watkins	1989–
Secretary of Veterans Affairs	Edward J. Derwinski	1989–

Supreme Court Justices

Name	Terms of Service[1]	Appointed by	Name	Terms of Service[1]	Appointed by
John Jay	1789–1795	Washington	Howell E. Jackson	1893–1895	B. Harrison
James Wilson	1789–1798	Washington	Edward D. White	1894–1910	Cleveland
John Rutledge	1790–1791	Washington	Rufus W. Peckham	1896–1909	Cleveland
William Cushing	1790–1810	Washington	Joseph McKenna	1898–1925	McKinley
John Blair	1790–1796	Washington	Oliver W. Holmes	1902–1932	T. Roosevelt
James Iredell	1790–1799	Washington	William R. Day	1903–1922	T. Roosevelt
Thomas Johnson	1792–1793	Washington	William H. Moody	1906–1910	T. Roosevelt
William Paterson	1793–1806	Washington	Horace H. Lurton	1910–1914	Taft
John Rutledge[2]	1795	Washington	Charles E. Hughes	1910–1916	Taft
Samuel Chase	1796–1811	Washington	Willis Van Devanter	1911–1937	Taft
Oliver Ellsworth	1796–1800	Washington	Joseph R. Lamar	1911–1916	Taft
Bushrod Washington	1799–1829	J. Adams	**Edward D. White**	1910–1921	Taft
Alfred Moore	1800–1804	J. Adams	Mahlon Pitney	1912–1922	Taft
John Marshall	1801–1835	J. Adams	James C. McReynolds	1914–1941	Wilson
William Johnson	1804–1834	Jefferson	Louis D. Brandeis	1916–1939	Wilson
Brockholst Livingston	1807–1823	Jefferson	John H. Clarke	1916–1922	Wilson
Thomas Todd	1807–1826	Jefferson	**William H. Taft**	1921–1930	Harding
Gabriel Duvall	1811–1835	Madison	George Sutherland	1922–1938	Harding
Joseph Story	1812–1845	Madison	Pierce Butler	1923–1939	Harding
Smith Thompson	1823–1843	Monroe	Edward T. Sanford	1923–1930	Harding
Robert Trimble	1826–1828	J. Q. Adams	Harlan F. Stone	1925–1941	Coolidge
John McLean	1830–1861	Jackson	**Charles E. Hughes**	1930–1941	Hoover
Henry Baldwin	1830–1844	Jackson	Owen J. Roberts	1930–1945	Hoover
James M. Wayne	1835–1867	Jackson	Benjamin N. Cardozo	1932–1938	Hoover
Roger B. Taney	1836–1864	Jackson	Hugo L. Black	1937–1971	F. Roosevelt
Philip P. Barbour	1836–1841	Jackson	Stanley F. Reed	1938–1957	F. Roosevelt
John Cartron	1837–1865	Van Buren	Felix Frankfurter	1939–1962	F. Roosevelt
John McKinley	1838–1852	Van Buren	William O. Douglas	1939–1975	F. Roosevelt
Peter V. Daniel	1842–1860	Van Buren	Frank Murphy	1940–1949	F. Roosevelt
Samuel Nelson	1845–1872	Tyler	**Harlan F. Stone**	1941–1946	F. Roosevelt
Levi Woodbury	1845–1851	Polk	James F. Byrnes	1941–1942	F. Roosevelt
Robert C. Grier	1846–1870	Polk	Robert H. Jackson	1941–1954	F. Roosevelt
Benjamin R. Curtis	1851–1857	Fillmore	Wiley B. Rutledge	1943–1949	F. Roosevelt
John A. Campbell	1853–1861	Pierce	Harold H. Burton	1945–1958	Truman
Nathan Clifford	1858–1881	Buchanan	**Frederick M. Vinson**	1946–1953	Truman
Noah H. Swayne	1862–1881	Lincoln	Tom C. Clark	1949–1967	Truman
Samuel F. Miller	1862–1890	Lincoln	Sherman Minton	1949–1956	Truman
David Davis	1862–1877	Lincoln	**Earl Warren**	1953–1969	Eisenhower
Stephen J. Field	1863–1897	Lincoln	John Marshall Harlan	1955–1971	Eisenhower
Salmon P. Chase	1864–1873	Lincoln	William J. Brennan, Jr.	1956–	Eisenhower
William Strong	1870–1880	Grant	Charles E. Whittaker	1957–1962	Eisenhower
Joseph P. Bradley	1870–1892	Grant	Potter Stewart	1958–1981	Eisenhower
Ward Hunt	1873–1882	Grant	Byron R. White	1962–	Kennedy
Morrison R. Waite	1874–1888	Grant	Arthur J. Goldberg	1962–1965	Kennedy
John M. Harlan	1877–1911	Hayes	Abe Fortas	1965–1970	Johnson
William B. Woods	1881–1887	Hayes	Thurgood Marshall	1967–	Johnson
Stanley Matthews	1881–1889	Garfield	**Warren E. Burger**	1969–1986	Nixon
Horace Gray	1882–1902	Arthur	Harry A. Blackmun	1970–	Nixon
Samuel Blatchford	1882–1893	Arthur	Lewis F. Powell, Jr.	1971–1988	Nixon
Lucious Q. C. Lamar	1888–1893	Cleveland	William H. Rehnquist	1971–1986	Nixon
Melville W. Fuller	1888–1910	Cleveland	John Paul Stevens	1975–	Ford
David J. Brewer	1890–1910	B. Harrison	Sandra Day O'Connor	1981–	Reagan
Henry B. Brown	1891–1906	B. Harrison	**William H. Rehnquist**	1986–	Reagan
George Shiras, Jr.	1892–1903	B. Harrison	Antonin Scalia	1986–	Reagan
			Anthony Kennedy	1988–	Reagan

Chief Justices in bold type

[1] The date on which the justice took his judicial oath is here used as the date of the beginning of his service, for until that oath is taken he is not vested with the prerogatives of his office. Justices, however, receive their commissions ("letters patent") before taking their oath—in some instances, in the preceding year.

[2] Acting Chief Justice; Senate refused to confirm appointment.

Admission of States Into the Union

State	Date of Admission	State	Date of Admission	State	Date of Admission
1. Delaware	December 7, 1787	18. Louisiana	April 30, 1812	35. West Virginia	June 20, 1863
2. Pennsylvania	December 12, 1787	19. Indiana	December 11, 1816	36. Nevada	October 31, 1864
3. New Jersey	December 18, 1787	20. Mississippi	December 10, 1817	37. Nebraska	March 1, 1867
4. Georgia	January 2, 1788	21. Illinois	December 3, 1818	38. Colorado	August 1, 1876
5. Connecticut	January 9, 1788	22. Alabama	December 14, 1819	39. North Dakota	November 2, 1889
6. Massachusetts	February 6, 1788	23. Maine	March 15, 1820	40. South Dakota	November 2, 1889
7. Maryland	April 28, 1788	24. Missouri	August 10, 1821	41. Montana	November 8, 1889
8. South Carolina	May 23, 1788	25. Arkansas	June 15, 1836	42. Washington	November 11, 1889
9. New Hampshire	June 21, 1788	26. Michigan	January 26, 1837	43. Idaho	July 3, 1890
10. Virginia	June 25, 1788	27. Florida	March 3, 1845	44. Wyoming	July 10, 1890
11. New York	July 26, 1788	28. Texas	December 29, 1845	45. Utah	January 4, 1896
12. North Carolina	November 21, 1789	29. Iowa	December 28, 1846	46. Oklahoma	November 16, 1907
13. Rhode Island	May 29, 1790	30. Wisconsin	May 29, 1848	47. New Mexico	January 6, 1912
14. Vermont	March 4, 1791	31. California	September 9, 1850	48. Arizona	February 14, 1912
15. Kentucky	June 1, 1792	32. Minnesota	May 11, 1858	49. Alaska	January 3, 1959
16. Tennessee	June 1, 1796	33. Oregon	February 14, 1859	50. Hawaii	August 21, 1959
17. Ohio	March 1, 1803	34. Kansas	January 29, 1861		

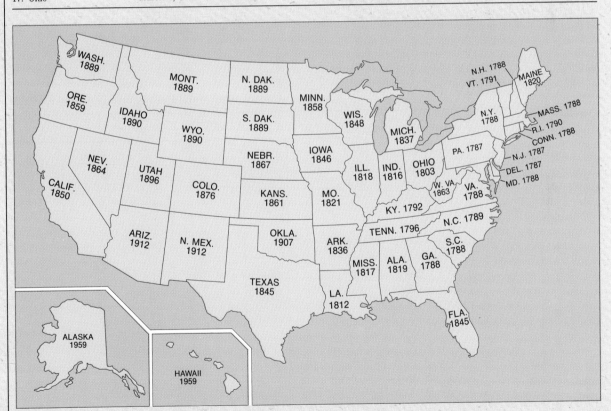

U.S. Population, 1790–1985

Year	Population	Percent Increase	Population Per Square Mile	Sex (rounded to nearest million) Male	Female	Median Age
1790	3,929,214		4.5	NA	NA	NA
1800	5,308,483	35.1	6.1	NA	NA	NA
1810	7,239,881	36.4	4.3	NA	NA	NA
1820	9,638,453	33.1	5.5	5	5	16.7
1830	12,866,020	33.5	7.4	7	6	17.2
1840	17,069,453	32.7	9.8	9	8	17.8
1850	23,191,876	35.9	7.9	12	11	18.9
1860	31,443,321	35.6	10.6	16	15	19.4
1870	39,818,449	26.6	13.4	19	19	20.2
1880	50,155,783	26.0	16.9	26	25	20.9
1890	62,947,714	25.5	21.2	32	31	22.0
1900	75,994,575	20.7	25.6	39	37	22.9
1910	91,972,266	21.0	31.0	47	45	24.1
1920	105,710,620	14.9	35.6	54	52	25.3
1930	122,775,046	16.1	41.2	62	61	26.4
1940	131,669,275	7.2	44.2	66	66	29.0
1950	150,697,361	14.5	50.7	75	76	30.2
1960	179,323,175	18.5	50.6	88	91	29.5
1970	203,302,031	13.4	57.4	99	104	28.0
1980	226,545,805	11.4	64.0	110	116	30.0
1985	237,839,000	5.0	64.0	117	123	31.3

NA = Not available.

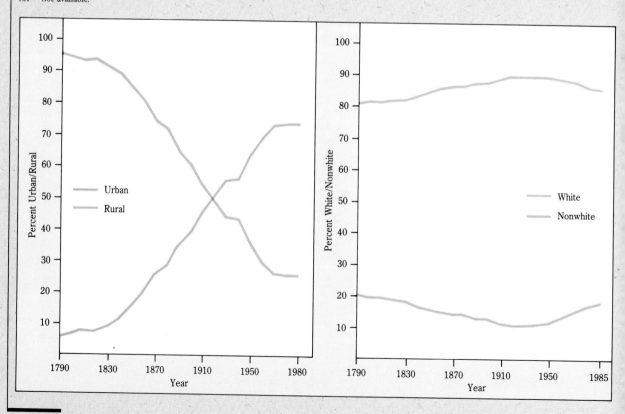

Employment, 1870–1985

Year	Number of Workers (in Millions)	Male/Female Employment Ratio	Percentage of Workers in Unions
1870	12.5	85/15	—
1880	17.4	85/15	—
1890	23.3	83/17	—
1900	29.1	82/18	3
1910	38.2	79/21	6
1920	41.6	79/21	12
1930	48.8	78/22	7
1940	53.0	76/24	27
1950	59.6	72/28	25
1960	69.9	68/32	26
1970	82.1	63/37	25
1980	108.5	58/42	23
1985	108.9	57/43	19

Unemployment

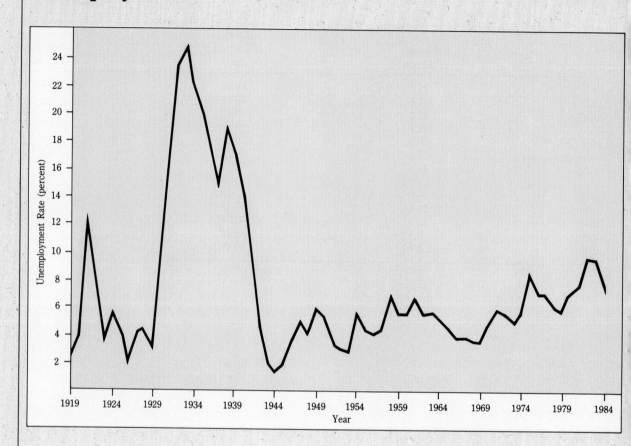

Regional Origins of Immigration

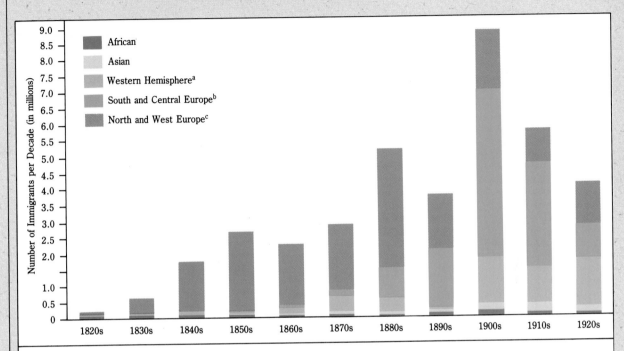

^aCanada and all countries in South America and Central America.
^bItaly, Spain, Portugal, Greece, Germany (Austria included, 1938-1945), Poland, Czechoslovakia (since 1920), Yugoslavia (since 1920), Hungary (since 1861), Austria (since 1861, except 1938-1945), U.S.S.R. (excludes Asian U.S.S.R. between 1931 and 1963), Latvia, Estonia, Lithuania, Finland, Romania, Bulgaria, Turkey (in Europe), and other European countries not classified elsewhere.
^cGreat Britain, Ireland, Norway, Sweden, Denmark, Iceland, Netherlands, Belgium, Luxembourg, Switzerland, France.
SOURCE: Stephan Thernstrom, ed., *Harvard Encyclopedia of American Ethnic Groups* (1980), p. 480; and U.S. Bureau of the Census, *Statistical Abstract of the United States, 1984* (1983), p. 9.

Total Federal Debt

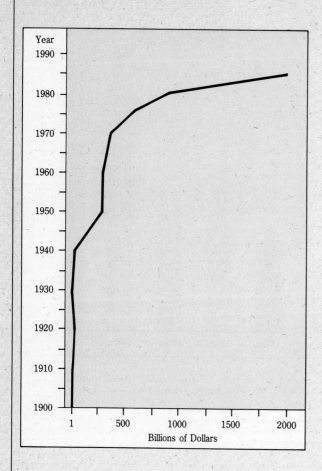

Credits

Contents
x Courtesy of the John Carter Brown Library, Brown University. **xi** Joslyn Art Museum, Omaha, Nebraska. **xiii, xiv** Library of Congress. **xvii** Photographer: Dev O'Neill. **xviii** Bob Adelman/Magnum Photos.

Comparative Chronologies
xxii(t) From the Codex Mendoza in Lord Kingsborough's *Antiquities of Mexico*, 1829, **(b)** Bettmann Archive. **xxiii** American Antiquarian Society. **xxiv(t)** *Harper's New Monthly Magazine*, **(bl)** John T. Hopf, **(br)** Library of Congress. **xxv** Bettmann Archive. **xxvi(t)** U.S. Bureau of Printing and Engraving, **(br)**Newberry Library, Chicago. **xxviii** Huckleberry Finn from *The Annotated Huckleberry Finn* by Michael Patrick Hearn, Clarkson N. Potter, Inc., Publishers, N.Y. **xxix(t)** *Frank Leslie's Illustrated Newspaper*, September 11, 1920, **(b)** Bettmann Newsphotos. **xxx** Courtesy Bell Laboratories. **xxxi** © G. B. Trudeau, Universal Press Syndicate.

Chapter Openers
Chapter 1 Arapaho buffalo skull: Museum of the American Indian, Heye Foundation. Christopher Columbus: The Metropolitan Museum of Art, Gift of J. Pierpont Morgan, 1900. "Falls at Colville": Royal Ontario Museum, Toronto. Corn: Arents Collection/New York Public Library, Astor, Lenox and Tilden Foundations.

Chapters 2-6 "Pilgrims Going to Church": The New-York Historical Society, New York City. Ad for colony of Virginia: Rare Books and Manuscripts Division/New York Public Library, Astor, Lenox and Tilden Foundations. Slave sale broadside: American Antiquarian Society. Section and plan of blockhouse: Thomas Anburey, *Travels Through the Interior Parts of America*, 1789. Plan of Philadelphia: Library of Congress (Map Division). "Mrs. Elizabeth Freake and Baby Mary": Worcester Art Museum, Worcester, Massachusetts. Declaration of Independence: National Archives. Slave ship: Library of Congress.

Chapters 7-12 National Bank of the United States: Stokes Collection, Prints Division/New York Public Library, Astor, Lenox and Tilden Foundations. North wing of the Capitol: Library of Congress. Plan of the City of Washington: Stokes Collection, Prints Division/New York Public Library, Astor, Lenox and Tilden Foundations. American sailor: The New-York Historical Society, New York City. "Fairview Inn": Maryland Historical Society, Baltimore. Hampton, the Seat of General Charles Ridgley, Maryland: Historical Society of Pennsylvania. Cotton plantation: Library of Congress. "Progress of Cotton": Yale University Art Gallery, Mabel Brady Garvan Collection. Pioneers: Denver Public Library, Western Collection. Ad for *Uncle Tom's Cabin*: The New-York Historical Society, New York City.

Chapters 13-15 Captured slave: Musée de l'Homme, Paris. Slave sale broadside: State Historical Society of Wisconsin. Slave nurse: Cook Collection/Valentine Museum, Richmond, Virginia. Robert E. Lee: Library of Congress. Union soldier: Chicago Historical Society. Pickett's Charge: Gettysburg National Military Park. Battle of the Crater: The Commonwealth Club, Richmond, Virginia. Ulysses S. Grant: Library of Congress. 1st Virginia Regiment: Cook Collection/Valentine Museum, Richmond, Virginia. Infantry at Fort Lincoln: Library of Congress. Ruins of Richmond, Virginia: Library of Congress. Elizabeth Cady Stanton: Culver Pictures. Susan B. Anthony: The Sophia Smith Collection (Women's History Archive), Smith College, Northampton, MA.

Chapters 18-21 Chinese fire hose team: Library of Congress. Cowboys: Montana Historical Society, Helena. Cattle brands: From *We Pointed Them North*, copyright 1954, University of Oklahoma Press. Sitting Bull: Library of Congress. George Custer: Library of Congress. Golden spike ceremony: Union Pacific Railroad Museum Collection. Cowboy: © Charles J. Belden, Whitney Gallery of Western Art, Cody, Wyoming. Football team: Steve Karchin Collection. Ferris wheel: Chicago Historical Society. Horse: *Treasury of American Design*. Skyscraper: The New-York Historical Society, New York City. Edison's electric light bulbs: Greenfield Village and Henry Ford Museum, Dearborn, Michigan. Immigrants: International Museum of Photography at George Eastman House. Schoolroom: Brown Brothers.

Chapters 22-26 Immigrant: International Museum of Photography at George Eastman House. Jack Johnson: Bettmann Archive. Lusitania ad: Culver Pictures. Henry Ford in Model T: UPI/Bettmann Newsphotos. Shell casing factory: National Archives. WW I soldier: Smithsonian Institution. WW I soldiers: Charlotte Iglarsh Collection. FDR and Eleanor: UPI/Bettmann Newsphotos. Charles Lindbergh: Bettmann Archive. Flappers:

Schomberg Collection/New York Public Library, Astor, Lenox and Tilden Foundations. Soldiers wearing gas masks: UPI/Bettmann Newsphotos. Wall Street, October 29, 1929: Brown Brothers. Mickey Mouse: © Walt Disney Productions. Hitler and Mussolini: National Archives. Woman kissing WW II soldier: U.S. Army. Blimp and bombers: U.S. Navy photo. U.S. at War headline: *San Francisco* Chronicle, December 8, 1941. WW II poster: Nastional Archives. Sailors: U.S. Navy photo. Mushroom cloud over Nagasaki: U.S. Air Force.

Chapters 27-30 Dwight Eisenhower: Library of Congress. Woman in kitchen: Bettmann Archive. Suburban homes: FPG. Noguchi table, Eames chair: © Herman Miller, Inc., Zeeland, Mich. Fabric samples: Alexander Girard, © Herman Miller, Inc., Zeeland, Mich. Martin Luther King, Jr.: Costa Manos/Magnum Photos. Kennedy-Nixon debate: Wide World Photos. Missiles: Cornell Capa/Magnum Photos. Helicopter, Vietnam: UPI/Bettmann Newsphotos. March on Washington, 1963: Robert W. Kelley, LIFE Magazine © 1970 Time Inc. Saturn rings photographed from Voyager 2: NASA. Woodstock Festival: Elliot Landy/Magnum Photos. Soldiers, Vietnam: Philip Jones Griffiths/Magnum Photos. Antiwar deomonstration: Jean-Claude Lejeune. Astronauts on moon: NASA. Betty Friedan: Michael Ginsburg/Magnum Photos. Sam Ervin, Senate Watergate Investigating Committee: Mark Godfrey/Archive Pictures. Richard Nixon: Hiroji Kubota/Magnum Photos. Student demonstration: Wayne Miller/Magnum Photos. Supreme Court Justice Sandra Day O'Connor: Owen Franken/Sygma. Space shuttle: UPI/Bettmann Newsphotos. Ronald Reagan and Mikhail Gorbachev: Sigma.

Chapter Photos
Chapter 1
5 Courtesy of the Pilgrim Society, Plymouth, Ma. **7(t)** Library of Congress **7(c)** The Peabody Museum, Harvard University, Photographed by Hillel Burger **7(b)** Robert Frerck/Odyssey Productions, Chicago **8(l)** Tony Linck **8(tr,br)** Glenn A. Black Laboratory of Archaeology, Indiana University **9** National Gallery of Canada, Ottawa **12** Holbein, *The Dance of Death* **13** The British Library **14** Ets J. E. Bulloz **15** Rare Book Room/New York Public Library, Astor, Lenox and Tilden Foundations **18** The Granger Collection, New York **19** Osterreichische Nationabibliothek **20** Collection Nuastra Senora de Copacabana, Lima, Photo Jose Casals/Aldus Archives **21** Johnson Collection, Philadelphia **22(t)** Thyssen-Bornemisza Collection **22(b)** National Portrait Gallery, London **23** Musee Historique de la Reformation, Geneva **24** National Maritime Museum, London **25** National Portrait Gallery, London **27** Courtesy of the Trustees of the British Museum **28** Library of Congress **30** Courtesy of the Newberry Library, Chicago, Edward E. Ayer Collection **32(l)** Holbein, *The Dance of Death* **32(r)** Rare Book Room/New York Public Library, Astor, Lenox and Tilden Foundations

Chapter 2
39 Duke University Library, Durham, NC **40** The Granger Collection, New York **41** Library of Congress **43(t)** National Maritime Museum, London **43(b)** National Portrait Gallery, London **44** Enoch Pratt Free Library **45** The Colonial Williamsburg Foundation **46** Society of Antiquaries of London **47** Courtesy of the Pilgrim Society, Plymouth, Ma. **48(l)** American Antiquarian Society **48(c)** Courtesy of the Pilgrim Society, Plymouth, Ma. **48(r)** Massachusetts State Art Commission **49** Massachusetts State Archives **51(t)** Courtesy of the Pilgrim Society, Plymouth, Ma. **51(b)** Culver Pictures **53(l)** Rare Book Room/New York Public Library, Astor, Lenox and Tilden Foundations **53(r)** The Huntington Library, San Marino, California **54** The Essex Institute, Salem, Ma. **55** Culver Pictures **56** National Library of Medicine **58** Courtesy of the Trustees of the British Museum **61** Collection of Tazwell Ellett III **62** The Granger Collection, New York **64** Arents Collection/New York Public Library, Astor, Lenox and Tilden Foundations **65** Abby Aldrich Rockefeller Folk Art Collection

Chapter 3
71 Charleston Library Society **72** City of Bristol Museum and Art Gallery **73** Picture Collection/New York Public Library, Astor, Lenox and Tilden Foundations **74** National Portrait Gallery, London **77** The Museum of the City of New York **78** Pennsylvania Academy of the Fine Arts, Gift of Mrs. Joseph Harrison, Jr. **79** Abby Aldrich Rockefeller Folk Art Collection **80** New York Public Library, Astor, Lenox and Tilden Foundations **83** Picture Collection/New York Public Library, Astor, Lenox and Tilden Foundations **86** Philadelphia Museum of Art **89(t)** *The Story of*

Chapter 13

407(l) Indiana Historical Society **407(r)** California State Library **411** Library of Congress **412** From: *Mathew Brady*, Time-Life Books **414** National Museum of American Art, Smithsonian Institution, Gift of William T. Evans **416** Library of Congress **417(t)** The New-York Historical Society, New York City **417(b)** The Metropolitan Museum of Art, Gift of I. N. Phelps Stokes, Edward S. Hawes, Alice Mary Hawes, Marion Augusta Hawes, 1937 **418** Historical Society of Philadelphia **420(l)** DeWolf Perry Collection **420(r)** Library of Congress **422** American Antiquarian Society **425** The Kansas State Historical Society, Topeka **426** Prints Division/New York Public Library, Astor, Lenox and Tilden Foundations **427** The New-York Historical Society, New York City **429(l)** Missouri Historical Society **429(r)** National Archives **433(l)** University of Hartford: Museum of American Political Life **433(r)** Historical Society of Pennsylvania

Chapter 14

441(l) Courtesy Georgia Dept. of Archives & History **441(r)** John L. McGuire Collection **442** New York Public Library, Astor, Lenox and Tilden Foundations **445** Library of Congress **447(t)** U.S. Army Photo **447(b)** Library of Congress **449** M. and M. Karolik Collection of American Watercolors and Drawings, 1800–1875, Courtesy, Museum of Fine Arts, Boston **451** Chicago Historical Society **452, 453(both)** Library of Congress **455** Collection of Oliver Jensen **459** Library of Congress **462** Historical Society of York County, Pennsylvania **463** Chicago Historical Society **463** Chicago Historical Society **466** Collection of Mrs. Nelson A. Rockefeller **467** Library of Congress **468** Henry Groskinsky **471** Cook Collection/Valentine Museum, Richmond, Virginia **472(l)** Courtesy The Museum of the Confederacy, Richmond, Va. **472(r)** The Bettmann Archive

Chapter 15

479 Brown Brothers **480** Brady Collection/Library of Congress **481** Cook Collection/Valentine Museum, Richmond, Virginia **482, 484** Library of Congress **485(l)** *Harper's Weekly* **485(r)** *Frank Leslie's Illustrated Newspaper*, May 21, 1864 **486** The Granger Collection, New York **488** Library of Congress **490** *Harper's Weekly*, October 27, 1866 **491** *Harper's Weekly* **493, 495** Culver Pictures **496** Library of Congress **498** Culver Pictures **499** *Harper's Weekly*, September 23, 1871 **500** Lightfoot Collection **501** *Harper's Weekly*, October 24, 1874 **504** Montana Historical Society **505** DeGolyer Library, S.M.U. **506** Braun Research Library/Southwest Museum, Los Angeles, Ca.

Chapter 16

513 Courtesy of the Carnegie Library of Pittsburgh **514** Library of Congress **515** Drake Well Museum **516** Chicago Historical Society **517** U.S. Dept. of the Interior, National Park Service Edison National Historic Site **518** Courtesy Metropolitan Life Ins. Co. **520** Mrs. Vincent Astor **521** The Museum of the City of New York **522(l)** Culver Pictures **522(r)** Library of Congress **523** The New-York Historical Society, New York City **527, 530** Culver Pictures **531** Library of Congress **533** Courtesy Caterpillar Tractor Co., Peoria **534** The Kansas State Historical Society, Topeka **535** Solomon D. Butcher Collection, Nebraska State Historical Society **536** Historical Pictures Service, Chicago **541(l)** Brown Brothers **541(r)** Library of Congress **542(l)** U.S. Dept. of the Interior, National Park Service, Edison National Historic Site **542(r)** Courtesy of Eastman Kodak Company

Chapter 17

547 Keystone-Mast Collection, California Museum of Photography, University of California, Riverside **548** Culver Pictures **550** Courtesy American Museum of Immigration, Statue of Liberty, National Park Service, U.S. Dept. of the Interior **551** Culver Pictures **553** Courtesy Archives Division/Texas State Library, Austin, Texas **556** *Harper's Weekly*, September 29, 1888 **557** Culver Pictures **559** International Museum of Photography at George Eastman House **561** *Puck*, March 17, 1886 **562** The Bettmann Archive **565** Photograph by Byron, The Byron Collection, The Museum of the City of New York **568** The Granger Collection, New York **569** Library of Congress **570** Pach/The Bettmann Archive **571(l)** Bettmann Archive **571(r)** Free Library of Philadelphia

Chapter 18

577(l) Culver Pictures **577(r)** American Antiquarian Society **581** Brown Brothers **582** Culver Pictures **583** Harry P. Lepman Collection/Smithsonian Institution **584** New York Public Library, Astor, Lenox and Tilden Foundations **585** *Puck*, December 9, 1887 **587** *Harper's Weekly* **590, 591** Culver Pictures **595** Solomon D. Butcher Collection/Nebraska State Historical Society **597** Courtesy of the Carnegie Library of Pittsburgh **598** New York Public Library, Astor, Lenox and Tilden Foundations **600** Library of Congress **601** Scott, Foresman and Company

Chapter 19

607, 609 The Bettmann Archive **610** Library of Congress **613** Library of Congress **615** Culver Pictures **618** UPI/Bettmann Newsphotos **620** Library of Congress **623** Culver Pictures **625** Chicago Historical Society **626** Library of Congress **631** National Archives **632** Library of Congress **633** The Bettmann Archive

Chapter 20

639 Culver Pictures **642** Chicago Historical Society **643** The Museum of the City of New York **645** Courtesy of the Carnegie Library of Pittsburgh **646(l)** International Museum of Photography at George Eastman House **646(r)** Brown Brothers **649** The Museum of the City of New York **650** UPI/Bettmann Newsphotos **651** Brown Brothers **652** Private Collection **653** The Metropolitan Museum of Art, The Alfred Stieglitz Collection, 1949 **654** Hogan Jazz Archives, Tulane University **656** The Granger Collection, New York **658** Library of Congress **660** Culver Pictures **663** The Museum of the City of New York **664** Photo from the collection of John W. Ripley, Topeka, Kansas **666** Frank Leslie's Illustrated Newspaper, July 1, 1865

Chapter 21

673 U. S. Dept. of the Interior, National Park Service **674** International Museum of Photography at George Eastman House **675** Culver Pictures **676** The Bettmann Archive **678(l)** The Bettmann Archive **678(r)** Culver Pictures **679** The Lawrence Lee Pelletier Library, Allegheny College **681** Chicago Historical Society **683** Wide World **684** NAACP **686** The Granger Collection, New York **687** Centers for Disease Control, Atlanta, Center for Professional Development & Training, Still Pictures Archives **688** UPI/Bettmann Newsphotos **689** Culver Pictures **691** Library of Congress **693(l)** Ship Ahoy Restaurant, Seabright, NJ **693(r)** Brown Brothers **694, 696** Library of Congress **697** The Bettmann Archive **699** Brown Brothers **701** Culver Pictures **705(l)** The Bettmann Archive **705(r)** Scott, Foresman and Company

Chapter 22

711 UPI/Bettmann Newsphotos **712** Cartoon by Rogers in the NEW YORK HERALD **714, 715** UPI/Bettmann Newsphotos **718** Imperial War Museum, London **721** The Archives of Labor and Urban Affairs, Wayne State University **722** New York Public Library, Music Division **723** LIFE, July 25, 1915 **724(t)** UPI/Bettmann Newsphotos **724(b), 725** National Archives **727** Imperial War Museum, London **729** National Archives **730** Robert Hunt Library **734** Brown Brothers **735** Historical Pictures Service, Chicago **737** CHICAGO TRIBUNE—N.Y. News Syndicate

Chapter 23

745 Culver Pictures **746** The New-York Historical Society **747** Wide World Photos **748** Brown Brothers **749** Courtesy VOGUE Copyright © 1925, (renewed 1953, 1981) by The Conde Nast Publications Inc. **750** Granger **754(l)** UPI/Bettmann Newsphotos **754(r)** Culver Pictures **755** Rollin Kirby, NEW YORK WORLD, May 19, 1925 **758, 759** Brown Brothers **760(l)** VANITY FAIR photograph by Breaker Copyright © 1928, 1956 by The Conde Nast Publications Inc. **760(r), 763(l)** Brown Brothers **763(r)** UPI/Bettmann Newsphotos **764** Museum of Modern Art/Film Stills Archive **765** LIFE, June 8, 1920 **769** Bureau of Engraving and Printing **770** NEW YORK TIMES, Oct. 25, 1929 **771** Brown Brothers **772** Library of Congress

Chapter 24

778 Culver Pictures **779** Library of Congress **781** Historical Pictures Service, Chicago **784** UPI/Bettmann Newsphotos **785** Wide World Photos **786** Library of Congress **789** The Bettmann Archive **791** Wide World Photos **793** Culver Pictures **795** UPI/Bettmann Newsphotos **797** © 1938 by Esquire, Inc. **799** Keystone/FPG **800** Courtesy Lou Erikson

Chapter 25

810 Brown Brothers **811, 813, 814, 816** UPI/Bettmann Newsphotos **818** Official U.S. Navy Photo **819, 821** Wide World Photos **824** UP FRONT by Bill Mauldin, published by Henry Holt & Co. **825(l)** Library of Congress **825(r)** Baker Library, Harvard Business School **829** Photograph by Dorothea Lange, War Relocation Authority in The National Archives **832** Imperial War Museum, London **836** U.S. Coast Guard Photo **837** Courtesy Franklin D. Roosevelt Library **840** UPI/Bettmann Newsphotos **842** U.S. Air Force Photo **844** U.S. Army Photo **845** Photographer: Dev O'Neill

Chapter 26

851(r) James Whitmore, Life Magazine © Time Inc. **853** Acme/The Bettmann Archive **855(b)** UPI/Bettmann Newsphotos **858** Wide World **860** Ferro Jacobs/Black Star **861(l)** Shoemaker **861(r)** Soufoto/Eastfoto **864, 865** UPI/Bettmann Newsphotos **866** Wide World **870(both)** Elliot Erwitt/Magnum Photos **871** UPI/Bettman Newsphotos **872** Alfred Eisenstaedt, Life Magazine © Time Inc. **875(t)** Wide World **875(b)** Film

Stills Archive/Museum of Modern Art **877(l)** Acme/The Bettmann Archive **877(r)** UPI/Bettmann Newsphotos

Chapter 27

883 Wide World **884(l)** Ralph Morse, Life Magazine © Time Inc. **884(r)** UPI/Bettmann Newsphotos **888** Cornell Capa/Magnum Photos **889, 890** UPI/Bettmann Newsphotos **892** Harold M. Talburt, Scripps–Howard Newspapers **895** Tass from Sovfoto **896** Costa Manos/Magnum Photos **898** UPI/Bettmann Newsphotos **900** Ed Clark, Life Magazine © 1949 Time Inc. **902, 903(both)** Wide World **904** Courtesy Life Picture Service/Life Magazine © Time Inc. **906** Cornell Capa/Magnum Photos **907** Don Wright, Life Magazine © Time Inc. **908** Wide World

Chapter 28

909, 914, 916 UPI/Bettmann Newsphotos **917** John Fitzgerald Kennedy Library **918** Charles Moore/Black Star **920** Leslie Illingworth, Courtesy The National Library of Wales **921(t)** N.Y. Daily News photo **921(b)** Courtesy Daniel Fitzpatrick/St. Louis *Post-Dispatch* **926** Fred Ward/Black Star **927(t)** J. Pavlovsky/Sygma **927(b)** C. Simonpietri/Sygma **930** Bob Fitch/Black Star **932(t)** Lee Lockwood/Black Star **932(b)** Roger Falconer/Black Star **933** Steve Schapiro/Black Star **934** Paul Sequeira **938** Kent State University News Service, photo by Jack Davis **940** Magnum Photos **942** Mark Godfrey/Archive Pictures, Inc. **943** Alex Webb/Magnum Photos

Chapter 29

949 Wide World **952, 953** UPI/Bettmann Newsphotos **956** Fred Ward/Black Star **957** Bob Adelman/Magnum Photos **960** Constantine Manos/Magnum Photos **962** Yoichi Okomoto/Photo Researchers **965** B. Bartholomew/Black Star **967** Wayne Miller/Magnum Photos **968** Peter Simon/Stock Boston **974** David Strick/Onyx **977(l)** Ira Wyman/Sygma **977(r)** Kathleen Foster/Black Star **979** Phil Degginger/Click/Chicago Ltd. **980** Herman Kokojan/Black Star **981** Michael Abramson/Black Star

Chapter 30

988 Anthony Loew © 1984 **991** Bill Fitz-Patrick/Courtesy The White House **993** Sipa/Special Features **994** Pete Souza/Courtesy The White House **996** Scrawls-Atlanta Constitution **997** Franklin-Sygma **998** Jason Bleibtreu/Sygma **999** Jack Higgins, With permissions of the Chicago Sun-Times, Inc., © 1986 **1000** Artstreet **1002** Bouvet-Duclos-Simon/Gamma-Liaison **1004** J.P. Laffont/Sygma **1005** Fred Ward/Black Star **1008** Reprinted Courtesy of Chicago Tribune

Popular Protest in Early America *following page 160*

1 Alexander Hamilton addressing the mob at Columbia College. *Harper's New Monthly Magazine*, October, 1884. **2** (t) Governor Sir William Berkeley confronting the insurgents. (b) "Nathaniel Bacon and his Followers Burning Jamestown," by Howard Pyle. Brown County Library. **3** (t) A handbill distributed in October, 1765. State Paper Office, London. (b) "Boston Tea Party," by Howard Pyle. Brown County Library. **4** "A New Method of Macaroni Making as Practised at Boston in North America," 1775. The Carnegie Museum of Art, Pittsburgh; Eavenson Fund, 1955. **5** (t) "General Anthony Wayne being attacked by the mutinous Pennsylvania regiments at Morristown, January 1, 1781. Library of Congress. (b) "The Wicked Statesman," cover of the *Massachusetts Calendar*, 1774. American Antiquarian Society. **6** (t) "Saints Driven from Jackson County, Missouri," by C.C.A. Christensen. Courtesy of Brigham Young University. All rights reserved. (b) "Our Peculiar Domestic Institutions," *Anti-Slavery Almanac*, 1840. The New-York Historical Society, New York City. **7** "Destruction by Fire of Pennsylvania Hall," May 17, 1838. The Historical Society of Pennsylvania. **8** (t) "A Sketch from The New Tragic Farce of 'Americans Shall Rule America,' as enacted by Mayor Swann of Baltimore, and his wonderful 'Star' Company," 1856. The Maryland Historical Society. (b) "Justice Meted Out to 'English Jim' by the Vigilantes, San Francisco Harbor," c. 1855. Collection of The Oakland Museum, gift of Concours d'Antiques.

The Changing American Landscape Part I *following page 320*

1 "Twilight in the Wilderness," by F.E. Church. The Cleveland Museum of Art, Mr. and Mrs. William H. Marlatt Fund, 65.233. **2**(t1) "Head of a Female Bighorn," by Karl Bodmer. Joslyn Art Museum, Omaha, Nebraska. (tr) "American Blue Crab," by Sesse and Mocino, 1787-1812. Torner Collection of Sesse and Mocino Biological Illustrations, Hunt Institute for Botanical Documentation, Carnegie-Mellon University, Pittsburgh, PA. **3**(t1) "Carolina Parroquet," 1825, by John James Audubon. The New-York Historical Society, N.Y.C. (tr) "Franklinia Altamaha," 1788, by William Bartram. The British Museum (Natural History). (b) "Schroon Mountain, Adi-

rondacks," 1828, by Thomas Cole. The Cleveland Museum of Art, Hinman B. Hurlbut Collection. **4**(t) "View from Bushongo Tavern, 5 miles from York Town on the Baltimore Road," 1788. Library of Congress (b) Redraft of the Castello Plan, New Amsterdam, 1660. The Phelps Stokes Collection, Prints Division, The New York Public Library, Astor, Lenox, and Tilden Foundation. **5**(t1) "Hope Estate Plantation," 1857-61, by Adrien Persac. Anglo-American Art Museum, Louisiana State University, Baton Rouge. (tr) "Military Plaza, San Antonio, Texas," 1857. Library of Congress (b) "New Haven Public Square," c. 1780, by William Giles Munson. New Haven Colony Historical Society. **6**(t) "Utica, New York," 1850. The Phelps Stokes Collection, Prints Division, The New York Public Library, Astor, Lenox and Tilden Foundation. (c) "Galena, Ill.," 1856. Courtesy Chicago Historical Society. (b) "View of Prairie du Chien looking North," 1848, by Seth Eastman. Minnesota Historical Society. **7** "Jefferson City, Mo.," 1855. Library of Congress. **8**(t) "City of San Francisco, Cal.," 1852. Library of Congress. (b) "Blackhawk Point, Colorado," 1862. Library of Congress.

Popular Protest Since the Civil War *following page 592*

1 Frank Leslie's Illustrated Newspaper, September 16, 1882. **2**(t1) Culver Pictures (tr) © 1983 Frank Johnson/Black Star (b) © Arthur Grace/Sygma **3**(t) © 1979 Charles Moore/Black Star (b) © J. L. Atlan/Sygma **4**(t) UPI/Bettmann Newsphotos (b) © 1985 John Troha/Black Star **5**(t,c) The Archives of Labor and Urban Affairs, Wayne State University (b) UPI/Bettmann Newsphotos **6**(t) Tom Zimberoff/Sygma (b) Ira Wyman/Sygma **7**(t) Kenneth Yimm for Insight magazine (c) Jean-Pierre Laffont/Sygma (b) © 1988 Jerome Friar **8** © 1980 Jim Anderson/Black Star

The Changing American Landscape Part II *following page 768*

1 "Central Park," 1863. The New-York Historical Society. **2** (t) The Dakota Apartments in New York City, 1889. (b) "Lower Manhattan and the Harbour," by Richard Rummell, 1911. The New-York Historical Society. **3** (t) "Roof Garden, Hotel Astor, Times Square, New York." Bella C. Landauer Collection, The New-York Historical Society. **4** (t) Garden apartments, Jackson Heights, New York, 1920s. Brown Brothers. (b) Wilshire Boulevard and Beverly Drive, looking East, Los Angeles, 1922. Spence Air Photos, UCLA. **5** (t1) Mineola, Long Island, New York, 1920s. Brown Brothers. (tr) Cincinnati, Ohio, slums, 1930s. Library of Congress. (b) Pittsburgh, PA., 1945. Allegheny Conference on Community Development, Pittsburgh. **6** (t) St. Albans Bay, Vermont, 1948, photo by L.L. McAllister. Special Collections, Bailey Library, University of Vermont. (c) Richards Drive-in, Cambridge, Mass., c. 1957. Cambridge Historical Commission. (b) Reston, Va., 1988. Milt & Joan Mann/CAMERAMANN INTERNATIONAL. **7** (c) Lenox Square Mall, Altanta, Ga. Ralph Krubner/H. Armstrong Roberts. (b) Along Second Street at Lombard, Society Hill, Philadelphia, Pa., 1988. Milt & Joan Mann/CAMERAMANN INTERNATIONAL **8** (t) San Francisco, Ca. copyright Baron Wolman. (b) Willard Clay.

In addition, the authors and publisher acknowledge with gratitude permission to reprint, quote from, or adapt the following materials. (The numbers shown below refer to pages of this text.)

648 From *Chicago: Growth of a Metropolis* by Harold M. Mayer and Richard C. Wade. Copyright © 1969 by The University of Chicago. Reprinted by permission of The University of Chicago Press. **733** data from G. M. Gathorne-Hardy, *The Fourteen Points and the Treaty of Versailles*, Oxford Pamphlets on World Affairs, no. 6, 1939 and Thomas G. Paterson, et al., *American Foreign Policy, A History Since 1900*, 2nd ed., vol. 2. **788** data from C. D. Premer, *American Bank Failures*, Columbia University Press, 1935. **893** From *An Atlas of World Affairs* by Andrew Boyd. Reprinted by permission of Metheum & Co., Ltd. **906** From "Little Boxes," words and music by Malvina Reynolds. Copyright © 1962 by Schroder Music Co. (ASCAP). Used by permission. All rights reserved. **907** From "Long Tall Sally" by Richard Penniman, Enntris Johnson, and Robert A. Blackwell and "Rip It Up" by Robert A. Blackwell and John S. Marascalo. Copyright © 1956, renewed 1984 by Venice Music Inc. All rights controlled and administered by SBK Blackwood Music Inc. under license from ATV Music (Venice). All rights reserved. International copyright secured. Used by permission. From "Roll Over Beethoven" by Chuck Berry. Used by permission of Isalee Music Company. **908** From "Shake, Rattle and Roll" by Charles Calhoun. Copyright © 1954 by Hill and Range Songs, Inc. (renewed). All rights reserved. Used by permission. **909** Excerpts from "Howl" by Allen Ginsberg. Copyright © 1955 by Allen Ginsberg. Excerpts from "America" by Allen Ginsberg Copyright © 1956, 1959 by Allen Ginsberg. Both from *Collected Poems 1947–1980* by Allen Ginsberg. Reprinted by permission of Harper & Row, Publishers, Inc. and Penguin Books Ltd.

Index

The World

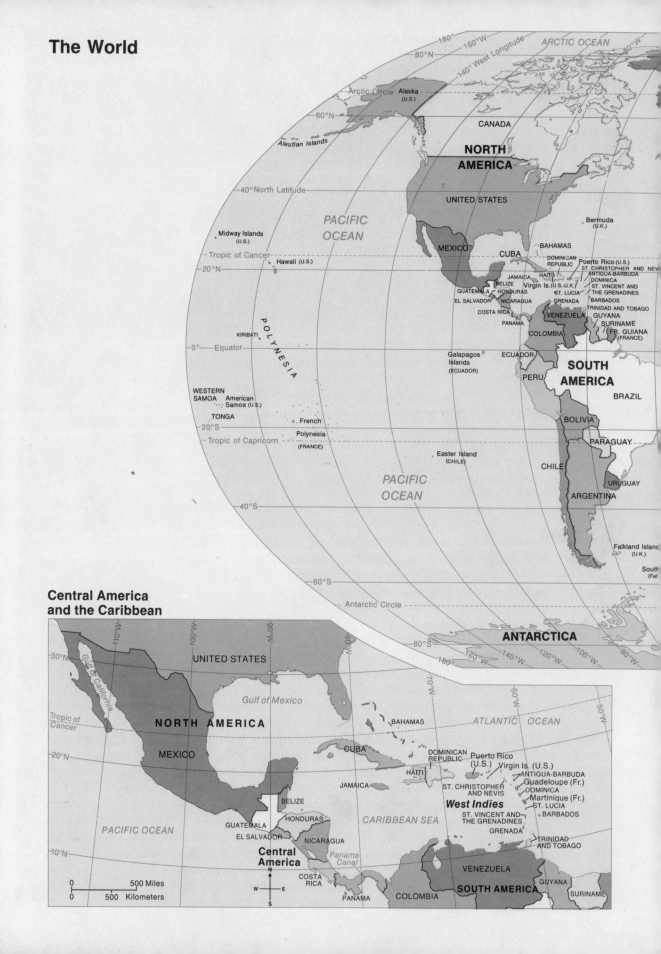

ARCTIC OCEAN

180°   160°W
140° West Longitude
80°N

Arctic Circle   Alaska
(U.S.)

60°N

CANADA

Aleutian Islands

**NORTH
AMERICA**

40° North Latitude

PACIFIC
OCEAN

UNITED STATES

Bermuda
(U.K.)

Midway Islands
(U.S.)

MEXICO   CUBA   BAHAMAS
DOMINICAN   Puerto Rico (U.S.)
REPUBLIC   ST. CHRISTOPHER AND NEV

Tropic of Cancer

HAITI   ANTIGUA-BARBUDA
DOMINICA

20°N   Hawaii (U.S.)   JAMAICA   Virgin Is. (U.S.-U.K.)   ST. VINCENT AND
BELIZE   THE GRENADINES
GUATEMALA   HONDURAS   ST. LUCIA   BARBADOS
EL SALVADOR   NICARAGUA   GRENADA   TRINIDAD AND TOBAGO
COSTA RICA   VENEZUELA   GUYANA
PANAMA   SURINAME
COLOMBIA   FR. GUIANA
(FRANCE)

KIRIBATI

0°   Equator   Galapagos   ECUADOR
Islands
(ECUADOR)   **SOUTH
AMERICA**

PERU   BRAZIL

WESTERN
SAMOA   American
Samoa (U.S.)

TONGA   BOLIVIA

20°S   French   PARAGUAY
Polynesia
Tropic of Capricorn   (FRANCE)

Easter Island   CHILE
(CHILE)   URUGUAY

PACIFIC
OCEAN   ARGENTINA

40°S

Falkland Island
(U.K.)

South
(Fal

60°S

Antarctic Circle

80°S   **ANTARCTICA**

160°W   140°W   120°W   100°W   80°W
180°

Central America
and the Caribbean

110°W   100°W   90°W   80°W   70°W

30°N   UNITED STATES

Gulf of California

Tropic of
Cancer   Gulf of Mexico

BAHAMAS   ATLANTIC   60°W
OCEAN

NORTH   AMERICA   50°W

20°N   CUBA   DOMINICAN   Puerto Rico
MEXICO   REPUBLIC   (U.S.)   Virgin Is. (U.S.)
HAITI   ANTIGUA-BARBUDA
JAMAICA   Guadeloupe (Fr.)
BELIZE   DOMINICA
ST. CHRISTOPHER   Martinique (Fr.)
HONDURAS   AND NEVIS   ST. LUCIA
West Indies
GUATEMALA   ST. VINCENT AND   BARBADOS
EL SALVADOR   CARIBBEAN SEA   THE GRENADINES
NICARAGUA   GRENADA
10°N   **Central
America**   TRINIDAD
AND TOBAGO
PACIFIC OCEAN   N
W   E   COSTA   Panama
S   RICA   Canal   VENEZUELA   GUYANA

0   500 Miles   PANAMA   COLOMBIA   **SOUTH AMERICA**   SURINAME
0   500   Kilometers